BUSINESS

Fourth Canadian Edition

BUSINESS

Fourth Canadian Edition

Ricky W. Griffin
Texas A&M University

Ronald J. Ebert
University of Missouri-Columbia

Frederick A. Starke
University of Manitoba

Prentice
Hall

Toronto

To Ann, Eric, and Grant

Canadian Cataloguing in Publication Data

Griffin, Ricky W.
   Business
4th Canadian ed.

ISBN 0-13-089696-9

1. Industrial management. 2. Business enterprises. 3. Industrial management – Canada. 4. Business enterprises – Canada. I. Ebert, Ronald J. II. Starke, Frederick A., 1942- . III. Title.

HD31.G75 2002   658   C00-932837-8

0-13-089696-9

Vice President, Editorial Director: Michael Young
Acquisitions Editor: Samantha Scully
Marketing Manager: James Buchanan
Developmental Editor: Suzanne Schaan
Production Editor: Mary Ann McCutcheon
Copy Editor: Susan Broadhurst
Production Coordinator: Deborah Starks
Page Layout: Joan M. Wilson
Permissions Research: Amanda McCormick
Photo Research: Lisa Brant, Beth McAuley
Art Director: Julia Hall
Interior and Cover Design: Amy Harnden
Cover Image: Masterfile/David Muir

1 2 3 4 5 06 05 04 03 02

Printed and bound in U.S.A.

OVERVIEW

CONTENTS

*Summary of Learning Objectives, Key Terms, Study Questions and Exercises, Building Your Business Skills, and Exploring the Net appear before the Concluding Cases in every chapter.

Part Five

Managing Marketing   455

Part Six

Appendices

This is the fourth Canadian edition of *Business*. As in previous editions, our intent is to excite and inform students about today's business world, and to support instructors with an interesting and attractive book that explains the basic ideas that beginning business students must learn. The fourth edition maintains the strengths that made the first three editions so successful; once again, we have kept in sight the fundamental objectives of being comprehensive, accurate, current, and readable. We believe that we have met all of these objectives, as this new edition of *Business* continues to offer significant coverage of both traditional topics and new ideas.

The Theme of Change

We have all heard the sentiment expressed that change is occurring at an accelerating pace. As we worked on the manuscript for this edition, we were struck by the truly stunning changes that are actually taking place in the practice of business. The rules of the game are constantly changing and new forces are at work. For example, companies come together on short notice for collaborative projects and then, just as quickly, return to their original shapes as separate—and often competing—entities. Employees and companies share new ideas about the nature of work, when and where it takes place, how it is done, and who determines roles and activities in the workplace. Communication technologies are rapidly breaking down the barriers of physical distance, and tightly knit teams with members positioned around the world share information as effectively as groups that meet together in the same room.

In nearly every aspect of business today there are totally new ways of doing things. These new ways are replacing traditional business practices, usually with surprising speed and often with better competitive results. Along with new practices come a host of unique legal and ethical issues to challenge the creativity and judgment of business managers. Given these developments, we as authors and teachers felt that our goal had to be to communicate the theme of change by describing how real-world business firms cope with organizational change and conflict in the modern business world. Thus, we have tried to capture the flavour and convey the excitement of the "new economy" in all of its rapidly evolving practices.

As a major thoroughfare along the information superhighway, the Internet has become a major new artery for e-commerce and e-business. More and more aspiring start-up companies are carving out niches and staking their claims to consumer dollars. But when the first crucial laps have been run, who will still be running, and who will be left at the side of the track? What will make the difference? How will traditional companies—the so-called "bricks-and-mortar" businesses—compete in this brave new world? Or are e-businesses going to have more problems?

Other Themes

In support of the overall theme of change, the organization and content of this fourth Canadian edition reflect five other trends that are important in today's businesses. These trends will likely accelerate as the twenty-first century unfolds.

- *The growth of international business*—Globalization of the economy is seen by many business people as the dominant challenge of the twenty-first century. To keep students aware of this challenge, we've based many of the examples and cases in this book on the experiences of global companies, and on the experiences of Canadian companies in the global marketplace. An entire chapter is also devoted to international business (Chapter 3, Understanding International Business).

- *The role of ethics and social responsibility*—Business ethics and social responsibility continue to generate a great deal of discussion and debate. Because ethical and social issues are so pervasive in the business world, we present them early in the text so students have a frame of ethical reference throughout the book. We also devote an entire chapter to these topics (Chapter 4, Conducting Business Ethically and Responsibly).

- *The significance of small business*—Since many students will not work for major corporations, we have provided coverage of both large and small companies throughout the text. In various chapters, the implications of the ideas for small business are discussed, and one full chapter is devoted to small business in Canada (Chapter 7, Understanding Entrepreneurship and Small Business).

- *The importance of information and communication technology*—In our information-based society, the people and organizations that learn how to obtain and use information will be the ones that succeed. The explosive growth and change in these systems is recognized as we devote an entire chapter to the management of information (Chapter 13, Managing Information Systems and Communication Technology).

- *The quality imperative*—Quality and productivity became the key to competitive recovery for many companies in the global marketplace during the 1990s. These topics continue to be of special interest in the twenty-first century, so we have devoted a full chapter to their coverage (Chapter 12, Increasing Productivity and Quality).

Changes in the Fourth Canadian Edition

The fourth Canadian edition of *Business* incorporates many of the changes suggested by professors and students who used the previous three editions. It also includes changes suggested by reviewers. The following major changes have been made:

- All of the opening cases are either new or updated.

- A new series of boxed inserts, It's a Wired World, has been introduced to discuss relevant Internet and technology issues within each chapter. Another boxed series, Business Today, looks at Canadian and international business.

- A new feature called WebConnexion provides real-world examples of businesses that practise the concepts discussed in the text, along with links to the companies' Web sites for more information.

- Many new examples of business practice have been included in each of the chapters; some of these examples are brief and some are more detailed.

- New cases are included at the end of each chapter.

■ New CBC video cases are included at the end of each major part of the text.

■ Major revisions have been made to several chapters, including Chapter 1 (Understanding the Canadian Business System), Chapter 3 (Understanding International Business), and Chapter 13 (Managing Information Systems and Communication Technology); substantial revisions have also been made in many other chapters.

■ The number of chapters has been reduced to 20 from 22, and material is presented in a more concise fashion.

■ Many examples of e-businesses are given to demonstrate how technology is affecting business practice.

Organization of the Text

The text is organized into six parts as follows:

Part One: Introducing the Contemporary Business World. This part introduces students to the basic ideas underlying business activity. Chapter 1 describes how business activity is oriented towards satisfying consumer needs and making a profit. Several types of economic systems are described, and the Canadian mixed economic system is analyzed (including important interactions between business and government). Chapter 2 presents a brief history of Canadian business and focuses on several types of business ownership—sole proprietorships, partnerships, corporations, and cooperatives. Chapter 3 describes the critical area of international business and free trade, and the importance of international business for Canada. Chapter 4 discusses the impact of business ethics and social responsibility.

Part Two: The Business of Managing. The chapters in this part focus on the general management activities that are necessary in business firms. Chapter 5 introduces the functions of management—planning, organizing, leading, and controlling—and the basic types of management skills that are required to carry out these functions. Chapter 6 focuses on the planning and organizing functions of management and the strategic decisions that business managers must make. In Chapter 7, general management principles are applied to small business activity.

Part Three: Understanding People in Organizations. The chapters in this part focus on the most important resource in business firms: people. Chapter 8 describes the activities that are required to recruit, hire, train, and compensate a company's human resources. Chapter 9 deals with managerial activities that are necessary to motivate and lead employees so they are both satisfied and productive. Chapter 10 presents information on Canadian labour unions and the way that unions affect management activity.

Part Four: Managing Operations and Information. This part describes the managerial activities that are necessary to convert raw materials into finished products and services that are needed by consumers. Chapter 11 focuses on the production of goods and services, while Chapter 12 deals with the crucial issues of productivity and quality. Chapter 13 presents information on how managers use information to make business decisions, and how the dynamic and rapidly developing area of computers affects the practice of management. Chapter 14 describes the accounting function and the financial statements that accountants develop for managers and investors.

Part Five: Managing Marketing. The chapters in this part explain the key activities that are carried out by marketing managers. Chapter 15 introduces the "4 Ps of marketing"—product, place, promotion, and price. Other activities such as marketing research and the study of consumer behaviour help marketing managers carry out the marketing function effectively. Chapter 16 explains new product development and the promotion of goods and services, and Chapter 17 focuses on pricing and distributing goods and services.

Part Six: Managing Financial Issues. The chapters in this part introduce students to the key financial activities of business firms. Chapter 18 explores the nature of money, the various financial intermediaries that exist in Canada, and the role of the Bank of Canada. Chapter 19 looks at securities markets and the buying and selling of stocks, bonds, and other investments. Chapter 20 explains why business firms need funds, and the way they go about acquiring these funds. The role of the financial manager is also described.

Major Features of the Text

The text contains the following features to stimulate student interest in, and understanding of, the material that is being presented about business.

Part Opener

At the beginning of each of the six parts of the book is a brief outline introducing the material that will be discussed in that part. By explaining the rationale for the structure of the part, these outlines give students a glimpse of the "big picture" as they head into a new area of the business world.

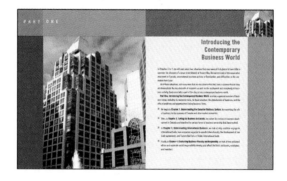

Chapter Materials

Each chapter contains several features that are designed to increase student interest in and understanding of the material being presented. These features are as follows:

Opening Case. Each chapter begins with a description of a situation that is faced by a real Canadian or international company. The subject matter of this opening case is relevant to the material presented in that chapter, helping students bridge the gap between theory and practice.

Learning Objectives. A list of learning objectives is presented at the beginning of each chapter. These objectives guide students in determining what is important in each chapter.

1. Trace the history of business in Canada.
2. Identify the *major forms of business ownership.*
3. Explain *sole proprietorships* and *partnerships* and discuss the advantages and disadvantages of each.

LEARNING OBJECTIVES

Boxed Inserts. Each chapter contains two boxed inserts: Business Today and It's a Wired World. The Business Today boxes describe activities in Canadian or international companies and show students how theoretical concepts are actually put into practice by business firms. The series entitled It's a Wired World describes the steps that businesses are taking to keep pace with competitors in the rapidly changing e-business environment. Each box describes the situation faced by a real firm, showing how challenges are being met by the introduction of technology.

WebConnexions. Every chapter contains two or three cyberspace field trips at the students' fingertips. Captioned screen shots provide examples of Canadian and international companies whose Web sites offer ready-made avenues for further study.

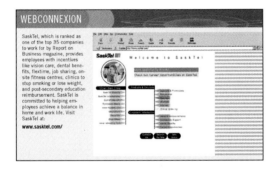

Examples. In addition to the boxed inserts, each chapter contains numerous examples of how businesses operate. These examples will further help students understand actual business practice in Canada and elsewhere.

Figures and Tables. The latest data available have been used to update tables and figures throughout the text. The Top 10 tables provide information on the largest Canadian companies in various industries.

Weblinks. Internet addresses are supplied throughout the text for many of the companies that are discussed.

End-of-Chapter Material

Several important pedagogical features are found at the end of each chapter. These are designed to help students better understand the material that is presented in the chapter.

Summary of Learning Objectives. The material in each chapter is concisely summarized to help students understand the main points that were presented in the chapter.

SUMMARY OF LEARNING OBJECTIVES

1. **Explain how individuals develop their personal *codes of ethics* and why ethics are important in the workplace.** Individual *codes of ethics* are derived from social standards of right and wrong. *Ethical behaviour* is behaviour that conforms to generally accepted social norms concerning beneficial and harmful actions. Because ethics affect the behaviour of individuals on behalf of the companies that employ them, many firms are adopting formal statements of ethics. Unethical behaviour can result in loss of business, fines, and even imprisonment.

2. **Distinguish *social responsibility* from *ethics*, identify *organizational stakeholders*, and trace the evolution of social responsibility in business.** *Social responsibility* refers to an organization's response to social needs. One way to understand social responsibility is to view it in terms of *stakeholders*—those groups, individuals, and organizations that are directly affected by the practices of an organization and that therefore have a stake in its performance. Until the second half of the nineteenth century, businesses often paid little attention to stakeholders. Since then, however, both public pressure and government regulation, especially as a result of the Great Depression of the 1930s and the social activism of the 1960s and 1970s,

Key Terms.   In each chapter, the key terms that students should know are highlighted and defined in the text, repeated in the margin, and listed at the end of the chapter (with page references).

Study Questions and Exercises.   There are three types of questions here: review questions (straightforward questions of factual recall), analysis questions (which require students to think beyond simple factual recall and apply the concepts), and application exercises (which require students to visit local businesses or managers and gather additional information that will help them understand how business firms operate).

Building Your Business Skills.   This feature is an in-depth exercise that allows students to examine some specific aspect of business in detail. The exercise may ask students to work individually or in a group to gather data about an interesting business issue and then develop a written report or a class presentation based on the information that was gathered.

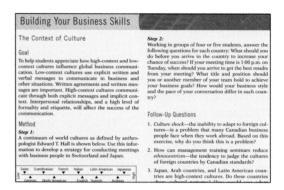

Exploring the Net.   This feature gives students the opportunity to carry out interesting, business-related assignments by using the Internet. By doing so, students gain important skills in locating and using information from Canadian and international Web sites.

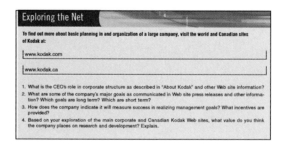

Concluding Cases.   Each chapter concludes with two case studies that focus on real Canadian or international companies. These cases are designed to help students see how the chapter material can be applied to a real company that is currently in the news. At the end of each case, several questions guide students in their analysis. Classic cases from previous editions are included in the Instructor's Resource Manual.

End-of-Part Material

At the end of each of the six major parts of the text, two recent CBC video cases are presented. The instructor can show the *Venture* episode in class and then either conduct a class discussion using the questions at the end of the written case as a guide or ask students to complete a written assignment that contains answers to the case questions. This approach to teaching adds a major new dynamic to classes because students will be able to relate text material to actual Canadian business situations. The cases are also available on the Companion Website for *Business*.

Supplementary Materials

For Instructors

Instructor's Resource Manual. This manual contains chapter outlines, teaching tips, and suggestions on how to use the text effectively. It includes material for classroom use, such as Careers in Business and additional cases (including the cases to accompany the Lands' End videos). The manual also provides answers to the end-of-chapter questions and cases (including Building Your Business Skills, Exploring the Net, and the CBC video cases).

Test Item File. With approximately 100 multiple choice, 35 true/false, and 15 essay questions per chapter, this supplement provides a total of over 3000 questions for class tests.

Test Manager. This new version of Pearson Education's computerized testing software is a comprehensive suite of tools for testing and assessment that comes loaded with all the questions from the Test Item File. It allows instructors to easily create and distribute tests for their courses, either by printing and distributing through traditional methods or by online delivery.

CBC Video Library. The CBC Video Library for *Business*, Fourth Canadian Edition, includes 13 segments from CBC's program *Venture*, which accompany the video cases found at the end of each part in the text. These cases focus on Canadian companies and discuss business issues from a Canadian point of view. The cases are also available on the Companion Website, and answers are discussed in the Instructor's Resource Manual. (Please contact your Pearson Education sales representative for details.)

On Location! Lands' End Videos. These six video segments focus on Lands' End Inc., a major catalogue retailer. These videos focus on the operations of a successful company that deals with both goods and services on a global scale. The written cases and answers are both provided in the Instructor's Resource Manual. The cases are also available on the Companion Website. (Please contact your Pearson Education sales representative for details.)

Electronic Transparencies in PowerPoint. The Electronic Transparencies, which are available for downloading from the Companion Website, offer an average of about 40 PowerPoint slides per chapter, outlining the key points in the text. The slides include lecture notes that provide page references to the text, summaries, and suggestions for student activities or related questions from the text.

Companion Website. In addition to the online study guide and other materials for students, the Companion Website includes supplementary cases focusing on e-businesses (with answers in a protected area for instructors). The Electronic Transparencies and Instructor's Resource Manual are also available for downloading from the site. Visit the site at www.pearsoned.ca/griffin.

For Students

Survival Guide to Business. This guide enables students to review the introductory business concepts presented in the text and understand their application. It provides summaries of the major sections within each chapter, as well as practice questions (multiple-choice, true/false, and essay) with answers. The guide also includes ongoing discussions of how to learn, study, and succeed in the course.

Companion Website The Companion Website includes a variety of resources for students. The site acts as an online study guide, with multiple choice, true/false, and short essay questions that can be submitted for grading. Internet exercises, live Weblinks, and a search function encourage students to explore the Web to find information relevant to their course and business interests. Careers in Business provides information about possible occupations, pointers on preparing a resume and interviewing for jobs, and other related career information. Supplementary cases include a series that focuses on e-business. Visit the site at www.pearsoned.ca/griffin.

Acknowledgments

We owe special thanks to Susan Broadhurst for her excellent copyediting; Mary Ann McCutcheon, Production Editor, for her efficient management of this project; and Lisa Brant for her fine photo research. Thanks are also due to Michael Young, Publisher; Samantha Scully, Acquisitions Editor; Suzanne Schaan, Developmental Editor; James Buchanan, Marketing Manager; and all the members of the Pearson Education Canada sales team.

In addition, we would like to acknowledge the contributions of Emmet Mellow, who researched the Weblinks, WebConnexions, and Exploring the Net exercises, and Beth McAuley, who acted as permissions editor for the WebConnexions.

We appreciate the insights and suggestions of the following individuals who provided feedback on the third edition or reviewed the manuscript for the new edition:

Laura Allan, Wilfrid Laurier University

Tim Carroll, University of Prince Edward Island

Michael A. Costa, Fanshawe College

Jane Haddad, Seneca College

Ibrahim Hayani, Seneca College

Kate Muller, Humber College

Barbara Smith, Niagara College

Fran Smyth, Seneca College

David Wicks, Saint Mary's University

Their comments were carefully considered and implemented wherever possible.

Frederick A. Starke
2001

Your Internet companion to the most exciting, state-of-the-art educational tools on the Web!

The Pearson Education Canada Companion Website is easy to navigate and is organized to correspond to the chapters in this textbook. The Companion Website comprises these distinct, functional features:

Customized Online Resources

Online Interactive Study Guide

Interactivities

Communication

Explore these areas in this Companion Website. Students and distance learners will discover resources for indepth study, research, and communication, empowering them in their quest for greater knowledge and maximizing their potential for success in the course.

A NEW WAY TO DELIVER EDUCATIONAL CONTENT

Course Management

Our Companion Websites provide instructors and students with the ability to access, exchange, and interact with material specially created for our individual textbooks.

- **Syllabus Manager** provides instructors with the option of creating online classes and constructing an online syllabus linked to specific modules in the Companion Website.

- **Grader** allows the student to take a test that is automatically marked by the program. The results of the test can be e-mailed to the instructor and then added to the student's record.

- **Help** includes an evaluation of the user's system and a tune-up area that makes updating browsers and plug-ins easier. This new feature will facilitate the use of our Companion Websites.

Instructor Resources

This section features modules with additional teaching material organized by chapter for instructors. Downloadable PowerPoint Presentations, Electronic Transparencies, and an Instructor's Manual are just some of the materials that may be available in this section. Where appropriate, this section will be password protected. To get a password, simply contact your Pearson Education Canada representative or call Faculty Sales and Services at 1-800-850-5813.

General Resources

This section contains information that is related to the entire book and that will be of interest to all users of the site. A Table of Contents and a Glossary are just two examples of the kind of information you may find in this section.

The General Resources section may also feature *Communication facilities* that provide a key element for distributed learning environments:

- **Message Board** – This module takes advantage of browser technology to provide the users of each Companion Website with a national newsgroup to post and reply to relevant course topics.

- **Chat Room** – This module enables instructors to lead group activities in real time. Using our chat client, instructors can display website content while students participate in the discussion.

Want some practice before an exam?

The Student Resources section contains the modules that form the core of the student learning experience in the Companion Website. The modules presented in this section may include the following:

- Learning Objectives
- Multiple-Choice Questions
- True/False Questions
- Essay Questions

- Internet Exercises
- Additional Cases
- Destinations
- Net Search

The question modules provide students with the ability to send answers to our grader and receive instant feedback on their progress through our Results Reporter. Coaching comments and references to the textbook may be available to ensure that students take advantage of all available resources to enhance their learning experience.

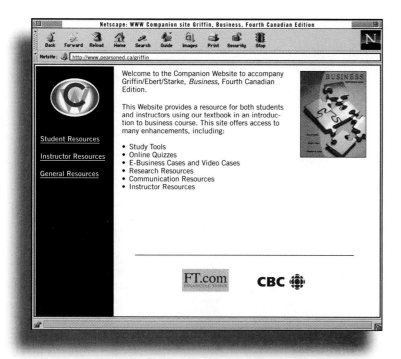

Companion Websites are currently available for:

- Dessler/Starke/Cyr: *Management*
- Solomon/Stuart/Carson/Smith: *Marketing*
- Kotler/Armstrong/Cunningham: *Principles of Marketing*

Note: Companion Website content will vary slightly from site to site depending on discipline requirements.

PEARSON EDUCATION CANADA

26 Prince Andrew Place
Toronto, Ontario M3C 2T8

To order:
Call: 1-800-567-3800
Fax: 1-800-263-7733

For samples:
Call: 1-800-850-5813
Fax: (416) 299-2539
E-mail:
phabinfo_pubcanada@pearsoned.com

The Companion Website for this text can be found at:
www.pearsoned.ca/griffin

Introducing the Contemporary Business World

In Chapters 1 to 4, you will read about four situations that may seem at first glance to have little in common: the discovery of a large nickel deposit at Voisey's Bay, the current state of the cooperative movement in Canada, international business activity at Bombardier, and difficulties at the animation firm Cinar.

All of these situations, and many more that are described in this text, have a common thread: they all demonstrate the key elements of business as well as the excitement and complexity of business activity. Each case tells a part of the story of our contemporary business world.

Part One, Introducing the Contemporary Business World, provides a general overview of business today, including its economic roots, its legal structure, the globalization of business, and the ethical problems and opportunities facing business firms.

- We begin in **Chapter 1, Understanding the Canadian Business System,** by examining the role of business in the economy of Canada and other market economies.

- Then, in **Chapter 2, Setting Up Business in Canada,** we review the history of business development in Canada and examine the various forms of business ownership that have evolved.

- In **Chapter 3, Understanding International Business,** we look at why countries engage in international trade, how companies organize to operate internationally, the development of free trade agreements, and factors that help or hinder international trade.

- Finally, in **Chapter 4, Conducting Business Ethically and Responsibly,** we look at how individual ethics and corporate social responsibility develop and affect the firm's customers, employees, and investors.

The Saga of Voisey's Bay

Inco Ltd., the giant Canadian mining company, held its annual meeting on April 19, 2000. The meeting, which was punctuated by angry questions from company shareholders, focused on the stalled Voisey's Bay project and the possibility of a strike by 3500 workers at Inco's Sudbury operation. Also present was a group of Indonesian citizens who expressed concern about growing social problems and unemployment difficulties near one of Inco's properties in their country.

This meeting was the latest in a series of unfortunate events for Inco. The current difficulties started in 1993, when two diamond prospectors under contract to Diamond Fields Resources (DFR) stumbled upon one of the world's richest nickel finds in the rolling hills of northeast Labrador. After word of the discovery got out, the price of DFR's stock rose from $4 per share to $41 per share.

In 1996, Inco decided to buy controlling interest in DFR for $4.3 billion to maintain Inco's dominant position in the world nickel mining business. Unfortunately, once Inco gained control of the nickel deposit, things began to go wrong. The price of nickel declined, dropping from $3.00 per pound in 1996 to $1.70 per pound by the end of 1998. Inco's stock price also dropped 50 percent, partly because of the decline in nickel prices and partly because Inco had issued additional shares to pay for the purchase of Voisey's Bay.

In 1997, Inco announced that it would have to delay development of the project because of a time-consuming and expensive environmental review process. The government of Newfoundland had also become involved, demanding that Inco build a smelter in the province to smelt the ore it mined. The Innu Nation then demanded a 3 percent smelter royalty and a guarantee that the mine would be in operation for 25 years.

At Inco's 1998 annual meeting, Chairman Michael Sopko had to cope with hostile questions from union and aboriginal leaders, shareholders, environmentalists, and political leaders. Rumours began to circulate that Inco would have to take a massive writedown on the Voisey's Bay project because a deal could not be worked out with the Newfoundland government.

By 1999, things were again looking up for Inco. Nickel prices (and Inco's stock price) had increased sharply since 1997, and Inco had returned to the bargaining table with provincial politicians to try to work out an agreement. With its improved financial condition, Inco was apparently now willing to talk about building the smelter in Newfoundland after all. As of late 1999, it looked like Inco was finally going to be able to begin production at Voisey's Bay sometime in 2000.

But in February 2000, Inco announced it was closing its Newfoundland office because it had been unable to reach an agreement with Newfoundland Premier Brian Tobin about the conditions under which Inco would be allowed to mine nickel at Voisey's Bay. Inco also announced it was shifting more than $1 billion to its nickel operations in the South Pacific. ◆

The forces of supply and demand that play such an important role in the financial future of companies like Diamond Fields Resources and Inco also dictate stories of success and failure for virtually every business enterprise. As you will see in this chapter, those forces define the Canadian market economy. You will also see that although the world's economic systems differ markedly, the standards for evaluating the success or failure of a system are linked to its capacity to achieve certain basic goals.

By focusing on the learning objectives of this chapter, you will better understand the Canadian business system and the mechanisms by which it not only pursues its goals but permits businesses large and small to pursue theirs. After reading this chapter, you should be able to:

LEARNING OBJECTIVES

1. Define the nature of Canadian *business* and identify its main goals.

2. Describe different types of global *economic systems* according to the means by which they control the *factors of production* through *input and output markets*.

3. Show how *demand* and *supply* affect resource distribution in Canada.

4. Identify the elements of *private enterprise* and explain the various *degrees of competition* in the Canadian economic system.

5. Explain the criteria for evaluating the success of an economic system in meeting its goals and show how the federal government attempts to manage the Canadian economy.

6. Discuss the current economic picture in Canada and summarize expert opinions about its future.

THE IDEA OF BUSINESS AND PROFIT

What do you think of when you hear the word *business*? Does it conjure up images of huge corporations like Canadian Pacific and Alcan Aluminum? Smaller companies like your local supermarket? One-person operations like the barbershop around the corner? Indeed, each of these firms is a **business**—an organization that produces or sells goods or services in an effort to make a profit. **Profit** is what remains after a business's expenses have been subtracted from its revenues. Profits reward the owners of businesses for taking the risks involved in investing their time and money. Canada's "Big Six" banks made profits totalling $9.1 billion in 1999.[1]

While most businesses will never earn anywhere near that much profit, the prospect of earning profits is what encourages people to open and expand businesses. Today businesses produce most of the goods and services that we consume, and they employ many of the working people in Canada. Profits from these businesses are paid to thousands of owners and shareholders. And business taxes help support governments at all levels. In addition, businesses help support charitable causes and provide community leadership.

In this chapter, we begin your introduction to Canadian business by looking at its role in our economy and society. Because a variety of economic systems are found around the world, we will first consider how the dominant ones operate. Once you have some understanding of different systems, you can better appreciate the workings of our own system. As you will see, the effect of economic forces on Canadian businesses and the effect of Canadian businesses on our economy produce dynamic and sometimes volatile results.

business
An organization that seeks to earn profits by providing goods and services.

profit
What remains (if anything) after a business's expenses are subtracted from its sales revenues.

GLOBAL ECONOMIC SYSTEMS

A Canadian business is different in many ways from one in China. And both are different from businesses in Japan, France, or Peru. A major determinant of how organizations operate is the kind of economic system that characterizes the country in which they do business. An **economic system** allocates a nation's resources among its citizens. Economic systems differ in terms of who owns and controls these resources, known as the "factors of production."

economic system
The way in which a nation allocates its resources among its citizens.

Factors of Production

The key difference between economic systems is the way in which they manage the **factors of production**—the basic resources that a country's businesses use to produce goods and services (see Figure 1.1). Traditionally, economists have focused on four factors of production: *labour, capital, entrepreneurs,* and *natural resources*. Newer perspectives, however, tend to broaden the idea of "natural resources" to include all *physical resources*. In addition, *information resources* are now often included as well.[2]

factors of production
The resources used to produce goods and services: labour, capital, entrepreneurs, and natural resources.

Natural resources

Human resources

Factors of production

Capital

Entrepreneurs

Figure 1.1
Factors of production are the basic resources a business uses to create goods and services. The four basic factors used are natural resources, labour, capital, and entrepreneurs.

The people who work for a company represent the first factor of production, **labour**. Sometimes called *human resources*, labour is the mental and physical capabilities of people. Carrying out the business of such a huge company as Imperial Oil, for example, requires a labour force with a wide variety of skills ranging from managers to geologists to truck drivers.

Obtaining and using material resources and labour requires **capital**, the funds needed to operate an enterprise. Capital is needed to start a business and to keep the business operating and growing. Imperial's annual drilling costs alone run into the millions of dollars. A major source of capital for most businesses is personal investment by owners. Personal investment can be made either by the individual entrepreneurs or partners who start businesses or by investors who buy stock in them. Revenues from the sale of products, of course, is another and important ongoing source of capital. Finally, many firms borrow funds from banks and other lending institutions.

Entrepreneurs are those people who accept the opportunities and risks involved in creating and operating businesses. They are the people who start new businesses and who make the decisions that allow small businesses to grow into larger ones. Conrad Black and Jimmy Pattison are well-known Canadian entrepreneurs.

Land, water, mineral deposits, and trees are good examples of **natural resources**. For example, Imperial makes use of a wide variety of natural resources. It obviously has vast quantities of crude oil to process each year. But Imperial also needs the land where the oil is located, as well as land for its refineries and pipelines.

While the production of tangible goods once dominated most economic systems, today **information resources** play a major role. Businesses themselves rely heavily on market forecasts, the specialized expertise and knowledge of people, and various forms of economic data for much of their work. Much of what they do results in either the creation of new information or the repackaging of existing information for new users and different audiences. AOL, for example, does not produce tangible products. Instead, it provides numerous online services for its millions of subscribers in exchange for monthly access fees. Essentially, then, AOL is in the information business.

labour
The mental and physical training and talents of people; sometimes called human resources.

capital
The funds needed to operate an enterprise.

Imperial Oil
www.imperialoil.ca

entrepreneur
An individual who organizes and manages labour, capital, and natural resources to produce goods and services to earn a profit, but who also runs the risk of failure.

natural resources
Items used in the production of goods and services in their natural state, including land, water, mineral deposits, and trees.

information resources
Information such as market forecasts, economic data, and specialized knowledge of employees that is useful to a business and that helps it achieve its goals.

Types of Economic Systems

Different types of economic systems manage the factors of production in different ways. In some systems, ownership is private; in others, the government owns the factors of production. Economic systems also differ in the way that decisions are made about production and allocation. A **command economy**, for example, relies on a centralized government to control all or most factors of production and to make all or most production and allocation decisions. In **market economies**, individuals—producers and consumers—control production and allocation decisions through supply and demand. We will describe each of these economic types and then discuss the reality of the *mixed market economy*.

command economy
An economic system in which government controls all or most factors of production and makes all or most production decisions.

market economy
An economic system in which individuals control all or most factors of production and make all or most production decisions.

Command Economies

The two most basic forms of command economies are communism and socialism. As originally proposed by the nineteenth-century German economist Karl Marx, **communism** is a system in which the government owns and operates all sources of production. Marx envisioned a society in which individuals would ultimately contribute according to their abilities and receive economic benefits according to their needs. He also expected government ownership of production factors to be only temporary: Once society had matured, government would "wither away" and the workers would gain direct ownership.

communism
A type of command economy in which the government owns and operates all industries.

Most Eastern European countries and the former Soviet Union embraced communist systems until very recently. During the early 1990s, however, one country after another renounced communism as both an economic and a political system. Today, Cuba, North Korea, Vietnam, and the People's Republic of China are among the few nations with avowedly communist systems. Even in these countries, however, command economic systems are making room for features of the free-enterprise system from the lowest to the highest levels.

In Cuba, for example, a variety of free-market activities are evident, even though they are technically illegal. Special shops that once were reserved for diplomats now sell goods to Cubans from all walks of life. These stores are surrounded by paid bicycle parking lots, car washes, and stalls selling homegrown produce and homemade handicrafts. This street-corner commerce reflects a rapid growth in private enterprise as a solution to problems that Cuba's centralized economy has long been unable to solve.[3]

China is another country where dramatic changes are taking place. Prior to 1979, people who sold watches on street corners were sentenced to years of hard labour. But in 1999, China's constitution was amended to elevate private enterprise to a place alongside the state sector in China's official economic ideology. The private sector in China now generates more than one-third of the country's gross domestic product.[4]

socialism
A kind of command economy in which the government owns and operates the main industries, while individuals own and operate less crucial industries.

In a less extensive command economic system called **socialism**, the government owns and operates only selected major industries. Smaller businesses such as clothing stores and restaurants may be privately owned. Although workers in socialist countries are usually allowed to choose their occupations or professions, a large proportion generally works for the government. Many government-operated enterprises are inefficient, since management positions are frequently filled based on political considerations rather than on ability. Extensive public welfare systems have also resulted in very high taxes. Because of these factors, socialism is generally declining in popularity.[5]

In Israel, even the kibbutz concept is being questioned. In a kibbutz, members contribute their services in producing goods and then share equally in the resources that are generated. The emphasis is on teamwork and absolute equality. But at Kibbutz Ein Ziwan, a monument to socialist values, several historic practices (communal cars, central dining facilities) have been abandoned because they are no longer affordable. In addition, the kibbutz will soon take a dramatic step: paying people based on how productive they are, rather than on the equal-sharing basis of the past. Other kibbutzim are also considering taking this step.[6]

Market Economies

A *market* is a mechanism for exchange between the buyers and sellers of a particular good or service. To understand how a *market economy* works, consider what happens when a customer goes to a fruit stand to buy apples. Let's say that while one vendor is selling apples for $1 per kilogram, another is charging $1.50. Both vendors are free to charge what they want, and customers are free to buy what they choose. If both vendors' apples are of the same quality, the customer will buy the cheaper ones. But if the $1.50 apples are fresher, the customer may buy them instead. In short, both buyers and sellers enjoy freedom of choice. The "It's a Wired World" box describes B2B in several industries.

Input and Output Markets.   Figure 1.2 provides a useful and more complete model for better understanding how the factors of production work in a pure market economy. According to this view, businesses and

While we can identify different types of economies, the distinctions between them are becoming increasingly blurred. Previous command economies in Eastern Europe, for example, are moving towards a market system. The woman shown here is selling decorated eggs on the street. China still uses a command economy, but more and more elements of capitalism are becoming evident. In Canada, capitalism has always allowed farmers to decide what they would grow and how much to sell it for. Of course, capitalists aren't protected from failure, a concern that people in command economies seldom have to confront.

households interact in two different market relationships.[7] In the **input market**, firms buy resources from households, which obviously then supply those resources. In the **output market**, firms supply goods and services in response to demand on the part of households. (We will provide a more detailed discussion of supply and demand later in this chapter.)

As you can see in Figure 1.2, the activities of these two markets create a circular flow. Ford Motor Co., for example, relies on various kinds of inputs. It buys labour directly from households, which may also supply capital from accumulated savings in the form of stock purchases. Consumer buying patterns provide information that help Ford decide which models to produce and which to discontinue. In turn, Ford uses these inputs in various ways and becomes a supplier to households when it designs and produces various kinds of automobiles, trucks, and sports utility vehicles and offers them for sale to consumers.

Individuals, meanwhile, are free to work for Ford or an alternative employer and to invest in Ford stock or alternative forms of saving or consumption. Similarly, Ford, can create whatever vehicles it chooses and price them at whatever value it chooses. But consumers are then free to buy their next car from Ford or Toyota or BMW. This process contrasts markedly with that of a planned economy, in which individuals may be told where they can and cannot

input market
Firms buy resources that they need in the production of goods and services.

output market
Firms supply goods and services in response to demand on the part of consumers.

Ford
www.ford.ca

IT'S A WIRED WORLD

Jumping on the B2B Bandwagon

A new term—B2B—has become popular in strategic business thinking. B2B stands for business-to-business electronic commerce. It involves businesses joining together to create e-commerce companies that make them more efficient when they purchase the goods and services they need.

When people talk about e-commerce, they usually think of business-to-consumer (B2C) transactions such as buying books over the Internet for personal use. These transactions are obviously important, but B2B transactions far exceed B2C transactions in dollar value. International Data Corp. Canada Ltd. (IDC) predicts that the value of B2B transactions in Canada will total $129 billion by 2004, while the value of B2C transactions will total only $19 billion. Dollar values in both of those categories are up sharply from the late 1990s. Worldwide, the numbers are even more staggering: B2B transactions are predicted to be about $2.2 trillion by 2004, while B2C transactions will total about $200 billion.

All of this B2B activity is good news for consumers, because businesses will become more efficient in their supply chain purchasing, which will allow them to reduce their costs. That, in turn, will allow them to reduce prices.

A good example of this trend is the recently announced partnership among some of the world's largest automobile manufacturers. It all started when various individual automakers began to create their own global purchasing Web sites. Ford Motor Co., for example, planned a site called Auto-Xchange. The company intended to post all of its global procurement needs on the site, and request that its suppliers post availability and prices for parts and equipment.

When it became apparent that other automakers were planning to do the same thing, major suppliers to the auto industry realized that they might soon be facing an unwieldy array of separate Web sites for each company—a situation that would potentially increase rather than reduce their own costs. Thus, a coalition of the largest suppliers approached Ford and General Motors with a novel proposal: Why not team up to create a single site that could be used by both automakers and their suppliers?

Ford and GM executives quickly saw the wisdom of this idea and then convinced DaimlerChrysler to join them.

Now the three companies plan to establish a single Web site to serve as a marketplace for all interested automobile manufacturers, suppliers, and dealers—essentially, a global virtual market including all firms in the industry. Almost immediately, France's Renault and Japan's Nissan, which is controlled by Renault, indicated a desire to join; Toyota also indicated strong interest. In addition, both Ford and GM indicated that they would encourage their foreign affiliates and strategic partners to participate as well. The partners who are building the Web site intend to establish it as a self-contained organization that will eventually offer shares to the public.

Many experts believe that the impact of this global electronic market will be tremendous. For example, it currently costs GM about $100 in ordering costs to buy parts or supplies in the traditional way—on paper, over the telephone, etc. But the firm estimates that its ordering costs will drop to less than $10 under the new system. Clearly, then, the automakers will realize substantial cost savings. Suppliers, too, will benefit in various ways. Besides having more information about the immediate needs of different customers, they will be able to buy and sell among themselves.

Companies in other industries are also jumping on the B2B bandwagon:

- In April 2000, six of the world's largest airlines joined forces to create an e-commerce company that connects them to their suppliers through a single Internet portal. The online company will handle the $32 billion in purchases the six airlines make annually in areas such as fuel, equipment, aircraft parts, and maintenance. The arrangement will lower transaction, processing, and inventory costs.

- Companies in the oil and chemical industry launched an electronic procurement exchange that will spend more than US$125 billion annually.

- A group of the world's largest defence contractors launched a company that will facilitate annual purchases of about $71 billion. The company will link 37 000 businesses.

- In September 2000, Bell Canada, the Canadian Imperial Bank of Commerce, the Bank of Nova Scotia, and Mouvement Desjardins announced that they were forming an e-commerce joint venture to help themselves and businesses cut purchasing costs.

work, companies are told what they can and cannot manufacture, and consumers may have little or no choice as to what they purchase or how much they pay for items. The economic basis of market processes is the law of demand and supply; the political basis is called *capitalism,* which we discuss next.

capitalism
An economic system in which markets decide what, when, and for whom to produce.

Capitalism.   **Capitalism** provides for the private ownership of the factors of production. It also encourages entrepreneurship by offering profits as

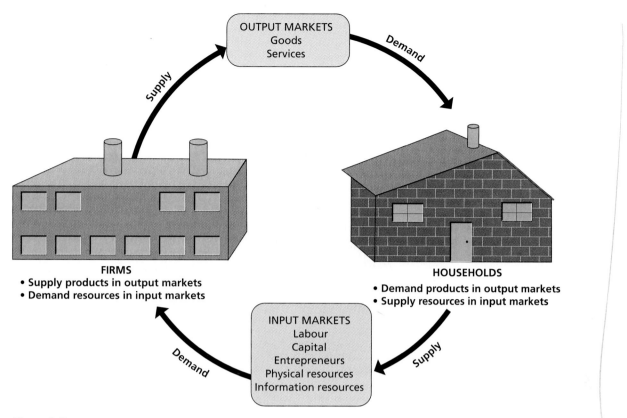

Figure 1.2
Circular flow in a market economy.

an incentive. Businesses can provide whatever goods and services they wish, and they can charge whatever prices they choose. Similarly, customers can choose how and where to spend their money. Consider, for example, the case of Intershop, a highly successful German start-up company. The firm, founded by three friends, buys and installs personal computers and software for individual consumers. It has also recently branched into numerous other forms of e-commerce and is quickly becoming a player in the global economy. But what really sets Intershop apart is the fact that it was started in *East* Germany. Formerly part of a rigid command economy, this area is now blossoming under the market system of unified Germany.[8]

Intershop
www.intershop.com

Mixed Market Economies

In their pure theoretical forms, command and market economies are often viewed as two extremes or opposites. In reality, however, most countries rely on some form of **mixed market economy**—a system featuring characteristics of both command and market economies. For example, most countries of the former Eastern bloc are now adopting market mechanisms through a process called **privatization**—the process of converting government enterprises into privately owned companies. In recent years this practice has also begun to spread to many other countries as well. For example, the postal system in most countries is government-owned and -managed, regardless of whether the country has a command or market economy. The Netherlands, however, recently began the process of privatizing its TNT Post Group N.V., already among the world's most efficient post office operations. Similarly, Canada has recently privatized its air traffic control system. In each case, the new enterprise reduced its payroll, boosted efficiency and productivity, and quickly became profitable.[9]

mixed market economy

An economic system with elements of both a command economy and a market economy; in practice, typical of most nations' economies.

privatization

The transfer of activities from the government to the public sector.

According to the model of circular flow in a market economy, this German Wal-Mart shopper plays a role in the *output market*: she demands goods that are supplied by a firm in the retailing business. Think of the German farmers from whom Wal-Mart buys the produce shown here as *households* that supply the input market with labour, time, skills, and investment in land.

CANADA'S MIXED ECONOMIC SYSTEM

In Canada's mixed economic system, there are many important interactions between business and government. The ways in which government influences business and business influences government are described below.

How Government Influences Business

Government plays several different roles in the Canadian economy, and each of these roles influences business activity in some way. As the "Business Today" box demonstrates, sometimes business people feel that government is unfair in the way it performs some of its roles. The roles government plays are as follows:

Government as a Customer

Government buys thousands of different products and services from business firms, including office supplies, office buildings, computers, battleships, helicopters, highways, water treatment plants, and management and engineering consulting services. Many businesses depend on government purchasing, if not for their survival at least for a certain level of prosperity. Government expenditures on goods and services amount to billions of dollars each year.

Government as a Competitor

Government also competes with business through Crown corporations, which are accountable to a minister of parliament for their conduct. Crown corporations exist at both the provincial and federal level, and account for a significant and wide variety of economic activity in Canada (see Table 1.1).

Government as a Regulator

Despite the move towards deregulation, federal and provincial governments in Canada still regulate many aspects of business activity. Government regulates business through many administrative boards, tribunals, or commissions. At the federal level, examples include the **Canadian Radio-television and Telecommunications Commission (CRTC)** (which issues and renews broadcast licences), the **Canadian Transport Commission (CTC)**

Canadian Radio-television and Telecommunications Commission (CRTC)
Regulates and supervises all aspects of the Canadian broadcasting system.

Canadian Transport Commission (CTC)
Makes decisions about route and rate applications for commercial air and railway companies.

BUSINESS TODAY

Business–Government Relations Gone Sour

Although government involvement in the Canadian economy is supposed to create a stable economic environment and level playing field, in the minds of some people it doesn't always work out that way. Consider the case of Gabe Magnotta, CEO of Magnotta Winery Corp., the third-largest vintner in Ontario. The company has achieved its status despite the fact that its products are shut out of the 600 provincially owned and operated liquor stores of the Liquor Control Board of Ontario (LCBO).

Against all odds, Magnotta's winery has flourished outside of the LCBO's rigidly controlled network. Magnotta is battling to succeed in an environment in which his competitor is also his regulator, and he doesn't think the playing field is level.

The story began in 1989 when Charal Winer Osterman Estates Inc. was put up for sale. It had both a coveted manufacturing licence and a retail permit to sell wine. Magnotta bought the company for $250 000 and changed its name to Magnotta Winery Estates. He claims that the LCBO assured him it would allow his newly named company to sell wine in provincial stores. However, when he tried to ship his first batch of wine, the stores told him there was no room for it on their shelves.

Magnotta decided that he had no alternative but to sell his wine at his own on-site store at the vineyard. Since he was not part of the LCBO system, he was free to set his own prices. He decided to charge $3.95 for a 750-ml bottle, undercutting the LCBO's price of $5.15.

Consumers immediately liked Magnotta's wines and his prices. Soon he was selling 10 000 cases per month. Positive word of mouth and press coverage helped, and sales continued to increase. The LCBO wasn't happy with this situation, because every bottle Magnotta sold was a bottle it did not. It invoked a rule known as "non-discriminatory ref-

erence price" (NDRP), which prohibited Magnotta from selling his products for less than the cheapest wine carried in an LCBO store. The LCBO argued that the rule was designed to discourage the sale of really inexpensive wine, which some people feel promotes irresponsible drinking behaviour. But a Mackenzie Institute report claimed that the LCBO's policy of higher prices was actually causing a black market for wine to develop.

In 1997, the LCBO introduced a promotion in which customers could buy a bottle of wine for $4.58 per bottle as long as they bought a minimum of 12 bottles. When Magnotta heard about this, he reduced the price of his wine to $4.58 per bottle. The LCBO promptly told him he couldn't do that because the LCBO had set a reduced price only for wine sold by the LCBO. This led one commentator to conclude that the LCBO was exempting itself from its own policy.

Magnotta has spent over $500 000 in legal fees fighting the LCBO. He argues that the LCBO is using its regulatory power to boost its competitive position, and that that is improper. He also states that the LCBO makes up the rules as it goes along. His contention seems to be supported by a report from the Ontario Law Reform Commission, which said that the LCBO should codify its policies to ensure consistency. (In July 2000, the province of Ontario stripped its government-owned liquor stores of their regulatory status to make competition fairer.)

The same sort of dispute is evident in Manitoba, where 6 privately owned wine stores sell over half the wine sold in Winnipeg, while 22 Manitoba Liquor Control Commission (MLCC) stores sell the rest. A Probe Research poll showed that 90 percent of Winnipeggers don't want the province to phase out private wine stores. More than half of those polled said that private wine stores have forced the MLCC stores to improve their service. The private wine sellers in Manitoba say the same thing that Magnotti says: the MLCC is in a conflict of interest because it has the power to regulate its competitors.

(which makes decisions about route and rate applications for commercial air and railway companies), and the **Canadian Wheat Board** (which regulates the prices of wheat). Provincial boards and commissions also regulate business through their decisions.

There are several important reasons for regulating business activity. These include protecting competition, protecting consumers, achieving social goals, and protecting the environment.

Canadian Wheat Board
A Crown corporation that regulates the price farmers receive for their wheat.

Table 1.1	The Top 10 Crown Corporations in Canada (ranked by revenues)

Company	Annual Revenues (in billions)
1. Caisse de dépôt et placement du Québec	$11.2
2. Hydro-Québec	9.5
3. Canada Post Corp.	5.3
4. Ontario Power Generation Inc.	4.3
5. The Canadian Wheat Board	4.0
6. Loto-Canada	3.1
7. British Columbia Hydro and Power Authority	3.0
8. Liquor Control Board of Ontario	2.3
9. Ontario Lottery Corp.	2.1
10. Bank of Canada	1.9

Hazardous Products Act
Regulates banned products and products that can be sold but must be labelled hazardous.

Tobacco Act
Prohibits cigarette advertising on billboards in retail stores, and assigns financial penalties to violators.

Weights and Measures Act
Sets standards of accuracy for weighing and measuring devices.

Textile Labelling Act
Regulates the labelling, sale, importation, and advertising of consumer textile articles.

Food and Drug Act
Prohibits the sale of food unfit for human consumption and regulates food advertising.

Canada Water Act
Controls water quality in fresh and marine waters of Canada.

Fisheries Act
Regulates the discharge of harmful substances into water.

Environmental Contaminants Act
Establishes regulations for airborne substances that are a danger to human health or to the environment.

deregulation
A reduction in the number of laws affecting business activity.

One of the reasons that government regulates business is to ensure that healthy competition exists among business firms, because competition is crucial to a market economy. Without restrictions, a large company with vast resources could cut its prices and drive smaller firms out of the market. In 1999, five international drug companies were fined $88.4 million for price fixing in the food additives and vitamins market. In 2000, both WestJet Airlines and CanJet Airlines filed complaints with the Competition Bureau, claiming that Air Canada was engaging in predatory pricing on routes that the two airlines were flying.[10]

Competition policy tries to eliminate restrictive trade practices and thereby stimulate maximum production, distribution, and employment. The guidelines for Canada's competition policy are contained in *The Competition Act* (see Table 1.2).

Protecting consumers is another reason for government regulation of business. The government has initiated many programs that protect consumers. Consumer and Corporate Affairs Canada administers many of these. Important legislation includes the **Hazardous Products Act** (which requires poisonous, flammable, explosive or corrosive products to be appropriately labelled), the **Tobacco Act** (which prohibits cigarette advertising on billboards and in stores), the **Weights and Measures Act** (which sets standards of accuracy for weighing and measuring devices), the **Textile Labelling Act** (which regulates the labelling, sale, importation, and advertising of consumer textile articles), and the **Food and Drug Act** (which prohibits the sale of food that contains any poisonous or harmful substances).

A third reason for regulation is the achievement of social goals, because these goals promote the well-being of our society. Social goals include universal access to health care, safe workplaces, employment insurance, and decent pensions. All of these goals require the interaction of business firms and government.

A final reason for regulation is to protect the environment. Here again, government legislation is important. Laws include the **Canada Water Act** (which controls water quality in fresh and marine waters), the **Fisheries Act** (which controls the discharge of any harmful substance into water), and the **Environmental Contaminants Act** (which establishes regulations for airborne substances that are a danger to human health or the environment).

In spite of all these regulations, there is actually a strong move towards **deregulation**—a reduction in the number of laws affecting business activity. Deregulation is evident in many industries, including airlines, pipelines, banking, trucking, and communications.

Table 1.2	The Competition Act

Section 32   Prohibits conspiracies and combinations formed for the purpose of unduly lessening competition in the production, transportation, or storage of goods. Persons convicted may be imprisoned for up to five years or fined up to $1 million or both.

Section 33   Prohibits mergers and monopolies that substantially lessen competition. Individuals who assist in the formation of such a monopoly or merger may be imprisoned for up to two years.

Section 34   Prohibits illegal trade practices. A company may not, for example, cut prices in one region of Canada while selling at a higher price everywhere else if this substantially lessens competition. A company may not sell at "unreasonably low prices" if this substantially lessens competition. (This section does not prohibit credit unions from returning surpluses to their members.)

Section 35   Prohibits giving allowances and rebates to buyers to cover their advertising expenses, unless these allowances are made available proportionally to other purchasers who are in competition with the buyer given the rebate.

Section 36   Prohibits misleading advertising including (1) false statements about the performance of a product, (2) misleading guarantees, (3) pyramid selling, (4) charging the higher price when two prices are marked on an item, and (5) referral selling.

Section 37   Prohibits bait-and-switch selling. No person can advertise a product at a bargain price if there is no supply of the product available to the consumer. (This tactic baits prospects into the store, where salespeople switch them to higher-priced goods.) This section also controls the use of contests to sell goods, and prohibits the sale of goods at a price higher than the advertised one.

Section 38   Prohibits resale price maintenance. No person who produces or supplies a product can attempt to influence upward, or discourage reduction of, the price of the good in question. It is also illegal for the producer to refuse to supply a product to a reseller simply because the producer believes the reseller will cut the price.

Government as a Taxation Agent

Taxes are imposed and collected by federal, provincial, and local governments. **Revenue taxes** (e.g., income taxes) are levied by governments primarily to provide revenue to fund various services and programs. **Progressive revenue taxes** are levied at a higher rate on higher-income taxpayers and at a lower rate on lower-income taxpayers. **Regressive revenue taxes** (e.g., sales tax) are levied at the same rate regardless of a person's income. They cause poorer people to pay a higher percentage of their income for these taxes than rich people pay. **Restrictive taxes** (e.g., taxes on alcohol, tobacco, and gasoline) are levied partially for the revenue they provide, but also because legislative bodies believe that the products in question should be controlled.

revenue taxes *(income tax)*
Taxes whose main purpose is to fund government services and programs.

progressive revenue taxes
Taxes levied at a higher rate on higher-income taxpayers and at a lower rate on lower-income taxpayers.

regressive revenue taxes *(sales tax)*
Taxes that cause poorer people to pay a higher percentage of income than richer people pay.

restrictive taxes
Taxes levied to control certain activities that legislators believe should be controlled.

Government as a Provider of Incentives

Federal, provincial, and municipal governments offer incentive programs that help stimulate economic development. In Quebec, for example, Hyundai Motors received $6.4 million to build a production facility and an additional $682 000 to train workers. Both Toyota and Hyundai have received millions of dollar in incentives from government in the form of training incentives, interest-free loans, and the suspension of custom duties.[11]

Governments also offer incentives through the many services they provide to business firms through government organizations. These include the Export Development Corporation (which assists Canadian exporters by offering export insurance against nonpayment by foreign buyers and long-term loans to foreign buyers of Canadian products), Energy, Mines and Resources Canada (which provides geological maps of Canada's potential mineral-producing areas), and Statistics Canada (which provides data and analysis on almost every aspect of Canadian society).

There are many other government incentive programs, including municipal tax rebates for companies that locate in certain areas, design assistance programs, and remission of tariffs on certain advanced technology production equipment. Government incentive programs may or may not have the desired effect of stimulating the economy.

Government as a Provider of Essential Services

The federal, provincial, and municipal governments facilitate business activity through the wide variety of services they supply. The federal government provides highways, the postal service, the minting of money, the armed forces, and statistical data on which to base business decisions. It also tries to maintain stability through fiscal and monetary policy.

Provincial and municipal governments provide streets, sewage and sanitation systems, police and fire departments, utilities, hospitals, and education. All of these activities create the kind of stability that encourages business activity.

How Business Influences Government

While government activity influences what businesses do, businesses also influence the government through lobbyists, trade associations, and advertising (see Figure 1.3). A **lobbyist** is a person hired by a company or industry to represent its interests with government officials. The Canadian Association of Consulting Engineers, for example, regularly lobbies the federal and provincial governments to make use of the skills possessed by private sector consulting engineers on projects like city water systems. Some business lobbyists have training in the particular industry, public relations experience, or a legal background. A few have served as legislators or government regulators.

The *Lobbyists Registration Act* came into effect in 1989. Lobbyists must register with the Registrar of Lobbyists so that it is clear which individuals are being paid for their lobbying activity. For many lobbying efforts, there are opposing points of view. The Canadian Cancer Society and the Tobacco Institute present very different points of view on cigarette smoking and cigarette advertising.

Employees and owners of small businesses that cannot afford lobbyists often join **trade associations**. Trade associations may act as an industry lobby to influence legislation. They also conduct training programs relevant to the particular industry, and they arrange trade shows at which members display their products or services to potential customers. Most publish newsletters featuring articles on new products, new companies, changes in ownership, and changes in laws affecting the industry.

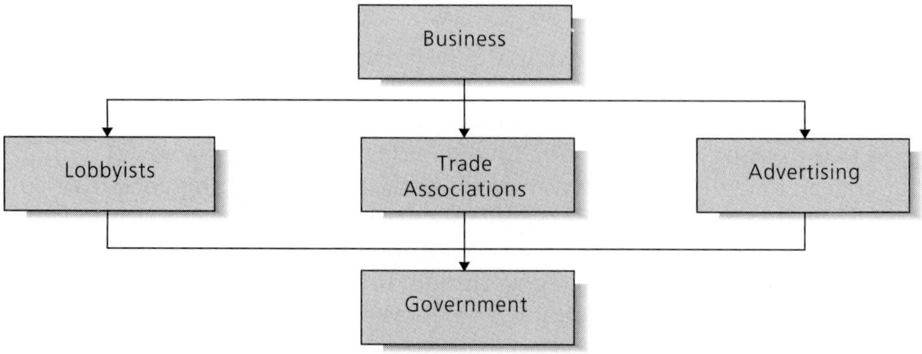

lobbyist

A person hired by a company or an industry to represent its interests with government officials.

trade association

An organization dedicated to promoting the interests and assisting the members of a particular industry.

Figure 1.3
Business influences the government in a variety of ways.

Corporations can influence legislation indirectly by influencing voters. A company can, for example, launch an advertising campaign designed to get people to write their MPs, MPPs, or MLAs demanding passage—or rejection—of a particular bill that is before parliament or the provincial legislature.

THE CANADIAN MARKET ECONOMY

Understanding the complex nature of the Canadian economic system is essential to understanding Canadian businesses. In the next few pages, we will examine the workings of our market economy in more detail. Specifically, we look at markets, demand, supply, the business cycle, private enterprise, and degrees of competition.

Markets, Demand, and Supply

In economic terms, a **market** is not a specific place, such as a supermarket, but an exchange process between buyers and sellers. Decisions about production in a market economy are the result of millions of exchanges. How much of what product a company offers for sale and who buys it depend on the laws of demand and supply.

market
An exchange process between buyers and sellers of a particular good or service.

The Laws of Demand and Supply

On all economic levels, decisions about what to buy and what to sell are determined primarily by the forces of demand and supply.[12] **Demand** is the willingness and ability of buyers to purchase a product (a good or a service). **Supply** is the willingness and ability of producers to offer a good or service for sale. Generally speaking, demand and supply follow basic "laws":

- The **law of demand**: Buyers will purchase (demand) more of a product as its price drops and less of a product as its price increases.

- The **law of supply**: Producers will offer (supply) more of a product for sale as its price rises and less as its price drops.

demand
The willingness and ability of buyers to purchase a product or service.

supply
The willingness and ability of producers to offer a good or service for sale.

law of demand
The principle that buyers will purchase (demand) more of a product as price drops.

law of supply
The principle that producers will offer (supply) more of a product as price rises.

The Demand and Supply Schedule. To appreciate these laws in action, consider the market for pizza in your town. If everyone in town is willing to pay $25 for a pizza (a high price), the town's only pizzeria will produce a large supply. If everyone is willing to pay only $5 (a low price), however, the restaurant will make fewer pizzas. Through careful analysis, we can determine how many pizzas will be sold at different prices. These results, called a **demand and supply schedule**, are obtained from marketing research and other systematic studies of the market. Properly applied, they help managers better understand the relationships among different levels of demand and supply at different price levels.

demand and supply schedule
Assessment of the relationships between different levels of demand and supply at different price levels.

Demand and Supply Curves. The demand and supply schedule, for example, can be used to construct demand and supply curves for pizza in your town. A **demand curve** shows how many products—in this case, pizzas—will be *demanded* (bought) at different prices. A **supply curve** shows how many pizzas will be *supplied* (cooked) at different prices.

Figure 1.4 shows hypothetical demand and supply curves for pizzas. As you can see, demand increases as price decreases; supply increases as price increases. When the demand and supply curves are plotted on the same graph, the point at which they intersect is the **market price** or **equilibrium price**—the price at which the quantity of goods demanded and the quantity of goods

demand curve
Graph showing how many units of a product will be demanded (bought) at different prices.

supply curve
Graph showing how many units of a product will be supplied (offered for sale) at different prices.

market price (or equilibrium price)
Profit-maximizing price at which the quantity of goods demanded and the quantity of goods supplied are equal.

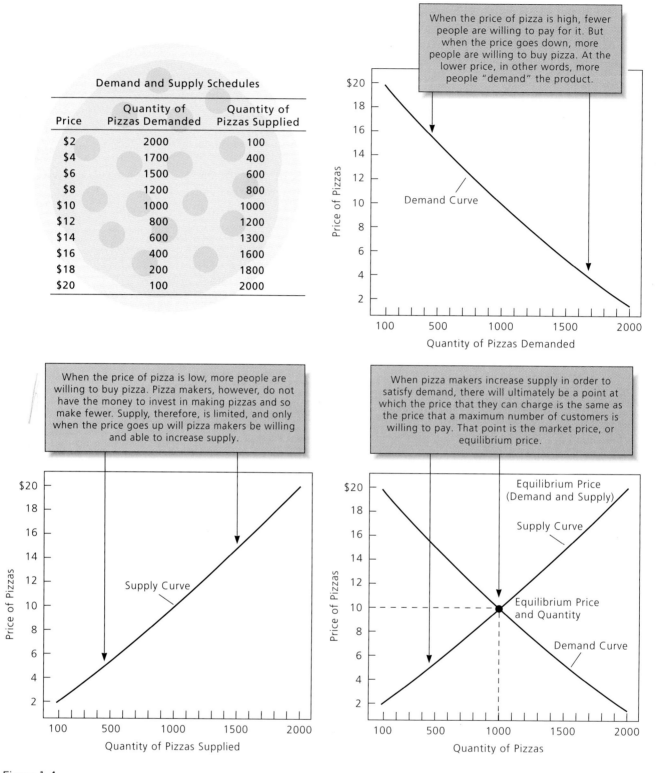

Demand and Supply Schedules		
Price	Quantity of Pizzas Demanded	Quantity of Pizzas Supplied
$2	2000	100
$4	1700	400
$6	1500	600
$8	1200	800
$10	1000	1000
$12	800	1200
$14	600	1300
$16	400	1600
$18	200	1800
$20	100	2000

When the price of pizza is high, fewer people are willing to pay for it. But when the price goes down, more people are willing to buy pizza. At the lower price, in other words, more people "demand" the product.

When the price of pizza is low, more people are willing to buy pizza. Pizza makers, however, do not have the money to invest in making pizzas and so make fewer. Supply, therefore, is limited, and only when the price goes up will pizza makers be willing and able to increase supply.

When pizza makers increase supply in order to satisfy demand, there will ultimately be a point at which the price that they can charge is the same as the price that a maximum number of customers is willing to pay. That point is the market price, or equilibrium price.

Figure 1.4
Demand and supply.

supplied are equal. Note in Figure 1.4 that the equilibrium price for pizzas in our example is $10. At this point, the quantity of pizzas demanded and the quantity of pizzas supplied are the same: 1000 pizzas per week.

Surpluses and Shortages. But what if the restaurant chooses to make some other number of pizzas? For example, what would happen if the owner tried to increase profits by making more pizzas to sell? Or what if the owner wanted to reduce overhead, cut back on store hours, and reduce the number of pizzas offered for sale? In either case, the result would be an inefficient use of resources—and perhaps lower profits. For example, if the restaurant supplies 1200 pizzas and tries to sell them for $10 each, 200 pizzas will not be purchased. The demand schedule clearly shows that only 1000 pizzas will be demanded at this price. The pizza maker will have a **surplus**—a situation in which the quantity supplied exceeds the quantity demanded. The restaurant will thus lose the money it spent making those extra 200 pizzas.

Conversely, if the pizzeria supplies only 800 pizzas, a **shortage** will result: the quantity demanded will be greater than the quantity supplied. The pizzeria will "lose" the extra money that it could have made by producing 200 more pizzas. Even though consumers may pay more for pizzas because of the shortage, the restaurant will still earn lower profits than it would have if it had made 1000 pizzas. In addition, it will risk angering customers who cannot buy pizzas. To optimize profits, therefore, all businesses must constantly seek the right combination of the price charged and the quantity supplied. This "right combination" is found at the equilibrium point.

This simple example, of course, involves only one company, one product, and a few buyers. The Canadian economy is far more complex. Thousands of companies sell hundreds of thousands of products to millions of buyers every day. In the end, however, the result is much the same: companies try to supply the quantity and selection of goods that will earn them the largest profits.

surplus
Situation in which quantity supplied exceeds quantity demanded.

shortage
Situation in which quantity demanded exceeds quantity supplied.

The Business Cycle

The **business cycle** is the fluctuation in the level of economic activity that an economy goes through over time (see Figure 1.5). It has four recognizable phases: peak, recession, trough, and recovery. Periods of expansion and contraction can vary from several months to several years. The

business cycle
The fluctuation in the level of economic activity that an economy goes through over time.

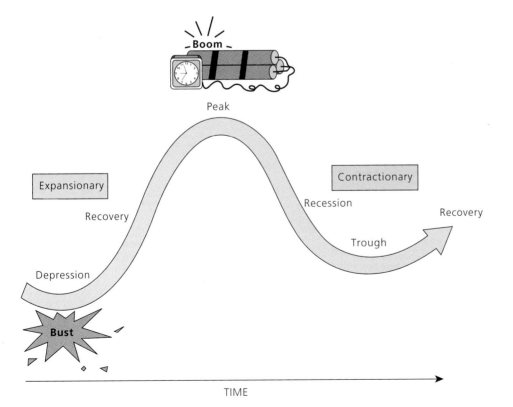

Figure 1.5
The business cycle.

1990s showed sustained expansion in the economy, leading some to believe that the ups and downs of the business cycle could be avoided. But by the end of 2000, warning signs were starting to appear that signalled an end to the boom times. Government and business leaders hoped for a "soft landing," that is, a decline in business activity that was not so bad that a recession occurred.

The belief that the business cycle could be avoided was particularly evident among investors in high-tech stocks. They accepted a number of myths: that tech companies could generate huge gains in earnings for years to come, that tech companies weren't subject to normal economic forces, that exponential Internet growth could be sustained, and that future prospects were more important than current earnings.[13] These myths were demonstrated as tech stocks crashed and economic growth slowed in 2000.

Private Enterprise

private enterprise
An economic system characterized by private property rights, freedom of choice, profits, and competition.

In his book *The Wealth of Nations,* first published in 1776, economist Adam Smith argued that a society's interests are best served by **private enterprise**—allowing individuals within that society to pursue their own interests without governmental regulation or restriction. He believed that because of self-interests, the "invisible hand of competition" would lead businesses to produce the best products they could as efficiently as possible and to sell them at the lowest possible price. Each business would unintentionally be working for the good of society as a whole.

Market economies have prospered in large part due to private enterprise. As Adam Smith first noted, private enterprise requires the presence of four elements: (1) private property rights, (2) freedom of choice, (3) profits, and (4) competition.[14] These elements are shown in Figure 1.6.

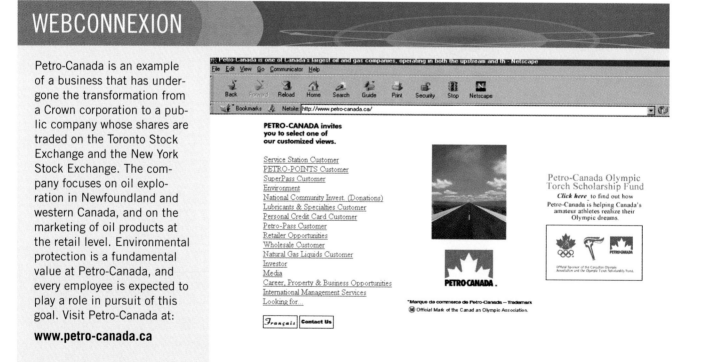

WEBCONNEXION

Petro-Canada is an example of a business that has undergone the transformation from a Crown corporation to a public company whose shares are traded on the Toronto Stock Exchange and the New York Stock Exchange. The company focuses on oil exploration in Newfoundland and western Canada, and on the marketing of oil products at the retail level. Environmental protection is a fundamental value at Petro-Canada, and every employee is expected to play a role in pursuit of this goal. Visit Petro-Canada at:

www.petro-canada.ca

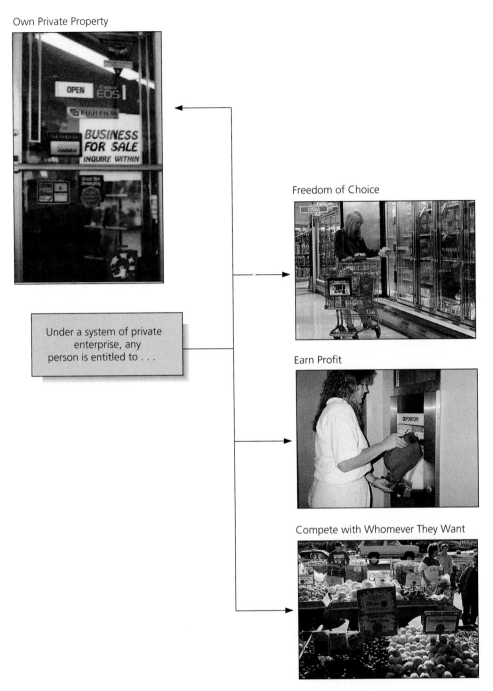

Own Private Property

Under a system of private enterprise, any person is entitled to . . .

Freedom of Choice

Earn Profit

Compete with Whomever They Want

Figure 1.6
A free enterprise system is based on four basic elements. In such a system, all people are entitled to own private property, to choose what to buy or sell, to earn profit, and to compete with whomever they want.

Private Property

Smith maintained that the creation of wealth should be the concern of individuals, not the government. Thus, he argued that the ownership of the resources used to create wealth must be in the hands of individuals, not the government. Individual ownership of property is part of everyday life in Canada. You or someone you know has bought and owned automobiles, homes, land, or stock. The right to **private property**—to buy, own, use, and sell almost any form of property—is one of the most fundamental aspects of capitalism. Most of us take private property for granted. Yet, in some countries you could not own a business even if you had the money to pay for it in cash.

private property
The right to buy, own, use, and sell an item.

Freedom of Choice

Freedom of choice means that you can try to sell your labour to whomever you choose. You can also choose which products to buy. Freedom of choice further means that producers of goods and services can usually choose whom to hire and what to make. The Canadian government, for example, normally does not tell The Bay what it can and cannot sell. We noted earlier the success being enjoyed by Intershop in Germany. A few years ago its founders would not have been permitted to launch such a business. In fact, the communist regime of East Germany had not even allowed Intershop's co-founder, Stephan Schambach, to study computers as he had wanted. But when the Soviet bloc collapsed and East Germany and West Germany were reunified, everything changed. "I had a choice," explains Schambach, whose start-up is now valued at $1.4 billion on Germany's equivalent of NASDAQ.[15]

Profits

What a company chooses to produce will, by definition, be affected by the *profits* it hopes to make. A business that fails to make a profit must eventually close its doors. The majority of small businesses fail within the first five years of their existence.[16] But the lure of profits leads some people to give up the security of working for someone else and assume the risks of entrepreneurship.

Competition

If profits motivate individuals to start businesses, competition motivates them to operate their businesses efficiently. **Competition** occurs when two or more businesses vie for the same resources or customers. For example, if you decide to buy a new pair of athletic shoes, you have a choice of several different stores in which to shop. After selecting a store, you may then choose between brands (for example, Nike, Reebok, or Adidas). If you intend to buy only one pair of shoes, these manufacturers are in competition with one another, as are all of the shoe retailers in your area, from mass marketers such as Sears to specialty outlets such as Foot Locker.

To gain an advantage over its competitors, a business must produce its goods or services efficiently and must be able to sell them at prices that earn reasonable profits. To achieve these goals, a business must convince customers that its products are either better than or less expensive than those of competitors. In this sense, competition benefits society: it forces all competitive businesses to make their products better or cheaper. Naturally, a company that produces inferior, expensive products is sure to be forced out of business.

Degrees of Competition

Not all industries are equally competitive. Economists have identified four basic degrees of competition within a private enterprise system—pure competition, monopolistic competition, oligopoly, and monopoly. Figure 1.7 illustrates these four degrees of competition.

Pure Competition

In order for **pure competition** to exist, firms must be small in size, but large in number. In such conditions, no firm is powerful enough individually to influence the price of its product in the marketplace.

First, in pure competition the products offered by each firm are so similar that buyers view them as identical to those offered by other firms. Second,

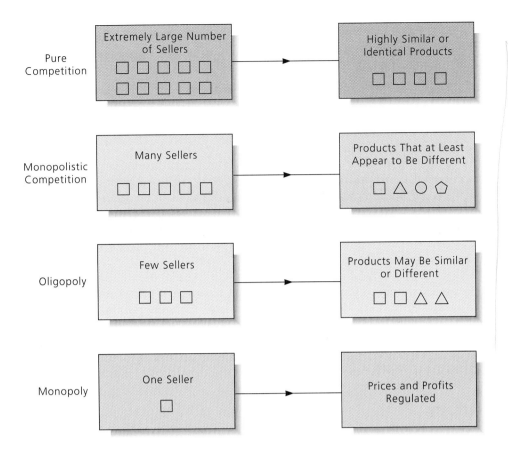

Figure 1.7
There are four basic degrees of competition in a private enterprise system.

both the buyers and the sellers know the price that others are paying and receiving in the marketplace. Third, the firms involved in a purely competitive situation are small, which makes it relatively easy for a firm to go into or out of business.

Under pure competition, price is set exclusively by supply and demand in the marketplace. Sellers and buyers must accept the going price. Despite some government price-support programs, agriculture is usually considered to be a good example of pure competition in the Canadian economy. The wheat produced on one farm is essentially the same as wheat produced on another farm. Both producers and buyers are well aware of prevailing market prices. Moreover, it is relatively easy to get started or to quit producing wheat.

Monopolistic Competition

In **monopolistic competition**, there are fewer sellers than in pure competition, but there are still many buyers. Sellers try to make their products at least appear to be slightly different from those of their competitors by tactics such as brand names (Tide and Cheer), design or styling (Ralph Lauren and Izod clothes), and advertising (as done by Coke and Pepsi).

Monopolistically competitive businesses may be large or small, because it is relatively easy for a firm to enter or leave the market. For example, many small clothing manufacturers compete successfully with large apparel makers. Product differentiation also gives sellers some control over the price they charge. Thus Ralph Lauren Polo shirts can be priced with little regard for the price of Eaton's shirts, even though the Eaton's shirts may have very similar styling.

monopolistic competition
A market or industry characterized by a large number of firms supplying products that are similar but distinctive enough from one another to give firms some ability to influence price.

Oligopoly

When an industry has only a handful of sellers, an **oligopoly** exists. As a general rule, these sellers are almost always very large. The entry of new competitors is restricted because a large capital investment is usually necessary to enter the industry. Consequently, oligopolistic industries—such as automobile, rubber, and steel—tend to remain oligopolistic. Other industries—music, semiconductors, pharmaceuticals, railroads, and soft drinks—are moving towards oligopoly.[17]

Oligopolists have even more control over their alternatives than do monopolistically competitive firms. However, the actions of any one firm in an oligopolistic market can significantly affect the sales of all other firms. When one reduces prices or offers some type of incentives to increase its sales, the others usually do the same to protect their sales. Likewise, when one raises its prices, the others generally follow suit. As a result, the prices of comparable products are usually quite similar.

Since substantial price competition would reduce every seller's profits, firms use product differentiation to attract customers. For example, the four major cereal makers (Kellogg, General Mills, General Foods, and Quaker Oats) control almost all of the cereal market. Each charges roughly the same price for its cereal as do the others. But each also advertises that its cereals are better tasting or more nutritious than the others.[18] Competition within an oligopolistic market can be fierce.

Monopoly

When an industry or market has only one producer, a **monopoly** exists. Being the only supplier gives a firm complete control over the price of its product. Its only constraint is how much consumer demand will fall as its price rises. Until 1992, the long-distance telephone business was a monopoly

Consumers often buy products under conditions of monopolistic competition. For example, there are few differences between different brands of toothpaste, cold tablets, detergents, canned goods, and soft drinks.

in Canada, and cable TV, which has had a local monopoly for years, will lose it when telephone companies and satellite broadcasters are allowed into the cable business.[19]

In Canada, laws such as the *Competition Act* forbid many monopolies. In addition, the prices charged by "natural monopolies" are closely watched by provincial utilities boards. **Natural monopolies** are industries in which one company can most efficiently supply all the product or service that is needed. For example, like most utilities, your provincial electric company is a natural monopoly because it can supply all the power (product) needed in an area. Duplicate facilities—such as two nuclear power plants, two sets of power lines, and so forth—would be wasteful.

A very high-profile legal battle began in 1998, when the U.S. government pursued a lawsuit against the software giant Microsoft, alleging practices designed to eliminate competition from firms such as Netscape and other software developers. Focusing on Microsoft's practices in the markets for Internet-browsing and Web-navigation software, the government charged that Microsoft's monopoly status (1) limited market entry for new competitors, (2) controlled channels of distribution, (3) inflated prices and restricted consumers' product choices, and (4) privileged it as the sole supplier of software to major computer manufacturers. Interestingly, while it may take years for the legal case to be settled, market forces have already altered Microsoft's competitive dominance. For example, new handheld devices such as Palm organizers are attracting some customers away from desktop software. In addition, the World Wide Web is becoming increasingly important, and firms like Sun Microsystems, America Online, and Yahoo! are already outpacing Microsoft in that arena. An alternative operating system called Linux is making significant inroads against Microsoft by offering much lower prices for its comparable software.[20]

natural monopoly
A market or industry in which having only one producer is most efficient because it can meet all of consumers' demand for the product.

Microsoft
www.microsoft.com

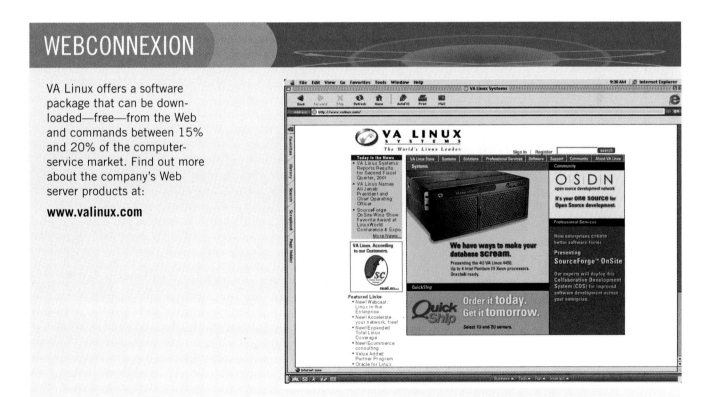

WEBCONNEXION

VA Linux offers a software package that can be downloaded—free—from the Web and commands between 15% and 20% of the computer-service market. Find out more about the company's Web server products at:

www.valinux.com

EVALUATING ECONOMIC SYSTEMS

Thus far we have noted that nations employ a variety of economic systems. We naturally think that our economic system works better than those used in other countries. We point with pride to our high standard of living and to our general prosperity. Yet, leaders in other countries believe just as strongly that their systems are best. So how do we really know that our system works as well as we think it does? To assess the effectiveness of an economic system objectively, we must consider the society's goals, its record in meeting those goals, and the interaction of governmental and non-governmental forces within the economy.

Economic Goals

Nearly every economic system has as its broad goals stability, full employment, and growth. Economies differ in the emphasis they place on each and in their approach to achieving them.

Stability

stability

A situation in which the relationship between the supply of money and goods, services, and labour remains constant.

inflation

A period of widespread price increases throughout an economic system.

consumer price index

Changes in the cost of a basket of goods and services that the typical family buys.

In economic terms, **stability** is a condition in which the balance between money available and goods produced remains about the same. As a consequence, prices for consumer goods, interest rates, and wages paid to workers change very little. Stability helps maintain equilibrium and predictability for business people, consumers, and workers.

The biggest threat to stability is **inflation**, a period of widespread price increases throughout the economic system. The most widely known measure of inflation is the **consumer price index**, which measures changes in the cost of a "basket" of goods and services that a typical family buys. Figure 1.8 shows how inflation has varied over the last 20 years in Canada.

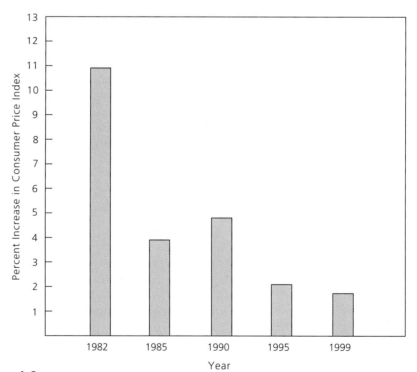

Figure 1.8
In the last few years the rate of price increases in Canada has dropped.

Yet inflation is not necessarily bad. Stability can cause stagnation and a decline in innovation. The onset of inflation is usually a sign of growth. Initially, higher prices cause businesses to expand, hire new workers, pump more dollars into advertising, and introduce new and exciting products and services. New businesses also start up to take advantage of the prosperity.

Inflation is not the only threat to economic stability. Suppose that a major factory in your town closes. Hundreds or even thousands of workers would lose their jobs. If other companies in the area do not have jobs for them, these unemployed people will reduce their spending. Other local businesses will thus suffer drops in sales—and perhaps cut their own workforces. The resulting **recession**, characterized by a decrease in employment, income, and production, may spread across the province and the nation. A particularly severe and long-lasting recession, such as the one that affected much of the world in the 1930s, is called a **depression**.

recession
The part of the business cycle characterized by a decrease in employment, income, and production.

depression
A particularly severe and long-lasting recession such as the one that affected the world in the 1930s.

Full Employment

Full employment means that everyone who wants to work has an opportunity to do so. In reality, full employment is impossible. There will always be people looking for work. These people generally fall into one of four categories.

Some people are out of work temporarily while looking for a new job, a situation known as *frictional unemployment*. A skilled engineer who has just quit her job but who will find a new job soon is in this category. Other people are out of work because of the seasonal nature of their jobs, a situation known as *seasonal unemployment*. Farm workers and construction workers, for example, may not work much in the winter. Sometimes people are out of work because of reduced economic activity, a situation known as *cyclical unemployment*. For example, many oil field workers in Alberta lost their jobs during the petroleum glut of the late 1980s. Some regained their jobs when stability returned, while many others moved to jobs in other industries. Finally, some people are unemployed because they lack the skills needed to perform available jobs, a situation known as *structural unemployment*. A steelworker laid off in a town looking for computer programmers falls into this category.

Because of the many reasons for unemployment, the rate of unemployment has varied greatly over the years, as Figure 1.9 shows. And because full employment is essentially impossible, our real goal is to minimize unemployment. High unemployment wastes talent and is a drain on resources that must be allocated to unemployment-associated welfare programs. Higher welfare costs, in turn, result in higher taxes for everyone.

Growth

A final goal of our economic system is **growth**, an increase in the amount of goods and services produced by our own resources. In theory, we all want our system to expand—more businesses, more jobs, more wealth for everyone. In practice, growth is difficult without triggering inflation and other elements of instability. However, an extended period of no growth may eventually result in an economic decline—business shutdowns, loss of jobs, a general decrease in overall wealth, and a poorer standard of living for everyone.

growth
An increase in the amount of goods and services produced using the same resources.

For many decades, Canada experienced growth rates in excess of most nations. More recently, however, countries such as South Korea, Taiwan, and Germany all had higher growth rates than Canada, in part because they became increasingly more efficient at producing goods and services.[21]

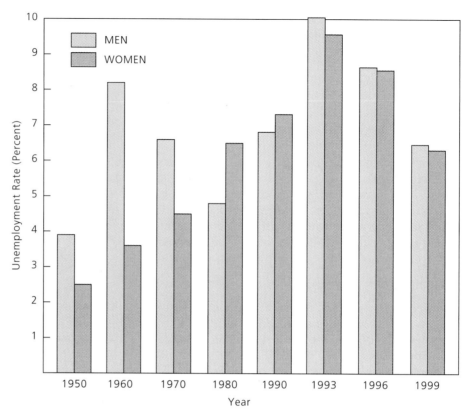

Figure 1.9
During the period 1950–93, there was a steady upward trend in unemployment rates, but the rate began to decline again during the last half of the 1990s.

Assessing Economic Performance

To judge how well an economic system is achieving its goals, economists use one or more of the following measures: standard of living, gross national product and gross domestic product, productivity, the balance of trade, and national debt.

Standard of Living

standard of living
A measure of a society's economic well-being.

The **standard of living** is a measure of a society's economic well-being. It helps us to observe the change in a society's well-being over time and to compare one society's well-being with that of another. Canadians have become used to expecting their living standards to increase as time goes on. But during the 1990s, the standard of living in Canada did not increase at all.

Gross National Product and Gross Domestic Product

gross domestic product (GDP)
The value of all goods and services produced in Canada during a one-year period.

gross national product (GNP)
The value of all goods and services produced by a country regardless of where the factors of production are located.

If we add up the total value of all goods and services produced in Canada during a one-year period, that value is known as **gross domestic product (GDP)**. Canada's GDP in 2000 was approximately $1 trillion. Another figure that is often computed by economists is **gross national product (GNP)**. GNP includes the value of all goods and services produced by a country regardless of where the factors of production are located. For example, the profits earned by a Canadian company abroad are included in GNP, but not in GDP. Conversely, profits earned by foreign firms in Canada *are* included in GDP.

GDP and GNP are useful measures of economic growth because they allow us to track an economy's performance over time. For example, the Exxon Valdez oil spill in 1986 increased GDP because the activities required

WEBCONNEXION

For the seventh consecutive year, the United Nations has ranked Canada as being first out of 174 countries in the Human Development Index (HDI), which measures a country's achievements in terms of life expectancy, educational attainment and adjusted real income. See the HDI in the Human Development Report 2000, published by the UN Development Programme, at www.undp.org/hdr2000/english/presskit/hdi.pdf. Visit the UN at:

www.un.org/english

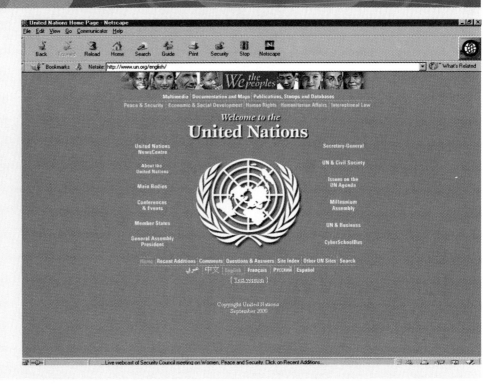

to clean up the mess were included in measurements of economic growth. An organization called Redefining Progress has proposed a more realistic measure to assess economic activity—the Genuine Progress Indicator (GPI). GPI treats activities that harm the environment or our quality of life as costs and gives them negative values. This new measure shows that while GDP has been increasing for many years, GPI has been falling since the 1970s.[22]

Per capita GDP allows us to compare GDP figures for different countries, taking into account their population size. GDP per capita in the United States is $30 200, followed by Japan ($24 500), Canada ($21 700), Norway ($21 400), and Germany ($20 800).

per capita GDP
Allows comparison of GDP figures for different countries, taking into account population size.

Productivity

As a measure of economic growth, **productivity** describes how much is produced relative to the resources used to produce it. That is, if Mind Computers can produce a personal computer for $1000 but Canon needs $1200 to produce a comparable computer, Mind is more productive. Chapter 12 provides a detailed look at productivity.

productivity
A measure of efficiency that compares how much is produced with the resources used to produce it.

Balance of Trade

Another commonly used measure of economic performance is the **balance of trade**, the total of a country's exports to other countries minus its imports from other countries. A positive balance of trade is generally considered to be favourable because new money flows into the country from the sales of exports. A negative balance is less favourable because money is flowing out of the country from the purchase of imports. Canada has enjoyed a favourable balance of trade since the mid-1970s, but the balance is favourable only because Canada exports so much to the United States. Our balance of trade with most other countries is unfavourable.

balance of trade
The total of a country's exports (sales to other countries) minus its imports (purchases from other countries).

This Fiat plant is the largest automotive factory in Brazil. The plant's payroll, the value of the 400 000 vehicles made here, and the profits earned by Fiat's Italian owners are produced domestically and therefore counted in the Brazilian gross domestic product. Because Brazilian labour costs are much lower than in their Western home countries, DaimlerChrysler, Honda, Toyota, Volkswagen, Mercedes, and Renault also build cars in Brazil.

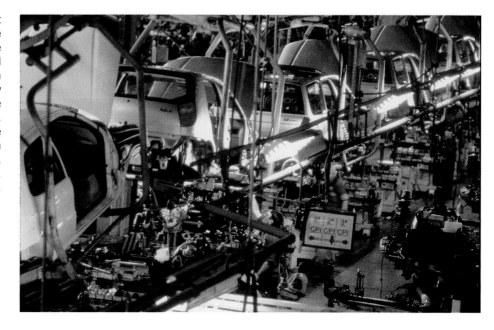

budget deficit

The result of the government spending more in one year than it takes in during that year.

national debt

The total amount of money that Canada owes its creditors (presently more than $500 billion).

National Debt

Like a business, the government takes in revenues (primarily in the form of taxes) and has expenses (military spending, social programs, and so forth). For many years, the government of Canada incurred annual **budget deficits**; that is, the government spent more money each year than it took in. These accumulated annual deficits have created a huge **national debt**—the amount of money that Canada owes its creditors.

Until the mid-1990s, annual budget deficits and the total national debt were increasing at an alarming rate. From Confederation (1867) to 1981, the *total* accumulated debt was only $85.7 billion, but in the period 1981–94, *annual deficits* were in the $20 to $40 billion range. Since 1994, however, things have changed dramatically. Annual deficits declined rapidly between 1994 and 1996, and in 1997 the first budget surplus in many years occurred. In the 1999–2000 fiscal year, the surplus was $12.3 billion.[23]

If the surplus is not used to reduce the national debt, that debt will obviously remain, and it will affect both Canadian consumers and Canadian business firms because the government must borrow money to finance the debt. In fact, Canada borrowed money more often in international markets than any other nation in the period 1989–94. Of all bonds issued in international markets during that period, Canada accounted for 31 percent of the total (the U.S., with its much larger economy, accounted for only 19 percent).[24]

fiscal policies

Policies by means of which governments collect and spend revenues.

monetary policies

Policies by means of which the government controls the size of the nation's money supply.

Bank of Canada
www.bank-banque-canada.ca

Managing the Canadian Economy

The government manages the economic system through two sets of policies. **Fiscal policies** refer to the collection and spending of government revenues. Tax policies, for example, can function as fiscal policy to increase revenues. Similarly, budget cuts (for example, closing military bases) function as fiscal policy when spending is decreased.

Monetary policies focus on controlling the size of the nation's money supply. Working primarily through the Bank of Canada (the nation's central bank), the government can influence the ability and willingness of banks throughout the country to lend money. It can also influence the supply of money by prompting interest rates to go up or down. A primary goal in recent years has been to adjust interest rates so that inflation is kept in check.

THE GLOBAL ECONOMY IN THE TWENTY-FIRST CENTURY

As we leave the twentieth century behind and cross the threshold of the twenty-first, it is useful to end our discussion of the Canadian business system with a look ahead. First, however, let's examine a variety of factors that, according to many experts, explain the booming economy that emerged in the 1990s. Table 1.3 summarizes one view of why things have gone so well for so many people in recent years.

Table 1.3	Ten Forces Driving Economic Expansion

1. New breakthroughs in technology and increased productivity
2. Deregulation of financial markets and institutions
3. Increased entrepreneurial activity and investment of venture capital
4. New approaches to inventory management
5. End of the Cold War
6. Consumer spending boom
7. Budget-deficit reduction
8. Soaring stock market
9. Business-friendly federal government monetary policies
10. Increased international trade

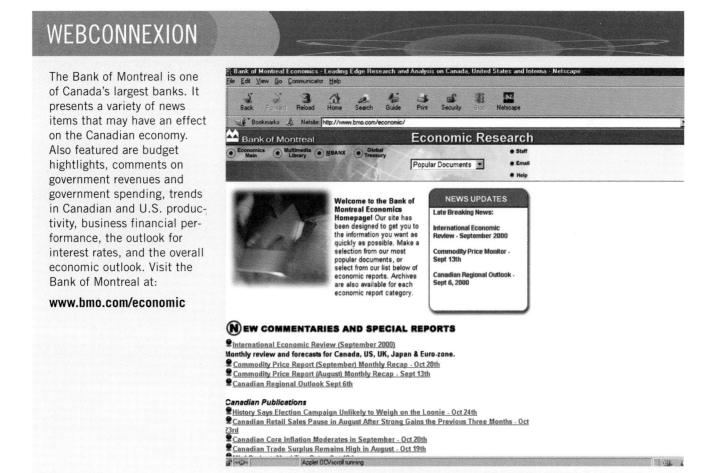

WEBCONNEXION

The Bank of Montreal is one of Canada's largest banks. It presents a variety of news items that may have an effect on the Canadian economy. Also featured are budget hightlights, comments on government revenues and government spending, trends in Canadian and U.S. productivity, business financial performance, the outlook for interest rates, and the overall economic outlook. Visit the Bank of Montreal at:

www.bmo.com/economic

Three Major Forces

So, what does the future hold? First of all, most experts see three major forces driving the economy for the next decade:

- The information revolution will continue to enhance productivity across all sectors of the economy, but most notably in such information-dependent industries as finance, media, and wholesale and retail trade.

- New technological breakthroughs in areas such as biotechnology will create entirely new industries.

- Increasing globalization will create much larger markets while also fostering tougher competition among global businesses; as a result, companies will need to focus even more on innovation and cost cutting.[25]

Figures 1.10 through 1.12 clearly illustrate the significance of these forces. Figure 1.10, for example, highlights the increased use of the Internet per 1000 people for the world and in North America, Western Europe, and the Asia-Pacific region during 1995. It also provides estimates for 2000 and 2005. The trends are clear and unambiguous: more and more people are using the Internet, and although North America still leads the way, Western Europe is catching up and the Asia-Pacific region is growing rapidly as well. Figure 1.11 amplifies these trends by isolating information-technology spending as a proportion of GDP for numerous countries. Again, while the United States continues to lead the way, other countries are clearly catching up.[26]

Finally, Figure 1.12 underscores the fact that world exports are again booming. Exports grew rapidly from the late 1980s through 1997 but then flattened and subsequently declined for two years. This downward trend was primarily attributable to the currency crisis and resultant economic downturn in Asia. Between 1999 and 2000, however, exports again began increasing. Taken together, then, these data—and many, many more—clearly reinforce the significance of information, technology, and globalization as the economic forces to be reckoned with in the twenty-first century.

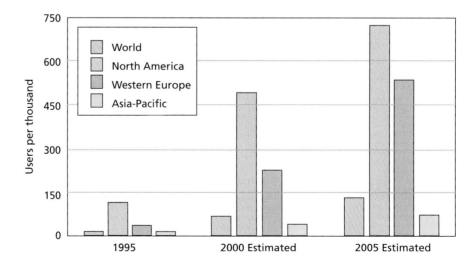

Figure 1.10
Internet users per 1000 people.

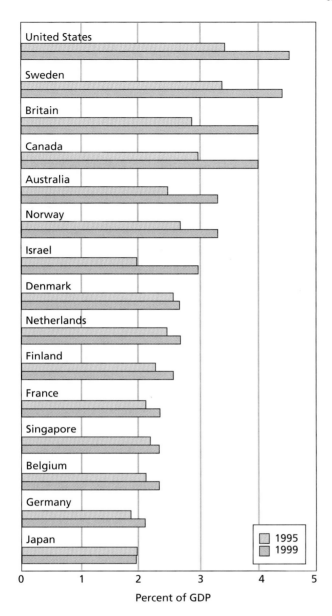

Figure 1.11
Information-technology spending.

Projected Trends and Patterns

As a result of these forces, economists also predict certain trends and patterns in economic indicators and competitive dynamics for at least the next few years. These include the following:

- The economy will maintain strong and consistent growth rates, perhaps exceeding 3 percent per year.

- Inflationary surges and large budget deficits will become less likely.

- Countries that encourage free trade, innovation, and open financial systems will prosper.

- The most successful businesses will be those that are able to master new technologies and keep abreast of their competitors.[27]

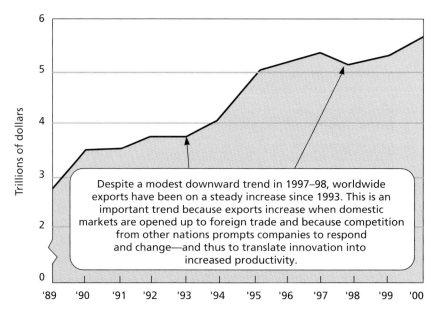

Figure 1.12
The export resurgence.

All things considered, both the Canadian domestic economy and the global economy are in excellent shape. Businesses and entrepreneurs will enjoy tremendous opportunities for growth and expansion for at least the next several years, and managers astute enough to navigate the competitive waters will probably arrive at greater prosperity. But don't forget the old saying: If it were easy, everyone would do it. Thus, it's important for all managers—both current and future—to develop and maintain a comprehensive understanding of business so they can take more effective advantage of the opportunities and better address the challenges they will face. This book will help you gain that understanding.

SUMMARY OF LEARNING OBJECTIVES

1. **Define the nature of Canadian *business* and identify its main goals.** *Businesses* are organizations that produce or sell goods or services to make a profit. *Profits* are the difference between a business's revenues and expenses. The prospect of earning profits encourages individuals and organizations to open and expand businesses. The benefits of business activities also extend to wages paid to workers and to taxes that support government functions.

2. **Describe different types of global *economic systems* according to the means by which they control the *factors of production* through *input and output markets*.** An *economic system* is a nation's system for allocating its resources among its citizens. Economic systems differ in terms of who owns or controls the five basic *factors of production*: labour, capital, entrepreneurs, physical resources, and information resources. In *command economies*, the government controls all or most of these factors. In *market economies*, which are based on the principles of *capitalism*, individuals and businesses control the factors of production and exchange them through *input and output markets*. Most countries today have *mixed market economies* that are dominated by one of these

systems but include elements of the other. The process of *privatization* is an important means by which many of the world's planned economies are moving towards mixed market systems.

3. **Show how *demand* and *supply* affect resource distribution in Canada.** The Canadian economy is strongly influenced by markets, demand, and supply. *Demand* is the willingness and ability of buyers to purchase a good or service. *Supply* is the willingness and ability of producers to offer goods or services for sale. Demand and supply work together to set a *market* or *equilibrium price*—the price at which the quantity of goods demanded and the quantity of goods supplied are equal.

4. **Identify the elements of *private enterprise* and explain the various *degrees of competition* in the Canadian economic system.** The Canadian economy is founded on the principles of *private enterprise: private property rights, freedom of choice, profits*, and *competition*. Degrees of competition vary because not all industries are equally competitive. Under conditions of *pure competition*, numerous small firms compete in a market governed entirely by demand and supply. An *oligopoly* involves a handful of sellers only. A *monopoly* involves only one seller.

5. **Explain the criteria for evaluating the success of an economic system in meeting its goals and show how the federal government attempts to manage the Canadian economy.** The basic goals of an economic system are *stability, full employment*, and *growth*. Measures of how well an economy has accomplished these goals include *gross national product, gross domestic product, productivity, balance of trade*, and *national debt*. The Canadian government uses *fiscal policies* to manage the effects of its spending and revenue collection and *monetary policies* to control the size of the nation's money supply.

6. **Discuss the current economic picture in Canada and summarize expert opinions about its future.** Canada is riding the crest of a long-term economic boom. Growth has been strong, and unemployment and inflation remain low. Experts believe that these trends will continue for at least another few years. Particularly important areas of the economy will include information technology, other forms of technological innovation, and globalization.

KEY TERMS

business, 5
profit, 5
economic system, 6
factors of production, 6
labour, 7
capital, 7
entrepreneur, 7
natural resources, 7
information resources, 7
command economy, 7
market economy, 7
communism, 7
socialism, 8
input market, 9
output market, 9
capitalism, 10

mixed market economy, 11
privatization, 11
Canadian Radio-television and Telecommunications Commission, 12
Canadian Transport Commission, 12
Canadian Wheat Board, 13
Hazardous Products Act, 14
Tobacco Act, 14
Weights and Measures Act, 14

Textile Labelling Act, 14
Food and Drug Act, 14
Canada Water Act, 14
Fisheries Act, 14
Environmental Contaminants Act, 14
deregulation, 14
revenue taxes, 15
progressive revenue taxes, 15
regressive revenue taxes, 15
restrictive taxes, 15
lobbyist, 16
trade association, 16
market, 17

demand, 17
supply, 17
law of demand, 17
law of supply, 17
demand and supply schedule, 17
demand curve, 17
supply curve, 17
market price (or equilibrium price), 17
surplus, 19
shortage, 19
business cycle, 19
private enterprise, 20
private property, 21
freedom of choice, 22

competition, 22
pure competition, 22
monopolistic
    competition, 23
oligopoly, 24
monopoly, 24
natural monopoly, 25

stability, 26
inflation, 26
consumer price index,
    26
recession, 27
depression, 27
growth, 27

standard of living, 28
gross domestic product
    (GDP), 28
gross national product
    (GNP), 28
per capital GDP, 29

productivity, 29
balance of trade, 29
budget deficit, 30
national debt, 30
fiscal policies, 30
monetary policies, 30

STUDY QUESTIONS AND EXERCISES

Review Questions

1. What are the five factors of production? Is one factor more important than the others? If so, which one? Why?
2. What is GDP? Per capita GDP? What does each measure?
3. Explain the differences between the four degrees of competition and give an example of each. (Do not use the examples given in the text.)
4. Why is inflation both good and bad? How does the government try to control it?

Analysis Questions

5. In recent years, many countries have moved from command economies to market economies. Why do you think this has occurred? Can you envision a situation that would cause a resurgence of command economies?
6. Identify a situation in which excess supply of a product led to decreased prices. Identify a situation in which a shortage led to increased prices. What eventually happened in each case? Why?

7. Explain how current economic indicators such as inflation and unemployment affect you personally. Explain how they will affect you as a manager.

Application Exercises

8. Choose a locally owned and operated business. Interview the owner to find out how the business uses the factors of production, and identify its sources for acquiring them.
9. Visit a local shopping mall or shopping area. List each store that you see and determine what degree of competition it faces in the immediate environment. For example, if there is only one store in the mall that sells shoes, that store represents a monopoly. Note the businesses with direct competitors (for example, two jewellery stores) and describe how they compete with each other.
10. Go to the library or on the Internet and research 10 different industries. Classify each according to degree of competition.

Building Your Business Skills

Analyzing the Price of Doing E-Business

Goal

To encourage students to understand how the competitive environment affects a product's price.

Situation

Assume that you own a local business that provides Internet access to individuals and businesses in your community. Yours is one of four such businesses in the local market. Each of the four companies charges the same price: $12 per month for unlimited dial-up service. Your business also provides users with e-mail service; two of your competitors also offer e-mail service. One of these same two competitors, plus the third, also provides the individual user with a free, basic personal Web page. One competitor just dropped its price to $10 per month, and the other two have announced their intentions to follow suit. Your break-even price is $7 per

customer. You are concerned about getting into a price war that may destroy your business.

Method

Divide into groups of four or five people. Each group is to develop a general strategy for handling competitors' price changes. In your discussion, take the following factors into account:

- how the demand for your product is affected by price changes
- the number of competitors selling the same or a similar product
- the methods—other than price—you can use to attract new customers and/or retain current customers

Analysis

Develop specific pricing strategies based on each of the following situations:

- Within a month after dropping the price to $10, one of your competitors raises its price back to $12.

- Two of your competitors drop their prices further—to $8 per month. As a result, your business falls off by 25 percent.

- One of your competitors that has provided customers with a free Web page has indicated that it will start charging an extra $2 per month for this optional service.

- Two of your competitors have announced that they will charge individual users $8 per month, but will charge businesses a higher price (not yet announced).

- All four providers (including you) are charging $8 per month. One goes out of business, and you know that another is in poor financial health.

Follow-Up Questions

1. Discuss the role that various inducements other than price might play in affecting demand and supply in the market for Internet service.

2. Is it always in a company's best interest to feature the lowest prices?

3. Eventually, what form of competition is likely to characterize the market for Internet service?

Exploring the Net

To learn more about how the music recording industry is adapting to the contemporary business environment, surf over to the Web site for LAUNCH Media Inc. at:

www.launch.com

Examine the various news features, interviews, downloads and "LAUNCHcast Radio." Then consider the following questions:

1. How effective is the LAUNCHcast feature as a marketing tool? Can you foresee any technical difficulties that might inhibit the use of this aspect of the site?

2. What feature did you find the most engaging? Least engaging?

3. Does the site work well as an introduction to those that are unfamiliar with popular music? What were your own initial reactions to the site, from the perspective of a seasoned/neophyte music fan?

4. Note that there is also a link for a LAUNCH Japan site that is, aesthetically, very different from the North American version. List some of the things that a company might take into consideration when recreating their product for a different market.

5. Explain how a feature like the one outlined in the "Affiliate Program" can be beneficial for LAUNCH Media.

Concluding Case 1-1

A Classic Case of Supply and Demand

Most people have never heard of palladium, a greyish metal produced primarily in Russia and South Africa. It is used in automobile catalytic converters, cellphones, fax machines, and dental bridgework. In the mid-1990s, when automobile manufacturers adopted tighter pollution emission standards, they switched from platinum to palladium in their catalytic converters. They did so because palladium does a better job of cleaning up auto emissions, and because it is cheaper than platinum (platinum then cost about $400 per ounce, palladium only $200).

The auto manufacturers knew that shifting to palladium would cause demand to exceed world production, which was about 5 million ounces per year. They expected that this would cause the price of palladium to increase somewhat, but they were not prepared for what happened next. Russian exports of palladium suddenly ceased in January 1997. The official reason given was that export quotas and licences were tied up in the infamous Russian bureaucracy.

The price of palladium immediately jumped. Speculators pushed prices even higher as the export delay continued, and the price quickly rose to $239 per ounce. By the spring of 1997, the bureaucracy problem was solved, exports increased, and prices dropped back to $200 per ounce.

However, in May 1998, palladium hit $417 per ounce as a new shortage blossomed. By summer, Russia was again selling palladium, and the price dropped, but only to $300 per ounce.

By this time, the auto manufacturers were becoming very concerned. Even though only small amounts of palladium are used in catalytic converters, price increases of this magnitude meant that the price of the average car would have to increase $100 to cover the cost of palladium. With competition very severe, automakers find it difficult to raise prices without losing sales. General Motors set up teams of experts to figure out how to use less palladium and still meet the tighter pollution standards.

In 1999, prices of palladium rose sharply again as buyers anticipated the annual routine of reduced exports from Russia. By February 2000, palladium prices had risen to over $700 per ounce. This concerned automakers so much that they took the unprecedented step of stipulating the maximum amount of palladium that would be allowed in engineers' car designs.

CASE QUESTIONS

1. What is profit? How does the price of palladium relate to the profits of automobile manufacturers?

2. Define supply and demand. What factors have influenced the supply of, and demand for, palladium?

3. What alternatives will automobile manufacturers likely consider as they try to solve their problems with palladium? Which alternatives are feasible and which are not? Explain.

4. Will the Russian firm producing palladium be pleased about its recent price increases? Explain. ◆

Concluding Case 1-2

Electronic Commerce

Electronic commerce is becoming a major part of every industry and marketplace these days. E-businesses such as Amazon.com and eBay are all less than 10 years old but have already become household names and major players in transforming our economy into an information-based one. Faced with this rapid and dynamic change, to remain vital and effective, staid older businesses have found it necessary to refocus their own operations to encompass the Internet and electronic commerce. Some have made successful transitions, while others have faltered.

The music industry is an especially interesting arena for e-commerce competition—one in which both newcomers and established firms continue to struggle to find just the right approach to integrating the Internet into their operations. Giants like Universal Music Group, Warner Music Group, Sony Music, BMG Entertainment, and EMI have long dominated the recorded-music business. But they are facing new and complex challenges as the Internet comes to play an increasingly significant role in their marketplace. New e-businesses pose both serious threats and significant opportunities for these media giants.

Consider, for example, the case of David Goldberg and Launch Media. When Goldberg, a music fanatic, was only 24 years old, he landed a plum job as director of new business development for Capitol Records. Goldberg was interested in extending the Capitol library of popular music, which ranged from Frank Sinatra to the Beatles, into new arenas. For example, he wanted to promote Capitol's music products on CD-ROM games and to focus heavily on new and emerging forms of electronic media for both promoting and delivering music to consumers.

But senior executives at Capitol weren't interested. They listened politely, but they adopted few of his ideas and gave him little encouragement in his efforts to push into new products and product lines. They apparently believed that the old tried-and-true method of recording music on compact discs and tapes, advertising and promoting new recordings in magazines and on the radio, and then distributing them through traditional retailing channels was never going to change.

Finally, Goldberg left Capitol in frustration and created Launch Media, which has quickly become one of the top five music-information sites on the Internet. When the firm went public in April 1999, the value of his personal stake mushroomed to US$12 million. But unlike some entrepreneurs in other industries and markets, Goldberg has never been interested in taking over the music business. What he wants to do is change it. And more and more industry experts are coming around to his point of view. "Our role," says one industry consultant who sees things Goldberg's way, "is to teach the industry to do things differently."

For example, some industry experts worried that Internet sites would render traditional recording companies obsolete—that consumers would simply download all the music they wanted directly from various Web sites controlled by artists and/or upstart Web outfits and that the recording companies would be squeezed out. But those in the know quickly realized that this isn't how things would work out. Instead, the Internet is emerging as a new catalyst for old and new music businesses alike. Web sites such as launch.com are becoming platforms for more and more interaction among consumers, performers, and recording labels.

The big companies still play a vital role in this information-related activity. For example, they still control most of the recordings, handle much of the advertising and promotion, and provide the "human contact" that remains an essential part of all entertainment enterprises. Consumers, meanwhile, can visit Web sites in the comfort of their own homes and download trial music cuts to sample music that they might want to buy. Then they can easily purchase CDs—in addition to concert tickets, posters, shirts, and other paraphernalia—directly from the same sites. Granted, performers can leverage bigger cuts of the profits, but Goldberg and others like to point out the obvious advantages of keeping everybody happy.

The challenge of building and sustaining a new business to meet changing and newly emerging customer needs is as common to small firms like Launch Media as it is to billion-dollar corporations like Warner Music Group or Sony Music. A changing marketplace creates a need for the kind of innovative responses that have long characterized business in Canada, the U.S., and other industrialized nations. Such responses require vision, careful attention to quality and customer service, substantial financial commitment, internal accounting controls, and well-defined marketing strategies designed to help businesses grow over time.

It is not clear how the music business itself will change in response to the growth of the Internet. One scenario calls for Web information sites to become a normal but separate part of the market—the recorded music giants will continue to produce music and the information sites will simply be part of the marketing process. According to a different scenario, the big music companies will eventually disappear and be replaced by Internet sites that make it easier and cheaper to get music. A third scenario sees the big music companies moving into the information business, either by initiating their own operations or by buying existing companies.

CASE QUESTIONS

1. Why is the recorded music market currently an oligopoly?
2. Explain how recorded-music companies and Internet information sites use the factors of production in different ways.
3. Discuss how pricing, demand, and supply affect both recorded-music companies and Internet information sites.
4. Which of the three scenarios posed at the end of the case do you regard as most likely? Why?
5. Suppose each of the five big recorded-music companies were to buy one of the Internet information businesses. Forecast the ways in which this turn of events would affect the industry. What would you expect to happen next? ◆

CHAPTER 2

Unsung Heroes of Canadian Business

The Calgary Co-operative Association Ltd., which has 354 000 dedicated customers and 16 retail outlets, controls nearly 30 percent of the grocery market in Calgary. It also operates gas bars, travel agencies, and liquor stores. Members receive regular discounts of between 5 and 15 percent on selected store items. Members who purchase goods from the co-op receive some of the surplus (sometimes called "patronage dividends") at the end of the year. The amount they receive is proportional to how much they purchased.

There are 10 000 co-ops in Canada, and 15 million Canadians are co-op members. Many of these members belong to more than one co-op. While private enterprise is valued in Canada, co-ops don't fit this mold. The shareholders are also customers, so they benefit from the efficiencies of the organization. As individual co-ops become larger and larger, some members worry that they may have difficulty maintaining the grassroots structure that has traditionally characterized co-ops.

The largest co-op in Canada is the Saskatchewan Wheat Pool. It has 74 000 members, 3000 employees, and annual revenues in excess of $4 billion. It resembles a private business because its class B non-voting investment shares are traded on the Toronto Stock Exchange. But because of its cooperative structure, all of the members of the board of directors are farmer-producers. Most of the members of the co-op have one Class A share, which costs just $25; that share allows them to participate in the election of delegates. Delegates, in turn, choose the board of directors.

Although co-ops are quite different than for-profit business firms, they do some things that are similar. For example, Manitoba Pool Elevators and Alberta Pool merged in 1998 to form a new company called Agricore. The newly merged co-op may also acquire other companies, such as Saskatchewan Wheat Pool did when it acquired 100 percent of Can-Oat Group and 45 percent of Fletcher's Fine Foods.

Co-ops can be found in almost every sector of the economy—insurance, farming, financial services, housing, forestry, and daycare. Financial co-ops such as credit unions are particularly popular, often springing up in areas where banks don't operate. Credit unions are the *only* financial institution in many small towns across Canada. There are well over 2000 financial co-ops in existence, including credit unions, caisse populaires, insurance companies, and trust companies. Collectively, they have more than $100 billion in total assets. Financial co-ops account for one-quarter of all co-ops and two-thirds of total co-op membership. Quebec alone has more than 5 million members, and the Desjardins-Laurentian Financial Corporation has over $10 billion in assets.

The first housing co-op was created in 1968. There are now over 2000 housing co-ops across Canada and nearly 90 000 units have been built to date. Co-ops fill a social need; members who cannot afford to rent units at market rates pay between 25 and 30 percent of their gross household income instead. ◆

Creative solutions to problems of business organization are becoming more common as firms struggle to enter markets or to remain competitive in rapidly changing markets. In this chapter, we examine the business structures that are used by both large and small businesses. By focusing on the learning objectives of this chapter, you will better understand the structural options open to Canadian businesses. After reading this chapter, you should be able to:

1. Trace the history of business in Canada.

2. Identify the *major forms of business ownership*.

3. Explain *sole proprietorships* and *partnerships* and discuss the advantages and disadvantages of each.

4. Describe *corporations* and discuss their advantages and disadvantages.

5. Describe the basic issues involved in creating and managing a corporation.

6. Identify recent trends and issues in corporate ownership.

7. Discuss *mergers, acquisitions, divestitures*, and *spinoffs*.

A BRIEF HISTORY OF BUSINESS IN CANADA

Canadian business has not always had a variety of complex structures. Indeed, a look at the history of business in Canada shows a steady development from sole proprietorships to the complex corporate structures of today. In this section, we will trace the broad outlines of the development of business in Canada. Table 2.1 highlights some of the specific events in Canadian business history.[1]

The Early Years

Business activity and profit from commercial fishing were the motivation for the first European involvement in Canada. In the late 1400s, ships financed by English entrepreneurs came to the coast of Newfoundland to fish for profit. By the late 1500s, the Newfoundland coast was being visited by hundreds of fishing vessels each year.

Beginning in the 1500s, French and British adventurers began trading with the native peoples. Items such as cooking utensils and knives were exchanged for beaver and other furs. One trading syndicate made over 1000 percent profit on beaver skins sold to a Paris furrier. Trading was aggressive and, over time, the price of furs rose as more and more Europeans bid for them. Originally the fur trade was restricted to eastern Canada, but by the late 1600s, *coureurs de bois* were travelling far to the west in search of new sources of furs.

European settlers who arrived in Canada in the sixteenth and seventeenth centuries initially had to farm or starve. Gradually, however, they began to produce more than they needed for their own survival. The governments of the countries from which the settlers came (notably England and France) were strong supporters of the mercantilist philosophy. Under *mercantilism*, colonists were expected to export raw materials like beaver pelts and lumber at low prices to the mother country. These raw materials were then used to produce finished goods such as fur coats, which were sold at high prices to settlers in Canada. Attempts to develop industry in Canada were thwarted by England and France, who enjoyed large profits from mercantilism. As a result, Canadian manufacturing was slow to develop.

Table 2.1		Some Important Dates in Canadian Business History

1490	English fishermen active off the coast of Newfoundland
1534	Account of first trading with native peoples written by Jacques Cartier
1669	*Nonsuch* returns to London with a cargo of furs from Hudson Bay area
1670	Hudson's Bay Company founded
1730–40	Hat-making industry arises in Quebec and is stifled by French home officials
1737	Compagnie des forges du St. Maurice formed to produce iron
1779	North West Company forms
1785	Molson brewery opens
1805	First Canadian paper mill built at St. Andrew's, Quebec
1809	First steamboat (the *Accommodation*) put into service on the St. Lawrence River by John Molson
1817	Bank of Montreal chartered
1821	Hudson's Bay Company and North West Company merge
1830–50	Era of canal building
1836	First railroad train pulled by a steam engine
1850–60	First era of railroad building
1855	John Redpath opens first Canadian sugar refinery in Montreal
1856	Railroad trains begin running between Toronto and Montreal
1857–58	First oil well in Canada drilled near Sarnia, Ontario
1861	Toronto Stock Exchange opens
1869	Eaton's opens for business in Toronto
1879	National Policy implemented; raised tariffs on foreign goods to protect and encourage Canadian manufacturers
1880–90	First western land boom
1885	Last spike driven to complete the Canadian Pacific Railroad
1896	First large pulp and paper mill in Canada opened at Sault Ste. Marie, Ontario
1897–99	Klondike gold rush
1907	First issue of *The Financial Post*
1917–22	Creation of Canadian National Railways
1920	First ship-plate steel mill in Canada opens in Sydney, Nova Scotia
1926	U.S. replaces Great Britain as Canada's largest trading partner
1927	Armand Bombardier sells first "auto-neige" (forerunner of the snowmobile)
1927	Canadian Tire begins operations in Toronto
1929	Great stock market crash
1929–33	Great Depression
1930	Canadian Airways Limited formed
1932	Canadian Radio Broadcasting Corporation formed. (It became the CBC in 1936.)
1935	Bank of Canada begins operations
1937	Canadian Breweries Limited is formed
1940	C.D. Howe appointed as Minister of Munitions and Supply
1945	Argus Corporation Limited formed
1947–51	Early computer built at the University of Toronto
1947	Leduc Number 1 oil well drilled in Alberta
1949	A.V. Roe (Avro) makes Canada's first commercial jetliner
1964	Volvo of Sweden begins assembling cars in Nova Scotia
1965	Auto Pact signed with the U.S.
1969	Canada becomes world's largest potash producer
1980–86	Dome, Canadair, and Massey-Ferguson receive financial assistance from the federal government
1989	Free trade agreement with U.S. comes into effect
1993	North American Free Trade Agreement comes into effect

The Factory System and the Industrial Revolution

Industrial Revolution
A major change in goods production that began in England in the mid-eighteenth century and was characterized by a shift to the factory system, mass production, and specialization of labour.

factory system
A process in which all the machinery, materials, and workers required to produce a good in large quantities are brought together in one place.

mass production
The manufacture of products of uniform quality in large quantities.

specialization
The breaking down of complex operations into simple tasks that are easily learned and performed.

British manufacturing took a great leap forward around 1750 with the coming of the **Industrial Revolution**. This revolution was made possible by advances in technology and by the development of the **factory system**. Instead of hundreds of workers turning out items one at a time in their cottages, the factory system brought together in one place all of the materials and workers required to produce items in large quantities, along with newly created machines capable of **mass production**.

Mass production offered savings in several areas. It avoided unnecessary duplication of equipment. It allowed firms to purchase raw materials at better prices by buying large lots. And most important, it encouraged **specialization** of labour. No longer did production require highly skilled craftspeople who could do all the different tasks required to make an item. A series of semiskilled workers, each trained to perform only one task and supported by specialized machines and tools, greatly increased output.

WEBCONNEXION

The Hudson's Bay Company was established in 1670 and is Canada's largest department store. Zellers is the mass retail brand of Hudson's Bay. The Web site includes a history of the company that traces its activities from the earliest years to the present. The site also presents information on careers and company finances. Visit Hudson's Bay at:

www.hbc.com

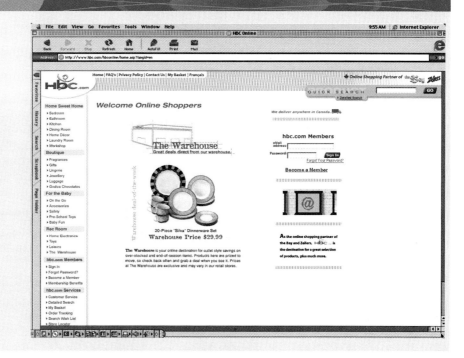

In spite of British laws against the export of technology and manufacturing in North America, Canadian manufacturing existed almost from the beginning of European settlement. Modest manufacturing operations were evident in sawmills, breweries, grist mills for grinding grain, tanneries, woollen mills, shoemakers' shops, and tailors' shops. These operations were so successful that by 1800, exports of manufactured goods were more important than exports of fur.

With the advent of steam power in the early 1800s, manufacturing activity began to increase rapidly. By 1850, more than 30 factories—employing more than 2000 people—lined the Lachine Canal alone. Exports of timber to England in 1850 were 70 times greater than what they had been in 1800. The demand for reliable transportation was the impetus for canal building in the mid-1800s and then the railroad-building boom in the mid- and late 1800s.

The Entrepreneurial Era

One of the most significant features of the last half of the nineteenth century was the emergence of entrepreneurs willing to take risks in the hope of earning huge profits. Adam Smith in his book *The Wealth of Nations* argued that the government should not interfere in the economy, but should let businesses function without regulation or restriction. This *laissez-faire* attitude was often adopted by the Canadian government. As a result, some individuals became immensely wealthy through their aggressive business dealings. Some railway, bank, and insurance executives made over $25 000 per year in the late 1800s, and their purchasing power was immense. Entrepreneurs such as Joseph Flavelle, Henry Pellatt, and John MacDonald lived in ostentatious mansions or castles.

The size and economic power of some firms meant that other businesses had difficulty competing against them. At the same time, some business executives decided that it was more profitable to collude than to compete.

In the eighteenth century, the home crafts industry provided our young nation with clothing and foodstuffs. During the nineteenth century, machinery such as the cotton gin changed the way the world worked. Today, automation continues to alter our work lives and the types of products that are available to us.

They decided among themselves to fix prices and divide up markets. Hurt by these actions, Canadian consumers called for more regulation of business. In 1889, the first anti-combines legislation was passed in Canada, and legislation regulating business has increased ever since.

The Production Era

The concepts of specialization and mass production that originated in the Industrial Revolution were more fully refined as Canada entered the twentieth century. The Scientific Management Movement focused management's attention on production. Increased efficiency via the "one best way" to accomplish tasks became the major management goal.

production era

The period during the early twentieth century when businesses focused almost exclusively on improving productivity and manufacturing methods.

Henry Ford's introduction of the moving assembly line in the U.S. in 1913 ushered in the **production era**. During the production era, less attention was paid to selling and marketing than to technical efficiency when producing goods. By using fixed workstations, increasing task specialization, and moving the work to the worker, the assembly line increased productivity and lowered prices, making all kinds of products affordable for the average person.

During the production era, large businesses began selling stock—making shareholders the owners—and relying on professional managers. The growth of corporations and improved production output resulting from assembly lines came at the expense of worker freedom. The dominance of big firms made it harder for individuals to go into business for themselves. Company towns run by the railroads, mining corporations, and forest products firms gave individuals little freedom of choice over whom to work for and what to buy. To restore some balance within the overall system, both government and labour had to develop and grow. Thus, this period saw the rise of labour unions and collective bargaining. We will look at this development in more detail in Chapter 10. The Great Depression of the 1930s and the Second World War caused the federal government to intervene in the economic system on a previously unimaginable scale.

Today, business, government, and labour are frequently referred to by economists and politicians as the three *countervailing powers* in our society. All are big. All are strong. Yet, none totally dominates the others.

The Sales and Marketing Eras

By the 1930s, business's focus on production had resulted in spectacular increases in the amount of goods and services for sale. As a result, buyers had more choices and producers faced greater competition in selling their wares. Thus began the so-called **sales era**. According to the ideas of this time, a business's profits and success depended on hiring the right salespeople, advertising heavily, and making sure products were readily available. Business firms were essentially production- and sales-oriented, and they produced what they thought customers wanted, or simply what the company was good at producing. This approach is still used by firms that find themselves with surplus goods that they want to sell (e.g., used-car dealerships).

Following the Second World War, pent-up demand for consumer goods kept the economy rolling. While brief recessions did occur periodically, the 1950s and 1960s were prosperous times. Production increased, technology advanced, and the standard of living rose. During the **marketing era**, business adopted a new philosophy of how to do business—use market research to determine what customers want, and then make it for them. Firms like Procter & Gamble and Molson were very effective during the marketing era, and continue to be profitable today. Each offers an array of products within a particular field (toothpaste or beer, for example), and gives customers a chance to pick what best suits their needs.

sales era
The period during the 1930s and 1940s when businesses focused on sales forces, advertising, and keeping products readily available.

marketing era
The period during the 1950s and 1960s when businesses began to identify and meet consumer wants in order to make a profit.

Procter & Gamble
www.pg.com

Molson
www.molson.com

The Finance Era

In the 1980s, emphasis shifted to finance. In the **finance era** there was a sharp increase in mergers and in the buying and selling of business enterprises. Some people now call it the "decade of greed." As we will see in the next chapter, during the finance era there were many hostile takeovers and a great deal of financial manipulation of corporate assets by so-called corporate raiders. Critics charged that these raiders were simply enriching themselves and weren't creating anything of tangible value by their activity. They also charged that raiders were distracting business managers from their main goals of running the business. The raiders responded that they were making organizations more efficient by streamlining, merging, and reorganizing them.

finance era
The period during the 1980s when there were many mergers and much buying and selling of business enterprises.

The Global Era

The last few years have seen the continuation of technological advances in production, computer technology, information systems, and communication capabilities. They have also seen the emergence of a truly global economy. Canadians drive cars made in Japan, wear sweaters made in Italy, drink beer brewed in Mexico, and listen to stereos made in Taiwan. But we're not alone in this. People around the world buy products and services from foreign companies.

While it is true that many Canadian businesses have been hurt by foreign imports, numerous others have profited by exploring new foreign markets themselves. And domestic competition has forced many businesses to work harder than ever to cut costs, increase efficiency, and improve product and service quality. We will explore a variety of important trends, opportunities, and challenges of the global era throughout this book.

The Internet Era

The turn of the century has been accompanied by what many experts are calling the Internet era of business. Internet usage in North America grew from about 100 users per 1000 people in 1995 to over 450 users per 1000 people in 2000. Projections call for this figure to grow to nearly 750 users per 1000 people by 2005. The growth rate in Western Europe, however, is expected to be even faster and, by 2005, will also become significant in the Asia-Pacific region.

How does the growth of the Internet affect business? In at least three different ways:

1. *The Internet will give a dramatic boost to trade in all sectors of the economy, especially services.* If the Internet makes it easier for all trade to grow, this is particularly true for trade in services on an international scale.

2. *The Internet will level the playing field, at least to some extent, between larger and smaller enterprises, regardless of what products or services they sell.* In the past, a substantial investment was typically needed to enter some industries and to enter foreign markets. Now, however, a small business based in central Alberta, southern Italy, eastern Malaysia, or northern Brazil can set up a Web site and compete quite effectively with much larger businesses located around the world.

3. *The Internet holds considerable potential as an effective and efficient networking mechanism among businesses.* So-called business-to-business (B2B) networks can link firms with all of their suppliers, business customers, and strategic partners in ways that make it faster and easier for them to do business together.

TYPES OF BUSINESS ORGANIZATIONS

All business owners must decide which form of legal organization—a sole proprietorship, a partnership, a corporation, or a cooperative—best suits them and their business. Few decisions are more critical, since the choice affects a host of managerial and financial issues, including income taxes and the owners' liability. In choosing a legal form of organization, the parties concerned must consider their likes, dislikes, and dispositions, their immediate and long-range needs, and the advantages and disadvantages of each form. Seldom, if ever, does any one factor completely determine which form is best.[2] The "It's a Wired World" box describes some of the strategic decisions that were made by Altec Lansing Technologies when it set up a new business.

IT'S A WIRED WORLD

Setting Up an Internet Marketing Business

You may not recognize the name Altec Lansing Technologies Inc., but you've probably heard its products. Altec designs, manufactures, and markets high-quality sound systems for personal computers and home entertainment. Its customers are mostly other companies—Compaq, Dell Computers, IBM, Gateway—that use Altec's products in making consumer products. Its marketing strength helped it build strategic partnerships with such leading companies such as Intel Corp., Dolby® Labs, and Texas Instruments. But moving into Internet marketing, Altec managers decided, was a venture with which they could use some outside help. They selected Agency.Com Ltd., experts in e-business marketing, to determine how they should establish Altec for competitive advantage on the Net.

The first step was to decide on an overall Internet strategy: that is, to identify the firm's marketing purpose in Internet marketing and then to determine a way to implement that strategy. The overall strategy had to recognize that Altec intends to maintain long-lasting relationships with its business customers. Another consideration was changing industry trends: at the time, there was convergence in the markets for home computing, office computing, and home entertainment, and the technology was changing from analog to digital audio. With these considerations in mind Altec and Agency.Com proposed a strategy featuring five elements:

1. Online commerce would be implemented and would emphasize relationship marketing to ensure ongoing relationships with customers.
2. Altec products would be positioned on quality—as providing the best audio experience possible.
3. Current customers would be secured and encouraged for further sales.
4. New customers would be captured.
5. Greater brand recognition would be built.

Implementation called for a Web site as the focal point for all online activity. The Altec site is a commerce centre that offers information pages and, along with e-mail, provides an online communication channel for building and maintaining customer relationships. Altec's online media strategy includes space purchased on third-party sites, content sponsorships and alliances, and co-marketing to bring new customers to the site. Customers can access a list of products, evaluate system requirements and performance specifications, download speaker-system software, be direct-linked to Altec's distributors, or make online purchases. Finally, the site includes sections devoted to customer support and "System Builders," which provides special services to companies that purchase Altec audio systems for use in building computers and sound systems.

Sole Proprietorships

As the very first legal form of business organization, **sole proprietorships** date back to ancient times. This is still the most numerous form of business in Canada. Despite their numbers, however, they account for only a small proportion of total business revenues in this country.

Because most sole proprietorships are small, often employing only one person, you might assume that all are small businesses. However, sole proprietorships may be as large as a steel mill or as small as a lemonade stand. Some of Canada's largest companies started out as sole proprietorships. Eaton's, for example, was originally a one-man operation founded by Timothy Eaton. One of Canada's biggest sole proprietorships is the Jim Pattison Group, with sales of $3 billion and 15 000 employees (see the boxed insert on page 201). Figure 2.1 summarizes the basic advantages and disadvantages of the sole proprietorship form of ownership.

sole proprietorship
A business owned (and usually operated) by one person who is personally responsible for the firm's debts.

Eaton's
www.eatons.com

ADVANTAGES

DISADVANTAGES

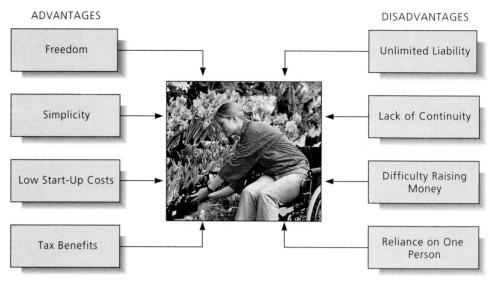

Freedom

Simplicity

Low Start-Up Costs

Tax Benefits

Unlimited Liability

Lack of Continuity

Difficulty Raising Money

Reliance on One Person

Figure 2.1

The most popular form of business ownership in Canada is the sole proprietorship. There are both advantages and disadvantages to this form of ownership.

Advantages

Freedom is the most striking feature of sole proprietorships. Because they alone own their businesses, sole proprietors need answer to no one but themselves. They can also maintain a high level of privacy, since they are not required to report information about their operations to anyone.

Sole proprietorships are simple to form. Sole proprietors often need only put a sign on their door to go into business for themselves. They are also easy to dissolve. Rock concerts or athletic events may be organized as sole proprietorships by individuals who then dissolve the business entity when the events are over.

Low start-up costs are yet another attractive feature of sole proprietorships. Legal fees are likely to be low, since some sole proprietorships need only register the business with the provincial government to ensure that no other business bears the same name. Some proprietorships do need to take out licences, however. For example, restaurants and pet shops need special licences.

Sole proprietorships also offer tax benefits for new businesses likely to suffer losses before profits begin to flow. Tax laws permit sole proprietors to treat the sales revenues and operating expenses of the business as part of their personal finances. Thus, a proprietor can cut taxes by deducting any operating losses from income earned from sources other than the business. Since most businesses lose money at the beginning, this tax situation is very helpful to entrepreneurs starting up. However, if a proprietor makes a lot of money running a business, a tax disadvantage may exist because personal tax rates are higher than small business corporation tax rates.

Disadvantages

unlimited liability

A person who invests in a business is liable for all debts incurred by the business; personal possessions can be taken to pay debts.

One major drawback of sole proprietorships is their **unlimited liability**. A sole proprietor is personally liable for all debts incurred by the business. Bills must be paid out of the sole proprietor's own pocket if the business fails to generate enough cash. Otherwise, creditors can step in and claim the proprietor's personal possessions, including a home, furniture, and automobile. (Actually, the law does protect some of the proprietor's assets, but many can be claimed.)

Another disadvantage is lack of continuity. A sole proprietorship legally dissolves when the owner dies. The business can, of course, be reorganized soon after the owner's death if a successor has been trained to take over the business. Otherwise, executors or heirs must **liquidate** (sell the assets of) the business.

Finally, a sole proprietorship is dependent upon the resources of a single individual. If the proprietor has unlimited resources and is a successful manager, this characteristic is not really a problem. In most cases, however, the proprietor's financial and managerial limits constrain what the organization can do. Sole proprietors often find it hard to borrow money not only to start up, but also to expand. Banks often reject such applications, fearing that they will not be able to recover the loan if the sole proprietor becomes disabled. Often, would-be proprietors must rely on personal savings and loans from family for start-up funds.

liquidate
Sell the assets of a business.

Partnerships

A **partnership** is established when two or more individuals agree to combine their financial, managerial, and technical abilities for the purpose of operating a company for profit. The partnership form of ownership was developed to overcome some of the more serious disadvantages of the sole proprietorship. **General partners** are actively involved in managing the firm and they have unlimited liability. **Limited partners** generally don't participate actively in the business, and their liability is limited to the amount they invested in the partnership. See Table 2.2.

Partnerships are often an extension of a business that began as a sole proprietorship. The original owner may want to expand, or the business may have grown too big for a single person to handle. Pentagram Design Inc., a now-prestigious architectural design partnership, was originally formed in London, England, by three prominent professionals who had previously worked alone. Realizing that they could attract more and larger clients by working together, the three agreed to form a partnership, which was originally called Fletcher Forbes Gill after its founders. Partnerships are common among professionals such as accountants, doctors, architects, lawyers, and engineers because law does not allow these professionals to incorporate. Figure 2.2 summarizes the advantages and disadvantages of the partnership form of organization.

partnership
A business with two or more owners who share in the operation of the firm and in financial responsibility for the firm's debts.

general partner
A partner who is actively involved in managing the firm and has unlimited liability.

limited partner
A partner who generally does not participate actively in the business, and whose liability is limited to the amount invested in the partnership.

Table 2.2	Types of Partnerships and Partners

Types of Partnerships

General partnership	All partners have unlimited liability for the firm's debts.
Limited partnership	This partnership has at least one general partner and one or more limited partners. The latter's liability is limited to their financial investment in the firm.

Types of Partners

General partner	Actively involved in managing the firm and has unlimited liability.
Secret partner	Actively participates in managing the firm and has unlimited liability. A secret partner's identity is not disclosed to the public.
Dormant partner	Does not actively participate in managing the firm. A dormant partner's identity is not disclosed to the public. Has unlimited liability.
Ostensible partner	Not an actual partner but his or her name is identified with the firm. Usually an ostensible partner is a well-known personality. Promotional benefits accrue from using his or her name for which the person is usually paid a fee. Has unlimited liability.
Limited partner	Liability is limited to the amount invested in the partnership.

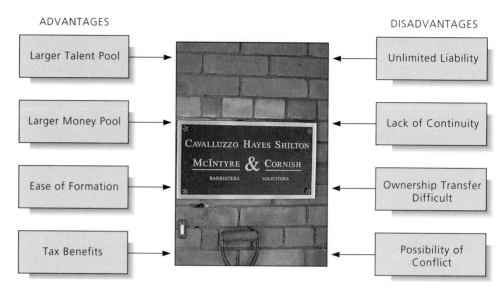

Figure 2.2
Partnerships are fairly common in professional organizations.

Advantages

The most striking feature of general partnerships is their ability to grow by adding talent and money. Partnerships also have a somewhat easier time borrowing funds than do sole proprietorships. Banks and other lending institutions prefer to make loans to enterprises that are not dependent on a single individual.

Like a sole proprietorship, a partnership is simple to organize, with few legal requirements. Even so, all partnerships must begin with an agreement of some kind. It may be written, oral, or even unspoken. Wise partners, however, insist on a written agreement to avoid trouble later. This agreement should answer such questions as

- Who invested what sums of money in the partnership?
- Who will receive what share of the partnership's profits?
- Who does what and who reports to whom?
- How may the partnership be dissolved? In that event, how would leftover assets be distributed among the partners?
- How would surviving partners be protected from claims by surviving heirs if a partner dies?
- How will disagreements be resolved?

Although it helps to clarify how partners relate to each other, the partnership agreement is strictly a private document. No laws require partners to file an agreement with some government agency. Nor are partnerships regarded as legal entities. In the eyes of the law, a partnership is nothing more than two or more persons working together. The partnership's lack of legal standing means that the partners are taxed as individuals.

Disadvantages

As with sole proprietorships, unlimited liability is the greatest drawback of general partnerships. By law, each partner may be held personally liable for all debts incurred in the name of the partnership. And if any partner incurs a debt, even if the other partners know nothing about it, they are all liable if the offending partner cannot pay up.

Lloyd's of London, one of the most famous insurance companies in the world, demonstrates the concept of unlimited liability. Until recently, the people who invested in Lloyd's (called "names") have always had unlimited liability, but they invested because historically such investments have yielded good returns. During the 1990s, however, Lloyd's ran into severe financial difficulties and lost billions of dollars. The names were called upon to make good the loss, but many of them simply could not afford to do so. Some committed suicide and others lost their personal property. Still others sued Lloyd's for financial negligence to prevent their personal assets from being seized. In the end, an agreement was reached that forgave the names their liability, and the names agreed to drop their lawsuit against Lloyd's.[3]

Another problem with partnerships is lack of continuity. When one partner dies or pulls out, a partnership may dissolve legally, even if the other partners agree to stay. The dissolving of a partnership, however, need not cause a loss of sales revenues. If they wish, the surviving partners can quickly form a new partnership to retain the business of the old firm.

A related drawback is the difficulty of transferring ownership. No partner may sell out without the other partners' consent. Also, a partner who wants to retire or to transfer his or her interest to a son or daughter must receive the other partners' consent. Thus, the life of a partnership may depend on the ability of retiring partners to find someone compatible with the other partners to buy them out. Failure to do so may lead to forced liquidation of the partnership.

Finally, a partnership provides little or no guidance in resolving conflict between the partners. For example, suppose one partner wants to expand the business rapidly and the other wants it to grow slowly. If under the partnership agreement the two are equal, it may be difficult for them to decide what to do. Conflicts can involve anything from personal habits like smoking to hours of operation to managerial practices.

Corporations

When you think of corporations you probably think of giant businesses such as General Motors of Canada or Nortel Networks (see Table 2.3). The very word **corporation** suggests bigness and power. Yet, the tiny corner newsstand has as much right to incorporate as does a giant oil refiner. And the

Lloyd's of London
www.lloydsoflondon.co.uk

corporation

A business considered by law to be a legal entity separate from its owners with many of the legal rights and privileges of a person; a form of business organization in which the liability of the owners is limited to their investment in the firm.

Nortel Networks
www.nortelnetworks.cm

Table 2.3	The Top 10 Corporations in Canada (ranked by annual sales)
Company	**Sales (in billions)**
1. General Motors of Canada	$39.6
2. Nortel Networks Corp.	32.9
3. Ford Motor Co. of Canada Ltd.	29.9
4. DaimlerChrysler Canada Inc.	22.4
5. George Weston Ltd.	20.8
6. Canadian Imperial Bank of Commerce	20.1
7. Royal Bank of Canada	19.6
8. The Seagram Co. Ltd.	18.5
9. Bank of Montreal	16.6
10. The Bank of Nova Scotia	16.6

newsstand and oil refiner have the same basic characteristics that all corporations share: legal status as a separate entity, property rights and obligations, and an indefinite lifespan.

A corporation has been defined as "an artificial being, invisible, intangible, and existing only in contemplation of the law."[4] As such, corporations may:

- Sue and be sued.

- Buy, hold, and sell property.

- Make and sell products to consumers.

- Commit crimes and be tried and punished for them.

Corporations can be found in both the private and the public sector in Canada, although our emphasis is on the private sector. We discussed Crown (government) corporations in Chapter 1.

Public Versus Private Corporations

public corporation
A business whose stock is widely held and available for sale to the general public.

private corporation
A business whose stock is held by a small group of individuals and is not usually available for sale to the general public.

Some corporations are public; others are private. A **public corporation** is one whose stock is widely held and available for sale to the general public. Anyone who has the funds to pay for them can buy shares of Brascan, George Weston, or Canadian Pacific. The stock of a **private corporation**, on the other hand, is held by only a few people and is not generally available for sale. The controlling group may be a family, employees, or the management group. Para Paints of Canada and Bata Shoes are private corporations.

Most new corporations start out as private corporations, because few investors will buy an unknown stock. As the corporation grows and develops a record of success, it may issue shares to the public as a way of raising additional money. This is called its initial public offering (IPO). Going public may not be easy. The Quebec weekly business magazine *Les Affaires* reported on seven companies that had decided to go public. Three of them gave up halfway through the process, another three reduced the size of their IPO, and one was successful with its original plan.[5] The process of going public usually takes six to nine months.

Mutual Life Assurance Co. of Canada and several other insurance companies "went public" in the late 1990s after they "demutualized" (see the "Business Today" box). WestJet went public in 2000, as did the Toronto Stock Exchange (TSE); this puts the TSE in the unusual position of being listed on itself.[6]

Just as companies can "go public," they can also "go private"; that is, a public corporation can be converted to a private corporation. In 1997, Jim Pattison, a well-known Canadian entrepreneur, was involved in negotiations to convert three companies to private corporation status: Westar Group Ltd., Great Pacific Enterprises Inc., and B.C. Sugar Refinery Ltd.[7]

Formation of the Corporation

The two most widely used methods to form a corporation are federal incorporation under the *Canada Business Corporations Act* and provincial incorporation under any of the provincial corporations acts. The former is used if the company is going to operate in more than one province; the latter is used if the founders intend to carry on business in only one province.

Except for banks and certain insurance and loan companies, any company can be federally incorporated under the *Canada Business Corporations Act*. To do so, Articles of Incorporation must be drawn up. These articles include such information as the name of the corporation, the type and number of shares to be issued, the number of directors the corporation will have,

BUSINESS TODAY

Demutualization and Going Public

The most dramatic event of 1999 in the Canadian financial services industry was "demutualization." This involved the conversion of five major Canadian life insurance companies from mutual enterprises owned by their voting policyholders to publicly traded companies owned by shareholders. The five companies are Canada Life Financial Corp., Manulife Financial Corp., Clarica Life Insurance Co., Sun Life Assurance Co. of Canada, and Industrial-Alliance Life Insurance Co. Their stock is now traded on the Toronto Stock Exchange (TSE), thereby adding five big financial services stocks to the TSE. These companies will attract investors and thus provide potent competition for other public financial companies such as banks and other publicly traded insurance companies. When all five of the new stocks have been traded for long enough to become part of the TSE 300 index, they will represent about one-quarter of the financial services sub-index.

These companies pursued demutualization because they wanted to tap into stock markets for badly needed expansion and acquisition capital. They also felt that it would help them retain executive talent by allowing them to start paying their executives at the same level as other private sector competitors.

Demutualization will also benefit the policyholders. The five companies, which will distribute between $20 and $25 billion in cash or shares to their approximately 3.7 million policyholders, are saying that the change in ownership form will result in the greatest transfer of wealth in Canadian history. Complex formulas were developed by the companies to determine how much each policyholder should get. The biggest portion of stock that Clarica doled out to an individual was 18 804 shares worth between $272 000 and $400 000. The bigger corporate clients received more than 100 000 shares worth between $1.45 and $2.25 million.

Policyholders aren't the only ones who benefited from demutualization. The deal was also a bonanza for investment dealers who received large commissions from the companies' initial public offerings of stock. For example, the Manulife IPO was $2.49 billion, and generated about $75 million in brokerage fees.

The road to demutualization was a long and rocky one, particularly for those companies that had foreign operations and had to get approval from foreign regulators before they could demutualize. Extensive communications were also carried out with policyholders to obtain their approval. Special meetings were held at which votes were taken, and at some of these meetings, tempers flared. At Clarica, for example, a small group of policyholder rights advocates turned one of its meetings into a bitter three-hour wrangle. After a Sun Life meeting, one insurance activist laid assault charges against two security guards, claiming that she had been injured when they forcibly removed her from the meeting.

and the location of the company's operations. All companies must attach the word "Limited" (Ltd./Ltée), "Incorporated" (Inc.), or Corporation (Corp.) to the company name to indicate clearly to customers and suppliers that the owners have limited liability for corporate debts. The same sorts of rules apply in other countries. British firms, for example, use PLC for "public limited company" and German companies use AG for "Aktiengesellschaft" (corporation).

Provincial incorporation takes one of two forms. In certain provinces (British Columbia, Alberta, Saskatchewan, Manitoba, Ontario, Newfoundland, Nova Scotia, and the three territories), the registration system or its equivalent is used. Under this system, individuals wishing to form a corporation are required to file a memorandum of association. This document contains the same type of information as required under the *Canada Business Corporations Act*. In the remaining provinces, the equivalent incorporation document is called the letters patent. In Quebec, a corporation may be formed either by issuing a letters patent or by drawing up articles of incorporation. The specific procedures and information required vary from province to province. The basic differences between these incorporation systems is that the registration system forms corporations by authority of parliament, while the letters patent system forms corporations by royal prerogative.

Corporate Governance

corporate governance

The relationship between shareholders, the board of directors, and other top managers in the corporation.

Corporate governance, which is specified for each firm in its bylaws, involves three distinct bodies. **Stockholders** (or **shareholders**) are the real owners of a corporation—investors who buy shares of ownership in the form of stock. The *board of directors* is a group of people elected by stockholders to oversee the management of the corporation. Corporate *officers* are top managers hired by the board to run the corporation on a day-to-day basis.

stockholders (or shareholders)

Those who own shares of stock in a company.

stock

A share of ownership in a corporation.

Stock Ownership and Stockholders' Rights. Corporations sell shares in the business (that is, **stock**) to investors, who then become stockholders, or shareholders. Profits are distributed among stockholders in the form of dividends, and corporate managers serve at their discretion. Stockholders, then, are the owners of a corporation. As noted earlier, in a closely held corporation, only a small number of people own the stock. In a publicly held corporation, on the other hand, large numbers of people own the stock.

The Initial Public Offering. An increasingly common practice today is for formerly closely held corporations to sell stock to individual investors as a way of raising cash. For example, suppose the ownership of a closely held corporation is spread across 1 000 000 shares of stock valued at $100 per share, and that each of four owners has 250 000 shares. If they believe that the stock will be of value to other investors, these owners might elect to sell some of it through a process called an **initial public offering (IPO)**. Usually working in concert with an investment banking firm, the owners make available a specified number of shares on a certain date at a certain price.[8]

initial public offering (IPO)

Selling shares of stock in a company for the first time to the general investing public.

Suppose that each owner sells 150 000 shares at $100 per share. To make the stock attractive to potential investors, the owners must commit to investing much of the money back into the business, rather than taking all of it in profits. As a result, 600 000 shares (150 000 x 4) are sold, reaping $60 million in new funds for the company. Moreover, because the owners still hold 40 percent of the stock, they effectively remain in control of the corporation. Finally, because they now have funds to invest in growth and new business opportunities for their firm, the value of the stock that they retained will—at least, theoretically—become more valuable in the future.

Even so, some analysts argue that too many firms, especially e-commerce businesses, are going public too quickly. IPOs are promoted by investment bankers who reap percentages of sale prices but are not responsible for postsale performance. A typical firm, for example, will spend 15 to 25 percent of the capital it raises through an IPO on the cost of the IPO itself.[9] Microsoft and AOL were IPOs, but so was Boston Chicken, which went public with stock valued at $10 per share, skyrocketed to $36 per share, and plummeted to under $1 per share before going bankrupt—all in less than five years. About half of all IPOs are now selling below their original offering prices.[10]

In the wake of an IPO, private investors do not have to share the company's wealth with its new public investors, but they forfeit a certain amount of control because outside investors gain voting control corresponding to their ownership shares. Occasionally, therefore, a publicly held corporation may choose to take the opposite path from an IPO—to reacquire its stock and become a closely held corporation. Levi Strauss, for example, was a publicly held company for many years. In 1985, however, the firm bought all of its own stock on the open market. Why? Levi's management reasoned that the firm could manage itself more effectively if control were more tightly held.

preferred stock

Shares whose owners have first claim on the corporation's assets and profits but who usually have no voting rights in the firm.

Preferred and Common Stock. Corporate stock may be either preferred or common. **Preferred stock** guarantees holders fixed dividends, much like the interest paid on savings accounts. Preferred stockholders are so called because they have preference, or priority, over common stockholders when dividends are distributed and, if a business liquidates, when the value of assets is distributed. Although many major corporations issue preferred stock, few small corporations do.

In contrast, **common stock** usually pays dividends only if the corporation makes a profit. Holders of common stock have the last claim to any assets if the company folds. Dividends on common stock, like those on preferred stock, are paid per share. Thus, a shareholder with 10 shares receives 10 times the dividend paid a shareholder with one share. Unlike preferred stock, however, common stock *must* be issued by every corporation, big or small.

There are two types of common stock—Class A and Class B. Class A common shares always have voting rights, but Class B common shares usually do not. Shareholder rights advocates argue that Class B common shares prevent democracy from working in companies because controlling shareholders hold most of the Class A stock and sell non-voting Class B stock to the general public. If Class B shareholders don't like what is going on in the company, they can't vote out the board of directors (see below).[11]

When investors cannot attend a shareholders' meeting, they can grant authority to vote the shares to someone who will attend. This procedure, called voting by **proxy**, is the way almost all individual investors vote.

Ownership of common stock does not automatically give an individual the right to act for the corporation or to share in its management. (Many management personnel do own stock, however.) The only way that most shareholders can influence the running of a corporation is to cast their votes for the board of directors of the corporation once a year. In most cases, however, shareholders' votes are meaningless, since corporations offer only one slate of directors for election.

Even when shareholders have choices, the number of shareholders may mean little real power for individual owners. For example, Noranda has thousands of shareholders, but only a handful of them have enough votes to have any effect on the way the company is run.

The Board of Directors

By law, the governing body of a corporation is its **board of directors**. The directors choose the president and other officers of the business and delegate the power to run the day-to-day activities of the business to those officers. The directors set policy on paying dividends, on financing major spending, and on executive salaries and benefits. For example, the board of directors can fire the CEO if the board does not agree with the CEO's business decisions. However, in most cases a board of directors will support the CEO.

Large corporations tend to have large boards with as many as 20 or 30 directors. Smaller corporations, on the other hand, tend to have no more than five directors. Usually, these are people with personal or professional ties to the corporation, such as family members, lawyers, and accountants.

Many boards have outside as well as inside directors. **Inside directors** are employees of the company and have primary responsibility for the corporation. That is, they are also top managers, such as the president and executive vice-president. **Outside directors** are not employees of the corporation in the normal course of its business. Attorneys, accountants, university officials, and executives from other firms are commonly used as outside directors. The basic responsibility of both inside and outside directors is the same, however—to ensure that the corporation is run in a way that is in the best interests of the shareholders.

The threat of liability suits from unhappy shareholders has motivated board members to ask corporations to provide liability insurance. Ten ex-directors at Peoples Jewellers Ltd. were involved in a $35 million lawsuit that alleged that the directors failed to disclose risks associated with a bond

common stock
Shares whose owners usually have last claim on the corporation's assets (after creditors and owners of preferred stock) but who have voting rights in the firm.

proxy
A legal document temporarily transferring the voting rights of a shareholder to another person.

board of directors
A group of individuals elected by a firm's shareholders and charged with overseeing, and taking legal responsibility for, the firm's actions.

inside directors
Members of a corporation's board of directors who are also full-time employees of the corporation.

outside directors
Members of a corporation's board of directors who are not also employees of the corporation on a day-to-day basis.

Corporations hold annual meetings with their shareholders. At such meetings, managers summarize what the corporation accomplished during the last year, announce plans for the coming year, and answer questions from individual shareholders. Shareholders also elect new members to the board of directors.

issue that was sold to the public. The directors could be forced to pay out of their own pocket if the judgment exceeds the $10 million in liability insurance that covers them.

Shareholder activism has also forced board members to take their responsibilities more seriously. Shareholders have, for example, shown an increased willingness to vote out board members if they feel they are doing a poor job. At Sherritt Gordon Ltd., one group of shareholders voted out existing board members because they failed to take proper steps to deal with potential problems of oversupply in the Canadian fertilizer industry.[12]

In an era of intense global competition, strategic leadership is absolutely essential. This will mean that big changes will have to occur in the way that boards operate. The "old code" of keeping the board in the background and letting management set strategy and operate the company will have to be replaced with a "new code" that requires board members to be actively involved in confronting problems the firm is facing.

Officers

chief executive officer (CEO)
The person responsible for the firm's overall performance.

Although board members oversee the corporation's operation, most of them do not participate in day-to-day management. Rather, they hire a team of top managers to run the firm. As we have already seen, this team, made up of officers, is usually headed by the firm's **chief executive officer**, or **CEO**, who is responsible for the firm's overall performance. Other officers typically include a president, who is responsible for internal management, and vice-presidents, who oversee various functional areas such as marketing or operations. Some officers may also be elected to serve on the board, and in some cases a single individual plays multiple roles. For example, one person might serve as board chairperson, CEO, and president. In other cases, a different person fills each slot.

Advantages of the Corporation

limited liability
Investor liability is limited to their personal investments in the corporation; courts cannot touch the personal assets of investors in the event that the corporation goes bankrupt.

Limited liability is the most striking feature of corporations. That is, the liability of investors is limited to their personal investments in the corporation. In the event of failure, the bankruptcy courts may seize a corporation's assets and sell them to pay debts, but the courts cannot touch the personal possessions of investors. Limited liability may be the main reason that many businesses incorporate, but limited liability is meaningless in some cases. For example, if all your personal assets are tied up in a business, then limited liability offers you little protection.

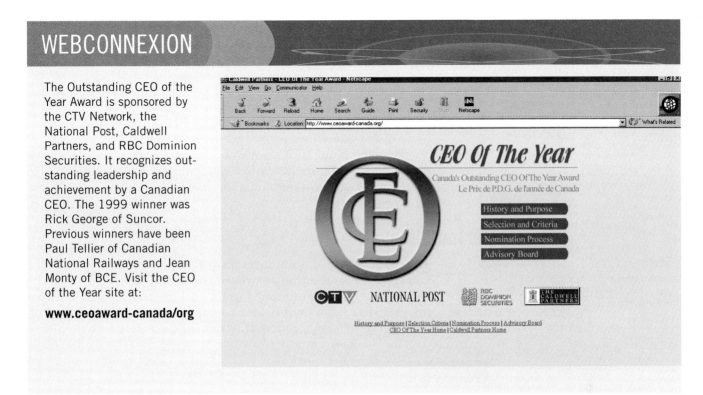

Another advantage of a corporation is continuity. Because it has a legal life independent of its founders, a corporation can continue to exist and grow long after the founders have retired or died. In theory, a corporation can go on forever.

Most corporations also benefit from professional management. In a sole proprietorship, a single person typically owns and manages the business. In most corporations, on the other hand, professional managers run the company but do not necessarily own any part of it.

Finally, corporations have a relatively easy time raising money. By selling more stock, they can expand the number of investors. In addition, the legal protections afforded corporations and the continuity of such organizations tend to make bankers more willing to grant loans.

Disadvantages of the Corporation

Ease of transferring ownership, one of the corporation's chief attractions, can also complicate the life of its managers. For example, one or more disgruntled shareholders in a small corporation can sell their stock to someone who wants to control the corporation and overthrow its top managers. Gaining control of a large corporation by this method is a complicated and expensive process, partially because of the large number of shareholders and partially because of the large sums of money involved. Amid the takeover environment of the 1980s, some shareholders of large firms succeeded. Philip Morris took over both General Foods and Kraft against their wishes and then combined them to form Kraft General Foods.[13] We discuss this interesting topic in more detail later in this chapter.

Forming a corporation also costs more than forming either a sole proprietorship or a partnership. The main reason is that someone who wants to incorporate must meet all the legal requirements of the province in which it incorporates. Corporations also need legal help in meeting government regulations. Corporations are far more heavily regulated than are proprietorships and general partnerships.

double taxation

A corporation must pay taxes on its profits, and the shareholders must pay personal income taxes on the dividends they receive.

The greatest potential drawback of the corporate form of organization, however, is **double taxation**. A corporation must pay income taxes on its profits, and then shareholders must pay income taxes on the dividends they receive from the corporation. Unlike interest expenses, dividends are not tax deductible for corporations. They come out of after-tax profits. So, from the shareholder's point of view, this procedure amounts to double taxation of the corporation's profits. By contrast, sole proprietorships and partnerships are taxed only once, since their profits are treated as the owner's personal income. The advantages and disadvantages of the corporate form of ownership are summarized in Figure 2.3. Table 2.4 compares the various forms of business ownership, using different characteristics.

Cooperatives

cooperative

An organization that is formed to benefit its owners in the form of reduced prices and/or the distribution of surpluses at year-end.

A **cooperative** is an organization that is formed to benefit its owners in the form of reduced prices and/or the distribution of surpluses at year-end. The process works like this: suppose some farmers believe they can get cheaper fertilizer prices if they form their own company and purchase in large volumes. They might then form a cooperative, which can be either federally or

Table 2.4	A Comparison of Three Forms of Business Ownership		
Characteristic	**Sole Proprietorship**	**Partnership**	**Corporation**
Protection against liability for bad debts	low	low	high
Ease of formation	high	high	medium
Permanence	low	low	high
Ease of ownership transfer	low	low	high
Ease of raising money	low	medium	high
Freedom from regulation	high	high	low
Tax advantages	high	high	low

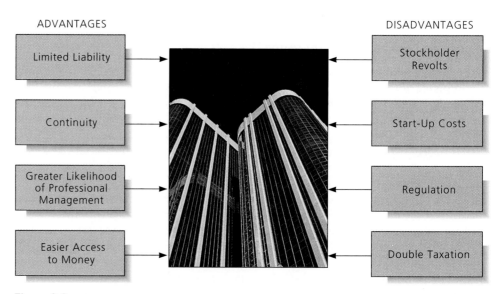

ADVANTAGES

Limited Liability

Continuity

Greater Likelihood of Professional Management

Easier Access to Money

DISADVANTAGES

Stockholder Revolts

Start-Up Costs

Regulation

Double Taxation

Figure 2.3
Corporations dominate the Canadian business system. Like sole proprietorships and partnerships, the corporate form of ownership has several advantages and disadvantages.

provincially chartered. Prices are generally lower to buyers and, at the end of the fiscal year, any surpluses are distributed to members on the basis of how much they purchased. If Farmer Jones bought 5 percent of all co-op sales, he would receive 5 percent of the surplus.

Voting rights are different from those in a corporation. In the cooperative, each member is entitled to one vote, regardless of how many shares he or she holds. This system prevents voting and financial control of the business by a few wealthy individuals. Table 2.5 shows the top 10 Canadian cooperatives.

Some large cooperatives have recently decided to become publicly traded companies. In 1994, SaskPool delegates voted 80 percent in favour of trading their shares on the Toronto Stock Exchange, thus giving up their status as a cooperative. United Grain Growers had made the same move a year earlier, and it was able to raise $34 million in its first year as a corporation. Other grain cooperatives like Manitoba Pool Elevators may follow suit. The ability to sell shares of stock will give the grain companies extra capital to invest in food processing, but farmers say they will lose control of the grain companies, and that more and more power will fall into the hands of managers.[14]

Types of Cooperatives

There are hundreds of different cooperatives, but they generally function in one of six main areas of business:

- Consumer cooperatives—These organizations sell goods to both members and the general public (e.g., co-op gasoline stations, agricultural implement dealers).

- Financial cooperatives—These organizations operate much like banks, accepting deposits from members, giving loans, and providing chequing services (e.g., credit unions).

- Insurance cooperatives—These organizations provide many types of insurance coverage, such as life, fire, and liability (e.g., the Cooperative Hail Insurance Company of Manitoba).

- Marketing cooperatives—These organizations sell the produce of their farm members and purchase inputs for the production process (e.g., seed and fertilizer). Some, like Federated Co-operatives, also purchase and market finished products.

- Service cooperatives—These organizations provide members with services, such as recreation.

Table 2.5	The Top 10 Cooperatives in Canada (ranked by annual revenues)

Company	Revenues (in billions)
1. Le Mouvement des caisses Desjardins	$5.4
2. Saskatchewan Wheat Pool	3.5
3. Agricore Cooperative Ltd.	3.0
4. Federated Co-operatives Ltd.	2.5
5. Cooperative fédérée de Québec	1.7
6. Agropur, cooperative Agro-alimentaire	1.4
7. Agrifoods International Cooperative Ltd.	1.2
8. XCAN Grain Pool	1.2
9. Calgary Co-operative Association Ltd.	0.5
10. Vancouver City Savings	0.4

Saskatchewan Wheat Pool
www.swp.com

■ Housing cooperatives—These organizations provide housing for members, who purchase a share in the cooperative, which holds the title to the housing complex.

In terms of the number of establishments in Canada, cooperatives are the least important form of ownership. However, they are of significance to society and to their members; they may provide services that are not readily available or that cost more than the members would otherwise be willing to pay.

TRENDS IN BUSINESS OWNERSHIP

Several trends in business ownership have become evident in recent years. Significant among these are acquisitions and mergers, divestitures and spin-offs, employee-owned corporations, strategic alliances, subsidiary and parent corporations, and institutional ownership.

Acquisitions and Mergers

In an **acquisition**, one firm simply buys another firm. For example, America Online bought Time Warner, Air Canada bought Canadian Airlines International, and BCE bought Teleglobe. The transaction is similar to buying a car that then becomes your property. In contrast, a **merger** is a consolidation of two firms, and the arrangement is more collaborative. For example, Canadian National Railways merged with the Illinois Central Railroad, Rogers Communication merged with Groupe Videotron Ltd., and Toronto Dominion Bank merged with Canada Trust.

As shown in Figure 2.4, mergers can take many forms. When the companies are in the same industry, as when Ford purchased Jaguar or Price and Costco merged, it is called a **horizontal merger**. When one of the companies is a supplier or customer to the other, it is called a **vertical merger**. Finally, when the companies are in unrelated businesses, it is called a **conglomerate merger**.

A merger or acquisition can take place in one of several different ways. In a **friendly takeover**, the acquired company welcomes the acquisition, perhaps because it needs cash or sees other benefits in joining the acquiring firm. But in a **hostile takeover**, the acquiring company buys enough of the other company's stock to take control even though the other company is opposed to the takeover.

A *poison pill* is a defence that management adopts to make a firm less attractive to an actual or potential hostile suitor in a takeover attempt. The objective is to make the "pill" so distasteful that a potential acquirer will not want to swallow it. In February 2000, BCE Inc. adopted a poison pill that allowed its shareholders to buy BCE stock at a 50 percent discount if another company announced its intention to acquire 20 percent or more of BCE's shares. BCE introduced the poison pill because it feared it might be a target of a hostile takeover, not because one was actually threatened. Its poison pill would flood the market with cheap shares and make the hostile bid unduly expensive.[15] BCE's poison pill is very similar to one adopted by Inco in the 1990s.

Divestitures and Spinoffs

A **divestiture** occurs when a company decides to sell part of its existing business operations to another corporation. For example, Unilever—the maker of Close-Up toothpaste, Dove soap, Vaseline lotion, and Q-tips—at one time

acquisition
The purchase of a company by another, larger firm, which absorbs the smaller company into its operations.

merger
The union of two companies to form a single new business.

horizontal merger
A merger of two firms that have previously been direct competitors in the same industry.

vertical merger
A merger of two firms that have previously had a buyer-seller relationship.

conglomerate merger
A merger of two firms in completely unrelated businesses.

friendly takeover
An acquisition in which the management of the acquired company welcomes the firm's buyout by another company.

hostile takeover
An acquisition in which the management of the acquired company fights the firm's buyout by another company.

divestiture
Occurs when a company sells part of its existing business operations to another company.

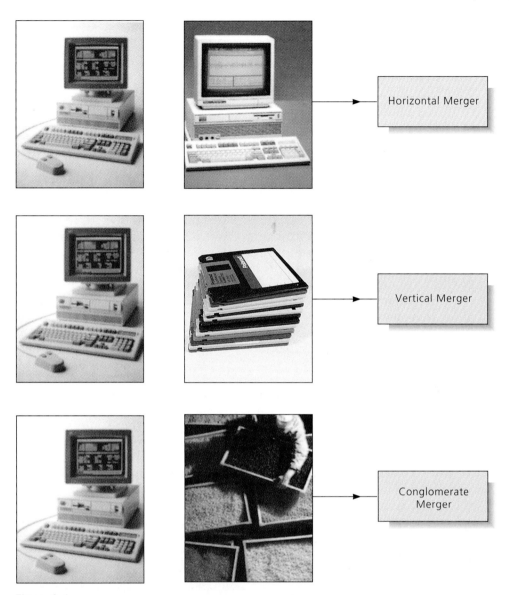

Figure 2.4
There are several different types of mergers. The three most common types are horizontal, vertical, and conglomerate mergers.

owned several specialty chemical businesses that made ingredients for its consumer products. The company decided that it had to focus more on the consumer products themselves, so it sold the chemical businesses to ICI, a European chemical company.

In other cases, a company might sell part of its operations to raise money. Seagram sold Tropicana Products Inc. to generate funds to help pay for its acquisition of Polygram. Kmart sold its profitable bookstore operations—Borders and Waldenbooks—to raise money to expand its discount chain. Such a sale is known as a spinoff. PepsiCo spun off Pizza Hut, KFC, and Taco Bell into a new, separate corporation called Tricon Global Restaurants, and BCE spun off Nortel Networks.

Employee-Owned Corporations

As we have discussed, corporations are sometimes owned by the employees who work for them. While many smaller corporations are owned by the

employee stock ownership plan (ESOP)

An arrangement whereby a corporation buys its own stock with loaned funds and holds it in trust for its employees. Employees "earn" the stock based on some condition such as seniority. Employees control the stock's voting rights immediately, even though they may not take physical possession of the stock until specified conditions are met.

individuals who founded them, there is a growing trend today for employees to buy significant stakes of larger corporations. The current pattern is for this ownership to take the form of **employee stock ownership plans**, or **ESOPs**.

An ESOP is essentially a trust established on behalf of the employees. A corporation might decide, for example, to set up an ESOP to stimulate employee motivation or to fight a hostile takeover attempt. The company first secures a loan, which it then uses to buy shares of its stock on the open market. A portion of the future profits made by the corporation is used to pay off the loan. The stock, meanwhile, is controlled by a bank or other trustee. Employees gradually gain ownership of the stock, usually on the basis of seniority. But even though they might not have physical possession of the stock for a while, they control its voting rights immediately.

A survey of 471 Canadian and U.S. companies conducted by Western Compensation & Benefits Consultants of Vancouver found that three-quarters of the companies that have adopted ESOPs have experienced improvement in both sales and profits. This result is not surprising, since companies with ESOPs must communicate their operating and financial results to employees. If employees know these things, they may be able to figure out how to improve their performance. Canadian companies such as Celestica and St. Laurent Paperboard Inc. have found that ESOPs give employees an increased sense of belonging in the company.[16]

Strategic Alliances   — Joint Venture

strategic alliance

An enterprise in which two or more persons or companies temporarily join forces to undertake a particular project.

A **strategic alliance**, or joint venture, involves two or more enterprises cooperating in the research, development, manufacture, or marketing of a product. For example, GM and Suzuki formed a strategic alliance at the Ingersoll, Ontario, plant where Trackers and Grand Vitaras are made.

Companies might choose to engage in, say, a joint venture for several reasons. One major reason is that it helps spread the risk. For example, the

WEBCONNEXION

Tembec, a forest products company, was created in Temiscaming, Quebec, when the community joined with employees to save a pulp mill that had been closed by its owners. The company encourages employee ownership, profit sharing, and employee participation in all issues reflecting company activities. Tembec's unique culture has stimulated innovation, entrepreneurship, and competitiveness, allowing it to grow into the international company it is today. Visit Tembec at:

www.tembec.ca

national oil company of Nigeria and Chevron Oil were both interested in building a new type of drilling platform to search for oil in swampy areas. The platform was so expensive, however, that the companies were afraid to build it on their own. They decided to contribute half the costs each and share in its use. Thus, each firm decreased its own risks.

Another reason for joint ventures is that each firm thinks it can get something from the other. For example, Toyota and General Motors recently agreed to jointly own and manage an automobile assembly plant in California. General Motors had not been able to operate the plant profitably alone, and had actually shut it down. But it eventually realized that it could learn more about the Japanese approach to management by working with Toyota. And the Japanese, in turn, got access to an assembly plant in the U.S. without having to invest millions of dollars in a new one.

Subsidiary and Parent Corporations

Sometimes corporations own other corporations. A **subsidiary corporation** is one that is owned by another corporation. The corporation that owns the subsidiary is called the **parent corporation**. For example, Unilever is the parent corporation of Lever Brothers, Lipton, Minnetonka, and Chesebrough-Ponds. Dylex was the parent corporation of Tip Top Tailors, Harry Rosen, Fairweather, Bi-Way, and Thrifty's, but it sold Tip Top Tailors in 2000 and is trying to sell some of its other retail chains as well.

subsidiary corporation
One that is owned by another corporation.

parent corporation
A corporation that owns a subsidiary.

Institutional Ownership

Most individual investors do not own enough stock to exert any influence on the management of big corporations. In recent years, however, more and more stock has been purchased by **institutional investors** such as mutual funds and pension funds. Because they control enormous resources, these investors can buy huge blocks of stock. Occasionally, institutional investors may expect to be consulted on major management decisions. Mutual funds are discussed in Chapter 19.

institutional investors
Organizations such as mutual and pension funds that purchase large blocks of company stock.

SUMMARY OF LEARNING OBJECTIVES

1. **Trace the history of business in Canada.** Modern business structures reflect a pattern of development over centuries. Throughout much of the colonial period, sole proprietors supplied raw materials to English manufacturers. The rise of the factory system during the Industrial Revolution brought with it mass production and specialization of labour. During the entrepreneurial era in the nineteenth century, huge corporations—and monopolies—emerged. During the production era of the early twentieth century, companies grew by emphasizing output and production. During the sales and marketing eras of the mid-1900s, businesses began focusing on sales staff, advertising, and the need to produce what consumers wanted. The most recent development has been towards a global perspective and using the Internet to boost business.

2. **Identify the *major forms of business ownership.*** The most common forms of business ownership are the *sole proprietorship*, the *partnership*, the *corporation*, and the *cooperative*. Each form has several advantages and disadvantages. The form under which a business chooses to organize is crucial because it affects both long-term strategy and day-to-day decision making. In addition to advantages and disadvantages, entrepreneurs must consider their preferences and long-range requirements.

3. **Explain *sole proprietorships* and *partnerships* and discuss the advantages and disadvantages of each.** *Sole proprietorships*, the most common form of business, consist of one person doing business. Although sole proprietorships offer freedom and privacy and are easy to form, they lack continuity and present certain financial risks. For one thing, they feature *unlimited liability*. The sole proprietor is liable for all debts incurred by the business. *General partnerships* are proprietorships with multiple owners. Partnerships have access to a larger talent pool and more investment money than do sole proprietorships, but may be dissolved if conflicts between partners cannot be resolved.

4. **Describe *corporations* and discuss their advantages and disadvantages.** *Corporations* are independent legal entities that are usually run by professional managers. In some corporations, stock is widely held by the public; in other firms, stock is held by individuals or small, private groups. The corporate form is used by most large businesses because it offers continuity and opportunities for raising money. It also features financial protection through *limited liability*: the liability of investors is limited to their personal investments. However, it is a complex legal entity subject to *double taxation*: In addition to taxes paid on corporate profits, investors must pay taxes on earned income.

5. **Describe the basic issues involved in creating and managing a corporation.** Creating a corporation generally requires legal assistance to file *articles of incorporation* and corporate *bylaws* and to comply with government regulations. Managers must understand shareholders' rights as well as the rights and duties of the *board of directors*.

6. **Identify recent trends and issues in corporate ownership.** Recent trends in corporate ownership include *strategic alliances* (in which two or more organizations collaborate); *employee stock ownership plans* (ESOPs) (by which employees buy large shares of their employer companies); *subsidiary and parent corporations* (where one corporation owns another); and *institutional ownership* of corporations (by groups such as mutual and pension funds).

7. **Discuss *mergers, acquisitions, divestitures.* and *spinoffs*.** Mergers and acquisitions are becoming increasingly popular strategies for firms today. Common forms of mergers include *horizontal, vertical,* and *conglomerate mergers*. Firms sometimes engage in *divestitures* to improve profitability and may create *spinoffs* to raise new capital.

KEY TERMS

Industrial Revolution, 42
factory system, 42
mass production, 42
specialization, 42
production era, 44
sales era, 45
marketing era, 45
finance era, 45
sole proprietorship, 47
unlimited liability, 48
liquidate, 49
partnership, 49
general partner, 49

limited partner, 49
corporation, 51
public corporation, 52
private corporation, 52
corporate governance, 54
stockholders (or
   shareholders), 54
stock, 54
initial public offering
   (IPO), 54
preferred stock, 54
common stock, 55
proxy, 55

board of directors, 55
inside directors, 55
outside directors, 55
chief executive officer
   (CEO), 56
limited liability, 56
double taxation, 58
cooperative, 58
acquisition, 60
merger, 60
horizontal merger, 60
vertical merger, 60
conglomerate merger, 60

friendly takeover, 60
hostile takeover, 60
divestiture, 60
employee stock
   ownership plan
   (ESOP), 62
strategic alliance, 62
subsidiary corporation,
   63
parent corporation, 63
institutional investors,
   63

STUDY QUESTIONS AND EXERCISES

Review Questions

1. Why is it important to understand the history of Canadian business?
2. What are the comparative advantages and disadvantages of the three basic forms of business ownership?
3. What are the primary benefits and drawbacks to serving as a limited partner in a partnership?
4. Why might a corporation choose to remain private? Why might a private corporation choose to go public?
5. Why have strategic alliances become more common in recent years?

Analysis Questions

6. Locate two annual reports and review them. Identify the specific points in the reports that the board of directors are communicating to the shareholders.

7. Go to the library and identify four major joint ventures beyond those discussed in the text. Is one of the parties likely to benefit more than the other?
8. What steps must be taken to incorporate a business in your province?

Application Exercises

9. Interview a manager in a sole proprietorship or general partnership. Based on your talks, what characteristics of that business form led the owner to choose it?
10. Interview the principal shareholder of a corporation. Based on your talks, what characteristics of that business form led the shareholder to choose it?

Building Your Business Skills

The Ups and Downs of Widget Ownership

Goal

To help students analyze the implications of corporate acquisitions and mergers for individual stockholders.

Situation

You own 500 shares of Widget International (WI). Although you like the company's products, you are disappointed with the current stock price. Analysts agree with you and warn that the company must drastically cut expenses or risk a takeover. Management begins to trim budgets, but its efforts are seen as too little too late. With the stock price continuing to drop, XYZ Corp. offers to buy WI. After successful negotiations, XYZ is set to acquire WI on January 1. When this happens, your 500 shares of WI will be converted into XYZ Corp. stock.

Method

Working in groups of four or five, analyze the ways in which this acquisition may affect your stock holdings. Research a similar corporate merger that took place in the past year as you consider the following factors:

- the nature of the acquiring company
- the fit between the products or services offered by the two companies
- the fiscal health of the acquiring company, as reflected in its stock price
- the stock market's long-term reaction to the acquisition. Does the market think it is a good move?
- changes in corporate leadership as a result of the acquisition
- changes in the way the acquired company's products are produced and marketed
- announced budgetary changes

Follow-Up Questions

1. After one company acquires another, what factors are likely to increase the stock price of the acquired firm?
2. After one company acquires another, what factors are likely to lower the stock price of the acquired firm?
3. Did your research identify any factors that are likely to trigger a corporate takeover?
4. In an acquisition, who is likely to be named CEO—the person in charge of the acquired or acquiring company? Who is likely to be named CEO in a merger of equals? What factors are likely to influence this decision?
5. How is the board of directors likely to change as a result of an acquisition? As a result of a merger?

Exploring the Net

Initial public offerings, or IPOs, are all the rage now. It seems as if the media are constantly discussing how this firm or that firm has just made its owners rich through an IPO. Investment bankers everywhere seem to be pointing their clients towards the latest IPO. Not surprisingly, there is an abundance of Internet sites now available to help observers and investors alike better navigate the IPO currents. With this in mind, begin this exercise by visiting and exploring each of the following Web sites:

www.ipo.com

www.ipocentral.com

www.ipomaven.com

www.ipospotlight.com

www.ipomonitor.com

Now, respond to the following questions:

1. Who is the target audience for each of these sites?
2. What are the strengths and weaknesses of each site?
3. As a potential investor, which site would you find most useful? Why?
4. Select one recent IPO discussed on all or most of these sites. Compare what you learn about the firm from the various sites. Explain any differences you observe.

Concluding Case 2-1

Trends in Corporate Governance

Corporate annual meetings are supposed to be occasions when shareholders ask important questions about company operations, find out how well their company is doing, and hear about its strategic plans for the future. But this frequently does not happen. Instead, annual meetings often seem to be a waste of time for everyone, and almost nothing is said or done that affects the corporation's activities.

Problems include carefully scripted shareholder meetings with prearranged questions, shareholder questions that are not very insightful, ritualized CEO speeches that stifle creativity and spontaneity, high-cost videos that are entertaining but have little real impact on corporate operations, and disruptions by dissident shareholders who object to things like excessive CEO pay or environmental insensitivity on the part of the company.

But things may be changing. The move towards increased corporate democracy in banks began in 1997, when a Quebec judge ruled that Royal Bank and National Bank must present shareholder proposals at their annual meetings. The banks resisted, claiming that the person who wanted to make proposals—Yves Michaud, a former Quebec politician and journalist—had a personal vendetta against them. The judge rejected the banks' argument, and two proposals—to cap the CEO's salary and to limit directors' terms to 10 years—were presented (but defeated by shareholders).

That court decision set the stage for a big change in the tenor of the banks' annual meetings, which had formerly been tightly controlled love-ins. They are now more oriented towards shareholder democracy and change. Banks have become less fearful of shareholder motions, largely because Michaud's court victory hasn't resulted in a flood of shareholder proposals.

At the Bank of Montreal's annual meeting in 2000, six proposals were presented to shareholders by Paul Lussier, president of the Association for the Protection of Quebec Savers and Investors. One of the proposals received majority support from the assembled shareholders, even though management recommended that shareholders vote against the motion. This is a departure from past practice.

At most of the major banks, proposals from shareholders are now being treated with much more respect than they formerly were. In early 2000, for example, shareholder motions were presented at the annual meetings of four major Canadian banks. The banks have been targets for activists and shareholder motions because bank stock is widely held and banks have a great deal of power.

CASE QUESTIONS

1. Does the corporate annual meeting serve any purpose? Defend your answer.

2. Why do the problems noted above occur at so many annual meetings?

3. What suggestions can you make for solving these problems?

4. Why have banks recently become more open to shareholder motions? ◆

Concluding Case 2-2

Employees Are Stockholders at WestJet

WestJet Airlines started operations on February 29, 1996. Its strategy is to sell tickets at bargain prices, offer good customer service, keep costs down by running a low-cost operation, and fly short-haul trips to carefully chosen markets. In just a few short years, WestJet's fleet has grown to 21 jets and sales revenues have grown to over $330 million annually. WestJet's share price on the Toronto Stock Exchange has increased 240 percent since its initial public offering (IPO) in 1999. WestJet's performance has made its founders rich, but they aren't the only ones who are benefiting.

WestJet's employees have been actively involved in buying up shares of the company's stock. For every dollar an employee invests, the company matches that amount. This means that employees are essentially able to buy shares of stock in WestJet at half the normal market price. Therefore, it isn't surprising that 83 percent of employees own shares in the company. The employees who bought in before the IPO now have an impressive portfolio. Some flight attendants now own more than $400 000 in stock, and some WestJet pilots are millionaires.

WestJet CEO Clive Beddoe has encouraged a corporate culture that aligns the interests of the employees with those of the company. He recognizes that in the commercial airline business employees are spread out all over the country as they work in various airports and on the airplanes. He knows that he has to encourage people to manage themselves. WestJet therefore gives a lot of latitude to workers to perform their jobs. This strategy means fewer layers of supervisors and a much higher level of productivity per worker. The strategy seems to be working: WestJet operates with fewer than 60 people per aircraft, while rival Air Canada uses more than 140 per aircraft.

Beddoe isn't so naïve as to assume that workers will automatically take ownership of their job. He realizes the value of incentives, so WestJet has instituted a profit-sharing plan that encourages employees to be interested in maximizing profits. The plan works as follows: If WestJet's profit margin is, say, 10 percent, then 10 percent of net income is given to employees (prorated by salary). If the profit margin is 15 percent, employees get 15 percent, and so on up to a maximum of 20 percent. On November 17, 2000, cheques totalling more than $8 million were handed out to employees. WestJet pays salaries that are slightly lower than the industry average, but when the profit sharing is added in, employees are better off than others in the industry.

WestJet receives more than 3000 résumés a week from people who want to join the company. Most of these people do not currently work in the airline industry. Beddoe views that positively, saying that it's

important to hire people who have new ideas and a new vision. WestJet is particularly interested in applicants who are enthusiastic and have a sense of humour, because Beddoe thinks that everyone should have fun while working.

An employee association called the Pro-Active Communication Team (PACT) is active at WestJet. It includes all employees in the company, and has chapters representing the various employee groups, such as pilots and flight attendants. Each of these groups has representatives who sit on a council. PACT helps management keep in touch with rank-and-file workers and address any concerns they may have. PACT provides workers many of the same services a union would, but without the adversarial environment that a union can create. PACT may make it very difficult for a union to get into WestJet because of the way PACT is organized. If an employee group (e.g., flight attendants) wants to leave PACT, it must receive approval from 75 percent of the members. That is not very likely to happen.

CASE QUESTIONS

1. Is WestJet a private corporation or a public corporation? Explain how the offering of an IPO affects whether a corporation is public or private.

2. How have WestJet employees benefited from owning shares in the company? Why would employees who bought stock before the IPO have benefited more than others who bought shares later?

3. What rights do WestJet employees have as stockholders? To what extent will these rights influence their day-to-day behaviour on the job?

4. What is an ESOP? Does WestJet have an ESOP, or doesn't it? Explain.

5. Consider the following statement: "When a company forms an employee association like PACT, it is just trying to get employees to do what management wants, but under the guise of consulting with employees. Management and workers have basically conflicting goals, and these conflicting goals can't be removed simply by forming an employee association." Do you agree or disagree with this statement? Explain. ◆

Next Stop: The World

Bombardier Inc. is a diversified Canadian company that specializes in transportation, recreational products, aerospace, financial, and real estate services. The company was founded in 1942 to manufacture a classic Canadian product—tracked vehicles for transportation across snow-covered terrain. Many of the original Bombardier snowmobiles that were manufactured decades ago can still be seen in remote areas of Canada. One such half-track sits on the windswept shores of Yathkyed Lake in the Northwest Territories, hundreds of kilometres from any town. It is a mute reminder of the important role Bombardier played in opening up Canada's remote North.

Bombardier has come a long way since its start. It is now the sixth-largest aviation company in the world and a major force in international aviation. It achieved its present size by acquiring several aviation firms, including Canadair, Learjet, Short Brothers PLC, and de Havilland. In 1996, Bombardier rolled out its Global Express jet, which can fly 12 000 kilometres at 850 kilometres per hour. The jet is designed to capture the interest of executives who must travel long distances in the newly globalized business world.

While Bombardier's headquarters are in Montreal, Bombardier employees work around the world. In 1999, 22 000 employees worked in Canada, 9000 worked in the U.S., 2000 worked in Mexico, 18 000 worked in Europe, and 2000 worked in the Middle East. More than 90 percent of company revenues come from outside Canada. Annual sales revenues exceed $5 billion, and company assets exceed $14 billion.

Bombardier is on a mission of expansion to accelerate growth in foreign markets. Bombardier's mandate is to:

- search for and identify new business opportunities in countries other than those in North America and Europe
- act as an intermediary with government authorities and business communities in foreign locations
- explore opportunities for acquisitions and strategic alliances

Although Bombardier has done well in international aviation markets, the competition is fierce. In the mid-1990s, Bombardier held two-thirds of the market for regional jets. But that was before Brazilian rival Embraer captured 45 percent of that market. Bombardier complained to the World Trade Organization (WTO) that the Brazilian government was unfairly subsidizing Embraer to the tune of $2.5 billion. In 1999, the WTO struck down Brazil's Pro-ex financing program, which gave buyers of Embraer jets reduced rates of interest. However, the WTO also struck down Canada's Technology Partnership Program (TPP), saying that it, too, was an illegal export subsidy program. In April 2000, the WTO endorsed Canada's revamped TPP program and ruled that Brazil had failed to fix its program. This was a major boost for Bombardier.

Other competitors are expected to loom in the market over the next few years. As it pursues its goals in the international marketplace, Bombardier will have to constantly monitor subsidies that other aviation companies receive from their governments to ensure that it does not find itself in an untenable competitive position. ◆

As Bombardier discovered, carrying on business outside of Canada can be a very complicated process that involves the company in more than simply business activities. Yet Canadian business firms are increasingly looking beyond the domestic Canadian market as they pursue customers, sales, and profit. By focusing on the learning objectives in this chapter, you will better understand the dynamics of international business management as well as some of the social, cultural, economic, legal, and political differences that make international trade a challenging enterprise. After reading this chapter, you should be able to:

LEARNING OBJECTIVES

1. Describe the rise of international business and identify the major world marketplaces.

2. Explain how different forms of *competitive advantage, import-export balances, exchange rates*, and *foreign competition* determine the ways in which countries and businesses respond to the international environment.

3. Discuss the factors involved in deciding to do business internationally and in selecting the appropriate *levels of international involvement* and *international organizational structure*.

4. Describe some of the ways in which *social, cultural, economic, legal,* and *political differences* act as barriers to international trade.

5. Explain how *free trade agreements* assist world trade.

THE RISE OF INTERNATIONAL BUSINESS

The total volume of world trade today is immense—around $8 trillion each year. As more and more firms engage in international business, the world economy is fast becoming a single interdependent system—a process called **globalization**. Even so, we often take for granted the diversity of goods and services available today as a result of international trade. Your television set, your shoes, and even the roast lamb on your dinner table may all be **imports**—that is, products made or grown abroad but sold in Canada. At the same time, the success of many Canadian firms depends in large part on **exports**—products made or grown domestically and shipped for sale abroad.

globalization
The integration of markets globally.

imports
Products that are made or grown abroad and sold in Canada.

exports
Products made or grown in Canada that are sold abroad.

The Contemporary Global Economy

International business is nothing new. Trade between nations can actually be traced back as far as 2000 B.C., when North African tribes took dates and clothing to Assyria and Babylonia in the Middle East and traded them for olive oil and spices. Christopher Columbus's voyages of discovery were motivated by the search for new trade routes. Still, there is a tendency for people to forget that international business has been around for a long time. An understanding of historical forces can significantly improve our understanding of the contemporary global economy—how it works, why it works, and what trends will likely shape its future.[1]

MIT professor Paul Krugman argues that what we now regard as an extremely active "global economy" is not as big a change as you might imagine. He points out that imports now represent only a slightly higher proportion of GDP than they did 100 years ago, and that capital mobility (the movement of money from country to country) is about the same as it was in 1914. At that time, moreover, England's trade surplus—4 percent of GDP—was the same as the surplus enjoyed by Japan during the peak decade of the 1980s.

On the other hand, it is also true that international trade is becoming increasingly central to the fortunes of most nations of the world, as well as to their largest businesses. Whereas in the past many nations followed strict polices to protect domestic business, today more and more countries are aggressively encouraging international trade. They are more freely opening their borders to foreign businesses, offering incentives for their own domestic businesses to expand internationally, and making it easier for foreign firms to partner with local firms through various alliances. Similarly, as more and more industries and markets become global, firms that compete in them are also becoming global.

Several forces have combined to spark and sustain globalization. For one thing, governments and businesses have simply become more aware of the benefits of globalization to their countries and shareholders. For another, new technologies make international travel, communication, and commerce increasingly easier, faster, and cheaper than ever before. Overseas phone calls and seaborne shipping costs per tonne have both declined over the last several decades. Likewise, transatlantic travel once required several days aboard a ship. Today, the Concorde can whisk people between North America and Europe in less than four hours; and even conventional transatlantic travel takes less than a day. Finally, there are competitive pressures: sometimes, a firm simply must enter foreign markets just to keep up with its competitors.

In this section, we examine some key factors that have shaped—and are shaping—today's global business environment. First, we identify and describe the *major world marketplaces*. Then we discuss some important factors that determine the ways in which both nations and their businesses respond to the international environment: the roles of different forms of *competitive advantage*, *import-export balances*, and *exchange rates*.

The Major World Marketplaces

The contemporary world economy revolves around three major marketplaces: North America, Europe, and Asia-Pacific. This is not to say that other regions are unimportant, nor is it to suggest that all countries in these three regions are equally important. However, these three geographic regions are

At booths run by Internet Perú, the nation's largest online service, native Ashaninkas line up to sell their traditional crafts over the Net. From fewer than 5 million users in 1998, Latin America will grow to 19 million by 2003. E-commerce sales will balloon from $167 million to $8 billion in the same period.

home to most of the world's largest economies, biggest multinational corporations, most influential financial markets, and highest-income consumers.

The World Bank, an agency of the United Nations, uses **per capita income**—the average income per person—as a measure to divide countries into one of three groups:[2]

- *High-income countries* are those with per capita income greater than US$9386. These include Canada, the United States, most countries in Europe, Australia, New Zealand, Japan, South Korea, Kuwait, the United Arab Emirates, Israel, Singapore, and Taiwan. Hong Kong, while technically no longer an independent nation, also falls into this category.

- *Middle-income countries* are those with per capita income of less than US$9386 but more than US$765. Some of the countries in this group are the Czech Republic, Greece, Hungary, Poland, most countries comprising the former Soviet Bloc, Turkey, Mexico, Argentina, and Uruguay. Some of these nations, most notably Poland, Argentina, and Uruguay, are undergoing successful industrialization and economic development and are expected to move into the high-income category very soon.

- *Low-income countries*, also called *developing countries*, are those with per capita income of less than US$765. Some of these, such as China and India, have huge populations and are seen as potentially attractive markets for international business. Due to low literacy rates, weak infrastructures, unstable governments, and related problems, other countries in this group are less attractive to international business. For example, the East African nation of Somalia, plagued by drought, civil war, and starvation, plays virtually no role in the world economy.

North America

The United States dominates the North American business region. It is the single largest marketplace and enjoys the most stable economy in the world. Canada also plays a major role in the international economy. Moreover, the U.S. and Canada are each other's largest trading partner. Many U.S. firms, such as General Motors and Procter & Gamble, have maintained successful Canadian operations for years, and many Canadian firms, such as Nortel Networks and Alcan Aluminum, are also major international competitors.

Mexico has also become a major manufacturing centre, especially along the southern U.S. border, where cheap labour and low transportation costs have encouraged many firms, from the United States and other countries, to build manufacturing plants. The auto industry has been especially active. For example, DaimlerChrysler, General Motors, Volkswagen, Nissan, and Ford have large assembly plants in this region. Moreover, several of their major suppliers have also built facilities in the area. From 1993 to 1999, exports of automobiles and automobile parts from Mexico increased from $7.2 billion to a stunning $20.4 billion, and the auto industry in Mexico employs 380 000 workers.

These three nations, which are shown in Figure 3.1, have enjoyed the benefits of the North American Free Trade Agreement (NAFTA). According to this agreement, over a 15-year period the three nations will gradually eliminate tariffs and other major trade barriers. Since its ratification in 1994, NAFTA has created several million new jobs in all three countries and substantially boosted mutual trade. There is speculation that NAFTA will eventually expand to include other Latin American countries, with Chile seen as the most likely new member.

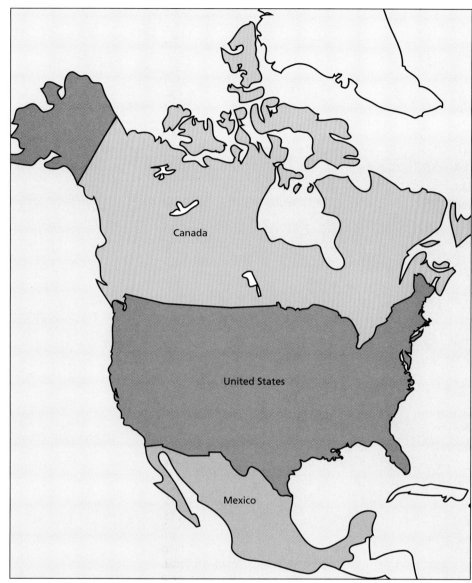

Figure 3.1
The North American marketplace.

Europe

Europe has often been regarded as two regions—Western Europe and Eastern Europe. Western Europe, dominated by Germany, the United Kingdom, France, and Italy, has long been a mature but fragmented marketplace. But the transformation of the European Union (EU) in 1992 into a unified marketplace has further increased the region's importance (see Figure 3.2). Major international firms such as Unilever, Renault, Royal Dutch/Shell, Michelin, Siemens, and Nestlé are all headquartered in Western Europe.

E-commerce and technology have also become increasingly important in this region.[3] There has been a surge in Internet start-ups in southeast England, the Netherlands, and the Scandinavian countries, and Ireland is now the world's number-two exporter of software (after the United States).[4] Strasbourg, France, is a major centre for biotech start-ups. Barcelona, Spain, has many flourishing software and Internet companies, and the Frankfurt region of Germany is dotted with both software and biotech start-ups.[5]

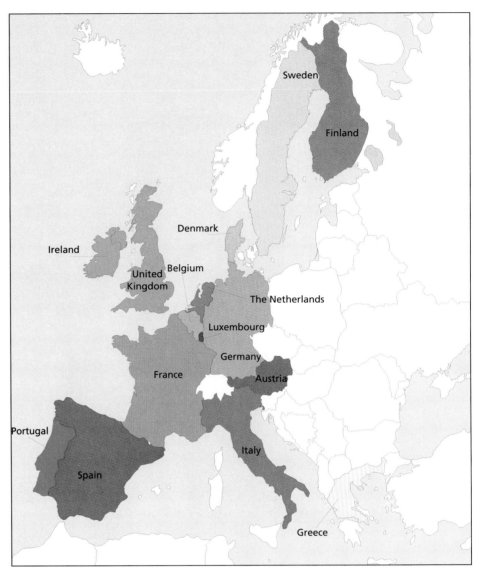

Figure 3.2
Europe and the nations of the European Union.

Eastern Europe, which was primarily communist until recently, has also gained in importance, both as a marketplace and as a producer. For example, such multinational corporations as Daewoo, Nestlé, General Motors, and ABB Asea Brown Boveri all have set up operations in Poland. Similarly, Ford, General Motors, Suzuki, and Volkswagen have all built new factories in Hungary. On the other hand, government instability has hampered economic development in Russia, Bulgaria, Albania, Romania, and other countries in this region.

Asia-Pacific

Asia-Pacific generally consists of Japan, China, Thailand, Malaysia, Singapore, Indonesia, South Korea, Taiwan, the Philippines, and Australia. Some experts still identify Hong Kong as a separate part of the region, although the former city-state is now actually part of China. Vietnam is sometimes included as part of the region. Fuelled by strong entries in the automobile, electronics, and banking industries, the economies of these countries grew rapidly in the 1970s and 1980s. Unfortunately, a currency

WEBCONNEXION

Letsbuyit.com is an Internet retailer founded and head-quartered in Sweden. It targets European customers with a retailing concept called "co-buying." To learn more about the idea of "the power of consumers joining in numbers"—and to find out more about the company's products and distribution process—visit its site at:

www.letsbuyit.com

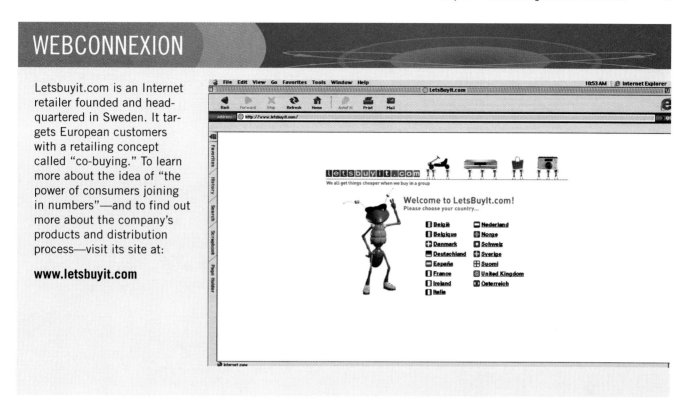

crisis in the late 1990s generally slowed growth in virtually every country of the region.

The currency crisis aside, however, Asia-Pacific is an important force in the world economy and a major source of competition for North American firms. Led by firms such as Toyota, Toshiba, and Nippon Steel, Japan dominates the region. In addition, South Korea (with such firms as Samsung and Hyundai), Taiwan (owner of Chinese Petroleum and manufacturing home of many foreign firms), and Hong Kong (a major financial centre) are also successful players in the international economy. China, the most densely populated country in the world, continues to emerge as an important market in its own right. In fact, most indicators suggest that the Chinese economy is now the world's third largest, behind the United States and Japan.

As in North America and Western Europe, technology promises to play an increasingly important role in this region. In Asia, however, the emergence of technology firms has been hampered by a poorly developed electronic infrastructure, slower adoption of computers and information technology, a higher percentage of lower-income consumers, and the aforementioned currency crisis. Thus, while the future looks promising, technology companies in this region are facing several obstacles as they work to keep pace with competitors based elsewhere.[6]

Figure 3.3 shows a map of the Association of Southeast Asian Nations (ASEAN) countries of Asia-Pacific. ASEAN (pronounced *OZZIE-on*) was founded in 1967 as an organization for economic, political, social, and cultural cooperation. In 1995, Vietnam became the group's first communist member. Today, the ASEAN group has a population of over 400 million and a GNP of approximately $350 billion.

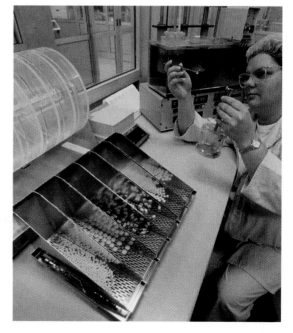

Egis is a Hungarian pharmaceutical company that has developed a number of new hypertension drugs. Because it hopes to sell these drugs in the United States and Europe, Hungarian membership in the European Union would be a plus for Egis, as well as for numerous start-ups and privatized companies in Eastern Europe.

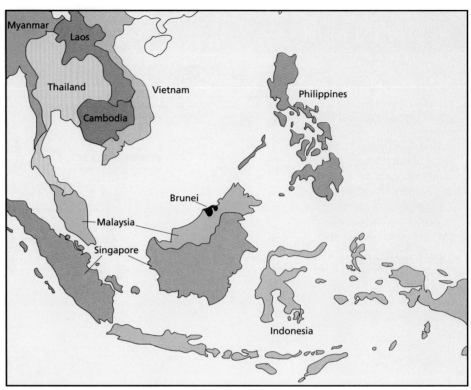

Figure 3.3
The nations of ASEAN.

Forms of Competitive Advantage

Why are there such high levels of importing, exporting, and other forms of international business activity? Because no country can produce all the goods and services that its people need. Thus, countries tend to export products that they can produce better or less expensively than other countries, using the proceeds to import products that they cannot produce as effectively.

Of course, this principle does not fully explain why various nations export and import *what* they do. Such decisions hinge partly on the kind of advantages a particular country may enjoy regarding its abilities to create and/or sell various products and resources.[7] Traditionally, economists focused on *absolute* and *comparative advantage* to explain international trade. But because this approach focuses narrowly on such factors as natural resources and labour costs, a perspective has emerged that focuses on a more complex view of *national competitive advantage*.

Absolute Advantage

absolute advantage

A nation's ability to produce something more cheaply or better than any other country.

An **absolute advantage** exists when a country can produce something more cheaply and/or of higher quality than any other country. Saudi oil, Brazilian coffee beans, and Canadian timber approximate absolute advantage, but examples of true absolute advantage are rare. In reality, "absolute" advantages are always relative. For example, most experts say that the vineyards of France produce the finest wines in the world. But the burgeoning wine business in California and Ontario attests to the fact that producers there can also produce very good values in wine—wines that are perhaps almost as good as French wines and that also are available in more varieties and at lower prices.

For thousands of years, the Indonesian islands held an absolute advantage in the kinds of spices—cinnamon, pepper, nutmeg, cloves—being sold in this market in the modern country's capital of Jakarta. The local market is still worth $1.5 billion a year, and although Indonesia no longer enjoys an absolute advantage, the cultivation of exotic natural resources still accounts for about 40 percent of the nation's jobs.

Comparative Advantage

A country has a **comparative advantage** in goods that it can produce more efficiently or better than other goods. For example, if businesses in a given country can make computers more efficiently than they can make automobiles, that nation's firms have a comparative advantage in computer manufacture. Canada has a comparative advantage in farming (because of fertile land and a temperate climate), while South Korea has a comparative advantage in electronics manufacturing (because of efficient operations and cheap labour). As a result, Canadian firms export grain to South Korea and import VCRs and stereos from South Korea. The "It's a Wired World" box describes how comparative advantage played a key role in the historical development of Finland's Nokia Corp.

comparative advantage
A nation's ability to produce some products more cheaply or better than it can others.

Nokia Corp.
www.nokia.com

National Competitive Advantage

In recent years, a theory of national competitive advantage has become a more widely accepted model of why nations engage in international trade.[8] Basically, **national competitive advantage** derives from four conditions:

1. *Factor conditions* are the factors of production that we identified in Chapter 1.

2. *Demand conditions* reflect a large domestic consumer base that promotes strong demand for innovative products.

3. *Related and supporting industries* include strong local or regional suppliers and/or industrial customers.

4. *Strategies, structures, and rivalries* refer to firms and industries that stress cost reduction, product quality, higher productivity, and innovative new products.

national competitive advantage
A country will be inclined to engage in international trade when factor conditions, demand conditions, related and supporting industries, and strategies/structures/ rivalries are favourable.

When all of these conditions exist, a nation will naturally be inclined to engage in international business. Japan, for instance, has an abundance of natural resources and strong domestic demand for automobiles. Its automobile producers have well-oiled supplier networks, and domestic firms have competed intensely with each other for decades. This set of circumstances

IT'S A WIRED WORLD

Nokia Puts the Finishing Touches on a Telecommunications Giant

On the surface, one would assume that the major industrialized countries—Canada, the United States, Germany, Japan—would obviously be leading the way in information technology. But while this is generally true, a surprising upstart (Nokia Corp.) in a relatively remote part of the world (Finland) is at the forefront of today's emerging global communication network.

Ironically, conditions in Finland actually provided a unique catalyst for the Nokia success story. Many parts of the Finnish landscape are heavily forested, and vast regions of the country are very sparsely populated. Creating, maintaining, and updating wired land-based communication networks is difficult and extremely expensive. But wireless digital systems are a relative bargain. As a result, conditions were virtually perfect for an astute, forward-looking company like Nokia to strike gold.

Nokia was formed in 1865 by Fredrik Idestam, a Finnish engineer. The company's early success is quite consistent with the theory of comparative advantage. Idestam's young company set up shop on the Nokia River in Finland to manufacture pulp and paper, using the area's lush forests as raw material. Nokia flourished in anonymity for about a century, focusing almost exclusively on its domestic market.

In the 1960s, however, management decided to expand regionally. In 1967, with the government's encouragement, Nokia took over two state-owned firms, Finnish Rubber Works and Finnish Cable Works. But it was in 1981 that a seminal event dramatically altered Nokia's destiny: Because it had done so well with the rubber and cable operations, the Finnish government offered to sell Nokia 51 percent ownership of the state-owned Finnish Telecommunications Co.

Because Nokia had already been developing competencies in digital technologies, the firm seized the opportunity and almost immediately pushed aggressively into a variety of telecommunications businesses. For example, Nokia created Europe's first digital telephone network in 1982. A series of other acquisitions and partnerships subsequently propelled Nokia into the number-one position in the global market for mobile telephones. Today, the firm commands a 27 percent market share in cellular telephones, comfortably ahead of second-place Motorola's 17 percent.

But Nokia hasn't been content to rest on its laurels. To the contrary, the company continues to expand into new and emerging markets. Foremost among these is technology to provide cellular phones with reliable and affordable Web content. Indeed, Nokia was first out of the gate in this area and quickly established its own innovation, WAP (an acronym for *wireless application protocol*), as the likely standard that other firms will have little choice but to license for their own use.

explains why Japanese automobile companies such as Toyota, Honda, Nissan, and Mazda are generally successful in foreign markets.

Import-Export Balances

Although international trade involves many advantages, trading with other nations can pose problems if a country's imports and exports do not strike an acceptable balance. In deciding whether an overall balance exists, economists use two measures: *balance of trade* and *balance of payments*.

Balance of Trade

balance of trade
The difference in value between a country's total exports and its total imports.

A nation's **balance of trade** is the total economic value of all products it imports minus the total economic value of all products it exports. Canada has enjoyed a favourable balance of merchandise trade since 1980 (see Figure 3.4). However, the trade balance is favourable only because Canada exports so much more to the U.S. than it imports from the U.S. Canada's trade balance with its other major trading partners (e.g., Japan, the U.K., and other EU countries) is unfavourable. Our trade balance with all remaining countries of the world taken together as a group is also unfavourable (see Table 3.1).

A study by the World Trade Organization (WTO) found that Canada's economic dependence on the U.S. is growing, and that this trend leaves Canada

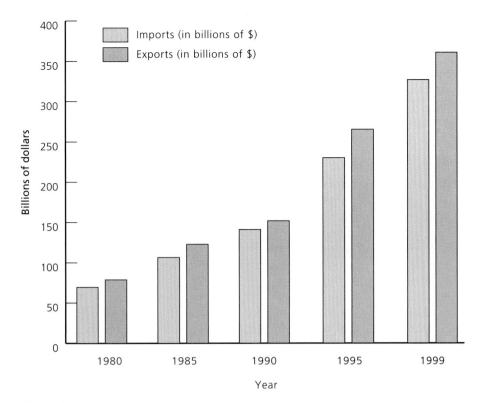

Figure 3.4
Canadian imports and exports of merchandise.

Table 3.1	Canadian Exports to, and Imports from, Selected Countries	
Country	**Exports to (billions)**	**Imports from (billions)**
United States	$252.3	$203.3
Japan	8.1	13.9
United Kingdom	4.1	6.2
Germany	2.4	6.1
South Korea	1.7	3.3
France	1.5	4.9
Taiwan	0.9	1.2
Mexico	1.3	7.6
Hong Kong	0.6	1.2

vulnerable. The U.S. accounts for 80 percent of Canada's merchandise exports and two-thirds of its imports. What's worse, only 50 companies operating in Canada account for nearly half of all merchandise exports, and these companies are often U.S.-owned. Canada has too many of its eggs in one basket.[9]

Trade Deficits and Surpluses.   When a country's imports exceed its exports—that is, when it has a negative balance of trade—it suffers a **trade deficit**. In short, more money is flowing out of the country than flowing in. A positive balance of trade occurs when a country's exports exceed its imports and it enjoys a **trade surplus**: more money is flowing into the country than flowing out of it. Trade deficits and surpluses are influenced by an array of factors, such as the absolute, comparative, or national competitive

World Trade Organization
www.wto.org

trade deficit
Occurs when a country imports more than it exports.

trade surplus
Occurs when a country exports more than it imports.

advantages enjoyed by the relevant trading partners, the general economic conditions prevailing in various countries, and the effect of trade agreements. For example, higher domestic costs, greater international competition, and continuing economic problems of some of its regional trading partners have slowed Japan's exports from the tremendous growth it enjoyed several years ago. But rising prosperity in both China and India have resulted in strong increases in both exports from and imports to those countries.

Balance of Payments

balance of payments
The difference between money flowing into and out of a country as a result of trade and other transactions.

The **balance of payments** refers to the flow of money into or out of a country. The money a nation pays for imports and receives for exports—that is, its balance of trade—comprises much of its balance of payments. Other financial exchanges are also factors. For example, money spent by tourists, money spent on foreign-aid programs, and money spent and received in the buying and selling of currency on international money markets all affect the balance of payments.

An unfavourable balance means that more money is flowing out than in. For Canada to have a favourable balance of payments for a given year, the total of our exports, foreign tourist spending in this country, foreign investments here, and earnings from overseas investments must be greater than the total of our imports, Canadian tourist spending overseas, our foreign aid grants, our military spending abroad, the investments made by Canadian firms abroad, and the earnings of foreigners from their investments in Canada. (See Figure 3.5.) Canada has had an unfavourable balance of payments for about the last 20 years.

Exchange Rates

exchange rate
The ratio of one currency to another.

The balance of imports and exports between two countries is affected by the rate of exchange between their currencies. An **exchange rate** is the rate at which the currency of one nation can be exchanged for that of another.[10] Suppose that the exchange rate between Canadian dollars and French francs is 5 to 1. This means that it costs one dollar to "buy" five francs; alternatively, it costs five francs to "buy" one dollar. In a more relevant purchasing example, this exchange rate means that one dollar or five francs should have exactly the same purchasing power.

At the end of the Second World War, the major nations of the world agreed to establish fixed exchange rates. Under *fixed exchange rates*, the value of any country's currency relative to that of another country remains constant. Today, however, *floating exchange rates* are the norm, and the value of one country's currency relative to that of another country varies with market conditions. For example, when many French citizens want to spend francs to buy Canadian dollars (or goods), the value of the dollar relative to the franc increases, or becomes "stronger"; *demand* for the dollar is high. In other words, a currency is said to be "strong" when demand for it is high. It is also "strong" when there is high demand for the goods manufactured at the expense of that currency. Thus, the value of the dollar rises with the demand for Canadian goods. In reality, exchange rates fluctuate by very small degrees on a daily basis. More significant variations usually occur over greater spans of time.

Fluctuation in exchange rates can have an important impact on the balance of trade. Suppose, for example, that you want to buy some French

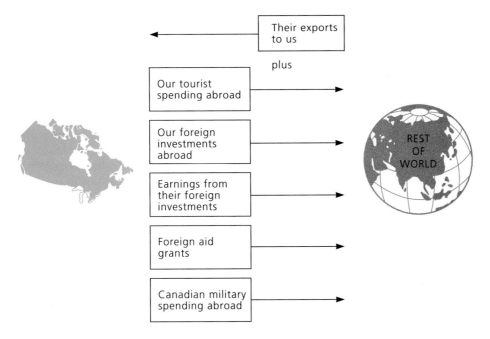

Figure 3.5
Requirements for Canada to have a favourable balance of payments. (The arrows indicate the direction of the flow.)

wine priced at 50 francs per bottle. At an exchange rate of 5 francs to the dollar, a bottle will cost you $10 (50 ÷ 5 = 10). But what if the franc is weaker? At an exchange rate of 10 francs to the dollar, that same bottle of wine would cost you only $5 (50 ÷ 10 = 5).

Changes in the exchange rate, of course, would affect more than just the price of wine. If the dollar were stronger in relation to the franc, the prices of all Canadian-made products would rise in France and the prices of all French-made products would fall in Canada. As a result, the French would buy fewer Canadian-made products, and Canadians would be prompted to spend more on French-made products. The result could conceivably be a Canadian trade deficit with France.

| Table 3.2 | Canadian vs. U.S. Prices |

With the strengthening of the American dollar, Americans are driving north to save money. All prices are in U.S. dollars and reflect August 1999 prices.

	Niagara Falls NY	Niagara Falls ON
Saturday stay at Days Inn, with Jacuzzi	$260.00	$165.00
Whopper with cheese at Burger King	$2.39	$2.18
	Seattle	**Vancouver**
Lauryn Hill CD	$17.99	$12.60
Nintendo 64 game system	$130.00	$119.00
Grande latte at Starbucks	$2.70	$2.29
Levi's 501 jeans at Original Levi's Store	$50.00	$45.00

Exchange Rates and Competition

Companies that conduct international operations must watch exchange-rate fluctuations closely because these changes affect overseas demand for their products and can be a major factor in international competition. In general, when the value of a country's domestic currency rises—becomes "stronger"— companies based there find it harder to export products to foreign markets and easier for foreign companies to enter local markets. It also makes it more cost-efficient for domestic companies to move production operations to lower-cost sites in foreign countries. When the value of a country's currency declines—becomes "weaker"—just the opposite patterns occur. Thus, as the value of a country's currency falls, its balance of trade should improve because domestic companies should experience a boost in exports. There should also be a corresponding decrease in the incentives for foreign companies to ship products into the domestic market.

A good case in point is the recent decline of the Canadian dollar relative to the U.S. dollar. In 1990, the Canadian dollar was relatively strong; as a result, Canadian consumers frequently drove south of the border to shop for bargains in the U.S. But during the 1990s, the Canadian dollar weakened, and it is now cheaper for U.S. consumers to do just what their Canadian counterparts used to do—drive across the border to shop. Table 3.2 illustrates the effects of this trend. For example, the same hamburger that costs US$2.39 in Niagara Falls, New York, sells for only US$2.18 just across the border in Ontario. Likewise, a caffe latte in Seattle costs US$2.70 but in Vancouver costs only US$2.29. As one Vancouver store owner puts it, "There has been an exact switch. Five years ago, we would go down to Seattle to get good deals. Now the Americans come here for shopping."[11]

Because the U.S. dollar is so strong compared to other currencies, some economists are recommending something called "dollarization." This means having countries outside the U.S. adopt the U.S. dollar as their currency. Ecuador and Panama have already done this, and half the money circulating in Peru is in U.S. dollars. Since Canada's currency has fallen against the U.S. dollar, some Canadians propose that Canada also adopt the U.S. dollar.[12] But others say that adopting the U.S. dollar will reduce Canadian policy flexibility and will mean a loss in our sovereignty.[13]

INTERNATIONAL BUSINESS MANAGEMENT

Wherever a firm is located, its success depends largely on how well it is managed. International business is so challenging because the basic management responsibilities—planning, organizing, directing, and controlling—are much more difficult to carry out when a business operates in several markets scattered around the globe.

Managing, of course, means making decisions. In this section, we examine the three most basic decisions that a company's management must make when faced with the prospect of globalization. The first decision is whether to "go international" at all. Once that decision has been made, managers must decide on the company's level of international involvement and on the organizational structure that will best meet its global needs.

"Going International"

The world economy is becoming globalized, and more and more firms are conducting international operations. This route, however, is not appropriate for every company. For example, companies that buy and sell fresh produce and fish may find it most profitable to confine their activities to a limited geographic area because storage and transport costs may be too high to make international operations worthwhile.

As Figure 3.6 shows, several factors enter into the decision to go international. One overriding factor is the business climate of other nations. Even experienced firms have encountered cultural, legal, and economic roadblocks. (These problems are discussed in more detail later in this chapter.) In considering international expansion, a company should also consider at least two other questions: Is there a demand for its products abroad? If so, must those products be adapted for international consumption?

Gauging International Demand

Products that are seen as vital in one country may be useless in another. Snowmobiles, for example, are not only popular for transportation and

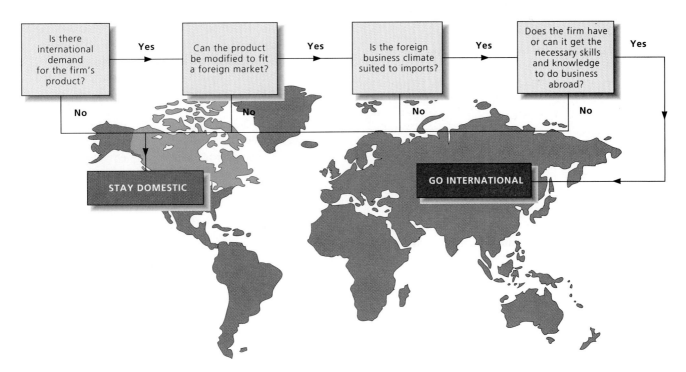

Figure 3.6
The decision to go international.

recreation in Canada and the northern United States, but actually revolutionized reindeer herding in Lapland. But there would be no demand at all for this product in Central America. Although this is an extreme example, the point is quite basic to the decision to go international: namely, that foreign demand for a company's product may be greater than, the same as, or weaker than domestic demand. The "Business Today" box describes some of the experiences of a Canadian company that decided to sell its products in foreign markets.

Adapting to Customer Needs

If there is international demand for its product, a firm must consider whether and how to adapt that product to meet the special demands and expectations of foreign customers. Movies, for example, have to be dubbed into foreign languages. Likewise, McDonald's restaurants sell wine in France, beer in Germany, and meatless sandwiches in India to accommodate local tastes and preferences. Ford products must have their steering wheels mounted on the right if they are to be sold in England and Japan. When Toyota launches upscale cars at home, it retains the Toyota nameplate; but those same cars are sold under the Lexus nameplate in Canada because the firm has concluded that Canadian consumers there will not pay a premium price for a "Toyota."

BUSINESS TODAY

Purdy's Goes International

Purdy's Chocolates is a Vancouver-based gourmet chocolate maker that is run by Karen Flavelle. It is the largest manufacturer of chocolate in B.C., and has 44 stores in B.C. and Alberta. Sales revenues exceed $20 million a year, and the firm employs 600 people.

The Purdy brand is well known in western Canada, but relatively unknown elsewhere. A couple of years ago Karen decided that Purdy's needed to break into some new markets if the firm had any hope of growing. She decided on Taipei, the capital of Taiwan, because the Taiwanese have a sweet tooth, and because Lei Mei How, a Taiwanese businesswoman, convinced her it would be a good idea.

How was so convinced that Purdy's Chocolates would be a hit in Taiwan that she paid for Neil Hastie, a vice-president at Purdy's, to fly to Taiwan and personally conduct some market research. Among other things, he discovered that there is a fascination with North American products in Taiwan, and a well-organized retail sector that does a good job of showcasing new products.

After hearing these positive comments, Purdy's formed a partnership with How to set up shop in a high-end department store (Mitsukoshi) in Taipei. Purdy's began selling in October 1995, expecting first-year sales to be in the $200 000 to $250 000 range. But even that modest target wasn't reached because several unexpected roadblocks were encountered.

Purdy's discovered, for example, that getting chocolate onto store shelves in a tropical climate was a problem, particularly when the chocolate was melting in the cargo hold of a plane as it sat baking on the tarmac under the tropical sun. Hiring and managing staff from a distance was also a lot more difficult than it was close to the home base in Vancouver.

Purdy's also assumed that products that sold well to Asians in Vancouver would sell well in Taipei, but found that was not the case. For example, ice cream dipped in chocolate and rolled in nuts wasn't nearly as popular in Taipei as it was in Vancouver.

The company also discovered many "little" things that slowed it down. For example, the rectangular package that is so common for chocolate in Canada was not well received in Taipei. There, customers prefer packages that are circular or triangular, which necessitated changes in packaging.

These difficulties were severe enough that the profitability of the Asian venture was in serious doubt. Karen decided to sign an agreement with a distributor—Konig Foods Ltd. of Taipei. Konig arranges to have the product picked up at Purdy's factory and delivered to Konig's facility. Purdy's Chocolates now functions solely as a wholesaler and lets Konig deal with the retailers that sell Purdy's chocolate. In December 1998, the company filled its biggest order yet in Taipei.

Levels of Involvement in International Business

After a firm decides to go international, it must decide on the level of its international involvement. Several different levels of involvement are possible. At the most basic level, a firm may act as an *exporter* or *importer*, organize as an *international firm*, or operate as a *multinational firm*. Most of the world's largest industrial firms are multinationals.

Exporters and Importers

An **exporter** is a firm that makes products in one country and then distributes and sells them in others. An **importer** buys products in foreign markets and then imports them for resale in its home country. Exporters and importers tend to conduct most of their business in their home nations. Both enterprises entail the lowest level of involvement in international operations and are excellent ways to learn the fine points of global business.

    Almost 40 percent of all goods and services produced in Canada are exported. Canada ranks first among the G7 countries in the proportion of its production that is exported.[14] McCain Foods, for example, is a formidable presence in Europe. It holds 75 percent of the "oven fries" market in Germany, and dominates the frozen french fry market in France and England.[15] MacMillan-Bloedel and Abitibi-Price sell newsprint and other forest products around the world. Small firms also export products and services. Seagull Pewter & Silversmiths Ltd., Magic Pantry Foods, and Lovat Tunnel Equipment Inc. have all recently won Canada Export Awards. Sabian Cymbals sells 90 percent of its products to 80 different countries outside Canada. Electrovert Ltd. does 95 percent of its business outside Canada. Other companies that export a high proportion of their output include Repap B.C. Inc. (95 percent), Pratt & Whitney Canada (86 percent), Noranda Inc. (86 percent), and General Motors of Canada (85 percent). These companies have little in common with firms that concentrate on the Canadian market and then unload what is left somewhere else.[16] Table 3.3 shows the top 10 importing and exporting countries.

International Firms

As firms gain experience and success as exporters and importers, they may move to the next level of involvement. An **international firm** conducts a

exporter
A firm that makes products in one country and then distributes and sells them in others.

importer
A firm that buys products in foreign markets and then imports them for resale in its home country.

international firm
A company that conducts a significant portion of its business abroad and maintains manufacturing facilities overseas.

Table 3.3	The World's Top 10 Importers and Exporters		
Country	**Exports (in billions)**	**Imports (in billions)**	**Trade Surplus (Deficit)**
1. United States	$683	$945	$(262)
2. Germany	540	467	73
3. Japan	388	281	107
4. France	307	287	20
5. United Kingdom	273	316	(43)
6. Italy	241	214	27
7. **Canada**	**214**	**205**	**9**
8. Netherlands	198	184	14
9. China	184	140	44
10. Hong Kong	174	189	(15)

Nestlé, a well-known multinational firm, gears its planning and decision making to international markets.

significant portion of its business abroad. International firms also maintain manufacturing facilities overseas. Wal-Mart, for instance, is an international firm. Most of the retailer's stores are still in the United States, but the company is rapidly expanding into Canada and other markets.

Although an international firm may be large and influential in the global economy, it remains basically a domestic firm with international operations: its central concern is its own domestic market. Despite its obvious presence (and impact) in Canada, Wal-Mart still earns 90 percent of its revenues from U.S. sales.

Multinational Firms

multinational firm
Controls assets, factories, mines, sales offices, and affiliates in two or more foreign countries.

Most **multinational firms** do not ordinarily think of themselves as having domestic and international divisions. Instead, planning and decision making are geared to international markets.[17] The locations of headquarters are almost irrelevant. Royal Dutch/Shell, Nestlé, IBM, and Ford are well-known multinationals.

The economic importance of multinational firms should not be underestimated. Consider, for example, the economic impact of the 500 largest multinational corporations. In 1998, these 500 firms generated $11.4 trillion in revenues and $440.3 billion in owner profits. They owned $38.9 trillion in assets, and they employed 39 685 624 people. In addition, they bought supplies, materials, parts, equipment, and materials from thousands of other firms and paid billions of dollars in taxes. Moreover, their products affected the lives of hundreds of millions of consumers, competitors, investors, and even protestors.[18] "Wealth," says Jürgen Schrempp, CEO of DaimlerChrysler (the number-two firm on the *Fortune* global 500 list), "is to add something to society materially and, ideally, over the long term. That's how I see my responsibility."

International Organizational Structures

Different levels of involvement in international business require different kinds of organizational structure. For example, a structure that would help coordinate an exporter's activities would be inadequate for the activities of a multinational firm. In this section, we briefly consider the spectrum of international organizational strategies, including *independent agents, licensing arrangements, branch offices, strategic alliances,* and *direct investment.*

Independent Agents

An **independent agent** is a foreign individual or organization that agrees to represent an exporter's interests in foreign markets. Independent agents often act as sales representatives: They sell the exporter's products, collect payment, and ensure that customers are satisfied. Independent agents often represent several firms at once and usually do not specialize in a particular product or market. Levi Strauss uses agents to market clothing products in many small countries in Africa, Asia, and South America.

independent agent
A foreign individual, or organization, who agrees to represent an exporter's interests in foreign markets.

Licensing Arrangements

Canadian companies seeking more substantial involvement in international business may opt for **licensing arrangements**. Firms give individuals or companies in a foreign country the exclusive right to manufacture or market their products in that market. In return, the exporter typically receives a fee plus ongoing payments called **royalties**.[19] Royalties are usually calculated as a percentage of the licence holder's sales. For example, Can-Eng Manufacturing, Canada's largest supplier of industrial furnaces, exports its furnaces under licensing arrangements with Japan, Brazil, Germany, Korea, Taiwan, and Mexico.

Franchising is a special form of licensing that is also growing in popularity.[20] McDonald's and Pizza Hut franchise around the world. Similarly, Accor SA, a French hotel chain, franchises its Ibis, Sofitel, and Novotel hotels. Allied-Lyons PLC, a British firm, owns and franchises Baskin-Robbins and Dunkin' Donuts stores in dozens of countries.

licensing arrangement
An arrangement by an owner of a process or product to allow another business to produce, distribute, or market it for a fee or royalty.

royalties
Fees that an exporter receives for allowing a company in a foreign company to manufacture or market the exporter's products.

Branch Offices

Instead of developing relationships with foreign companies or independent agents, a firm may simply send some of its own managers to overseas **branch offices**. A company has more direct control over branch managers than over agents or licence holders. Branch offices also give a company a more visible public presence in foreign countries. Potential customers tend to feel more secure when a business has branch offices in their country.

When a business operates branches, plants, or subsidiaries in several countries, it may assign to one plant or subsidiary the responsibility for researching, developing, manufacturing, and marketing one product or line of products. This is known as **world product mandating**.

At Nortel Networks, for example, the company's Belleville, Ontario, plant was chosen as the one to produce a new business telephone system designed for the world market. The plant won out in a competition with two other Nortel plants, one in Calgary and one in Santa Clara, California. The Belleville plant also has global mandates for several other product lines.

branch office
A location that an exporting firm establishes in a foreign country in order to sell its products more effectively.

world product mandating
The assignment by a multinational of a product responsibility to a particular branch.

Nortel Networks
www.nortelnetworks.com

Strategic Alliances

In a **strategic alliance**, a company finds a partner in the country in which it would like to conduct business. Each party agrees to invest resources and capital in a new business or else to cooperate in some way for mutual benefit. This new business—the alliance—is then owned by the partners, who divide its profits. Such alliances are sometimes called **joint ventures**.[21] As we saw in Chapter 2, however, the term *strategic alliance* has arisen because of the

strategic alliance
An enterprise in which two or more persons or companies temporarily join forces to undertake a particular project.

joint venture
Another name for a strategic alliance.

increasingly important role that such partnerships play in the larger organizational strategies of many major companies.

The number of strategic alliances among major companies has increased significantly over the last decade and is likely to grow even more. In many countries, including Mexico, India, and China, laws make alliances virtually the only way to do international business within their borders. Mexico, for example, requires all foreign firms investing there to have local partners. Similarly, Disney's new theme park currently under construction near Hong Kong is a joint venture with local partners.

In addition to easing the way into new markets, alliances give firms greater control over their foreign activities than independent agents and licensing arrangements. (At the same time, of course, all partners in an alliance retain some say in its decisions.) Perhaps most important, alliances allow firms to benefit from the knowledge and expertise of their foreign partners. Microsoft, for example, relies heavily on strategic alliances as it expands into new international markets. This approach has successfully enabled the firm to learn the intricacies of doing business in China and India, two emerging markets that are difficult to crack.

Foreign Direct Investment

foreign direct investment (FDI)
Buying or establishing tangible assets in another country.

The term **foreign direct investment (FDI)** means buying or establishing tangible assets in another country.[22] Dell Computer, for example, is building a new assembly plant in Europe, and Volkswagen is building a new factory in Brazil.

As we've seen, many Canadian firms export goods and services to foreign countries; they also set up manufacturing operations in other countries. But a debate has been going on for many years in Canada about how FDI here affects Canadians. The **Foreign Investment Review Agency (FIRA)**, which was established in 1973, was designed to ensure that FDI benefited Canadians. After FIRA was established, the proportion of various industries controlled by foreign firms declined from a high of 38 percent in the early 1970s to a low of 25.7 percent in 1988 (just before NAFTA took effect).

Foreign Investment Review Agency (FIRA)
Established in 1973 to screen new foreign direct investment in Canada; supposed to ensure that significant benefits accrued to Canada.

Investment Canada
Replaced FIRA in 1985; designed primarily to attract and facilitate foreign investment in Canada.

In 1985, FIRA's title was changed to **Investment Canada**, and its mandate was changed to focus on attracting foreign investment to Canada. Since the late 1980s, foreign ownership of Canadian industry has again been on the rise, and in the late 1990s it reached 31.5 percent. But foreign ownership may in fact be higher than it appears since many firms that seem to be Canadian are actually multinational companies. For example, before it was bought by a French company, Seagram had been run from New York City, and Nortel Networks runs all of its business divisions from Dallas, Texas. Table 3.4 lists the top 10 foreign-owned companies in Canada.

Over 200 major Canadian companies trade their stock on the New York Stock Exchange, and more than half of the trading in many of those companies' stock takes place in the U.S.[23] A *Globe and Mail* study in 1998 showed that in just one 12-month period, 10 companies with a total market value of $39 billion disappeared from the Toronto Stock Exchange (TSE) because they were purchased by foreign firms. These firms accounted for 6 percent of the value of the TSE 300 index.[24]

Canadian business leaders are beginning to sound the warning that the Canadian operations of multinational firms are being "hollowed out" and that Canadian firms are vulnerable to takeovers by foreign companies.[25] This concern is a bit ironic, since business leaders have generally been the ones most in favour of free trade.

Table 3.4	The Top 10 Foreign-Owned Companies in Canada (ranked by revenues)

Company	Annual Canadian Revenues (in billions)
1. General Motors of Canada Ltd.	$39.6
2. Ford Motor Co. of Canada Ltd.	29.9
3. DaimlerChrysler Canada Inc.	22.4
4. Imperial Oil Ltd.	9.0
5. Imperial Tobacco Canada Ltd.	9.0
6. Sears Canada Inc.	6.1
7. Honda Canada Inc.	5.9
8. Shell Canada Ltd.	5.2
9. Canada Safeway Ltd.	4.9
10. Canadian Ultramar Co.	4.3

WEBCONNEXION

Founded by two young entrepreneurs—one from Pennsylvania and one from Bulgaria—the Shenyang Shawnee Cowboy Food company sells candy directly to Chinese wholesalers and retailers. To find out more about the company's factory operations, which are located in the city of Shenyang, and its 32-city distribution network, contact Cowboy Candy at:

www.cowboycandy.com

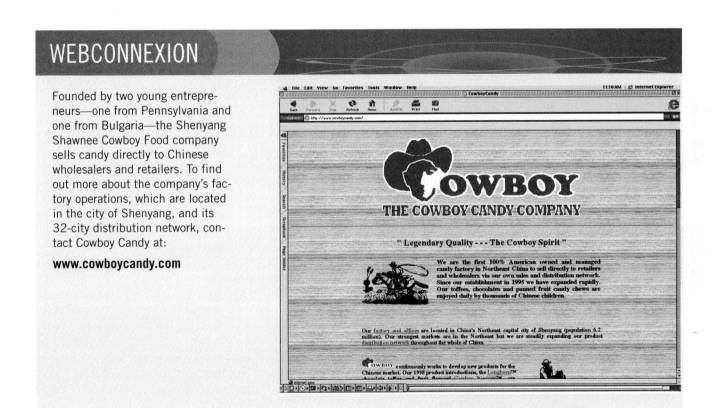

Matching Strategies and Opportunities

Multinational firms often use whatever approach seems best suited to a particular situation in their search for worldwide business opportunities. In some cases, they opt for independent agents. In other cases, they prefer licensing arrangements, strategic alliances, or direct investments. Consider, for example, the case of ABB Asea Brown Boveri Ltd., one of the world's most globally oriented businesses. Jointly owned by a Swedish firm and a Swiss firm, ABB is the world's largest electrical engineering company. It has

200 000 employees, of whom only 176 work at its Zurich headquarters. ABB consists of 1300 separate companies functioning in 140 countries. The CEO is Swedish and other corporate officers hail from Germany, France, Australia, and the United States.

BARRIERS TO TRADE

Whether a business is selling to just a few foreign markets or is a true multinational, a number of differences between countries will affect its international operations. How a firm responds to social, economic, and political issues will go a long way towards determining its success.

Social and Cultural Differences

Any firm involved in international business needs to understand something about the society and culture of the countries in which it plans to operate. Unless a firm understands these cultural differences—either itself or by acquiring a partner that does—it will probably not be successful in its international business activities.

Some differences are relatively obvious. Language barriers can cause inappropriate naming of products. In addition, the physical stature of people in different countries can make a difference. For example, the Japanese and French are slimmer and shorter on average than Canadians, an important consideration for firms that intend to sell clothes in these markets.

Differences in the average ages of the local population can also have an impact on product development and marketing. Countries with growing populations tend to have a high percentage of young people. Thus, electronics and fashionable clothing would likely do well. Countries with stable or declining populations tend to have more old people. Generic pharmaceuticals might be more successful in such markets.

In addition to such obvious differences, a wide range of subtle value differences can have an important impact on international business. For example, many Europeans shop daily. To Canadians used to weekly trips to the supermarket, the European pattern may seem like a waste of time. But for Europeans, shopping is not just "buying food." It is also meeting friends, exchanging political views, gossiping, and socializing.

What implications does this kind of shopping have for firms selling in European markets? First, those who go shopping each day do not need the large refrigerators and freezers common in North America. Second, the large supermarkets one sees in Canada are not appropriate retail outlets in Europe. Finally, the kinds of food Europeans buy differ from those Canadians buy. While in Canada prepared and frozen foods are important, Europeans often prefer to buy fresh ingredients to do their own food preparation "from scratch." These differences are gradually disappearing, however, so firms need to be on the lookout for future opportunities as they emerge.

Even more subtle behavioural differences that can influence business activity exist. For example, crossing your legs in a business meeting in Saudi Arabia is inappropriate, because showing the sole of your foot is viewed as an insult to the other people in the room. In Portugal, it is considered rude to discuss business during dinner, and in Taiwan, tapping your fingers on the table is a sign of appreciation for a meal. Knowledge of local dos and don'ts is important in international business activity.

Economic Differences

Although cultural differences are often subtle, economic differences can be fairly pronounced. In dealing with economies like those of France and Sweden, for example, firms must be aware of when—and to what extent—the government is involved in a given industry. The French government, for example, is heavily involved in all aspects of airplane design and manufacturing.

Similarly, a foreign firm doing business in a command economy must understand the unfamiliar relationship of government to business, including a host of idiosyncratic practices. General Motors, which entered a $100 million joint venture to build pickup trucks in China, found itself faced with an economic system that favoured state-owned companies over foreign investors. So, while its Chinese suppliers passed on inflation-based price increases for steel and energy, GM could not in turn pass increases on to Chinese consumers. With subsidized state-owned automakers charging considerably less per truck, GM had no choice but to hold its own prices—and lose money on each sale.

Despite such problems, however, not all companies have had entirely negative experiences. For example, when Motorola opened a factory in China to manufacture paging devices, it planned to export most of the pagers because it forecasted limited internal demand. In a pleasant surprise, Motorola was forced to reassess the Chinese market after repeatedly selling out its weekly output of 10 000 units. This experience helped convince Motorola to build a $120 million plant in the northern port city of Tianjin to manufacture pagers, simple integrated circuits, and cellular phones. As part of the largest manufacturing venture in Canada, it will also involve Chinese technicians in the production process. Chinese designers and engineers will play key roles in creating an operation that integrates manufacturing, sales, research, and development.

Motorola
www.motorola.com

Legal and Political Differences

Closely linked to the structure of the economic systems in different countries are the legal and political issues that confront businesses as they try to expand internationally. These issues include tariffs and quotas, local-content laws, and business-practice laws. An awareness of differences in these areas can be crucial to a business's success.

Quotas, Tariffs, and Subsidies

Even free-market economies often use some form of quota and/or tariff that affects the prices and quantities of foreign-made products in those nations. A **quota** restricts the total number of certain products that can be imported into a country. It indirectly raises the prices of those imports by reducing their supply.

The ultimate form of quota is an **embargo**: a government order forbidding exportation and/or importation of a particular product—or even all products—of a particular country. For example, many countries control bacteria and disease by banning certain plants and agricultural products.

In contrast, a **tariff** is a tax charged on imported products. Tariffs directly affect the prices of products, effectively raising the price of imports to consumers who must pay not only for the products but also for the tariff. Tariffs may take either of two forms. A **revenue tariff** is imposed strictly to raise money for the government. But most tariffs in effect today are **protectionist tariffs** meant to discourage the import of a particular product.

quota
A restriction by one nation on the total number of products of a certain type that can be imported from another nation.

embargo
A government order forbidding exportation and/or importation of a particular product. from a particular country.

tariff
A tax levied on imported products.

revenue tariff
A tariff imposed solely to raise money for the government that imposes it.

protectionist tariff
A tariff imposed at least in part to discourage imports of a particular product.

Governments impose quotas and tariffs for a wide variety of reasons. For example, the U.S. government restricts the number of Japanese automobiles that can be imported into that country. Italy imposes high tariffs on imported electronic goods. Consequently, Sony Walkmans cost almost $150, and CD players are prohibitively expensive. Canada also imposes tariffs on many imported goods.

subsidy
A government payment to help domestic business compete with foreign firms.

A **subsidy** is a government payment to help a domestic business compete with foreign firms. Many European governments subsidize farmers to help them compete with U.S. grain imports. In 1999, the World Trade Organization ruled that the governments of both Canada and Brazil were illegally subsidizing regional jet manufacturers in their respective countries. The ruling struck down Brazil's Pro-ex financing program, which reduced the interest rate that purchasers of Embraer's regional jet had to pay on loans. It also struck down Canada's Technology Partnership Program (TPP), saying that it was essentially an illegal export subsidy on planes built by Bombardier.[26]

In April 2000, the WTO endorsed Canada's revamped TPP program and ruled that Brazil had failed to fix its financing program. The ruling will give Bombardier a major boost, but it could also start a trade war since Brazil did not agree with the WTO's decision.[27]

protectionism
Protecting domestic business at the expense of free market competition.

Protectionism—the practice of protecting domestic business at the expense of free market competition—has both advocates and critics. Supporters argue that tariffs and quotas protect domestic firms and jobs. In particular, they protect new industries until they are truly able to compete internationally. Some claim that, since other nations have such measures, so must we. Still others justify protectionism in the name of national security. They argue that a nation must be able to produce goods needed for its survival in the event of war and that advanced technology should not be sold to potential enemies.

But opponents of protectionism are equally vocal. They note that protectionism reduces competition and drives up prices to consumers. They cite it as a cause of friction between nations. They maintain that, while jobs in some industries would be lost if protectionism ceased, jobs in other industries would expand if all countries abolished tariffs and quotas.

Local-Content Laws

local-content laws
Laws requiring that products sold in a particular country be at least partly made in that country.

A country can affect how a foreign firm does business there by enacting local-content laws. **Local-content laws** require that products sold in a particular country be at least partly made in that country. These laws typically mean that firms seeking to do business in a country must either invest directly in that country or have a joint-venture partner from that country. In this way, some of the profits from doing business in a foreign country are shared with the people who live there.

Many countries have local-content laws. In a fairly extreme case, Venezuela forbids the import of any product if a like product is made in Venezuela. Even when an item is not made in Venezuela, many companies choose to begin making their product in Venezuela both to drive out competitors and to prevent being forced out by local firms.

Local-content laws may even exist within a country; when they do, they act just like trade barriers. In Canada, for example, a low bid on a bridge in British Columbia was rejected because the company that made the bid was from Alberta. The job was given to a B.C. company. A New Brunswick window manufacturer lost a contract in Nova Scotia despite having made the lowest bid; the job went to a Nova Scotia company. Recognizing that these interprovincial barriers are not helping Canada's international competitiveness, the federal government has committed itself to removing such barriers.

The 1994 Agreement on Internal Trade (AIT) required all 10 Canadian provinces to remove barriers to agricultural trade by September 1997. But when Quebec—which has a strong dairy lobby—prohibited margarine coloured to look like butter, it was in violation of the agreement.[28] In January 2000, Prince Edward Island ignored a dispute panel ruling that stated P.E.I.'s milk import restrictions also violated the AIT.[29] If provincial governments do not honour their obligations, the AIT will become meaningless.

A Quebec customs official seizing illegal butter-coloured margarine. The dairy industry in Quebec has been successful in maintaining the legislation that makes it illegal to make margarine the same colour as butter.

Business-Practice Laws

A final influence on how a company does business abroad stems from laws both abroad and in the firm's home nation. Sometimes, what is legal—and even accepted—business practice in one country is illegal in another. For example, in some countries it is legal to obtain business by paying bribes to government officials.

Transparency International, an organization devoted to stamping out global corruption, says that Canadian business firms operating abroad are least likely to pay bribes to win business. As well, Canada is a country that has little tolerance for corruption at home. But as more Canadian companies do business abroad, they are finding themselves competing against companies from other countries that are not so reluctant to pay bribes in order to get business. As a result, Canadian companies are losing business to these companies.[30]

Transparency International says that bribery is most devastating and common in developing countries because government officials in those countries are poorly paid. Bribing of government officials is most likely in the construction, defence, and energy sectors, and least likely in the banking and agriculture sectors. In an attempt to create fairer competition among multinational companies, ministers from 29 member countries of the Organization for Economic Cooperation and Development (OECD) agreed in 1997 to criminalize bribery of foreign public officials.[31]

A **cartel** is an association of producers whose purpose is to control the supply and price of a commodity. The most famous cartel is the Organization of Petroleum Exporting Countries (OPEC). It has given oil-producing countries considerable power in the last 25 years. In 1994, the major aluminum producing countries, including Canada, worked out a deal to curb world aluminum production in an attempt to raise prices.[32] The diamond and shipping cartels have also been successful in keeping the prices they charge artificially high.[33] In 2000, the world's coffee-producing countries formed an OPEC-style cartel to control the price of coffee. They immediately raised coffee prices by 37 percent, which increased the price of a cup of coffee by about 15 cents. Surprisingly, most coffee buyers were sympathetic to the cartel, since coffee prices had been at their lowest level in seven years and coffee farmers in developing countries were struggling.[34]

Many countries forbid **dumping**—selling a product abroad for less than the comparable price charged at home. Antidumping legislation typically views dumping as occurring if products are being sold at prices less than fair value, or if the result unfairly harms domestic industry. In 2000, the

cartel
Any association of producers whose purpose is to control supply of and prices for a given product.

dumping
Selling a product for less abroad than in the producing nation; illegal in Canada.

Canada Customs and Revenue Agency determined that refrigerators, dishwashers, and dryers produced by Whirlpool and Frigidaire in the U.S. were being "dumped" in Canada.[35] In 1997, the Canadian International Trade Tribunal renewed antidumping duties on bicycle imports from Taiwan and China. Canadian manufacturers argued that cheap foreign bicycles were damaging the Canadian industry, and that China and Taiwan would continue to "dump" bicycles on the Canadian market if the duties were not continued.[36]

OVERCOMING BARRIERS TO TRADE

Despite the barriers described so far, world trade is flourishing. A number of world organizations and treaties have as their primary reason for being the promotion of international business.

Trade Agreements

General Agreement on Tariffs and Trade (GATT)

An international trade accord in which the 92 signatories agreed to reduce tariffs; often ignored by signatories.

European Union (EU)

An agreement among Western European nations to eliminate quotas and keep tariffs low on products traded among themselves, but to impose high tariffs and low quotas on goods imported from other nations.

Virtually every nation in the world has formal treaties with other nations regarding trade. One of the largest such treaties, the **General Agreement on Tariffs and Trade (GATT)**, was signed shortly after the end of the Second World War. But while the 92 countries that have signed GATT have agreed to reduce taxes on imported goods to 5 percent, not all have complied. One of the worst offenders is the United States.

Other GATT signatories who often do not live up to the terms of this treaty include the members of the **European Union (EU)**. The EU includes most Western European nations, most notably Belgium, Denmark, France, Greece, Ireland, Italy, Luxembourg, the Netherlands, the United Kingdom, and Germany. These nations continue to place quotas and high tariffs on goods imported from nonmember nations. But they have eliminated most quotas and set uniform tariff levels on products imported and exported within their group, encouraging intracontinental trade. In 1992, virtually all internal trade barriers were eliminated, making Western Europe the largest free marketplace in the world.

On January 1, 1995, the World Trade Organization (WTO) came into existence as the successor to GATT (often humorously referred to as the General Agreement to Talk and Talk). The WTO will oversee a one-third reduction in import duties on thousands of products that are traded between countries. The reductions will be phased in over the next few years. Canada, the U.S., and the European Union are founding members of the WTO.[37]

Unlike GATT, the WTO's decisions are binding, and many people feared that it would make sweeping decisions and boss countries around. But the WTO is off to a slow start. It has not been very successful in toppling global barriers to trade in three critical areas—world financial services, telecommunications, and maritime markets—because political leaders from various countries are fearful of the consequences of freer trade.[38]

On several occasions when the WTO has held talks on trade liberalization, protestors have disrupted the meetings. The WTO meetings in Seattle and Prague, for example, were disrupted by protestors who resent the power of the WTO and who are concerned about what world trade is doing to both the environment and the developing countries that were not sharing in its benefits. Protestors included labour unions (who regard Third World imports as unfair), environmentalists (who are concerned about business activity harming the environment), social activists (who are concerned about poor working conditions in developing countries), and farmers (who are concerned about the effect of free trade on grain prices).

The Canada–U.S. Free Trade Agreement

On January 1, 1989, the far-reaching **Canada–U.S. Free Trade Agreement (FTA)** came into effect. The FTA has as its goal the elimination over time of tariffs on products and services that move between the two countries. By January 1, 1998, tariffs were eliminated on almost all goods and services traded between Canada and the U.S.

The FTA is the culmination of a long series of trade agreements made with the U.S. over the last 100 years. The first trade agreement was signed in 1854, and in 1935 a "most favoured nation" agreement came into effect with the U.S. In 1965, the Auto Pact provided for duty-free trade in cars, trucks, buses, and auto parts at the manufacturing level. However, in 1999 the WTO ruled that Canada had to scrap the Auto Pact because it was essentially an export subsidy program, which is prohibited.[39]

Canada–U.S. Free Trade Agreement (FTA)
An agreement to eliminate over time tariffs on goods and services that move between the two countries.

The North American Free Trade Agreement

On January 1, 1994, the **North American Free Trade Agreement (NAFTA)** took effect. The objective of NAFTA is to create a free trade area for Canada, the U.S., and Mexico. It eliminates trade barriers, promotes fair competition, and increases investment opportunities.

Surveys conducted during the early 1990s showed that the majority of Canadians were opposed to free trade. They feared that (1) jobs would be lost to other countries, (2) Canada would be flooded with products manufactured in lower-wage countries such as Mexico, (3) Canada would lose the right to control its own environmental standards, (4) the U.S. might take our natural resources, and (5) Canadian cultural sovereignty would be lost.

Supporters of free trade, by contrast, argued that (1) access to U.S. markets is guaranteed by free trade and is therefore crucial to protecting Canadian employment, (2) Canadian exports would increase because of free trade, (3) the environment is not covered in free trade agreements, (4) there is nothing

North American Free Trade Agreement (NAFTA)
A trade agreement signed by Canada, the U.S., and Mexico whose purpose is to create a free trade area.

WEBCONNEXION

The Canadian Trade Commissioner Service helps Canadian companies that have selected their target markets and are committed to be involved in international business. It provides market study data that allow companies to determine the potential of their selected target market. It also provides information about key contacts such as lawyers, business partners, and government officials. Visit the Canadian Trade Commissioner Service at:

www.infoexport.gc.ca/ menu-e.asp

in the free trade agreements that threatens Canada's control over its energy resources, and (5) the free trade agreements are about trade and tariffs, not cultural sovereignty.

What has actually happened since NAFTA took effect? Canada is shedding its image as a country whose people are "hewers of wood and drawers of water" and is becoming an exporting powerhouse. Trade between the U.S. and Canada has risen 37 percent since 1994, and Canada enjoyed a $22 billion trade surplus with the U.S. in 1996. Before free trade, exports accounted for about one-quarter of GDP, but now exports account for 40 percent. In the manufacturing sector, 60 percent of output is now exported, compared to just 30 percent in 1988. Canada is the most trade-intensive country in the G7 group. One job in three is now devoted to producing goods and services for export.[40]

Individual provinces are doing well, too. In the period 1990–96, for example, Manitoba's exports to the U.S. doubled to nearly $4.3 billion, and wheat is no longer its number-one export. One Manitoba company—Digital Chameleon—colours and digitizes *Superman* comics for New York–based DC Comics. And Palliser Furniture, which used to export about 10 percent of its output to the U.S., is now exporting more than 50 percent. Nearly 2500 jobs have been created in Winnipeg alone.[41]

Canadians may be surprised to learn that there is now much more opposition to NAFTA in the U.S. than there is in Canada. A report issued in 1997 by a coalition of U.S. labour and environmental groups says that NAFTA has been bad for the U.S. and good for Canada. The report claims that NAFTA has caused the loss of 420 000 U.S. jobs, an increasing trade deficit with Canada and Mexico, a flight of industry to Mexico, and a decline in the standard of living of U.S. citizens.[42] It is difficult to tell how much effect NAFTA has had compared to many other major changes that have occurred during the same time period—globalization, rapid changes in information technology, and the Bank of Canada's actions to stop inflation, to name just a few. One of the biggest concerns about free trade was what it would do to Canadian jobs. The latest evidence shows that factory employment as a proportion of all jobs in Canada has continued to drop (as it has for decades), but that there was little difference between industries affected most by NAFTA and those affected least.[43]

Other Free Trade Agreements in the Americas

The Canada–U.S. Free Trade Agreement and NAFTA are the most publicized trade agreements in the Americas, but there has recently been a flurry of activity among other countries as well. On January 1, 1995, a free trade agreement known as Mercosur went into effect between Argentina, Brazil, Uruguay, and Paraguay. By 2005, tariffs will be eliminated on 80 percent of the goods traded between those four countries. Brazil has proposed enlarging Mercosur into a South American Free Trade Area (SAFTA), which might eventually negotiate with NAFTA to form an Americas Free Trade Area (AFTA).

There are several other free trade areas already in existence in the Americas: The Andean Pact (Bolivia, Ecuador, Colombia, Peru, and Venezuela), The Central American Common Market (Costa Rica, El Salvador, Guatemala, Honduras, and Nicaragua), the G-3 group (Columbia, Mexico, and Venezuela), and The Caribbean Common Market (many of the island nations of the Caribbean).[44] The population of the various free trade areas of the Americas totals nearly 900 million. The economies of many of these nations are growing rapidly, and they will become increasingly important to Canada during the next decade.

The Palliser furniture showroom in Winnipeg, Manitoba. Employment at Palliser has surged due to the company's success in exporting its products to U.S. markets.

Free Trade Agreements in Other Areas of the World

Free trade agreements are not restricted to the Americas. A high level of activity is evident around the world as groups of nations band together to form regional trade associations for their own benefit. Some examples are the ASEAN Free Trade Area (Brunei, Indonesia, Malaysia, the Philippines, Singapore, Thailand, and Vietnam), the Asia-Pacific Economic Cooperation (many nations of the Pacific Rim, as well as the U.S., Canada, and Mexico), the Economic Community of Central African States (many nations in equatorial Africa), and the Gulf Cooperation Council (Bahrain, Kuwait, Oman, Qatar, Saudi Arabia, and United Arab Emirates).

SUMMARY OF LEARNING OBJECTIVES

1. **Describe the rise of international business and identify the major world marketplaces.** More and more business firms are engaged in international business. The term *globalization* refers to the process by which the world economy is fast becoming a single interdependent entity. The global economy is characterized by a rapid growth in the exchange of information and trade in services. The three major marketplaces for international business are *North America* (the United States, Canada, and Mexico), *Western Europe* (which is dominated by Germany, the United Kingdom, France, and Italy), and *Asia-Pacific* (where the dominant country, Japan, is surrounded by such rapidly advancing nations as South Korea, Taiwan, Hong Kong, and China).

2. **Explain how different forms of** *competitive advantage, import-export balances, exchange rates,* **and** *foreign competition* **determine the ways in which countries and businesses respond to the international environment.** With an absolute advantage, a country engages in international trade because it can produce a good or service more efficiently than any other nation. But more often countries trade because they enjoy comparative advantages, that is, they can produce some items more efficiently than they can produce other items. A country that exports more than it imports has a favourable balance of trade,

while a country that imports more than it exports has an unfavourable balance of trade. If the exchange rate decreases (the value of the Canadian dollar falls), our exports become less expensive for other countries so they will buy more of what we produce. The reverse happens if the value of the Canadian dollar increases. Changes in the exchange rate therefore have a strong impact on our international competitiveness.

3. **Discuss the factors involved in deciding to do business internationally and in selecting the appropriate *levels of international involvement* and *international organizational structure*.** In deciding whether to do business internationally, a firm must determine whether a market for its product exists abroad, and if so, whether the firm has the skills and knowledge to manage such a business. It must also assess the business climates of other nations to ensure that they are conducive to international operations.

   A firm must also decide on its level of international involvement. It can choose to be an *exporter* or *importer*, to organize as an *international firm*, or to operate as a *multinational firm*. The choice will influence the organizational structure of its international operations, specifically, its use of *independent agents, licensing arrangements, branch offices, strategic alliances*, and *direct investment*.

4. **Describe some of the ways in which *social, cultural, economic, legal*, and *political differences* act as barriers to international trade.** *Social* and *cultural differences* that can serve as barriers to trade include language, social values, and traditional buying patterns. Differences in economic systems may force businesses to establish close relationships with foreign governments before they are permitted to do business abroad. *Quotas, tariffs, subsidies*, and *local-content laws* offer protection to local industries. Differences in *business-practice laws* can make standard business practices in one nation illegal in another.

5. **Explain how *free trade agreements* assist world trade.** Several *trade agreements* have attempted to eliminate restrictions on free trade internationally. The *General Agreement on Tariffs and Trade* (GATT) was instituted to eliminate tariffs and other trade barriers among participating nations. The *European Union* (EU) has eliminated virtually all trade barriers among the 12 principal Western European nations. The *North American Free Trade Agreement* (NAFTA) eliminates many of the barriers to free trade that exist among the United States, Canada, and Mexico.

KEY TERMS

globalization, 70
imports, 70
exports, 70
per capita income, 72
absolute advantage, 76
comparative advantage, 77
national competitive
   advantage, 77
balance of trade, 78
trade deficit, 79
trade surplus, 79
balance of payments, 80
exchange rate, 80
exporter, 85

importer, 85
international firm, 85
multinational firm, 86
independent agent, 87
licensing arrangement, 87
royalties, 87
branch office, 87
world product
   mandating, 87
strategic alliance, 87
joint venture, 87
foreign direct investment
   (FDI), 88

Foreign Investment
   Review Agency (FIRA),
   88
Investment Canada, 88
quota, 91
embargo, 91
tariff, 91
revenue tariff, 91
protectionist tariff, 91
subsidy, 92
protectionism, 92

local-content laws, 92
cartel, 93
dumping, 93
General Agreement on
   Tariffs and Trade
   (GATT), 94
European Union (EU), 94
Canada–U.S. Free Trade
   Agreement (FTA), 95
North American Free
   Trade Agreement
   (NAFTA), 95

STUDY QUESTIONS AND EXERCISES

Review Questions

1. Explain the difference between a nation's balance of trade and balance of payments.
2. What are the possible ways that Canadian firms can be involved in international business?
3. What are the advantages and disadvantages of multinational corporations?
4. How does the economic system of a country affect foreign firms interested in doing business there?

Analysis Questions

5. Make a list of all the major items in your bedroom. Identify the country in which each item was made. Give possible reasons why that nation might have a comparative advantage in producing this good.
6. Do you support protectionist tariffs for Canada? If so, in what instances and for what reasons? If not, why not?
7. Is the Canada–U.S. Free Trade Agreement good for Canada? Give supporting reasons for your answer.

8. Do you think that a firm that is operating internationally is better advised to adopt a single standard of ethical conduct or to adapt to local conditions? Under what kinds of conditions might each approach be preferable?

Application Exercises

9. Interview the manager of a local firm that does at least some business internationally. Identify reasons why the company decided to "go international," as well as the level of the firm's international involvement and the organizational structure it uses for its international operations.
10. Select a product familiar to you. Using library references, learn something about the culture of India and identify the problems that might arise in trying to market this product to India's citizens.

Building Your Business Skills

The Context of Culture

Goal

To help students appreciate how high-context and low-context cultures influence global business communication. Low-context cultures use explicit written and verbal messages to communicate in business and other situations. Written agreements and written messages are important. High-context cultures communicate through both explicit messages and implicit context. Interpersonal relationships, and a high level of formality and etiquette, will affect the success of the communication.

Method

Step 1:

A continuum of world cultures as defined by anthropologist Edward T. Hall is shown below. Use this information to develop a strategy for conducting meetings with business people in Switzerland and Japan.

Step 2:

Working in groups of four or five students, answer the following questions for each country: What should you do before you arrive in the country to increase your chance of success? If your meeting time is 1:00 p.m. on Tuesday, when should you arrive to get the best results from your meeting? What title and position should you or another member of your team hold to achieve your business goals? How would your business style and the pace of your conversation differ in each country?

Follow-Up Questions

1. *Culture shock*—the inability to adapt to foreign cultures—is a problem that many Canadian business people face when they work abroad. Based on this exercise, why do you think this is a problem?

2. How can management training seminars reduce *ethnocentrism*—the tendency to judge the cultures of foreign countries by Canadian standards?

3. Japan, Arab countries, and Latin American countries are high-context cultures. Do these countries share cultural patterns? How would you adapt your business style from country to country?

Exploring the Net

The Internet has immense potential value for anyone who is interested in the global environment of business. An excellent source of information regarding international business is a Web site called "International Business Resources on the WWW. Log on to this site at:

http://ciber.bus.msu.edu/busres.htm

First, browse the site according to what interests you most. Then consider the following questions:

1. Select one country in each of the following areas: Asia and Oceania, Central and South America, and Europe. Find out as much as you can about the social/cultural and legal/political factors affecting business.

2. Briefly review the textbook discussions of exporting and licensing. Identify two or three sites that might be especially relevant to someone considering these forms of international business.

3. Select one of the following sites:
   - "World Stock Exchanges"
   - "Banking and Finance"
   - "Government Resources"

On the section that you explored, what further information is available to the Canadian business person who is interested in learning more about the global environment of business today?

Concluding Case 3-1

Ricardo.de AG

Because U.S. business got such a big head start in electronic commerce, some experts believed that most European e-businesses would end up being copies of successful American enterprises. For example, the dominance of eBay Inc.—one of the most visible dot-com businesses—in the online auction market seemed to prove this point. But don't tell that to Ricardo.de AG, an upstart German auction firm that is creating a growing international presence for itself and gaining on the U.S.-based industry leader in Europe.

eBay, of course, is a very young firm itself. Essentially started as a cyberspace flea market in 1995, the company adopted its present name in 1997, went public in 1998, and acquired the up-scale auction house Butterfield & Butterfield in 1999. It currently boasts 1600 different product categories and about 4 million registered users. And unlike many dot-com businesses, eBay is also already quite profitable—it takes a percentage of each sale from

every successful auction transaction. Not surprisingly, then, eBay has attracted new competitors. Both Amazon.com and Yahoo.com, for example, have launched auction sites.

In Europe, however, Ricardo.de has emerged as one of eBay's most formidable challengers. The three young German entrepreneurs behind Ricardo.de—Stefan Glaenzer, Christoph Linkwitz, and Stefan Wiskemann—actually started out by creating a publishing business in 1997. But when they auctioned off a new Mercedes A-Class car on the Internet to promote an online business directory they had just published, the overwhelming response caught their attention. "We figured it's better to do e-commerce than write about it," quips Wiskemann. They named their new enterprise after the eighteenth-century English economist David Ricardo, an early champion of free markets.

But just after the firm's mid-1998 launch, one problem after another arose. First, some potential investors expressed concerns that Ricardo.de lacked a clear strategy for differentiating itself from eBay. Moreover, eBay appeared to get the inside track in Germany when it acquired Alando.de, a Berlin-based online auction firm that was already up and running. Alando.de also had the local advantage of being a partner with T-Online, Europe's largest Internet-access provider.

Ricardo.de's owners dealt with the first concern by formalizing and announcing their strategy. Rather than concentrate (like eBay) on used articles and collectibles, they would sell only new merchandise—mostly discontinued or overstocked electronics, appliances, and computers bought at bargain prices from both wholesalers and retailers. Ricardo.de also promised to hold regular five-minute "live" auctions with a moderator calling the action, chatting with bidders, and congratulating winners.

The approach seemed to make sense to local investors, who started lining up for the initial public offering (IPO). But the optimism surrounding the venture began to melt under the heat of two more setbacks. First, a group of traditional auctioneers filed suit, citing a 100-year-old German law making it illegal to sell new goods at public auction. Second, on the eve of the IPO, a major underwriter backed out because of a dispute with the lead investment banker.

As the old adage goes, sometimes it's darkest right before the dawn. Clearly, the founders of Ricardo.de must have felt like that in mid-1999. eBay was gobbling market share and Ricardo.de's own IPO was in trouble because a major banker had withdrawn from the deal. Moreover, a lawsuit threatened to nullify the very idea on which the business planned to build. But just as the future looked bleakest for the three young Germans, things started turning in their favour.

First, in a surprise move a judge dismissed the auctioneers' lawsuit, opening the door for the online auction company to proceed with its business plan.

Second, eBay inexplicably decided not to renew its exclusive deal with T-Online. Ricardo.de quickly stepped in to take its place. Finally, Deutsche Bank agreed to pick up the part of the stock deal that the other investment banker had abandoned. This series of events spurred new optimism about the potential for the new company. After the IPO, Ricardo.de's share price increased slowly at first but then soared by over 500 percent by the end of 1999.

By mid-2000, Ricardo.de was off and running, picking up significant growth in terms of both sellers and buyers. It also launched operations in Britain, bought the top Dutch auction site, and announced plans to expand into France and Italy by the end of the year. Most impressively, it had signed up 500 000 registered users in Germany alone, putting it right behind eBay's customer base of 580 000. Finally, to prepare for a full-fledged global assault, the firm hired a professional executive to run its operations—Eckard Pfeiffer, the former head of Compaq Computer.

CASE QUESTIONS

1. Explain how e-businesses may define the geographic boundaries of their markets differently than traditional firms.

2. How do various forms of competitive advantage relate to e-businesses engaged in international commerce?

3. In what ways are exchange rates relevant to online auction houses like eBay and Ricardo.de?

4. On what level of international involvement are eBay and Ricardo.de currently operating? In what ways might this change in the future?

5. What are some of the barriers to international trade that an online auction business might confront? ◆

Concluding Case 3-2

The Story of McDonald's Canada in Russia

Starting a business in another country can be a huge challenge, as George Cohon, senior chairman of McDonald's Restaurants of Canada Ltd., discovered when he decided to introduce the famous fast-food to Russia. In a country known for its communist ideology, the introduction of a restaurant that symbolized Western capitalism was viewed with considerable suspicion.

Negotiations began in 1976 and took 12 years to complete. The first McDonald's outlet finally opened in Moscow in 1990. However, there were several key problems that had to be solved along the way:

- Local processors could not meet McDonald's exacting standards for milk and beef, so the company had to build a huge complex to process the food that serves as the inputs for its restaurants; at the beginning, about one-half of the food items had to be imported.

- Getting inputs to the right place at the right time was a major problem in a country that had one of the worst-run agricultural sectors in the world; at one point, McDonald's workers actually had to go out and harvest potatoes.
- The idea of private enterprise was ridiculed in Russia (one critic said, "the trouble with Russia is that no one ever had a paper route").
- Russian workers had to learn to be consumer-oriented and to be polite to customers; in the beginning, Western managers were brought in to provide training and direction to Russian workers.

McDonald's had to face other uncertainties as well. For example, it was not clear whether Western-style food would appeal to Russians, or whether they would have enough money to purchase McDonald's hamburgers, fries, and shakes. A Big Mac is priced at $2.80, which doesn't sound like much unless you understand that the average monthly wage of Russian workers is only $200. This is equivalent to asking Canadians to pay about $35 for a Big Mac. In spite of this, demand was high from the start, and McDonald's Canada is now making profits in Russia.

The restaurant in Moscow's Pushkin Square, for example, was an instant success. It now serves about 40 000 customers per day, making it the busiest McDonald's in the world. The restaurant on the Old Arbat is the second busiest, serving about 20 000 people per day. The three biggest restaurants in Moscow serve as much food as 30 average-sized McDonald's restaurants in North America. Cohon has

since expanded operations to other Russian cities, and in 1999 there were 49 McDonald's restaurants operating in Russia.

Most of the problems that were initially encountered have now been solved. In the early days, about 80 percent of the managers were from the West. However, with the right coaching the Russian staff gained skills and management expertise. Now only a handful of Western managers remain. In addition, almost all of McDonald's ingredients are provided by 150 local businesses.

Although there are still problems with high taxes and excessive government red tape, this is a Canadian success story. It proves that opportunities exist in the global economy for Canadians who are willing to take calculated risks, who are persistent, and who are willing to adapt to local cultures and circumstances.

CASE QUESTIONS

1. How does the activity of McDonald's in Russia affect Canada's balance of trade? How does it affect Canada's balance of payments?

2. In deciding to "go international," how did McDonald's answer each of the basic questions shown in Figure 3.6 (see page 83)?

3. What level of involvement has McDonald's Canada decided on as it pursues business in Russia?

4. What skills must an expatriate manager possess to work effectively with local managers and employees?

5. Explain how the various barriers to trade (social/cultural, economic, legal/political) affected McDonald's Canada as it tried to establish itself in Russia. ◆

Visit the *Business* Website at www.pearsoned.ca/griffin
for up-to-date e-business cases!

CHAPTER 4

CONDUCTING BUSINESS ETHICALLY AND RESPONSIBLY

The Bubble Bursts at Cinar

Micheline Charest and Ronald Weinberg were the driving force behind Cinar Corp., the company that produces children's shows like *Arthur*, *The Adventures of Paddington Bear*, and *Wimzie's House*. The shows, which have a non-violent, social conscience, made Cinar one of the world's most successful animation companies. Both Weinberg and Charest tirelessly promoted their company to the media and to the financial markets.

But on March 7, 2000, Charest and Weinberg abruptly resigned as co-chief executives of the company amid allegations that over $100 million had been invested without proper approval from Cinar's board of directors. Earlier, Hasanain Panju, vice-president of finance, had been fired after he was charged with making unauthorized investments for Cinar. At the time, he claimed that he had done so with the approval of the company. A few weeks later, a Cinar spokesperson admitted that one of the co-founders and the former controller (who left the company in 1999) had actually approved $122 million in investments. This contradicted earlier claims by Cinar that Panju had acted alone.

J. Richard Finlay, chairman of the Centre for Corporate & Public Governance, offered the view that Cinar's top management and board structure were rather peculiar and likely contributed to the company's difficulties. The husband-wife team of Charest and Weinberg functioned as co-CEOs, one acting as president and the other chairing the board to which both reported. The corporate governance guidelines of the Toronto Stock Exchange, where the stock is listed, call for a non-executive and independent director as chairperson of the board.

A related problem was the composition of Cinar's board. While it was composed of both inside and outside directors, the outside directors had a majority of only one. And none of the board's outside directors was on the powerful Management Committee, which oversees succession planning, financial strategies, and the evaluation of top executives. The Options Committee, which grants options to senior management members who are on the board, was also a problem. It was made up of only one member—the president and co-CEO.

When asked by five independent members of the board of directors to resign from the board in August 2000, Charest and Weinberg refused. They said they would resign only if the other board members joined them to make way for a new slate. The NASDAQ Stock Market delisted Cinar's shares over concerns about the governance of the company. Cinar was also suspended from the Toronto Stock Exchange. Weinberg and Charest own 62 percent of the company's stock.

The issue of $100 million in unauthorized investments was not Cinar's only problem. In October 1999, it was alleged in parliament that Cinar had fraudulently obtained Canadian tax credits by putting the names of Canadians on television scripts actually written by Americans. (To qualify for subsidies under Canadian content rules, either the director or the screenwriter must be Canadian, along with the lead or second lead performer.)

And that wasn't all. In March 2000, the Ontario and Quebec securities commissions announced that they were launching an investigation to determine whether Cinar breached securities rules with its financial statements and other disclosure documents. ◆

Issues of fairness, ethics, and social responsibility are becoming increasingly important as companies around the world enter an era of intense competition, not only for public and consumer support, but also for the support of employees and stockholders. By focusing on the learning objectives of this chapter, you will see that many firms establish policies on business ethics and social responsibility to stipulate exactly how managers and employees should act with regard to the environment, customers, fellow employees, and investors. After reading this chapter, you should be able to:

LEARNING OBJECTIVES

1. Explain how individuals develop their personal *codes of ethics* and why ethics are important in the workplace.

2. Distinguish *social responsibility* from *ethics*, identify *organizational stakeholders*, and trace the evolution of social responsibility in business.

3. Show how the concept of social responsibility applies both to environmental issues and to a firm's relationships with customers, employees, and investors.

4. Identify four general *approaches to social responsibility* and describe the four steps a firm must take to implement a *social responsibility program*.

5. Explain how issues of social responsibility and ethics affect small businesses.

In this chapter, we look at the issues of individual ethics in business and the social responsibility of business as a whole. Remember that these issues were not always considered important in business philosophy or practice. Today, however, the ethical implications of business practices are very much in the spotlight. Managers must confront a variety of ethical problems, and companies must address many issues of social responsibility.

ETHICS IN THE WORKPLACE

ethics
Individual standards or moral values regarding what is right and wrong or good and bad.

ethical behaviour
Behaviour that conforms to individual beliefs and social norms about what is right and good.

unethical behaviour
Behaviour that individual beliefs and social norms define as wrong and bad.

business ethics
Ethical or unethical behaviours by a manager or employee of an organization.

Just what is *ethical behaviour*? **Ethics** are beliefs about what is right and wrong or good and bad. An individual's personal values and morals and the social context in which they occur determine whether a particular behaviour is perceived as ethical or unethical. In other words, **ethical behaviour** is behaviour that conforms to individual beliefs and social norms about what is right and good. **Unethical behaviour** is behaviour that individual beliefs and social norms define as wrong and bad. **Business ethics** is a term often used to refer to ethical or unethical behaviours by a manager or employee of an organization.

Because ethics are based on both individual beliefs and social concepts, they vary from person to person, from situation to situation, and from culture to culture. Social standards, for example, tend to be broad enough to support certain differences in beliefs. Without violating the general standards of the culture, therefore, individuals may develop personal codes of ethics that reflect a fairly wide range of attitudes and beliefs. Thus, what constitutes ethical and unethical behaviour is determined partly by the individual and partly by culture.

Influences on Ethics

Aside from situational factors, what makes different people's codes of ethics vary so much? The most common influences on an individual's ethics and behaviour are family, peers, and experiences.

Families—especially parents—have the first chance to influence a child's ethics. Parents usually put a high priority on teaching their children certain values. In many families, these values include religious principles. Most parents also try to teach their children to obey society's rules and to behave well towards other people. The so-called *work ethic*—the belief and practice that hard work brings rewards—is learned in the home. Children who see their parents behaving ethically are more likely to adopt high ethical standards for themselves than are the children of parents who behave unethically. Teenagers are particularly likely to reject the verbal messages of parents who do not practise what they preach.

As children grow and are exposed more to other children, peers begin to have more influence on ethical behaviour. Indeed, the values of the group may become far more important than those of the larger society. Although such beliefs and behaviour are most talked about in the case of juvenile delinquent gangs, they also apply to the business world. Many unethical (and even criminal) business behaviours are fostered by a company environment in which such practices are acceptable (at least until the company gets caught).

Finally, experiences can increase or decrease certain types of ethical behaviour and beliefs about what is right and wrong. A child punished for telling lies learns that telling lies is wrong. Likewise, a company president who goes to jail for misrepresenting the company's financial position will probably have a new understanding of business ethics. But the manager who gets away with sexually harassing an employee will be more likely to see nothing wrong with it and do it again.

The "Business Today" box describes another influence on individual ethics.

Assessing Ethical Behaviour

By definition, what distinguishes ethical behaviour from unethical behaviour is often subjective and subject to differences of opinion.[1] So, how does one go about deciding whether a particular action or decision is ethical? Figure 4.1 presents a simplified three-step model for applying ethical judgments to situations that may arise during the course of business activities:

1. Gather the relevant factual information.

2. Determine the most appropriate moral values.

3. Make an ethical judgment based on the rightness or wrongness of the proposed activity or policy.

Unfortunately, the process does not always work as smoothly as the scheme in Figure 4.1 suggests. What if the facts are not clear-cut? What if there are no agreed-upon moral values? Nevertheless, a judgment and a decision must be made. Experts point out that, otherwise, trust is impossible; and trust, they add, is indispensable to any business transaction.

To assess more fully the ethics of a particular behaviour, we need a more complex perspective. To illustrate this perspective, let's consider a common dilemma faced by managers involving their *expense accounts*. Companies routinely provide managers with accounts to cover work-related expenses when they are travelling on company business and/or entertaining clients for business purposes. Common examples of such expenses include hotel bills, meals, rental cars or taxis, and so forth. Employees, of course, are expected to claim only those expenses that are accurate and work-related. For example, if a manager takes a client to dinner while travelling on business and spends $100, submitting a receipt for that dinner to be reimbursed for $100 is clearly accurate and appropriate. Suppose, however, that the manager then

BUSINESS TODAY

Ethics and the Internet

The rapid expansion of the Internet into the workplace has created great opportunities for businesses, but also a number of ethical dilemmas for employees. Consider the following questions:

- Is it acceptable for employees to use their company's Internet connections to obtain stock quotations, or to buy and sell stock for their personal portfolios?
- Is it acceptable for employees to use the company's e-mail system to send e-mails that deal with non-business subjects (e.g., supporting political candidates, promoting charities, gossiping, etc.)?
- Is it acceptable for employees to do online shopping during their lunch hour?
- Is it acceptable for employees to look for a new job on the Internet while they are at work?

These and many other questions have arisen because the Internet is providing opportunities that did not formerly exist. These ethical dilemmas are the modern version of the question: "Can an employee use the company's phone for personal business?"

Companies are reacting in various ways as they try to cope with this new technology. Some seem to have accepted the inevitable, and allow employees to use the company's fax, e-mail, and Internet for personal reasons, as long as the usage is of reasonable duration and frequency and does not cause embarrassment to the company. Chain letters, obscenity, and religious and political solicitation are typically prohibited.

Other companies do not set specific guidelines, but warn employees that they should not expect privacy for personal matters if they use the company's e-mail system. They also indicate that the company has the right to check on employees at any time, and that employees will be disciplined if unacceptable usage occurs. And unacceptable usage does occur. One employee used his company's computer to run his own business on the side. Another employee was fired after he sent an e-mail promoting a religious holiday to so many people that it disabled the company's e-mail system for six hours.

What does the general public think about some of these ethical dilemmas? A poll conducted by the *Wall Street Journal* revealed the following:

- 34 percent of those polled felt that it is wrong to use the company's e-mail for personal business.
- 37 percent felt that it is wrong to use office equipment to help a child or spouse do school work.
- 49 percent felt that it is wrong to play computer games on office equipment.
- 54 percent said that it is wrong to do Internet shopping while at work.
- 87 percent said that it is wrong to visit pornographic Web sites while at work.

Here's another Internet ethics question: Should alcohol be sold on the Internet? In 2000, the liquor commissions of Manitoba, Ontario, and Quebec all began selling liquor on the Internet. Some of the potential problems with selling alcohol over the Internet include the following: Might delivery people inadvertently hand over liquor to a minor when delivering it? Or to someone who is already drunk? Will delivery people be tempted to take a few sips while they're delivering the goods?

---

has a $100 dinner the next night in that same city with a good friend for purely social purposes. Submitting that receipt for full reimbursement would be unethical. A few managers, however, will rationalize that it is acceptable to submit a receipt for dinner with a friend. They will argue, perhaps, that they are underpaid and are simply increasing the income due to them.

Other principles that come into play in a case like this include various *ethical norms*. Consider four such norms and the issues that they entail:

- *Utility*: Does a particular act optimize what is best for those who are affected by it?

- *Rights*: Does it respect the rights of the individuals involved?

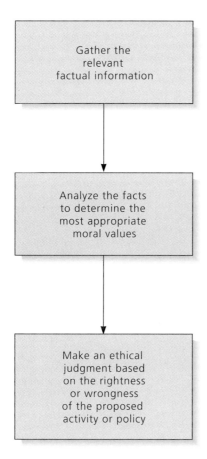

Figure 4.1
Steps in making ethical judgments.

■ *Justice*: Is it consistent with what we regard to be fair?

■ *Caring*: Is it consistent with people's responsibilities to each other?

Figure 4.2 is an expanded version of Figure 4.1 that incorporates the consideration of these ethical norms.

Now, let's return to the case of the inflated expense account. While the utility norm would acknowledge that the manager benefits from padding an expense account, others, such as co-workers and owners, do not. Likewise, most experts would agree that it does not respect the rights of others. Moreover, it is clearly unfair and compromises the manager's responsibilities to others. This particular act, then, appears to be clearly unethical.

Figure 4.2, however, also provides mechanisms for considering unique circumstances—those that apply only in certain limited situations. Suppose, for example, that the manager loses the receipt for the legitimate dinner but retains the receipt for the social dinner. Some people will argue that it is acceptable to submit the illegitimate receipt because the manager is only doing so to be reimbursed for what he or she is entitled to. Others, however, will continue to argue that submitting the other receipt is wrong under any circumstances. We won't pretend to arbitrate the case. For our purposes, we will simply make the following point: Changes in the situation can make issues more or less clear-cut.

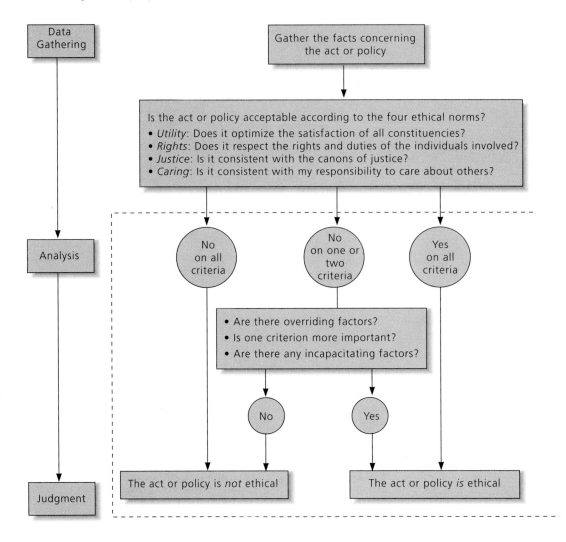

Figure 4.2
Expanded model of ethical judgments.

Company Practices and Business Ethics

Organizations try to promote ethical behaviour and discourage unethical behaviour in numerous ways. As unethical and even illegal activities by both managers and employees plague more and more companies, many firms have taken additional steps to encourage ethical behaviour in the workplace. Many, for example, establish codes of conduct and develop clear ethical positions on how the firm and its employees will conduct its business. An increasingly controversial area regarding business ethics and company practices involves the privacy of e-mail and other communications that take place inside an organization. The "It's a Wired World" box discusses these issues more fully.

Perhaps the single most effective step a company can take is to demonstrate top management support. A classic illustration of the power of ethical commitment involves Johnson & Johnson. In 1982, it was discovered that capsules of the company's Tylenol pain reliever had been laced with cyanide. Managers at J&J quickly recalled all Tylenol bottles still on retailers' shelves and then went public with candid information throughout the crisis. J&J's ethical choices proved to be a crucial factor in its campaign to rescue its product: both the firm and the brand bounced back much more quickly than most observers had thought possible.

IT'S A WIRED WORLD

When It Comes to Privacy, It's a Small World After All

E-mail has virtually become the standard method of communication in the business world. Most people enjoy its speed, ease, and casual nature. But e-mail also has its share of problems and pitfalls. One challenge is privacy. Many people assume that the contents of their e-mail are private, but there may in fact be any number of people authorized to see it. Some experts have likened e-mail to postcards sent through the regular mail: they pass through a lot of hands and before a lot of eyes, and, theoretically, many people can read them.

The courts, for example, have held that e-mail messages sent and/or received during working hours and on company equipment are the property of the business. Compaq Computer has one full-time employee who does nothing but randomly scan e-mail messages that pass through the company's servers and monitor Internet usage among employees. Although many businesses do not have formal electronic communication policies, they do have the power of the law behind them when they do eventually establish policies or procedures.

Aside from organizational scrutiny, people also face the threat of hackers breaking into and wreaking havoc with the company's computer network, including its e-mail system. Indeed, e-mail is one of the easiest routes for hackers to use to gain access to other parts of a firm's computer system. Once inside, they can read sensitive e-mail messages, destroy them, or forward them to other people.

Finally, many users have good reason to regard themselves as the worst enemies to their own privacy. A surprisingly common error is inadvertently sending e-mail to the wrong address—even to a large group of people. More than one starry-eyed e-mailer has dispatched a love note to the wrong person. Even worse, a simple inadvertent click of the mouse can send a sensitive or inflammable message intended for a single recipient to everyone in the company.

But e-mail is actually only part of the privacy issue. Other concerns have arisen concerning general privacy over the Internet and cellular telephones. For consumers, Internet privacy is an especially important issue. Companies, for instance, have the capacity to monitor which Web sites individuals visit, how long they stay there, what they buy, and how frequently they return. They can use this information to make referrals to other companies who might then want to target advertising to those individuals. Cellular and cordless telephones are not nearly as private as hard-wired phones—indeed, tapping into or eavesdropping on a cellular conversation is amazingly easy. Not surprisingly, then, concerns about the shrinking world in which we can enjoy privacy are beginning to assume an increasingly higher profile with each passing day.

WEBCONNEXION

Privada offers "the infrastructure to secure privacy in a digital world." To find out how to send private electronic mail (via "Messaging incognito"™) and conduct private Web browsing (via "Web Incognito"™) contact the company at:

www.privada.net

In 1999, some Belgian school-children got sick after drinking Coke. The problem was a bad batch of carbon dioxide, and there was no health hazard. At first, Coke saw no reason to take action. But then the company got caught in the middle of Belgian political infighting over the incident, and Coke was removed from retail shelves for several days. Finally, Coke CEO Douglas Ivester apologized to Belgian consumers in a series of full-page newspaper ads, adding contritely, "I should have spoken with you earlier."

A more recent example involves the operations of Coca-Cola in Europe. First, some Belgian schoolchildren suffered minor illnesses after drinking Coke made from a bad batch of carbon dioxide. Then Coke cans shipped from the company's plant in Dunkirk, France, were found to have some fungicide on their bottoms. Neither problem was serious, but the two events combined to create a public relations problem. Coke CEO Douglas Ivester flew directly to Brussels and made a straightforward public apology: "My apologies to the consumers of Belgium." The furor died down almost immediately, primarily due to the top manager's quick, forthright response.[2]

In addition to demonstrating an attitude of honesty and openness, as in the case of Coca-Cola, firms can also take specific and concrete steps to formalize their commitment to ethical business practices. Two of the most common approaches to formalizing commitment are *adopting written codes* and *instituting ethics programs*.

Adopting Written Codes

Many companies, including Johnson & Johnson, McDonald's, Starbucks, and Dell Computer have adopted written codes of ethics that formally acknowledge their intent to do business in an ethical manner. Figure 4.3 shows the code of ethics adopted by Great-West Life Assurance. Most codes of ethics are designed to perform one or more of four functions:

1. They may increase public confidence in a firm or its industry.

2. They may help stem the tide of government regulation—that is, aid in self-regulation.

3. They may improve internal operations by providing consistent standards of both ethical and legal conduct.

4. They can help managers respond to problems that arise as a result of unethical or illegal behaviour.

A 1997 survey by KPMG found that two-thirds of Canada's largest corporations have codes of ethics (90 percent of large U.S. firms do). More and more regulatory and professional associations in Canada are recommending that corporations adopt codes of ethics. The Canada Deposit Insurance

GUIDING PRINCIPLES — THE GREAT-WEST LIFE ASSURANCE COMPANY

1. Great-West Life's management recognizes that, to prosper, the company must serve its clients, staff members and sales representatives, shareholders, and the community at large, with integrity and according to the highest standards of conduct.

2. We will maintain an environment of trust in, and respect for, the dignity of the individual. We will strive to select superior people. We will build and maintain a dynamic organization through an open and participative style of management. We will give staff members and sales personnel every opportunity to make the most of their abilities and reward them according to their contribution to meeting our objectives.

3. We will distribute our products and services in the best interests of our clients through distribution systems that are contemporary, innovative, and socially responsible.

4. Our investment program will carefully balance the quality, terms, and rate of return on our investments. We will strive to achieve a consistently superior rate of return to meet our overall financial objectives and obligations to our clients.

5. We will find new and better ways to serve our clients by offering products and services that are both contemporary and innovative to satisfy their changing needs and desires. We will maintain their goodwill by meeting our commitments to them both in spirit and letter with particular emphasis upon the financial management and security of their funds.

6. We will work to increase the long-term value of shareholders' investment to maintain our reputation as a sound and growing financial institution.

Figure 4.3
Ethical principles at Great-West Life Assurance Co.

Corp., for example, requires that all deposit-taking institutions have a code of conduct that is periodically reviewed and ratified by the board of directors. The Canadian Competition Bureau, the Canadian Institute of Chartered Accountants, and the Ontario Human Rights Commission all are pushing for the adoption of codes of ethics by corporations.[3]

Figure 4.4 illustrates the essential role that corporate ethics and values should play in corporate policy. You can use it to see how ethics statements might be structured most effectively. Basically, it suggests that although business strategies and practices can change frequently and business objectives may change occasionally, an organization's core principles and values should remain steadfast. Hewlett-Packard, for example, has had the same written code of ethics, called *The HP Way*, since 1957, and it has served the firm well for over 40 years. "No one," claims CEO Carly Fiorina, "would say this company doesn't have a shining soul."[4] The essential elements of *The HP Way* are as follows:

- We have trust and respect for individuals.
- We focus on a high level of achievement and contribution.
- We conduct our business with uncompromising integrity.
- We achieve our common objectives through teamwork.
- We encourage flexibility and innovation.

Teaching Ethics

Instances like the Tylenol case suggest that ethical responses can be learned through experience. But can business ethics be "taught," either in the workplace or in schools? While business schools have become important players in the debate about ethics education, most analysts agree that companies must take the chief responsibility for educating employees. In fact, more and more firms are doing so. Imperial Oil, for example, conducts workshops for employees that emphasize ethical concerns. The purpose of these workshops is to help employees put Imperial's ethics statement into practice.

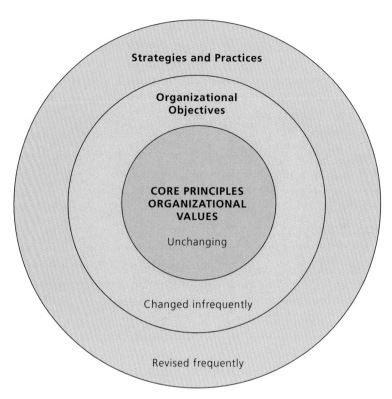

Strategies and Practices

Organizational Objectives

CORE PRINCIPLES ORGANIZATIONAL VALUES

Unchanging

Changed infrequently

Revised frequently

Figure 4.4
Core principles and organizational values.

Nike
www.nike.com

Some firms, however, struggle with ethical dilemmas. International business can make matters even more complicated. A good case in point is Nike, the giant athletic shoe and apparel firm. Like other businesses, Nike exists to make a profit. To help boost profitability, Nike manufactures most of its products overseas, subcontracting in areas of the world where labour costs are low. But how far can a company take this practice before running into problems? A recent scathing report investigating Nike's manufacturing partners in Asia called it just short of slave labour. In 1996, for example, 40 Vietnamese workers were forced to kneel with their hands in the air as punishment for poor performance. In 1997, another group of workers was forced to run around a factory in stifling heat because they had not worn regulation shoes to work that day. Dozens of similar problems were uncovered.

Nike responded to this report by acknowledging its mistakes and systematically working to improve the plight of offshore workers. Nike plants in Asia, for example, can no longer force employees to work on Sundays. Wages have been increased, and supervisors are now forbidden to practise many of the more extreme forms of punishment they once doled out. Air ventilation and circulation have been improved, and a senior Nike executive has been placed in charge of monitoring the working conditions of workers in subcontractors' factories. Says Dusty Kidd, Nike's head of global labour practices: "People now know that if they don't accept responsibility [for the welfare of their offshore workers], they may not have consumers in the [future]." While some critics complain that Nike has not gone far enough, most would agree that the company is at least moving in the right direction.[5]

SOCIAL RESPONSIBILITY

Ethics affect individual behaviour in the workplace. **Social responsibility**, however, refers to the way in which a business tries to balance its commitments to certain groups and individuals in its social environment. **Organizational stakeholders** are those groups, individuals, and organizations that are directly affected by the practices of an organization and that therefore have a stake in its performance.[6] Major stakeholders are identified in Figure 4.5.

The Stakeholder Model of Responsibility

Most companies that strive to be responsible to their stakeholders concentrate on five main groups: *customers, employees, investors, suppliers*, and the *local communities* in which they do business. They may then select other stakeholders that are particularly relevant or important to the organization and try to address their needs and expectations as well.

The Evolution of Social Responsibility

Canadian society and Canadian business have changed dramatically in the last two centuries. Not surprisingly, so have views about social responsibility. The late nineteenth century was characterized by the entrepreneurial spirit and the laissez-faire philosophy. During this era of labour strife and predatory business practices, both individual citizens and the government first became concerned about unbridled business activity. This concern was translated into laws regulating basic business practices.

During the Great Depression of the 1930s, many people blamed the failure of businesses and banks and the widespread loss of jobs on a general climate of business greed and lack of restraint. Out of the economic turmoil emerged new laws that described an increased expectation that business should protect and enhance the general welfare of society.

social responsibility
A business's collective code of ethical behaviour towards the environment, its customers, its employees, and its investors.

organizational stakeholders
Groups, individuals, and organizations that are directly affected by the practices of an organization and that therefore have a stake in its performance.

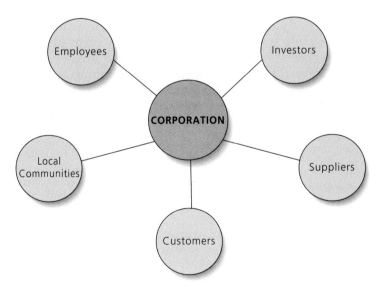

Figure 4.5
Major stakeholders.

WEBCONNEXION

Mountain Equipment Co-op was founded in 1971 as a not-for-profit business venture. It sells gear for mountaineering, rock climbing, and hiking. Its mission statement includes the following core values: to conduct business ethically and with integrity, to respect others in words and actions, to act in the spirit of community and cooperation, and to respect and protect the natural environment. Visit Mountain Equipment Co-op at:

www.mec.ca

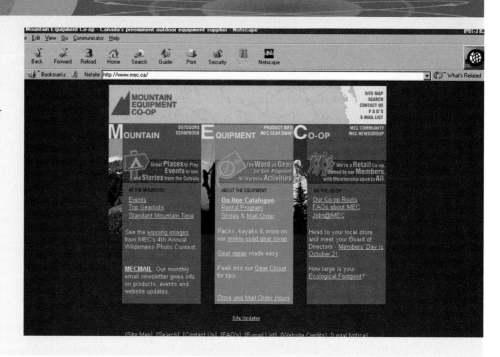

During the social unrest of the 1960s and 1970s, business was often characterized as a negative social force. Eventually, increased activism prompted increased government regulation in a variety of areas. Health warnings, for example, were placed on cigarettes, and stricter environmental protection laws were enacted.

Contemporary Social Consciousness

Social consciousness and views towards social responsibility continue to evolve in the twenty-first century. Today's attitudes seem to be moving towards an enlightened view stressing the need for a greater social role for business. An increased awareness of the global economy and heightened campaigning on the part of environmentalists and other activists have combined to make many businesses more sensitive to their social responsibilities.

For example, retailers such as Sears have policies against selling handguns and other weapons, and toy retailer Toys "R" Us refuses to sell toy guns that look too realistic. Firms in numerous other industries have also integrated socially conscious thinking into their production plans and marketing efforts. The production of environmentally safe products, for example, has become a potential boom area, as many companies introduce products designed to be "environmentally friendly."

Electrolux, a Swedish appliance maker, has developed a line of water-efficient washing machines, a solar-powered lawnmower, and, for Brazil, the first refrigerators that are free of ozone-depleting refrigerants. Herman Miller, a Michigan-based office-furniture business, uses recycled materials and focuses on products that are simple in design, more durable, and recyclable. Ford has set up an independent brand called Think to develop and market low-pollution and electric-powered vehicles.[7]

Electrolux
www.electrolux.com

Herman Miller
www.hermanmiller.com

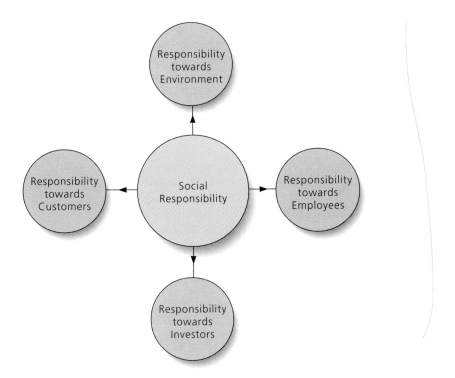

Figure 4.6
There are four basic areas of social responsibility.

Areas of Social Responsibility

In defining its sense of social responsibility, most firms must confront four is-sues. As Figure 4.6 shows, these issues concern an organization's responsibility towards its environment, its customers, its employees, and its investors.

Responsibility Towards the Environment

One critical area of social responsibility involves how the business relates to its physical environment. Although noise pollution is attracting increased concern, air pollution, water pollution, and land pollution are the subjects of most anti-pollution efforts by business and governments.[8] The Kyoto Summit in 1997 was an attempt by various governments to reach agreement on ways to reduce the threat of pollution.

Air Pollution. Air pollution results when a combination of factors converges to lower air quality. Large amounts of chemicals such as the carbon monoxide emitted by automobiles contribute to air pollution. Smoke and other chemicals emitted by manufacturing plants also help to create air pollution.

Legislation has gone a long way towards controlling air pollution. Under new laws, many companies have had to install special devices to limit the pollutants they expel into the atmosphere. Such clean-up efforts are not with-out costs, however. The bill to private companies for air pollution control devices runs into billions of dollars.

Even with these devices, however, acid rain remains a problem. **Acid rain** occurs when sulphur pumped into the atmosphere mixes with natural moisture and falls as rain. Much of the acid rain damage to forests and streams in the eastern United States and Canada has been attributed to heavy manufacturing and power plants in the midwestern United States.

acid rain
A form of pollution affecting the eastern United States and Canada as a result of sulphur expelled into the air by midwestern power and manufacturing plants.

Acid rain poses a dilemma in social responsibility for businesses. Current technologies to greatly reduce sulphur pollution are so costly that they would force many businesses to close. Such a move would cause major financial losses for investors and for laid-off employees, not to mention the loss of crucial services. The business challenge is to find ways to significantly reduce the sulphur—and thus the acid rain—without incurring costs that are too high to bear.

Water Pollution.   For years, businesses and municipalities dumped their waste into rivers, streams, and lakes with little regard for the effects. Thanks to new legislation and increased awareness on the part of businesses, water quality is improving in many areas. Millar Western Pulp Ltd. built Canada's first zero-discharge pulp mill at Meadow Lake, Saskatchewan. There is no discharge pipe to the river, no dioxin-forming chlorine, and next to no residue. Dow Chemical built a plant at Fort Saskatchewan that will not dump any pollutants into the nearby river.[9] However, water pollution problems remain. In 2000, seven people died in Walkerton, Ontario, after the town's water supply was contaminated with E. coli bacteria.

Land Pollution.   Two key issues are associated with land pollution. The first issue is how to restore the quality of land damaged and abused in the past. In 1998, 5 million cubic litres of toxic waste escaped from a holding pond at a zinc mine in Spain that was operated by the Canadian firm Boliden Ltd. Thousands of hectares of agricultural land were contaminated.[10]

A second issue is how to prevent such problems in the future. Changes in foresting practices, limits on types of mining, and new forms of solid waste disposal are all attempts to address this issue, although such changes are often opposed. A whole new industry—**recycling**—has developed as part of increased consciousness about land pollution. RBW Graphics, for example, uses a process that cleanses paper fibres and other impurities from ink recovered from printing presses. The system saves the company 35 000 kilograms of ink annually. This ink used to be transported to a dump. Instead, recycling saves the company $175 000 each year.[11]

Other business firms are also reducing what they send to city dumps. The Royal York Hotel in Toronto, for example, installed machinery that extracts 70 percent of the moisture from organic waste. The hotel reduced the amount it sends to the dump by 50 percent. Ramada Renaissance in Toronto bought a refrigerator that stores waste that will ultimately become animal food. The hotel has reduced the waste it sends to the dump by 75 percent.[12] Bell Canada has reduced the amount of garbage it generates each day from 800 kilograms to 22 kilograms at its Etobicoke, Ontario, location.[13]

Dow Chemical
www.dow.com

recycling
The reconversion of waste materials into useful products.

Toxic waste disposal and clean-up have become increasingly important areas of debate and concern in recent years.

An especially controversial problem centres on toxic waste disposal. **Toxic wastes** are dangerous chemical and/or radioactive byproducts of various manufacturing processes. Because toxic waste cannot usually be processed into harmless material or destroyed, it must be stored somewhere. The problem is—where? Few people want a toxic waste storage facility in their town.

Various organizations aggressively monitor business activity that might lead to pollution. For example,

- Greenpeace sent a letter to 60 Canadian and foreign investment dealers making the case that the dealers should advise their clients not to invest in Canadian Mining and Energy Corp. because of environmental concerns.[14]

- A group of Canadian shareholders has criticized Placer Dome Inc. for its open pit copper mine on Marinduque Island in the Philippines.[15]

- The Task Force on the Churches and Corporate Responsibility (TFCCR) and Probe International have publicly criticized Canadian firms such as Atomic Energy of Canada Ltd. (selling a food irradiator to Thailand), Petro-Canada (road building in the Ecuadorian rain forest), and Brascan Ltd. (exploration rights for tin in areas of Ecuador conflicting with native land claims).[16]

- Because those who own the land can be forced to pay to clean it up, the Royal Bank refuses to lend money to some types of companies (e.g., waste oil firms) until an environmental audit has been carried out. When Dominion Barrel and Drum went bankrupt, for example, it left behind thousands of contaminated barrels on 21 hectares of land. The firm's creditor, the Federal Business Development Bank, decided not to foreclose on the land when it found that it would cost over $1 million—more than what the land was worth—to clean it up.[17]

Many business firms are now acting to reduce various forms of pollution. Under the Canadian and Ontario environmental protection acts, liability for a business firm can run as high as $2 million per day. To protect themselves, companies must prove that they showed diligence in avoiding an environmental disaster such as an oil or gasoline spill.[18] The Environmental Choice program, sponsored by the federal government, licenses products that meet environmental standards set by the Canadian Standards Association. Firms whose products meet these standards can put the logo—three doves intertwined to form a maple leaf—on their products.[19]

An interesting problem that highlights some of the complexities in both waste disposal and recycling involves the proliferation of wooden pallets—those splintery wooden platforms used to store and transport consumer goods. Pallets are popular because they provide an efficient method for stacking and moving large quantities of smaller items. Boxes of canned goods, batteries, hair dryers, cans of paint, bags of fertilizer, and bundles of roofing shingles can all be stacked on pallets and wrapped with plastic or other binding material. Pallets of merchandise can be easily and efficiently forklifted from factories to trucks, from trucks to warehouses, from warehouses to different trucks, and, finally, to Wal-Mart, Home Depot, and Safeway storerooms.

Granted, pallets are eminently recyclable, but the cost of new ones is still generally lower than the cost of returning and/or redistributing used ones. As a result, many companies just toss used pallets aside and collect more. Some entrepreneurs have tried to sell them for firewood, but because the wood is thin and tends to be quite dry, it burns both too quickly and too hot for most applications. Because they are both heavy and prone to dangerous splintering, pallets are also hard to handle without a forklift. Thus, many landfills refuse to take them, and others assess surcharges for recycling them. They eventually biodegrade after several decades. Ironically, some environmentalists argue that abandoned pallets actually serve a useful purpose: in urban areas, they often become refuge for animals such as raccoons, rats, and abandoned pets.[20]

toxic waste

Pollution resulting from the emission of chemical and/or radioactive byproducts of various manufacturing processes into the air, water, or land.

Greenpeace
www.greenpeacecanada.org

Responsibility Towards Customers

Social responsibility towards customers generally falls into one of two categories: providing quality products and pricing those products fairly. As with the environment, firms differ in their level of concern about responsibility to customers. Yet unlike environmental problems, customer problems do not require expensive technological solutions. Most such problems can be avoided if companies obey the laws regarding consumer rights, avoid illegal pricing practices, and behave ethically when advertising their products.

Rights of Consumers.   Much of the current interest in business responsibility towards customers can be traced to the rise of consumerism. **Consumerism** is a form of social activism dedicated to protecting the rights of consumers in their dealings with businesses.

Consumers have several rights. First, they have the right to safe products. For example, when you buy a new paint sprayer, it must be safe to use for spraying paint. It must come with instructions on how to use it, and it must have been properly tested by its manufacturer. Dow Corning Corp. halted production of silicone breast implants after questions were raised about the product's safety. When the British government announced a possible link between "mad cow disease" and Creutzfeld-Jakob disease, McDonald's and Burger King suspended the sale of all British beef products. Both firms took this action to maintain consumer confidence in their products.

Second, consumers have the right to be informed about all relevant aspects of a product. Food products must list their ingredients. Clothing must be labelled with information about its proper care. And banks must tell you exactly how much interest you are paying on a loan. Cereal companies have come under fire recently for some of the claims they have made about the oat bran content of their cereals, as well as its likely effects.

Third, consumers have a right to be heard. Many companies today have complaints offices. Retailers like Kmart offer a money-back guarantee if consumers aren't satisfied. Procter & Gamble puts a toll-free number on many of its products that consumers can call if they have questions or complaints. When companies refuse to respond to consumer complaints, consumer protection agencies such as the Better Business Bureau and consumer interest groups such as the Airline Passengers Association may intervene.

Finally, consumers have a right to choose what they buy. Central to this right is free and open competition among companies. In times past, "gentlemen's agreements" were often used to avoid competition or to divide up a market so that firms did not have to truly compete against each other. Such practices are illegal today and any attempts by business to block competition can result in fines or other penalties.

Unfair Pricing.   Interfering with competition can also mean illegal pricing practices. **Collusion** among companies—getting together to "fix" prices—is against the law. Polar Plastic Ltd. of Montreal pled guilty to conspiring to fix prices of disposable cups, glasses, and cutlery in the U.S. market. Although secret meetings and phone conversations took place between executives of competing companies as they tried to fix prices, the conspiracy was not successful.[21]

Recently, the U.S. Justice Department charged three international pharmaceutical firms with illegally controlling worldwide supplies and prices of vitamins. France's Rhone-Poulenc cooperated with the investigation, helped break the case several months earlier than expected, and was not fined. Switzerland's F. Hoffmann-LaRoche was fined US$500 million, and one of its senior executives was sentenced to four months in a U.S. prison. Germany's BASF was fined US$225 million.[22]

Under some circumstances, firms can also come under attack for *price gouging*—responding to increased demand with overly steep (and often unwarranted) price increases. For example, when BMW launched its Z3

---

consumerism

A social movement that seeks to protect and expand the rights of consumers in their dealings with businesses.

collusion

An illegal agreement among companies in an industry to "fix" prices for their products.

Roadsters, demand for the car was so strong that some dealers sold Z3s only to customers willing to pay thousands of dollars over sticker prices. Volkswagen dealers adopted a similar practice when the new Beetle was launched.

Ethics in Advertising.   In recent years, increased attention has been given to ethics in advertising and product information. Because of controversies surrounding the potential misinterpretation of words and phrases such as "light," "reduced calorie," "diet," and "low fat," food producers are now required to use a standardized format for listing ingredients on product packages. Similarly, controversy arose over a commercial aired during the 2000 Super Bowl game. The ad featured Christopher Reeve, a quadriplegic actor, apparently standing up from his wheelchair and walking to a podium. In reality, the images were computer altered and were intended to convey a message of hope and optimism for a foundation supporting spinal cord research. However, many viewers were confused by the ads, and the day after the game, dozens of quadriplegics called their doctors and hospitals to inquire about the procedure that had evidently cured the actor. The ad was quickly pulled after widespread media criticism.

Another issue concerns advertising that some consumers consider to be morally objectionable. Benetton, for example, aired a series of commercials featuring inmates on death row. The ads, dubbed "We, on Death Row," prompted such an emotional outcry that Sears dropped the Benetton USA clothing line.[23] Other ads receiving criticism include Victoria's Secret models in skimpy underwear and campaigns by tobacco and alcohol companies that are accused of targeting young people.

Benetton
www.benetton.com

Responsibility Towards Employees

Organizations also need to employ fair and equitable practices with their employees. Later, in Chapter 8, we describe the human-resource management activities essential to a smoothly functioning business. These same activities—recruiting, hiring, training, promoting, and compensating—are also the basis for social responsibility towards employees. A company that provides its employees with equal opportunities for rewards and advancement without regard to race, sex, or other irrelevant factors is meeting its social responsibilities. Firms that ignore their responsibility to employees leave themselves open to lawsuits. They also miss the chance to hire better and more highly motivated employees.

Some progressive companies go well beyond these legal requirements, hiring and training the so-called hard-core unemployed (people with little education and training and a history of unemployment) and those who have disabilities. The Bank of Montreal, for example, sponsors a community college skills upgrading course for individuals with hearing impairments. The Royal Bank provides managers with discrimination awareness training. Rogers Cablesystems Ltd. has begun to provide individuals with mobility restrictions with telephone and customer-service job opportunities.[24] Bell Canada employs more than 1000 people with disabilities (2 percent of its permanent workforce). But, in Canada, over 50 percent of those with physical disabilities are still unemployed.[25]

The safety of workers is an important consideration for all organizations. The required use of hardhats, for example, is designed to protect workers from head injuries.

Privacy →

Canadian National Railways
www.cn.ca

whistle-blower
An individual who calls attention to an unethical, illegal, and/or socially irresponsible practice on the part of a business or other organization.

In addition to their responsibility to employees as resources of the company, firms have a social responsibility to their employees as people. Firms that accept this responsibility ensure that the workplace is safe, both physically and emotionally. They would no more tolerate an abusive manager or one who sexually harasses employees than they would a gas leak.

Business firms also have a responsibility to respect the privacy of their employees. While nearly everyone agrees that companies have the right to exercise some level of control over their employees, there is great controversy about exactly how much is acceptable in areas such as drug testing and computer monitoring. When Canadian National Railways instituted drug testing for train, brake, and yard employees, 12 percent failed. Trucking companies have found that nearly one-third of truckers who have been involved in an accident are on drugs.[26]

Employees are often unaware that they are being monitored by managers who are using new computer technology. Computer software firms even sell programs called "Spy" and "Peek" to facilitate monitoring. This type of monitoring increases employee stress levels because they don't know exactly when the boss is watching them. A lawsuit was brought against Nortel Networks by employees who charged that the firm installed telephone bugs and hidden microphones in one of its plants.[27]

Respecting employees as people also means respecting their behaviour as ethically responsible individuals. Employees who discover that their company has been engaging in practices that are illegal, unethical, and/or socially irresponsible should be able to report the problem to higher-level management and be confident that managers will stop the questionable practices. If no one in the organization will take action, the employee might decide to inform a regulatory agency or perhaps the media.

At this point, the person becomes what is popularly known as a **whistle-blower**—an employee who discovers and tries to put an end to a company's unethical, illegal, and/or socially irresponsible actions by publicizing them.[28] The recent Al Pacino–Russell Crowe movie *The Insider* featured the story of a tobacco-industry whistle-blower named Jeffrey Wigand, who was fired when he made his accusations public. Wigand says, "I went from making $300 000 a year, plus stock options, plus, plus, plus—to making $30 000. Yes, there is a price I've paid."[29]

Ross Gray, formerly a vice-president at Standard Trustco Ltd., was dismissed from his position after he "blew the whistle" on illegal activities at the company. The company claimed that Gray had participated in the illegal activities. He filed a wrongful dismissal suit against the firm.[30]

When Phillip Adams worked in the computer industry, he discovered a flaw in the chip-making process that, under certain circumstances, could lead to data being randomly deleted or altered. He reported the flaw to manufacturers, but several years later found that one company, Toshiba, had ignored the problem and continued to make flawed chips for 12 years. He went on to report the problem and became actively involved in a class-action lawsuit based heavily on his research. Toshiba eventually agreed to a $2.1 billion settlement. Adams' share was kept confidential, but he did receive a substantial reward for his efforts.[31] Not surprisingly, the prospect of large cash "rewards" has also generated a number of false or questionable accusations.[32]

Responsibility Towards Investors

It may sound odd to say that a firm can be irresponsible towards investors, since they are the owners of the company. But if the managers of a firm abuse its financial resources, the ultimate losers are the owners, since they do not receive the earnings, dividends, or capital appreciation due them.

The Bre-X stock market scandal (see Chapter 19) clearly shows how investors can be hurt when individuals in a business firm behave irresponsibly. This behaviour can take several forms.

Improper Financial Management. Occasionally, organizations are guilty of financial mismanagement. In other cases, executives have been "guilty" of paying themselves outlandish salaries, spending huge amounts of company money for their own personal comfort, and similar practices. Creditors can do nothing. Even shareholders have few viable options. Trying to force a management changeover is not only difficult, it can drive down the price of the stock, a penalty shareholders are usually unwilling to assign themselves.

Cheque Kiting. Other practices are specifically illegal. **Cheque kiting**, for instance, involves writing a cheque against money that has not yet arrived at the bank on which it is drawn. In 1993, E.F. Hutton and Co. was convicted of violating kiting laws on a massive scale: in a carefully planned scheme, company managers were able to use as much as $250 million every day that did not belong to the firm. Managers would deposit customer cheques for, say, $1 million into the company account. Knowing that the bank would collect only a percentage of the total deposit over the course of several days, they proceeded to write cheques against the total $1 million.

Insider Trading. Another area of illegal and socially irresponsible behaviour by firms towards investors is the practice of **insider trading**. Insider trading occurs when someone uses confidential information to gain from the purchase or sale of stocks. In July 2000, an Ontario court found Glen Harper, president of Golden Rule Resources Ltd., guilty of insider trading. He had sold $4 million worth of shares in his company after he found out that its supposedly huge gold find in Ghana was in doubt. When Harper sold his shares, the price of Golden Rule's stock was trading at about $13 per share. After the bad news became public, the stock fell to $2.50 per share, and eventually to 10 cents a share. Harper was sentenced to one year in prison and fined $3.95 million.[33]

Misrepresentation of Finances. Irresponsible and unethical behaviour regarding financial representation is also illegal. All corporations are required to conform to generally accepted accounting practices in maintaining and reporting their financial status. Sometimes, though, managers project profits far in excess of what they truly expect to earn. When the truth comes out, investors are almost always bitter. Occasionally, companies are found guilty of misrepresenting their finances to outsiders.

cheque kiting
The illegal practice of writing cheques against money that has not yet arrived at the bank on which the cheque has been written, relying on that money arriving before the cheque clears.

insider trading
The use of confidential information to gain from the purchase or sale of stock.

IMPLEMENTING SOCIAL RESPONSIBILITY PROGRAMS

Thus far, we have discussed social responsibility as if a consensus exists on how firms should behave in most situations. In fact, dramatic differences of opinion exist as to the appropriateness of social responsibility as a business goal. As you might expect, some people oppose any business activity that cuts into profits to investors. Others argue that responsibility must take precedence over profits.

Even people who share a common attitude towards social responsibility by businesses may have different reasons for their beliefs. Some opponents of such activity fear that if businesses become too active in social concerns, they will gain too much control over how those concerns are addressed. They point to the influence many businesses have been able to exert on the government agencies that are supposed to regulate their industries.

Other critics of business-sponsored social programs argue that companies lack the expertise needed. They believe that technical experts, not businesses, should decide how best to clean up a polluted river, for example.

Supporters of social responsibility believe that corporations are citizens just like individuals and therefore need to help improve our lives. Others point to the vast resources controlled by businesses and note that since businesses often create many of the problems social programs are designed to alleviate, they should use their resources to help. Still others argue that social responsibility is wise because it pays off for the firm.

Max Clarkson, formerly a top-level business executive, is now the director of the Centre for Corporate Social Performance and Ethics at the University of Toronto. He says that business firms that have a strong consciousness about ethics and social responsibility outperform firms that do not. After designing and applying a social responsibility rating system for companies, he found that companies that had the highest marks on questions of ethics and social responsibility also had the highest financial performance.[34]

Approaches to Social Responsibility

Given these differences of opinion, it is little wonder that corporations have adopted a variety of approaches to social responsibility. As Figure 4.7 illustrates, the four stances an organization can take concerning its obligations to society fall along a continuum ranging from the lowest to the highest degree of socially responsible practices.

Obstructionist Stance

obstructionist stance
A company does as little as possible to solve social or environmental problems.

The few organizations that take what might be called an **obstructionist stance** to social responsibility usually do as little as possible to solve social or environmental problems. When they cross the ethical or legal line that separates acceptable from unacceptable practices, their typical response is to deny or cover up their actions. Firms that adopt this position have little regard for ethical conduct and will generally go to great lengths to hide wrongdoing.

Defensive Stance

defensive stance
An organization does only what is legally required and nothing more.

One step removed from the obstructionist stance is the **defensive stance**, whereby the organization will do everything that is required of it legally but nothing more. This approach is most consistent with arguments against corporate social responsibility. Managers who take a defensive stance insist that their job is to generate profits. Such a firm, for example, would install

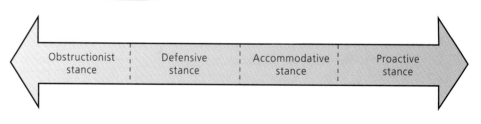

| Obstructionist stance | Defensive stance | Accommodative stance | Proactive stance |

LOWEST LEVEL OF SOCIAL RESPONSIBILITY

HIGHEST LEVEL OF SOCIAL RESPONSIBILITY

Figure 4.7
Spectrum of approaches to corporate social responsibility.

pollution-control equipment dictated by law, but would not install higher-quality equipment even though it might further limit pollution.

Tobacco companies generally take this position in their marketing efforts. In Canada and the United States, they are legally required to include warnings to smokers on their products and to limit advertising to prescribed media. Domestically, they follow these rules to the letter of the law but use more aggressive marketing methods in countries that have no such rules. In many Asian and African countries, for example, cigarettes are heavily promoted, contain higher levels of tar and nicotine than those sold in Canada and the U.S., and carry few or no health warning labels. Firms that take this position are also unlikely to cover up wrongdoing, will generally admit to mistakes, and will take appropriate corrective actions.

Accommodative Stance

A firm that adopts an **accommodative stance** meets its legal and ethical requirements, but will also go further in certain cases. Such firms voluntarily agree to participate in social programs, but solicitors must convince them that these programs are worthy of their support. Many organizations respond to requests for donations to community hockey teams, Girl Guides, youth soccer programs, and so forth. The point, however, is that someone has to knock on the door and ask; accommodative organizations do not necessarily or proactively seek avenues for contributing.

accommodative stance
A company meets all of its legal and ethical requirements, and in some cases even goes beyond what is required.

Proactive Stance

The highest degree of social responsibility a firm can exhibit is the **proactive stance**. Firms that adopt this approach take to heart the arguments in favour of social responsibility. They view themselves as citizens in a society and proactively seek opportunities to contribute. The most common—and direct—way to implement this stance is by setting up a foundation through which to provide direct financial support for various social programs.

proactive stance
An organization actively seeks opportunities to be socially responsible.

These stances are not sharply distinct; they merely label stages along a continuum of social responsibility. Organizations do not always fit neatly into one category or another. The Ronald McDonald House program has been widely applauded, for example, but McDonald's has also come under fire for allegedly misleading consumers about the nutritional value of its food products. Likewise, while UPS has sincere motives for helping Olympic athletes, the company will also benefit by featuring their photos on its envelopes and otherwise promoting its own benevolence.

Corporate Charitable Donations.   Donating money to different "causes" is one way that business firms try to show that they are socially responsible. Many groups that used to receive government funding (but no longer do because of government spending cuts) are increasingly seeking corporate support for their activities. More and more corporations are being asked to donate money to educational institutions, welfare agencies, service clubs, arts and culture groups, and athletic organizations.

A Decima Research survey found that 80 percent of Canadians think that businesses should give some of their profits to social causes.[35] An Environics survey of people in 23 different countries found that two-thirds of them thought that business was not doing enough if it simply abided by the law and provided employment. Instead, these people think that companies should also contribute to the broader goals of society.[36] A third survey, conducted by the Centre for Philanthropy, found that Canadian corporations contributed less than 2 percent of all charitable revenue. Canadians *think* that this number is closer to 20 percent, and that it should be 30 percent.[37]

Ronald McDonald House helps the families of children who are in hospital care. It is supported by McDonald's and is an excellent example of socially responsible behaviour by a business corporation.

Although the typical corporation gives less than half of 1 percent of its pre-tax profits to charity, many corporations have demonstrated a willingness to give money and products when disasters strike. When 11 people died in Walkerton, Ontario, as a result of drinking contaminated water, companies such as Petro-Canada, Shoppers Drug Mart, Sobeys, and Zellers contributed products such as bleach and bottled water. Companies generally receive favourable publicity when they make contributions like these.

Most large business firms in Canada have clear procedures for dealing with requests from charities and community organizations. The company first determines how much money it will give each year, usually stated as a percentage of profit. It then decides which specific organizations will receive the money and the amount each will receive. These decisions are made by the board of directors after it receives a recommendation from a committee that has been set up to consider charitable requests. Companies are increasingly taking a community-based approach to giving; they try to determine how they can achieve value for the community (and the company) with their donations.

Managing Social Responsibility Programs

Making a company truly socially responsible in the full sense of the proactive stance takes an organized and managed program. In particular, managers must take four steps to foster social responsibility, as shown in Figure 4.8.

First, social responsibility must start at the top. Without this support, no program can succeed. Top managers must make the decision that they want to take a stronger stand on social responsibility and develop a policy statement outlining their commitment.

Second, a committee of top managers needs to develop a plan detailing the level of support to be directed towards social responsibility. Some companies set aside a percentage of profits for social programs. Levi Strauss, for example, has a policy of giving 2.4 percent of its pre-tax earnings to worthy causes. Managers also need to set specific priorities. Should the firm train the hard-core unemployed or support the arts, for example?

Third, one specific executive needs to be given the authority to act as director of the firm's social agenda. Whether this is a separate job or an additional responsibility, this individual must monitor the program and ensure that its implementation is consistent with the policy statement and the strategic plan.

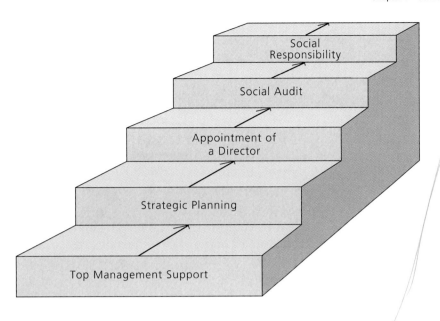

Figure 4.8
Establishing a social responsibility program involves four basic steps.

Finally, the organization needs to conduct occasional social audits. A **social audit** is a systematic analysis of how a firm is using funds earmarked for its social-responsibility goals. Consider the case of a company whose strategic plan calls for spending $100 000 to train 200 hard-core unemployed people and subsequently to place 180 of them in jobs. If at the end of one year the firm has spent $98 000, trained 210 people, and placed 175 into jobs, an audit will confirm the program as a success. But if the program cost $150 000, trained only 90 people, and placed only 10 of them in jobs, the audit will reveal the program's failure. A failure should signal the director and the committee to rethink the program's implementation and/or their choice of priorities.

social audit
A systematic analysis of how a firm is using funds earmarked for social-responsibility goals and how effective these expenditures have been.

Social Responsibility and the Small Business

Although many of the examples in this chapter illustrate responses to social responsibility and ethical issues by big business, small businesses face many of the same questions.

As the owner of a garden supply store, how would you respond to a building inspector's suggestion that a cash payment would expedite your application for a building permit? As the manager of a nightclub, would you call the police, refuse service, or sell liquor to a customer whose ID card looks forged? Or as the owner of a small laboratory, would you actually call the board of health to make sure that it has licensed the company you want to contract with to dispose of the lab's medical waste? Is the small manufacturing firm justified in overcharging a customer by 5 percent whose purchasing agent is lax? Who will really be harmed if a small firm pads its income statement to help get a much-needed bank loan?

Can a small business afford a social agenda? Should it sponsor hockey teams, make donations to the United Way, and buy light bulbs from the Lion's Club? Is joining the Chamber of Commerce and supporting the Better Business Bureau too much or just good business? Clearly, ethics and social responsibility are decisions faced by all managers in all organizations, regardless of rank or size. One key to business success is to decide in advance how to respond to these issues.

SUMMARY OF LEARNING OBJECTIVES

1. **Explain how individuals develop their personal *codes of ethics* and why ethics are important in the workplace.** Individual *codes of ethics* are derived from social standards of right and wrong. *Ethical behaviour* is behaviour that conforms to generally accepted social norms concerning beneficial and harmful actions. Because ethics affect the behaviour of individuals on behalf of the companies that employ them, many firms are adopting formal statements of ethics. Unethical behaviour can result in loss of business, fines, and even imprisonment.

2. **Distinguish *social responsibility* from *ethics*, identify *organizational stakeholders*, and trace the evolution of social responsibility in business.** *Social responsibility* refers to an organization's response to social needs. One way to understand social responsibility is to view it in terms of *stakeholders*—those groups, individuals, and organizations that are directly affected by the practices of an organization and that therefore have a stake in its performance. Until the second half of the nineteenth century, businesses often paid little attention to stakeholders. Since then, however, both public pressure and government regulation, especially as a result of the Great Depression of the 1930s and the social activism of the 1960s and 1970s, have forced businesses to consider public welfare, at least to some degree. A trend towards increased social consciousness, including a heightened sense of environmental activism, has recently emerged.

3. **Show how the concept of social responsibility applies both to environmental issues and to a firm's relationships with customers, employees, and investors.** Social responsibility towards the environment requires firms to minimize pollution of air, water, and land. Social responsibility towards customers requires firms to provide products of acceptable quality, to price products fairly, and to respect consumers' rights. Social responsibility towards employees requires firms to respect workers both as resources and as people who are more productive when their needs are met. Social responsibility towards investors requires firms to manage their resources and to represent their financial status honestly.

4. **Identify four general *approaches to social responsibility* and describe the four steps a firm must take to implement a *social responsibility program*.** An *obstructionist stance* on social responsibility is taken by a firm that does as little as possible to address social or environmental problems and that may deny or attempt to cover up problems that may occur. The *defensive stance* emphasizes compliance with legal minimum requirements. Companies adopting the *accommodative stance* go beyond minimum activities, if asked. The *proactive stance* commits a company to actively seek to contribute to social projects. Implementing a social responsibility program entails four steps: (1) drafting a policy statement with the support of top management, (2) developing a detailed plan, (3) appointing a director to implement the plan, and (4) conducting *social audits* to monitor results.

5. **Explain how issues of social responsibility and ethics affect small businesses.** Managers and employees of small businesses face many of the same ethical questions as their counterparts at larger firms. Small businesses face the same issues of social responsibility and the same need to decide on an approach to social responsibility. The differences are primarily differences of scale.

KEY TERMS

ethics, 104
ethical behaviour, 104
unethical behaviour, 104
business ethics, 104
social responsibility, 113
organizational
   stakeholders, 113

acid rain, 115
recycling, 116
toxic waste, 117
consumerism, 118
collusion, 118
whistle-blower, 120
cheque kiting, 121

insider trading, 121
obstructionist stance,
   122
defensive stance, 122

accommodative stance,
   123
proactive stance, 123
social audit, 125

STUDY QUESTIONS AND EXERCISES

Review Questions
1. What basic factors should be considered in any ethical decision?
2. Who are an organization's stakeholders? Who are the major stakeholders with whom most businesses must be concerned?
3. What are the major areas of social responsibility with which businesses should be concerned?
4. What are the four basic approaches to social responsibility?
5. In what ways do you think your personal code of ethics might clash with the operations of some companies? How might you try to resolve these differences?

Analysis Questions
6. What kind of wrongdoing would most likely prompt you to be a whistle-blower? What kind of wrongdoing would be least likely? Why?

7. In your opinion, which area of social responsibility is most important? Why? Are there areas other than those noted in the chapter that you consider to be important?
8. Identify some specific ethical or social responsibility issues that might be faced by small-business managers and employees in each of the following areas: environment, customers, employees, and investors.

Application Exercises
9. Develop a list of the major stakeholders of your college or university. As a class, discuss the ways in which you think the school prioritizes those stakeholders. Do you agree or disagree with this prioritization?
10. Using newspapers, magazines, and other business references, identify and describe at least three companies that take a defensive stance to social responsibility, three that take an accommodative stance, and three that take a proactive stance.

Building Your Business Skills

Developing a Corporate Code of Ethics

Goal
To encourage students to apply general concepts of business ethics to specific business situations.

Situation
As the head of human resources of a large bank, you are in the process of developing a corporate code of ethics that will be issued to every bank employee. Among the major sections in the document are those that deal with the following sensitive topics:

• Discrimination against minority employees
• Discrimination against minority customers
• Sexual harrassment

• Conflicts of interest
• Accepting gifts from clients
• Privacy and confidentiality
• Accounting irregularities
• Lying to clients and fellow employees

Method
Step 1:
Working with four other students, determine your company's ethical stance on each of the topics listed above. This part of the project may require additional research. In your analysis, be certain to distinguish between your company's ethical and legal responsibilities. For example, while discriminating against minority mortgage applicants on the basis of race is clearly illegal, lying to

fellow employees may violate ethical, rather than legal, rules.

Step 2:

Using the information gathered in your research, draft a corporate code of ethics that explains the bank's position in each area. The code should define what the bank will do in each of the following situations:

- A mortgage officer refuses to grant mortgages to qualified minority clients.
- A female employee is sexually harassed by a male supervisor.
- A lending officer grants a million-dollar loan to his wife's business associate even though the associate fails to meet appropriate qualifications.
- A supplier of computer equipment receives special treatment after he gives gifts to bank employees responsible for computer purchases.
- False data are included in accounting reports to stockholders.

- Employees are regularly caught lying to clients and fellow employees in order to enhance their own positions in the company.

Follow-Up Questions

1. Do your responses to the ethics situations presented here have a common thread? If so, does this thread represent a values-based approach to corporate ethics? Explain.

2. What measures would you suggest for making your written code of ethics a living document that influences the way in which every employee conducts business?

3. In your opinion, is the need for corporate codes of ethics greater than it was five years ago? Explain your answer.

Exploring the Net

In this chapter, we note that some organizations develop codes of conduct or written statements that convey to interested parties how the firm views ethics and social responsibility. One firm, The Body Shop, is highly rated by sustainability for the United Nations Environmental Program. The Body Shop has drawn up written statements of its ethics and values. For a summary of the company's principles, visit its Web site at:

www.the-body-shop.com

1. Four business approaches to social responsibility are offered in the chapter. Which best describes The Body Shop? Explain.

2. Is The Body Shop's mission statement achievable? How could its success be measured?

3. What difficulties might The Body Shop have living up to company values and ethics when dealing with suppliers in less developed areas of the world? Research newspaper, magazine, or online sources to find out if any such problems have occurred for The Body Shop.

4. Based on the Web site, would you want to work for The Body Shop? Explain why or why not.

Concluding Case 4-1

Nortel Changes Its Corporate Giving Policy

Like many companies, Nortel Networks used to make contributions to a variety of charitable organizations. It also used to match employee contributions to the United Way. But its new corporate giving strategy means no more matching contributions to the United Way and a more focused giving strategy for the contributions it does make. In the future, Nortel will focus on education efforts that have a direct relationship to its business objectives and bottom line.

CEO John Roth is the force behind the new policy. He believes that it makes sense for companies to fund programs that benefit them. Roth has some allies in this thinking; they argue that profit generated by a company is the property of shareholders, not corporate managers, and that shareholders should decide where it goes. Not surprisingly, Nortel's new policy has alarmed some charitable organizations, most obviously the United Way.

Nortel's new policy was developed because of concerns about the effectiveness of its traditional giving patterns. Like most major corporations in Canada, Nortel was bombarded with requests to sponsor events such as art exhibits, ballet companies, the United Way, and hospital fundraisers. But the traditional corporate citizenship model of scattering contributions among many different good causes may not be effective, so Nortel will now concentrate on three areas of giving: business fundamentals, science and technology education, and community support.

Specifically, Nortel will fund scholarships and research initiatives that link back to the company's corporate objectives. For example, $18 million will be given to establish an Institute in Advanced Information Technology at Waterloo University, and $14 million will be given to fund 7000 students in engineering and computer science. These programs benefit Nortel both directly and indirectly.

Nortel recognizes that its new approach is a departure from the traditional social responsibility model that has been evident in corporate philanthropy in Canada for many years. The company says it is "reinventing corporate citizenship for a connected world." Nortel will continue to encourage its employees to donate time and money on a voluntary basis, but the company will pursue its new strategy as well. It argues that its new approach makes sense because education benefits everyone by providing access to rewarding careers, decent wages, and opportunities for growth. It also increases the talent pool and helps industry by providing educated students.

CASE QUESTIONS

1. In general, what are the arguments for and against corporate philanthropy?

2. What are the arguments for and against Nortel's new policy?

3. "Corporate profits are the property of shareholders and should not be given to charity." Do you agree or disagree? Explain. ◆

Concluding Case 4-2

Questionable Behaviour

José Ignacio López de Arriotua has had an interesting business career, including being the chief purchasing agent for General Motors' huge purchasing operations, and later, for Volkswagen. But in May 2000, López was charged by the U.S. Justice Department with stealing secret General Motors documents and turning them over to rival Volkswagen. The Justice Department said it would try to extradite López from Spain to stand trial in the U.S.

The story began in 1993, when López was the head of GM's purchasing. His job put him at the centre of key strategy decisions and financial forecasts. For one thing, López handled on a daily basis the kind of top secrets that would in large part determine GM's success throughout the 1990s. Indeed, two days before announcing his resignation, López had attended an international strategy meeting at GM's Opel subsidiary in Germany. During the meeting, he was introduced to GM Europe's model plans, sales projections, and financial forecasts up to the year 2000.

Fearing that López had taken confidential information away from the European strategy meeting, GM demanded written confirmation that López "had not taken any documents" with him "pertaining to [GM's] present and future corporate plans." Fueling GM's deepest fears were Volkswagen's subsequent efforts to lure away other GM employees. With López's help, Volkswagen had tried to recruit more than 40 managers at Opel and GM, often enticing them with offers of doubled salaries. Before an injunction put a stop to its recruiting forays, VW had succeeded in hiring away seven key GM executives.

Although VW denied allegations of industrial espionage and corporate raiding, the charges left both López and the German carmaker under a legal and ethical cloud. That cloud became heavier when the district attorney of Darmstadt, Germany, discovered confidential GM documents at the home of a former GM executive who had, like López, defected to VW. At stake for Volkswagen was the public's perception of company ethics—an intangible factor that could affect the firm's sales. When a German polling organization asked 1000 Germans what they thought of the López affair, 65 percent believed that there was "something to" the allegations, while only 7 percent deemed them unfounded.

GM filed a civil suit against Volkswagen claiming that López stole GM's plans for new cars, parts lists, price lists, and plans for a secret manufacturing plant. It claimed that VW used this information to lower its costs and to gain market share at GM's expense.

In early 1997, Volkswagen agreed to give GM $100 million in cash and to purchase $1 billion in parts from GM through 2004. López also resigned from VW, and GM agreed to drop its civil suit.

CASE QUESTIONS

1. As a result of López's resignation, GM decided to require all top officers to sign formal contracts restricting their ability to work for a competing company for three years after leaving GM. How do you feel about this contract provision?

2. Does an employee have an ethical responsibility to maintain the confidentiality of information gained on the job with one company when taking a job with a competing firm?

3. Should Volkswagen be concerned with the public's reaction to the López affair?

4. GM allowed López to reveal suppliers' proprietary information in order to elicit lower bids. Considering its behaviour, did GM demonstrate a double standard in its reaction to the López affair?

5. The ethics of both VW and GM were called into question by the López affair. How will the ethical misjudgments of both companies affect their relationship with customers, suppliers, and employees?

Visit the *Business* Website at www.pearsoned.ca/griffin
for up-to-date e-business cases!

CBC Video Case

I-1   CBC

New Ideas in Newfoundland

At a recent job fair in St. John's, Newfoundland, recruiters from Ireland were looking for top Newfoundland grads. Why? Because (1) Ireland is the ancestral home of 40 percent of Newfoundlanders, and (2) Ireland's economy is booming.

An economic miracle has taken place in Ireland. Its economy is growing at the phenomenal rate of 10 percent per year, and Ireland is now the world's leading exporter of computer software. Irish businesses need 40 000 new workers each year to keep up with demand. Canadian-based Saturn, for example, is in Dublin, where it manufactures software CDs. Ireland has been called the Silicon Valley of Europe.

Only a decade ago, Ireland was struggling just as Newfoundland has always done. In Ireland, it was farming, not fishing, that failed, and young people—who were educated for free at university—were leaving the country in droves. Drastic action was needed to turn the country around, so representatives from labour, business, and government devised a dramatic plan to solve the problem. Labour agreed to accept wage stability for three years, and government agreed to slash personal income tax rates. The European Union did its part, giving Ireland billions in transfer payments. This allowed the Irish government to cut corporate tax rates to 10 percent, the lowest in the world.

New high-tech industries were targeted for development. Since Ireland had never really been very industrialized, it was able to capitalize on this new wave of industrial development without having to cope with the fallout from declining "old economy" industries. High-tech manufacturing plants rose out of potato fields, and Ireland's prosperity rose with them. Young people are returning to Ireland by the thousands, and the country's population is actually increasing.

Newfoundland, fed up with its legendary unemployment problems, is determined to create a new economic miracle. How is it going to do this? By recreating Ireland's economic miracle. If successful, this will give Newfoundland's children a reason to come home. Because the economies of Newfoundland and Ireland are similar, it might just work.

Newfoundland is already the fastest-growing province in Canada, thanks largely to oil developments such as Hibernia. However, Newfoundland is a province, not a sovereign country, and it doesn't have the freedom that Ireland had to cut taxes. All it can do is cut provincial taxes. As well, transfer payments are clawed back in Canada. So, Newfoundland will have to create a miracle on its own terms. Part of the process involves sending trade missions to Ireland to develop partnerships with Irish businesses. Development is targeted in three sectors: information technology, cultural industries, and environmental industries. Some progress is already evident. XWAVE, Newfoundland's biggest information technology company, has grown from 300 to 2300 employees. Among other things, it provides specialized software to Dublin University.

Newfoundland has other advantages, such as being the second-cheapest place to do business in North America. It is also isolated, but that isolation has motivated it to become the most-wired province in Canada. It plans to export to the U.S. just as Ireland exports to Europe. Newfoundland is going to push hard to keep opportunities coming its way.

STUDY QUESTIONS

1. Compare a pure market system and a mixed market system. How do the economies of Ireland and Newfoundland demonstrate the mixed market economy?

2. What are the factors of production? Explain how these factors worked together to generate the Irish economic miracle.

3. What type of economy does Ireland have? How do the economies of Ireland and Newfoundland differ? How are they similar?

4. In Chapter 1, three major forces that will be evident in the future are noted. Explain how each of these forces is evident in the economies of Ireland and Newfoundland.

5. Briefly describe the barriers to trade. To what extent will these barriers affect Newfoundland's plan to export goods and services?

Video Resource: "Looking for a Miracle," *Venture* #764 (November 14, 2000).

CBC Video Case

I-2   CBC 🍁

The Risk of Global Business Operations

More and more Canadian companies are doing business in dangerous countries around the world. Ranger Oil, for example, is exploring for oil in politically volatile countries such as Angola, Libya, Ivory Coast, and Iraq. And Ranger is not alone. Increasing numbers of small and medium-sized Canadian companies are doing business in politically volatile regions, where they encounter things such as extortion in the former Soviet Union, armed attacks in Africa, and kidnapping in South America.

Unfortunately, the number of violent incidents is increasing. In 1999, Edmonton's United Pipelines sent eight oil workers to Ecuador as part of an investment opportunity there. The workers were kidnapped by local rebels and held for 99 days before finally being released. This incident was traumatic for the workers, and it created a serious disruption in the business activity of United Pipelines because the company had no experience in managing this type of incident.

Hunting for "big finds" is risky, and an industry that provides "political risk insurance" to Canadian companies operating in risky global markets is growing. Many companies have decided to buy political risk insurance to protect themselves. Such insurance commonly covers things like:

- war and civil strife
- expropriation (where the host country seizes the assets of the Canadian firm without paying for them)
- contract frustration (where the host country makes it impossible to carry out business by imposing bureaucratic or other barriers)
- inconvertibility (where the Canadian company is paid in a currency that it cannot convert into Canadian dollars)
- kidnapping and ransom insurance (the latter is not made public for obvious reasons)

The federal government is one of the top political risk insurers in Canada through the activities of the Export Development Corp. (EDC). Its risk portfolio is valued at $2.5 billion. Companies like to buy political risk insurance from the EDC because it places the weight of the federal government behind its projects. However, this type of insurance is not cheap. Tracer Petroleum, which is looking at an investment opportunity in Iran, found that the insurance premium can be as much as 5 percent of the total value of the project.

Even when a company carries political risk insurance, it may find that problems arise that require specialized expertise. Kroll Associates is one company that provides such expertise, selling everything from market intelligence to armoured limousines. It is free of the public policy restraints that hinder governments in their attempts to help their countries' business firms when problems arise. For example, when Kroll is called on to retrieve kidnapped employees unharmed, it doesn't have to shy away from grey areas such as paying "commissions" in order to achieve its goal.

Some companies choose not to buy political risk insurance. Canadian Occidental Petroleum, for example, operates in high-risk areas such as Yemen, Nigeria, Indonesia, and Colombia. Instead of buying risk insurance, the company attempts to manage risk by involving the local community in company activities (by providing jobs, for example). The company feels that good business practice is the best insurance, and they have published a list of ethical guidelines for doing business in high-risk areas. The risks are still there, however, such as the car bomb that exploded and blew the door off the company's office.

When Canadian companies are deciding whether to start doing business in a risky area of the world, they must ask the following question: Is the risk to company employees and property worth the rewards of sales and profits? In practice, this is a very difficult question to answer because local situations are so complex and unpredictable.

STUDY QUESTIONS

1. Figure 3.6 (see page 83) describes some key questions that managers must ask before deciding to "go international." Develop some additional questions that managers should ask, based on the information provided in this case.

2. What are the main barriers to international trade? Which of these barriers are particularly relevant for the firms described in this case? Explain.

3. Can socially responsible business behaviour really reduce the risk of operating in global markets? Defend your answer.

4. What alternative ways are available to help companies cope with financial risk? What is the relationship between political risk and financial risk? How do companies cope with political risk? (It will be helpful to read the section "Coping with Risk" in Chapter 20—see page 663—before answering this question.)

Video Resource: "Risky Business," *Venture* #738 (February 8, 2000).

The Business
of Managing

Seagrams, Bata Shoes, and Cuddy International are three of the business firms you will read about
in the opening cases of Chapter 5 to 7. Each of these companies must be managed effectively if they
are to grow and prosper. Regardless of the size of the business, managers in all companies—indeed,
in any kind of organization—must carry out the basic management functions of planning, organizing,
leading, and controlling.

   Part Two, The Business of Managing, provides an overview of business management today. It includes a look at the various types of managers that business firms need, the special concerns of managing small businesses, the ways in which managers set goals for their companies, and how a
business's structure affects its management and goals.

■ We begin in **Chapter 5, Managing the Business Enterprise**, by describing how managers set goals
   and choose corporate strategies. The basic functions of management—planning, organizing,
   leading, and controlling—are examined, as are the different types and levels of managers that
   are found in business firms, and the corporate culture that is created in each firm.

■ In **Chapter 6, Organizing the Business Enterprise**, we look at the basic organizational structures that companies have adopted, and the different kinds of authority that managers can
   have. The impact of the informal organization is also analyzed.

■ Finally, in **Chapter 7, Understanding Entrepreneurship and Small Business**, we explore the
   role of small business and franchises in the Canadian economy—what they do, why they succeed or fail, and how they are owned and managed.

Seagram's Final Strategy

On June 20, 2000, the French conglomerate Vivendi SA purchased Montreal-based Seagram Co. for approximately $33 billion in stock. Seagram was started in the 1920s by Sam Bronfman, who sold liquor by mail order. His son, Edgar Bronfman, Sr. became CEO in 1957. Until the early 1990s, the company's activities focused largely on the production of wine, distilled spirits, and orange juice. But in the mid-1990s, the company, led by Edgar Bronfman, Jr., began making some dramatic strategic moves that took it away from its traditional products and moved it towards the high-risk entertainment business.

Edgar Bronfman, Jr. has both an artistic and a business temperament. He is friends with some well-known show business people, including Michael Douglas, and he is fascinated with Hollywood. Bronfman was well aware that more than a few third-generation heirs had dissipated family fortunes, and he was determined that he would not make those mistakes. But he also refused to simply make cautious investments.

Some of his decisions were startling. For example, he paid more than $2 billion for 15 percent of Time Warner in 1993, leading some to think that he might try a hostile takeover of that company. But then he sold those shares, as well as a large block of DuPont shares that Seagram had held for many years. In 1995, he bought MCA Inc. (now Universal) for $5.7 billion.

In 1997, Seagram decided to begin processing orange juice in China through its Tropicana Beverages Group. The plan was to form a joint venture with a Chinese organization to finance and build an orange juice processing plant. But in 1998, Seagram sold Tropicana to PepsiCo Inc. for $3.3 billion in cash. Also in 1998, Bronfman took a giant step into the world of entertainment with the $10.6 billion acquisition of Polygram NV, a company whose artists are as diverse as Elton John, U2, and The Three Tenors. With the acquisition of Polygram, Seagram instantly became the world's largest music company.

Were all of these strategic moves a good idea? Critics noted that the DuPont stock that Bronfman sold for $8.8 billion in 1995 would have been worth $20 billion in 1998 if the dividends had been reinvested. They also said that in selling Tropicana Seagram had waved goodbye to a steady source of income and traded it for the uncertain revenue of the music business. But in 1999, Bronfman countered these criticisms by noting that Seagram's stock was at its highest level in a year, and that an investment in Seagram made at the same time it sold off its DuPont stock was worth more than an investment made in DuPont.

The sale of Seagram to Vivendi brought financial vindication for Bronfman. Vivendi handed over stock worth about $75 per Seagram share, which was well above the high $40s that Seagram stock was trading for just prior to the sale. However, in the process, one of Canada's largest and most famous companies has suddenly disappeared. ◆

Edgar Bronfman is one of millions of managers worldwide. In this chapter, we explain how these managers differ from industrial engineers, accountants, market researchers, production workers, secretaries, and other people who work in business firms. Although we will focus on managers in business firms, managers are necessary in many other kinds of organizations—colleges and universities, charities, social clubs, churches, labour unions, and governments. The president of the University of Toronto, the prime minister of Canada, and the executive director of the United Way are just as much managers as the president of MacMillan Bloedel.

By focusing on the learning objectives of this chapter, you will better understand the nature of managing, the meaning of corporate culture, and the range of skills that managers like Edgar Bronfman need if they are to work effectively. After reading this chapter, you should be able to:

1. Explain the importance of setting *goals* and formulating *strategies* as the starting points of effective management.

2. Describe the four activities that constitute the *management process*.

3. Identify *types of managers* by level and area.

4. Describe the five basic *management skills*.

5. Describe the development and explain the importance of *corporate culture*.

> LEARNING OBJECTIVES

SETTING GOALS AND FORMULATING STRATEGY

The starting point in effective management is setting **goals**, objectives that a business hopes (and plans) to achieve. Every business needs goals, and we begin by discussing the basic aspects of organizational goal setting. However, deciding what it *intends* to do is only step one for an organization. A company's managers must also make decisions about actions that will and will not achieve its goals. From this perspective, *strategy* is the broad program that underlies those decisions; the basic steps in formulating strategy are discussed later in the chapter.

goals
Objectives that a business hopes and plans to achieve.

Setting Business Goals

Goals are performance targets, the means by which organizations and their managers measure success or failure at every level. In this section, we identify the main purposes for which organizations establish goals, classify the basic levels of business goals, and describe the process by which goals are commonly set.

The Purposes of Goal Setting

An organization functions systematically because it sets goals and plans accordingly. Indeed, an organization functions as such because it commits its resources on all levels to achieving its goals. Specifically, we can identify four main purposes in organizational goal setting:

1. *Goal setting provides direction, guidance, and motivation for all managers.* For example, each of the managers at Kanke Seafood Restaurants Ltd. is required to work through a goal setting exercise each year. Setting and achieving goals is the most effective form of self motivation.[1]

2. *Goal setting helps firms allocate resources.* Areas that are expected to grow, for example, will get first priority. Thus 3M allocates more resources to new projects with large sales potential than to projects with low growth potential.

3. *Goal setting helps to define corporate culture.* General Electric's goal, for instance, is to push each of its divisions to number one or number two in its industry. The result is a competitive, often stressful, environment and a culture that rewards success and has little tolerance for failure.

4. *Goal setting helps managers assess performance.* If a company sets a goal to increase sales by 10 percent in a given year, managers in units who attain or exceed the goal can be rewarded. Units failing to reach the goal will also be compensated accordingly.

Kinds of Goals

Naturally, goals differ from company to company, depending on the firm's purpose and mission. Every enterprise, of course, has a purpose—a reason for being. Businesses seek profit, universities work to discover and transmit new knowledge, and government agencies exist to provide service to the public. A company's purpose is fairly easy to identify. Reebok, for example, attempts to make a profit by making and selling athletic shoes and related merchandise. IBM's purpose is to make and sell computers and computer technology.

Every enterprise also has a **mission statement**—a statement of how it will achieve its purpose. Bell Canada's mission, for example, is to be a world leader in helping communicate and manage information. DaimlerChrysler's mission statement emphasizes "delighted customers." Atco Ltd.'s mission is to provide products and services to the energy and resource industries, and to invest principally in energy-related assets in North America. The mission of Investor's Group is to satisfy clients who are in need of general and comprehensive financial planning.

Two business firms can have the same purpose—for example, to sell watches at a profit—yet they have very different missions. Timex sells low-cost, reliable watches in outlets ranging from department stores to corner drugstores. Rolex, on the other hand, sells high-quality, high-priced fashion watches through selected jewellery stores.

Regardless of a company's purpose and mission, every firm needs long-term, intermediate, and short-term goals:

- **Long-term goals** relate to extended periods of time—typically five years or more into the future. Mastercard, for example, might set a long-term goal of doubling the number of participating merchants during the next 10 years. Similarly, Kodak might adopt a long-term goal to increase its share of the 35-mm film market by 10 percent during the next eight years.

- **Intermediate goals** are set for a period of one to five years into the future. Companies usually have intermediate goals in several areas. For example, the marketing department's goal might be to increase sales by 3 percent in two years. The production department might want to decrease expenses by 6 percent in four years. Human resources might seek to cut turnover by 10 percent in two years. Finance might aim for a 3 percent increase in return on investment in three years.

- Like intermediate goals, **short-term goals**—which are set for one year or less—are developed for several different areas. Increasing sales by 2 percent this year, cutting costs by 1 percent next quarter, and reducing turnover by 4 percent over the next six months are all short-term goals.

mission statement
An organization's statement of how it will achieve its purpose in the environment in which it conducts its business.

long-term goals
Goals set for extended periods of time, typically five years or more into the future.

intermediate goals
Goals set for a period of one to five years.

short-term goals
Goals set for the very near future, typically less than one year.

Who Sets Goals?

Within any company, managers at different levels are responsible for setting different kinds of goals. The firm's purpose is largely determined by the context in which it operates—that is, the environment in which it markets its products. The board of directors generally defines the firm's mission. Working in conjunction with the board, top managers then usually set long-term goals. These same managers typically work closely with middle managers to set intermediate goals. Finally, middle managers work with first-line managers to set and achieve short-term goals.

Formulating Strategy

Planning is concerned with the nuts and bolts of setting goals, choosing tactics, and establishing schedules. In contrast, strategy tends to have a wider scope. It is by definition a "broad program" that describes an organization's intentions. A business strategy outlines how it intends to meet its goals, and includes the organization's responsiveness to new challenges and new needs. **Strategy formulation** involves three basic steps:

strategy formulation
Creation of a broad program for defining and meeting an organization's goals.

1. setting strategic goals

2. analyzing the organization and its environment

3. matching the organization and its environment.[2]

Setting Strategic Goals

Strategic goals are long-term goals derived directly from the firm's mission statement. General Electric Co., for example, is pursuing four strategic goals to ensure continued success for the company: an emphasis on quality control, an emphasis on selling services and not just products, concentrating on niche acquisitions, and expansion globally.[3]

strategic goals
Long-term goals derived directly from a firm's mission statement.

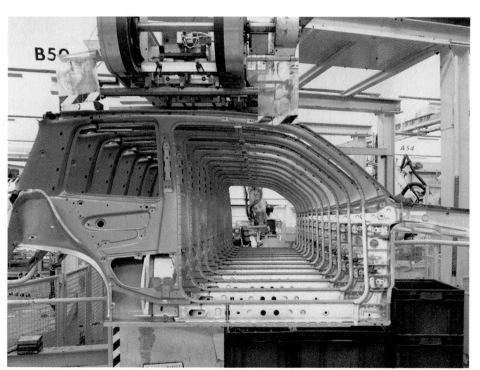

Since Ferdinand Piech became chairman of Volkswagen in 1993, productivity at plants like this one in Wolfsburg, Germany, have increased sales to 4.7 million vehicles per year and enabled VW to catch Toyota as the world's third-largest carmaker. Piech (who calls his management style "democratic dictatorship") requires all new projects to be self-financing and gives designers free rein to create new models only as long as they buy parts off a preset purchasing list. Current long-term goals call for matching Audi in quality and marketing high-end VWs against Audi and Mercedes models.

General Electric
www.ge.com

environmental analysis
The process of scanning the environment for threats and opportunities.

Virgin Atlantic
www.virgin.com

organizational analysis
The process of analyzing a firm's strengths and weaknesses.

Similarly, Ferdinand Piech, CEO of Volkswagen, has clear strategic goals for the European automaker. When Piech took over in 1993, Volkswagen was only marginally profitable, and regarded as an also-ran in the industry. Over the next few years, however, Piech totally revamped the firm and now it is making big profits. Volkswagen is now a much more formidable force in the global automobile industry. It currently competes with Toyota for the number-three spot in the industry (behind only General Motors and Ford), but Piech is clearly not finished. "For the moment," he reports, "we are happy with the bronze medal. But we want to step up the stairway."[4]

Analyzing the Organization and Its Environment

The term **environmental analysis** means scanning the environment for threats and opportunities. Changing consumer tastes and hostile takeover offers are *threats*, as are new government regulations. Even more important threats come from new products and new competitors. *Opportunities*, meanwhile, are areas in which the firm can potentially expand, grow, or take advantage of existing strengths.

Consider, for example, the case of British entrepreneur Richard Branson and his company, Virgin Group Ltd. Branson started the firm in 1968, when he was 17, naming it in acknowledgement of his own lack of experience in the business world. Over the years, he has built Virgin into one of the world's best-known brands, comprising a conglomeration of over 200 entertainment, media, and travel companies worldwide. Among the best known of his enterprises are Virgin Atlantic (an international airline), Virgin Megastores (retailing), and V2 Music (record labels). Branson sees potential threats from other competitors such as British Airways and KLM for Virgin Atlantic, Tower Records for retailing, and the EMI Group for recorded music.

But he also sees significant opportunities because of his firm's strong brand name (especially in Europe). Indeed, one of his most recent ventures is a new e-commerce firm. The business is called Virgin Mobile and operates like a cellular telephone company. But in addition to providing conventional cellular service, the Virgin telephone permits the user to press a red button to go directly to a Virgin operator who can sell products, make airline and hotel reservations, and provide numerous other services. A companion Web site also complements the cellular service and its related programs. Virgin Mobile is signing up new customers at a rate of 100 000 per month.[5]

In addition to performing environmental analysis, which is analysis of *external* factors, managers must also examine *internal* factors. The purpose of **organizational analysis** is to better understand a company's strengths and weaknesses. Strengths might include surplus cash, a dedicated workforce, an ample supply of managerial talent, technical expertise, or weak competition. The absence of any of these strengths could represent an important weakness.

Branson, for example, started up Virgin Mobile in part because he saw so many of his current operations as old-line, traditional businesses that might be at future risk from new forms of business and competition. One strength he has employed has been the widespread name recognition that his businesses enjoy. Another strength relates to finances. Branson sold 49 percent of Virgin Atlantic to Singapore Airlines for almost $1 billion in cash, retaining ownership control but raising all of the funds he needed to launch his new venture. On the other hand, he also admits that neither he nor most of his senior managers have much experience in or knowledge about e-commerce, which may be a significant weakness.

WEBCONNEXION

British-based Virgin operates businesses ranging from an airline to a chain of mega-media stores to a financial services company. Only recently, however, has its strategy included the expansion of its Web site into an international e-commerce portal. While some critics say the move is too late, Virgin counters that because it already has so many of its own products, it's well-suited to make the entrepreneurial move. To find out more about Virgin's diverse product line, contact the company at:

www.virgin.com

Matching the Organization and Its Environment

The final step in strategy formulation is matching environmental threats and opportunities with corporate strengths and weaknesses. The matching process is the heart of strategy formulation: More than any other facet of strategy, matching companies with their environments lays the foundation for successfully planning and conducting business.[6] This is exactly the perspective adopted by Leroy Keith, CEO of Carson Inc., a firm that specializes in personal-care products for blacks. Because Keith and his top managers are all black, their own familiarity with the personal-care products and preferences of ethnic minorities constituted a distinctive strength. They knew, for example, that black women spend about three times as much per capita on personal-care products as do white women. Because few other firms were aggressively pursuing this market, Carson managers rightly regarded this untapped market as a major opportunity.[7]

A Hierarchy of Plans

Figure 5.1 shows how plans can be viewed on three general levels: *strategic* (SP), *tactical* (TP), and *operational* (OP). Each level reflects plans for which managers at that level are responsible. These levels constitute a hierarchy because implementing plans is practical only when there is a logical flow from one level to the next.

- **Strategic plans** reflect decisions about resource allocations, company priorities, and the steps needed to meet strategic goals. They are usually set by the board of directors and top management. General Electric's decision that viable products must be number one or number two within their respective categories is a matter of strategic planning.

strategic plans
Plans that reflect decisions about resource allocations, company priorities, and steps needed to meet strategic goals.

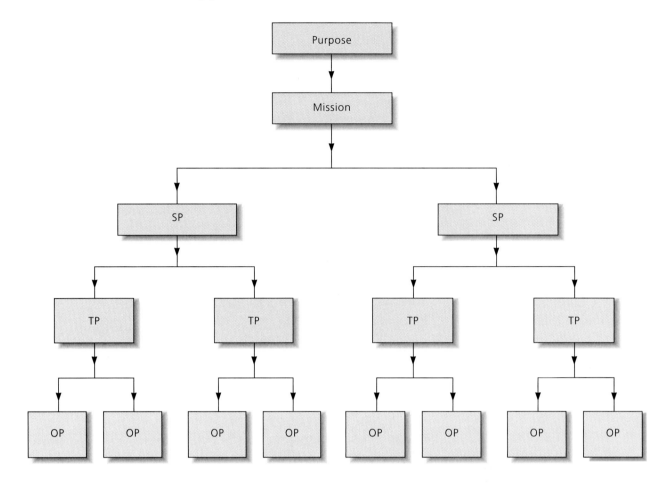

Figure 5.1
A hierarchy of plans.

tactical plans
Generally, short-range plans concerned with implementing specific aspects of a company's strategic plans.

operational plans
Plans setting short-term targets for daily, weekly, or monthly performance.

corporate-level strategy
Identifies the various businesses that a company will be in, and how these businesses will relate to each other.

business-level (competitive) strategy
Identifies the ways a business will compete in its chosen line of products or services.

functional strategies
Identify the basic courses of action that each department in the firm will pursue so that it contributes to the attainment of the business's overall goals.

■ **Tactical plans** are shorter-range plans concerned with implementing specific aspects of the company's strategic plans. They typically involve upper and middle management. Coca-Cola's decision to increase sales in Europe by building European bottling facilities is an example of tactical planning.

■ Developed by middle and lower-level managers, **operational plans** set short-term targets for daily, weekly, or monthly performance. McDonald's, for example, establishes operational plans when it explains precisely how Big Macs are to be cooked, warmed, and served.

Levels of Strategies

There are three levels of strategy in a business firm. A **corporate-level strategy** identifies the various businesses that a company will be in, and how these businesses will relate to each other. A **business-level (competitive) strategy** identifies the ways a business will compete in its chosen line of products or services. **Functional strategies** identify the basic courses of action that each department in the firm will pursue so that it contributes to the attainment of the business's overall goals. Each of these strategies is discussed below.

Corporate-Level Strategies

There are several different corporate-level strategies that a company might pursue, including concentration, growth, integration, diversification, and investment reduction.

Concentration. A **concentration strategy** involves focusing the company on one product or product line. Organizations that have successfully pursued a concentration strategy include McDonald's and Canadian National Railway. The main advantage of a concentration strategy is that the company can focus its strengths on the one business it knows well. The main disadvantage is the risk inherent in putting all of one's eggs in one basket.

concentration strategy
Involves focusing the company on one product or product line.

Growth. Companies have several growth strategies available to them, including **market penetration** (boosting sales of present products by more aggressive selling in the firm's current markets), **geographic expansion** (expanding operations in new geographic areas or countries), and **product development** (developing improved products for current markets).

market penetration
Boosting sales of present products by more aggressive selling in the firm's current markets.

geographic expansion
Expanding operations in new geographic areas or countries.

product development
Developing improved products for current markets.

Integration. There are two basic integration strategies. **Horizontal integration** means acquiring control of competitors in the same or similar markets with the same or similar products. For example, Hudson's Bay Company purchased Kmart and Zellers. **Vertical integration** means owning or controlling the inputs to the firm's processes and/or the channels through which the products or services are distributed. Thus, major oil companies like Shell not only drill and produce their own oil, but also sell it through company-controlled outlets across Canada.

horizontal integration
Acquiring control of competitors in the same or similar markets with the same or similar products.

vertical integration
Owning or controlling the inputs to the firm's processes and/or the channels through which the products or services are distributed.

Diversification. **Diversification** means expanding into related or unrelated products or market segments. Diversification helps the firm avoid the problem of having all of its eggs in one basket by spreading risk among several products or markets. *Related diversification* means adding new, but related, products or services to an existing business. For example, CN diversified into trucking, an activity that is clearly related to railway operations. Maple Leaf Gardens Ltd., which already owned the Toronto Maple Leafs, also acquired the Toronto Raptors basketball team. *Conglomerate diversification* means diversifying into products or markets that are not related to the firm's present businesses. For example, Bell Canada diversified by forming BCE Inc., which then acquired interests in such unrelated businesses as trust companies, pipelines, and real estate.

diversification
Expanding into related or unrelated products or market segments.

Investment Reduction. **Investment reduction** means reducing the company's investment in one or more of its lines of business. One investment-reduction strategy is *retrenchment*, which means the reduction of activity or operations. For example, Federal Industries formerly was a conglomerate with interests in trucking, railways, metals, and other product lines, but it has now retrenched and focuses on a more limited set of products and customers. *Divestment* is another investment-reduction strategy; it involves selling or liquidating one or more of a firm's businesses.

investment reduction
Reducing the company's investment in one or more of its lines of business.

Business-Level (Competitive) Strategies

Whatever corporate-level strategy a firm decides on, it must also have a competitive strategy. A **competitive strategy** is a plan to establish a profitable and sustainable competitive position against the forces that determine industry

competitive strategy
A plan to establish a profitable and sustainable competitive position against the forces that determine industry competition.

competition.[8] Michael Porter identifies three competitive strategies: cost leadership, differentiation, and focus.

Cost Leadership. **Cost leadership** means becoming *the* low cost leader in an industry. Wal-Mart is an industry cost leader. Its distribution costs are minimized through a satellite-based warehousing system, its store-location costs are minimized by placing stores on low-cost land, and the stores themselves are very plain.

Differentiation. In a **differentiation** strategy, a firm seeks to be unique in its industry along some dimension that is valued by buyers. For example, Caterpillar Tractor emphasizes durability, Volvo stresses safety, Apple Computer stresses user-friendly products, and Mercedes-Benz emphasizes quality.

Focus. A **focus** strategy means selecting a market segment and serving the customers in that market niche better than competitors. For example, Fraser, Inc. focuses on producing high-quality, durable, lightweight paper that is used in bibles.

Functional Strategies

Each business's choice of competitive strategy (cost leadership, differentiation, or focus) is translated into supporting functional strategies for each of its departments to pursue. A **functional strategy** is the basic course of action that each department follows so that the business accomplishes its overall goals. To implement its cost-leadership strategy, for example, Wal-Mart's distribution department pursued a functional strategy of satellite-based warehousing that ultimately drove distribution costs down to a minimum.

CONTINGENCY PLANNING AND CRISIS MANAGEMENT

Because business environments are often difficult to predict, and because the unexpected can create major problems, most managers recognize that even the best-laid plans sometimes become impractical. For instance, when Walt Disney Co. announced plans to launch a cruise line replete with familiar Disney characters and themes, managers also began aggressively developing and marketing packages linking three- and four-day cruises with visits to Disney World in Florida. The first sailing was scheduled for early 1998, and the company began to book reservations a year in advance. However, the shipyard constructing Disney's first ship (the *Disney Magic*) notified the company in October 1997 that it was behind schedule and that the ship would be delivered several weeks late. When similar problems befall other cruise lines, they can offer to rebook passengers on alternative itineraries. But because Disney had no other ship, it had no choice but to refund the money it had collected as prebooking deposits for its first 15 cruises.

The 20 000 displaced customers were offered substantial discounts if they rebooked on a later cruise. Many of them, however, could not rearrange their schedules and requested full refunds. Moreover, quite a few blamed Disney, and a few expressed outrage at what they perceived to be poor planning by the entertainment giant. Fortunately, *Disney Magic* was eventually launched and has now become both very popular and very profitable.[9]

Because managers know that such things can happen, they often develop alternative plans in case things go awry. Two common methods of dealing with the unknown and unforeseen are *contingency planning* and *crisis management*.

---

cost leadership
Becoming the low cost leader in an industry.

differentiation
A firm seeks to be unique in its industry along some dimension that is valued by buyers.

focus
Selecting a market segment and serving the customers in that market niche better than competitors.

functional strategy
The basic course of action that each department follows so that the business accomplishes its overall goals.

Contingency Planning

Contingency planning takes into account the need to find solutions for specific aspects of a problem. By its very nature, a contingency plan is a hedge against changes that might occur. **Contingency planning**, then, is planning for change: it attempts to identify in advance important aspects of a business or its market that might change. It also identifies the ways in which a company will respond to changes. Today, many companies use computer programs for contingency planning.

Suppose, for example, that a company develops a plan to create a new business. It expects sales to increase at an annual rate of 10 percent for the next five years and develops a marketing strategy for maintaining that level. But suppose that sales have increased by only 5 percent by the end of the first year. Does the company abandon the business, invest more in advertising, or wait to see what happens in the second year? Any of these alternatives is possible. However, things will go more smoothly if managers have decided in advance what to do in the event of lower sales. Contingency planning can help them do exactly that.

Disney learned from its mistake with its first ship, and when the second ship (the *Disney Wonder*) was launched a year later, managers did several things differently. First, they allowed for an extra two weeks between when the ship was supposed to be ready for sailing and its first scheduled cruise. They also held open a few cabins on *Disney Magic* as a backup for any especially disgruntled customers who might need to be accommodated due to unexpected delays launching *Disney Wonder*.

contingency planning
Identifying aspects of a business or its environment that might entail changes in strategy.

Crisis Management

A crisis is an unexpected emergency requiring immediate organizational response. **Crisis management** involves an organization's methods for dealing with emergencies. In May 2000, for example, a virus that was quickly dubbed the "Love Bug" hit millions of computers around the world. The virus came disguised as an e-mail attachment with a tag line indicating that the receiver should open it to see a love note. But once opened, the virus-laden file began damaging files on the receiver's computer and transmitting itself to others via e-mail and the Internet. Numerous organizations had to shut down their electronic communications networks for hours in order to set up new and more effective security procedures. Some organizations were able to get back up and running very quickly, but others took much longer. Warns Steve White, a computer-virus expert at IBM: "Everybody now needs e-mail. Somebody shuts it down and we are significantly out of business."[10]

To prepare for emergencies better, many organizations maintain crisis plans. These plans, designed to enable employees to cope when disasters do occur, typically outline who will be in charge in different kinds of circumstances, how the organization will respond, and so forth. In addition, they typically lay out plans for assembling and deploying crisis-management teams.

crisis management
An organization's methods for dealing with emergencies.

THE MANAGEMENT PROCESS

Management is the process of planning, organizing, leading, and controlling an enterprise's financial, physical, human, and information resources in order to achieve the organization's goals of supplying various products and services. Thus, the CEO of Walt Disney Productions is a manager

management
The process of planning, organizing, leading, and controlling a business's financial, physical, human, and information resources in order to achieve its goals.

because he regularly carries out these four functions as films are being made. Actors such as Julia Roberts or Tom Cruise, while they may be the stars of the movies, are not managers because they don't carry out the four functions of management. The "Business Today" box explains the dynamic nature of managerial jobs.

The planning, organizing, leading, and controlling aspects of a manager's job are interrelated. While these activities generally follow one another in a logical sequence, sometimes they are performed simultaneously or in a different sequence altogether. In fact, any given manager is likely to be engaged in all these activities during the course of any given business day.

Planning

planning
That portion of a manager's job concerned with determining what the business needs to do and the best way to achieve it.

Determining what the organization needs to do and how best to get it done requires planning. **Planning** has three main components. As we have seen, it begins when managers determine the firm's goals. Next, they develop a comprehensive strategy for achieving those goals. After a strategy is developed, they design tactical and operational plans for implementing the strategy.

BUSINESS TODAY

What Do Managers Actually Do?

Henry Mintzberg of McGill University conducted a detailed study of the work of five chief executive officers and found the following:

1. Managers work at an unrelenting pace.
2. Managerial activities are characterized by brevity, variety, and fragmentation.
3. Managers have a preference for "live" action, and emphasize work activities that are current, specific, and well-defined.
4. Managers are attracted to the verbal media.

Mintzberg believes that a manager's job can be described as 10 roles that must be performed. The manager's formal authority and status give rise to three **interpersonal roles**: (1) *figurehead* (duties of a ceremonial nature, such as attending a subordinate's wedding); (2) *leader* (being responsible for the work of the unit); and (3) *liaison* (making contact outside the vertical chain of command). These interpersonal roles give rise to three **informational roles**: (1) *monitor* (scanning the environment for relevant information); (2) *disseminator* (passing information to subordinates); and (3) *spokesperson* (sending information to people outside the unit).

The interpersonal and informational roles allow the manager to carry out four **decision-making roles**: (1) *entrepreneur* (improving the performance of the unit); (2)

disturbance handler (responding to high-pressure disturbances, such as a strike at a supplier); (3) *resource allocator* (deciding who will get what in the unit); and (4) *negotiator* (working out agreements on a wide variety of issues, such as the amount of authority an individual will be given).

Insight into what managers actually do can also be gained by looking at the so-called *functions* of management (planning, organizing, leading, and controlling). Consider the work of Marina Pyo, who is a Publisher, School Division, at Pearson Education Canada, a publisher of textbooks for elementary and secondary schools, colleges, and universities. Her job is to manage the activities that are necessary to develop resources in math and science for the Canadian elementary school market. Her work is at times intense, fragmented, rewarding, frustrating, and fast-paced. In short, she is a typical manager.

Pyo carries out the *planning* function when she drafts a plan for a new book. She is *organizing* when she develops a new organization chart to facilitate goal achievement. She is *leading* when she meets with a subordinate to discuss that person's career plans. And she is *controlling* when she checks sales prospects for a book before ordering a reprint.

Some of Pyo's activities do not easily fit into this "functions of management" model. For example, it is not clear which function she is performing when she negotiates the size of a reprint run with the manager of the sales division, or when she talks briefly with the president of her division about recent events in Pyo's area of responsibility.

When Yahoo! was created, for example, the company's top managers set a strategic goal of becoming a top firm in the then-emerging market for Internet search engines. But then came the hard part—figuring out how to do it. They started by assessing the ways in which people actually use the Web. They also studied ways in which they would probably use it in the future, analyzed the successful strategies of other growing firms, and assessed the ways in which big companies were using the Internet. They concluded that people wanted an easy-to-understand Web interface. They also wanted to be able to satisfy a wide array of needs, preferences, and priorities by going to as few sites as possible to find what they were looking for.

Managers usually work together to set goals and determine corporate strategy. These activities take a great deal of time but are critical to the success of any organization.

Yahoo!
www.yahoo.com

One key component of Yahoo!'s strategy, therefore, was to foster partnerships and relationships with other companies so that potential Web surfers could draw upon several sources through a single portal—which would, of course, be Yahoo! Thus, the goal of partnering emerged as one set of tactical plans for moving forward.

Yahoo! managers then began fashioning alliances with such diverse partners as Reuters, Standard & Poor's, and the Associated Press (for news coverage), RE/Max (for real estate information), and a wide array of information providers specializing in sports, weather, entertainment, shopping, travel, and so forth. The creation of individual partnership agreements with each of these companies represents a form of operational planning.

Organizing

The portion of a manager's job that is concerned with mobilizing the necessary resources to complete a particular task is known as **organizing**. The importance of the organizing function of management can be seen by considering what happened at Hewlett-Packard, which lost some of its lustre in the 1990s. One of the major reasons for its slide could be traced back to what had once been a major strength. Specifically, HP had long prided itself on being little more than a corporate confederation of individual businesses. Sometimes these businesses even ended up competing against themselves. This approach had been beneficial for much of the firm's history: it was easier for each business to make its own decisions quickly and efficiently, and the competition kept each unit on its toes. By 1998, however, problems started to become apparent, and no one could quite figure out what was going on.

Enter Ann Livermore, then head of the firm's software and services business. Livermore realized that it was the structure that had served so well in the past that was now holding the firm back. Specifically, to regain its competitive edge HP needed an integrated, organization-wide Internet strategy. Unfortunately, the company's highly decentralized organization made that impossible. Livermore led the charge to create one organization to drive a single Internet plan. "I felt we could be the most powerful company in the industry," she says, "if we could get our hardware, software, and services aligned." In fact, a reorganized HP has bounced back and is quickly regaining its competitive strength.[11]

organizing

That portion of a manager's job concerned with mobilizing the necessary resources to complete a particular task.

Hewlett-Packard
www.hewlett-packard.com

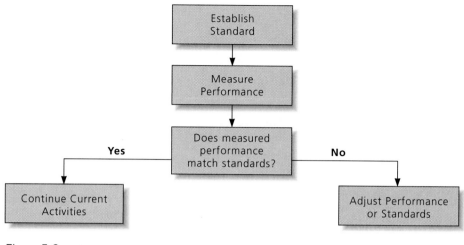

Figure 5.2
Steps in the control process.

Leading

The activities involving interactions between managers and their subordinates to meet the firm's objectives are known as **leading** (or directing). By definition, managers have the power to give orders and demand results. Leading, however, goes beyond merely giving orders. Leaders attempt to guide and motivate employees to work in the best interests of the organization. We discuss leadership more fully in Chapter 9.

Controlling

The fourth basic managerial activity, **controlling**, means monitoring the firm's performance to ensure that it stays on track towards its goals. Figure 5.2 shows the basic control process. The process begins with standards, or goals, the company wants to meet. For example, if the company wants to increase sales by 20 percent over the next 10 years, an appropriate standard might be an increase of around 2 percent each year. Managers must then measure actual performance regularly and compare this performance to the standard. If the two figures agree, the organization will continue its present activities. If they vary significantly, though, either the performance or the standard needs to be adjusted.

TYPES OF MANAGERS

Although all managers plan, organize, lead, and control, not all managers have the same degree of responsibility for each activity. Moreover, managers differ in the specific application of these activities. Thus we can divide managers by their *level* of responsibility or by their *area* of responsibility.

Levels of Management

The three basic levels of management are top, middle, and first-line management. As Figure 5.3 shows, in most firms there are more middle managers than top managers and more first-line managers than middle managers. Moreover, as the categories imply, the power of managers and the complexity of their duties increase as we move up the pyramid.

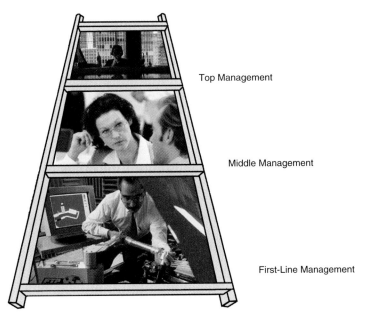

Figure 5.3
Most organizations have three basic levels of management.

Top Managers

The fairly small number of executives who guide the fortunes of most companies are **top managers**. Common titles for top managers include President, Vice-President, Treasurer, Chief Executive Officer (CEO), and Chief Financial Officer (CFO). Top managers are responsible to the board of directors and shareholders of the firm for its overall performance and effectiveness. They set general policies, formulate strategies, oversee all significant decisions, and represent the company in its dealings with other businesses and government.[12]

top managers
Those managers responsible for a firm's overall performance and effectiveness and for developing long-range plans for the company.

Middle Managers

Although below the ranks of the top executives, **middle managers** occupy positions of considerable autonomy and importance. Titles such as Plant Manager, Operations Manager, and Division Manager are typical of middle-management slots. In general, middle managers are responsible for implementing the strategies, policies, and decisions of the top managers. For example, if top management decides to bring out a new product in 12 months or to cut costs by 5 percent, middle management will have to decide to increase the pace of new product development or to reduce the plant's workforce.

middle managers
Those managers responsible for implementing the decisions made by top managers.

First-Line Managers

Those who hold titles such as Supervisor, Office Manager, and Group Leader are **first-line managers**. Although they spend most of their time working with and supervising the employees who report to them, first-line managers' activities are not limited to that arena. At a building site, for example, the Project Manager not only ensures that workers are carrying out construction as specified by the architect, but also interacts extensively with materials suppliers, community officials, and middle and top managers at the home office. The manager of an Old Navy store and the flight-services manager for a specific Air Canada flight would also be considered first-line managers.

first-line managers
Those managers responsible for supervising the work of employees.

Areas of Management

Within any large company, the top, middle, and first-line managers work in a variety of areas, including marketing, finance, operations, human resources, and information.

Marketing Managers

Marketing includes the development, pricing, promotion, and distribution of a product or service. **Marketing managers** are responsible for getting products and services to buyers. Marketing is especially important for firms dealing in consumer products, such as Procter & Gamble, Coca-Cola, and Roots. These firms often have large numbers of marketing managers at various levels. For example, a large firm will probably have a vice-president for marketing (top manager), regional marketing managers (middle managers), and several district sales managers (first-line managers). A marketing person often rises to the top of this type of corporation.

In contrast, firms that produce industrial products such as machinery and janitorial supplies tend to put less emphasis on marketing and to have fewer marketing managers. However, these firms do not ignore marketing altogether. In recent years, law firms and universities have also come to recognize the value and importance of marketing. For a detailed look at marketing, see Chapters 15 to 17.

marketing managers
Those managers responsible for developing, pricing, promoting, and distributing goods and services to buyers.

Financial Managers

Management of a firm's finances, including its investments and accounting functions, is extremely important to its survival. Nearly every company has **financial managers** to plan and oversee its financial resources. Levels of financial management may include a vice-president for finance (top), division controller (middle), and accounting supervisor (first-line). For large financial institutions such as the Bank of Montreal, First City Trust, and Burns Fry, effective financial management is the company's reason for being. No organization, however, can afford to ignore the need for management in this area. Chapters 18 to 20 cover financial management in detail.

financial managers
Those managers responsible for planning and overseeing the financial resources of a firm.

Operations Managers

A firm's operations are the systems by which it creates goods and services. **Operations managers** are responsible for production control, inventory control, and quality control, among other duties. Manufacturing companies like Steelcase, Bristol Aerospace, and Sony need operations managers at many levels. Such firms typically have a vice-president for operations (top), plant managers (middle), and foremen or supervisors (first-line). In recent years, sound operations management practices have also become increasingly important to service organizations, hospitals, universities, and the government. Operations management is the subject of Chapters 11 and 12.

operations managers
Those managers responsible for controlling production, inventory, and quality of a firm's products.

Bristol Aerospace
www.bristol.ca

Human Resource Managers

Every enterprise uses human resources. Most companies have **human resource managers** to hire employees, train them, evaluate their performances, decide how they should be compensated, and, in some cases, deal with labour unions. Large firms may have several human resource departments, each dealing with specialized activities. Imperial Oil, for example, has separate departments to deal with recruiting and hiring, wage and salary levels, and labour relations. Smaller firms may have a single department, while very small organizations may have a single person responsible for all human resource activities. Chapters 8 to 10 address issues involved in human resource management.

human resource managers
Those managers responsible for hiring, training, evaluating, and compensating employees.

Information Managers

A new type of managerial position appearing in many organizations is **information manager**. These managers are responsible for designing and implementing various systems to gather, process, and disseminate information. Dramatic increases in both the amount of information available to managers and the ability to manage it have led to the emergence of this important function. While relatively few in number now, the ranks of information managers are increasing at all levels. Federal Express, for example, has a Chief Information Officer. Middle managers engaged in information management help design information systems for divisions or plants. Computer systems managers within smaller businesses or operations are first-line managers. Information management is discussed in Chapter 13.

information managers
Those managers responsible for the design and implementation of systems to gather, process, and disseminate information.

Other Managers

Some firms have more specialized managers. Chemical companies such as CIL have research and development managers, for example, whereas companies such as Petro-Canada and Apple have public relations managers. The range of possibilities is endless; the areas of management are limited only by the needs and imagination of the firm.

BASIC MANAGEMENT SKILLS

While the range of managerial positions is almost limitless, the success that people enjoy in those positions is often limited by their skills and abilities. Effective managers must possess several skills: *technical, human relations, conceptual, decision-making,* and *time management skills.*

Technical Skills

Skills associated with performing specialized tasks within a company are called **technical skills**. A secretary's ability to type, an animator's ability to draw a cartoon, and an accountant's ability to audit a company's records are all technical skills. People develop their technical skills through education and experience. The secretary, for example, probably took a keyboarding course and has had many hours of practice both on and off the job. The animator may have had training in an art school and probably learned a great deal from experienced animators on the job. The accountant earned a university degree and, possibly, professional certification.

technical skills
Skills associated with performing specialized tasks within a firm.

As Figure 5.4 shows, technical skills are especially important for first-line managers. Most first-line managers spend considerable time helping employees solve work-related problems, monitoring their performance, and training them in more efficient work procedures. Such managers need a basic understanding of the jobs they supervise.

As a manager moves up the corporate ladder, however, technical skills become less and less important. Top managers, for example, often need only a cursory familiarity with the mechanics of basic tasks performed within the company. Michael Eisner, for example, freely admits that he can't draw Mickey Mouse or build a ride for Disney World.

Human Relations Skills

A few years ago, Hyatt Hotels checked 379 corporate employees into the chain's 98 hotels. They were not, however, treated as guests. Rather, they were asked to make beds, carry luggage, and perform the other tasks

Hyatt Hotels
www.hyatt.com

TOP MANAGEMENT

MIDDLE MANAGEMENT

FIRST-LINE MANAGEMENT

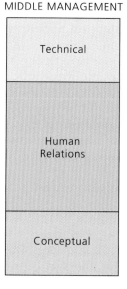

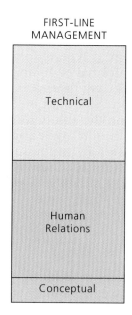

Figure 5.4
Different levels in an organization require different combinations of managerial skills.

necessary to make a big hotel function. Top management at Hyatt believes that learning more about the work of lower-level employees will allow executives to understand them better as human beings (and as co-workers).

human relations skills

Skills in understanding and getting along with people.

The Hyatt experiment was designed to test and improve the **human relations skills** of upper-level managers—that is, skills in understanding and getting along with other people. A manager with poor human relations skills may have trouble getting along with subordinates, cause valuable employees to quit or transfer, and contribute to poor morale.

While human relations skills are important at all levels, they are probably most important for middle managers, who must often act as bridges between top managers, first-line managers, and managers from other areas of the organization. Managers should possess good communication skills. Many managers have found that being able to understand others—and to get them to understand—can go far towards maintaining good relations in an organization.

Conceptual Skills

conceptual skills

Abilities to think in the abstract, diagnose and analyze different situations, and see beyond the present situation.

Conceptual skills refer to a person's ability to think in the abstract, to diagnose and analyze different situations, and to see beyond the present situation. Conceptual skills help managers recognize new market opportunities (and threats). They can also help managers analyze the probable outcomes of their decisions. The need for conceptual skills differs at various management levels: top managers depend most on conceptual skills, first-line managers least. Although the purposes and everyday needs of various jobs differ, conceptual skills are needed in almost any job-related activity.

In many ways, conceptual skills may be the most important ingredient in the success of executives in e-commerce businesses. For example, the ability to foresee how a particular business application will be affected by or can be translated to the Internet is clearly conceptual in nature. The "It's a Wired World" box discusses this idea in more detail.

Decision-Making Skills

decision-making skills

Skills in defining problems and selecting the best courses of action.

Decision-making skills include the ability to define problems and select the best course of action. Figure 5.5 illustrates the basic steps in decision making.

IT'S A WIRED WORLD

How to Spot the E-CEO

Top managers, especially CEOs, have always moved in a fast-paced, stress-filled work environment. But the job of CEO for an e-commerce company seems to be setting new standards for pace, complexity, and stress. CEOs in traditional businesses are generally accustomed to dealing with either tangible products (such as automobiles, shoes, or computer hardware) or relatively well-defined services (accounting, transportation, or retailing operations). Moreover, the "rules of the game," established over a period of decades, are relatively clear: Businesses are supposed to make profits, stock price is based on earnings, and so forth.

But the world of electronic commerce has put a few bumps in this well-worn road. Managers in this area clearly believe that the pace of their work is faster, more complex, and more ambiguous than that of their traditional counterparts. They attribute some of these conditions to the nature of their business (which is based almost solely on information), some to the pace of change in their industries (it occurs very, very quickly), and some to a new set of business rules (for example, market valuation based more on intuition than on reality). But all agree on one fundamental thing: they operate at breakneck speed with little or no margin for error. Table 5.1 highlights some of the fundamental differences between the work of a traditional CEO and an e-CEO.

Table 5.1	Traditional CEOs vs. E-CEOs
Traditional CEO	**E-CEO**
Encouraging	Evangelizing
Alert	Paranoid
Cordial	Brutally frank
Infotech semiliterate (at best)	Infotech literate (at least)
Clearly focused	Intensely focused
Fast moving	Faster moving
Anti-ambiguity	Pro-Ambiguity
Technology-confrontation-anxiety sufferer	Bandwidth-separation-anxiety sufferer
Paragon of good judgment	Paragon of good judgment
Age: 57	Age: 38
Rich	Really rich

A traditional CEO, for example, is generally expected to be encouraging, cordial, and fast moving; he or she is said to dislike ambiguity. This person might also have some anxiety about confronting technology-related issues, and his or her average age is 57. The e-CEO, on the other hand, is more prone to evangelizing, is often brutally frank, and apparently thrives on ambiguity. Furthermore, the e-CEO exhibits more anxiety when he or she is deprived of technology, and has an average age of 38. Finally, while all CEOs are presumed to be rich, well to do, or comfortable, successful e-CEOs are likely to be very wealthy.

1. *Define the problem, gather facts, and identify alternative solutions*. Current managers at bicycle maker Schwinn, for instance, realized that their predecessors had made some serious errors in assuming that mountain bikes were just a fad. The opposite had proved to be true, and Schwinn's share of the bicycle market had dropped dramatically.

2. *Evaluate each alternative and select the best one*. Managers at Schwinn acknowledged that they had to take corrective action. They discussed such alternatives as buying a mountain bike maker, launching their own line of mountain bikes, or refocusing on other product lines. They chose to develop their own line of mountain bikes and did so in 1994.

3. *Implement the chosen alternative, periodically following up and evaluating the effectiveness of that choice*. Schwinn's actions turned out to be right on

Figure 5.5
The decision-making process.

track: The firm's revenues began to increase steadily after its first mountain bikes went on the market. At first, true mountain bike enthusiasts were wary of the new products because they still associated Schwinn with recreational bicycles for casual or occasional riders. But after a few professional mountain bike racers started using Schwinn's products, these concerns evaporated. Today, Schwinn is once again pre-eminent in every market in which it competes.

Time Management Skills

time management skills

Skills associated with the productive use of time.

Time management skills refer to the productive use that managers make of their time. In 1999, for example, General Electric CEO Jack Welch was paid $13 325 000 in salary. Assuming that he worked 50 hours a week and took 2 weeks of vacation, Welch earned $5330 an hour—about $89 per minute. (Actually, this example substantially underestimates Welch's earnings; he also received another $79 million in deferred compensation such as stock options and retirement benefits.)[13] Any amount of time that Welch wastes clearly represents a large cost to GE and its stockholders. Most managers receive much smaller salaries than does Welch; however, their time is still valuable and poor use of it translates into costs and reduced productivity.

To manage time effectively, managers must address four leading causes of wasted time:

- *Paperwork*. Some managers spend too much time deciding what to do with letters and reports. Most documents of this sort are routine and can be handled quickly. Managers must learn to recognize those documents that require more attention.

- *The telephone*. Experts estimate that managers are interrupted by the telephone every five minutes. To manage time more effectively, they suggest having a secretary screen all calls and setting aside a certain block of time each day to return the important ones.

- *Meetings*. Many managers spend as much as four hours per day in meetings. To help keep this time productive, the person handling the meeting should specify a clear agenda, start on time, keep everyone focused on the agenda, and end on time.

- *E-mail*. Increasingly, of course, more and more managers are also relying heavily on e-mail and other forms of electronic communication. Like memos and telephone calls, many e-mail messages are not particularly important; some are even trivial. As a result, time is wasted when managers have to sort through a variety of electronic folders, in-baskets, and archives. As the average number of electronic messages grows, the potential time wasted also increases.

Management Skills for the Twenty-First Century

Managers face some major challenges as they prepare to enter the twenty-first century. We will touch on two of the most significant challenges: *global management* and *technology*.

Global Management Skills

Tomorrow's managers must equip themselves with the special tools, techniques, and skills necessary to compete in a global environment. They will need to understand foreign markets, cultural differences, and the motives and practices of foreign rivals.

On a more practical level, businesses will need managers who are capable of understanding international operations. In the past, most Canadian businesses hired local managers to run their operations in the various countries in which they operated. More recently, however, the trend has been to transfer Canadian managers to foreign locations. This practice helps firms better transfer their corporate cultures to foreign operations. In addition, foreign assignments help managers become better prepared for international competition as they advance within the organization.[14]

Management and Technology Skills

Another significant issue facing tomorrow's manager is technology, especially as it relates to communication. Managers have always had to deal with information. In today's world, however, the amount of information has reached staggering proportions. New forms of technology have added to a manager's ability to process information while simultaneously making it even more important to organize and interpret an ever-increasing wealth of input.

Technology has also begun to change the way the interaction of managers shapes corporate structures. Computer networking, for example, exists because it is no longer too expensive to put a computer on virtually every desk in the company. In turn, this elaborate network controls the flow of the firm's lifeblood—information. Information no longer flows strictly up and down through hierarchies. It now flows to everyone at once. As a result, decisions are made more quickly—and more people are directly involved. With e-mail, teleconferencing, and other forms of communication, neither time nor distance—nor such corporate "boundaries" as departments and divisions—can prevent people from working more closely together. More than ever, bureaucracies are breaking down, while planning, decision making, and other activities are beginning to benefit from group building and teamwork.

BECOMING A MANAGER

The skills of management are not easily acquired by would-be managers. Nor can organizations easily identify people who possess these skills. As you will see in this section, both the training and the recruiting of managers are complex operations.

Preparing for Management

At one time, managers simply started at the "bottom" (in many cases, a plant or warehouse) and worked their way to the "top." While such a career path is still possible, the increasing complexity of management makes people who follow it a rare breed. Today more than ever before, managers are acquiring their skills and abilities through a cyclical process of education, experience, and then more education.

Education

The most common starting point for contemporary Canadian managers is a B. Comm. degree from a university or a college diploma in business administration. Many people leave school with this credential and start their careers. Their learning, however, is not complete. More and more people eventually return to school to get a masters of business administration (MBA) degree.[15] Even managers who do not earn an MBA usually go through corporate training programs. Many attend management development programs and seminars sponsored by universities, colleges, or private training companies. Learning is a lifelong process for most managers.

Experience

Education is not the only route into management. In some companies, managers—especially first-line managers—may have little or no advanced education. They have earned their positions strictly on the basis of experience. This pattern is common in heavy manufacturing industries such as steel and automobile production.

Experience is also necessary for those with degrees or diplomas who want to get ahead. After completing their degree(s) or diploma(s), most people today accept an entry-level position in a large company, go to work in a family-owned business, or start their own business. As their careers progress, they gain much valuable experience. In larger companies, for example, most management trainees go through formal training programs and work in a variety of areas to gain a broader perspective.

Where Organizations Find Managers

Just as there are different paths to management, companies acquire new managers in different ways. Firms have three basic sources of new managers: the academic world, the company itself, and other companies.

Recruiting from Colleges and Universities

Colleges and universities are a major source of new managers. Large firms such as Sears, the Bank of Montreal, Canadian Pacific, and Noranda hire hundreds of new graduates as managers every year. Often they start graduates from community colleges and universities as first-line managers. MBAs may be able to start at the lower levels of middle management.

The primary advantages of this source are that the managers are young and have been exposed to the latest ideas. On the other hand, they frequently lack experience and a proven track record. Businesses that adopt this strategy must invest in effective campus recruiting strategies and be prepared to develop future managers over a longer period of time.

Promoting from Within

Another common source of managers is the firm itself, especially one or two layers below where the new managers are needed. Promotion from within offers many advantages. Recognizing that they have a chance to advance within the company motivates lower-level employees to do their best. Employees who are promoted from within also come with a track record. The firm has its own data on the individual's performance and accomplishments.

Of course, if someone from middle management is promoted to an executive position, someone else must be found to fill the middle-management position. Promotion from within tends to perpetuate current practices and ideas, providing less opportunity for innovation. In addition, these promotion decisions

Most managers start learning their basic skills in university or college classrooms

are sometimes seen as being too political, making other employees resentful or damaging their morale.

Hiring Away from Other Organizations

Finally, some managers are hired away from other businesses. Contacts with talented managers willing to consider alternative opportunities can come from a manager's own network or through professional recruiting firms, commonly referred to as "headhunters."

As with the other options, hiring away from other firms has both advantages and disadvantages. The company may be able to get more talented people than are available internally. Already-trained managers mean a savings to the organization. Hiring from outside may inject fresh ideas and creativity. On the other hand, insiders passed over in favour of an outsider may feel resentful and leave. The newcomer may not fit into the company. Thus, the managers in charge of attracting human resources need to consider carefully the pros and cons of each source as they develop their human resource strategy.

MANAGEMENT AND THE CORPORATE CULTURE

Every organization—big or small, more successful or less successful—has an unmistakable "feel" to it. Just as every individual has a unique personality, every company has a unique identity, called **corporate culture**: the shared experiences, stories, beliefs, and norms that characterize an organization. This culture helps define the work and business climate that exists in an organization.

A strong corporate culture serves several purposes. First, it directs employees' efforts and helps everyone work towards the same goals. Some cultures, for example, stress financial success to the extreme, while others focus more on quality of life. Second, corporate culture helps newcomers learn accepted behaviours. If financial success is the key to a culture, newcomers quickly learn that they are expected to work long, hard hours and that the "winner" is the one who brings in the most revenue. But if quality of life is more fundamental, newcomers learn that it's more acceptable to spend less time at work and that balancing work and non-work is encouraged.

Magna International, a large Canadian producer of auto parts, is a firm with a strong culture. Its founder, Frank Stronach, is well known for his views about employees, working conditions, daycare centres, unions, the free enterprise system, and profit distribution.[16] Four Seasons Hotels and Resorts has a different, but equally strong, culture. Managers are judged by deeds, not words, and act as role models; employees take their cues from the managers.[17] At Toyota's Cambridge, Ontario, plant the corporate culture stresses values, principles, and trust. The culture is one of continuous improvement.[18] At WestJet Airlines the corporate culture emphasizes profit maximization. Most of the employees own shares in the company, and all of them get to keep some of the profits. This is a powerful incentive for them to work productively.[19]

corporate culture
The shared experiences, stories, beliefs, and norms that characterize a firm.

Magna International
www.magna.com

Forces Shaping Corporate Culture

A number of forces shape corporate cultures. First, the values held by top management help set the tone of the organization and influence its business goals and strategies. Frank Stronach (Magna International), Timothy Eaton (Eaton's), Max Ward (Wardair), Larry Clark (Spar Aerospace), and Jean de Grandpre (BCE) are just a few of the leaders who have had a profound impact on the culture of their respective organizations. Even a large, long-time firm

Mainframe Entertainment of Vancouver has one of the lowest turnover rates in the animation business. Its culture emphasizes giving young artists and designers opportunities to acquire new skills and develop leadership potential—opportunities not available in the bigger Los Angeles studios.

like Ford still bears the traces of founder Henry Ford.

The firm's history also helps shape its culture. Championship banners line the Molson Centre, reinforcing the message that the Montreal Canadiens are winners. Maintaining a corporate culture draws on many dimensions of business life. Shared experiences resulting from norms sustain culture. Thus, working long hours on a special project becomes a shared experience for many employees. They remember it, talk about it among themselves, and wear it as a badge of their contribution to the company.

Stories and legends are also important. Walt Disney has been dead for many years now, but his spirit lives on in the businesses he left behind. Quotations from Disney are affixed to portraits of him throughout the company's studios. And Disney's emphasis on family is still visible in corporate benefits such as paying for spouses to accompany employees on extended business trips. In fact, employees are often called "the Disney family."

Finally, strong behavioural norms help define and sustain corporate cultures. For example, a strong part of the culture at Hewlett-Packard Canada is that everyone wears a name tag and that everyone is called by his or her first name. And at Sony Corporation every employee wears a corporate smock.

Communicating the Culture and Managing Change

Corporate culture influences management philosophy, style, and behaviour. Managers, therefore, must carefully consider the kind of culture they want for their organization, then work to nourish that culture by communicating with everyone who works there. Wal-Mart, for example, is acutely conscious of the need to spread the message of its culture as it opens new stores in new areas. One of the company's methods is to regularly assign veteran managers to lead employees in new territories. At Continental Airlines, Gordon Bethune delivers weekly messages to all employees to update them on what's going on in the firm; the employees can either listen to it on a closed-circuit broadcast or else call an 800 telephone number and hear a recorded version at their own convenience.

Communicating the Culture

To use its culture to a firm's advantage, managers must accomplish several tasks, all of which hinge on effective communication. First, managers themselves must have a clear understanding of the culture. Second, they must transmit the culture to others in the organization. Communication is thus one aim in training and orienting newcomers. A clear and meaningful statement of the organization's mission is also a valuable communication tool. Finally, managers can maintain the culture by rewarding and promoting those who understand it and work towards maintaining it.

Managing Change

Not surprisingly, organizations must sometimes change their cultures. Ontario Hydro, for example, had an "engineering" culture for many years.

This meant that everything was planned and analyzed down to the last detail before any action was taken. But Ontario Hydro's culture is changing towards a more consumer-oriented, risk-taking culture as it tries to cope with large debt and changes in its markets. The RCMP is also much different now than it was in the days when military tradition dominated the organization. It recently completed a "visioning process" that resulted in a new mission statement, a new set of core values, and a commitment to the communities in which it works.[20]

Individual managers can have a big impact on a company's culture. James Bonini was only 33 years old when he was named manager of Chrysler's van plant in Windsor, Ontario. He quickly concluded that he was going to have to change the culture at the plant, which was characterized by quality problems, managers who acted like drill sergeants, and workers who were demoralized. Bonini took several actions, including dealing with the disappointed individuals who thought they should have gotten his job, spending a lot of time on the production floor, boosting the sale of vans by ensuring that the plant was responsive to special customer orders, and giving workers much more authority to make production decisions.[21]

When cultural change is required, the process usually goes through three stages:

1. At the highest level, analysis of the company's environment highlights extensive change as the most effective response to its problems. This period is typically characterized by conflict and resistance.

2. Top management begins to formulate a vision of a new company. Whatever that vision is, it must include renewed focus on the activities of competitors and the needs of customers.

3. The firm sets up new systems for appraising and compensating employees that enforce its new values. The purpose is to give the new culture solid shape from within the firm.

Procter & Gamble is in the midst of a major overhaul designed to remake its corporate culture into one better suited to today's competitive global business environment. Because its brands have been dominant for such a long time, managers at P&G have been criticized for having tunnel vision— focusing only on the ways they've done things in the past and then trying to repeat them. Its popular Tide laundry detergent, for example, has been through more than 60 formula upgrades since it was first introduced. CEO Durk Jager, however, is working to shake things up by advocating new approaches, new ways of thinking, and new models of product development.[22]

SUMMARY OF LEARNING OBJECTIVES

1. **Explain the importance of setting *goals* and formulating *strategies* as the starting points of effective management.** *Goals*—the performance targets of an organization—can be *long-term, intermediate,* and *short-term.* They provide direction for managers, they help managers decide how to allocate limited resources, they define the corporate culture, and they help managers assess performance. *Strategies*—the methods that a company uses to meet its stated goals—involve three major activities: setting strategic goals, analyzing the organization and its environment, and matching the organization and its environment. These strategies are translated into *strategic, tactical,* and *operational plans.* To deal with crises or major environmental changes, companies develop *contingency plans* and plans for *crisis management.*

2. **Describe the four activities that constitute the *management process*.** *Management* is the process of planning, organizing, leading, and controlling an organization's financial, physical, human, and information resources to achieve the organization's goals. *Planning* means determining what the company needs to do and how best to get it done. *Organizing* means determining how best to arrange a business's resources and the necessary jobs into an overall structure. *Leading* means guiding and motivating employees to meet the firm's objectives. *Controlling* means monitoring the firm's performance to ensure that it is meeting its goals.

3. **Identify *types of managers* by level and area.** Managers can be differentiated in two ways: by level and by area. By level, *top managers* set policies, formulate strategies, and approve decisions. *Middle managers* implement policies, strategies, and decisions. *First-line managers* usually work with and supervise employees. Areas of managers include marketing, financial, operations, human resource, and information. Managers at all levels may be found in every area of a company.

4. **Describe the five basic *management skills*.** Most managers agree that five basic management skills are necessary for success. *Technical skills* are associated with performing specialized tasks ranging from typing to auditing. *Human relations skills* are associated with understanding and getting along with other people. *Conceptual skills* are the abilities to think in the abstract, to diagnose and analyze different situations, and to see beyond present circumstances. *Decision-making skills* allow managers to define problems and to select the best course of action. *Time management skills* refer to managers' ability to make productive use of the time available to them.

5. **Describe the development and explain the importance of *corporate culture*.** *Corporate culture* is the shared experiences, stories, beliefs, and norms that characterize an organization. A strong, well-defined culture can help a business reach its goals and can influence management styles. Culture is determined by several factors, including top management, the organization's history, stories and legends, and behavioural norms. If carefully communicated and flexible enough to accommodate change, corporate culture can be managed for the betterment of the organization.

KEY TERMS

goals, 137
mission statement, 138
long-term goals, 138
intermediate goals, 138
short-term goals, 138
strategy formulation, 139
strategic goals, 139
environmental analysis, 140
organizational analysis, 140
strategic plans, 141
tactical plans, 142

operational plans, 142
corporate-level strategy, 142
business-level (competitive) strategy, 142
functional strategies, 142
concentration strategy, 143
market penetration, 143
geographic expansion, 143
product development, 143

horizontal integration, 143
vertical integration, 143
diversification, 143
investment reduction, 143
competitive strategy, 143
cost leadership, 144
differentiation, 144
focus, 144
functional strategy, 144
contingency planning, 145

crisis management, 145
management, 145
planning, 146
organizing, 147
leading, 148
controlling, 148
top managers, 149
middle managers, 149
first-line managers, 149
marketing managers, 150
financial managers, 150
operations managers, 150
human resource managers, 150

STUDY QUESTIONS AND EXERCISES

Review Questions

1. What are the four main purposes of setting goals in an organization?
2. Identify and explain the three basic steps in strategy formulation.
3. Relate the five basic management skills to the four activities in the management process. For example, which skills are most important in leading?
4. What is corporate culture? How is it formed? How is it sustained?

Analysis Questions

5. Select any group of which you are a member (your company, your family, or a club or organization, for example). Explain how planning, organizing, leading, and controlling are practised in that group.
6. Identify managers by level and area at your college or university.
7. In what kind of company would the technical skills of top managers be more important than human relations or conceptual skills? Are there organizations in which conceptual skills are not important?
8. What differences might you expect to find in the corporate cultures of a 100-year-old manufacturing firm based in Winnipeg and a one-year-old e-commerce firm based in Ottawa?

Application Exercises

9. Interview the manager at any level of a local company. Identify that manager's job according to level and area. Show how planning, organizing, leading, and controlling are part of this person's job. Inquire about the manager's education and work experience. Which management skills are most important for this manager's job?
10. Compare the corporate cultures of two companies that do business in most communities. Be sure to choose two companies in the same industry—for example, a Bay department store and a Wal-Mart discount store.

Building Your Business Skills

Skilful Talking

Goal

To encourage students to appreciate effective speaking as a critical human relations skill.

Situation

A manager's ability to understand and get along with supervisors, peers, and subordinates is a critical human relations skill. At the heart of this skill, says Harvard University professor of education Sarah McGinty, is the ability to speak with power and control. McGinty defines "powerful speech" in terms of the following characteristics:

- the ability to speak at length and in complete sentences
- the ability to set a conversational agenda
- the ability to deter interruptions
- the ability to argue openly and to express strong opinions about ideas, not people
- the ability to make statements that offer solutions rather than pose questions
- the ability to express humour

Taken together, says McGinty, "all this creates a sense of confidence in listeners."

Method

Step 1:

Working alone, compare your own personal speaking style with McGinty's description of powerful speech by taping yourself as you speak during a meeting with classmates or during a phone conversation. (Tape both sides of the conversation only if the person to whom you are speaking gives permission.) Listen for the following problems:

- unfinished sentences
- an absence of solutions
- too many disclaimers (e.g., "I'm not sure I have enough information to say this, but . . .")
- the habit of seeking support from others instead of making definitive statements of personal conviction (e.g., say, "I recommend consolidating the medical and fitness functions," instead of, "As Emily stated in her report, I recommend consolidating the medical and fitness functions")

- language fillers (saying, "you know," "like," and "um" when you are unsure of your facts or uneasy about expressing your opinion)

Step 2:
Join with three or four other classmates to evaluate each other's speaking styles. Finally:

- Have a 10-minute group discussion on the importance of human relations skills in business.

- Listen to other group members and take notes on the "power" content of what you hear.

- Offer constructive criticism by focusing on what speakers say rather than on personal characteristics (e.g., say, "Bob, you sympathized with Paul's position, but I still don't know what you think," instead of, "Bob, you sounded like a weakling").

Follow-Up Questions

1. How do you think the power content of speech affects a manager's ability to communicate? Evaluate some of the ways in which effects may differ among supervisors, peers, and subordinates.

2. How do you evaluate yourself and group members in terms of powerful and powerless speech? List the strengths and weaknesses of the group.

3. Do you agree or disagree with McGinty that business success depends on gaining insight into your own language habits? Explain your answer.

4. In our age of computers and e-mail, why do you think that personal presentation continues to be important in management?

5. McGinty believes that power language differs from company to company and that it is linked to the corporate culture. Do you agree, or do you believe that people express themselves in similar ways no matter where they are?

Exploring the Net

To find out more about basic planning in and organization of a large company, visit the world and Canadian sites of Kodak at:

www.kodak.com

www.kodak.ca

1. What is the CEO's role in corporate structure as described in "About Kodak" and other Web site information?

2. What are some of the company's major goals as communicated in Web site press releases and other information? Which goals are long term? Which are short term?

3. How does the company indicate it will measure success in realizing management goals? What incentives are provided?

4. Based on your exploration of the main corporate and Canadian Kodak Web sites, what value do you think the company places on research and development? Explain.

Concluding Case 5-1

Starbucks

Starbucks Corp. is one of the fastest-growing and highest-profile food and beverage companies in North America. Starbucks was started in Seattle in 1971 by three coffee aficionados. Their primary business at the time was buying premium coffee beans, roasting them, and then selling the coffee by the pound. The business performed modestly well and soon grew to nine stores, all in the Seattle area. But when they thought their business growth had stalled in 1987, the three partners sold Starbucks to a former employee named Howard Schultz. Schultz promptly reoriented the business, trading in bulk coffee sales for retail coffee sales through the firm's coffee bars.

Today, the firm has over 2800 stores, revenues of over US$1.3 billion a year, annual profits of almost US$70 million, and a workforce of over 26 000 employees.

What is the key to Starbucks phenomenal growth and success? One important ingredient is its well-conceived and implemented strategy. Starbucks is on a phenomenal growth pace, opening a new coffee shop almost every day. But this growth is planned and coordinated at each step through careful site selection. In addition, through its astute promotional campaigns and commitment to quality, the firm has elevated the coffee-drinking tastes of millions and fuelled a significant increase in demand.

Its phenomenal growth rate notwithstanding, Starbucks is also continually on the alert for new business opportunities. One area of growth is the international market. In 1996, for example, the firm opened two stores in Japan and one in Singapore. Another growth area is brand extension through ventures with other companies. Dreyer's, for example, now distributes five flavours of Starbucks coffee ice cream to grocery freezers across the U.S. Capitol Records has produced two jazz CDs that are available only in Starbucks stores.

Starbucks has become almost synonymous with coffee—indeed, people sometimes talk about stopping for some "Starbucks" rather than stopping for "coffee." The firm plans to open 500 stores in Europe and Asia by the end of 2003. Starbucks also plans to partner with Kraft Foods to distribute its coffee in grocery stores. To maintain high levels of quality control, Starbucks also refuses to franchise—it owns and operates every one of its stores.

But a firm like Starbucks is not without problems. It has been the target of protests at some sites because it buys most of its beans from coffee corporations and plantations in less-developed countries instead of from small independent growers. Other critics take issue with the extra "packaging" that Starbucks uses for a hot cup of coffee—double cups or corrugated bands, large plastic lids, plastic stirring sticks, and so forth. Still others lump Starbucks in with other megaretailers, such as Barnes & Noble and Wal-Mart, criticizing them all for overwhelming independent family-owned businesses.

CASE QUESTIONS

1. Briefly describe what is involved in carrying out each of the management functions at a company like Starbucks.

2. What types of managers and areas of management exist in a firm like Starbucks? How would these differ from those found in a local competitor of Starbucks?

3. What differences, if any, are likely to exist between the key management skills needed at Starbucks and the key management skills needed at a small, local competitor?

4. What corporate strategy does Starbucks seem to be pursuing?

5. What kinds of contingency plans should a company like Starbucks develop? ◆

Concluding Case 5-2

Big Changes in the Airline Industry

Throughout the 1990s, Canada's two premier airlines—Air Canada and Canadian Airlines International—were locked in a bitter competitive struggle for supremacy in the domestic airline market. Industry observers agreed that significant changes were needed and that the market could not support two national airlines in Canada. Other suggested charges were reducing costs, cutting employees, increasing revenues, reducing baggage handling mistakes, and generally improving service.

Canadian Airlines, which was continuously on the brink of bankruptcy, considered several alternatives in an attempt to solve its problems, including asking for a federal bailout, merging with Air Canada, and partnering with a larger U.S. airline. In 1999, Onex Corporation made a surprise bid to buy Canadian, and intended to follow that up with a bid for Air Canada so the two airlines could be merged. But a Quebec court ruled against that idea. Soon after, Air Canada made its own offer to buy Canadian and run it as a separate company. In January 2000, Air Canada announced that it had successfully completed the purchase of Canadian. The federal government and the Competition Bureau approved the deal.

The outcome probably means greater stability and security for employees of the newly merged company, since Air Canada will now control about 80 percent of all domestic air traffic. But consumers are worried that this dominance will result in higher airfares and reduced service. The federal government immediately responded to this concern by passing new price-gouging legislation. The legislation included a maximum prison sentence of five years and fines of up to $10 million if Air Canada did not live up to its promises to ensure competition in the industry. As well, the Canadian Transportation Agency has the power to reject or roll back fare increases, and it can order the airline to give refunds to customers. The government also indicated that if new domestic competitors don't emerge in the industry, U.S. airlines would be invited into Canada to ensure that competition continues to exist.

What does the future hold? If Air Canada does not provide reasonably priced service, other new airlines will no doubt start up to compete in certain market niches. Discount airline WestJet is already planning significant expansion because it sees new opportunities in the market. Like everything else these days, the airline business is in a constant state of change.

CASE QUESTIONS

1. What three steps are involved in strategy formulation? To what extent did Air Canada follow these steps as it took over Canadian Airlines?

2. What strategic options are available to business firms? Which of these strategic options is Air Canada apparently pursuing?

3. What is contingency planning? What kinds of contingency plans will a company like Air Canada have?

4. What is corporate culture? What difficulties might be evident in merging the cultures of Air Canada and Canadian Airlines International? ◆

Visit the *Business* Website at www.pearsoned.ca/griffin
for up-to-date e-business cases!

Restructuring at Bata Shoe Ltd.

Toronto-based Bata Shoe Ltd. is a privately held company that employs 52 000 people worldwide, operates in 69 countries, and sells 250 million pairs of shoes each year. The company has been departmentalized by territory, with divisions in Europe, Africa, the Far East, and South America. Its products vary from region to region in accordance with the local population's wants and needs. Each subsidiary operates more or less autonomously.

However, big changes are planned because Bata is suffering from intense competition amid a flood of cheap imports from competitors. These companies manufacture shoes in low-cost areas like Korea, Taiwan, and China, and then use a central office to market and distribute them. Bata, by contrast, operates factories around the world, and this has led to poor integration of its operations. Bata will close some of its factories, cut $60 million in costs, and revamp its organizational structure. In the future, each remaining plant will specialize in one type of footwear for the global market.

Bata's retail stores will also be enlarged and updated to attract younger middle-income family shoppers. The company will give top priority to expansion in the U.S. market, where its absence is glaring. Industry observers note that U.S. consumers set global trends, and if a company is going to be world class, it must have a presence in the U.S. Bata will also improve its stores in Canada, which operate under the names Bata, Athletes World, and Out There.

This is not the first attempt made by Bata to improve its operations. During the last decade, a succession of non-family members held the top jobs while trying to turn the company around. But these efforts failed, say managers, because Thomas Bata, the son of the company's founder, did not give them sufficient authority to do the things that were necessary to overcome the company's problems. Ironically, one of the problems was that Bata's authority structure was very decentralized at the production level, with operations in each country acting as virtually independent companies with no overall coordination. ◆

Bata Shoe Ltd.
www.bata.com

The need to fit structure to operations is common to all companies, large and small. Whether a company employs five people or 500 000, it needs organization to function. In this chapter, we consider the nature of business organization and the structures that firms have traditionally chosen. By focusing on the learning objectives of this chapter, you will better understand the importance of business organization and the ways in which both formal and informal aspects of its structure affect the decisions a business makes. After studying this chapter, you should be able to:

LEARNING OBJECTIVES

1. Discuss the elements that influence a firm's *organizational structure*.

2. Describe *specialization* and *departmentalization* as the building blocks of organizational structure.

3. Distinguish between *responsibility* and *authority* and explain the differences in decision making in *centralized* and *decentralized organizations*.

4. Explain the differences between *functional, divisional, project*, and *international organization structures*.

5. Define the *informal organization* and discuss *intrapreneuring*.

THE STRUCTURE OF BUSINESS ORGANIZATIONS

Exactly what do we mean by the term *organizational structure*? In many ways, a business is like an automobile. All automobiles have an engine, four wheels, fenders and other structural components, an interior compartment for passengers, and various operating systems including those for fuel, braking, and climate control. Each component has a distinct purpose but must also work in harmony with the others. Automobiles made by competing firms all have the same basic components, although the way they look and fit together may vary.

Similarly, all businesses have common structural and operating components, each of which has a specific purpose. Each component must fulfil its own purpose while simultaneously fitting in with the others. And, just like automobiles made by different companies, how these components look and fit together varies from company to company. Thus, **organizational structure** is the specification of the jobs to be done within a business and how those jobs relate to one another.

organizational structure
The specification of the jobs to be done within a business and how those jobs relate to one another.

Every institution—be it a for-profit company, a not-for-profit organization, or a government agency—must develop the most appropriate structure for its own unique situation. What works for Air Canada will not work for Canada Customs and Revenue. Likewise, the structure of the Red Cross will not work for the University of Toronto.

Determinants of Organization Structure

How is an organization's structure determined? Does it happen by chance or is there some logic that managers use to create structure? Does it develop by some combination of circumstance and strategy? Ideally, managers carefully assess a variety of important factors as they plan for and then create a structure that will allow their organization to function efficiently.

Many elements work together to determine an organization's structure. Chief among these are the organization's *purpose, mission*, and *strategy*. A dynamic and rapidly growing enterprise, for example, achieved that position because of its purpose and successful strategies for achieving it. Such a firm will need a structure that contributes to flexibility and growth. A stable organization with only modest growth will function best with a different structure.

WEBCONNEXION

This San Francisco–based company once called itself AllApartments because it merely provided an online listing of apartments available across the country. But then its mission, purpose, and strategy—and its organization—changed. Now the firm calls itself SpringStreet, and it also quotes prices on furniture and moving services, in addition to a host of other services related to finding a place to live. To get a better idea of this range of services, log on at:

www.homestore.com

Size, technology, and changes in environmental circumstances also affect structure. A large manufacturer operating in a strongly competitive environment requires a different structure than a local barbershop or video store. Moreover, even after a structure has been created, it is rarely free from tinkering—or even outright recreation. Indeed, most organizations change their structures on an almost continuing basis.

Organizing is a function that is conducted with an equal awareness of a firm's external and internal environments. Since it was first incorporated in 1903, for example, Ford Motor Co. has undergone literally dozens of major structural changes, hundreds of moderate changes, and thousands of minor changes. In the last 10 years alone, Ford has initiated several major structural changes. In 1994, the firm announced a major restructuring plan called *Ford 2000*, which was intended to integrate all of Ford's vast international operations into a single, unified structure by 2000. By 1998, however, midway through implementation of the plan, top Ford executives announced major modifications, indicating that (1) additional changes would be made, (2) some previously planned changes would not be made, and (3) some recently realigned operations would be changed again. In early 1999, managers announced yet another sweeping set of changes intended to eliminate corporate bureaucracy, speed decision making, and improve communication and working relationships among people at different levels of the organization.[1] The "It's a Wired World" box explains how Ford's e-commerce initiatives are affecting its structure in still other ways.

Chain of Command

Most businesses prepare **organization charts** that illustrate the company's structure and show employees where they fit into the firm's operations. Figure 6.1 shows the organization chart for a hypothetical company. Each box represents a job within the company. The solid lines that connect the boxes

organization chart
A physical depiction of the company's structure showing employee titles and their relationship to one another.

IT'S A WIRED WORLD

Hot-Wiring Ford

Imagine going to a Web page to buy a new car. You specify the car online just as you want it—colour, engine size, options—and electronically negotiate the price. Then you click on "okay." Your simple action transmits a slew of information directly to a local dealer, a financial broker, your insurance agent, the factory that will build your car, the suppliers who provide the components, and the Ford designers working on next year's models. A few days later, your new car is delivered to your home.

Fantasy? Not if Ford CEO Jacques Nasser has his way. Nasser and his managers at Ford are rushing headlong towards his vision of the automobile-buying future. To get there, Nasser is convinced that Ford must systematically absorb the Internet into every element of its organization. Indeed, experts agree that Ford stands at the forefront of old-line manufacturers who are working to absorb Web technology. Recall, for instance, the "It's a Wired World" box in Chapter 1, in which we described Ford's partici-

pation in an electronic marketplace for auto parts and supplies.

Another major initiative at Ford is its comprehensive and integrated corporate intranet. One official goes so far as to describe it as the backbone of Ford's business today. To weave one major strand in the Ford intranet, managers are strongly encouraged to create all reports online. Nasser wants to deliver a clear message: namely, Ford manages itself on the intranet and interacts with stakeholders on the Internet.

Nasser also believes that if Ford is to embrace the Internet fully, each and every one of its employees must "think Internet." To that end, Ford announced in early 2000 that it would provide all of its 350 000 global employees with a home computer, a printer, and $5 per month for Internet access.

Ford is also working to integrate Web technology into its cars. Designers are trying to figure out the best way to wire cars for e-mail and news, voice-recognition systems, and satellite phone services. Nasser and Ford are clearly gambling on the future. If they're right, they may well become the car of choice for the Internet generation.

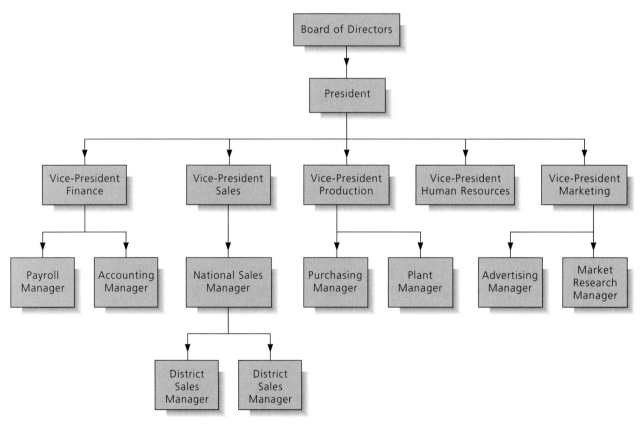

Figure 6.1
An organization chart shows key positions in the organization and interrelationships among them.

define the **chain of command**, or the reporting relationships within the company. Thus, each plant manager reports directly to the vice-president for production who, in turn, reports to the president. When the chain of command is not clear, many different kinds of problems can result.

An actual organization chart would, of course, be far more complex and include individuals at many more levels. Indeed, because of their size, larger firms cannot easily draw a diagram with everyone on it.

THE BUILDING BLOCKS OF ORGANIZATIONAL STRUCTURE

The first step in developing the structure of any business, large or small, is twofold:

- *Specialization*: determining who will do what

- *Departmentalization*: determining how people performing certain tasks can best be grouped together

These two tasks are the basic building blocks of all business organization.

Specialization

The process of identifying the specific jobs that need to be done and designating the people who will perform them leads to **job specialization**. In a sense, all organizations have only one major "job"—for example, making a profit by manufacturing and selling men's and boys' shirts. But this job, of course, is broken into smaller components. In turn, each component is assigned to an individual. Consider the manufacture of men's shirts. Because several steps are required to produce a shirt, each job is broken down into its component parts—that is, into a set of tasks to be completed by a series of individuals or machines. One person, for example, cuts material for the shirt body, another cuts material for the sleeves, and a third cuts material for the collar. Components are then shipped to a sewing room, where a fourth person assembles the shirt. In the final stage, a fifth person sews on the buttons.[2]

Specialization and Growth

In a very small organization, the owner may perform every job. As the firm grows, however, so does the need to specialize jobs so that others can perform them. To see how specialization can evolve in an organization, consider the case of Mrs. Fields Cookies. When Debbi Fields opened her first store, she did everything herself: bought the equipment, negotiated the lease, baked the cookies, operated the store, and kept the records. As the business grew, however, Fields found that her job was becoming too much for one person. She first hired a bookkeeper to

Whether they are produced manually or digitally, the drawings that comprise a full-length Nelvana cartoon are the result of highly coordinated job specialization. A lead animator, for example, may provide a rough pencil sketch that is then refined by one or more artists. Other teams scan clean drawings into a computer and colour them according to a plan devised by the art director. Finally, to achieve hand-drawn movement, a team of so-called "in-betweeners" completes all the drawings needed to give fluid motion to one or two key frames drawn by the lead animator.

Mrs. Fields Cookies
www.mrsfields.com

handle her financial records. She then hired an in-store manager and a cookie baker. She herself concentrated on advertising and promotions. Her second store required another set of employees—another manager, another baker, and some salespeople. While Fields focused her attention on other expansion opportunities, she turned promotions over to a professional advertising director. Thus the job that she once did all by herself was increasingly broken down into components and assigned to different individuals.

Job specialization is a natural part of organizational growth. It is neither a new idea nor limited to factory work. In the ancient art of winemaking, for example, a high degree of specialization has existed for centuries. The activities necessary to make wine—picking and crushing grapes, fermenting the juice, aging and clarifying the wine, and selling it through specialized intermediaries—are performed by individuals with years of experience.

Job specialization carries with it certain advantages—individual jobs can be performed more efficiently, the jobs are easier to learn, and it is easier to replace people who leave the organization. On the other hand, if job specialization is carried too far and jobs become too narrowly defined, people get bored, derive less satisfaction from their jobs, and often lose sight of how their contributions fit into the overall organization.

Departmentalization

departmentalization
The process of grouping jobs into logical units.

After jobs are specialized, they must be grouped into logical units. This process is called **departmentalization**. Departmentalized companies benefit from the division of activities. Control and coordination are narrowed and made easier, and top managers can see more easily how various units are performing.

profit centre
A separate company unit responsible for its own costs and profits.

For example, departmentalization allows the firm to treat a department as a **profit centre**—a separate unit responsible for its own costs and profits. Thus, by assessing profits from sales in a particular area—for example, men's clothing—Sears can decide whether to expand or curtail promotions in that area.

In an effort to improve competitiveness, Lucent Technologies, the world's largest telephone equipment maker, recently created four new departments. These departments represent activities that have grown so large within existing departmental arrangements that they now warrant separate units. One department will focus on optical networking, another on wireless communication, a third on semiconductor operations, and a fourth on Lucent's e-business initiatives. Lucent managers believe that these new departments will sharpen the company's focus on these four high-growth areas.[3] "This new organization," explains one Lucent executive, "will allow Lucent to move forward in a more aggressive and flexible way as we continue to expand into new markets."

Lucent Technologies
www.lucent.com

Managers do not group jobs randomly. They group them logically, according to some common thread or purpose. In general, departmentalization may occur along *customer, product, process, geographic,* or *functional* lines (or any combination of these).

The Bay
www.hbc.com/bay

customer departmentalization
Departmentalization according to the types of customers likely to buy a given product.

Customer Departmentalization

Stores like Sears and The Bay are divided into departments—a men's department, a women's department, a luggage department, and so on. Each department targets a specific customer category (men, women, people who want to buy luggage). **Customer departmentalization** makes shopping easier by providing identifiable store segments. Thus, a customer shopping for a baby's playpen can bypass Lawn and Garden Supplies and head straight for Children's Furniture. Stores can also group products in locations designated for deliveries, special sales, and other service-oriented purposes. In general, the store is more efficient and customers get better service—in part because salespeople tend to specialize and gain expertise in their departments.[4]

Product Departmentalization

Both manufacturers and service providers often opt for **product depart-mentalization**—dividing an organization according to the specific product or service being created. A bank, for example, may handle consumer loans in one department and commercial loans in another. On a larger scale, 3M Corp., which makes both consumer and industrial products, operates different divisions for Post-it brand tape flags, Scotch-Brite scrub sponges, and the Sarns 9000 perfusion system for open-heart surgery.

product departmentalization
Departmentalization according to the products being created.

3M Corp.
www.3m.com

Process Departmentalization

Other manufacturers favour **process departmentalization**, in which the organization is divided according to production processes. This principle, for example, is logical for the pickle maker Vlasic, which has separate departments to transform cucumbers into fresh-packed pickles, pickles cured in brine, and relishes. Cucumbers destined to become fresh-packed pickles must be packed into jars immediately, covered with a solution of water and vinegar, and prepared for sale. Those slated for brined pickles must be aged in brine solution before packing. Relish cucumbers must be minced and combined with a host of other ingredients. Each process requires different equipment and worker skills.

process departmentalization
Departmentalization according to the production process used to create a good or service.

Geographic Departmentalization

Some firms may be divided according to the area of the country—or even the world—they serve. This is known as **geographic departmentalization**. The Personal Services division of Montreal Trust, for example, is organized around four regions—Atlantic, Quebec, Central, and BC/Western.

geographic departmentalization
Departmentalization according to the area of the country or world supplied.

Many department stores are departmentalized by product. Concentrating different products in different areas of the store makes shopping easier for customers.

Functional Departmentalization

Many service and manufacturing companies develop departments according to a group's functions or activities—a form of organization known as **functional departmentalization**. Such firms typically have production, marketing and sales, human resource, and accounting and finance departments. Departments may be further subdivided. For example, the marketing department might be divided geographically or into separate staffs for market research and advertising.

Because different forms of departmentalization have different advantages, larger companies tend to adopt different types of departmentalization for various levels. For example, the company illustrated in Figure 6.2 uses functional departmentalization at the top level. At the middle level, production is divided along geographic lines. At a lower level, departmentalization is based on product groups.

ESTABLISHING THE DECISION-MAKING HIERARCHY

A major question that must be asked about any organization is this: *Who makes which decisions?* The answer almost never focuses on an individual or even on a small group. The more accurate answer usually refers to the decision-making hierarchy. The development of this hierarchy generally results from a three-step process:

1. *Assigning tasks*: determining who can make decisions and specifying how they should be made

2. *Performing tasks*: implementing decisions that have been made

3. *Distributing authority*: determining whether the organization is to be centralized or decentralized

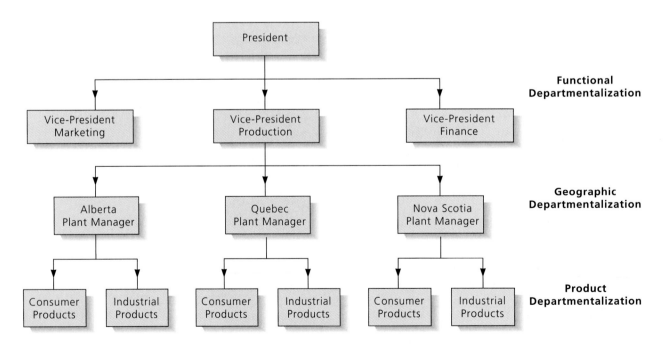

Figure 6.2
Most organizations use multiple bases of departmentalization. This organization, for example, is using functional, geographic, and product departmentalization.

Assigning Tasks

The question of who is supposed to do what and who is entitled to do what in an organization is complex. In any company with more than one person, individuals must work out agreements about responsibilities and authority. **Responsibility** is the duty to perform an assigned task. **Authority** is the power to make the decisions necessary to complete the task.

For example, imagine a mid-level buyer for The Bay who encounters an unexpected opportunity to make a large purchase at an extremely good price. Let's assume that an immediate decision is absolutely necessary—a decision that this buyer has no authority to make without confirmation from above. The company's policies on delegation and authority are inconsistent, since the buyer is responsible for purchasing the clothes that will be sold in the upcoming season but lacks the authority to make the needed purchases.

responsibility
The duty to perform an assigned task.

authority
The power to make the decisions necessary to complete a task.

Performing Tasks

Trouble occurs when appropriate levels of responsibility and authority are not clearly spelled out in the working relationships between managers and subordinates. Here, the issues become delegation and accountability. **Delegation** begins when a manager assigns a task to a subordinate. **Accountability** falls to the subordinate, who must then complete the task. If the subordinate does not perform the assigned task properly and promptly, he or she may be reprimanded or punished, possibly even dismissed.

Subordinates sometimes cannot complete a task because their managers have not also delegated the necessary authority. Such employees face a dilemma: they cannot do what the boss demands, but that boss will probably still hold them accountable. Successful managers surround themselves with a team of strong subordinates and then delegate sufficient authority to those subordinates to get the job done.

Experts pinpoint certain reasons why some small business managers may have trouble delegating effectively:

delegation
Assignment of a task, a responsibility, or authority by a manager to a subordinate.

accountability
Liability of subordinates for accomplishing tasks assigned by managers.

■ The feeling that employees can never do anything as well as they can

■ The fear that something will go wrong if someone else takes over a job

■ The lack of time for long-range planning because they are bogged down in day-to-day operations

■ The sense of being in the dark about industry trends and competitive products because of the time they devote to day-to-day operations

To overcome these tendencies, small business owners must admit that they can never go back to running all aspects of the business and that they can, in fact, prosper—with the help of their employees—if they learn to let go. But this problem isn't always confined to small businesses. Some managers in big companies also don't delegate as much or as well as they should. There are several reasons for this problem:

■ The fear that subordinates don't really know how to do the job

■ The fear that a subordinate might "show the manager up" in front of others by doing a superb job

■ The desire to keep as much control as possible over how things are done

■ A simple lack of ability as to how to effectively delegate to others

The remedies in these instances are a bit different. First, managers should recognize that they cannot do everything themselves. Second, if subordinates cannot do a job, they should be trained so that they can assume more responsibility in the future. Third, managers should recognize that if a subordinate performs well, it reflects favourably on that employee's manager. Finally, a manager who simply does not know how to delegate might need specialized training in how to divide up and assign tasks to others.

Distributing Authority

centralization

Occurs when top managers retain most decision-making rights for themselves.

decentralization

Occurs when lower- and middle-level managers are allowed to make significant decisions.

In every organization, management must decide how to distribute authority throughout the hierarchy. **Centralization** occurs when top management retains the right to make most decisions that need to be made. In a highly centralized organization, the CEO makes most of the decisions, and subordinates simply carry them out. For example, Cedric Ritchie, the CEO of the Bank of Nova Scotia, knew all the details of the bank's operations and made many decisions that CEOs of other banks delegated to subordinates.[5]

Decentralization occurs when top managers delegate the right to make decisions to the middle and lower levels of the management hierarchy. At General Electric's Bromont, Quebec, plant, for example, every effort has been made to involve employees in a wide range of decision making.[6] Traditional jobs like supervisor and foreman do not exist at the plant, and all hiring is done by committees made up of workers. Some workers spend only 65 percent of their time on production work; the other 35 percent is spent on training, planning, and in meetings. At Hymac Ltée., a Laval, Quebec, producer of pulp processing machinery, managers encourage employees to meet with customers to determine how Hymac can serve them more effectively.[7]

Tall and Flat Organizations

Related to the concept of centralized or decentralized authority is the concept of tall or flat organizational structures. With relatively fewer layers of

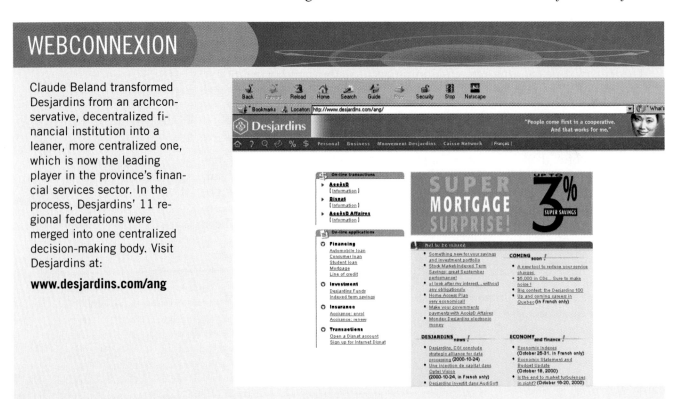

WEBCONNEXION

Claude Beland transformed Desjardins from an archconservative, decentralized financial institution into a leaner, more centralized one, which is now the leading player in the province's financial services sector. In the process, Desjardins' 11 regional federations were merged into one centralized decision-making body. Visit Desjardins at:

www.desjardins.com/ang

management, decentralized firms tend to have a **flat organizational structure** such as the one shown in Figure 6.3. In contrast, companies with centralized authority systems typically require multiple layers of management and thus have a **tall organizational structure**. The Canadian Forces is an example of such an organization. Because information, whether upward or downward bound, must pass through so many organizational layers, tall structures are prone to delays in information flow.

Of course, as organizations grow in size it is both normal and necessary that they become at least somewhat taller. For instance, a small firm with only an owner-manager and a few employees is likely to have two layers—the owner-manager and the employees who report to that person. But as the firm grows, more layers will be needed. Born Information Services, for instance, is a small consulting firm created and run by Rick Born. At first, all employees reported to him. But when his firm grew to more than 20 people, he knew he needed help in supervising and coordinating projects.

flat organizational structure
An organization with relatively few layers of management.

tall organizational structure
An organization with many layers of management.

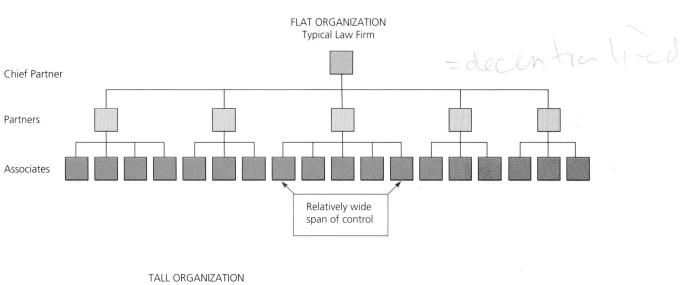

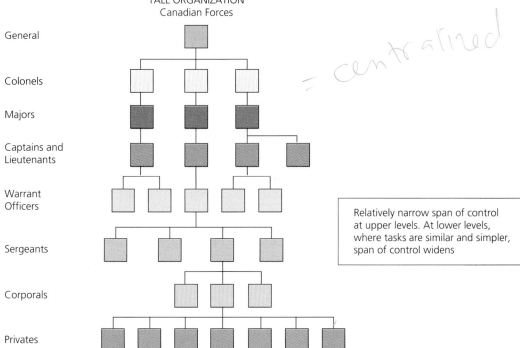

Figure 6.3
Organizational structure and span of control.

As a result, he added a layer of management consisting of what he called "staff managers" to serve as project coordinators. This move freed him up to seek new business clients.[8] Like other managers, however, Born must ensure that he has only the number of layers his firm needs. Too few layers can create chaos and inefficiency, while too many layers can create rigidity and bureaucracy.

Span of Control

span of control
The number of people managed by one manager.

The number of people managed by one supervisor is called the **span of control**. Employees' abilities and the supervisor's managerial skills help determine whether the span of control is wide or narrow. So do the similarity and simplicity of tasks performed under the manager's supervision and the extent to which they are interrelated. For example, by eliminating two layers of management, the president of the Franklin Mint recently increased his own span of control from 6 to 12.

When several employees perform either the same simple task or a group of interrelated tasks, a wide span of control is possible and often desirable. For instance, because all of the jobs are routine, one supervisor may well control an entire assembly line. Moreover, each task depends on another: if one station stops, everyone stops. Having one supervisor ensures that all stations receive equal attention and function equally well. In contrast, when jobs are not routine, or when they are prone to change, a narrow span of control is preferable.

Three Forms of Authority

In an organization, it must be clear who will have authority over whom. As individuals are delegated responsibility and authority in a firm, a complex web of interactions develops. These interactions may take one of three forms of authority: *line*, *staff*, or *committee and team*. In reality, like departmentalization, all three forms may be found in a given company, especially a large one.

Line Authority

line authority
An organizational structure in which authority flows in a direct chain of command from the top of the company to the bottom.

line department
A department directly linked to the production and sales of a specific product.

Line authority is authority that flows up and down the chain of command (refer back to Figure 6.1 on page 168). Most companies rely heavily on **line departments**—departments directly linked to the production and sales of specific products. For example, Clark Equipment Corp. has a division that produces forklifts and small earthmovers. In this division, line departments include purchasing, materials handling, fabrication, painting, and assembly (all of which are directly linked to production) along with sales and distribution (both of which are directly linked to sales).

Each line department is essential to an organization's success. Line employees are the "doers" and producers in a company. If any line department fails to complete its task, the company cannot sell and deliver finished goods. Thus, the authority delegated to line departments is important. A bad decision by the manager in one department can hold up production for an entire plant. For example, say that the painting department manager at Clark Equipment changes a paint application on a batch of forklifts, which then show signs of peeling paint. The batch will have to be repainted (and perhaps partially reassembled) before the machines can be shipped.

Staff Authority

staff authority
Authority that is based on expertise and that usually involves advising line managers.

Most companies also rely on **staff authority**. Staff authority is based on special expertise and usually involves counselling and advising line managers.

Common **staff members** include specialists in areas such as law, accounting, and human resource management. A corporate attorney, for example, may be asked to advise the marketing department as it prepares a new contract with the firm's advertising agency. Legal staff, however, do not actually make decisions that affect how the marketing department does its job. Staff members, therefore, aid line departments in making decisions but do not have the authority to make final decisions.

Suppose, for example, that the fabrication department at Clark Equipment has an employee with a drinking problem. The manager of the department could consult a human resource staff expert for advice on handling the situation. The staff expert might suggest that the worker stay on the job but enter a counselling program. But if the line manager decides that the job is too dangerous to be handled by a person whose judgment is often impaired by alcohol, that decision will most likely prevail.

Typically, the separation between line authority and staff responsibility is clearly delineated. As Figure 6.4 shows, this separation is usually shown in organization charts by solid lines (line authority) and dotted lines (staff responsibility). It may help to understand this separation by remembering that while staff members generally provide services to management, line managers are directly involved in producing the firm's products.

Committee and Team Authority

Recently, more and more organizations have started to use **committee and team authority**—authority granted to committees or work teams that play central roles in the firm's daily operations. A committee, for example, may consist of top managers from several major areas. If the work of the committee is especially important, and if the committee will be working together for an extended time, the organization may even grant it special authority as a decision-making body that goes beyond the individual authority possessed by each of its members.

At the operating level, many firms today are also using *work teams*—groups of operating employees empowered to plan and organize their own work and to perform that work with a minimum of supervision. As with

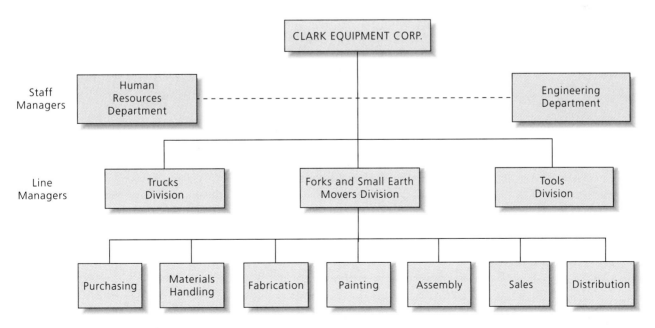

Figure 6.4
Line-and-staff organization: Clark Equipment Corp.

Business firms are increasingly using work teams and allowing groups of employees to plan and organize their own work with a minimum of supervision. This contributes to employee empowerment.

permanent committees, the organization will usually find it beneficial to grant special authority to work teams so that they may function more effectively.[9]

BASIC ORGANIZATIONAL STRUCTURES

A glance at the organization charts of many organizations reveals what appears to be an infinite variety of structures. However, closer examination shows that it is possible to identify four basic forms: functional, divisional, project, and international. These structures are described below.

The Functional Structure

functional structure

Various units are included in a group based on functions that need to be performed for the organization to reach its goals.

The functional structure is the oldest and most commonly used. In the **functional structure**, the various units in the organization are formed based on the functions that must be carried out to reach organizational goals. The functional structure makes use of departmentalization by function. An example of a functional structure is shown in Figure 6.1 (see page 168). The advantages and disadvantages of the functional structure are summarized in Table 6.1.

The Divisional Structure

divisional structure

Divides the organization into divisions, each of which operates as a semi-autonomous unit.

The functional structure's disadvantages can make it inappropriate for some companies. Many companies have found that the divisional structure is more suited to their needs. The **divisional structure** divides the organization into several divisions, each of which operates as a semi-autonomous unit and profit centre. Divisions in organizations can be based on products, customers,

Table 6.1	Advantages and Disadvantages of a Functional Structure
Advantages	**Disadvantages**
1. Focuses attention on the key activities that must be performed.	1. Conflicts may arise among the functional areas.
2. Expertise develops within each function.	2. No single function is responsible for overall organizational performance.
3. Employees have clearly defined career paths.	3. Employees in each functional area have a narrow view of the organization.
4. The structure is simple and easy to understand.	4. Decision making is slowed because functional areas must get approval from top management for a variety of decisions.
5. Eliminates duplication of activities.	5. Coordinating highly specialized functions may be difficult.

or geography. Whatever basis is used, divisional performance can be easily assessed each year because the division operates as a separate company. Firms with this structure are often called *conglomerates*.

H.J. Heinz, for example, is one of the world's largest food-processing companies. Heinz makes thousands of different products and markets them around the world. The firm is organized into seven basic divisions: food service (selling small packaged products such as mustard and relish to restaurants), infant foods, condiments (Heinz ketchup, steak sauce, and tomato sauce), Star-Kist tuna, pet foods, frozen foods, and miscellaneous products, including both new lines being test-marketed and soups, beans, and pasta products. Because of its divisional structure, Heinz can evaluate the performance of each division independently. Until recently, for example, Heinz also had a division for its Weight Watchers business. But because this business was performing poorly, the company sold the Weight Watchers classroom program and folded its line of frozen foods into its existing frozen-foods division.[10] Because divisions are relatively autonomous, a firm can take such action with minimal disruption to its remaining business operations.

Like Heinz, other divisionalized companies are free to buy, sell, create, and disband divisions without disrupting the rest of their operations. Divisions can maintain healthy competition among themselves by sponsoring separate advertising campaigns, fostering different corporate identities, and so forth. They can also share certain corporate-level resources (such as market research data). Of course, if too much control is delegated to divisional managers, corporate managers may lose touch with daily operations. Competition between divisions has also been known to become disruptive, and efforts of one division may be duplicated by those of another.

The advantages and disadvantages of the divisional structure are summarized in Table 6.2.

Project Organization

A typical line or line-staff organization is characterized by unchanging vertical authority relationships. It has such a setup because the organization produces a product or service in a repetitive and predictable way. Procter & Gamble, for example, produces millions of tubes of Crest toothpaste each year using standardized production methods. The company has done this for years and intends to do so indefinitely.

But some organizations find themselves faced with new product opportunities or with projects that have a definite starting and end point. These organizations often use a project structure to deal with the uncertainty encountered in new situations. **Project organization** involves forming a team of specialists from different functional areas of the organization to work on

project organization
An organization that uses teams of specialists to complete specific projects.

Table 6.2	Advantages and Disadvantages of a Divisional Structure	
Advantages	**Disadvantages**
1. Accommodates change and expansion.	1. Activities may be duplicated across divisions.
2. Increases accountability.	2. A lack of communication among divisions may occur.
3. Develops expertise in the various divisions.	3. Adding diverse divisions may blur the focus of the organization.
4. Encourages training for top management.	4. Company politics may affect the allocation of resources.

Hydro-Québec
www.hydro.qc.ca

Manitoba Hydro
www.hydro.mb.ca

---

matrix organization

A project structure in which the project manager and the regular line managers share authority until the project is concluded.

---

international organizational structure

An organizational structure that is designed to help a company succeed in international markets. International departments, international divisions, or an integrated global organization are all variations of the international organizational structure.

a specific project.[11] A project structure may be temporary or permanent; if it is temporary, the project team disbands once the project is completed and team members return to their regular functional area or are assigned to a new project.

Project organization is used extensively by Canadian firms, for example, in the construction of hydroelectric generating stations like those developed by Hydro-Québec on La Grande River, and by Manitoba Hydro on the Nelson River. Once the generating station is complete, it becomes part of the traditional structure of the utility. Project organization is also used at Genstar Shipyards Ltd. in Vancouver. Each ship that is built is treated as a project and supervised by a project manager; the project manager for a given ship is responsible for ensuring that the ship is completed on time and within budget.[12] Project organization has also proven useful for coordinating the many elements needed to extract oil from the tar sands. Project management is also used in other kinds of tasks, including shipbuilding, construction, military weapons, aerospace, and health care delivery.[13]

Some companies use a **matrix organization**, which is a variation of project structure in which the project manager and the regular line managers share authority. When a project is concluded, the matrix is disbanded. Ford, for example, uses a matrix organization to design new models, such as the Ford Thunderbird that was launched in 2001. A design team composed of people from engineering, marketing, operations, and finance was created to design the new car. After the team's work was done, team members moved back to their permanent functional jobs.

A problem with the matrix structure is that employees have two bosses—their regular line boss *and* the project manager. Employees may therefore receive conflicting orders. These and other problems have caused some firms that used to like the matrix structure to move away from it. For example, Digital Equipment Company's president, Robert Palmer, announced in 1994 that "matrix management at our company is dead."[14]

International Organization

As we saw in Chapter 3, many businesses today manufacture, purchase, and sell in the world market. Thus, several different **international organizational structures** have emerged. Moreover, as competition on a global scale becomes more complex, companies often find that they must experiment with the ways in which they respond.

For example, when Wal-Mart opened its first store outside the United States in 1992, it set up a special projects team to handle the logistics. As more stores were opened abroad in the mid-1990s, the firm created a small international department to handle overseas expansion. By 1999, however, international sales and expansion had become such a major part of Wal-Mart's operations that the firm created a separate international division headed up by a senior vice-president. Interestingly, Wal-Mart now envisions the day when this separate division may no longer be needed, simply because international operations will have become so thoroughly integrated in the firm's overall business.

Wal-Mart typifies the form of organization outlined in Figure 6.5. Other firms have also developed a wide range of approaches to international organizational structure. The French food giant Danone Group, for instance, has three major product groups: dairy products (Danone yogurt), bottled water (Evian), and cookies (Pim's). Danone's structure does not differentiate internationally, but rather integrates global operations within each product group.[15] In contrast, U.S. entertainment companies are finding it advantageous to create more local identity when they enter foreign markets. For in-

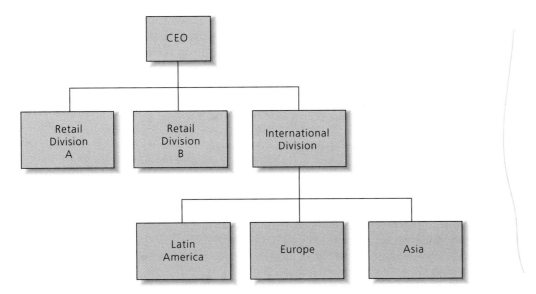

Figure 6.5
International division structure.

stance, Columbia TriStar, known for such U.S. television programs as *Seinfeld* and *Mad About You*, recently launched *Chinese Restaurant*, a sitcom filmed and shown only in China. Universal and HBO are also getting in on the act by setting up new television-production businesses in Germany and Japan.[16]

Finally, some companies adopt a truly global structure in which they acquire resources (including capital), produce goods and services, engage in research and development, and sell products in whatever local market is appropriate, without any consideration of national boundaries. Until a few years ago, for example, General Electric kept its international business operations as separate divisions. Now, however, the company functions as one integrated global organization. GE businesses around the world connect and interact with each other constantly, and managers freely move back and forth among them. This integration is also reflected in the top management team: the head of its audit team is French, the head of quality control is Dutch, and a German runs one of GE's core business groups.[17]

ORGANIZATIONAL DESIGN FOR THE TWENTY-FIRST CENTURY

As the world grows increasingly complex and fast paced, organizations continue to seek new forms of organization that permit them to compete effectively. Among the most popular of these new forms are the *boundaryless organization*, the *team organization*, the *virtual organization*, and the *learning organization*.

Boundaryless Organization

The *boundaryless organization* is one in which traditional boundaries and structures are minimized or eliminated altogether. For example, General Electric's fluid organization structure, in which people, ideas, and information flow freely between businesses and business groups, approximates this concept. Similarly, as firms partner with their suppliers in more efficient ways, external boundaries disappear. Some of Wal-Mart's key suppliers are tied directly into the retailer's vaunted information system. As a result, when Wal-Mart distribution centres start running low on, say, Wrangler blue jeans, the manufacturer receives the information as soon as the retailer. Wrangler proceeds to manufacture new inventory and restock the distribution centre without Wal-Mart having to place a new order.

Team Organization

Team organization relies almost exclusively on project-type teams, with little or no underlying functional hierarchy. People "float" from project to project as dictated by their skills and the demands of those projects. At Cypress Semiconductor, units or groups that become large are simply split into smaller units. Not surprisingly, the organization is composed entirely of small units. This strategy allows each unit to change direction, explore new ideas, and try new methods without having to deal with a rigid bureaucratic superstructure. Although few large organizations have actually reached this level of adaptability, Apple Computer and Xerox are among those moving towards it.

Virtual Organization

Closely related to the team organization is the virtual organization. A *virtual organization* has little or no formal structure. Typically, it has only a handful of permanent employees, a very small staff, and a modest administrative facility. As the needs of the organization change, its managers bring in temporary workers, lease facilities, and outsource basic support services to meet the demands of each unique situation. As the situation changes, the temporary workforce changes in parallel, with some people leaving the organization and others entering it. Facilities and subcontracted services also change. In other words, the virtual organization exists only in response to its own needs.

Global Research Consortium (GRC) is a virtual organization. GRC offers research and consulting services to firms doing business in Asia. As clients request various services, GRC's staff of three permanent employees subcontracts the work to an appropriate set of several dozen independent consultants and/or researchers with whom it has relationships. At any given time, therefore, GRC may have several projects underway and 20 or 30 people working on various projects. As the projects change, so too does the composition of the organization. Figure 6.6 illustrates a hypothetical virtual organization.

Learning Organization

The so-called *learning organization* works to integrate continuous improvement with continuous employee learning and development. Specifically, a learning organization works to facilitate the lifelong learning and personal development of all of its employees while continually transforming itself to respond to changing demands and needs.

While managers might approach the concept of a learning organization from a variety of perspectives, the most frequent goals are improved quality, continuous improvement, and performance measurement. The idea is that the most consistent and logical strategy for achieving continuous

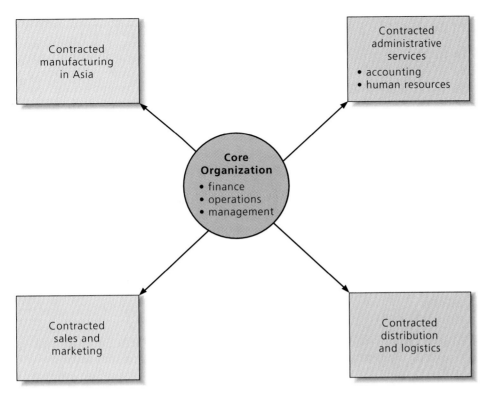

Figure 6.6
A virtual organization.

improvement is constantly upgrading employee talent, skill, and knowledge. For example, if each employee in an organization learns one new thing each day and can translate that knowledge into work-related practice, continuous improvement will logically follow. Indeed, organizations that wholeheartedly embrace this approach believe that only through constant employee learning can continuous improvement really occur.

In recent years, many different organizations have implemented this approach on various levels. Shell Oil Co., for example, recently purchased an executive conference centre called the Shell Learning Center. The facility boasts state-of-the-art classrooms and instructional technology, lodging facilities, a restaurant, and recreational amenities, such as a golf course, swimming pool, and tennis courts. Line managers at the firm rotate through the centre and serve as teaching faculty. Teaching assignments last anywhere from a few days to several months. At the same time, all Shell employees routinely attend training programs, seminars, and related activities, all the while gathering the latest information they need to contribute more effectively to the firm. Recent seminar topics have included time management, balancing work and family demands, and international trade theory.

THE INFORMAL ORGANIZATION

Much of our discussion so far has focused on the organization's *formal* structure—its "official" arrangement of jobs and job relationships. In reality, however, all organizations also have another dimension—an *informal* organization within which people do their jobs in different ways and interact with other people in ways that do not follow formal lines of communication.

Formal versus Informal Organizational Systems

The formal organization of a business is the part that can be seen and represented in chart form. The structure of a company, however, is by no means limited to the organization chart and the formal assignment of authority. Frequently, the **informal organization**—everyday social interactions among employees that transcend formal jobs and job interrelationships—effectively alters a company's formal structure. Indeed, this level of organization is sometimes just as powerful, if not more powerful, than the formal structure.

On the negative side, the informal organization can reinforce office politics that put the interests of individuals ahead of those of the firm. Likewise, a great deal of harm can be caused by distorted or inaccurate information communicated without management input or review. For example, if the informal organization is highlighting false information about impending layoffs, valuable employees may act quickly (and unnecessarily) to seek other employment. Among the more important elements of the informal organization are *informal groups* and the *organizational grapevine*.

informal organization

A network of personal interactions and relationships among employees unrelated to the firm's formal authority structure.

Informal Groups

Informal groups are simply groups of people who decide to interact among themselves. They may be people who work together in a formal sense or who simply get together for lunch, during breaks, or after work. They may talk about business, the boss, or nonwork-related topics such as families, movies, or sports. For example, at the New York Metropolitan Opera, musicians and singers play poker during the intermissions. Most pots are in the $30 to $40 range. Luciano Pavarotti, the famed tenor, once played and lost big. The impact of informal groups on the organization may be positive (if they work together to support the organization), negative (if they work together in ways that run counter to the organization's interests), or neutral (if what they do is unrelated to the organization).

Organizational Grapevine

grapevine

An informal communications network that carries gossip and other information throughout an organization.

The **grapevine** is an informal communication network that can run through an entire organization.[18] Grapevines are found in all organizations except the very smallest, but they do not always follow the same patterns as formal channels of authority and communication, nor do they necessarily coincide with them. The Internet is a worldwide grapevine. Formerly, when people gathered around the water cooler or on the golf course to exchange gossip and pass on information, they had names and faces. But with the Internet, you may not know who you are talking to and how reliable the person is who is providing the information.[19]

Because the grapevine typically passes information orally, messages often become distorted in the process. Attempts to eliminate the grapevine are fruitless, but managers do have some control over it. By maintaining open channels of communication and responding vigorously to inaccurate information, they can minimize the damage the grapevine can do. In fact, the grapevine can actually be an asset. By getting to know the key people in the grapevine, for example, the manager can partially control the information they receive and use the grapevine to determine employee reactions to new ideas (e.g., a change in human resource policies or benefit packages). The manager can also receive valuable information from the grapevine and use it to improve decision making. The "Business Today" box provides more information on this important feature of organizations.

The grapevine is a powerful informal communications network in most organizations. These workers may be talking about any number of things—an upcoming deadline on an important project, tonight's football game, the stock market, rumours about an impending takeover, gossip about forthcoming promotions, or the weather.

BUSINESS TODAY

Heard It Through the Grapevine

Faster than a speeding bullet—that's the office grapevine. But how accurate is it? Should you listen to it, or is it just so much gossip?

Today many experts advise tuning in to the grapevine's message. They note that the grapevine is often a corporate early warning system. Ignoring this valuable source of information can leave you the last to know that you're about to get a new boss, or that you have a potentially fatal image problem. Even personal information about co-workers and superiors can be useful in helping you interact positively with these individuals.

Do consider both the source and the message carefully, though. Most office gossip has at least some kernel of truth to it. But as "facts" are passed down from person to person, they can get twisted out of shape. In other cases, those passing on news will deliberately alter it, either to advance their own goals or to submarine someone else's chances. Experts also warn that listening to and passing on information damaging to someone's reputation can backfire, harming your credibility and making you a target for similar gossip.

In general, the more detailed the information, the less likely it is to be true. Likewise, beware the hush-hush "don't quote me on this" rumour. (Cynics claim that the better the news, the less likely it is to be true, too.) The higher the source, the greater the likelihood that the grapevine has the real story. Don't reject information from "lower" sources, however. Many an executive assistant can provide valuable insights into a corporation's plans.

An interesting phenomenon of office communication occurs when individuals responsible for formal information systems, such as newsletters, press briefings, and memoranda, spread a somewhat different story on the grapevine. Which should you believe? Today it is so common for a corporate executive to publicly deny rumours of layoffs one day and hand out pink slips the next that no one even raises an eyebrow. The grapevine, unconcerned with public image and long-range schemes, cuts to the heart of the matter.

The grapevine is not infallible, however. In addition to miscommunication and attempts by some people to manipulate it for their own ends, it may carry rumours with absolutely no basis in fact. Such rumours are most common when there is a complete lack of information. Apparently, human nature abhors such a vacuum and fills it. Baseless rumours can be very hard to kill, however.

Intrapreneuring

Sometimes organizations actually take steps to encourage the informal organization. They do so for a variety of reasons, two of which we have already discussed. First, most experienced managers recognize that the informal organization exists whether they want it or not. Second, many managers know how to use the informal organization to reinforce the formal organization. Perhaps more important, however, the energy of the informal organization can be harnessed to improve productivity.

intrapreneuring
The process of creating and maintaining the innovation and flexibility of a small business environment within the confines of a large organization.

Many firms, including Compaq Computer, Rubbermaid, 3M, and Xerox, are supporting a process called **intrapreneuring**: creating and maintaining the innovation and flexibility of a small-business environment within the confines of a large, bureaucratic structure. The concept is basically sound. Historically, most innovations have come from individuals in small businesses (see Chapter 7). As businesses increase in size, however, innovation and creativity tend to become casualties in the battle for higher sales and profits. In some large companies, new ideas are even discouraged, and champions of innovation have been stalled in mid-career.

Compaq is an excellent example of how intrapreneuring works to counteract this trend. The firm has one major division called the New Business Group. When a manager or engineer has an idea for a new product or product application, he or she takes it to the New Business Group and "sells" it. The managers in the group are then encouraged to help the innovator develop the idea for field testing. If the product takes off and does well, it is then spun off into its own business group or division. If it doesn't do as well as hoped, it may be maintained as part of the New Business Group or phased out.

SUMMARY OF LEARNING OBJECTIVES

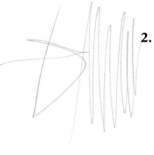

1. **Discuss the elements that influence a firm's *organizational structure*.** Every business needs structure to operate. *Organizational structure* varies according to a firm's mission, purpose, and strategy. Size, technology, and changes in environmental circumstances also influence structure. In general, while all organizations have the same basic elements, each develops the structure that contributes to the most efficient operations.

2. **Describe *specialization* and *departmentalization* as the building blocks of organizational structure.** The building blocks of organizational structure are *job specialization* and *departmentalization*. As a firm grows, it usually has a greater need for people to perform specialized tasks (specialization). It also has a greater need to group types of work into logical units (departmentalization). Common forms of departmentalization are *customer, product, process, geographic,* and *functional*. Large businesses often use more than one form of departmentalization.

3. **Distinguish between *responsibility* and *authority* and explain the differences in decision making in *centralized* and *decentralized organizations*.** *Responsibility* is the duty to perform a task; *authority* is the power to make the decisions necessary to complete tasks. *Delegation* begins when a manager assigns a task to a subordinate; *accountability* means that the subordinate must complete the task. *Span of control* refers to the number of people who work for any individual manager. The more people supervised by

a manager, the wider his or her span of control. Wide spans are usually desirable when employees perform simple or unrelated tasks. When jobs are diversified or prone to change, a narrower span is generally preferable.

In a *centralized organization*, only a few individuals in top management have real decision-making authority. In a *decentralized organization*, much authority is delegated to lower-level management. Where both *line* and *line-and-staff systems* are involved, *line departments* generally have authority to make decisions while *staff departments* have a responsibility to advise. A relatively new concept, *committee and team authority*, empowers committees or work teams involved in a firm's daily operations.

4. **Explain the differences between** *functional, divisional, project,* **and** *international organization structures.* In a *functional organization*, authority is usually distributed among such basic functions as marketing and finance. In a *divisional organization*, the various divisions of a larger company, which may be related or unrelated, operate in a relatively autonomous fashion. In *project organization*, in which individuals report to more than one manager, a company creates teams to address specific problems or to conduct specific projects. A company that has divisions in many countries may require an additional level of *international organization* to coordinate those operations.

5. **Define the** *informal organization* **and discuss** *intrapreneuring.* The informal organization consists of the everyday social interactions among employees that transcend formal jobs and job interrelationships. To foster innovation and flexibility, some large companies encourage *intrapreneuring*— creating and maintaining the innovation and flexibility of a small business environment within the confines of a large bureaucratic structure.

KEY TERMS

organizational structure, 166
organization chart, 167
chain of command, 169
job specialization, 169
departmentalization, 170
profit centre, 170
customer department-
  alization, 170
product department-
  alization, 171
process department-
  alization, 171

geographic department-
  alization, 171
functional department-
  alization, 172
responsibility, 173
authority, 173
delegation, 173
accountability, 173
centralization, 174
decentralization, 174
flat organizational
  structure, 175

tall organizational
  structure, 175
span of control, 176
line authority, 176
line department, 176
staff authority, 176
staff members, 177
committee and team
  authority, 177
functional structure,
  178

divisional structure, 178
project organization,
  179
matrix organization, 180
international
  organizational
  structure, 180
informal organization,
  184
grapevine, 184
intrapreneuring, 186

STUDY QUESTIONS AND EXERCISES

Review Questions
1. What is an organization chart? What purpose does it serve?
2. Explain the significance of size as it relates to organizational structure. Describe the changes that are likely to occur as an organization grows.

3. What is the difference between responsibility and authority?
4. Why do some managers have difficulties in delegating authority? Why does this problem tend to plague smaller businesses?
5. Why is a company's informal organization important?

Analysis Questions

6. Draw up an organization chart for your college or university.
7. Describe a hypothetical organizational structure for a small printing firm. Describe changes that might be necessary as the business grows.
8. Compare the matrix and divisional approaches to organizational structure. How would you feel about working in a matrix organization in which you were assigned simultaneously to multiple units or groups?

Application Exercises

9. Interview the manager of a local service business—for example, a fast-food restaurant. What types of tasks does this manager typically delegate? Is the appropriate authority also delegated in each case?
10. Using books, magazines, or personal interviews, identify a person who has succeeded as an intrapreneur. In what ways did the structure of the intrapreneur's company help this individual succeed? In what ways did the structure pose problems?

Building Your Business Skills

Getting with the Program

Goal

To encourage students to understand the relationship between organizational structure and a company's ability to attract and retain valued employees.

Situation

You are the founder of a small but growing high-technology company that develops new computer software. With your current workload and new contracts in the pipeline, your business is thriving except for one problem: you cannot find computer programmers for product development. Worse yet, current staff members are being lured away by other high-tech firms. After suffering a particularly discouraging personnel raid in which competitors captured three of your most valued employees, you schedule a meeting with your director of human resources to plan organizational changes designed to encourage worker loyalty. You already pay top dollar, but the continuing exodus tells you that programmers are looking for something more.

Method

Working with three or four classmates, identify some ways in which specific organizational changes might improve the working environment and encourage employee loyalty. As you analyze the following factors, ask yourself the obvious question: If I were a programmer, what organizational changes would encourage me to stay?

- *Level of job specialization.* With many programmers describing their jobs as tedious because of the focus on detail in a narrow work area, what changes, if any, would you make in job specialization? Right now, for instance, few of your programmers have any say in product design.
- *Decision-making hierarchy.* What decision-making authority would encourage people to stay? Is expanding worker authority likely to work better in a centralized or decentralized organization?
- *Team authority.* Can team empowerment make a difference? Taking the point of view of the worker, describe the ideal team.
- *Intrapreneuring.* What can your company do to encourage and reward innovation?

Follow-Up Questions

1. With all competitive firms paying top dollar, why might organizational issues be critical in determining employee loyalty?
2. If you were a programmer, what organizational factors would make a difference to you? Why?
3. As the company founder, how willing would you be to make major organizational changes in light of the shortage of qualified programmers?

Exploring the Net

Chapter 6 describes the increasing importance of intrapreneurship in many organizations today. The following Web site is a useful starting point in learning more about this concept:

www.pinchot.com:80/

Browse this site, and then consider the following questions:

1. Review "The Intrapreneur's Ten Commandments." Do these principles seem reasonable to you? Which would be the most difficult for you personally to adopt?

   • What is your first reaction to the advice that you should "come to work each day willing to be fired"? What is your reaction upon further reflection?

   • If there is one theme that is more insistent than the others in this list, what is it?

2. Take the quiz entitled "Leading Growth Through Innovation Questionnaire." Basing your ideas on these questions, draw up a brief "personality profile" of someone who would make a good intrapreneur. To what extent do you fit this profile?

3. Review the feature entitled "Five People of Innovation" and draw up brief thumbnail sketches to characterize each of the five types described here. In what ways can people from these five groups be expected to work together successfully? In what ways might they encounter difficulties in working together?

4. Study the "Innovation Climate Survey." Judging from the questions asked here, list five important characteristics of a climate that is conducive to innovation in an organization.

Concluding Case 6-1

Construction: Putting the Pieces Together

Construction is among the world's oldest jobs. Ever since they lived in caves, people have been continually crafting newer, bigger, safer, and more functional places to live, work, and play. But if any industry seems tailor-made for the Internet, it just might be construction.

Construction has always been a job that encourages specialization. Very different kinds of skills and expertise, for example, are needed to create a foundation from concrete; erect walls from brick, wood, or steel; build networks of pipes for plumbing and wire for electricity; construct a weather-proof roof; and complete an interior with a high-quality appearance. There are even craft specialists within specialties—building a wall from steel, for example, or a roof from shingles is far different from building a wooden wall or a metal roof.

Putting all these pieces together, then, can be a big and complicated job. Consider just a few of the complexities in building a simple wood-frame house. Shortly after the concrete foundation has been poured and set, a supplier should deliver a load of wooden studs for constructing the frame. If the wood is delivered too early, it may become damaged, scattered, or even stolen. If it comes too late, delays will result. Quantity, of course, is also important. Too much wood means needless cost overruns; too little wood means more delays. The contractor faces the same issues with regards to the framing crew. Crew members need to arrive on a certain day and finish on a certain day. Complicating things even further, of course, is the homeowner. As the project takes shape, he or she may decide to move a wall, add a door, or change the colour of the walls.

Someone has to organize the overall process, ensuring that the right materials in the right quantities and the right people are at the job site at the right time. This individual is generally called the *contractor*. Each of the specialists hired to perform specific tasks required by the overall project—roofers, plumbers, electricians, painters, and so forth—is called a *subcontractor*.

A house like the one we described above will probably need a dozen or more subcontractors. But what about a major construction project—for example, a high-rise building or an office complex? These projects require hundreds of subcontractors working at different times over periods spanning several months or even years. The complexities of organizing such a massive project are significant indeed. And a well-organized project can mean the difference between profit and loss for the contractor.

Until recently, organizing most building projects relied on paper—architects drew up blueprints, contractors drew up schedules, and paperwork flowed freely between contractors and subcontractors as materials were requested and ordered, work was completed and billed, and so forth. But a simple change (e.g., a redesigned doorway) or one delay (e.g., one late order of materials) could have a domino effect on dozens of other subcontractors. On top of everything else, someone had to monitor the project continually, make scheduling and delivery adjustments as needed and then notifying suppliers and subcontractors.

Slowly but surely, Internet technology is creeping into the construction industry. As it does, it's revolutionizing the way contractors and subcontractors work and interact. It's also showing signs of enormous potential for lowering costs, shortening schedules, and improving overall efficiency. Indeed, large construction firms like Turner Corp. and Bechtel Group have begun partnering with such e-commerce companies as Cephren and Bidcom to use Web technology to communicate with suppliers and subcontractors.

Cephren has created a software network that serves as a communication system for the contractors and subcontractors that are working together on a project. Clients pay a start-up fee of $750 and a monthly fee of $1250 to use the Cephren system, plus an initial $1500 training fee. Each part of the construction team receives passwords that allow them access to the facet of the project relevant to its work. Thus a middle manager working at the construction site might need access to blueprints but not to the minutes of the senior management team's last meeting.

While Cephren focuses primarily on organizing construction projects more efficiently, Bidcom focuses on linking contractors and suppliers. Using the Bidcom system, for example, a contractor can put out a call for bids on, say, 100 steel doors or 500 windows, with corresponding specifications and delivery details. Suppliers, meanwhile, can review the call and submit bids directly to the contractor. This overall improvement in efficiency can potentially save thousands of dollars on a big construction project. Now, blueprints can be posted online; each supplier and each subcontractor can review his or her part of the project, including scheduling details, online. E-mail can be sent to everyone involved, work schedules can be issued, and bid requests can be sent to potential suppliers, all with the push of a button or the click of a mouse. The advent of newer hand-held computers is also accelerating change because these devices allow contractors, subcontractors, supervisors, and workers to access information at the construction project.

Of course, not everyone is rushing to this new way of doing business. However, all of the major construction companies are at least taking steps in this direction. Indeed, experts forecast that by 2004 at least 10 percent of all construction-industry business will be conducted online. One major construction firm, WebCor, indicates that in two years it will do business only with subcontractors and suppliers who are able to work online. We may never live and work in virtual buildings, but, increasingly, the construction of bricks-and-mortar facilities is taking place in cyberspace.

CASE QUESTIONS

1. What elements of organizational structure are most relevant to the construction industry?

2. Why do you think some firms are so eager and some are reluctant to adopt this new technology?

3. What new pitfalls might exist for a construction project being managed completely online?

4. Are the organizational effects of new technology more likely to be felt within a given construction company or in the way that construction companies relate to one another? Why?

5. In what ways, if any, might new technology affect the informal organization that exists at a construction site? ◆

Concluding Case 6-2

Jersak Holdings Ltd.

Vaclav Jersak was born in Prague, Czechoslovakia, in 1930. His family had long been active in the retail trade in that city. The Jersak family was very close, but the 1930s and 1940s were a time of great turbulence in central Europe. In 1938, Hitler's troops invaded Czechoslovakia and five years of war followed. After the war, Czechoslovakia came under the influence of the Soviet Union, and capitalistic ventures that had been such an integral part of the Jersak family were severely restricted. By the early 1960s, there were some hints of a return to a more capitalistic economy. To Jersak's dismay, these were snuffed out by the Soviet Union's invasion of Czechoslovakia in 1968.

The invasion was the last straw for Jersak, who had felt for some years that the environment for private business activity was very poor. At age 38, he decided to leave Czechoslovakia for a better life in Canada. He arrived in Toronto in December 1968, determined to apply his entrepreneurial talents in a more promising business environment.

Jersak quickly discovered the freedom that entrepreneurs had in Canada. He started a small gas station, and over the next three years he opened several more. In 1971, he purchased a franchise of a major fast-food outlet, and by 1977 he owned four fast-food restaurants. His entrepreneurial instincts led him into a wide variety of business operations after that. From 1977 to 1991, he expanded his activity into the manufacture of auto parts, microcomputers, textiles, and office furniture. He purchased five franchises of a retail auto parts store, two automobile dealerships, and a carpet business that sells to both residential and commercial users. A mining company, a soft drink bottling plant, and a five-store chain of shoe stores are also part of Jersak Holdings Ltd.

As each new business venture was added, Jersak hired a person to manage the operating company. He also added individuals with expertise in accounting, finance, marketing, and production in his head office. Currently, Jersak Holdings Ltd. contain 17 operating companies, each headed by a manager (see Figure 6.7). Employment ranges from five to ten people in each company. In 1999, sales totalled $37 million and profits were $4.7 million.

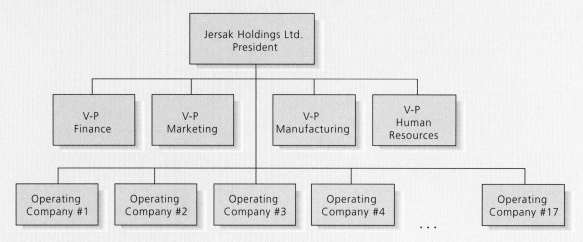

Figure 6.7
Organization of Jersak Holdings Ltd.

Head office staff make most of the strategic decisions in the firm. Jersak and the other top executives have frequent informal meetings to discuss matters of importance to the firm. Discussions usually continue until a consensus is reached on a course of action. The operating managers are expected to put into practice the strategic plans that are made at head office.

As Vaclav Jersak looks back on the last 30 years, he feels a great sense of satisfaction that he has accomplished so much. He has been thinking that the top management group operates smoothly because the people have worked together for many years. But he feels that areas of authority should be more clearly defined so that when changes occur in top management because of retirements, the new people will know exactly what they are responsible for.

Some of Jersak's business acquaintances are of the view that he should delegate considerably more authority to the managers of the operating companies. In effect, they recommend that he turn these operating managers into presidents of their own firms, each of them being responsible for making a profit in their particular enterprise. His acquaintances point out that giving the managers of the operating companies this level of responsibility will motivate them to achieve much more than they are now. Also, it should motivate the employees in these firms because they will have more discretion as well. Jersak sees some real benefits in this approach, but worries that the current managers of the operating companies haven't had much experience in making important decisions. He also fears that head office will lose control of the operating companies. Jersak feels that it is important for head office staff to know some of the details of each operating company. Without this knowledge, he feels that the head office staff will be unable to make good decisions regarding the operating companies.

Other friends of Jersak argue that the time has come to centralize control at head office because the firm has gotten so large and is so diverse. Only in this way, they argue, will top management be able to effectively control all of the activities of Jersak Holdings Ltd.

Jersak is uncertain about what to do, but he feels he must do something to ensure that his life's work will not disappear when he retires.

CASE QUESTIONS

1. Discuss the advantages and disadvantages of centralization and decentralization as they relate to Jersak Holdings Ltd.

2. Which basic approach—centralization or decentralization—should Jersak Holdings Ltd. adopt? Defend your answer.

3. What problems are evident in the current organizational structure of Jersak Holdings Ltd.? Design a new organization chart for the company that will solve these problems. ◆

A Divided Family

Cuddy International Corp. is the largest turkey breeding and hatching company in Canada, with revenues of more than $350 million annually. It also holds the lucrative contract to supply chicken products to McDonald's. The company's founder, Mac Cuddy, is known as "the turkey king of Canada." The saga of Cuddy International is a rags-to-riches story of a brilliant entrepreneur who created a great company, but then couldn't manage it. Mac Cuddy also experienced difficulty getting along with his five sons and one daughter.

In spite of the success of the business, the Cuddy family is badly divided. Gordon Pitts, the author of *In the Blood,* a book about family businesses, says that the Cuddy case is a classic example of all the things that can go wrong in a family business—a control-oriented founding father, no succession plan, untrained children who have worked only in the business, and a lack of trained and talented managers from outside the family. As a result of these problems, Cuddy International has been suffering. The company had five CEOs between 1994 and 1999, and sales have declined sharply from their former level of $500 million annually.

Mac Cuddy's sons have all worked in the business at one time or another, but Mac was always doubtful about their capabilities. He decided to bring in outsiders for the top management positions in the company because he felt that his sons did not have the

management skills to run a large company. Three of his sons—Peter, Bruce, and Brian—made several attempts to take control of the business, but failed. Eventually, Mac fired Peter and Brian, and demoted Bruce. Bruce quit the business and is now a competitor to his father.

In 1997, Peter Cuddy sued the company for $11.5 million, claiming that he was not being provided with the financial information to which he was entitled. He also alleged that his father and one of his brothers were misspending company funds. He eventually dropped his lawsuit, but was then sued by Cuddy International for allegedly making defamatory comments at a press conference. Oddly enough, his father is helping him set up a new snack food company.

Numerous other upheavals have occurred at Cuddy International over the years. While the specific things that have happened may be unusually severe, the fact is that many family businesses experience the same general kinds of problems as those the Cuddy family has suffered through. ◆

Cuddy International Corp.
www.cuddyfarms.com

*Data on various aspects of small business in Canada were provided by Robert W. Sexty of Memorial University.

Every year, thousands of Canadians launch new business ventures. These individuals, called entrepreneurs, are essential to the growth and vitality of the Canadian economic system. Entrepreneurs develop or recognize new products or business opportunities, secure the necessary capital, and organize and operate businesses.

In this chapter we first define the term *small business*, describe the role of the entrepreneur, and note the advantages and disadvantages of owning a small business. Alternative approaches to becoming a small business owner (including franchising) are noted, as are the challenges facing entrepreneurs. The chapter concludes with a description of the various sources of assistance that are available to small business owners.

If you are aware of the challenges you will encounter as an entrepreneur, you are more likely to avoid the classic problems that small business owners face. It is easy to start a business, but to operate one at a profit over a period of years requires the knowledge and application of the fundamentals of management. This chapter is designed to give you realistic expectations about small business management.

When you have completed this chapter, you should be able to:

LEARNING OBJECTIVES

1. Define *small business* and explain its importance to the Canadian economy.

2. Define *entrepreneurship* and describe some basic *entrepreneurial characteristics*.

3. Describe the *start-up decisions* made by small businesses.

4. Identify the advantages and disadvantages of *franchising*.

5. Identify the key reasons for the success and failure of small businesses.

6. Describe the sources of financial and management advice that are available to small businesses.

SMALL BUSINESS IN CANADA

What Is a Small Business?

The term *small business* is not easy to define. Locally owned and operated restaurants, hair salons, service stations, and accounting firms are obviously small businesses, while giant corporations such as Canadian National Railways and Noranda are obviously big businesses. Between these two extremes fall thousands of companies that cannot be easily categorized.

In terms of form of business ownership, a small business may be a corporation, a sole proprietorship, or a partnership. Small businesses can be found in every industry and are particularly prominent in the retail trade. In terms of numbers, small business is the dominant type of business in Canada. Of the approximately 2.2 million businesses in Canada, 58 percent consist of self-employed individuals, while 41 percent employ fewer than 50 persons. Less than 1 percent of all businesses have between 50 and 499 employees, and less than 0.1 percent employ more than 500.[1]

The degree of small business varies across different industries. As shown in Figure 7.1, small business firms are dominant in the construction and retailing industries, but not as dominant in manufacturing. About 6 of every 10 Canadians employed in the private sector work in a firm with fewer than 500 employees.

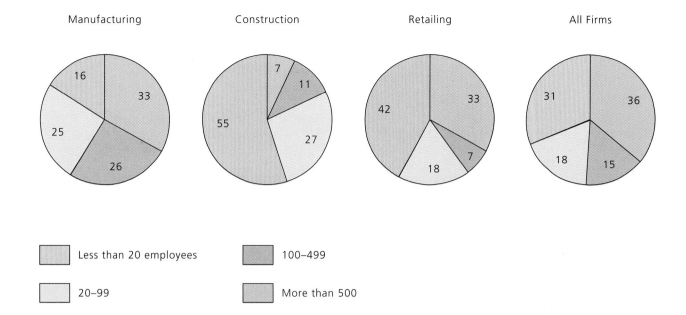

Figure 7.1
Employment distribution by enterprise size.

There are almost as many definitions of small business as there are books on the topic. Two approaches will be used here to define a small business: one based on characteristics and the other based on size. A **small business** is one that is independently owned and operated and is not dominant in its field of operations. It possesses most of the following characteristics:

- Management of the firm is independent. Usually the managers are also the owners.

- An individual or a small group supplies the capital and holds the ownership.

- The area of operations is usually local, and the workers and owners live in the same community. However, the markets are not always local.

- The enterprise is smaller than others in the industry. This measure can be in terms of sales volume, number of employees, or other criteria. It is free of legal or financial ties to large business enterprises.

- The enterprise qualifies for the small business income tax rate under the Canada *Income Tax Act*.

small business
An independently owned and operated business not dominant in its field of operations.

The size of a small business and how the size should be measured are matters of debate. Two common measures are sales revenues and the number of employees. The Canadian government's Small Business Office in conjunction with Statistics Canada defines a small business as having less than $2 million in annual sales. Various government agencies also use numbers of employees to define small business. However, this number differs widely among government agencies: the federal Ministry of State for Small Business stipulates 50 or fewer, the Federal Business Development Bank says 75 or fewer, and Statistics Canada uses numbers ranging from 100 to 1500 for manufacturing industries, and 50 for service industries.

For our purposes, a small business is one that is independent and smaller than the main enterprises in an industry, generally employing 1 to 1500 people.

A common type of small business in Canada is the convenience store. It attracts customers from its immediate area with its long hours of operation and the product lines it carries.

The Importance of Small Business in the Canadian Economy

On the basis of numbers alone, then, small business is a strong presence in the Canadian economy. And the situation in Canada is not unique. In Germany, for example, companies with fewer than 500 employees produce two-thirds of the nation's gross national product, train 9 out of 10 apprentices, and employ 4 of every 5 workers. Small businesses also play major roles in the economies of Italy, France, and Brazil. In addition, experts agree that small businesses will be quite important in the emerging economies of countries such as Russia and Vietnam. The contribution of small business can be measured in terms of its effects on key aspects of an economic system. These aspects include *job creation*, *innovation*, and *importance to big business*.

WEBCONNEXION

Ingenuity.com is a Winnipeg-based small business that was started by Lisa Bako and Sigfrid Froese, two marketing graduates from the University of Manitoba. The company has developed content-filtering software for the Internet and for private intranets that allows information to be customized to user needs and has just signed a major integration deal with the Boston-based subsidary of a Swiss technology firm. Visit Ingenuity.com at:

www.phtsuite.com

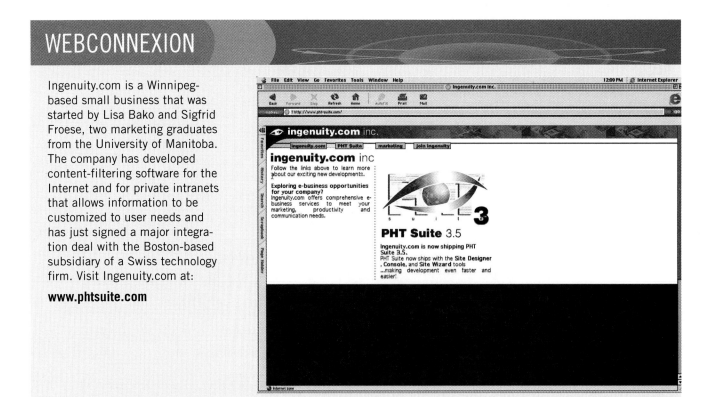

Job Creation

In the early 1980s, a widely circulated study proposed that small businesses create 8 of every 10 new jobs. This contention initiated considerable interest in the fostering of small business as a matter of public policy. As we will see, relative job growth among businesses of different sizes is not easy to determine. It is clear, however, that small business—especially in certain industries—is an important source of new (and often well-paid) jobs in this country.

Although small businesses certainly create many new jobs each year, the importance of big businesses in job creation should not be overlooked. While big businesses eliminated thousands of jobs in the late 1980s and early 1990s, the booming Canadian economy resulted in large-scale job creation in many larger businesses beginning in the mid-1990s. Figure 7.2 details the changes in the number of jobs at 16 large U.S. companies during the 10-year period of 1990 to 1999. As you can see, General Motors eliminated 181 100 jobs and General Mills and Kmart eliminated over 86 000 jobs each. Wal-Mart alone, however, created 639 000 new jobs during the same period and Dayton Hudson (which operates Target stores) created an additional 100 000.

But even these data have to be interpreted with care. PepsiCo, for example, "officially" eliminated 116 000 jobs. However, most of those losses came in 1997, when the firm sold its restaurant chains (KFC, Pizza Hut, and Taco Bell) to Tricon. In reality, therefore, many of the jobs were not eliminated but simply "transferred" to another employer. Likewise, while most of Wal-Mart's 639 000 new jobs are indeed "new," some were added when the company acquired other businesses and thus were not net new jobs.

At least one message is clear: Business *success*, more than business *size*, accounts for most new job creation. Whereas successful retailers such as Wal-Mart have been adding thousands of new jobs, struggling chains such as Kmart have been eliminating thousands. At the same time, flourishing high-tech giants such as Nortel Networks, Dell, Intel, and Microsoft continue to add jobs at a constant pace. It is also essential to take a long-term view when analyzing job growth. Figure 7.2, for example, shows that IBM has eliminated 92 153 jobs. However, the firm actually cut a total of 163 381 jobs between 1990 and 1994. Since 1995, it has created 71 228 new jobs as it has recovered from an economic slump that caused the original job cuts to be so severe.

Kmart
www.kmart.com

Wal-Mart
www.walmart.com

Target Corp.
www.targetcorp.com

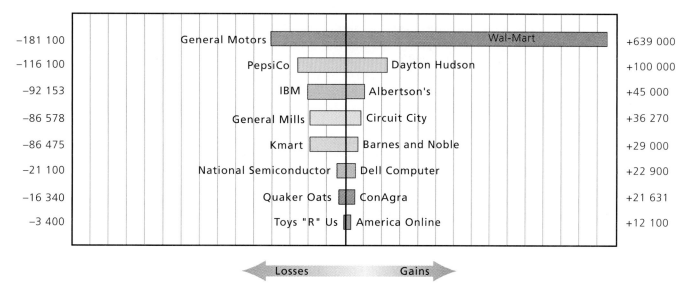

Figure 7.2
Big business: Jobs created and lost.

The reality, then, is that jobs are created by companies of all sizes, all of which hire workers and lay them off. Although small firms often hire at a faster rate than large ones, they are also likely to eliminate jobs at a far higher rate. Small firms are also the first to hire in times of economic recovery; large firms are the last to hire. Conversely, however, big companies are also the last to lay off workers during economic downswings.

Innovation

History has shown that major innovations are as likely to come from small businesses (or individuals) as from big businesses. For example, small firms and individuals invented the personal computer, the stainless-steel razor blade, the transistor radio, the photocopying machine, the jet engine, and the self-developing photograph. They also gave us the helicopter, power steering, automatic transmissions, air conditioning, cellophane, and the ballpoint pen.

Not surprisingly, history is repeating itself infinitely more rapidly in the age of computers and high-tech communication. For example, much of today's most innovative software is being written at new start-up companies such as Trilogy Software Inc. Trilogy's products help optimize and streamline complicated sales and marketing processes for big-business customers such as IBM. Yahoo! and Netscape brought the Internet into the average Canadian living room, and online companies such as Chapters are using it to redefine our shopping habits. Each of these firms started out as a small business. So did Alain Rossmann's Phone.com, a new but growing enterprise that helps big companies provide wireless access to the Internet. Similarly, eToys, Inc., another dotcom start-up, is also making major inroads in the toy retailing business.

Importance to Big Business

Most of the products made by big manufacturers are sold to consumers by small businesses. For example, the majority of dealerships selling Fords, Chevrolets, Toyotas, and Volvos are independently owned and operated. Moreover, small businesses provide big businesses with many of the services, supplies, and raw materials they need. As we noted, for example, Trilogy Software has become an important supplier to big businesses. Likewise, Microsoft relies heavily on small businesses in the course of its routine operations. For example, the software giant outsources much of its codewriting functions to hundreds of sole proprietorships and other small firms. It also outsources much of its packaging, delivery, and distribution to smaller companies. Dell Computer uses this same strategy, buying most of the parts and components used in its computers from small suppliers around the world.

The value of small business to Canada's economy has been recognized by the federal and provincial governments with the establishment of small business departments and lending institutions catering to these enterprises. Government agencies sponsor awards to recognize entrepreneurs or enterprises that have performed in an outstanding manner. An example of one such award is the Canada Awards for Business Excellence. Begun in 1984 by the federal government, these awards were created to acknowledge exceptional business achievements, ones that contribute to Canada's competitiveness in national and international business. The awards are given each year to honour extraordinary performance in various categories of business activity, including entrepreneurship and small business.

Dell Computer
www.dell.com

ENTREPRENEURSHIP

Although the concepts of *entrepreneurship* and *small business* are closely related, there are some important, though often subtle, differences between them.

The Distinction Between Entrepreneurship and Small Business

Entrepreneurs are individuals who assume the risk of business ownership with the primary goal of growth and expansion. A study by the Global Entrepreneurship Monitor (GEM) rated Canada as sixth out of 21 countries for entrepreneurial activity. Brazil ranked first. About 1 in 16 Canadians tried to start a new business in 2000.[2]

There is a distinction between entrepreneurship and small business. A person may be a small business person only, an entrepreneur only, or both. Consider an individual who starts a small pizza parlour with no plans other than to earn enough money from the restaurant to lead a comfortable lifestyle. That individual is clearly a small business person. With no plans to grow and expand, however, the person is not really an entrepreneur. In contrast, an entrepreneur may start with one pizza parlour and turn it into a national chain. Although this individual may have started with a small business, the growth of the firm resulted from entrepreneurial vision and activity.

entrepreneur
A business person who accepts both the risks and the opportunities involved in creating and operating a new business venture.

Describing the Entrepreneur

In general, most successful entrepreneurs have characteristics that set them apart from most other business owners—for example, resourcefulness and a concern for good, often personal, customer relations. Most successful entrepreneurs also have a strong desire to be their own bosses. Many express a need to gain control over their lives or build for their families, and believe that building successful businesses will help them do that. They can also handle ambiguity and deal with surprises. Table 7.1 provides an interesting contrast between some of the characteristics and stereotypes that typified entrepreneurs in the past and those that describe many of today's most successful entrepreneurs.

Yesterday's entrepreneur was stereotyped as "the boss"—someone who was self-reliant and male and who made snap decisions. In contrast, today's entrepreneur is seen more as an inquisitive, open-minded leader who relies on networks, business plans, and consensus. While today's entrepreneur may be male, there is an almost equal likelihood that she will be female. Past and present entrepreneurs also have fundamentally different views as to why they succeeded, the role of automation in business, and the importance of trade versus business knowledge.[3]

The typical entrepreneur is about 42 years old, as compared with the typical employee, who is about 34 years old. An increasing number of women are becoming entrepreneurs. A Royal Bank of Canada study estimates that one-quarter to one-third of all businesses worldwide are owned by women, and that women now account for half the increase in new businesses each year. Between 1991 and 1994, firms led by women created jobs four times faster than the average of all Canadian companies. Women are more conservative than men in running a small business, and their failure rate is lower than that of men.[4]

Dozens of studies have identified common traits among entrepreneurs. A researcher at the University of Western Ontario compiled a list of many of the characteristics identified by these studies, including assertiveness, challenge seeking, charismatic, coping, creative, improvising, opportunistic, preserving, risk taking, self-confident, tenacious, venturesome, and oriented towards achievement and action.[5]

An Ontario government report, *The State of Small Business*, found that the main reasons entrepreneurs started businesses were:

■ The need to achieve or the sense of accomplishment. Entrepreneurs believe that they can make a direct contribution to the success of the enterprise.

Women Business Owners of Manitoba
www.wbom.mb.ca

Table 7.1		Entrepreneurs: Past and Present
Then		**Now**
Small business founder		True entrepreneur
Boss		Leader
Lone ranger		Networker
Secretive		Open
Self-reliant		Inquisitive
Seat-of-the-pants		Letter of the business plan
Snap decisions		Consensus decisions
Male ownership		Mixed ownership
Idea		*Execution*
In 1982, 80% of *Inc.* 500 CEOs believed their companies' success was based on novel, unique, or proprietary ideas		In 1992, 80% of *Inc.* 500 CEOs said that the ideas for their companies were ordinary and that they owed their success to superior execution
Knows the Trade		*Knows the Business*
Eastern, one of the first airlines in the United States, was founded by pilot Eddie Rickenbacker		Federal Express, an overnight delivery service using airplanes, was developed from a business plan written by Fred Smith while he was studying for his M.B.A.
Automation		*Innovation*
Technology lets business automate the work that people had always done		Technology lets people do things that they've never done before

- The need to be their own boss and to control their time.
- The perceived opportunity in the marketplace to provide a product or service.
- The wish to act in their own way or have the freedom to adapt their own approach to work.
- The desire to experience the adventure of independence and a variety of challenges.
- The desire to make money.
- The need to make a living.[6]

More and more women are starting and successfully operating their own small businesses; they now account for half of all new businesses that are formed.

The motivations of successful entrepreneurs include having fun, building an organization, making money, winning in business, earning recognition, and realizing a sense of accomplishment.[7] The "Business Today" box describes the career of one of Canada's best-known entrepreneurs.

Costs and Benefits of Entrepreneurship

Entrepreneurship has both benefits and costs. On the positive side, entrepreneurs get a tremendous sense of satisfaction from being their own boss. They also enjoy successfully bringing together the factors of production (land,

Chapter 7 Understanding Entrepreneurship and Small Business 201

BUSINESS TODAY

Jimmy Pattison—Canadian Entrepreneur Extraordinaire

Most 65-year-old Vancouverites like to have a relaxed breakfast and read the newspaper. Not Jimmy Pattison, one of Canada's most famous entrepreneurs. It's 9 a.m., and he has been in his office since 6 a.m. He has already gone through his mail and phone messages, solved a potential crisis, and talked to a businessman from Thailand who wants to do a deal. In spite of his great wealth, Pattison has no intention of slowing down.

The Jim Pattison Group, one of Canada's largest sole proprietorships, employs 15 000 people and has sales in excess of $3 billion. Jimmy Pattison started out in the 1950s selling pots and pans door to door. He knew he could make enough money to live on if he sold just one set of pots and pans each day. He also learned that he could sell one set if he could just get three evening appointments to make his sales pitch. To get those three evening appointments, he had to knock on about 30 doors. Then he discovered that if he whistled while going door to door, he only had to make 22 house calls to get three appointments. So that's what he did.

In 1961, he began selling cars. Over the years he became involved in numerous other ventures. Now his one-man conglomerate owns 12 car franchises, a Caribbean bank, Ripley's Believe-It-Or-Not, Overwaitea food stores, outdoor signs, Gold Seal fishery products, and Westar

Group Ltd., to name just a few. The company's biggest investments in the next few years will be in B.C. and Alberta. Expansion into the U.S. is also planned. In the 1980s, the company did no business in the U.S., but now the U.S. accounts for 20 percent of company sales. He is also thinking of expanding into Mexico.

Pattison is obviously in charge of the company. His inner circle includes six executives specializing in law, tax, accounting, insurance/administration, cash management, and deal making. He says that being a private company allows him to take a long-run perspective. He says that as long as he keeps his banker happy, things run smoothly. One of Pattison's biggest recent challenges has been to "renew" the company by recruiting a younger generation to replace his colleagues. Most of the new top executives come from the operating divisions. One is only 29 years old.

Pattison says he has only sales skills, but those have served him well throughout his career. He notes that sales requires hard work, and it forces you to relate to people. Those two elements are crucial for success. He also learned in selling that having the door slammed in your face teaches you to handle setbacks and disappointments. He learned not to take no for an answer.

Like many entrepreneurs, Pattison is an incurable optimist. He is a devout Pentecostal Christian, and he is also very generous. In May 1999, he donated $20 million to Vancouver General Hospital, and he funded the private Christian Pacific Academy.

labour, and capital) to make a profit. Perhaps the greatest benefit, however, is that entrepreneurs can make a fortune if they have carefully planned what the business will do and how it will operate.

On the negative side, entrepreneurs can go bankrupt if their business fails. Customers can demand all sorts of services or inventory that small businesses cannot profitably supply. Entrepreneurs must work long hours and often get little in return in the first few years of operation. An entrepreneur may find that he or she is very good at one particular aspect of the business—for example, marketing—but knows little about managing the overall business. This imbalance can cause serious problems. In fact, poor management is the main reason that businesses fail.

STARTING AND OPERATING A SMALL BUSINESS

The Internet is rewriting virtually all of the rules for starting and operating a small business. Getting into business is easier and faster than ever before, there are many more potential opportunities than at any time in history, and the ability to gather and assimilate information is at an all-time high. Even so, would-be entrepreneurs must still make the right decisions when they start. They must decide, for example, precisely *how* to get into business. Should they buy an existing business or build from the ground up? In addition, would-be entrepreneurs must find appropriate sources of financing and decide when and how to seek the advice of experts.

An old Chinese proverb suggests that a journey of a thousand miles begins with a single step. This is also true of a new business. The first step is the individual's commitment to becoming a business owner. Next comes choosing the goods or services to be offered—a process that means investigating one's chosen industry and market. Making this choice also requires would-be entrepreneurs to assess not only industry trends but also their own skills. Like the managers of big businesses, small business owners must be sure that they understand the true nature of their enterprises.

Most people become involved in a small business in one of four ways: they take over a family business, they buy out an existing firm, they start their own firm, or they buy a franchise. There are pros and cons to each approach.

Taking Over a Family Business

Taking over and operating one's own family business poses many challenges. There may be disagreement over which family member assumes control. If the parent sells his or her interest in the business, the price paid may be an issue. The expectation of other family members is typical of how managing such an organization can be difficult. Some may consider a job, promotion, and impressive title their birthright, regardless of their talent or training. Choosing an appropriate successor and ensuring that he or she receives adequate training, and disagreements among family members about the future of the business are two problem areas. Sometimes the interests of the family and those of the enterprise conflict. As a result, family enterprises often fail to respond to changing market conditions. The challenges faced in running such an organization are summarized in Figure 7.3.

A family business also has some strengths. It can provide otherwise unobtainable financial and management resources because of the personal sacrifices of family members; family businesses often have a valuable reputation or goodwill that can result in important community and business relationships; employee loyalty is often high; and an interested, unified family management and shareholders group may emerge.

Buying an Existing Enterprise

Because a family-run business and other established firms are already operating, they have certain advantages for the purchaser: the clientele is established, financing might be easier because past performance and existing assets can be evaluated, experienced employees may already be in place, and lines of credit and supply have been established. An entrepreneur who buys someone else's business, however, faces more uncertainty about the exact conditions of the organization than does a person who takes over his or her family's operation.

The acquisition of an existing enterprise may have other drawbacks: the business may

Martha Billes, president of Canadian Tire. Billes' father and uncle co-founded Canadian Tire in 1927.

Canadian Tire
www.canadiantire.ca

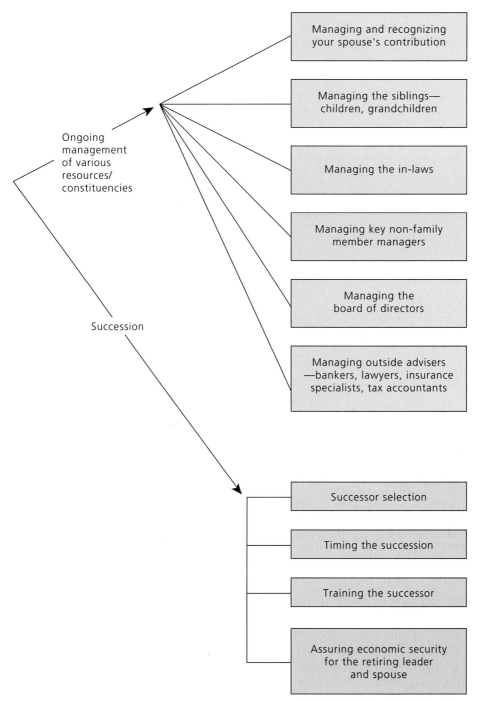

Figure 7.3
Family-owned business leader's key challenges.

have a poor reputation, the location may be poor, and an appropriate price may be difficult to ascertain.

Starting a Business from Scratch

Some people seek the satisfaction that comes from planting an idea, nurturing it, and making it grow into a strong and sturdy business. There are also practical reasons to start a business from scratch. A new business does not suffer the ill effects of a prior owner's errors. The start-up owner is also free to choose lenders, equipment, inventories, locations, suppliers, and workers, unbound by a predecessor's commitments and policies. A good business plan is essential for those individuals who wish to start a small business. The contents of such a plan are shown in Table 7.2.

Not surprisingly, the risks of starting a business from scratch are greater than those of buying an existing firm. Founders of new businesses can only make predictions and projections about their prospects. Success or failure thus depends heavily on identifying a genuine business opportunity—a product for which many customers will pay well but that is currently unavailable to

Table 7.2	A Business Plan

The contents of a business plan vary depending upon the information required by the financial institutions or government agencies. Some entrepreneurs develop plans as a personal guide to check on where they are or want to be. The following are the components that might be included in such a plan:

Cover Page

Contains the enterprise's name, address, telephone numbers, and key contacts.

Table of Contents

Executive Summary

A brief statement, usually about one page long, summarizing the plan's contents.

Background/History of the Enterprise

A concise outline of when and how the enterprise got started, the goods or services it sells, and its major suppliers and customers.

Management

Background information on the entrepreneur and other employees, especially other managers (if there are any).

Marketing Assessment

Descriptions of the products or a service profile, the results of any market research, a market description and analysis, an identification of competition, and an account of the marketing strategy.

Production Assessment

A brief description of the production process, the technological process employed, quality requirements, location and physical plant, and details of machinery and equipment.

Financial Assessment

A review of the capital structure and the money needed to finance the business. Usually includes a projected balance sheet, profit and loss statement, and a cash flow forecast. Lenders may also require details of loan collateral and a repayment proposal.

Research and Development (R&D)

For many enterprises, R&D is important and a statement of what is planned would be included. There may also be an assessment of the risks anticipated with any new products or ventures.

Basic Data

Data on the enterprise's bankers, accountants, lawyers, shareholders (if any), and details of incorporation (if applicable).

Appendices

The following might be attached to a plan: detailed management biographies, product literature, evaluation of assets, detailed financial statements and cash flow forecast, and a list of major contracts.

WEBCONNEXION

Amsdell Inc. is an Ontario-based company that has developed an innovative power protection system that protects personal computers from damage or loss of information. Amsdell's product was touted as "best new technology" at the PC Week Comdex 97 trade show. Amsdell's System Integration Division financed the research and development necessary to come up with the new product. Visit Amsdell at:

www.amsdell.com

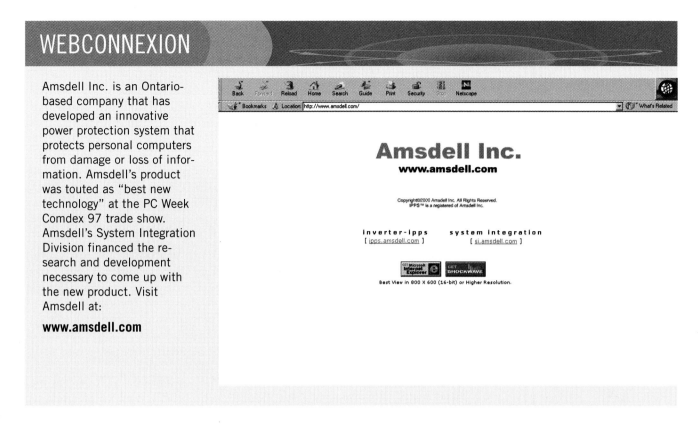

them. To find openings, entrepreneurs must study markets and answer the following questions:

- Who are my customers?

- Where are they?

- At what price will they buy my product?

- In what quantities will they buy?

- Who are my competitors?

- How will my product differ from those of my competitors?

Finding answers to these questions is a difficult task even for large, well-established firms. But where can the small business owner get the necessary information? Other sources of assistance are discussed later in this chapter, but we briefly describe three of the most accessible here:

- The best way to gain knowledge about a market is to work in it before going into business in it. For example, if you once worked in a bookstore and now plan to open one of your own, you probably already have some idea about the kinds of books people buy.

- A quick scan of the local Yellow Pages or an Internet search will reveal many potential competitors, as will advertisements in trade journals. Personal visits to these establishments and Web sites can give you insights into their strengths and weaknesses.

- Studying magazines, books, and Web sites aimed specifically at small businesses can also be of help, as can hiring professionals to survey the market for you.

microenterprise
An enterprise that the owner operates part-time from the home while continuing regular employment elsewhere.

Many new businesses start as **microenterprises**—enterprises operated from the home part-time while the entrepreneur continues to work as a regular employee of another organization. Sometimes such a business is operated in partnership with others. The obvious advantage of beginning as a microenterprise is that the entrepreneur can test his or her idea before quitting regular employment. This approach is being used increasingly by Canadians.

An example of a microenterprise or home office business is Lori M Consulting in Toronto. It was formed by Lori Molmar, an executive with the Federation of Women Teachers' Association of Ontario. She left that job to set up a business in her home as an interior designer and environmental gerontologist. The cost of operating from her home is lower than renting office space.

Buying a Franchise

When you drive or walk around any Canadian town, you will notice retail outlets with names like McDonald's, Pizza Pizza, Swiss Chalet, Yogen Fruz, 7-Eleven, Re/Max, Comfort Inn, Blockbuster Video, Sylvan Learning Centre, and Super Lube. What do all these businesses have in common? They are all franchises, operating under licences issued by parent companies to local entrepreneurs who own and manage them.

Franchising became very visible in the 1950s with fast-food franchisers like McDonald's, but it actually started in the early 1800s. In 1898, General Motors began franchising retail dealerships, and similar systems were created by Rexall (pharmacies) in 1902, and by Howard Johnson (restaurants and motels) in 1926. Franchising continues to increase in importance as we begin the twenty-first century. Depending on how it is defined, franchising now accounts for up to 50 percent of retail sales in Canada. There are thousands of franchise establishments in Canada, and they generate approximately $30 billion in annual sales revenue.

franchise
An arrangement that gives franchisees (buyers) the right to sell the product of the franchiser (the seller).

franchising agreement
Stipulates the amount and type of payment that franchisees must make to the franchiser.

A **franchise** is an arrangement that gives franchisees (buyers) the right to sell the product of the franchiser (the seller). A **franchising agreement** stipulates the amount and type of payment that franchisees must make to the franchiser. Franchisees usually make an initial payment for the right to operate a local outlet of the franchise; they also make royalty payments to the franchiser ranging from 2 to 30 percent of the franchisee's annual revenues or profits. The franchisee also pays an advertising fee so that the franchiser can advertise in the franchisee's local area. At Burger King, for example, the original franchise fee might be as much as $1 million, with the royalty fee being 3.5 percent and the advertising fee 4 percent.

The Benefits of Franchising

Both franchisers and franchisees benefit from the franchising way of doing business (see Table 7.3). However, franchising is not without problems, particularly from the franchisee's perspective. Over the years, certain problems have been noted with some frequency:

- franchisers may impose policy changes without consulting with their franchisees
- the local market may be saturated with too many outlets of one franchise; this reduces the profits that each franchisee is able to make
- payments must be made to the franchiser even if profits are low
- the franchisee has little room to develop a unique identity in the local community because the head office of the franchise stipulates how the business must be run and how the product must be made
- the franchiser might be financially strapped and unable to help individual franchisees

Table 7.3	The Benefits of Franchising

For the Franchiser

- the franchiser can attain rapid growth for the chain by signing up many franchisees in many different locations
- franchisees share in the cost of advertising
- the franchiser benefits from the investment money provided by franchisees
- advertising money is spent more efficiently (the franchiser teams up with local franchisees to advertise only in the local area)
- the franchiser benefits because franchisees are motivated to work hard for themselves; the more revenue the franchisee generates, the more money the franchiser makes
- the franchiser is freed from all details of a local operation, which are handled by the franchisee

For the Franchisee

- franchisees own a small business that has access to big business management skills
- the franchisee does not have to build up a business from scratch
- franchisee failure rates are lower than when starting one's own business
- a well-advertised brand name comes with the franchise and the franchisee's outlet is recognizable because it looks like all other outlets in the chain
- the franchiser may send the franchisee to a training program run by the franchiser (e.g., the Canadian Institute of Hamburgerology run by McDonald's)
- the franchiser may visit the franchisee and provide expert advice on how to run the business
- economies in buying allow franchisees to get lower prices for the raw materials they must purchase
- financial assistance is provided by the franchiser in the form of loans; the franchiser may also help the franchisee obtain loans from local sources
- franchisees are their own bosses and get to keep most of the profit they make

---

- bad behaviour of some franchisees may damage the image of the entire franchise
- start-up cost can be large for well-known franchises
- franchise agreements can be difficult to terminate, or they can be terminated by the franchiser even if the franchisee wants to continue
- there is no guarantee of success for the particular outlet that the franchisee operates, or for the chain as a whole
- published failure rates for franchises may be understated

Is Franchising for You?

Do you think you would be happy being a franchisee? The answer depends on a number of factors, including your willingness to work hard, your ability to find a good franchise to buy, and the financial resources you possess. If you are thinking seriously of going into franchising, you should consider several areas of costs that you will incur:

- the franchise sales price
- expenses that will be incurred before the business opens
- training expenses
- operational expenses for the first six months
- personal financial needs for the first six months
- emergency needs

Franchising is very popular in Canada. It offers individuals who want to run their own business an opportunity to establish themselves quickly in a local market.

For further information about franchising, consult the Canadian Franchising Association at www.cfa.ca. Concluding Case 7-1 also contains more information on franchising.

CHALLENGES FOR THE ENTREPRENEUR

Starting and operating a business enterprise is challenging. The enterprise must be carefully managed, financing must be obtained, and transitions in management must be planned.

Managing the Small Enterprise

Information on Small Business

Many sources of information on small business are available. The following represent the main resources.

Small Business Textbooks. There are several Canadian textbooks on small business and entrepreneurship.[8] And, of course, many others are written in other countries, especially the United States.

Books Profiling Canadian Entrepreneurs. Many books have been published on successful (and some unsuccessful) Canadian entrepreneurs. Examples include Gould's *The New Entrepreneurs: 80 Canadian Success Stories*, Barnes and Banning's *Money Makers: The Secrets of Canada's Most Successful Entrepreneurs*, and Fraser's *Quebec Inc.: French Canadian Entrepreneurs and the New Business Elite*.[9]

Magazines. Two Canadian publications are devoted to small business and entrepreneurship. *Profit: The Magazine for Canadian Entrepreneurs*, published nine times a year by CB Media Ltd., is a practical magazine oriented towards business people. A more academic publication is the *Journal of Small Business and Entrepreneurship*, published quarterly by the Centre for Entrepreneurship, Faculty of Management, University of Toronto, for the International Council for Small Business Canada. In addition, many magazines and journals are published in the United States.

Small Business Centres or Institutes. Dozens of centres and institutes, usually located at colleges or universities, provide assistance to small businesses. Examples are the P.J. Gardiner Small Business Institute at Memorial University of Newfoundland, the Centre for Entrepreneurship at the University of Toronto, and Business Consulting Services at the University of Saskatchewan.

Small Business Organizations. Several organizations have been formed to represent the interests of small business. The largest is the **Canadian Federation of Independent Business (CFIB)**, a non-profit, nonpartisan political action group, or lobby, representing the interests of small and medium-sized business to governments. The CFIB has about 75 000 members. Its stated objectives are to promote and protect a system of free competitive enterprise in Canada and to give the independent entrepreneur a voice in laws governing business and the nation. A similar organization is the Canadian Organization for Small Business, operating in western Canada. Numerous provincial groups also exist.

Canadian Federation of Independent Business (CFIB)
A non-profit, nonpartisan lobby group representing small and medium-sized businesses.

Government and Private Agencies. Information is also available from government and private bodies including small business departments in provincial governments, the "Small Business Network" in Willowdale, Ontario, and the Business Information Centre of the Federal Business Development Bank. The Canadian Youth Business Foundation (CYBF) is a non-profit, private-sector initiative to provide mentoring, business support, and loans to young entrepreneurs ages 18 to 29 who are interested in starting a business. Many chartered banks have booklets and brochures on various topics related to small business.

Assistance for Entrepreneurs and Small Business Enterprises

In the Canadian economic system, the existence of small enterprises is considered desirable for a number of reasons, including the employment it provides, the innovations it introduces, and the competition it ensures. To help entrepreneurs through the hazards of starting up and operating a new business, substantial assistance is available. Government is the main source of assistance, but other sources are also available. Various sources of assistance are summarized in Table 7.4.

In spite of the numerous government assistance programs, small business owners are not happy with government involvement in small business. A *Financial Post* survey revealed that just 5 percent of small business owners felt that a government program had helped them start their business. By contrast, 46 percent felt that government policies and regulations (e.g., excessive paper work requirements and red tape) have caused them to cut back their business operations. Small business owners also said that government assistance programs are not as effective as they used to be. Small business owners rank managerial competence as most important in promoting growth. Government assistance is ranked last.[10]

The Financial Post
www.canoe.ca/FP

Financing the Small Enterprise

The amount of capital needed to start a small business prevents some people from becoming entrepreneurs. However, sources of funding are available (see the list in Table 7.5). It should be noted that some sources are more likely than others to provide money. Lenders may or may not lend money to entrepreneurs, depending on whether the enterprise is just beginning or is ongoing.

Table 7.4   Summary of Assistance for Small Business

Government Assistance	Private Sector
Industry Canada is the department in the federal government responsible for small business and has many programs to promote entrepreneurship. Provincial governments also have numerous programs. The National Entrepreneurship Development Institute was established as a non-profit organization to serve as a clearing house for information about entrepreneurship. Taxation policy allows small business to pay lower levels of taxes than other enterprises. The Federal Business Development Bank (FBDB) administers the Counselling Assistance for Small Enterprises (CASE) program, which offers one-on-one counselling by experienced people to thousands of entrepreneurs each year. The *Small Business Loans Act* (SBLA) encourages the provision of term loan financing to small enterprises by private sector institutions by guaranteeing the loans. The Program for Export Market Development shares the cost of efforts by business to develop export markets. Incubators and technology centres operate across Canada. Incubators are centres where entrepreneurs can start their businesses with the assistance of shared secretarial staff, counselling services, office equipment, legal advice, and financial contact. The Industry Partnership Facility (IPF) is a government-run incubator at the National Research Council of Canada. When it opened in 1998, it housed 13 tenants with a total of 25 employees. In 2000, those same companies employed a total of 130 people. Schools for entrepreneurs funded by government but operated by the private sector prepare prospective entrepreneurs by training them in all aspects of small business. An example is the Regina Business and Technology Centre.	The Canada Opportunities Investment Network (COIN) is a computerized national investment match making service operated through Chambers of Commerce. This service brings potential entrepreneurs together with people who might be willing to supply them with capital. Banks and other financial institutions not only lend money but also provide advice to entrepreneurs. Venture capital companies are groups of small investors seeking to make profits on companies with rapid growth potential. Most of these firms do not lend money, but rather invest it, supplying capital in return for stock. Venture capital companies may also demand a representative on the board of directors. In some cases, managers may even need approval from venture capital companies before making major decisions. Business angels are a special category of private venture capitalists. They invest in new, high-risk enterprises that they feel should be supported even though no one else will lend support. For example, Dr. Drew Pinsky, co-host of MTV's *Loveline*, recently received venture capital funding to extend his program to the Internet from a group of investors collectively known as Garage.com. Garage.com is composed of several individuals and other investors who specialize in financing Internet start-ups. All companies, even those that do not legally need boards of directors, can benefit from the problem-solving abilities of advisory boards. Thus, some small businesses create boards to provide advice and assistance. For example, an advisory board might help an entrepreneur determine the best way to finance a plant expansion or to start exporting products to foreign markets. Management consultants are experts who charge fees to help managers solve problems. They often specialize in one area, such as international business, small business, or manufacturing. Thus, they can bring an objective and trained outlook to problems and provide logical recommendations. They can be quite expensive, however, as some consultants charge $1000 or more for a day of assistance. Like other professionals, consultants should be chosen with care. They can be found through major corporations that have used their services and can provide references and reports on their work. Not surprisingly, they are most effective when the client helps (for instance, by providing schedules and written proposals for work to be done). The Canadian Federation of Independent Business (CFIB) is the largest of the organizations formed to protect the interests of small business. It is a non-profit, nonpartisan group, or lobby, that represents the interests of about 75 000 small and medium-sized enterprises.

Funds for Starting a Business

The most likely sources of financing are the personal funds of individuals, in particular, the entrepreneurs themselves. Some government agencies may provide assistance funds for start-up and so may chartered banks if they think that the proposed business has promise.

Funds for an Ongoing Business

After the enterprise has operated for some time, other services are more likely to be used, if a good financial reputation has been established. Sources include trade credit (that is, the delayed payment terms offered by suppliers), chartered banks, trust companies, and venture capitalists. Another source of funds is profits from the business. Entrepreneurs seldom pay themselves all the profits generated by the enterprise. Some profits are reinvested in the enterprise and are called **retained earnings**.

retained earnings
Profits reinvested in an enterprise.

Table 7.5	Principal Sources of Funds for Small Business Enterprises

Debt Sources

These are funds borrowed by the enterprise. They may come from:

The entrepreneur, who may loan money to the enterprise

Private lenders, that is, individuals or corporations

Financial institutions such as banks, credit unions, trust companies, and finance companies. Such borrowing may be by the enterprise but guaranteed by the entrepreneur or secured against other nonbusiness assets of the entrepreneur

Trade credit, that is, the delayed payment terms offered by suppliers

Government agencies, for example, the Federal Business Development Bank

The selling of bonds or debentures (usually only done when the enterprise is larger)

Equity Sources

This money is invested in the enterprise and represents an ownership interest. It comes from:

The entrepreneur's personal funds

Partners, either individuals or corporations

Family and friends

Venture capitalists

Governments

The selling of shares to the public (usually only done when the enterprise is larger)

Employees who may participate in a stock purchase plan or simply invest in the enterprise.

Retained Earnings

Profits, that is, funds generated from the operation of the business, can be either paid to the owners in dividends or reinvested in the enterprise. If retained or reinvested, profits are a source of funds.

Managing Funds

In Table 7.5, each source is identified as debt or equity. **Debt** refers to borrowed funds that require interest payments and must be repaid. **Equity** refers to the money, or capital, invested in the enterprise by individuals or companies who become owners, and to profits reinvested. In the case of small enterprises, the entrepreneur is often the sole owner. The challenge for entrepreneurs is to keep the amount of funds borrowed and funds invested in ownership in balance. If an enterprise relies on debt too heavily, interest payments might become burdensome and could lead to the failure of the enterprise.

Investors who invest equity obtain ownership and have some influence on the firm's operations. If investors own 51 percent or more of the firm's equity, they could control the enterprise. As enterprises require funds to grow, this diminishing of control frequently cannot be avoided.

debt
Borrowed funds that require interest payments and must be repaid.

equity
Money invested in the enterprise by individuals or companies who become owners.

Transitions in Management

Changes in how a business is managed occur as the enterprise grows. Models of small business growth have been developed that help explain these changes in management.[11] Table 7.6 gives examples of the shift in management approaches necessary as a small enterprise develops.

The launch stage covers the preparatory activities as well as the actual start-up, while the survival stage is the initial period of operation (up to five

Table 7.6				Growth Model for Small Enterprises
Characteristics	**Launch**	**Survival**	**Expansion**	**Maturity**
Key Issues	Development of business "idea" Raising funds Obtaining customers	Generating revenues Breaking even	Managing and funding growth Obtaining resources Maintaining control	Expense control Productivity Consideration of diversification and other expansion
Management Style	Entrepreneurial, individualistic, direct supervision	Entrepreneurial, allows others to administer but supervises closely	Delegation, coordinative but still entrepreneurial Monitoring	Decentralization, reliance on others
Organizational Structure	Unstructured	Simple	Functional, centralized	Decentralized functional/product
Product/Market	Single line and single market	Single line and market but increasing diversity	Wider product range and multiple markets	Several product lines, multimarket and channels
Main Sources of Funds	Owners, friends, and relatives	Owners, suppliers (trade credit), banks	Banks, new partners, retained earnings, secured long-term debt	Retained earnings, long-term debt, shareholders

years) in which many enterprises fail. During expansion, the organization passes the break-even point, and success appears to be more likely. Finally, the maturity stage involves slowed or slight growth and might be referred to as a "comfort" stage during which success is assured. Maturity is not necessarily the end of growth for a business. Expansion opportunities are still sought and diversification is considered, sometimes through taking over or merging with other enterprises.

During these stages, the firm changes from being entrepreneurial to being professionally managed. This change usually happens once the business employs between 50 and 100 people. That is, the entrepreneurial approach to management in which one individual dominates shifts to a professional management style with several top, middle, and supervisory managers necessary to operate the enterprise.

THE SURVIVAL OF SMALL BUSINESS

Numerous statistics on the survival rate of small businesses have been compiled. The following data are representative:

- About 13 to 15 percent of all business enterprises disappear each year.
- One-half of new businesses fail in the first three years. After that the failure rate levels off.
- After 10 years, only 25 percent of businesses are still in existence.
- The average lifespan of small enterprises is 7.25 years.
- Female entrepreneurs have a survival rate about twice as high as that of males.[12]

The low survival rate need not be viewed as a serious problem, since failures are natural in a competitive economic system. In some cases, enterprises are poorly managed and are replaced by more efficient and innovative ones. In recent years, more enterprises have started than have failed, indicating the resiliency of small business and entrepreneurs.

Reasons for Success

Four factors are typically cited to explain the success of small business owners:

1. *Hard work, drive, and dedication.* Small business owners must be committed to succeeding and be willing to put in the time and effort to make it happen. Long hours and few vacations generally characterize the first few years of new business ownership.

2. *Market demand for the product or service.* If the area around a college has only one pizza parlour, a new pizzeria is more likely to succeed than if there are already 10 in operation. Careful analysis of market conditions can help small business people assess the reception of their products in the marketplace.

3. *Managerial competence.* Successful small business people have a solid understanding of how to manage a business firm. They may acquire competence through training (by taking courses in small business management at a local college), experience (by learning the ropes in another business), or by using the expertise of others.

4. *Luck.* Luck also plays a role in the success of some firms. For example, after one entrepreneur started an environmental clean-up firm, he struggled to keep his business afloat. Then the government committed a large sum of money for toxic waste clean-up. He was able to get several large contracts, and his business is now thriving.

Reasons for Failure

Small businesses collapse for a number of reasons (see Table 7.7). The entrepreneur may have no control over some of these factors (for example, weather, fraud, accidents), but he or she can influence most items on the list. This is the main reason an entrepreneur should learn as much as possible about management.

IT'S A WIRED WORLD

Palm Pilot or Filofax?

How do you keep track of your appointments and "to-do" lists? There are two basic alternatives, one old-fashioned and the other high-tech. The six-ring Filofax binder, one of the many legendary products to come out of Britain, typifies the old-fashioned approach. It was a "must-have" for British vicars and army officers during the 1920s and then a status symbol for yuppies during the 1980s. Now, its users are typically women who are trying to cope with a busy schedule of family and work.

Filofax grew slowly over many years. Sales were less than $200 000 per year in the early 1980s, when David Collischon bought the company. Soon the company was offering a wide array of new binders. When Filofax binders became popular among yuppies, Collischon found that he could raise prices and still increase sales. At one point, Filofax binders were selling for twice as much as other functionally equivalent binders. By the mid-1990s, annual sales revenue had jumped to $40 million.

The Palm Pilot is the high-tech alternative to the Filofax. Introduced in the mid-1990s, the hand-held electronic device keeps track of meetings, expenses, addresses, and billing hours. A foldable keyboard can be attached so the user can type documents. Many software programs have been written for use with the Palm Pilot, and users can exchange information through the air on infrared waves with the "beaming" future. Many people originally were attracted to the product because it is a high-tech toy, but most find that it is actually very useful.

Sales of Palm Pilot and its clones jumped 70 percent between 1999 and 2000. Many companies are now buying them for their employees, and some employees consider them to be important perks. Glaxo Wellcome Inc., for example, purchased Palm Pilots for its sales staff and law firms such as McCarthy Tetrault and Lang Michener have also bought them for their employees.

Table 7.7	Causes of Small Business Failure

Poor management skills

- poor delegation and organizational ability
- lack of depth in management team
- entrepreneurial incompetence, such as a poor understanding of finances and business markets
- lack of experience

Inadequate marketing capabilities

- difficulty in marketing product
- market too small, nonexistent, or declines
- too much competition
- problems with distribution systems

Inadequate financial capabilities

- weak skills in accounting and finance
- lack of budgetary control
- inadequate costing systems
- incorrect valuation of assets
- unable to obtain financial backing

Inadequate production capabilities

- poorly designed production systems
- old and inefficient production facilities and equipment
- inadequate control over quality
- problems with inventory control

Personal reasons

- lost interest in business
- accident, illness
- death
- family problems

Disasters

- fire
- weather
- strikes
- fraud by entrepreneur or others

Other

- mishandling of large project
- excessive standard of living
- lack of time to devote to business
- difficulties with associates or partners
- government policies change

SUMMARY OF LEARNING OBJECTIVES

1. **Define *small business* and explain its importance to the Canadian economy.** A *small business* is independently owned and managed and does not dominate its market. Small businesses are crucial to the economy because they create new jobs, foster entrepreneurship and innovation, and supply goods and services needed by larger businesses.

2. **Define *entrepreneurship* and describe some basic *entrepreneurial characteristics*.** *Entrepreneurs* are small business owners who assume the risk of business ownership. Unlike small business owners, growth and expansion are their primary goals. Most successful entrepreneurs share a strong desire to be their own bosses and believe that building businesses will help them gain control over their lives and build for their families. Many also enjoy taking risks and committing themselves to the necessary time and work. Finally, most report that freedom and creative expression are important factors in the decision to own and operate their own businesses.

3. **Describe the *start-up decisions* made by small businesses.** The Internet is rewriting the rules of business start-up. But in deciding to go into business, the entrepreneur must still first choose between buying an existing business and starting from scratch. Both approaches involve practical advantages and disadvantages. A successful existing business has working relationships with other businesses and has already proved its ability to make a profit. New businesses, on the other hand, allow owners to plan and work with clean slates, but it is hard to make projections about the business's prospects.

4. **Identify the advantages and disadvantages of *franchising*.** *Franchising* has become a popular form of small business ownership because the *franchisor* (parent company) supplies the financial, managerial, and marketing assistance to the *franchisee*, who buys the right to sell the franchisor's product. Franchising also enables small businesses to grow rapidly. Finally, the risks in franchising are lower than those involved in opening a new business from scratch. However, the costs of purchasing a franchise can be quite high, and the franchisee sacrifices independence and creativity. In addition, franchises offer no guarantee of success.

5. **Identify the key reasons for the success and failure of small businesses.** There are four key factors that contribute to small business failure: *managerial incompetence or inexperience; neglect; weak control systems*; and *insufficient capital*. Similarly, four key factors contribute to small business success: *hard work, drive, and dedication; market demand for the products or services being provided; managerial competence*; and *luck*. Among the *entrepreneurial characteristics* that are also important are resourcefulness, a concern for positive customer relations, a willingness to take risks, and a strong need for personal freedom and opportunity for the type of creative expression that goes with running one's own company.

6. **Describe the sources of financial and management advice that are available to small businesses.** Financial and management advice for small businesses is available from several private and government sources. The private sources include The Canada Opportunities Investment Network, banks, venture capitalists, the Federation of Independent Businesses, and the Canadian Youth Business Foundation. Government sources include Industry Canada, The Federal Business Development Bank, and incubators and technology centres.

KEY TERMS

small business, 195
entrepreneur, 199
microenterprise, 206

franchise, 206
franchising agreement, 206

Canadian Federation of Independent Business (CFIB), 209

retained earnings, 2101
debt, 211
equity, 211

STUDY QUESTIONS AND EXERCISES

Review Questions

1. Why are small businesses important to the Canadian economy?
2. What are the characteristics of a small business?
3. What are the characteristics of an entrepreneur?
4. What are the advantages and disadvantages of the following ways of becoming involved in a small business: taking over a family business, buying out an existing business, starting a business from scratch, and buying a franchise?
5. What are the causes of small business failure?

Analysis Questions

6. Do you think you would be a successful entrepreneur? Why or why not?
7. Why would a person want to become involved in a microenterprise instead of going into business full-time?

8. Why do small businesses fail despite all the assistance available? Should we be concerned about these failures?

Application Exercises

9. Interview a person who is involved in a family business to identify the management challenges he or she faces. Check your findings against the key challenges identified in Figure 7.3 (see page 203). Write the Canadian Association of Family Enterprises for more information at 10 Prince Street, 3rd Floor, Toronto, ON, M4W 1Z4.
10. Research a business that you are interested in and prepare a plan for starting it. Use the contents of a business plan listed in Table 7.2 (see page 204).

Building Your Business Skills

Working the Internet

Goal

To encourage students to define opportunities and problems for small companies doing business on the Internet.

Situation

Suppose you and two partners own a gift basket store, specializing in special occasion baskets for individual and corporate clients. Your business is doing well in your community, but you believe there may be opportunity for growth through a virtual storefront on the Internet.

Method

Step 1:

Join with two other students and assume the role of business partners. Start by researching Internet businesses. Look at books and articles at the library and contact the following Web sites for help:

- Federal government resources for small business: www.cbsc.org
- Small Business Administration: www.sba.gov
- IBM Small Business Center: www.businesscenter.ibm.com
- Apple Small Business Home Page: www.smallbusiness.apple.com

These sites may lead you to other sites, so keep an open mind.

Step 2:

Based on your research, determine the importance of the following small business issues:

- An analysis of changing company finances as a result of expansion to the Internet
- An analysis of your new competitive marketplace (the world) and how it affects your current marketing approach, which focuses on your local community
- Identification of sources of management advice as the expansion proceeds
- The role of technology consultants in launching and maintaining the Web site
- Customer service policies in your virtual environment

Follow-Up Questions

1. Do you think your business would be successful on the Internet? Why or why not?
2. Based on your analysis, how will Internet expansion affect your current business practices? What specific changes are you likely to make?
3. Do you think that operating a virtual storefront will be harder or easier than doing business in your local community? Explain your answer.

Exploring the Net

A valuable information source for small businesspersons is the Online Small Business Workshop. You can reach the Web site at the following address:

www.cbsc.org/osbw/workshop.html

1. Review the outline of a business plan in the text. Within the Web site, where would you find the information to help you complete a business plan? For example, where in the Web site would you find information or tools to assist you in completing the market assessment section of a business plan?
2. Write down a type of business you'd like to start. In the "Financing Your Business" section of the Web site, investigate small business loan opportunities for your new business. List the loans you qualify for because of the nature of your proposed business, your geographic region, or other criteria.
3. Review the possible ups and downs of starting your own small business as described in the "Planning Fundamentals" section. Assess your own weaknesses in possible areas that are controllable (e.g., a weather disaster is beyond your control). What resources could help you overcome these shortcomings?
4. Evaluate the usefulness of the "Sample Business Plan."

Concluding Case 7-1

The Ever-Changing World of Franchising

Franchising is a very popular form of business in Canada. But in the last few years, a recurring theme has been evident: conflict between franchisees and franchisers. Consider the difficulties at three franchises: Subway, Grower Direct, and Pizza Pizza.

Subway. Chris Downer, the owner of a Subway franchise in Etobicoke, Ontario, arrived one day at his store and found the locks changed and a security guard inside. Subway Franchise Systems had repossessed his store because he had missed a royalty payment of $4800. Downer broke a window to get in and sent the security guard home. He paid the money four days later, but was then hit with a $4600 legal bill from Subway to cover costs they had incurred when trying to get him to pay up.

Some analysts feel that Subway has opened so many new outlets that existing franchisees are going to suffer. John Sotos, a Toronto franchise lawyer, fears that Subway's all-out expansion drive is putting franchisees at risk. He wonders what basis the Subway chain is using to reach the conclusion that it can sustain so many franchises. Ned Levitt, also a franchise lawyer, notes that the chain's low franchising fee ($10 000) may allow undercapitalized franchisees into the business. If they run into difficulty, these franchisees are more likely to be unable to keep up the necessary payments. Fred DeLuca, Subway's CEO, says the chain does not open new stores without taking current franchisees' well-being into account. If the chain determines that the opening of a new outlet will have severe impact on an existing franchisee, the new outlet will not be opened. He notes that about one-third of proposed new outlets are not opened because of objections from existing franchisees.

Grower Direct. This company is Canada's largest importer of roses, with sales of $25 million. It sells roses for $9.99 per dozen in stores across Canada. Owner Skip Kerr is able to sell roses at this low price because the firm is vertically integrated all the way back to the farm where the roses are grown. The company has grown rapidly by selling franchises for $20 000. In return, franchisees receive an exclusive territory.

While the franchising concept has allowed Grower Direct to rapidly increase its sales, there are problems. In Toronto and Vancouver, for example, several franchisees broke away from the company, claiming that they had to pay too much for their flowers from the franchiser and could buy them more cheaply in Toronto. But, as long as they were part of the franchise, they were forced to buy their flowers from Grower Direct.

Kerr agrees that franchisees can get flowers cheaper elsewhere, but he says these flowers are of much lower quality. One Toronto franchisee discovered that she could buy flowers on the local market for about half the price that Grower Direct was charging her as a franchisee. She now owns a non-franchised store.

One franchisee who owns 11 Grower Direct franchise outlets says that being a franchisee is very restricting. Franchisees often have ideas about how to improve the business, but they must operate the way the franchiser dictates. Other franchisees accept the restrictions because they want to run a business outlet where they can be their own bosses.

Pizza Pizza. Darlene Thiele owned two Pizza Pizza franchises. Because she had an outstanding balance of $28 000 with the franchiser, she was fearful that her stores would be taken away. To prevent a situation like the one facing Chris Downer, she hired a locksmith to change the locks on her store, and she slept in the store overnight. The next morning the police arrived at the front door, accompanied by two managers from Pizza Pizza headquarters. Soon after, the chain filed a lawsuit against Thiele, alleging breach of the franchise agreement. Then they stopped deliveries to her store.

Thiele was not alone in her run-ins with the franchiser. In 1992, several franchisees who had experienced difficulties with Pizza Pizza formed the Southern Ontario Pizza Franchisee Association (SOPFA). The franchisees began to grow bolder as they recognized that others had the same concerns they had. They eventually hired a lawyer who filed a $7.5 million lawsuit against Pizza Pizza, demanding that it produce certain financial statements, stop interfering with the regular operations of franchisees, and stop terminating franchise agreements without cause.

The case was eventually turned over to an arbitrator in the spring of 1994. He handed down a decision that supported some of the franchisees' claims, but didn't go as far as they would have liked. Pizza Pizza was told it owed the franchisees a total of $821 495. It paid this out in the summer of 1995. But more than one-third of the franchisees involved in the lawsuit were eventually terminated or bought out.

New Legislation. In the fall of 2000, new legislation came into effect in Ontario that governs the relationships between franchisers and franchisees. The new law is the culmination of a 29-year effort to regulate the franchise sector. The final version of the legislation was weaker than franchisees wanted, but stronger than franchisers wanted. The new law:

- requires franchisers to disclose basic information to franchisees at least two weeks before the franchisee agreement is signed
- prohibits franchisers from punishing franchisees who participate in franchisee associations
- imposes a "duty of fair dealing" on both franchisees and franchisers

Critics of the new legislation point out that it addresses only the "bottom feeders" in the business (those who lie, swindle, and intimidate) and doesn't deal at all with the numerous business issues that have caused so many problems in the industry. These business issues were raised in public hearings that featured numerous tales of franchisee woes such as cannibalization, anti-competitive practices, kickbacks, arbitrary termination of franchises, and forfeiture of deposits.

However, the new law does require franchise agreements to include many statements that will make new franchisees aware of the realities of the franchising industry. For example, franchisees will now be made aware that they may not get the best price available on the goods and services they buy from the franchiser.

The wording of the new legislation is based on regulations set by the U.S. Federal Trade Commission. If recent U.S. court interpretations are any indication, some business operators who do not consider themselves to be franchisers may find, to their dismay,

that the new law applies to them. The new law's definition of a franchise contains three elements:

- direct or indirect payments of a fee to engage in a business
- the right to sell goods that are "substantially associated" with the franchiser's trademark
- the franchiser's exercise of "significant control" over the franchisee's operations

Companies particularly at risk are those whose agents, dealers, or distributors use the organization's trademarks or advertising. For example, consider the situation in which a company gets involved in a dispute with one of its distributors. Might the distributor claim that the relationship falls under the franchise law and that the "franchiser" hasn't met the new disclosure requirements? Might the distributor then rescind the distributorship agreement and demand compensation for everything the distributor has paid the company over and above the wholesale cost of the goods?

This possibility has many business owners seeking legal advice on whether they fall under the new law. Unfortunately, the answer is not clear. For example, does supplying a distributor with promotional giveaways for customers mean that the company is a franchiser? Franchise lawyer Paul Jones says that if a company is simply teaching its dealers how its product works or how to repair the product, that likely would not make the company a franchiser under the law. But if the company is training dealers to sell the product and do point-of-purchase displays, there may be a problem.

CASE QUESTIONS

1. Do franchisees really own their own businesses?

2. What difficulties in franchising have led to the formulation of new legislation in Ontario? (Look at the source notes for this case and read about specific problems that franchisees have identified.)

3. "In a free society, we should not have laws governing the way that franchises can operate. Everyone who gets involved in a franchise is responsible for assessing the reasonableness of the deal. Government interference simply inhibits efficient business practices." Do you agree or disagree with this statement? Defend your answer. ◆

Concluding Case 7-2

Financing a Small Business

Sebastian Yoon is an artist who runs a high-end glass art gallery in Calgary. He is successful in gallery terms, but now he has taken a big financial risk because he wants to grow. He has over $500 000 tied up at the site formerly occupied by Coconut Joe's on Electric Avenue in Calgary. Yoon bought the property with a loan from a relative that must be repaid in eight months. He says people think he's nuts when they hear what he wants to do with the place—turn it into a fancy restaurant that surrounds a glassed-in glass-blowing studio. He wants to provide food with living art for entertainment.

Yoon's projected budget is $1 million, with $500 000 for the purchase of the building, and another $500 000 to renovate it. His original plan was to borrow the money from a bank, but every bank he visited said no. He's now trying to drum up private investors. At the moment, he's trying to get $100 000 from Brad, a friend who operates a bar and who has indicated an interest in Yoon's project. Yoon badly needs this infusion of cash because his bills are piling up. Architect fees alone will soon reach $30 000.

The grand opening is scheduled for November, and the longer Yoon delays, the more the project will cost. He has called Brad many times in a single day, but has still been unable to reach him. Finally, Yoon goes to Brad's bar in the hopes of finding him. No luck. Yoon then goes to Brad's home, but Brad is not there, either. Eventually, Yoon does receive a cheque from Brad, but it bounces. Brad is out of the picture.

During his busy day, Yoon visits his father, who runs an art school. Yoon's parents know generally what he is doing and that he is trying to raise money, but that's about it. Yoon thinks his parents don't understand what he is trying to do.

Yoon has reduced his budget to $800 000 because of his inability to raise money. He is becoming exhausted and his energy level is way down. On today's schedule, Yoon has lunch with a friend who says he wants in on the deal. Yoon receives $5000, with a promise for an additional $5000. With the money, Yoon pays his lawyer and accountant

first. He has found a bank that is willing to discuss a loan. A few days later, he meets with the banker, explains his idea, and asks for $200 000. The banker grills Yoon on his cash flow projections and his estimated costs (banks aren't eager to fund restaurants). The banker wants to use the building as collateral for the loan, but Sebastian's wealthy relative won't allow him to borrow against the building. The banker then wonders whether Yoon's backers would be willing to put up their personal assets as collateral. Yoon doesn't think this will work, but reassures himself with the fact that the banker didn't give him a flat refusal on the loan request.

It is now August and the building renovations are underway. Yoon has just three months to pay off the loan from his relative. Because he has been giving so much attention to this new project, his art gallery business has gone downhill, and the bills keep coming in. His lawyer is a friend, but he doesn't work for nothing.

Yoon is ready to throw in the towel. It is now October and the grand opening is supposed to be in two weeks. Just when all seems lost, a buyer expresses interest in buying Yoon's building for $875 000. Luck has just rescued Yoon from his dilemma. He accepts the deal and pockets a $300 000 capital gain on the sale of the building. He still plans to build a glass-blowing studio some day.

CASE QUESTIONS

1. Is Sebastian Yoon a small business owner, an entrepreneur, or both? Explain your answer.

2. Describe the costs and benefits of entrepreneurship from Yoon's perspective.

3. What are the various ways in which a person can get involved in a small business? Which alternative has Yoon chosen? Why might he have chosen this route?

4. Would Yoon be happy as a franchisee? Why?

5. What are the main debt and equity sources of money for small business owners? To what extent have these sources been used by Yoon? ◆

Visit the *Business* Website at www.pearsoned.ca/griffin
for up-to-date e-business cases!

CBC Video Case

Building an Empire

Morey Chaplick knows where he's headed—he wants to create an empire in the video game store business. He is the entrepreneurial equivalent to Super Mario. Chaplick has always had an entrepreneurial bent. At age 19, he and a friend started selling stereos and ended up with a chain of 23 retail stores. He then left that business and started Beamscope, which grew into the biggest distributor of software in Canada. But he sold his stake in Beamscope and took a year off because he was feeling burned out.

But he couldn't stay away from business. His newest company is Hip Interactive Corp. Chaplick's plan is to put together a group of companies that will cover every aspect of the video games business and corner a big chunk of the market. To achieve his goal, Hip has been on a buying binge and has acquired seven different companies in the space of a couple of months. Chaplick has also raised $26 million on the stock market.

Chaplick hopes his strategy will work as follows: the video arcades will generate traffic to Hip's Games Mania Web site, which will direct customers to the retail and e-tail stores that sell video games. These retail stores will, in turn, buy products from distributors owned by Hip. This strategy will create new gamers who will spend more money at the arcades and the process will start all over again. To be successful with this corporate strategy, Chaplick has to convince competitors to hang up their gloves and to work with him instead of against him. It is the sales job of his life. One of his most aggressive competitors, SJS, is finally enticed to join the Chaplick empire by an offer of cash and shares in Hip. Another competitor, the former CEO of a video games retail chain, also decides to join the company.

Chaplick gets immense satisfaction from convincing people to do things his way. The core of Chaplick's idea is a group of franchise video stores he bought cheap from Microplay, a retail chain that had 85 stores in Canada and the U.S. The chain had been badly managed, but he thinks he can turn Microplay's uninspired stores into a powerful market force by putting good management behind the Microplay brand. The first step is to weed out "loser" stores and get the remaining franchisees on side. It's not an easy sell. Microplay franchisees are skeptical because several previous franchisers had promised a lot of things but did not deliver on their promises. Chaplick must also create a new look for the Microplay stores and spend a lot of money on advertising and sales promotion. He is developing radio, television, and print media advertising, as well as a national quiz contest that will increase Microplay's visibility. Overall, Chaplick will spend a million dollars on the advertising campaign.

On the organization front, head office is putting together a buyers group for the franchisees to meet the anticipated boom in sales. The buyers group will give the franchisees lower prices because it will buy in volume. But there is trouble here because only 40 percent of franchisees have signed up. They don't want to sign the personal financial guarantee that is required. Chaplick keeps pushing them, and says that if they don't join the buyers group, they may have trouble getting product to sell, and will likely have to pay higher wholesale prices for the products they are able to buy. Since Hip increasingly controls distribution of video games in Canada, this argument is powerful. Within a few months, the reluctant franchisees have agreed to join the buyers group.

Like all entrepreneurs, Chaplick is constantly on the lookout for new opportunities. He is already looking beyond Hip to the next big idea just around the corner. He doesn't want to overstay his welcome at any one company. He is driven to build a business as fast as he can, create value, and then move on.

STUDY QUESTIONS

1. What are the *functions* of management? Describe some daily activities in Morey Chaplick's work that illustrate these management functions in action. What are the *skills* of management? Which of these are particularly important for Chaplick? Why?

2. Is Chaplick a small business owner, an entrepreneur, or both? Explain.

3. What corporate-level business strategy does Chaplick seem to be pursuing? Explain.

4. What is franchising? How does the franchising concept facilitate Chaplick's corporate strategy?

5. What are the key challenges facing entrepreneurs? How has Morey Chaplick met these challenges?

Video Resource: "The Operator," *Venture* #761 (October 24, 2000).

CBC Video Case

II-2   CBC

Wheelchair Access

Marco Ferrara's company, Universal Motion (UM), sells lifts that move people in wheelchairs in and out of vans. Ferrara has first-hand experience with this problem: twelve years ago he broke his back in an automobile accident. His strategy is to make friends with his competition and to use competitors and other manufacturers to leverage his own company's sales. He says, "We sell their product to finance our own."

In this very demanding marketplace, Ferrara's disability is a real plus. He says that when a person in a wheelchair makes a product for other people in a wheelchair, there is a "poster-child" quality to his company. In its first year, UM had sales of $60 000; second-year sales were $300 000. UM's product was demonstrated at the People in Motion show in Toronto in 1999. It is a specialty product for a specialty market. UM's lift stows in a pocket between the van floor and the undercarriage. Van conversion for the disabled is a quarter-billion dollar business in North America. Whether it's lifts or ramps, each conversion costs between $6000 and $20 000 per van.

The van conversion market is dominated by a few large U.S. firms like Vantage Mobility International (VMI). A VMI salesman at the People in Motion show introduced VMI's ramp to Canada. A large company like VMI has the money to advertise its products extensively, but a small company like UM has to rely on its ingenuity. So, UM signs on as a VMI dealer to sell Vantage ramps in the Toronto area. UM thereby becomes a full-line dealership because it can sell several different VMI products. But a big company like VMI may have trouble keeping track of its dealers. UM discovers to its dismay that VMI already has a dealer in southern Ontario, and what's worse, that dealer has a booth right next to UM's booth at the People in Motion show. This is really bad form, and Ferrara is understandably upset, but he doesn't lose his cool.

He cuts VMI some slack over this foul-up and continues to work things out. At the UM plant, UM's inventor is working on the next generation of lifts. But solving engineering kinks takes a lot of money, which is something UM does not have. Ferrara knows that selling a VMI product makes UM twice as much money as selling their own, so he is interested in strong sales volume. VMI made a commitment to provide sales referrals to UM from the People in Motion show, but UM is still waiting for these sales referrals. Apparently VMI is having some problems

getting its act together because Toronto is a bigger market than VMI expected.

A few weeks later, a VMI salesman comes to Canada to showcase UM as a Vantage dealer. He is happy to learn that Ferrara has already closed a deal for VMI's product. At the Bloorview MacMillan Rehab Centre for disabled children, Ferrara demonstrates the product. But Ferrara's poster-child quality doesn't necessarily translate into business respect. The VMI sales rep repeats some information that Ferrara has already provided and gives the impression that he wasn't listening when Ferrara was talking.

In spite of situations like this, Ferrara persists and it pays off. By late 2000, the relationship with VMI is going well, and UM sales have topped $1 million. Most of the revenue comes from the sale of VMI's products. UM's next big partner may be one of the "Big 3" automobile companies because an aging population means a big increase in the demand for van conversions. It is estimated that somewhere between 30 000 and 50 000 vans will need to be converted each year. While talking to a Ford supplier, Ferrara learns that GM might also be interested. A commitment from a company the size of Ford or GM could mean major research and development money from the government of Canada because 90 percent of these products will be exported.

The lesson here is this: you can't beat persistence when it comes to making friends with your competitors.

STUDY QUESTIONS

1. Explain what was involved in carrying out each of three basic steps in strategy formulation at Universal Motion.

2. What corporate-level strategy is Universal Motion pursuing?

3. Briefly describe what is involved in each of the basic functions of management. Which of these functions has Marco Ferrara emphasized most to date?

4. What is the difference between small business and entrepreneurship? Is Marco Ferrara a small businessperson, an entrepreneur, or both? Explain.

5. Briefly describe the main challenges facing entrepreneurs. Which of these challenges are most significant for Marco Ferrara?

Video Resource: "Wheelchair," *Venture* #764 (November 14, 2000).

Understanding People in Organizations

You will read about several timely and complex human resource management issues in the opening cases of the chapters in this section—the increasing success of women in top management positions in Canadian businesses, motivating and leading employees at PanCanadian Petroleum, and a changing approach to labour relations at GM Canada. The intense competition that Canadian business firms face at the start of the twenty-first century means that it is very important that human resources be managed effectively.

Part Three, Understanding People in Organizations, provides an overview of the relationship between managers and their employees, including managers' attitudes, the activities of managers responsible for human resource management, the special relationship between management and labour unions, and the role of the government in labour-management issues.

- We begin in **Chapter 8, Managing Human Resources**, by exploring the wide range of activities that are necessary to effectively manage employees, including assessing employee needs and training, promoting, and compensating employees.

- Then, in **Chapter 9, Motivating and Leading Employees**, we examine the reasons why firms should establish good relationships with their employees, and how managers' attempts to maintain productivity can affect their relations with employees.

- Finally, in **Chapter 10, Understanding Labour–Management Relations**, we look at the development of the union movement in Canada, why and how workers organize, and how government legislation has affected workers' rights and abilities to organize.

CHAPTER 8

More Cracks in the Glass Ceiling

During the 1990s, much was written about the "glass ceiling," the invisible barrier that prevents women from moving into the very top jobs in business firms. But in the early years of the new millennium, the winds of change are blowing, and women have achieved more breakthroughs. Some particularly dramatic changes have occurred in the automobile industry, which has been dominated by men since its inception. Consider this: the CEOs of two of the three North American auto manufacturers are now women. Maureen Kempston Darkes, CEO and president of General Motors of Canada, started with GM in 1975 and worked her way up through the legal and government affairs side of the company. Bobbie Gaunt, CEO of Ford Motor of Canada (pictured), is a 25-year veteran of Ford and a world-class marketer. New Brunswick native Cynthia Trudell is president of Saturn Corp., a subsidiary of GM. She is the first woman ever to head up a fully integrated subsidiary of a North American automaker.

The success of women in top management jobs is not restricted to the automobile industry. Carly Fiorino, CEO of Hewlett-Packard, is the first woman to head a company in the Dow Jones Industrial average. Fiorino says that there really is not a glass ceiling any more, and that women who believe they are limited by their gender will end up actually limiting their careers.

Fiorino's opinions may not be widely accepted just yet, but the fact is that more and more women are earning high-level leadership positions. The Canadian CEOs of Home Depot, Xerox, General Foods, and Kraft are all women. Linda Hasenfratz is the president of Linamar Corp. and Nancy Southern is deputy CEO of Atco Ltd. Other women who have reached the top are Joy Calkin (CEO of Extendicare), Eleanor Clitheroe (CEO of Ontario Hydro Services), Colleen Moorehead (CEO of E*Trade Canada), and Barbara Stymiest (president of the Toronto Stock Exchange).

A survey of 461 female executives found that four strategies were important for women to break through the glass ceiling:

- consistently exceeding performance expectations
- developing a style with which male managers are comfortable
- seeking difficult or high-visibility work assignments
- having an influential mentor

The same survey found that male CEOs thought that women didn't advance to the very top ranks of management because they lacked general management experience, and because women had not been "in the pipeline" long enough. Women, on the other hand, felt that the key barriers to their success were male stereotyping of women, the exclusion of women from informal networks, and an inhospitable corporate culture.

The trend towards more women in the very top jobs is clearly going to continue because women are also increasingly holding jobs just below the top level. Gail McGovern is the head of AT&T's $25 billion consumer business, and Lois Juliber is the head of North American and European operations for Colgate-Palmolive. Both of these women have a chance to become CEO in a few years.

These specific examples suggest that the situation for women in management is improving. But if we look at the overall picture, there are still many problems. A 2000 study released by Catalyst found that women occupied only 6.4 percent of line management positions and 3.4 percent of top corporate jobs (executive vice-president and above) in Canada's largest companies. Nearly half of Canada's largest companies had no women at all in corporate officer jobs. Sheila Wellington, president of Catalyst, argues that looking at who is in top management gives a pretty good idea of what is going on in the lower ranks and how women are viewed.

Some companies are promoting women to top jobs at a substantial rate. At the Bank of Montreal, for example, women fill 20 of the top 70 jobs in the company. Ford Motor of Canada has women in 5 of its 11 top jobs. And at Johnson & Johnson, women hold 3 of the 4 top spots.

The appointment of increasing numbers of women to top management jobs is no accident. Rather, it is the result of careful assessment of the human resources that a firm has available to it. The strategies used at Ford Canada and General Motors of Canada are typical of systems that businesses use to develop and maintain an effective workforce. These systems focus on defining the jobs that need to be done; ensuring that appropriate people are hired and oriented to their new jobs; training, appraising, and compensating employees; and providing appropriate human resource services to employees.

By focusing on the learning objectives for this chapter, you will better understand the key issues in contemporary human resource management. After reading this chapter, you will be able to:

LEARNING OBJECTIVES

1. Define *human resource management,* discuss its strategic significance, and explain how managers plan for human resources.

2. Identify the issues involved in *staffing* a company, including *internal* and *external recruiting* and *selection.*

3. Discuss different ways in which organizations go about developing the capabilities of employees and managers.

4. Explain ways in which organizations evaluate employee performance.

5. Discuss the importance of *wages and salaries, incentives*, and *benefit programs* in attracting and keeping skilled workers.

6. Describe some of the key legal issues involved in hiring, compensating, and managing workers in today's workplace.

7. Discuss *workforce diversity,* the management of *knowledge workers,* and the use of *contingent and temporary workers* as important changes in the contemporary workplace.

THE FOUNDATIONS OF HUMAN RESOURCE MANAGEMENT

human resource management (HRM) = personnel

The development, administration, and evaluation of programs to acquire and enhance the quality and performance of people in a business.

Human resource management (HRM) is the set of organizational activities directed at attracting, developing, and maintaining an effective workforce. Human resource management takes place within a complex and ever-changing environmental context and is increasingly being recognized for its strategic importance.[1]

The Strategic Importance of HRM

Human resources are critical for effective organizational functioning. HRM (or *personnel,* as it is sometimes called) was once relegated to second-class status in many organizations, but its importance has grown dramatically in the last two decades. This new importance stems from increased legal complexities, the recognition that human resources are a valuable means for improving productivity, and the awareness today of the costs associated with poor human resource management.

Indeed, managers now realize that the effectiveness of their HR function has a substantial impact on a firm's bottom-line performance. Poor human resource planning can result in spurts of hiring followed by layoffs—costly in terms of unemployment compensation payments, training expenses, and morale. Haphazard compensation systems do not attract, keep, and motivate good employees, and outmoded recruitment practices can expose the firm to expensive and embarrassing legal action. Consequently, the chief human resource executive of most large businesses is a vice-president directly accountable to the CEO, and many firms are developing strategic HR plans that are integrated with other strategic planning activities.

Even organizations with as few as 200 employees usually have HR managers and HR departments charged with overseeing these activities. Responsibility for HR activities, however, is typically shared between HR departments and line managers. The HR department may recruit and initially screen candidates, but managers in the department where the new employee will work usually make the final selection. Similarly, although the HR department may establish performance-appraisal policies and procedures, the actual evaluating and coaching of employees is done by immediate superiors.

Human Resource Planning

The starting point in attracting qualified human resources is planning. In turn, HR planning involves *job analysis* and *forecasting* the demand for and supply of labour (see Figure 8.1).

Job Analysis

job analysis
A detailed study of the specific duties in a particular job and the human qualities required for that job.

job description
The objectives, responsibilities, and key tasks of a job; the conditions under which it will be done; its relationship to other positions; and the skills needed to perform it.

job specification
The specific skills, education, and experience needed to perform a job.

Job analysis is a systematic analysis of jobs within an organization. A job analysis is made up of two parts:

- The **job description** lists the duties of a job, its working conditions, and the tools, materials, and equipment used to perform it.

- The **job specification** lists the skills, abilities, and other credentials needed to do the job.

Job analysis information is used in many HR activities. For instance, knowing about job content and job requirements is necessary to develop appropriate selection methods and job-relevant performance appraisal systems and to set equitable compensation rates.

Forecasting HR Demand and Supply

After managers fully understand the jobs to be performed within an organization, they can start planning for the organization's future HR needs. The manager starts by assessing trends in past HR usage, future organizational plans, and general economic trends. A good sales forecast is often the foundation, especially

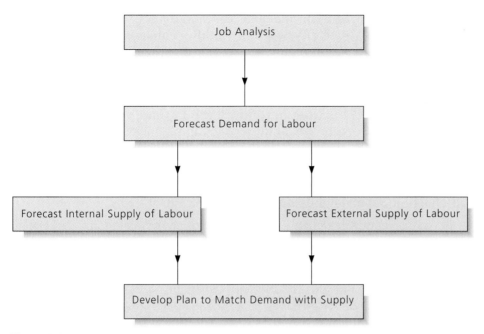

Figure 8.1
Planning for human resources.

for smaller organizations. Historical ratios can then be used to predict demand for types of employees, such as operating employees and sales representatives. Large organizations, of course, use much more complicated models to predict HR needs. Human resource consulting firms can help with forecasting HR demand and supply.

Forecasting the supply of labour involves two tasks:

■ Forecasting *internal supply*—the number and type of employees who will be in the firm at some future date

■ Forecasting *external supply*—the number and type of people who will be available for hiring from the labour market at large.

The simplest approach merely adjusts present staffing levels for anticipated turnover and promotions. Large organizations use extremely sophisticated models to keep track of the present and future distributions of professionals and managers. This allows the company to spot areas where there will eventually be too many qualified professionals competing for too few promotions or, conversely, too few good people available to fill important positions.

Replacement Charts. At higher levels of the organization, managers plan for specific people and positions. The technique most commonly used is the **replacement chart**, which lists each important managerial position, who occupies it, how long he or she will probably stay in it before moving on, and who (by name) is now qualified or soon will be qualified to move into it. This technique allows ample time to plan developmental experiences for people identified as potential successors to critical managerial jobs.

Skills Inventories. To facilitate both planning and identifying people for transfer or promotion, some organizations also have **employee information systems**, or **skills inventories**. These systems are usually computerized and

replacement chart
An HR technique that lists each important managerial position, who occupies it, how long he or she will probably stay in it before moving on, and who (by name) is now qualified or soon will be qualified to move into it.

employee information systems (skills inventories)
Computerized systems that contain information on each employee's education, skills, work experience, and career aspirations.

contain information on each employee's education, skills, work experience, and career aspirations. Such a system can quickly locate every employee who is qualified to fill a position requiring, say, a degree in chemical engineering, three years of experience in an oil refinery, and fluency in Spanish.

Forecasting the external supply of labour is a different problem altogether. How does a manager, for example, predict how many electrical engineers will be seeking work in Ontario or B.C. three years from now? To get an idea of the future availability of labour, planners must rely on information from outside sources, such as government reports and figures supplied by colleges and universities on the number of students in major fields.

Matching HR Supply and Demand

After comparing future demand and internal supply, managers can make plans to manage predicted shortfalls or overstaffing. If a shortfall is predicted, new employees can be hired, present employees can be retrained and transferred into understaffed areas, individuals approaching retirement can be convinced to stay on, or labour-saving or productivity-enhancing systems can be installed.

If the organization needs to hire, the external labour-supply forecast helps managers plan how to recruit according to whether the type of person needed is readily available or scarce in the labour market. The use of temporary workers also helps managers in staffing by giving them extra flexibility. If overstaffing is expected to be a problem, the main options are transferring the extra employees, not replacing individuals who quit, encouraging early retirement, and laying people off.

STAFFING THE ORGANIZATION

Once managers have decided what positions they need to fill, they must find and hire individuals who meet the job requirements. A 1996 study by the Canadian Federation of Independent Business found that the top three characteristics employers are looking for when they hire people are a good work ethic, reliability, and willingness to stay on the job.[2] Staffing of the corporation is one of the most complex and important aspects of good human resource management. The top 10 employers in Canada are listed in Table 8.1.

In this section, we will describe both the process of acquiring staff from outside the company (*external staffing*) and the process of promoting staff from within (*internal staffing*). Both external and internal staffing, however, start with effective recruiting.

Recruiting Human Resources

Once an organization has an idea of its future HR needs, the next phase is usually recruiting new employees. **Recruiting** is the process of attracting qualified persons to apply for the jobs that are open. Where do recruits come from? Some recruits are found internally; others come from outside the organization.

Internal Recruiting

Internal recruiting means considering present employees as candidates for openings. Promotion from within can help build morale and keep high-

Canadian Federation of
Independent Business
www.cfib.ca

recruiting
The phase in the staffing of a company in which the firm seeks to develop a pool of interested, qualified applicants for a position.

internal recruiting
Considering present employees as candidates for job openings.

Table 8.1	The Top 10 Employers in Canada (ranked by number of employees)

Company	Number of Employees
1. George Weston Ltd.	119 000
2. Onex Corp.	83 000
3. Nortel Networks Corp.	77 000
4. Laidlaw Inc.	71 300
5. Hudson's Bay Co.	65 000
6. Quebecor Inc.	60 000
7. Magna International Inc.	58 000
8. Bombardier Inc.	56 000
9. BCE Inc.	55 000
10. Royal Bank of Canada	51 891

quality employees from leaving. In unionized firms, the procedures for notifying employees of internal job-change opportunities are usually spelled out in the union contract. For higher-level positions, a skills inventory system may be used to identify internal candidates or managers may be asked to recommend individuals who should be considered.

External Recruiting

External recruiting involves attracting people outside the organization to apply for jobs. External recruiting methods include advertising, campus interviews, employment agencies or executive search firms, union hiring halls, referrals by present employees, and hiring "walk-ins" or "gate-hires" (people who show up without being solicited). Of course, a manager must select the most appropriate method for each job. Private employment agencies can be a good source of clerical and technical employees, and executive search firms specialize in locating top-management talent. Newspaper ads are often used because they reach a wide audience and thus allow minorities "equal opportunity" to learn about and apply for job openings.

The old-fashioned job fair has survived in spite of Internet career postings and the proliferation of employment agencies and headhunters. At a job fair, candidates browse through the positions available and employers can see a sample of the skills candidates have. While job postings on the Internet are impersonal, at job fairs candidates and recruiters can talk to each other face to face. Job fairs are also cheaper than posting jobs with an employment agency or headhunter.

Sears Canada held a three-day job fair at the Marriott Hotel in Toronto's Eaton Centre in 2000 because it was looking for hundreds of new employees. When IBM Canada held a job fair at its Markham, Ontario, office, nearly 5000 people came hoping to snap up one of the 500 jobs that were available. IBM was looking for senior people, while Sears Canada was looking for entry-level people.[3]

Some companies carry on recruiting in non-traditional ways. For example, Brampton-based Nortel Networks recruits at rock concerts outside Boston, near one of its new manufacturing facilities. David Lucey heads up

external recruiting
Attracting people outside the organization to apply for jobs.

a team of "talent acquisition" specialists who work the crowds as they enter the concert venue. One night in the summer of 2000, the team members handed out lip balm, ran a raffle, and chatted about Nortel to people who were arriving to hear Counting Crows and Live.

These recruiting tactics are designed to raise the profile of Nortel in the Boston area. Nortel is trying to hire about 2000 new employees for its facility in nearby Billerica, Massachusetts. The company also has a booth at the Boston Marathon, and a company tour bus parked at restaurants, commuter rail stations, and shopping malls. High-tech workers are in short supply, and unusual recruiting methods are necessary to attract qualified workers.[4]

Selecting Human Resources

Once the recruiting process has attracted a pool of applicants, the next step is to select someone to hire. The intent of the selection process is to gather information from applicants that will predict their job success and then to hire the candidates likely to be most successful. Of course, the organization can only gather information about factors that are predictive of future performance. The process of determining the predictive value of information is called **validation**.

To reduce the element of uncertainty, managers use a variety of selection techniques, the most common of which are shown in Figure 8.2. Each organization develops its own mix of selection techniques and may use them in almost any order.

validation
The process of determining the predictive value of information.

Applications Forms

The first step in selection is usually asking the candidate to fill out an application form. An application form is an efficient method of gathering information about the applicant's previous work history, educational

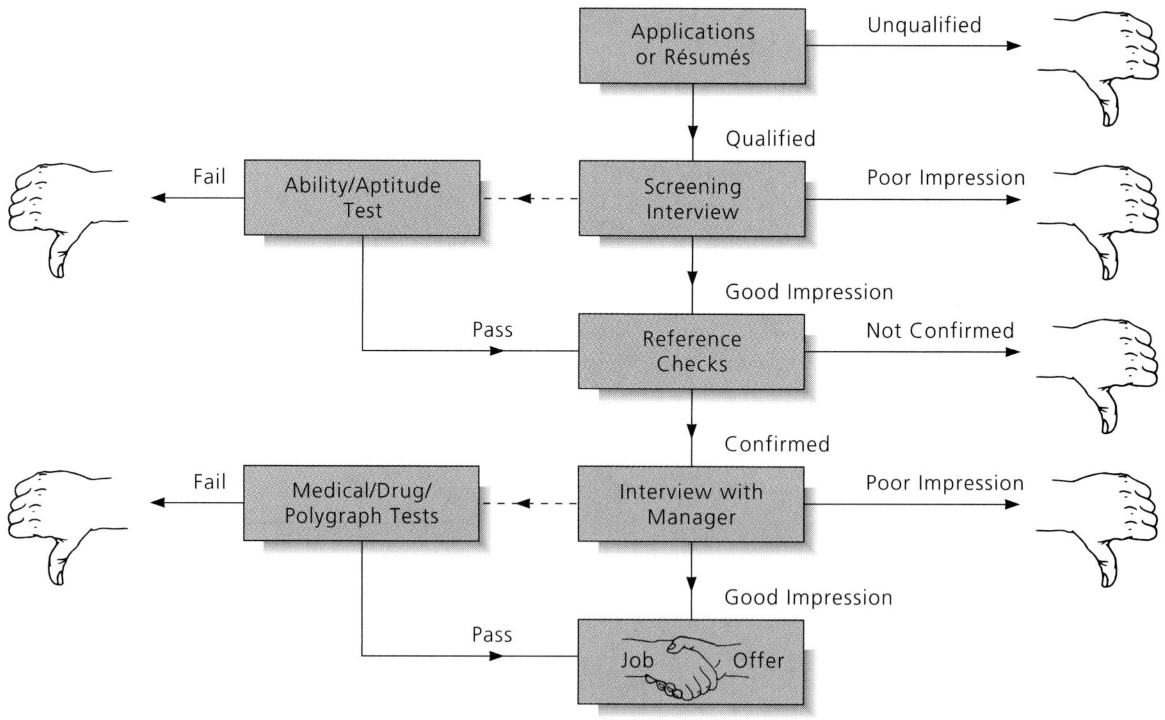

Figure 8.2
General steps in the selection process.

background, and other job-related demographic data. It should not contain questions about areas unrelated to the job, such as gender, religion, or national origin. Application-form data are generally used informally to decide whether a candidate merits further evaluation, and interviewers use application forms to familiarize themselves with candidates before interviewing them.

Tests

Tests of ability, skill, aptitude, or knowledge that is relevant to a particular job are usually the best predictors of job success, although tests of general intelligence or personality are occasionally useful as well. In addition to being validated, tests should be administered and scored consistently. All candidates should be given the same directions, allowed the same amount of time, and offered the same testing environment (e.g., temperature, lighting, distractions).

For some positions, ability or aptitude tests may be part of the initial screening process. When Toyota hired workers for its Cambridge, Ontario, plant, applicants were put through a series of tests to determine their math, verbal, and communication skills and their ability to work on a team. Even though most of the workers had never worked for an automobile firm before, they are now producing the highest-rated car in North America.

An **assessment centre** is a series of exercises in which candidates perform realistic management tasks under the watchful eye of expert appraisers. A typical assessment centre might be set up in a large conference room and go on for two or three days. During this time, potential managers might take selection tests, engage in management simulations, make individual presentations, and conduct group discussions. Assessors check to see how each participant reacts to stress or to criticism by colleagues.

A relatively new type of test is **video assessment** (see the "It's a Wired World" box). Regardless of the type of test that is used, it must be job-related (i.e., it must not serve as a basis for discriminating against anyone for reasons unrelated to the job) and it must be a valid predictor of performance (i.e., it must provide evidence that people who score well on it are more likely to perform well in the job than are people who score poorly on it).

assessment centre
A series of exercises in which management candidates perform realistic management tasks while being observed by appraisers.

video assessment
Involves showing potential hires videos of realistic work situations and asking them to choose a course of action to deal with the situation.

Interviews

The interview is a popular selection device, but it is sometimes a poor predictor of job success because biases inherent in the way people perceive and judge others on first meeting affect subsequent evaluations. Interview validity can be improved by training interviewers to be aware of potential biases and by increasing the structure of the interview. In a structured interview, questions are written in advance and all interviewers follow the same question list with each candidate. Such structure introduces consistency into the interview procedure and allows the organization to validate the content of the questions. For interviewing managerial or professional candidates, a somewhat less structured approach can be used. Although question areas and information-gathering objectives are still planned in advance, specific questions vary with the candidates' backgrounds.

Other Techniques

Organizations also use other selection techniques that vary with the circumstances. A manufacturer afraid of injuries to workers on the job might require new employees to have a physical examination. This gives the company some information about whether the employees are physically fit to do the work and what (if any) pre-existing injuries they might have.

IT'S A WIRED WORLD

Screen Test

Finding, screening, and hiring new employees can be a big expense for companies. It can cost $5000 to $10 000 to hire a clerical person, and much more to hire a top manager. In this cost-conscious era, companies are always ready to consider alternatives to the traditional hiring techniques.

One such promising new technique is video assessment. Potential new hires view videos that show a series of realistic work situations (portrayed by actors). For example, one scenario shows an assistant to a department manager who is trying to convince the supervisor of the word-processing pool to give his job top priority because the boss wants some last-minute changes made in a report. The supervisor refuses and the assistant asks the boss to intercede. At the end of each situation the viewers choose one of four courses of action to resolve the problem shown in the video. The test administrator then uses the computer to score candidate choices (much like a university or college instructor would grade student exams).

Video assessment is fast, reliable, cheap, and versatile. It also allows managers to screen more extensively for jobs at the lower levels in the organization. Improving selection at entry-level jobs should mean better customer service and greater chances for promotion from within. Video assessment can also give management greater insight into employee strengths and weaknesses before they are hired, and this can help the company solve long-standing problems like high turnover.

Video assessment evolved from assessment centres, which have been in use for more than 30 years. While assessment centres do get results, they are high-cost operations (up to $5000 for each person who is assessed). Videos are cheap by comparison. They take about an hour to complete and cost between $25 and $100. Canadian firms using video assessment include Weyerhaeuser, Reebok, Nortel, and B.C. Hydro.

But care must be taken when using video assessment. If a company simply buys a ready-made video from a consulting firm, it may get lax about doing its homework—stating the specific knowledge, skills, and motivation needed to do various jobs. Mindlessly using video assessment could, for example, cause a company to hire a salesperson who is good at "cold calls" when what it really needs is a salesperson who is good at maintaining existing accounts.

Another potential problem is that managers don't have a stake in selection criteria the way they do when they interview people. Some companies overcome these limitations by using multiple methods. Weyerhaeuser used both video assessment and an assessment centre to hire a supervisor for a sawmill. Some companies also use video assessment for ongoing training purposes. At Reebok, employees view the videos on a regular basis in training and development sessions.

An in-depth interview with a prospective employee is often part of the recruiting process, particularly for managerial jobs.

WEBCONNEXION

At the Taylor Group, a systems integrator located in Bedford, New Hampshire, hiring new employees is serious business. It's also a methodical—indeed, intensive—process designed to make just the right person-job fit. To find out more about Taylor—and to hear from some employees who were hired after as many as eight interviews—log on at:

www.taylornet.com

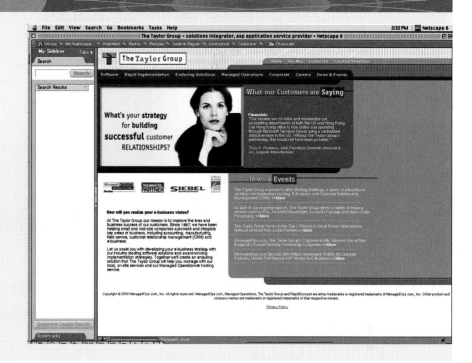

Polygraph (lie detector) tests are largely illegal now, and drug tests are also coming under fire. In 1998, for example, the Ontario Divisional Court decided that Imperial Oil Ltd.'s drug policy (which included pre-employment drug testing that made offers of work conditional on a negative result) was unlawful because Imperial failed to prove that a positive drug test would indicate a failure to perform essential duties. Imperial's policy also required random drug and alcohol testing, but that was also judged to be discriminatory because the company could not prove that such testing was necessary to deter alcohol or drug impairment on the job.[5] The Toronto Dominion Bank wanted to give drug tests to all new employees because it wanted to have the public's trust. However, a federal court ruled that the bank's policy was discriminatory and that it wasn't related closely enough to job performance.[6]

DEVELOPING HUMAN RESOURCES

Regardless of how effective a selection system is, most employees need additional training if they are to grow and develop in their jobs. This process begins with *orientation* and then proceeds to the *assessment of training and development needs* (including the performance of a *needs analysis*) and the selection of the best *training techniques and methods*.

New Employee Orientation

An important part of an organization's training and development program is new employee orientation. **Orientation** is the process of introducing new employees to the organization so that they can more quickly become effective contributors. Poor orientation can result in disenchantment, dissatisfaction, anxiety, turnover, and other employee problems. But effective

orientation
The initial acquainting of new employees with the company's policies and programs, personnel with whom they will interact, and the nature of the job.

orientation can play a key role in job satisfaction, performance, and retention. An effective orientation program will help newcomers feel like part of a team, introduce them quickly to co-workers, supervisors, and other new employees, and in a variety of other ways ease the transition from outsider to insider.

Some organizations also find it appropriate to include as a part of their orientation a general overview of and introduction to the business itself. This introduction may include such things as information about the firm's history, its evolution, its successes, and perhaps even some of its failures. Organizations with strong corporate cultures are especially likely to include such information because it is quick and efficient in helping to provide information about the firm's culture to new hires. This makes it easier for them to understand the culture and to know how to function within it.

Assessing Training and Development Needs

Beyond orientation for new employees, most organizations also find it effective to continue training and development on a regular basis. In other words, employees must be continually trained and developed in order to enhance and otherwise improve the quality of the contributions they make to the organization.

Needs Analysis

The starting point in assessing training and development needs is conducting a *needs analysis*—determining the organization's true needs and the training programs necessary to meet them. This analysis generally focuses on two things: the organization's job-related needs and the capabilities of the current workforce. The organization's needs are determined by the nature of the work that the organization needs to be done. That is, what knowledge, skills, and abilities does the organization need to compete? What skills must its workforce possess in order to perform the organization's work effectively?

Statistics Canada reports that 16 percent of Canadian adults cannot read the majority of written material they encounter in everyday life, and that 22 percent lack the reading skills necessary to deal with complex instructions. Because the equipment that workers use is increasingly complex, it is important that they have strong literacy skills. Companies like Nortel Networks and CCL Manufacturing have to train workers to use complex equipment, and they can do that only if their workers have good literacy skills.[7]

The actual design of training programs is the foundation of effective training and development. Without solid and relevant content, training and development efforts are pointless. The usual approach to content development starts with outlining program content and then expanding the outline into fully formed programs. Selecting the most appropriate instructors completes the process.

Training and Development Techniques and Methods

Depending on both the content of the program and the instructors selected to present it, a number of techniques and methods can be used for the actual delivery of information. We examine some of the more popular techniques and methods in this section.

Work-Based Programs

One major family of techniques and methods consists of various **work-based programs** that tie training and development activities directly to task performance. The most common method of work-based training is **on-the-job training**. The employee is placed in the actual work situation and is shown how to perform a task by a supervisor or an experienced employee. Much on-the-job training is informal, as when one employee shows another how to operate the photocopy machine.

Another work-based program is **vestibule training**, which involves a work simulation in which the job is performed under conditions closely simulating the actual work environment. Commercial airline pilots, for example, regularly undergo training and assessment in a flight simulator. Likewise, machine operators in a factory might be trained on simulated equipment that is comparable to that which they would use in the actual job setting.

Another method of work-based training program is **systematic job rotations and transfers**. This method is most likely to be used for lower-level managers or for operating employees being groomed for promotions to supervisory management positions. As the term suggests, the employee is systematically rotated or transferred from one job to another. The employee thus learns a wider array of tasks, acquires more abilities, and develops a more comprehensive view of the work of an organization or a particular subunit.

Instructional-Based Programs

A second family of techniques and methods involves **instructional-based programs**. The most commonly used of these programs is the **lecture or discussion approach**. In these situations, a trainer presents material in a descriptive fashion to those attending a trainee program. Just as a professor lectures students on a particular subject matter, an organizational trainer "lectures" trainees. Depending on the situation and the size of the training class, the instructor may opt for a pure lecture method or may include discussion with trainees. Sometimes lectures are on video or audio tapes so that various individuals in the organization can receive the same training at different times and/or at different locations.

Off-the-job training is performed at a location away from the work site. It may be at a classroom within the same facility or at a different location altogether. For example, refresher courses are offered to managers of McDonald's 600 Canadian restaurants at the Canadian Institute of Hamburgerology; in addition, training videotapes are shown to restaurant workers.[8] Coffee College is a two-week cram course run by Second Cup Ltd., Canada's largest retailer of specialty coffee. During their stay at Coffee College, franchisees and managers learn how to hire workers, keep the books, detect employee theft, and boost Christmas sales.[9]

Another instructional-based program is computer-assisted instruction. A trainee sits at a personal computer and operates software that has been specifically developed to teach certain material. The actual training materials are stored on the computer's hard drive, a CD-ROM, or a Web site. One major advantage of this method is that it allows self-paced learning and immediate feedback.

Training Technology

In recent years, the technology used for training has changed dramatically. Until just a few years ago, virtually all training involved paper and pencil, individual instruction, and mechanical reproduction of tasks. More recently,

work-based programs
A technique that ties training and development activities directly to task performance.

on-the-job training
Those development programs in which employees gain new skills while performing them at work.

vestibule training
A work simulation in which the job is performed under conditions closely simulating the actual work environment.

systematic job rotations and transfers
A technique in which an employee is systematically rotated or transferred from one job to another.

instructional-based programs
Training workers through the use of classroom-based programs such as the lecture approach.

lecture or discussion approach
An instructional-based program in which a trainer presents material in a descriptive fashion to those attending a trainee program.

off-the-job training
Those development programs in which employees learn new skills at a location away from the normal work site.

Second Cup Ltd.
www.secondcup.com

however, new technology has reshaped the way many companies deliver training. As we already noted, for example, computer-assisted instruction has become more popular. Obviously, computer-assisted instruction was impossible before the advent of computers, but it has only been within the last few years with the widespread adoption of personal computers that computer-assisted instruction has become widely used.

Video Teleconferencing.   Video teleconferencing is also used increasingly as a training tool. Companies find that when trainers in centralized locations deliver material live by satellite hookup to remote sites, training can be delivered just as effectively as transporting people to common training sites while saving travel costs. In the early days of video teleconferencing, communication tended to be one way: both the trainer and trainees simply saw the material as it was presented on a monitor. Now, however, there is considerably more interaction. Trainees usually have the ability to interact verbally or electronically.

Interactive Video.   Yet another new training tool is interactive video, which is essentially a combination of standard video and computer-based instruction. The material is presented via videotechnology on a monitor from a central serving mechanism, a videodisk, CD-ROM, or Web site. The trainee interacts with the system through a mouse or keyboard. Feedback can be provided when inadequate responses or improper answers are given, and the trainee can also skip over material that has already been learned.

Team Building and Group-Based Training

Also increasingly popular in recent years are various team-building and group-based methods of training. As more and more organizations are using teams as a basis for doing their jobs, it should not be surprising that many of the same companies are developing training programs specifically designed to facilitate intragroup cooperation among team members.

One popular method involves various outdoor training exercises. Some programs, for example, involve a group going through a physical obstacle course that requires climbing, crawling, and other physical activities. Outward Bound and several other independent companies specialize in offering these

Outward Bound
www.outwardbound.org

By using video teleconferencing, training of new employees involves considerably more interaction between trainer and trainee.

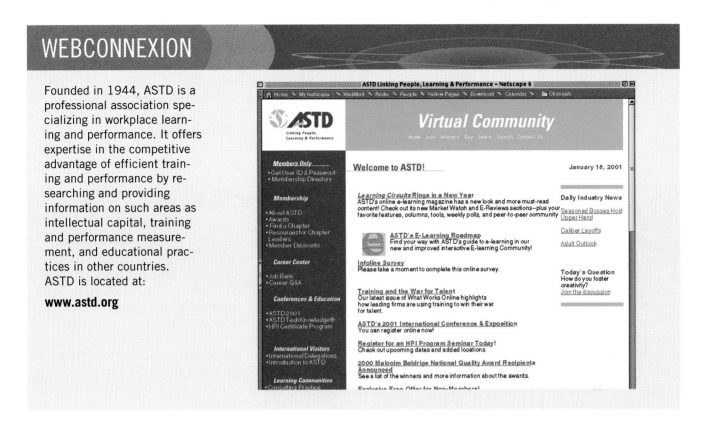

kinds of programs, and their clients include such firms as General Foods, Xerox, and Burger King. Participants, of course, must see the relevance of such programs if they are to be successful. Firms don't want employees returning from team-building programs to report merely that the experience "was childlike and fun and fairly inoffensive."[10]

EVALUATING EMPLOYEE PERFORMANCE

Another important part of human resource management is **performance appraisal**: the specific and formal evaluation of an employee to determine the degree to which he or she is performing effectively. Appraisals are important because they provide a benchmark to assess the extent to which recruiting and selection processes are adequate. In other words, performance appraisals help managers assess the extent to which they are recruiting and selecting the best employees. They also contribute to effective training, development, and compensation.

performance appraisal
A formal program for comparing employees' actual performance with expected performance; used in making decisions about training, promoting, compensating, and firing.

The Performance Appraisal Process

Several questions must be answered as part of the performance appraisal process. These questions generally relate to who conducts the performance appraisal and provides feedback to the individual whose performance is being evaluated.

Conducting the Performance Appraisal

The individual's supervisor is the person most likely to conduct a performance appraisal. Supervisors usually have both the most knowledge of the job requirements and the most opportunity to observe employees performing their jobs. In addition, the supervisor is usually responsible for the performance of his or her subordinates. Thus, the supervisor is both responsible for employees' high performance and accountable for their inadequate performance.

Sources of Information.   One possible source of information in the performance appraisal process is the subordinates of the individual being appraised. Subordinates are an especially important source of information when the performance of their own managers is being evaluated. Their input is perhaps most useful when the performance appraisal focuses on the manager's leadership potential. Another source of information is self-evaluation. In many professional and managerial situations, individuals occasionally may be asked to evaluate their own performance.

A final source of information is customers. Restaurants such as Red Lobster, for example, place feedback forms in the envelopes in which customers receive their cheques. These types of forms typically ask customers to rate their servers, the cook, and so forth on various characteristics.

Managers must recognize that each source of information is subject to various weaknesses and shortcomings. As a result, many organizations find it effective to rely on a variety of different information sources in the conduct of appraisals. They may, for example, gather information not merely from supervisors or peers, but from both. Indeed, some organizations gather information from every source described in this section. This comprehensive approach is called **360-degree feedback**.

Providing Performance Feedback

After the performance appraisal, the next major activity is providing feedback, coaching, and counselling. Many managers do a poor job in this area, in part because they don't understand how to do it properly and in part because they don't enjoy it. Almost by definition, performance appraisal in many organizations tends to focus on negatives. As a result, managers may have a tendency to avoid giving feedback because they know that an employee who receives negative feedback may be angry, hurt, discouraged, or argumentative. But clearly, if employees are not told about their shortcomings, they will have no concrete reason to try to improve and receive no guidance as to *how* to improve. It is critical, therefore, that managers follow up on appraisals by providing feedback.

Methods for Appraising Performance

Because of the nature of many jobs today, especially managerial work, most methods for appraising performance rely on judgments and ratings. A great deal of effort has therefore been expended trying to make relatively subjective evaluations as meaningful and useful as they can be. While some of the methods are based on relative rankings, others are based on ratings. In this section, we examine a few of the more popular methods, which we have categorized as either *ranking* or *rating methods*.

Ranking Methods

The **simple ranking method** requires a manager to rank-order from top to bottom or from best to worst each member of a particular work group or department. The individual ranked first is the top performer, the individual ranked second is the second-best performer, and so forth. The basis for the ranking is generally global or overall performance.

Red Lobster
www.redlobster.com

360-degree feedback
Gathering information from a manager's subordinates, peers, and superiors when assessing the manager's performance.

simple ranking method
A method of performance appraisal that requires a manager to rank-order from top to bottom or from best to worst each member of a particular work group or department.

Another ranking method, the **forced distribution method**, involves grouping employees into predefined frequencies of performance ratings. Those frequencies are determined in advance and are imposed on the rater. A decision might be made, for instance, that 10 percent of the employees in a work group will be grouped as "outstanding," 20 percent as "very good," 40 percent as "average," 20 percent as "below average," and the remaining 10 percent as "poor." The forced distribution method is familiar to many students because it is the principle used by professors who grade on a so-called "bell curve" or "normal curve."

forced distribution method
A method of performance appraisal that involves grouping employees into predefined frequencies of performance ratings.

Rating Methods

One of the most popular and widely used methods is the **graphic rating scale**, which consists simply of a statement or question about some aspect of an individual's job performance. Following the statement or question is a series of answers or possible responses from which the rater must select the one that fits best. For example, one common set of responses to a graphic rating scale with five possible alternatives is *strongly agree, agree, neither agree nor disagree, disagree*, and *strongly disagree*. These responses, or "descriptors," are usually arrayed along a bar, line, or similar visual representation marked with numbers or letters corresponding to each descriptor. Figure 8.3 shows a sample graphic rating scale.

graphic rating scale
A statement or question about some aspect of an individual's job performance for which the rater must select the response that fits best.

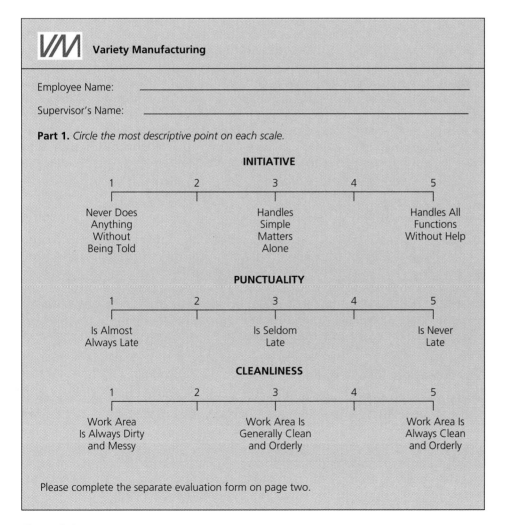

Figure 8.3
Performance rating scale.

Graphic rating scales are appealing because they are relatively easy to develop. A manager simply "brainstorms" or otherwise develops a list of statements or questions that are presumably related to relevant indicators of performance. Moreover, a wide array of performance dimensions can be tapped with various rating scales on the same form. As we noted, a number or a letter accompanies each descriptor on the rating form. Most rating scales have ranges of one to five or one to seven. To develop a performance measure, the manager simply adds up the "points" for a particular employee's responses to obtain an overall index of performance.

critical incident method

A technique of performance appraisal in which raters recall examples of especially good or poor performance by an employee and then describe what the employee did (or did not do) that led to success or failure.

Somewhat different is the **critical incident method**. A *critical incident* is simply an example of especially good or poor performance on the part of the employee. Organizations that rely on this method often require raters to recall such instances and then describe what the employee did (or did not do) that led to success or failure. This technique not only provides information for feedback but defines performance in fairly clear, behavioural terms. In other cases, managers keep logs or diaries in which they record examples of critical incidents.

PROVIDING COMPENSATION AND BENEFITS

compensation

What a firm offers its employees in return for their labour.

Employees do not work for free—they expect to be compensated for the time, talent, and effort they devote to their jobs and to helping the organization achieve its goals. In this section, we explore basic compensation, incentives and performance-based rewards, and employee benefits and services. **Compensation** is the set of rewards that organizations provide to individuals in return for their willingness to perform various jobs and tasks within the organization. As we shall see, compensation includes a number of different elements, including base salary, incentives, bonuses, benefits, and other rewards. Compensation should never be a random decision, but rather the result of a careful and systematic strategic process. The "Business Today" box lists the annual compensation of selected entertainers and top managers.

Determining Basic Compensation

wages

Dollars paid based on the number of hours worked.

salary

Dollars paid at regular intervals in return for doing a job, regardless of the amount of time or output involved.

Basic compensation means the base level of wages or salary paid to an employee. **Wages** generally refer to hourly compensation paid to operating employees. Most of the jobs that are paid on an hourly wage basis are lower-level and/or operating-level jobs. Rather than expressing compensation on an hourly basis, the organization may instead describe compensation on an annual or monthly basis. Many college and university graduates, for example, compare job offers on the basis of annual **salary**, such as $36 000 versus $38 000 a year.

Pay Surveys in Compensation

pay survey

A survey of compensation paid to employees by other employers in a particular geographic area, an industry, or an occupational group.

One common source of information that many organizations use to determine base compensation is **pay surveys**—surveys of compensation paid to employees by other employers in a particular geographic area, an industry, or an occupational group. Pay surveys provide the information that an organization needs to avoid an imbalance between its own pay scale and those of comparable organizations. Some pay surveys are conducted by professional associations. For example, the Canadian Federation of Business School Deans publishes an annual summary of salaries for professors teaching in business schools in Canadian universities.

In general, then, a pay survey simply asks other organizations what they pay people to perform various jobs. Most organizations participate in such surveys because they will have access to the resulting data. There is, for example,

BUSINESS TODAY

Some Highly Paid Canadians

The average family income in Canada is less than $60 000 per year. The chief justice of the Supreme Court of Canada makes over $200 000 and the dean of the Faculty of Management at the University of Toronto makes more than $300 000. Most Canadians would find these salaries very comfortable. But even they are insignificant when compared to what some other Canadians earn per year.

- Shania Twain (singer), $70 million
- Jim Carrey (actor), $66 million
- Celine Dion (singer), $60 million
- Michael J. Fox (actor), $44 million
- Frank Stronach (Magna International), $34.2 million
- J.R. Shaw (Shaw Communications), $26.6 million
- Larry Walker (baseball player), $17 million
- Paul Kariya (hockey player), $14 million
- Gerald Schwartz (Onex), $11.1 million
- John Hunkin (CIBC), $6.1 million
- John Roth (Nortel Networks), $5.1 million
- Edgar Bronfman (Seagram), $3.7 million
- Laurent Beaudoin (Bombardier), $3.1 million

The managers included in this list not only earn high compensation when they work for a company, but also receive sizeable compensation when they retire. An executive who earned a large salary during his or her time with a company may represent a liability to the company of more than $5 million (assuming that the executive lives for 15 years after retirement). In spite of these seemingly large numbers, the compensation of Canadian executives is not out of line compared to the annual earnings of CEOs in other countries. Canadian salaries are higher than those of top executives in Japan and Germany, but they are much lower than those in the U.S.

Statistics Canada data show that CEOs earn 20, 50, and even 100 times what hourly workers earn. Are these large differences warranted? Critics argue that it is unethical to pay top executives $1 million or $5 million per year for what they do. Professor Henry Mintzberg of McGill University says that these salary levels send a terrible message to the average working person, particularly since many top managers frequently talk about how important employees are. Mintzberg says that real leadership qualities are shown by top managers who take salaries in the range of $250 000 to $500 000.

Supporters of high executive salaries argue that we can determine what a top executive is worth by comparing top managers with top professional athletes or successful entertainers. In professional sports, one superstar can make a team, and a similar argument might be made that a CEO can make a company. If a professional athlete or entertainer can make millions of dollars in one year, surely a CEO of a large company is worth millions as well.

---

a consortium of eight large electronic companies in the United States that routinely survey one another to determine what each pays new engineers and other professional employees who are hired directly out of college or university. The companies alternate the responsibility for conducting surveys from year to year, with the responsible organization sharing its results with the other members.

A study by Statistics Canada shows that the average earnings of U.S. workers in 1997 was about $36 500 (in 1995 Canadian dollars), and that the average Canadian worker earned about $28 300. In the period 1985–97, earnings of U.S. workers rose 14.6 percent, while earnings of Canadian workers rose only 5.9 percent.[11]

Statistics Canada
www.statcan.ca

Job Evaluation

Another means of determining basic compensation is *job evaluation,* which should not be confused with *job analysis.* Recall that managers use job analysis to understand the requirements and nature of a job and its performance so that appropriate individuals can be recruited and selected. **Job evaluation** is a method for determining the relative value or worth of a job to the organization so that individuals who perform it can be appropriately compensated. In other words, it is mostly concerned with establishing internal pay equity. A number of well-established job evaluation techniques and methods have been established.

job evaluation
A method for determining the relative value or worth of a job to the organization so that individuals who perform it can be appropriately compensated.

Establishing a Pay Structure

A third method for determining basic compensation is establishing a *pay structure*. Compensation for different jobs is based on the organization's assessment of the relative value to the organization of each job class. Thus, there should be a logical rank ordering of compensation levels from the most valuable to the least valuable jobs throughout the organization. The organization, of course, may also find it necessary to group certain jobs together; thus, two or more jobs that are valued relatively equally will be compensated at approximately the same level. In addition, the organization decides on minimum and maximum pay ranges for each job or job class. Managers might use performance, *seniority* (a system that gives priority in promotions to employees with greater length of service), or a combination of the two to determine how much a person can be paid for doing a particular job.

Because of today's tight labour market, many job seekers are finding it possible to demand higher salaries than ever before. The Internet is also playing a key role in this trend, because job seekers and current employees can more easily get a sense of what their true market value is. If they can document the claim that their value is higher than what their current employer now pays or is offering, they are in a position to demand higher salaries. One manager who met with a subordinate to discuss her raise was surprised when she produced data from five different Web sites to support her request for a bigger raise than he had intended to offer.

Performance-Based Compensation

Besides basic compensation, many organizations also offer performance-based rewards. The reason is obvious: When rewards are associated with higher levels of performance, employees will presumably be motivated to work harder in order to reap those awards.

Merit Pay Plans

merit pay
Pay awarded to employees according to the relative value of their contributions.

merit pay plans
Compensation plans that formally base at least some meaningful portion of compensation on merit.

Merit pay refers to pay awarded to employees according to the relative value of their contributions. Employees who make greater contributions receive higher pay than those who make lesser contributions. **Merit pay plans**, then, are compensation plans that base at least some meaningful portion of compensation on merit. The most general form of a merit pay plan is the *raise*—an annual salary increase granted to an employee because of his or her relative merit. In such plans, merit is usually determined or defined according to individual performance and overall contribution to the organization.

skill-based pay
Pay awarded to employees not for any specific level of performance, but for the acquisition of job-related skills.

knowledge-based pay
Pay awarded to employees for learning.

Skill- and Knowledge-Based Pay Systems. Although these systems are usually not strictly viewed as merit systems, it is worth noting how **skill-based pay** or **knowledge-based pay** systems focus employee attention on different areas but still rely on similar motivational processes. Instead of rewarding employees for increased performance, such systems reward them for the acquisition of more skills or knowledge. Skill-based pay systems reward employees not for any specific level of performance, but for the acquisition of job-related skills. Knowledge-based pay systems reward employees for learning, because presumably, as they acquire more and more skills and knowledge, employees become more valuable to the organization.

Incentive Compensation Systems

Incentive compensation systems are among the oldest forms of performance-based rewards. Indeed, some companies were using individual piece-rate incentive plans over 100 years ago. Under a **piece-rate incentive plan**, the organization pays an employee a certain amount of money for every unit produced. An employee might, for example, be paid $1 for every 12 units of a product successfully completed. But such simplistic systems fail to account for such factors as minimum wage levels and rely on two questionable assumptions: (1) that performance is totally under an individual's control, and (2) that the individual employee does a single task continuously during the course of his or her work time. Today, therefore, incentive compensation systems tend to be much more sophisticated.

Incentive Pay Plans. Generally speaking, **individual incentive plans** reward individual performance on a real-time basis. That is, rather than increasing a person's base salary at the end of the year, an employer gives an individual a salary increase or some other financial reward for outstanding performance immediately or shortly after the performance occurred. For example, many baseball players have clauses in their contracts that pay them bonuses for hitting more than .300 over a season.

Individual incentive systems are most common where performance can be assessed objectively (e.g., by the number of units of output) rather than subjectively by a superior. Perhaps the most common form of individual incentive is the **sales commission** paid to people engaged in sales work.

Other Forms of Incentives. Occasionally organizations use other forms of incentives. For example, a non-monetary incentive, such as additional time off or a special perk, might be useful. At Nortel Networks, recognition is given

piece-rate incentive plan
A compensation system in which an organization pays an employee a certain amount of money for every unit produced.

individual incentive plans
A compensation system in which an employer gives an individual a salary increase or some other financial reward for outstanding performance immediately or shortly after the performance occurred.

sales commission
Paying salespeople based on the number of units they sell or the dollar value of sales they generate for the company.

WEBCONNEXION

The Cheesecake Factory operates upscale restaurants across the country and actually serves about 200 different menu items (including, of course, cheesecake). The company is also known for its efforts to remain productive by retaining employees. Salaries, for instance, are above market rates, and general managers all get stock options. To find out more about The Cheesecake Factory's employee incentives, log on at:

www.thecheesecakefactory.com

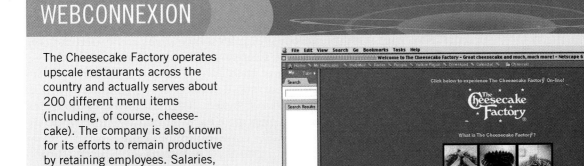

to employees in the form of special points that are awarded on the recommendation of a supervisor. Recipients can convert their points into money or they can use them to buy merchandise or trips from a special online catalogue.[12]

Team and Group Incentive Systems

The merit compensation and incentive compensation systems described in the preceding sections deal primarily with reward plans for individuals. There are also performance-based reward programs for teams and groups. Given today's increasing trend towards team- and group-based methods of work, such programs are growing in importance.

gainsharing program
An incentive program in which employees receive a bonus if the firm's costs are reduced because of greater worker efficiency and/or productivity.

Palliser Furniture Ltd.
www.palliser.com

Gainsharing.   Many organizations use **gainsharing programs**, which are designed to share with employees the cost savings from productivity improvements. Palliser Furniture Ltd., for example, introduced a gainsharing plan that rewards employees for increasing production. Any profit resulting from production above a certain level is split 50–50 between the company and the employees.[13] The underlying assumption is that employees and the employer have the same goals and should therefore share in incremental economic gains. In general, organizations start by measuring team- or group-level productivity. The team or work group itself is then charged with lowering costs and otherwise improving productivity through any measures that members develop and their manager approves. Any resulting cost savings or productivity gains are then quantified and translated into dollar values. According to a predetermined formula, these dollar savings are then allocated to both employer and employees.

Performance Increases.   Some companies use true incentives at the team or group level. Just like individual incentives, some team or group incentives tie rewards directly to performance increases. Like individual incentives, team or group incentives are also paid as they are earned rather than added to base salaries.

profit-sharing plan
An incentive program in which employees receive a bonus depending on the firm's profits.

Profit Sharing.   Other team- or group-level incentives go beyond the contributions of a specific work group. These are generally organization-wide incentives. One long-standing type of incentive program is called a **profit-sharing plan**. At the end of the year, some portion of the company's profits is paid into a profit-sharing pool that is then distributed to all employees. In 2000, Dofasco's profit-sharing plan gave each worker $7906 beyond his or her regular pay. Dofasco annually contributes 14 percent of its pre-tax profits to the profit-sharing plan.[14] Ipsco Steel of Regina introduced a profit-sharing plan that gives all workers an identical year-end bonus. In one recent year, over $9 million was distributed to employees.[15]

Indirect Compensation and Benefits

In addition to financial compensation, most organizations provide employees with an array of other indirect compensation in the form of benefits. **Benefits** generally refer to various rewards, incentives, and other things of value that an organization gives employees in addition to wages, salaries, and other forms of direct financial compensation. Because these benefits have tangible value, they represent a meaningful form of compensation even though they are not generally expressed in financial terms.

benefits
What a firm offers its workers other than wages and salaries in return for their labour.

Mandated Protection Plans

Protection plans protect employees when their income is threatened or reduced by illness, disability, death, unemployment, or retirement. A number of these plans are required by law, but others are optional. One mandated benefit is **employment insurance**, which provides a basic subsistence payment to employees who are between jobs. It is intended for people who have stopped working for one organization but who are assumed to be actively seeking employment with another. Both employers and employees pay premiums to an employment insurance fund.

Also mandated are Canada Pension Plan payments. The original purpose of this program was to provide some limited income to retired individuals to supplement personal savings, private pensions, part-time work, and so forth. It is funded through employee and employer taxes that are withheld from payroll.

Workers' compensation is mandated insurance that covers individuals who suffer a job-related illness or accident. Employers bear the cost of workers' compensation insurance. The exact premium is related to each employer's past experience with job-related accidents and illnesses. For example, a steel company might pay $20 per $100 of wages, while an accounting firm might pay only 10 cents per $100 of wages.

protection plan
A plan that protects employees when their income is threatened or reduced by illness, disability, death, unemployment, or retirement.

employment insurance
A protection plan that provides a basic subsistence payment to employees who are between jobs.

workers' compensation
Mandated insurance that covers individuals who suffer a job-related illness or accident.

Optional Protection Plans

Another major category of employee benefits consists of various optional protection plans. These plans provide protection in many of the same areas as those discussed above, except that organizations can choose whether to provide them. Perhaps the most common optional protection plan is insurance coverage. Health insurance is probably the most important type of coverage. In recent years, it has been expanded by many organizations to include such things as special programs for prescription drugs, vision care products, mental health services, and dental care. Other kinds of coverage include life insurance, long-term disability insurance, and so forth.

Paid Time Off

Paid vacations are usually for periods of one, two, or more weeks during which an employee can take time off from work and continue to be paid. Most organizations vary the amount of paid vacation with an individual's seniority. Another common paid time off plan is *sick leave*. This benefit is provided when an individual is sick or otherwise physically unable to perform his or her job. Most organizations allow an individual to accumulate sick time according to a schedule, such as one sick day per month.

Sometimes an organization will allow an employee to take off a small number of days simply for "personal business." This benefit is usually called *personal leave*. Occasions might include funerals, religious observances, weddings, birthdays, or simply personal holidays. Finally, organizations are usually required by law to allow employees to miss work if they are called for jury duty.

Other Types of Benefits

In addition to protection plans and paid time off, many organizations offer a growing number of other benefit programs. **Wellness programs**, for example, concentrate on preventing illness in employees rather than simply paying their expenses when they become sick. In some organizations, these

wellness program
A program that concentrates on preventing illness in employees rather than simply paying their expenses when they become sick.

programs are simple and involve little more than organized jogging or walking during lunch breaks. More elaborate programs include smoking cessation, blood pressure and cholesterol screening, and stress management. Some organizations maintain full-fledged health clubs on site and provide counselling and programs for fitness and weight loss.

Child-care benefits are also becoming extremely popular. In fact, any organization that wants to be considered "family-friendly" must have some type of child-care benefits, and being a "family-friendly" company is increasingly becoming a competitive advantage. These plans might include scheduling help, referrals to various types of services, or reimbursement accounts for child-care expenses. In many cases, they actually include company-paid daycare. Elder care is also going to become increasingly common as the population ages and workers care for their elderly parents. Concluding Case 9-1 on page 287 gives additional examples of benefits that are sometimes provided by Canadian companies.

Cafeteria-Style Benefit Plans

cafeteria-style benefit plans
A flexible approach to providing benefits in which employees are allocated a certain sum to cover benefits and can "spend" this allocation on the specific benefits they prefer.

Most benefit programs are designed for all employees in an organization. Although the exact benefits may vary according to the employee's level in the organization, within those levels plans are generally "one size fits all." In contrast, **cafeteria-style benefit plans** allow employees to choose the benefits they really want. Under these plans, the organization typically establishes a budget, indicating how much it is willing to spend, per employee, on benefits. Employees are then presented with a list of possible benefits and the cost of each. They are free to put the benefits together in any combination they wish. Employees at Toyota's Cambridge, Ontario, plant are given the opportunity once each year to restructure their benefit packages. For example, they can give more weight to dental coverage if they have young children, or to life insurance or disability coverage, depending on their circumstances.[16]

THE LEGAL CONTEXT OF HRM

As much or more than any area of business, HRM is heavily influenced by federal law, provincial law, and judicial review. In this section, we summarize some of the most important and far-reaching areas of HR regulation.

Equal Employment Opportunity

equal employment opportunity
Regulations to protect people from unfair or inappropriate discrimination in the workplace.

The basic goal of all **equal employment opportunity** regulations is to protect people from unfair or inappropriate discrimination in the workplace. Let's begin by noting that discrimination in itself is not illegal. Whenever one person is given a pay raise and another is not, or when one person is hired and another is not, the organization has made a decision to distinguish one person from another. As long as the basis for this discrimination is purely job-related (made, for instance, on the basis of performance or qualifications) and is applied objectively and consistently, the action is legal and appropriate. Problems arise when distinctions among people are not job-related. In such cases, the resulting discrimination is illegal.

Anti-Discrimination Laws

Canadian Human Rights Act
Ensures that any individual who wishes to obtain a job has an equal opportunity to apply for it.

When recruiting, firms must be careful not to violate anti-discrimination laws. The key federal anti-discrimination legislation is the ***Canadian Human Rights Act*** of 1977. The goal of this act is to ensure that any individual who wishes to obtain a job has an equal opportunity to compete for it. The act applies to all federal agencies, federal Crown corporations, any employee of the federal government, and business firms that do business interprovincially. Thus, it applies to such firms as the Bank of Montreal, Air Canada, Telecom Canada, Canadian National Railways, and many other public and private sector organizations that operate across Canada. Even with such wide application, the act affects only about 10 percent of Canadian workers; the rest are covered under provincial human rights acts.

The *Canadian Human Rights Act* prohibits a wide variety of practices in recruiting, selecting, promoting, and dismissing personnel. The act specifically prohibits discrimination on the basis of age, race and colour, national and ethnic origin, physical handicap, religion, gender, marital status, or prison record (if pardoned). Some exceptions to these blanket prohibitions are permitted. Discrimination cannot be charged if a blind person is refused a position as a train engineer, bus driver, or crane operator. Likewise, a firm cannot be charged with discrimination if it does not hire a deaf person as a telephone operator or as an audio engineer.

These situations are clear-cut, but many others are not. For example, is it discriminatory to refuse women employment in a job that routinely requires carrying objects with a mass of more than 50 kilograms? Difficulties in determining whether discrimination has occurred are sometimes dealt with by using the concept of "**bona fide occupational requirement**." An employer may choose one person over another based on overriding characteristics of the job in question. If a fitness centre wants to hire only women to supervise its women's locker room and sauna, it can do so without being discriminatory because it established a bona fide occupational requirement.

bona fide occupational requirement
When an employer may choose one applicant over another based on overriding characteristics of the job.

Enforcement of the federal act is carried out by the Canadian Human Rights Commission. The commission can either respond to complaints from individuals who believe they have been discriminated against, or launch an investigation on its own if it has reason to believe that discrimination has occurred. During an investigation, data are gathered about the alleged discriminatory behaviour and, if the claim of discrimination is substantiated, the offending organization or individual may be ordered to compensate the victim.

Each province has also enacted human rights legislation to regulate organizations and businesses operating in that province. These provincial regulations are similar in spirit to the federal legislation, with many minor variations from province to province. All provinces prohibit discrimination on the basis of race, national or ethnic origin, colour, religion, sex, and marital status, but some do not address such issues as physical handicaps, criminal record, or age. Provincial human rights commissions enforce provincial legislation.

The ***Employment Equity Act of 1986*** addresses the issue of discrimination in employment by designating four groups as employment disadvantaged—women, visible minorities, aboriginal people, and people with disabilities. Companies covered by the act are required to publish statistics on their employment of people in these four groups.

Employment Equity Act of 1986
Federal legislation that designates four groups as employment disadvantaged— women, visible minorities, aboriginal people, and people with disabilities.

The Bank of Montreal recently became the first company outside the U.S. to win a prestigious award for promoting women's careers. Women represented over half of executive level promotions at the bank in 1993. The Bank of Montreal has introduced initiatives such as flexible working hours, a mentoring program, a national career information network, and a gender awareness workshop series.[17]

Companies are increasingly making provisions for disabled employees. At Rogers Cablevision, a division of Rogers Communications Inc., a large workplace area was completely redesigned to accommodate workers who were either visually disabled or in wheelchairs. Special equipment was also installed—a large-print computer for workers with partial sight, and a device that allows blind workers to read printed materials.[18]

Comparable Worth

In spite of recent advances, the average woman still earns only about three-quarters of what the average man earns; the average *single* woman, however, earns 99 percent of what single men earn. The most recent gains by women have occurred because men lost four of every five jobs that disappeared during the 1990s. The opening case described the advances that women are making in top-level management jobs, but most top jobs in the public and private sector continue to be held by men.[19]

Comparable worth is a legal concept that aims at paying equal wages for jobs that are of comparable value to the employer. This might mean comparing dissimilar jobs, such as those of nurses and mechanics or secretaries and electricians. Proponents of comparable worth say that all the jobs in a company must be evaluated and then rated in terms of basic dimensions such as the level of skill they require. All jobs could then be compared based on a common index. People in different jobs that rate the same on this index would be paid the same. Experts hope that this will help to reduce the gap between men's and women's pay.

Critics of comparable worth object on the grounds that it ignores the supply and demand aspects of labour. They say, for example, that legislation forcing a company to pay people more than the open market price for their labour (which may happen in jobs where there is a surplus of workers) is another example of unreasonable government interference in business activities. They also say that implementing comparable worth will cost business firms too much money. A study prepared for the Ontario Ministry of Labour estimated that it would cost approximately $10 billion for the public and private sectors in Ontario to establish equitable payment for jobs of equal value. Yet the cost defence cannot be easily used. In one case, the Quebec Human Rights Commission ruled that 24 female office employees of the Quebec North Shore Paper Company were performing work of equal value to that done by male production workers. The company was required to increase the secretaries' salaries by $701 annually and give them over $1000 in back pay.[20]

In 1999, the Canadian Human Rights Tribunal ruled that the federal government must pay a total of more than $3 billion to thousands of civil servants because it discriminated against workers in female-dominated job classifications. About 85 percent of these workers were women.

There is one very interesting fact in this debate about comparable worth: Male earning power has been declining for decades. Young males who are now entering the labour market, regardless of their education, will likely earn dramatically less than their predecessors did. Young, female university graduates, on the other hand, have recently earned more than their predecessors.[21]

Sexual Harassment

Within the job context, sexual harassment refers to requests for sexual favours, unwelcome sexual advances, or verbal or physical conduct of a sexual nature that creates an intimidating or hostile environment for a given employee. The *Canadian Human Rights Act* takes precedence over any policies that a company might have developed on its own to deal with sexual harassment problems.

If a manager is found guilty of sexual harassment, the company is also liable because the manager is an agent of the company. In fact, even if one employee makes another employee feel uncomfortable, the instigator may be guilty of sexual harassment. At Levac Supply Ltd. of Kingston, Ontario, for

comparable worth
A legal idea that aims to pay equal wages for work of equal value.

Ontario Ministry of Labour
www.gov.on.ca/LAB/main.htm

example, one employee harassed another over a period of many years. A board of inquiry ruled that the company was jointly responsible for the harassment with the employee who had done the harassing. The woman who was harassed received a settlement of $448 273.[22]

To deal effectively with the potential for sexual harassment, managers should:

- develop clear and enforceable policies dealing with sexual harassment
- inform all employees about the existence of these policies
- train employees to recognize and refrain from sexual harassment
- take complaints about sexual harassment seriously
- establish a procedure for dealing with harassment complaints
- take action against those who are involved in sexual harassment.

Employee Safety and Health

Employee safety and health programs help to reduce absenteeism and turnover, raise productivity, and boost morale by making jobs safer and more healthful.

Government regulations about employee safety are becoming stricter. Ontario, which loses more than 7 million working days yearly because of on-the-job injuries, has passed amendments to the Ontario *Occupational Health and Safety Act*. Officers and directors of companies are held personally responsible for workplace health and safety and are punishable by jail terms and fines for permitting unsafe working conditions.[23]

Some industrial work—logging, construction, fishing, and mining—can put workers at risk of injury in obvious ways. But other types of work—such as typing or lifting—can also cause painful injuries. **Repetitive strain injuries** (RSIs) occur when workers perform the same functions over and over again. These injuries disable more than 200 000 Canadians each year and account for nearly half of all work-related time loss claims.

In Canada, each province has developed its own workplace health and safety regulations. The purpose of these laws is to ensure that employees do not have to work in dangerous conditions. These laws are the direct result of undesirable conditions that existed in many Canadian businesses at the close of the nineteenth century. While much improvement is evident, Canada still has some problems with workplace health and safety. In one study of six Western industrialized nations, Canada had the worst safety record in mining and construction and the second-worst record in manufacturing and railways.

The Ontario *Occupational Health and Safety Act* illustrates current legislation in Canada. It requires all employers to ensure that equipment and safety devices are used properly. Employers must also show workers the proper way to operate machinery. At the job site, supervisors are charged with the responsibility of ensuring that workers use equipment properly. The act also requires workers to behave appropriately on the job. Employees have the right to refuse to work on a job if they believe it is unsafe; a legal procedure exists for resolving any disputes in this area.

In most provinces, the Ministry of Labour appoints inspectors to enforce health and safety regulations. If the inspector finds a sufficient hazard, he or she has the authority to clear the workplace. Inspectors can usually arrive at a firm unannounced to conduct an inspection.

repetitive strain injuries
Injuries that occur when workers perform the same functions over and over again.

Retirement

Some employees are ready for retirement earlier than others. But because many retirement plans are based on an employee's age, some workers who should retire earlier stay on the job while others, who are still useful workers, leave before they would like to. This policy is shortsighted. A compromise is to grant year-to-year extensions to productive employees who want to continue working past the traditional retirement age.

Canadian courts have typically upheld 65 as the mandatory retirement age, but there have been many complaints from older workers who want to continue working past this age. As a result, the Ontario Human Rights Commission has launched a review of age discrimination and mandatory retirement. The commission is also studying downsizing practices that may push older workers into early retirement.[24] The commission is going ahead with the study even though Canadians generally are retiring earlier than they used to. In the period 1976–80, for example, the median retirement age in Canada was 64.9 years, but in the period 1991–95 that figure dropped to 62.3 years.[25] Two other interesting facts: Workers over age 65 are nearly four times as likely to die from work-related causes than younger workers, and older workers have double the health care costs that workers in their forties do.[26]

NEW CHALLENGES IN THE CHANGING WORKPLACE

As we have seen throughout this chapter, HR managers face several ongoing challenges in their efforts to keep their organizations staffed with effective workers. To complicate matters, new challenges arise as the economic and social environments of business change. We conclude this chapter with a discussion of several of the most important HRM issues facing business today: managing workforce diversity, managing knowledge workers, and managing contingent and temporary workers.

Managing Workforce Diversity

workforce diversity

The range of workers' attitudes, values, beliefs, and behaviours that differ by gender, race, age, ethnicity, physical ability, and other relevant characteristics.

One extremely important set of human resource challenges centres on **workforce diversity**—the range of workers' attitudes, values, beliefs, and behaviours that differ by gender, race, age, ethnicity, physical ability, and other relevant characteristics. In the past, organizations tended to work towards homogenizing their workforces, getting everyone to think and behave in similar ways. Partly as a result of affirmative action efforts, however, many organizations are now creating more diverse workforces by embracing more women, ethnic minorities, and foreign-born employees than ever before.

Today, organizations are recognizing not only that they should treat everyone equitably, but also that they should acknowledge the individuality of each person they employ. They are also recognizing that diversity can be a competitive advantage. For example, by hiring the best people available from every group rather than hiring from just one or a few groups, a firm can develop a higher-quality workforce. Similarly, a diverse workforce can bring a wider array of information to bear on problems and can provide insights on marketing products to a wider range of consumers. Says the head of workforce diversity at IBM: "We think it is important for our customers to look inside and see people like them. If they can't . . . the prospect of them becoming or staying our customers declines."

Managing Knowledge Workers

Traditionally, employees added value to organizations because of what they did or because of their experience. In the "information age," however, many employees add value because of what they know.[27]

The Nature of Knowledge Work

These employees are usually called **knowledge workers**, and the skill with which they are managed is a major factor in determining which firms will be successful in the future. Knowledge workers, including computer scientists, engineers, and physical scientists, provide special challenges for the HR manager. They tend to work for high-tech firms and are usually experts in some abstract knowledge base. They often prefer to work independently and tend to identify more strongly with their professions than with any organization—even to the extent of defining performance in terms recognized by other members of their professions.

As the importance of information-driven jobs grows, the need for knowledge workers continues to grow as well. But these employees require extensive and highly specialized training, and not every organization is willing to make the human capital investments necessary to take advantage of these jobs. In fact, even after knowledge workers are on the job, training updates are critical to prevent their skills from becoming obsolete. It has been suggested, for example, that the "half-life" of a technical education in engineering is about three years. The failure to update such skills will not only result in the loss of competitive advantage but also increase the likelihood that the knowledge worker will move to another firm that is more committed to updating his or her knowledge.

knowledge workers
Workers who are experts in specific fields like computer technology and engineering, and who add value because of what they know, rather than how long they have worked or the job they do.

Knowledge Worker Management and Labour Markets

In recent years, the demand for knowledge workers has been growing at a dramatic rate. As a result, organizations that need these workers must introduce regular market adjustments (upward) in order to pay them enough to keep them. This is especially critical in areas in which demand is growing, as even entry-level salaries for these employees are skyrocketing. Once an employee accepts a job with a firm, the employer faces yet another dilemma. Once hired, workers are subject to the company's internal labour market, which is not likely to be growing as quickly as the external market for knowledge workers as a whole. Consequently, the longer an employee remains with a firm, the further behind the market his or her pay falls—unless, of course, it is regularly adjusted upward.

Every year the toy industry sells about 10 million scientific toys, such as chemistry sets. It also sells about 30 million electronic toys. These discrepancies help account for the fact that more and more science-minded students—like this Power PC chip builder at Intel Corp—are opting for computer-industry jobs instead of jobs in the traditional hard sciences, such as chemistry. Many experts predict that the current lure of quick financial solvency will result in a future shortage of science researchers and teachers.

Not surprisingly, the growing demand for these workers has inspired some fairly extreme measures for attracting them in the first place.[28] High starting salaries and sign-on bonuses are common. British Petroleum Exploration was recently paying starting petroleum engineers with undersea platform-drilling knowledge—not experience, just knowledge—salaries in the six figures, plus sign-on bonuses of over US$50 000 and immediate profit sharing. Even with these incentives, HR managers complain that in the Gulf Coast region, they cannot retain specialists because young engineers soon leave to accept sign-on bonuses from competitors. Laments one HR executive: "We wind up six months after we hire an engineer having to fight off offers for that same engineer for more money."[29]

Managing Contingent and Temporary Workers

A final contemporary HR issue of note involves the use of contingent and/or temporary workers. Indeed, recent years have seen an explosion in the use of such workers by organizations.

Trends in Contingent and Temporary Employment

In recent years, the number of contingent workers has increased dramatically. A contingent worker is a person who works for an organization on something other than a permanent or full-time basis. Categories of contingent workers include independent contractors (freelancers), on-call workers, temporary employees (usually hired through outside agencies), and contract and leased employees. Another category is part-time workers. The financial services giant Citigroup, for example, makes extensive use of part-time sales agents to pursue new clients. (See Concluding Case 8.1 at the end of this chapter for more information on freelancing.)

Managing Contingent and Temporary Workers

Given the widespread use of contingent and temporary workers, HR managers must understand how to use such employees most effectively. That is, they need to understand how to manage contingent and temporary workers.

This young woman is one of 1500 temporary workers at Sola Optical. Sola keeps at least 100 temps working at all times, because human resources managers like both the scheduling flexibility and the opportunity to try potential permanent employees.

One key is careful planning. Even though one of the presumed benefits of using contingent workers is flexibility, it still is important to integrate such workers in a coordinated fashion. Rather than having to call in workers sporadically and with no prior notice, organizations try to bring in specified numbers of workers for well-defined periods of time. The ability to do so comes from careful planning.

A second key is understanding contingent workers and acknowledging both their advantages and their disadvantages. That is, the organization must recognize what it can and cannot achieve by using contingent and temporary workers. Expecting too much from contingent workers, for example, is a mistake that managers should avoid.

Third, managers must carefully assess the real cost of using contingent workers. Many firms adopt this course of action to save labour costs. The organization should be able to document precisely its labour-cost savings. How much would it be paying people in wages and benefits if they were on permanent staff? How does this cost compare with the amount spent on contingent workers? This difference, however, could be misleading. Contingent workers might be less effective performers than permanent and full-time employees. Comparing employees on a direct-cost basis, therefore, is not necessarily valid. Organizations must learn to adjust the direct differences in labour costs to account for differences in productivity and performance.

Finally, managers must fully understand their own strategies and decide in advance how they intend to manage temporary workers, specifically focusing on how to integrate them into the organization. On a very simplistic level, for example, an organization with a large contingent workforce must make some decisions about the treatment of contingent workers relative to the treatment of permanent, full-time workers. Should contingent workers be invited to the company holiday party? Should they have the same access to such employee benefits as counselling services and child care? Managers must understand that they need to develop a strategy for integrating contingent workers according to some sound logic and then follow that strategy consistently over time.[30]

SUMMARY OF LEARNING OBJECTIVES

1. **Define *human resource management*, discuss its strategic significance, and explain how managers plan for human resources.** *Human resource management,* or *HRM*, is the set of organizational activities directed at attracting, developing, and maintaining an effective workforce. HRM plays a key strategic role in organizational performance. Planning for human resource needs entails several steps. Conducting a *job analysis* enables managers to create detailed, accurate job descriptions and specifications. After analysis is complete, managers must *forecast* demand and supply for both the numbers and types of workers they will need. Then they consider steps to match supply with demand.

2. **Identify the issues involved in *staffing* a company, including *internal* and *external recruiting* and *selection*.** *Recruiting* is the process of attracting qualified persons to apply for jobs that an organization has open. *Internal recruiting* involves considering present employees for new jobs. This approach helps build morale and rewards an organization's best employees. *External recruiting* means attracting people from outside the organization to apply for openings. When organizations are actually selecting people for jobs,

they generally use such selection techniques as *application forms, tests, interviews*, and other techniques. Regardless of what selection techniques are used, they must be valid predictors of an individual's expected performance in the job.

3. **Discuss different ways in which organizations go about developing the capabilities of employees and managers.** If a company is to get the most out of its workers, it must develop both those workers and their skills. Nearly all employees undergo some initial *orientation* process that introduces them to the company and to their new jobs. Many employees are given the opportunity to acquire new skills through various *work-based* and/or *instructional-based programs*.

4. **Explain ways in which organizations evaluate employee performance.** *Performance appraisals* help managers decide who needs training and who should be promoted. Appraisals also tell employees how well they are meeting expectations. Although a variety of alternatives are available for appraising performance, employee supervisors are most commonly used. No matter who does the evaluation, however, feedback to the employee is very important. Managers can select from a variety of ranking and rating methods for use in performance appraisal.

5. **Discuss the importance of *wages and salaries, incentives*, and *benefit programs* in attracting and keeping skilled workers.** *Wages and salaries, incentives*, and *benefit packages* may all be parts of a company's *compensation program*. By paying its workers as well as or better than competitors, a business can attract and keep qualified personnel. Incentive programs can also motivate people to work more productively. *Indirect compensation* also plays a major role in effective and well-designed compensation systems.

6. **Describe some of the key legal issues involved in hiring, compensating, and managing workers in today's workplace.** In hiring, compensating, and managing workers, managers must obey a variety of federal and provincial laws. *Equal employment opportunity* and *equal pay* laws forbid discrimination other than action based on legitimate job requirements. The concept of *comparable worth* states that equal wages should be paid for jobs that are of comparable value to the employer. Firms are also required to provide employees with safe working environments, as set down by the guidelines of provincial occupational health and safety acts. *Sexual harassment* is another key contemporary legal issue in business.

7. **Discuss *workforce diversity*, the management of *knowledge workers*, and the use of *contingent and temporary workers* as important changes in the contemporary workplace.** *Workforce diversity* refers to the range of workers' attitudes, values, beliefs, and behaviours that differ by gender, race, ethnicity, age, and physical ability. Today, many businesses are working to create workforces that reflect the growing diversity of the population as it enters the labour pool. Although many firms see the diverse workforce as a competitive advantage, not all are equally successful in or eager about implementing diversity programs.

Many firms today also face challenges in managing *knowledge workers*. The recent boom in high-tech companies has led to rapidly increasing salaries and high turnover among the workers who are best prepared to work in those companies. *Contingent workers* are temporary and part-time employees hired to supplement an organization's permanent workforce. Their numbers have grown significantly since the early 1980s and are expected to rise further. The practice of hiring contingent workers is gaining in popularity because it gives managers more flexibility and because temps are usually not covered by employers' benefit programs.

KEY TERMS

human resource management (HRM), 225
job analysis, 226
job description, 226
job specification, 226
replacement chart, 227
employee information systems (skills inventories), 227
recruiting, 228
internal recruiting, 228
external recruiting, 229
validation, 230
assessment centre, 231
video assessment, 231
orientation, 233
work-based programs, 235
on-the-job training, 235

vestibule training, 235
systematic job rotations and transfers, 235
instructional-based programs, 235
lecture or discussion approach, 235
off-the-job training, 235
performance appraisal, 237
360-degree feedback, 238
simple ranking method, 238
forced distribution method, 239
graphic rating scale, 239
critical incident method, 240
compensation, 240

wages, 240
salary, 240
pay survey, 240
job evaluation, 241
merit pay, 242
merit pay plans, 242
skill-based pay, 242
knowledge-based pay, 242
piece-rate incentive plan, 243
individual incentive plans, 243
sales commission, 243
gainsharing program, 244
profit-sharing plan, 244
benefits, 244
protection plan, 245
employment insurance, 245

workers' compensation, 245
wellness program, 245
cafeteria-style benefit plans, 246
equal employment opportunity, 246
Canadian Human Rights Act, 246
bona fide occupational requirement, 247
Employment Equity Act of 1986, 247
comparable worth, 248
repetitive strain injuries, 249
workforce diversity, 250
knowledge workers, 251

STUDY QUESTIONS AND EXERCISES

Review Questions

1. What are the advantages and disadvantages of internal and external recruiting? Under what circumstances is each more appropriate?
2. Why is the formal training of workers so important to most employers? Why don't employers simply let people learn about their jobs as they perform them?
3. What different forms of compensation do firms typically use to attract and keep productive workers?
4. What are some of the most significant laws affecting human resource management?

Analysis Questions

5. What are your views on drug testing in the workplace? What would you do if your employer asked you to submit to a drug test?

6. Have you or anyone you know ever suffered discrimination in a hiring decision? Did you or the person you know do anything about it?
7. What training do you think you are most likely to need when you finish school and start your career?
8. How much will benefit considerations affect your choice of an employer after graduation?

Application Exercises

9. Interview an HR manager at a local company. Focus on a position for which the firm is currently recruiting applicants and identify the steps in the selection process.
10. Identify some journals in your library that might be useful to an HR manager. What topics have been covered in recent features and cover stories?

Building Your Business Skills

Getting Online for a Job

Goal

To introduce students to career-search resources available on the Internet.

Situation

If companies are on one side of the external staffing process, people looking for work are on the other. Companies need qualified candidates to fill job openings and candidates need jobs that are right for them. The challenge, of course, is to make successful matches. Increasingly, this matchmaking is being conducted on the Internet. Companies are posting jobs in cyberspace, and job seekers are posting resumés in response. The number of job postings has grown dramatically in recent years. On a typical Sunday, you might find as many as 50 000 postings on the Monster Board, a leading job site. With so many companies looking for qualified candidates online, it makes good business sense to learn how to use the system.

Method

Using Internet career resources means locating job databases and preparing and posting a resumé. (You will therefore need access to the Internet to complete this exercise.)

Step 1:

Team up with three classmates to investigate and analyze specific job databases. In each case, write a short report describing the database (which you and other group members may use during an actual job search). Summarize the site and its features as well as its advantages, disadvantages, and costs. Start with the following sites and add others you may find on your own:

- The Monster Board, www.monster.com
- CareerMosaic, www.careermosaic.com
- College Grad Job Hunter, www.collegegrad.com

Step 2:

Investigate the job opportunities listed on the home pages of various companies. Consider trying the following companies:

- Air Canada, www.aircanada.ca
- Dofasco, www.dofasco.ca
- Royal Bank, www.royalbank.com

- IBM, www.can.ibm.com
- Wal-Mart, www.walmartstores.com
- McDonald's, www.mcdonalds.com
- Bombardier, www.bombardier.com

Write a summary of the specific career-related information you find on each site.

Step 3:

Working with group members, research strategies for composing effective cyber resumés. The following Web sites provide some helpful information on formats and personal and job-related information that should be included in your resumé. They also offer hints on the art of creating a scannable resumé:

- E-Span, www.espan.com
- JobSource, www.jobsource.com
- Career Magazine, www.careermag.com

Two books by Joyce Lain Kennedy, *Electronic Job Search Revolution* and *Electronic Résumé Revolution*, also contain valuable information.

Step 4:

Working as a group, create an effective electronic resumé for a fictitious college or university graduate looking for a first job. Pay attention to format, language, style, and the effective communication of background and goals.

Step 5:

Working as a group, learn how to post your resumé online. (Do not submit the resumé you created for this exercise, which is, after all, fictitious.) The databases provided will guide you in this process.

Follow-Up Questions

1. Why is it necessary to learn how to conduct an electronic job search? Do you think it will be more or less necessary in the years ahead?

2. Why do you think more computer-related jobs than nontechnical jobs are posted online? Do you think this situation will change?

3. Why is it a waste of time to stylize your resumé with different fonts, point sizes, and centred headings?

4. What is the advantage of e-mailing your resumé directly to a company rather than applying for the same job through an online databank?

Exploring the Net

To find out what a real-world company would like you to know about its human resources policies and programs, log on to Nortel Networks, Careers, at:

www.nortelnetworks.com/employment

After you have read the material, including the extensive "Global Operations" section, consider the following questions:

1. Which of the skills listed by Nortel Networks that are not specific to technology would you list under your own strong or weak points? What are one or two skills important for any position at Nortel Networks?

2. Why do you think Nortel Networks devotes so much space solely to Global Operations? How effective did you find the anecdotal remarks from current employees that were included on the site?

3. How important are terms like "mission" and "vision" in the description of the Nortel Networks jobs? What sense of the company are they trying to convey to prospective employees?

Concluding Case 8-1

Freelancing

When people think about careers, they usually think of going to work full-time for a company and, if they like it, staying at that company for many years. In fact, until recently the notion of "lifetime employment" was touted as the wave of the future. Even if a person didn't stay at one firm, the idea still was that the person would work full-time for a company for at least a few years.

But times are changing. A growing number of workers are becoming freelancers—individuals who contract with a company for a set period of time, usually until a specific project is completed. After the project is completed, the freelancer moves on to another project in the firm, or to another firm. Statistics Canada estimates that 30 percent of working adults are doing non-standard work such as freelancing.

Why is this happening? The main reason is that competitive pressures are forcing firms to reduce their costs and increase their productivity. The current buzzword is "flexibility" and this can often be achieved by hiring freelancers to solve specific company problems. This allows a firm to maintain a minimum number of full-time workers and then supplement them with freelancers.

Some people freelance because they can't get full-time work with one company, but others freelance by choice. Accomplished freelancers can control their own destiny, make above-average incomes, and have a strong sense of flexibility and freedom. Typically, freelancers aren't paid company benefits like full-time workers, but pressures are building to change this. In 1994, the province of Saskatchewan became the first in Canada to require companies to pay contract and part-time workers at least some benefits.

Many banks and insurance companies have trouble seeing the needs of contract workers. To them, it may appear that the contract worker is not really employed on a steady basis because they work for so many different companies. Creative Arts Management Service is a firm that fills this void. It offers business advice, financial planning, budgeting, and legal services for contract workers. The firm takes the view that freelancing, if properly planned and executed, is the best security in the new economy of the 1990s.

While the work of technical or professional employees is often contracted out to freelancers, the management of various functions may also be contracted out. The Halifax District School Board contracted out the management of custodial services for the district's 42 schools to ServiceMaster Canada Ltd. The school district expects to save more than $500 000 each year. And Manpower Temporary Services manages a packaging department for a pharmaceutical firm that sometimes numbers as many as 130 people, and sometimes as few as 70, depending on demand. A Manpower manager is on site at the pharmaceutical firm; she recruits the temporary workers, does some of the necessary training, conducts performance appraisals of temporary workers, and handles the payroll.

Management experts predict that freelancing will increase in importance. With the massive layoffs that have been evident in recent years, workers are beginning to realize that large firms do not provide job security. Rather, security comes from having confidence in your own knowledge and skills, and marketing yourself in innovative ways. The recent advances in information technology have facilitated freelancing, since workers do not necessarily have to be at the workplace to do their work.

There are both positive and negative aspects to the idea of non-standard work. From the worker's perspective, those with marketable skills will find that non-standard work will result in high pay and satisfying work. For those without marketable skills, non-standard work will likely mean part-time work in low-paying service jobs. Those individuals who lack either the ability or interest to capitalize on non-standard work will find that there is much uncertainty in their careers.

From the organization's perspective, a conclusion about the value of non-standard work means weighing the value of long-term employee loyalty and commitment against the benefits of the increased flexibility that is possible with part-time freelancers.

CASE QUESTIONS

1. What kind of people are most likely to want freelance work?

2. What are the pros and cons of freelance work from the individual's perspective? From the organization's perspective?

3. Is it unethical to hire freelancers to avoid paying them company benefits? ◆

Concluding Case 8-2

Monster.com: Can a Firm Outsource Its Recruiting?

Most Canadians became familiar with Monster.com when the company ran its famous advertisements during the 2000 Super Bowl. The advertisements challenged viewers to take stock of their careers with its "When I Grow Up" spots. The ads featured children musing about what they wanted to be when they grew up. Each child described a particularly distasteful aspect of a job, saying "I want to file all day," or "I want to claw my way up to middle management." The spots have been successful in building a brand identity for Monster.com, the online recruitment leader.

Behind the successful image campaign at Monster.com is a well-organized corporate entity. The company is a subsidiary of TMP Worldwide, the world's largest yellow page advertising agency and a highly respected provider of direct marketing services. The "Monster" subsidiary, a natural extension of their advertising business, is drawing 9.6 million unique visits per month to its job-search Web site. Independent research has estimated that Monster.com's share of the Web job-search market is over 40 percent.

For job seekers, Monster.com can form a career network, providing instantaneous access to many progressive companies. The firm also offers interactive, personalized tools to facilitate the job search process, including résumé planning and management, a personal job search agent, chats and message boards, privacy options, and expert advice on job seeking. In high turnover industries it is conceivable that an individual could use Monster.com as a life-long career agent.

One of the most attractive features for employers is the ability to attract high-tech employees. Only candidates with a computer, a browser, and access to the Internet are likely to use the forum. There are other benefits as well. The Internet can provide instantaneous information, allowing firms to post last-minute openings. A firm can also provide links to its own Web site, offering a prospective employee far more information than is available in a print ad. Monster.com can also offer résumé-screening services, routing, and searching. Currently, Monster.com has over 1 million active résumés from job seekers in its database.

The more traditional method of recruiting employees is to place an advertisement in a local or regional paper. National publications like trade magazines often require 30-day lead times for ads. Once the ads have gone out, the company needs to allow time for potential employees to respond. It is not uncommon for an organization to wait 60 days before it begins the interview process. Delays like this could prove costly in highly competitive industries.

It is common for companies to outsource areas that are not part of their core competence or areas in which they have difficulty being competitive. Given that Monster.com already has over 1 million résumés in its database and the ability to instantly post for jobs, will more and more companies outsource their recruiting to Monster.com?

CASE QUESTIONS

1. What strengths does Monster.com bring to the recruiting process that a company might not have?

2. Why might a company outsource its recruiting to Monster.com?

3. Why would a company decide to keep its recruiting "in house"; that is, what are the limitations of Monster.com? ◆

Visit the *Business* Website at www.pearsoned.ca/griffin
for up-to-date e-business cases!

Motivating and Leading at PanCanadian Petroleum Ltd.

When PanCanadian Petroleum Ltd. took a close look at how well it was training its employees, it discovered that it was providing ample training for new recruits such as geologists, engineers, and accountants, all of whom did very technical work. However, it wasn't providing any management training to people who worked their way up from these technical positions to management positions, so they weren't trained to lead and motivate workers.

Terry Lawrence, who started out as a reservoir engineer (a person who evaluates the amount of oil underground), is now vice-president of human resources. He has come to the realization that many of the managers in the company really don't know anything about management. And before they were promoted to management, the company sometimes didn't even check to see whether they had people skills, a crucial element in leadership success.

To remedy these problems, the company established the PanCanadian Management Institute in cooperation with the University of Calgary. At the Institute, executives of PanCanadian receive basic training in management. Lawrence says that employees think that the training they receive is a very good experience. Employees not only improve their performance and take on more challenges, the training itself is a reward and recognition. As such, it is very motivating.

The company also sends employees to other executive development programs such as the Banff School of Management and the Niagara Institute Leadership Development Program. Lawrence has taken some training himself, and has attended an intensive two-week course in strategic human resources at the University of Michigan. The company spends 5 to 7 percent of its operating budget on training, compared to the Canadian average of 2 to 3 percent.

In addition to training people with managerial potential, PanCanadian also trains employees who make a difference in the technical side of the business. Lawrence recognizes that the best engineers and geologists are not necessarily the best managers.

David Tuer, president and CEO of PanCanadian, observes that the oil and gas the company produces looks just like the oil and gas produced by competitors, so the company has to distinguish itself on the basis of the quality of the decisions its managers make. PanCanadian therefore plans to put all of its 1600 employees, especially those identified as having "high potential," through training programs that will prepare them for the rapid changes ahead. ◆

PanCanadian Petroleum Ltd.
www.pcp.ca

As you will see in this chapter, people work for reasons other than money. They want interesting work that makes them feel part of a team and that satisfies their intellectual, social, and emotional needs. They also want to be well rewarded for their talents and their contributions to the success of a business. But organizations also want certain things from their employees—things like hard work and dedication. All of these mutual—and sometimes conflicting—needs affect psychological contracts, attitudes and morale, employee motivation, and leadership in the workplace.

By focusing on the learning objectives of this chapter, you will better understand why employee behaviour, attitudes, and motivation are important to all types of businesses. You will also understand the role of leadership in motivating employees—or team members—to high levels of achievement. After reading this chapter, you should be able to:

1. Describe the nature and importance of *psychological contracts* in the workplace.

2. Discuss the importance of *job satisfaction* and *employee morale* and summarize their roles in human relations in the workplace.

3. Identify and summarize the most important *theories of employee motivation*.

4. Describe some of the strategies used by organizations to improve *job satisfaction* and *employee motivation*.

5. Discuss different managerial styles of *leadership* and their impact on human relations in the workplace.

LEARNING OBJECTIVES

The foundation of good **human relations**—the interactions between employers and employees and their attitudes towards one another—is a satisfied and motivated workforce. But satisfaction and motivation usually are based on what some people call the "psychological contract" that exists between organizations and employees. Thus, we begin our discussion by examining the nature and meaning of *psychological contracts*.

human relations
Interactions between employers and employees and their attitudes towards one another.

PSYCHOLOGICAL CONTRACTS IN ORGANIZATIONS

Whenever we buy a car or sell a house, both buyer and seller sign a contract that specifies the terms of the agreement—who pays what to whom, when it's paid, and so forth. In some ways, a psychological contract resembles a legal contract. On the whole, however, it's less formal and less rigidly defined. A **psychological contract** is the set of expectations held by an employee concerning what he or she will contribute to an organization (referred to as *contributions*) and what the organization will provide the employee (referred to as *inducements*) in return.

If either party perceives an inequity in the contract, that party may seek a change. The employee, for example, might ask for a pay raise, promotion, or a bigger office. He or she might put forth less effort or look for a better job elsewhere. The organization can also initiate change by training workers to improve their skills, transferring them to new jobs, or terminating them.

All organizations face the basic challenge of managing psychological contracts. They want value from their employees, and they must give employees the right inducements. Valuable but underpaid employees, for instance, may perform below their capabilities or leave for better jobs. Conversely, overpaying employees who contribute little incurs unnecessary costs.

psychological contract
The set of expectations held by an employee concerning what he or she will contribute to an organization (contributions) and what the organization will provide the employee (inducements) in return.

The massive wave of downsizing and cutbacks that swept the Canadian economy in the 1980s and early 1990s has complicated the process of managing psychological contracts. Many organizations, for example, used to offer at least reasonable assurances of job permanence as a fundamental inducement to employees. Now, however, because job permanence is less likely, alternative inducements—such as lavish benefits packages—may be needed instead.

If psychological contracts are created, maintained, and managed effectively, the result is likely to be workers who are satisfied and motivated. On the other hand, poorly managed psychological contracts may result in dissatisfied, unmotivated workers. Although most people have a general idea of what "job satisfaction" is, both job satisfaction and high morale can be elusive in the workplace. Because they are critical to an organization's success, we now turn our attention to discussing their importance.

THE IMPORTANCE OF JOB SATISFACTION AND MORALE

job satisfaction
The pleasure and feeling of accomplishment employees derive from performing their jobs well.

morale
The generally positive or negative mental attitude of employees towards their work and workplace.

Broadly speaking, **job satisfaction** is the degree of enjoyment that people derive from performing their jobs. If people enjoy their work, they are relatively satisfied; if they do not enjoy their work, they are relatively dissatisfied. In turn, satisfied employees are likely to have high **morale**—the overall attitude that employees have towards their workplace. Morale reflects the degree to which they perceive that their needs are being met by their jobs. It is determined by a variety of factors, including job satisfaction and satisfaction with such things as pay, benefits, co-workers, and promotion opportunities.[1]

Why Businesses Need Satisfied Employees

When workers are enthusiastic and happy with their jobs, the organization benefits in many ways. Because they are committed to their work and the organization, satisfied workers are more likely to work hard and try to make useful contributions to the organization. They will also have fewer grievances and are less likely to engage in negative behaviours (e.g., complaining, deliberately slowing their work pace, etc.). Satisfied workers are also more likely to come to work every day and are more likely to remain with the organization. So, by ensuring that employees are satisfied, management gains a more efficient and smooth-running company.

Just as the rewards of high worker satisfaction and morale are great, so are the costs of job dissatisfaction and poor morale. Dissatisfied workers, for example, are far more likely to be absent due to minor illnesses, personal reasons, or a general disinclination to go to work. Low morale may also result in high turnover. Some turnover is a natural and healthy way to weed out low-performing workers in any organization. But high levels of turnover have many negative consequences, including numerous vacancies, disruption in production, decreased productivity, and high retraining costs.

empowerment
Motivating employees to produce high-quality products.

Empowerment of employees was the buzzword of the 1990s. It means motivating and energizing employees to create high-quality products and to provide bend-over-backwards service to customers so that the firm is more competitive. It means eliminating entire layers of traditional management that exist simply to control people. Properly used, it can reduce absenteeism and turnover and increase quality and productivity.[2]

Job Satisfaction and Dissatisfaction Trends

Canadian industry shows mixed results when companies try to give employees what they want and to keep them on the job. Consider the following:

■ A survey of 2300 workers by the Wyatt Co. of Vancouver found that three-quarters of Canadian workers are satisfied with the content of their job, but fewer than half are happy with the way they are managed. Workers felt that management did not show genuine interest in them and did not treat them with dignity. Managers, on the other hand, felt that they did treat workers with dignity. Perhaps most disconcerting of all, fewer than one-third of those surveyed felt that promotions were based on merit. The longer they had been with a company, the more cynical they were about this issue.[3]

■ Another survey of 1631 employees from 94 companies across Canada and the U.S. found that, while employees are optimistic and committed to their work, they also feel frustrated because they have no control over what happens in their job. Most employees feel that their abilities are not used to the fullest extent. They want direction and measurable goals.[4]

■ Based on responses from 7000 private- and public-sector workers, a Conference Board of Canada survey found the following:
  • One-third of employees felt that caring for children or elderly parents limited their career advancement.
  • One-eighth had left an employer because of family responsibilities.
  • Seventeen percent had turned down promotions.
  • Twenty-five percent had turned down transfers.
  • Women were four times as likely as men to report conflicts in home and work responsibilities.[5]

■ A report by the Business and Economic Roundtable on Mental Health concluded that employee stress is costing Canadian industry about $60 billion each year, and more than half of that is in lost productivity. The top sources of stress for employees were identified as too much (or too little) work to do, lack of two-way communication up and down the hierarchy, being unappreciated, inconsistent performance review processes, career uncertainty, unclear company policies, and office politics.[6]

MOTIVATION IN THE WORKPLACE

Although job satisfaction and morale are important, employee motivation is even more critical to a firm's success. As we saw in Chapter 5, motivation is one part of the managerial function of directing. Broadly defined, **motivation** is the set of forces that cause people to behave in certain ways. For example, while one worker may be motivated to work hard to produce as much as possible, another may be motivated to do just enough to get by. Managers must understand these differences in behaviour and the reasons for them.

Over the years, many theories have been proposed to address the issues of motivation. In this section, we will focus on three major approaches to motivation in the workplace that reflect a chronology of thinking in the area: *classical theory and scientific management, behaviour theory,* and *contemporary motivation theories*.

motivation
The set of forces that causes people to behave in certain ways.

The ideas of Frederick Taylor, the founder of scientific management, had a profound impact on the way manufacturing activities were carried out in the early twentieth century. His basic ideas are still used today.

Classical Theory and Scientific Management

According to the so-called **classical theory of motivation**, workers are motivated solely by money. In his book *The Principles of Scientific Management* (1911), industrial engineer Frederick Taylor proposed a way for both companies and workers to benefit from this widely accepted view of life in the workplace.[7] If workers are motivated by money, Taylor reasoned, then paying them more would prompt them to produce more. Meanwhile, the firm that analyzed jobs and found better ways to perform them would be able to produce goods more cheaply, make higher profits, and thus pay—and motivate—workers better than its competitors.

Taylor's approach is known as **scientific management**. His ideas captured the imagination of many managers in the early twentieth century. Soon, plants across Canada and the U.S. were hiring experts to perform **time-and-motion studies**. Industrial-engineering techniques were applied to each facet of a job to determine how to perform it most efficiently. These studies were the first "scientific" attempts to break down jobs into easily repeated components and to devise more efficient tools and machines for performing them.

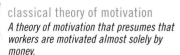
classical theory of motivation
A theory of motivation that presumes that workers are motivated almost solely by money.

scientific management
Analyzing jobs and finding better, more efficient ways to perform them.

time-and-motion studies
The use of industrial-engineering techniques to study every aspect of a specific job to determine how to perform it most efficiently.

Behaviour Theory: The Hawthorne Studies

One of the first challenges to the classical theory of human relations management came about by accident. In 1925, a group of Harvard researchers began a study at the Hawthorne Works of Western Electric. Their intent was to examine the relationship between changes in the physical environment and worker output, with an eye to increasing productivity.

The results of the experiment at first confused, then amazed, the scientists. Increasing lighting levels improved productivity, but so did lowering lighting levels. And against all expectations, raising the pay of workers failed to increase their productivity. Gradually they pieced together the puzzle. The explanation for the lighting phenomenon lay in workers' response to attention. In essence, they determined that almost any action on the part of management that made workers believe they were receiving special attention caused worker productivity to rise. This result, known as the **Hawthorne effect**, had a major influence on human relations management, convincing many businesses that paying attention to employees is indeed good for business.

Hawthorne effect
The tendency for workers' productivity to increase when they feel they are receiving special attention from management.

Contemporary Motivation Theories

Following the Hawthorne studies, managers and researchers alike focused more attention on the importance of good human relations in motivating employee performance. Stressing the factors that cause, focus, and sustain workers' behaviour, most motivation theorists are concerned with the ways in which management thinks about and treats employees. The major motivation theories include *the human-resources model*, the *hierarchy of needs model*, *two-factory theory, expectancy theory, equity theory*, and *goal-setting theory*.

The Hawthorne studies were an important step in developing an appreciation for the human factor at work. These women worked under different lighting conditions as researchers monitored their productivity. To the researchers' amazement, productivity increased regardless of whether the light was increased or decreased.

The Human-Resources Model: Theories X and Y

In an important study, behavioural scientist Douglas McGregor concluded that managers had radically different beliefs about how best to use the human resources at a firm's disposal. He classified these beliefs into sets of assumptions that he labelled "Theory X" and "Theory Y."[8] The basic differences between these two theories are highlighted in Table 9.1.

Managers who subscribe to **Theory X** tend to believe that people are naturally lazy and uncooperative and must therefore be either punished or rewarded to be made productive. Managers who incline to **Theory Y** tend to believe that people are naturally energetic, growth-oriented, self-motivated, and interested in being productive.

McGregor generally favoured Theory Y beliefs. Thus he argued that Theory Y managers are more likely to have satisfied, motivated employees. Of course, Theory X and Y distinctions are somewhat simplistic and offer little concrete basis for action. Their value lies primarily in their ability to highlight and analyze the behaviour of managers in light of their attitudes towards employees.

Theory X
A management approach based on the belief that people must be forced to be productive because they are naturally lazy, irresponsible, and uncooperative.

Theory Y
A management approach based on the belief that people want to be productive because they are naturally energetic, responsible, and cooperative.

Table 9.1	Beliefs about People at Work

Theory X and Theory Y convey very different assumptions about people at work.

Theory X	Theory Y
1. People are lazy.	1. People are energetic.
2. People lack ambition and dislike responsibility.	2. People are ambitious and seek responsibility.
3. People are self-centred.	3. People can be selfless.
4. People resist change.	4. People want to contribute to business growth and change.
5. People are gullible and not very bright.	5. People are intelligent.

Maslow's Hierarchy of Needs Model

Psychologist Abraham Maslow proposed that people have a number of different needs that they attempt to satisfy in their work. He classified these needs into five basic types and suggested that they are arranged in the hierarchy of importance shown in Figure 9.1. According to Maslow, needs are hierarchical because lower-level needs must be met before a person will try to satisfy those on a higher level.[9]

■ *Physiological needs* are necessary for survival; they include food, water, shelter, and sleep. Businesses address these needs by providing both comfortable working environments and salaries sufficient to buy food and shelter.

■ *Security needs* include the needs for stability and protection from the unknown. Many employers thus offer pension plans and job security.

■ *Social needs* include the needs for friendship and companionship. Making friends at work can help to satisfy social needs, as can the feeling that you "belong" in a company.

■ *Esteem needs* include the need for status and recognition as well as the need for self-respect. Respected job titles and large offices are among the things that businesses can provide to address these needs.

■ Finally, *self-actualization needs* are needs for self-fulfilment. They include the needs to grow and develop one's capabilities and to achieve new and meaningful goals. Challenging job assignments can help satisfy these needs.

According to Maslow, once one set of needs has been satisfied, it ceases to motivate behaviour. This is the sense in which the hierarchical nature of lower- and higher-level needs affects employee motivation and satisfaction.

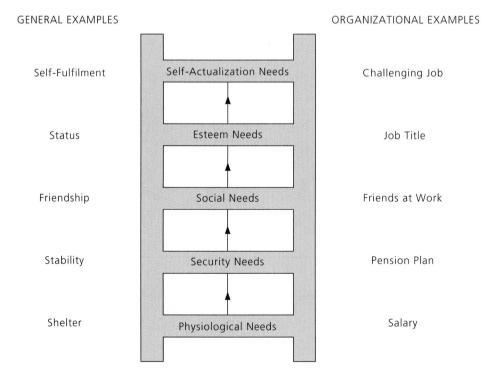

Figure 9.1
Maslow's hierarchy of human needs provides a useful categorization of the different needs people have.

For example, if you feel secure in your job, a new pension plan will probably be less important to you than the chance to make new friends and join an informal network among your co-workers. If, however, a lower-level need suddenly becomes unfulfilled, most people immediately refocus on that lower level. Suppose, for example, that you are seeking to meet your esteem needs by working as a divisional manager at a major company. If you learn that your division—and consequently your job—may be eliminated, you might very well find the promise of job security at a new firm as motivating as a promotion once would have been at your old company.

Maslow's theory recognizes that because different people have different needs, they are motivated by different things. Unfortunately, research has found that the hierarchy varies widely, not only for different people but across different cultures.

Two-Factor Theory

After studying a group of accountants and engineers, psychologist Frederick Herzberg concluded that job satisfaction and dissatisfaction depend on two factors: *hygiene factors*, such as working conditions, and *motivating factors*, such as recognition for a job well done.[10]

According to **two-factor theory**, hygiene factors affect motivation and satisfaction only if they are *absent* or *fail* to meet expectations. For example, workers will be dissatisfied if they believe that they have poor working conditions. If working conditions are improved, however, they will not necessarily become *satisfied*; they will simply be *not dissatisfied*. On the other hand, if workers receive no recognition for successful work, they may be neither dissatisfied nor satisfied. If recognition is provided, they will likely become more satisfied.

Figure 9.2 illustrates two-factor theory. Note that motivation factors lie along a continuum from *satisfaction* to *no satisfaction*. Hygiene factors, on the other hand, are likely to produce feelings that lie on a continuum from dissatisfaction to no dissatisfaction. While motivation factors are directly related to the work that employees actually perform, hygiene factors refer to the environment in which they perform it.

two-factor theory
A theory of human relations developed by Frederick Herzberg that identifies factors that must be present for employees to be satisfied with their jobs and factors that, if increased, lead employees to work harder.

Rewards and recognition are an important determinant of employee motivation. *The Financial Post* recognized Theresa Butcher, its head librarian, as an Unsung Hero for all of her help to reporters and editors over many years.

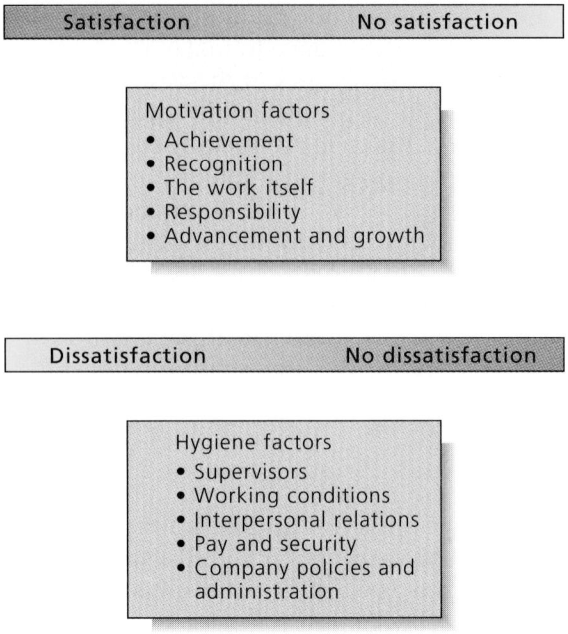

Satisfaction	No satisfaction

Motivation factors
- Achievement
- Recognition
- The work itself
- Responsibility
- Advancement and growth

Dissatisfaction	No dissatisfaction

Hygiene factors
- Supervisors
- Working conditions
- Interpersonal relations
- Pay and security
- Company policies and administration

Figure 9.2
According to two-factor theory, job satisfaction depends on two factors.

This theory thus suggests that managers should follow a two-step approach to enhancing motivation. First, they must ensure that hygiene factors—working conditions, clearly stated policies—are acceptable. This practice will result in an absence of dissatisfaction. Then they must offer motivating factors—recognition, added responsibility—as means of improving satisfaction and motivation.

Research suggests that two-factor theory works in some professional settings, but it is not as effective in clerical and manufacturing settings. (Herzberg's research was limited to professionals—accountants and engineers only.) In addition, one person's hygiene factor may be another person's motivating factor. For example, if money represents nothing more than pay for time worked, it may be a hygiene factor for one person. For another person, however, money may be a motivating factor because it represents recognition and achievement.

Expectancy Theory

expectancy theory
The theory that people are motivated to work towards rewards that they want and that they believe they have a reasonable chance of obtaining.

Expectancy theory suggests that people are motivated to work towards rewards that they want and that they believe they have a reasonable chance—or expectancy—of obtaining.[11] A reward that seems out of reach, for example, is not likely to be motivating even if it is intrinsically positive.

Figure 9.3 illustrates expectancy theory in terms of issues that are likely to be considered by an individual employee. Consider the case of an assistant department manager who learns that her firm needs to replace a retiring division manager two levels above her in the organization. Even though she wants the job, she does not apply because she doubts that she will be selected. In this case, she raises the *performance–reward issue*: for some reason, she believes that her performance will not get her the position. Note that she may think that her performance merits the new job but that performance alone will not be enough; perhaps she expects the reward to go to someone with more seniority.

Assume that our employee also learns that the firm is looking for a production manager on a later shift. She thinks that she could get this job, but

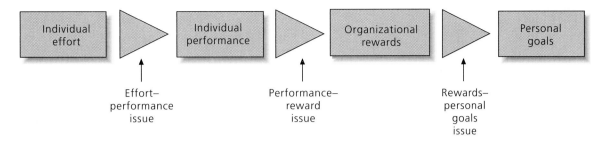

Figure 9.3
Expectancy theory model.

does not apply because she does not want to change shifts. In this instance, she raises the *rewards–personal goals issue*. Finally, she learns of an opening one level higher—department manager—in her own division. She may well apply for this job because she both wants it and thinks that she has a good chance of getting it. In this case, her consideration of all the issues has led to an expectancy that she can reach a given goal.

Expectancy theory helps explain why some people do not work as hard as they can when their salaries are based purely on seniority. Paying employees the same whether they work very hard or just hard enough to get by removes the financial incentive for them to work harder. In other words, they ask themselves, "If I work harder, will I get a pay raise?" and conclude that the answer is no. Similarly, if hard work will result in one or more *undesirable* outcomes—say, a transfer to another location or a promotion to a job that requires unpleasant travel—employees will not be motivated to work hard. The "It's a Wired World" box examines ways in which the expectancy theory of motivation has been instrumental at dot-com business TixToGo.

TixToGo
www.tixtogo.com

Equity Theory

Equity theory focuses on social comparisons—people evaluating their treatment by the organization relative to the treatment of others. This approach says that people begin by analyzing *inputs* (what they contribute to their jobs in terms of time, effort, education, experience, and so forth) relative to *outputs* (what they receive in return—salary, benefits, recognition, security). The result is a ratio of contribution to return. Then they compare their own ratios with those of other employees: They ask whether their ratios are *equal to, greater than,* or *less than* those of the people with whom they are comparing themselves. Depending on the outcome of their assessments, they experience feelings of equity or inequity. Figure 9.4 illustrates the three possible results of such an assessment.

For example, suppose that a new graduate gets a starting job at a large manufacturing firm. His starting salary is $25 000 per year, he gets a compact company car, and he shares an office with another new employee. If he later learns that another new employee has received the same salary, car, and office arrangement, he will feel equitably treated. If the other newcomer, however, has received $30 000, a full-size company car, and a private office, he may experience feelings of inequity.

Note, however, that the two ratios do not have to be the *same*—they need be only *fair*. Let's assume, for instance, that our new employee has a bachelor's degree and two years of work experience. Perhaps he learns subsequently that the other new employee has an advanced degree and 10 years of work experience. After first feeling inequity, our new employee may now conclude that his comparison person is actually contributing more to the organization. The other employee is equitably entitled, therefore, to receive more in return.

equity theory
The theory that people compare (1) what they contribute to their job with what they get in return, and (2) their input/output ratio with that of other employees.

IT'S A WIRED WORLD

The Future of Compensation?

What would it take to get someone to work for free? Let's rephrase the question in more realistic terms: What would it take to get someone to work for no income today but with the potential for a big payoff in the future? That's the question that a Silicon Valley start-up company recently asked. The answers it received may be surprising. The company found that the right people would actually be quite enthusiastic about this prospect—as long as the potential rewards were substantial and the probability of receiving them was within reason.

The company in question is TixToGo, which sells events and activities, such as tours and programs, for other vendors. The firm was actually a fledgling Internet site when its founder approached Lu Cordova, head of a consulting company and acting director of another Internet start-up firm, with an offer to become CEO. The founder wanted Cordova to run the firm while he devoted more time to looking for new funding. The only problem was that TixToGo only had US$12 000 in the bank and, with four other full-time employees, had no money to pay Cordova. Although Cordova was intrigued by the firm's prospects, she wasn't excited about working for free. So, she devised her own compensation plan, which revolved around the promise that she would be given an attractive salary retroactive to her start date, payable in cash and/or equity, if the firm was successful in obtaining new funding.

However, just because Cordova was willing to buy into this plan, it did not follow that anyone else at TixToGo was interested. The skeptics were quickly proven wrong, however, when Cordova was able to attract six full-time employees, two part-timers, and eight outside consultants and contractors—all for deferred pay. Moreover, each individual was given the option of taking his or her deferred pay in cash or stocks. Actually, *deferred pay* might have been a misnomer. After all, if TixToGo never found the funding it needed, no one, including Cordova, will ever be paid a cent, deferred or otherwise.

Why would someone accept this deal? One major reason is the potential payoff. Most of the new TixToGo employees decided to take their future compensation in stock. The number of shares received by each employee is determined by dividing the dollar amount of his or her salary by the per-share valuation used in determining the venture capitalists' stake (US$11 per share). As a result, an individual could end up with several thousand shares of stock. If the firm then subsequently goes public, a truly big payoff would be in the offing.

Outside consultants and contractors also bought in. Each took part of his or her fees in cash, generally just enough to cover costs, and the rest in stock. One contractor, for example, produced a television ad for TixToGo. The normal fee would have been US$250 000. In this instance, however, the contractor took US$70 000 in cash and US$20 000 in stock. Like the company's employees, contractors stand to make a bundle if the stock price takes off.

At this point, we are left with one significant question: How realistic is it for employees and contractors to expect a big payday in the future? Given the recent spate of successful high-tech public offerings and the initial interest shown by investors, TixToGo appears to have a promising future. One investor, for example, wrote Cordova a cheque for US$50 000 on the basis of its compensation system alone—without even seeing a business plan. Because TixToGo also seems to be attracting the attention of several other big-time investment groups, the prospects for success are quite promising.

When people feel that they are being inequitably treated, they may do various things to restore fairness. For example, they may ask for raises, reduce their effort, work shorter hours, or just complain to their bosses. They may also rationalize their situation ("management succumbed to pressure to promote a woman"), find different people with whom to compare themselves, or leave their jobs altogether.

Good examples of equity theory at work can be found in professional sports. Each year, for example, rookies are signed to lucrative contracts. No sooner is the ink is dry than veteran players start grumbling about raises or revised contracts.

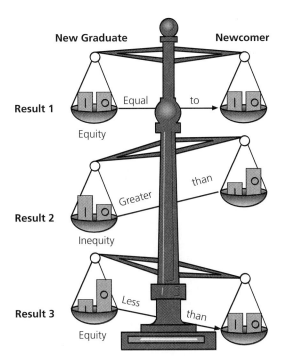

Figure 9.4
Equity theory: Possible assessments.

Goal-Setting Theory

Goal-setting theory describes the kinds of goals that better motivate employees. In general, effective goals tend to have two basic characteristics. First, they are moderately difficult: While a goal that is too easy does little to enhance effort and motivation, a goal that is too difficult also fails to motivate people. Second, they are specific. A goal of "do your best," for instance, does not motivate people nearly as much as a goal such as "increase profits by 10 percent." The specificity and clarity of this goal serves to focus attention and energy on exactly what needs to be done.[12]

An important aspect of goal setting is the employee's participation in the goal-setting process. When people help select the goals they are to work towards, they tend to accept them more readily and are more committed to achieving them. On the other hand, when goals are merely assigned to people with little or no input on their part, they are less likely to adopt them.

goal-setting theory
The theory that people perform better when they set specific, quantified, time-framed goals.

STRATEGIES FOR ENHANCING JOB SATISFACTION AND MORALE

Deciding what motivates workers and provides job satisfaction is only part of the manager's battle. The other part is to apply that knowledge. Experts have suggested—and many companies have instituted—a wide range of programs designed to make jobs more interesting and rewarding and the work environment more pleasant. In this section, we will consider five of the most common types of programs: reinforcement/behaviour modification theory, management by objectives, participative management, job enrichment and job redesign, and modified work schedules.

WEBCONNEXION

SaskTel, which is ranked as one of the top 35 companies to work for by *Report on Business* magazine, provides employees with incentives like vision care, dental benefits, flextime, job sharing, on-site fitness centres, clinics to stop smoking or lose weight, and post-secondary education reimbursement. SaskTel is committed to helping employees achieve a balance in home and work life. Visit SaskTel at:

www.sasktel.com/

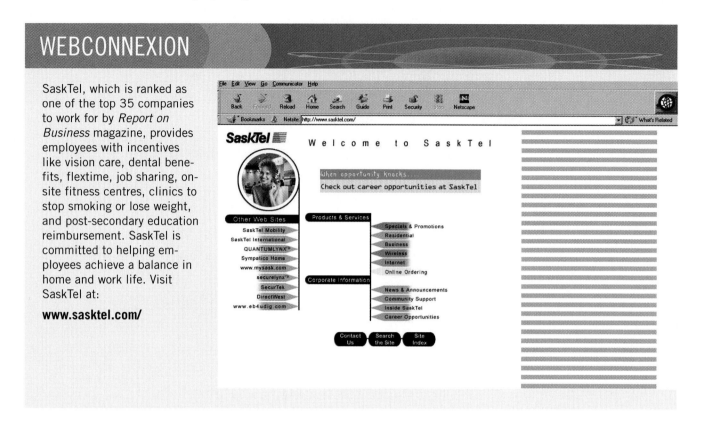

Reinforcement/Behaviour Modification Theory

Many companies try to control, and even alter or modify, workers' behaviour through systematic rewards and punishments for specific behaviours. In other words, they first try to define the specific behaviours they want their employees to exhibit (working hard, being courteous to customers, stressing quality) and the specific behaviours they want to eliminate (wasting time, being rude to customers, ignoring quality). Then they try to shape employee behaviour by linking reinforcement with desired behaviours and punishment with undesired behaviours.

Reinforcement is used, for example, when a company pays *piecework* rewards—when workers are paid for each piece or product completed. In reinforcement strategies, rewards refer to all of the positive things people receive for working (pay, praise, promotions, job security, and so forth). When rewards are tied directly to performance, they serve as *positive reinforcement*. For example, paying large cash bonuses to salespeople who exceed quotas prompts them to work even harder during the next selling period. John Deere has recently adopted a new reward system based on positive reinforcement. The firm now gives pay increases when its workers complete college or university courses and demonstrate mastery of new job skills. As well, incentive reward systems at B.C. Tel, Drexis Inc., and Toronto's SkyDome all rely on positive reinforcement (see the "Business Today" box).

Punishment is designed to change behaviour by presenting people with unpleasant consequences if they fail to change in desirable ways. Employees who are repeatedly late for work, for example, may be suspended or have their pay docked. When the National Hockey League or Major League Baseball fines or suspends players found guilty of substance abuse, the organization is seeking to change players' behaviour.

reinforcement
Controlling and modifying employee behaviour through the use of systematic rewards and punishments for specific behaviours.

BUSINESS TODAY

Incentives and Motivation

Canadian companies have begun to realize that offering incentives beyond the normal benefits can result in creative ideas as well as large increases in employee productivity. These incentives may be monetary or nonmonetary. Consider the following:

- At B.C. Tel, a suggestion system was implemented that gives cash rewards to employees for ideas that generate revenue or save the company money. The employee receives 10 percent of the money saved or the revenue generated. Employees have received up to $20 000 for ideas.

- Drexis Inc. recently flew 12 employees and their families to Disney World as a reward for increasing sales by over 100 percent in one year.

- Proctor & Redfern Ltd., a consulting engineering firm, lets high achievers serve on committees with senior executives, represent the firm at outside functions, or enrol in development courses for which the company pays the bill.

- Avatar Communications Inc. sent employees on a week-long Outward Bound expedition into the wilderness. The trip had both reward and motivational components.

- Pitney Bowes Canada Ltd. sent 60 of its top salespeople and their spouses to Hong Kong after they achieved 135 percent of their sales quota; salespeople who achieved 112 percent received a trip to San Diego.

- At Cloverdale Paint, employees who come up with innovative ideas to improve customer service receive a personal letter from the president and a coffee mug or T-shirt bearing the company logo. The best idea submitted each quarter earns the originator a restaurant gift certificate worth $50. The employee who makes the best suggestion of the year receives $200 and an engraved plaque presented at a workplace ceremony.

- Manitoba Telephone System instituted a suggestion system called IDEA$PLUS, which gives employees cash awards of up to $10 000 for good ideas.

- Employees at Toronto's SkyDome are given coupons for exceptional service, such as finding a lost child or repairing a broken seat. The coupons can be used to accumulate points, which can be redeemed for prizes.

- Emery Apparel Canada Inc. conducts an annual "Oscar" awards ceremony. With great hoopla, the CEO asks for the envelope with the name of the winner of the top award. Last year, a 12-year employee won the award for figuring out (on her own time) how to satisfy a customer's difficult request.

- At Ford Motor Company, workers are rewarded for suggestions that save the company money. For example, when a metal press operator found a way to save on the amount of sheet metal used in floor panels, the company gave back to the worker $14 000 of the $70 000 saved. A recent study shows that activity like this has an effect—it takes workers at Ford one-third less time to build a car than workers at GM.

Incentives are important for top managers as well. The higher a manager is placed in a firm, the more likely it is that a good chunk of the manager's pay will be performance-based. A Conference Board of Canada study of executive compensation in Canada showed that up to 40 percent of top executives' total compensation comes in the form of incentives. For lower-level managers, the figure was 20 percent, and for other employees it was 10 percent. Top managers in the U.S. often receive up to 60 percent of their total compensation in the form of incentives. Most Canadian companies have set up some type of incentive plan for their senior executives.

Incentive systems must be carefully developed or they will not motivate employee behaviour in the desired direction. In addition to the usual sales and profit goals, firms are beginning to look at incentive systems that reward managers for achieving goals such as effective downsizing, increasing environmental consciousness, and improving the corporate culture. A decision must also be made about whether the incentive system will be directed at individual employees or groups. Historically, incentives have been directed at individuals, but with the new emphasis on teamwork in organizations, this is changing. Now, a group may receive an incentive if it manages to launch a new product on time.

Incentive systems must be used with care because they may unintentionally motivate employees to engage in undesirable behaviour. For example, stockbrokers are often given bonuses for making sales of mutual funds. Super salespeople may be given trips to exotic locations in return for making their sales goals. This may motivate the salesperson to push a product or service that really doesn't meet the customers' needs.

Pitney Bowes Canada Ltd.
www.pitneybowes.ca

Manitoba Telephone System
www.mts.mb.ca

Cloverdale Paint
www.cloverdalepaint.com

Extensive rewards work best when people are learning new behaviours, new skills, or new jobs. As workers become more adept, rewards can be used less frequently. Because such actions contribute to positive employer–employee relationships, managers generally prefer giving rewards and placing positive value on performance. Conversely, most managers dislike punishing employees, partly because workers may respond with anger, resentment, hostility, or even retaliation. To reduce this risk, many managers couple punishment with rewards for good behaviour.

Management by Objectives

management by objectives (MBO)
A system of collaborative goal setting that extends from the top of an organization to its bottom.

Management by objectives (MBO) is a system of collaborative goal setting that extends from the top of an organization to its bottom. As a technique for managing the planning process, MBO is concerned mainly with helping managers implement and carry out their plans. As you can see in Figure 9.5, MBO involves managers and subordinates in setting goals and evaluating progress. Once the program is set up, the first step is establishing overall organizational goals. It is also these goals that will ultimately be evaluated to determine the success of the program. At the same time, however, collaborative activity—communicating, meeting, controlling, and so forth—is the key to MBO. Therefore, it can also serve as a program for improving satisfaction and motivation. (Note, too, that MBO represents an effort to apply throughout an entire organization the goal-setting theory of motivation that we discussed earlier.)

Indeed, according to many experts, motivational impact is the biggest advantage of MBO. When employees sit down with managers to set goals, they learn more about company-wide objectives, feel that they are an important part of a team, and see how they can improve company-wide performance by achieving their own goals. If an MBO system is used properly, employees should leave meetings not only with an understanding of the value of their contributions, but also with fair rewards for their performances. They should also accept and be committed to the moderately difficult and specific goals they have helped set for themselves.

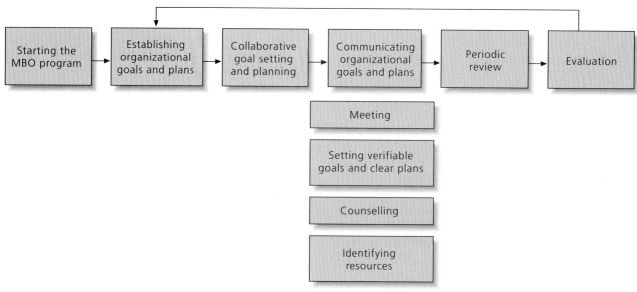

Figure 9.5
Management by objectives.

Investors Group Financial Services has used MBO since 1974 to motivate its sales force in selling financial services. The MBO process begins when the vice-president of sales develops general goals for the entire sales force. This sets the stage for Planning Week, which is held annually in 73 regional centres across Canada. Sales reps review their financial accomplishments and think through their personal and financial goals for the coming year. During Planning Week, sales reps meet with their division managers and reach a consensus about the specific goals the sales reps will pursue during the next year. Each division manager then forwards the proposed objectives for his or her division to the appropriate regional manager. This process continues all the way up to the vice-president of sales, who gives final approval to the overall sales objectives of the company for the coming year.[13]

Participative Management

Another popular technique for promoting human relations is **participative management**. Simply stated, participative management involves giving employees a voice in how they do their jobs and how the company is managed. Such participation should make employees feel more committed to the goals of the organization because they help shape them.

Some employees prefer a democratic, or supportive, leader. A survey at B.C. Telecom, for example, showed that people with a supportive boss missed less work, were less tense, felt more secure, and were more confident about their ability to get ahead in the company. Supervisors who received negative ratings usually were inflexible, supervised their workers too closely, and didn't communicate useful information to them.[14]

Japanese companies like Honda have been especially effective at practising participative management. And participative management has become more popular in recent years in Canada, partly from imitating the Japanese and partly as businesses and labour unions have become increasingly cooperative. At CP Express and Transport, for example, truck drivers were allowed to decide how to spend $8 million on new equipment.[15]

Although some employees thrive in participative programs, these programs are not for everyone. Many people will be frustrated by responsibilities they are not equipped to handle. Moreover, participative programs may actually result in dissatisfied employees if workers see the invitation to participate as more symbolic than substantive. One key, say most experts, is to invite participation only to the extent that employees want to have input and only if participation will have real value for an organization.

Managers should remember that teams are not for everyone. Levi Strauss, for example, has encountered major problems in its efforts to use teams. Previously, individual workers performed repetitive, highly specialized tasks, such as sewing zippers into jeans, and were paid according to the number of jobs they completed each day. In an attempt to boost productivity, company management reorganized everyone into teams of 10 to 35 workers and assigned tasks to the entire group. Each team member's pay was determined by the team's level of productivity. In practice, faster workers became resentful of slower workers because they reduced the group's total output. Slower workers, meanwhile, resented the pressure put on them by faster coworkers. As a result, motivation, satisfaction, and morale all dropped, and Levi Strauss eventually abandoned the teamwork plan altogether.[16]

By and large, however, participative management continues to be widely used as an enhancer of employee motivation and company performance. Although teams are often less effective in traditional and rigidly structured bureaucratic organizations, they often help smaller, more flexible organizations

participative management
A method of increasing employees' job satisfaction by giving them a voice in how they do their jobs and how the company is managed.

Levi Strauss
www.levi.com

make decisions more quickly and effectively, enhance company-wide communication, and encourage employees to feel more like a part of an organization. In turn, these attitudes usually lead to higher levels of both employee motivation and job satisfaction.[17]

Job Enrichment and Job Redesign

While MBO programs and participative management can work in a variety of settings, *job enrichment* and *job redesign* programs are generally used to increase satisfaction in jobs significantly lacking in motivating factors.[18]

Job Enrichment Programs

job enrichment
A method of increasing employees' job satisfaction by extending or adding motivating factors such as responsibility or growth.

Job enrichment is designed to add one or more motivating factors to job activities. At Continental Airlines, for example, flight attendants now have more control over their own scheduling. The jobs of flight service managers were enriched when they were given more responsibility and authority for assigning tasks to flight crew members.

Job Redesign Programs

job redesign
A method of increasing employees' job satisfaction by improving the worker–job fit through combining tasks, creating natural work groups, and/or establishing client relationships.

Job redesign acknowledges that different people want different things from their jobs. By restructuring work to achieve a more satisfactory fit between workers and their jobs, **job redesign** can motivate individuals with strong needs for career growth or achievement. Job redesign is usually implemented in one of three ways: through *combining tasks, forming natural work groups,* or *establishing client relationships*.

Combining Tasks. The job of combining tasks involves enlarging jobs and increasing their variety to make employees feel that their work is more meaningful. In turn, employees become more motivated. For example, the job done by a programmer who maintains computer systems might be redesigned to include some system design and system development work. While developing additional skills, then, the programmer also becomes involved in the overall system package.

Forming Natural Work Groups. People who do different jobs on the same projects are candidates for natural work groups. These groups are formed to help employees see the place and importance of their jobs in the total structure of the firm. They are valuable to management because the people working on a project are usually the most knowledgeable about it, and thus the most capable problem solvers.

Establishing Client Relationships. Establishing client relationships means allowing employees to interact with customers. This approach increases job variety. It gives workers both a greater sense of control and more feedback about performance than they get when their jobs are not highly interactive.

For example, software writers at Microsoft watch test users work with programs and discuss problems with them directly rather than receive feedback from third-party researchers. In Fargo, North Dakota, Great Plains Software has employee turnover of less than 7 percent, compared with an industry average of 15 to 20 percent. The company recruits and rewards in large part according to candidates' customer service skills and their experience with customer needs and complaints.

Microsoft
www.microsoft.com

Great Plains Software
www.greatplains.com

Modified Work Schedules

As another way of increasing job satisfaction, many companies are trying out different approaches to working hours and the workweek. Several types of modified work schedules have been tried, including *flextime, the compressed workweek, telecommuting,* and *workshare programs.*

Flextime

Some modifications involve adjusting a standard daily work schedule. **Flextime** allows people to pick their working hours. Figure 9.6 illustrates how a flextime system might be arranged and how different people might use it. The office is open from 6 a.m. until 7 p.m. Core time is 9 a.m. until 11 a.m. and 1 p.m. until 3 p.m. Joe, being an early riser, comes in at 6 a.m., takes an hour lunch between 11 and 12, and finishes his day by 3 p.m. Sue, on the other hand, prefers a later day. She comes in at 9 a.m., takes a long lunch from 11 a.m. to 1 p.m., and then works until 7 p.m. Pat works a more traditional day from 8 a.m. until 5 p.m.

> **flextime**
>
> *A method of increasing employees' job satisfaction by allowing them some choice in the hours they work.*

Flextime programs give employees more flexibility in their professional and personal lives. Such programs allow workers to plan around the work schedules of spouses and the school schedules of young children, for example. The increased feeling of freedom and control over their work life also reduces individuals' levels of stress.

Companies can also benefit from flextime programs. In large urban areas, flextime programs reduce traffic congestion that contributes to lost work time. Companies benefit from the higher levels of commitment and job satisfaction among workers in such programs. 3M Canada and National Cash Register are among the companies that have adopted some form of flextime. A survey of 1600 Canadian companies showed that nearly half of them had some type of flextime program.

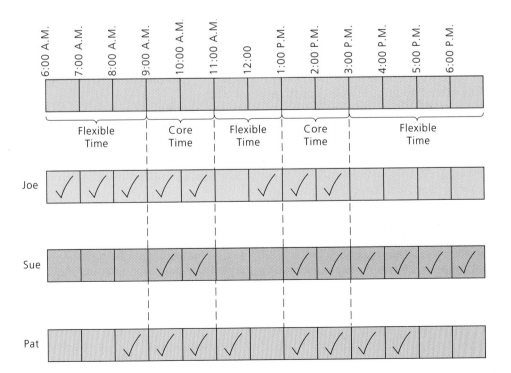

Figure 9.6
Flextime schedules include core time, when everyone must be at work, and flexible time, during which employees can set their own working hours.

The Compressed Workweek

compressed workweek
Employees work fewer days per week, but more hours on the days they do work.

In the **compressed workweek**, employees work fewer days per week, but more hours on the days they do work. The most popular compressed workweek is 4 days, 10 hours per day, but some companies have also experimented with 3 days, 12 hours per day. The "weekend worker" program at 3M Canada in London, Ontario, offers workers 12-hour shifts on Saturdays and Sundays only, and pays them the same wage as if they had worked normal hours Monday through Friday. There is a long waiting list to transfer to weekend work.[19]

Tellers at the Bank of Montreal in Oakville Place work long days (up to 14 hours), but enjoy a short workweek. Some tellers work 7 a.m. to 9 p.m. Thursdays and Fridays, and 7:30 a.m. to 5:30 p.m. Saturdays. Others work Mondays to Wednesdays for 14 hours each day. Employees like the system because it allows them to do personal errands during the day on the weekdays they do not have to be at work.[20]

Telecommuting

telecommuting
Allowing employees to do all or some of their work away from the office.

A third variation in work design is **telecommuting**, which allows people to do some or all of their work away from their office. The availability of networked computers, fax machines, cellular telephones, and overnight delivery services makes it possible for many independent professionals to work at home or while travelling. Statistics Canada estimates that 1.3 million Canadians were telecommuting in 2001.[21] As an extreme example, David Longstaff, a software developer, "commutes" from Waterloo, Ontario, to Leeds, England, each day to provide support for computer programs he has written for the company.[22]

While employees like telecommuting because it saves them time and money, the federal government is concerned that holes may be developing in the health and safety net because employers may not extend workplace health and safety coverage to telecommuters who work at home. That is not the only problem with telecommuting. Workers often report feeling isolated and lonely. To avoid this problem, B.C. Tel and Bentall Development Inc. jointly developed a satellite telecommuting office in Langley, B.C. It allows workers who used to commute to Burnaby or Vancouver to reduce their travel time considerably and still be able to interact with other workers.[23]

But telecommuting may not be for everyone. Would-be telecommuters must ask themselves several important questions: Can I meet deadlines even when I'm not being closely supervised? What will it be like to be away from the social context of the office five days a week? Can I renegotiate family rules, so my spouse doesn't come home expecting to see dinner on the table just because I've been home all day?

Another obstacle to establishing a telecommuting program is convincing management that it will be beneficial for everyone involved. Telecommuters may have to fight the perception—from both bosses and co-workers—that if they are not being supervised, they are not working. Managers are often very suspicious about telecommuting, asking "How can I tell if someone is working when I can't see them?"

Workshare Programs

worksharing (job sharing)
A method of increasing employee job satisfaction by allowing two people to share one job.

NOVA Corp.
www.nova.ca

A fourth type of modified work schedule, **worksharing** (also called **job sharing**), benefits both employee and employer. This approach allows two people to share one full-time job. For example, Kim Sarjeant and Loraine Champion, who are staff lawyers at NOVA Corp. in Calgary, share a position advising the human resources department. Sarjeant works Mondays through Wednesdays, and Champion works Wednesdays through Fridays.[24] A Statistics

Canada survey showed that 8 percent of all part-time workers in Canada share a job with someone. People who share jobs are more likely to be women, to be university educated, and to have professional occupations such as teaching and nursing. In addition, job sharers earned more than regular part-time workers.[25]

Short-run worksharing programs can help ease experienced workers into retirement while training their replacements. Worksharing can also allow students in university co-op programs to combine academic learning with practical experience.

Long-run worksharing programs have proven a good solution for people who want only part-time work. For example, five people might decide to share one reservationist's job at Air Canada with each working one day a week. Each person earns some money, remains in the job market, and enjoys limited travel benefits.

MANAGERIAL STYLES AND LEADERSHIP

In trying to enhance morale, job satisfaction, and motivation, managers can use many different styles of leadership. **Leadership** is the process of motivating others to work to meet specific objectives. Leading is also one of the key aspects of a manager's job and an important component of the directing function.

Joe Liemandt started a software company in Austin, Texas, in 1990. As part of his strategy, he was determined to develop and maintain a workforce of creative people who worked well in teams, adapted to rapid change, and felt comfortable taking risks. A decade later, people with these qualities—now numbering nearly 1000—have helped build Liemandt's company, Trilogy Software Inc., into a rapidly growing maker of industry-leading software for managing product pricing, sales plans, and commissions.

When Trilogy hires a new group of employees, Liemandt himself oversees their training. He sees himself as the firm's leader and believes that, as such, it is his responsibility to ensure that every employee shares his vision and understands his way of doing business. Training takes several weeks, starting with a series of classes devoted to the technical aspects of Trilogy's products and methods of software development. Then recruits move into areas in which Liemandt truly believes they make a real difference—developing risk-taking skills and the ability to recognize new opportunities.

Recruits are formed into teams, and each team is given three weeks to complete various projects, ranging from creating new products to developing marketing campaigns for existing products. Teams actually compete with one another and are scored on such criteria as risk and innovation, goal setting, and goal accomplishment. Evaluations are completed by Liemandt, other Trilogy managers, and some of the firm's venture capital backers. Winners receive free trips to Las Vegas. Losers go straight to work.

Liemandt's leadership doesn't stop there, even with regards to those employees who go to Las Vegas, where Liemandt challenges everyone to place a $2000 bet at the roulette wheel. He argues that $2000 is a meaningful sum, and one that can cause real pain, but not so much pain that it will cause financial disaster for anyone. Actually, Liemandt puts up the money, which losers pay back through payroll deductions of $400 over five months. Not everyone, of course, decides to take the chance, but enough do to make the message clear: Liemandt aims to succeed by taking chances, and he expects employees to share the risks. Those who do stand to earn bigger returns on more intrepid investments.[26]

leadership

The process of motivating others to work to meet specific objectives.

Managerial Styles

Early theories of leadership tried to identify specific traits associated with strong leaders. For example, physical appearance, intelligence, and public speaking skills were once thought to be "leadership traits." Indeed, it was once believed that taller people made better leaders than shorter people. The trait approach, however, proved to be a poor predictor of leadership potential. Ultimately, attention shifted from managers' traits to their behaviours, or **managerial styles**—patterns of behaviour that a manager exhibits in dealing with subordinates. Managerial styles run the gamut from autocratic to democratic to free rein. These three major styles involve very different kinds of responses to human relations problems. Any given style or combination of styles may prove appropriate, depending on the situation.

managerial styles

Patterns of behaviour that a manager exhibits in dealing with subordinates.

autocratic style

A managerial style in which managers generally issue orders and expect them to be obeyed without question.

democratic style

A managerial style in which managers generally request input from subordinates before making decisions but retain final decision-making power.

free-rein style

A managerial style in which managers typically serve as advisers to subordinates who are allowed to make decisions.

- Managers who adopt an **autocratic style** generally issue orders and expect them to be obeyed without question. The military commander prefers and usually needs the autocratic style on the battlefield. Because no one else is consulted, the autocratic style allows for rapid decision making. It therefore may be useful in situations that test a firm's effectiveness as a time-based competitor.

- Managers who adopt a **democratic style** generally request input from subordinates before making decisions but retain final decision-making power. For example, the manager of a technical group may ask other group members to interview and offer opinions about job applicants. The manager, however, will ultimately make the hiring decision.

- Managers who adopt a **free-rein style** typically serve as advisers to subordinates who are allowed to make decisions. The chairperson of a volunteer committee to raise funds for a new library may find a free-rein style most effective.

According to many observers, the free-rein style of leadership is currently giving rise to an approach that emphasizes broad-based employee input into decision making and to the fostering of workplace environments in which employees increasingly determine what needs to be done and how.

Regardless of theories about the ways in which leaders should lead, the relative effectiveness of any leadership style depends largely on the desire of subordinates to share input or exercise creativity. Whereas some people are frustrated by autocratic managers, others prefer them because they do not want to participate in making decisions. The democratic approach, meanwhile, can be disconcerting both to people who want decision-making responsibility and to those who do not. A free-rein style lends itself to employee creativity, and thus to creative solutions to pressing problems. This style also appeals to employees who prefer to plan their own work. Not all subordinates, however, have the necessary background or skills to make creative decisions. Others are not sufficiently self-motivated to work without supervision.

Canadian vs. American Management Styles

The management style of Canadian managers might look a lot like that of Americans, but there are several notable differences. Most fundamentally, Canadian managers are more subtle and subdued than are American managers. Canadian managers also seem more committed to their companies, less willing to mindlessly follow the latest management fad, and more open to different cultures because of the multicultural nature of Canada. All of these characteristics may be advantageous for Canadian companies that will increasingly be competing in global markets.[27]

In August 2000, Manitoba-born Don McCaw was named CEO of William M. Mercer Inc. in the U.S. Mercer is a leading human resource consulting firm, with 5000 employees and 130 offices around the world. The U.S. division had revenues of over $700 million in 1999 (Canadian revenues were $210 million). McCaw previously had been the CEO of Mercer's Canadian operation. He is described as loyal, pleasant, and able to collaborate with others. He built a strong team in Canada because of his management style, and the U.S. operation wants him to do the same thing there. The collaborative skills of Canadian managers are legendary in the eyes of many U.S. managers.

McCaw recognizes that being able to delegate authority and to work with a diverse workforce is an increasingly valued skill in the so-called New Economy. Managers simply cannot order people around any more. McCaw isn't alone in being successful in team building. In July 2000, Tom O'Neill was appointed CEO of the U.S. operation of PricewaterhouseCoopers. He had been the CEO of the Canadian operations before that. O'Neill credits his rise to his appreciation of the contributions that teams make to corporate success.[28]

The Contingency Approach to Leadership

Because each managerial style has both strengths and weaknesses, most managers vary their responses to different situations. Flexibility, however, has not always characterized managerial style or responsiveness. For most of the twentieth century, in fact, managers tended to believe that all problems yielded to preconceived, pretested solutions. If raising pay reduced turnover in one plant, for example, it followed that the same tactic would work equally well in another.

More recently, however, managers have begun to adopt a **contingency approach** to managerial style. They have started to view appropriate managerial behaviour in any situation as dependent, or contingent, on the elements unique to that situation. This change in outlook has resulted largely from an increasing appreciation of the complexity of managerial problems and solutions. For example, pay raises may reduce turnover when workers have been badly underpaid. The contingency approach, however, recognizes that raises will have little effect when workers feel adequately paid but ill-treated by management. This approach also recommends that training managers in human relations skills may be crucial to solving the latter problem.[29]

The contingency approach also acknowledges that people in different cultures behave differently and expect different things from their managers. A certain managerial style, therefore, is more likely to be successful in some countries than in others. Japanese workers, for example, generally expect managers to be highly participative and to allow them input in decision making. In contrast, many South American workers actually balk at participation and want take-charge leaders. The basic idea, then, is that managers will be more effective when they adapt their styles to the contingencies of the situations they face.[30]

contingency approach
An approach to managerial style holding that the appropriate behaviour in any situation is dependent (contingent) on the elements unique to that situation.

Motivation and Leadership in the Twenty-First Century

Motivation and leadership remain critically important areas of organizational behaviour. As times change, however, so do the ways in which managers motivate and lead their employees.

Changing Patterns of Motivation

From the motivational side, today's employees want rewards that are often quite different from those valued by earlier generations. Money, for example, is no longer the prime motivator for most people. In addition, because businesses today cannot offer the degree of job security that many workers want, motivating employees to strive towards higher levels of performance requires skilful attention from managers.

One recent survey asked workers to identify the things they most wanted at work. Among the things noted were flexible working hours (67 percent), casual dress (56 percent), unlimited Internet access (51 percent), opportunities to telecommute (43 percent), nap time (28 percent), massages (25 percent), daycare (24 percent), espresso machines (23 percent), and the opportunity to bring pets to work (11 percent).[31] In another study focusing on fathers, many men also said they wanted more flexible working hours in order to spend more time with their families.[32] Managers, then, must recognize that today's workers have a complex set of needs and must be motivated in increasingly complicated ways.

As we saw in Chapter 8, the diversity inherent in today's workforce also makes motivating behaviour more complex. The reasons why people work reflect more varying goals than ever before, and the varying lifestyles of diverse workers mean that managers must first pay closer attention to what their employees expect to receive for their efforts and then try to link rewards with job performance.

Changing Patterns of Leadership

Leadership, too, is taking different directions as we head into the twenty-first century. For one thing, today's leaders are finding it necessary to change their own behaviour. As organizations become flatter and workers become more empowered, managers naturally find it less acceptable to use the autocratic approach to leadership. Instead, many are becoming more democratic—functioning more as "coaches" than as "bosses." Just as an athletic coach teaches athletes how to play and then steps back to let them take the field, many leaders now try to provide workers with the skills and resources to perform at their best before backing off to let them do their work with less supervision.

Diversity, too, is affecting leadership processes. In earlier times, most leaders were white males who were somewhat older than the people they supervised—people who were themselves relatively similar to one another. But as organizations become more and more diverse, leaders are also becoming increasingly diverse. They are also increasingly likely to be younger than some of the people they are leading. Leaders, therefore, must have greater sensitivity to the values, needs, and motives of a diverse group of people as they examine their own behaviour in relation to other people.

Finally, leaders must also adopt a "network" mentality rather than a "hierarchical" one. When people worked in the same place at the same time, the organizational hierarchy had a clear vertical chain of command and lines of communication. But now people work in different places

WEBCONNEXION

Located in Mountain View, California, the Growth & Leadership Center offers professional and psychological assistance to Silicon Valley executives who are feeling the pressures of increasing workloads and stress levels. Using a variety of techniques, the company helps managers from such companies as Lucent Technologies, Sun Microsystems, Netscape, and Intel develop the patterns of behaviour and communication that make them more valuable to their employers as leaders. You can take a closer look at GLC at:

www.glcweb.com

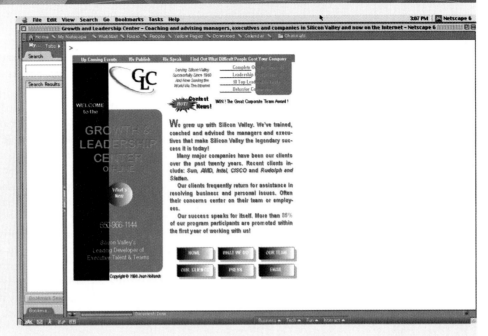

and at different times. New forms of organization design may call for a person to be the leader on one project and a team member on another. Thus, people need to become comfortable with leadership based more on expertise than on organizational position and with interaction patterns that are not tied to specific places or times. The leader of tomorrow, then, will need a different set of skills and a different point of view than did the leader of yesterday.

SUMMARY OF LEARNING OBJECTIVES

1. **Describe the nature and importance of *psychological contracts* in the workplace.** A *psychological contract* is the set of expectations held by an employee concerning what he or she will contribute to an organization (referred to as *contributions*) and what the organization will provide in return to the employee (referred to as *inducements*). Until the last decade or so, businesses generally offered their employees high levels of job security and employees were very loyal to their employers. More recently, however, new psychological contracts have been created in many sectors. Now, organizations offer less security but more benefits. In turn, employees are often willing to work longer hours but also more willing to leave an employer for a better opportunity elsewhere.

2. **Discuss the importance of *job satisfaction* and *employee morale* and summarize their roles in human relations in the workplace.** Good *human relations*—the interactions between employers and employees and their attitudes towards one another—are important to business because

they lead to high levels of *job satisfaction* (the degree of enjoyment that workers derive from their jobs) and *morale* (workers' overall attitudes towards their workplaces). Satisfied employees generally exhibit lower levels of absenteeism and turnover. They also have fewer grievances and engage in fewer negative behaviours.

3. **Identify and summarize the most important *theories of employee motivation*.** Views of employee motivation have changed dramatically over the years. The *classical theory* holds that people are motivated solely by money. *Scientific management* tried to analyze jobs and increase production by finding better ways to perform tasks. The *Hawthorne studies* were the first to demonstrate the importance of making workers feel that their needs were being considered. The *human resources model* identifies two kinds of managers—*Theory X managers*, who believe that people are inherently uncooperative and must be constantly punished or rewarded, and *Theory Y managers*, who believe that people are naturally responsible and self-motivated to be productive.

   Maslow's *hierarchy of needs model* proposes that people have several different needs (ranging from physiological to self-actualization), which they attempt to satisfy in their work. People must fulfil lower-level needs before seeking to fulfil higher-level needs. *Two-factor theory* suggests that if basic hygiene factors are not met, workers will be dissatisfied. Only by increasing more complex motivation factors can companies increase employees' performance.

   Expectancy theory holds that people will work hard if they believe that their efforts will lead to desired rewards. *Equity theory* says that motivation depends on the way employees evaluate their treatment by an organization relative to its treatment of other workers.

4. **Describe some of the strategies used by organizations to improve *job satisfaction* and *employee motivation*.** Managers can use several strategies to increase employee satisfaction and motivation. The principle of *reinforcement*, or *behaviour modification theory*, holds that rewards and punishment can control behaviour. *Rewards*, for example, are positive reinforcement when they are tied directly to desired or improved performance. *Punishment* (using unpleasant consequences to change undesirable behaviour) is generally less effective.

   Management by objectives (a system of collaborative goal setting) and *participative management* (techniques for giving employees a voice in management decisions) can improve human relations by making an employee feel like part of a team. *Job enrichment, job redesign*, and *modified work schedules* (including *workshare programs, flextime, compressed workweeks*, and *telecommuting*) can enhance job satisfaction by adding motivation factors to jobs in which they are normally lacking.

5. **Discuss different managerial styles of *leadership* and their impact on human relations in the workplace.** Effective *leadership*—the process of motivating others to meet specific objectives—is an important determinant of employee satisfaction and motivation. Generally speaking, managers practise one of three basic managerial styles. *Autocratic managers* generally issue orders that they expect to be obeyed. *Democratic managers* generally seek subordinates' input into decisions. *Free-rein managers* are more likely to advise than to make decisions. The *contingency approach* to leadership views appropriate managerial behaviour in any situation as dependent on the elements of that situation. Managers thus need to assess situations carefully, especially to determine the desire of subordinates to share input or exercise creativity. They must also be aware of the changing nature of both motivation and leadership as we enter the twenty-first century.

KEY TERMS

human relations, 261
psychological contract, 261
job satisfaction, 262
morale, 262
empowerment, 262
motivation, 263
classical theory of motivation, 264
scientific management, 264

time-and-motion studies, 264
Hawthorne effect, 264
Theory X, 265
Theory Y, 265
two-factor theory, 267
expectancy theory, 268
equity theory, 269
goal-setting theory, 271
reinforcement, 172

management by objectives (MBO), 174
participative management, 275
job enrichment, 276
job redesign, 276
flextime, 277
compressed workweek, 278
telecommuting, 278

worksharing (job sharing), 278
leadership, 279
managerial styles, 280
autocratic style, 280
democratic style, 280
free-rein style, 280
contingency approach, 281

STUDY QUESTIONS AND EXERCISES

Review Questions

1. Describe the psychological contract you currently have or have had in the past with an employer. If you have never worked, describe the psychological contract that you have with the instructor in this class.
2. Do you think that most people are relatively satisfied or dissatisfied with their work? Why are they mainly satisfied or dissatisfied?
3. Compare Maslow's hierarchy of needs with the two-factor theory of motivation.
4. How can participative management programs enhance employee satisfaction and motivation?s

Analysis Questions

5. Some evidence suggests that recent college and university graduates show high levels of job satisfaction. Levels then drop dramatically as they reach their late twenties, only to increase gradually once they get older. What might account for this pattern?

6. As a manager, under what sort of circumstances might you apply each of the theories of motivation discussed in this chapter? Which would be easiest to use? Which would be hardest to use? Why?
7. Suppose you realize one day that you are dissatisfied with your job. Short of quitting, what might you do to improve your situation?
8. List five managers who you think would also qualify as great leaders.

Application Exercises

9. At the library, research the manager or owner of a company in the early twentieth century and the manager or owner of a company in the 1990s. Compare the two in terms of their times in history, leadership styles, and views of employee motivation.
10. Interview the manager of a local manufacturing company. Identify as many different strategies for enhancing job satisfaction at that company as you can.

Building Your Business Skills

Too Much of a Good Thing

Goal

To encourage students to apply different motivational theories to a workplace problem involving poor productivity.

Situation

Consider a small company that makes its employees feel as if they were members of a large family. Unfortunately, this company is going broke because too few members are working hard enough to make money for it. They are happy, comfortable, complacent—and lazy. With sales dropping, the company brings in management consultants to analyze the situation and make recommendations. The outsiders quickly identify a motivational

problem affecting the sales force: sales reps are paid a handsome salary and receive automatic year-end bonuses regardless of performance. They are also treated to bagels every Friday and regular group birthday lunches that cost as much as $200 each. Employees feel satisfied, but have little incentive to work very hard. Eager to return to profitability, the company's owners wait to hear your recommendations.

Method

Step 1:

In groups of four, step into the role of management consultants. Start by analyzing your client's workforce motivation problems from the following perspectives (the questions focus on key motivational issues):

- *Job satisfaction and morale*. As part of a long-standing family-owned business, employees are happy and loyal, in part, because they are treated so well. Can high morale have a downside? How can it breed stagnation, and what can managers do to prevent stagnation from taking hold?

- *Theory X versus Theory Y*. Although the behaviour of these workers seems to make a case for Theory X, why is it difficult to draw this conclusion about a company that focuses more on satisfaction than on sales and profits?

- *Two-factor theory*. Analyze the various ways in which improving such motivational factors as recognition, added responsibility, advancement, and growth might reduce the importance of hygiene factors, including pay and security.

- *Expectancy theory*. Analyze the effect on productivity of redesigning the company's sales force compensation structure: namely, by paying lower base salaries while offering greater earnings potential through a sales-based incentive system. How would linking performance with increased pay that is achievable through hard work motivate employees? How would the threat of job loss motivate greater effort?

Step 2:
Write a short report based on your analysis, and make recommendations to the company's owners. The goal of your report is to change the working environment in ways that will motivate greater effort and generate greater productivity.

Follow-Up Questions

1. What is your group's most important recommendation? Why do you think it is likely to succeed?

2. Changing the corporate culture to make it less paternalistic may reduce employees' sense of belonging to a family. If you were an employee, would you consider a greater focus on profits to be an improvement or a problem? How would it affect your motivation and productivity?

3. What steps would you take to improve the attitude and productivity of long-time employees who resist change?

Exploring the Net

This chapter stresses the fact that employee satisfaction and morale are important to any organization. However, it is also quite difficult for managers to know for sure just how satisfied and motivated their employees actually are. In most cases, managers interested in assessing satisfaction and/or morale do so with surveys. Employees are asked to respond to various questions about how they feel about their work, and their responses are scored to provide an indication of their satisfaction and morale. To examine such a survey, visit the Web site at:

www.fdgroup.co.uk/neo/djassoc/dj_jdq.html

After you have examined the satisfaction questionnaire at this site, consider the following questions:

1. For whose use is this questionnaire meant? After studying the explanatory headnote, can you identify two or three key principles of instruments like this one?

2. At face value, how valid does this survey instrument seem to be? Is it likely to meet the objectives outlined in the headnote?

3. Complete the survey yourself, and then analyze your responses.

4. What appear to be the biggest strengths and weaknesses of this particular survey? Assuming this questionnaire to be typical, what would you judge to be the strengths and weaknesses of job satisfaction surveys in general?

5. Try writing a survey yourself. Focus it on job satisfaction in your present job, in a previous job, or in this class. What information do you most want to elicit? What aspect of this information is hardest to elicit? Why?

Concluding Case 9-1

A New Era in Employee Perks

In the increasingly competitive labour market of the past decade, companies are offering more and more perks to both current and prospective employees. Companies are doing this because they recognize the importance of retaining productive current employees and hiring promising new employees. Emphasizing a richer mix of employee perks makes it necessary for managers to adopt the view that employees can be trusted to do what is beneficial for the company and don't have to be watched all the time to ensure they're doing the right things.

Trimark Investment Management Inc. is just one example of the new era in employee perks. When the company moved from downtown Toronto to the suburbs in 1998, it wanted to make sure it kept valued employees who liked being close to big-city amenities. So it built the Energy Zone, an on-site facility that offers aerobics, self-defence, and yoga classes. It also includes a weight room, massage room, pool tables, a big-screen TV, and an Internet café. The Energy Zone gives employees some diversions from work, but it also acts as a place where they can meet and interact with people from other departments. Trimark also has a Recovery Room for employees who feel under the weather while at work.

A study done for *Report on Business Magazine* found that many of the traditional things that managers have assumed are important to employees—for example, fair pay, financial incentives such as share ownership plans, and the opportunity for further training and education—are, in fact, important. However, employees also want to work for a company where the culture values people, where their opinions count, and where their judgment is trusted.

Surveys also show that it is important for today's employees to be able to balance work and life activities. Employers are increasingly willing to accommodate these wishes because employee commitment and retention rise when a company recognizes that employees have a life outside work. If a company does nothing to help employees balance work and life concerns, and if it simply assumes that people are going to be totally devoted to the company, the bottom line is negatively affected because of the stress employees will experience.

A Canada @ Work study done by Aon Consulting found that when employers recognize employee needs outside the workplace, the company's employees are more likely to stay with the company, and are more likely to recommend the company as a good place to work. Overall, companies need to have a "people-first" attitude about their employees.

Flexible work arrangements such as job sharing, flextime, compressed workweeks, and work-at-home opportunities are examples of "people-first" attitudes. Consider the case of Nicole Black, who returned to her job at the Royal Bank three months after having her first child. She quickly found that she didn't have as much time with her new baby as she wanted. As a result, the bank arranged for a compressed workweek so she could work four days per week. When she became pregnant a second time, she reduced her work hours even further and started job sharing with another employee. She now works only on Mondays and Tuesdays.

A study by Hewitt Associates showed that companies that are recognized on lists such as "The 100 Best Companies to Work For" have almost twice the number of job applications and half the annual turnover as non-ranked companies. A study by the Gallup Organization showed that there was a strong correlation between employee satisfaction and company profitability.

CASE QUESTIONS

1. What is the difference between *job satisfaction* and *morale*? How do employee perks affect each of these concepts?

2. What do the various motivation factors discussed in this chapter say about the impact on employee satisfaction and motivation of things such as job sharing, compressed workweek, and flextime?

3. What are the various managerial styles that managers can use? What do the employee perks mentioned above imply about the most effective managerial style?

4. What strategies are available to managers to enhance employee job satisfaction? How are strategies such as compressed workweeks, job sharing, and flextime different from participative management and job enrichment?

5. Are there any potential problems with a company implementing the perks mentioned above? If so, what are they? ◆

Concluding Case 9-2

Has Levi's Lost Its Touch?

Levi Strauss & Co. is not only the world's leading maker of branded clothing and one of *Fortune* magazine's most admired companies. It is also a leader in creating a supportive work environment based on worker loyalty and trust.

The average length of service at the legendary blue jeans maker is more than 10 years, and management turnover at its headquarters in San Francisco is a mere 1.5 percent a year. Pay and bonuses are generous, and Levi's stock has risen with its fortunes, from US$2.53 in 1984 to US$265 in 1996, a record most firms would envy. This is the firm that's paying children in Bangladesh to stay in school full-time until they are old enough to reclaim the guaranteed jobs in Levi's factories that await them when they turn 14. Under the leadership of CEO Robert Haas, whose great-great-granduncle started the firm, Levi's seems to have figured out how to be ethical and make money at the same time.

Employee motivation has been high during Haas's tenure, sustained by his vision of the firm. "I believe that if you create an environment that your people identify with, that is responsible to their sense of values, justice, fairness, ethics, compassion, and appreciation, they will help to be successful. There's no guarantee, but I will stake my chips on this vision."

The company sets great store in its Aspirations Statement, which invokes teamwork, trust, diversity, recognition, and ethics, and is backed by required courses in leadership, diversity, and ethical decision making. Employees are assured that these values are real. Managers' bonuses, which can be as much as twice their salaries, depend directly on how well they achieve "aspirational behaviour," as judged by their subordinates and others. To compensate for ending its ESOP plan, Levi's has conscientiously promised an extra year's pay to each of its 37 000 employees if cash flow goals for 1997-2001 are met. Says Clive Smith, who works at the new plant in Cape Town, South Africa, "When we tell people what it's like working here, they think we're lying.... You'll have to fish the cops to get me out of here."

Yet the company is dealing with a possible threat to its sterling employee relations: a layoff affecting 6000 jobs was announced in 1997. Partly the result of debt incurred in massive buyback of company stock in 1996, the layoffs seem to go against everything the company stood for in its dealings with employees, although job security was never promised. Ironically, another contributing factor to the loss of jobs was an expensive plan to improve Levi's service to retailers that depended on developing new computer systems and software, not the firm's core business. The effort failed.

Layoffs are not the only problem Levi's employees are facing. Workers in Levi's factories have traditionally been paid on a piece work system that pays a certain amount of money for each zipper they sew or each belt loop they attach. In Levi's U.S. factories, this system has been replaced with a groupwork system where workers share tasks and are paid on the basis of how productive the *group* is. The company hoped this shift in emphasis from the individual to the group would relieve worker boredom and also reduce repetitive stress injuries that were caused by workers pushing themselves too hard.

But the new system has created unanticipated problems. Skilled workers feel that their wages are being lowered because slower workers reduce the overall productivity of the team. Morale has dropped, there is infighting among employees, and faster workers have tried to banish slower workers from their teams. In one factory, when a team found out that one of its members was going to have hand surgery, they voted the worker off the team because they feared team productivity would suffer when she returned after her surgery. One executive said that Levi's has created a lot of pain and anxiety for its employees, and nothing positive has been accomplished.

CASE QUESTIONS

1. How can Levi's minimize the damages its uncharacteristic actions might cause to employee morale and motivation? What specific strategies should management use?

2. CEO Haas has accepted responsibility for the situation that created the need for layoffs and plans to adhere to the firm's aspirational values. How can he use his position to focus employees on the positive aspects of working for Levi's?

3. Levi's president Peter Jacobi sees the company's unusual commitment to teamwork and trust as "a business strategy, pure and simple." Do you agree? Why?

4. Jacobi says, "We're not in business to create world peace." Is there a downside to the aspirational approach?

5. Would you be satisfied working at Levi's. Why or why not? ◆

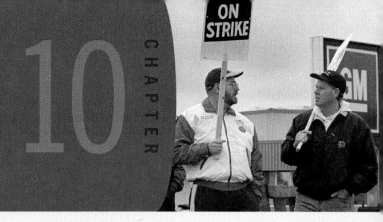

A Changing Approach to Labour Relations?

On October 19, 1999, the negotiating team for General Motors of Canada walked into the Royal York Hotel's Tudor Room and received a standing ovation from the Canadian Auto Workers (CAW) who were assembled there. The GM managers then applauded the workers. This type of behaviour is very unusual, particularly since CAW president Buzz Hargrove had said that CAW's relationship with GM of Canada was the worst among the "Big Three" domestic automakers. But even Hargrove admits that the atmosphere was positive during the negotiations.

And, indeed, it was clear early in the negotiating process that something was different. GM's first offer met the pattern of wages and benefits that the CAW had already negotiated with DaimlerChrysler Canada and Ford Motor of Canada. A cost of living allowance was also given, as were generous improvements in pensions. GM also agreed to drop its plan to contract out 1300 jobs (it was this issue that led to a 1996 strike). GM also settled hundreds of outstanding grievances at the Oshawa and St. Catharines plants. The two sides reached a tentative agreement seven hours before the deadline. A union official says it was obvious that GM was determined not to have another strike.

This turnaround comes on the heels of serious disputes between the CAW and GM of Canada. In 1996, 26 000 CAW workers went on strike and shut down all of GM's Canadian operations. GM also experienced strikes at its Dayton, Ohio, and Flint, Michigan, plants in the late 1990s. All of this contributed to a continuing decline in GM's stock price and its market share in North America. Those strikes apparently convinced both workers and management that they had to begin working together if GM hoped to become as efficient as Ford and DaimlerChrysler.

How were the improvements in union–management relations actually achieved? For one thing, GM's chief negotiator, Al Green, spent a lot of time getting to know union boss Buzz Hargrove. The union and the company also spent a lot of time exchanging information about the business challenges each of them was facing. GM has more capacity than it has market share, and industry analysts say that it will have to close more manufacturing plants to bring its output in line with its market share. Another problem is increasing foreign competition from companies such as Honda and Toyota.

The union has potential problems, too. Although overall membership in the CAW has grown (because the union has merged with other unions and diversified into the airline industry), the number of unionized autoworkers has declined because the automakers continue to downsize. These declines in union membership at automobile plants are not being offset by increased union membership at auto parts makers.

Has a new era really dawned at GM of Canada? Some observers are skeptical. They think that the new, more cooperative approach will continue only as long as GM doesn't have to make tough decisions. But tough decisions will be needed in the future. When the red-hot car market cools off, as it inevitably will, GM will be under considerable pressure to cut costs, and closing manufacturing plants will surely be considered. But what happens to the positive labour–management relations if a tough decision like that is made? ◆

In this chapter, we will examine various aspects of labour–management relations in Canada. We will begin by considering how and why workers have chosen to band together in the past, as well as the laws that regulate labour–management relations. We will then explore the interaction of worker organizations and management in areas such as compensation, employee performance, and workers' grievances. Finally, we will look at the future of labour organizations in Canada.

By focusing on the learning objectives for this chapter, you will better understand the formation of unions as a result of workers' fundamental concerns about workplace conditions, the legal and regulatory basis for labour–management relations, and the collective bargaining process. After reading this chapter, you will be able to:

LEARNING OBJECTIVES

1. Explain why workers unionize.

2. Trace the evolution of and discuss trends in *unionism* in Canada.

3. Describe the *major laws governing labour–management relations*.

4. Describe the union *certification* and *decertification processes*.

5. Identify the steps in the *collective bargaining process*.

WHY DO WORKERS UNIONIZE?

Over 2000 years ago, the Greek poet Homer wrote, "There is a strength in the union even of very sorry men." There were no labour unions in Homer's time, but his comment is a particularly effective expression of the rationale for unions. A **labour union** is a group of individuals working together to achieve shared job-related goals, such as higher pay, shorter working hours, more job security, greater benefits, or better working conditions.[1] **Labour relations** describes the process of dealing with employees who are represented by a union.

Labour unions grew in popularity in Canada in the nineteenth and early twentieth centuries. The labour movement was born with the Industrial Revolution, which also gave birth to a factory-based production system that carried with it enormous economic benefits. Job specialization and mass production allowed businesses to create ever-greater quantities of goods at ever-lower costs.

But there was also a dark side to this era. Workers became more dependent on their factory jobs. Eager for greater profits, some owners treated their workers like other raw materials: as resources to be deployed with little or no regard for the individual worker's well-being. Many businesses forced employees to work long hours; 60-hour weeks were common, and some workers were routinely forced to work 12 to 16 hours per day. With no minimum-wage laws or other controls, pay was also minimal and safety standards were virtually nonexistent. Workers enjoyed no job security and received few benefits. Many companies, especially textile mills, employed large numbers of children at poverty wages. If people complained, nothing prevented employers from firing and replacing them at will.

Unions appeared and ultimately prospered because they constituted a solution to the worker's most serious problem: They forced management to listen to the complaints of all their workers rather than to just the few who were brave (or foolish) enough to speak out. The power of unions, then, comes from collective action. **Collective bargaining** is the process by which union leaders and managers negotiate common terms and conditions of employment for the workers represented by unions. Although collective bargaining does not often occur in small businesses, many mid-size and larger businesses must engage in the process, which we will discuss in more detail later in this chapter.

labour union
A group of individuals who work together to achieve shared job-related goals.

labour relations
The process of dealing with employees who are represented by a union.

collective bargaining
The process through which union leaders and management personnel negotiate common terms and conditions of employment for those workers represented by the union.

THE DEVELOPMENT OF CANADIAN LABOUR UNIONS

The earliest evidence of labour unions in Canada comes from the maritime provinces early in the nineteenth century. Generally, these unions were composed of individuals with a specific craft (e.g., printers, shoemakers, barrelmakers). Most of these unions were small and had only limited success. However, they laid the foundation for the rapid increase in union activity that occurred during the late nineteenth and early twentieth centuries.

A succession of labour organizations sprang up and just as quickly faded away during the years 1840–70. In 1873, the first national labour organization was formed—the Canadian Labour Union. By 1886, the Knights of Labour (a U.S.-based union) had over 10 000 members in Canada. The Canadian labour movement began to mature with the formation of the Trades and Labour Congress (TLC) in 1886. The TLC's purpose was to unite all labour organizations and to work for the passage of laws that would ensure the well-being of the working class.

The growth of labour unions began in earnest early in the twentieth century as the concept of organized labour gradually came to be accepted. Various disputes arose that resulted in numerous splits in labour's ranks. For example, there was concern that U.S.-based unions would have a detrimental effect on Canadian unions. The Canadian Federation of Labour was formed in 1908 to promote national (Canadian) unions over U.S. unions. These and other disputes (such as how communists in the movement should be handled) often led to the creation of rival union organizations that competed for membership. By 1956, these disputes had been largely resolved, and the two largest congresses of affiliated unions—the Trades and Labour Congress and the Canadian Congress of Labour—merged to form the Canadian Labour Congress. This amalgamation brought approximately 80 percent of all unionized workers into one organization. Table 10.1 highlights some of the important events in Canadian labour history.

Canadian Labour Congress
www.clc-ctc.ca

The Canadian Labour Congress (CLC), formed in 1956, brought the majority of unionized workers in Canada into one organization.

Table 10.1		Some Important Dates in Canadian Labour History

1827	First union formed: boot and shoemakers in Quebec City
1840–70	Many new unions formed; influenced by U.S. and British unions
1871	Formation of Toronto Trades Assembly; composed of five craft unions; went out of existence a few years later
1873	Canadian Labour Union formed; objective was to unite unions across Canada
1879	First coal miners union in North America formed in Nova Scotia
1881	The U.S.-based Knights of Labor enter Canada
1883	Canadian Labour Congress formed; lasted until 1886
1886	Canadian Trades and Labour Congress formed; later became known as the Trades and Labour Congress of Canada (TLC)
1902	Knights of Labor expelled from TLC
1902	Expelled unions form the National Trades and Labour Congress (became the Canadian Federation of Labour [CFL] in 1908); purpose was to promote national unions instead of international ones
1902–20	Rapid growth of union membership in both major unions (TLC and CFL)
1919	One Big Union formed; organized in opposition to the TLC
1919	Winnipeg General Strike
1921	Canadian Brotherhood of Railway Employees (CBRE) expelled from TLC
1921	Confédération des Travailleurs Catholiques du Canada (CTCC) organized by the Roman Catholic clergy in Quebec; goal was to keep French-Canadian workers from being unduly influenced by English-speaking and American trade unions
1927	All-Canadian Congress of Labour (ACCL) formed; objective was to achieve independence of the Canadian labour movement from foreign control; made up of One Big Union, the CFL, and the CBRE
1939	TLC expels industrial unions; Canadian Congress of Industrial Organization (CIO) Committee formed
1940	ACCL and the Canadian CIO Committee unite to form the Canadian Congress of Labour (CCL)
1956	TLC and CCL merge to form the Canadian Labour Congress; remnants of One Big Union join new organization
1960	CTCC drops association with Roman Catholic Church and chooses a new name— Confédération des Syndicats Nationaux (CSN); in English, the Confederation of National Trade Unions (CNTU)
1960–69	Rapid growth of CNTU in Quebec
1971	Centre for Democratic Unions formed as a result of secession from the CNTU by dissident members
1981	International building trades unions suspended from CLC
1982	Founding convention of Canadian Federation of Labour (CFL)
1985	Formation of United Auto Workers of Canada; formerly part of international UAW
1989	Merger of Canadian Union of Postal Workers (CUPW) and Letter Carriers Union of Canada
1992	First-ever strike of NHL players
1994	Major league baseball players strike; no World Series played; NHL players also locked out; only half of hockey season played
1997	Strike of primary and secondary school teachers in Ontario
1999	Quebec nurses strike

UNIONISM TODAY

While understanding the historical context of labour unions is important, so too is appreciating the role of unionism today, especially trends in union membership, union–management relations, and bargaining perspectives.

Trends in Union Membership

Since the mid-1970s, Canadian labour unions have experienced increasing difficulties in attracting new members. As a result, although millions of workers still belong to labour unions, union membership *as a percentage of the total workforce* has begun to decline. As shown in Figure 10.1, union membership peaked in the 1980s and began to decline in the 1990s. Currently,

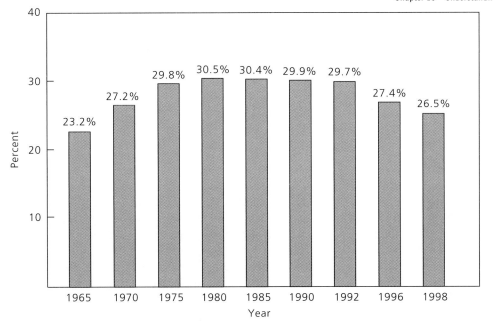

Figure 10.1
Union members as a proportion of the total workforce.

less than 27 percent of the total Canadian workforce is unionized. If the thousands of unionized public sector employees are excluded, an even smaller percentage of the Canadian workforce is unionized.

Over the years, unions have experienced ups and downs in terms of their success at becoming certified at new locations. In the years following the Second World War, unions routinely won certification votes. In recent years, however, unions have been experiencing increased opposition from management of companies that are trying to remain flexible in a fiercely competitive and global environment.

From most indications, then, the power and significance of labour unions, while still quite formidable, are also measurably lower than they were just a few decades ago. Two factors help to explain the decline in union membership.

Composition of the Workforce

Traditionally, union members have been predominantly white males in blue-collar jobs. But today's workforce is increasingly composed of women and ethnic minorities. Because these groups have much weaker traditions of union affiliation, their members are less likely to join unions when they enter the workforce. In a related trend, the workforce is increasingly employed in the service sector, which traditionally has been less heavily unionized.

Anti-Unionization Activities

A second reason for declining union membership is more aggressive anti-unionization activity on the part of employers. Although federal and provincial labour legislation restricts what management of a company can do to keep out a union, companies are free to pursue certain strategies to minimize unionization. As we saw in Chapter 9, for example, many companies have tried to create a much more employee-friendly work environment and are increasingly treating workers with more respect and dignity. One goal of this approach is to minimize the attractiveness of labour unions for employees (see the "Business Today" box, which describes that company's attempts to keep out a union).

BUSINESS TODAY

Giving Up at Wal-Mart

In 1996, Wal-Mart management first began hearing rumours that employees at the Windsor store were being approached about joining a union. Wal-Mart employees are supposed to be one big, happy family, but the prospect of a union caused squabbling among employees at the store. One anti-union employee gave a speech exhorting other employees not to join the union, and when pro-union employees asked for the opportunity to respond, they were denied the right to do so.

Wal-Mart had never had a union in any of its stores in the U.S., Canada, Puerto Rico, Argentina, Brazil, or Mexico. It had been able to resist unions partly by promoting its family-like culture. The company argued that forcing employees to work under a collective agreement would reduce their motivation and damage the company's successful formula for keeping consumers happy. The company had also resisted unionization in more direct ways. For example, when it purchased 122 Woolco stores in Canada, it pointedly did not buy the 9 stores that were unionized.

On May 5, 1996 (four days before the certification vote was to be held), the Windsor store manager told at least one employee that unionization would mean a lot of changes at the store, and that employees might lose certain benefits they currently had. When the certification vote was held, the union lost by a margin of 151–43. In spite of this, the Ontario Labour Relations Board (OLRB) certified the union as the bargaining agent for employees at the Windsor store, ruling that Wal-Mart had used intimidation tactics to try to prevent unionization.

In December 1997, the first collective agreement seemed to be approved by workers in a 109–39 vote. However, a group of 80 employees then signed a petition claiming that they did not vote in favour of the contract.

In April 1998, a majority of workers at the store filed an application with the OLRB to have the union decertified, claiming that there were irregularities in voting on the first collective agreement. The decertification application also claimed that the union had only minority support at the store.

In April 2000, the union was decertified and the Canadian Auto Workers decided to abandon its efforts to represent workers at the only unionized Wal-Mart store in the world.

Many Japanese manufacturers who have set up shop in North America have avoided unionization efforts by the United Auto Workers (UAW) by providing job security, higher wages, and a work environment in which employees are allowed to participate and be actively involved in plant management. The Toyota plant in Cambridge, Ontario, is just one example.

Trends in Union–Management Relations

The gradual decline in unionization in Canada has been accompanied by some significant trends in union–management relations. In some sectors of the economy, perhaps most notably in the automobile and steel industries, labour unions remain quite strong. In these areas, unions have large memberships and considerable power in negotiating with management. The CAW, for example, is still a strong union.

In most sectors, however, unions are clearly in a weakened position. As a result, many have taken much more conciliatory stances in their relations with management. This situation contrasts sharply with the more adversarial relationship that once dominated labour relations in this country. Increasingly, for instance, unions recognize that they don't have as much power as they once held and that it is in their own best interests, as well as in the best interests of the workers they represent, to work with instead of against management. Ironically, then, union–management relations in many ways are better today than they have been in several years. Admittedly, the improvement is attributable in large part to the weakened power of unions. Even so, most experts agree that improved union–management relations have benefited both sides.

Trends in Bargaining Perspectives

Given the trends described in the two previous sections, we should not be surprised to find changes in bargaining perspectives as well. In the past, for example, most union–management bargaining situations were characterized by union demands for dramatic increases in wages and salaries. A secondary issue was usually increased benefits for members. Now, however, unions often bargain for different benefits, such as job security. Of particular interest in this area is the trend towards relocating jobs to take advantage of lower labour costs in other countries. Unions, of course, want to restrict job movement, whereas companies want to save money by moving facilities—and jobs—to other countries.

As a result of organizational downsizing and several years of relatively low inflation in Canada, many unions today find themselves able to achieve only modest wage increases for their members. A common goal of union strategy is to preserve what has already been won. Unions also place greater emphasis on improved job security. A trend that has become especially important in recent years is towards improved pension programs for employees.

In North America, unions have also begun to increasingly set their sights on preserving jobs for workers in the face of business efforts to relocate production to countries where labour costs are lower. In the U.S., for example, the AFL-CIO has been an outspoken opponent of efforts to normalize trade relations with China, fearing that more businesses might be tempted to move jobs there. General Electric has been targeted by union protests recently because of its strategy to move many jobs—and those of key suppliers—to Mexico.[2]

General Electric
www.ge.com

The Future of Unions

Despite declining membership and loss of power, labour unions remain a major factor in Canadian business. The labour organizations in the Canadian Labour Congress and independent major unions such as the International Brotherhood of Teamsters and the Canadian Union of Public Employees can disrupt the economy by refusing to work. The votes of their members are still sought by politicians at all levels. In addition, the concessions they have won for their members—better pay, shorter working hours, safer working conditions—now cover many non-unionized workers as well.

Canadian Union of Public Employees
www.cupe.ca

Some unions still wield considerable clout, especially in the traditional strongholds of goods-producing industries. Consider the recent clash between labour and management at General Motors. In June 1998, the UAW had threatened to shut down a GM metal-stamping plant in Flint, Michigan, over a contract dispute. GM was concerned because the plant was being set up to make fenders and bumpers for a new truck model with the potential to become the best-selling and highest-profit-margin vehicle in GM's 1999 lineup. GM simply could not risk losing production time to a strike and felt that extreme measures were necessary to protect its interests. Thus, on a Sunday afternoon when the plant was closed, GM hauled away a dozen two-tonne metal dies that were critical to building the new trucks. These were then shipped secretly to another stamping plant in Mansfield, Ohio. Because the Ohio plant had a contract with GM that prohibited a strike, GM planned to produce the needed truck parts there if the Flint plant was shut down. Not surprisingly, the UAW was outraged, and a strike was called immediately. All told, 25 000 workers walked out of GM's Flint plant. The strike lasted 54 days and cost GM US$2.2 billion in lost revenues.

United Auto Workers (UAW)
www.uaw.org

GM did get its trucks out on time from its Ohio plant, but the dispute in Flint was so bitter, and the concessions ultimately made by GM so sweeping, that it's still not clear who, if anyone, ultimately "won." Thus, despite predictions that unions are slowly dying and calls for a "new unionism" in which cooperation replaces conflict, the reality of union–management relationships often remains harsh. Costly strikes are not a thing of the past, and companies operating under collective bargaining agreements must still find ways to deal with and co-exist with labour unions.[3]

While there are examples of labour–management relationships that are less antagonistic (as we saw in the opening case of this chapter), a big question remains: Will unions be able to cope with the many challenges that are currently facing them, or will their power continue to dwindle? The challenges facing unions are many, including:

- the decline of the so-called "smokestack industries," where union power has traditionally been very strong

- employment growth in service industries, where union power has traditionally not been strong

- deregulation, which has led to mergers and layoffs and to the emergence of new, non-unionized companies

- free trade and the globalization of business, which has raised the very real possibility of many jobs being moved to areas of the world with lower labour costs

- technological change, which allows telecommuting and increases the difficulty of organizing workers

Unions are increasingly aware that they must cooperate with employers if both companies and unions are to survive and prosper. The goal is to create effective partnerships in which managers and workers share the same goals: profitability, growth, and effectiveness, with equitable rewards for everyone.

In fact, a new wave of unionism may be about to sweep across Canada. This movement may be fuelled by young people (including college and university graduates) who fear they will be stuck in low-wage jobs and who hope that unions can help them avoid that fate. In 1997, for example, unions were certified at nine Starbucks Coffee locations.

Other changes are also occurring, including the increased number of women as union members. In 1967, women accounted for less than 20 percent of union membership in Canada, but by 1997 they represented nearly half of all union workers. These unionized women are highly concentrated in the public sector, which provides jobs for only 19 percent of the workforce, but accounts for 43 percent of all union members.[4]

THE LEGAL ENVIRONMENT FOR UNIONS IN CANADA

Political and legal barriers to collective bargaining existed until well into the twentieth century. Courts held that some unions were conspirators in restraint of trade. Employers viewed their employees' efforts to unionize as attempts to deprive the employers of their private property. The employment contract, employers contended, was between the individual worker and the employer—not between the employer and employees as a group. The balance of bargaining power was very much in favour of the employer.

The employer–employee relationship became much less direct as firms grew in size. Managers were themselves employees. Hired managers dealt with other employees. Communication among owners, managers, and workers became more formalized. Big business had more power than workers. Because of mounting public concern, laws were passed to place the worker on a more even footing with the employer.

In 1900, government concern about labour disputes resulted in the passage of the *Conciliation Act*. The act was designed to help settle labour disputes through voluntary conciliation and was a first step in creating an environment more favourable to labour. A more comprehensive law, the 1907 **Industrial Disputes Investigation Act**, provided for compulsory investigation of labour disputes by a government-appointed board before a strike was allowed. However, this act was later found to violate a fundamental provision of the *BNA Act* (see below).

Industrial Disputes Investigation Act (1907)
Provided for compulsory investigation of labour disputes by a government-appointed board before a strike was allowed.

The current positive environment for labour did not come into being until 1943 when **Privy Council Order 1003** was issued. This order recognized the right of employees to bargain collectively, prohibited unfair labour practices on the part of management, established a labour board to certify bargaining authority, and prohibited strikes and lockouts except in the course of negotiating collective agreements. Approximately 45 years of dealings among labour, management, and government were required before the labour movement achieved its fundamental goal of the right to bargain collectively.

Privy Council Order 1003 (1943)
Recognized the right of employees to bargain collectively.

The **Constitution Act** (originally the *BNA Act*), passed in 1867, has also affected labour legislation. This act allocated certain activities to the federal government (e.g., labour legislation for companies operating interprovincially) and others to individual provinces (labour relations regulations in general). Thus, labour legislation emanates from both the federal and provincial governments but is basically a provincial matter. That is why certain groups of similar employees might be allowed to go on strike in one province but not in another.

Constitution Act, 1867
Divided authority over labour regulations between the federal and provincial governments.

Federal Legislation—The Canada Labour Code

The **Canada Labour Code** is a comprehensive piece of legislation that applies to the labour practices of firms operating under the legislative authority of parliament. The code is composed of four major sections:

Canada Labour Code
Legislation that applies to the labour practices of firms operating under the legislative authority of parliament.

Fair Employment Practices

This section prohibits an employer from either refusing employment on the basis of a person's race or religion or using an employment agency that discriminates against people on the basis of their race or religion. These prohibitions apply to trade unions as well, but not to non-profit, charitable, and philanthropic organizations. Any individual who believes that a violation has occurred may make a complaint in writing to Labour Canada. The allegation will then be investigated and if necessary, an Industrial Inquiry Commission will be appointed to make a recommendation in the case. (Since 1982, fair employment practices have been covered by the *Canadian Human Rights Act*; they are also covered by the Canadian Charter of Rights and Freedoms.)

Standard Hours, Wages, Vacations, and Holidays

This section deals with a wide variety of mechanical issues such as standard hours of work (8-hour days and 40-hour weeks), maximum hours of work per week (48), overtime pay (at least one and a half times the regular pay), minimum wages, equal wages for men and women doing the same jobs,

WEBCONNEXION

The Canada Labour Code is a comprehensive piece of legislation that specifies labour requirements in the areas of safety legislation, minimum age to work, dispute resolution, labour standards, wages, sick leave, vacations, etc. It is divided into three main sections: industrial relations regulations, occupational health and safety regulations, and labour standards. Visit the Canada Labour Code at:

www.hrdc-drhc.gc.ca/dept/ guide/labour-5.shtn

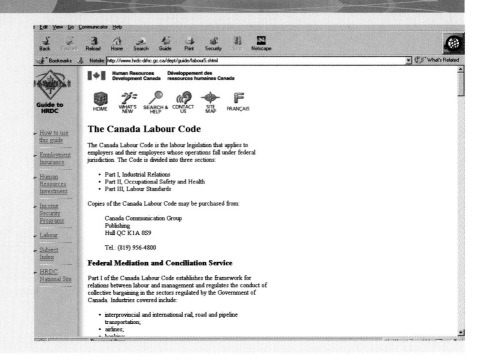

vacations, general holidays, and maternity leave. The specific provisions are changed frequently to take into account changes in the economic and social structure of Canada, but their basic goal is to ensure consistent treatment of employees in these areas.

Safety of Employees

This section requires that every person running a federal work project do so in a way that will not endanger the health or safety of any employee. It also requires that safety procedures and techniques be implemented to reduce the risk of employment injury. This section requires employees to exercise care to ensure their own safety; however, even if it can be shown that the employee did not exercise proper care, compensation must still be paid. This section also makes provisions for a safety officer whose overall duty is to assure that the provisions of the code are being fulfilled. The safety officer has the right to enter any federal project "at any reasonable time."

Canada Industrial Relations Regulations

The final major section of the *Canada Labour Code* deals with all matters related to collective bargaining. It is subdivided into seven divisions:

- Division I—gives employees the right to join a trade union and gives employers the right to join an employers association.

- Division II—establishes the Canada Labour Relations Board whose role is to make decisions on a number of important issues (e.g., certification of trade unions).

- Division III—stipulates the procedures required to acquire or terminate bargaining rights.

- Division IV—establishes the rules and regulations that must be adhered to during bargaining; also presents guidelines for the content and interpretation of collective agreements.

- Division V—states the requirement that the Minister of Labour must appoint a conciliation officer if the parties in the dispute cannot reach a collective agreement.

- Division VI—stipulates the conditions under which strikes and lockouts are permitted.

- Division VII—a general conclusion giving methods that might be used to promote industrial peace.

Provincial Labour Legislation

Each province has enacted legislation to deal with the personnel practices covered in the *Canada Labour Code*. These laws vary across provinces and are frequently revised; however, their basic approach and substance is the same as in the *Canada Labour Code*. Certain provinces may exceed the minimum code requirements on some issues (e.g., minimum wage).

Each province also has a labour relations act. To give an indication of what these acts cover, the *Ontario Labour Relations Act* is briefly described below.

The Ontario Labour Relations Act

The *Ontario Labour Relations Act* is a comprehensive document dealing with the conduct of labour relations in that province. Some illustrative provisions of the Ontario law are noted below.

- A trade union may apply at any time to the Ontario Labour Relations Board (OLRB) for certification as the sole bargaining agent for employees in a company.

- The OLRB has the right to call for a certification vote. If more than 50 percent of those voting are in favour of the trade union, the board certifies the union as the bargaining agent.

- Following certification, the union gives the employer written notification of its desire to bargain, with the goal being the signing of a collective agreement. The parties are required to begin bargaining within 15 days of the written notice.

- On request by either party, the Minister of Labour appoints a conciliation officer to confer with the parties and to help achieve a collective agreement. On joint request, the Minister of Labour can appoint a mediator.

- The parties may jointly agree to submit unresolved differences to voluntary binding arbitration. The decision of the arbitrator is final.

- Employers are required to deduct union dues from the union members and remit these dues directly to the union.

- Every agreement must include a mechanism for settling grievances—differences between the parties arising from interpretation, application, or administration of the collective agreement.

■ If a person objects to belonging to a labour union because of religious beliefs, he or she is allowed to make a contribution equal to the amount of the union dues to a charitable organization.

■ If a trade union is not able to negotiate a collective agreement with management within one year of being certified, any of the employees in the union can apply to the OLRB for decertification of the union.

■ No employer can interfere with the formation of a union. The employer is, however, free to express an opinion about the matter.

■ No employer shall refuse to employ an individual because he or she is a member of a trade union.

The basic provisions of the *Ontario Labour Relations Act* are found in one form or another in the labour relations acts of all provinces, but the details and procedures vary from province to province. It is obvious that administering labour relations activity is complex and time-consuming. Company management, the union, and the government all expend much time and energy in an attempt to ensure reasonable relations between management and labour.

UNION ORGANIZING STRATEGY

A union might try to organize workers when a firm is trying to break into a new geographical area, when some workers in a firm are members and it wants to cover other workers, or when it is attempting to outdo a rival union. In some cases, a union might try to organize workers for purposes other than helping a group of employees to help themselves.

Management often becomes aware of a union organizing effort through gossip from the company grapevine. In 1999, management at Honda of Canada's Alliston, Ontario, plant and at Toyota Canada's Cambridge, Ontario,

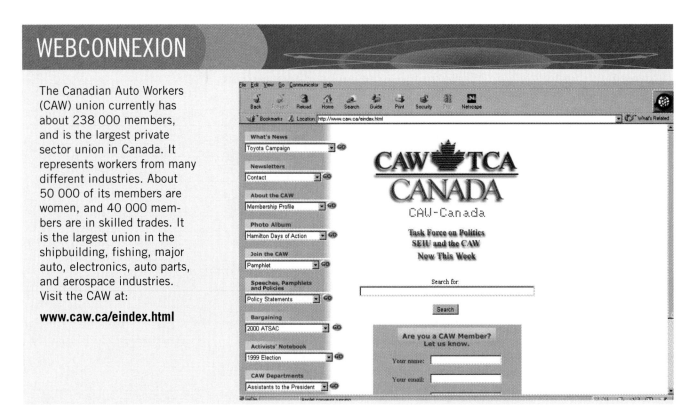

WEBCONNEXION

The Canadian Auto Workers (CAW) union currently has about 238 000 members, and is the largest private sector union in Canada. It represents workers from many different industries. About 50 000 of its members are women, and 40 000 members are in skilled trades. It is the largest union in the shipbuilding, fishing, major auto, electronics, auto parts, and aerospace industries. Visit the CAW at:

www.caw.ca/eindex.html

plant learned that the CAW had launched organizing drives at their plants. The CAW distributed leaflets at plant gates and contacted groups of workers inside the plant as part of its organizing drive.[5]

When management discovers that an organizing drive is underway, it may try to counteract it. However, management must know what it can legally do to discourage the union. In Quebec, McDonald's has been the target of union organizing drives at several of its restaurants. In 1998, the McDonald's restaurant in St. Hubert closed when it appeared that the teamsters union might be successful in getting certified as the bargaining agent for the employees. Critics immediately called for a government investigation into the possibility of unfair labour practices on the part of the company.[6]

Certifying a Union: An Example

Suppose that a union is trying to organize employees of a Manitoba company. If it can show that at least 50 percent of the employees are members of the union, it can apply to the Manitoba Labour Board (MLB) for certification as the bargaining agent for the employees.

A problem may arise regarding the right of different types of workers to join or not join the union. For example, supervisors may or may not be included in a bargaining unit along with nonmanagement workers. The **bargaining unit** includes those individuals deemed appropriate by the province. The MLB has final authority in determining the appropriateness of the bargaining unit. Professional and nonprofessional employees are generally not included in the same bargaining unit unless a majority of the professional employees wish to be included.

Once the MLB has determined that the unit is appropriate, it may order a **certification vote**. If a majority of those voting are in favour of the union, it is certified as the sole bargaining agent for the unit. The "It's a Wired World" box describes how unions are using the Internet to achieve their goals.

bargaining unit
Individuals grouped together for purposes of collective bargaining.

certification vote
A vote supervised by a government representative to determine whether a union will be certified.

Types of Unions

The two basic types of union are craft and industrial unions.

Craft unions are organized by crafts or trades—plumbers, barbers, airline pilots, etc. Craft unions restrict membership to workers with specific skills. In many cases, members of craft unions work for several different employers during the course of a year. For example, many construction workers are hired by their employers at union hiring halls. When the particular job for which they are hired is finished, these workers return to the hall to be hired by another employer.

Craft unions have a lot of power over the supply of skilled workers because they have apprenticeship programs. A person who wants to become a member of a plumber's union, for example, must go through a training program. He or she starts out as an apprentice. After the training, the apprentice is qualified as a journeyman plumber.

Industrial unions are organized according to industries, for example, steel, auto, clothing. Industrial unions include semiskilled and unskilled workers. They were originally started because industrial workers were not eligible to join craft unions. Industrial union members typically work for a particular employer for a much longer period of time than do craft union members. An industrial union has a lot of say regarding pay and human resource practices within unionized firms.

The **local union** (or local) is the basic unit of union organization. A local of a craft union is made up of artisans in the same craft in a relatively

craft unions
Unions organized by trades; usually composed of skilled workers.

industrial unions
Unions organized by industry; usually composed of semiskilled and unskilled workers.

local union
The basic unit of union organization.

IT'S A WIRED WORLD

The Web as a Bargaining Tool

It's no secret that the Internet now plays a key role in the plans and operations of many businesses. A bit less obvious, though certainly no less important, is the approach that organized labour is taking to the Internet. There are at least three different areas in which labour is taking advantage of the Internet to promote various agendas.

First, just like many if not most businesses, many unions have Web sites. Some of these sites are posted by national and international unions; others are posted by local unions. Web sites provide information for members, promote the union's current agenda, and contain links to other relevant sites. Some of the more aggressive union Web sites go so far as to provide warnings and directives to management as to what it can and cannot do during ongoing organizing and/or collective bargaining periods—even pointing out that the Web site itself is a union organizing location and thus off-limits to managers.

The Internet is also important to unions as a source of information and means of research. A critical part of effective collective bargaining—for both sides—is having the right information. Both sides, for example, need to know such statistics as employment rates, cost-of-living changes and projections, and so forth. They also need to know what contract terms have been negotiated in similar industries and settings. The Internet makes this information more accessible.

The Internet also makes it easier for a union to learn more about a company, especially when it is a privately held corporation. A long-time union practice has been to obtain employment for what is called a "salt"—essentially, an employee planted for espionage purposes. These individuals try to find out whatever they can about the lifestyles and wealth of business owners. Learning, for instance, that a business owner has expensive hobbies, travels in lavish style, and maintains a fleet of expensive cars makes it easier for the union to argue for higher wages. The Internet makes it easier to locate this same information more quickly and more easily.

Finally, the Internet is used more and more frequently as a recruiting tool during organizing campaigns. Whereas organizers once had little choice but to hang out in company parking lots or neighbourhood bars to strike up conversations with a business's employees, they can now do most of their work electronically. Today, for example, they can put up Web sites at the start of a campaign. All they have to do is recruit a few people and then wait for the recruits to pass along the Web address to co-workers. Interested parties can visit the site, review what the union says it can and will do, and post e-mails with questions and comments. One day soon, certification elections may even be conducted online.

---

small geographical area. A local of an industrial union is made up of workers in a given industry or plant in a relatively small geographical area. Thus, plumbers in a local labour market may be members of the local plumbers' union. Truck drivers and warehouse workers in that same area may be members of a teamsters' local.

The functions of locals vary, depending not only on governance arrangements but also on bargaining patterns in particular industries. Some local unions bargain directly with management regarding wages, hours, and other terms and conditions of employment. Many local unions are also active in disciplining members for violations of contract standards and in pressing management to consider worker complaints.

national union
A union with members across Canada.

A **national union** has members across Canada. These members belong to locals affiliated with the national union. There are many national unions in Canada, including the Canadian Union of Public Employees, the National Railway Union, and the Canadian Airline Pilots Union. About two-thirds of unionized Canadian workers belong to national unions.

international union
A union with members in more than one country.

An **international union** is a union with members in more than one country. One example is the United Steelworkers of America, made up of locals in the United States and Canada. About 30 percent of unionized workers in Canada belong to international unions.

Table 10.2	The Top 10 Labour Unions in Canada

Union	Members (thousands)
1. Canadian Union of Public Employees	389.3
2. National Union of Public and General Employees	309.0
3. National Automobile, Aerospace, and Agricultural Implement Workers	222.5
4. United Food and Commercial Workers	200.0
5. United Steelworkers of America	180.0
6. Communication, Energy, and Paperworkers Union of Canada	144.3
7. Public Service Alliance of Canada	142.3
8. Fédération de la santé et des services sociaux (CSN)	97.0
9. International Brotherhood of Teamsters, Chauffeurs, Warehousemen, and Helpers of America	94.0
10. Fédération des enseignantes des commissions	82.6

An **independent local union** is one that is not formally affiliated with any labour organization. It conducts negotiations with management at a local level, and the collective agreement is binding at that location only. The University of Manitoba Faculty Association is an independent local union. Less than 5 percent of unionized workers in Canada belong to independent local unions. Table 10.2 lists the 10 largest unions in Canada.

independent local union
One not formally affiliated with any labour organization.

Union Structure

Just as each organization has its own unique structure, so too does each union create a structure that best serves its own needs. As Figure 10.2 shows, however, there is a general structure that characterizes most national and international unions. A major function of unions is to provide service and support to both members and local affiliates. Most of these services are carried out by the types of specialized departments shown in Figure 10.2.

Officers and Functions

Each department or unit represented at the local level elects a **shop steward**—a regular employee who acts as a liaison between union members and supervisors. For example, if a worker has a grievance, he or she takes it to the steward, who tries to resolve the problem with the supervisor. If the local is very large, the union might hire a full-time **business agent** (or **business representative**) to play the same role.

shop steward
A regular employee who acts as a liaison between union members and supervisors.

business agent
In a large union, the business agent plays the same role as a shop steward.

Within a given union, the main governing bodies are the national union (or international union when members come from more than one country) and its officers. Among their other duties, national and international unions charter local affiliates and establish general standards of conduct and procedures for local operations. For example, they set dues assessments, arrange for the election of local officers, sanction strikes, and provide guidance in the collective bargaining process. Many national unions also engage in a variety of political activities, such as lobbying. They may also help coordinate organizing efforts and establish education programs.

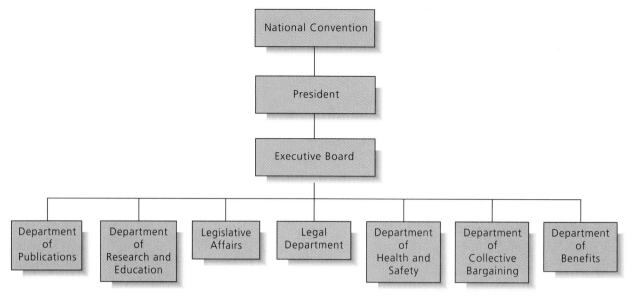

Figure 10.2
Organization of a large national union.

Given the magnitude of their efforts, it is little wonder that unions often take on many of the same characteristics as the companies for which their members work. For example, almost all large unions have full-time administrators, formal organizational structures (see Figure 10.2), goals and strategic plans, and so forth.

Union Security

The growing security consciousness of Canadian workers is reflected in union goals. The seniority provision in most contracts spells out the workers' rights when layoffs, transfers, and promotions occur. Employees are ranked by length of service. Those with longer service receive better treatment.

Much conflict exists regarding seniority. For example, women and members of minority groups typically have less seniority and are the first to be laid off and the last to move up to higher jobs. These workers tend to oppose the tradition of seniority.

Union security refers to the means of ensuring the union's continued existence and the maintenance of its membership so that it can continue to meet the criteria for certification. There is always a danger—particularly in bad economic times—that the membership may drop below the required absolute majority. The union may then lose its certification.

The greatest union security is found in the closed shop. In a **closed shop**, an employer can hire only union members. For example, a plumbing or electrical contractor who hires workers through a union hiring hall can hire only union members.

In a **union shop**, an employer may hire nonunion workers even if the employer's current employees are unionized. New workers, however, must join the union within a stipulated period of time (usually 30 days).

In an **agency shop**, all employees for whom the union bargains must pay dues, but they need not join the union. This compromise between the union shop and the open shop is called the Rand Formula after the judge who proposed it. In the *Quebec Labour Code*, the Rand formula applies to all unions certified under this code.

In an **open shop**, an employer may hire union and/or nonunion labour. Employees need not join or pay dues to a union in an open shop.

union security

The maintenance of a union's membership so that it can continue to meet the criteria for certification.

closed shop

An employer can hire only union members.

union shop

An employer can hire nonunionized workers, but they must join the union within a certain period.

agency shop

All employees for whom the union bargains must pay dues, but they are not required to join the union.

open shop

An employer may hire union or nonunion workers.

COLLECTIVE BARGAINING

Too often, people associate collective bargaining with the signing of a contract between a union and a company or industry. In fact, collective bargaining is an ongoing process involving not only the drafting but also the administering of the terms of a labour contract.

Reaching Agreement on the Contract's Terms

The collective bargaining process begins with the recognition of the union as the exclusive negotiator for its members. The bargaining cycle begins when union leaders meet with management representatives to agree on a new contract. By law, both parties must sit down at the bargaining table and negotiate "in good faith." When each side has presented its demands, sessions focus on identifying the *bargaining zone*. This process is shown in Figure 10.3. For example, although an employer may initially offer no pay raise, it may expect to grant a raise of up to 6 percent. Likewise, the union may initially *demand* a 10 percent pay raise while *expecting* to accept a raise as low as 4 percent. The bargaining zone, then, is a raise between 4 and 6 percent. Ideally, some compromise is reached between these levels and the new agreement is submitted for a ratification vote by union membership.

Sometimes, this process goes quite smoothly. At other times, however, the two sides cannot—or will not—agree. The speed and ease with which such an impasse is resolved depend in part on the nature of the contract issues, the willingness of each side to use certain tactics, and the prospects for mediation or arbitration.

Contract Issues

The labour contract itself can address an array of different issues. Most of these issues concern demands that unions make on behalf of their members. In this section we will survey the categories of issues that are typically most important to union negotiators: *compensation*, *benefits*, and *job security*. Although few issues covered in a labour contract are company sponsored, we will also describe the kinds of management rights that are negotiated in most bargaining agreements.

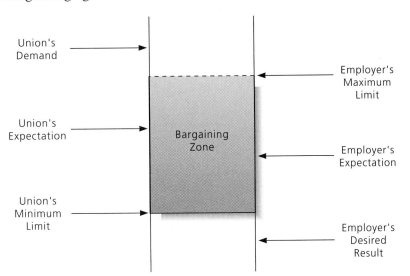

Figure 10.3
The bargaining zone.

First, note that bargaining items generally fall into two categories:

- *Mandatory items* are matters over which both parties must negotiate if either wants to. This category includes wages, working hours, and benefits.

- *Permissive items* may be negotiated if both parties agree. For example, a union demand for veto power over the promotion of managerial personnel would be a permissive bargaining item.

Neither party may bring illegal items to the table. For example, a management demand for a nonstrike clause would be an illegal item.

Compensation

The most common issue is compensation. One aspect of compensation is current wages. Obviously, unions generally want their employees to earn higher wages and try to convince management to raise hourly wages for all or some employees.

Of equal concern to unions is future compensation: wage rates to be paid during subsequent years of the contract. One common tool for securing wage increases is a **cost-of-living adjustment (COLA)**. Most COLA clauses tie future raises to the *consumer price index (CPI)*, a government statistic that reflects changes in consumer purchasing power. The premise is that as the CPI increases by a specified amount during a given period of time, wages will automatically increase.

Wage reopener clauses may also be included. Such a clause allows wage rates to be renegotiated at preset times during the life of the contract. For example, a union might be uncomfortable with a long-term contract based solely on COLA wage increases. A long-term agreement might be more acceptable, however, if management agrees to renegotiate wages every two years.

cost-of-living adjustment (COLA)
A contract clause specifying that wages will increase automatically with the rate of inflation.

wage reopener clause
A contract clause that allows wage rates to be renegotiated at preset times during the life of the contract.

Benefits

Employee benefits are also an important component of most labour contracts. Unions typically want employers to pay all or most of the costs of insurance for employees. Other benefits commonly addressed during negotiations include retirement benefits and working conditions.

Job Security

Job security is an increasingly important agenda item in bargaining sessions today. In some cases, demands for job security entail the promise that a company will not move to another location. In others, the contract may dictate that if the workforce is reduced, seniority will be used to determine which employees lose their jobs.

Other Union Issues

Other possible issues might include such things as working hours, overtime policies, rest period arrangements, differential pay plans for shift employees, the use of temporary workers, grievance procedures, and allowable union activities (dues collection, union bulletin boards, and so forth).

Management Rights

Management wants as much control as possible over hiring policies, work assignments, and so forth. Unions, meanwhile, often try to limit management

WEBCONNEXION

Founded in 1992, the Labor Project for Working Families works with unions to develop family-oriented policies—including family leave, flexible hours, dependent care, and domestic partner benefits—at the workplace. The organization then helps unions negotiate contracts that reflect the needs of working families. To find out more, log on at:

violet.berkeley.edu/~iir/ workfam/home.html

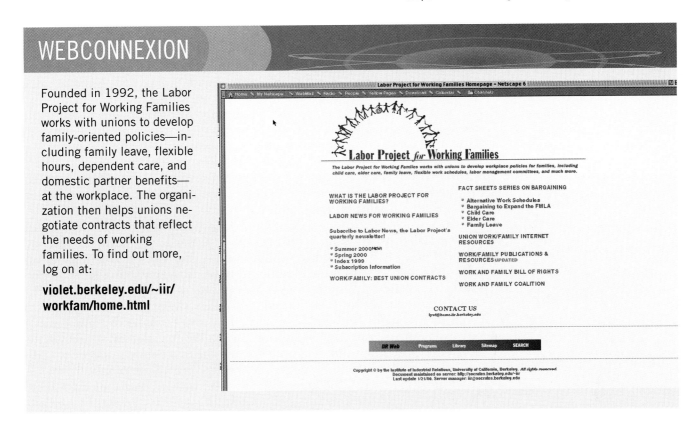

rights by specifying hiring, assignment, and other policies. At one DaimlerChrysler plant, for example, the contract stipulates that three workers are needed to change fuses in robots: a machinist to open the robot, an electrician to change the fuse, and a supervisor to oversee the process. As in this example, contracts often bar workers in one job category from performing work that falls within the domain of another. Unions try to secure jobs by defining as many different categories as possible (the DaimlerChrysler plant has over 100). Of course, management resists this practice, which limits flexibility and makes it difficult to reassign workers.

When Bargaining Fails

An impasse occurs when, after a series of bargaining sessions, management and labour fail to agree on a new contract or a contract to replace an agreement that is about to expire. Although it is generally agreed that both parties suffer when an impasse is reached and action is taken, each side can employ several tactics to support its cause until the impasse is resolved.

Union Tactics

Unions can take a variety of actions when their demands are not met. Chief among these tactics is the **strike**. Strikes triggered by impasses over mandatory bargaining items are called economic strikes, even if they occur over noneconomic issues such as working hours. Most strikes in Canada are economic strikes. The strikes by National Hockey League players in 1992, by major league baseball players in 1994, by Canada Safeway workers in 1997, by Quebec nurses in 1999, and by B.C. forestry workers in 2000 were largely over economic issues.

During a strike, workers are not paid and the business is usually unable to produce its normal range of products and services. During this time,

strike
A tactic of labour unions in which members temporarily walk off the job and refuse to work in order to win concessions from management.

the union may try to convince the general public that the company is being unfair. When Canada Safeway workers went on strike in Alberta in 1997, they were very successful at convincing the general public not to shop at Safeway. So many people refused to cross the union's picket lines that sales at some Safeway stores fell by as much as 70 percent.[7]

After a strike is over, employees may exhibit low morale, anger, increased absenteeism, and decreased productivity. In these situations, care must be taken to improve communications between management and workers.[8]

Strikes may occur in response to an employer's unfair labour practices. A firm that refuses to recognize a duly certified union may find itself with a striking workforce and having to explain its refusal to the provincial labour relations board. Such strikes are rare, however.

Not all strikes are legal. The Ontario primary and secondary school teachers strike in 1997 against the province of Ontario was illegal because the teachers had not gone through the necessary steps prior to going out on strike. The teachers voluntarily returned to work after striking for only two weeks. Nurses in Quebec and Saskatchewan also carried out illegal strikes in 1999. *Sympathy strikes* (also called secondary strikes), where one union strikes in sympathy with strikes initiated by another labour organization, may violate the sympathetic union's contract. Wildcat strikes, strikes unauthorized by the union that occur during the life of a contract, deprive strikers of their status as employees and thus of the protection of labour laws.

Unions are more reluctant to use the strike weapon than they used to be. There are several reasons for this: more and more workers are in profit-sharing plans and therefore receive a portion of company profits, workers' own shares of the company's stock and their personal payoffs are tied to the success of the company, union membership continues to decline, strikes are bad publicity and hurt union efforts to recruit new union members, and technology and globalization mean that companies can easily displace highly paid but low-skilled workers.[9]

As part of or instead of a strike, unions faced with an impasse may picket or launch a boycott. **Picketing** involves having workers march at the entrance to the company with signs explaining their reasons for striking. A **boycott** occurs when union members agree not to buy the product of the firm that employs them. Workers may also urge other consumers to shun their firm's product. Another alternative to striking is a work **slowdown**: Instead of striking, workers perform their jobs at a much slower pace than normal. A variation is the "sickout," during which large numbers of workers call in sick.

Management Tactics

Management can also respond forcefully to an impasse. To some extent, **lockouts** are the flip side of the strike coin. Lockouts occur when employers physically deny employees access to the workplace. Lockouts are illegal if they are used as offensive weapons to give the firm an economic advantage in the bargaining process. They might be used, for example, if management wants to avoid a buildup of perishable inventory or in similar circumstances. The lockout is not widely used, but almost half of the 1998–99 NBA season was lost when team owners locked out their players over contract issues.[10]

As an alternative to a lockout, firms faced with a strike can hire temporary or permanent replacements (**strikebreakers**) for the absent employees. When players in the National Football League went out on strike during the 1987 season, the team owners hired free agents and went right on playing. In 1992, National Hockey League owners planned to use minor

picketing
A tactic of labour unions in which members march at the entrance to the company with signs explaining their reasons for striking.

boycott
A tactic of labour unions in disputes with management in which members refuse to buy the products of the company and encourage other consumers to do the same.

slowdown
Instead of striking, workers perform their jobs at a much slower pace than normal.

lockout
A tactic of management in which the firm physically denies employees access to the workplace in order to pressure workers to agree to the company's latest contract offer.

strikebreaker
An individual hired by a firm to replace a worker on strike; a tactic of management in disputes with labour unions.

league hockey players if they could not reach an agreement with striking NHL players.

In extreme cases, management may simply close down a plant if they cannot reach agreement with the union. In 1997, Maple Leaf closed its Edmonton hog processing plant when the workers went on strike. This cost 850 workers their jobs. Ipsco Steel of Regina is expanding its operations, but not in Canada, because it feels that Canada's labour laws are too restrictive. The company is constructing new steel mills in U.S. states where workers can opt out of a union.[11]

Postal workers picket Queen's Park.

National Hockey League
www.nhl.com

More and more firms are contracting out work as a way to blunt their unions' effects. Instead of doing all the assembly work they used to do themselves, many firms now contract out work to nonunion contractors. This lessens the impact the unions can have and results in fewer union workers.

Employers' associations are especially important in industries that have many small firms and one large union that represents all workers. Member firms sometimes contribute to a strike insurance fund. Such a fund could be used to help members whose workers have struck. They are similar in purpose to the strike funds built up by unions.

Employers are also increasingly using what unions refer to as "union-busting" consultants. These consultants assist management in improving their communications with the shop floor. They help management identify and eliminate the basic pressures that led to the pro-union vote in the first place.

The same law that grants employees the right to unionize also allows them to decertify. **Decertification** is the process by which employees legally terminate their union's right to represent them. A labour dispute over job security and safety that arose at Goldcorp Inc.'s gold mine near Red Lake, Ontario, led to a strike involving 100 workers that began in June 1996. The strike was settled in April 2000 when workers agreed to decertify their union in return for severance pay that was four times the rate mandated by Ontario law.[12] The first union ever at a McDonald's outlet was certified in 1998 in B.C., but decertified by its members in 1999.

Decertification campaigns do not differ much from certification campaigns (those leading up to the initial election). The union organizes membership meetings, house-to-house visits, and other tactics to win the election. The employer uses meetings, letters, and improved working conditions to try to obtain a decertification vote.

decertification
The process by which employees terminate their union's right to represent them.

Mediation and Arbitration

Rather than using weapons on one another, labour and management can agree to call in a third party to help resolve the dispute. In **mediation**, the neu-

mediation
A method of settling a contract dispute in which a neutral third party is asked to hear arguments from both the union and management and offer a suggested resolution.

tral third party (a mediator) can only advise—not impose—a settlement on the parties. In **voluntary arbitration**, the neutral third party (an arbitrator) dictates a settlement between two sides who have agreed to submit to outside judgment.

In some cases, arbitration is legally required to settle bargaining disputes. Such **compulsory arbitration** is used to settle disputes between government and public employees such as firefighters and police officers.

Administering a Labour Agreement

Once a labour agreement has been reached, its details are written down in the form of a contract that is legally enforceable in the courts. Labour contracts almost always have precise agreements as to how the agreement will be enforced. In some cases, of course, enforcement is quite clear. If the two sides agree that the company will increase wages by 2 percent per year over the next three years according to a prescribed schedule, then there is little opportunity for disagreement because wage increases can be mathematically calculated and union members will see its effects in their paycheques. However, other provisions may be much more prone to misinterpretation and different perceptions.

Suppose, for example, that a labour contract specifies the process for allocating overtime assignments. Such strategies are often complex, and the employer may have to take into account a variety of factors, such as seniority, previous overtime allocations, the hours or days in which the overtime work is needed, and so forth. Now suppose that a factory supervisor is trying to follow the labour contract and offers overtime to a certain employee. This employee, however, indicates that before he or she can accept the overtime, it may be necessary to check with the individual's spouse or partner about other obligations and commitments. The supervisor may feel the pressure of a deadline and instead award the overtime opportunity to someone else. If the first employee objects to this course of action, he or she may file a complaint with the union.

When such differences of opinions arise, the union member takes the complaint to the shop steward. The shop steward may advise the employee that the supervisor handled things properly, but there are other appeal mechanisms, and the employee, even if refuted by the shop steward, still has channels for appeal.

Of course, if the shop steward agrees with the employee, prescribed methods for pursuing the complaint are followed. The prescribed methods might include talking with the supervisor to hear the other side of the story and then providing for lines of appeal further up the hierarchy of both the union and the company. In some cases, mediation or arbitration may be tried, as may other efforts to resolve the dispute. The overtime, for example, may be reassigned to the employee to whom it was first offered. Or the overtime may remain with the second employee while the first employee is also paid.

A **grievance** is a complaint by a worker that a manager is violating the contract. Figure 10.4 traces a typical grievance procedure. The union generally promises not to strike over disputes about contract interpretation. In return, unions get the right to file grievances in a formal procedure that culminates in binding arbitration. Most grievance arbitrations take place over disputes regarding the discipline or discharge of employees, but safety issues are a cause for arbitration in some industries.

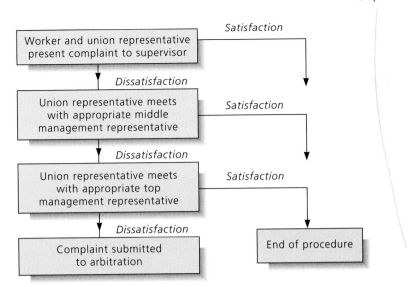

Figure 10.4
A typical grievance procedure.

SUMMARY OF LEARNING OBJECTIVES

1. **Explain why workers unionize.** The Industrial Revolution and the emergence of a factory based production system made many workers dependent on continuing factory employment. The treatment of labour as a raw material led to such abuses as minimal pay, long workdays and workweeks, unsafe working conditions, and even child labour. Individuals had little recourse in rectifying problems. By organizing into labour unions, however, workers are able to act collectively to improve work conditions. Most importantly, acting as a group, they can engage in *collective bargaining* for higher wages, greater benefits, or better working conditions.

2. **Trace the evolution of and discuss trends in *unionism* in Canada.** The first unions were formed in the early nineteenth century in the maritime provinces. Many labour organizations sprang up and then faded away during the nineteenth century. In the twentieth century, unions began to develop in earnest. In 1943, *Privy Council Order 1003* gave unions the right to bargain collectively with employers.

    Since the mid-1970s, labour unions in Canada have experienced increasing difficulties in attracting new members. While millions of workers still belong to labour unions, union membership as a percentage of the total workforce has begun to decline. Increasingly, unions recognize that they do not have as much power as they once held and that it is in their own best interests, as well as the best interests of the workers they represent, to work with management instead of against it. Bargaining perspectives have also altered in recent years.

3. **Describe the *major laws governing labour–management relations.*** *Privy Council Order 1003* gave unions the right to collectively bargain in Canada. The *Constitution Act of 1867* allows the federal government to pass labour legislation (e.g., the *Canada Labour Code*) for companies that operate interprovincially, and allows the provincial governments to pass legislation (e.g., the Ontario *Labour Relations Act*) for companies that operate in only one province.

4. **Describe the union *certification* and *decertification processes.*** If a union can show that a certain percentage (usually 50 percent) of employees of a company are members of the union, it can apply to a provincial labour relations board for certification as the sole bargaining agent for the employees. A certification vote is then held. If a majority of the employees is in favour of the union, it is certified. To decertify a union, employees must vote to do so.

5. **Identify the steps in the *collective bargaining process.*** Once certified, the union engages in collective bargaining with the organization. The initial step in collective bargaining is reaching agreement on a *labour contract.* Contract demands usually involve wages, job security, or management rights.

   Both labour and management have several tactics that can be used against the other if negotiations break down. Unions may attempt a *strike* or a *boycott* of the firm or may engage in a *slowdown.* Companies may hire replacement workers (*strikebreakers*) or *lock out* all workers. In extreme cases, mediation or arbitration may be used to settle disputes. Once a contract has been agreed on, union and management representatives continue to interact to settle worker *grievances* and interpret the contract.

KEY TERMS

labour union, 290
labour relations, 290
collective bargaining, 290
*Industrial Disputes
   Investigation Act
   (1907),* 297
*Privy Council Order 1003
   (1943),* 297
Constitution Act, 1867,
   297
Canada Labour Code,
   297

bargaining unit, 301
certification vote, 301
craft unions, 301
industrial unions, 301
local union, 301
national union, 302
international union, 302
independent local union,
   303
shop steward, 303
business agent, 303

union security, 304
closed shop, 304
union shop, 304
agency shop, 304
open shop, 304
cost-of-living adjustment
   (COLA), 306
wage reopener clause,
   306
strike, 307
picketing, 308

boycott, 308
slowdown, 308
lockout, 308
strikebreaker, 308
decertification, 309
mediation, 309
voluntary arbitration,
   310
compulsory arbitration,
   310
grievance, 310

STUDY QUESTIONS AND EXERCISES

Review Questions

1. Why do workers in some companies unionize while workers in other companies do not?
2. Why did it take so many years for the union movement to mature in Canada? Describe some of the key events along the way.
3. The proportion of the Canadian workforce that is unionized has been constant for more than 15 years. Why hasn't the proportion increased or decreased?
4. Describe the kinds of employment issues that the Canada Labour Code deals with.
5. How are craft and industrial unions different? How are international, national, and local unions different?

Analysis Questions

6. Workers at the Canadian plants of Ford, General Motors, and DaimlerChrysler are represented by the Canadian Auto Workers. Why are automobile workers at Toyota's Cambridge, Ontario, plant—who are

doing exactly the same kind of work—not unionized?

7. Suppose that you are a manager in a nonunionized company. You have just heard a rumour that some of your workers are discussing forming a union. What would you do? Be specific.
8. What are the implications for management of a closed shop, a union shop, and an agency shop?

Application Questions

9. Interview the managers of two local companies, one unionized and one nonunionized. Compare the wage and salary levels, benefits, and working conditions of workers at the two firms.
10. With your instructor playing the role of management and a student playing the role of a union organizer, role play the processes involved in trying to form a union.

Building Your Business Skills

A Little Collective Brainstorming

Goal
To encourage students to understand why some companies unionize and others do not.

Situation
You've been working for the same nonunion company for five years. Although there are problems in the company, you like your job and have confidence in your ability to get ahead. Recently, you've heard rumblings that a large group of workers want to call for a union election. You're not sure how you feel about this because none of your friends or family members are union members.

Method

Step 1:
Come together with three other "co-workers" who have the same questions as you do. Each person should target four companies to learn their union status. Avoid small businesses; choose large corporations such as Canadian National Railways, General Motors, and Wal-Mart. As you investigate, answer the following questions:

- Is the company unionized?
- Is every worker in the company unionized or only selected groups of workers? Describe the groups.
- If a company is unionized, what is the union's history in that company?
- If a company is unionized, what are the main labour–management issues?
- If a company is unionized, how would you describe the current status of labour–management relations? For example, is it cordial or strained?
- If a company is not unionized, what factors are responsible for its nonunion status?

To learn the answers to these questions, contact the company, read corporate annual reports, search the company's Web site, contact union representatives, or do research on a computerized database.

Step 2:
Go to the Web site of the CUPE (www.cupe.org) to learn more about the current status of the union movement. Then, with your co-workers, write a short report about the advantages of union membership.

Step 3:
Research the disadvantages of unionization. A key issue to address is whether unions make it harder for companies to compete in the global marketplace.

Follow-Up Questions

1. Based on everything you have learned, are you sympathetic to the union movement? Would you want to be a union member?
2. Are the union members you spoke with satisfied or dissatisfied with their union's efforts to achieve better working conditions, higher wages, and improved benefits?
3. What is the union's role when layoffs occur?
4. Based on what you have learned, do you think the union movement will stagnate or thrive in the years ahead?

Exploring the Net

Labour-management issues play an important role in determining the business climate of Canada. The Canadian Union of Public Employees is an example of one labour organization. Visit its Web site at:

www.cupe.ca

1. What are the most important issues facing CUPE and its members? Where do you stand on these issues? Why?
2. Where in the Web site could you go to find the management position on these issues? What is the management position?
3. What do the facts and statistics in "About CUPE" tell you about the union? About life as a public employee?

Concluding Case 10-1

Labour Relations at Canada Post

Relations between Canada Post and the Canadian Union of Postal Workers (CUPW) have been troubled for nearly two decades. Canada Post wants to introduce technological improvements in the way work is done, and this action will reduce the number of employees it needs. CUPW has vigorously opposed these ideas from the start. During 1997, the long-simmering dispute between workers and management heated up again as the two sides tried to sign a new collective agreement.

Bargaining dragged on for many months without much progress. A mediator was then appointed in the hope that he could get the disputing parties to reach an agreement and avert a strike. But after a few days of talks, the mediator concluded that the two sides were not willing to bargain seriously, and he gave up. CUPW then went on strike, and its 45 000 members began walking the picket line.

Tensions were high, and during the strike CUPW workers delayed some commercial airline flights by preventing cargo and food from reaching the planes. They also snarled traffic in some locations, and picketed Preston Manning's official Ottawa residence to show their displeasure. Manning's Reform party viewed the postal service as "essential," and thought that strikes should not be allowed in essential services.

About two weeks after the strike started, the Liberal Minister of Labour, Lawrence MacAuley, introduced back-to-work legislation that forced the postal workers to return to work. The imposed agreement gave the workers a 5.15 percent wage increase over three years (they had been hoping for a 10 percent increase over two years). The legislation also levied fines of $1000 per day against workers who defied the back-to-work order. Union leaders could be fined up to $50 000 per day, and CUPW could face fines of up to $500 000 if it defied the back-to-work order.

MacAuley said he felt compelled to introduce the legislation since so many Canadians were suffering during the labour dispute. Many businesses and charities, for example, were being hurt by the strike since they could not carry on their usual activities without mail service. While MacAuley scolded both Canada Post and CUPW for failing to reach a new agreement, the Reform party criticized the Liberal government for not having acted sooner.

CUPW immediately condemned the legislation, and promised large-scale civil disobedience if the workers were forced back to work. Darrell Tingley, CUPW president, claimed that the Canadian Direct Marketing Association was putting pressure on the government to get the postal workers back on the job.

On December 4, 1997, the defiant postal workers grudgingly returned to work. Tingley suggested that postal workers disrupt normal Canada Post activities by purposely misdirecting business mail, and by sending mail through the system without stamps. Canada Post president Georges Clermont said that it was unbelievable that the postal workers would listen to advice like this, because it would mean hurting Canada Post's customers—the very people who are responsible for the workers having jobs in the first place. Clermont said the workers who followed Tingley's suggestions would be disciplined. But Tingley said that Canada Post could expect a campaign of workplace defiance for the remainder of the three-year agreement.

CASE QUESTIONS

1. When the postal workers went on strike, many businesses and charities were hurt. Is this an argument for abolishing the right to strike for postal workers? Should postal workers have the right to strike? Defend your answer.

2. What is mediation? Why do you think mediation was not effective in this situation?

3. Read newspaper accounts of the postal strike and the events leading up to it (consult papers dated November 15 through December 5, 1997). How do these accounts illustrate how the collective bargaining process works? ◆

Concluding Case 10-2

Teamwork or Dirty Work?

To proponents, it's a chance for Canadian firms to increase productivity and become more competitive in global markets and for workers to use their brains as well as their backs. But to opponents, it's just another management attempt to speed up production at the expense of workers' jobs, earnings, and health. It's the latest in Japanese imports: the team concept.

Actually, the idea of using teams of workers trained in all phases of constructing a product is not original to Japan. British, Swedish, and American firms have experimented with the team concept for over 40 years.

In a traditional assembly line, an individual worker performs only one specified task. Over the years, the worker builds up seniority and is then allowed to apply for better-paying or easier jobs in the company. Assembly-line workers, in turn, are supervised very closely by first-line managers.

In contrast, the team concept breaks down job distinctions. All members of a team are "cross-trained" to perform every necessary function to produce a good or service. Teams also solve minor problems as they arise. Individuals who show the most leadership within the team—not necessarily those with the most seniority—are promoted.

These radical departures disturb both managers and workers in many companies. First and foremost on the minds of both groups is the issue of power. Managers in industries such as automobiles and steel—which are trying hardest to institute teamwork—are accustomed to giving orders and having them carried out. The need to share power and ask for suggestions instead of issuing commands is difficult for many managers. First-line managers are particularly likely to resist such changes since, under the team concept, fewer such managers are needed.

On the other side of the fence, some workers perceive the team concept as transferring responsibility but not authority. In many places, team managers dictate the problem to be solved and the parameters for solving it. Teams may be put in a position of choosing to increase production either by using less safe methods or by rejecting fewer flawed pieces.

Part of this problem no doubt stems from differences between Japanese and Canadian workers. Japanese workers do not expect a voice in management and the teamwork system devised in Japan makes no provision for it. To get Canadian workers to "buy into" working harder for their employers, companies have had to face worker demands for greater input into management. Any shift of this kind will take years to effect.

Even the job rotation aspect of the team concept has been called into question. Some workers like the chance to change assignments: "I used to switch jobs for half a day with one of my buddies just because we were bored. [Job rotation] makes the day go by faster." But others disagree sharply: "Being able to do six monotonous jobs is no more fulfilling than being able to do one."

Although some labour unions support the team concept when management is willing to link it to guarantees of job security, a very vocal minority sees it as another in a long series of union-busting attempts by industry. The Canadian Auto Workers, for example, opposes teamwork partnerships between labour and management. In particular, it dislikes the fact that unions are being forced to bid against each other for jobs. It points to General Motors' decision to close a more productive non-team plant and keep open a less productive pro-team plant.

CASE QUESTIONS

1. What are the differences between the new team concept and the old assembly-line concept?
2. What problems might a company encounter when it tries to implement the team concept?
3. Can labour and management ever really be a team, or is there a fundamental difference in goals between workers and managers?
4. Is the team concept simply a gimmick to allow management to get more work out of workers or to "bust" unions? Even if it is a gimmick, might there be advantages for workers? ◆

Visit the *Business* Website at www.pearsoned.ca/griffin
for up-to-date e-business cases!

CBC Video Case

III-1   CBC ◈

Raiders

They're like cattle rustlers. They are drawn to big companies and they try to entice away their key employees. They are called raiders, or headhunters, and they connect companies that need new employees with workers in other companies who want to change jobs. Headhunting is a $50 billion a year business. The boom in Canada's economy has caused a labour shortage, and this in turn has caused raiding because there aren't enough skilled people to go around. Companies are stealing staff from each other and they are using raiders to do it.

Who hires headhunters? High-tech companies like Silicon Access, which needs 20 new employees immediately, is offering perks such as stock options, better pay, and advancement opportunities in the hope of attracting the people they need. They're using five different firms to find people, one of which is Ottawa's TalentLab. TalentLab looks to big companies like Nortel or Alcatel for prospects because they have a large supply of skilled high-tech workers. For example, TalentLab recently talked to a chip designer at Nortel who had grown bored and wanted a new challenge at a smaller company. TalentLab's president, Alex Kearns, makes no apologies for taking restless employees from big companies. He says that TalentLab does not intend to hurt the big companies; rather, his firm helps start-ups to grow. He says that firms like TalentLab are viewed as a threat, and they should be. TalentLab is considering an alliance with another recruiter to more effectively work the market. As long as the labour market remains tight, firms like TalentLab will grow.

All of this is well and good for firms like TalentLab, but what about the firms that are being raided? For them, the experience can be exasperating. Ask Investors Group, for example, which has recently lost many of its salespeople to other firms. It claims that Berkshire Group has targeted members of its sales force to the point that Investors Group's business is actually being threatened. Investors Group has filed suit against Berkshire Group, seeking an injunction to prevent it from recruiting any more of its people. Berkshire Group denies raiding Investors Group and claims it has done nothing illegal.

Companies who fear being raided are turning to people like David Cohen, who teaches human resource employees how to defend against attacks by raiders. Cohen points out that it is much cheaper to retain good employees than to find new ones after someone has left the company. Aventis hired Cohen after it discovered that it cost $42 500 for every employee it lost. Cohen says that only unhappy people are easily lured away, so companies should pay attention to morale and salary if they want to keep raiders at bay. Aventis knows that raiders are going to win some battles, so it is streamlining the process of replacing the people it loses.

Some companies have taken even more drastic action to deal with raiding and to cope with the general labour shortage. Tundra Semiconductors is growing so quickly that it cannot hire new staff fast enough to keep up with both business growth and the losses from raiding. As a result, Tundra bought a U.S. company to get its hands on that firm's engineers.

STUDY QUESTIONS

1. Is the behaviour of firms like TalentLab ethical? Defend your answer.

2. Briefly describe the basic compensation systems that companies use. The case describes a software designer who wanted to work for a small company. In what kind of compensation would this person most likely be interested?

3. In Chapter 8, several new challenges in the changing workplace are discussed. Relate these challenges to the raiding activity described in the case.

4. What is a psychological contract? How does this concept help you understand the movement of people from one organization to another? How has downsizing affected the psychological contract?

5. David Cohen argues that companies can fend off raiders by paying attention to the morale and job satisfaction of workers. What can managers do to enhance the morale and job satisfaction of workers? Be specific.

Video Resource: "The Raiders," *Venture* #765 (November 21, 2000).

CBC Video Case

Keepers

In Canadian high-tech companies, 60-hour weeks are not uncommon. Couple that with demanding bosses and customers, and families that are unseen for days, and you have a recipe for employee turnover. Anne Graham is vice-president of Human Resources at Kanata-based Dy4 Systems, a company that builds specialized computers for use in deserts, oceans, and battlefields. One of her important goals is to keep employees from leaving Dy4 and moving to the competition. Turnover is high in this industry—25 percent—and rapid growth in many firms is stretching employees to the breaking point.

Dy4 has hired Daniel O'Connor of Keepers Inc., a firm that specializes in helping employees determine what is causing friction and unhappiness in their lives and how to resolve that friction. O'Connor, who has spent more than 12 years looking deeply into workers' lives, strives to practise what he preaches about balance. Currently, he is writing a romantic comedy that is set in a business firm.

O'Connor first meets with employees one-on-one and tries to determine what is bothering them. He has found a common theme: employees have lost their sense of control in the workplace. As a result, they feel disempowered and subject to the whims of others.

At Dy4, O'Connor meets three typical employees. *Grant* manages one of Dy4's product lines. O'Connor meets with him and listens to his concerns. Grant feels overwhelmed and anxious because he has so many meetings that he must attend. O'Connor asks Grant if perhaps he is allowing this to happen. This week's "assignment" is for Grant to think about that possibility and what he might do about it.

Michelle manages Dy4's Human Resources department. She feels that demands from her bosses have pulled her in too many directions. She also feels frustrated, chasing after people to ensure they do what they are supposed to. For her, cutting back hours has been difficult. She leaves the building at the end of the day feeling she should have done more.

Ernie is a veteran engineer at Dy4. He feels that he doesn't have enough time with his family and that he needs a better work-family balance. Ernie's "assignment" is to keep track of his time for a week.

After a period of time has passed, O'Connor meets again with the three individuals to check on their progress. After two months, *Grant's* situation has somewhat improved. The company has allowed him to hire an assistant, and this has made a noticeable difference. But he is still looking for ways to get more control over his schedule, because he continues to spend a great deal of time in meetings. He also notes that he had to work three 12-hour days just to be able to take a week's vacation. O'Connor emphasizes the need for Grant to make change happen.

O'Connor takes the data that *Ernie* provided and converts it into a pie chart so he can clearly see where Ernie is spending his time. Ernie learns that seeing his life mapped out in pie chart form can be very startling (he spent 61 hours at work one week, leaving little time for his family). Ernie sees a new perspective on what overcommitment means and the importance of balancing home and work life.

When *Michelle* meets with O'Connor again, she decides to resolve her dilemma by setting a goal to at least do the tasks that are necessary so that other people who are counting on her are not let down. She will cut back on some other things that do not impact other people.

After two months of O'Connor's coaching, the employees at Dy4 seem to be slowly turning their lives around. They are now focusing on maintaining their new "life rules" after O'Connor leaves. Dy4 is counting on it to keep their talent under its roof.

STUDY QUESTIONS

1. What is the psychological contract? How might this concept give managers at Dy4 insights into the problems being experienced by Grant, Michelle, and Ernie?

2. Explain how Dy4 could use an assessment centre to resolve some of the difficulties it is having with turnover.

3. What role might orientation and training play in helping employees cope with the rapid pace of change and the heavy workload at Dy4?

4. Consider the data on employee job satisfaction and dissatisfaction that is presented in Chapter 9. How well do those general findings match the specific concerns that Grant, Michelle, and Ernie have at Dy4?

5. Besides hiring a counselor like Daniel O'Connor, what can managers at Dy4 do to enhance the morale and satisfaction of their employees? Be specific.

Video Resource: "Keepers Inc.," *Venture* #742 (March 7, 2000).

PART FOUR

Managing Operations and Information

To be effective, Canadian business firms must produce high-quality goods and services. They must also have good information on which to base business decisions. The opening cases in the chapters in this section show how business firms such as Interface Inc., Coca-Cola, Playdium Entertainment Corp., and Nortel Networks have focused on more effectively managing their operations and information functions.

Part Four, Managing Operations and Information, provides an overview of four aspects of business that are important to a firm's survival: the efficient production of goods and services, increasing productivity and quality, managing information systems, and understanding principles of accounting.

- We begin in **Chapter 11, Producing Goods and Services**, by examining how firms manage the production of goods and services, and how they control both the cost and the quality of their output.

- Then, in **Chapter 12, Increasing Productivity and Quality**, we consider the various approaches companies take to improve the productivity and the quality of their output, and thus their competitive position.

- Next, in **Chapter 13, Managing Information Systems and Communication Technology**, we describe the concept of management information systems, and how modern electronic technologies have revolutionized the work of managers. Included in this discussion is an analysis of the key elements of the information system, the concept of databases and application programs, and the importance of telecommunications and networks in the effective management of information.

- Finally, in **Chapter 14, Understanding Principles of Accounting**, we examine the role of accountants in gathering, assembling, and presenting financial information about a firm. We also look at the tools accountants use and the statements they prepare to report a firm's financial standing.

CHAPTER 11

PRODUCING GOODS AND SERVICES

Natural Capitalism

Interface Inc.'s Belleville, Ontario, plant is a popular destination for government officials, academics, and corporate executives. They want to find out how this carpet manufacturing plant manages to be so efficient and at the same time so environmentally friendly. When they talk to Rahumathulla Marikkar, the plant's director of technology and environment, they learn about some fascinating new developments in the production of goods and services.

In the old days, Interface's Belleville plant produced not only carpets, but also 500 000 litres of dirty waste water every month. Solving that problem—by eliminating a printing process that used a lot of water—saved the company $15 000 a month. Interface then examined other waste, such as the 474 tonnes of carpet remnants it had to dispose of each year. After making some design changes, that remnant waste was reduced to only 39 tonnes per year. Environmentally friendly substitutes were also found to replace the toxic goo that had formerly been used to make carpets fireproof. Several other innovations, such as smaller motors, were used to reduce the company's utility bills by 70 percent. All of these actions made the plant so efficient that it now exports 60 percent of its output to the U.S. In the process, sales have more than tripled. Company CEO Ray Anderson calls it "doing well by doing good."

Interface wants to become the first company to lease floor coverings. If your carpet wears out, the company will replace the used portion and recycle it instead of taking it to a landfill, where it would take 20 000 years to degrade. This idea can be extended to many different consumer products such as cars, refrigerators, and washing machines.

Interface's actions are not isolated exceptions. More and more Canadian companies are pursuing something called "natural capitalism" or "eco-efficiency." Gord Lambert, Suncor's director of sustainable development, calls it the triple bottom line: economic, en-

vironmental, and social performance. Unlike the traditional production methods used in the Industrial Revolution (which polluted earth and sky), natural capitalism is dedicated to improving the bottom line by respecting Mother Nature. The key tenet of natural capitalism is doing more with fewer resources. Amory Lovins, co-CEO of the Rocky Mountain Institute, says that businesses will have to reduce their energy and resource use by 90 percent in the next 20 years just to protect Canadians' current quality of life.

Other companies are jumping on the natural capitalism bandwagon. Kuntz Electroplating in Kitchener, Ontario, started recycling chrome-plating solution more than 30 years ago to save money. Now the company also ships 32 tonnes of nickel-bearing sludge to Inco Ltd. each week instead of sending it to a landfill. This nickel recycling has saved the company more than $2 million in disposal costs. Energy costs and water consumption have also been reduced by 50 percent. Employees get awards for cost or environmental improvements.

Canfor Corp. of Vancouver became interested in natural capitalism partly out of exasperation with incessant pressure by environmental groups like Greenpeace. The company studied all the environmental costs associated with making a newspaper, from the forest to the consumer's doorstep. It found that the "hot spots" in newspaper production were heavy energy use and heavy metals. The report motivated the company to do research on how to eliminate heavy metals from the process. Canfor is also pushing energy-saving strategies at its pulp mills.

The case for natural capitalism has gradually become stronger as environmental regulations have become stricter, and as banks and insurance companies have paid increasing attention to environmental liabilities. David Kerr, CEO of Noranda, says that companies that ignore these trends simply cannot remain competitive. Noranda is practising what it preaches. Its latest project involves "mining" magnesium from asbestos tailings at its Magnola site in Quebec. Noranda now produces 15 percent of the world's supply of magnesium and is the industry's lowest cost producer.

But getting natural capitalism to be widely used will still require a lot of effort. Much of that effort will have to go into changing the mindset of workers and managers. At Interface, employees are trained not only in continuous improvement initiatives; they are also actively rewarded for waste-fighting practices. When Interface's Belleville plant started its energy-saving incentive in the late 1990s, it encouraged employees to get involved in energy audits so they could see how they were doing. Since then, the company has saved $3 million. ◆

Interface Inc.
www.interfaceinc.com

The opening case gives some idea of just how complex, dynamic, and innovative the Canadian manufacturing sector is. In this chapter, we will consider how firms involved in the production of goods and services deal with this complexity and with the rapid change and new ideas that are continually emerging. By focusing on the learning objectives of this chapter, you will better understand the complexity of production processes for physical goods and intangible services. After reading this chapter, you will be able to:

1. Explain the meaning of the term *production* or *operations* and describe the four kinds of *utility* it provides.

2. Describe and explain the three classifications of *operations processes*.

3. Identify the characteristics that distinguish *service operations* from *goods production* and explain the main differences in the *service focus*.

4. Describe the factors involved in *operations planning*.

5. Explain some of the activities involved in *operations control*, including *materials management* and the use of certain *operation control tools*.

> **LEARNING OBJECTIVES**

Everywhere you go today, you encounter business activities that provide goods and services to their customers. You wake up in the morning, for example, to the sound of your favourite radio station. You stop at the corner newsstand for a newspaper on your way to the bus stop, where you catch the bus to work or school. Your instructors, the bus driver, the clerk at the 7-Eleven store, and the morning radio announcer are all examples of people who work in **service operations**. They provide you with tangible and intangible service products, such as entertainment, transportation, education, and food preparation. Firms that make tangible products—radios, newspapers, buses, textbooks—are engaged in **goods production**.

service operations
Production activities that yield intangible products.

goods production
Production activities that yield tangible products.

A SHORT HISTORY OF PRODUCTION OPERATIONS

Before the Industrial Revolution began in England in the eighteenth century, the typical workplace was the small shop and the home. Leather and cloth were handmade, as were needles and other tools; clothing, harnesses, and other goods were made one at a time by craftspeople. In the late 1770s, however, a new institution emerged: Using machines, materials, industrial workers, and managers, the factory produced greater quantities of goods in an organized fashion. Throughout the nineteenth century, the factory remained the central institution for commerce. By then, it was using water, and then electricity, for power sources. The factory also relied on heavy machinery that was cumbersome, powerful, and often operated by children.

In the early 1900s in the U.S., two major developments took place: Frederick W. Taylor began his "scientific management" studies and Henry Ford revolutionized industry with the Ford "mass production" system. Production had become—at least in theory—the "science" of making products economically on a massive scale. Using specialization of labour for efficiency, the assembly line became the new tool for gaining economies of scale. Through the 1940s, the assembly line still depended heavily on human labour. By the 1960s, however, when mass production had reached its zenith, the factory culture had matured socially as well as commercially. As consumers continued to rely on access to the material goods that flooded from factories, attitudes towards production and production workers were changing. Children, of course, were no longer a part of the workforce, and such "radical" ideas as gender equality and ethnic diversity were soon to become accepted goals. Environmental concerns were also gaining in prominence.

Although the term *production* has historically referred to companies engaged in goods production, the concept as we now use it means services as well as goods. An abundance of necessities and conveniences on which we rely, from fire protection and health care to mail delivery and fast food, are all produced by service operations. Traditionally, service sector managers have focused less on such manufacturing-centred goals as equipment and technology. Rather, they have stressed the human element in their activities. Why? Because success or failure depends on contact with the customer during service delivery. The service provider's employees—its human resources—who deal directly with its customers affect the customer's feelings about the service. As we will see throughout this chapter, one of the main differences between production and service operations is the customer's involvement in the latter.

Today, customers are increasingly involved in both goods and services production because electronic communications and the Internet are vital components in the effort to win and keep customers in a huge range of competitive industries. Customers place orders faster, production schedules are accelerated, and delivery times are shrinking. Internet consumers can be linked electronically to the production floor itself, where their orders for products ranging from cellphones and CDs to automobiles are launched into production in real time. Business-to-business customers also expect real-time responses and online fast delivery, rather than traditional offline methods.

The Growth of Global Operations

Many countries have joined in the global competition that has reshaped production into a faster-paced, more complex business activity. Although the factory remains the centrepiece for manufacturing, it is virtually unrecognizable when compared with its counterpart of just a decade ago. The smoke, grease, and danger have been replaced in many companies by glistening high-tech machines, computers, and "clean rooms" that are contaminant-free and carefully controlled for temperature.

Instead of the need to maintain continuous mass production, firms today face constant change. New technologies are allowing machines to run cleaner, faster, and safer and to operate on a global scale. The "Business Today" box describes one important element of the modern factory. In online manufacturing, industrial machines can log on to the Internet, adjust their own settings, and make minor decisions without human help. They can communicate both with other machines in the company (via an intranet) and with other companies' machines (via the Internet). So-called "smart" equipment stores performance data that become available at desktops around the

BUSINESS TODAY

Industrial Robots Are Coming on Strong

At Honda Canada's minivan plant in Alliston, Ontario, a giant robot with huge arms grasps an automobile chassis and welds the floor, roof, and sides in one motion. The robot is part of a $345 million investment made by Honda in the Alliston plant. Harber Manufacturing of Fort Erie, Ontario, uses five arc-welding robot systems to make wood-burning stoves, and Canadian National Railways runs a fully computerized robotic paint shop for railroad cars in Winnipeg.

A 1999 report by a United Nations economic commission found that orders for industrial robots soared 60 percent over one year earlier. The increase points to an acceleration in the drive towards automation of manufacturing facilities. When robots were first introduced in the 1970s, it was thought that they would quickly be adopted and would revolutionize the workplace by performing all sorts of mundane and dangerous tasks. But progress was slowed for a time by the high cost of robots, and by the large amount of time that was needed to do studies to determine just exactly what robots could do best.

The initial purchase price is the cheapest part of a robot. Exhaustive studies must be performed by company personnel to determine the precise task that can be accomplished by a robot. Workers must be trained to operate and work with robots, and computer scientists are needed to program and reprogram the robots.

The UN report says that we have seen only the first phase of industrial robots, and that they will increasingly be used in manufacturing and other industries. A sharp drop in the price of robots is one of the reasons for their increased adoption. The price of robots at the end of the 1990s was as much as 40 percent less than it was at the beginning of the decade. This drop in prices, coupled with increasing human labour costs, has motivated more and more companies to consider the purchase of an industrial robot.

Human beings are still superior to robots in a great many ways, especially in tasks requiring sensory input and adaptation. For example, the most sophisticated robots can recognize about 20 slightly different shapes as airplanes, but humans can identify thousands of slightly different shapes as planes. As one researcher notes, the human eye has about 100 million vision cells and four layers of neurons, all capable doing about 10 billion calculations a second. In other words, it would take 100 000 supercomputers to imitate the visual calculations of a one-eyed human being.

Still, robots are making progress in Canadian industry. Already, they are used in fields that are dangerous to humans. Submersible robots, for example, are replacing divers in offshore oil and gas operations. And they toil for hours in areas of nuclear power plants where humans once worked in very short relays to minimize their exposure to radiation.

---

world, where designers can click on machine data, simulate machine action, and evaluate performance before the machines themselves ever swing into action. With the Internet, producers of both services and goods are integrating their production activities with those of far-off suppliers and customers. IBM's growing Internet activities, for example, include designs for new services, outsourcing, research, and even running Web businesses for other firms.[1]

CREATING VALUE THROUGH PRODUCTION

To understand the production processes of a firm, you need to understand the importance of products—both goods and services. Products provide businesses with both economic results (profits, wages, goods purchased from other companies) and noneconomic results (new technology, innovations, pollution). And they provide consumers with what economists call **utility**—want satisfaction.

Four basic kinds of utility would not be possible without production. By making a product available at a time when consumers want it, production creates **time utility**, as when a company turns out ornaments in time for Christmas. By making a product available in a place convenient for

utility
The power of a product to satisfy a human want; something of value.

time utility
That quality of a product satisfying a human want because of the time at which it is made available.

place utility
That quality of a product satisfying a human want because of where it is made available.

ownership (possession) utility
That quality of a product satisfying a human want during its consumption or use.

form utility
That quality of a product satisfying a human want because of its form; requires raw materials to be transformed into a finished product.

operations (production) management
The systematic direction and control of the processes that transform resources into finished goods.

consumers, production creates **place utility**, as when a local department store creates a "Trim-A-Tree" section. By making a product that consumers can take pleasure in owning, production creates **ownership (possession) utility**, as when you take a box of ornaments home and decorate your tree.

But above all, production makes products available in the first place. By turning raw materials into finished goods, production creates **form utility**, as when an ornament maker combines glass, plastic, and other materials to create tree decorations.

Because the term *production* has historically been associated with manufacturing, it has been replaced in recent years by *operations*, a term that reflects both services and goods production. **Operations** (or **production**) **management** is the systematic direction and control of the processes that transform resources into finished goods and services. Thus production managers are ultimately responsible for creating utility for customers.

As Figure 11.1 shows, production managers must bring raw materials, equipment, and labour together under a production plan that effectively uses all the resources available in the production facility. As demand for a good increases, they must schedule and control work to produce the amount required. Meanwhile, they must control costs, quality levels, inventory, and plant and equipment.

Not all production managers work in factories. Farmers are also production managers. They create form utility by converting soil, seeds, sweat, gas, and other inputs into beef cattle, tobacco, wheat, milk, cash, and other outputs. As production managers, farmers have the option of employing many workers to plant and harvest their crops. Or they may decide to use automated machinery or some combination of workers and machinery. These decisions affect farmers' costs, the buildings and equipment they own, and the quality and quantity of goods they produce. Table 11.1 shows examples of different types of production management.

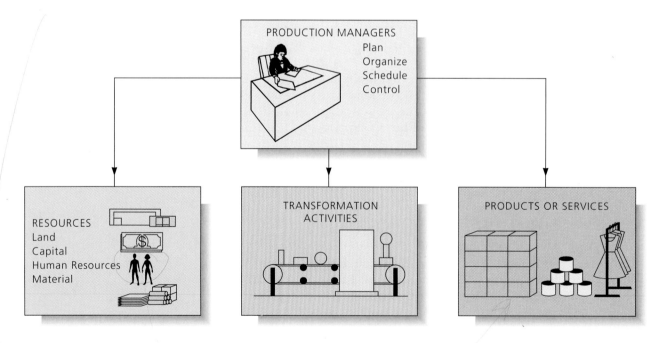

Figure 11.1
The transformation system.

Table 11.1			Inputs, Transformation, and Outputs in Production Systems
Production System	**Inputs**	**Transformation**	**Outputs**
Farm	Land, tractors and equipment, labour, buildings, fertilizer, farmer's management skills	Cultivation of plants and livestock	Food products, profit for owner, jobs for farmer's family
Jewellery store	Fashion-conscious customers, merchandise, sales clerks, showroom, fixtures, and equipment	Exchange of merchandise between buyer and seller	Satisfied jewellery customers
Tire producer	Rubber and chemical compounds, blending equipment, tire molds, factory, and human skills	Chemical reactions of raw materials	Tires for autos, airplanes, trucks, trailers, and other vehicles
Furniture manufacturer	Woodworking equipment fabrics, wood, nails and screws, factory, woodworking skills	Fabrication and assembly of materials	Furniture for homes and offices

Operations Processes

An **operations process** is a set of methods and technologies used in the production of a good or a service. We classify various types of production according to differences in their operations processes. In other words, we can describe goods according to the kind of *transformation technology* they require, or according to whether their operations process combines resources or breaks them into component parts. We can describe services according to the *extent of customer contact* required.

operations process
A set of methods and technologies used in the production of a good or a service.

Goods-Manufacturing Processes

All goods-manufacturing processes can be classified in two different ways: by the *type of transformation technology* that transforms raw materials into finished goods and by the *analytic or synthetic nature of the transformation process.*

Types of Transformation Technology. Manufacturers use the following types of transformation processes to turn raw materials into finished goods:

- In *chemical processes*, raw materials are chemically altered. Such techniques are common in the aluminum, steel, fertilizer, petroleum, and paint industries.

- *Fabrication processes* mechanically alter the basic shape or form of a product. Fabrication occurs in the metal forming, woodworking, and textile industries.

- *Assembly processes* put together various components. These techniques are common in the electronics, appliance, and automotive industries.

- In *transport processes*, goods acquire place utility by being moved from one location to another. For example, bicycles are routinely moved by trucks from manufacturing plants to consumers through warehouses and discount stores.

- *Clerical processes* transform information. Combining data on employee absences and machine breakdowns into a productivity report is a clerical process. So is compiling inventory reports at a retail outlet.

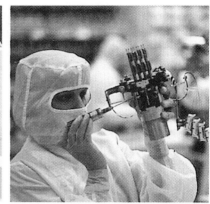

As these photos show, various industries use different transformation techniques: (from left, top) chemical, fabrication, assembly; (bottom) transport, clerical.

analytic process

Any production process in which resources are broken down.

synthetic process

Any production process in which resources are combined.

Analytic versus Synthetic Processes.   A second way of classifying production processes is by the way in which resources are converted into finished goods. An **analytic process** breaks down the basic resources into components. For example, Alcan manufactures aluminum by extracting it from an ore called bauxite. The reverse approach, a **synthetic process**, combines a number of raw materials to produce a finished product such as fertilizer or paint.

Service Processes: Extent of Customer Contact

One way of classifying services is to ask whether a given service can be provided without the customer being part of the production system. In answering this question, services are classified according to the extent of *customer contact*.

high-contact system

A system in which the service cannot be provided without the customer being physically in the system (e.g., transit systems).

High-Contact Processes.   Think for a moment about the service provided by your local public transit system. When you purchase transportation, you must board a bus or train, so public transit is a **high-contact system**. For this reason, transit managers must worry about the cleanliness of the trains and buses and the appearance of the stations. This is usually not the case in low-contact systems. Large industrial concerns that ship coal in freight trains, for example, are generally not concerned with the appearance inside those trains.

low-contact system

A system in which the service can be provided without the customer being physically in the system (e.g., lawn care services).

Low-Contact Processes.   Consider the cheque-processing operations at your bank. Workers sort the cheques that have been cashed that day and dispatch them to the banks on which they were drawn. This operation is a **low-contact system** because customers are not in contact with the bank while the service is performed. They receive the service—their funds are transferred to cover their cheques—without ever setting foot in the cheque-processing centre. Gas and electric utilities, auto repair shops, and lawn care services are also low-contact systems.

Differences Between Service and Manufacturing Operations

Service and manufacturing operations both transform raw materials into finished products. In service production, however, the raw materials, or inputs, are not glass or steel. Rather, they are people who choose among sellers because they have either unsatisfied needs or possessions for which they require some form of care or alteration. In service operations, then, "finished products" or "outputs" are people with needs met and possessions serviced.

Focus on Performance

One very obvious difference exists between service and manufacturing operations: Whereas goods are produced, services are performed. Therefore, customer-oriented performance is a key factor in measuring the effectiveness of a service company.

Wal-Mart, for example, sells to millions of people from California to China to Winnipeg to Argentina out of nearly 4000 stores. Its superstar status stems from an obsession with speedy product delivery that it measures not in days or even in hours, but in minutes and seconds. Wal-Mart's keen customer focus emphasizes avoiding unnecessary inventories, getting fast responses from suppliers, streamlining transaction processes, and knowing accurately the sales and restocking requirements for keeping the right merchandise moving from warehouses to store shelves. To implement this strategy, Wal-Mart has made technology—namely, its vaunted computer and telecommunications system—a core competency.[2]

Wal-Mart
www.walmart.com

In many ways, the focus of service operations is more complex than that of goods production. First, service operations feature a unique link between production and consumption—between process and outcome. Second, services are more intangible and more customized and less storable than most products. Finally, quality considerations must be defined, and managed, differently in the service sector than in manufacturing operations.

Focus on Process and Outcome

As we saw earlier, manufacturing operations focus on the outcome of the production process. The products offered by most service operations, however, are actually combinations of goods and services. Services, therefore, must focus on both the transformation *process* and its outcome—both on making a pizza and on delivering it to the buyer. Service operations thus require different skills from manufacturing operations. For example, local gas company employees may need the interpersonal skills necessary to calm and reassure frightened customers who have reported gas leaks. The job, therefore, can mean more than just repairing defective pipes. Factory workers who install gas pipes while assembling mobile homes are far less likely to need such skills.

Focus on Service Characteristics

Service companies' transactions always reflect the fact that service products are characterized by three key qualities: *intangibility, customization,* and *unstorability*.

Intangibility. Often services cannot be touched, tasted, smelled, or seen. An important value, therefore, is the *intangible* value that the customer experiences in the form of pleasure, satisfaction, or a feeling of safety. For example, when you hire an attorney to resolve a problem, you purchase not only the intangible quality of legal expertise but also the equally intangible reassurance that help is at hand. Although all services have some degree of intangibility, some provide tangible elements as well. Your attorney, for example, can draw up the living will that you want to keep in your safe deposit box.

Customization. When you visit a physician, you expect to be examined for your symptoms. Likewise, when you purchase insurance, have your pet groomed, or have your hair cut, you expect these services to be designed for your needs. Typically, therefore, services are *customized*.

Unstorability. Services such as rubbish collection, transportation, child care, and house cleaning cannot be produced ahead of time and then stored. If a service is not used when it is available, it is usually wasted. Services, then, are typically characterized by a high degree of *unstorability*.

Focus on the Customer-Service Link

Because they transform customers or their possessions, service operations often acknowledge the customer as part of the operations process itself. For example, to purchase a haircut you must usually go to the barbershop or beauty salon.

As physical participants in the operations process, service consumers have a unique ability to affect that process. In other words, as the customer, you expect the salon to be conveniently located, to be open for business at convenient times, to offer needed services at reasonable prices, and to extend prompt service. Accordingly, the manager adopts hours of operation, available services, and an appropriate number of employees to meet the requirements of the customer.

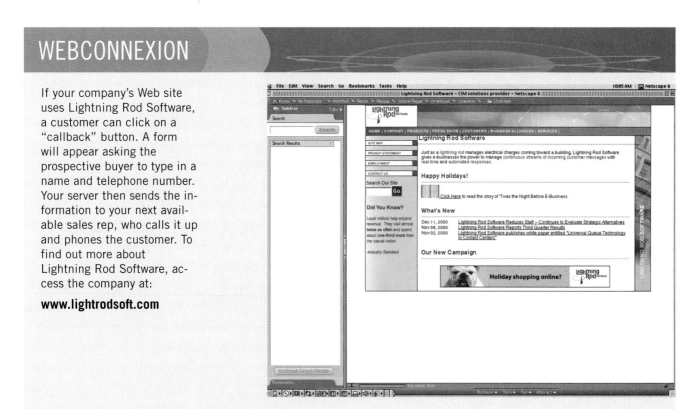

WEBCONNEXION

If your company's Web site uses Lightning Rod Software, a customer can click on a "callback" button. A form will appear asking the prospective buyer to type in a name and telephone number. Your server then sends the information to your next available sales rep, who calls it up and phones the customer. To find out more about Lightning Rod Software, access the company at:

www.lightrodsoft.com

E-Commerce: The "Virtual Presence" of the Customer. The growth of e-commerce has introduced a "virtual presence," as opposed to a physical presence, of customers in the service system. Consumers interact electronically, in real time, with sellers, collecting information about product features, delivery availability, and after-sales service. They have around-the-clock access to information via automated call centres, and those who want human interaction can talk with live respondents or enter chat rooms. Many companies have invited "the virtual customer" into their service systems by building customer-communications relationships. The online travel agency Expedia.ca responds to your personalized profile with a welcome e-mail letter, presents you with a tailor-made Web page the next time you sign on, offers chat rooms in which you can compare notes with other customers, and notifies you of upcoming special travel opportunities.

Internet technology also enables firms to build relationships with industrial customers. Electronic Data Systems (EDS), for example, helps client firms develop networks among their many desktop computers. In managing more than 700 000 desktops for clients throughout the world, EDS has created a special service called Renascence that links clients, suppliers, and employees in a private 500 000–computer electronic marketplace. Some 2000 software products can be viewed, purchased, tracked, and delivered if you are a member of the network.[3]

Electronic Data Systems
www.eds.com

Focus on Service Quality Considerations

Consumers use different criteria to judge services and goods. Service managers must understand that quality of work and quality of service are not necessarily synonymous. For example, although your car may have been flawlessly repaired, you might feel dissatisfied with the service if you were forced to pick it up a day later than promised.

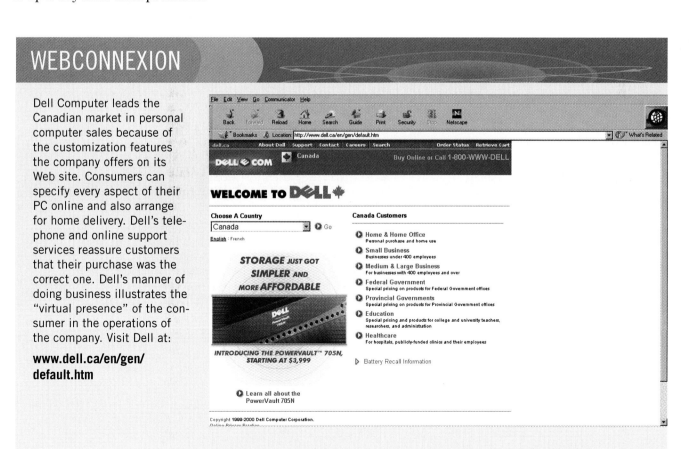

WEBCONNEXION

Dell Computer leads the Canadian market in personal computer sales because of the customization features the company offers on its Web site. Consumers can specify every aspect of their PC online and also arrange for home delivery. Dell's telephone and online support services reassure customers that their purchase was the correct one. Dell's manner of doing business illustrates the "virtual presence" of the consumer in the operations of the company. Visit Dell at:

www.dell.ca/en/gen/ default.htm

OPERATIONS PLANNING

Now that we've contrasted goods and services we can return to a more general consideration of production that encompasses both goods and services. Like all good managers, we start with planning. Managers from many departments contribute to the firm's decisions about operations management. As Figure 11.2 shows, however, no matter how many decision makers are involved, the process can be described as a series of logical steps. The success of any firm depends on the final result of this logical sequence of decisions.

The overall business plan developed by a company's top executives guides operations planning. This plan outlines the firm's goals and objectives, including the specific products and services it will offer in the upcoming years. In this section, we will survey each of the major components of the business plan that directly affect operations planning. First, we will describe forecasting and then we will discuss the key planning and forecasting activities that fall into one of five major categories: capacity, location, layout, quality, and methods planning.

Forecasting

forecasts
Estimates of future demand for both new and existing products.

In addition to the business plan, managers develop the firm's long-range production plan through **forecasts** of future demand for both new and existing products. This plan covers a two- to five-year period. It specifically details the number of plants or service facilities, as well as labour, machinery, and transportation and storage facilities, that will be needed to meet demand. It also specifies how resources will be obtained.

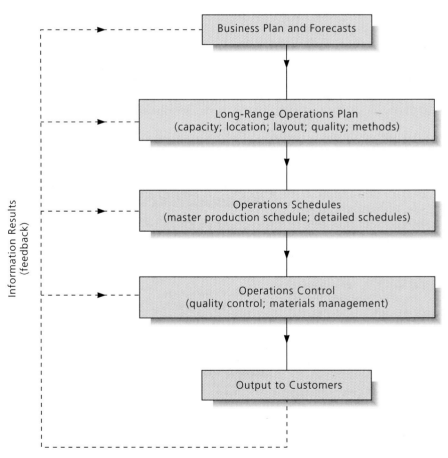

Figure 11.2
Operations planning and control.

Forecasting uses both qualitative and quantitative methods. *Qualitative forecasts* may come from an expert or group of experts who basically use judgment and experience. *Quantitative forecasts* are statistical methods to project future demand from past demand patterns. For example, in developing a new line of Memorex videotapes, Memtek Products might use quantitative methods to calculate demand three years hence at 4 million cassettes per year. Its long-range production plan might translate this demand into a need to build three new plants, lease another warehouse, acquire four new tape-filling machines, and hire 2500 new employees.

Capacity Planning

The amount of a product that a company can produce under normal working conditions is its **capacity**. The capacity of a goods or service firm depends on how many people it employs and the number and size of its facilities. Long-range planning must take into account both current and future capacity.

capacity
The amount of a good that a firm can produce under normal working conditions.

Capacity Planning for Producing Goods

Capacity planning for goods means ensuring that a manufacturing firm's capacity slightly exceeds the normal demand for its product. To see why this policy is best, consider the alternatives. If capacity is too small to meet demand, the company must turn away customers—a situation that not only cuts into profits but also alienates both customers and salespeople. If capacity greatly exceeds demand, the firm is wasting money by maintaining a plant that is too large, by keeping excess machinery on-line, or by employing too many workers.

The stakes are high in the company's capacity decisions. While expanding fast enough to meet future demand and to protect market share from competitors, it must also weigh the increased costs of expanding. One reason that Intel Corp. enjoys more than 70 percent market share in the worldwide semiconductor business is the $11 billion it invested in capacity expansion between 1991 and 1995. Will demand for semiconductors continue to grow even further? With so much invested thus far, Intel must decide whether the risks of additional capacity are worth the potential gains.[4]

Capacity Planning for Producing Services

In low-contact processes, maintaining inventory allows managers to set capacity at the level of *average demand*. For example, a catalogue sales warehouse may hire enough order fillers to handle 1000 orders per day. When daily orders exceed this average demand, some orders are placed in inventory—set aside in a "to-be-done" file—to be processed on a day when fewer than 1000 orders are received.

In high-contact processes, managers must plan capacity to meet *peak demand*. A supermarket, for instance, has far more cash registers than it needs on an average day; but on a Saturday morning or during the three days before Thanksgiving, all registers will be running at full speed.

Location Planning

Because the location of a factory, office, or store affects its production costs and flexibility, sound location planning is crucial. Depending on the site of its facility, a company may be capable of producing a low-cost product or may find itself at an extreme cost disadvantage relative to its competitors.

Location Planning for Producing Goods

Managers in goods-producing operations must consider many factors in location planning. Their location decisions are influenced by proximity to raw materials and markets, availability of labour, energy and transportation costs, provincial and municipal regulations and taxes, and community living conditions.

In 1998, for example, General Motors announced it would build new plants in North America to increase productivity and competitiveness. These agile, highly efficient assembly plants will rely on outside producers to supply large components such as fully assembled dashboards, stamped hoods, and other body parts. GM intends for production efficiencies to arise from a system in which each supplier specializes in making just one major component. To resupply GM assembly plants quickly and to reduce transportation costs, suppliers will locate factories nearby.[5]

Some location decisions are now being simplified by the rise of industrial parks. Created by cities interested in attracting new industry, these planned sites come with the necessary zoning, land, shipping facilities, utilities, and waste disposal outlets already in place. Such sites offer flexibility, often allowing firms to open new facilities before competitors can get started in the same area. The ready-made site also provides faster construction start-ups because it entails no lead time in preparing the chosen site.

Location Planning for Producing Services

In planning low-contact services, companies have some options. Services can be located near resource supplies, labour, or transportation outlets. For example, the typical Wal-Mart distribution centre is located near the hundreds of Wal-Mart stores it supplies, not near the companies that supply the distribution centre. Distribution managers regard Wal-Mart stores as their customers. To better serve them, distribution centres are located so that truckloads of merchandise flow quickly to the stores.

On the other hand, high-contact services are more restricted. They must locate near the customers who are a part of the system. Accordingly, fast-food restaurants such as Taco Bell, McDonald's, and Burger King have begun moving into nontraditional locations with high traffic—dormitories, hospital cafeterias, museums, and shopping malls.

Layout Planning

Once a site has been selected, managers must decide on plant layout. Layout of machinery, equipment, and supplies determines whether a company can respond quickly and efficiently to customer requests for more and different products or finds itself unable to match competitors' production speed or convenience of service.

Layout Planning for Producing Goods

In facilities that produce goods, layout must be planned for three different types of space:

- *Productive facilities*: workstations and equipment for transforming raw materials, for example

- *Nonproductive facilities*: storage and maintenance areas

- *Support facilities*: offices, restrooms, parking lots, cafeterias, and so forth

In this section, we focus on productive facilities. Alternatives for layout planning include *process*, *cellular*, and *product layouts*.

Process Layouts. In a **process layout**, which is well suited to job shops specializing in custom work, equipment and people are grouped according to function. In a woodworking shop, for example, machines cut the wood in an area devoted to sawing, sanding occurs in a dedicated area, and jobs that need painting are taken to a dust-free area where all the painting equipment is located. The various tasks are each performed in specialized locations.

The job shop produces many one-of-a-kind products, and each product, as you can see in Figure 11.3(a), requires different kinds of work. Whereas Product X needs only three production steps prior to packaging, Product Y needs four. When there is a large variety of products, there will be many flow paths through the shop and potentially much congestion. Machine shops, custom bakeries, and dry cleaning shops often feature process layouts.

Cellular Layouts. Another workplace arrangement for some applications is called the **cellular layout**. Cellular layouts are used when a family of products (a group of similar products) follows a fixed flow path. A clothing manufacturer, for example, may establish a cell, or designated area, dedicated to making a family of pockets—for example, pockets for shirts, coats, blouses, trousers, and slacks. Although each type of pocket is unique in shape, size, and style, all go through the same production steps. Within the cell, therefore, various types of equipment (for cutting, trimming, and sewing) are arranged close together in the appropriate sequence. All pockets pass stage by stage through the cell from beginning to end, in a nearly continuous flow.

In plants that produce a variety of products, there may be one or two high-volume products that justify separate manufacturing cells. Figure 11.3(b) shows two production cells, one each for Products X and Y, while all other smaller-volume products are produced elsewhere in the plant.

process layout
A way of organizing production activities such that equipment and people are grouped together according to their function.

cellular layout
Used to produce goods when families of products can follow similar flow paths.

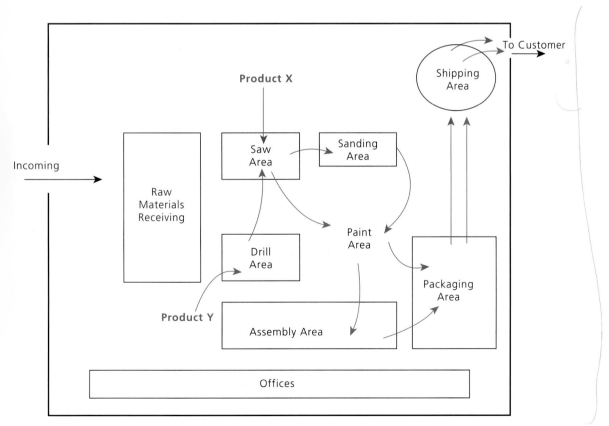

Figure 11.3 (a)
Process layout for wood shop: Arrows indicate unique path of work flow for each product.

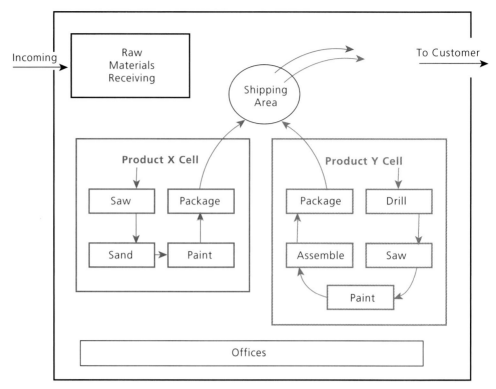

Figure 11.3 (b)
Cellular layout for wood shop: Arrows indicate the fixed path of work flow for each product.

Cellular layouts have several advantages. Because similar products require less machine adjustment, equipment setup time in the cell is reduced, as compared with setup times in process layouts. Because flow distances are usually shorter, there is less material handling and transit time. Finally, inventories of goods in progress are lower and paperwork is simpler because material flows are more orderly. A disadvantage of cells is the duplication of equipment. Note, for example, in Figure 11.3(b) that two saws are needed (one in each cell) as well as two paint areas, but only one of each is needed in the process layout (see Figure 11.3(a)).

Product Layouts. In a **product layout**, equipment and people are set up to produce one type of product in a fixed sequence of steps and are arranged according to its production requirements. Product layouts are efficient for producing large volumes of product quickly and often use **assembly lines**. A partially finished product moves step by step through the plant on conveyor belts or other equipment, often in a straight line, until the product is completed. Figure 11.3(c), for example, shows the sequence of production steps performed identically, from start to finish, on all units of Product Z as they move through the line. Automobile, food processing, and television assembly plants use product layouts.

Product layouts are efficient because the work skill is built into the equipment; simplified work tasks can then use unskilled labour. However, product layouts tend to be inflexible because, traditionally, they have required heavy investment in specialized equipment that is hard to rearrange for new applications. In addition, workers are subject to boredom, and when someone is absent or overworked, those farther down the line cannot help out.

Today, however, the assembly-line layout is much more flexible because of the new possibilities provided by computers. Tools and machine sequences can now be switched economically from position to position on the line by computers connected to the Internet, to an intranet, or to both.

With the **flexible manufacturing system (FMS)**, a single factory can produce a wide variety of products. Using computer information systems,

product layout
A way of organizing production activities such that equipment and people are set up to produce only one type of good.

assembly line
A type of product layout in which a partially finished product moves through a plan on a conveyor belt or other equipment.

flexible manufacturing system (FMS)
A production system that allows a single factory to produce small batches of different goods on the same production line.

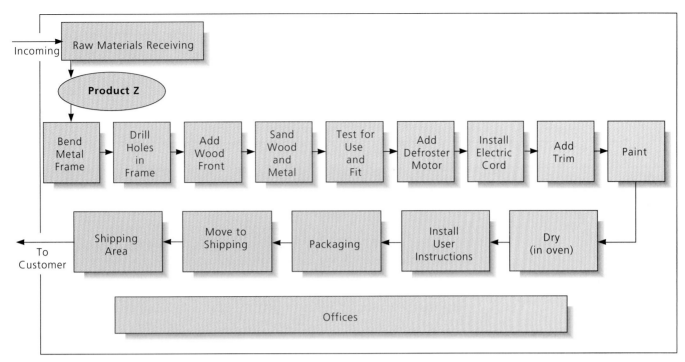

Figure 11.3 (c)
Product layout for wood shop: Arrows indicate the fixed path of work flow for all units of Product Z.

production for each product is adapted rapidly to changes in customer demand by integrating sales information with the factory's production activities. At Toshiba, for example, workers can make 9 different desktop computers and 20 different laptop computers on adjacent assembly lines. At each post, a computer screen displays a drawing and gives instructions for the appropriate product. The goal is to produce sufficient numbers of products that are in high demand, while avoiding overproduction of products that are not in as high demand.

But flexible manufacturing is being replaced by an even newer development. **Soft manufacturing (SM)** emphasizes computer software and computer networks instead of production machines. Soft manufacturing recognizes that complete automation of production processes may not be advisable, and that humans are actually better at certain things than machines are. SM plants can turn out customized products at mass-production speeds. Hewlett-Packard, for example, embarrassed its Japanese rival NEC by beating it to the market with an ink-jet colour printer. H-P's product was so good that the Japanese withdrew theirs a few months later.

soft manufacturing (SM)
Emphasizes computer software and computer networks instead of production machines.

Layout Planning for Producing Services

Service firms use some of the same layouts as goods-producing firms. In a low-contact system, for instance, the facility should be arranged to enhance the production of the service. A mail-processing facility at UPS or Federal Express, therefore, looks very much like a product layout in a factory: machines and people are arranged in the order in which they are used in the mass processing of mail. In contrast, Kinko's Copy Centres use process layouts for different custom jobs: specific functions such as photocopying, computing, binding, photography, and laminating are performed in specialized areas of the store.

High-contact systems should be arranged to meet customer needs and expectations. For example, Piccadilly Cafeterias focuses both layout and services on the groups that constitute its primary market: families and elderly people. As you can see in Figure 11.4, families enter to find an array of

Kinko's Copy Centres
www.kinkos.com

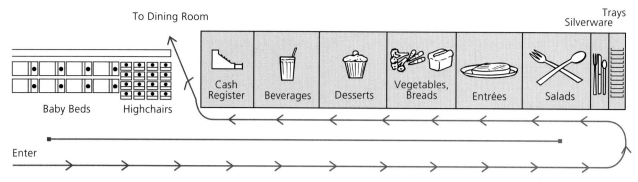

To Dining Room

Trays
Silverware

Baby Beds   Highchairs

Cash Register | Beverages | Desserts | Vegetables, Breads | Entrées | Salads

Enter

Figure 11.4
Layout of a typical Piccadilly cafeteria.

highchairs and rolling baby beds that make it convenient to wheel children through the lineup. Servers are willing to carry trays for elderly people and for those pushing strollers. Note, too, that customers must pass by the entire serving line before making selections. Not only does this layout help them make up their minds; it also tempts them to select more.

Quality Planning

In planning production systems and facilities, managers must keep in mind the firm's quality goals.[6] Thus any complete production plan includes systems for ensuring that goods are produced to meet the firm's quality standards. The issues of productivity and quality are discussed in detail in Chapter 12.

Methods Planning

In designing operations systems, managers must clearly identify every production step and the specific methods for performing them. They can

Employees at the Toyota manufacturing plant in Cambridge, Ontario, discuss a production problem. At this plant, employees are responsible not only for making automobiles, but also for monitoring quality control and for maintaining and cleaning the work area.

then work to reduce waste, inefficiency, and poor performance by examining procedures on a step-by-step basis—an approach sometimes called *methods improvement*.

Methods Improvement in Goods

Improvement of production for goods begins when a manager documents the current method. A detailed description, often using a diagram called the *process flow chart*, is usually helpful for organizing and recording all information. The process flow chart identifies the sequence of production activities, movements of materials, and work performed at each stage as the product flows through production. The flow can then be analyzed to identify wasteful activities, sources of delay in production flows, and other inefficiencies. The final step is implementing improvements.

Mercury Marine, for example, used methods improvement to streamline the production of stern-drive units for powerboats. Examination of the process flow from raw materials to assembly (the final production step) revealed numerous waste and inefficiencies. Each product passed through 122 steps, travelled nearly 7 kilometres in the factory, and was handled by 106 people. Analysis revealed that only 27 steps actually added value to the product (for example, drilling, painting). Work methods were revised to eliminate nonproductive activities. Mercury ultimately identified potential savings in labour, inventory, paperwork, and space requirements. Because production lead time was also reduced, customer orders were filled more quickly.

Methods Improvement in Services

In a low-contact process, managers can use methods improvements to speed services ranging from mowing lawns to filling prescriptions and drawing up legal documents. Dell Computer, for example, sells its computers online and over the phone, mostly to medium and large companies. Methods analysis eliminates unnecessary steps so that orders can be processed quickly for production and delivery. Dell's emphasis on efficient selling by means of electronic technology speeds its response time to provide customers with a specific value—extremely fast delivery service.

Service-Flow Analysis. By showing the flow of processes that make up a given service, **service flow analysis** helps managers decide whether all those processes are necessary. Moreover, because each process is a potential contributor to good or bad service, analysis also helps identify and isolate potential problems (known as *fail points*). In Figure 11.5, for instance, the manager of a photo-finishing shop has determined that the standard execution time for developing a roll of film is 48.5 minutes. She has also found that the "develop film" stage is the one most likely to delay service because it is the most complex. Thus, she has marked it as a potential fail point, as a reminder to give special attention to this stage of operations.

Designing to Control Employee Discretion in Services. Thus far, we have stressed the importance of the human factor in service activities—that is, the direct contact of server and customer. In some cases, however, the purpose of service design is to limit the range of activities of both employees and customers. By careful planning—and sometimes even by automating to control human discretion—managers can make services more customer-oriented because they can ensure product consistency.

service flow analysis

An analysis that shows the process flows that are necessary to provide a service to customers; it allows managers to determine which processes are necessary.

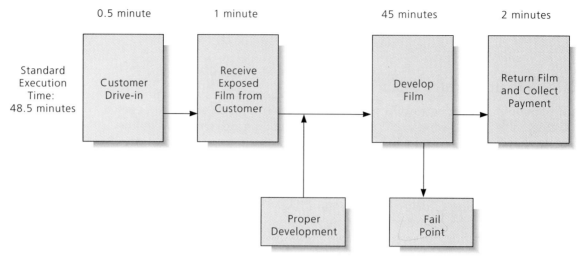

Figure 11.5
Service flow analysis.

McDonald's, for example, has done an outstanding job of designing the fast-food business as a mass-production system. By automating processes that would otherwise rely on judgment, McDonald's has been able to provide consistent service from a staff with little specialized training. At a central supply house, for instance, hamburger patties are automatically measured and packed. Specially designed scoops measure the same amount of french fries and other items into standard-sized containers. In addition, all drawers, shelves, and bins are designed to hold the ingredients for McDonald's standard product mixes only.

Sometimes, firms design ways to transfer discretion from employees to customers. For example, hospital patients connected to special equipment can administer their own pain-relieving drugs. This procedure offers more control to the patient and frees up nurses for other duties. Of course, there are safeguards: once a predetermined limit of drugs has been used, the source shuts down.

Design for Customer Contact in Services. In a high-contact service, the demands on system designs are somewhat different. Here, managers must develop procedures that clearly spell out the ways in which workers interact with customers. These procedures must cover such activities as exchanging information or money, delivering and receiving materials, and even making physical contact. The next time you visit your dentist's office, for instance, notice the way dental hygienists scrub up and wear disposable gloves. They also scrub after patient contact, even if they intend to work on equipment or do paperwork, and they rescrub before working on the next patient. The high-contact system in a dental office consists of very strict procedures designed to avoid contact that can transmit disease.

OPERATIONS SCHEDULING

Once plans identify needed resources and how they will be used to reach a firm's goals, managers must develop timetables for acquiring resources for production. This aspect of operations is called *scheduling*.

Scheduling Goods Operations

Scheduling of goods production occurs on different levels within the firm. First, a top-level or master production schedule shows which products will be produced, when production will occur, and what resources will be used during specified time periods.

Consider the case of Logan Aluminum Inc. Logan produces coils of aluminum that its main customers, Atlantic Richfield and Alcan Aluminum, use to produce aluminum cans. Logan's master schedule extends out to 60 weeks and shows how many coils will be made during each week. For various types of coils, the master schedule specifies how many of each will be produced. "We need this planning and scheduling system," says material manager Candy McKenzie, "to determine how much of what product we can produce each and every month."

This information, however, is not complete. For example, manufacturing personnel must also know the location of all coils on the plant floor and their various stages of production. Start and stop times must be assigned, and employees must be given scheduled work assignments. Short-term detailed schedules fill in these blanks on a daily basis. These schedules use incoming customer orders and information about current machine conditions to update the sizes and variety of coils to make each day.

Scheduling Service Operations

Service scheduling may involve both work and workers. In a low-contact service, work scheduling may be based either on desired completion dates or on the time of order arrivals. For example, several cars may be scheduled for repairs at a local garage. Thus, if your car is not scheduled for work until 3:30 p.m., it may sit idle for several hours even if it was the first to be dropped off. In such businesses, reservations and appointments systems can help smooth ups and downs in demand.

In contrast, if a hospital emergency room is overloaded, patients cannot be asked to make appointments and come back later. As we have seen, in high-contact services, the customer is part of the system and must be accommodated. Thus, precise scheduling of services may not be possible in high-contact systems.

In scheduling workers, managers must also consider efficiency and costs. McDonald's, for example, guarantees workers that they will be scheduled for at least four hours at a time. To accomplish this goal without having workers be idle, McDonald's uses overlapping shifts—the ending hours for some employees overlap the beginning hours for others. The overlap provides maximum coverage during peak periods. McDonald's also trains employees to put off minor tasks, such as refilling napkin dispensers, until slow periods.

A 24-hour-a-day service operation, such as a hospital, can be an even greater scheduling challenge. Nurses, for example, must be on duty around the clock, seven days a week. Few nurses, however, want to work on weekends or during the early hours of the morning. Similarly, although enough nurses must be scheduled to meet emergencies, most hospitals are on tight budgets and cannot afford to have too many on-duty nurses. Thus, incentives are often used to entice nurses to work at times they might not otherwise choose. For example, would you choose to work 12 hours per day, 7 days a week? Probably not, but what if you were entitled to have every other week off in exchange for working such a schedule? A number of hospitals use just such a plan to attract nurses.

OPERATIONS CONTROL

operations control
Managers monitor production performance by comparing results with plans and schedules.

follow-up
Checking to ensure that production decisions are being implemented.

Once long-range plans have been put into action and schedules have been drawn up, **operations control** requires production managers to monitor production performance by comparing results with detailed plans and schedules. If schedules or quality standards are not met, these managers must take corrective action. **Follow-up**—checking to ensure that production decisions are being implemented—is an essential and ongoing facet of operations control. The "It's a Wired World" box describes what happened when Hershey Foods was not able to exercise control over its production processes.

Operations control features *materials management* and *production process control*. Both activities ensure that schedules are met and that production goals are fulfilled, both in quantity and in quality. In this section, we consider the nature of materials management and look at some important methods of process control.

Materials Management

Both goods-producing and service companies use materials. For many manufacturing firms, material costs account for 50 to 75 percent of total product

---

IT'S A WIRED WORLD

Hershey Kisses Off Profits

By 1999, Hershey Foods Corp.—manufacturers of such well-known candies as Hershey Kisses, Reese's Peanut Butter Cups, and Hershey chocolate bars—had spent three years and US$112 million to implement a new information technology (IT) system called Enterprise 12 with which it planned to enter the e-commerce arena. The core of the new technology is SAP, a complex software system that electronically links all of a firm's main business functions, including manufacturing, material flows, inventories, material purchasing, production scheduling, warehousing, order entry, billing, and accounting. By integrating all of these activities, SAP's unified database offers powerful up-to-the-minute information sharing throughout the firm and generates efficient flows of incoming raw materials into production and on through to deliveries to customers. A fine-tuned SAP application can reduce inventories, shorten cycle times, and lower costs. To get up and running, however, Hershey had a lot to do. For one thing, 5000 outdated desktop computers had to be upgraded and standardized. In addition, employees in every department had to be trained to use the new system. During the installation, a flock of expert consultants roamed the company, and, after 30 months, Hershey's SAP system began running in July 1999.

In the same month, retailers began ordering candy for the back-to-school and Halloween seasons. Unfortunately, the new system required big changes in the way that Hershey employees did their jobs, and they weren't ready for peak demand. By mid-September, the company was already having trouble pushing orders through the new system. Shipments were delayed, and it wasn't long before management realized that Hershey couldn't make enough candy for the Halloween season. By missing one of its prime shipping seasons, Hershey was hit with a 19 percent drop in third-quarter profits. Although no one announced the exact cause of the failure, it seemed to revolve around the way that information flowed—or didn't flow—from department to department through the IT system. In particular, there was a breakdown in order processing. Analysts attributed the problem to the attempt to implement an intricate system in one fell swoop. The new system should have been tested gradually, they concluded, to confirm that each piece was working properly and that every piece was properly integrated.

Meanwhile, as Hershey's six plants kept producing its well-known products, chocolate continued to pile up in warehouses instead of getting to retail shelves. As retailers were saddled with partial deliveries, customer relations naturally became strained. Typical delivery times escalated from 5 days to 12, inventory costs increased 29 percent, and sales for the fourth quarter dropped another 12 percent. While Hershey employees continued to master their new system, inefficient order processing took another bite out of Hershey's sales during the 1999 Christmas season.

Hershey
www.hersheys.com

costs. For goods whose production uses little labour, such as petroleum refining, this percentage is even higher. Thus, companies have good reasons to emphasize materials management.

The process of **materials management** not only controls but also plans and organizes the flow of materials. Even before production starts, materials management focuses on product design by emphasizing materials **standardization**—the use of standard and uniform components rather than new or different components. Law firms, for example, maintain standardized forms and data files for estate wills, living wills, trust agreements, and various contracts that can be adjusted easily to meet your individual needs. In manufacturing, Ford's engine plant in Romeo, Michigan, uses common parts for several different kinds of engines rather than unique parts for each. Once components were standardized, the total number of different parts was reduced by 25 percent. Standardization also simplifies paperwork, reduces storage requirements, and eliminates unnecessary material flows.

Once the product has been designed, materials managers purchase the necessary materials and monitor the production process through the distribution of finished goods. There are five major areas in materials management:

- **Transportation** includes the means of transporting resources to the company and finished goods to buyers.

- **Warehousing** is the storage of both incoming materials for production and finished goods for physical distribution to customers.

- **Purchasing** is the acquisition of all the raw materials and services that a company needs to produce its products; most large firms have purchasing departments to buy proper materials in the amounts needed.

- **Supplier selection** means finding and choosing suppliers of services and materials to buy from. It includes evaluating potential suppliers, negotiating terms of service, and maintaining positive buyer–seller relationships.

- **Inventory control** includes the receiving, storing, handling, and counting of all raw materials, partly finished goods, and finished goods. It ensures that enough materials inventories are available to meet production schedules.

Managers in each area of materials management are constantly on the lookout for cost savings. Consider the cost-cutting possibilities in just one area—purchasing. Industrial buyers are banding together on the Internet. By forming online buying groups, they can purchase equipment and supplies in huge quantities for big discounts. Purchasing-Center.com, for example, is a brokerage site that brings together buyers and sellers into a single Internet marketplace, where it is easier for companies to contact and negotiate with each other on prices.[7]

Tools for Operations Process Control

Numerous tools assist managers in controlling operations. Chief among these are worker training, just-in-time production systems, material requirements planning, and quality control.

Worker Training

Customer satisfaction is closely linked to the employees who provide the service. Effective customer relationships do not come about by accident: Service workers can be trained and motivated in customer-oriented atti-

materials management
Planning, organizing, and controlling the flow of materials from purchase through distribution of finished goods.

standardization
Using standard and uniform components in the production process.

transportation
The means of transporting resources to the company and finished goods to buyers.

warehousing
The storage of both incoming materials for production and finished goods for physical distribution to customers.

purchasing
The acquisition of all the raw materials and services that a company needs to produce its products.

supplier selection
Finding and determining suppliers to buy from.

inventory control
The receiving, storing, handling, and counting of all resources, partly finished goods, and finished goods.

tudes and behaviour. In service-product design, it is important to remember that most services are delivered by people; that is, service system employees are both the producers of the product and the salespeople. Thus, human relations skills are vital in anyone who has contact with the public. More and more human resource experts now realize that without employees' trained relationship skills for pleasing their clients, businesses such as airlines, employment agencies, and hotels can lose customers to better-prepared competitors.

Managers realize how easily service employees with a poor attitude can reduce sales. Conversely, the right attitude is a powerful sales tool. The Walt Disney Co. has long recognized the vital link between its employees and its business success. Its methods for employee development are widely recognized by other firms who send managers to the Disney Institute to learn "The Disney Approach to People Management." Disney does an excellent job of remembering that no matter what their jobs, service employees are links to the public. Of the 35 000 employees at Disney World Resort in Buena Vista, Florida, 20 000 have direct contact with guests. For example, Disney World has a team of sweepers constantly at work picking up bits of trash as soon as they fall to the ground. When visitors have questions about directions or time, they often ask one of the sweepers. Because their responses affect visitors' overall impressions of Disney World, sweepers are trained to respond in appropriate ways. Their work is evaluated and rewarded based on strict performance appraisal standards. A pleased customer is more likely to return.[8]

Just-in-Time Production Systems

To minimize manufacturing inventory costs, some managers use **just-in-time (JIT) production systems**. JIT brings together all the needed materials and parts at the precise moment they are required for each production stage, not before. All resources are continuously flowing, from their arrival as raw materials to subassembly, final completion, and shipment of finished products. JIT reduces to practically nothing the number of goods in process (that is, goods not yet finished) and saves money by replacing stop-and-go production with smooth movement. Once smooth movements become the norm, disruptions become more visible and thus are resolved more quickly. Finding and eliminating disruptions by continuous improvement of production is a major objective of JIT.

By implementing JIT, Harley-Davidson reduced its inventories by over 40 percent, improved production work flows, and reduced its costs of warranty work, rework, and scrap by 60 percent. In addition, Harley-Davidson motorcycles have retained their coveted quality reputation: the annual number of shipments more than doubled from 1988 to 1996. With the help of JIT, the company's Plan 2003 calls for another doubling of production for Harley's 100th anniversary in 2003.[9]

Mount Sinai Hospital in Toronto has also introduced JIT. Individual suppliers no longer go to Mount Sinai to deliver the items they have sold to the hospital. Rather, all suppliers deliver their products to Livingston Healthcare Services Inc. Livingston stores these items and fills Mount Sinai's order once each day; therefore, Mount Sinai no longer keeps any inventory. Once the goods are delivered, they are sent directly to the various departments in the hospital; the former centralized storeroom at the hospital no longer exists. In the first year using the new system, the hospital saved about $200 000.[10]

Walt Disney Co.
www.disney.go.com

just-in-time (JIT) production systems
A method of inventory control in which materials are acquired and put into production just as they are needed.

Mount Sinai Hospital
www.mtsinai.on.ca

At Toyota's Cambridge, Ontario, plant, delivery trucks constantly pull in to unload tires, batteries, steering wheels, seats, and many other items needed in the JIT production system.[11] And when General Motors of Canada's Oshawa assembly plant needs seats for cars, it sends the order electronically to a local supplier. The supplier has four hours to make the seats and ship them to the plant. The supplier loads the truck in reverse order so that the last seat loaded is the first one that will be used on the assembly line. The supplier knows, for example, that the plant will be making a certain number of one model and then a certain number of another model of car.[12]

Material Requirements Planning

Like JIT, **material requirements planning (MRP)** seeks to deliver the right amount of materials at the right place and the right time for goods production. MRP uses a bill of materials that is basically a recipe for the finished product. It specifies the necessary ingredients (raw materials and components), the order in which they should be combined, and the quantity of each ingredient needed to make one batch of the product (say, 2000 finished telephones). The recipe is fed into a computer that controls inventory and schedules each stage of production. The result is fewer early arrivals, less frequent stock shortages, and lower storage costs. MRP is most popular among companies whose products require complicated assembly and fabrication activities, such as automobile manufacturers, appliance makers, and furniture companies.

    Manufacturing resource planning (MRP II) is an advanced version of MRP that ties all parts of the organization into the company's production activities. For example, MRP inventory and production schedules are translated into cost requirements for the financial management department and into personnel requirements for the human resources department; information about available capacity for new orders goes to the marketing department.

material requirements planning (MRP)
A method of inventory control in which a computerized bill of materials is used to estimate production needs so that resources are acquired and put into production only as needed.

manufacturing resource planning (MRP II)
An advanced version of MRP that ties together all parts of the organization into the company's production activities.

Quality Control

Another operation control tool is **quality control**—the management of the production process in order to manufacture goods or supply services that meet specific quality standards. United Parcel Service Inc. (UPS), for instance, delivers 13 million packages every day, and all of them are promised to arrive on strict delivery schedules, mostly for business clients. Quality control is essential because delivery reliability—namely, avoiding late deliveries—is critical for customer satisfaction. UPS

When North American manufacturers turned to leaner operations to counter foreign competition in the 1990s, they shifted to just-in-time inventory methods and cut workforces—and capacity. Today, economic good times mean accelerated demand and hard-pressed, understaffed assembly lines at many firms. At General Electric's locomotive plant in Erie, Pennsylvania, managers have tried to head off problems by relying on certified parts supplied on time and in full quantities only by carefully monitored subcontractors.

UPS
www.ups.com

quality control
The management of the production process so as to manufacture goods or supply services that meet specific quality standards.

tracks the locations, time schedules, and on-time performance for some 500 aircraft and 150 000 vehicles as they carry packages through the delivery system.

Special Production Control Problems in Service Operations

The unique characteristics of services—customization, unstorability, and the presence of customers within the production process—create special challenges. In this final section, we will consider some techniques for meeting these challenges.

Customization

The customized nature of services often makes scheduling difficult or impossible. This difficulty is one reason why you often have to wait at your doctor's office even though you have an appointment. Because the patients ahead of you also purchased customized services, the receptionist who schedules appointments can never know exactly when service will be completed.

Because scheduling is harder in high-contact services, it can often be improved by reducing customer contact. Routine transactions, such as approval for small loans, for example, can be handled by telephone or mail; only exceptions need to be handled on a face-to-face basis. Locating drop-off points away from main facilities also reduces the level of customer contact. Consider the success of automatic teller machines; not only are they more convenient for customers, but they free bank tellers from processing routine deposits and withdrawals.

Scheduling can also be improved by separating information gathering from provision of the service itself. For example, a well-run medical office will give you a medical history form to fill out while you wait. This system frees all office personnel, including the doctor, for other duties.

Unstorability

As we noted earlier, the unstorability of services creates a potential for waste. Many hotels therefore accept more reservations than they can accommodate on a given night. If some customers fail to keep reservations, the hotel's ability to provide rooms has not been wasted (although it does risk offending customers who must be turned away if everyone shows up). Likewise, airlines overbook flights because they can usually count on no-shows.

Customer Involvement

We have already seen that having customers as part of the process complicates the production of services. But some managers have found a way to turn customer presence into an advantage. They actually get the customer more involved in the process. Direct long-distance dialling, for example, allows the customer to do the work that long-distance operators used to do. Some car washes provide the basic necessary equipment, but require the consumer to actually wash the car.

Shifting some of the productive effort to the customer frees employees for the tasks that require their special abilities. However, some customers reject the idea of doing the work and paying for it, too. Offering financial incentives, such as reduced prices for self-service gasoline or bag-your-own groceries, may solve this problem.

SUMMARY OF LEARNING OBJECTIVES

1. **Explain the meaning of the term *production* or *operations* and describe the four kinds of *utility* it provides.** *Production* (or *operations*) refers to the processes and activities for transforming resources into finished services and goods for customers. Resources include knowledge, physical materials, equipment, and labour that are systematically combined in a production facility to create four kinds of *utility* for customers: *time utility* (which makes products available when customers want them), *place utility* (which makes products available where they are convenient for customers), possession or *ownership utility* (by which customers benefit from possessing and using the product), and *form utility* (which results from the creation of the product).

2. **Describe and explain the three classifications of *operations processes*.** Operations managers in manufacturing use one of two classifications to describe operations processes. Criteria include the *type of technology* used (chemical, fabrication, assembly, transport, or clerical) to transform raw materials into finished goods and whether products are submitted to *analytic or synthetic processes* (that is, whether the process breaks down resources into components or combines raw materials into finished products). Service operations are classified according to the *extent of customer contact*, as either high-contact systems (the customer is part of the system) or low-contact (customers are not in contact while the service is provided).

3. **Identify the characteristics that distinguish *service operations* from *goods production* and explain the main differences in the *service focus*.** Although the creation of both goods and services involves resources, transformations, and finished products, service operations differ from goods manufacturing in several important ways. In service production, the raw materials are not, say, glass or steel, but rather people who choose among sellers because they have unsatisfied needs or possessions that require care or alteration. Therefore, whereas services are typically performed, goods are physically produced. In addition, services are largely *intangible*, more likely than physical goods to be *customized* to meet the purchaser's needs, and more *unstorable* than most products. Service businesses therefore focus explicitly on these characteristics of their products. Because services are intangible, for instance, providers work to ensure that customers receive value in the form of pleasure, satisfaction, or a feeling of safety. Often, they also focus on both the transformation process and the final product (say, making the loan interview a pleasant experience as well as providing the loan itself). Finally, service providers typically focus on the *customer-service link*, often acknowledging the customer as part of the operations process.

4. **Describe the factors involved in *operations planning*.** *Operations planning* involves the analysis of six key factors. *Forecasts* of future demand for both new and existing products provide information for developing

production plans. In *capacity planning*, the firm analyzes how much of a product it must be able to produce. In high-contact services, managers must plan capacity to meet peak demand. Capacity planning for goods means ensuring that manufacturing capacity slightly exceeds the normal demand for its product. *Location planning* for goods and for low-contact services involves analyzing proposed facility sites in terms of proximity to raw materials and markets, availability of labour, and energy and transportation costs. Location planning for high-contact services, in contrast, involves locating the service near customers, who are part of the system. *Layout planning* involves designing a facility so that customer needs are supplied for high-contact services and so as to enhance production efficiency. Layout alternatives include product, process, and cellular configurations. In *quality planning*, systems are developed to ensure that products meet a firm's quality standards. Finally, in *methods planning*, specific production steps and methods for performing them are identified. *Service flow analysis* and *process flow charts* are helpful for identifying all operations activities and eliminating wasteful steps from production.

5. **Explain some of the activities involved in *operations control*, including *materials management* and the use of certain *operation control tools*.** *Operations control* requires production managers to monitor production performance, by comparing results with detailed plans and schedules, and then to take corrective action as needed. *Materials management* is the planning, organizing, and controlling of the flow of materials. It focuses on the control of *transportation* (transporting resources to the manufacturer and products to customers), *warehousing* (storing both incoming raw materials and finished goods), *purchasing* (acquiring the raw materials and services that a manufacturer needs), *supplier selection*, and *inventory control*. To control operations processes, managers use various methods. For example, *worker training* programs can assist in quality control, the management of the operations process so as to ensure that services and goods meet specific quality standards. *Just-in-time (JIT) production systems* bring together all materials and parts needed at each production stage at the precise moment they are required. JIT reduces manufacturing inventory costs and reveals production problems that need improvement. *Material requirements planning (MRP)* is another method for ensuring that the right amounts of materials are delivered to the right place at the right time for manufacturing. It uses computer-controlled schedules for moving inventories through each stage of production.

KEY TERMS

STUDY QUESTIONS AND EXERCISES

Review Questions

1. What are the four different kinds of production-based utility?
2. What are the major differences between goods production operations and service operations?
3. What are the major differences between high-contact and low-contact service systems?
4. What are the six major categories of operations planning?

Analysis Questions

5. What are the resources and finished products in the following services?
   - real estate firm
   - child-care facility
   - bank
   - city water and electric department
   - hotel
6. Analyze the location of a local firm where you do business (perhaps a restaurant, a supermarket, or a manufacturing firm). What problems do you see with this location? What recommendations would you make to management?
7. Find good examples of a synthetic production process and an analytic process. Then classify each according to whether it is chemical, fabrication, assembly, transport, or clerical. Explain your analysis.
8. Develop a service flow analysis for some service that you use frequently, such as buying lunch at a cafeteria, having your hair cut, or riding a bus. Identify areas of potential quality or productivity failures in the process.

Application Exercises

9. Interview the manager of a local service business, such as a laundry or dry-cleaning shop. Identify the major decisions that were involved in planning its service operations. Prepare a class report suggesting areas for improvement.
10. Select a high-contact industry. Write an advertisement seeking workers for this business. Draw up a plan for motivating workers to produce high-quality services for the firm.

Building Your Business Skills

The One-on-One Entrepreneur

Goal

To encourage students to apply the concept of customization to an entrepreneurial idea.

Situation

Imagine that you are an entrepreneur with the desire to start your own service business. You are intrigued by the idea of creating some kind of customized one-on-one service that would appeal to baby boomers, who traditionally have been pampered, and working women, who have little time to get things done.

Method

Step 1:

Get together with three or four other students to brainstorm business ideas that would appeal to harried working people. Among the ideas to consider are the following:

- A concierge service in office buildings that would handle such personal and business services as arranging children's birthday parties and booking guest speakers for business luncheons.
- A personal image consultation service aimed at helping clients improve their appearance, personal etiquette, and presentation style.
- A mobile pet-care network in which veterinarians and personal groomers make house calls.

Step 2:

Choose an idea from these or others you might think of. Then write a memo explaining why you think your idea will succeed. Research may be necessary as you target any of the following:

- A specific demographic group or groups. (Who are your customers and why would they buy your service?)
- The features that make your service attractive to this group.
- The social factors in your local community that would lead to success.

Follow-Up Questions

1. Why is the customization of and easy access to personal services so attractive as we enter the twenty-first century?
2. As services are personalized, do you think quality will become more or less important? Why?
3. Why does the trend towards personalized, one-on-one service present unique opportunities for entrepreneurs?
4. In a personal one-on-one business, how important are the human relations skills of those delivering the service? Can you make an argument that they are more important than the service itself?

Exploring the Net

At a time when rigorous competition has driven some Canadian companies out of the steel-making business, Dofasco has survived. To learn more about production operations, log on to the Dofasco Web site at:

www.dofasco.ca

1. How would you describe Dofasco's operations process? What type of transformation technology does it use?
2. What are the major inputs to the production process? What are its outputs?
3. What are Dofasco's traditional markets? What are some major emerging markets?
4. Using specific information from the Dofasco Web site, what can you conclude about this company's position on environmental issues? Are any environmental considerations evident in the company's production activities?
5. Visit the "Technology" section of the Web site. Summarize how the company is using computer technology to improve operational efficiency.

Concluding Case 11-1

Toyota's Production System: Still the Standard

Why do executives from Ford, Chrysler, and GM want to take plant tours of Toyota manufacturing facilities? To try to figure out how Toyota is able to make cars so efficiently, that's why. Toyota doesn't charge its competitors for these tours, and it doesn't keep anything secret from them. This seems odd; would Coke let Pepsi see its secret formula? But Toyota doesn't seem worried that competitors will see its operations up close, because it knows that those competitors have been trying (unsuccessfully) for years to match its productivity.

The Toyota Production System (TPS) is designed to mobilize all human and capital resources in such a way that peak efficiency, productivity, and quality will be achieved in the assembly of automobiles. Mercedes-Benz may have sophisticated engineering, Honda great engine technology, and Chrysler great styling, but Toyota has the most efficient production system.

The Big 3 domestic automobile manufacturers have all adopted parts of TPS, but none of them has been able to match the efficiency produced by the total TPS system. The system *looks* simple enough: maximize flow, eliminate waste, and respect people. But the implementation requires huge amounts of effort and insight. For example, lots of manufacturing plants have adopted the idea that any worker who sees something wrong can pull a cord and stop the production line. But Toyota is the only company that has actually been able to drive the right philosophies about quality down to the worker level.

A key aspect of TPS is consistent, smooth production. In many manufacturing plants, workers work hard during the first few hours on the job to meet their quota, and then relax later in the day. This leads to uneven production. At Toyota, overproduction at any time is considered bad practice. Work flows are designed to move from process to process with no ups or downs. Another example: In the typical automobile plant, visitors will see stacks of half-finished parts and idle workers standing along assembly lines that are temporarily shut down for one reason or another. But at Toyota plants, workers are constantly in motion and almost look like dancers in a choreographed production.

TPS requires that experienced managers work with a highly motivated and well-trained workforce. The TPS system also involves dependence on outside suppliers who must run their own operations completely in sync with Toyota's. Because Toyota produces just 30 percent of the parts it needs (GM produces almost two-thirds of its own parts), suppliers are an integral part of Toyota's production system and often have an ownership stake in the company.

Toyota is famous for pioneering the just-in-time parts delivery system. Suppliers deliver parts up to eight times daily to Toyota factories, allowing the company to maintain inventory levels that are only one-quarter those at GM. Toyota's suppliers are also physically much closer to Toyota production plants than GM's suppliers are to its plants—an average of 100 kilometres for Toyota versus 700 kilometres for GM.

Suppliers are involved in every aspect of Toyota's production so that they can be an effective part of the team that produces cars. If the supplier has problems, Toyota helps it to improve. Two Toyota engineers once spent seven months at a supplier improving its operations so it could meet Toyota's standards. All this took place while the supplier was under contract to a Toyota competitor.

The TPS system is not restricted to just the production line. It also works in important areas like new product development. With TPS, Toyota can develop a new car model in 18 months, a much shorter time than is typical in this industry. In 1996 and 1997, the company introduced 18 new or redesigned models. It also introduced a new engine—partly battery-powered—that gets 66 miles per gallon. The 120-horsepower engine in the 1998 Corolla uses one-quarter fewer parts than its predecessor, making it lighter, cheaper, and more fuel-efficient.

With all of this good news, are there any problems on the horizon for Toyota? Yes. The company will have to find more foreign markets for its cars because of limited demand within Japan. Unfortunately, Toyota has not been able to completely export its TPS system to its manufacturing facilities outside Japan. Its North American plants, for example, still require 30 to 50 percent more time to build a car than its Japanese plants do. These difficulties have arisen because of a lack of middle managers with TPS experience, and because so much time has to be spent bringing supplies up to Toyota's standards.

CASE QUESTIONS

1. What is *utility*? What are the various kinds of utility? What kind of utility is Toyota providing with its automobiles?

2. What are the different kinds of transformation technologies that are used to turn raw materials into finished goods? Which one(s) does Toyota use? Explain.

3. Explain the just-in-time (JIT) inventory system. How does JIT help Toyota in its pursuit of productivity and quality?

4. Why has Toyota had difficulties exporting its TPS system to its North American production plants? What can it do to overcome these problems? ◆

Concluding Case 11-2

Efficiency and Flexibility at Honda Motors

Honda Motor Co. Ltd. is the ninth-largest automobile manufacturer in the world, producing about 2.5 million vehicles each year. It ranks second in the world in terms of profit generated from each vehicle it produces. The company is betting that new manufacturing technology and smaller, more flexible factories will help it to thrive even though its resources are far smaller than those of its competitors.

Honda Canada's president says that the company must be speedy, efficient, and flexible if it hopes to remain competitive. These three elements are obvious at Honda's twin production facilities in Alliston, Ontario. There, about 4000 workers turn out nearly one-third of Honda's total North American production.

Efficiency at the Alliston plant has been increased with the introduction of a device known as a general welder. Under the old production system, body parts sat on assembly line fixtures called jigs until they were welded together. The jigs held welding guns that performed the 100 to 200 welds that held the car's chassis together. When model changes took place, it took about 15 minutes to switch the jigs. Under the new system, robots weld roofs and body panels to the car's floor in about one minute, and if the plant wants to change over from making, say, Odysseys to making MDXs, it takes only a matter of minutes to make the switch. With that kind of flexibility, Honda is able to react quickly to changes in the market. It can therefore redesign and develop new vehicles when customer needs change.

Honda is building duplicate plants around the world that can make different vehicles using the same "platform"—the frame on which the car sits. Honda doesn't have the resources to build a different platform for each model it produces, so it puts different models on basically the same platform. Honda plans, for example, to make seven new models of the Accord on a single innovative platform. The platform can be shrunk or expanded to accommodate car bodies of varying sizes. The cars will range from a mid-sized North American sedan to a sporty Japanese compact to a narrow European model, a minivan, a sport utility vehicle, and two luxury models. By customizing the Accord, Honda hopes to increase market share worldwide. By 2003, when all Honda plants will be converted, assembly costs will be cut by $1.4 billion.

The newest plant at Alliston is smaller than the first one and this saves Honda money in terms of bricks and mortar. Since 1986, the total investment at the two Alliston plants has been about $1.3 billion; this has yielded production capacity of about 340 000 vehicles per year. In contrast, DaimlerChrysler spent $1.2 billion at its Windsor plant just to prepare to produce 350 000 minivans for the 2001 model year.

CASE QUESTIONS

1. Explain the input-transformation-output process as it relates to the production of automobiles. What role do managers play in this process?

2. What kind of layout is used in the manufacture of automobiles? How have Honda's innovations increased the flexibility of the traditional automobile production line?

3. Would you expect other competitors to try to adapt Honda's new production technology in their own bid to build a global car? Why or why not?

4. What alternative strategies might competitors use instead of customization? What are their advantages and disadvantages?

5. North American automakers have been less successful at cutting costs than either Toyota or Honda. How might Honda promote its efficient cost management as a marketing strategy? Why might such a strategy also be risky? ◆

Visit the *Business* Website at www.pearsoned.ca/griffin for up-to-date e-business cases!

CHAPTER 12

INCREASING PRODUCTIVITY AND QUALITY

Coke's Quality Controls Fizzle

In May 1999, a pub owner near Antwerp, Belgium, reported that several patrons had become ill after drinking bad-smelling Coca-Cola. In early June, children at a school in Bornem, Belgium, also became ill after drinking Coke. In the next few days, additional reports of illnesses caused by Coke began popping up. In early June, the Belgian health minister, who was trying to cope with a scandal over dioxin in the poultry industry, called in Wim Zijerveld, a senior Coke executive, for an explanation of what was going on. In the middle of their meeting, information was received that yet another group of schoolchildren had become ill after drinking Coke. The minister then decided to ban the sale of Coke products made in the Antwerp, Belgium, and Dunkirk, France, production facilities. Coke now had a full-fledged crisis on its hands.

How could this happen to a company that is famous for its quality control? The answer is human error. Lapses in quality control procedures at Coke's bottling plants in Antwerp and Dunkirk allowed contaminated carbon dioxide (the gas that puts the fizz in soft drinks) to get into Coke's products. The carbon dioxide was contaminated with carbonyl sulphide and hydrogen sulphide, both of which are highly toxic. In violation of procedures, employees at the Antwerp plant did not require certificates of analysis from the Swedish supplier of the carbon dioxide gas (these certificates guarantee the purity of the gas). Workers at the Antwerp plant also failed to carry out a routine test for purity after the carbon dioxide was pumped into holding tanks.

Human errors continued as the crisis progressed. When the director of a parochial school called Coke on June 14 to inquire about the safety of its product, he was told that there were no real problems, but that cans with certain codes should be removed from vending machines just to be on the safe side. The school did so, but after the morning break, many children began to report feeling ill after drinking Coke products. Only then did the director of the school learn that the codes he had been given were only a partial list of suspected batches.

Eventually, 14 million cases of Coke products were recalled in five different European countries. There was some dispute about how serious the contamination was, with Coke saying that the amounts were so small that no significant health effects would occur. Indeed, no deaths were reported. But Coke did suffer a major public relations disaster, and profits were reduced by $35 million. Critics observed that a company like Coke, which is so good at marketing and advertising, did a very poor job of communicating to the public about the crisis and how serious it was. Coke has now put in place new quality assurance personnel to ensure that the problem doesn't happen again. ◆

It is no secret that productivity and quality are watchwords in today's business. Companies are not only measuring productivity and insisting on improvements, but also insisting that quality means bringing to market products that satisfy customers, improve sales, and boost profits. By focusing on the learning objectives of this chapter, you will better understand the increasingly important concepts of productivity and quality. After reading this chapter, you should be able to:

1. Describe the connection between *productivity* and *quality*.

2. Understand the importance of increasing productivity.

3. Explain *total* and *partial measures of productivity* and show how they are used to keep track of national, industry-wide, and company-wide productivity.

4. Identify the activities involved in *total quality management* and describe six tools that companies can use to achieve it.

5. Discuss four ways in which companies can compete by improving productivity and quality.

> LEARNING OBJECTIVES

THE PRODUCTIVITY-QUALITY CONNECTION

As we saw in Chapter 1, **productivity** is a measure of economic performance. It measures how much is produced relative to the resources used to produce it. The more we are able to produce the right things while using fewer resources, the more productivity grows and everyone—the economy, businesses, and workers—benefits.

    Productivity considers both the amounts and the quality of what is produced. By using resources more efficiently, the quantity of output will be greater. But unless the resulting goods and services are of satisfactory quality (the "right things"), consumers will not want them. **Quality**, then, means fitness for use—offering features that consumers want.

productivity
A measure of efficiency that compares how much is produced with the resources used to produce it.

quality
A product's fitness for use in terms of offering the features that consumers want.

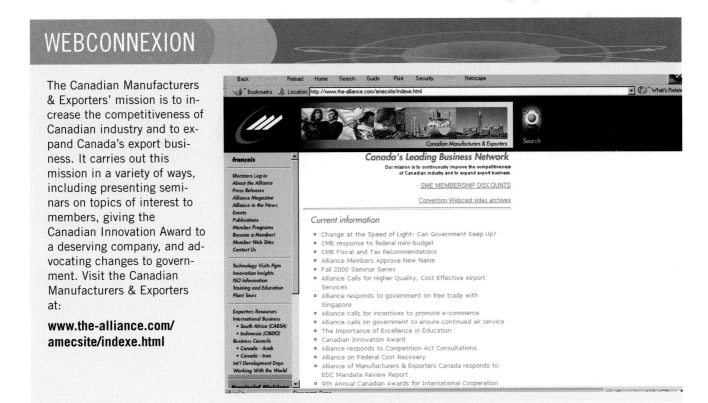

WEBCONNEXION

The Canadian Manufacturers & Exporters' mission is to increase the competitiveness of Canadian industry and to expand Canada's export business. It carries out this mission in a variety of ways, including presenting seminars on topics of interest to members, giving the Canadian Innovation Award to a deserving company, and advocating changes to government. Visit the Canadian Manufacturers & Exporters at:

www.the-alliance.com/ amecsite/indexe.html

The importance of quality in productivity cannot be overstated. Poor quality has created competitive problems for Canadian firms that have focused only on efficiency (quantity). Businesses in other countries have emphasized both efficiency and quality and consequently have increased productivity more rapidly than Canadian companies.

MEETING THE PRODUCTIVITY CHALLENGE

Productivity is an international issue with major domestic effects. A nation's productivity determines how large a piece of the global economic resource pie it gets. A country with more resources has more wealth to divide among its citizens. A country whose productivity fails to increase as rapidly as that of other countries will see its people's standard of living fall relative to the rest of the world.

Productivity among Global Competitors

Figure 12.1 shows productivity comparisons among several Organization for Economic Cooperation and Development (OECD) countries, including the leader, Belgium, whose economic output per hour worked is 28 percent higher than the average output for all OECD countries. Canada's output is 3 percent below the average, while New Zealand's, at 31 percent below the average, is lowest among the nations listed in the figure.

Why are there such differences from nation to nation? The answer lies in many factors: technologies, human skills, economic policies, natural resources, and even traditions. Consider, for example, just one industrial sector—food production. In Japan, the food-production industry employs more workers than the automotive, computer, consumer-electronics, and machine-tool industries combined. It is a fragmented, highly protected industry and an

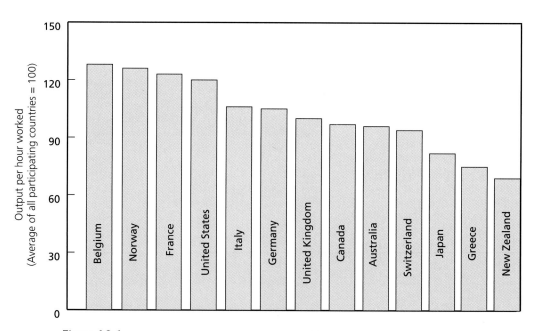

Figure 12.1
Competitive Canadian productivity.

extremely inefficient one. The average U.S. worker, for example, produces 3.5 times as much food as his or her Japanese counterpart. What about overall productivity, with all industries taken together? In the time that it takes a U.S. worker to produce $100 worth of goods, Japanese workers produce about $68 worth. In contrast, Belgian workers produce $107 worth.[1]

According to Michael Porter, a Harvard University expert on international competitiveness, Canada's competitiveness is a concern because we have been living off our rich diet of natural resources. In Porter's view, Canada will have to start emphasizing innovation and develop a more sophisticated mix of products if it hopes to be successful in international markets. Porter criticizes Canadian business, government, and labour for failing to abandon outdated ways of thinking regarding productivity and innovation.[2]

Domestic Productivity

Nations must care about domestic productivity regardless of their global standing. A country that improves its ability to make something out of its existing resources can increase the wealth of all its inhabitants. Conversely, a decline in productivity shrinks a nation's total wealth. Therefore, an increase in one person's wealth comes only at the expense of others with whom he or she shares a social economic system.

For example, additional wealth from higher productivity can be shared among workers (as higher wages), investors (as higher profits), and customers (as stable prices). When productivity drops, however, wages can be increased only by reducing profits (penalizing investors) or by increasing prices (penalizing customers). It is understandable, then, that investors, suppliers, managers, and workers are all concerned about the productivity of specific industries, companies, departments, and even individuals. Accordingly, we next survey recent trends in productivity on various levels: national, industry-wide, company-wide, and departmental and individual.

The United States is the most productive nation in the world. In 1997, for example, the value of goods and services produced by each U.S. worker was US$65 400. This **level of productivity** is higher than that of any other country. In second place, Norwegian workers produced US$62 300 per worker, followed by Swiss workers at US$56 700. Canadian workers produced US$51 100.[3]

level of productivity
The dollar value of goods and services produced versus the dollar value of resources used to produce them.

Productivity Growth Rates

Productivity growth is a key indicator of a country's living standards. In 1999, Canada's productivity rose 1.4 percent over 1998, but productivity in the U.S. increased 3.2 percent in the same period. Generally, output per worker in the U.S. is about one-third higher than output per worker in Canada. In the last two decades, Canada's productivity growth has consistently been lower than that in the U.S., and this has led to a decline in living standards in Canada.

Why has this happened? Some economists think that the low Canadian dollar has reduced the incentive for Canadian manufacturers to increase productivity because they are able to sell their products in the U.S. more cheaply because of the lower value of the Canadian dollar.[4]

Manufacturing versus Service Productivity

Manufacturing productivity is higher than service productivity. Thus, manufacturing is primarily responsible for recent rises in the nation's overall productivity. With services growing as a proportion of Canadian businesses, productivity must increase more rapidly in that sector in the years ahead if Canada is to keep its edge.

Industry Productivity

In addition to differences between the manufacturing and service sectors, industries within these sectors differ vastly in terms of productivity. Agriculture is more productive in Canada than in many other nations because we use more sophisticated technology and superior natural resources. Technological advances have also given the computer industry a productivity edge in many areas. Steel manufacturing, which experienced significant problems in the 1970s and 1980s, has improved recently. For example, in the early 1980s, about 10 hours of labour were required to produce a tonne of steel. Now, only about four hours of labour are needed. One reason for the improvement is a new technology called continuous casting. Today, machines can turn molten metal into slabs that can be processed while still red-hot. It is no longer necessary to cool the steel, strip off the molding, and then reheat it for processing. This new process has meant immense savings in both labour and energy.[5]

In an effort to increase productivity, Canfor Corp. developed a system called Genus, which it is using to manage its forestry operations. Genus, a computerized database containing geographic information and other essential data about Canfor's vast lumber and pulp operations in B.C. and Alberta, will be used as a strategic planning tool to determine how the company should adjust its logging plans to reflect both market demand and logging regulations laid down by B.C.'s *Forest Practices Code*.[6]

The productivity of specific industries concerns many people for different reasons. Labour unions need to take it into account in negotiating contracts, since highly productive industries can give raises more easily than can less productive industries. Investors and suppliers consider industry productivity when making loans, buying securities, and planning their own future production. Areas that have long depended on steel and auto plants have experienced economic and social devastation as a result of plant closings, layoffs, and closings of related businesses.

Canfor Corp.
www.canfor.com

Company Productivity

High productivity gives a company a competitive edge because its costs are lower. As a result, it can offer its product at a lower price (and gain more customers), or it can make a greater profit on each item sold. Increased productivity also allows companies to pay workers higher wages without raising prices.

As a result, the productivity of individual companies is also important to investors, workers, and managers. Comparing the productivity of several companies in the same industry helps investors in buying and selling stocks. Employee profit-sharing plans are often based on the company's productivity improvements each year. And managers use information about productivity trends to plan for new products, factories, and funds to stay competitive in the years ahead.

Department and Individual Productivity

Within companies, managers are concerned with the productivity of various divisions, departments, workstations, and individuals. Improved

productivity in any of these areas can improve a firm's overall productivity. An overemphasis on the performance of individuals and departments, however, tends to discourage working together as a team for overall company improvement. For this reason, many companies are cautious about using departmental and individual productivity measures.

MEASURING PRODUCTIVITY

To improve productivity, we must first be able to measure it. Otherwise, we cannot determine whether a given program has increased productivity. In this section we will describe several standard measures of productivity. Each measure is an equation, or *ratio*, and each compares goods and services produced with the resources required to produce them.

Total and Partial Measures of Productivity

Every productivity measure is a ratio of outputs to inputs. *Outputs* are goods and services produced. *Inputs* are the resources used to create outputs. In selecting a productivity measure, managers must first decide which inputs, or factors, are most important for their businesses. In other words, the choice of inputs determines the specific measure a manager will use.

    In some cases, all inputs are equally important. Managers thus use a **total factor productivity ratio**, which is calculated as follows:

total factor productivity ratio
A measure of a firm's overall productivity calculated as outputs divided by all inputs.

$$\text{Total factor productivity} = \frac{\text{Outputs}}{\substack{\text{Labour} + \text{Capital} + \text{Materials} + \\ \text{Energy inputs} + \text{Purchased business services}}}$$

For example, if an insurance company sold $10 million in policies and used $2 million worth of resources, its total factor productivity would be 5.

    Sometimes a single input resource is so important for production that it deserves special attention and control. For some purposes, therefore, **partial productivity ratios** are used because they are designed to concentrate on just one factor.

    For example, **materials productivity**, although a partial productivity ratio, may be a fairly good measure of overall productivity in non–labour-intensive industries, where materials and equipment, not labour, constitute over 90 percent of operating costs. Material productivity is calculated thus:

partial productivity ratio
A measure of a firm's overall productivity based on the productivity of its most significant input; calculated as total outputs divided by the selected input.

materials productivity
A partial productivity ratio calculated as total outputs divided by materials inputs.

$$\text{Materials productivity} = \frac{\text{Outputs}}{\text{Materials}}$$

For instance, if a chemical plant uses 8 tonnes of chemicals to produce 2 tonnes of insecticide, its materials productivity is 0.25 (2/8).

Measures of Labour Productivity

When we examine productivity on a national or industry-wide level, we see that a major input is labour. We can thus analyze productivity by calculating a ratio designed to determine **labour productivity**. Most countries use partial ratios of labour productivity to measure national productivity. In general, labour productivity is calculated as follows:

labour productivity
A partial productivity ratio calculated as total outputs divided by labour inputs for a company and as gross domestic product divided by the total number of workers for a nation.

$$\text{Labour productivity} = \frac{\text{Outputs}}{\text{Labour}}$$

A country's labour productivity is usually calculated this way:

$$\text{Labour productivity of a country} = \frac{\text{GDP}}{\text{Total number of workers}}$$

In this equation, total number of workers represents the nation's total labour input. (This figure could also be total hours worked.) Recall our definition in Chapter 1 of *gross domestic product* (*GDP*) as the value of all goods and services produced in an economy in a given period of time, *excluding foreign earnings and income*. This figure represents the nation's total output. (In contrast, *gross national product* is the value of all goods and services produced by an economy, including foreign earnings and income.)

Labour productivity measures are popular because they are easy to calculate and compare. Thus, the Canadian government keeps records on gross domestic product. Such figures are typically adjusted to erase the effects of inflation. The resulting data permit reliable year-to-year comparisons of national productivity—changes that, in turn, can be compared with the productivity of other countries. However, as labour-intensive industries become less important in many national economies, other measures, such as materials productivity, energy productivity, and even total factor productivity, are coming into wider use.

Canada has not fared well in either total factor or labour productivity. A 1996 study by the OECD showed that Canada ranked near the bottom of a list of 22 countries in both total factor and labour productivity.[7]

WEBCONNEXION

Siemens Telecom Innovation Centre in Kanata, Ontario, is proactive not only in recruiting highly educated employees but also in providing them with advanced training. As a result, its labour force is highly productive and focused on quality. To find out more about Siemens employees and how they contribute to the company's productivity, visit TIC's "Our People" page at:

www.tic.siemens.ca/20.html

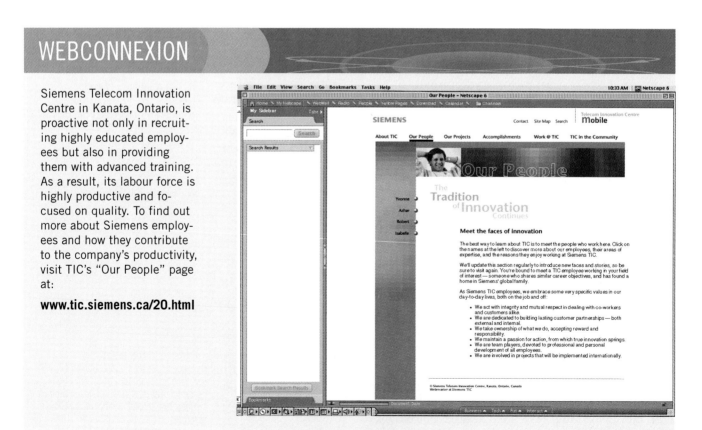

Measures of Company Productivity

Many companies have established productivity measures for individual divisions, plants, departments, and even jobs. Goals for productivity improvement are set in the areas of greatest importance. They serve as guidelines for workplace changes and performance evaluations. For example, an automated, petroleum-fuelled factory may place high priority on energy productivity. Its major goal, therefore, might be to raise the level of its sales per barrel of consumed fuel from $200 to $220. Employees would thus seek ways to conserve fuel while maintaining or increasing production and sales.

By contrast, retailers such as The Bay and Wal-Mart have been successful in using sales per square foot of space and sales per employee as their main productivity measures. Similarly, a labour-intensive restaurant will use the dollar amount of food served per server. If it offers servers incentives to increase sales, they will encourage customers to order tempting (and highly profitable) specialties, drinks, and desserts.

A number of companies use a traditional measure of sales per employee: If the company can boost revenues without a corresponding increase in labour costs, it is more productive. Mentor Graphics Corp., a software tools developer, has increased sales productivity more than 20 percent since adopting new methods that standardize the sales process. At Stryker Osteonics Corp., a surgical instrument manufacturer, sales per employee have more than doubled since the company initiated closer cooperation between sales and production activities.[8]

Ford, Westinghouse, Control Data, and TRW Inc. are among the growing number of companies profiting from the development of major productivity programs. As part of their programs, these companies have established tailor-made productivity measures to reflect their own performances. Measures at TRW, a diversified leader in space, defence, and information technology, provide guidelines for evaluating the productivity of each of the company's inputs (labour, materials, capital, and energy). Using these measures, TRW can identify which resources are being overused and decide how to correct problems to gain higher productivity in each area.

TOTAL QUALITY MANAGEMENT

It is no longer enough for businesses to simply measure productivity in terms of the numbers of items produced. They must also take into account quality. But Canadian business has not always recognized the importance of quality.

In the decades after the Second World War, American business consultant W. Edwards Deming tried to persuade U.S. firms that they needed to improve quality at least as much as quantity. Like many a prophet, he was not honoured in his homeland. But his arguments won over the Japanese. Through years of meticulous hard work, Japan's manufacturers have changed "Made in Japan" from a synonym for cheap, shoddy merchandise into a hallmark of reliability.

Quality advocates such as Joseph Juran and Kaoru Ishikawa introduced methods and tools for implementing quality. Juran's "Quality Trilogy"—quality planning, quality control, and quality improvement—was the first structured process for managing quality. It identifies management steps for ensuring quality. In addition to management actions, Juran, like Deming and Ishikawa, championed the idea of company-wide employee participation. These theorists also developed quality tools for day-to-day work activities because they knew that without employee participation, real quality improvement would never happen. Ishikawa, for example, developed so-called "fishbone diagrams," also known as "cause-and-effect diagrams" or "Ishikawa diagrams," that help teams of employees investigate and track down causes of quality problems in their work areas. The diagram in Figure 12.2, for instance, was designed to help

W. Edwards Deming

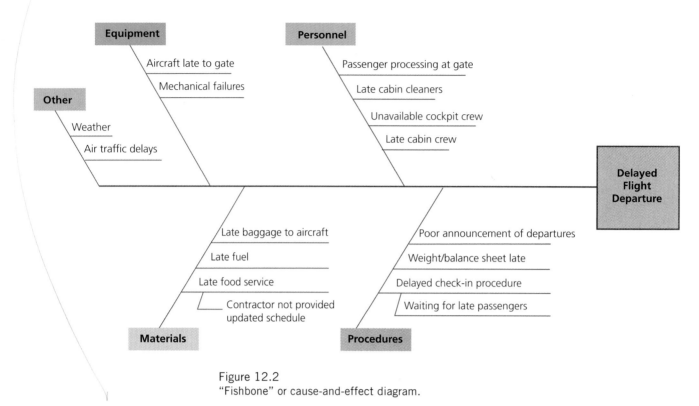

Figure 12.2
"Fishbone" or cause-and-effect diagram.

an airport manager find out why his facility had so many delayed departures. Focusing on five major categories of possible causes, he then noted several potential causes of the problem in each. (It turns out that there weren't enough tow trucks to handle baggage transfers.)[9]

Managing for Quality

total quality management (TQM)

A concept that emphasizes that no defects are tolerable and that all employees are responsible for maintaining quality standards.

Toyota
www.toyota.ca

Total quality management (TQM) (sometimes called *quality assurance*) includes all the activities necessary for getting high-quality goods and services into the marketplace. It must consider all parts of the business, including customers, suppliers, and employees. TQM emphasizes that no defects are tolerable, and that employees are responsible for maintaining quality standards. At Toyota's Cambridge, Ontario, plant, for example, workers can push a button or pull a rope to stop the production line when something is not up to standard.[10]

The strategic approach for TQM in any company begins with leadership and the desire for TQM. This approach involves getting people's attention, getting them to think in an entirely new way about what they do, and then getting them to improve things. Sometimes managers have to confront thoroughly entrenched mindsets before quality orientation can begin. On his first day in office, for example, one new CEO gave a less than subtle hint that a new quality orientation was underway when he took a pile of airsickness bags from his briefcase and placed them at each seat around the conference table. Holding up a bag, he opened the meeting by saying, "The quality of our products makes me want to puke."

Customer focus is the starting point; it includes using methods for determining what customers want, and then causing all the company's activities and people to be directed towards fulfilment of those needs to gain greater customer satisfaction. Total participation, as Deming noted years ago, is mandatory; if all employees are not working towards improved quality, the firm is wasting potential contributions from its human resources, and is missing a chance to become a stronger competitor in the marketplace. TQM in today's competitive markets demands unending and continuous improvement of products, after-sales services, and all of the company's internal processes, such as accounting, delivery, billing, and information flow.

Says John Kay, director of Oxford University's School of Management: "You can't run a successful company if you don't care about customers and employees, or if you are systematically unpleasant to suppliers."[11] To bring the interests of all these stakeholders together, TQM involves planning, organizing, directing, and controlling.

Successful use of TQM requires a high level of commitment from all members of the organization. Consider the case of Standard Aero in Winnipeg, which is in the business of aircraft overhaul. When the company instituted TQM, the process began with the formation of a "change council" consisting of the CEO and five senior managers. This council ensured that the TQM initiative received the money, equipment, and support it needed for success. Next, a nine-person task force was formed that consisted of employees who had done the full range of jobs on one of Standard's major overhaul contracts. Its first job was to find out what the customer wanted. It did this by designing a questionnaire and visiting customer plants around the world to gather information. The task force also worked within Standard Aero to determine exactly how the company did its aircraft overhaul work. After weeks of analysis, the task force was able to significantly reduce the time required for overhaul work. For example, the number of times a certain gearbox was handled as it moved through the repair process was reduced by 84 percent.[12]

Planning for Quality

Planning for quality should begin before products are designed or redesigned. Managers need to set goals for both quality levels and quality reliability in the beginning. **Performance quality** refers to the features of a product and how well it performs. For example, Maytag gets a price premium because its washers and dryers offer a high level of performance quality. Customers perceive Maytags as having more advanced features and being more durable than other brands. (Everyone knows that the Maytag repairman is a lonely and idle person.)

Performance quality may or may not be related to quality reliability in a product. **Quality reliability** refers to the consistency or repeatability of performance. Toyota's small cars may not equal the overall quality level or have the luxury features of Rolls Royce; consequently, Toyota's prices are much lower. But Toyotas have high quality reliability. The firm has a reputation for producing very few "lemons."

Some products offer both high quality reliability and high performance quality. Kellogg has a reputation for consistent production of cereals made of good-quality ingredients. To achieve any form of high quality, however, managers must plan for production processes—equipment, methods, worker skills, and materials—that will result in quality products, as discussed in Chapter 11.

Organizing for Quality

Perhaps most important to the quality concept is the belief that producing quality goods and services requires an effort from all parts of the organization. The old idea of a separate "quality control" department is no longer enough. Everyone from the chairperson of the board to the part-time clerk—purchasers, engineers, janitors, marketers, machinists, and

performance quality
The overall degree of quality; how well the features of a product meet consumers' needs and how well the product performs.

Maytag
www.maytag.com

quality reliability
The consistency of quality from unit to unit of a product.

other personnel—must work to assure quality. In Germany's Messerschmitt-Boelkow-Blohm aerospace company, for example, all employees are responsible for inspecting their own work. The overall goal is to reduce eventual problems to a minimum by making the product correctly from the beginning. The same principle extends to teamwork practice at Heinz Co., where teams of workers are assigned to inspect virtually every activity in the company. Heinz has realized substantial cost savings by eliminating waste and rework.

At Motorola, the concept of teamwork as a key to organizational quality has resulted in an international event called the Total Customer Satisfaction Team Competition. Teams are composed of Motorola employees and also include customers and outside suppliers. Teams are judged on their success not only in promoting productivity but in sharing innovative ideas with people both inside and outside the company.

Although everyone in a company contributes to product quality, responsibility for specific aspects of total quality management is often assigned to specific departments and jobs. In fact, many companies have quality assurance, or quality control, departments staffed by quality experts. These people may be called in to help solve quality-related problems in any of the firm's other departments. They keep other departments informed of the latest developments in equipment and methods for maintaining quality. In addition, they monitor all quality control activities to identify areas for improvement.

Leading for Quality

Too often, firms fail to take the initiative to make quality happen. Leading for quality means that managers must inspire and motivate employees throughout the company to achieve quality goals. They need to help employees see how they affect quality and how quality affects their jobs and their company. Leaders must continually find ways to foster a quality orientation by training employees, encouraging their involvement and tying wages to quality of work. If managers succeed, employees will ultimately accept **quality ownership**—the idea that quality belongs to each person who creates or destroys it while performing a job.

General Electric Co. has recently embarked on a strong quality control initiative. Top management commitment to the program is assured by tying executive bonuses to actual implementation of the quality control program. The program involves training managers to be "Black Belts" in quality improvement. These Black Belts then spend their time in GE plants setting up quality improvement projects. Young managers have been told that they won't have much of a future at GE unless they become Black Belts.

Controlling for Quality

By monitoring its products and services, a company can detect mistakes and make corrections. To do so, however, managers must first establish specific quality standards and measurements. Consider the following control system for a bank's teller services. Observant supervisors periodically evaluate transactions against a checklist. Specific aspects of each teller's work—appearance, courtesy, efficiency, and so on—are recorded. The results, reviewed with employees, either confirm proper performance or indicate changes that are needed to bring performance up to standards.

quality ownership
The concept that quality belongs to each employee who creates or destroys it in producing a good or service; the idea that all workers must take responsibility for producing a quality product.

TOOLS FOR QUALITY ASSURANCE

By monitoring its products and services, a company can detect mistakes and make corrections.

In managing for quality, many leading companies rely on assistance from proven tools. Often, ideas for improving both the product and the production process come from *competitive product analysis*. For example, Toshiba will take apart a Xerox photocopier and test each component. Test results help Toshiba's managers decide which Toshiba product features are satisfactory (in comparison to the competition), which product features need to be upgraded, or whether Toshiba's production processes need improvement.

Methods such as value-added analysis, statistical process control, quality/cost studies, quality circles, benchmarking, getting closer to the customer, ISO 9000, and re-engineering provide different routes to quality. Each of these approaches is discussed briefly below.

Value-Added Analysis

One effective method of improving quality and productivity is **value-added analysis**: the evaluation of all work activities, material flows, and paperwork to determine the value that they add for customers. Value-added analysis often reveals wasteful or unnecessary activities that can be eliminated without harming (and even improving) customer service. When Hewlett-Packard, for example, simplified its contracts and reduced them from 20 pages to as few as 2 pages for all customers, computer sales rose by more than 18 percent.

value-added analysis
The evaluation of all work activities, material flows, and paperwork to determine the value they add for customers.

Statistical Process Control

Every business experiences unit-to-unit variations in its products and services. Although every company would like complete uniformity in its outputs, this is an impossible quest. Companies can gain better control, however, by understanding the sources of variation. **Statistical process control (SPC)** methods—especially process variation studies and control charts—allow managers to analyze variations in production data.

statistical process control (SPC)
Statistical analysis techniques that allow managers to analyze variations in production data and to detect when adjustments are needed to create products with high quality reliability.

Process Variation

Variations in a firm's products may arise from the inputs in its production process. As people, materials, work methods, and equipment change, so do production outputs. While some amount of **process variation** is acceptable, too much can result in poor quality and excessive operating costs.

Consider the box-filling operation for Honey Nuggets cereal. Each automated machine fills two 400-gram boxes per second. Even under proper conditions, slight variations in cereal weight from box to box are normal. Equipment and tools wear out, the cereal may be overly moist, machinists make occasional adjustments. But how much variation is occurring? How much is acceptable?

process variation
Any change in employees, materials, work methods, or equipment that affects output quality.

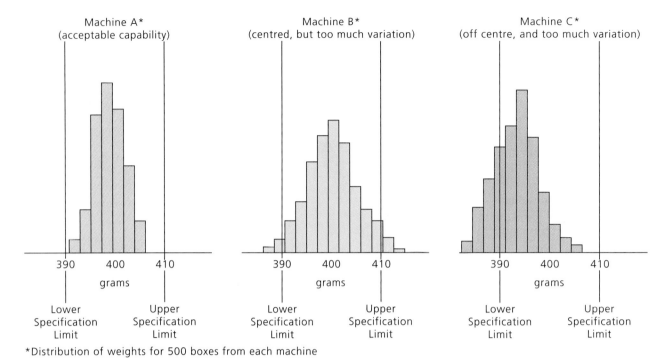

*Distribution of weights for 500 boxes from each machine

Figure 12.3
Process variation in box filling for Honey Nuggets cereal.

process capability study

A statistical process control method in which samples of the product are measured to determine the amount of process variation; shows the outputs' conformity with or deviation from specification limits.

specification limits

Limits defining acceptable and unacceptable quality in production of a good or service.

Information about variation in a process can be obtained from a **process capability study**. Boxes are taken from the filling machines and weighed. The results are plotted, as in Figure 12.3, and compared with the upper and lower **specification limits** (quality limits) for weight. These limits define good and bad quality for box filling. Boxes with more than 410 grams are a wasteful "giveaway." Underfilling has a cost because it is unlawful.

Looking at the results of the capability study, we see that none of machine A's output violates the quality limits. In fact, most of the boxes from machine A are very close to the desired weight of 400 grams. The shape of machine A's graph, high at the centre and dropping sharply at the margins, is typical of many production processes. Machine A, then, is fully capable of meeting the company's quality standards.

But machines B and C have problems. In their present condition, they are "not capable." They cannot reliably meet Honey Nuggets' quality standards. The company must take special—and costly—actions to sort the good from the bad boxes before releasing the cereal for shipment. Unless machines B and C are renovated, substandard production quality will plague Honey Nuggets.

Control Charts

control chart

A statistical process control method in which results of test sampling of a product are plotted on a diagram that reveals when the process is beginning to depart from normal operating conditions.

control limit

The critical value on a control chart that indicates the level at which quality deviation is sufficiently unacceptable to merit investigation.

Knowing that a process is capable of meeting quality standards is not enough. Managers must still monitor the process to prevent its drifting astray during production. To detect the beginning of bad conditions, managers can check production periodically and plot the results on a **control chart**. For example, several times a day a machine operator at Honey Nuggets might weigh several boxes of cereal together to ascertain the average weight.

Figure 12.4 shows the control chart for machine A, in which the first five points are randomly scattered around the centre line, indicating that the machine was operating well. However, the points for samples 5 through 8 are all above the centre line, indicating that something was causing the boxes to overfill. The last point falls outside the upper **control limit**, confirming that the process is out of control.

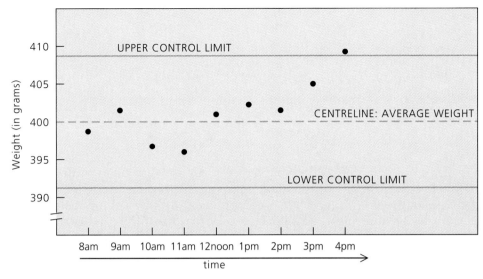

Figure 12.4
Honey Nuggets cereal process control chart for machine A.

At this point, the machine must be shut down so that a manager and/or the operator can investigate what is causing the problem—equipment, people, materials, or work methods. Control is completed by correcting the problem and restoring the process to normal.

Quality/Cost Studies for Quality Improvement

Statistical process controls help keep operations up to existing capabilities. But in today's competitive environment, firms must consistently raise quality capabilities. Any improvement in products or production processes means additional costs, however, whether for new facilities, equipment, training, or other changes. Managers thus face the challenge of identifying those improvements that offer the greatest promise. **Quality/cost studies** are useful because they not only identify a firm's current costs but also reveal areas with the largest cost-savings potential.

Quality costs are associated with making, finding, repairing, or preventing defective goods and services. All of these costs should be analyzed in a quality/cost study. For example, Honey Nuggets must determine its costs for **internal failures**. These are expenses—including the costs of overfilling boxes and the costs of sorting out bad boxes—incurred during production and before bad products leave the plant. Studies indicate that many manufacturers incur very high costs for internal failures—up to 50 percent of total costs.

Despite quality control procedures, however, some bad boxes may get out of the factory, reach the customer, and generate complaints from grocers and cereal eaters. These are **external failures** that occur outside the factory. The costs of correcting them—refunds to customers, transportation costs to return bad boxes to the factory, possible lawsuits, factory recalls—should also be tabulated in the quality/cost study.

The percentage of costs in the different categories varies widely from company to company. Thus every firm must conduct systematic quality/cost studies to identify the most costly—and often the most vital—areas of its operations. Not surprisingly, these areas should be targets for improvement. Too often, however, firms substitute hunches and guesswork for data and analysis.

quality/cost study
A method of improving product quality by assessing a firm's current quality-related costs and identifying areas with the greatest cost-saving potential.

internal failures
Expenses incurred during production and before bad product leaves the plant.

external failures
Allowing defective products to leave the factory and get into consumers' hands.

Quality Circles

One proven technique for improving quality is the use of **quality circles**, groups of employees who work in teams to improve their job environment. Meeting on company time in the facility, quality circles are a forum for quality improvement. Although the format varies in different companies, quality circle members are deeply involved in initiating changes in their work environment.

Quality circles organize their own efforts, choose a leader, and establish rules for discussion. Within the group, members identify aspects of their jobs that pose problems or are barriers to better quality and overall productivity. They gather data to evaluate the severity of problems and to identify improvement projects. The group's problem solving emphasizes brainstorming, group discussions, and tools such as process capability studies and cost analysis. Ultimately, the quality circle makes recommendations to management, identifying expected benefits, costs, and implementation timetables.

Perhaps the greatest benefit of quality circles, however, is not any direct cost savings, but their effect on employees' attitudes. Rather than viewing themselves as passive resources for production, employees develop a sense of self-worth and quality ownership. The talents and job knowledge of circle members are put to active, constructive use instead of lying dormant.

Benchmarking

A powerful TQM tool that has been effective for some firms is called **benchmarking**. To improve its own products or its business procedures, a company compares its current performance against its own past performance, or one company finds and implements the best practices of others. With *internal benchmarking*, a firm tracks its own performance over time to evaluate its progress and to set goals for further improvement. As an example, the percentage of customer phone calls with more than two minutes of response time may be 15 percent this month. Compared with past months, this percentage may be high or low. In short, past performance is the benchmark for evaluating recent results.

External benchmarking begins with a critical review of competitors (or even companies in other lines of business) to determine which goods or services perform the best; these activities and products are called *best practices*. For example, Toronto Hospital gathered performance data on 26 indicators from various Canadian hospitals so it could determine how well it was performing compared to other organizations in the health care industry.[13] Executives from Ford, DaimlerChrysler, and General Motors frequently tour Toyota manufacturing facilities as they try to figure out how Toyota makes cars so efficiently.

Getting Closer to the Customer

As one advocate of quality improvement has put it, "Customers are an economic asset. They're not on the balance sheet, but they should be." One of the themes of this chapter has been that struggling companies have often lost sight of customers as the driving force for all business activity. Perhaps they waste resources designing products that customers do not want. Sometimes they ignore customer reactions to existing products or fail to keep up with changing consumer tastes. By contrast, the most successful businesses keep close to their customers and know what they want in the products they consume.

At Greyhound Lines of Canada, the marketing and operations vice-president wanted to drive home the point to managers that clean restrooms are important to customers. He warned regional managers that he would

Greyhound
www.greyhound.ca

visit bus depots on one-hour's notice to see if the restrooms were clean enough to eat dinner in. Within weeks, photos of regional managers having dinner in spotless restrooms began pouring in to the vice-president's office.[14]

MBNA, a credit-card company, has learned that speed of service is vital for serving 4300 groups with custom Visas and MasterCards. These premium customers want good service, and they want it now. MBNA was one of the first in the industry to make service representatives available 24 hours per day. Furthermore, MBNA continually monitors its own performance using 15 measures, many of them relating to speed of service. The phone must be picked up within two rings, incoming calls at the switchboard must be transferred within 21 seconds to the correct party, and customer address changes must be processed in one day. The company-wide goal on the 15 standards is 98.5 percent. That means, for example, that responses to credit-line inquiries will be answered in 30 minutes 98.5 percent of the time, and the phone will be answered within two rings 98.5 percent of the time. Results are posted daily on 60 scoreboards throughout the company. By placing the customer at the head of its organizational culture, MBNA is able to retain a remarkable 98 percent of its profitable customers, and its common stock price has increased 600 percent in five years.

ISO 9000

Consider the following case in quality control diagnosis and correction. DuPont Co. had a problem: A molding press used to make plastic connectors for computers had a 30 percent defect rate. Efforts to solve the problem went nowhere until, as part of a plant-wide quality program, press operators were asked to submit detailed written reports describing how they did their jobs. After comparing notes, operators realized that they were incorrectly measuring the temperature of the molding press; as a result, temperature adjustments were often wrong. With the mystery solved, the defect rate dropped to 8 percent.

The quality program that led to this solution is called *ISO 9000*—a certification program attesting to the fact that a factory, a laboratory, or an office has met the rigorous quality management requirements set by the International Organization for Standardization. ISO 9000 (pronounced *ICE-o nine thousand*) originated in Europe as an attempt to standardize materials received from suppliers in such high-tech industries as electronics, chemicals, and aviation. Today, more than 90 countries have adopted ISO 9000 as a national standard, and 128 000 certificates have been issued in 99 countries. Companies that are certified are, in turn, requiring certification from their own suppliers, including employment agencies.

ISO 9000 standards allow firms to demonstrate that they follow documented procedures for testing products, training workers, keeping records, and fixing product defects. To become certified, companies must document the procedures that workers follow during every stage of production. The purpose of ISO 9000 is to ensure that a manufacturer's product is exactly the same today as it was yesterday and as it will be tomorrow. The goal of standardization is to guarantee that goods will be produced at the same level of quality even if all the employees are replaced by a new set of workers.

Companies seeking ISO 9000 certification are audited by an elite group of quality system registrars. Not surprisingly, the certification process is time consuming and costly; it can take up to 18 months for a manufacturing plant employing 300 workers and can cost up to $200 000. More than 600 Canadian firms have been certified. After Toronto Plastics was awarded the designation, its defect rate dropped from 15 percent to 1.5 percent.[15] More information is contained in the "Business Today" box.

ISO 9000: Seeking the Standard in Quality

ISO 9000 standards enable firms to demonstrate that they follow documented procedures for testing products, training workers, keeping records, and fixing product defects. To become certified, companies must document the procedures that workers follow during every stage of production. They must also show that they have incorporated mechanisms to ensure that workers actually follow accepted practices. Not surprisingly, this approach leads to more reliable products with fewer defects. The purpose of ISO 9000 is "to ensure that a manufacturer's product is exactly the same today as it was yesterday, as it will be tomorrow." The goal of standardization is to guarantee that "goods will be produced at the same level of quality even if all the employees were replaced by a new set of workers."

Companies seeking ISO 9000 certification are audited by an elite group of quality-systems "registrars."

These registrars focus on 20 different functions including design control, contract review, purchasing, inspection and testing, and training. For example, to pass order-processing requirements, a company must demonstrate procedures for guaranteeing on-time deliveries.

Despite the interest in ISO 9000, however, it is not a cure-all for quality ailments. On the contrary, certification standards have little to do with customer satisfaction. Instead of imposing guarantee procedures, they focus on documenting a company's commitment to its own procedures. "With ISO 9000 you can still have terrible processes and products," complains Richard Buetow, director of corporate quality at Motorola. "You can certify a manufacturer that makes life jackets from concrete," says Buetow, "as long as those jackets are made according to the documented procedures and the company provides the next of kin with instructions on how to complain about defects. That's absurd."

Re-engineering

re-engineering

The process of rethinking and redesigning business processes to achieve dramatic improvements in productivity and quality.

Re-engineering is the process of rethinking and redesigning business processes to achieve dramatic improvements in productivity and quality. In effect, those engaged in re-engineering ask, "If this were a new company, how would we run it?" The bottom line in every re-engineering process is redesigning systems to better serve the needs of customers.

Figure 12.5 shows the six steps involved in the re-engineering process. The process starts with a statement justifying the proposed re-engineering based on benefits envisioned for customers and the company. The company's vision statement is a key resource for step 1; it provides guidance, as does management's awareness of the competition's capabilities. The process then flows logically through these five steps:

1. Identify the business activity that will be changed.

2. Evaluate information and human resources to see if they can meet the requirements for change.

3. Diagnose the current process to identify its strengths and weaknesses.

4. Create the new process design.

5. Implement the new design.

Key resources in each step are essential for performing the activities required by that stage. As you can see, re-engineering is a broad undertaking that requires know-how in technical matters, depends on leadership and management skills, and must be based on knowledge about what customers want and how well their needs are being met by the company and its competition.

The bottom line in every re-engineering process is redesigning systems to serve the needs of customers better and to adopt a customer-first value

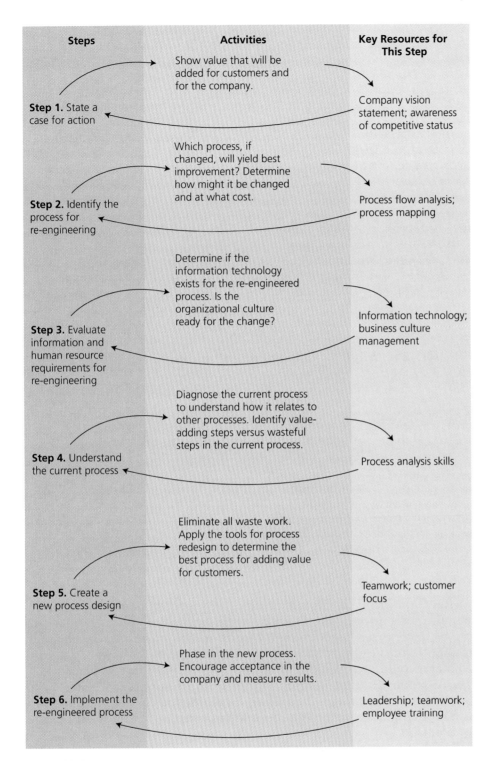

Steps	Activities	Key Resources for This Step

Step 1. State a case for action — Show value that will be added for customers and for the company. — Company vision statement; awareness of competitive status

Step 2. Identify the process for re-engineering — Which process, if changed, will yield best improvement? Determine how might it be changed and at what cost. — Process flow analysis; process mapping

Step 3. Evaluate information and human resource requirements for re-engineering — Determine if the information technology exists for the re-engineered process. Is the organizational culture ready for the change? — Information technology; business culture management

Step 4. Understand the current process — Diagnose the current process to understand how it relates to other processes. Identify value-adding steps versus wasteful steps in the current process. — Process analysis skills

Step 5. Create a new process design — Eliminate all waste work. Apply the tools for process redesign to determine the best process for adding value for customers. — Teamwork; customer focus

Step 6. Implement the re-engineered process — Phase in the new process. Encourage acceptance in the company and measure results. — Leadership; teamwork; employee training

Figure 12.5
Re-engineering process.

system throughout the company. Redesign is dominated by a desire to improve operations so that goods and services are produced at the lowest possible cost and at the highest value for the customer. As the "It's a Wired World" box shows, a company may have difficulty convincing employees to work in ways that give the highest value to the customer.

IT'S A WIRED WORLD

Selling the Idea of Culture Shift

When a firm decides to trade in its traditional operations for high-tech processes, there's more involved than just financial and technical considerations. Consider, for example, a company with successful sales procedures established long before today's electronic-sales processes were available. What problems does it face in moving from its established (and highly personalized) sales process into the realm of Internet sales?

That's the issue at Mercury Marine, the market leader in recreational boat engines. With various choices of engine types, horsepower ratings, and "salt water" versus "blue water" options, Mercury sells about 400 different outboard engines and enjoys a substantial market share in both the Canadian and the U.S. markets. Sales are even better for inboard engines and stern drives, where Mercury's market share is over 70 percent. Needless to say, Mercury's $1.4 billion annual sales are vital to its parent company, Brunswick Corp.

Mercury's markets consist of two kinds of customers:

1. Outboard motors are sold mainly to distributors and boat dealers, who resell them.
2. Inboard engines and stern drives are sold to boat builders.

In addition to its current person-to-person selling process, Mercury wants to sell motors to outboard dealers and boat builders over the Internet. In other words, Mercury wants to use technology as a competitive weapon by making it easier for customers to do business with Mercury. Internet access can increase sales productivity and promote better service quality for customers. So what's the problem? Resistance from the sales department. With person-to-person sales, Mercury's salespeople get to know the customers, and *up-selling* and *cross-selling* are important sales tools that would be threatened by the changeover. Currently, salespeople can explain to customers the advantages of upgrading to a more expensive motor (up-selling), thus increasing Mercury's sales revenues. They can also talk customers into buying some of Mercury's complementary products (cross-selling), such as propellers, inflatable boats, and other accessories, which increases sales revenues. Admits Geof Storm, Mercury's chief information officer: "There are a lot of culture changes involved when tightening the supply chain." Although the sales department still prefers the more personal touch, some of its resistance is being overcome—Mercury has decided to proceed with Internet sales of inboard engines to boat builders. However, until the climate changes further, the decision to sell outboards on the Internet is likely to remain on hold.

Mercury Marine
www.mercurymarine.com

Re-engineering has also taken place at Novacor Chemicals in Sarnia. When the company acquired four different businesses, each with its own style, technology, and processes, it had to rethink how it produced about 2 million tonnes of petrochemicals each year. In the process, it discovered that it could save millions of dollars by having the four businesses operate in a coordinated fashion rather than as separate entities. For example, when plants were shut down for maintenance, each one hired its own maintenance teams. Now, one team is hired and rotated among the four plants.[16]

PRODUCTIVITY AND QUALITY AS COMPETITIVE TOOLS

A company's ability to compete by improving productivity and quality depends on participation by all parts of the firm. And total firm involvement stems from having company-wide strategies that we consider in this section: the company's willingness to invest in innovation, its long-run perspective on its goals, its concern for the quality of work life, and the improving of its service operations.

Invest in Innovation and Technology

Many firms that have continued to invest in innovative technology have enjoyed rising productivity and rising incomes. For example, while Steinway & Sons' piano factory is just as concerned as ever about maintaining the highest quality in its products, it's using newer technology to help the woodworkers do their jobs more efficiently and precisely. "It still takes us a year to craft one of these things," says Steinway president Bruce Stevens, "but technology is assisting us in making more precise parts that our people can assemble. It's helping us create a better instrument."[17]

Adopt a Long-Run Perspective

Part of the decline in innovation among Canadian firms reflects a common short-run perspective. Shareholders prefer short- and intermediate-term (less than five years), "sure thing" paybacks. Many companies reward managers with salaries and bonuses based on their quarterly or yearly performance. With owners and managers unwilling to wait for financial returns, many buildings, tools, and equipment have become old or obsolete. Canada is still a creative hothouse, but many businesses are shying away from long-term risks and are failing to convert their good new ideas into actual products.

By contrast, instead of emphasizing short-run results, many quality-oriented firms are committed to a long-run perspective for **continuous improvement**—the ongoing commitment to improving products and processes, step by step, in pursuit of ever-increasing customer satisfaction. Motorola is a good example of a company that emphasizes continuous, long-run improvement. Its Six Sigma program called for the unheard-of target of having only three defects per million parts; for all practical purposes this would be zero defects. In 1981, Motorola started by adopting a five-year goal of a 90 percent reduction of errors. In 1986, it extended that goal to a 99 percent reduction of errors by 1992. In only five years, the defect rate dropped from 6000 defects per million to just 40. When, by 1996, Six Sigma quality had been achieved, Motorola began planning for errors per *billion* rather than errors per million quality levels. As of 1999, the company had reduced errors to an unimaginable two defects per billion parts.[18]

continuous improvement
The ongoing commitment to improve products and processes, step by step, in pursuit of ever-increasing customer satisfaction.

Motorola
www.motorola.com

Operators at Dofasco monitor the production of steel products with the latest in high-tech monitoring devices.

Emphasize Quality of Work Life

The products and services of businesses represent such a large part of total national output that the well-being and participation of their workers is central to improving national productivity. How can firms make their employees' jobs more challenging and interesting? Many companies are enhancing workers' physical and mental health through recreational facilities, counselling services, and other programs. In addition, more and more firms have started programs to empower and train employees.

Employee Empowerment

Many firms are replacing the environments of yesterday, based on the principle of management-directed mass production, with worker-oriented environments that foster loyalty, teamwork, and commitment. Trident Precision Manufacturing has a program for full employee involvement. Over 95 percent of employee recommendations for process improvements have been accepted since the program started. As a result, employee turnover has fallen from 41 percent to less than 5 percent. Sales per employee have more than doubled.

Firms using this approach have found success in the concept of *employee empowerment*—the principle that all employees are valuable contributors to a business and should be entrusted with certain decisions regarding their work. The Hampton Inns motel chain, for example, initiated a program of refunds to customers who were dissatisfied with their stays for any reason. Managers were pleased, and the refund policy created far more additional business than it cost. A surprise bonus was the increased morale when employees—everyone from front-desk personnel to maids—were empowered to grant refunds. With greater participation and job satisfaction, employee turnover was reduced to less than one-half its previous level. Such confidence in employee involvement contrasts sharply with the traditional belief that managers are the primary source of decision making and problem solving.

Employee Training

For employee involvement to be effective, it must be implemented with preparation and intelligence. Training is one of the proven methods for avoiding judgments and actions that can lead to impaired performance. In a recent survey, for example, insufficient training was the most common barrier reported by work teams. The study reconfirms the belief that training is a key to implementing a successful quality management program. At Heath Tecna Aerospace Co., for example, team members are taught how to work in groups, as well as trained in job skills, work flow planning, and basic knowledge about the company's markets and operations. With increased training and experience, the rate of material waste has diminished and product quality has increased.

Improve the Service Sector

As important as employee attitudes are to goods production, they are even more crucial to service production, since employees often *are* the service. The service sector has grown rapidly but this growth has often come at a cost of high inefficiency. Many newly created service jobs have not been streamlined. Some companies operate effectively, but many others are very inefficient, dragging down overall productivity. As new companies enter these markets, however, the increased need to compete should eventually force service producers to operate more productively.

Quality begins with listening to customers to determine what services they want. Companies in the temporary-services industry, for example, have long emphasized the needs of clients for clerical and light-industrial employees. More recently, however, temp services have realized the need for highly skilled, specialized temps such as nurses, accountants, and scientists.

In trying to offer more satisfactory services, many providers have discovered five criteria that customers use to judge service quality:[19]

- *Reliability*: Perform the service as promised, both accurately and on time.

- *Responsiveness*: Be willing to help customers promptly.

- *Assurance*: Maintain knowledgeable and courteous employees who will earn the trust and confidence of customers.

- *Empathy*: Provide caring, individualized attention to customers.

- *Tangibles*: Maintain a pleasing appearance of personnel, materials, and facilities.

SUMMARY OF LEARNING OBJECTIVES

1. **Describe the connection between *productivity* and *quality*.** *Productivity* is a measure of economic performance; it compares how much is produced with the resources used to produce it. *Quality* is a product's fitness for use. However, an emphasis solely on productivity or solely on quality is not enough. Profitable competition in today's business world demands high levels of both productivity and quality.

2. **Understand the importance of increasing productivity.** During the 1980s, the growth rate of Canadian productivity slowed down. In recent years, Canada's growth rate of productivity has lagged behind that of countries like Japan, South Korea, and France. It is important that Canadian business firms increase their rate of productivity growth so that they can be competitive in world markets. As the productivity of Canadian business firms increases, they will be able to produce a greater quantity of goods without using more resources.

3. **Explain *total* and *partial measures of productivity* and show how they are used to keep track of national, industry-wide, and company-wide productivity.** Productivity measures are ratios of *outputs* (goods and services produced) and *inputs* (the resources needed to produce outputs). *Total factor productivity* includes all types of input resources: materials, labour, capital, energy, and purchased business services. In contrast, *partial productivity measures* focus on certain key input factors while ignoring others. Thus *materials productivity* focuses on the productivity of materials and is especially important in non–labour-intensive industries. *Labour productivity*, the most common national productivity measure, focuses on labour as an input. *Capital productivity* focuses on money and investment as input factors.

4. **Identify the activities involved in *total quality management* and describe six tools that companies can use to achieve it.** *Total quality management (TQM)* is the planning, organizing, leading, and controlling of all the activities needed to get high-quality goods and services into the marketplace. Managers must set goals for and implement the processes needed to achieve high quality and reliability levels. *Value-added analysis* evaluates all work activities, materials flows, and paperwork to determine what value

they add for customers. *Statistical process control methods*, such as *process variation studies* and *control charts*, can help keep quality consistently high. *Quality/cost studies*, which identify potential savings, can help firms improve quality. *Quality improvement teams* also can improve operations by more fully involving employees in decision making. *Benchmarking*—studying the firm's own performance and the best practices of other companies to gather information for improving a company's own goods and services—has become an increasingly common TQM tool. *Getting closer to the customer* provides a better understanding of what customers want so that firms can satisfy them more effectively. *ISO 9000* is a certification program attesting to the fact that a factory, a laboratory, or an office has met the rigorous quality management requirements set by the International Organization for Standardization. Finally, *re-engineering* is the process of rethinking and redesigning business processes to achieve improvements in productivity.

5. **Discuss four ways in which companies can compete by improving productivity and quality.** To increase quality and productivity, business must invest in innovation and technology, adopt a long-run strategy for continuous improvement, place greater emphasis on the quality of work life for employees, and improve the service sector.

KEY TERMS

productivity, 353
quality, 353
level of productivity, 355
total factor productivity
    ratio, 357
partial productivity
    ratio, 357
materials productivity,
    357

labour productivity, 357
total quality
    management (TQM),
    360
performance quality, 361
quality reliability, 361
quality ownership, 362
value-added analysis,
    363

statistical process
    control (SPC), 363
process variation, 363
process capability study,
    364
specification limits, 364
control chart, 364
control limit, 364

quality/cost study, 365
internal failures, 365
external failures, 365
quality circle, 366
benchmarking, 366
re-engineering, 368
continuous
    improvement, 371

STUDY QUESTIONS AND EXERCISES

Review Questions

1. What is the relationship between productivity and quality?
2. Why do labour unions care about the productivity of an industry?
3. How do total factor productivity ratios differ from partial factor ratios?
4. What activities are involved in total quality management?
5. What are the essential steps in process engineering?

Analysis Questions

6. How would you suggest that benchmarking be used to increase productivity in the service sector?
7. Why is employee empowerment essential to successful quality improvement teams?

8. Why is high productivity in the service sector so difficult to achieve?

Application Exercises

9. Using a local company as an example, show how you would conduct a quality/cost study. Identify the cost categories and give some examples of the costs in each category. Which categories do you expect to have the highest and lowest costs? Why?
10. Select a company of interest to you and consider the suggestions for competing that are detailed in this chapter. Which of these suggestions apply to this company? What additional suggestions would you make to help this company improve its overall quality and productivity?

Building Your Business Skills

Making Your Benchmark in the Business World

Goal

To encourage students to understand ways in which benchmarking can improve quality and productivity.

Situation

As the director of maintenance for a regional airline, you are disturbed to learn that the cost of maintaining your 20-plane fleet is skyrocketing. A major factor is repair time; when maintenance or repairs are required, work often proceeds slowly. As a result, additional aircraft are required to meet the schedule. To address the problem, you decide to use a powerful total quality management tool called benchmarking. You will approach your problem by studying ways in which other companies have successfully managed similar problems. Your goal is to apply the best practices to your own maintenance and repair operation.

Method

Step 1:
Working with three or four other students, choose your benchmarking target from among the following choices:

- The maintenance and repair operations of a competing airline
- The pit crew operations of a race car team
- The maintenance and repair operations of a national trucking company

Write a memo explaining the reasons for your choice.

Step 2:
Write a list of benchmarking questions that will help you learn the best practices of your targeted company. Your goal is to ask questions that will help you improve your own operation. These questions will be asked during on-site visits.

Step 3:
As part of a benchmarking project, you will be dealing with your counterparts in other companies. You have a responsibility to prepare for these encounters, and you must remember that what you learn during the exchange process is privileged information. Given these requirements, describe the steps you would take before your first on-site visit and outline your benchmarking code of ethics.

Follow-Up Questions

1. Why is benchmarking an important method for improving quality?

2. Why did you make your benchmarking choice? Explain why the company you selected holds more promise than other companies in helping you solve your internal maintenance problems.

3. What kind of information would help you improve the efficiency of your operations? Are you interested in management information, technical information, or both?

4. In an age of heightened competition, why do you think companies are willing to benchmark with each other?

Exploring the Net

The Productivity Improvement Centre trains and consults with organizations to help them achieve quality and productivity goals. Visit their Web site at:

http://www.pic-northamerica.com

1. Survey the "Supplier Quality Resources" section. What aspects of the quality control procedure surprised you? Do you find this program comprehensive?

2. Read the "Quality Assurance Related Subjects." Compare your perspective on quality control before and after having read these.

3. Based on what you have seen at this Web site, why is it important for companies to meet certain quality control standards?

Concluding Case 12-1

Harley-Davidson

Harley-Davidson represents a true riches-to-rags/back-to-riches story. Harley-Davidson motorcycles enjoyed decades of distinguished history as police bikes and dispatch vehicles during both world wars. (Of course, they also became notorious as the vehicles of choice for motorcycle "clubs" such as the Hell's Angels.) At one time, Harley's competition included more than 140 companies. But when the Indian Motorcycle Co. of Springfield, Massachusetts, went out of business in 1953, Harley emerged the sole surviving American motorcycle manufacturer. Then, during the 1960s, as Honda and other aggressive Japanese competitors began exporting high-quality, low-priced motorcycles to Canada and the United States, Harley itself teetered on the brink of extinction.

In 1969, Harley-Davidson was acquired by American Machine and Foundry Inc. (AMF), a recreational equipment conglomerate. AMF's strategy called for capitalizing on the explosion in market demand caused by Japan's successful marketing efforts. The new parent firm countered the competition by increasing production from 15 000 units to 52 000 units per year. The plan failed. Among other consequences of stepped-up quantity, Harley's once-touted quality began to plummet. About half of the motorcycles coming off the assembly line were actually missing parts, but problems with a new model, the Cafe Racer, best typified Harley's production woes: the first 100 Cafe Racers to roll off the assembly line required a total of $100 000 in rework before they could be shipped to dealers. Not surprisingly, Harley found itself at a distinct disadvantage in its road wars with the Japanese.

In 1981, Vaughn Beals, AMF's Harley division manager, led a successful management bid to buy the company back from AMF. Beals was determined to revamp Harley's image and marketing strategy. More importantly, he was determined to improve reliability and quality—above even Harley's original standards. Even classic Harleys, for example, were legendary for leaking oil, and Harley had become the butt of such insider jokes as "What do hound dogs and Harleys have in common? They both like to ride in the back of a truck."

Beals understood, first of all, that many potential buyers lacked the backyard-mechanic skills traditionally needed to keep Harleys on the road. He thus instituted a number of internal changes. For example, quality circles and an employee-involvement program were established to improve product quality through employee input. A new inventory system called Materials as Needed (MAN) was instituted to reduce inventory costs, shorten manufacturing setup times, and contribute overall quality improvement. A third change involved training employees in problem solving and statistical methods for detecting defects on the assembly line.

Taken together, these steps soon produced significant results: a 36 percent reduction in warranty costs, a 46 percent increase in defect-free motorcycles delivered to dealers, and a 50 percent increase in employee productivity. CEO Richard Teerlink says that the turnaround resulted from a combination of improvements in operations and human resources: "If we can get people to focus on doing the right things and then doing the things right," he says, "we will be in good shape on the productivity issue." On the human resource front, Teerlink has recently turned his attention to Harley's organization chart. For instance, two executive positions—senior vice-presidents in marketing and operations—have been eliminated because "they didn't add value to our products. The people were auditors," explains Teerlink. "They were checkers. People would go up to one boss and that boss would go to another boss and he would go to still another boss. And we wondered why the Japanese beat us on the issue of time." Now Harley employees are organized in teams: a team to create demand, a production team, and a product-support team.

By improving quality and productivity, Harley-Davidson has become profitable once again. Its share of the super-heavyweight market, for example, has jumped to 64 percent from a low of 28 percent in 1985. Moreover, Harley not only has reclaimed its market position but also has experienced significant export growth. It seems that the cornerstones of Harley's image—ruggedness and high quality—have great global appeal. In England, dealers put potential buyers on a six-month waiting list, and Harley is the best-selling import in Japan. The new Harley, however, carefully limits production increases to maintain Harley's hard-won reputation for quality—and, of course, to keep the product supply limited in relation to demand. Production is currently running at merely 350 units per day because, as one Harley executive puts it, "Enough motorcycles is too many motorcycles."

CASE QUESTIONS

1. Identify some of the productivity and quality issues described in this case.

2. What role has employee empowerment played in Harley's comeback?

3. What specific tools of total quality management are integral to the quality/productivity effort at Harley?

4. Do you agree with Harley's strategy of intentionally limiting the supply of motorcycles it produces? ◆

Harley-Davidson
www.harley-davidson.com

Concluding Case 12-2

Where the Rubber Hits the Road

In the summer of 2000, Bridgestone/Firestone Inc. announced that it was recalling 6.5 million Wilderness AT and Firestone ATX tires. Most of these had been installed as original equipment on Ford Explorer SUVs. Hints that there were problems with Firestone tires began cropping up in the early 1990s. There was often a pattern: the tread of a rear tire on a heavily loaded Explorer travelling at high speed separated, and the vehicle swerved out of control and flipped over. These reports generally came from warmer parts of the U.S. (California, Arizona, Texas, and Florida), and from Venezuela and the Persian Gulf. The investigation revealed that about 100 people had been killed in these kinds of accidents in the U.S., and about 50 people had been killed overseas.

Transport Canada launched a probe to determine if there were similar problems in Canada, but no hard evidence of tire defects was found, even though as many as 500 000 of these tires are on vehicles in Canada. One million Firestone tires were eventually recalled in Canada.

Both Ford and Firestone tested the suspect tires, but no particular problems were found. In public, the two companies portrayed themselves as working together to solve the mystery, but there was tension behind the scenes. Ford noted that it didn't have any problem with blown tires or rollovers with any of its vehicles except Explorers, and those vehicles had the suspect Firestone tires on them. Firestone, on the other hand, accused Ford of contributing to the problem by recommending tire pressures of only 26 pounds when Firestone recommended 30 pounds of pressure. (Lower tire pressure improves the ride of a vehicle, but underinflation leads to heat build-up and an increased chance of tire failure.) Firestone also claimed that Ford had made design changes in the Explorer that increased the chance that rear tires would fail. Firestone noted that the suspect tires were on other types of vehicles and that the tires on those vehicles had not failed.

What was the problem? Experts thought there were several possibilities: (1) the quality of the material that was used to make the glue that holds the tire's steel belts together wasn't up to standard; (2) the raw materials that were used to make the glue weren't sufficiently well mixed; (3) the steel wires that form the belts may have rusted due to high humidity during manufacturing; (4) the tire wasn't properly cured (vulcanized); (5) too much adhesive was used to bond the steel belts to the rubber, and this actually made the treads more likely to separate.

After a four-month investigation, Bridgestone/Firestone finally concluded that there were quality problems at its plant in Decatur, Illinois. Apparently, that plant did not properly process the rubber that was used to make the tires. However, Firestone also put some of the blame on the Ford Explorer, arguing that higher load limits and lower inflation pressures were part of the problem.

Firestone spent $450 million recalling the problem tires. In the aftermath of the crisis, Firestone's sales plummeted 40 percent, and its stock lost half its value. What is Bridgestone/Firestone doing now to recover its public image? Several steps have been taken:

A new senior vice-president was appointed and given a mandate to impose strict production standards and fix operating problems at the company's U.S. unit.

Since Firestone expects to lose all of its business at Ford (about $350 million annually), it wants to start rebuilding the market share it has lost. It may abandon the original equipment market and focus instead on the retail tire replacement market. It will also launch a racing-oriented image campaign with race-car drivers serving as spokesmen for the company.

A new method of examining product performance data will be introduced to address the criticism that the company was unaware it had quality problems with its tires.

U.S. factories will be brought more into line with the higher standards of Bridgestone's Japanese operation. Quality assurance controls will be introduced that will make it easier for information about tire failures to be shared throughout the company.

CASE QUESTIONS

1. What is total quality management? To what extent was total quality management pursued at Bridgestone/Firestone? At Ford?

2. What are the various tools for quality assurance that are available? Which ones are appropriate for helping to resolve this problem?

3. The plant where the faulty tires were made was ISO-certified. How could problems like these arise at such a plant?

4. How is quality a competitive tool?

5. Can Firestone gets its quality image back? How? ◆

Visit the *Business* Website at www.pearsoned.ca/griffin
for up-to-date e-business cases!

High-Tech Information Processing

Playdium Entertainment Corp. opened a 33 000-square-foot game park in Mississauga, Ontario, in 1996. The park has every kind of simulated sport imaginable, including hang gliding, car racing, and mogul skiing. It also features an outdoor go-cart track and an IMAX Ridefilm with hydraulic motion simulators. As you might expect, Playdium is a hot spot for the 18 to 35 age group. But the game park has captured the interest of everyone from adolescents to accountants, and it is very popular with business groups.

A group of 69 sales staff from Ralston Purina Canada is typical of the business groups that visit Playdium. For the Ralston Purina staff, it's the first night of a three-day software training session, and the group is out on the town to have some fun and learn something about high-tech equipment. The company is introducing some new technology of its own, and wants the sales staff to have some face-to-face time with simulation games to ease their concerns about working with such equipment in their jobs. The Ralston Purina manager, who has accompanied the group, says that technology might seem scary at first but after you become familiar with it, it becomes fun. Business groups account for 40 percent of Playdium's annual revenues.

There is also an important behind-the-scenes development at Playdium—a sophisticated management information system. To entice business groups and other adults to come and play video games, Playdium had to create an environment that was radically different from the one commonly associated with arcades—which is teenage boys with dirty coins in their pocket. So Playdium devised an internal debit card system. Customers pay a flat fee at the door and in return they receive a Playcard. These Playcards are inserted into whatever game the patron wants to play, and they are "reloaded" when necessary by purchasing more time.

Every game is wired into a central computer that files vast amounts of detailed information each time a customer inserts a Playcard into a game. This has allowed Playdium to develop an elaborate demographic profile on the more than 150 000 people who have become "virtual citizens" by joining the Playdium membership club. Playdium knows which customers are playing what games at what times of the day, how often they play, and how much they spend.

This information helps Playdium with its marketing strategy. For example, the information systems shows that fighting games are most interesting to 15- and 16-year-old males, while the IMAX Ridefilm has a much broader demographic interest. Since the lighting, laser, and sound technology at Playdium can be changed to create different atmospheres, a "nightclub" atmosphere can be created on Friday nights, and a "family atmosphere" can be created on Saturday mornings.

Playdium has built new game parks in Burnaby, B.C., Edmonton, and downtown Toronto. There is a continuing emphasis on corporate clients. The new four-storey, 54 000-square-foot Playdium in Toronto has meeting rooms with more versatility than the Mississauga location. Playdium staff are trained to work with corporate clients to design events to suit specific purposes like team building, product launches, or entertaining clients. ◆

Playdium Entertainment Corp.
www.playdium.com

In today's complex business environment, the need to manage information efficiently and quickly is crucial. Information can take many forms: information about customers' locations and order patterns, information about supplies and finished goods on hand, information about workers' pay and productivity, information about products in development, and information about competitors and customers.[1]

By focusing on the learning objectives of this chapter, you will better understand why the list is so long—and getting longer all the time. You will also appreciate the role of the computer at the forefront of contemporary information management. After reading this chapter, you should be able to:

1. Explain why businesses must manage *information* and show how computer systems and communication technologies have revolutionized *information management*.

2. Identify and briefly describe three elements of *data communication networks*—the Internet, the World Wide Web, and intranets.

3. Describe five *new options for organizational design* that have emerged from the rapid growth of information technologies.

4. Discuss different information-systems *applications* that are available for users at various organizational levels.

5. Identify and briefly describe the *main elements of an information system*.

INFORMATION MANAGEMENT: AN OVERVIEW

Today's businesses rely on information management in ways that we could not foresee as recently as just a decade ago. Managers now turn to digital technology as an integral part of organizational resources and as a means of conducting everyday business. Every major firm's business activities—designing services, ensuring product delivery and cash flow, evaluating personnel, creating advertising—are linked to information systems. Thus the management of information systems is a core business activity that can no longer be delegated to technical personnel.

In addition, most businesses regard their information as a private resource—an asset that they plan, develop, and protect. It is not surprising, then, that companies have **information managers**, just as they have production, marketing, and finance managers. **Information management** is an internal operation that arranges the firm's information resources to support business performance and outcomes.

To find the information they need to make critical decisions, managers must often sift through a virtual avalanche of reports, memos, magazines, and phone calls. Thus the question that faces so many businesses today is how to get useful information to the right people at the right time. In this section, we will explore the ways in which companies manage information with computers and related information technologies. First, however, in order to understand information management, you must understand what information is and what it is not. Only then can you appreciate what computers do and how they do it.

Data versus Information

Although business people often complain that they receive too much information, they usually mean that they get too much data. **Data** are raw facts and figures. **Information** is based on data, but it is a meaningful, useful interpretation of that data (see Figure 13.1).

information manager
The manager responsible for the activities needed to generate, analyze, and disseminate information that a company needs to make good decisions.

information management
An internal operation that arranges the firm's information resources to support business performance and outcomes.

data
Raw facts and figures.

information
A meaningful, useful interpretation of data.

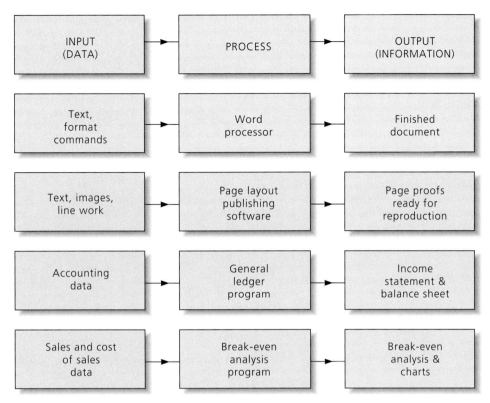

Figure 13.1
From data to information and knowledge.

Consider the following data: 50 million tubes of toothpaste were sold last year; the birth rate is rising; 35 million tubes of toothpaste were sold the year before last; advertising for toothpaste increased 57 percent; a major dentists' group recently came out in favour of brushing three times a day. If all these data can be put together in a meaningful way, they may produce information about what sells toothpaste and whether manufacturers should build new plants. The challenge for businesses is to turn a flood of data into information and to manage that information to their best advantage.

Information Systems

One response to this challenge has been the growth of **information systems (IS)** designed to transform data into information that can be used for decision making. Those charged with the company's IS services must determine what information will be needed, then gather the data and provide ways to convert them into the desired information. They must also control the flow of information so that only those who need or are entitled to certain information receive it. Information supplied to employees and managers varies, depending on the functional area in which they work (such as accounting or marketing) and on their level in management.

First-line managers need information for the day-to-day operations of the business. Middle managers need summaries and analyses to help them set intermediate- and long-range goals and to plan strategies for reaching these goals. Top management needs even more sophisticated analyses to meet its responsibilities for long-range and corporate planning.

Consider the needs of various managers of a flooring manufacturer. Sales managers (first-line managers) supervise salespeople, assign territories to the sales force, and handle customer-service and delivery problems. To

information systems (IS)
An organized method of transforming data into information that can be used for decision making.

do their job well, they need current and accurate information on the sales and delivery of flooring products to customers in their branches. Regional managers (middle managers) set sales quotas for each sales manager, prepare budgets, and plan staffing needs for the next year. They need total monthly sales by product and by branch, as opposed to an itemized sales report. Finally, top management will need sales data summarized by product, customer type, and geographic region, and analyzed in comparison to previous years' and competitors' sales. Environmental (external) information such as consumer behaviour patterns, the competition's record, and related economic forecasts are as important as internal operations information.

Figure 13.2 illustrates the need for information at the different levels of management. As you can see, information is increasingly condensed and summarized as it moves up through the management hierarchy.

National Sales Manager
(top management)

Consumer preference trends

Federal regulations

Competitor product development

Internal sales summary
by product and by the region

Regional Sales Manager
(middle management)

Monthly sales summary by product and by branch
Competitor's sales by product line in each district

Branch Sales Manager
(first-line management)

Daily sales and deliveries per salesperson
Weekly sales for branch and for competition

Figure 13.2
Different information needs at various managerial levels.

Information systems are becoming increasingly important as managers try to cope with the flood of data they are confronted with.

NEW BUSINESS TECHNOLOGIES IN THE INFORMATION AGE

Employees at every level in the organization, ranging from operational specialists to the top executive, use information systems to improve performance. Information systems assist in scheduling day-to-day vehicle trips, evaluating prospective employees, and formulating the firm's business strategy. The widening role of IS results from rapid developments in electronic technologies that allow faster and broader flows of information and communications. As we shall see, however, the networked enterprise is more than a firm equipped with the latest technology. Technology has inspired new organizational designs, innovative relationships with other organizations, and new management processes for improved competitiveness.

The top 10 information technology companies in Canada are listed in Table 13.1, and the "It's a Wired World" box describes the merger of two technology companies.

The Expanding Scope of Information Systems

The relationship between information systems and organizations is among the fastest-changing aspects of business today. At one time, IS applications were narrow in scope and technically focused—processing payroll data, simulating new engineering designs, compiling advertising expenditures. But as you can see in Figure 13.3, managers soon began using IS systems not merely to solve technical problems, but to analyze management problems, especially for control purposes—applying quality-control standards to production, comparing costs against budgeted amounts, keeping records on employee absences and turnover.

Today, information systems are also crucial in planning. Managers routinely use IS to decide on a firm's products and markets for the next 5 to 10 years. The same database that helps marketing analyze demographics for millions of customers is also used for such higher-level applications as financial planning, managing materials flows, and setting up electronic funds transfers with suppliers and customers around the globe.

Table 13.1	The Top 10 Information Technology Companies (ranked by revenues)
Company	**Annual Revenues (in billions)**
1. Hewlett-Packard Canada Ltd.	$1.9
2. Compaq Canada	1.8
3. CGI Group Inc.	1.4
4. DMR Consulting Group Inc.	1.3
5. EDS Systemhouse Inc.	1.3
6. Geac Computer Corp. Ltd.	0.7
7. Cognos Inc.	0.5
8. Corel Corp.	0.3
9. Oracle Corp. Canada Inc.	0.3
10. McDonald, Dettwiler and Associates Ltd.	0.2

IT'S A WIRED WORLD

"These Two Companies Are a Natural Fit"

Even a high-tech giant cannot be an expert in every new development in the digital world. Consider, for example, America Online (including its CompuServ service)—the United States' largest online Internet service provider (ISP), with 22 million subscribers. AOL's customers have Internet access through traditional phone lines, but AOL is thinking about ways to give them even faster Internet service by means of high-speed cable lines. Traditional phone lines are slower than cables in connecting to the Internet. They're also slower in downloading information and slower in reading graphics files.

Not surprisingly, AOL already knows that if it's going to remain competitive, it will need to offer customers faster Internet connections. On one level, the problem is fairly simple: How do you get from phone lines to cables? One approach—replacing all of those phone lines with cables—is more than prohibitively expensive: it simply can't be done. Because AOL doesn't own the lines it uses (the phone company does), it can't replace them. A more feasible approach involves cable service providers. They already have the capability, but they haven't yet exploited their cable technology in the Internet market.

Now consider the situation at Time Warner Inc.—a cable service provider that also happens to be the world's top media and entertainment company. Time Warner wants to harness the power of the Internet, which it sees as the future avenue for distributing its entertainment products. Unfortunately, Time Warner cannot deliver magazines such as *Time*, *People*, and *Sports Illustrated* online without Internet technology. Nor can Time Warner deliver movies and music for downloading. Time Warner's problem, then, is how to become digital when it isn't skilled at the technology. Ultimately, doing things internally turned out to be too costly: When Time Warner tried to reinvent its own Internet capabilities, it spent US$500 million (in 1999 alone) in a less-than-successful effort to rework its online approach.

In early 2000, AOL and Time Warner announced a permanent partnering conceived to give each company a much needed lift in overcoming their respective problems. Internet giant AOL is joining with media behemoth Time Warner in a corporate merger valued at US$166 billion—the largest ever. The new firm, AOL Time Warner Inc., gains the advantages of each partner's technological expertise and resources. AOL, of course, has Internet expertise. It also has 22 million customers who can purchase and download Time Warner's entertainment products from the Internet. Meanwhile, Time Warner brings not only 13 million cable TV subscribers to the merger, but also expertise in the high-speed cable lines that AOL needs for faster Internet services. This large base of cable-ready households will be a big boost for AOL because only 6 percent of Web users currently have the high-speed (cable-modem) access that can be up to 100 times faster than modems on traditional phone lines. Thus two giants, each wanting to grow but hindered by technology shortcomings, believe that, as one firm, they'll grow much faster than either could have grown alone. "These two companies," says Time Warner chairman Gerald Levin, "are a natural fit."

Another basic change in organizations is an increased interdependence between a company's business strategy and its IS. Today, the choice of a business strategy—say, to be the low-cost provider or the most flexible provider or the high-quality provider—requires an information system that can support that strategy. As Figure 13.4 shows, a given strategy will fail if a system's software, hardware, and other components are not integrated to support it.

Scope of IS Application

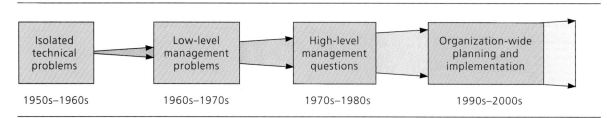

Figure 13.3
The evolution of IS.

Organizational System **Information System**

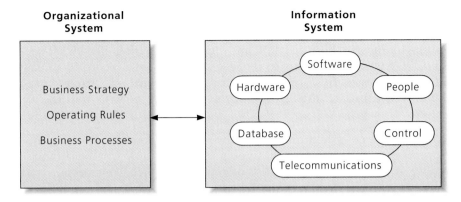

Figure 13.4
Aligning strategy with the IS.

Consider, for example, a strategy that calls for the rapid receipt of customer orders and fast order fulfilment. Unless the systems' components are specifically designed to handle these tasks, the best-laid plans are probably doomed to failure.

Electronic Business and Communications Technologies

The pressures to maintain better communications and information systems are increasing as competition intensifies and as organizations expand into global and e-business operations. Firms like Ralston Purina Co., for instance, need instantaneous communications among managers in those countries in which they either sell products or buy raw materials, including Canada, China, Columbia, Brazil, and the U.S. The needs of such companies are being met by new electronic information technologies and more advanced data communication networks.

Ralston Purina Co.
www.ralston.com

Electronic Information Technologies

Electronic information technologies (EIT) are IS applications based on telecommunications technologies. EITs use networks of appliances or devices (such as cellphones and computers) to communicate information by electronic means. EITs enhance the performance and productivity of general business activities by performing two functions:

electronic information technologies (EIT)

IS applications based on telecommunications technologies.

1. Providing coordination and communication within the firm, and

2. Speeding up transactions with other firms.

In this section, we will survey six of the most widely used innovations in today's digital business systems: *fax machines, voice mail, e-mail, electronic conferencing, groupware,* and *digital information services.*

Fax Machines. The **fax machine** (short for *facsimile machine*) can transmit and receive digitized images of text documents, drawings, and photographs over telephone lines in a matter of seconds, thus permitting written communication over long distances. Fax machines are popular with both large and small firms because of speed and low cost.

fax machine

A machine that can quickly transmit a copy of documents or graphics over telephone lines.

Voice Mail. **Voice mail** refers to a computer-based system for receiving and delivering incoming telephone calls. Incoming calls are never missed because a voice responds to the caller, invites a message, and stores it for later retrieval. A company with voice mail networks each employee's phone for receiving, storing, and forwarding calls.

voice mail

A computer-based system for receiving and delivering incoming telephone calls.

Voice mail software links the communication device (telephone) with a computer. The input from the telephone is sent to the computer, which uses software to digitize the voice data and stores it on a disk. The employee can then call the voice mail centre to retrieve from storage a recording of waiting calls and messages. By combining technologies, voice mail can receive and store an incoming fax message until the recipient requests that the fax be printed.

electronic mail (e-mail) system
Electronic transmission of letters, reports, and other information between computers.

E-Mail. An **electronic mail** (or **e-mail**) **system** electronically transmits letters, reports, and other information between computers, whether in the same building or in another country. It is also used for voice transmission and for sending graphics and videos from one computer to another. E-mail thus substitutes for the flood of paper and telephone calls that threatens to engulf many offices.

electronic conferencing
Allows people to communicate simultaneously from different locations via telephone, video, or mail group software.

Electronic Conferencing. **Electronic conferencing** is becoming increasingly popular because it eliminates travel and thus saves money. It is also increasingly accessible and speeds up information flows. Teleconferencing allows people to communicate simultaneously from various locations via e-mail group software or via telephone. One form of electronic conferencing, *dataconferencing*, allows people in remote locations to work simultaneously on the same document. Working as a team, they can modify part of a database, revise a marketing plan, or draft a press release. Another form of electronic conferencing, *videoconferencing*, allows participants to see one another on a video screen while the teleconference is in progress.

groupware
A system that allows two or more individuals to communicate electronically between desktop PCs.

Groupware. Collaborative work by teams and other groups is facilitated by **groupware**: software that connects members of the group for e-mail distribution, electronic meetings, message storing, appointments and schedules, and group writing. Linked by groupware, members can work together on their own desktop computers even if they are remotely located. Groupware is especially useful when members work together regularly and rely on intensive information sharing. Groupware products include Lotus Development Corp.'s Lotus Notes, Netscape Communicator, and Microsoft's Office 2000 software suite, which uses Web technology.

Digital Information Services. Information from outside a company can be linked to its electronic network and the information can be made available at every workstation. Commercial electronic information services provide online information for both special-purpose and general topics. Lexis, for example, is specifically a source for legal-research information. In contrast, America Online offers a variety of business information as well as general-interest information.

Data Communication Networks

data communication networks
Global networks that permit users to send electronic messages quickly and economically.

Popular on both home and business information systems are public and private **data communication networks**: global networks that carry streams of digital data (electronic messages, documents, and other forms of video and sound) back and forth quickly and economically on telecommunication systems. The most prominent network, the Internet, and its companion system, the World Wide Web, have emerged as powerful communication technologies. Let's look a little more closely at each of these networks.

Internet
A gigantic network of networks that serves millions of computers, offers information on business, science, and government, and provides communication flows among more than 170 000 separate networks around the world.

The Internet. The **Internet**—the largest public data communications network—is a gigantic network of networks that serves millions of computers, offers information on business, science, and government, and provides communication flows among more than 170 000 separate networks around the world. Originally commissioned by the U.S. military as a communication tool for use during war, the Internet allows personal computers in virtually any location to be linked together. The Internet has gained in popularity because it is an efficient tool for information retrieval that makes available an immense wealth of academic, technical, and business information. Because it can transmit information quickly and at low cost—lower than long-distance phone service, postal delivery, and overnight delivery—the Internet has also become the most important e-mail system in the world. For thousands of businesses, therefore, the Internet has joined—and is even replacing—the telephone, fax machine, and express mail as a standard means of communication.

Although individuals cannot connect directly to the Internet, for small monthly usage fees they can subscribe to the Internet via an **Internet service provider (ISP)**, such as Prodigy, America Online, or Earthlink. An ISP is a commercial firm that maintains a permanent connection to the Internet and sells temporary connections to subscribers.[2]

The Internet's popularity continues to grow for both business and personal applications. In 2000, more than 302 million Internet users were active on links connecting more than 180 countries. Its power to change the way business is conducted has been amply demonstrated in both large and small firms.

The World Wide Web. Thanks to the **World Wide Web** (or simply "the Web"), the Internet is easy to use and allows users around the world to communicate electronically with little effort. The World Wide Web is a system with universally accepted standards for storing, retrieving, formatting, and displaying information.[3] It provides the "common language" that enables us to "surf" the Internet and makes the Internet available to a general audience, rather than merely to technical users such as computer programmers. To access a Web site, for example, the user must specify the *Uniform Resource Locator (URL)* that points to the resource's unique address on the Web. For example, Air Canada's URL is www.aircanada.ca—a designation that specifies the storage location of Air Canada's Web pages.

Internet service provider (ISP)
A commercial firm that maintains a permanent connection to the Internet and sells temporary connections to subscribers.

World Wide Web
A system with universally accepted standards for storing, retrieving, formatting, and displaying information on the Internet.

WEBCONNEXION

The name pretty much tells the story: CandyCommerce.com is the B2B marketplace of the confection industry. Among other pages, the Web site includes an "Auction House" at which sellers can list products for sale and a "Product Showcase" that allows members to shop the organization's listing of online confectionery-supplier catalogues. You can visit the National Confectioners Association Web site at:

www.candycommerce.com

Each Web site opens with a *home page*—a screen display that welcomes the visitor with a greeting that may include graphics, sound, and visual enhancements introducing the user to the site. Additional *pages* provide details on the sponsor's products and explain how to contact help in using the site. Often, sites furnish URLs for related Web sites that the user can link to by simply pointing and clicking. The person responsible for maintaining an organization's Web site is usually called a *Webmaster*. Large Web sites use dedicated work stations—large computers—known as **Web servers** that are customized for managing, maintaining, and supporting Web sites.

With hundreds of thousands of new Web pages appearing each day, cyberspace is now serving up billions of pages of publicly accessible information. Sorting through this maze would be frustrating and inefficient without access to a Web **browser**—software that enables the user to access information on the Web. A browser runs on the user's PC and supports the graphics and linking capabilities needed to navigate the Web. Netscape Navigator has enjoyed as much as an 80 percent market share, although its dominance is now being challenged by other browsers, including its own Netscape Communicator and Microsoft's Internet Explorer.

The Web browser offers additional tools—Web site directories and search engines—for navigating the Web. Among the most successful cyberspace enterprises are companies such as Yahoo! that maintain free-to-use **directories** of Web content. When Yahoo! is notified about new Web sites, it classifies them in its directory. The user enters one or two key words (for example, "compact disc") and the directory responds by retrieving a list of Web sites with titles containing those words.

In contrast to a directory, a **search engine** will search cyberspace's millions of Web pages without pre-classifying them into a directory. It searches for Web pages that contain the same words as the user's search terms. Then it displays addresses for those that come closest to matching, those that are the next closest, and so on. A search engine, such as AltaVista or Lycos, may respond to more than 10 million inquiries per day. It is thus no surprise that both directories and search engines are packed with paid ads. At the beginning of 1999, Yahoo! was the leader in *portal sites*—sites used by Net surfers as primary home pages—although Lycos was closing fast in the race for most users.[4]

Intranets. The success of the Internet has led some companies to extend its technology internally, so that employees can browse internal Web sites containing information. These private networks, or **intranets**, are accessible only to employees via entry through electronic firewalls. **Firewalls** are hardware and software security systems that are not accessible to outsiders.[5] Compaq Computer Corp.'s intranet allows employees to shuffle their retirement savings among various investment funds. Ford Motor Co.'s intranet connects 120 000 workstations in Asia, Europe, and the U.S. to thousands of Ford Web sites containing private information on Ford activities in production, engineering, distribution, and marketing. Sharing such information has helped reduce the lead time for getting new models into production from 36 to 24 months. Ford's latest project in improving customer service through internal information sharing is called *manufacturing on demand*. Now, for example, the Mustang that required 50 days' delivery time in 1996 is available in less than two weeks. The savings to Ford, of course, will be billions of dollars in inventory and fixed costs.[6]

Extranets. Sometimes firms allow outsiders access to their intranets. These so-called **extranets** allow outsiders limited access to a firm's internal information system. The most common application allows buyers to enter the seller's system to see which products are available for sale and delivery, thus providing product-availability information quickly to outside buyers. Industrial suppliers, too, are often linked to their customers' intranets so that they can see planned production schedules and ready supplies as needed for customers' upcoming operations.

Web servers
Dedicated work stations—large computers—that are customized for managing, maintaining, and supporting Web sites.

browser
Software that enables a user to access information on the Web.

directories
Features that help people find the content they want on the Web. The user types in key words and the directory retrieves a list of Web sites with titles containing those words.

search engine
Software for searching Web pages that does not pre-classify them into a directory.

intranet
A company's private network that is accessible only to employees via entry through electronic firewalls.

firewall
Hardware and software security systems that are not accessible to outsiders.

extranet
A network that allows outsiders limited access to a firm's internal information system.

New Options for Organizational Design: The Networked Enterprise

The rapid growth of information technologies has changed the very structure of business organizations. We begin this section with a discussion of changes wrought by technology in the workforce and organizational structures of many organizations. We then examine ways in which electronic networks are contributing to greater flexibility in dealing with customers. After discussing the growing importance of collaboration in the workplace, we look at the ways in which information networks can help make the workplace independent of a company's physical location. Finally, we describe new management processes inspired by the availability of electronic networks.

Leaner Organizations

Information networks are leading to leaner companies with fewer employees and simpler organizational structures. Because today's networked firm can maintain information linkages among both employees and customers, more work can be accomplished with fewer people. As a bank customer, for example, you can dial into a 24-hour information system and find out your current balance from a digital voice. You no longer need bank tellers or phone operators. In the industrial sector, assembly workers at an IBM plant used to receive instructions from supervisors or special staff. Now instructions are delivered electronically to their workstations.

Widespread reductions in middle-management positions and the shrinkage of layers in organizational structure are possible because information networks now provide direct communications between the top managers and workers at lower levels. The operating managers who formerly communicated company policies, procedures, or work instructions to lower-level employees are being replaced by electronic information networks.

More Flexible Operations

Electronic networks allow businesses to offer customers greater variety and faster delivery cycles. Custom-tailored rehabilitation programs designed with integrated information systems, for example, expedite recovery after heart surgery. Each personalized program integrates the patient's history with information from physicians and rehabilitation specialists and then matches the patient with an electronically monitored exercise regimen. Products such as cellular phones, PCs, and audio systems can be custom-ordered, too, with your choice of features and options and next-day delivery. The principle is called **mass-customization**: although companies produce in large volumes, each unit features the unique variations and options that the customer prefers. As you can see in Figure 13.5, flexible production and fast delivery depend on an integrated network to coordinate all the transactions, activities, and process flows necessary to make quick adjustments in the production process. The ability to organize and store massive volumes of information is crucial, as are the electronic linkages between customers, manufacturers, materials suppliers, and shippers.

mass-customization

Producing large volumes of products or services, but giving customers the choice of features and options they want.

Increased Collaboration

Collaboration, not only among internal units but with outside firms as well, is on the rise because networked systems make it cheaper and easier to contact everyone, whether other employees or outside organizations. Aided by intranets, more companies are learning that complex problems can be solved better by means of collaboration, either in formal teams or through spontaneous interaction. In the new networked organization, decisions that were

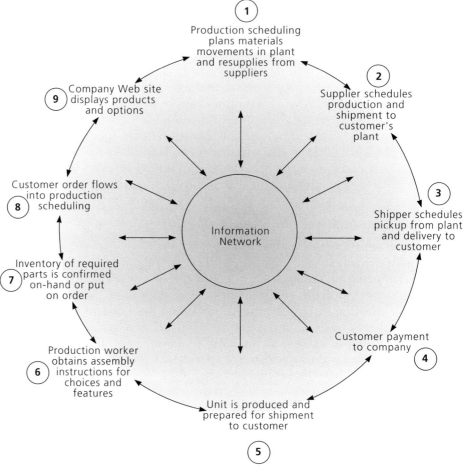

Figure 13.5
Networking for mass-customization.

once the domain of individuals are now shared as both people and departments have become more interdependent. The design of new products, for example, was once an engineering responsibility. Now, in contrast, it can be a shared responsibility because so much information is accessible for evaluation from various perspectives. Marketing, finance, production, engineering, and purchasing can share their different stores of information and determine a best overall design.

Naturally, networked systems are also helpful in business-to-business relationships. Increasingly, organizational buyers and suppliers are becoming so closely networked that they sometimes seem to be working for one organization. In the financial services industry, for example, institutional investors are networked with investment bankers, thus allowing efficient buying and selling of initial stock

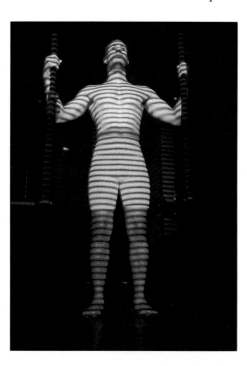

Thanks to networking technology, customers can give manufacturers information that manufacturers can feed into production systems at relatively little cost. The result is so-called mass-customization. At Levi Strauss & Co. new technologies can take an apparel buyer's body measurements and transfer the information, via the Web, to a manufacturing plant. There, the data is fed into equally advanced machines designed to handle one-of-a-kind items on an assembly line.

WEBCONNEXION

Because "a one-size-fits-all vitamin can't supply you with optimal nutrition," Acumins will customize the precise blend of vitamins, minerals, and herbs that each customer wants. To find out how the process works—and how the Net is essential to businesses in the world of mass-customization, log on at:

www.acumins.com

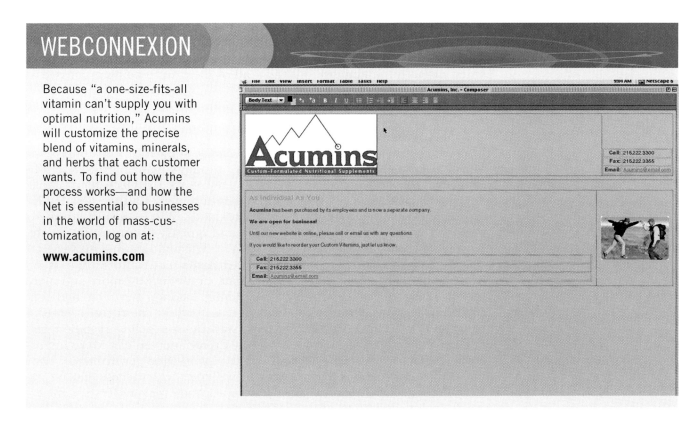

offerings. In manufacturing, Ford Motor Co.'s parts suppliers are linked to Ford's extranet. Because they know Ford's current production schedule and upcoming requirements, they can move materials into Ford plants more quickly and more accurately.

A step towards even greater collaboration between companies—the so-called *virtual company*—has become possible through networking. A virtual company can be a temporary team assembled by a single organization, or when several firms join forces. Each contributes different skills and resources that, collectively, result in a competitive business that would not be feasible for any of the collaborators acting alone. A company with marketing and promotional skills, for example, may team up with firms that are experts in warehousing and distribution, engineering, and production. Networking allows collaborators to exchange ideas, plan daily activities, share customer information, and otherwise coordinate their efforts, even if their respective facilities are far apart.

Greater Independence of Company and Workplace

Geographic separation of the workplace from the company headquarters is more common than ever because of networked organizations. Employees no longer work only at the office or the factory, nor are all of a company's operations performed at one location. The sales manager for an advertising agency may visit the company office in Toronto once every two weeks, preferring instead to work over the firm's electronic network from her home office in Montreal. A medical researcher for the Calgary Clinic may work at a home office networked into the clinic's system.

A company's activities may also be geographically scattered but highly coordinated, thanks to a networked system. Many e-businesses, for example, do not conduct any activities at one centralized location. When you order products from an Internet storefront—say, a chair, a sofa, a table, and two lamps—the chair may come from a cooperating warehouse in Windsor and the lamps from a manufacturer in Toronto, while the sofa and table may be direct-shipped from two manufacturers in North Carolina. All of these activities are launched instantaneously by the customer's order and coordinated through the network, just as if all of them were being processed at one location.

Improved Management Processes

Networked systems have changed the very nature of the management process. The activities, methods, and procedures of today's manager differ significantly from those that were common just a few years ago. Once, for example, upper-level managers did not concern themselves with all the detailed information that filtered upward in the workplace. Why? Because it was expensive to gather and slow in coming and quickly became out of date. Workplace management was delegated to middle and first-line managers.

With networked systems, however, instantaneous information is accessible in a convenient and usable format. Consequently, more and more upper managers use it routinely for planning, leading, directing, and controlling operations. Today, a top manager can find out the current status of any customer order, inspect productivity statistics for each workstation, and analyze the delivery performance of any driver and vehicle. More importantly, managers can better coordinate company-wide performance. They can identify departments that are working well together and those that are creating bottlenecks. The networked system at candy maker Hershey, for example, includes SAP—an enterprise-resource-planning model—that identifies the current status of any order and traces its progress from order entry to customer delivery and receipt of payment. Progress and delays at intermediate stages—materials ordering, inventory availability, production scheduling, packaging, warehousing, distribution—can be checked continuously to determine which operations should be more closely coordinated with others to improve overall performance.

TYPES OF INFORMATION SYSTEMS

In a sense, the phrase *information system* may be a misnomer. It suggests that there is one system when, in fact, a firm's employees will have different interests, job responsibilities, and decision-making requirements. One information system cannot accommodate such a variety of information requirements. Instead, "the information system" is a complex of several information systems that share information while serving different levels of the organization, different departments, or different operations.

User Groups and System Requirements

knowledge workers
Employees whose jobs involve the use of information and knowledge as the raw materials of their work.

Four user groups, each with different system requirements, are identified in Figure 13.6, which also indicates the kinds of systems best suited to each user level. Among users we include **knowledge workers**—employee whose jobs involve the use of information and knowledge as the raw materials of their work. Knowledge workers are specialists, usually professionally trained and certified—engineers, scientists, information technology specialists, psychologists—who rely on information technology to design new products or create new business processes.

System User/Level   **Kind of Information System**

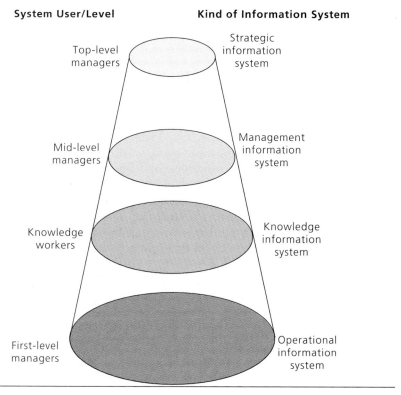

Figure 13.6
Matching users and systems.

Managers at Different Levels

Because they work on different kinds of problems, top managers, middle managers, knowledge workers, and first-line managers have different information needs. First-line (or operational) managers, for example, need information to oversee the day-to-day details of their departments or projects. Knowledge workers need special information for conducting technical projects. Meanwhile, middle managers need summaries and analyses for setting intermediate and long-range goals for the departments or projects under their supervision. Finally, top management analyzes broader trends in the economy, the business environment, and overall company performance to conduct long-range planning for the entire organization.

Consider the various information needs of a flooring manufacturer. Sales managers (first-level managers) supervise salespeople, assign territories to the sales force, and handle customer service and delivery problems. They need current information on the sales and delivery of products: lists of incoming customer orders and daily delivery schedules to customers in their territories. Regional managers (middle managers) set sales quotas for each sales manager, prepare budgets, and plan staffing needs for the upcoming year. They need information on monthly sales by product and region. Knowledge workers developing new flooring materials need information on the chemical properties of adhesives and compression strengths for floor structures. Finally, top managers need both external and internal information. Internally, they use sales data summarized by product, customer type, and geographic region, along with comparisons to previous years. Equally important is external information on consumer behaviour patterns, the competition's performance, and economic forecasts.

Functional Areas and Business Processes

Each business *function*—marketing, human resources, accounting, production, finance—has its own information requirements. In addition, as we saw in Chapter 6, many businesses are organized according to various business processes, and these process groups also need special information. Each of these user groups and departments, then, is represented by an information system. When we add to these systems the four systems needed by the four levels of users that we just discussed, we see that the total number of information systems and applications increases significantly. Each cell in Figure 13.7 describes a potential information system associated with a particular user group. Top-level finance managers, for example, are concerned with long-range planning for capital expenditures for future facilities and equipment and with determining sources of capital funds. In contrast, the arrows on the right side of Figure 13.7 indicate that a business-process group will include users, both managers and employees, drawn from all organizational levels. The supply-chain management group, for instance, may be in the process of trimming the number of suppliers. The information system supporting this project would contain information ranging across different organization functions and management levels because the group will need information and expert knowledge on marketing, warehousing and distribution, production, communications technology, purchasing, suppliers, and finance. It will also need different perspectives on operational, technical, and managerial issues: determining technical requirements for new suppliers, specifying task responsibilities for participating firms, and determining future financial requirements.

Major Systems by Level

In this section, we discuss different kinds of systems that provide applications at some organizational levels but not at others. For any routine, repetitive, highly structured decision, a specialized application will suffice. System re-

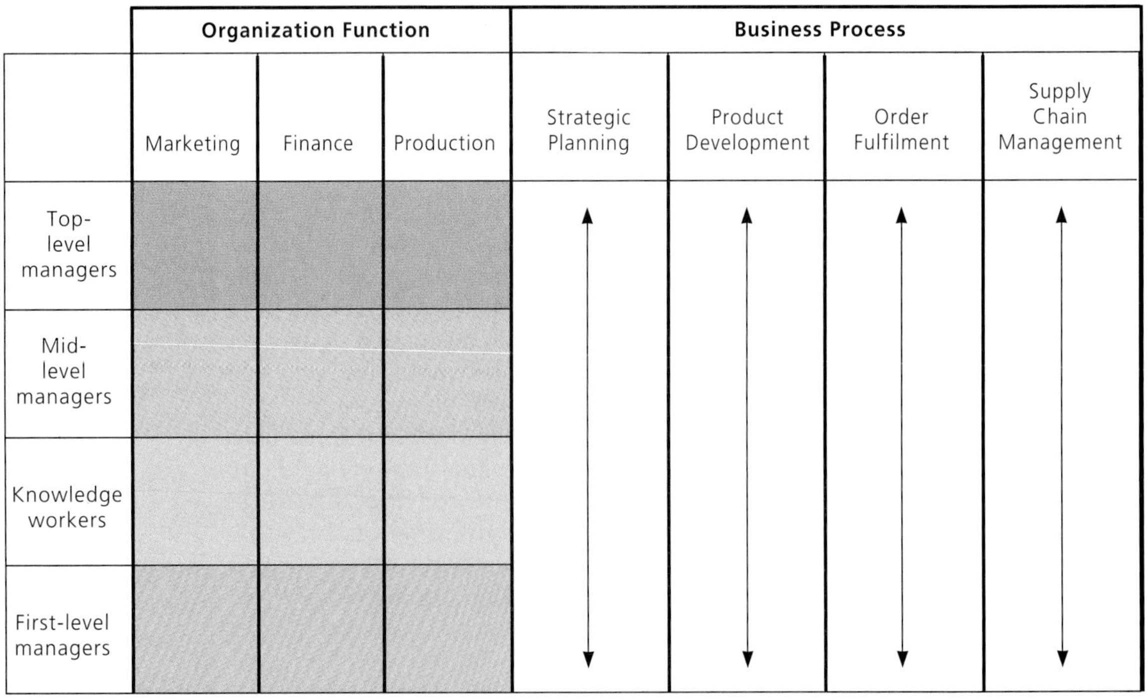

	Organization Function			Business Process			
	Marketing	Finance	Production	Strategic Planning	Product Development	Order Fulfilment	Supply Chain Management
Top-level managers				↑	↑	↑	↑
Mid-level managers							
Knowledge workers							
First-level managers				↓	↓	↓	↓

Figure 13.7
Matching user levels with functional areas and processes.

quirements for knowledge workers, however, will probably vary because knowledge workers often face a variety of specialized problems. Applications of information systems for middle or top-level management decisions must also be flexible, though for different reasons. In particular, they will use a broader range of information collected from a variety of sources, both external and internal.

Transaction Processing Systems

Transaction processing systems (TPS) are applications of information processing for basic day-to-day business transactions. Customer order-taking by online retailers, approval of claims at insurance companies, receiving and confirming reservations by airlines, payroll processing and bill payment at almost every company—all are routine business processes. Typically, the TPS for first-level (operational) activities is well defined, with predetermined data requirements, and follows the same steps to complete all transactions in the system.

A diagram representing the TPS for a customer-billing process is shown in Figure 13.8. The process begins when finished products for a customer's order are packed and ready for shipment. Using data stored in the company's master files, billing staffers match the customer's identification number (from the billing master file) with code numbers for products (from the products master file). The system instantly tallies the payment amount due (including

transaction processing systems (TPS)

Applications of information processing for basic day-to-day business transactions.

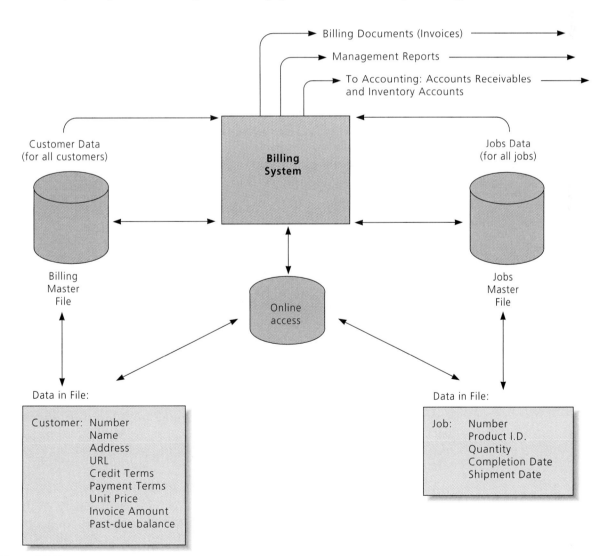

Figure 13.8
Customer billing TPS.

the bill of the current shipment plus any past-due payments), creates the billing document (invoice), and provides status reports to first-level managers and other system users with online access. Information from the billing and products master files flows electronically to the accounting system for updating accounts receivables and inventory accounts.

Systems for Knowledge Workers and Office Applications

Systems for knowledge workers and office applications support the activities of both knowledge workers and employees in clerical positions. They provide assistance for data processing and other office activities, including the creation of communications documents. Like other departments, the IS department includes both knowledge workers and data workers.

IS Knowledge Workers. IS knowledge workers include both systems analysts (and designers) and application (or systems) programmers:

- *Systems analysts and designers* deal with the entire computer system. They represent the IS group in working with users to learn users' requirements and to design systems that meet them. Generally, they decide on the types and sizes of computers and on how to set up links among computers to form a network of users.

- Using various language programs, *programmers* write the software instructions that tell computers what to do. Application programmers, for example, write instructions to address particular problems. Systems programmers ensure that a system can handle the requests made by various application programs.

Operations Personnel (Data Workers). People who run the company's computer equipment are called **system operations personnel**. They ensure that the right programs are run in the correct sequence and monitor equipment to ensure that it is operating properly. Many organizations also have personnel for entering data into the system for processing.

system operations personnel
People who run a company's computer equipment.

Knowledge-Level and Office Systems

Needless to say, the explosion of new support systems—word processing, document imaging, desktop publishing, computer-aided design, simulation modelling—has increased the productivity of both office and knowledge workers. We will discuss word processing—systems for formatting, editing, and storing documents—later in this chapter. Desktop publishing, also discussed later, combines graphics and word-processing text to publish professional-quality print and Web documents. Document imaging systems can scan paper documents and images, convert them into digital form for storage on disks, retrieve them, and transmit them electronically to workstations throughout the network.

World-class firms are using system applications for knowledge workers to reduce product-design times, reduce production-cycle times, and make faster deliveries to customers. Knowledge-level systems include *computer-aided design (CAD)*, *computer-aided manufacturing (CAM)*, and *computer operations control*.

computer-aided design (CAD)
Computer analysis and graphics programs that are used to create new products.

Computer-Aided Design. **Computer-aided design (CAD)** assists in designing products by simulating the real product and displaying it in three-dimensional graphics. Immersion's MicroScribe-3D software, for example, uses a penlike tool to scan the surface of any three-dimensional object, such as a football helmet, and electronically transforms it into a 3D graphic. The helmet designer can then try different shapes and surfaces in the computer and analyze the new designs on a video monitor.[7] Products ranging from cellphones to auto parts are created using CAD because it creates faster designs at lower cost than manual modelling methods. The older method—making handcrafted prototypes (trial models) from wood, plastic, or clay—is replaced with *rapid prototyping (RP)*: the CAD system electronically transfers instructions to a computer-controlled machine that then automatically builds the prototype.[8]

Immersion
www.immersion.com

Computer-Aided Manufacturing. **Computer-aided manufacturing (CAM)** is used to design the manufacturing equipment, facilities, and plant layouts for better product flows and productivity. *Computer operations control* refers to any system for managing the day-to-day production activities for either goods or service production. Hospitals, for instance, use computer-based scheduling for preparing patients' meals, just as manufacturers do for making cars, clocks, and paper products.

computer-aided manufacturing (CAM)
Computer systems used to design and control all the equipment and tools for producing goods.

Management Information Systems

Management information systems (MIS) support an organization's managers by providing daily reports, schedules, plans, and budgets. Each manager's information activities vary according to his or her functional area (say, accounting or marketing) and management level. Whereas mid-level managers focus mostly on internal activities and information, higher-level managers are also engaged in external activities. Middle managers, the largest MIS user group, need networked information to plan such upcoming activities as personnel training, materials movements, and cash flows. They also need to know the current status of the jobs and projects being carried out in their departments: What stage is it at now? When will it be finished? Is there an opening so the next job can be started? Many of a firm's management information systems—cash flow, sales, production scheduling, shipping—are indispensable for helping managers find answers to such questions.

management information systems (MIS)
Systems that support an organization's managers by providing daily reports, schedules, plans, and budgets.

Decision Support Systems (DSS)

Middle and top-level managers receive decision-making assistance from a **decision support system (DSS)**: an interactive system that locates and presents information needed to support the decision-making process. Whereas some DSSs are devoted to specific problems, others serve more general purposes, allowing managers to analyze different types of problems. Thus a firm that often faces decisions on plant capacity, for example, may have a *Capacity DSS* in which the manager inputs data on anticipated levels of sales, working capital, and customer-delivery requirements. Then the system's built-in transaction processors manipulate the data and make recommendations on the best levels of plant capacity for each future time period.

decision support system (DSS)
Computer systems used to help managers consider alternatives when making decisions on complicated problems.

In contrast, a general-purpose system, such as a marketing DSS, might respond to a variety of marketing-related problems. It may be programmed to handle "what-if" questions, such as "When is the best time to introduce a new product if my main competitor introduces one in 3 months, our new product has an 18-month expected life, demand is seasonal with a peak in the autumn, and my goal is to gain the largest possible market share?" The DSS can assist in decisions for which predetermined solutions are unknown by using sophisticated modelling tools and data analysis.

Executive Support Systems

An **executive support system (ESS)** is a quick-reference, easy-access application of information systems specially designed for upper-level managers.

executive support system (ESS)
A quick-reference, easy-access application of information systems specially designed for upper-level managers.

ESSs are designed to assist with executive-level decisions and problems, ranging from "What lines of business should we be in five years from now?" to "Based on forecasted developments in electronic technologies, to what extent should our firm be globalized in five years? In 10 years?" An ESS also uses a wide range of both internal information and external sources, such as industry reports, global economic forecasts, and reports on competitors' capabilities.

Because senior-level managers do not usually possess advanced computer skills, they prefer systems that are easily accessible and adaptable. Accordingly, ESSs are not designed to address only specific, predetermined problems. Instead, they allow the user some flexibility in addressing a variety of problem situations. They are easily accessible by means of simple keyboard strokes or even voice commands.

Artificial Intelligence and Expert Systems

artificial intelligence (AI)
The construction and/or programming of computers to imitate human thought processes.

Artificial intelligence (AI) can be defined as the construction of computer systems, both hardware and software, to imitate human behaviour—in other words, systems that perform physical tasks, use thought processes, and learn. In developing AI systems, knowledge workers—business specialists, modellers, information-technology experts—try to design computer-based systems capable of reasoning so that computers, instead of people, can perform certain business activities.

One example is a credit-evaluation system that decides which loan applicants are creditworthy and which ones are risky and then composes acceptance and rejection letters accordingly. Another example is an applicant-selection system that receives interviewees' job applications, screens them, and then decides which applicants are best matched for each of several job openings.

robotics
The use of computer-controlled machines that perform production tasks.

Robotics—the combination of computers with industrial robots—is a category of AI. With certain "reasoning" capabilities, robots can "learn" repetitive tasks such as painting, assembling components, and inserting screws. They also avoid repeating mistakes by "remembering" the causes of past mistakes and, when those causes reappear, adjusting or stopping until adjustments are made.

Robotics is a category of artificial intelligence. Robots can "learn" repetitive tasks and "remember" the causes of past mistakes.

There are also designed AI systems that possess sensory capabilities, such as lasers that "see," "hear," and "feel." In addition, as machines become more sophisticated in processing natural languages, humans can give instructions and ask questions merely by speaking to a computer.

AND Corp. of Toronto has developed a software program—called Hnet—that can learn to recognize faces. This may seem like a simple thing, but millions of dollars had been spent on this problem without success until AND Corp. developed the software. The system can be used to improve airport security and to track terrorists.[9]

A special form of AI program, the **expert system**, is designed to imitate the thought processes of human experts in a particular field.[10] Expert systems incorporate the rules that an expert applies to specific types of problems, such as the judgments a physician makes when diagnosing illnesses. In effect, expert systems supply everyday users with "instant expertise."

expert system
A form of artificial intelligence in which a program draws on the rules an expert in a given field has laid out in order to arrive at a solution for a problem.

General Electric's Socrates Quick Quote, for example, imitates the decisions of a real estate expert and then places a package of recommendations about real estate transactions at the fingertips of real estate dealers on GE's private computer network. Nortel Networks uses an expert system called Engineering Change Manager, which simplifies and speeds up product design changes by suggesting redesigns to meet product requirements. Campbell Soup developed an expert system to mimic complex decision processes and save the expert knowledge that was going to be lost when a long-time expert soup maker announced his intention to retire.[11]

ELEMENTS OF THE INFORMATION SYSTEM

We now know that an *information system* is a group of interconnected devices at several different locations that can exchange information. We also know that *networking*—connecting these devices—allows otherwise decentralized computers to exchange data quickly and easily. Obviously, a key component of the information system is its **computer network**: all of the computer and information technology devices that, working together, drive the flow of digital information throughout the system.

computer network
A form of computer system architecture in which computers at different locations can function independently but are also interconnected and able to exchange information with one another.

Although the computer is a powerful machine, it is only one part of the information system. Every system has six components:

- Hardware
- Software
- Control
- Database
- People
- Telecommunications

In this section, we will describe each of the first four components in detail. We have already described the fifth element, the people at various levels who use and prepare the system. We will reserve our discussion of telecommunications for the next section. Remember that all six of these components must be present and properly coordinated for a networked information system to function effectively.

Hardware

Figure 13.9 shows the various systems and components that make up IS **hardware**: the physical components of a computer system. The functioning

hardware
The physical components of a computer system.

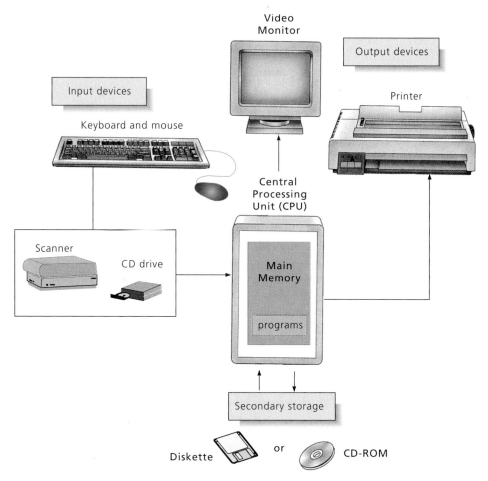

Figure 13.9
IS hardware.

of a computer's hardware is not as complicated as it looks. To get a bird's-eye view of how the system works, suppose that you are a very simple piece of data (say, the number 3).

Inputting

input device
Hardware that gets data into the computer in a form the computer can understand.

To get into the computer, data must be entered by an **input device**. Optical scanners, voice pickups, CD-ROM drives, and computer mice are all input devices, but let's assume that you are entered by a friend using the most common input device, a keyboard. When your friend presses the number 3 on the keyboard, an electronic signal is sent to the computer's **central processing unit (CPU)**, where the actual processing of data takes place.

central processing unit (CPU)
Hardware in which the actual transforming of data into information takes place; contains the primary storage unit, the control unit, and the arithmetic logic unit.

Main Memory

main memory
The part of a computer's CPU that stores those programs that it needs in order to operate.

You are now inside the CPU in a form that the computer can understand. What happens now? As a piece of data, you must go first to **main memory**—the part of the computer's CPU that stores those programs that it needs in order to operate.

Programs

program
Any sequence of instructions to a computer.

At this point, the CPU searches through its memory for instructions—**programs**—on what to do with you. Using the appropriate instructions, it then performs the calculations (addition, subtraction, multiplication, and division) and comparisons as directed by the program. Then, the CPU sends the results to one or more **output devices**: a video monitor, a printer, or a voice output.

output device
That part of a computer's hardware that presents results to users; common forms include printers and video monitors.

Secondary Storage

If someone turned off the computer at this point, it would forget both the data (you) and the information that resulted. Why? The computer's active memory is a short-term form of memory that lasts only as long as the computer stays on. It is called **random access memory (RAM)** because any part of it can be called on for processing at any time.

random access memory (RAM)
The computer's short-term active memory that lasts only as long as the computer stays on.

Disks, CD-ROMs, and CD-Rs. For long-term memory, however, we need **secondary storage**, that is, any medium for storing data or information outside the computer's CPU. Magnetic tape, hard disks, diskettes, and CD-ROMs can all be used for secondary storage. Digital data that are stored can later be retrieved (that is, read) from secondary storage by the user. **Hard disks** are rigid metal disks permanently enclosed in the computer. **Diskettes** are portable and can be easily inserted and removed.

secondary storage
Any medium that can be used to store computerized data and information outside the computer's primary storage mechanism; magnetic tape, hard disks, diskettes, and CD-ROMs are common forms.

CD-ROMs (for *compact disc read-only memory*) look just like music CDs and can hold as much data as 400 regular diskettes. They are convenient for storing sound and video images, but do not allow users to write new data onto them. A newer disk, the CD-R (for *compact disc-recordable*) can accept new written data from a CD recorder. The recorder uses special software to laser-cut grooves into the CD. Popular CD-ROMs include large-volume materials such as encyclopedias. *Encyclopaedia Britannica*, for example, is available in a CD-ROM Multimedia Edition, which includes the entire text of the 32 volumes, 72 000 articles, 8000 photos and illustrations, sound clips, animation and video, *Webster's Collegiate® Dictionary*, and 15 000 related Internet links. CD-ROMs are especially useful for storing multimedia technical presentations that use overhead projections, videos, voice, and sound.

hard disks
Rigid metal disks permanently enclosed in the computer.

diskettes
Portable disks that can be easily inserted into and removed from the computer.

CD-ROMs
Look like music CDs but can hold as much data as 400 regular diskettes.

Encylopedia Britannica
www.britannica.com

Once the Hardware Takes Over

Now that you have an inside view of computer hardware operations, let's look at things from the outside. Suppose that you have a part-time job in the registrar's office at your school. Let's say that a student requests information about an introductory accounting class. You insert a diskette and type the request on your keyboard—your link to the CPU. Although the keyboard does no processing itself, it lets you issue commands to the CPU.

Next, the CPU takes over. It issues an electronic command that finds data about accounting classes in secondary storage and copies it into the main memory. A program in the CPU tells the computer how to search through the lists for the introductory course requested by the student. Finally, the CPU transfers the results to your video display. In a matter of seconds, you can tell the student that the class meets at 8:30 a.m. every day and that three seats are still open.

Software

Although hardware is a vital component of a computer system, it is useless without the other components. As we have just seen, hardware needs programs—**software**—to function. There are basically two types of software programs: system and application.

software
Programs that instruct the computer in what to do and how to do it.

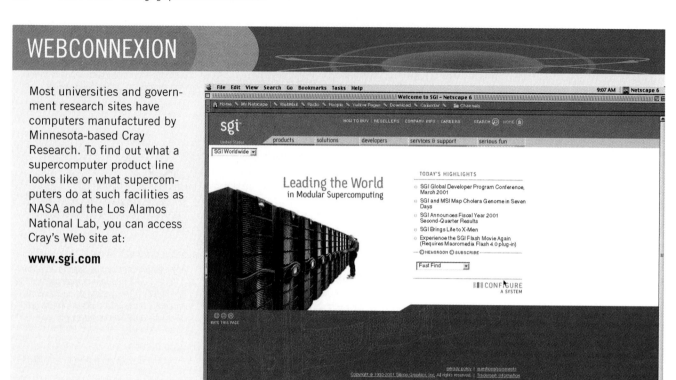

System Programs

system program
A program that tells a computer what resources to use and how to use them.

System programs tell the computer what resources to use and how to use them. For example, an operating system program tells the computer how and when to transfer data from secondary storage to primary storage and to return information to the user. You have probably heard of **DOS**, the disk operating system. It is called **DOS** because a disk is used to store the operating system software.

language program
A program that allows computer users to write specialized instructions for their computers.

Another type of system program, the **language program**, allows computer users to write specialized instructions for their computers. For example, FORTRAN (for *formula translator*), one of the first languages, is used in engineering and the sciences because it is designed for the rapid calculation of large numbers. Visual Basic and Visual C++ are popular general-purpose languages for specialists who like to write their own programs. Many educators prefer PASCAL because it teaches good programming habits and makes both reviewing and debugging fairly simple.

Application Programs

application program
A program that actually processes data according to a particular user's specific needs.

Most computer users do not write programs but rather use **application programs**: software packages written by others. Each different type of application (such as financial analysis, word processing, or Web browsing) uses a program that meets that need. Thus, a computer system usually has many application programs available, such as Lotus 1-2-3, Quicken, and WordPerfect. We review some of these later in this chapter.

Graphical User Interface

graphical user interface (GUI)
The user-friendly display that helps users select from among the many possible applications of the computer.

One of the most helpful software developments is the **graphical user interface (GUI)**: the user-friendly visual display that helps users select from among the many possible applications on the computer. Typically, the screen displays numerous **icons** (small images) representing such choices as word processing, graphics, DOS, fax, printing, CD, or games. The user tells the computer what to do by moving a pointing device (usually an arrow) around the screen to activate the desired icon. Printed text presents simple instructions for using activated features. Today, Microsoft Windows is the most popular GUI because it simplifies computer use while actually making it fun.

icons
Small images on a computer screen that represent various applications.

Control

Control ensures that the system is operating according to specific procedures and within specific guidelines. These procedures include guidelines for operating the system, responsibilities of the personnel involved with it, and plans for dealing with system failure. For example, a key aspect of information management is controlling two groups of people: those who have access to input or change the system's data and those who receive output from it. Thus, for example, most firms limit access to salary information. Another aspect of control is management surveillance of employees as they work (see the "Business Today" box).

BUSINESS TODAY

The Keystroke Cops

Recent developments in computer surveillance have made it possible for bosses to monitor employees without their knowledge. The latest innovations allow for the monitoring of every keystroke employees make while working at their computers. These silent monitoring programs—with names like Spy, Peek, Silent Watch, and Investigator—cost as little as US$99. Some companies display an on-screen notice that employees' work is being monitored. This acts as a deterrent, even if monitoring is not actually being done.

The Investigator program does not appear as an icon on the computer screen, and it is hard to find among computer files even when someone searches for it. It is usually installed on a worker's computer after-hours. The program allows a manager to choose "alert" words such as "boss" or "union." Any time these words appear in the text of an e-mail, a copy is automatically sent to the employee's supervisor.

One company bought the Silent Watch program after concerns developed about what a computer programmer was actually doing on the job. The program was installed on the worker's computer, and within a few days it became clear that he was spending considerable time visiting pornographic Web sites. The worker was immediately fired.

These monitoring programs are very effective at intercepting all work that employees do, even work that is erased by the employee before it is sent. Suppose that you type a nasty letter to your boss on your computer while at work. After you calm down, you decide not to send the letter and erase it. Can your boss find out what you wrote? Yes. Your boss can read your unsent draft because it has been intercepted and stored in the computer's memory.

Companies do not restrict their monitoring to keystrokes. They also use other types of monitoring, including listening in on employee conversations with customers to see how well the employee is performing. This monitoring can improve the effectiveness of employees, but it can also increase their stress levels, because they don't know exactly when the boss is listening in on their conversations.

The employer's desire for more information may conflict with the employee's need for privacy. Some studies show that computer monitoring has a negative effect on employee health. A study of telephone operators, for example, showed that those who were monitored had more headaches, back pain, severe fatigue, shoulder soreness, anxiety, and sore wrists than those who were not monitored.

An increasing number of lawsuits are being brought against companies by employees who charge that the firms overstepped the bounds of decency when they monitored their work. The most extensive case is the one against Nortel Networks. The employees' union claims that Nortel installed telephone bugs and hidden microphones in one of its plants and used them to spy on employees over a period of 13 years.

Problems of Privacy and Security

"Breaking and entering" no longer refers merely to physical intrusions into one's home or business. Today, it applies to IS intrusions as well. In this section, we will describe one of the most common forms of intrusion: *privacy invasion*. We will also discuss some of the methods that companies use to provide *security* for their information systems.[12]

Privacy Invasion.   With information systems, privacy invasion occurs when intruders (hackers) gain unauthorized access, either to steal information, money, or property or to tamper with data. You have probably read or heard about computer enthusiasts who have gained access to school systems to change grades. A 16-year-old British hacker, for example, made 150 intrusions into the U.S. Air Force's top command-and-control facility. He then used those entries to gain access to the computers of several defence contractors and the South Korean Atomic Research Institute.

Security.   Security measures for protection against intrusion are a constant challenge. To gain entry into most systems, IS users have protected passwords that guard against unauthorized access, but many firms rely on additional protective software for safeguards. To protect against intrusions by unauthorized outsiders, companies use security devices, called electronic *firewalls*, in their systems. Firewalls allow employees access to both the Internet and the company's internal computer network while barring entry by outsiders.

Security for electronic communications is an additional concern. Electronic transmissions can be intercepted, altered, and read by intruders. To prevent unauthorized access, many firms rely on encryption—the use of a secret numerical code to scramble the characters in the message, so that the message is not understandable during transmission. Only personnel with the deciphering codes can read them. Protection for preserving data files and databases is not foolproof and typically involves making backup copies to be stored outside the computer system, usually in a safe. Thus, damaged system files can be replaced by backup.

Finally, the most important security factor is the people in the system. At most firms, personnel are trained in the responsibilities of computer use and warned of the penalties for violating system security. For example, each time a computer boots up, a notice displays the warning that software and data are protected and spells out penalties for unauthorized use.

Databases and Application Programs

As we have noted, all computer processing is the processing of data. This processing is carried out by programs—instructions that tell the system to perform specified functions. In this section we begin by briefly describing the nature of computer data and databases. We then discuss a few of the specialized applications programs designed for business use.

Data and Databases

Computers convert data into information by organizing them in some meaningful manner. Within a computer system, chunks of data—numbers, words, and sentences—are stored in a series of related collections called *fields*, *records*, and *files*. Taken together, all of these data files constitute a **database**: a centralized, organized collection of related data.

Processing.   Once data are entered into the database, they can be manipulated, sorted, combined, or compared. In **batch processing**, data are col-

database
A centralized, organized collection of related data.

batch processing
A method of transforming data into information in which data are collected over a period of time and then processed as a group or batch.

lected and stored over some time period and then processed as groups or batches. Payrolls, for example, are usually run in batches. Because most employees are paid on either a weekly or a biweekly basis, the data (the hours worked) are accumulated over the pay periods and processed at one time.

Batch processing was once the only type of computer processing. Although it is still widely used, companies today more often use **online processing**, in which data are entered and processed immediately. This system is always used when the results of each entry affect subsequent entries. For example, if you book seat 16D on WestJet flight 253 on December 23, the computer must thereafter prevent other passengers from booking the same seat.

online processing
A method of transforming data into information in which data are entered and processed immediately.

Application Programs

Increasingly inexpensive equipment and software have made computers an irresistible option for businesses of all types and sizes. Moreover, programs are available for a huge variety of business-related tasks. Some of these programs address such common, long-standing needs as accounting, payroll, and inventory control. Others have been developed for application to an endless variety of specialized needs. Most business application programs fall into one of four categories—*word processing, spreadsheets, database management,* and *graphics*.[13] Of all PC software applications, 70 percent are designed for the first three types of programs.

Microsoft
www.microsoft.com

Corel Corp.
www.corel.com

Lotus Development Corp.
www.lotus.com

Word Processing. Popular **word-processing programs**, such as Microsoft Word for Windows, Corel WordPerfect, and Lotus Development Corp.'s Word Pro for Windows, allow computer users to store, edit, display, and print documents. Sentences or paragraphs can be added or deleted without retyping or restructuring an entire document, and mistakes are easily corrected.

word-processing programs
Application programs that allow the computer to act as a sophisticated typewriter to store, edit, and print letters and numbers.

Spreadsheets. Electronic spreadsheets spread data across and down the page in rows and columns. Users enter data, including formulas, at row and column intersections and the computer automatically performs the necessary calculations. Payroll records, sales projections, and a host of other financial reports can be prepared in this manner.

Spreadsheets are useful planning tools because they allow managers to see how making a change in one item will affect related items. For example, a manager can insert various operating cost percentages, tax rates, or sales revenues into the spreadsheet. The computer will automatically recalculate all the other figures and determine net profit. Three popular spreadsheet packages are Lotus 1-2-3, Quattro Pro, and Microsoft Excel for Windows.

electronic spreadsheets
Application programs that allow the user to enter categories of data and determine the effect of changes in one category (e.g., sales) on other categories (e.g., profits).

Database Management. In addition to word processing and spreadsheets, another popular type of personal productivity software is **database management systems**. Such programs as Microsoft Access for Windows, and, from Borland, Paradox for Windows and dBase are popular desktop applications. IBM's DB2 software for mainframe systems can keep track of all of a firm's relevant data. Oracle8i is a popular database for Internet computing. These systems can store, sort, and search through data and integrate a single piece of data into several different files.

database management systems
Application programs that keep track of and manipulate the relevant data of a business.

Figure 13.10 shows how a database management program might be used at a company called Artists' Frame Service. In this case, the program is integrating the file for customer orders with the company's inventory file. When sales to Jones and Smith are entered into the customer orders file, the database system automatically adjusts the frame inventory file; the quantities of materials B5 and A3 are reduced because those materials were used to make the frames for Jones and Smith.

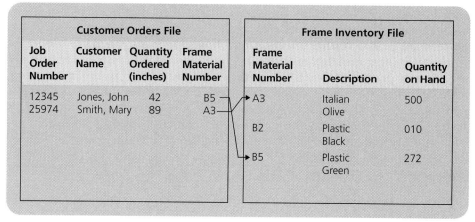

Figure 13.10
Artists' Frame Service.

computer graphics programs

Application programs that convert numerical and character data into pictorial forms.

Graphics. **Computer graphics programs** convert numeric and character data into pictorial information such as charts, graphs, and cartoon characters. These programs make computerized information easier to use and understand in two ways. First, graphs and charts summarize data and allow managers to detect problems, opportunities, and relationships more easily. Second, graphics are valuable in creating clearer and more persuasive reports and presentations.

Two of the most common graphics displays are the pie chart and the bar graph. As Figure 13.11 shows, both types of graphics can convey different kinds of information—in this case, the types of materials that should be ordered by a framing shop like Artists' Frame Service. Both types of graphs are more likely to help a manager make decisions than the raw numbers on which they are based.

presentation graphics software

Application programs that offer choices for assembling graphics for visual displays, slides, video, and even sound splices for professional presentations.

Presentation graphics software, such as CorelDraw, Microsoft PowerPoint for Windows, Corel Presentations, and Microsoft Vision 2000

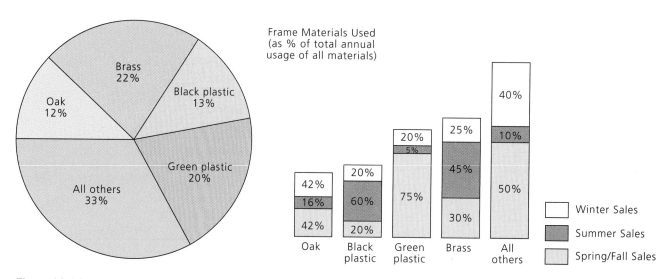

Figure 13.11
Both the pie chart and the bar graph show that four frame materials are the most used, but the bar graph also shows that brass and oak are most popular in winter.

The realism of the space creatures in *Star Wars* is due to special effects created with computer graphics.

offer choices for assembling graphics for visual displays, slides, video, and even sound splices for professional presentations. The ability to vary colour and size and to use pictures and charts with three-dimensional effects, shadows, and shading with animation and sound is more visually interesting than static presentations.

Computer graphics capabilities extend beyond mere data presentation. They also include stand-alone programs for artists, designers, and special effects designers. Everything from simple drawings to fine art, television commercials, and motion picture special effects are now created by computer graphics software. The realism of the boat sinking in *Titanic* and the physical appearance of the space creatures in *Star Wars*, *Episode One* and *Terminator 2* are due to special effects created with computer graphics.

Some software allows firms to publish their own sales brochures, in-house magazines, and annual reports. The latest of these **desktop publishing** packages combines word processing and graphics capability to produce type-set-quality text with stimulating visual effects from personal computers. Quark Xpress, for example, is able to manipulate text, tables of numbers, graphics, and full-colour photographs. Desktop publishing eliminates costly printing services for reports and proposals, and Quark is also used by ad agencies whose computer-generated designs offer greater control over colour and format. Other desktop publishing packages include Microsoft Publisher and Adobe Systems PageMaker Plus.

desktop publishing
Combines word processing and graphics capability in producing typeset-quality text from personal computers.

Quark Xpress
www.quark.com

TELECOMMUNICATIONS AND NETWORKS

Although communications systems are constantly evolving, some of the fundamental elements are well established: computers, communications devices, and networking. The most powerful vehicle for using these elements to their full potential is the marriage of computers and communication technologies. Thanks to lower-cost, higher-capacity networks, the joining of computers, communication, and mass media is changing the nature of information and the ways in which business is conducted.

A network is a means of organizing telecommunications components into an effective system. When a company decides how to organize its equipment and facilities, it also determines how its information resources will be shared, controlled, and applied for users in its network. In this section, we will first discuss *multimedia communications technologies* and the devices found in today's systems. We will then describe different ways of organizing information resources into effective systems.

Multimedia Communication Systems

multimedia communication systems

Connected networks of communication appliances such as faxes, televisions, sound equipment, cellphones, printers, and photocopiers that may also be linked by satellite with other remote networks.

Today's information systems include not only computers but also **multimedia communication systems**. These systems are connected networks of communication appliances such as faxes, televisions, sound equipment, cellphones, printers, and photocopiers that may also be linked by satellite with other remote networks. Not surprisingly, the integration of these elements is changing the ways in which we live our lives and manage our businesses. A good example is the modern grocery store. The checkout scanner reads the bar code on the product you buy. Data are then transmitted to the store's inventory-control system, which updates the number of available units. If inventory falls below a given level, more product is ordered electronically. Meanwhile, the correct price is added to your bill and checkout coupons are printed automatically according to the specific product you bought. Your debit card transfers funds, sales reports are generated for the store's management, and all the while, satellite transmissions are dispatching a remote truck to begin loading replacement supplies for the store.

Multimedia Technology

Multimedia communication technology is profoundly expanding the applications of PCs. Today's programs incorporate sound, animation, and photography as well as ordinary graphics and text. Communication power has multiplied through online information services that provide subscribers with instant access to financial and news data. Electronic discussion groups and business meetings via videoconferencing display interactive dialogue for conference callers in widespread locations. Equipped with audio and video devices, today's PCs allow you to tune in your favourite TV show on your computer monitor, watch movies from digital video disks (DVDs), and listen to your favourite music.

Communication Devices. The explosion in personal communications devices now permits people to conduct business across large distances and from territories where communications were not available before. *Global-positioning-systems (GPS)*, for example, use satellite transmissions to track and identify the geographic location of a target, such as a boat or even a person. When you're linked to a GPS network, your firm can know your whereabouts at all times. *Personal digital assistants (PDAs)* are tiny hand-held computers with wireless telecommunications capabilities. Several of these palm-top devices are capable of accessing the Internet, including receiving and sending e-mail messages from the most primitive locations. *Paging systems* and *cellular telephones* provide instant fingertip connections with one or more communications networks.

Communication Channels. Communication channels are the media that make all of these transmissions possible. These include wired and wireless transmission. Microwave systems, for example, transmit straight-line radio (wireless) signals through the air between transmission stations. Another system—satellite communications—has also gained popularity in the growing

Demonstrating how computers have changed communications, these engineers at GE's corporate research and development centre can monitor engines in flight from the ground via satellite. The new system can diagnose potential engine problems, plan for maintenance or overhaul, and resolve problems more quickly than ever.

demand for wireless transmission. GE's Technical Response Center, for example, demonstrates the value of satellites for improving aircraft-engine maintenance and safety. Relying on wireless systems instead of underground cables, laser beams and radio waves transmit signals from satellite to satellite.

Accessible through satellite networks, the Internet is available in remote areas where underground cable is not feasible. The entire world is within the instant reach of the Internet. Most of us use communication channels when we use some type of telephone system. Even today, however, the bulk of telephone transmissions are data, not conversations.

Smart Software.   Software for many multimedia components actually permits them to perform some activities automatically. Smart modems perform such functions as dialling, answering the phone, and transmitting. Smart TVs remember your program preferences, remind you of upcoming programs, and even make suggestions for your viewing pleasure. Similar software is available for watches, ovens, automobiles, airplanes, and air conditioners. Software is also available for integrating the activities of multimedia hardware. Microsoft at Work, for example, can be installed in office equipment hardware (phones, fax machines, copiers) so that they can all be controlled by PCs.

System Architecture

There are several ways to organize the components in computer and communications networks. One way to classify networks is according to *geographic scope*. Another is according to the *pattern of connections* among the system's devices.

Local and Wide Area Networks

Networked systems classified according to geographic scope may be either local or wide area networks. Computers may be linked province-wide or even nationwide through telephone lines, microwave, or satellite communications, as in a **wide area network (WAN)**. Firms can lease lines from communications vendors or maintain private WANs. Wal-Mart, for example, depends heavily on a private satellite network that links more than 2000 retail stores to its Bentonville, Arkansas, headquarters.

wide area network (WAN)

A system to link computers across the country through telephone wires or satellites.

Internal networks covering limited distances may link all of a firm's nearby computers, as in a **local area network (LAN)**. Computers within a building, for example, can be linked by cabling (fibre optic, coaxial, or twisted wire) or by wireless technology. Internally networked computers share processing duties, software, storage areas, and data. On the Home Shopping Network, hundreds of operators seated at monitors in a large room are united by a LAN to enter call-in orders from customers. This arrangement allows the use of a single computer system with one database and software system. To exchange information with other networks, any LAN can be connected to other outside communications via a *network gateway*—a communications processor that connects the LAN to a public telephone network or to the networks of other companies.

Connecting the Hardware. Combination systems using local and wide area networks are also possible. Separate plants or offices, for example, might handle orders locally while electronically transmitting sales summaries to a corporate office. Computer networks thus give companies the advantages of both centralized and decentralized processing. Through a personal computer with a **modem**—a computer-to-computer link over telephone wires—users can conduct searches in a remote database and exchange messages.

The materials used to make local and wide area networks are changing rapidly. *Fibre optic cable* is made from thousands of strands of ultra-thin glass fibres that not only carry data faster, but are lighter and less expensive than older copper media, such as *coaxial cable* (as used in cable television) and *twisted-wire cable* (as used in telephone wires). Whereas copper-wire cables carry data as electrical signals, fibre optic cable carries data as laser-generated light beams.[14] Wire cables throughout the world are being replaced daily with fibre optic cable, but the change will require many years to complete. Tele Danmark, Denmark's leading telecommunications company, is leading the way. In 1996, it installed the 400-kilometre BALTICA submarine cable between Poland, Denmark, and Sweden and a 725-kilometre underwater cable in Brazil.

Client–Server Systems. An obvious advantage of networks is the sharing of resources—and thus the avoidance of costly and unnecessary duplication. In a **client–server network**, **clients** are the users of services. They are the points of entry, usually laptop computers, workstations, or desktop computers. The **server** provides the services shared by network users. The powerful *minicomputer* at the network hub, for example, which is larger and more sophisticated than your PC, or *microcomputer*, may be the server for the surrounding client PCs in an office network.

More specifically, the server may act as a file server, a print server, and a fax server. As a *file server*, the minicomputer has a large-capacity disk for storing the programs and data shared by all of the PCs in the network. It contains customer files plus the database, word-processing, graphics, and spreadsheet programs that may be used by clients. As a *print server*, the minicomputer controls the printer, stores printing requests from client PCs, and routes jobs to the printer as it becomes available. As the *fax server*, the minicomputer receives, sends, and otherwise controls the system's fax activities. Only one disk drive, one printer, and one fax, therefore, are needed for an entire system of users. Internet computing uses the client–server arrangement.

By linking and sharing computing resources, client–server LANs have replaced many stand-alone minicomputers and *mainframes* (which are even bigger and faster than minicomputers). At University Medical Center, Stony Brook, New York, for instance, a wireless LAN helps respiratory therapists capture more accurate information faster than ever before, so that they will have more time for patient treatment. Each therapist carries a hand-held tablet-sized portable terminal (the client) from room-to-room. The server is a Dell computer that provides the Windows NT operating system to all clients, allowing therapists to record notes while visiting patients instead of first returning to the nursing stations.[15]

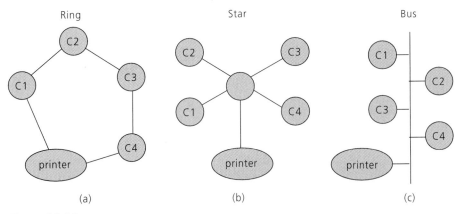

Figure 13.12
Three network patterns.

Network Patterns

A second way to classify networks is according to the pattern of connections among the system's devices. We discuss the three patterns—the *ring*, the *star*, and the *bus*—shown in Figure 13.12. Each pattern has its own technical and management requirements.

The Ring. In the *ring network* (see Figure 13.12(a)), each computer performs its own applications independently and can communicate directly with every other computer. The network cable is connected to all devices, including the shared printer. Cable connections are both extensive and expensive. If any computer fails, however, the others continue operating because each computer is connected to every other one.

The Star. In the *star network* (see Figure 13.12(b)), a central host computer is connected to every other computer. Because all computer-to-computer communications must pass through the host, the entire system is interrupted when the host shuts down. The star pattern is useful in organizations that must do both centralized processing and independent processing at local computers.

The Bus. The simplest network is the *bus network* (see Figure 13.12(c)), in which a single length of cable is shared by every network device. As in the ring, computers perform independently, without a central host computer. Although it has the advantage of simplicity, a drawback to the bus is the risk of a cable break. Workstations cannot communicate across the break point.

SUMMARY OF LEARNING OBJECTIVES

1. **Explain why businesses must manage *information* and show how computer systems and communication technologies have revolutionized *information management*.** Because businesses are faced with an overwhelming amount of *data* and *information* about customers, competitors, and their own operations, the ability to manage this input can mean the difference between success and failure. The management of its information system is a core activity because all of a firm's business activities are linked to it. New digital technologies have taken an integral place among an organization's resources for conducting everyday business.

2. **Identify and briefly describe three elements of *data communication networks*—the Internet, the World Wide Web, and intranets.** *Data com-*

munication networks, both public and private, carry streams of digital data (electronic messages) back and forth quickly and economically via *telecommunication systems*. The largest public communications network, the *Internet*, is a gigantic network of networks linking millions of computers and offering information on business around the world. The Internet is the most important e-mail system in the world. Individuals can subscribe to the Internet via an *Internet service provider (ISP)*. The *World Wide Web* is a system with universally accepted standards for storing, formatting, retrieving, and displaying information. It provides the common language that enables users around the world to "surf" the Internet using a common format. *Intranets* are private networks that any company can develop to extend Internet technology internally—that is, for transmitting information throughout the firm. Intranets are accessible only to employees, with access to outsiders prevented by hardware and software security systems called *firewalls*.

3. **Describe five** *new options for organizational design* **that have emerged from the rapid growth of information technologies.** Information networks are leading to *leaner* organizations—businesses with fewer employees and simpler organizational structures—because networked firms can maintain electronic, rather than human, information links among employees and customers. Operations are *more flexible* because electronic networks allow businesses to offer greater product variety and faster delivery cycles. Aided by intranets and the Internet, *greater collaboration* is possible, both among internal units and with outside firms. *Geographic separation* of the workplace and company headquarters is more common because electronic links are replacing the need for physical proximity between the company and its workstations. *Improved management processes* are feasible because managers have rapid access to more information about the current status of company activities and easier access to electronic tools for planning and decision making.

4. **Discuss different information-systems** *applications* **that are available for users at various organizational levels.** *Transaction processing systems (TPS)* are applications for basic day-to-day business transactions. They are useful for routine transactions, such as taking reservations and meeting payrolls, that follow predetermined steps. Systems for *knowledge workers and office applications* include personal productivity tools such as *word processing, document imaging, desktop publishing, computer-aided design (CAD)*, and *simulation modelling. Management information systems (MIS)* support an organization's managers by providing daily reports, schedules, plans, and budgets. Middle managers, the largest MIS user group, need networked information to plan upcoming activities and track current activities. *Decision support systems (DSS)* are interactive applications that assist the decision-making processes of middle and top-level managers. *Executive support systems (ESS)* are quick-reference, easy-access programs to assist upper-level managers. *Artificial intelligence (AI)* and *expert systems* are designed to imitate human behaviour and provide computer-based assistance in performing certain business activities.

5. **Identify and briefly describe the** *main elements of an information system.* Hardware is the physical devices and components, including the computer, in the *information system (IS)*. It consists of an input device (such as a keyboard), a central processing unit (CPU), a main memory, disks for data storage, and output devices (such as video monitors and printers). *Software* includes the computer's operating system, application programs (such as word processing, spreadsheets, and Web browsers), and a graphical user interface (GUI) that helps users select among the computer's many possible applications.

Control is important to ensure not only that the system operates correctly but also that data and information are transmitted through secure channels to people who really need them. Control is aided by the use of electronic security measures, such as firewalls, that bar entry to the system by unauthorized outsiders. The *database* is the organized collection of all the data files in the system. *People* are also part of the information system. IS *knowledge workers* include systems analysts who design the systems and programmers who write software instructions that tell computers what to do. System users, too, are integral to the system. *Telecommunications* components include multimedia technology that incorporates sound, animation, video, and photography along with ordinary graphics and text. Electronic discussion groups, videoconferencing, and other forms of interactive dialogue are possible with communication devices (such as global positioning systems and personal digital assistants) and communication channels (such as satellite communications).

KEY TERMS

information manager, 380

information management, 380

data, 380

information, 380

information systems (IS), 381

electronic information technologies (EIT), 385

fax machine, 385

voice mail, 385

electronic mail (e-mail) system, 386

electronic conferencing, 386

groupware, 386

data communication networks, 386

Internet, 386

Internet service provider (ISP), 387

World Wide Web, 387

Web servers, 388

browser, 388

directories, 388

search engine, 388

intranet, 388

firewall, 388

extranet, 388

mass-customization, 389

knowledge workers, 392

transaction processing systems (TPS), 395

systems operations personnel, 396

computer-aided design (CAD), 396

computer-aided manufacturing (CAM), 397

management information systems (MIS), 397

decision support systems (DSS), 397

executive support system (ESS), 397

artificial intelligence (AI), 398

robotics, 398

expert system, 399

computer network, 399

hardware, 399

input device, 400

central processing unit (CPU), 400

main memory, 400

program, 400

output device, 401

random access memory (RAM), 401

secondary storage, 401

hard disks, 401

diskettes, 401

CD-ROMs, 401

software, 401

system program, 402

language program, 402

application program, 402

graphical user interface (GUI), 402

icons, 403

database, 404

batch processing, 404

online processing, 405

word-processing programs, 405

electronic spreadsheets, 405

database management systems, 405

computer graphics programs, 406

presentation graphics software, 406

desktop publishing, 407

multimedia communication systems, 408

wide area network (WAN), 409

local area network (LAN), 410

modem, 410

client–server network, 410

client, 410

server, 410

STUDY QUESTIONS AND EXERCISES

Review Questions

1. Why does a business need to manage information as a resource?
2. How can an e-mail system increase office productivity and efficiency?
3. Why do the four levels of user groups in an organization need different kinds of information from an information system?
4. In what ways are local area networks (LANs) different from or similar to wide area networks (WANs)?
5. What are the main types of electronic information technologies being applied in business information systems?

Analysis Questions

6. Give two examples (other than those provided in this chapter) for each of the major types of application programs used in business.

7. Describe three or four activities in which you regularly engage that might be made easier by multimedia technology.

8. Give three examples (other than those provided in this chapter) of how a company can become leaner by adopting a networked information system.

Application Exercises

9. Describe the information system at your college or university. Identify its components and architecture.

Identify the features that either promote or inhibit collaboration among system users.

10. Visit a small business in your community to investigate the ways it is using communication technologies and the ways it plans to use them in the future. Prepare a report for presentation in class.

11. Identify two businesses, one locally in your community and one located elsewhere (perhaps one that you have read about or seen on television), that you think might be able to combine their efforts effectively in a new business venture. Describe what each company would contribute (in terms of services, skills, and business processes), and then explain how they can use the Internet and the World Wide Web to coordinate their activities.

Building Your Business Skills

The Art and Science of Point-and-Click Research

Goal

To introduce students to World Wide Web search sites.

Situation

In a recent survey of nearly 2000 Web users, two-thirds stated that they used the Web to obtain work-related information. With an estimated 320 million pages of information on the Web, the challenge for business users is fairly obvious: how to find what they're looking for.

Method

You'll need a computer and access to the World Wide Web to complete this exercise.

Step 1:

Get together with three other classmates and decide on a business-related research topic. Choose a topic that interests you, for example, "Business Implications of the Year 2000 Census," "Labour Disputes in Professional Sports," or "Marketing Music Lessons and Instruments to Parents of Young Children."

Step 2:

Search the following sites for information on your topic. Divide the sites among group members to speed the process:

- Yahoo! www.yahoo.com
- Hotbot, www.hotbot.com
- Alta Vista, www.altavista.net
- Excite, www.excite.com
- Infoseek, www.infoseek.com
- Lycos, www.lycos.com
- Metacrawler, www.metacrawler.com

- Dogpile, www.dogpile.com
- Ask Jeeves, www.askjeeves.com
- Northern Light, www.nlsearch.com
- Internet Sleuth, www.isleuth.com

Take notes as you search so that you can explain your findings to other group members.

Step 3:

Working as a group, answer the following questions about your collective search:

1. Which sites were the easiest to use?

2. Which sites offered the most helpful results? What specific factors made these sites better than the others?

3. Which sites offered the least helpful results? What were the problems?

4. Why is it important to learn the special code words or symbols, called operators, that target a search? (Operators are words like *and*, *or*, and *not* that narrow search queries. For example, using *and* in a search tells the system that all words must appear in the results—certified *and* management *and* accountants.)

Follow-Up Questions

1. Research the differences between search *engines* and search *directories*. Then place the sites listed above in each category. Did you find search engines or directories more helpful in this exercise?

2. Why is it important to learn to use a search site's "Help" function?

3. Based on your personal career goals, how do you think mastering Web research techniques might help you in the future?

4. How has the World Wide Web changed the nature of business research?

Exploring the Net

Most firms rely on expert assistance to get started on network development and buy the technology they need for their Internet systems. Cisco Systems Inc. is the worldwide leader in Internet networking, providing most of the systems that make the Internet work. By looking at Cisco's products, including hardware, software, and services, we can get an idea about both the needs of Internet users and some of the leading-edge solutions that are available. To learn about Cisco, its products, and its customers, visit its Web site at

www.cisco.com

Spend some time navigating through the home page. To get an idea of the variety of Cisco's products and services, enter each of the subject gates (point the mouse to the title and click) located up, down, and across the page. Scroll down the page and select "Services" and "Solutions" titles that seem interesting to you. Be sure to note the different kinds of customers at whom each product is directed. After becoming acquainted with the site, consider the following items:

1. Under "Solutions for Your Network," look at Cisco's "Internet Communications Software." From the description, identify the company's software products, the purpose of those products, the way in which they work, and the benefits of using them.

2. Under Cisco's "Internet Business Solutions," look at the company's approach to "E-Commerce" and its approach to "Business-to-Business E-Commerce." Explain how these approaches differ from one another. Describe the purpose of "E-Commerce" and contrast it with "Business-to-Business E-Commerce."

3. Look at "Employee Productivity" for small to medium-sized businesses. What Internet tools does Cisco offer? Explain the ways in which those tools could improve productivity and identify the kinds of organizational conditions under which they would be most appropriate.

4. Suppose that you have questions about which products are best suited for your firm's Internet requirements and about how certain products would apply to your situation. Where, in the Cisco Web site, would you turn for help?

Concluding Case 13-1

Is Your Computer a Television? Or Is Your TV a Computer?

Picture yourself watching the World Series on TV and using a wireless keyboard to open a window on the television screen. Now you can download the pitcher's career stats from the team's home page on the Internet without even missing an out.

There is little doubt in most observers' minds that some day soon the functions of the family television and the home office computer will be joined in a single machine. Whether that machine will be a computer that picks up TV feeds from the Internet, or a TV with computer and Internet capabilities, is a question that threatens to shake up both the computer and television manufacturing industries, with broadcasters caught in the middle.

In an escalating series of news conferences, product introductions, and sweeping statements about the future as they see it, executives of consumer electronics firms and computer makers have been squaring off for several years. Neither has had much success breaking into the other's market yet, but neither is giving up any time soon. Gateway 2000 Inc., which makes PCs, also sells a big-screen computer television under the brand name Destination. Several electronics firms have marketed Web TV devices that allow users to access the Internet on conventional TVs. Sales of both products have been disappointing.

Most Canadian and U.S. households own one or more TVs, and about 40 percent own a personal computer. Both industries are assuming that with the arrival of digital or high-definition television (HDTV) technology, people will be forced to replace their TVs before the scheduled end of conventional broadcasting in 2006. With the prospect of $150 billion in revenues just from sales of new TV sets, the stakes are high for what may be the biggest market stakeout of the computer age.

PC makers want to produce their television pictures in a format incompatible with the one that broadcasters use, which uses 525 lines per screen but achieves higher resolution than normal with extra channel capacity. TV manufacturers, anticipating the announced plans of major broadcasters who lobbied hard for—and secured—the right to broadcast HDTV, expect to produce high-definition TVs or PC/TVs that accept 1080 lines per screen. The Federal Communication Commission (FCC) in the U.S. has urged an agreement over technology and doesn't want to arbitrate the coming clash.

The computer industry is counting on the decline of television viewing and the rise of the Internet to change the way in which people use their TVs. It's already clear that most browsing on the Internet occurs during television's traditional prime time hours. And "we think it is much easier to have a PC do television than to add personal computer capabilities to TVs," says Intel executive Rob Siegal. "The PC has just got to migrate from the home office to the family room." In fact, within the next year, every new PC sold in the United States will include a digital TV receiver as standard equipment, and computer industry executives expect to sell 1 million PCs with digital TV decoders by 2002.

Consumer electronics firms, even while they explore the interactive potential, defend the simplicity and single function of their traditional product, the television set. "I think people will buy these (digital) TVs for entertainment—a great high-definition picture on a big screen," say Richard Kraft, president of Matsushita Electric's U.S. subsidiary, which makes the Panasonic and Quasar brands. And broadcasters have slowed their drive towards HDTV as well. Says Michael Jordan, chairperson of Westinghouse Electric Corp., which owns CBS, "All of a sudden we got this thing approved, and nobody has a clue what they are going to do."

Those in the computer camp counter that with the new digital technology, the "PC theatre," a computer that combines traditional TV programming with computer functions, will be transparently easy to use. But is it what the customer ordered? Jim Meyer, vice-president of Thomson Consumer Electronics, which makes the RCA and Proscan brands, doesn't think so. He says he is not convinced that interactivity is going to be the service that drives this product. "Interactivity may be popular in Silicon Valley, but it may not be popular elsewhere."

CASE QUESTIONS

1. The combination of broadcast and computer functions in a single machine is known in the communication industry as convergence. Do you think convergence is an idea whose time has come? Why or why not?

2. Do you think consumers place greater value on simplicity of use or on functionality? Which do you prefer?

3. Television networks are concentrating on perfecting digital high-definition programming and getting it on the air by 1999, as mandated by the FCC in the U.S. For now they are not planning the kind of interactive programming that computer makers want to offer with their PC/TVs. How might a change in the networks' plans affect the computer and consumer electronics industry? How do you think the networks should use whatever power they have to influence the outcome?

4. Do you foresee any way in which computer and television makers can successfully divide the consumer computer and entertainment markets between them? What would this mean for the consumer?

5. Why might the FCC be unwilling to mandate a solution to the problem of incompatible technologies? Do you agree with the FCC's decision to force the market to choose? ◆

Concluding Case 13-2

Computing Flower Power

G.A. Vantreight & Sons has grown daffodils on Vancouver Island's Saanich peninsula since the 1930s. Each spring, seasonal labourers pick about 12 million yellow daffodils. Vantreight sells about half of its daffodils to the Canadian Cancer Society, which uses them for its fundraiser that kicks off its annual April campaign. Other flowers grown by Vantreight are sold to Canada Safeway, wholesale florists, and other retailers.

As serene and slow moving as this business might seem, it has been changed dramatically by computers in the last few years. The big change is a recently introduced automated payroll system that tracks each worker's production in the field. With the new system, the average worker's output has doubled, labour and production costs have declined, and profits are up.

The system uses 12 portable hand-held computers, bar-coded packaging tags, bar-coded employee identification badges, and a customized software package called FieldManager designed especially for the company. Under the old system, the names of workers were scribbled on notepads before they were sent to various fields to pick. Errors in keeping track of workers were common. And when it rained (which was often), the notepads got soaked. At the end of the day, the notepads were turned in to the office staff so they could figure out how much each worker should be paid.

With the new system, most of these problems have disappeared. Supervisors now record the output of each worker right in the field by scanning the bar-coded identification attached to each bunch of flowers the worker picks. By 3 p.m. each day, the company knows how many flowers have been picked. Under the old system, all the company could do was make an educated guess.

The new system has also meant a change in the way workers are paid. Previously paid a flat $6.50 per hour, workers are now paid 14 cents per bunch of 10 flowers they pick. A fast worker can pick enough flowers to earn the equivalent of $11.50 per hour, a big improvement over the flat-wage amount. This payment system has reduced the number of pickers employed, but those that do work are much more productive. It has also reduced the farm's unit costs—from 22 cents to 18 cents per bunch.

The use of computers is just beginning at Vantreight. The next step is to start tracking bulb production and relate it to actual flower production.

CASE QUESTIONS

1. How has computerization improved productivity and profits at Vantreight?

2. From the workers' perspective, what are the disadvantages of the new computer system?

3. What kinds of attitudes towards computer technology might exist in the minds of field workers as they consider the introduction of the new computer system? What attitudes might supervisors and office workers have? How will these attitudes facilitate or inhibit the acceptance of the new system? ◆

Visit the *Business* Website at www.pearsoned.ca/griffin for up-to-date e-business cases!

CHAPTER 14

The Arcane Art of Accounting in Russia

In Russia, the word *profit* does not mean the same thing it does in the West. Some companies in Russia—major oil companies, the natural gas monopoly, and some large corporations—have been producing Western-style financial statements for a few years. But most enterprises still stick to the old ways. For example, the chief accountant at the Moscow Electrode Factory, Nadezhda Belobrovkina, learned her trade many years ago. She has never heard of generally accepted accounting principles (GAAP), and she still keeps records by hand in a big white ledger. The factory has trouble paying its staff, has fallen heavily into debt, and is way behind in paying its energy bills. But according to Belobrovkina's calculations, the factory still makes money.

The accounting software department at 1C, a Russian computer company, designs software to help other companies convert their raw financial data into two different sets of accounts, one Russian and one Western. Even though the Soviet era is long gone, the Russian accounting system has not been reformed. It was never designed to account for things like profit.

The Russian Finance Ministry would like to see a change, as would the International Monetary Fund, which gave Russia a $22.6 billion assistance package in 1998. Among other things, the money is to be used to institute changes in Russia's outdated accounting system.

Russia's Chart of Accounts is the framework for corporate bookkeeping. But it is designed to help the state's central planners (and more recently the tax police) to prevent people from stealing by keeping close tabs on inventories. It is not designed to help managers develop their businesses. Under the old system, accountants focused on production and tracking of inputs and outputs. They could not say whether value had been added, or whether profit had been made.

Another problem: Accountants were not allowed to set realistic depreciation rates. Rather, the state's published guidelines, which stipulated the lifespan of everything from chairs to machine tools, discouraged replacement of obsolete equipment and buildings. Western accountants, for example, usually set the useful life of a building at 30 years; in Russia they are decreed to last up to 100 years.

The problems with the Russian accounting system are nicely illustrated at Bratsk Aluminum, Russia's largest aluminum producer. The company claimed it made $37 million in profit in 1997, but when Arthur Andersen Company audited the books it reported that the company had actually lost more than $7 million. Profit is not the only area of disagreement. Andersen estimated depreciation at Bratsk at about $56 million, while the company put the figure at only $19 million. The company said that its buildings last 40 to 50 years; Andersen said 15 to 30 years.

The Russian accounting system creates other problems, too. The old Soviet system never accounted for advertising or for employee travel and training costs. But these cost are an important part of doing business in the modern world. Russian authorities seem to view these activities as simply another possibility for tax fraud and therefore put strict limits on deductions.

But changes are in the air, and in the long run an emerging new breed of accountants will help Russia make the transition to a market economy. The head of the Russian Finance Ministry's Department of Accounting Methodology, Alexander Bakaev, is also pushing for more Western-style accounting. He has drafted various reform guidelines and says that Russia must adopt International Accounting Standards. However, he faces an uphill battle. Companies try to avoid value-added tax by shunning accrual accounting in favour of cash accounting. This means that they record transactions not when goods are delivered, but when they receive payment. However, in the Russian system bad debts are endemic, which means that some transactions are never recorded because they are never paid.

Russia's outdated accounting system will also change as eager new Russian entrepreneurs try to attract foreign capital. They realize that they cannot be successful unless they have reasonable accounting records. ◆

This chapter will introduce you to the work performed by accountants and to the basic financial reports of economic activity that are the primary reason for accounting. As you will see in this chapter, accounting goes hand in hand with information management. In today's complex business environment, the need to manage information efficiently and quickly is crucial. Information, of course, can take many forms—information about expenses and assets, information about customers' locations and order patterns, information about supplies and finished goods on hand, information about workers' pay and productivity, information about products in development, and information about competitors and customers. After reading this chapter, you should be able to:

LEARNING OBJECTIVES

1. Explain the role of accountants and distinguish between the kinds of work done by *public* and *private accountants*.

2. Explain how the *accounting equation* and *double-entry accounting* are used in record keeping.

3. Describe the three basic *financial statements* and show how they reflect the activity and financial condition of a business.

4. Discuss the importance of *budgets* in internal planning and control.

5. Explain how computing key *financial ratios* can help in analyzing the financial strengths of a business.

6. Explain some of the special issues facing accountants at firms that do international business.

WHAT IS ACCOUNTING?

Accounting is a comprehensive information system for collecting, analyzing, and communicating financial information. As such, it is a system for measuring business performance and translating those measures into information for management decisions. Accounting also uses performance measures to prepare performance reports for owners, the public, and regulatory agencies. To meet these objectives, accountants keep records of such transactions as taxes paid, income received, and expenses incurred, and they analyze the effects of these transactions on particular business activities. By sorting, analyzing, and recording thousands of transactions, accountants can determine how well a business is being managed and how financially strong it is.

> **accounting**
> *A comprehensive system for collecting, analyzing, and communicating financial information.*

   Bookkeeping, a term that is sometimes confused with accounting, is just one phase of accounting—the recording of accounting transactions. Clearly, accounting is much more comprehensive than bookkeeping because accounting involves more than just the recording of information.

> **bookkeeping**
> *Recording accounting transactions.*

   Because businesses engage in many thousands of transactions, ensuring consistent, dependable financial information is mandatory. This is the job of the **accounting system**: an organized procedure for identifying, measuring, recording, and retaining financial information so that it can be used in accounting statements and management reports. The system includes all the people, reports, computers, procedures, and resources for compiling financial transactions.[1]

> **accounting system**
> *An organized procedure for identifying, measuring, recording, and retaining financial information so that it can be used in accounting statements and management reports.*

Users of Accounting Information

Noranda Inc., Canada's biggest natural resource company, faced an accounting challenge when it announced plans to refocus on the mining and metals side of its activities by selling its forest products and oil and natural gas interests. In preparation for the announcement, corporate officers relied on accounting to provide information for everyone who might be interested in the firm's activities. Its 49 percent ownership of Norcen Energy Resources Ltd. would be sold. Its oil and gas subsidiary, Canadian Hunter Exploration Ltd., would be distributed as a dividend to Noranda shareholders, as would its interest in Noranda Forest Inc., a forest products company. A statement was issued to shareholders and the public to show clearly how much each of the three segments contributed to Noranda's overall sales, expenses, and earnings. Current and potential stockholders also had to be told how the new stock shares would be distributed.[2]

Noranda accountants had to tabulate financial projections for the separation because stakeholders would have important questions about each of the three companies destined for separation: Do the business prospects indicate that as separate companies they are good credit risks? As investments, would they pay sufficient financial returns to owners? Have adequate arrangements been made for employee retirement funds and benefits? Do their business prospects look healthy enough to support current employment levels? Upon receiving accounting answers to questions such as these, different information users (owners, employees, regulatory agencies, lenders, and the public) are better prepared to make decisions for themselves and for their organizations.

As the Noranda story illustrates, there are numerous users of accounting information:

- *Business managers* use accounting information to set goals, develop plans, set budgets, and evaluate future prospects.

- *Employees and unions* use accounting information to get paid and to plan for and receive such benefits as health care, insurance, vacation time, and retirement pay.

- *Investors and creditors* use accounting information to estimate returns to stockholders, to determine a company's growth prospects, and to decide if it is a good credit risk before investing or lending.

- *Taxing authorities* use accounting information to plan for tax inflows, to determine the tax liabilities of individuals and businesses, and to ensure that correct amounts are paid in a timely fashion.

- *Government regulatory agencies* rely on accounting information to fulfil their duties; the provincial securities commissions, for example, require firms to file financial disclosures so that potential investors have valid information about a company's financial status.

Noranda Inc.
www.noranda.ca

WHO ARE ACCOUNTANTS AND WHAT DO THEY DO?

controller
The individual who manages all the firm's accounting activities.

At the head of the accounting system is the **controller**, who manages all the firm's accounting activities. As chief accounting officer, the controller ensures that the accounting system provides the reports and statements needed for planning, controlling, and decision-making activities. This broad range of activities requires different types of accounting specialists. In this section, we will begin by distinguishing between the two main fields of ac-

A financial report is an integral component of the financial accounting system.

counting, *financial* and *managerial*. Then we will discuss the different functions and activities of *chartered accountants* and *private accountants*. The "Business Today" box describes the various careers open to students interested in these areas.

Financial and Managerial Accounting

In any company, two fields of accounting—financial and managerial—can be distinguished by the different users they serve. As we have just seen, it is both convenient and accurate to classify users of accounting information as users outside the company and users inside the company. This same distinction allows us to categorize accounting systems as either *financial* or *managerial*.

Financial Accounting

A firm's **financial accounting system** is concerned with *external* users of information—consumer groups, unions, shareholders, and government agencies. It prepares and publishes income statements and balance sheets at regular intervals. All of these documents focus on the activities of *the company as a whole*, rather than on individual departments or divisions.

    In reporting data, financial accountants must conform to standard reporting formats and procedures imposed by both the accounting profession and government regulatory agencies. This requirement helps ensure that users can clearly compare information, whether from many different companies or from the same company at different times. The information in such reports is mostly *historical*: That is, it summarizes financial transactions that have occurred during past accounting periods.

financial accounting system
The process whereby interested groups are kept informed about the financial condition of a firm.

Managerial Accounting

In contrast, **managerial** (or **management**) **accounting** serves *internal* users. Managers at all levels need information to make decisions for their departments, to monitor current projects, and to plan for future activities. Other employees, too, need accounting information. Engineers, for instance, want to

managerial accounting
Internal procedures that alert managers to problems and aid them in planning and decision making.

BUSINESS TODAY

Certification Programs in Accounting and Finance

Not too long ago, a professional certificate in accounting meant the CA or Chartered Accountant. To become a CA, a person must earn a university degree, complete an accounting-oriented education program, and then pass a national exam. About half of all CAs work in public accounting firms (CA firms). These firms give external opinions on their clients' financial statements. The other half work in business, government, and non-profit organizations. The main emphasis in CA work is on financial accounting, auditing, and taxation accounting.

In recent years, accounting and financial skills have become increasingly specialized. In addition to the CA, the following certification programs are now available.

- *Certified General Accountant (CGA).* To become a CGA, a person must complete an education program and pass a national exam. To be eligible, a person must have an accounting job with a company. There are fewer CGAs than CAs, and in some provinces they are not allowed to give opinions on financial statements of publicly held companies. Almost all CGAs work in private companies, but there are a few CGA firms. Some CGAs work in CA firms.

- *Certified Management Accountant (CMA).* The goal of the CMA program is to train accountants for industry. To become a CMA, a person must have an accounting position with a company and must complete an education program. Unlike CAs, CMAs have management accounting as their focus. That is, they are concerned about internal uses of accounting data rather than their external uses, as are CAs.

- *Certified Financial Analyst (CFA).* To earn the CFA designation, a person must complete a three-year self-study program and pass a series of three national exams of increasing difficulty. These exams deal with securities regulations, investments, and related topics. The CFA designation is granted only to people who hold jobs in the securities industry (e.g., investment bankers, stockbrokers, securities analysts, etc.).

- *Certified Financial Planner.* This is a two-year course of studies that is relevant for those who will be advising clients with respect to retirement planning, tax planning, and the setting up of investment programs. There are six courses at six levels that must be taken. There is an exam at the end of each course, as well as a national exam at the end of the six courses. Courses can be taken by correspondence or in-class.

- *Canadian Securities Course (CSC).* The CSC is a mandatory licensing requirement for people training to become investment advisers. Courses are offered by correspondence for people in the financial services industry (e.g., mutual fund salespeople, financial planners, bank employees, etc.). The course is designed to increase the competency levels of people working in the securities and financial services industry. To complete the one-year course, students must pass a three-hour exam.

- *Registered Financial Planner.* This designation is offered by the Canadian Association of Financial Planners, and is relevant for individuals who are helping people with financial planning needs. The course, which is open only to individuals who are members of the Association, is a self-study course. A six-hour exam must be passed before the designation is granted. No formal classes are required, but the Association does offer a series of financial planning seminars that are helpful in studying for the exam. The time required to earn the designation varies depending on how much experience and knowledge the person has.

know costs for materials and production so they can make product or operations improvements. To set performance goals, salespeople need data on past sales by geographic region. Purchasing agents use information on materials costs to negotiate terms with suppliers.

Reports to these users serve *the company's individual units*, whether departments, projects, plants, or divisions. Internal reports may be designed in any form that will assist internal users in planning, decision making, and controlling. Furthermore, as *projections and forecasts* of both financial data and business activities, internal reports are an extremely important part of the management accounting system: They are forward-looking rather than historical in nature.

Professional Accountants

Users of financial statements want to be confident that the accountants who have prepared them have a high level of expertise and credibility. Three professional accounting organizations have developed in Canada to certify accounting expertise.

The Canadian Institute of Chartered Accountants (CICA) grants the **chartered accountant (CA)** designation. To achieve this designation, a person must earn a university degree, then complete an educational program and pass a national exam. About half of all CAs work in CA firms that offer accounting services to the public; the other half work in government or industry. CA firms typically provide audit, tax, and management services (see Table 14.1 for a list of the 10 largest CA firms in Canada). CAs focus on external financial reporting, that is, certifying for various interested parties (shareholders, lenders, Canada Customs and Revenue Agency, etc.) that the financial records of a company accurately reflect the true financial condition of the firm.

The Certified General Accountants' Association of Canada grants the **certified general accountant (CGA)** designation. To achieve the designation, a person must complete an education program and pass a national exam. Some CGAs work in private industry and others work in CGA firms. CGAs also focus on external financial reporting, and emphasize the use of the computer as a management accounting tool.

The Society of Management Accountants of Canada grants the **certified management accountant (CMA)** designation. To achieve the designation, a person must complete an education program. Unlike CAs or CGAs, CMAs typically work in industry and focus on internal management accounting, that is, they provide information for management decision making within the firm. CMAs emphasize the role of accountants in the planning and overall strategy of the firm in which they work.

Auditing

In an **audit**, the accountant examines a company's accounting system to determine whether the company's financial reports fairly present its financial operations. Companies normally must provide audited financial reports when applying for loans or when selling stock.

chartered accountant (CA)
An individual who has met certain experience and education requirements and has passed a licensing examination; acts as an outside accountant for other firms.

certified general accountant (CGA)
An individual who has completed an education program and passed a national exam; works in private industry or a CGA firm.

Canadian Institute of Chartered Accountants
www.cica.ca

Certified General Accountants' Association of Canada
www.cga-canada.org

certified management accountant (CMA)
An individual who has completed an education program; works in industry and focuses on internal management accounting.

audit
An accountant's examination of a company's financial records to determine if it used proper procedures to prepare its financial reports.

Table 14.1	The Top 10 Accounting Firms in Canada (ranked by revenues)
Company	**Annual Revenues (in millions)**
1. PricewaterhouseCoopers LLP	$845
2. Deloitte & Touche LLP	750
3. KPMG LLP	735
4. Ernst & Young LLP	616
5. Grant Thornton Canada	227
6. Arthur Andersen	203
7. BDO Dunwoody LLP	172
8. Collins Barrow/Mintz & Partners	56
9. Richter, Usher & Vineberg	54
10. HLB/Schwartz Zlevitsky Feldman	37

CMA Canada grants professional designations in management accounting. It serves more than 31 000 Certified Management Accountants and more than 10 000 CMA students. It offers online workshops, career advice, and designation requirements, and produces a number of publications, products, and services. Visit CMA Canada at:

www.cma-canada.org

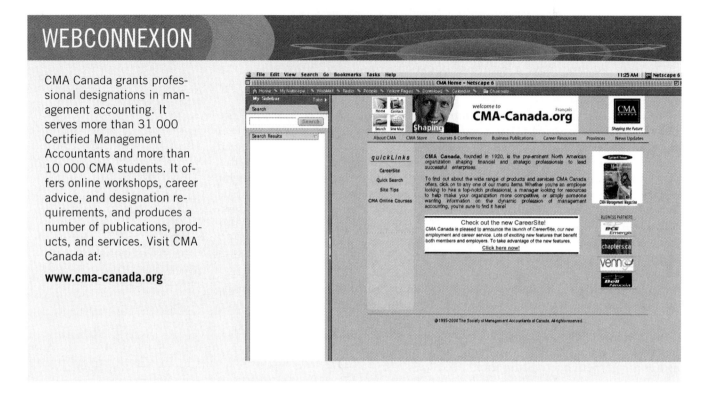

The audit will determine if the firm has controls to prevent errors or fraud from going undetected. Auditors also examine receipts such as shipping documents, cancelled cheques, payroll records, and cash receipts records. In some cases, an auditor may physically check inventories, equipment, or other assets, even if it means descending 200 metres underground in a lead mine.

Forensic accountants are special types of accountants who track down hidden funds in business firms. Because white-collar crime is on the increase, the number of forensic accountants has increased in recent years. They were used to unravel the Daiwa Bank and Barings Bank scandals. They are also examining Swiss bank accounts for assets deposited by victims of Nazi persecution during the Second World War.[3] Al Rosen is a well-known Canadian forensic accountant (see Video Case IV-2 on page 453).

One of the auditor's responsibilities is to ensure that the client's accounting system adheres to generally accepted accounting principles. **Generally accepted accounting principles (GAAP)** are a body of theory and procedure developed and monitored by the CICA, a professional accounting organization. At the end of an audit, the auditor will certify whether the client's financial reports comply with GAAP.

Recently, some non-profit organizations such as churches and universities have said that they felt pressured by their auditors to use GAAP. They argue, however, that GAAP principles are designed for profit-seeking business firms, not non-profit organizations. Non-profits should be judged on how well they meet their goals—for example, helping people—rather than on a financial criterion like profit.[4]

forensic accountant
An accountant who tracks down hidden funds in business firms, usually as part of a criminal investigation.

generally accepted accounting principles (GAAP)
Standard rules and methods used by accountants in preparing financial reports.

Tax Services

Tax services include helping clients not only with preparing their tax returns but also in their tax planning. Tax laws are complex. A CA's advice can help a business structure (or restructure) its operations and investments and save millions of dollars in taxes. To serve their clients best, of course, accountants must stay abreast of changes in tax laws—no simple matter.

Management Services

Management services range from personal financial planning to planning corporate mergers. Other services include plant layout and design, marketing studies, production scheduling, computer feasibility studies, and design and implementation of accounting systems. Some CA firms even assist in executive recruitment. Small wonder that the staffs of CA firms include engineers, architects, mathematicians, and even psychologists.

Private Accountants

To assure the fairness of their reports, CAs and CGAs must be independent of the firms they audit. They are employees of accounting firms and provide services for many clients. But businesses also hire their own **private accountants** as salaried employees to deal with the company's day-to-day accounting needs.

Private accountants perform a variety of accounting jobs. An internal auditor at Petro-Canada, for example, might fly to the Hibernia site to confirm the accuracy of oil-flow meters on the offshore drilling platform. But a supervisor responsible for $200 million in monthly accounts payable to vendors and employees may travel no further than the executive suite. The nature of the accounting job thus depends on the specific business and the activities needed to make that business a success.

Large businesses employ specialized accountants in such areas as budgets, financial planning, internal auditing, payroll, and taxation. Each accounting area has its own challenges and excitement. In small businesses, a single individual may handle all accounting tasks—and approve credit terms, too!

The "It's a Wired World" box describes an interesting dilemma for accounting firms that wish to provide auditing and management consulting services to new dot-com firms.

private accountant
An accountant hired as a salaried employee to deal with a company's day-to-day accounting needs.

TOOLS OF THE ACCOUNTING TRADE

All accountants, whether public or private, rely on record keeping. Private accountants use journals and ledgers to enter and keep track of business transactions for their company. Underlying these records are the two key concepts of accounting: the accounting equation and double-entry bookkeeping.[5]

Record Keeping with Journals and Ledgers

As Figure 14.1 shows, record keeping begins with initial records of the firm's financial transactions. Examples include sales orders, invoices for incoming materials, employee time cards, and customer payments on instalment purchases. Large companies receive and process tens of thousands of these documents every day. But unless they are analyzed and classified in an orderly fashion, managers cannot keep track of the business's progress.

As *initial records* are received, they are sorted and entered into a **journal**: a chronological record of financial transactions, including a brief description of each. They are now *intermediate records*. Most companies keep specialized journals for different transactions, such as cash receipts, sales, and purchases.

Journal transactions are summarized, usually on a monthly basis, in a *final record* called the **ledger**. In the phrase *auditing the books*, the *book* is the ledger. Like specialized journals, the ledger is divided into *accounts*, such as

journal
A chronological record of a firm's financial transactions along with a brief description of each transaction.

ledger
Summations of journal entries, by category, that show the effects of transactions on the balance in each account.

IT'S A WIRED WORLD

A Roundabout Look at Conflicting Interests

With all the new dot-com companies popping up, things are looking up for accounting firms. Because all those e-businesses need accounting services—setting up accounting systems, preparing taxes and financial reports, conducting audits—prospects are good for an upsurge of new clients. Or are they? Two factors are getting in the way, one having to do with the lean purses of the dot-com companies, and the other having to do with the structure of today's large accounting firms. As a result, accounting firms are running into roadblocks in trying to pursue dot-com clients.

Many dot-coms are short on cash; most of them are operating in the red even though prospects may be bright for future earnings. Some of today's financially strapped dot-coms will prosper and become tomorrow's e-commerce giants. Naturally, public accounting firms would like them to become giant clients in need of accounting services for years to come. PricewaterhouseCoopers, for example, expects that about half of its consulting revenues will eventually come from e-businesses. Unfortunately, would-be e-giants need accounting services now, including management advisory services to help formulate focused strategies, target desirable markets, and improve operations now, while they're getting started, instead of later. The problem is that they can't pay now.

The solution? Increasingly, accounting firms are accepting equity positions instead of cash payment. In return for its services, the accounting firm becomes part-owner of the dot-com company. Generally speaking, it's a good arrangement. While the accounting firm gets a new client (and stands to gain future revenues from its ownership position), the dot-com gets timely professional management help without laying out badly needed cash.

But there's a problem. What the accounting firm gains in a present consulting client it may lose in a future auditing client. Accounting firms are not allowed to make the kind of ownership-investment arrangement described above *and* provide auditing (or other financial accounting) services for the same client because there is a potential conflict of interest. Rules require that auditors have no investment stake in the companies they audit. In fact, it stands to reason that allowing an accounting firm to audit a company in which it has an ownership interest is an invitation to financial mischief. It would be like asking a bank to audit itself rather than hiring an independent auditor.

Nor do the problems stop there. As part-owner, the accounting firm must also steer away from other part-owners in the company. Suppose, for example, that a number of other firms, such as a shipping company, an investment firm, a wholesaler, and a computer supplier, also have ownership interests in the same dot-com. The accounting firm must also decline to audit those firms. Again, there is a potential conflict of interest: The accounting firm could make the dot-com's financial position look good in order to improve the appearance of its fellow part-owners' financial positions.

At present, therefore, it appears that the dot-com explosion that looks like such a terrific opportunity for accounting firms may turn out to be much more limited. Currently, an accountant is forced to make a choice: to take on the dot-com as a client for auditing services or as a client for management advisory services. Accountants can't have it both ways. And whatever choice the accountant makes, the accounting firm also has to ensure that its auditors and management consultants know what its accountants are doing.

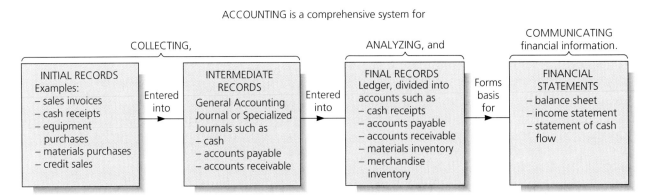

ACCOUNTING is a comprehensive system for

COLLECTING,   ANALYZING, and   COMMUNICATING financial information.

INITIAL RECORDS
Examples:
– sales invoices
– cash receipts
– equipment purchases
– materials purchases
– credit sales

Entered into →

INTERMEDIATE RECORDS
General Accounting Journal or Specialized Journals such as
– cash
– accounts payable
– accounts receivable

Entered into →

FINAL RECORDS
Ledger, divided into accounts such as
– cash receipts
– accounts payable
– accounts receivable
– materials inventory
– merchandise inventory

Forms basis for →

FINANCIAL STATEMENTS
– balance sheet
– income statement
– statement of cash flow

Figure 14.1
Accounting and record keeping.

cash, inventories, and *receivables*. The cash account, for example, is a detailed record of all the firm's changes in cash. Other accounts record changes in each type of asset and liability. Ledgers also feature an important column labelled "balance," which shows the current total dollar amount in each account. If a balance in a given account is unexpectedly high or low, tracking backwards to the corresponding journal entry should reveal the cause of the unexpected figure.

Financial Reports and the Fiscal Year

At the end of the year, all of the accounts in the ledger are totalled, and the firm's financial status is assessed. This summation is the basis for annual financial reports. With the preparation of reports, the old accounting cycle ends and a new cycle begins. The timing of the annual accounting cycle is called the **fiscal year**: the 12-month period used for financial reporting purposes. Although most companies adopt the calendar year as their fiscal year, many companies use 12-month periods that reflect the seasonal nature of their industries. For example, to close its fiscal year at the completion of harvesting, a fruit orchard may select the period from September 1 to August 31.

> **fiscal year**
> The 12-month period used for financial reporting purposes.

As an example of the record-keeping process, consider Figures 14.2 and 14.3, which illustrate a portion of the process for Perfect Posters Inc., a hypothetical wholesaler. In Figure 14.2, a cheque from Eye-Poppers (an initial record) is entered in Perfect Posters' general accounting journal (an intermediate record).

In Figure 14.3, this entry eventually turns up in Perfect Posters' general ledger, where it becomes a final record showing a cash account balance of $98 808.43. In the next section we see how this entry is ultimately reflected in the financial reports that Perfect Posters submits to its stockholders and its bank.

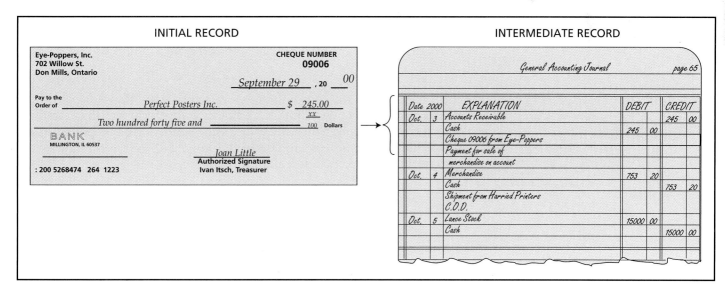

Figure 14.2
Entering a cheque in the general journal. The transaction begins when Perfect Posters receives a cheque from Eye-Poppers. Along with a brief explanation, the amount of the cheque is entered on the *debit* side of Perfect Posters' general accounting journal. Note that the amount, $245, has also been entered on Oct. 4 as an *accounts receivable*. The accountant has noted both a *decrease* in the company's assets (money owed Perfect by Eye-Poppers) and an *increase* (money paid to Perfect Posters by Eye-Poppers). As we will see, these entries will be balanced in the firm's general ledger (Figure 14.3).

General Ledger						page 19	
Accounts Receivable Account							
Date 2000			DEBIT		CREDIT	BALANCE	
Sept.	30					7436	61
Sept.	30	No Blond Books			324 46	4222	15
Oct.	3	Eye Poppers			245 00	3977	15
Oct.	6	Walls R Us	5131 32			9106	47
Oct.	10	Cover Ale			123 45	8985	02

General Ledger							
Cash Account							
Date 2000			DEBIT		CREDIT	BALANCE	
Oct.	3					98 563	43
Oct.	3	Eye Poppers	245 00			98 808	43
Oct.	4	Harried Printers			753 20	98 055	23
Oct.	5	Lance			15 000 00	83 055	23
Oct.	5	Walls R Us			5131 20	77 924	03

Figure 14.3
Entering a cheque in the general ledger. Perfect Posters' accountant now transfers the entry from the general journal to the general ledger. The ledger is divided into two accounts: *accounts receivable* and *cash*. Note that a new column, *balance*, also appears; total dollar amounts for each type of account are entered here. As we will see, the accountant has used the *double-entry accounting system*. The $245 cheque from Eye-Poppers decreased Perfect Posters' accounts receivable account (it is no longer owed the money) *and* increases its cash account. On the company's balance sheet (Figure 14.4), both balances will appear as *current assets*.

The Accounting Equation

At various points in the year, public and private accountants balance the data in journals and ledgers by using the following accounting equation:

$$\text{Assets} = \text{Liabilities} + \text{Owners' equity}$$

To understand why this equation is important, you must first understand what accountants mean by assets, liabilities, and owners' equity.

You are probably familiar with the first two terms in their general sense. Charm and intelligence are often said to be "assets." Someone who cannot swim may be a "liability" on a boat trip. Accountants apply these terms more narrowly, focusing on items with quantifiable value. Thus an **asset**, in the accounting sense, is anything of economic value owned by the firm. Examples include land, buildings, equipment, inventory, and payments due the company. In contrast, a **liability** is a debt owed by the firm to others.

You may have heard people speak of the "equity" they have in their home, meaning the amount of money they would get if they sold the house and paid off the mortgage. Similarly, **owners' equity** refers to the amount of money a firm's owners would receive if they sold all the company's assets and paid off all its liabilities (liquidated the company). We can rewrite the accounting equation to show this definition:

$$\text{Assets} - \text{Liabilities} = \text{Owners' equity}$$

If a company's assets exceed its liabilities, owners' equity is positive: If the company goes out of business, the owners will receive some cash (a gain) after selling assets and paying off liabilities. If liabilities outweigh assets, however, owners' equity is negative: There are insufficient assets to pay off all debts. If the company goes out of business, the owners will get no cash and some creditors will not be paid. Finally, owners' equity is also a meaningful number of both investors and lenders. For example, before lending money to owners, lenders want to know the amount of owners' equity existing in a business.

asset
Anything of economic value owned by a firm or individual.

liability
Any debt owed by a firm or individual to others.

owners' equity
Any positive difference between a firm's assets and its liabilities; what would remain for a firm's owners if the company were liquidated, all its assets were sold, and all its debts were paid.

Owners' equity consists of two sources of capital:

- the amount the owners originally invested
- profits earned by and reinvested in the company.

When a company operates profitably, its assets increase faster than its liabilities. Owners' equity, therefore, will increase if profits are kept in the business instead of paid out as dividends to shareholders. Owners' equity can also increase if owners invest more of their own money to increase assets. However, owners' equity can shrink if the company operates at a loss or if the owners withdraw assets.

Double-Entry Accounting

If your business purchases inventory with cash, you do two things: (1) decrease your cash and (2) increase your inventory. Similarly, if you purchase supplies on credit, you (1) increase your supplies and (2) increase your accounts payable. If you invest more money in your business, you (1) increase your cash and (2) increase your owners' equity. In other words, *every transaction affects two accounts*. Accountants thus use a **double-entry accounting system** to record the *dual effects* of financial transactions.

Recording dual effects ensures that the accounting equation always balances. As the term implies, the double-entry system requires at least two bookkeeping entries for each transaction. This practice keeps the accounting equation in balance.

double-entry accounting system
A bookkeeping system, developed in the fifteenth century and still in use, that requires every transaction to be entered in two ways—how it affects assets and how it affects liabilities and owners' equity—so that the accounting equation is always in balance.

FINANCIAL STATEMENTS

As we noted earlier, the primary purpose of accounting is to summarize the results of a business's transactions and to issue reports that can help managers and others make informed decisions. Some of the most important reports, called **financial statements**, fall into several broad categories: balance sheets, income statements, and statements of cash flows. Balance sheets are sometimes called statements of financial position because they show the financial condition of a firm at one time. Other financial statements summarize the economic activities that have occurred during a specified period, usually one year. Together, these statements provide a picture of a business's financial health: what it is worth, how much it earns, and how it spends its resources.[6] Misleading financial statements can be very costly to investors.

financial statement
Any of several types of broad reports regarding a company's financial status; most often used in reference to balance sheets, income statements, and/or statements of cash flows.

Balance Sheets

Balance sheets supply detailed information about the accounting equation factors: assets, liabilities, and owners' equity. Because they also show a firm's financial condition at one point in time, balance sheets are sometimes called *statements of financial position*. Figure 14.4 shows the balance sheet for Perfect Posters.

balance sheet
A type of financial statement that summarizes a firm's financial position on a particular date in terms of its assets, liabilities, and owners' equity.

Assets

As we have seen, an asset is any economic resource that a company owns and from which it can expect to derive some future benefit. From an accounting standpoint, most companies have three types of assets: *current, fixed*, and *intangible*.

❑❑❑❑❑❑❑❑❑ **Perfect Posters, Inc.**
555 Riverview, Toronto, Ontario

Perfect Posters, Inc.
Balance Sheet
As of December 31, 2000

Assets

Current Assets:
Cash		$7,050
Marketable securities. . . .		2,300
Accounts receivable.	$26,210	
Less: Allowance of.		
doubtful accounts.	(650)	25,560
Merchandise inventory.		21,250
Prepaid expenses		1,050
Total current assets		**$57,210**

Fixed Assets:
Land		18,000
Building	65,000	
Less: Accumulated		
depreciation	(22,500)	42,500
Equipment	72,195	
Less: Accumulated		
depreciation	(24,815)	47,380
Total fixed assets. . .		**107,880**

Intangible Assets:
Patents	7,100	
Trademarks	900	
Total intangible		
assets		**8,000**
Total assets		**$173,090**

Liabilities and Owners' Equity

Current liabilities:
Accounts payable.	$16,315	
Wages payable.	3,700	
Taxes payable.	1,920	
Total current liabilities		**$21,935**

Long-term liabilities:
Notes payable, 8%		
due 2001	10,000	
Bonds payable, 9%		
due 2003	30,000	
Total long-term		
liabilities		**40,000**
Total liabilities		**$61,935**

Owners' Equity
Common stock, $5 par	40,000	
Additional paid-in capital	15,000	
Retained earnings	56,155	
Total owners' equity		**111,155**
Total liabilities and owners' equity . . .		**$173,090**

Figure 14.4
Perfect Posters' balance sheet shows clearly that the firm's total assets equal its total liabilities and owners' equity.

current assets
Cash and other assets that can be converted into cash within a year.

liquidity
The ease and speed with which an asset can be converted to cash; cash is said to be perfectly liquid.

accounts receivable
Amounts due to the firm from customers who have purchased goods or services on credit; a form of current asset.

merchandise inventory
The cost of merchandise that has been acquired for sale to customers but is still on hand.

Current Assets. **Current assets** include cash and assets that can be converted into cash within a year. They are normally listed in order of **liquidity**: the ease with which they can be converted into cash. Business debts, for example, can usually be satisfied only through payments of cash. A company that needs but cannot generate cash—in other words, a company that is not liquid—may thus be forced to sell assets at sacrifice prices or even go out of business.

By definition, cash is completely liquid. *Marketable securities* purchased as short-term investments are slightly less liquid but can be sold quickly if necessary. Marketable securities include stocks or bonds of other companies, government securities, and money market certificates. There are three other important nonliquid assets held by many companies: *accounts receivable, merchandise inventory*, and *prepaid expenses*.

Accounts receivable are amounts due from customers who have purchased goods on credit. Most businesses expect to receive payment within 30 days of a sale. In our hypothetical example, the entry labelled *Less: Allowance of doubtful accounts* in Figure 14.4 indicates $650 in receivables that Perfect Posters does not expect to collect. Total accounts receivable assets are decreased accordingly.

Following accounts receivable on the Perfect Posters balance sheet is **merchandise inventory**—the cost of merchandise that has been acquired for sale to customers and is still on hand. Accounting for the value of inventories on the balance sheet is difficult because inventories are flowing in and out throughout the year. Therefore, assumptions must be made about which ones were sold and which ones remain in storage.

The **LIFO (last-in-first-out) method** assumes that inventories received last (most recently) are sold first, thus leaving older inventories on hand for future use. In contrast, the **FIFO (first-in-first-out) method** assumes that older inventories (first in) are sold first and newer inventories are held for later use. The method used in calculating inventory (LIFO or FIFO) must be disclosed in a firm's financial statements. It must also be used consistently year after year.

Prepaid expenses include supplies on hand and rent paid for the period to come. They are assets because they have been paid for and are available to the company. In all, Perfect Posters' current assets as of December 31, 2000, totalled $57 210.

Fixed Assets. The next major classification on the balance sheet is usually **fixed assets**. Items in this category have long-term use or value (for example, land, buildings, and equipment). As buildings and equipment wear out or become obsolete, their value decreases. To reflect decreasing value, accountants use **depreciation** to spread the cost of an asset over the years of its useful life. Depreciation means calculating an asset's useful life in years, dividing its worth by that many years, and subtracting the resulting amount each year. Each year, therefore, the asset's remaining value decreases on the books. In Figure 14.4, Perfect Posters shows fixed assets of $107 880 after depreciation.

Intangible Assets. Although their worth is hard to set, intangible assets have monetary value. **Intangible assets** usually include the cost of obtaining rights or privileges such as patents, trademarks, copyrights, and franchise fees. **Goodwill** is the amount paid for an existing business beyond the value of its other assets.

A purchased firm, for example, may have a particularly good reputation or location. In fact, a company's goodwill may be worth more than its tangible assets. For example, when AT&T proposed its buyout of cable operator MediaOne Group for US$60.5 billion, US$40 billion was recorded as goodwill because the fair market value of MediaOne's assets was estimated at only US$20.5 billion.[7] Similarly, when Ford purchased Jaguar for US$2.5 billion, US$2 billion was recorded as goodwill.

Perfect Posters has no goodwill assets; however, it does own trademarks and patents for specialized storage equipment. These are intangible assets worth $8000. Larger companies, of course, have intangible assets that are worth much more.

Liabilities

Like assets, liabilities are often separated into different categories. **Current liabilities** are debts that must be paid within one year. These include **accounts payable**: unpaid bills to suppliers for materials as well as wages and taxes that must be paid in the coming year. Perfect Posters has current liabilities of $21 935.

Long-term liabilities are debts that are not due for at least one year. These normally represent borrowed funds on which the company must pay interest. Perfect Posters' long-term liabilities are $40 000.

LIFO (last-in-first-out) method
Inventories received last (most recently) are sold first, thus leaving older inventories on hand for future use.

FIFO (first-in-first-out) method
Older inventories (first in) are sold first and newer inventories are held for later use.

prepaid expense
Includes supplies on hand and rent paid for the period to come.

fixed assets
Assets that have long-term use or value to the firm such as land, buildings, and machinery.

depreciation
Distributing the cost of a major asset over the years in which it produces revenues; calculated by each year subtracting the asset's original value divided by the number of years in its productive life.

intangible assets
Nonphysical assets such as patents, trademarks, copyrights, and franchise fees, that have economic value but whose precise value is difficult to calculate.

goodwill
The amount paid for an existing business beyond the value of its other assets.

AT&T
www.att.com

MediaOne Group
www.mediaone.com

current liabilities
Any debts owed by the firm that must be paid within one year.

accounts payable
Amounts due from the firm to its suppliers for goods and/or services purchased on credit; a form of current liability.

long-term liabilities
Any debts owed by the firm that are not due for at least one year.

Owners' Equity

paid-in capital
Any additional money invested in the firm by the owners.

retained earnings
A company's net profits less any dividend payments to shareholders.

The final section of the balance sheet in Figure 14.4 shows owners' equity broken down into *common stock, paid-in capital,* and *retained earnings.* When Perfect Posters was formed, the declared legal value of its common stock was $5 per share. By law, this $40 000 ($5 x 8000 shares) cannot be distributed as dividends. **Paid-in capital** is additional money invested in the firm by its owners. Perfect Posters has $15 000 in paid-in capital.

Retained earnings are net profits minus dividend payments to stockholders. Retained earnings accumulate when profits, which could have been distributed to stockholders, are kept instead for use by the company. At the close of 2000, Perfect Posters had retained earnings of $56 155.

Income Statements

income (profit-and-loss) statement
A type of financial statement that describes a firm's revenues and expenses and indicates whether the firm has earned a profit or suffered a loss during a given period.

The **income statement** is sometimes called a **profit-and-loss statement**, because its description of revenues and expenses results in a figure showing the firm's annual profit or loss. In other words,

$$\text{Revenues} - \text{Expenses} = \text{Profit (or loss)}$$

□□□□□□□□□□□□ Perfect Posters, Inc.		
555 Riverview, Toronto, Ontario		
Perfect Posters, Inc.		
Income Statement		
Year ended December 31, 2000		
Revenues (gross sales)..........		**$256,425**
Costs of goods sold:		
Merchandise inventory,		
January 1, 2000..............	$22,380	
Merchandise purchases		
during year................	103,635	
Goods available for sale........		$126,015
Less: Merchandise inventory,		
December 31, 2000.........		21,250
Cost of goods sold		**104,765**
Gross profit		**151,660**
Operating expenses:		
Selling and repackaging expenses:		
Salaries and wages........	49,750	
Advertising..............	6,380	
Depreciation-warehouse and..		
repackaging equipment......	3,350	
Total selling and repackaging		
expenses.................		59,480
Administrative expenses:		
Salaries and wages..........	55,100	
Supplies...................	4,150	
Utilities....................	3,800	
Depreciation-office equipment.	3,420	
Interest expense.................	2,900	
Miscellaneous expenses..........	1,835	
Total administration expenses......		71,205
Total operating expenses......		**130,685**
Operating income (income before taxes)...		20,975
Income taxes...................		8,390
Net income....................		**$12,585**

Figure 14.5
Perfect Posters' income statement. The final entry on the income statement, the bottom line, reports the firm's profit or loss.

Popularly known as "the bottom line," profit or loss is probably the most important figure in any business enterprise. Figure 14.5 shows the 2000 income statement for Perfect Posters, whose bottom line that year was $12 585. The income statement is divided into three major categories: *revenues*, *cost of goods sold*, and *operating expenses*.

Revenues

When a law firm receives $250 for preparing a will or when a supermarket collects $65 from a customer buying groceries, both are receiving **revenues**: the funds that flow into a business from the sale of goods or services. In 2000, Perfect Posters reported revenues of $256 425 from the sale of art prints and other posters.

revenues
Any monies received by a firm as a result of selling a good or service or from other sources such as interest, rent, and licensing fees.

Cost of Goods Sold

In Perfect Posters' income statement, the **cost of goods sold** category shows the costs of obtaining materials to make the products sold during the year. Perfect Posters began 2000 with posters valued at $22 380. Over the year, it spent $103 635 to purchase posters. During 2000, then, the company had $126 015 worth of merchandise available to sell. By the end of the year, it had sold all but $21 250 of those posters, which remained as merchandise inventory. The cost of obtaining the goods sold by the firm was thus $104 765.

cost of goods sold
Any expenses directly involved in producing or selling a good or service during a given time period.

Gross Profit (or Gross Margin). To calculate **gross profit** (or **gross margin**), subtract the cost of goods sold from revenues. Perfect Posters' gross profit in 2000 was $151 660 ($256 425 – $104 765). Expressed as a percentage of sales, gross profit is 59.1 percent ($151 660 / $256 425).

Gross profit percentages vary widely across industries. In retailing, for example, gross margins might be about 30 percent, but in manufacturing they may be somewhat higher, and in pharmaceuticals higher still. For companies with low gross margins, product costs are a big expense. If a company has a high gross margin, it probably has low cost of goods sold but high selling and administrative expenses.

gross profit (gross margin)
A firm's revenues (gross sales) less its cost of goods sold.

Operating Expenses

In addition to costs directly related to acquiring goods, every company has general expenses ranging from erasers to the president's salary. Like cost of goods sold, **operating expenses** are resources that must flow out of a company for it to earn revenues. As you can see in Figure 14.5, Perfect Posters had 2000 operating expenses of $130 685. This figure consists of $59 480 in selling and repackaging expenses and $71 205 in administrative expenses.

Selling expenses result from activities related to selling the firm's goods or services. These may include salaries for the sales force, delivery costs, and advertising expenses. General and administrative expenses, such as management salaries, insurance expenses, and maintenance costs, are expenses related to the general management of the company.

operating expenses
Costs incurred by a firm other than those included in cost of goods sold.

Operating Income and Net Income. Sometimes managers must determine **operating income**, which compares the gross profit from business operations against operating expenses. This calculation for Perfect Posters ($151 660 – $130 685) reveals an operating income, or *income before taxes*, of $20 975. Subtracting income taxes from operating income ($20 975 – $8390) reveals **net income** (also called **net profit** or **net earnings**). In 2000, Perfect Posters' net income was $12 585.

operating income
Compares the gross profit from business operations against operating expenses.

net income (net profit or net earnings)
A firm's gross profit less its operating expenses and income taxes.

Statement of Cash Flows

Some companies prepare only balance sheets and income statements. However, many firms also report a **statement of cash flows**. This statement describes a company's yearly cash receipts and cash payments. It shows the effects on cash of three business activities:

- *Cash flows from operations*. This part of the statement is concerned with the firm's main operating activities: the cash transactions involved in buying and selling goods and services. It reveals how much of the year's profits result from the firm's main line of business (for example, Jaguar's sales of automobiles) rather than from secondary activities (for example, licensing fees a clothing firm paid to Jaguar for using the Jaguar logo on shirts).

- *Cash flows from investing*. This section reports net cash used in or provided by investing. It includes cash receipts and payments from buying and selling stocks, bonds, property, equipment, and other productive assets.

- *Cash flows from financing*. The final section reports net cash from all financing activities. It includes cash inflows from borrowing or issuing stock as well as outflows for payment of dividends and repayment of borrowed money.

The overall change in cash from these three sources provides information to lenders and investors. When creditors and stockholders know how firms obtained and used their funds during the course of a year, it is easier for them to interpret the year-to-year changes in the firm's balance sheet and income statement.

The Budget: An Internal Financial Statement

In addition to financial statements, managers need other types of accounting information to aid in internal planning, controlling, and decision making. Probably the most crucial *internal* financial statement is the budget. A **budget** is a detailed statement of estimated receipts and expenditures for a period of time in the future. Although that period is usually one year, some companies also prepare budgets for three- or five-year periods, especially when considering major capital expenditures.

Budgets are also useful for keeping track of weekly or monthly performance. Procter & Gamble, for example, evaluates all of its business units monthly by comparing actual financial results with monthly budgeted amounts. Discrepancies in "actual versus budget" totals signal potential problems and initiate action to get financial performance back on track.

Although the accounting staff coordinates the budget process, it requires input from many people in the company regarding proposed activities, needed resources, and input sources.[8] Figure 14.6, for example, is a sample sales budget. In preparing such a budget, the accounting department must obtain from the sales group both its projections for units to be sold and expected expenses for each quarter of the coming year. Accountants then draw up the final budget, and throughout the year, the accounting department compares the budget to actual expenditures and revenues.

Reporting Standards and Practices

Accountants follow numerous standard reporting practices and principles when they prepare external reports, including financial statements. The

Figure 14.6
Perfect Posters, Inc. sales budget, First Quarter 2001.

common language dictated by standard practices is designed to give external users confidence in the accuracy and meaning of the information in any financial statement. Spelled out in great detail in GAAP, these principles cover a wide range of issues, such as when to recognize revenues from operations, the so-called "matching" of revenues and expenses, and full public disclosure of financial information to the public. Without agreed-upon practices in these and many other accounting categories, users of financial statements would be unable to compare financial information from different companies and thus misunderstand—or be led to misconstrue—a given company's true financial status.

Revenue Recognition

As we noted earlier, revenues are funds that flow into a business as a result of its operating activities during the accounting period. *Revenue recognition* is the formal recording and reporting of revenues in the financial statements. Although any firm earns revenues continuously as it makes sales, earnings are not reported until the earnings cycle is completed. This cycle is complete under two conditions:

1. The sale is complete and the product has been delivered

2. The sale price to the customer has been collected or is collectable (accounts receivable).

The completion of the earning cycle, then, determines the timing for revenue recognition in the firm's financial statements. Revenues are recorded for the accounting period in which sales are completed and collectable (or collected). This practice assures the reader that the statement gives a fair comparison of what was gained for the resources that were given up.

Matching

Net income is calculated by subtracting expenses from revenues. The matching principle states that expenses will be matched with revenues to determine net income for an accounting period.[9] Why is this principle important? It permits the user of the statement to see how much net gain resulted from the assets that had to be given up in order to generate revenues during the period covered in the statement. Consequently, when we match revenue recognition with expense recognition, we get net income for the period.

Consider the hypothetical case of Little Red Wagon Co. Let's see what happens when the books are kept in two different ways:

1. Revenue recognition is matched with expense recognition to determine net income when the earnings cycle is *completed* (the correct method).

2. Revenue recognition occurs *before* the earnings cycle is completed (an incorrect method).

Suppose that 500 red wagons are produced and delivered to customers at a sales price of $20 each during 2000. In the next year, 600 red wagons are produced and delivered. In part (A) of Table 14.2, the correct matching method has been used: Revenues are recorded for the accounting period in which sales are completed and collectable from customers, as are the expenses of producing and delivering them. The revenues from sales are matched against the expenses of completing them. By using the matching principle, we see clearly how much better off the company is at the end of each accounting period as a result of that period's operations: It earned $2000 net income for the first year and did even better in 2001.

In part (B) of Table 14.2, revenue recognition and the matching principle have been violated. Certain activities of the two accounting periods are disguised and mixed together rather than separated for each period. The result is a distorted performance report that incorrectly shows that 2000 was a better year than 2001. Here's what Red Wagons' accountants did wrong: The sales department sold 200 red wagons (with revenues of $4000) to a customer late in 2000. Those *revenues* are included in the $14 000 for 2000. But because the 200 wagons were produced and delivered to the customer in 2001, the *expenses* are recorded, as in (A), for 2001. The result is a distorted picture of operations. It looks as if expenses for 2001 are out of line for such

Table 14.2	Revenue Recognition and the Matching Principle

(A) The correct method reveals each accounting period's activities and results

	Year ended December 31, 2000	Year ended December 31, 2001
Revenues	$10,000	$12,000
Expenses	8,000	9,000
Net income	2,000	3,000

(B) The incorrect method disguises each accounting period's activities and results

	Year ended December 31, 2000	Year ended December 31, 2001
Revenues	$14,000	$8,000
Expenses	8,000	9,000
Net income	6,000	(1,000)

a low sales level, and it looks as if expenses (as compared to revenues) were kept under better control during 2000. The firm's accountants violated the matching principle by ignoring *the period during which the earnings cycle was completed*. Although $4000 in sales of wagons occurred in 2000, the earnings cycle for those wagons was not completed until they were produced and delivered, which occurred in 2001. Accordingly, both the revenues and expenses for those 200 wagons should have been reported in the same period—namely, in 2001, as was reported in part (A). There, we can see clearly what was gained and what was lost on activities that were completed *in an accounting period*. By requiring this practice, the matching principle provides consistency in reporting and avoids financial distortions.

Full Disclosure

Full disclosure means that financial statements should include not just numbers, but also interpretations and explanations by management so that external users can better understand information contained in the statements. Because they know more about inside events than outsiders, management prepares additional useful information that explains certain events or transactions or discloses the circumstances underlying certain financial results. For example, MCI WorldCom Inc.'s 1999 balance sheet reports long-term debt totalling $13.1 billion. In a supporting note, additional details identify the different kinds of debt (commercial paper, notes, senior notes, debentures, etc.), debt sources, due dates for repayment, and a listing of debt in each category.[10] The additional disclosure helps financial experts more accurately estimate MCI's debt commitments and ability to repay the debt when it comes due.

Management's Discussion and Analysis. Another requirement for full disclosure in financial statements is called **management's discussion and analysis (MD&A)**. MD&A goes beyond the numbers in financial reports and provides an interpretation "as seen through the eyes of management." Managers' qualitative interpretations, together with their detailed knowledge of a firm's activities, give them a valuable perspective on past events and probable future events. Their explanation of items in financial statements allow investors to judge the "quality" of earnings, debt, and assets to determine if past performance is a reliable indicator of future earnings and cash flows. The 1999 Philip Morris annual report, for example, presents an MD&A discussion of operating revenues and expenses for 1999 versus 1998. Managers explain that 1999's $4.2 billion increase in operating revenues was due primarily to settlement-related price increases (related to tobacco-litigation settlements) from domestic tobacco operations.[11] Without such an explanation, the reader might conclude—erroneously—that more cigarettes were being sold when, in reality, the company was charging higher prices. In this case, then, MD&A clears up potential misconceptions and furnishes investors with a more accurate explanation of a year-to-year increase in revenues.

management's discussion and analysis (MD&A)
A type of full disclosure that in financial reports provides an interpretation "as seen through the eyes of management."

ANALYZING FINANCIAL STATEMENTS

Financial statements present a great deal of information, but what does it all mean? How, for example, can statements help investors decide what stock to buy or help managers decide whether to extend credit? Statements provide data, which in turn can be applied to various ratios (comparative numbers). These ratios can then be used to analyze the financial health of one or more companies. They can also be used to check a firm's progress by comparing current and past statements.

Ratios are normally grouped into three major classifications:

- **Solvency ratios**, both short-term and long-term, estimate risk.
- **Profitability ratios** measure potential earnings.
- **Activity ratios** reflect management's use of assets.

Depending on the decisions to be made, a user may apply none, some, or all the ratios in a particular classification.

Short-Term Solvency Ratios

In the short run, a company's survival depends on its ability to pay its immediate debts. Such payments require cash. Short-term solvency ratios measure a company's relative liquidity and thus its ability to pay immediate debts. The higher a firm's **liquidity ratios**, then, the lower the risk involved for investors. The two most commonly used liquidity ratios are the *current* and *quick* (or *acid-test*) *ratio*.

Current Ratio

The current ratio has been called the "banker's ratio" because it focuses on a firm's creditworthiness. The **current ratio** measures a company's ability to meet current obligations out of current assets. It thus reflects a firm's ability to generate cash to meet obligations through the normal, orderly process of selling inventories and collecting accounts receivable. It is calculated by dividing current assets by current liabilities.

As a rule, a current ratio is satisfactory if it is 2:1 or higher—that is, if current assets are more than double current liabilities. A smaller ratio may indicate that a company will have difficulty paying its bills. Note, however, that a larger ratio may imply that assets are not being used productively and should be invested elsewhere.

How does Perfect Posters measure up? Look again at the balance sheet in Figure 14.4 (see page 430). Judging from its current assets and current liabilities at the end of 2000, we see that

$$\frac{\text{Current assets}}{\text{Current liabilities}} = \frac{\$57\ 210}{\$21\ 935} = 2.61$$

How does Perfect Posters' ratio compare with those of other companies? It's lower than O'Reilly Automotive's ratio (3.17) and higher than those of Gillette (1.56), Cisco Systems (1.54), and Starwood Hotels & Resorts Worldwide (0.23). Although Perfect Posters may be holding too much uninvested cash, it looks like a good credit risk.

Working Capital. A related measure is **working capital**: the difference between the firm's current assets and its current liabilities. Working capital indicates the firm's ability to pay off short-term debts (liabilities) that it owes to outsiders. At the end of 2000, Perfect Posters' working capital was $35 275 ($57 210 – $21 935). Because current liabilities must be paid off within one year, current assets are more than enough to meet current obligations.

Quick (Acid-Test) Ratio

The current ratio represents a company's ability to meet expected demands for cash. In contrast, the **quick** (or **acid-test**) **ratio**, which divides quick assets by current liabilities, measures a firm's ability to meet emergency demands for cash. **Quick assets** include cash and assets one step removed from cash: marketable securities and accounts receivable. Inventory is excluded from this measure because it can be liquidated quickly only at sacrifice prices. Thus, the quick ratio is a more stringent test of liquidity than is the current ratio.

As a rule, a quick ratio of 1.0 or more is satisfactory, although it varies from industry to industry. Whirlpool Corp., for example, has a quick ratio of 0.92. Anheuser-Busch, meanwhile, with a very low ratio of only 0.4, is still regarded by many as a safe bet for meeting emergency demands for short-term obligations.

If we consider Perfect Posters' position at the end of 2000 (again using data from Figure 14.4), we see that

$$\frac{\text{Quick assets}}{\text{Current liabilities}} = \frac{\$7050 + 2300 + 26\ 210 - 650}{\$21\ 935} = 1.59$$

In an emergency, the firm apparently can pay off all current obligations without having to liquidate inventory.

Long-Term Solvency Ratios

To survive in the long run, a company must be able to meet both its short-term (current) debts and its long-term liabilities. These latter debts usually involve interest payments. A firm that cannot meet them is in danger of collapse or takeover—a risk that makes creditors and investors quite cautious. The 1998 Asian financial crisis was fuelled by a loss of confidence by investors in large firms in Japan and Korea that could not meet their long-term cash obligations.

Debt-to-Owners' Equity Ratio

To measure the risk that a company may encounter this problem, analysts use long-term solvency ratios called **debt ratios**. The most commonly used debt ratio is the **debt-to-owners'-equity ratio** (or debt-to-equity ratio), which describes the extent to which a firm is financed through borrowed money. It is calculated by dividing **debt**—total liabilities—by owners' equity.

This ratio is commonly used to compare a given company's status with industry averages. For example, companies with debt-to-equity ratios above 1.0 are probably relying too much on debt. Such firms may find themselves owing so much that they lack the income needed to meet interest payments or to repay borrowed money.

In the case of Perfect Posters, we can see from the balance sheet in Figure 14.4 that the debt-to-equity ratio calculates as follows:

$$\frac{\text{Debt}}{\text{Owners' equity}} = \frac{\$61\ 935}{\$111\ 155} = 0.56$$

Leverage. Note that a fairly high debt-to-equity ratio may sometimes be not only acceptable but desirable. Borrowing funds provides **leverage**: the ability to make otherwise unaffordable purchases. In *leveraged buyouts (LBOs)*, firms have willingly taken on huge debt to buy out other companies. When the purchased company allows the buying company to earn profits above the cost of the borrowed funds, leveraging makes sound financial sense, even if it raises the buyer's debt-to-equity ratio. Unfortunately, many buyouts have led to financial trouble when actual profits fell short of anticipated levels or when rising rates increased interest payments on the debt acquired by the buyer.

debt ratios
Measures of a firm's ability to meet its long-term debts; used to analyze the risks of investing in the firm.

debt-to-owners'-equity ratio
A form of debt ratio calculated as total liabilities divided by owner's equity.

debt
A company's total liabilities.

leverage
Using borrowed funds to make purchases, thus increasing the user's purchasing power, potential rate of return, and risk of loss.

Profitability Ratios

Although it is important to know that a company is solvent in both the long term and the short term, safety or risk alone is not an adequate basis for investment decisions. Investors also want some measure of the returns they can expect. *Return on sales, return on equity,* and *earnings per share* are three commonly used profitability ratios.

Return on Sales

return on sales (net profit margin)
A form of profitability ratio calculated as net income divided by net sales.

Also called the **net profit margin**, **return on sales** is calculated by dividing net income by sales. This ratio indicates the percentage of income that is profit to the company. There is no single correct net profit margin. The figure for any one company must be compared with figures for other firms in the industry to determine how well a business is doing. Typical return on sales ratios are 1 percent for meat-packing plants, 3 percent for wholesalers such as Perfect Posters, and 6 percent for machinery manufacturers.

Using data from Figure 14.5 (see page 432), we see that return on sales for Perfect Posters in 2000 was:

$$\frac{\text{Net income}}{\text{Sales}} = \frac{\$12\ 585}{\$256\ 425} = 0.049 = 4.9\%$$

In other words, the business realized profit of 4.9 cents on each dollar of sales—well above the 3 percent standard for its industry.

Return on Equity

return on equity
A form of profitability ratio calculated as net income divided by total owners' equity.

Owners are interested in the net income earned by a business for each dollar invested. **Return on equity** measures this performance by dividing net income (recorded in the income statement, Figure 14.5) by total owners' equity (recorded in the balance sheet, Figure 14.4).[12] For Perfect Posters, the return-on-equity ratio in 2000 can be calculated as follows:

$$\frac{\text{Net income}}{\text{Total owners' equity}} = \frac{\$12\ 585}{\$111\ 155} = 11.3\%$$

Is this figure good or bad? There is no set answer. If Perfect Posters' ratio for 2000 is higher than in previous years, owners and investors should be encouraged. But if 11.3 percent is lower than the ratios of other companies in the same industry, they should be concerned.

Earnings per Share

earnings per share
A form of profitability ratio calculated as net income divided by the number of common shares outstanding.

Defined as net income divided by the number of shares of common stock outstanding, **earnings per share** determines the size of the dividend a company can pay to its shareholders. Investors use this ratio to decide whether to buy or sell a company's stock. As the ratio gets higher, the stock value increases, because investors know that the firm can better afford to pay dividends. Naturally, stock will lose market value if the latest financial statements report a decline in earnings per share. For Perfect Posters, we can use the net income total from the income statement in Figure 14.5 to calculate earnings per share as follows:

$$\frac{\text{Net income}}{\text{Number of common shares outstanding}} = \frac{\$12\ 585}{8000} = \$1.57 \text{ per share}$$

As a baseline for comparison, note that Gucci's recent earnings were $3.48 per share. The Walt Disney Co. earned $0.62.

Activity Ratios

The efficiency with which a firm uses resources is linked to profitability. As a potential investor, then, you want to know which company gets more mileage from its resources. Activity ratios measure this efficiency. For example, suppose that two firms use the same amount of resources or assets. If Firm A generates greater profits or sales, it is more efficient and thus has a better activity ratio.

Inventory Turnover Ratio

Certain specific measures can be used to explain how one firm earns greater profits than another. One of the most important measures is the **inventory turnover ratio**, which calculates the average number of times that inventory is sold and restocked during the year—that is, how quickly inventory is produced and sold.[13] First, a company needs to know its *average inventory*: the typical amount of inventory on hand during the year. Average inventory can be calculated by adding end-of-year inventory to beginning-of-year inventory and dividing by 2. The company can then calculate the inventory turnover ratio, which is expressed as the cost of goods sold divided by average inventory:

inventory turnover ratio
An activity ratio that measures the average number of times inventory is sold and restocked during the year.

$$\frac{\text{Cost of goods sold}}{\text{Average inventory}} = \frac{\text{Cost of goods sold}}{(\text{Beginning inventory} + \text{Ending inventory}) \div 2}$$

A high inventory turnover ratio means efficient operations. Because a smaller amount of investment is tied up in inventory, the company's funds can be put to work elsewhere to earn greater returns. However, inventory turnover must be compared with both prior years and industry averages. An inventory turnover rate of 5, for example, might be excellent for an auto supply store, but it would be disastrous for a supermarket, where a rate of about 15 is common. Rates can also vary within a company that markets a variety of products. To calculate Perfect Posters' inventory turnover ratio for 2000, we take the merchandise inventory figures for the income statement in Figure 14.5. The ratio can be expressed as follows:

$$\frac{\$104\,765}{(\$22\,380 + \$21\,250) \div 2} = 4.8 \text{ times}$$

In other words, new merchandise replaces old merchandise every 76 days (365 days ÷ 4.8). The 4.8 ratio is below the average of 7.0 for comparable wholesaling operations, indicating that the business is slightly inefficient.

INTERNATIONAL ACCOUNTING

McCain Foods
www.mccain.com

As we saw in Chapter 3, companies such as McCain Foods, Sabian Cymbals, and MacMillan-Bloedel receive large portions of their operating revenues from foreign sales. Many Canadian companies also purchase components from foreign countries. Retailers such as The Bay and Sears buy merchandise from other countries for sale in Canada. In addition, more and more companies own subsidiaries in foreign countries. With all this international activity, there is obviously a need to keep track of foreign transactions. One of the most basic accounting needs is translating the values of the currencies of different countries.

Foreign Currency Exchange

A unique consideration in international accounting is the value of currencies and their exchange rates. As we saw in Chapter 3, the value of any country's currency is subject to occasional change. Political and economic conditions, for instance, affect the stability of a nation's currency and its value relative to the currencies of other countries. Whereas the Swiss franc, for example, has a long history of stability, the Brazilian real has a history of instability.

As it is traded each day around the world, any currency's value is determined by market forces: what buyers are willing to pay for it. The resulting values are called **foreign currency exchange rates**. How volatile are such rates? Table 14.3 shows the changes in exchange rates for some foreign currencies during a one-year period. Each table entry shows the value of one unit of that nation's currency expressed in U.S. dollars. For example, one French franc was worth US$0.173 in January 2000. When a nation's currency becomes unstable—that is, when its value changes frequently—it is regarded as a *weak* currency. The value of the Brazilian real, for example, fluctuated between US$0.55 and US$0.93—a variation range of 70 percent in U.S. dollars—during the period 1997–99. On the other hand, the Swiss franc is said to be a strong currency because its value historically rises or holds steady in comparison to the U.S. dollar. Accountants must consider exhange rate fluctuations when recording a firm's international transactions. These fluctuations will have an impact, perhaps a profound one, on the amount a firm pays for foreign purchases and the amount it gains from sales to foreign buyers.

International Transactions

International purchases, sales on credit, and accounting for foreign subsidiaries all involve accounting transactions that include foreign currency exchange rates. When a U.S. company called Village Wine and Cheese Shops imports Bordeau wine from a French company called Pierre Bourgeois, its accountant must be sure that Village's books reflect its true costs. The amount owed to Pierre Bourgeois changes daily along with the exchange rate between francs and dollars. Thus our accountant must identify the actual rate on the day that payment in francs is made so that the correct U.S.-dollar cost of the purchased wine is recorded.

Sales on credit to customers in other countries should also be recorded to reflect foreign currency exchange rates. In this case, the sale is made at one time and payment by the customer is made at another. Say, for example, that Motorola sells cellular phones on credit to Japanese distributor Hirotsu, with payment due in 30 days. If payment is made in yen, Motorola's books must be updated and yen must be converted to U.S. dollars according to the dollar–yen exchange rate on the date of payment. Only then will Motorola's accounting accurately reflect its cash inflow in terms of U.S. dollars.

Table 14.3				Foreign Currency Exchange Rates
Country	Monetary Unit	Dollar Value January 31, 1999	Dollar Value January 31, 2000	% Change in Value
Canada	dollar	0.6900	0.6600	−4.3
China	yuan	0.1200	0.1200	0.0
France	franc	0.1480	0.1730	+16.9
Japan	yen	0.0093	0.0086	−7.5
Switzerland	franc	0.6000	0.7100	+18.3

Suppose that your firm purchases a foreign company and your investors want to know the overall value of your new firm. The so-called "consolidated" balance sheet should reflect the combined assets of the parent company and the subsidiary. If, for example, you buy a Brazilian coffee company, day-to-day fluctuations in Brazilian currency will cause a reporting problem for your accountant. The coffee subsidiary's assets that are worth US$1 million today may be worth only US$800 000 next week, even though no assets have been bought or sold. The apparent change in value is due solely to the changing exchange rate between U.S. dollars and Brazilian reals. Although the exact method is beyond the scope of this book, accountants have formulated adjustments that deal with such changes and explain the situation to investors.

International Accounting Standards

Professional accounting groups in about 80 countries are members of the International Accounting Standards Committee (IASC), which is trying to eliminate differences in financial reporting across countries.[14] Bankers, investors, and managers would like to see financial reporting that is comparable from country to country and across all firms regardless of home nation.

Standardization is occurring in some areas but is far from universal. The financial statements required by the IASC, for example, include an income statement, a balance sheet, and statement of cash flows similar to those issued by Canadian and U.S. accountants. International standards, however, do not require a uniform format, and variety abounds. Differences are evident in other areas as well, especially among accounting principles in specific areas, such as methods for valuing assets and liabilities. For inventory valuation, for instance, LIFO is not allowed in the United Kingdom and Australia. Similarly, Japan and Canada allow different methods for revenue recognition—determining the time period in which to report revenues in the financial statement. Major differences exist also in accounting for benefit and pension plans, including methods for updating data to keep information current.

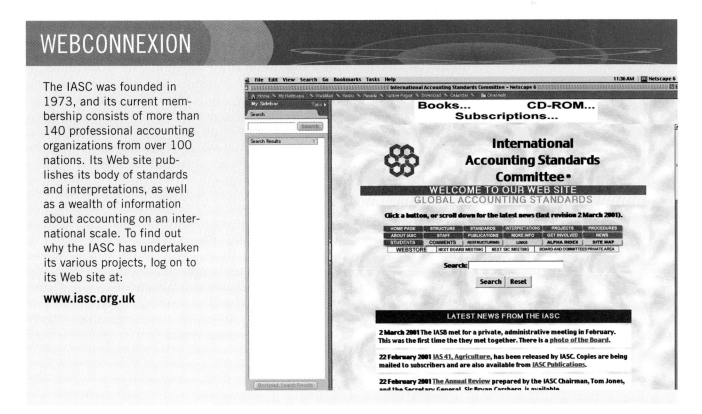

WEBCONNEXION

The IASC was founded in 1973, and its current membership consists of more than 140 professional accounting organizations from over 100 nations. Its Web site publishes its body of standards and interpretations, as well as a wealth of information about accounting on an international scale. To find out why the IASC has undertaken its various projects, log on to its Web site at:

www.iasc.org.uk

SUMMARY OF LEARNING OBJECTIVES

1. **Explain the role of accountants and distinguish between the kinds of work done by *public* and *private accountants*.** By collecting, analyzing, and communicating financial information, accountants provide business managers and investors with an accurate picture of the firm's financial health. Chartered accountants (CAs) are licensed professionals who provide auditing, tax, and management advisory services for other firms and individuals. Public accountants who have not yet been certified perform similar tasks. Private accountants provide diverse specialized services for the specific firms that employ them.

2. **Explain how the *accounting equation* and *double-entry accounting* are used in record keeping.** The *accounting equation* (assets = liabilities + owners' equity) is used to balance data in both journals and ledgers. *Double-entry accounting* acknowledges the dual effects of financial transactions and ensures that the accounting equation always balances. These tools enable accountants not only to enter but to track transactions.

3. **Describe the three basic *financial statements* and show how they reflect the activity and financial condition of a business.** The *balance sheet* summarizes a company's assets, liabilities, and owners' equity at a given point in time. The *income statement* details revenues and expenses for a given period of time and identifies any profit or loss. The *statement of cash flows* reports cash receipts and payments from operating, investing, and financing activities.

4. **Discuss the importance of *budgets* in internal planning and control.** To ensure the overall efficient use of resources, accountants and other managers develop *budgets*. A budget shows where funds will be obtained (the sources) and where they will be spent (the uses). Throughout the year, the budget is monitored to ensure that costs are not exceeding revenues.

5. **Explain how computing key *financial ratios* can help in analyzing the financial strengths of a business.** Drawing upon data from financial statements, ratios can help creditors, investors, and managers assess a firm's finances. The *liquidity, current, quick* (or *acid-test*), and *debt-to-equity ratios* all measure solvency—a firm's ability to pay its debt in both the short run and the long run. *Return on sales, return on investment*, and *earnings per share* are all ratios that measure profitability. *Inventory turnover ratios* show how efficiently a firm is using its funds.

6. **Explain some of the special issues facing accountants at firms that do international business.** Accounting for foreign transactions involves some special procedures. First, accountants must consider the fact that the *exchange rates* of national currencies change. Accordingly, the value of a foreign currency at any given time—its *foreign currency exchange rate*—is what buyers are willing to pay for it. Exchange rates will affect the amount of money a firm pays for foreign purchases and the amount it gains from foreign sales. Canadian accountants, therefore, must always translate foreign currencies into the value of the dollar. Then, in recording a firm's transactions, they must make adjustments to reflect shifting exchange rates over time.

KEY TERMS

STUDY QUESTIONS AND EXERCISES

Review Questions

1. Identify the three types of services that CAs and CGAs perform.
2. How does the double-entry system reduce the chances of mistakes or fraud in accounting?
3. What are the three basic financial statements and what major types of information does each contain?
4. Identify the four major classifications of financial statement ratios and give an example of one ratio in each category.
5. Explain how financial ratios allow managers to monitor their own efficiency and effectiveness.

Analysis Questions

6. Suppose that Inflatables Inc., makers of air mattresses for swimming pools, has the following transactions in one week:
   - Sale of three deluxe mattresses to Al Wett (paid cash—$75) on 7/16
   - Received cheque from Ima Flote in payment for mattresses bought on credit ($90) on 7/13
   - Received new shipment of 200 mattresses from Airheads Mfg. (total cost $2000) on 7/17
   Construct a journal for Inflatables Inc.

7. If you were planning to invest in a company, which of the three types of financial statements would you most want to see? Why?

8. Dasar Company reports the following data in its September 30, 2000, financial statements:
   - Gross sales $225 000
   - Current assets   40 000
   - Long-term assets   100 000
   - Current liabilities   16 000
   - Long-term liabilities   44 000
   - Owners' equity   80 000
   - Net income   7 200
   a. Compute the current ratio.
   b. Compute the debt-to-equity ratio.
   c. Compute the return on sales.
   d. Compute the return on owners' equity.

Application Exercises

9. Interview an accountant at a local manufacturing firm. Trace the process by which budgets are developed in that company. How does the firm use budgets? How does budgeting help its managers plan business activities? How does budgeting help them control business activities? Give examples.
10. Interview the manager of a local retail or wholesale business about taking inventory. What is the firm's primary purpose in taking inventory? How often is it done?

Building Your Business Skills

Putting the Buzz in Billing

Goal
To encourage students to think about the advantages and disadvantages of using an electronic system for handling accounts receivable and accounts payable.

Method

Step 1:
Study Figure 14.7. The outside cycle depicts the seven steps involved in issuing paper bills to customers, payment of these bills by customers, and handling by banks of debits and credits for the two accounts. The inside

cycle shows the same bill issuance and payment process handled electronically.

Step 2:
As the chief financial officer of a provincial hydroelectric utility, you are analyzing the feasibility of switching from a paper to an electronic system of billing and bill payment. You decide to discuss the ramifications of the choice with three business associates (choose three classmates to take on these roles). Your discussion requires that you research electronic payment systems now being developed. Specifically, using online and library research, you must find out as much as you can about the electronic bill-paying systems being developed by Visa International, Intuit, IBM, and the

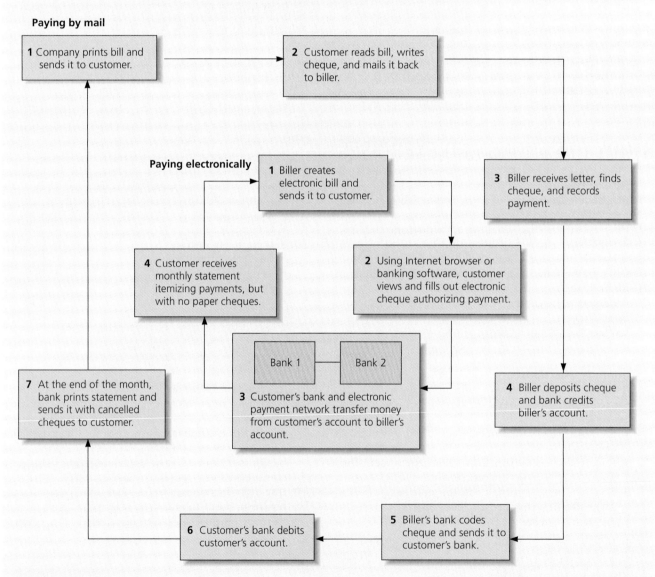

Figure 14.7
Managing operations and information.

Checkfree Corp. After you have researched this information, brainstorm the advantages and disadvantages of using an electronic bill-paying system in your company.

Follow-Up Questions

1. What cost savings are inherent in the electronic system for both your company and its customers? In your answer, consider such costs as handling, postage, and paper.

2. What consequences would your decision to adopt an electronic system have on others with whom you do business, including manufacturers of cheque-sorting equipment, Canada Post, and banks?

3. Switching to an electronic bill-paying system would require a large capital expenditure for new computers and computer software. How could analyzing the company's income statement help you justify this expenditure?

4. How are consumers likely to respond to paying bills electronically? Are you likely to get a different response from individuals than you get from business customers?

Exploring the Net

To get a feel for real-world accounting activity, visit the Accounting Management Solutions site at:

http://www.a-managementsolution.com

After examining the different aspects of the Web site, consider the following questions:

1. Which of the "Tax Tips and Traps" did you find surprising? Which of these tips could be useful for a small business?

2. Read the article titled "Change." How is this article meaningful for those involved in accounting?

3. Evaluate this site in terms of its ability to inform those unfamiliar with accounting practices. What could be done to improve the site?

Concluding Case 14-1

High-Tech Accounting Under Review

David Brown, the chairman of the Ontario Securities Commission (OSC), has recently criticized accounting practices in Canada. He says that "creative accounting" is an addictive practice that is increasingly being used by companies who want to avoid disappointing the stock market and then seeing their stock price drop. Creative accounting often involves overstating sales revenue, which yields a distorted picture of how much product or service a company is actually selling.

There are different ways that sales revenue can be overstated. For example, some software makers sell a lot of product at the end of a quarter and then count all those sales as revenue without taking into account the future costs the firm will incur to support the software or to provide the free upgrades they promised. Or, a company that acts as a sales agent for an airline might include the ticket price, plus the commission it earns, as revenue. When the airline firm is paid, the cost goes on the expense line. This approach vastly overstates revenue (but not profit). The company should have included only its sales commissions as revenue. This practice is worrisome because we are in an era when many high-tech firms are judged on their *revenue* growth, rather than their actual *profits*.

There is a general concern that high-tech firms are too liberal in recording revenues on their financial statements. The OSC has therefore asked 70 of these companies to explain in detail what policies they follow in reporting revenue. In the U.S., very specific guidelines exist about what can be included in revenue, but here in Canada things are a lot less well defined, so there is room for interpretation. As part of this process, the OSC is shifting its emphasis from examining prospectuses to analyzing the way companies report income. It has set up a continuous disclosure team to review the financial reports of corporations in a systematic manner.

To get a better understanding of the revenue problem, the OSC is also asking companies how they account for revenue from things like service contracts, and whether they benchmark their accounting practices against those used by other firms in their industry. Forensic accountant Al Rosen (see Video Case IV-2 on page 453) considers the OSC's move as desirable because companies have discovered that it's pretty easy to fool around with revenue figures. Rosen says that the OSC should issue its own guidelines about how revenue should be reported and should not wait for the professional accounting groups to do so.

CASE QUESTIONS

1. Who are the various users of accounting information? How will each of these users be influenced if sales revenues are overstated?

2. What are the three basic financial statements that accountants generate for business firms? What does each one show? How will overstating sales revenue affect each of these statements?

3. Read the sections in the chapter on revenue recognition and matching. How is the material in those sections helpful in dealing with the overstating of revenue problem noted in the case?

4. Consider the following statement: "Since sales revenues are measured in dollars, and since dollars are easy to quantify, it should be very clear what sales revenue a firm had in a given period. It is therefore unnecessary to have policies about how revenue should be reported." Do you agree or disagree? Explain. ◆

Concluding Case 14-2

There's No Business Like Show Business

When Ethel Merman belted out the famous refrain, "There's no business like show business," she wasn't singing about the business of accounting in Hollywood. But she probably should have been. That's because the accounting rules in Hollywood are like no other accounting rules in the world. According to critics, the rules make it difficult—if not impossible—for investors to determine the real financial condition of movie studios and their products.

Under existing rules, for example, studios can treat advertising costs as an asset (an economic resource) instead of an expense. This practice enables studios to inflate both assets and short-term profits. Studios can also choose to add to a film's costs millions in studio "overhead" charges and millions more in start-up costs of unrelated failed projects. Like advertising costs, these costs can be treated as assets and depreciated over a given number of years from the studio's balance sheet.

The following illustration (adapted from an article in *Business Week*) demonstrates how Hollywood's accounting system works. Using the unique system suggested above, studios manipulate balance sheet entries to paint a rosy financial picture that leaves investors in the dark about expenses and profits.

1. Let's say that Bigwig Pictures makes *Violent Death*, spending $50 million to acquire the story, hire actors, and film the movie.
2. The studio spends another $40 million to advertise and release *Violent Death*. This money is added to the movie's reported cost. This cost, moreover, climbs when Bigwig adds another $10 million to cover expenses from other films that were never released—plus costs related to everything from Bigwig salaries to paper clips. The total cost of *Violent Death* now stands at $100 million.
3. Now let's thicken the plot (albeit in a perfectly plausible way). Let's say that Bigwig is facing a depressed stock price and investor pressure to

raise the value of shares by improving its performance. Bigwig management thus decides to project that *Violent Death* will bring in $1 billion over the next 20 years. This revenue will come not only from the film's theatrical release, but from its release to home video, to pay TV and regular TV, and to laser disks, not to mention licensing in foreign markets. Because the studio states that *Violent Death* will be making money for 20 years, Bigwig can take the full two decades to subtract the film's bloated $100 million cost from its books.
4. Let's now say that *Violent Death* does well, taking in $200 million in box office and video revenue in the first year of its release. After deducting $20 million—that year's share of expenses—Bigwig shows an immediate profit of $180 million. Naturally, the studio's earnings—and stock price—jump. What about the remaining $80 million that the studio spent on the film? That sum remains on Bigwig's books for years—as an asset, not a liability.

Studios argue that this system makes sense. Because a movie has value that lasts long beyond the year in which it is made, it is reasonable to estimate profit margins over the lifetime of a movie. Profits, meanwhile, can be reported as such *as soon as box office dollars begin rolling in*. Why is this bookkeeping mechanism so important in the movie-making business? Studio executives point out that even a runaway hit has virtually no chance of making money *during its first distribution year*. In most cases, *first-year box office receipts* cannot cover the average $65 million cost required to make and market a Hollywood film. (For one thing, only 40 percent of the box office gross goes to the studio, with the remaining 60 percent going to theatres.)

However, this unique accounting system makes it extremely difficult for people with a so-called "net profit" interest in a movie to make any money from that interest. *Net profits* are the revenues that big studios agree to distribute among writers, actors, and others *after expenses, including salaries and distribution fees, have been paid*. Net profit arrangements are typically negotiated as part of individual contracts. Interestingly, however, only 5 to 20 percent of all films pay any net profits. "For most films," charges Philip Hacker, a consultant to plaintiffs in lawsuits against studios, "net profit participants don't receive anything." Thus, even though the blockbuster *Forrest Gump* grossed approximately $650 million, it has paid no money to anyone with a net profit interest in the film. So, too, with such successful releases as *JFK, Coming to America*, and *Batman*.

The estate of Jim Garrison, the late New Orleans prosecutor whose book was the basis for the 1991 Warner Brothers movie *JFK*, has initiated a federal class-action suit over the net profit issue. Joining in the suit are thousands of people who signed net profits contracts with movie studios since 1988. All the studios involved, including Disney, Universal, Warner Brothers, Twentieth Century Fox, Paramount, Columbia-TriStar, and MGM-UA, use the same accounting practices. If successful, the Garrison *JFK* suit could force payments of more than $1 billion and redefine Hollywood's approach to accounting.

A task force reporting to the Financial Accounting Standard Board (FASB) is now taking a close look at the way Hollywood studios determine their balance sheets. Its goal is to reform many of the unorthodox practices that give investors a distorted view of studio finances. The toughest practice to change involves the capitalizing of advertising costs (treating them as assets rather than expenses). The FASB, which determines the accounting rules by which U.S. companies must generally live, objects to this practice. The movie industry, however, is determined to maintain the status quo. "Most of us think that how we do the accounting makes sense," says Peter Cyffka, a task

force member and the senior vice-president of finance at Twentieth Century Fox Film Corp.

Even if the task force succeeds in changing Hollywood's accounting practices, its reforms will not affect the disbursement of net profits to those who help create movies. Any change in the studios' net profit system must come from the studios themselves in the process of contracting with creative artists. Dreamworks, the production company founded by Steven Spielberg, Jeffrey Katzenberg, and David Geffen, was the first studio to initiate a change. Screenwriters, animators, and other artists working for Dreamworks now sign contracts guaranteeing that they will share in the success of the films they help create.

CASE QUESTIONS

1. In your opinion, are Hollywood's current accounting practices fair to investors?

2. What changes would you suggest to make Hollywood's accounting system fair to both studios and investors?

3. Why is the contractual agreement to share in a film's net profits usually an empty agreement?

4. If you were a screenwriter, what accounting-related questions would you ask before agreeing to a movie deal?

5. Why is the Financial Accounting Standards Board involved in reforming Hollywood's accounting practices? ◆

Twentieth Century Fox Film Corp.
www.fox.com/white.html

CBC Video Case

How's the Oil Supply?

During 2000, gasoline prices rose in Canada from about 55 cents to nearly 80 cents per litre. Consumers are grumbling about high gas prices, and truckers have protested in some European cities. However, our society is dependent on oil—the world consumes 75 million barrels each day—so consumers really don't have much choice but to pay the price. We need oil, but it is scarcer and scarcer. Some analysts say this is the beginning of the end for conventional oil as we know it.

In the 1950s, a geologist named M.K. Hubbert predicted that a steep decline in oil supplies was coming and that this would be the end of cheap oil. He made this prediction based on a curve he developed that later came to be called Hubbert's Curve. This curve (think of a normal, or bell, curve) proposed that the supply of oil would rise, peak, then begin to decline. He predicted, for example, that the production of oil in the U.S. would peak in 1971, and that is exactly what happened. More ominously for us in the early twenty-first century, Hubbert also predicted that the world's supply of oil would peak by 2005.

Because oil prices increased so quickly in 2000, Hubbert's ideas are hot again. An analysis of the world's oil situation confirms that the oil map is shrinking. Oil production in the U.S., Canada, and Russia has already peaked, and the North Sea field is close to peaking. Worse, new oil discoveries are not occurring at the rate they used to. For every four barrels of oil that are used today, only one new barrel is found. This will inevitably lead to permanently higher oil prices.

Colin Campbell, currently the world's leading pessimist on oil prices, thinks that prices will never again drop below $20 a barrel, and that oil may in fact become much more expensive than it is now. Campbell is a geologist who has drilled a lot of wells in a lot of places during his career. He likens the current oil situation to the tremors that are evident in the weeks before an earthquake actually hits. Like Hubbert, he is convinced that the world's supply of oil is about to peak, and then will start to decline. More people are starting to listen to Campbell as oil prices rise, even though what he is saying is not pleasant. There is still a real sense of denial about the situation, given how reliant we are on oil.

Soon the Western industrialized countries will realize that a power shift has already occurred in world oil production, and that OPEC is now in the driver's seat because it controls half of the world's oil. We have already seen various countries essentially begging OPEC to produce more oil to drive the price back down. If OPEC is in the driver's seat, we had better hope they are good drivers.

Is there any good news on the oil front? Well, new seismic technologies can pinpoint where new oil pools are, but the technology can also pinpoint where oil is not. It is this latter point that is leading many experts to the conclusion that a decline in oil production is coming.

What about the often-heard argument that for the right price, technology can find more oil? This argument is sound up to a point, but in any case it will mean higher (and maybe much higher) prices for oil.

What about recent new oil finds like Hibernia? Won't they provide a lot of new oil? Not really. Hibernia's production, for example, will satisfy world demand for only a few months. What about the tar sands? There is obviously a lot of oil in the tar sands, but extracting oil there is expensive. If we have to rely on the tar sands, the price of oil will be much higher than it is now.

What about alternate fuels? There is increasing talk—even among oil company executives—that we are going to have to develop new power sources. Solar and hydrogen power seem to be most promising. The editor of *Petroleum Review* says that companies are seeing the writing on the wall, and that they are starting to prepare for the day when oil becomes less important to the world economy.

STUDY QUESTIONS

1. Explain the production process for oil using the concepts presented in Figure 11.1 (see page 324).

2. Is the manufacturing of gasoline an analytic or synthetic process? Explain. What type of plant layout is used in the production of oil?

3. Explain the current oil price situation in terms of the supply and demand ideas presented on pages 17–19. What will happen to the price of oil if new, alternative fuels become available?

4. Re-read Concluding Case 1-1 on page 38. How is the situation for oil similar to that for palladium? How is it different?

Video Resource: "Hubbert's Curve," *Venture* #759 (October 10, 2000).

CBC Video Case

IV-2 CBC

Forensic Accounting

We've just gotten over the Livent scandal and then along comes Cinar, the Quebec animation house, with all of its various problems. Who's watching the numbers? Is anyone trying to do something? As it turns out, someone is. It is Al Rosen, Canada's leading forensic accountant (also known as "The Enforcer"). He has been busy ferreting out fast and loose accounting practices that make a company look better than it actually is. He is working hard to alert the world to these scam artists. Rosen is a frequent expert witness in court cases, and he has given so much information about questionable accounting practices at various firms to *Canadian Business* magazine that he is now on their masthead.

People have described Rosen as hard-nosed, a corporate muckraker, tough, arrogant, bitter, dark, and gloomy. He isn't deterred, he says, because these people haven't seen the evidence he has seen. If a client is caught playing fast and loose with accounting rules, lawyers rush to Rosen's office for advice.

Rosen is an expert at explaining how a company can play with numbers to make its dismal financial statement glow. Rosen's concern is that this can be easily achieved using Generally Accepted Accounting Principles (GAAP), the accountant's "Bible." He says that "crooked" companies look at GAAP and say, "Wow, I can use this stuff to make my company look good."

Rosen wants to blow the whistle on suspicious accounting, and one of the ways he is doing so is by writing a monthly exposé for mutual fund managers. So far he has examined 20 companies in detail. He gives an opinion on whether a given company is on the level, whether it should be watched carefully, or whether it is already a disaster. In the early 1990s, he offered the view that the accounting numbers generated by Cott Corp., the generic cola maker, were not telling the whole story, and the company was not as strong as it appeared. Cott, which was then a stock-market darling, blasted Rosen for his views, but time has proved Rosen right. Cott's stock dropped from nearly $40 per share in 1994 to just $10 per share in 1999.

Another company that's unhappy with Rosen is ski-resort operator Intrawest. The company complained that Rosen's newsletter caused its stock to drop by 20 percent. It claims it was rock-solid, but that it was "bushwhacked" by Rosen, simply because Rosen has a vendetta against standard accounting practices.

Rosen's mutual fund clients seek his advice regarding which companies are good and which ones are questionable. And, indeed, Rosen says that there are many strong Canadian companies that are perfectly good investments. Still, he will continue to do everything he can to make sure that people receive his message that accounting numbers many not be what they seem. At York University, he tells aspiring accountants not to "play the game." He suggests thinking beyond the numbers, and encourages them to think in non-traditional ways about accounting. He warns that a business deal can easily fall prey to slippery accounting practices.

Rosen is keen to be a source for the media. One of his favourite words in describing manipulators is "scumbag." He recognizes that many people think that his perspective is too negative, but he says there are plenty of cheerleaders for companies and someone needs to do serious analyses of their soundness. He says there are 1000 cheerleaders, but no one (except him) is taking care of the other side.

So, corporate Canada beware: The Enforcer is watching.

STUDY QUESTIONS

1. List and briefly describe the various groups that are users of accounting information. How might the concerns raised by Al Rosen influence each of these groups?

2. What are generally accepted accounting principles (GAAP) designed to do? Why is it that Al Rosen thinks GAAP can be used to make a company's financial condition look stronger than it really is?

3. How might the concepts of *revenue recognition*, *matching*, and *full disclosure* be relevant for the concerns that Al Rosen has raised?

4. Consider the following observation: "The existence of generally accepted accounting principles makes it very difficult for accountants to present a distorted picture of a company's true financial condition. When this fact is coupled with the fact that there are many checks and balances during an audit, it becomes very unlikely that anyone could 'cook the books' so that a company will look like it is in better financial shape than it actually is." Do you agree or disagree? Explain.

5. Critics of Al Rosen charge that he is unreasonably stirring up trouble for managers who are working hard and doing the best they can. Do you agree or disagree? Defend your answer.

Video Resource: "On the Case with Al Rosen," *Venture* #745 (March 28, 2000).

Managing Marketing

What is the first thing you think of when you hear the names Coffee Crisp, Post-It, Crest, and Eno? If you grew up in Canada, you probably didn't hesitate at all before picturing candy, little slips of paper with one sticky edge, toothpaste, and something to calm your stomach. Your rapid association of company names and the goods or services they provide is a tribute to the effectiveness of the marketing managers of the firms that produce these goods. These and many other names have become household words because companies have developed the right products to meet customers' needs, have priced those products appropriately, have made prospective customers aware of the products' existence and qualities, and have made the products readily available.

Part Five, Managing Marketing, provides an overview of the many elements of marketing, including developing, pricing, promoting, and distributing various types of goods and services.

■ We begin in **Chapter 15, Understanding Marketing Processes and Consumer Behaviour**, by examining the ways in which companies distinguish their products, determine customer needs, and otherwise address consumer buying preferences.

■ Then, in **Chapter 16, Developing and Promoting Goods and Services**, we explore the development of different types of products, the effect of brand names and packaging, how promotion strategies help a firm meet its objectives, and the advantages and disadvantages of several promotional tools.

■ Finally, in **Chapter 17, Pricing and Distributing Goods and Services**, we look at the strategies firms use to price their products. We also consider the various outlets business firms use to distribute their products, and we discuss the problems of storing goods and transporting them to distributors.

Tracking Web Users and Television Watchers

Business firms spend millions of dollars each year on market research as they try to figure out their customers' habits and preferences. Various companies have sprung up to provide this information (for a price, of course). The question is this: How much confidence can companies place in the market research they purchase? Consider the uncertainties that exist in measuring consumer responses to the Internet and to television.

Internet usage. As use of the Internet skyrockets, various groups—Internet companies, advertisers, and investors—are desperate for accurate information about how many people visit Web sites. Media Metrix Inc., an Internet measurement company, is the leader in this business, and it is also a hot Web stock. But some of the companies that buy the services of Media Metrix are beginning to have doubts about the accuracy of its measurements. When Media Metrix reported that the number of visitors at Yahoo!'s site decreased 5 percent in one time period, Yahoo!'s director of research said the data were just plain wrong, and that Yahoo!'s own research showed that there were actually substantial increases in visits.

This dispute is interesting, because the Internet is supposedly the most measurable medium ever, able to record millions of clicks. But the fact is that most Internet measurement companies still use very traditional methods to gather data. Internet usage is often tracked by getting people to agree to install special software that monitors their online activity. Media Metrix also makes telephone calls to determine how many users are on the Internet during a particular period. This approach is very similar to the one used by Nielsen Media Research (discussed below).

Online merchants are beginning to question these methods and the results they generate. Family Education Network (FEN), for example, was startled when it received data from Media Metrix showing that the number of its Web pages requested by users dropped 40 percent between August and September in one recent year. FEN's own data showed an increase of 5 percent. Given that the back-to-school season is typically the strongest for an education Web site, the large drop in "hits" didn't seem believable.

Media Metrix says that companies that do their own market research may fail to distinguish between "unique" visitors and those who may log on twice a day from different computers. As well, the online companies' data may include hits by "crawlers" used by search engines, which may make it look as if there is traffic even when no one is actually looking.

Television usage. Nielsen Media Research is a well-known company that has reported on the television-viewing habits of North Americans. For many years, there was widespread acceptance that its market research was accurate. But everything changed in 1996, when Nielsen reported a significant drop in the number of people watching television. The networks immediately claimed the data were unreliable, and cited the fact that the numbers being generated were from a sample of households that was different from those used in the past. Nielsen had, in fact, expanded the number of households it gathered data from, but it was not clear that its data were inaccurate.

The traditional way to gather data about people's television habits is to use the classic "paper diary." Viewers note their viewing habits for each quarter-hour, including the station they are watching, the channel number, and who is watching. This is a lot of work, and in some markets less than one-quarter of the targeted homes send in their diaries. One study showed that these diaries contained many errors. Electronic meters are also attached to household TVs to gather data. These meters determine what channel is being watched and who is watching. Viewers must punch in a pre-assigned number on their remote control whenever they start to watch. When people forget to do this the data are inaccurate. ◆

Media Metrix
www.mediametrix.com

Nielsen Media Research
www.nielsenmedia.com

Certain businesses rely heavily on organizations like Media Metrix and Nielsen Media Research to provide data about their customers. But all businesses need information about their customers, and this important aspect of marketing will be discussed in the next three chapters. We begin in this chapter by exploring the nature of marketing. As you will see, the marketing process is complex, requiring marketers to understand the nature of their product (and its place in the market) and the nature of their customers. The special problems of marketing internationally and of marketing for the small business are also addressed.

By focusing on the learning objectives of this chapter, you will gain a better understanding of such marketing activities and the ways in which marketing influences consumer purchases. After reading this chapter, you will be able to:

1. Define *marketing.*

2. Describe the five forces that constitute the *external marketing environment.*

3. Explain *market segmentation* and show how it is used in *target marketing.*

4. Explain the purpose and value of *market research.*

5. Describe the key factors that influence the *consumer buying process.*

6. Discuss the three categories of *organizational markets* and explain how *organizational buying behaviour* differs from *consumer buying behaviour.*

> LEARNING OBJECTIVES

WHAT IS MARKETING?

What do you think of when you think of marketing? If you are like most people, you probably think of advertising for something like detergent or soft drinks. But marketing is a much broader concept. **Marketing** is "the process of planning and executing the conception, pricing, promotion, and distribution of ideas, goods, and services to create exchanges that satisfy individual and organizational objectives."[1] In this section, we will dissect this definition to see what it encompasses.

marketing
Planning and executing the development, pricing, promotion, and distribution of ideas, goods, and services to create exchanges that satisfy both buyers' and sellers' objectives.

Marketing: Goods, Services, and Ideas

Marketing of tangible goods is obvious in our everyday life. You walk into a department store and a woman with a clipboard asks if you'd like to try a new cologne. A pharmaceutical company proclaims the virtues of its new cold medicine. Your local auto dealer offers an economy car at an economy price. These

consumer goods
Products purchased by individuals for their personal use.

industrial goods
Products purchased by companies to use directly or indirectly to produce other products.

consumer goods are products that you, the consumer, buy for personal use. Firms that sell their products to the end user are engaged in *consumer marketing*.

Marketing is also applied to industrial goods. **Industrial goods** are items that are used by companies for production purposes or further assembly. Conveyors, lift trucks, and earthmovers are all industrial goods, as are components and raw materials such as transistors, integrated circuits, coal, steel, and plastic. Firms that sell their products to other manufacturers are engaged in *industrial marketing*.

Marketing techniques can also be applied to services. *Service marketing* has become a major area of growth in the Canadian economy. Insurance companies, airlines, investment counsellors, clinics, and exterminators all engage in service marketing to consumers. Some firms market their services to other companies, for example, security guards, janitors, and accountants.

Finally, marketing can be applied to *ideas* as well as to goods and services. Television advertising and other promotional activities have made "participaction" a symbol of a healthy lifestyle.

Relationship Marketing

relationship marketing
A type of marketing that emphasizes lasting relationships with customers and suppliers.

Although marketing often focuses on single transactions for products, services, or ideas, a longer-term perspective has become equally important for successful marketing. Rather than emphasizing a single transaction, **relationship marketing** emphasizes lasting relationships with customers and suppliers. Not surprisingly, stronger relationships—including stronger economic and social ties—can result in greater long-term satisfaction and retention of customers.[2]

For example, Harley-Davidson offers social incentives through the Harley Owners Group (H.O.G.)—the largest motorcycle club in the world, with 500 000 members and approximately 900 dealer-sponsored chapters worldwide. H.O.G., explain Harley marketers, "is dedicated to building customers for life. H.O.G. fosters long-term commitments to the sport of motorcycling by providing opportunities for our customers to bond with other riders and develop long-term friendships."

WEBCONNEXION

The 500 000-member Harley Owners Group (H.O.G.) is a club for Harley-Davidson motorcycle enthusiasts. You can examine the latest Harley models and related merchandise, check out upcoming motorcycle events, and, of course join H.O.G. at:

www.harleydavidson ofdallas.com/hog.html

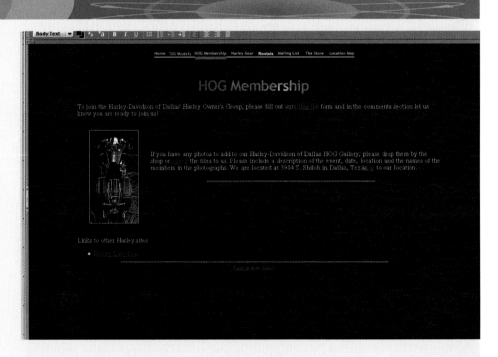

The Marketing Environment

Marketing plans, decisions, and strategies are not determined unilaterally by any business—not even by marketers as experienced and influential as Coca-Cola and Procter & Gamble. Rather, they are strongly influenced by powerful outside forces. As you can see in Figure 15.1, any marketing program must recognize the outside factors that comprise a company's **external environment**. In this section, we will describe five of these environmental factors: the *political/legal, social/cultural, technological, economic*, and *competitive environments*.

external environment
Outside factors that influence marketing programs by posing opportunities or threats.

Political and Legal Environment

Political activities, both foreign and domestic, have profound effects on business (refer back to Chapter 1 for a discussion of how government influences business).

To help shape their companies' futures, marketing managers try to maintain favourable political/legal environments in several ways. For example, to gain public support for their products and activities, marketing uses advertising campaigns for public awareness on issues of local, regional, or national importance. They also lobby and contribute to political candidates (although there are legal restrictions on how much they can contribute). Such activities sometimes result in favourable laws and regulations and may even open new international business opportunities.

Social and Cultural Environment

More women are entering the workforce, the number of single-parent families is increasing, food preferences and physical activities reflect the growing concern for healthful lifestyles, violent crimes are on the increase, and the growing recognition of cultural diversity continues. These and other issues reflect the values, beliefs, and ideas that form the fabric of Canadian society today. Obviously, these broad attitudes towards issues have direct effects on

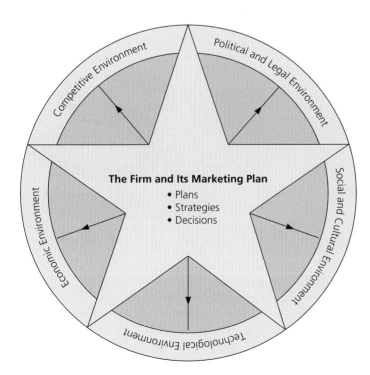

Figure 15.1
The external marketing environment.

Each of these advertisements provides information about a specific product, service, or idea. The President's Choice line, for example, is a consumer food product that can be consumed. The advertisement for the Toronto Zoo promotes a service that can be enjoyed. The safer sex advertisement promotes the idea of changing behaviour as a way of combatting sexually transmitted diseases.

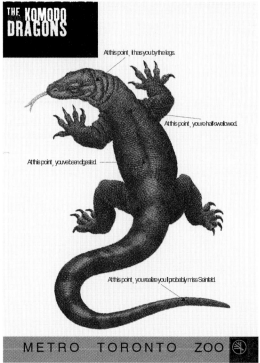

business. Today, for example, as we continue to insist on a "greener" Canada, we have seen the demise of freon in air conditioners and increased reliance on recycling materials in the goods that we consume.

By the same token, the need to recognize social values stimulates marketers to take fresh looks at the ways they conduct their business—say, developing and promoting new products for both consumers and industrial customers. Spalding, for example, has introduced a line of golf gear designed specifically for women. Naturally, such equipment requires new methods for advertising, promoting, and distributing products to meet the emerging preferences of women golfers.[3]

Technological Environment

Consider the phenomenon of DNA "fingerprinting." The O.J. Simpson trial and the Guy Paul Morin case have made just about everyone aware of its availability to law-enforcement officials. Bear in mind, however, that it is also the focal point of a new industry—one that involves biological science and laboratory analysis and instrumentation as well as criminology. DNA fingerprinting, then, is a product. Along with its technical developments, therefore, it involves marketing decisions—such as pricing and promotion. This has been the case with literally thousands of technological breakthroughs in such fields as genetics, electronics, aeronautics, medicine, information sciences, communications systems, and transportation.

New technologies affect marketing in several ways. Obviously, they create new goods (say, the satellite dish) and services (home television shopping). New products make some existing products obsolete (compact discs are replacing audiotapes), and many of them change our values and lifestyles. In turn, they often stimulate new goods and services not directly related to the new technology itself. Cellular phones, for example, not only facilitate business communication but free up time for recreation and leisure.

Economic Environment

Economic conditions determine spending patterns by consumers, businesses, and governments. Thus they influence every marketer's plans for product offerings, pricing, and promotional strategies. Among the more significant economic variables, marketers are concerned with inflation, interest rates, recession, and recovery. In other words, they must monitor the general business cycle, which typically features a pattern of transition from periods of prosperity to recession to recovery (return to prosperity). Not surprisingly, consumer spending increases as "consumer confidence" in economic conditions grows during periods of prosperity. Conversely it decreases during low-growth periods, when unemployment rises and purchasing power declines.

Traditionally, analysis of economic conditions focused on the national economy and the government's policies for controlling or moderating it. Increasingly, however, as nations form more and more economic connections, the "global economy" is becoming more prominent in the thinking of marketers everywhere. With pacts like the 1993 North American Free Trade Agreement and the 1994 General Agreement on Tariffs and Trade now in place, global economic conditions—indeed, conditions from nation to nation—will directly influence the economic fortunes of all trading partners (see Chapter 3). Certainly, marketers must now consider this new—and perhaps unpredictable—economic variable in developing both domestic and foreign marketing strategies.

Competitive Environment

In a competitive environment, marketers must convince buyers that they should purchase their products rather than those of some other seller. In a broad sense, because both consumers and commercial buyers have limited resources to spend, every dollar spent to buy one product is no longer available for other purchases. Each marketing program, therefore, seeks to make its product the most attractive; theoretically, a failed program loses the buyer's dollar forever (or at least until it is time for the next purchase decision).

By studying the competition, marketers determine how best to position their own products for three specific types of competition:

substitute product
A product that is dissimilar from those of competitors but that can fulfil the same need.

brand competition
Competitive marketing that appeals to consumer perceptions of similar products.

international competition
Competitive marketing of domestic against foreign products.

■ **Substitute products** are dissimilar from those of competitors but can fulfil the same need. For example, your cholesterol level may be controlled with either a physical-fitness program or a drug regimen; the fitness program and the drugs compete as substitute products.

■ **Brand competition** occurs between similar products, such as the auditing services provided by large accounting firms like Ernst & Young and KPMG Peat Marwick. The competition is based on buyers' perceptions of the benefits of products offered by particular companies.

■ **International competition** matches the products of domestic marketers against those of foreign competitors—say, a flight on Swissair versus Air Canada. The intensity of international competition has been heightened by the formation of alliances such as the European Union and NAFTA.

Planning and Executing Marketing Strategy

As a business activity, marketing requires management. Although many individuals also contribute to the marketing of a product, a company's **marketing managers** are typically responsible for planning and implementing all the marketing-mix activities that result in the transfer of goods or services to its customers. These activities culminate in the **marketing plan**: a detailed and focused strategy for gearing marketing activities to meet consumer needs and wants. Marketing, therefore, begins when a company identifies a consumer need and develops a product to meet it. One way of identifying those needs, market research, is explored later in this chapter. Here, however, we begin by noting two important aspects of the larger market-planning process: developing the marketing plan and setting marketing goals.

marketing managers
Responsible for planning and implementing all the marketing-mix activities that result in the transfer of goods or services to customers.

marketing plan
A detailed strategy for gearing the marketing mix to meet consumer needs and wants.

Developing the Marketing Plan

Marketing managers must realize that planning takes time. Indeed, the marketing-planning process may begin years before a product becomes available for sale. For example, the Dutch electronics firm Philips (its major label is Magnavox) developed such products as VCRs and compact discs years before these products actually hit the market. And although Philips has recently invested $1 billion in the planning and development of advanced semiconductor memory chips, the company is not assured of success. Without such planning and preparation, however, the electronics line would have little or no chance of success in a highly competitive market.[4]

Philips
www.philips.com

Setting Goals for Performance

Marketing managers—like all managers—must set objectives and goals and then establish ways to evaluate performance. An insurance company, for example, might establish a goal of increasing sales by 10 percent in its western and central Canadian sales districts. The district sales managers' performances will be evaluated against that goal. Or, a consumer products company might set a goal to reduce by 30 percent the time it takes to bring a new product to market.

The Marketing Concept

Increased competition and the growth of consumer discretionary income have given added impetus to an idea that had its beginnings early in the twentieth century. This idea or philosophy, known as the **marketing concept**, means that the whole firm is coordinated to achieve one goal—to serve its present and potential customers and to do so at a profit. This concept means that a firm must get to know what customers really want and follow closely the changes in tastes that occur. The various departments of the firm—marketing, production, finance, and human resources—must operate as a system, well coordinated and unified in the pursuit of a common goal—customer satisfaction.

The importance of customer satisfaction has been recognized at IBM, which introduced a scheme that influences the pay of 350 managers. Up to 15 percent of their pay is tied to how satisfied their customers are. Bell Canada has a similar scheme; team awards are based partly on customer satisfaction.[5] Japan Air Lines' 747s are equipped with video monitors in the armrests so that passengers may choose exactly what they want to watch from a movie library. At Air France, a passenger who purchases a first-class ticket to Paris can upgrade to the Concorde at no extra cost.[6]

marketing concept
The idea that the whole firm is directed towards serving present and potential customers at a profit.

The Marketing Mix

In planning and implementing their marketing strategies, managers rely on the four principal elements of marketing. These four elements, often called the Four Ps of marketing, are product (including developing goods, services, and ideas), pricing, promotion, and place (distribution).[7] Together, these elements are known as the **marketing mix**, depicted in Figure 15.2.

There are many possible combinations of the four elements in the marketing mix. Price might play a large role in selling fresh meat but a very small role in selling newspapers. Distribution might be crucial in marketing gasoline but not as important for lumber. Promotion could be vital in toy marketing but of little consequence in marketing nails. The product is important in every case but probably less so for toothpaste than for cars.

marketing mix
The combination of product, pricing, promotion, and distribution strategies used in marketing a product.

Product

Clearly, no business can undertake marketing activities without a **product**—a good, service, or idea that attempts to fulfil consumers' wants. The conception or development of new products is a continual challenge. Businesses must take into account changing technology, consumer wants and needs, and economic conditions, among other factors. A 1997 Statistics Canada study showed the percentage of Canadian households that owned the following items: VCR (85 percent), microwave oven (86.3 percent), compact disc player (25 percent), personal computer (33 percent), and dishwasher (48.5 percent). Most of these products did not even exist 25 years ago.[8]

Having the product that consumers desire may mean changing existing products. For example, in the clothing industry, manufacturers must be alert to changes in fashion, which often occur rapidly and unpredictably. And as computer technology changes, so must many computer products. Consider, for

product
A good, service, or idea that satisfies buyers' needs and demands.

Figure 15.2
Choosing the marketing mix for a business.

example, the current debate about the wisdom of replacing current PCs with an entirely new product. Not surprisingly, advocates of the existing PC include "establishment" PC firms, such as Intel Corp., and, of course, PC makers. Working towards a different concept for PCs is Sun Microsystems Inc., which proposes a simpler, less expensive desktop unit more intimately connected to the Internet. With Sun's unit, computer users would not buy expensive operating systems and other software, nor would your computer need the powerful computing capacity it needs today. Instead, when it needs software or added capacity, the unit would "borrow" them instantly from powerful networked servers that can be accessed over the Internet.[9]

Companies may also develop new products and enter markets in which they have not previously competed. For example, the German company SAP AG has been quite successful with its R/3 business software system. This so-called "enterprise software" (also known as ERP, for enterprise resource planning) manages all of a company's internal operations through a single powerful network. It ties together the basic processes of taking customer orders, checking credit, ordering materials, scheduling production, distributing products, verifying payments, and balancing the books. Used by more than 12 000 customers, including Microsoft and Nestlé, SAP's annual software revenues have grown rapidly, reaching more than $4 billion per year.[10]

Producers may develop new or "improved" goods and services for the sake of product differentiation. **Product differentiation** is the creation of a product or product image that differs enough from existing products to attract consumers. Product differentiation does not always mean a change in how a product functions. But when successful, it always means a change in how customers react. For example, early kitchen and laundry appliances were available only in white. Frigidaire capitalized on this situation, offering comparably priced and performing appliances, but in different colours. Procter & Gamble is a master at product differentiation, working to make its products not only different from those of other firms but also from its own competing goods.

product differentiation
The creation of a product or product image that differs enough from existing products to attract consumers.

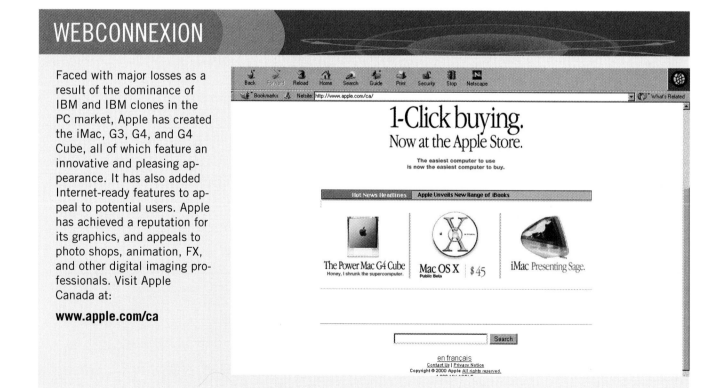

WEBCONNEXION

Faced with major losses as a result of the dominance of IBM and IBM clones in the PC market, Apple has created the iMac, G3, G4, and G4 Cube, all of which feature an innovative and pleasing appearance. It has also added Internet-ready features to appeal to potential users. Apple has achieved a reputation for its graphics, and appeals to photo shops, animation, FX, and other digital imaging professionals. Visit Apple Canada at:

www.apple.com/ca

Services can also be sources of differentiation. One company has developed a computer system so that its customers at retail home centres and lumberyards can purchase custom-designed decks and shelving. As a result, the company has differentiated its commodity two-by-fours by turning them into premium products. We discuss product development in Chapter 16.

Pricing

The second element of the marketing mix is the **pricing** of products. Deciding on the most appropriate price is often a balancing act. On the one hand, prices must support a variety of costs—the organization's operating, administrative, and research costs as well as marketing costs such as advertising and sales salaries. On the other hand, prices cannot be so high that consumers turn to competitors. Successful pricing means finding a profitable middle ground between these two requirements. An appliance retailer, for instance, sells refrigerators and washing machines at prices that are both profitable and attractive to customers. The same products, however, are priced lower when customers buy sets of kitchen or laundry appliances to furnish new homes. The retailers' lower transaction costs enable them to reduce their selling prices.

Whereas some firms succeed by offering lower prices than competitors, others price successfully on the high side. Both low-price and high-price strategies can be effective in different situations. Low prices, for example, generally lead to larger sales volumes. High prices usually limit market size but increase profits per unit. High prices may also attract customers by implying that a product is of especially high quality. We discuss pricing in more detail in Chapter 17.

pricing
That part of the marketing mix concerned with choosing the appropriate price for a product to meet the firm's profit objectives and buyers' purchasing objectives.

Promotion

The most visible component of the marketing mix is **promotion**—those techniques designed to sell a product to consumers. Promotional tools include advertising, personal selling, sales promotions, and public relations. Chapter 16 explores the promotion of products in more depth.

In marketing terms, **advertising** is any form of paid, nonpersonal communication used by an identified sponsor to persuade or inform certain audiences about a good, service, or idea. Advertising may be done through television, radio, magazines, newspapers, billboards or any other type of broadcast or print media.

Automobiles, appliances, and stereo equipment are often promoted through the use of **personal selling**—person-to-person sales. However, the bulk of personal selling occurs with industrial goods. Purchasing agents and other members of a business who require information about a product's technical qualities and price are usually referred to the selling company's sales representatives.

Less expensive items are often marketed through the use of **sales promotions**. Sales promotions can take many forms. Premiums (gifts included with the product), trading stamps, coupons, and package inserts are all sales promotions meant to tempt consumers to buy more of a product. Free samples, exhibits, and trade shows give customers an opportunity to try the product or talk with company representatives. The prevalence of self-service retail outlets has led marketers to think about package design—the "silent seller"—as an important sales promotion.

Public relations includes all promotional activities directed at building good relations with various sectors of the population. Many public relations activities are good deeds paid for by companies. Sponsorship of softball teams, Special Olympics, and automobile racing teams are examples of public relations efforts. Companies may also use public relations activities to boost employee morale.

promotion
That part of the marketing mix concerned with selecting the appropriate technique for selling a product to a consumer.

advertising
Any promotional technique involving paid, nonpersonal communication used by an identified sponsor to persuade or inform a large number of people about a product.

personal selling
A promotional technique involving the use of person-to-person communication to sell products.

sales promotion
A promotional technique involving one-time direct inducements to buyers (such as coupons, sales displays, and contests) to purchase a product.

public relations
Any promotional activity directed at building good relations with various sectors of the population of buyers.

By providing both distribution and advertising for Levi's, this truck plays a dual role in the company's marketing.

publicity

A promotional technique that involves unpaid communication about a product or firm and that is outside the control of the firm.

Publicity also refers to a firm's efforts to communicate to the public, usually through mass media. The firm, however, does not pay for publicity, nor does it control the content of publicity. Publicity, therefore, can sometimes hurt a business. For example, Dun & Bradstreet received considerable negative publicity when newspapers and magazines reported that it was billing its customers for financial reports they did not need.

Place (Distribution)

distribution

That part of the marketing mix concerned with getting products from the producer to the buyer, including physical transportation and choice of sales outlets.

Getting a product into a retail store requires transportation, decisions about direct sales, and a number of other **distribution** processes. Transportation options include moving merchandise by air, land, or pipeline, and, more specifically, by railroad, truck, air freight, or steamship.

WEBCONNEXION

High Road Communications is a public relations firm that helps high-tech companies build their businesses. It does this by publicizing the credibility of its clients and by building public awareness of its existence. In early 2000, High Road was acquired by Fleishman Hilliard, one of the largest public relations firms in the world. Visit High Road at:

www.highroad.com

Decisions about direct sales can affect a firm's overall marketing strategy. Many manufacturers sell their products to other companies who, in turn, distribute the goods to retailers. Some companies sell directly to major retailers such as Sears, Kmart, and Safeway. Still others sell directly to the final consumer. Chapter 17 presents more detail on distribution decisions.

TARGET MARKETING AND MARKET SEGMENTATION

Marketing managers long ago recognized that they cannot be "all things to all people." People have different tastes, different interests, different goals, different lifestyles, and so on. The marketing concept's recognition of consumers' various needs and wants led marketing managers to think in terms of target marketing. **Target markets** are groups of people with similar wants and needs.

Target marketing clearly requires **market segmentation**, dividing a market into categories of customer types or "segments." For example, Mr. Big-and-Tall sells to men who are taller and heavier than average. Certain special interest magazines are oriented towards people with specific interests (see Table 15.1). Once they have identified market segments, companies may adopt a variety of product strategies. Some firms decide to provide a range of products to the market in an attempt to market their products to more than one segment. For example, General Motors of Canada offers compact cars, vans, trucks, luxury cars, and sports cars with various features and prices. Its strategy is to provide an automobile for nearly every segment of the market.

In contrast, some businesses restrict production to one market segment. Rolls-Royce understands that only a relatively small number of people are willing to pay $310 000 for exclusive touring limousines. Rolls, therefore, makes no attempt to cover the entire range of possible products; instead, it markets only to a very small segment of the total automobile buyers market.

target market

Any group of people who have similar wants and needs and may be expected to show interest in the same product(s).

market segmentation

Dividing a market into categories according to traits customers have in common.

Rolls-Royce
www.rolls-royce.com

Table 15.1	Magazines with Specific Target Audiences

Accounting	**Fishing/Hunting**
CA Magazine	*Western Canada Outdoors*
CGA Magazine	*The Atlantic Salmon Journal*
CMA Update	*B.C. Outdoor Fishing Guide*
Agriculture	**Automotive**
Agro-Nouvelles	*Aftermarket Canada*
Canada Poultry	*Bodyshop*
Country Life in B.C.	*Canadian Automotive Trade*
Sports	**Boating**
B.C. Athletics Record	*Boating Business*
Canadian Squash	*Canadian Boating*
Athletics Canada	*Porthole Magazine*
Gardening	**Music**
Canadian Gardening News	*Billboard*
Prairie Landscape Magazine	*Guitar Player*
Landscape Ontario	*Rolling Stone*

positioning
The process of fixing, adapting, and communicating the nature of the product.

Table 15.2 shows how a marketer of home-electronic equipment might segment the radio market. Note that segmentation is a strategy for analyzing consumers, not products. The analysis in Table 15.2, for example, identifies consumer-users—joggers, commuters, travellers. Only *indirectly*, then, does it focus on the uses of the product itself. In marketing, the process of fixing, adapting, and communicating the nature of the product itself is called **positioning**.

Identifying Market Segments

By definition, the members of a market segment must share some common traits or behaviours that will affect their purchasing decisions. In identifying market segments, researchers look at geographic, demographic, psychographic, and product-use variables.

Geographic Variables

In some cases, where people live affects their buying decisions. The heavy rainfall in British Columbia prompts its inhabitants to purchase more umbrellas than does Arizona's desert. Urban residents have less demand for four-wheel drive vehicles than do their rural counterparts. Sailboats sell better along both coasts than they do in the prairie provinces.

These patterns affect marketing decisions about what products to offer, at what price to sell them, how to promote them, and how to distribute them. For example, consider marketing down parkas in rural Saskatchewan. Demand will be high, price competition may be limited, local newspaper advertising may be very effective, and the best location may be one easily reached from several small towns.

Table 15.2	Possible Segmentation of the Radio Market
Segmentation	**Product/Target Market**
Age	Inexpensive, unbreakable, portable models for young children
	Inexpensive equipment—possibly portable—for teens
	Moderate-to-expensive equipment for adults
Consumer attitude	Sophisticated components for audio buffs
	All-in-one units in furniture cabinets for those concerned with room appearance
Product use	Miniature models for joggers and commuters
	"Boom box" portables for taking outdoors
	Car stereo systems for travelling
	Components and all-in-one units for home use
Location	Battery-powered models for use where electricity is unavailable
	AC current for North American users
	DC current for other users

Demographic Variables

A variety of demographic characteristics are important to marketers. As we noted in earlier chapters, demographics include traits such as age, income, gender, ethnic background, marital status, race, religion, and social class. Many marketers, for example, have discovered that university and community college students are an important market segment. Students across Canada have discretionary income totalling $4 to $5 billion. Ford Motor of Canada has marketed to students since the mid-1980s, and gives graduates a $750 rebate on their first-time purchase of a car. Table 15.3 lists some demographic market segments. Note that these are objective criteria that cannot be altered. Marketers must work with or around them.

Demographics affect how a firm markets its products. For example, marketing managers may divide a market into age groups such as 18–25, 26–35, and 36–45 because general consumption characteristics can be attributed to these age groups. For example, managers at Binney & Smith Canada Ltd., the makers of Crayola crayons, discovered that the number of children ages 3 to 7—the top users of crayons—was declining. They also noticed that the size of the age group 8 to 12 was increasing. This latter group, called "tweens" by demographers because they are between the ages of children and teenagers, is much more sophisticated and brand conscious than younger children. They have very distinct preferences, and don't like crayons much, viewing them as "babyish." Tweens prefer coloured pencils, so Binney & Smith introduced a new line of coloured pencils called "Crayola IQ" aimed at the tweens group. They abandoned the famous yellow-and-green Crayola package and replaced it with a new all-green package. Sales jumped 44 percent.[11]

Crayola
www.crayola.com

Other major changes are also occurring in the 8–12 age group. Basically, children of younger and younger ages are starting to behave in ways that older children did in earlier generations. Take the case of the Barbie doll. Formerly, the demographic group that was targeted for this product ranged from ages 2 to 8. But Mattel Inc. says that 7- and 8-year-old girls are less

Table 15.3	Demographic Market Segmentation
Age	Under 5; 5–11; 12–19; 20–34; 35–49; 50–64; 65+
Education	Grade school or less; some high school; graduated high school; some college or university; college diploma or university degree; advanced degree
Family life cycle	Young single; young married without children; young married with children; older married with children under 18; older married without children under 18; older single; other
Family size	1, 2–3, 4–5, 6+
Income	Under $9000; $9000–$14 999; $15 000–$25 000; over $25 000
Nationality	Including but not limited to African, Asian, British, Eastern European, French, German, Irish, Italian, Latin American, Middle Eastern, and Scandinavian
Race	Including but not limited to Inuit, Asian, Black, and White
Religion	Including but not limited to Buddhist, Catholic, Hindu, Jewish, Muslim, and Protestant
Sex	Male, female
Language	Including but not limited to English, French, Inuktitut, Italian, Ukrainian, and German

and less interested in Barbie dolls and see them as something that "little kids" play with. However, these dolls can be marketed to girls age 7 to 10 as collectibles.[12]

Another demographic group that is becoming increasingly important in Canada is the over-50 age group. Francine Tremblay recognized this trend some years ago and launched *Le Bel Age*, a French-language magazine for "mature" Canadians. Soon after, she began producing *Good Times*, an English-language magazine aimed at the same age group. The two magazines sell about 150 000 copies each per month.[13]

Like most other industries, Major League Baseball Enterprises (MLB) tracks demographics trends to set marketing goals for its $6 billion-a-year business. Two decades ago, for instance, the typical fan was a child, but today's average fan is about 37 years old. With teens more interested in basketball and football, many baseball executives are worried about the aging of the game's core fan base. The numbers (demographics) gathered by market research conducted by MLB support the perception of a shift away from a youthful audience. Among 12- to 18-year-olds, 67 percent call themselves baseball fans, while 78 percent declare football loyalty and 82 percent favour basketball. "We'd love to get in the high seventies," admits MLB vice-president Jim Masterson. "The value of the young fan is . . . very important, because it not only represents fans for today but for thirty to forty years from now." By the same token, former major league player John Young sees the current downturn as an opportunity: "Baseball's got a great chance to turn it around. Kids watch a lot of television and now they're seeing Ken [Griffey, Jr.], and Sammy [Sosa], and Mark [McGwire] instead of lockouts and strikes." Unfortunately, the demographics point to a problem with TV as well: viewers under age 18 seldom watch an entire game and are more apt to watch highlights and recaps.[14] The "Business Today" box describes the importance of another demographic group and notes the similarities in this group across different countries.

Psychographic Variables

psychographic variables
Psychological traits that a group has in common, including motives, attitudes, activities, interests, and opinions.

Members of a market can also be segmented according to such **psychographic variables** as lifestyles, opinions, interests, and attitudes. One company that is using psychographic variables to revive its brand is Burberry, whose plaid-lined gabardine raincoats have been a symbol of British tradition since 1856. After a recent downturn in sales, Burberry is repositioning itself as a global luxury brand, like Gucci and Louis Vuitton. The strategy calls for luring top-of-the-line, fashion-conscious customers. Burberry pictures today's luxury-product shopper as a world traveller who identifies with prestige fashion brands and monitors social and fashion trends in *Harper's Bazaar*.[15]

Psychographics are particularly important to marketers because, unlike demographics and geographics, they can sometimes be changed by marketing efforts. For example, many companies have succeeded in changing at least some consumers' opinions by running ads highlighting products that have been improved directly in response to consumer desires. Many companies in Poland have succeeded in overcoming consumer resistance by promoting the safety and desirability of using credit rather than depending solely on cash for family purchases. One product of such changing attitudes is a booming economy and the emergence of a growing and robust middle class. The increasing number of Polish households that own televisions, appliances, automobiles, and houses is fuelling the status of Poland's middle class as the most stable in the former Soviet bloc.[16]

BUSINESS TODAY

Teenagers: An International Market Segment

We all know that trends spread rapidly through the ranks of teenagers. But that tendency is now accelerating internationally. Teens around the world have amazingly similar preferences for consumer products. BSB Worldwide, an advertising agency, videotaped teenagers' rooms in 25 different countries. From the items on display, it was hard to tell whether a room was in Mexico City, Tokyo, or Los Angeles.

The biggest beneficiary of this trend appears to be U.S. companies. The hot new trends in the U.S. often pop up in many other countries as well. Because the populations of Asia and Latin America are much younger than the population of North America, the teen market is big business. For example, the total number of 10- to 19-year-olds in Brazil, Argentina, and Mexico is 57 million; in the U.S., the total is only 35 million.

The most unifying force among teenagers is television. Satellite TV is helping to unify patchworks of domestic markets, and companies can mount Europe- or Asia-wide campaigns. No network is more popular than MTV, which is a monster hit in Europe and is watched by more households there than in the U.S. It broadcasts news and socially conscious programming, and is creating a Euro-language of simplified English.

MTV also promotes little-known European musicians and has the power to make them big stars in other countries. For example, it helped the Danish group Aqua sell over 12 million copies of its debut album worldwide and have a top-10 hit in countries such as Australia, Switzerland, Belgium, and Malaysia. MTV has a roster of 200 advertisers, including Levi Strauss, Procter & Gamble, Johnson & Johnson, Apple Computer, and Pepsi Cola. These firms advertise on MTV because it reaches the market segment they want.

MTV may cause a revolution in worldwide marketing. At present, it is difficult to sell the same products to 35-year-olds in different countries because they never were exposed to anything but products from the country in which they were raised. Not so for the upcoming generation of teenagers. They see (and buy) products from various countries and will probably continue to do so as they get older. Two famous brand names, Coke and Pepsi, are already competing vigorously to attract international teens to use their product.

Fashion fads are also spreading around the world. Hip-hop, first popularized by African-Americans, means wearing loose-fitting urban street wear, baggy jeans, sweat shirts, hiking boots, athletic shoes, and baseball caps (worn backwards). Within this fashion category, certain brands have become very popular. Levi jeans, Nike or Reebok athletic shoes, and Timberland boots are some of the brands that have profited.

Sports is the other universal language of teenagers. Basketball stars like Michael Jordan and Shaquille O'Neal have high name recognition overseas. In a poll of Chinese students in rural Shaanxi province, Michael Jordan tied with former Chinese premier Zhou En-lai for the title "World's Greatest Man." Not surprisingly, testimonial advertisements by big-name sports stars have a big impact on potential buyers. It is not uncommon for students to own multiple pairs of Nike Air Jordans.

Teen tastes in consumer electronics are also similar across countries. Kodak is developing an advertising campaign directed specifically at teenagers in the hope that when they have their own children they will use Kodak products to take pictures of them. Teens are also more comfortable with personal computers than their parents are. So, even if the parents are buying the machine, the teen determines what brand is purchased.

MTV
www.mtv.com

Product-Use Variables

This fourth way of segmenting looks at how group members use a good or service, their brand loyalty, and why they purchase the product. A woman's shoemaker, for example, might find three segments—athletic, casual, and dress shoes. Each market segment is looking for different benefits in a shoe. A woman buying an athletic shoe will probably not care much about its appearance, but she will care a great deal about arch support, traction offered by the sole, and sturdiness. In contrast, a woman buying a casual shoe will want it to look good but be comfortable, while a woman buying a dress shoe may require a specific colour or style and accept some discomfort and a relatively fragile shoe.

Market Segmentation: A Caution

Segmentation must be done carefully. A group of people may share an age category, income level, or some other segmentation variable, but their spending habits may be quite different. Look at your friends in school. You may all be approximately the same age, but you have different needs and wants. Some of you may wear cashmere sweaters while others wear sweatshirts. The same holds true for income. University professors and truck drivers frequently earn about the same level of income. However, their spending patterns, tastes, and wants are generally quite different.

In Canada, the two dominant cultures—English and French—show significant differences in consumer attitudes and behaviour. Researchers have found, for example, that compared to English Canadians, French Canadians are more involved with home and family, attend ballet more often, travel less, eat more chocolate, and are less interested in convenience food. Obviously, prudent marketers should take these differences into account when developing marketing plans. This is, however, easier said than done.

It is one thing to know that consumers in Quebec buy large quantities of certain products; it is quite another to capitalize on these differences. One problem is that differences may not continue over time. Change is continually occurring in consumption patterns across Canada, and data may quickly become outdated. Another problem is that consumption patterns differ from

IT'S A WIRED WORLD

Better Health Through Cyberspace Demographics

In an era of heightened concern for costly health care, many insurers are converting demographic and lifestyle information into personal health assessments for employees of their client companies. One way to gather personal information is by paper and pencil, but with online access the process is fast, convenient, and confidential. The online approach was developed by Network Health Systems™ (NHS). First, the employee fills out a personal questionnaire with items on physical characteristics, lifestyle practices, dietary patterns, work environment, emotional feelings, medical status, and health history. This information forms the individual's personal demographics package. Online subscribers at NHS's Web site can conveniently access the questionnaire, answer the questions, receive instantaneous feedback in the form of a personal report, and pay for the service.

The NHS system evaluates the individual's data using statistical models that determine the chances of experiencing various diseases or ailments. A personalized report is created instantaneously. Based on the individual's response demographics and lifestyle practices, it shows which of some 52 possible conditions and diseases—such as nerve disorders, benign tumours, pregnancy complications, and suicide—may be expected. The report then offers comments and suggestions about the individual's

future health, including recommendations for specific lifestyle changes that can be made for improvement.

The assessment system is based on a vast database of mortality and hospitalization data for 52 diseases and 24 age, sex, and race categories. Data are updated using medical research and national statistics from such sources as the Centers for Disease Control and the National Center for Health Statistics. The database also incorporates information from a panel of health professionals whose clinical judgments indicate correlations among demographics and various health problems. When an individual's demographics and lifestyle items are entered online, they are assessed against the database using the statistical model. Processing reports via the Internet saves time and money for NHS, and it provides results to clients more quickly.

In addition to individuals, business marketers for various health products benefit from the NHS system. Suppose, for example, that a marketer of an insulin product wants to target specific geographic areas with high sales potential. Using demographic data, NHS will search its database to locate concentrations of population, by postal codes, that are predisposed to diabetes. Perhaps results will show that while 40 percent of the population is predisposed in one region, just 10 percent is predisposed in another. NHS can report this information to health care providers who can, in turn, use it to deliver services to areas most in need of help.

region to region in Canada even where culture is not the main cause. The buying behaviour of Quebec and Ontario consumers may be more similar than the behaviour of British Columbia and Newfoundland consumers.

In summary, demographic, geographic, and lifestyle variables are useful in identifying market segments for effective target marketing. The "It's a Wired World" box describes another situation where market segmentation variables can be useful.

MARKET RESEARCH

Market research can greatly improve the accuracy and effectiveness of market segmentation.[17] **Market research**, the study of what buyers need and how best to meet those needs, can address any element in the marketing mix.

The relationship of marketing research in the overall marketing process is shown in Figure 15.3. Ultimately, its role is to increase the firm's competitiveness by understanding the relationship among the firm's customers, its marketing variables, and its marketing decisions. Marketing researchers use a variety of methods to obtain, interpret, and use information about customers. They determine the kinds of information that are needed for decisions on marketing strategy, goal setting, and target-market selection. In doing so, they may conduct studies on how customers will respond to proposed changes in the current marketing mix. One researcher, for example, might study consumer response to an experimental paint formula (new product). Another might explore the response to a price reduction (new price) on calculators. A third might check response to a proposed advertising campaign (new promotion). Marketers can also try to learn whether customers are more likely to purchase a given product in a specialty shop or on the Internet (new place).

market research
The systematic study of what buyers need and how best to meet those needs.

Figure 15.3
Market research and the marketing process.

Moreover, the importance of selling products in today's international markets is expanding the role of marketing research into new areas. For example, when companies decide to sell goods or services in other countries, they must decide whether to standardize products or to specialize them by offering different versions for each new market.

Most companies will benefit from market research, but they need not do the research themselves. O-Pee-Chee Co. Ltd. of London, Ontario (the bubble gum and candy manufacturer) does no market research and no product testing, yet it continues to be successful in a market where products change at a dizzying pace. By signing a licensing agreement with two U.S. giants, O-Pee-Chee simply has to look at what's hot in the U.S. and then start manufacturing those lines in Canada.[18]

The Research Process

Market research can occur at almost any point in a product's existence. Most commonly, however, it is used when a new or altered product is being considered. To see why, you need to understand the steps in performing market research illustrated in Figure 15.4.

The process begins with a *study of the current situation*. In other words, what is the need and what is being done to meet it at this point? Such a study should note how well the firm is or is not doing in meeting the need.

The second step is to *select a research method*. As you will see shortly, marketing managers have a wide range of methods available. In choosing a method, marketers must bear in mind the effectiveness and costs of different methods.

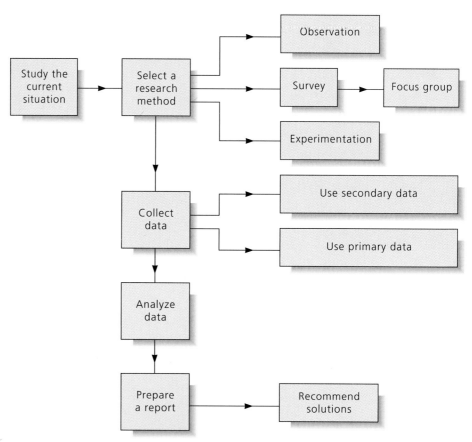

Figure 15.4
Steps in performing market research.

The next step is to *collect data*. **Secondary data** are information already available as a result of previous research by the firm or other agencies. For example, Statistics Canada publishes a great deal of data that are useful for business firms.

Using secondary data can save time, effort, and money. But in some cases secondary data are unavailable or inadequate, so **primary data**—new research by the firm or its agents—must be obtained. Hostess Frito-Lay, the maker of Doritos, spent a year studying how to best reach its target market—teenagers. The researchers hung around shopping malls, schools, and fast-food outlets to watch them.[19]

Once data have been collected, marketers need to *analyze the data*. As we saw in Chapter 13, data are not useful until they have been organized into information.

Marketing personnel then need to share their analysis with others by *preparing a report*. This report should include a summary of the study's methodology and findings. It should also identify alternative solutions (where appropriate) and make recommendations for the appropriate course of action.

secondary data
Information already available to market researchers as a result of previous research by the firm or other agencies.

primary data
Information developed through new research by the firm or its agents.

Research Methods

The four basic types of methods used by market researchers are observation, survey, focus groups, and experimentation.

Observation

Probably the oldest form of market research is simple **observation** of what is happening. A store owner notices that customers are buying red children's wagons, not green ones. The owner reorders more red wagons, the manufacturer's records show high sales of red wagons, and marketing concludes that customers want red wagons. Today, computerized systems allow marketers to "observe" consumers' preferences rapidly and with tremendous accuracy. For example, electronic scanners in supermarkets enable store owners to see what is and is not selling without having to check the shelves. Observation is also a popular research method because it is relatively low in cost, often drawing on data that must be collected for some other reason, such as reordering, anyway.

observation
A market research technique involving viewing or otherwise monitoring consumer buying patterns.

Survey

Sometimes, however, observation of current events is not enough. In many cases, marketers need to ask questions about new marketing ideas. One way to get answers is by conducting a **survey**. The heart of any survey is a questionnaire that is mailed to individuals for their completion or is used as the basis of telephone or personal interviews. Surveys can be expensive to carry out and may vary widely in their accuracy. Because no firm can afford to survey everyone, marketers must be careful to get a representative group of respondents. They must also construct their questions so that they get honest answers that address the specific issue being researched.

When United Parcel Service (UPS) surveyed customers to find out how it could improve service, it found that clients wanted more interaction with drivers because they can offer practical advice on shipping. UPS thus added extra drivers, freeing up some time for drivers to get out of their trucks and spend time with customers.

survey
A market research technique based on questioning a representative sample of consumers about purchasing attitudes and practices.

Focus Groups

Many firms also use **focus groups**, where 6 to 15 people are brought together to talk about a product or service. A moderator leads the group's

focus group
A market research technique involving a small group of people brought together and allowed to discuss selected issues in depth.

Focus groups, used by many firms, bring people together to talk about a product or service. This market research technique allows selected issues to be discussed in depth.

discussion, and employees from the sponsoring company may observe the proceedings from behind a one-way mirror. The people in the focus group are not usually told which company is sponsoring the research. The comments of people in the focus group are taped, and then researchers go through the data looking for common themes.

In 1999, Sears Canada bought some of Eaton's best stores after Eaton's went bankrupt. Sears then reopened these stores with a new image, but retained the Eaton's name. Before doing so, however, Sears conducted focus groups using former Eaton's customers to determine if the new ideas it had for the revamped Eaton's stores would be viewed favourably.[20]

At John Deere Company, focus groups have suggested many improvements in farm tractors, including being able to turn the tractor off with a key, different ways to change the oil filter, and making the steps to the tractor cab wider.[21]

At their best, focus groups allow researchers to explore issues too complex for questionnaires and can produce creative solutions. But because a focus group is small, its responses may not represent the larger market. Focus groups are most often used as a prelude to some other form of research.

Experimentation

experimentation

A market research technique in which the reactions of similar people are compared under different circumstances.

The last major form of market research, experimentation, also tries to get answers to questions that surveys cannot address. As in science, **experimentation** in market research attempts to compare the responses of the same or similar individuals under different circumstances. For example, a firm trying to decide whether to include walnuts in a new candy bar probably would not learn much by asking people what they thought of the idea. But if it made some bars with nuts and some without and then asked people to try both, the responses could be very helpful. Experimentation is, however, very expensive. In deciding whether to use it or any other research method, marketers must carefully weigh the costs against the possible benefits.

UNDERSTANDING CONSUMER BEHAVIOUR

Market research in its many forms can be of great help to marketing managers in understanding how the common traits of a market segment affect consumers' purchasing decisions. Why do people buy VCRs? What desire are they fulfilling? Is there a psychological or sociological explanation for why consumers purchase one product and not another? These questions and many others are addressed in the area of marketing known as consumer behaviour. **Consumer behaviour** focuses on the decision process by which customers come to purchase and consume a product or service.

consumer behaviour
The study of the process by which customers come to purchase and consume a product or service.

Influences on Consumer Behaviour

According to the not-so-surprising title of one classic study, we are very much "social animals."[22] To understand consumer behaviour, then, marketers draw heavily on the fields of psychology and sociology. The result is a focus on four major influences on consumer behaviour: psychological, personal, social, and cultural. By identifying the four influences that are most active, marketers try to explain consumer choices and predict future purchasing behaviour:

- *Psychological influences* include an individual's motivations, perceptions, ability to learn, and attitudes.

- *Personal influences* include lifestyle, personality, economic status, and life-cycle stage.

- *Social influences* include family, opinion leaders (people whose opinions are sought by others), and reference groups such as friends, co-workers, and professional associates.

- *Cultural influences* include culture (the "way of living" that distinguishes one large group from another), subculture (smaller groups, such as ethnic groups, with shared values), and social class (the cultural ranking of groups according to criteria such as background, occupation, and income).

All these factors can have a strong impact on the products that people purchase—often in complex ways.

The purchase of some products is not influenced by psychosocial factors. Consumers with high brand loyalty are less subject to such influences—they stick with the brand of their preference. However, the clothes you wear, the food you eat, and the dishes you eat from often reflect social and psychological influences on your consuming behaviour.

The Consumer Buying Process

Researchers who have studied consumer behaviour have constructed models that help marketing managers understand how consumers come to purchase products. Figure 15.5 presents one such model. At the base of this and similar models is an awareness of the psychosocial influences that lead to consumption. Ultimately, marketing managers use this information to develop marketing plans.

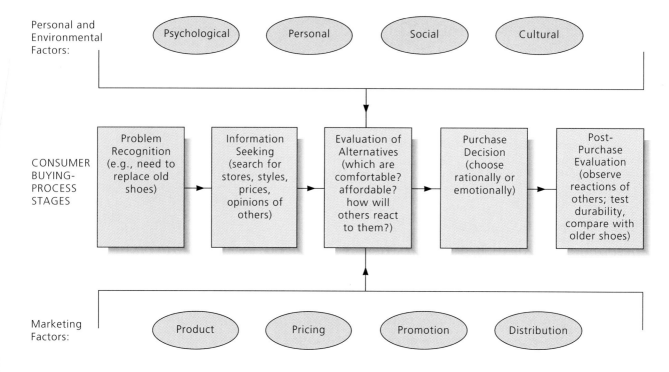

Figure 15.5
A model of the consumer buying process.

Problem/Need Recognition

The buying process begins when a consumer becomes aware of a problem or need. After strenuous exercise, you may recognize that you are thirsty and need refreshment. After the birth of twins, you may find your one-bedroom apartment too small for comfort. After standing in the rain to buy movie tickets, you may decide to buy an umbrella.

Need recognition also occurs when you have a chance to change your purchasing habits. For example, the income from your first job after graduation will allow you to purchase items that were too expensive when you were a student. You may also discover a need for professional clothing, apartment furnishings, and cars. Visa and The Bay recognize this shift and market their credit cards to graduates.

Information Seeking

Having recognized a need, consumers seek information. This search is not always extensive. If you are thirsty, you may ask where the pop machine is, but that may be the extent of your information search. Other times you simply rely on your memory for information.

Before making major purchases, however, most people seek information from personal sources, marketing sources, public sources, and experience. For example, if you move to a new town, you will want to find out who is the best local dentist, physician, hair stylist, butcher, or pizza maker. To get this information, you may check with personal sources such as acquaintances, co-workers, and relatives. Before buying an exercise bike, you may go to the library and read the latest *Consumer Reports*—a public source of consumer ratings—on such equipment. You may also ask market sources such as the salesclerk or rely on direct experience. For example, you might test ride the bike to learn more before you buy.

Consumer Reports
www.Consumer-Reports.org

What information is this shopper looking for to decide on his purchase? Marketers would like to know how and why he makes his choices.

Some sellers treat information as a value to be added to their products. For example, Body Shop International, a cosmetics manufacturer and retailer with no marketing or advertising department, has nevertheless been cited as a model of how to sell in the 1990s. The company's philosophy includes giving the customer product information rather than the traditional sales pitch. What makes this strategy work? The typical Body Shop customer is a skeptical consumer who generally distrusts advertising and sales hype, demands more product information, and is loyal to companies that, like the Body Shop, are perceived to be socially and environmentally responsible.[23]

Evaluation of Alternatives

The next step in the consumer decision process is to evaluate your alternatives. If you are in the market for a set of golf clubs, you probably have some idea of who produces clubs and how they differ. You may have accumulated some of this knowledge during the information-seeking stage and combined it with what you knew before. Based on product attributes such as colour, taste, price, prestige, quality, and service record, you will decide which product meets your needs most satisfactorily.

Purchase Decision

Ultimately, you make a purchase decision. You may decide to defer the purchase until a later time or you may decide to buy now. "Buy" decisions are based on rational and emotional motives. **Rational motives** involve a logical evaluation of product attributes: cost, quality, and usefulness. **Emotional motives** can lead to irrational decisions. Many spur-of-the-moment decisions are emotionally driven, though not all irrational decisions are sudden. Emotional motives include fear, sociability, imitation of others, and aesthetics. You might buy mouthwash to avoid ostracism. You might buy the same brand of jeans as your friends. And you might buy a chocolate milkshake because you like the taste.

Note that by *irrational* we do not mean insane or wrong, merely a decision based on nonobjective factors. Gratifying a sudden urge for ice cream may not require much thought and may produce a lot of enjoyment. However, in some cases, irrational decisions are bad. We have all purchased items, taken them home, and then wondered, "Why in the world did I buy this thing?"

rational motives
Those reasons for purchasing a product that involve a logical evaluation of product attributes such as cost, quality, and usefulness.

emotional motives
Those reasons for purchasing a product that involve nonobjective factors.

Body Shop International, which has no marketing or advertising department, is viewed by its loyal customers as socially and environmentally responsible.

Post-Purchase Evaluations

Marketing does not stop with the sale of a product or service, but includes the process of consumption. What happens *after* the sale is very important. A marketer wants consumers to be happy after the consumption of the product so that they will buy the product again. In fact, since consumers do not want to go through a complex decision process for every purchase, they often choose a product they have used and liked.

Not all consumers are satisfied with their purchases, of course. Dissatisfied consumers may complain, file a lawsuit, or publicly criticize the product and the company. They are unlikely to purchase the product again. In addition, dissatisfied customers are much more likely to speak about their experience with a product than are satisfied customers. Dissatisfied customers can have a very negative impact on a company's marketing effort. In fact, word of mouth can be the most influential marketing tool and also the most devastating, since businesses cannot control it.[24]

Doubts about the rationality of a purchase decision can cause **purchase anxiety**, sometimes called buyer's remorse. If you feel purchase anxiety after remodelling your home, you probably will not buy the services of the same interior designer again. Doing so would only perpetuate your anxiety. Reduction of purchase anxiety is important to marketers, particularly for expensive items such as furniture and major appliances.

purchase anxiety
A fear on the part of people who have made a purchase that their selection was wrong.

ORGANIZATIONAL MARKETING AND BUYING BEHAVIOUR

Buying behaviour is observable daily in the consumer market, where marketing activities, including buying-selling transactions, are visible to the public. Equally important, however, but far less visible, are *organizational* (or *commercial*) *markets*—organizations that buy goods and services to be used in creating and delivering consumer products. Marketing to these buyers involves different kinds of organizational markets and buying behaviours that are quite different from those found in consumer markets.

Organizational Markets

Organizational or commercial markets fall into three categories: *industrial, reseller,* and *government/institutional markets.*

Industrial Market

The **industrial market** includes businesses that buy goods falling into one of two categories: goods to be converted into other products and goods that are used up during production. This market includes farmers, manufacturers, and some retailers. For example, Seth Thomas purchases electronics, metal components, and glass to make clocks for the consumer market. The company also buys office supplies, tools, and factory equipment—items never seen by clock buyers—to be used during production.

industrial market
Businesses that buy goods to be converted into other products that will be sold to ultimate consumers.

Reseller Market

Before products reach consumers, they pass through a **reseller market** consisting of intermediaries, including wholesalers and retailers, who buy the finished goods and resell them (wholesalers and retailers are discussed in Chapter 17). Retailers like department stores, drugstores, and supermarkets buy clothing, appliances, foods, medicines, and other merchandise for resale to the consumer market. Retailers also buy such services as maintenance, housekeeping, and communications.

reseller market
Intermediaries like wholesalers and retailers who buy finished products and resell them.

Government and Institutional Market

Federal, provincial, and municipal governments purchase millions of dollars worth of computer equipment, buildings, paper clips and other items. The **institutional market** consists of nongovernmental organizations, such as hospitals, churches, museums, and charitable organizations, that also comprise a substantial market for goods and services. Like organizations in other commercial markets, these institutions use supplies and equipment, as well as legal, accounting, and transportation services.

institutional market
Nongovernment organizations such as hospitals, churches, and schools.

Organizational Buying Behaviour

In many respects, industrial buying behaviour bears little resemblance to consumer buying practices. For example, industrial product demand is stimulated by demand for consumer products and is less sensitive to price changes. Other differences include the buyers' purchasing skills, their decision-making activities, and buyer-seller relationships.

Differences in Demand

Recall our definition of *demand* in Chapter 1: the willingness and ability of buyers to purchase a good or service. There are two major differences in demand between consumer and industrial products: *derived demand* and *inelasticity of demand.* The term **derived demand** refers to the fact that demand for industrial products often results from demand for related consumer products (that is, industrial demand is frequently *derived from* consumer demand). **Inelasticity of demand** exists when a price change for a product does not have much effect on demand. Take, for instance, the demand for cardboard used to package file cabinets. Because cardboard packaging is such a small part of the manufacturer's overall cabinet cost, an increase in cardboard

derived demand
Demand for industrial products caused by (derived from) demand for consumer products.

inelasticity of demand
Exists when a price change for a product does not have much effect on demand.

prices will not lessen the demand for cardboard. In turn, because cabinet buyers will see little price increase, demand for filing cabinets—and for their accompanying cardboard packaging—will remain at about the same level.

Differences in Buyers

Unlike most consumers, organizational buyers are professional, specialized, and expert (or at least well informed):

- As *professionals*, organizational buyers are trained in arranging buyer-seller relationships and in methods for negotiating purchase terms. Once buyer-seller agreements have been reached, industrial buyers also arrange for formalized contracts.

- As a rule, industrial buyers are company *specialists* in a line of items. As one of several buyers for a large bakery, for example, you may specialize in food ingredients such as flour, yeast, butter, and so on.

- Industrial buyers are often *experts* about the products they are buying. On a regular basis, organizational buyers learn about competing products and alternative suppliers by attending trade shows, reading trade magazines, and conducting technical discussions with sellers' representatives.

Differences in Decision Making

Recall that we illustrated the five stages in the consumer buying process in Figure 15.5 (see page 478). The organizational buyer's decision process differs in three important respects—*developing product specifications, evaluating alternatives*, and *making postpurchase evaluations*.

Following problem recognition, the first stage of the buying process, industrial buying takes an additional step—developing product specifications. A document is drawn up to describe the detailed product characteristics that are needed by the buyer and must be met by the supplier. These specifications are then used in the information-seeking stage, when buyers search for products and suppliers capable of meeting their specific needs.

In evaluating alternatives, buyers carefully measure prospective suppliers against the product specifications developed earlier. Only suppliers that can meet those requirements are considered further. Only thereafter are prospective vendors evaluated according to other factors, such as price, reliability, and service reputation.

The final stage, post-purchase evaluation, is more systematic in organizational buying than in consumer buying. The buyer's organization examines the product and compares it, feature by feature, for conformance to product specifications. Buyers retain records on product and service quality received from suppliers as the basis for evaluating suppliers' performance. These performance ratings become important considerations for selecting suppliers in the future.

Differences in the Buyer-Seller Relationship

Consumer-seller relationships are often impersonal and fleeting—short-lived, one-time interactions. In contrast, industrial situations often involve frequent, enduring buyer-seller relationships. Accordingly, industrial sellers emphasize personal selling by trained representatives who can better understand the needs of each customer. Through extensive interaction with numerous buyers, sellers are better prepared to make suggestions for improving products and services that will benefit their customers.

THE INTERNATIONAL MARKETING MIX

Marketing products internationally means mounting a strategy to support global business operations. Obviously, this is no easy task. Foreign customers, for example, differ from domestic buyers in language, customs, business practices, and consumer behaviour. When they decide to go global, marketers must reconsider each element of the marketing mix: product, pricing, promotion, and place.

International Products

Some products, of course, can be sold abroad with virtually no changes. Budweiser, Coca-Cola, and Marlboros are exactly the same in Toronto, Tokyo, and Timbuktu. In other cases, firms have been obliged to create products with built-in flexibility—for example, electric shavers that adapt to either 115- or 230-volt outlets.

At times only a redesigned—or completely different—product will meet the needs of foreign buyers, however. To sell the Macintosh in Japan, for example, Apple had to develop a Japanese-language operating system. Whether they are standard domestic products or custom-made products for foreign markets, however, the most globally competitive products are usually reliable, low-priced products with advanced features.

International Pricing

When pricing for international markets, marketers must handle all the considerations of domestic pricing while also considering the higher costs of transporting and selling products abroad. Some products cost more overseas than in Canada because of the added costs of delivery. Due to the higher costs of buildings, rent, equipment, and imported meat, a McDonald's Big Mac that sells for $2.99 in Canada has a price tag of over $10 in Japan. In contrast, products like jet airplanes are priced the same worldwide because delivery costs are incidental; the huge development and production costs are the major considerations regardless of customer location.

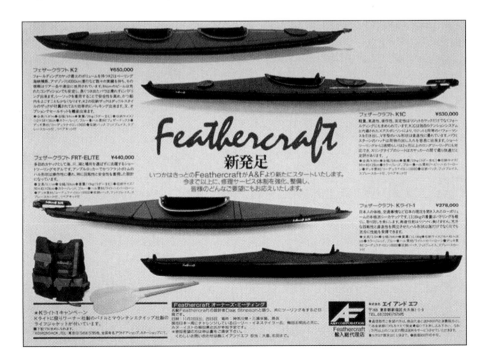

Feathercraft is a small British Columbia manufacturer that has been successful selling kayaks in the Japanese market.

International Promotion

Some standard Canadian promotional devices do not always succeed in other countries. In fact, many Europeans believe that a product must be inherently shoddy if a company does *any* advertising.

International marketers must also be aware that cultural differences can cause negative reactions to products that are advertised improperly. Some Europeans, for example, are offended by television commercials that show weapons or violence. Advertising practices are regulated accordingly. Consequently, Dutch commercials for toys do not feature the guns and combat scenes that are commonplace on Saturday morning television in North America. Meanwhile, liquor and cigarette commercials that are banned from Canadian and U.S. television are thriving in many Asian and European markets.

Symbolism, too, is a sometimes-surprising consideration. In France, for instance, yellow flowers suggest infidelity. In Mexico, they are signs of death—an association made in Brazil by the colour purple. Clearly, product promotions must be carefully matched to the customs and cultural values of each country.

International Distribution

Finally, international distribution presents several problems. In some industries, delays in starting new distribution networks can be costly. Therefore, companies with existing distribution systems often enjoy an advantage over new businesses. Several companies have gained advantages in time-based competition by buying existing businesses. Procter & Gamble, for example, saved three years of start-up time by buying Revlon's Max Factor and Betrix cosmetics, both of which are well established in foreign markets. P&G can thus immediately use these companies' distribution and marketing networks for selling its own brands in the United Kingdom, Germany, and Japan.

Other companies contract with foreign firms or individuals to distribute and sell their products abroad. Foreign agents may perform personal selling and advertising, provide information about local markets, or serve as exporters' representatives. But having to manage interactions with foreign personnel complicates a marketing manager's responsibilities. In addition, packaging practices in Canada must sometimes be adapted to withstand the rigours of transport to foreign ports and storage under conditions that differ radically from domestic conditions.

Given the need to adjust the marketing mix, success in international markets is hard won. Even experienced firms can err in marketing to other countries. International success requires flexibility and a willingness to adapt to the nuances of other cultures. Whether a firm sells products in domestic or international markets, however, the basic principles of marketing still apply. It is only the implementation of those principles that changes.

SMALL BUSINESS AND THE MARKETING MIX

As we noted in Chapter 7, far more small businesses fail than succeed. Yet many of today's largest firms were yesterday's small businesses. McDonald's began with one restaurant, a concept, and one individual (Ray Kroc) who had foresight. Behind the success of many small firms lies a skilful application of the marketing concept and careful consideration of each element in the marketing mix.

Small Business Products

Some new products—and firms—are doomed at the start simply because few consumers want or need what they have to offer. Too often, enthusiastic entrepreneurs introduce products that they and their friends like, but they fail to estimate realistic market potential. Other small businesses offer new products before they have clear pictures of their target segments and how to reach them. They try to be everything to everyone, and they end up serving no one well. In contrast, sound product planning has paid off for many small firms. "Keep it simple" is a familiar key to success—that is, fulfil a specific need and do it efficiently.

Small Business Pricing

Haphazard pricing that is often little more than guesswork can sink even a firm with a good product. Most often, small business pricing errors result from a failure to project operating expenses accurately. Owners of failing businesses have often been heard to utter statements like "I didn't realize how much it costs to run the business!" and "If I price the product high enough to cover my expenses, no one will buy it!" But when small businesses set prices by carefully assessing costs, many earn very satisfactory profits—sometimes enough to expand or diversify.

Small Business Promotion

Many small businesses are also ignorant when it comes to the methods and costs of promotion. To save expenses, for example, they may avoid advertising and rely instead on personal selling. As a result, too many potential customers remain unaware of their products.

Successful small businesses plan for promotional expenses as part of start-up costs. Some hold down costs by taking advantage of less expensive promotional methods. Local newspapers, for example, are sources of publicity when they publish articles about new or unique businesses. Other small businesses have succeeded by identifying themselves and their products with associated groups, organizations, and events. Thus a custom-crafts gallery might join with a local art league and local artists to organize public showings of their combined products.

Small Business Distribution

Problems in arranging distribution can also make or break small businesses. Perhaps the most critical aspect of distribution is facility location, especially for new service businesses. The ability of many small businesses—retailers, veterinary clinics, gourmet coffee shops—to attract and retain customers depends partly on the choice of location.

In distribution, as in other aspects of the marketing mix, however, smaller companies may have advantages over larger competitors, even in highly complex industries. They may be quicker, for example, in applying service technologies. Everex Systems Inc. sells personal computers to wholesalers and dealers through a system the company calls "Zero Response Time." Phone orders are reviewed every two hours so that the factory can adjust assembly to match demand.

SUMMARY OF LEARNING OBJECTIVES

1. **Define *marketing*.** *Marketing* is the process of planning and executing the conception, pricing, promotion, and distribution of ideas, goods, and services to create exchanges that satisfy individual and organizational objectives.

2. **Describe the five forces that constitute the *external marketing environment*.** The *external environment* consists of the outside forces that influence marketing strategy and decision making. The *political/legal environment* includes laws and regulations, both domestic and foreign, that may define or constrain business activities. The *social/cultural environment* is the context within which people's values, beliefs, and ideas affect marketing decisions. The *technological environment* includes the technological developments that affect existing and new products. The *economic environment* consists of the conditions, such as inflation, recession, and interest rates, that influence both consumer and organizational spending patterns. Finally, the *competitive environment* is the environment in which marketers must persuade buyers to purchase their products rather than their competitors'.

3. **Explain *market segmentation* and show how it is used in *target marketing*.** *Market segmentation* is the process of dividing markets into categories of customers. Businesses have learned that marketing is more successful when it is aimed towards specific *target markets*—groups of consumers with similar wants and needs. Markets may be segmented by *geographic, demographic, psychographic*, or *product-use variables*.

4. **Explain the purpose and value of *market research*.** *Market research* is the study of what buyers need and of the best ways to meet those needs. This process involves a study of the current situation, the selection of a research method, the collection of data, the analysis of data, and the preparation of a report that may include recommendations for action. The four most common research methods are *observation, surveys, focus groups*, and *experimentation*.

5. **Describe the key factors that influence the *consumer buying process*.** A number of personal and psychological considerations, along with various social and cultural influences, affect consumer behaviour. When making buying decisions, consumers first determine or respond to a problem or need and then collect as much information as they think necessary before making a purchase. *Postpurchase evaluations* are also important to marketers because they influence future buying patterns.

6. **Discuss the three categories of *organizational markets* and explain how *organizational buying behaviour* differs from *consumer buying behaviour*.** The *industrial market* includes firms that buy goods falling into one of two categories: (1) goods to be converted into other products, and (2) goods that are used up during production. Farmers and manufacturers are members of the industrial market. Members of the *reseller market* (mostly wholesalers) are intermediaries who buy and resell finished goods. Besides governments and agencies at all levels, the *government and institutional market* includes such nongovernmental organizations as hospitals, museums, and charities.

There are four main differences between consumer and organizational buying behaviour. First, the nature of *demand* is different in organizational markets: it is often *derived* (resulting from related consumer demand), *inelastic* (largely unaffected by price changes), or both. Second, organizational buyers are typically professionals, specialists, or experts. Third, organizational buyers develop product specifications, evaluate alternatives more thoroughly, and make more systematic postpurchase evaluations. Finally, they often develop enduring buyer-seller relationships.

KEY TERMS

marketing, 457
consumer goods, 458
industrial goods, 458
relationship marketing, 458
external environment, 459
substitute product, 462
brand competition, 462
international competition, 462
marketing managers, 462

marketing plan, 462
marketing concept, 463
marketing mix, 463
product, 463
product differentiation, 464
pricing, 465
promotion, 465
advertising, 465
personal selling, 465
sales promotion, 465
public relations, 465
publicity, 466

distribution, 466
target market, 467
market segmentation, 467
positioning, 468
psychographic variables, 470
market research, 473
secondary data, 475
primary data, 475
observation, 475
survey, 475

focus group, 475
experimentation, 476
consumer behaviour, 477
rational motives, 479
emotional motives, 479
purchase anxiety, 480
industrial market, 481
reseller market, 481
institutional market, 481
derived demand, 481
inelasticity of demand, 481

STUDY QUESTIONS AND EXERCISES

Review Questions
1. What are the similarities and differences between consumer marketing and industrial marketing?
2. Explain how and why market segmentation is used in target marketing.
3. Identify the steps in the consumer buying process.
4. What elements of the marketing mix may need to be adjusted to market a product internationally? Why?

Analysis Questions
5. Using examples of everyday products, explain why marketing plans must consider the marketing mix.
6. Pick an everyday product such as books, dog food, or shoes. Using your product as an example, show how different versions of it are aimed towards different market segments. Show how the marketing mix differs for each of the segments.
7. Select a readily available product and describe the steps you would expect to find in the consumer de-

cision process about buying that product.
8. If you were starting your own new small business, what are the major pitfalls you would try to avoid as you put together your marketing plans?

Application Exercises
9. Interview the owner of a local retail business. Determine if the store has a clear market segment it is trying to appeal to, and what that market segment is.
10. Select a product made by a foreign company and sold in Canada. Compare it to a similar product made domestically in terms of its product features, price, promotion, and distribution. Which one of the two products do you believe will be more successful with Canadian buyers? Why?

Building Your Business Skills

Dealing in Segments and Variables

Goal
To encourage students to analyze the ways in which various market segmentation variables affect business success.

Situation
You and four partners are thinking of purchasing a heating and air conditioning (H/AC) dealership that specializes in residential applications priced between $2000 and $40 000. You are now in the process of deciding where that dealership should be. You are considering four locations: Miami, Florida; Toronto, Ontario; Vancouver, B.C.; and Dallas, Texas.

Method

Step 1:
Working with four classmates (your partnership group), do library research to learn how H/AC makers market their residential products. Check for articles in *The Globe and Mail, Canadian Business, The Wall Street Journal,* and other business publications.

Step 2:
Continue your research. This time, focus on the specific marketing variables that define each prospective location. Check Statistics Canada data at your library and on the Internet and contact local chambers of commerce (by phone and via the Internet) to learn about the following factors for each location:

- geography
- demography (especially age, income, gender, family status, and social class)
- psychographic variables (lifestyles, interests, and attitudes)

Step 3:
Meet with group members to analyze which location holds the greatest promise as a dealership site. Base your decision on your analysis of market segment variables and their effects on H/AC sales.

Follow-Up Questions

1. Which location did you choose? Describe the market segmentation factors that influenced your decision.

2. Identify the two most important variables you believe will have the greatest impact on the dealership's success. Why are these factors so important?

3. Which factors were least important in your decision? Why?

4. When equipment manufacturers advertise residential H/AC products, they often show them in different climate situations (in winter, summer, or high-humidity conditions). Which market segments are these ads targeting? Describe these segments in terms of demographic and psychographic characteristics.

Exploring the Net

To find out about some of the marketing methods used by a world-class company, log on to the Marriott Hotels Web site at

www.marriott.com

In the left column of the Marriott home page, click on "Marriott Hotels, Resorts & Suites." Next, return to the home page. From there, explore the Web site and read the general description of the company's lodging business. Finally, return to the home page and click on "Our Hotels." One at a time, study each of Marriott's various hotel brands. Consider the following issues, all of which pertain to the company's marketing processes:

1. Identify a Marriott product that seems oriented towards the consumer market and one that is directed more at the commercial market. What are some specific services that you found that are different for the two markets?

2. Consider the way in which Marriott has identified market segments for five brands:

   - Marriott Hotels, Resorts, and Suites
   - Courtyard by Marriott
   - Residence Inn
   - Fairfield Inn
   - Renaissance Hotels and Resorts.

   Can you find an example of segmentation by geographic variables? By demographic variables? By psychographic variables? By product use variables?

3. Cite examples of incentives that Marriott uses and services that it offers to build relationships with its clients.

Concluding Case 15-1

JNCO Jeans

Adults don't know how to pronounce "JNCO" jeans, and, more importantly, they have no idea why teenagers like to wear them. With billowing 100-centimetre bottoms and cavernous 45-centimetre-deep pockets, JNCO has made wide legs fashionable, albeit no easier to wear. Ever try climbing stairs with pants that wide? And what about the dirt and chewing gum that collect at the cuff?

Nevertheless, boys ages 12 to 15 recently rated JNCO the sixth-"coolest" brand, right behind Tommy Hilfiger and Adidas. Strength in this market translates into millions of consumer dollars. According to *Tactical Retail Monitor*, the market for wide-leg jeans has recently grown five times as fast as the entire men's jeans category. That's why Revatex, the Los Angeles firm that manufactures JNCO, pays serious attention to marketing research that tells them what teenagers want and how they are likely to spend their consumer dollars.

Conscious of the independent, rebellious spirit of their target audience, Revatex marketers take a stealth approach to cultivating JNCO's cool image. They don't buy billboards or place GAP-style ads in popular magazines. Instead, Revatex supplies free clothes to trendsetting DJs and band members who play at all-night dance parties. It advertises in such magazines as *Electric Ink* and *Thrasher*, which target skateboarders and extreme rollerbladers. Recording artist J-Smooth will be wearing JNCO clothes in targeted ads in *Spin*, *Vibe*, *Blaze*, and *Urb*.

With wholesale revenues somewhere between US$100 and $200 million, Revatex is hitting Levi Strauss and other mainstream jeans makers where it hurts—in the wallet. Nicholas Lynch, who owns 11 pairs of JNCOs, says he'll never own a pair of Levi's: "Levi's came out with wide jeans," he admits, "but it just isn't the same because of who wears them." Translation: Baby boomers (also known as *losers*) wear Levi's, but those on the cutting edge wear JNCOs.

Finding and defining the cutting edge in teen taste is the work of marketing researchers who specialize in the teen market. Companies pay a high price for this research to attract a share of the roughly US$4 billion that teens spend every year on clothes, cosmetics, CDs, and other personal and fashion items. According to Teen-Age Research Unlimited, one of the most respected marketing research firms

in this segment, understanding teen buying behaviour means identifying and targeting teen decision makers known as *influencers*. A dream-come-true category for marketers, influencers spend money on fashion trends before they are popular and then influence *conformers* to follow suit. Conformers, explains one researcher, "make up the bulk of the teenage population. They're looking for brands and badges to ... get them to the next level."

As a group, teenagers have more money and more control over spending than any teen generation before it. With both parents working and their spending habits learned from self-gratifying baby-boomer parents, today's teens are worth studying.

However, teenagers aren't the only youths with discretionary cash. To the delight of marketers, 4- to 12-year-olds now spend millions (of their parents' money) on food and drink, clothes, movies, games, and toys. Both this surge in children's spending power and their maturing tastes are linked to the ways in which dual-career parents raise their kids. "The style of child rearing today," suggests one child psychologist, "is to empower very young children and give them choices about everything. When you give small children power, they act like adolescents."

With newfound maturity and anchored buying decisions, children are now viewed as a prime marketing target. It's no coincidence that retail stores for sophisticated children are opening in malls throughout the country. The Limited Too, Abercrombie & Fitch, Gap Kids, and Gymboree are stocking clothes and gear for 6- to 12-year-olds and doing land-office business.

Even when parents make the final buying decision, marketers now realize the influence exerted by children. That's why Ford's Lincoln Mercury division launched its new Mercury Villager minivan to coincide with the 1998 premiere of the first *Rugrats* movie. Some marketers are thriving because of the maturity shift, but others are being forced to rethink long-standing strategies. Mattel Inc., manufacturer of the Barbie doll, can no longer count on 7- to 8-year-old buyers. "We're losing them sooner," laments Mattel president Bruce Stein, whose core Barbie market has been trimmed to 2- to 6-year-olds. "They're in sensory overload.... There are too many things competing for their interests."

Other marketers have decided to cater to the special needs of the youngest sophisticates. When the Limited Too opened in 1991, it targeted girls ages 2 to 16. Six years later, it narrowed its focus to 6- to 14-year-olds, because it recognized preteens as a special market segment. The preteen girl, explains the chain's vice-president of marketing, is "moving out of the fantasy play world. She's kind of caught between Barbie and a driver's license."

CASE QUESTIONS

1. What social and cultural factors have influenced the growth of the teen and preteen markets?

2. How would you define the teenage target market? Why is it growing in importance?

3. What characteristics would you include in a psychographic profile of teenagers and preteenagers?

4. Do you agree or disagree with Revatex's stealth marketing tactics to reach teenage influencers? How do influencers affect consumer buying behaviour?

5. If you worked in Mattel's marketing department, how would you reattract 7- to 8-year-old buyers? What spinoff Barbie products might interest this market segment? ◆

Concluding Case 15-2

Which Washer Is Best?

There are basically two types of washing machines—top loaders and front loaders. The former dominates the market in Canada and the U.S., and the latter dominates the market in Europe. In front loaders, clothes spin around a horizontal axis, with the clothes tumbling in and out of a pool of detergent-rich water. The clothes are rinsed repeatedly. By contrast, North American top loaders swirl clothes around in a tub of water that dilutes the detergent.

Europeans argue front loaders are better because:
• they get clothes cleaner
• they use less water and are more energy efficient
• they are easier on clothes because there is no centre shaft for the clothes to hit during the wash cycle
• they spin more water out of the clothes during the wash cycle, which means less time in the dryer

North Americans see several disadvantages of front loaders:
• they take three times as long to complete the wash cycle
• they are much more expensive than top loaders because they must have watertight doors
• clothes cannot be added during the wash cycle as they can in top loaders
• front loaders don't have the capacity of top loaders
• front loaders are not as easy to load as top loaders

In spite of these back-and-forth arguments, front loaders may be getting a foothold in North America. In 1997, both Maytag and Amana announced that they would begin producing front loaders. At the moment, front loaders have only a 2 percent market share in North America. The key reasons are price (front loaders sell for as much as $3000, while top loaders often go for as little as $500) and efficiency (front loaders take much longer to complete the wash cycle).

The marketing strategy used by Europeans is to tout their washers as upscale products like fancy cars. Producers often try to get home builders to install them as a home is being built, and then the homeowner adds the price to the mortgage.

CASE QUESTIONS

1. Consider the detailed activities that must be carried out when washing clothes. What would the typical consumer find attractive about front loaders? About top loaders?

2. What would the typical consumer find unattractive about front loaders? About top loaders?

3. What kind of consumers in Canada and the U.S. are likely to purchase a front-loading machine?

4. How can the perceived (and real) disadvantages of front loaders be overcome by manufacturers? Be specific. ◆

Visit the *Business* Website at www.pearsoned.ca/griffin
for up-to-date e-business cases!

Clodhoppers

Krave Candy Co. was started in 1996 by two Winnipeg entrepreneurs—Chris Emery and Larry Finnson. Their company produces a food product that was originally made by Emery's grandmother and was popular with their friends. The product is called Clodhoppers, a popcorn-sized cluster of cashew nuts, white chocolate, and graham wafers. In just four years, Emery and Finnson have turned Clodhoppers into a promising new product that produced sales revenue of $1 million in 1999. They hope to double sales revenue in 2000.

As a new company with a low profile, Krave is spending a large chunk of money on marketing. But the entrepreneurs know they have a long way to go before their product will become as well known as Turtles or Skittles. In the company's first year, Clodhoppers were packaged in plastic peanut butter jars and sold locally in Winnipeg. The market segment that was being targeted was boxed chocolates, but the jar and the packaging didn't stand out next to competitors' products. Since the candy was visible in the jar, retailers often mistakenly placed it in the snack section instead of with other boxed chocolates.

The solution was to put the jar in a box. In 1998, the packaging was revamped and the product was put in a foil pouch in a classy-looking black carton with gold embossed lettering and a coating that kept the packaging looking shiny. Those changes helped Clodhoppers get a contract with Wal-Mart. During the 1999 Christmas season, Wal-Mart sold out its supply of Clodhoppers and ordered more for Easter and Mother's Day. The Wal-Mart contract gave Krave credibility and other orders followed. Clodhoppers are now carried by Shoppers Drug Mart and Zellers as well. Krave was also given a big boost when it was featured on a segment of the CBC's *Venture*.

In January 2000, Emery and Finnson attended The Fancy Food Show and met with buyers from several U.S. chain stores. Nieman Marcus indicated its interest in stocking Clodhoppers in all 31 of its stores. Costco also expressed interest. And in June 2000, Emery and Finnson signed an agreement to test Clodhoppers in 50 Sam's Club warehouses in the U.S. during the Christmas 2000 season.

Krave's promotion strategy has been to forego television advertising and instead put money into a national sampling blitz that hits stores around the holiday season. This gives shoppers a chance to actually taste the product. Krave also launched its second product— milk chocolate Clodhoppers—in March 2000. It also tested a Clodhopper Blizzard at Dairy Queens in Manitoba, Saskatchewan, and B.C. in August 2000. In the spring of 2001, Krave Candy became the first Canadian candy company to own a Blizzard flavour at Dairy Queen Canada. The product is available at all 538 Dairy Queen locations across Canada. Getting equal billing with other Blizzard flavours such as Oreo Cookies, Reese's Pieces, and Crispy Crunch gives Clodhoppers instant credibility.

Emery and Finnson are looking for an additional $1 million in capital to fund plant expansion. They would eventually like to go public and attack the U.S. market. If they get the money, their top priority will be doubling the 5000-square-foot production facility in Winnipeg, which currently produces only 500 pounds of Clodhoppers per hour. ◆

Krave Candy Co.
www.kraves.com

In the last chapter, we introduced the four components of the marketing mix: product, promotion, price, and distribution. In this chapter, we will look at the complex issue of what a *product* is and how it can best be promoted to customers. The opening case shows that developing a new product is a risky and time-consuming activity, but it must be done if a company is to survive and prosper in the long run.

By focusing on the learning objectives of this chapter, you will better understand new product development and promotion. After reading this chapter, you should be able to:

LEARNING OBJECTIVES

1. Identify a *product* and distinguish between *consumer* and *industrial products*.

2. Trace the stages of the *product life cycle* and explain the *growth-share matrix*.

3. Discuss the importance of *branding* and *packaging*.

4. Identify the important objectives of *promotion* and discuss the considerations in selecting a *promotional mix*.

5. Discuss the most important *advertising strategies* and describe the key *advertising media*.

6. Outline the tasks involved in *personal selling* and list the steps in the *personal selling process*.

7. Describe the various types of *sales promotions*.

WHAT IS A PRODUCT?

In developing the marketing mix for any products—whether ideas, goods, or services—marketers must consider what consumers really buy when they purchase products. Only then can they plan their strategies effectively. We will begin this section where product strategy begins—with an understanding of product *features* and *benefits*. Next, we will describe the major *classifications of products*, both consumer and industrial. Finally, we will discuss the most important component in the offerings of any business—its *product mix*.

Features and Benefits

Customers do not buy products simply because they like the products themselves; they buy products because they like what the products can do for them, either physically or emotionally. To succeed, then, a product must include the right features and offer the right benefits. Product **features** are the qualities, both tangible and intangible, that a company builds into its products, such as a 12-horsepower motor on a lawn mower. To be saleable, a product's features also must provide *benefits*. The lawn mower must provide an attractive lawn.

features
The qualities, both tangible and intangible, that a company builds into its products.

Obviously, features and benefits play extremely important roles in the pricing of products. If you look carefully at the Diners Club ad in Figure 16.1, you will realize that products are much more than just visible features and benefits. In buying a product, customers are also buying an image and a reputation. The marketers of the credit card advertised here are well aware that brand name, labelling, and postpurchase satisfaction are indispensable facets of their product. The ad is designed to remind customers—especially business customers—that such features as extended billing periods, hands-on service, bonus air miles, and widespread acceptance go hand in hand with the familiar plastic card.

AFTER 30 DAYS, MOST CHARGE CARD COMPANIES GIVE YOU A WARNING.

WE GIVE YOU ANOTHER 30 DAYS.

There must be a catch, right? Actually, no. We understand that sometimes a three-day business trip turns into three weeks and, by necessity, you could use some extra time to pay your bill. That's why we always give you the convenience of an extra billing period to pay when you need it, interest-free. Another difference is having a real person answer your calls and help you, 24 hours a day. We also give you an award-winning rewards program that allows you to earn miles that can be redeemed on every major U.S. airline. And, of course, the Diners Club Card is welcomed by airlines, hotels, car rental companies and millions of other places you go. Call us at 1 800 2 DINERS. We'll answer all of your questions, no extra charge.

BREAKING THE PLASTIC MOLD.

CITIBANK

© 2000 Citicorp Diners Club Inc.   www.dinersclubus.com

Figure 16.1
The product: Features and benefits.

Classifying Goods and Services

One way to classify a product is according to expected buyers. Buyers fall into two groups: buyers of *consumer* products and buyers of *industrial* products. As we saw in Chapter 15, the consumer and industrial buying processes differ significantly. Not surprisingly, then, marketing products to consumers is vastly different from marketing them to other companies.

Classifying Consumer Products

Consumer products are commonly divided into three categories that reflect buyers' behaviour: convenience, shopping, and specialty products.

convenience goods/services
Relatively inexpensive consumer goods or services that are bought and used rapidly and regularly, causing consumers to spend little time looking for them or comparing their prices.

■ **Convenience goods** (such as milk and newspapers) and **convenience services** (such as those offered by fast-food restaurants) are consumed rapidly and regularly. They are relatively inexpensive and are purchased frequently and with little expenditure of time and effort.

■ **Shopping goods** (such as stereos and tires) and **shopping services** (such as insurance) are more expensive and are purchased less frequently than convenience goods and services. Consumers often compare brands, sometimes in different stores. They may also evaluate alternatives in terms of style, performance, colour, price, and other criteria.

shopping goods/services
Moderately expensive consumer goods or services that are purchased infrequently, causing consumers to spend some time comparing their prices.

■ **Specialty goods** (such as wedding gowns) and **specialty services** (such as catering for wedding receptions) are extremely important and expensive purchases. Consumers usually decide on precisely what they want and will accept no substitutes. They will often go from store to store, sometimes spending a great deal of money and time to get a specific product.

specialty goods/services
Very expensive consumer goods or services that are purchased rarely, causing consumers to spend a great deal of time locating the exact item desired.

Classifying Industrial Products

Depending on how much they cost and how they will be used, industrial products can be divided into two categories: *expense items* and *capital items*.

Expense items are any materials and services that are consumed within a year by firms producing other goods or supplying services. The most obvious expense items are industrial goods used directly in the production process, for example, bulkloads of tea processed into tea bags. In addition, *support materials* help keep a business running without directly entering the production process. Oil, for instance, keeps the tea-bagging machines running but is not used in the tea bags. Similarly, *supplies*—pencils, brooms, gloves, and paint—are consumed quickly and regularly by every business. Finally, *services* such as window cleaning, equipment installation, and temporary office help are essential to daily operations. Because these items are used frequently, purchases are often automatic or require little decision making.

expense items
Relatively inexpensive industrial goods that are consumed rapidly and regularly.

Capital items are "permanent"—that is, expensive and long lasting—goods and services. All these items have expected lives of more than a year—typically up to several years. Expensive buildings (offices, factories), fixed equipment (water towers, baking ovens), and accessory equipment (computers, airplanes) are capital goods. Capital services are those for which long-term commitments are made. These may include purchases for employee food services, building and equipment maintenance, or legal services. Because capital items are expensive and purchased infrequently, they often involve decisions by high-level managers.

capital items
Expensive, long-lasting industrial goods that are used in producing other goods or services and have a long life.

The Product Mix

The group of products a company has available for sale, be it consumer or industrial, is known as the firm's **product mix**. Black and Decker, for example, makes toasters, vacuum cleaners, electric drills, and a variety of other appliances and tools. 3M makes everything from Post-its to laser optics.

product mix
The group of products a company has available for sale.

Most companies begin with a single product. Over time, successful companies may find that the initial product does not suit all consumers shopping for the product type. So they often introduce similar products designed to reach other consumers. Apple computer introduced the first successful personal computer. Shortly thereafter, Apple produced a range of personal computers for various applications—for example, the Apple 2C, 2E, 2GS, Macintosh Plus, and Macintosh SE. A group of similar products intended for a similar group of buyers who will use them in similar fashions is known as a **product line**.

product line
A group of similar products intended for a similar group of buyers who will use them in a similar fashion.

Companies may also extend their horizons and identify opportunities outside of their existing product line. The result—multiple (or diversified) product lines—is evident in firms like Procter & Gamble. This firm began by making soap, but it now also produces paper products, foods, coffee, and baby products. Multiple product lines allow a company to grow more rapidly and minimize the consequences of slow sales in any one product line.

DEVELOPING NEW PRODUCTS

To expand or diversify product lines—indeed, just to survive—firms must develop and successfully introduce streams of new products. Faced with competition and shifting consumer preferences, no firm can count on a single successful product to carry it forever. Even basic products that have been widely purchased for decades require nearly constant renewal. Consider the unassuming facial tissue. The white tissue in the rectangular box has been joined (if not replaced) by tissues of many different colours and patterns. They arrive in boxes shaped and decorated for nearly every room in the house, and they are made to be placed or carried not only in the bathroom but also in the purse, the briefcase, and the car.

Technology plays an important role in the development of new products. **Technology** is the application of science that enables people to do entirely new things or to perform established tasks in a new and better ways. Consider the following examples:

After studying the movement of the human foot in minute detail, Canstar Sports Inc. developed the Micron Mega skate, which is now worn by 70 percent of NHL players.

Alcan developed a ceramic and aluminum composite called Duralcan. A mountain bike built with Duralcan weighs half as much as a bike built with a standard steel frame.

Toyota Motor Corp. has demonstrated an experimental car that monitors driver alertness with a pulse sensor worn on the wrist. The car sounds a chime to wake up a drowsy driver.

Business firms must embrace technology so that their products and product features will not become obsolete. If a firm is aggressive, it will be the first to introduce a new and cheaper way to make its Product X. It might also introduce Product X—Mark II with features that make a competitor's Product Y obsolete. Any of these objectives require substantial investment in research and development (R&D).

R&D refers to those activities that are necessary to provide new products, services, and processes. It usually requires a large investment in laboratories, equipment, and scientific talent. In Canada, only 0.5 percent of GDP is spent on R&D; in Japan, the U.S., and Germany, the figure is between 1.5 and 2.0 percent of GDP. When we take into account the smaller size of Canada's GDP, it is clear that Canada spends far fewer dollars on R&D than these other countries. Only a small number of firms do R&D in Canada, and the top 25 firms account for over half of all R&D that is carried out.

R&D does not automatically guarantee success, because it may be difficult to find a market for a new product that has been developed. Terry Knight and Al Robinson, the owners of Inuktun Services Ltd., developed small, submersible, remotely operated vehicles (ROVs) equipped with lights and a video camera. The idea was that boat owners could guide these devices down into the water and view the bottom of their boat on a TV monitor. Boat owners weren't interested, but the nuclear industry was. Now Inuktun's ROVs travel up and down stairs, around corners, over obstacles, in water up to 30 metres deep, and through ducts and pipes as little as 15 centimetres in diameter.[1]

technology
The application of science that enables people to do entirely new things or to perform established tasks in a new and better way.

R&D
Those activities that are necessary to provide new products, services, and processes.

The New Product Development Process

Companies often face multi-year time horizons and high risks when developing new products. In 1989, discussions about the possibility of manufacturing a new long-range executive jet began at Bombardier Inc. of Montreal. Over the next few years, the company spent millions of dollars developing the product, which finally became available in 1998. Automobile manufacturers also face a long time horizon as they try to develop a new engine to replace the internal combustion engine that has powered automobiles for over 100 years. In the late 1990s, Ford invested $420 million in an alliance with DaimlerChrysler and Ballard Power Systems to produce cars powered by fuel cells by 2004.[2]

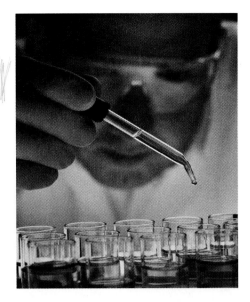

Pharmaceutical companies spend large amounts of money on research and development, yet bring relatively few products to market.

Ballard Power Systems
www.ballard.com

High-definition television (HDTV) is another example of a new product that has taken much longer than expected to develop. Because HDTV gives much-improved picture quality, it was originally assumed that consumers would quickly accept it. But HDTV has been plagued by a classic chicken-and-egg problem: broadcasters haven't decided to offer high-definition programs (because they require special transmitters and cameras) and manufacturers of HDTVs have been holding back because they don't know whether broadcasters are going to produce high-definition programs for consumers to watch. HDTV should be available in Canada by late 2001 or early 2002.[3]

Many firms maintain research and development departments or divisions for exploring new product possibilities. Why do they devote so many resources to thinking about products and exploring their possibilities, rejecting many seemingly good ideas along the way? How do they conduct these early explorations into new product possibilities?

We address these questions in this section. You will see, for instance, that the high mortality rate for new ideas means that only a few new products eventually reach the market. Moreover, for many companies, speed to market with a product is often as important as care in developing it. Finally, product development is a long, complex, and expensive process. Companies do not dream up new products one day and ship them to retailers the next. In fact, new products usually involve carefully planned and sometimes risky commitments of time and resources.

Product Mortality Rates

Typically, new products move through a series of stages, beginning with the search for ideas and culminating in introduction to consumers. At each stage of this process, potential products fall from further consideration as the company pursues more attractive alternatives. In fact, it is estimated that it takes 50 new product ideas to generate one product that finally reaches the marketplace. Even then, of course, only a few of those survivors become *successful* products. Many seemingly great *ideas* have failed as *products*. Indeed, creating a successful new product has become more and more difficult.

WEBCONNEXION

IDEO is a design consulting firm. To find out what sort of products the company has designed and engineered—and to get an idea of how its designers go about the process of prompting and realizing commercial inspirations—log on to IDEO's Web site at:

www.ideo.com

Speed to Market

A product's chances for success are also better if it beats its competition to market. The principle applies to products in every industry:

- SINA.com, a Web portal that functions as an online service provider, is a Chinese-language network of Web sites providing news, finance, lifestyle, sports, e-mail, and online shopping to global users. It started in 1995, but its founders estimated that by the year 2001, more than 19 million people would be surfing the Web in Chinese and that Sinanet would be the first to have established a loyal following. Today, SINA.com is the market leader, targeting the 1.3 billion potential Internet surfers of Chinese descent worldwide.

- A classic example of the advantage of getting a competitive head start is Miller Lite beer. Miller dominated the light beer market for years because it established itself with consumers before its competitors even got started. Miller was one year ahead of Schlitz Light, two years ahead of Anheuser-Busch Natural Light, and three years ahead of some 22 other brands. After years of expensive advertising, Bud Light finally made up lost ground to take the lead in market share.

The principle reflected in these two cases is simple: The more rapidly a product moves from the laboratory to the marketplace, the more likely it is to survive. By introducing new products ahead of competitors, companies quickly establish market leaders. They become entrenched in the market before being challenged by late-arriving competitors. How important is **speed to market**—that is, a firm's success in responding to customer demand or market changes? One study has estimated that a product that is only three months late to market (that is, three months behind the leader) sacrifices 12 percent of its lifetime profit potential. A product that is six months late will lose 33 percent.

speed to market
Strategy of introducing new products to respond quickly to customer and/or market changes.

The Seven-Step Development Process

To increase their chances of developing a successful new product, many firms adopt some variation on a basic seven-step process (see Figure 16.2).

1. Product ideas. Product development begins with a search for ideas for new products. Product ideas can come from consumers, the sales force, research and development people, or engineering personnel. The key is to actively seek out ideas and to reward those whose ideas become successful products.

2. Screening. This second stage is an attempt to eliminate all product ideas that do not mesh with the firm's abilities, expertise, or objectives. Representatives from marketing, engineering, and production must have input at this stage.

3. Concept testing. Once ideas have been culled, companies use market research to solicit consumers' input. In this way, firms can identify benefits that the product must provide as well as an appropriate price level for the product.

4. Business analysis. This stage involves developing an early comparison of costs versus benefits for the proposed product. Preliminary sales projections are compared with cost projections from finance and production. The aim is not to determine precisely how much money the product will make but to see whether the product can meet minimum profitability goals.

5. Prototype development. At this stage, product ideas begin to take shape. Using input from the concept-testing phase, engineering and/or research and development produce a preliminary version of the product. Prototypes can be extremely expensive, often requiring extensive hand crafting, tooling, and development of components. But this phase can help identify potential production problems.

6. Product testing and test marketing. Using what it learned from the prototype, the company goes into limited production of the item. The product is then tested internally to see if it meets performance requirements. If it does, it is made available for sale in limited areas. This stage is very costly, since promotional campaigns and distribution channels must be established for test markets. But test marketing gives a company its first information on how consumers will respond to a product under real market conditions.

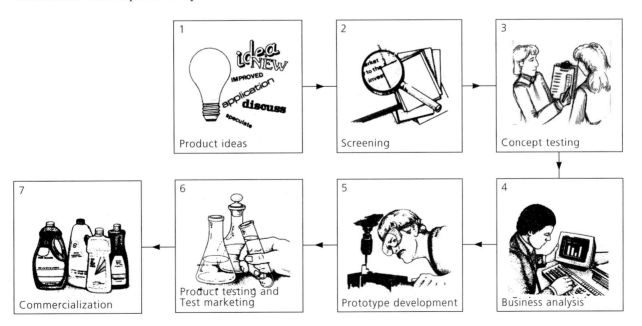

Figure 16.2
The new product development process.

7. Commercialization. If test-marketing results are positive, the company will begin full-scale production and marketing of the product. Gradual commercialization, with the firm providing the product to more and more areas over time, prevents undue strain on the firm's initial production capabilities. But extensive delays in commercialization may give competitors a chance to bring out their own version.

The development of services (both for consumers and industrial buyers) involves many of the same stages as goods development. Basically, Steps 2, 3, 4, 6, and 7 are the same. There are, however, some important differences in Steps 1 and 5:

definition of the service package
Identification of the tangible and intangible features that define the service.

- *Service Ideas.* The search for service ideas includes a task called **definition of the service package**, which involves identification of the tangible and intangible features that define the service (see Chapter 11).[4] This definition includes *service specifications*. For example, a firm that wants to offer year-end cleaning services to office buildings might commit itself to the following specifications: "The building interior will be cleaned by midnight, January 5, including floor polishing of all aisles, carpets swept free of all dust and debris, polished washbowls and lavatory equipment, with no interruption or interference to customer."

service process design
Selecting the process, identifying worker requirements, and determining facilities requirements so that the service can be effectively provided.

- *Service Process Design.* Instead of prototype development, services require a **service process design**. This step involves selecting the process, identifying worker requirements, and determining facilities requirements so that the service can be provided as promised in the service specifications. *Process selection* identifies each step in the service, including the sequence and the timing. *Worker requirements* specify employee behaviours, skills, capabilities, and interactions with customers during the service encounter. *Facilities requirements* designate all of the equipment that supports delivery of the service. All three of these areas must be coordinated.[5]

THE PRODUCT LIFE CYCLE

product life cycle (PLC)
The concept that the profit-producing life of any product goes through a cycle of introduction, growth, maturity (levelling off), and decline.

Products that reach the commercialization stage begin a new series of stages known as the product life cycle. **Product life cycle (PLC)** is the concept that products have a limited profit-producing life for a company. This life may be a matter of months, years, or decades, depending on the ability of the product to attract customers over time. Strong products such as Kellogg's Corn Flakes, Coca-Cola, Ivory soap, Argo cornstarch, and Caramilk candy bars have had extremely long productive lives.

Stages in the Product Life Cycle

The product life cycle is a natural process in which products are born, grow in stature, mature, and finally decline and die. The life cycle is typically divided into four states through which products pass as they "age" on the market:

1. *Introduction.* The introduction stage begins when the product reaches the marketplace. During this stage, marketers focus on making potential consumers aware of the product and its benefits. Because of extensive promotional and development costs, profits are nonexistent.

2. *Growth.* If the new product attracts and satisfies enough consumers, sales begin to climb rapidly. During this stage, the product begins to show a profit. Other firms in the industry move rapidly to introduce their own versions.

3. *Maturity.* Sales growth begins to slow. Although the product earns its highest profit level early in this stage, increased competition eventually leads to price cutting and lower profits. Towards the end of the stage, sales start to fall.

4. *Decline.* During this final stage, sales and profits continue to fall. New products in the introduction stage take away sales. Companies remove or reduce promotional support (ads and salespeople) but may let the product linger to provide some profits.

Figure 16.3 shows the four stages of the cycle—not yet complete—for VCRs. The product was introduced in the late 1970s and is, of course, widely used today. (Notice that profits lag behind sales because of the extensive costs of developing new products.) If the market becomes saturated, sales will begin to decline. Sales will also fall if new products, such as DVDs, send the VCR the way of the eight-track audio player.

Service products also have life cycles. Consider the management advice offered by consulting firms. Most major companies purchase advice for designing and implementing new management practices. For example, advice on appropriate wage-incentive systems flourished through the 1950s and then went into decline by the 1970s. Advice on how to implement "Management by Objectives" (see Chapter 5) was introduced in the 1960s, passed through the maturity stage during the 1970s, and today is in the decline stage. A more recent product, advice on "Total Quality Management" (see Chapter 12), has been introduced for firms that want assistance in implementing TQM.

Adjusting Marketing Strategy During the Life Cycle

As a product passes from stage to stage, marketing strategy changes, too. Each aspect of the marketing mix—product, price, promotion, place (distribution)—is re-examined for each stage of the life cycle. Changes in strategy for all four life-cycle stages are summarized in Table 16.1.

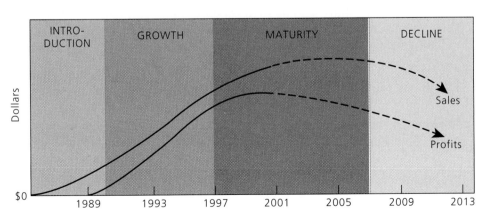

Figure 16.3
The product life cycle for VCRs. Note that profits lag behind sales due to the extensive development costs to create the new product.

Table 16.1				Marketing Strategy over the Life Cycle
Stage	**Introduction**	**Growth**	**Maturity**	**Decline**
Product Strategy	Develop market for product	Increase market share of product	Defend market share of product	Maintain efficiency in exploiting product
Pricing Strategy	High price, unique product/cover introduction costs	Lower price with passage of time	Price at or below competitors	Set price to stay profitable or decrease to liquidate
Promotion Strategy	Mount sales promotion for product awareness	Appeal to mass market; emphasize features, brand	Emphasize brand differences, benefits, loyalty	Reinforce loyal customers; reduce promotion expenditures
Place Strategy	Distribute through selective outlets	Build intensive network of outlets	Enlarge distribution network	Be selective in distribution; trim away unprofitable outlets

Extending Product Life

Not surprisingly, companies wish they could maintain a product's position in the maturity stage for longer periods of time. Many creative companies have successfully and profitably achieved this feat.[6] Cheez-Whiz experienced a rapid increase in sales when its maker used the popularity of microwave ovens to promote it as a "one-minute cheese sauce." Sales of television sets have been revitalized time and time again by introducing changes such as colour, portability, and stereo capability.

The beginning of a sales downturn in the maturity stage is not necessarily the time to start abandoning a product. Often, it is a time to realize that the old approach is starting to fade and to search for a new approach.

The Growth-Share Matrix

Companies with multiple product lines typically have various products at each point in the PLC. To decide how best to market each product, many marketers rely on the growth-share matrix, which classifies products according to market share and growth potential. Figure 16.4 shows the four categories into which products may be grouped: *question marks, stars, cash cows*, and *dogs*.

- Most products start as *question marks*—low market share, high growth potential—because they are entering new markets that may grow but have not yet captured consumers' attention.

- During the growth stage, products often become *stars* with high market share and high growth potential. Stars have large shares of still-growing markets.

- In the maturity stage, products serve as *cash cows*—high market share, low growth potential—because their large market share makes them profitable even while market growth slows.

- Products in the decline stage are *dogs*—low market share, low growth potential—whose profits and sales signal that the life cycle is nearly complete.

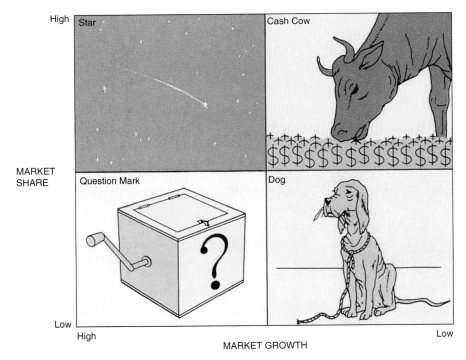

Figure 16.4
Growth-share matrix.

When developing marketing plans, managers must consider not only the product's location on the growth-share matrix but also the direction in which it is moving. For example, while a question mark with increasing market share may be headed for stardom, a question mark with decreasing market share may require major changes or elimination.

In addition, companies always seek balance and continuity in the product mix. A company loaded with cash cows, for example, has a great present but may have a questionable future. Because they require a lot of attention, a firm loaded with stars may be focusing its managers' energies too narrowly. On the other hand, a firm with mostly cash cows and stars, some question marks, and a couple of unavoidable dogs has developed a strong product pipeline and a balanced product mix.

IDENTIFYING PRODUCTS

As noted earlier in the chapter, developing the features of a product is only part of a marketer's battle. Identifying that product in consumers' minds through the use of brand names, packaging, and labelling is also important.

Branding Products

Coca-Cola is the best-known brand in the world. In fact, the *name* is so valuable that its executives like to say that if all of the company's other assets were obliterated, they could walk over to the bank and borrow $100 billion for rebuilding, just on the strength of the brand name. Brand names such as Coca-Cola and McDonald's are symbols for characterizing products and distinguishing them from one another. They were originally introduced to simplify the process when consumers are faced with a wealth of purchase

Coca-Cola
www.coca-cola.com

decisions. Branding, then, is a process of using symbols to communicate the qualities of a particular product made by a particular producer. Brands are designed to signal uniform quality. Customers who try and like a product can return to it by remembering its name.[7]

E-Business Branding

Managers have to be concerned about the branding of their company as well as the products the company sells. It takes a long time to establish national or global brand recognition. The expensive, sometimes fierce struggle for brand recognition is perhaps nowhere more evident than in the current branding battles among dot-com firms. Paying up to US$1.3 million for 30-second ads, dot-com companies dominated the advertising spots for the Super Bowl in January 2000. Currently, they are spending more than US$1.7 billion annually on national ad campaigns. Why so much expensive promotional activity? Says priceline.com vice-chairman Jay S. Walker, "A lot of companies are saying, 'We have to make it big, fast, or we're not going to make it at all.'" Collectively, the top Internet brands—America Online, Yahoo!, and Amazon.com—spent more than US$2 billion in 2000 even though they are just beginning to crack the ranks of the top 60 global brands. Even so, advertising alone is not enough. If a dot-com brand identity is going to emerge, it will be through an accumulation of customer contacts and experiences with products and brands. As the cost of building brand identity increases, it seems increasingly likely that many would-be e-businesses will not make it.[8]

It's not just e-businesses that are trying to catch the attention of consumers. Even traditional retailers are choosing attention-getting names such as Gadzooks, Wet Seal, Noodle Kidoodle, Koo Koo Roo, and Ugly Duckling.[9]

Firms that sell products internationally face an issue of growing importance in branding strategy. They must consider how product names will translate in various languages. In Spanish, for example, the name of Chevrolet's now-defunct Nova simply became *no va*— "it does not go." Sales were particularly poor in South America. Similarly, Rolls Royce was once going to name a new touring car "Silver Mist." Rolls changed the name to "Silver Shadow" when it discovered that *mist* is German for "manure."[10] Naturally, foreign companies hoping to sell in Canada must be equally careful.

Although domestic growth has been sluggish, McDonalds has taken advantage of its worldwide name recognition to pursue a long-term strategy of international expansion. In a variety of far-flung markets, McDonald's has also succeeded in finding local sources for the ingredients that go into products that, as necessary, it redesigns to appeal to local palates. Thus, the McOz Burger (Australia), the Chicken Tatsuta (Japan), and the Maharajah Mac (India).

McDonalds
www.mcdonalds.com

Types of Brands

Virtually every product has a brand name of some form. However, different types of brand names tell the alert consumer something about the product's origin.

National Brands

Brand name products that are produced and distributed by the manufacturer are called **national brands**. These brands, such as Scotch tape, are often widely recognized by consumers because of large national advertising campaigns. The costs of developing a positive image for a national brand are high, so some companies use their national brand on several related products. Procter & Gamble now markets Ivory shampoo, capitalizing on the widely recognized name of its soaps.

national brands
Products distributed by and carrying a name associated with the manufacturer.

Licensed Brands

More and more nationally recognized companies and personalities have sold other companies the right to place their names on products, which are **licensed brands**. Licensing has become big business. Franklin the Turtle, the subject of 26 books and an animated television series produced by Nelvana, is a Canadian product that is also popular in the U.S. In 2000, Nelvana and U.S.-based Sears Roebuck & Co. signed a licensing agreement allowing Sears to set up Franklin boutiques at its more than 850 stores. These boutiques will market Franklin clothing and accessories that will be available exclusively at Sears.[11]

licensed brands
Selling the right to use a brand name, a celebrity's name, or some other well-known identification mark to another company to use on a product.

Private Brands

When a wholesaler or retailer develops a brand and has the manufacturer place that brand name on the product, the resulting product name is a **private brand**. One of the best-known purveyors of private brands is Sears, with its Craftsman tools and Kenmore appliances.

J. Sainsbury PLC, the largest supermarket chain in Britain, recently introduced its own private brand of cola in a can that looks strikingly like the one used by Coke. The two products are stocked side by side on store shelves, and Sainsbury's offering is noticeably cheaper than Coke. The product is

private brands
Products promoted by and carrying a name associated with the retailer or wholesaler, not the manufacturer.

The Toronto Raptors benefit both from the licensing fees they receive as well as from the free advertising whenever these products are used.

Cott Corp.
www.cott.com

made by Cott Corp. of Toronto. The story is much the same in North America. Under the Sam's American Choice label, Cott sells a billion cans of soft drinks each year at Wal-Mart.

Loblaw Cos. Ltd., owned by George Weston, has created a line of upscale private brands called *President's Choice*. Clever advertising, fancy labels, and exotic product names differentiate the line and draw consumer attention to items such as peanut butter and cookies. Another Weston-owned company, Holt Renfrew, emphasizes its private brand. A stylish Prada suit sells for $2000 to $4000, but the Holt Renfrew equivalent is priced at only $300 to $700.[12]

Generic Products

generic products
Products carrying no brand or producer name and sold at lower prices.

"No-name" products in very plain packages with black lettering describing the contents were first introduced in the 1970s. For a while their lower prices attracted consumers. Supermarkets began devoting entire aisles to **generic products** such as paper towels, green beans, and shampoo. But concern over consistent product quality has resulted in a de-emphasis of generic products in recent years.

Trademarks, Patents, and Copyrights

trademark
The exclusive legal right to use a brand name.

Because brand development is very expensive, a company does not want another company using its name and confusing consumers into buying a substitute product. Many companies apply to the Canadian government and receive a **trademark**, the exclusive legal right to use a brand name. Trademarks are granted for 15 years and may be renewed for further periods of 15 years, but only if the company continues to protect its brand name.

Just what can be trademarked is not always clear, however. If the company allows the name to lapse into common usage, the courts may take away protection. Common usage occurs when the company fails to use the ® symbol for its brand. It also occurs if the company fails to correct those who do not acknowledge the brand as a trademark. Recently Windsurfer (a popular brand of sailboards by WSI Inc.) lost its trademark. Like the trampoline, yo-yo, and thermos, the brand name has become the common term for the product and can now be used by any sailboard company. But companies like Xerox, Coke, Jello, and Scotch tape have successfully defended their brand names.

patent
Protects an invention or idea for a period of 20 years.

Companies want to be sure that both product brands and new product ideas are protected. A **patent** protects an invention or idea for a period of 20 years. The cost is $1000 to $1500; it takes nine months to three years to secure a patent from the Canadian Patent Office.[13]

Copyrights give exclusive ownership rights to the creators of books, articles, designs, illustrations, photos, films, and music. Computer programs and even semiconductor chips are also protected. Copyrights extend to creators for their entire lives and to their estates for 50 years thereafter. Copyrights apply to the tangible expressions of an idea, not to the idea itself. For example, the idea of cloning dinosaurs from fossil DNA cannot be copyrighted, but Michael Crichton, the author of *Jurassic Park*, could copyright his novel because it is the tangible result of the basic idea.

Brand Loyalty

brand loyalty
Customers' recognition of, preference for, and insistence on buying a product with a certain brand name.

Companies that spend the large amount of money it takes to develop a brand are looking for one thing from consumers: **brand loyalty**. That is, they want to develop customers who, when they need a particular item, will go back to the same brand and buy the company's products.

Brand loyalty is measured in three stages. First, the company wants *brand recognition*. By putting the brand in front of consumers many times and associating it with a type of product, the producer hopes that consumers will become aware of its existence.

Recognition is not enough, however. The owner of the brand wants consumers to start showing *brand preference* when they make a purchase. Brand preference requires not only awareness that the brand exists but also a favourable attitude towards the ability of the brand to provide benefits.

Finally, because a brand may be unavailable in a store from time to time, companies seek *brand insistence*. Brand insistence is highly valued by brand owners, but it is very difficult to achieve. For all convenience and many shopping products, consumers will freely substitute another brand when they need a product. Usually, only specialty products have much potential for developing brand insistence in a large group of consumers. For example, a family wanting to buy or sell a home might insist on using a trusted local realtor.

Packaging Products

With a few exceptions, including fresh fruits and vegetables, structural steel, and some other industrial products, products need some form of **packaging** in which to be carried to the market. A package also serves as an in-store advertisement that makes the product attractive, clearly displays the brand, and identifies product features and benefits.

A growing number of companies are shifting their promotional spending from advertising to packaging. The trend is to lighter, brighter colours that stand out more on grocery store shelves. The package is the marketer's last chance to say "buy it" to the consumer.[14]

Packaging reduces the risk of damage, breakage, or spoilage, and it increases the difficulty of stealing smaller products. But once a product is opened and used, expensive packaging may become waste.

packaging
The physical container in which a product is sold, including the label.

Labelling Products

Every product has a **label** on its package. Packaging and labelling can help market the product. The information on package labels is regulated by the federal government. The ***Consumer Packaging and Labelling Act*** has two main purposes: the first is to provide a comprehensive set of rules for packaging and labelling of consumer products, and the second is to ensure that the manufacturer provides full and factual information on labels. All prepackaged products must state in French and English the quantity enclosed in metric and imperial units. The name and description of the product must also appear on the label in both French and English.

label
That part of a product's packaging that identifies the product's name and contents and sometimes its benefits.

Consumer Packaging and Labelling Act
A federal law that provides comprehensive rules for packaging and labelling of consumer products.

PROMOTING PRODUCTS AND SERVICES

As we noted in Chapter 15, **promotion** is any technique designed to sell a product. It is part of the communication mix: the total message a company sends to consumers about its product. Promotional techniques, especially advertising, must communicate the uses, features, and benefits of products. Sales promotions also include various programs that add value beyond the benefits inherent in the product. For example, it is nice to get a high-quality product at a reasonable price but even better when the seller offers a rebate or a bonus pack with "20 percent more *free*." In promoting products, then, marketers have an array of tools at their disposal.

promotion
Any technique designed to sell a product.

In this section, we will look at the different objectives of and approaches to promotion. We will show when and why companies use particular strategies and tools and then describe the special promotional problems faced by both international and small businesses. First, however, we will explain the two general values to be gained from any promotional activity, regardless of the particular strategy or tools involved: *communicating information* and *creating satisfying exchanges*.

Communicating Information and Creating Satisfying Exchanges

In free-market systems, a business uses promotional methods to communicate information about itself and its products to consumers and industrial buyers. The purpose, of course, is to influence purchase decisions. From an information standpoint, promotions seek to accomplish four things with potential customers:

- Make them aware of products
- Make them knowledgeable about products
- Persuade them to like products
- Persuade them to purchase products

In terms of the exchange relationship, the firm hopes that marketing promotions will make its product more attractive. The buyer therefore gains more from the exchange (a more attractive product), as does the seller (more unit sales or higher prices). Additionally, as part of relationship marketing, promotions help to build lasting relationships with consumers.

Successful promotions therefore provide communication about the product and create exchanges that satisfy both the customer's and the organization's objectives. However, because promotions are expensive, choosing

WEBCONNEXION

To find out how a team of young Swedish entrepreneurs went from running a publishing house to creating the world's third-largest online bookstore to starting up a company whose aim is to be "the world's largest online retailer of fashion and sportswear," log on at:

www.boo.com

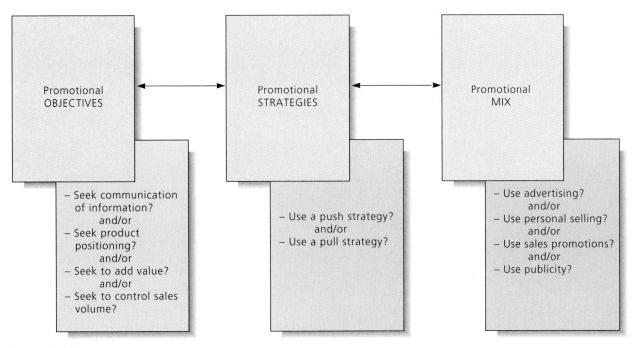

Figure 16.5
Developing the promotional plan.

the best promotional mix becomes critical. The promotional program, then, whether at the introduction stage (promoting for new product awareness) or the maturity stage (promoting brand benefits and customer loyalty), can determine the success or failure of any business or product.

Developing a promotional plan requires making decisions about promotional objectives, promotional strategies, and the promotional mix. These decisions are summarized in Figure 16.5 and discussed below.

Promotional Objectives

The ultimate objective of any promotion is to increase sales. However, marketers also use promotion to communicate information, position products, add value, and control sales volume.[15]

Communication of Information

Consumers cannot buy a product unless they have been informed about it. Information can advise customers about the availability of a product, educate them on the latest technological advances, or announce the candidacy of someone running for a government office. Information may be communicated in writing (newspapers and magazines), verbally (in person or over the telephone), or visually (television, a matchbook cover, or a billboard). Today, the communication of information regarding a company's products or services is so important that marketers try to place it wherever consumers may be. If you are an average consumer, you come in contact with approximately 1500 bits of promotional communication per day![16]

Product Positioning

Another objective of promotion, **product positioning**, is to establish an easily identifiable image of a product in the minds of consumers. For example, by selling only in department stores, Estée Lauder products have positioned

product positioning
The establishment of an easily identifiable image of a product in the minds of consumers.

themselves as more upscale than cosmetics sold in drugstores. With product positioning, the company is trying to appeal to a specific segment of the market rather than to the market as a whole.

Adding Value

Today's value-conscious customers gain benefits when the promotional mix is shifted so that it communicates value-added benefits in its products. Burger King, for instance, shifted its promotional mix by cutting back on advertising dollars and using those funds for customer discounts. Receiving the same food at a lower price is "value-added" for Burger King's customers.

Customers must be given information about the value-adding characteristics—for example, warranties, repair contracts, and after-purchase service—by which a product provides greater value than its competitors. Lexus, for example, prides itself on adding value by providing superb treatment of customers. Sales representatives don't pry, solicit, or hover over buyers in the showroom. The first two scheduled maintenances are free. Waiting customers can use offices, desks, or phones and can borrow cars or get rides.

Controlling Sales Volume

Many companies, such as Hallmark Cards, experience seasonal sales patterns. By increasing promotional activities in slow periods, these firms can achieve more stable sales volume throughout the year. They can thus keep production and distribution systems running evenly. Promotions can even turn slow seasons into peak sales periods. For example, greeting card companies and florists together have done much to create Grandparents' Day. The result has been increased consumer demand for cards and flowers in the middle of what was once a slow season for both industries.

Promotional Strategies

Once a firm's promotional objectives are clear, it must develop a promotional strategy to achieve these objectives. Promotional strategies may be of the push or pull variety. A company with a **push strategy** will aggressively "push" its product through wholesalers and retailers, who persuade customers to buy it. In contrast, a company with a **pull strategy** appeals directly to customers, who demand the product from retailers, who in turn demand the product from wholesalers. Advertising "pulls" while personal selling "pushes." In rare cases, a company may purposely do very little promotion of its products. For example, Langlitz Leathers makes leather jackets that cost as much as $800. They are worn by rebels like Hell's Angels, rockers like Bruce Springsteen, and actors like Sylvester Stallone. Even though the company does virtually no advertising, customers who want a Langlitz have to wait seven months to get one after they place their order.[17]

Makers of industrial products most often use a push strategy, and makers of consumer products most often use a pull strategy. Many large firms use a combination of the two strategies. For example, General Foods uses advertising to create consumer demand (pull) for its cereals. It also pushes wholesalers and retailers to stock these products.

Burger King
www.burgerking.com

Hallmark Cards
www.hallmark.com

push strategy
A promotional strategy in which a company aggressively pushes its product through wholesalers and retailers, which persuade customers to buy it.

pull strategy
A promotional strategy in which a company appeals directly to customers, who demand the product from retailers, which demand the product from wholesalers.

The Promotional Mix

As we noted in Chapter 15, there are four basic types of promotional tools: advertising, personal selling, sales promotions, and publicity and public relations. Figure 16.6 shows the relative usage of these tools by consumer- and industrial-goods businesses.

The best combination of these tools—the best **promotional mix**—depends on many factors. The company's product, the costs of different tools versus the promotions budget, and characteristics in the target audience all play a role. Figure 16.7 shows different combinations of products, promotional tools, and target consumers.

promotional mix
That portion of marketing concerned with choosing the best combination of advertising, personal selling, sales promotions, and publicity to sell a product.

The Product

The nature of the product being promoted affects the mix greatly. For example, advertising can reach a large number of widely dispersed consumers. It is used by makers of products that might be bought by anyone, such as sunglasses, radios, and snack foods. Companies introducing new products also favour advertising because it reaches a large number of people quickly and can repeat a message many times. Personal selling, on the other hand, is important when the product appeals to a specific audience, such as piping or pressure gauges for industrial customers.

Cost of the Tools

The cost of communication tools is important. Because personal selling is an expensive communication tool, it is most appropriate in marketing high-priced goods such as computers for industrial customers and homes for consumers. In contrast, advertising reaches more customers per dollar spent.

A promotional mix that is good for one company may not be good for another. A large firm can afford to spend millions of dollars on national advertising, but a local firm must rely on personal selling and publicity to promote its products.

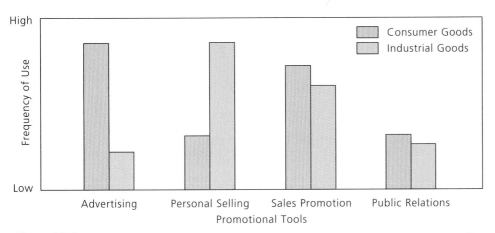

Figure 16.6
The relative importance of promotional tools.

Goods Promotion: House
    (real estate)
Tool: Personal selling
Consumer: House buyer

Organizational Promotion:
    Boy Scouts of Canada
Tool: Publicity
Consumer: Young men

Service Promotion: Weight-loss program
Tool: Sales promotion (coupon)
Consumer: Overweight person

Event Promotion: Rock
    concert
Tool: Advertising
Consumer: Cheering fan

Person or Idea Promotion: Candidate for Prime Minister
Tool: Publicity/advertising/personal sales
Consumer: Voter

Figure 16.7
Each promotional tool should be properly matched with the product being promoted and the
target customer.

Promotion and the Buyer Decision Process

Another consideration in establishing the promotional mix is the stage of
the buyer decision process that customers are in. As noted in Chapter 15,
customers must first recognize the need to make a purchase. At this stage,
marketers need to ensure that the buyer is aware that their products exist.
Thus, advertising and publicity, which can reach a large number of people
quickly, are important.

At the next stage, customers want to learn more about possible products.
Advertising and personal selling are important because they both can educate
the customer about the product.

During the third stage, customers will evaluate and compare competing products. Personal selling is vital at this point because sales representatives can demonstrate their product's quality and performance in direct relation to the competition's product.

Next, customers decide on a specific product and buy it. Sales promotion is effective at this stage because it can give consumers an incentive to buy. Personal selling can also help by bringing the product to convenient locations for the consumer.

Finally, consumers evaluate the product after buying it. Advertising, or even personal selling, is sometimes used after the sale to remind consumers that they made wise and prudent purchases. Figure 16.8 summarizes effective promotional tools for each stage of the consumer buying process.

The Promotional Mix Budget

Choosing the promotional mix begins by determining the promotional budget—one of the marketing manager's most difficult decisions. The budget specifies how much of the firm's total resources will be spent on promotions. The combined costs of personal selling, advertising, sales promotion, and public relations must fall within the budgeted amount. Moreover, the elements of the mix, collectively, must be *balanced* if they are to have the desired effect on attitudes and purchasing decisions.

The stage in the product's life cycle influences the promotional balance. New product introductions, for instance, may call for expensive personal sales promotions concentrated on a limited audience of early adopters and dealers. Personal sales may also be combined with direct mail to instil product awareness in the selected audience. The maturity stage, on the other hand, may call for mass-media advertising that emphasizes brand features and lower prices. Advertising may be used with sales promotions—for example, coupons to get buyers to try the seller's product instead of competitors'.

Now that you have a general understanding of promotional tools, let's look more closely at each.

ADVERTISING PROMOTIONS

What candy bar is "a nice light snack"? What soap is "99 and 44/100% pure"? What is the store where "the lowest price is the law"? What product is "only available in Canada? Pity"? If you are like most Canadians, you can answer these questions because of advertising. (The answers are Coffee Crisp, Ivory Soap, Zellers, and Red Rose Tea.) Figure 16.9 shows the top 10 advertisers in Canada.

Consumers remember brand names more easily if the company has a catchy advertising slogan. Buckley's Mixture, a well-known product in Canada,

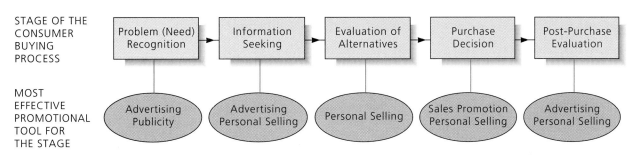

Figure 16.8
The promotional mix and the consumer buying process.

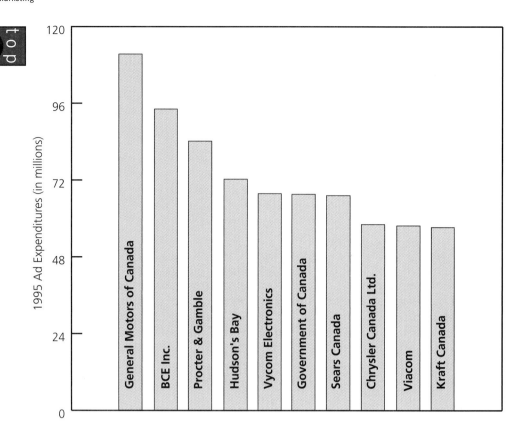

Figure 16.9
The top 10 advertisers in Canada.

is trying to crack the U.S. market. In an advertisement in 1999 on *The Price is Right*, the announcer intoned "Buckley's Mixture, the famous Canadian cough remedy, is now available here. It tastes awful, and it works."[18]

As important and high profile as advertising is, it has limits. Both Eaton's and Canadian Airlines were enthusiastic advertisers, but this didn't keep them in business. Advertising can convince customers to try your product or service, but it is the customer's experience with the product or service that determines whether they will give you repeat business. Just before Eaton's went bankrupt, for example, it launched a glitzy advertising campaign in an attempt to transform itself into an upscale store. But when customers walked through an Eaton's store, they saw a lot of clearance merchandise. That was clearly inconsistent with the message Eaton's advertising was sending.[19]

Advertising Strategies

informative advertising
An advertising strategy, appropriate to the introduction stage of the product life cycle, in which the goal is to make potential customers aware that a product exists.

persuasive advertising
An advertising strategy, appropriate to the growth stage of the product life cycle, in which the goal is to influence the customer to buy the firm's product rather than the similar product of a competitor.

Advertising strategies most often depend on which stage of the product life cycle their product is in. During the introduction stage, **informative advertising** can help develop an awareness of the company and its product among buyers and can establish a primary demand for the product. For example, before a new textbook is published, instructors receive direct-mail advertisements notifying them of the book's contents and availability.

As products become established, advertising strategies must change. During the growth stage, **persuasive advertising** can influence consumers to buy the company's products rather than those of its rivals. Persuasive advertising is also important during the maturity stage to maintain the product's level of sales. **Comparative advertising** involves comparing the sponsoring company's brand name with a competitor's brand name in such a way that the competitor's brand looks inferior. For example, Procter & Gamble aired advertisements claiming that its Bounty brand had more absorbency than Scott Paper's competing product. Scott retaliated by producing an advertisement that said that Scott Clean Ultra was 60 percent more absorbent than P&G's Bounty.[20]

In many countries (for example, Japan), advertisements that knock a competitor's product are frowned on. But this is not so in Canada or the U.S. In the European Union comparative advertising became legal in 1993, but advertisers must meet several limiting conditions.[21]

During the latter part of the maturity stage and all of the decline stage, **reminder advertising** keeps the product's name in front of the consumer.

Whatever the product's life cycle stage, advertising strategies must consider timing. Should the organization advertise continually throughout the year or seasonally? Companies such as banks space ads evenly throughout the year. In contrast, H&R Block Inc. runs advertisements in one major spurt during the tax season.

comparative advertising
An advertising strategy, appropriate to the growth stage of the product life cycle, in which the goal is to influence the customer to switch from a competitor's similar product to the firm's product by directly comparing the two products.

reminder advertising
An advertising strategy, appropriate to the latter part of the maturity stage of the product life cycle, in which the goal is to keep the product's name in the minds of customers.

Advertising Media

In developing advertising strategies, marketers must consider the best **advertising medium** for their message. IBM, for example, uses television ads to keep its name fresh in consumers' minds. But it also uses newspaper and magazine ads to educate consumers on products' abilities and trade publications to introduce new software.

An advertiser selects media with a number of factors in mind. The marketer must first ask: Which medium will reach the people I want to reach? If a firm is selling hog breeding equipment, it might choose *Playboar*, a business magazine read mostly by hog farmers. If it is selling silverware, it might choose a magazine for brides. If it is selling toothpaste, the choice might be a general audience television program or a general audience magazine such as *Reader's Digest* (or *Sélection*, for exposure to a similar audience of francophones).

advertising medium
The specific communication device—television, radio, newspapers, direct mail, magazines, billboards—used to carry a firm's advertising message to potential customers.

Newspapers

Newspapers remain the most widely used advertising medium. They offer excellent coverage, since each local market has at least one daily newspaper, and many people read the paper every day. This medium offers flexible, rapid coverage, since ads can change from day to day. It also offers believable coverage, since ads are presented side by side with news. However, newspapers are generally thrown out after one day, often do not print in colour, and have poor reproduction quality. Moreover, newspapers do not usually allow advertisers to target their audience well.

Television

Television allows advertisers to combine sight, sound, and motion, thus appealing to almost all of the viewer's senses. Information on viewer demographics for a particular program allows advertisers to promote to their target audiences. National advertising is done on television because it reaches more people than any other medium.

One disadvantage of television is that too many commercials cause viewers to confuse products. Most people, for example, can't recall whether

a tire commercial was sponsored by Firestone, Goodyear, or B.F. Goodrich. In addition, VCR viewers often fast-forward past the ads of TV shows they have recorded. Moreover, because "commercial spots" last only a short time (usually 30 seconds), the impact of the commercial is lost if the viewer is not paying attention. The brevity of TV ads also makes television a poor medium in which to educate viewers about complex products. Finally, television is the most expensive medium in which to advertise. A 30-second commercial during the NFL Super Bowl costs more than US$2 million.

Direct Mail

direct mail
Printed advertisements, such as flyers, mailed directly to consumers' homes or places of business.

Direct mail involves fliers or other types of printed advertisements mailed directly to consumers' homes or places of business. Direct mail allows the company to select its audience and personalize its message. Although many people discard "junk mail," targeted recipients with stronger-than-average interest are more likely to buy. Although direct mail involves the largest advance costs of any advertising technique, it does appear to have the highest cost effectiveness. Particularly effective have been "fax attacks," in which advertisers send their "mail" messages electronically via fax machines and get higher response rates than they would if they used Canada Post.

Radio

A tremendous number of people listen to the radio each day, and radio ads are inexpensive. In addition, since most radio is programmed locally, this medium gives advertisers a high degree of customer selectivity. For example, radio stations are already segmented into listening categories such as rock and roll, country and western, jazz, talk shows, news, and religious programming.

Like television, however, radio ads are over quickly. And radio permits only an audio presentation. As well, people tend to use the radio as "background" while they are doing other things, paying little attention to advertisements.

Magazines

The many different magazines on the market provide a high level of consumer selectivity. The person who reads *Popular Photography* is more likely to be interested in the latest specialized lenses from Canon than is a *Gourmet* magazine subscriber. Magazine advertising allows for excellent reproduction of photographs and artwork that not only grab buyers' attention but also may convince them of the product's value. And magazines allow advertisers plenty of space for detailed product information. Magazines have a long life and tend to be passed from person to person, thus doubling and tripling the number of exposures. The latest gimmick in print advertising is to catch the reader's eye by having the top half of an advertisement printed right side up and the bottom half printed upside down.[22]

One problem with magazine advertising is that ads must be submitted well in advance to be included in a certain issue. Often there is no guarantee of where within a magazine an ad will appear. Naturally, a company prefers to have its advertisement appear near the front of the magazine or within a feature article.

Outdoor

Outdoor advertising—billboards, signs, and advertisements on buses, taxis, and subways—is relatively inexpensive, faces little competition for customers' attention, and is subject to high repeat exposure. Unfortunately, companies have little control over who will see their advertisements. Because roadside billboards are prohibited on some major Ontario arteries, Moving Impressions Inc. has introduced "rolling billboards"—advertisements attached to the sides of large freight trucks. The truck companies get a piece of the action.[23]

Word of Mouth

Consumers form very strong opinions about products as a result of conversations with friends and acquaintances. If **word of mouth** says that a product is good, higher product sales are very likely. Of course, word of mouth will also spread bad news about a product.

Some companies rely heavily on word-of-mouth advertising. Big Rock Brewery does no advertising, but relies on word of mouth to expand its market share. It already has a 7 percent share of Alberta's draft beer market, and its exports to the U.S. are increasing rapidly.[24] Kiehl's makes and sells hair and skin care products. It gives away many samples to customers who come into its one and only retail outlet, but it doesn't do any advertising. It relies instead on simple word of mouth.[25]

word of mouth
Opinions about the value of products passed among consumers in informal discussions.

The Internet

The most recent advertising medium to arise is the Internet, where thousands of well-known and lesser-known firms have all placed ads. Although Internet advertising is still in its infancy and offers high potential, most marketers recognize that it also has limitations. In particular, consumers don't want to wade through electronic pages looking at details about hundreds of products. One expert offers the disappointing opinion that most of the commercial advertisements on the Internet may never be read by anyone.

Targeted advertising, however, is meeting with success because, unlike print or television ad buyers, Internet advertisers can measure the success of each ad they place. They receive a count of how many people see each ad and they can track the number of "click-throughs" by users looking for more information from the advertiser's own Web page. Electronic tracking devices are available for market analysis and relate such information as which ads generate more purchases, the sales margins resulting from each sale, and which ads attract the most attention from each target audience. DoubleClick, for example, was one of the first companies to help other advertisers take advantage of the Web's unique opportunities for linking up with users, tracking their behaviour online, and tailoring ad messages to them. Acting as an agent, DoubleClick sells ad space that allows advertisers to reach as many as 31 million unique users per month on 1500 Web sites, such as AltaVista and Travelocity. In addition to ad sales, DoubleClick also provides ad servicing—generating real-time reports on an ad's success—that the advertiser eventually uses to decide when to rerun an ad and whom to target.

Doubleclick
www.doubleclick.com

Data Mining. The Internet allows efficient targeting because volumes of data can be gathered electronically from Internet users. User behaviour patterns can be traced by analyzing files of information, gathered over time, from millions of users. Called *data mining*, this efficient searching, sifting, and reorganizing of vast pools of data on user purchase behaviour reveals who has bought which products; how many, when, and over what Web site; how they paid; and so on. By analyzing what customers actually do, the e-marketer can determine what subsequent purchases they are likely to make and then send them tailor-made ads.

To reach its full potential, e-commerce is going to have to improve its image. An Angus Reid/*Globe and Mail* poll of 1500 Canadians found that their main concern about e-commerce was security. People who had made at least one purchase on the Internet were more likely to list security as their top concern than were those who had never purchased anything on the Internet. People were concerned that their credit card number might end up the wrong hands, and that their privacy would be invaded if they purchased on the Internet.[26]

Virtual Advertising

An even newer method of advertising, called *virtual advertising*, uses digital implants of brands or products onto live or taped programming, giving the illusion that the product is part of the show. With this technique, an advertiser's product can appear as part of the television show, when viewers are paying more attention, instead of during commercial breaks. In a televised basketball game, for example, the digital image of a brand—for example, the round face of a Rolex watch or an Acura hubcap—can be electronically enlarged and superimposed on centre court without physically changing the playing floor. The image will be seen for the duration of the whole game. For videotaped movies, digital images can be inserted easily. A K-Mart shopping bag can be digitally added to the table in a kitchen scene, a Philips Flat TV can be superimposed on the wall for display during a dramatic scene in the den, and your favourite stars can be digitally dressed to display Polo and other brands on their shirts and sweaters. In addition to television applications, virtual advertising shows promise for use in radio and outdoor media.[27]

Other Advertising Channels

A combination of many additional media, including catalogues, sidewalk handouts, *Yellow Pages*, skywriting, telephone calls, special events, and door-to-door communications, make up the remaining advertisements to which Canadians are exposed. The "It's a Wired World" box describes how high-tech advertising works.

IT'S A WIRED WORLD

Advertising in a Wireless World

Before long, advertisements will be popping up on all kinds of wireless devices, including hand-held computers, cellphones, and pagers. This technological breakthrough is of great interest to advertisers, because it allows them access to consumers any time and anyplace.

Advertisers are interested in wireless advertising for several reasons. First, cellphone owners are typically young and affluent; in short, they are just the kind of consumers with whom advertisers want to communicate. Second, the market for wireless devices is growing rapidly. In 2000, there were nearly 100 million cellphones in Canada and the U.S. Third, advertisers can target their sales pitches to the consumers who are most likely to buy their products or services because they can obtain data about the age, gender, and buying preferences of people who own wireless devices. Companies will even be able to deliver ads based on

the cellphone user's location. For example, a clothing store could advertise a big sale to cellphone users who live or work near the store.

The technology is still in its early stages, and ads will initially consist mostly of a simple text message on the cellphone or pager screen. Some ads will have an audio component as well. Eventually, commercials will be received on cellphones.

It is quite possible that cellphone owners will not want to receive advertisements because they may view them as the wireless equivalent of "junk mail." Advertisers are therefore planning to deliver wireless ads only to those cellphone users who want them. In return for providing information on their carrier, type of phone, age, gender, and cellphone number, cellphone users will be offered free information such as sports scores, weather reports, and the daily horoscope delivered to their cellphone. Some advertisers are actually paying cellphone owners for agreeing to receive ads.

Table 16.2			Media Mix by Industry		
Industry	Magazines	Newspapers	Outdoor	Television	Radio
Retail stores	4.2%	61.1%	1.9%	27.8%	5.0%
Industrial materials	29.3	7.8	0.3	52.8	9.8
Insurance and real estate	11.1	53.5	2.2	29.3	3.9
Food	14.9	0.7	0.3	80.5	3.6
Apparel	50.5	1.8	0.5	45.8	1.4

The combination of media that a company chooses to advertise its products is called its **media mix**. Although different industries use different mixes, most depend on multiple media to advertise their products and services (see Table 16.2).

media mix
The combination of media through which a company chooses to advertise its products.

Types of Advertising

Regardless of the media used, advertisements fall into one of several categories. **Brand advertising** promotes a specific brand, such as Kodak 126 film, Air Canada, or Nike Air Jordan basketball shoes. A variation on brand advertising, **product advertising** promotes a general type of product or service such as dental services and milk. The "Got Milk?" advertisements are an example of product advertising. **Advocacy advertising** promotes a particular candidate or viewpoint, as in ads for political candidates at election time and antidrug commercials. **Institutional advertising** promotes a firm's long-term image rather than a specific product.

In consumer markets, local stores usually sponsor **retail advertising** to encourage consumers to visit the store and buy its products and services. Larger retailers, such as Kmart and The Bay, use retail advertising both locally and nationally. Often retail advertising is actually **cooperative advertising**, with the cost of the advertising shared by the retailer and the manufacturer.

In industrial markets, to communicate with companies that distribute its products, some firms use **trade advertising** publications. For example, a firm that makes plumbing fixtures might advertise in *Hardware Retailer* to persuade large hardware stores to carry its products. And to reach the professional purchasing agent and managers at firms buying raw materials or components, companies use **industrial advertising**.

Preparing the Campaign with an Advertising Agency

An **advertising campaign** is the arrangement of ads in selected media to reach target audiences. It includes several activities that, taken together, constitute a program for meeting a marketing objective, such as introducing a new product or changing a company's image in the public mind. A campaign typically includes six steps:

1. Identifying the target audience
2. Establishing the advertising budget
3. Defining the objectives of the advertising messages
4. Creating the advertising messages
5. Selecting the appropriate media
6. Evaluating advertising effectiveness

brand advertising
Advertising that promotes a specific brand-name product.

product advertising
A variation on brand advertising that promotes a general type of product or service.

advocacy advertising
Advertising that promotes a particular viewpoint or candidate.

institutional advertising
Advertising that promotes a firm's long-term image, not a specific product.

retail advertising
Advertising by retailers designed to reach end-users of a consumer product.

cooperative advertising
Advertising in which a manufacturer together with a retailer or a wholesaler advertise to reach customers.

trade advertising
Advertising by manufacturers designed to reach potential wholesalers and retailers.

industrial advertising
Advertising by manufacturers designed to reach other manufacturers' professional purchasing agents and managers of firms buying raw materials or components.

advertising campaign
The arrangement of ads in selected media to reach target audiences.

The Fido advertisement is an example of brand advertising because it promotes a specific brand. The Imagine advertisement is an example of advocacy advertising because it promotes a particular viewpoint about charitable giving.

advertising agency
A firm that specializes in creating and placing advertisements in the media for clients.

Advertising agencies assist in the development of advertising campaigns by providing specialized services. They are independent companies that provide some or all of their clients' advertising needs. The agency works together with the client company to determine the campaign's central message, create detailed message content, identify advertising media, and negotiate media purchases.[28]

The advantage offered by agencies is expertise in developing advertising themes, message content, and artwork, as well as in coordinating advertising production and advising on relevant legal matters. Today, even more specialized agencies have emerged to cater to clients with very specific goals in specific industries or market segments. Some agencies, for example, specialize in the marketing of pharmaceuticals.

As payment for its services, the agency usually receives a percentage, traditionally 15 percent of the media purchase cost. For example, if an agency purchases a $1 million television commitment for a client's campaign, it would receive $150 000 for its services. (See Table 16.3 for a list of the top 10 advertising agencies in Canada.)

Table 16.3	The Top 10 Advertising Agencies in Canada (ranked by revenues)
Company	**Annual Revenues (in millions)**
1. Envoy Communications Group Inc.	$138
2. Cossette Communications Group Inc.	94
3. MacLaren McCann	71
4. The Young & Rubicam Group of Cos. Ltd.	68
5. BBDO Canada Inc.	62
6. Wolf Group Integrated Communications Ltd.	46
7. Ogilvy & Mather Canada Ltd.	39
8. Palmer Jarvis DDB Inc.	33
9. Publicis Canada Inc.	32
10. FCB Worldwide Canada Ltd.	32

The globalization of business has affected advertising agencies, both in Canada and elsewhere. In 1994, IBM abandoned its practice of using over 40 different advertising agencies around the world and replaced them with one single agency—Ogilvy & Mather. Since IBM spends over $400 million on advertising each year, this was a major windfall for Ogilvy & Mather. Other large U.S.-based multinational advertisers such as Ford and Coca-Cola have also dropped Canadian agencies. By giving all their advertising business to one agency, these firms hope to cut costs and deliver a uniform global message about their products.[29]

The 18-member Association of Quebec Advertising Agencies says that big U.S. companies often bypass Montreal-based advertising agencies when they are developing advertising campaigns for Quebec. The group says that it is pointless to try to simply translate into French a campaign that is developed by a New York or Toronto agency for the rest of Canada. As an example of the right way to do it, consider advertisements for Pepsi. In the rest of English-speaking North America, big name singers and movie stars were used to promote the product, but in Quebec, successful commercials featured popular local comedian Claude Meunier to make Pepsi the number one soft drink in the province.[30]

All the news is not bad, however. The "Business Today" box describes several Canadian success stories in the field of advertising.

BUSINESS TODAY

Canadian Successes in Advertising

Amoeba Corp. is a newcomer to the advertising agency scene. Formed by Mike Richardson, Michael Kelar, and Ryan Smolkin, the company is suddenly having successes in spite of warnings from friends and relatives that Amoeba couldn't make it in Canada with its avant-garde advertising style. When it started in 1996, Amoeba had no cash and no clients; by 2000, it had $1.5 million in billings from clients such as Nike Canada, the Toronto Maple Leafs, YTV, and Molson.

Perhaps Amoeba's most visible work is that done for Molson, which asked it to help modernize Molson's "I Am Canadian" ad campaign. The most popular ad features a guy named Joe ranting and raving about the correct way to pronounce the last letter of the alphabet, and saying that he speaks English and French, but not American. Amoeba has also redesigned Molson's "I Am" logo, and has produced a commercial for the Export brand that is designed to give it more appeal to the youth market.

Originally, Amoeba functioned as an intermediary between traditional advertising agencies and clients. But then they decided to compete with advertising agencies and pitch their work directly to clients. Their first success was with YTV, which was looking for an advertising agency to handle its print account. This specific area was right up Amoeba's alley, and they successfully landed the account. However, the three partners who run Amoeba do not want their company to become a traditional advertising agency. They simply want to remain a creative company that produces good ads.

Richardson, Kelar, and Smolkin are not the only Canadians who are successful in the advertising business. In the past decade several Canadians have worked their way to the top of traditional U.S. advertising agencies. Frank Anfield, for example, became CEO of Young & Rubicam, Steve Brown became executive management director at J. Walter Thompson, and Julian Clopet became president of Ogilvy & Mather's North American operations.

Why are Canadians so popular in U.S. advertising agencies? There are several reasons. First, globalization has meant a more homogeneous business world where managers can move from country to country. Second, Canada is close to the U.S. and there is increasing control of Canadian advertising firms by U.S. companies. Third, Canadians are perceived as having a more worldly view than Americans. Their experience with a bilingual culture, for example, is a plus for agencies that are pursuing cross-cultural and global marketing strategies. Ironically, Canada's much-lamented "branch plant economy" has helped Canadian managers because Canada is seen as a great training ground for the best and the brightest. Finally, the challenging business climate in Canada means that managers benefit from working in Canada because it is harder to succeed here. Those managers who do well have finely honed their business skills.

PERSONAL SELLING PROMOTIONS

Virtually everyone has done some personal selling. Perhaps you had a lemonade stand or sold candy for the drama club. Or you may have gone on a job interview, selling your abilities and service as an employee to the interviewer's company. In personal selling, a salesperson communicates one-to-one with a potential customer to identify the customer's need and match that need with the seller's product.

Personal selling—the oldest form of selling—provides the personal link between seller and buyer. It adds to a firm's credibility because it provides buyers with someone to interact with and to answer their questions. Because it involves personal interaction, personal selling requires a level of trust between the buyer and the seller. When a buyer feels cheated by the seller, that trust has been broken and a negative attitude towards salespeople in general can develop.

Personal selling is the most expensive form of promotion per contact because presentations are generally made to one or two individuals at a time. Personal selling expenses include salespeople's compensation and their overhead, usually travel, food, and lodging. The average cost of an industrial sales call has been estimated at nearly $300.[31]

Such high costs have prompted many companies to turn to **telemarketing**: using telephone solicitations to carry out the personal selling process. Telemarketing can be used to handle any stage of the personal selling process or to set up appointments for outside salespeople. Because it saves the cost of personal sales visits to industrial customers, telemarketing is growing in importance.

telemarketing
The use of the telephone to carry out many marketing activities, including sales and research.

Types of Personal Selling Situations

Managers of both telemarketing and traditional personal salespeople must always consider how personal sales are affected by the differences between consumer products and industrial products that we discussed earlier in this chapter. **Retail selling** involves selling a consumer product for the buyer's own personal or household use. **Industrial selling** deals with selling products to other businesses, either for manufacturing other products or for resale. For example, Levi Strauss wholesales its jeans to the retail clothing operation The Gap (industrial selling). Consumers purchase these jeans at one of The Gap's stores (retail selling).

Each situation has its own distinct characteristics. In retail selling the buyer usually comes to the seller. The industrial salesperson almost always goes to the prospect's place of business. The industrial decision process also may take longer than a retail decision because more money, decision makers, and weighing of alternatives are involved. And industrial buyers are professional purchasing agents accustomed to dealing with salespeople. Salespeople, on the other hand, may intimidate consumers in retail stores.

Sales force management means setting goals at top levels of the organization, setting practical objectives for salespeople, organizing a sales force that can meet those objectives, and implementing and evaluating the success of the overall sales plan. Obviously, then, sales management is an important factor in meeting the marketing objectives of any large company.

retail selling
Selling a consumer product for the buyer's own personal or household use.

industrial selling
Selling products to other businesses, either for manufacturing other products or for resale.

sales force management
Setting goals at top levels of an organization; setting practical objectives for salespeople; organizing a sales force to meet those objectives; implementing and evaluating the success of a sales plan.

Personal Selling Tasks

Improving sales efficiency requires marketers to consider salespeople's tasks. Three basic tasks are generally associated with selling: order processing, creative selling, and missionary selling. Sales jobs usually require salespeople to perform all three tasks to some degree, depending on the product and the company.

Order Processing

At selling's most basic level, **order processing**, a salesperson receives an order and oversees the handling and delivery of that order. Route salespeople are often order processors. They call on regular customers to check the customer's supply of bread, milk, snack foods, or soft drinks. Then, with the customer's consent, they determine the size of the reorder, fill the order from their trucks, and stack the customer's shelves.

order processing
In personal sales, the receiving and follow-through on handling and delivery of an order by a salesperson.

Creative Selling

When the benefits of a product are not clear, **creative selling** may persuade buyers. Most industrial products involve creative selling because the buyer has not used the product before or may not be familiar with the features and uses of a specific brand. Personal selling is also crucial for high-priced consumer products, such as homes, where buyers comparison shop. Any new product can benefit from creative selling that differentiates it from other products. Finally, creative selling can help to create a need.

creative selling
In personal sales, the use of techniques designed to persuade a customer to buy a product when the benefits of the product are not readily apparent or the item is very expensive.

Missionary Selling

A company may also use **missionary selling** to promote itself and its products. Drug company representatives promote their companies' drugs to doctors who, in turn, prescribe them to their patients. The sale is actually made at the drugstore. In this case, the goal of missionary selling is to promote the company's long-term image rather than to make a quick sale.

missionary selling
In personal sales, the indirect promotion of a product by offering technical assistance and/or promoting the company's image.

The Personal Selling Process

Although all three sales tasks are important to an organization using personal selling, perhaps the most complicated is creative selling. It is the creative salesperson who is responsible for most of the steps in the personal selling process described here.

Prospecting and Qualifying

To sell, a salesperson must first have a potential customer or *prospect*. **Prospecting** is the process of identifying potential customers. Salespeople find prospects through past company records, customers, friends, relatives, company personnel, and business associates. Prospects must then be **qualified** to determine whether they have the authority to buy and the ability to pay.

prospecting
In personal sales, the process of identifying potential customers.

qualifying
In personal sales, the process of determining whether potential customers have the authority to buy and the ability to pay for a product.

Approaching

The first few minutes that a salesperson has contact with a qualified prospect are called the *approach*. The success of later stages depends on the prospect's

These customers have raised some questions that the salesperson is answering before they reach an agreed price for closing the sale of this car.

first impression of the salesperson, since this impression affects the salesperson's credibility. Salespeople need to present a neat, professional appearance and to greet prospects in a strong, confident manner.

Presenting and Demonstrating

Next, the salesperson must *present* the promotional message to the prospect. A presentation is a full explanation of the product, its features, and its uses. It links the product's benefits to the prospect's needs. A presentation may or may not include a *demonstration* of the product. But it is wise to demonstrate a product whenever possible, since most people have trouble visualizing what they have been told.

Handling Objections

No matter what the product, prospects will have some *objections*. At the very least, prospects will object to a product's price, hoping to get a discount. Objections show the salesperson that the buyer is interested in the presentation and which parts of the presentation the buyer is unsure of or has a problem with. They tell the salesperson what customers feel is important and, essentially, how to sell them.

Closing

closing
In personal sales, the process of asking the customer to buy the product.

The most critical part of the selling process is the **close**, in which the salesperson asks the prospective customer to buy the product. Successful salespeople recognize the signs that a customer is ready to buy. For example, prospects who start to figure out monthly payments for the product are clearly indicating that they are ready to buy. The salesperson should then attempt to close the sale.

Salespeople can ask directly for the sale or they can indirectly imply a close. Questions such as "Could you take delivery Tuesday?" and "Why don't we start you off with an initial order of 10 cases?" are implied closes. Such indirect closes place the burden of rejecting the sale on the prospect, who will often find it hard to say no.

Following Up

The sales process does not end with the close of the sale. Most companies want customers to come back again. Sales *follow-up* activities include fast processing of the customer's order and on-time delivery. Training in the proper care and use of the product and speedy service if repairs are needed may also be part of the follow-up.

SALES PROMOTIONS

Sales promotions are short-term promotional activities designed to stimulate consumer buying or cooperation from distributors, sales agents, or other members of the trade. They are important because they increase the likelihood that buyers will try products. They also enhance product recognition and can increase purchase size and amount. For example, soap is often bound into packages of four with the promotion, "Buy three and get one free."

> **sales promotion**
> *Short-term promotional activities designed to stimulate consumer buying or cooperation from distributors and other members of the trade.*

To be successful, sales promotions must be convenient and accessible when the decision to purchase occurs. If Harley-Davidson has a one-week motorcycle promotion and you have no local dealer, the promotion is neither convenient nor accessible to you, and you will not buy. But if The Bay offers a 20-percent-off coupon that you can save for use later, the promotion is convenient and accessible.

Types of Sales Promotions

The best known sales promotions are coupons, point-of-purchase displays, purchasing incentives (such as free samples, trading stamps, and premiums), trade shows, and contests and sweepstakes.

Coupons

Any certificate that entitles the bearer to stated savings off a product's regular price is a **coupon**. Coupons may be used to encourage customers to try new products, to attract customers away from competitors, or to induce current customers to buy more of a product. They appear in newspapers and magazines and are often sent through direct mail. Coupons are very popular with consumers. When Procter & Gamble decided to end all coupons in three New York cities on a test basis, it was surprised by the aggressive negative reaction from consumers. P&G ended the test in 1997 and began distributing coupons again.[32]

> **coupon**
> *A method of sales promotion featuring a certificate that entitles the bearer to stated savings off a product's regular price.*

Point-of-Purchase Displays

To grab customers' attention as they walk through a store, some companies use **point-of-purchase (POP) displays**.[33] Displays located at the end of the aisles or near the checkout in supermarkets are POP displays. POP displays often coincide with a sale on the item(s) being displayed. They make it easier for customers to find a product and easier for manufacturers to eliminate competitors from consideration. The cost of shelf and display space, however, is becoming more and more expensive.[34]

> **point-of-purchase (POP) display**
> *A method of sales promotion in which a product display is so located in a retail store as to encourage consumers to buy the product.*

Purchasing Incentives

Purchasing incentives such as free samples, trading stamps, and premiums are used by many manufacturers and retailers. Free samples allow customers to try a product for a few days without any risk. They may be given out at local retail outlets or sent by manufacturers to consumers via direct mail.

WEBCONNEXION

Many Internet sites offer coupons that help shoppers save money. FabulousSavings.com asks shoppers for their city and country and then provides them with information on coupon offers in many different product categories, including food, sporting goods, and automotive products. Site visitors can choose from thousands of possible coupons that provide 10 to 15 percent off purchases or "buy-one-get-one-free" offers. From time to time, users are given the opportunity to participate in surveys or to enter contests. Visit the site at:

www.fabuloussavings.com

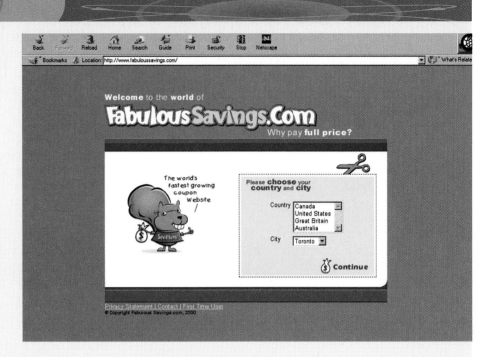

Although the use of free samples is commonplace in Canada, it is very unusual in some other countries, especially those that are changing over to free-market economies. Procter & Gamble's marketing team was greeted with thanks and even tears when it gave free shampoo samples to grateful shoppers in Warsaw, who were stunned to receive a valued product without having to pay for it or even wait in a long line.[35]

Some retail outlets offer trading stamps as a bonus for patronizing a particular store. Finally, **premiums** are gifts, such as pens, pencils, calendars, and coffee mugs, that are given away to consumers in return for buying a specified product. Retailers and wholesalers also receive premiums for carrying some products.

premium
A method of sales promotion in which some item is offered free or at a bargain price to customers in return for buying a specified product.

Trade Shows

Periodically, industries sponsor **trade shows** for their members and customers. Trade shows allow companies to rent booths to display and demonstrate their products to customers who have a special interest in the products or who are ready to buy. Trade shows are relatively inexpensive and are very effective, since the buyer comes to the seller already interested in a given type of product. International trade shows are becoming more important.

trade shows
A method of sales promotion in which members of a particular industry gather for displays and product demonstrations designed to sell products to customers.

Contests and Sweepstakes

Customers, distributors, and sales representatives may all be persuaded to increase sales of a product through the use of contests. Distributors and sales agents may win a trip to Hawaii for selling the most pillows in the month of March. Although sweepstakes cannot legally require consumers to buy a product to enter, they may increase sales by stimulating buyers' interest in a product.

PUBLICITY AND PUBLIC RELATIONS

Much to the delight of marketing managers with tight budgets, **publicity** is free. Moreover, because it is presented in a news format, consumers see publicity as objective and highly believable. Thus, it is an important part of the promotional mix. However, marketers often have little control over publicity.

For example, in 1995 Silken Laumann and her rowing teammates were stripped of their gold medals at an international competition because Laumann had inadvertently used a little-known product called Benadryl that contained a banned substance. The maker of Benadryl, Warner Wellcome, suddenly saw its product mentioned prominently on national newscasts, and it didn't have to pay a cent for the advertising. However, the company is not sure that it wants its product to be associated with an unfortunate incident.

The Miss Canada International organization also received negative publicity when the 1996 beauty contest winner was stripped of her title after being involved in a fight with a woman in a Newfoundland bar. Then, the first runner-up was denied the title because the pageant's organizer claimed she was not performing her duties. The first runner-up disputed these claims and accused the pageant's organizer of lying about her. All of this negative publicity was widely reported in newspapers across Canada.[36]

On a more positive note, the hottest-selling toy in 1996 was Tickle Me Elmo, a doll that says, "That Tickles" when you press on its chest. The craze started partly because a publicist at Freeman Public Relations sent one of the dolls to the son of TV personality Rosie O'Donnell. Two hundred Elmos were also sent to the show's producers. One day on her show, O'Donnell said she would toss an Elmo into the audience each time one of her guests used the word "wall." After that publicity, retail sales of the doll skyrocketed, and Tyco sold more than twice as many Elmos as they had predicted.[37]

In contrast to publicity, **public relations** is company-influenced publicity. It attempts to establish a sense of goodwill between the company and its customers through public-service announcements that enhance the company's image. For example, a bank may announce that senior citizens' groups can have free use of a meeting room for their social activities. Corporate sponsorships of athletic events also help promote a company's image. Corporate sponsorship was very much in evidence at the 1998 Winter Olympics in Nagano, Japan, with Nike Canada supporting Canada's snowboarding and hockey teams, Labatt Brewing and Ford Motor Co. supporting curling, and the Bank of Montreal supporting figure skating. Roots Canada has been particularly noticeable at the Olympics (remember the red hat that Ross Rebagliati wore at Nagano? Roots sold more than 500 000 of those hats after the games). At the 2000 Summer Olympics, Roots provided red-and-white hats to athletes, who wore them throughout the games. Roots has also been successful in getting other high-profile individuals to wear its products. At the Asia-Pacific Economic Cooperation group summit in 1997, for example, Canada's finance minister was seen wearing a Roots jacket in a publicity photo.[38]

In spite of doping and bribery scandals at the Olympic Games, big-name sponsors such as McDonald's, Coca-Cola, and UPS have continued to sponsor Olympic athletes. Most of them have even extended their agreements for the Olympic Games in 2002 and 2004. The marketing rights for the 2000 Olympic Games in Sydney, Australia, generated well over $2 billion for the Olympics.[39]

Most large firms have a department to manage their relations with the public and to present desired company images. As well, company executives may make appearances as guest speakers representing their companies at professional meetings and civic events. They may also serve as leaders in

publicity
Information about a company that is made available to consumers by the news media; not controlled by the company, but it does not cost the company any money.

public relations
Public-service announcements by the company designed to enhance the company's image.

civic activities like the United Way campaign and university fundraising. Through PR offices, many companies produce audio-visual materials about company activities and make them available to interested groups, other companies, or the general public.

Companies can also take steps to exercise some control over publicity by press releases and press conferences. A *press release* is a written announcement sent to news agencies describing a new product, an event, or information about the company that may be of interest to the general public. In a press conference, a firm's representative meets face to face with the press to communicate information that the media may then publish or broadcast publicly.

INTERNATIONAL PROMOTIONAL STRATEGIES

As we saw in Chapter 3, recent decades have witnessed a profound shift from "home-country" marketing to "multi-country" marketing and now to "global" marketing. Nowhere is this rapidly growing global orientation more evident than in marketing promotions, especially advertising.

Growth of Worldwide Advertising

In the mid–twentieth century, companies began exporting to other countries when domestic sales stagnated. Advertising played a key role in these efforts because it was the best tool for creating product awareness in each country—that is, for stimulating sales by explaining a product's benefits to new consumers. Today, worldwide advertising is a large part of many companies' promotional expenditures. The top 10 global advertising spenders are listed in Table 16.4.

Emergence of the Global Perspective

Every company that markets its products in several countries faces a basic choice: use a *decentralized approach* with separate marketing management for each country or adopt a *global perspective* with a coordinated marketing program directed at one worldwide audience. The **global perspective**, therefore, is actually a company philosophy that directs marketing towards a worldwide rather than a local or regional market.

global perspective
Company's approach to directing its marketing towards worldwide rather than local or regional markets.

Table 16.4				Top 10 Global Advertising Spenders
Advertiser	Headquarters	Primary Business	Worldwide Spending ($ millions)	Non-U.S. Spending as % of Worldwide
Proctor & Gamble	U.S.A.	Consumer products	4,747.5	63.6
Unilever	Netherlands	Consumer products	3,428.5	79.8
General Motors	U.S.A.	Automotive	3,193.5	32.5
Ford Motor Co.	U.S.A.	Automotive	2,229.5	47.1
Nestlé	Switzerland	Food	1,833.1	85.0
Toyota Motor Corp.	Japan	Automotive	1,692.4	61.1
Coca-Cola Co.	U.S.A.	Food	1,327.3	76.2
Volkswagen	Germany	Automotive	1,325.8	80.7
L'Oréal	France	Cosmetics	1,244.0	67.6
Peugeot Citroen	France	Automotive	854.9	100.0

The truly global perspective means designing products for multinational appeal—that is, genuinely *global products*. Brands like Coca-Cola, McDonald's, Revlon, Rolex, and Xerox, which are approaching global recognition in a huge variety of countries and cultures, are thus becoming truly *global brands*. Not surprisingly, then, globalization is affecting many firms' promotional activities. In effect, they have already posed the question "Is it possible to develop global advertising?" Certainly one universal advertising program would be more efficient and cost-effective than developing different programs for each of many countries. For several reasons, however, global advertising is not feasible for most companies. There are four factors that make global advertising a difficult proposition: *language differences, product variations, cultural receptiveness,* and *image differences.*

Language Differences

Perhaps the most obvious barrier to the global ad is language. Compared with those in other languages, for example, ads in English require less print space and air time because English is an efficient language with greater precision of meaning than most. More importantly, translations from one language to another are often inexact and lead to confusion and misunderstanding. When Coca-Cola first went to China, the translation of its name read "Bite the wax tadpole." For these reasons, acquisitions and mergers of advertising agencies have resulted in the growth of worldwide agency networks that can coordinate an ad campaign's central theme and yet allow regional variations.

Product Variations

Even if a basic product has universal appeal, at least modest *product variations*—slightly different products—are usually preferred in different cultures. To communicate product variations and their features (and, of course, their advantages), advertising must reflect these differences. In the magazine business, for example, Hearst Corp. has expanded to 33 editions of *Cosmopolitan* magazine, including one for Central America, English and Spanish editions for the United States, and local editions for Italy, Turkey, Russia, Hong Kong, and Japan. *Reader's Digest* has 48 editions in 19 languages.

Cultural Receptiveness

Another variable is cultural receptiveness to alien ideas and products. For example, there is considerable difference across nations regarding the acceptability of mass advertising for "sensitive" products or those that cause social discomfort (for example, underwear, condoms, and feminine-hygiene products), not to mention those for which advertising may be legally restricted (pharmaceuticals, alcohol, and cigarettes). Generally speaking, European countries have more liberal advertising environments than countries in North America, Asia, the Middle East, and Latin America. For worldwide advertising, magazines are the most popular medium for sensitive products because clear messages can be demographically targeted.

Image Differences

Each company's overall *image* can vary from nation to nation, regardless of any advertising appeals for universal recognition and acceptance. For example, a recent study comparing well-known global brands in the United States and the United Kingdom found that American Express, IBM, and Nestlé had higher-ranking images in the U.S. than in the U.K. In contrast, Heinz, Coca-Cola, and Ford had higher-ranking images in the U.K.[40]

The Coca-Cola Co. earns no less than 80 percent of its profits from markets outside North America. The company's marketing strategy is essentially the same everywhere: Coke (which is really little more than flavoured, carbonated, sweetened water) is positioned as unique. Something better than the next soft drink. "The real thing." The product itself, however, is not necessarily uniform. Its taste, for example, is often altered to suit local preferences.

Firms that are concerned about image and visibility use advertising to present desirable corporate images and to boost public awareness of themselves and their products. For example, Bayer, the German chemical conglomerate whose products include Aspirin and over-the-counter and prescription medicines, uses a worldwide image campaign. Advertising agency DDB Worldwide conducts the ad program in Europe and Asia, with the goal of informing consumers of Bayer's wide product range in an easy-to-understand way. While the theme is consistent across different regions, DDB uses local offices to ensure that the ad specifics in each country are focused on the common image theme.

In a different industry, Nickelodeon Latin America has launched its first image campaign in São Paolo, Brazil. The goal is to introduce Nickelodeon as the favourite television channel for kids. Created by J. Walter Thompson Co., the campaign uses TV spots, bus backs and windows, and outdoor boards aimed especially at 5- to 14-year-olds. The campaign features a slogan, "*Se nicka nessa*," which is a play on a popular saying among local kids, "*Se liga nessa*" ("Get with it"). In the TV spots, kids sing, dance, and play with Nickelodeon's animated characters and featured stars. In carrying the same image campaign to other countries, the choice of message content can be adapted for greater appeal to each regional audience.[41]

PROMOTIONAL PRACTICES IN SMALL BUSINESS

From our discussion so far, you might think that only large companies can afford to promote their goods and services. Although small businesses generally have fewer resources, cost-effective promotions can improve sales and enable small firms to compete with much larger firms.

Small Business Advertising

Advertising in non-prime-time slots on local television or cable TV offers great impact at a cost that many small firms can afford. More commonly, though, small businesses with a local market use newspaper and radio advertising and, increasingly, direct mail. Billboards are beyond the means of many small businesses, but outdoor store signs can draw a strong response from passers-by.

The timing of advertising can be critical for generating revenues for a small business. For year-round advertising, the *Yellow Pages* are a widely used medium for advertising both industrial and consumer products in local markets. However, many small businesses, especially those selling to consumer markets, rely more on seasonal advertising. Retail stores advertise for the holidays, ads for lawn care and home maintenance services begin to appear in the early spring, and ads for tax preparation services become more visible at the beginning of the year.

Television, radio, and newspapers are seldom viable promotional options for reaching international markets because of their high costs and their limited availability. The market research needed to determine the best message and style for reaching the target audience is costly. Additional costs are incurred in developing broadcast and newsprint advertisements with the necessary variations in language and cultural appeal. Limited availability—the inaccessibility of the intended audience—is a problem in nations that have underdeveloped mass media or high illiteracy rates, or that place severe restrictions on advertising by private companies. In these situations, broadcast and newsprint media will not be feasible options for the international advertising mix. Instead, most small firms find direct mail and carefully targeted magazine advertising the most effective promotional tools.

The Role of Personal Selling in Small Business

Some small firms maintain a sales force to promote and sell their products locally. Your local newspapers and television and radio stations, for example, use personal selling to attract advertisements by individuals and businesses. As part of the personal selling process, they provide complete information about the audiences ads will reach. Other small firms prefer not to do their own selling, but instead contract with a sales agency—a company that handles the products of several companies—to act on their behalf. Insurance agents who sell insurance for several different companies are sales agencies.

Because of the high costs of operating a national sales force, many small companies have established telemarketing staffs. By combining telemarketing with a catalogue or other educational product literature, small companies can sell their products nationally and compete against much larger companies.

Most small companies cannot afford to establish international offices, though some entrepreneurs, such as Art de Fehr of Palliser Furniture, do visit prospective customers in other countries. However, for most small businesses, even sending sales representatives overseas is expensive. Thus many small companies have combined telemarketing with direct mail in order to expand internationally.

Small Business Promotions

Small companies use the same sales promotion incentives that larger companies use. The difference is that larger firms tend to use more coupons, POP displays, and sales contests. Smaller firms rely on premiums and special sales, since coupons and sales contests are more expensive and more difficult to manage. For example, some automobile dealerships offer fishing reels at a bargain price if you just "come on down and road-test" a new four-wheel-drive vehicle. Gas stations use premiums by offering a free car wash with each fillup. Many service companies, including martial arts centres, remodelling companies, and dry cleaners, commonly offer special sales prices.

Small Business Publicity

Publicity is very important to small businesses with local markets. Small firms often have an easier time getting local publicity than do national firms. Readers of local papers like to read about local companies, so local papers like to write about such businesses. However, fierce competition for coverage in national and international publications limits the access small businesses have to those markets.

SUMMARY OF LEARNING OBJECTIVES

1. **Identify a *product* and distinguish between *consumer* and *industrial products*.** *Products* are a firm's reason for being: *Product features*—the tangible qualities that a company builds into its products—offer *benefits* to buyers whose purchases are the main source of the company's profits. In developing products, firms must decide whether to produce *consumer goods* for direct sale to consumers or industrial goods for sale to other firms. Marketers must recognize that buyers will pay less for common, rapidly consumed *convenience goods* than for less frequently purchased *shopping* and *specialty goods*. In industrial markets, *expense items* are generally less expensive and more rapidly consumed than such *capital items* as buildings and equipment.

2. **Trace the stages of the *product life cycle* and explain the *growth-share matrix*.** New products have a life cycle that begins with *introduction* and progresses through states of *growth, maturity*, and *decline*. Profits rise through the early maturity period; sales rise through the late maturity period. In the *growth-share matrix*, products are classified according to market share and growth potential. *Question marks* are new products with low market share but high potential. *Stars* have both high market share and high potential, while *dogs* rate low in both categories. *Cash cows* are mature products with high market share but low potential.

3. **Discuss the importance of *branding* and *packaging*.** Each product is given an identity by its brand and by the way it is packaged and labelled. The goal in developing *brands*—symbols to distinguish products and to signal their uniform quality—is to increase the preference consumers have for a product with a particular brand name. *Trademarks* grant exclusive legal rights to a brand name. *Packaging* provides an attractive container and advertises features and benefits.

4. **Identify the important objectives of *promotion* and discuss the considerations in selecting a *promotional mix*.** Although the ultimate goal of a *promotion* is to increase sales, other goals include *communicating information, positioning a product, adding value*, and *controlling sales volume*.

In deciding on the appropriate *promotional mix*, marketers must consider the good or service being offered, characteristics of the target audience and the buyer's decision process, and the promotional mix budget.

5. **Discuss the most important *advertising strategies* and describe the key *advertising media*.** *Advertising strategies* often depend on the *product life cycle stage*. In the introductory stage, *informative advertising* helps to build awareness. As a product passes through the growth and maturity stages, *persuasive advertising, comparative advertising*, and *reminder advertising* are often used. *Advertising media* include the Internet, newspapers, television, direct mail, radio, magazines, and outdoor advertising, as well as other channels such as *Yellow Pages*, special events, and door-to-door selling. The combination of media that a company chooses is called its *media mix*.

6. **Outline the tasks involved in *personal selling* and list the steps in the *personal selling process*.** *Personal selling* tasks include *order processing, creative selling* (activities that help persuade buyers), and *missionary selling* (activities that promote firms and products rather than simply close sales). The personal selling process consists of six steps: *prospecting and qualifying* (identifying potential customers with the authority to buy), *approaching* (the first moments of contact), *presenting and demonstrating* (presenting the promotional message that explains the product), *handling objections, closing* (asking for the sale), and *following up* (processing the order and ensuring after-sale service).

7. **Describe the various types of *sales promotions*.** *Coupons* provide savings off the regular price of a product. *Point-of-purchase (POP) displays* are intended to grab attention and help customers find products in stores. Purchasing incentives include *samples* (which let customers try products without buying them) and *premiums* (rewards for buying products). At *trade shows*, sellers rent booths to display products to customers who already have an interest in buying. *Contests* are intended to increase sales by stimulating buyers' interest in products.

KEY TERMS

STUDY QUESTIONS AND EXERCISES

Review Questions

1. What are the various classifications of consumer and industrial products? Give an example of a good and a service for each category different from the examples given in the text.
2. List the four stages in the product life cycle and discuss some of the ways in which a company can extend product life cycles.
3. Explain how brand names can be used to foster brand loyalty.
4. What are the differences between push and pull strategies? Why would a firm choose one over the other?
5. Compare the advantages and disadvantages of different advertising media.
6. What are the advantages of personal selling over other promotional tools?
7. Which promotional tools have proven most useful in mounting global advertising campaigns? Why?
8. Is publicity more or less available to small firms than to larger firms? Why?

Analysis Questions

9. How would you expect the branding, packaging, and labelling of convenience shopping and specialty goods to differ? Why? Give examples to illustrate your answers.
10. Take a look at some of the advertising conducted by businesses based in your area. Choose two campaigns—one that you think is effective and one that you think is ineffective. What differences in the campaigns make one better than the other?
11. Select a good or service that you have purchased recently. Try to retrace the relevant steps in the buyer decision process as you experienced it. Which steps were most important to you? Least important?
12. Find examples of publicity about some business, either a local firm or a national firm. Did the publicity have, or is it likely to have, positive or negative consequences for the business? Why?

Application Exercises

13. Interview the manager of a local manufacturing firm. Identify the company's different products according to their positions in the product life cycle.
14. Select a product that is sold nationally. Identify as many media used in its promotion as you can. Which medium is used most often? On the whole, do you think the campaign is effective? Why or why not?
15. Interview the owner of a local small business. Identify the company's promotional objectives and strategies, and the elements in its promotional mix. What, if any, changes would you suggest? Why?
16. Check out your college or university's Web site and determine how effective it is as a tool for promoting your school.

Building Your Business Skills

What's Brand News?

Goal

To encourage students to evaluate the ways in which branding affects their personal awareness of products available in the marketplace.

Method

Step 1:
Working individually, examine a recent Saturday newspaper from a large city. Focusing on paid advertisements, list the brands of various products that you see. Draw up a selective list of the various brands that are featured in the ads. Include only those that attract your attention for one reason or another. Then, divide the items on your list into two columns—national brands and private brands.

Step 2:
Join with three or four classmates to compare your lists. Analyze the extent to which private brands versus national brands are more prominent in that newspaper. Which brands are more familiar to you? Less familiar?

Discuss the reasons for your familiarity or non-familiarity with specific brands.

Follow-Up Questions

1. What do you think motivated the national brands (companies) on your list to advertise in this newspaper rather than elsewhere? For those brands, are you influenced by brand reputation or advertising?

2. Can you say what attracted you to select the private brands that you put on your list? Were you influenced mainly by price? By visual appeal? Were other factors involved?

3. Find a national brand that appears on the list of just one group member. Given the fact that only one group member listed a certain national brand that other group members ignored, what factors were responsible for the different choices?

4. Based on this exercise, are you likely to change the way you look at brands? Will you be attracted more to national brands or to private brands? Explain your answer.

Exploring the Net

Each e-commerce Web site is itself a product that competes in the marketplace. Some are new entrants while others are more established and well known. Each site offers a product line, a "get-acquainted" tour, and pricing information for the products it sells. To consider these variables and compare them in greater detail, visit each of the following sites:

www.ebay.com

www.priceline.com

www.nextag.com

www.amazon.com

Look first at the contents of the home page for an overview of each site. Click on some of the browse categories (e.g., "Products," "How to Enter the Store," "How to Buy"). Then consider the following questions:

1. Compare the product offerings across the sites. What percentage of the products offered are consumer products? How many are industrial products?

2. What percentage of advertised products are convenience items? Shopping items? How many are specialty items? Explain the similarities and differences among the sites in terms of product offerings.

3. On each site, how many product lines can you identify? What distinguishes any given product line from the others?

4. Compare the pricing methods of Priceline.com versus the way prices are determined at NexTag.com. Explain the similarities and differences.

5. Explore the Amazon.com and eBay.com sites, noting the ranges of products and pricing choices that are available. Describe the ways in which they are similar and the ways in which they differ from one another.

Concluding Case 16-1

Web Promotions

Please forgive us for using a phrase that most students love to hate, but it's the best way we know to describe how traditional product-promotion strategies are changing in the era of the Internet: There has been a *paradigm shift*—the emergence of a new world view—in the way companies promote products in the virtual world. It is a shift that combines traditional promotional methods with new approaches geared to the interactivity of the Web.

Advertisers have discovered (often the hard way) that tried-and-true promotional tactics don't work online. For example, an emotion-filled vignette may be just right for television, but it has no impact in cyberspace, where online customers won't take the time to get involved. "You're not allowed to say or market anything online unless the customer wants to hear it," explains Chan Suh, CEO of Agency.com Ltd., an interactive consulting company. "In [cyberspace] marketing, the customer is in charge."

According to research, the best way to reach online customers is through something called *rational marketing*—product promotions that provide concrete, interactive services. Consider a recent theme promoted on the MasterCard International Web site. "Shop Smart" is a program that guides online shoppers to retail sites with state-of-the-art credit card security systems. In contrast, the company's traditional marketing message for television uses the emotional tag line "Priceless" and shows Mark McGwire hitting his sixty-second home run in a single season. Debra Coughlin, a member of MasterCard's Internet marketing team, explains the thinking behind the different approaches: "The TV user is looking for entertainment. The Internet user is online for more practical reasons. Our brand efforts reflect that end-user goal."

Marketers at General Motors' Saturn division use television and other traditional media to introduce consumers to the help they'll receive online. The Saturn Web site includes a lease-price calculator, a purchase-payment calculator, an interactive method for choosing options and seeing how they look on different cars, a dealer locator, and an online order form. The Web site is featured on a humorous television commercial that shows a college student ordering a Saturn from his dorm room as easily as he might order a pizza. The synergy created through the television and virtual promotions has tripled the number of annual visitors to the Saturn Web site.

Not all products are equally promotable on the Web, as packaged-goods manufacturers have learned. Although marketers for Tide laundry detergent, Ragú sauces, and Clairol hair-care products have filled their sites with practical interactive help, they still use traditional channels for the bulk of their promotions. Fast-food companies are also taking a cautious promotional approach. Although McDonald's does some marketing on the Web, marketing executives are waiting for the technology that allows full-motion video and audio programming before they make a greater commitment. As a promotional medium, explains David G. Green, McDonald's senior vice-president for international marketing, the Internet "is more difficult for those of us who do not have a good or service that is transferable to a virtual experience."

Even though the Internet may be the most effective sales tool since the telephone, it also has the potential to throw a monkey wrench into traditional sales and distribution channels. Naturally, this prospect worries marketers who are aware that traditional methods, which rely on armies of sales representatives and retail partners, still account for at least 90 percent of most companies' orders.

Granted, online selling eliminates paperwork and sales commissions and can potentially reduce costs by as much as 15 percent. These savings, however, come out of the pockets of sales reps and distributors, many of whom wonder if they will survive the cybernetic future. As a result, companies wanting to maintain their current sales and distribution networks while simultaneously venturing onto the Web find themselves walking on eggshells. "In some cases," reports one business journalist, companies are "launching Web commerce sites with no publicity or limited merchandise offerings. In other cases, [they are] keeping online prices high, so traditional vendors can lead the way in offering discounts. Some manufacturers are even trying to placate dealers and salespeople with a cut of each Internet sale, regardless of whether they played a role in generating it."

Software maker Intuit Inc., wary of alienating its traditional distribution network by discounting Quicken, TurboTax, and other software programs on the Web, is leaving discounting to the retailers who are responsible for most of its sales. "We could decide to market aggressively on the Web," explains CEO William Harris, "but we don't do that in deference to our third-party resellers." Marketers at 3M Corp. also see the danger of Web-based selling and use the Web for promotion only, not for sales. Although the company's Web site lists hundreds of 3M products, it posts no order form—a policy that suits the traditional distribution network just fine. "We are very concerned about our distribution-channel structure," says a 3M Internet specialist. "We take care not to damage those relationships." In any case, most online orders would be relatively small by comparison with those brought in through current distributors (whereas a consumer might order a box of 10 floppy disks, a retailer like Staples will order in bulk). Obviously, 3M is also acting in its own economic best interest.

Meanwhile, however, other companies are moving rapidly into online discounting, despite the impact on traditional channels. When Compaq began selling computers at discounted prices on the Web, dealers saw a dramatic sales drop. "It's taking a chunk out of our business," admits Richard Wong, head of San Francisco–based Sefco Computers Inc. "We still have people ask us for bids on small business installations, but we don't win the orders anymore." The reason, says Wong, is pricing: Compaq's online site sells each machine for about $50 less than companies like Sefco can afford to sell them.

As the Internet becomes more sophisticated and its use becomes more widespread, companies that are now resisting online sales and distribution may be forced to find ways to keep traditional network members happy as they move onto the Web. "We'll learn as we go," says James Cyrier, head of medical sales and marketing for Hewlett-Packard. His hospital customers want the convenience of online shopping, but what does Cyrier do with the 500 H-P sales reps and distributors who bring in more than US$1 billion a year worldwide? There are no easy answers.

CASE QUESTIONS

1. What do you think of rational marketing as an approach to reaching Internet consumers?

2. Why is it necessary for marketers to introduce Internet sites on television and other media? Can marketers plan promotional strategies for one medium without considering others?

3. Why are sales representatives so concerned about Web-based marketing? Do you agree or disagree with their concerns? Explain.

4. Do you envision a changing role for direct mail in this era of online marketing? How do you think direct mail will be used in this new environment?

5. Argue for or against this statement: Marketers will always look to traditional sales and distribution channels for the bulk of their orders. ◆

Concluding Case 16-2

Walker Digital

Walker Digital has invested millions of dollars and years of effort to develop, fine-tune, and implement priceline.com—the world's first buyer-driven electronic commerce system. Led by founder and vice-chairman Jay Walker, the company observed an unfilled "open" consumer demand for such "perishable" products as airline tickets at prices below retail. "That demand creates a 'catch-22' for sellers," explains a Walker spokesperson. "On the one hand, sellers want the increased sales revenue. However, if they publicly discount their retail prices, or sell their products through a liquidator, sellers risk harming their retail channels and profitability." In other words,

otherwise unsold tickets could be sold at discount prices, but sellers needed a channel that did not disrupt those through which they did the great majority of their business at regular retail prices.

Walker's answer was priceline.com, a brand-name system that allows individual consumers to submit their own prices for products or services to various sellers via the World Wide Web or toll-free phones. Every electronic offer is privately presented to sellers, who then decide if it is worth accepting. The transaction is confidential—no other retail customer knows about any offer or deal—and costs nothing unless the seller accepts the buyer's offer in writing.

In 1998, priceline.com launched its "name your own price" service in the leisure airline ticket market. Fifteen major domestic and international carriers signed up in an effort to fill some of the 500 000 seats that are left empty each day. This is how the system works: Customers submit the prices they are willing to pay, guaranteeing offers with credit cards. Priceline.com then finds an airline that is interested in each potential deal and informs all buyers, within 1 hour for domestic flights and 24 hours for international flights, that they have purchased a nonrefundable ticket. Buyers with Internet access are notified electronically. Others call a toll-free number to find out if their offers have been accepted. "Priceline.com," says Walker, "lets consumers communicate the price they want with potential sellers in a quick and powerful way."

The idea of buyer-driven commerce caught on quickly, thanks to an aggressive advertising campaign featuring former Star Trek captain William Shatner that turned priceline.com into a national brand. By early 2000, the company was selling more than 30 000 tickets per week and had emerged as one of the Internet's leading sellers of leisure airline tickets.

Within months of introducing its buyer-driven service for airline tickets, priceline.com began offering hotel rooms, rental cars, and new cars and trucks on a "name your own price" basis. Like airline tickets, hotel rooms and rental cars constitute time-sensitive services and are subject to so-called "perishability losses": if they are not sold before a given date, the hotel cannot recover any portion of the room price or any profit for that date.

New cars and trucks are the first nonperishable products in the priceline.com system. Launched first in New York, New Jersey, and Connecticut, the service permits Internet consumers to buy new vehicles without ever talking to salespeople—and without haggling. Although there are other car-buying services on the Internet, including Auto-by-Tel and Microsoft CarPoint, they operate in a more traditional marketplace than priceline.com: they pay for the right to contact prospective customers and try to sell them vehicles. According to Gary Arlen, president of Arlen Communications, a research firm specializing in electronic media, "Priceline turns the car-buying process upside down. It takes advantage of the Web's capabilities by letting the buyer name the price and inviting dealers to take it or leave it."

How does priceline.com earn money? It charges customers $25 and dealers $75 once a sale is completed. To discourage browsing, consumers face a $200 penalty if they walk away after a dealer accepts an offer. Buyers who cannot break the haggling habit can use priceline.com to purchase vehicles and then argue with dealers about financing and trade-ins.

CASE QUESTIONS

1. Priceline.com plans to expand its buyer-driven electronic commerce system into the rental car and home mortgage markets. How will the introduction of these new products be affected by the public's recognition of other priceline.com brands?

2. Why was an aggressive promotional campaign especially important during the introduction of priceline.com? What marketing advantages—and burdens—do innovative products face?

3. Why is priceline.com described as a "buyer-driven" electronic commerce system? Can you think of any other buyer-driven pricing systems?

4. Why is it important for sellers to keep priceline.com deals private?

5. Why would an airline reject any offer from a priceline.com customer on the day of a flight if the seat is likely to remain empty? Isn't selling inventory a primary pricing goal? ◆

Visit the *Business* Website at www.pearsoned.ca/griffin
for up-to-date e-business cases!

PRICING AND DISTRIBUTING GOODS AND SERVICES

17

CHAPTER

Reinventing Canadian Retailing

The wrenching changes that have taken place in Canadian retailing during the last decade are continuing. One event—the bankruptcy of Eaton's—is illustrative of the kinds of changes that are occurring. Eaton's failure opened up a lot of underperforming real estate for other Canadian (and perhaps U.S.) retailers who wanted to get their hands on the prime space that Eaton's stores have been occupying for years. Many of these spaces will be replaced with new tenants, including big-box retailers, fashion boutiques, restaurants, and movie theatres.

From the bankruptcy of Eaton's to the dominance of U.S.-based Wal-Mart, Canadian retailers are struggling with vast changes in the retailing landscape. Stated most simply, customers have less money to spend, less time to spend it, and more places to spend it. To compete in this environment, a retailer simply must stand out. The gap between winners and losers is widening, and consumers are the beneficiaries.

What exactly do winning retailers do? What they *don't* do is pursue the old strategy of trying to be all things to all people—like Eaton's did and The Bay still does. That strategy is simply not going to work very well in the future. Instead, winning retailers do the following:

- they focus on profits, not revenues
- they find out exactly who their customers are
- they offer the right selection
- they have the most convenient location
- they treat staff well so that staff will treat customers well
- they deliver what their customers value most

- they embrace change
- they provide customers with the best "shopping experience"

These tactics can be seen at success stories like Canadian Tire, which has faced the full-frontal assault from Home Depot and Wal-Mart and yet has prospered. It did so by brightening aisles, improving product displays, smoothing internal relations between head office and retail outlets, and becoming an agenda-setter rather than a follower. Canadian Tire decided that it wouldn't try to be all things to all people. Instead, it picked the categories it wanted to dominate. It now focuses on three main categories: sports and leisure, auto parts, and home products. It also intends to create up to 4000 jobs at its new "PartSource" stores, which provide a broad selection of auto parts at low prices, expert salespeople, and speedy service.

Shoppers Drug Mart is another winner. It conducted 20 focus groups and 3000 interviews before it decided to forget the price-conscious shopper and emphasize better store layouts, more locations, and offering more food and convenience items.

The three Quebec outlets of The Wings of Fashion (Les Ailes de la Mode) also show winning form. Each store has leather couches, newspaper racks, a coat check, a concierge, and a private room for nursing mothers. The company spends three times the national average per square foot on customer service, but it also sells three times the value of goods as stores like The Bay. The company operates its own shuttle bus service, and it occasionally runs promotions with VIA Rail Canada to bring in customers from the outlying regions of the province so they can shop. ◆

In this chapter, we complete our look at the marketing function by examining the role of pricing and distribution. The opening case describes how Canadian retailing is changing because of increased competition and changes in consumer tastes.

The first part of the chapter examines the pricing objectives of business firms, as well as the various methods they use to decide what to charge for the goods and services they produce. The second part of the chapter describes how producers get their goods and services into consumers' hands. Should the company sell directly to consumers? Or should some type of intermediary such as a retailer be used? How will the merchandise be moved from the factory to the consumer?

By focusing on the learning objectives of this chapter, you will consider questions like these and better understand the importance of distribution in the marketing process. After reading this chapter, you should be able to:

<table>
<tr><td>LEARNING OBJECTIVES</td></tr>
</table>

1. Identify the various *pricing objectives* that govern pricing decisions and describe the price-setting tools used in making these decisions.

2. Discuss *pricing strategies* and tactics for existing and new products.

3. Identify the different *channels of distribution* and explain different *distribution strategies*.

4. Explain the differences between *merchant wholesalers* and *agents/brokers*.

5. Identify the different types of *retailing* and *retail stores*.

6. Describe the major activities in the *physical distribution process*.

7. Compare the five basic forms of *transportation* and identify the types of firms that provide them.

PRICING OBJECTIVES AND TOOLS

Price is becoming an increasingly important part of the marketing mix. During the last 10 years, companies have increased their emphasis on quality, so quality across products is now very similar. As a result, consumers now focus more on price as a way to decide which products to buy. Consider these examples:

- In grocery stores, private brands are increasingly successful because they sell for 15 to 40 percent less than brand-name products.

- Wal-Mart has adopted an "everyday low price" (EDLP) policy.[1]

- McDonald's announced in 1997 that they were dropping prices to keep competitors like Burger King from stealing market share from them.[2]

pricing
Deciding what the company will receive in exchange for its product.

In **pricing**, managers decide what the company will receive in exchange for its products. In this section, we first discuss the objectives that influence a firm's pricing decisions. Then we describe the major tools that companies use to meet those objectives.

Pricing to Meet Business Objectives

Companies often price products to maximize profits. But sellers hope to attain other pricing objectives when selling products. Some firms, for example, are more interested in dominating the market or securing high market share than in maximizing profits. Pricing decisions are also influenced by the need to survive in competitive marketplaces, by social and ethical concerns, and even by corporate image.

Profit-Maximizing Objectives

Pricing to maximize profits is tricky. If prices are set too low, the company will probably sell many units of its product. But it may miss the opportunity to make additional profit on each unit—and may indeed lose money on each exchange. Conversely, if prices are set too high, the company will make a large profit on each item but will sell fewer units. Again, the firm loses money. In addition, it may be left with excess inventory and may have to reduce or even close production operations. To avoid these problems, companies try to set prices to sell the number of units that will generate the highest possible total profits.

In calculating profits, managers weigh receipts against costs for materials and labour to create the product. But they also consider the capital resources (plant and equipment) that the company must tie up to generate that level of profit. The costs of marketing (such as maintaining a large sales staff) can also be substantial. Concern over the efficient use of these resources has led many firms to set prices so as to achieve a targeted level of return on sales or capital investment.[3]

Coca-Cola is testing an innovative way to avoid some of the traditional problems of what the price of a product should be. It is looking at two possibilities: a vending machine that automatically raises the price of a Coke as the temperature climbs, and setting prices at different vending machines at different levels depending on how many customers use the machine.[4]

Pricing for E-Business Objectives. Marketers pricing for sales on the Internet must consider different kinds of costs and different forms of consumer awareness than those pricing products to be sold conventionally. Many e-businesses are lowering both costs and prices because of the Internet's unique marketing capabilities. Because the Web, for example, typically provides a more direct link between producer and ultimate consumer, buyers avoid the costs entailed by wholesalers and retailers. Another factor in lower Internet prices is the ease of comparison shopping. Obviously, point-and-click shopping is much more efficient than driving from store to store in search of the best price. In addition, both consumers and businesses can force lower prices by joining together in the interest of greater purchasing power. Numerous small businesses, for instance, are joining forces on the Internet to negotiate lower prices on the health care services offered by employee benefits plans.[5]

Market-Share Objectives

In the long run, a business must make a profit to survive. Nevertheless, many companies initially set low prices for new products. They are willing to accept minimal profits—even losses—to get buyers to try products. In other words, they use pricing to establish **market share**: a company's percentage of the total market sales for a specific product. Even with established products, market share may outweigh profits as a pricing objective. For a product like Philadelphia Brand Cream Cheese, dominating a market means that consumers are more likely to buy it because they are familiar with a well-known, highly visible product.

market share
A company's percentage of the total market sales for a specific product.

Other Pricing Objectives

In some instances, neither profit maximizing nor market share is the best objective. During difficult economic times, for instance, loss containment and survival may become a company's main objectives. Thus in the mid-1980s, John Deere priced agricultural equipment low enough to ensure the company's survival in a severely depressed farm economy.

Still another objective might be to provide a benefit to customers. To introduce its services to industrial clients, for example, International Graffiti Control (IGC) offered a set-fee pricing system (typically charging $60 per month per building) to owners who needed graffiti removed from building walls. This method shifted the risk from the customer to IGC. It appeals to customers who never know from day to day how much new graffiti will appear but who do know that removal is covered by a fixed fee.

Price-Setting Tools

Whatever a company's objectives, managers must measure the potential impact before deciding on final prices. Two basic tools are often used for this purpose: *cost-oriented pricing* and *break-even analysis*. As a rule, these tools are combined to identify prices that will allow the company to reach its objectives.

Cost-Oriented Pricing

Cost-oriented pricing considers the firm's desire to make a profit and takes into account the need to cover production costs. A music store manager, for instance, would begin to price CDs by calculating the cost of making them available to shoppers. Included in this figure would be store rent, employee wages, utilities, product displays, insurance, and, of course, the cost of buying CDs from the manufacturer. The "Business Today" box presents an interesting case where costs are not considered in pricing.

Let's assume that the cost from the manufacturer is $8 per CD. If the store sells CDs for this price, it will not make any profit. Nor will it make a profit if it sells CDs for $8.50 each or even for $10 or $11. The manager must account for product and other costs and set a figure for profit. Together, these figures constitute markup. In this case, a reasonable markup of $7 over costs would result in a $15 selling price. Markup is usually stated as a percentage of selling price. Markup percentage is thus calculated as follows:

$$\text{Markup percentage} = \frac{\text{Markup}}{\text{Sales price}}$$

BUSINESS TODAY

How Much Should a Movie Ticket Cost?

Think about this: When you go to a first-run movie theatre, you pay the same price for each film you see. But it may cost as little as $2 million or as much as $200 million to make a film. Shouldn't the admission price be based on how much the film cost to make? After all, you pay a lot more for a Lincoln Continental than you do for a Ford because the Lincoln costs more to make. Shouldn't the same pricing system apply to Hollywood?

At an entertainment industry conference in 1998, Edgar Bronfman, then CEO of Seagram Co. Ltd., argued that the movie industry's current pricing model makes no sense. He made the case for a new approach to pricing, and openly said that movie studios must look at ways to increase revenues in order to cope with the skyrocketing cost of movie production. In 1997, the average price for producing a Hollywood movie was a record $53.4 million; distribution costs added another $22.2 million to the final studio outlay.

It is interesting that Bronfman's pricing idea met with a very cool reception from movie industry people. Tom Sherak, chairman of Twentieth Century Fox, said that Bronfman's idea would not work in the movie business. Sherak also feared that Bronfman's idea would cause filmmakers to demand that their films be priced higher at the box office so they could make more expensive films like *Titanic*.

In the case of our CD retailer, the markup percentage is 46.7:

$$\text{Markup percentage} = \frac{\$7}{\$15} = 46.7\%$$

In other words, out of every dollar taken in, 46.7 cents will be gross profit for the store. From this profit the store must still pay rent, utilities, insurance, and all other costs. Markup can also be expressed as a percentage of cost: The $7 markup is 87.5 percent of the $8 cost of a CD ($7/$8).

Break-Even Analysis: Cost-Volume-Profit Relationships

Using cost-oriented pricing, a firm will cover its **variable costs**—costs that change with the number of goods or services produced or sold. It will also make some money towards paying its **fixed costs**—costs that are unaffected by the number of goods or services produced or sold. But how many units must the company sell before all of its fixed costs are covered and it begins to make a profit? To determine this figure, it needs a **break-even analysis**.[6]

To continue our music store example, suppose again that the variable cost for each CD (in this case, the cost of buying the CD from the producer) is $8. This means that the store's annual variable costs depend on how many CDs are sold—the number of CDs sold multiplied by $8 cost per CD. Say that fixed costs for keeping the store open for one year are $100 000. These costs are unaffected by the number of CDs sold; costs for lighting, rent, insurance, and salaries are steady whether the store sells any CDs. Therefore, how many CDs must be sold to cover both fixed and variable costs and to generate some profit? The answer is the **break-even point**, which is 14 286 CDs. We arrive at this number through the following equation:

$$\text{Break-even point (in units)} = \frac{\text{Total fixed costs}}{\text{Price} - \text{Variable cost}}$$

$$= \frac{\$100\,000}{\$15 - \$8} = 14\,286 \text{ CDs}$$

Figure 17.1 shows the break-even point graphically. If the store sells fewer than 14 286 CDs, it loses money for the year. If sales exceed 14 286 CDs, profits grow by $7 for each CD sold. If the store sells exactly 14 286 CDs, it will cover all of its costs but will earn zero profit.

variable costs
Those costs that change with the number of goods or services produced or sold.

fixed costs
Those costs unaffected by the number of goods or services produced or sold.

break-even analysis
An assessment of how many units must be sold at a given price before the company begins to make a profit.

break-even point
The number of units that must be sold at a given price before the company covers all of its variable and fixed costs.

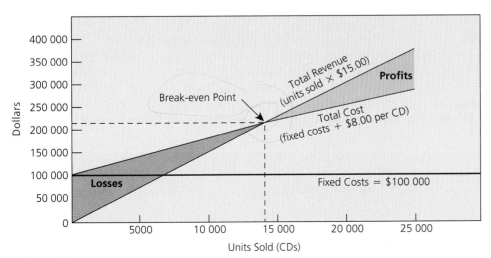

Figure 17.1
Break-even analysis.

Table 17.1	Comparative Breakthrough Quantities
Price ($)	**Number of CDs for Break-even Quantity**
8.00	—
10.00	50 000
12.00	25 000
14.00	16 667
15.00	14 286
16.00	12 500
18.00	10 000
20.00	5 000

Zero profitability at the break-even point can also be seen by using the profit equation:

Profit = Total revenue − (Total fixed cost + Total variable cost)
   = (14 286 CDs x $15) − ($100 000 + [14 286 CDs x $8])
$0 = ($214 290) − ($100 000 + $114 288)
   (rounded to the nearest whole CD)

In reality, managers calculate break-even points for each of several possible price levels. As the price per CD increases, the number of units that must be sold to reach the break-even point decreases. As prices fall, the number of units that must be sold before reaching the break-even point increases. Table 17.1 shows this relationship for a variety of prices. Prices below $8 are not considered; if the price does not exceed the item's variable cost, the break-even point will never be reached.

The store owner would certainly like to hit the break-even point as early as possible; after all, that is when profits will start rolling in. Why not charge $20 per CD, therefore, and break even earlier? Because at $20 per CD, unit sales would drop. In setting a price, the manager must consider how much buyers will pay for a CD and what the store's local competitors charge.

PRICING STRATEGIES AND TACTICS

The pricing tools discussed in the previous section provide a valuable guide for managers trying to set prices on specific goods. But they do not provide general direction for managers trying to set a pricing philosophy for their company. In this section, we discuss *pricing strategy*—that is, pricing as a planning activity that affects the marketing mix. We then describe some basic *pricing tactics*—ways in which managers implement a firm's pricing strategies.

Pricing Strategies

Let's begin this section by asking two questions. First: Can a manager really identify a single "best" price for a product? The answer is: probably not. For example, a study of prices for popular nonaspirin pain relievers (such as Tylenol and Advil) found variations of 100 percent.[7] In this market, in other words, some products sold for *twice* the price of other products with similar properties.

Granted, such differences may reflect some differences in product costs. The issue, however, is a little more complex. Such wide price differences reflect differing brand images that attract different types of customers. In turn, these images reflect vastly different pricing philosophies and strategies.

Our second question is this: Just how important is pricing as an element in the marketing mix? As we have already seen, it is a mistake to try to isolate any element in the marketing mix from the others. Nevertheless, because pricing has a direct and visible impact on revenues, it is extremely important to overall marketing plans. Moreover, it is a very flexible tool. It is certainly easier to change prices than to change products or distribution channels. In this section, we will focus on the ways in which pricing strategies for both new and existing products can result in widely differing prices for very similar products.

Whatever price strategy a company is using, it must be clearly communicated to buyers. Wal-Mart clearly communicates a low price strategy to consumers, but Eaton's strategy was not clear. For many years, Eaton's had a high-price strategy, coupled with a generous return policy. In 1991, Eaton's switched to an "everyday low price" strategy, but then slowly drifted back to a high-price strategy with occasional sales. Industry experts think that consumers were confused by this strategy, and that this contributed to Eaton's demise.

Pricing Existing Products

A firm basically has three options available in pricing its existing products. It can set prices for its product above prevailing market prices charged for similar products. It can set prices below market. Or it can set prices at or near the market price.

Companies pricing above the market play on customers' beliefs that higher price means higher quality. Curtis Mathes, a maker of televisions, VCRs, and stereos, promotes itself as the most expensive television set, "but worth it." Companies such as Godiva chocolates and Rolls Royce have also succeeded with this pricing philosophy.

In contrast, both Budget and Dollar car rental companies promote themselves as low-priced alternatives to Hertz and Avis. Ads for Suave hair-care products argue that "Suave does what theirs does—for a lot less." Pricing below the prevailing market price can succeed if the firm can offer a product of acceptable quality while keeping costs below those of higher-priced options.

A company can use different strategies for different customers. Airlines, for example, use a technique called yield management to predict precisely how many last-minute business travellers will want to get on a flight and be willing to pay a very high price. As a result, prices for leisure travel (which must be booked weeks in advance) may be as little as one-fifth the price of business travel.[8] This type of pricing system has allowed airlines to boost their profits significantly.

Finally, in some industries, a dominant firm establishes product prices and other companies follow along. This is called **price leadership**. (Don't confuse this approach with *price fixing*, the illegal process of producers agreeing among themselves what prices will be charged.) Price leadership is often evident in products such as structural steel, gasoline, and many processed foods. These products differ little in quality from one firm to another. Companies compete through advertising campaigns, personal selling, and service, not price.

Curtis Mathes
www.curtismathes.com

price leadership
The dominant firm in the industry establishes product prices and other companies follow suit.

Pricing New Products: Skimming and Penetration Pricing

Companies introducing new products into the market have to consider two contrasting pricing policy options: coming in with either a very high price or

price-skimming strategy
The decision to price a new product as high as possible to earn the maximum profit on each unit sold.

penetration-pricing strategy
The decision to price a new product very low to sell the most units possible and to build customer loyalty.

a very low one. The former is known as a **price-skimming strategy** and the latter is a **penetration-pricing strategy**.

Price Skimming. Price skimming may allow a firm to earn a large profit on each item sold. The cash income is often needed to cover development and introduction costs. Skimming works only if marketers can convince consumers that a product is truly different from those already on the market. Today's expensive high-definition television (HDTV) is an example. Moreover, the initial high profits will eventually attract competition. Like HDTVs, microwave ovens, calculators, video games, and video cameras were all introduced at high skim prices. Naturally, prices fell as soon as new companies entered the market.

Fixed versus Dynamic Pricing for E-Business. The electronic marketplace has introduced a highly variable pricing system as an alternative to more conventional—and more stable—pricing structures for both consumer and business-to-business products. So-called *dynamic pricing* is feasible because the flow of information on the Internet notifies millions of buyers around the world of instantaneous changes in product availability. In addition, to attract sales that might be lost under traditional fixed-price structures, sellers can alter prices privately, on a one-to-one, customer-to customer basis.[9] At present, *fixed pricing* remains the most widely available option for cybershoppers. E-tail giant Amazon.com, for example, has maintained the practice as the pricing strategy for its 16 million retail items. That situation, however, is beginning to change as dynamic-price challengers, such as eBay—the online person-to-person auction Web site—and Priceline.com—the online clearing house for person-to-business price negotiation—grow in popularity.

In questioning which way to go—fixed versus dynamic pricing—the answer among e-retailers and other experts is mixed. Although eBay epitomizes dynamic pricing, many recently polled eBay members said that they wanted to see some fixed-price auctions. Conversely, Amazon.com is starting to supplement fixed prices with auctions, thus competing head-to-head with eBay. Currently, however, there is a clear trend: dynamic pricing now garners 15 percent of all consumer e-business spending. Why? For one thing, close interaction between buyers and sellers at eBay seems to foster a "sense of community" that results in customer loyalty and more time at the Web site. The "It's a Wired World" box describes how one company saved a great deal of money by having its suppliers bid for contracts on the Internet.

eBay
www.ebay.ca

Penetration Pricing. In contrast to price skimming, penetration pricing seeks to generate consumer interest and stimulate trial purchase of new products. For example, new food products (convenience foods, cookies, and snacks) are often promoted at special low prices to stimulate early sales. Penetration pricing provides for minimal (if any) profit. Thus, it can succeed only if sellers can raise prices as consumer acceptance grows. Of course, increases must be managed carefully to avoid alienating customers.

Pricing Tactics

No matter what philosophy a company uses to price existing or new products, its managers may adopt one or more pricing tactics such as *price lining, psychological pricing,* or *discounting.*

Price Lining

Companies selling multiple items in a product category use price lining. For example, a department store carries literally thousands of products. To set a separate price for each brand and style of suit, plate, or couch would take

IT'S A WIRED WORLD

The World of Cyberspace Bidding

Sometimes a company getting into e-business is better off outsourcing some e-activities rather than doing them all itself. Consider, for example, the experience of United Technologies Corp. (UTC). The Connecticut-based conglomerate needed to renew contracts for printed circuit boards it was buying from eight suppliers to be used in UTC elevators, air conditioners, and other products. What prices would various suppliers charge? Before accepting estimates from suppliers, UTC hoped to reduce overall prices by 4 percent and, based on the going rate, expected to pay out US$74 million. At that point UTC decided to outsource the entire bidding process to FreeMarkets Inc., an Internet auction company. The results were stunning. FreeMarkets received bids from 29 circuit-board companies in the United States, Europe, and Asia. The winning suppliers signed contracts for US$42 million—some 43 percent below UTC's projection.

The Internet has created an auction marketplace for industrial goods that makes price setting an art and a gamble for industrial buyers and sellers, just as it did earlier with auction sites for consumer items (such as CyberBuyer.com). The existence of such a marketplace changes the entire method for price setting by firms selling to industrial customers. The conventional price-setting method generally follows established patterns:

- Incumbent suppliers have the inside edge for the new contracts.
- Closed bids prohibit suppliers from knowing competitors' prices.
- Only a few suppliers are invited to submit bids.
- If a firm's bid is not accepted, it has no opportunity to revise it.

FreeMarkets is changing all of that, and in doing so, it saves client companies an average of 15 percent on the costs of their purchases. The savings potential in the $5 trillion industrial-parts market is obvious.

To get suppliers to participate, FreeMarkets does not charge them fees for bidding. Instead, industrial buyers (large companies) pay fixed subscription fees of up to US$4 million a year. The auction infrastructure includes not just the software and computer technology necessary to conduct the bidding, but the standardizing of relevant technical requirements: delivery quantities and schedules, inventory quantities, and quality standards are all clarified before bidding starts. In a recent auction for a parts contract, the client set the most recent price, US$745 000, as the starting point. The 25 suppliers at remote locations instantly saw each bid as it was received and posted at FreeMarkets' communications headquarters. With an official 20-minute total time deadline for submitting a better price, the low bid dropped to US$612 000 after 10 minutes and then to US$585 000 with 30 seconds left. When a bid is received in the last minute of regulation time, the auction kicks into a 60-second overtime period. After 13 minutes of overtime bidding, the final price landed at US$518 000—which was 31 percent below the client's expectations. In this environment, the fixed-price approach to selling industrial goods is quickly becoming a thing of the past.

United Technologies Corp.
www.utc.com

FreeMarkets Inc.
www.freemarkets.com

---

many hours. By using **price lining**, the store can predetermine three or four price points at which a particular product will be sold. For men's suits, the price points might be $175, $250, and $400. All men's suits in the store will be priced at one of these three points. Buyers for the store must choose suits that can be purchased and sold profitably for one of these three prices.

price lining
The practice of offering all items in certain categories at a limited number of predetermined price points.

Psychological Pricing

Another pricing tactic, **psychological pricing**, takes advantage of the fact that customers are not completely rational when making buying decisions.[10] **Odd-even psychological pricing** proposes that customers prefer prices that are not stated in even dollar amounts. That is, customers see prices of $1000, $100, $50, and $10 as much higher than prices of $999.95, $99.95, $49.95, and $9.95, respectively. One common explanation for this widely recognized process is that the consumer looks at the whole dollar figure, ignores the cents, and rounds down.

psychological pricing
The practice of setting prices to take advantage of the nonlogical reactions of consumers to certain types of prices.

odd-even psychological pricing
A form of psychological pricing in which prices are not stated in even dollar amounts.

Closely related to odd-even pricing, **threshold pricing** argues that consumers set maximum prices they will pay for a particular item. Many gift shops, for example, will carry a supply of gifts in the $20-or-under price range. The feeling is that gift-givers often place an upper limit of $20 on gifts they buy.

Discounting

The price that is eventually set for a product is not always the price at which all items are sold. Many times a company has to offer a price reduction—a **discount**—to stimulate sales. Cash, seasonal, trade, and quantity discounts are the most common forms.

In recent years, **cash discounts** have become popular, even at retail stores. Stores may offer **seasonal discounts** to stimulate the sales of products during times of the year when most customers do not normally buy the product. Travellers can find low prices on summer trips to tropical islands and July shoppers can get sale prices on winter coats thanks to seasonal discounts. **Trade discounts** are available only to those companies or individuals involved in a product's distribution. Thus, wholesalers, retailers, and interior designers pay less for fabric than the typical consumer does. Related to trade discounts are **quantity discounts**—lower prices for purchases in large quantities. Case price discounts for motor oil or soft drinks at retail stores are examples of quantity discounts.

THE DISTRIBUTION MIX

We have already seen that a company needs an appropriate product mix. But the success of any product also depends in part on its **distribution mix**: the combination of distribution channels a firm selects to get a product to end-users. In this section, we will consider some of the many factors that enter into the distribution mix. First, we will explain the need for *intermediaries*. We will then discuss the basic *distribution strategies*. Finally, we will consider some special issues in channel relationships—namely, conflict and leadership.

These teens are as concerned with the price tags as with the style of the clothing they might buy on this shopping trip.

As you are reading the material on the next few pages, keep in mind one key point: intermediaries must provide added value to customers to stay in business. Over the next decade, traditional intermediaries may become smaller or disappear altogether as the Internet increasingly provides more and more products and services to customers in a more efficient way.[11]

Intermediaries and Distribution Channels

Once called *middlemen*, **intermediaries** are the individuals and firms who help distribute a producer's goods. They are generally classified as wholesalers or retailers. **Wholesalers** sell products to other businesses, which resell them to final consumers. **Retailers** sell products directly to consumers. While some firms rely on independent intermediaries, others employ their own distribution networks and sales forces. The decision normally hinges on three factors:

- the company's target markets

- the nature of its products

- the costs of maintaining distribution and sales networks.

We examine these factors more closely below by describing some of the distribution decisions that go into the marketing of consumer products.

intermediary
Any individual or firm other than the producer who participates in a product's distribution.

wholesalers
Intermediaries who sell products to other businesses, which in turn resell them to the end-users.

retailers
Intermediaries who sell products to end-users.

Distribution of Consumer Products

Figure 17.2 shows eight primary **distribution channels** aimed at different target audiences and product types. Note that all channels must begin with a producer and end with a consumer or an industrial user. Channels 1 through 5 are most often used for the distribution of consumer goods and services.

distribution channel
The path a product follows from the producer to the end-user.

WEBCONNEXION

With the introduction of the *National Post* as a competing national daily newspaper, the *Globe and Mail* has stepped up its advertising, including door-to-door campaigns, telephone solicitations, handing out free papers, and TV and Internet advertising. Along with the traditional home delivery and newspaper boxes, the Globe and Mail has developed a Web site that adds news stories as they occur. This channel of distribution gives readers almost instantaneous updates on breaking news. Visit the *Globe and Mail* at:

www.globeandmail.com

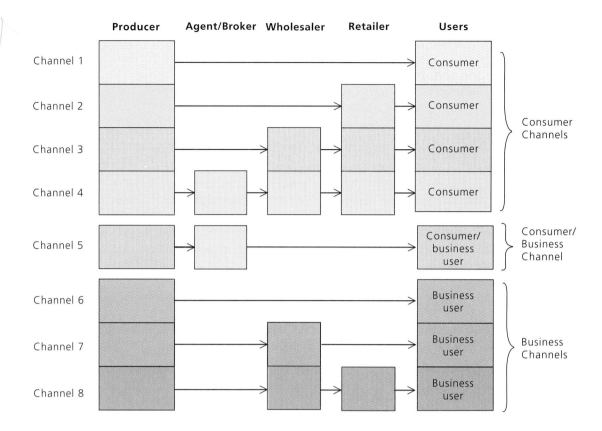

Figure 17.2
Channels of distribution: How the product travels from producer to consumer or user.

Channel 1

direct channel

A distribution channel in which the product travels from the producer to the consumer without passing through any intermediary.

In this **direct channel**, the product travels from the producer to the consumer with no intermediaries. Companies such as Avon, Fuller Brush, Tupperware, and many encyclopedia distributors use this channel. Direct channel distribution is also popular with craftspeople who sell their wares through word-of-mouth reference or from booths at local flea markets or craft shows. Roadside vegetable stands also use the direct channel. This direct channel is also prominent on the Internet for thousands of products ranging from books and automobiles to insurance and vacation packages sold directly by producers to consumers. A leader in direct sales of computer products, for example, the Gateway 2000 Internet storefront generates annual sales of US$9 billion in computers and related products for PC users at home and at the workplace.

Channel 2

In Channel 2, producers distribute products through retailers. Goodyear, for example, maintains its own system of retail outlets. Levi Strauss has its own outlets but also produces jeans for other retailers such as The Gap. On the other hand, Liz Claiborne, in addition to its own 200 retail outlets, relies on more than 9300 retailers to sell its apparel worldwide. Claiborne uses a sales force to sell products to retailers, which then sell them over the counter to consumers.

Channel 3

Until the mid-1960s, Channel 2 was a widely used method of retail distribution. But that channel requires a large amount of floor space both for storing merchandise and for displaying it in retail stores. As the cost of retail space rose, retailers found that they could not afford to buy space to store goods.

Thus wholesalers have increasingly entered the distribution network. They have taken over more and more of the storage service. A good example of this philosophy in practice is convenience food/gas stores. Approximately 90 percent of the space in these stores is devoted to merchandise displays. Only about 10 percent is used for storage and office facilities.

Wholesalers are prominent in e-commerce because Internet stores can provide customers with access to information and product displays 24 hours per day. They also make it possible to place orders electronically and confirm delivery commitments almost instantaneously. In the diamond industry, for example, retail companies can access wholesalers such as Diasqua Group, visually examine diamonds for grade and quality, place orders, and receive delivery dates.

Wholesalers have always played a role in distributing some products. Many manufacturers only distribute their products in large quantities. Small businesses that cannot afford to purchase large quantities of goods rely on wholesalers to hold inventories of such products and to supply them on short notice. For example, a family-owned grocery store that sells only 12 cases of canned spinach in a year cannot afford to buy a truckload (perhaps 500 cases) in a single order. Instead, it orders one case a month from a local wholesaler, which buys large lots of spinach and other goods from the makers, stores them, and resells them in small quantities to various retailers.

Channel 4

This complex channel uses **sales agents**, or **brokers**, which represent manufacturers and sell to wholesalers, retailers, or both. They receive commissions based on the price of goods they sell. Agents generally deal in the related product lines of a few producers, serving as their sales representatives on a relatively permanent basis. Travel agents, for example, represent the airlines, car-rental companies, and hotels. In contrast, brokers are hired to assist in buying and selling temporarily, matching sellers and buyers as needed. This channel is often used in the food and clothing industries. The real estate industry and the stock market also rely on brokers for matching buyers and sellers.

Indirect distribution channels do mean higher prices to the end consumer. The more members involved in the channel, the higher the final price to the purchaser. After all, each link in the distribution chain must charge a markup or commission to make a profit. Figure 17.3 shows typical markup growth through the distribution channel.

Ernst & Young conducted a study of the competitiveness of distribution channels that showed that Canada often has an extra layer of wholesale distribution compared to American distribution channels and higher markups at the retail level. But the Canadian retail sector is becoming more like the U.S., with larger stores, more items, and fewer intermediaries.[12]

agent/broker
An independent business person who represents a business and receives a commission in return, but never takes legal possession of the product.

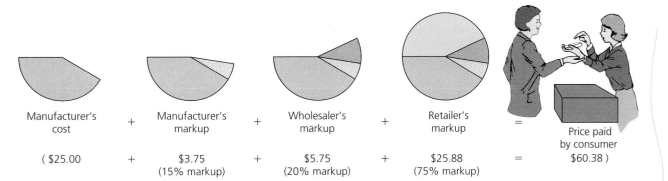

Manufacturer's cost	+	Manufacturer's markup	+	Wholesaler's markup	+	Retailer's markup	=	Price paid by consumer
($25.00	+	$3.75 (15% markup)	+	$5.75 (20% markup)	+	$25.88 (75% markup)	=	$60.38)

Figure 17.3
Where your dollar goes in the distribution channel for an electronic calculator.

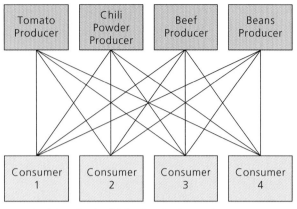
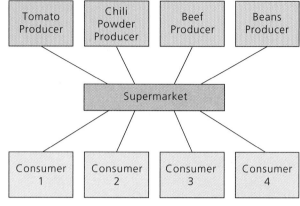

PURCHASE OF GOODS WITHOUT INTERMEDIARIES   PURCHASE OF GOODS WITH INTERMEDIARIES

Figure 17.4
Advantages of intermediaries.

Intermediaries add to the visible dollar cost of a product but, in many ways, they save the consumer time and thus money. A manufacturer would not sell you one calculator for the same price it charges wholesalers who buy truckloads of them. In other ways, intermediaries actually save you money.

Consider Figure 17.4, which illustrates the problem of making chili without an intermediary—the supermarket. You would probably spend a lot more time (and a lot of money on gas) if you had to get all the necessary ingredients on your own. In fact, intermediaries can add form, place, and time utility by making the right quantities available where and when you need them.

Channel 5

Channel 5 differs from the previous channels in two ways: (1) it includes an agent as the sole intermediary, and (2) it distributes to both consumers and business customers. Consider Vancouver-based Uniglobe Travel International, a travel agent that represents airlines, car rental companies, and hotels. Uniglobe books flight reservations and provides arrangements for complete packages of recreational travel services for consumers. It also provides services to companies whose employees need lodging and transportation for businesses travel.

Expansion into e-commerce is well suited to this distribution channel because it allows more people to find out directly about products. Uniglobe, for example, expanded its traditional services by implementing a new online strategy. Now an online subsidiary combines a high-tech Web site with an old-fashioned human touch in a specialty market—booking cruises. Customers can scan for destinations, cruise lines, restaurants, deck plans, and cabin locations on any of the 70 ships that the firm represents. Moreover, with Uniglobe's online chat function, customers can simply open a window to chat in real time with any of 75 cruise specialists. The strategy has paid off: Uniglobe.com is the market leader in online cruise bookings.[13]

Distribution of Industrial Products

Industrial channels are important because each company is itself a customer that buys other companies' products. The Kellogg Co. buys grain to make breakfast cereals, Stone Container Corp. buys rolls of paper and vats of glue to make corrugated boxes, and Victoria Hospital buys medicines and other supplies to provide medical services. **Industrial distribution**, therefore,

industrial distribution
The network of channel members involved in the flow of manufactured goods to industrial customers.

refers to the network of channel members involved in the flow of manufactured goods to industrial customers. Unlike consumer products, industrial products are traditionally distributed through Channels 6 to 8 (refer back to Figure 17.2)

Channel 6

Most industrial goods are sold directly by the manufacturer to the industrial buyer. For example, Lawless Container Corp. produces packaging containers that are sold directly to such industrial customers as Fisher-Price (toys), Dirt Devil (vacuum cleaners), and Mr. Coffee (coffee makers). As contact points with their customers, manufacturers maintain **sales offices**. These offices provide all services for the company's customers and serve as headquarters for its salespeople.

E-commerce technologies have intensified the use of Channel 6. For example, Dell Computer Corp., a pioneer in direct Internet sales, now gets about two-thirds of its $25 billion in sales from other businesses, governments, and schools. Armed with the ever-expanding reach of the Internet, Dell is trying to establish a foothold in the massive Chinese market.

sales offices
Offices maintained by sellers of industrial goods to provide points of contact with their customers.

Channel 7

Wholesalers function as intermediaries between manufacturers and users in only a very small percentage of industrial channels. Brokers and agents are even rarer. Channel 7 is most often used for accessory equipment (computer terminals, office equipment) and supplies (floppy disks, copier paper). While manufacturers produce these items in large quantities, companies buy them in small quantities. Few companies, for example, order truckloads of paper clips. As with consumer goods, then, intermediaries help end-users by representing manufacturers or by breaking down large quantities into smaller sales units.

Channel 8

For some industries, the roles of channel members are changing. In the office-products industry, for instance, Channel 7 is being displaced by the emergence of a newer channel that looks very much like Channel 3 for consumer products. Instead of buying office supplies from wholesalers (Channel 7), many buyers are now shopping at office discount stores such as Staples, Office Depot, and Office Max. Before selling to large companies, these warehouse-like superstores originally targeted retail consumers and small and mid-size businesses that bought supplies at retail stores (at retail prices). Today, however, small business buyers stroll down the aisles of what are in effect discount stores for industrial users, selecting from 7000 items at prices 20 to 75 percent lower than manufacturers' suggested retail.

Superstores can get merchandise either from wholesalers or directly from manufacturers. Thus the supply chain in this channel sometimes includes wholesalers and sometimes bypasses them. As a result, the superstore that buys directly from the manufacturer can sell to retail consumers while simultaneously serving as wholesalers to large business customers.

E-commerce is fuelling the rapid growth in the office-superstore industry. In Japan, for example, the largest office supplier, Askul, doubled its sales volume in just a three-month period. Askul's customers can use the Internet to shop in real time and have orders delivered within 24 hours. Low prices are possible because Askul's high-tech distribution warehouses can be located on cheap land and because electronic transactions eliminate the workforce needed to conduct face-to-face selling. In the United States, Staples Inc., the office superstore pioneer, also relies on e-business for continued rapid growth. In addition to shopping electronically from the home or office, in-store customers can access new e-business services at special-order kiosks located in Staples' stores. They can save money, for example, by customizing their own PCs by using Staples' build-to-order offerings from Compaq or Hewlett-Packard. Customers get the equipment they want and Staples doesn't have to carry shelves of computers waiting for buyers who may or may not show up.[14]

Distribution Strategies

Choosing a distribution network is a vital consideration for a company. It can make the firm succeed or fail. The choice of distribution strategy determines the amount of market exposure the product gets and the cost of that exposure.

The appropriate strategy depends on the product class. The goal is to make a product accessible in just enough locations to satisfy customers' needs. Milk can be purchased at many retail outlets (high exposure). But there is only one distributor for Rolls Royce in a given city.

Different degrees of market exposure are available through intensive distribution, exclusive distribution, and selective distribution. **Intensive distribution** means distributing a product through as many channels and channel members (using both wholesalers and retailers) as possible. For example, as Figure 17.5 shows, Caramilk bars flood the market through all suitable outlets. Intensive distribution is normally used for low-cost consumer goods such as candy and magazines.

In contrast, **exclusive distribution** occurs when a manufacturer grants the exclusive right to distribute or sell a product to one wholesaler or retailer in a given geographic area. Exclusive distribution agreements are most

intensive distribution
A distribution strategy in which a product is distributed in nearly every possible outlet, using many channels and channel members.

exclusive distribution
A distribution strategy in which a product's distribution is limited to only one wholesaler or retailer in a given geographic area.

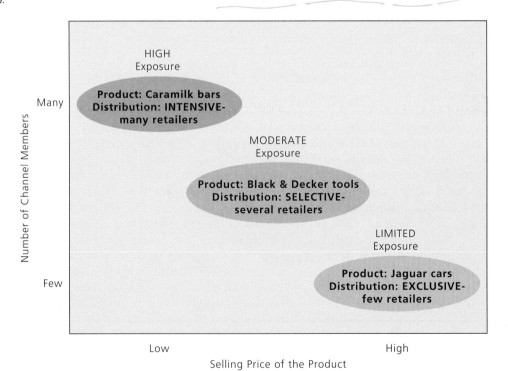

Figure 17.5
Amounts of market exposure from three kinds of distribution.

common for high-cost, prestige products. For example, Jaguar automobiles are sold by only a single dealer servicing a large metropolitan area.

Selective distribution falls between intensive and exclusive distribution. A company that uses this strategy carefully selects only wholesalers and retailers who will give special attention to the product in terms of sales efforts, display position, etc. Selective distribution policies have been applied to virtually every type of consumer product. It is usually embraced by companies like Black & Decker whose product lines do not require intense market exposure to increase sales.

Para Paints uses an interesting selective distribution policy. It keeps its high-end paint products out of the "big-box" stores such as Canadian Tire and Home Depot. Doing so has increased Para's margins (because big-box stores demand steep discounts), and has also increased sales by 15 to 20 percent because the independent stores that sell Para paint have remained loyal to Para. The company repeatedly turns down requests from big-box stores to carry its paints because it doesn't want to harm its good relations with independent dealers.[15]

selective distribution

A distribution strategy that falls between intensive and exclusive distribution, calling for the use of a limited number of outlets for a product.

Channel Conflict and Channel Leadership

Manufacturers can choose to distribute through more than one channel or wholesaler. They can also choose to make new uses of existing channels. Similarly, most retailers are free to strike agreements with as many producers as capacity permits. In such cases, *channel conflict* may arise. Conflicts are resolved when members' efforts are better coordinated. A key factor in coordinating the activities of independent organizations is *channel leadership*. Another strategy for improving coordination is known as the *vertical marketing system*.

Channel Conflict

Channel conflict occurs when members of the channel disagree over the roles they should play or the rewards they should receive. John Deere, for example, would no doubt object if its dealers began distributing Russian and Japanese tractors. Similarly, when a manufacturer-owned factory outlet store discounts the company's apparel or housewares, it runs the risk of alienating the manufacturer's retail accounts. Channel conflict may also arise if one member has more power than others or is viewed as receiving preferential treatment. Needless to say, such conflicts defeat the purpose of the system by disrupting the flow of goods to their destinations.

John Deere
www.johndeere.com

Consider the case of IBM, which sells both through wholesalers and retailers and directly to major corporations. When IBM makes a direct sale, its dealers point out that they have lost a chance to earn money by making the sale themselves. If this pattern repeatedly frustrates one particular dealer, that dealer may take action—switching, for example, from IBM to Apple products.[16]

The intense competition between IBM and Apple has led to rapid technological advances in personal computers.

Channel Leadership

Usually, one channel member is most powerful in determining the roles and rewards of other members. That

channel captain
The channel member that is the most powerful in determining the roles and rewards of organizations involved in a given channel of distribution.

vertical marketing system (VMS)
A system in which there is a high degree of coordination among all the units in the distribution channel so that a product moves efficiently from manufacturer to consumer.

IGA
www.igainc.com

merchant wholesaler
An independent wholesaler that buys and takes legal possession of goods before selling them to customers.

full-service merchant wholesaler
A merchant wholesaler that provides storage and delivery in addition to wholesaling services.

limited-function merchant wholesaler
An independent wholesaler that provides only wholesaling—not warehousing or transportation—services.

drop shipper
A type of wholesaler that does not carry inventory or handle the product.

member is the **channel captain**. Often, the channel captain is a manufacturer, particularly if the manufacturer's product is in high demand. In some industries, an influential wholesaler or a large retailer such as Wal-Mart or Sears may emerge as channel captain because of large sales volumes.

Vertical Marketing Systems

To overcome problems posed by channel conflict and issues of channel leadership, the **vertical marketing system (VMS)** has emerged. In a VMS, separate businesses join to form a unified distribution channel, with one member coordinating the activities of the whole channel. There are three types of VMS arrangements:

- In a *corporate VMS*, all stages in the channel are under single ownership. The Limited, for example, owns both the production facilities that manufacture its apparel and the retail stores that sell it.

- In a *contractual VMS*, channel members sign contracts agreeing to specific duties and rewards. The Independent Grocers' Alliance (IGA), for example, consists of independent retail grocers joined with a wholesaler who contractually leads—but does not own—the VMS. Most franchises are contractual VMSs.

- In an *administered VMS*, channel members are less formally coordinated than in a corporate or contractual VMS. Instead, one or more of the members emerge as leader(s) and maintain control as a result of power and influence. Although the administered VMS is more fragile than the corporate and contractual forms, it is more unified than channels relying on independent members.

WHOLESALING

Now that you know something about distribution channels, we can consider the broader role played by intermediaries. Wholesalers provide a variety of functions for their customers, who are buying products for resale or for business use. In addition to storing products and providing an assortment of products for their customers, wholesalers offer delivery, credit, and information about products. Not all wholesalers provide all of these functions. The specific services they offer depend on the type of intermediary involved: merchant wholesalers or agents/brokers.

Merchant Wholesalers

Most wholesalers are independent operators who derive their income from sales of goods produced by a variety of manufacturers. All **merchant wholesalers** take title to merchandise. That is, merchant wholesalers buy and own the goods they resell to other businesses. They usually provide storage and a means of delivery.

A **full-service merchant wholesaler** provides credit, marketing, and merchandising services. Approximately 80 percent of all merchant wholesalers are full-service wholesalers.

Limited-function merchant wholesalers provide only a few services, sometimes merely storage. Their customers are normally small operations that pay cash and pick up their own goods. One such wholesaler, the **drop shipper**, does not even carry inventory or handle the product. Drop shippers receive orders from customers, negotiate with producers to supply goods, take title to them, and arrange for shipment to customers. The drop shipper bears the risks of the transaction until the customer takes title to the goods.

Other limited-function wholesalers, known as **rack jobbers**, market consumer goods—mostly nonfood items—directly to retail stores.[17] Procter & Gamble, for example, uses rack jobbers to distribute products like Pampers diapers. After marking prices, setting up display racks, and displaying diapers in one store, the rack jobber moves on to another outlet to check inventories and shelve products.

rack jobber
A full-function merchant wholesaler specializing in nonfood merchandise that sets up and maintains display racks of some products in retail stores.

Agents and Brokers

Agents and brokers serve as sales forces for various manufacturers. They are independent representatives of many companies' products. They work on commissions, usually about 4 to 5 percent of net sales. Unlike merchant wholesalers, they do not take title to—that is, they do not own—the merchandise they sell. Rather, they serve as the sales and merchandising arms of manufacturers that do not have their own sales forces.

Consider, for instance, the role of On Air Digital Audio as an *e-agent* (or *shopping agent*). Corporate clients need the right kind of voices for radio ads; likewise, voice talents are looking for jobs. As the intermediary between clients and artists, On Air Digital transmits ad scripts and artists' readings electronically and, in doing so, saves clients time. Samples from On Air's voice bank are transmitted digitally to clients who scan and select the best voices. On Air then arranges for the artist to record the message, receives it electronically, and sends it electronically to the client, thus avoiding the cost entailed in mailing CDs and tapes back and forth.[18]

The value of agents and brokers lies primarily in their knowledge of markets and their merchandising expertise. They also provide a wide range of services, including shelf and display merchandising and advertising layout. Finally, they maintain product saleability by removing open, torn, or dirty packages, arranging products neatly, and generally keeping them attractively displayed. Many supermarket products are handled through brokers.

On Air Digital Audio
www.onair.ca

The Advent of the E-Intermediary

The ability of e-commerce to bring together millions of widely dispersed consumers and businesses continues to change the types and roles of intermediaries in distribution channels. **E-intermediaries** are Internet-based distribution-channel members that perform one or both of two functions: (1) they collect information about sellers and present it in convenient form to consumers, or (2) they help deliver Internet products to consumers. Internet intermediaries such as Chapters.com and Amazon.com account for sales to millions of consumers who otherwise might walk into traditional retail outlets instead of shopping online. In addition to these well-known examples, however, other major intermediaries are emerging for both consumers and business customers. We will examine three types of emerging e-intermediaries: *syndicated sellers, shopping agents,* and *business-to-business brokers.*

e-intermediaries
Internet-based distribution-channel members that collect information about sellers and present it in convenient form to consumers and/or help deliver Internet products to consumers.

Syndicated Sellers

The early years of the Internet spawned widely held expectations that traditional intermediaries would be eliminated by producers selling directly to consumers. The resulting shorter supply chains would lower costs and consumers would benefit from lower prices. Although this has happened in some cases, new and unexpected cyber-intermediaries also have emerged. One of these new marketing developments, called **syndicated selling**, occurs when

syndicated selling
Occurs when a Web site offers other Web sites a commission for referring customers.

a Web site offers other Web sites a commission for referring customers. In effect, the site receiving the commission is a new type of intermediary that channels customers to an end site for their purchases. One such company is Expedia.com, which, with 7.5 million users, was the most-visited Web site for travel services in 1999. Expedia has given Uniglobe.com, the online travel agent described earlier, a special cruise section on its Web page. When Expedia customers click on the Uniglobe banner ad, they are transferred from the Expedia site to the Uniglobe site. Uniglobe pays a fee to Expedia for each booking that comes through this channel. Although the new intermediary increases the cost of Uniglobe's supply chain, it adds value for customers who avoid endless searches in cyberspace and are efficiently guided to experts specializing in recreational cruises.[19]

Shopping Agents

shopping agent (e-agent)
A type of intermediary that helps Internet consumers by gathering and sorting information they need to make purchases.

Another new type of intermediary is the **shopping agent** (or **e-agent**). Shopping agents help Internet consumers by gathering and sorting information they need to make purchases. They do not, however, take possession of any products. The e-agent knows which Web sites and stores to visit, shows accurate comparison prices, identifies product features, and helps consumers complete transactions by pulling information from worldwide sites, sorting it, and presenting it, in a usable format, in a matter of seconds. PriceScan is a well-known shopping agent for computer products. For CDs and tapes, evenbetter.com will search for vendors, do price comparisons (including shipping costs), list the prices from low to high, and then transfer you to the Web sites of up to 50 different e-stores.[20]

Business-to-Business Brokers

E-commerce intermediaries have also emerged for business customers. Consider the start-up Internet company efdex (which stands for *electronic food and drink*

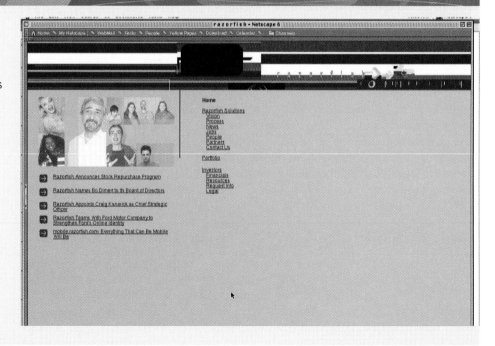

WEBCONNEXION

Boasting a client list that includes Time Warner, Charles Schwab, and the Smithsonian, Razorfish is a consulting firm for companies that conduct or want to conduct e-commerce. To find out how the company promotes digital technology in the building of new business models, including new channels and new value chains, log on to its Web site at:

www.razorfish.com

exchange). The concept is a massive food exchange to buy and sell foodstuffs that are needed (on the buyers' side) by food manufacturers, restaurants, grocers, and farmers and (on the sellers' side) by a wide variety of agri-businesses. Established first in the United Kingdom in early 2000, efdex plans to be operating soon in North America and Europe. Like a stock exchange, its Web site provides up-to-date market information and price and product data from both suppliers and buyers—all listed by type and size of business. Efdex enables businesses to buy and sell from one another and confirm transactions electronically. As a broker, Efdex does not take possession of products. Rather, it functions to bring together timely information and business-to-business exchange linkages.[21]

RETAILING

You probably have had little contact with merchant wholesalers, merchandise brokers, or manufacturers. If you are like most Canadians, you buy nearly all the goods and services you consume from retailers. Most retailers are small operations, often consisting of just the owners and part-time help. But there are a few very large retailers, and these account for billions of dollars of sales each year (see Table 17.2 for a top 10 list of retailers in Canada).

In the past few years, U.S. retailers have become very aggressive in expanding into Canada. American Eagle Outfitters Inc. bought the Braemar Women's Wear chain in 2000. It converted 35 Braemar stores to American Eagle stores, which sell mid-priced basics to the 16 to 34 age group. It also purchased Dylex's 115 Thrifty's outlets and changed their name to Bluenotes.[22] Old Navy, the discount division of California-based Gap Inc., also set up shop in Canada in 2001.

Types of Retail Outlets

Retail operations in Canada vary as widely by type as they do by size. They can be classified in various ways: by pricing strategies, location, range of services, or range of product lines. Choosing the right types of retail outlets is a crucial aspect of every seller's distribution strategy. Consider the experience of the Sara Lee Corp., whose name usually conjures visions of cheesecake and chocolate brownies. The Sara Lee of the twenty-first century, however, has as much to do with pantyhose as it does with pies. To achieve broad distribution on its pantyhose line, Sara Lee had to design product lines that

Table 17.2	The Top 10 Retailers in Canada (ranked by revenues)
Company	**Annual Revenues (in billions)**
1. Hudson's Bay Co.	$7.2
2. Sears Canada Inc.	6.1
3. Canadian Tire Corp. Ltd.	4.7
4. Costco Canada Inc.	3.0
5. Liquor Control Board of Ontario	2.3
6. Future Shop Ltd.	1.9
7. The Katz Group	1.5
8. Société des alcools du Québec	1.2
9. Dylex Ltd.	1.0
10. Hartco Enterprises Inc.	0.8

Note: Wal-Mart is the largest retailer in Canada, but it has no Canadian subsidiary.

appealed to a variety of retailers. To appeal to food retailers, Sara Lee developed two inexpensive hosiery lines: L'Eggs and Just My Size. In this section, we describe retail stores by using two classifications: *product line retailers* and *bargain retailers*.

Product Line Retailers

Retailers that feature broad product lines include *department stores, supermarkets,* and *hypermarkets; specialty stores* are typified by narrow product lines.

Department Stores.   As the name implies, **department stores** are organized into specialized departments: shoes, furniture, women's petite sizes, and so on. Department stores are usually large and handle a wide range of goods. In addition, they usually offer a variety of services, such as generous return policies, credit plans, and delivery.

High-end department stores offer attractive surroundings, sometimes with entertainment, that create the atmosphere that affluent shoppers seem to demand. Others offer rock-bottom pricing as their distinguishing feature. But those in between, without distinctive differentiating features, are at risk of failure. For example, the collapse of Eaton's, one of Canada's most famous department stores, occurred due to lack of a clear identity.

Supermarkets.   The shift from the small corner grocery to supermarkets began in the 1930s. Like department stores, **supermarkets** are divided into departments of related products: food products, household products, and so forth. The emphasis is on low prices, self-service, and wide selection. The largest supermarkets are chain stores such as Safeway and Loblaws.

Online supermarkets are now in the infancy stage. Shoppers like the convenience of e-shopping: logging onto a Web site, browsing electronic "aisles," choosing grocery categories—soups, snacks, baby foods, etc.—filling a grocery cart, paying online, and receiving delivery at home. But most shoppers still prefer the bricks-and-mortar store that is more familiar and easier to navigate. They want to test first-hand the freshness, colour, and texture of food products before selecting them.[23]

department stores
Large retail stores that offer a wide variety of high-quality items divided into specialized departments.

supermarkets
Large retail stores that offer a variety of food and food-related items divided into specialized departments.

Although supermarkets are beginning to feel pressure from such Internet retailers as WebVan Group and priceline.com, they are responding with technology-oriented conveniences of their own. At this Stop & Shop supermarket in Massachusetts, a customer uses a handheld price scanner to speed her trip through the checkout line; when she gets to the cashier, she will simply hand over the scanner and a credit card. Stop & Shop is owned by a Dutch firm called Royal Ahold, which is the fourth-largest food retailer in the United States.

Hypermarkets. A phenomenon begun in the 1970s, **hypermarkets** are much larger than supermarkets (up to 200 000 square feet) and sell a much wider variety of products. They also practice **scrambled merchandising**: carrying any product, whether similar or dissimilar to the store's original product offering, that promises to sell. Hypermarché Laval near Montreal is an example of a hypermarket.

Specialty Stores. **Specialty stores** are small stores that carry one line of related products. They serve clearly defined market segments by offering full product lines in narrow product fields and often feature knowledgeable sales personnel. Sunglass Hut International, for example, has 1600 outlets carrying a deep selection of sunglasses at competitive prices. Its stores in Canada, the U.S., Europe, and Australia are located in malls, airports, and anywhere else that is convenient for quick, one-stop shopping. "People's time," contends CEO Jack Chadsey, "is so limited, they don't want to walk through a maze of categories. If they're looking for electronics, they're going to go to an electronics specialty store. Sunglasses are no different."

Particularly in the apparel industry, the 1980s were the decade of the specialty store. Between 1980 and 1990, retailers such as The Gap, The Limited, and Ann Taylor spearheaded the growth spurt of a multibillion-dollar industry in stylish upscale clothing. More apparel manufacturers are entering the retail industry. Companies such as Timberland (outdoor wear), Tommy Hilfiger (casual clothing), OshKosh B'Gosh (children's clothes), and Speedo (swim and athletic wear) have all opened showcase outlets in specialty shopping centres and large malls.

Retailers who carry an extremely deep selection of goods in a relatively narrow product line and hire technical experts to give customers advice are called **category killers**. They are so named because they carry virtually everything within a certain category. Home Depot is an example of a category killer. It sells building materials, lawn and garden supplies, and home improvement products.

Bargain Retailers

Bargain retailers carry a wide range of products and come in many forms. Included in this category are *discount houses, catalogue showrooms, factory outlets, warehouse clubs*, and *convenience stores*.

Discount Houses. After the Second World War, some retailers began offering discounts to certain customers. These first **discount houses** sold large numbers of items such as televisions and other appliances by featuring substantial price reductions. As name-brand items became more plentiful in the early 1950s, discounters offered even better product assortments while still embracing a philosophy of cash-only sales conducted in low-rent facilities. As they became more firmly entrenched, they began moving to better locations, improving decor, and selling better-quality merchandise at higher prices. They also began offering a few department store services, such as credit plans and noncash sales. Zellers and Wal-Mart are discount houses.

Catalogue Showrooms. Another form of bargain store that has grown dramatically in recent years is the **catalogue showroom**. These firms mail out catalogues with colour pictures, product descriptions, and prices to attract customers into their showrooms. Once there, customers view display samples, place orders, and wait briefly while clerks retrieve orders from attached warehouses.

Factory Outlets. **Factory outlets** are manufacturer-owned stores that avoid wholesalers and retailers by selling merchandise directly from the factory to consumers. The first factory outlets featured apparel, linens, food, and furniture. Because they were usually located in warehouse-like facilities next to the factories, distribution costs were quite low. Lower costs were passed on to customers as lower prices.

Warehouse Clubs.   The **warehouse club** (or **wholesale club**) offers large discounts on brand-name clothing, groceries, appliances, automotive supplies, and other merchandise. Unlike customers at discount houses and factory outlets, club customers pay annual membership fees. The first warehouse club, Price Club, opened in 1976. It merged with rival Costco in 1993, and today the sales of the combined company, called Costco, total US$24 billion each year—tops among warehouse clubs. Selling everything from salmon to diamonds, Costco isn't complacent with its current success. It has expanded into e-retailing with CostcoOnline, where you can take out a club membership, chat with other members, and shop electronically. Expanding beyond the United States, Costco buys in bulk for its warehouse stores in Canada, South Korea, Japan, Taiwan, and Britain. When its Watford, England, store opened, the Costco concept surprised local customers: "At first people said, 'Huh? You don't buy rubber boats where you buy baked beans,'" recalls Jim Murphy, manager of seven stores in the U.K. locations.[24]

Traditional retailers such as Canada Safeway generate 80 percent of their sales from just 20 percent of the products they carry. By contrast, warehouse clubs stock only the 20 percent and sell huge volumes of it at low margins. Supermarkets carry about 20 000 items, but warehouse clubs carry only about 3500. The typical warehouse club margin is 8 percent, while at more traditional discount stores the margin can be up to 40 percent. By carrying only the top-selling brands, warehouse clubs have been able to expand their product lines into non-grocery items such as appliances, consumer electronics, tools, and office supplies.

Convenience Stores.   Neighbourhood food retailers such as 7-Eleven and Circle K stores are successful convenience store chains. As the name suggests, **convenience stores** offer ease of purchase. They stress easily accessible locations with parking, extended store hours (in many cases 24 hours), and speedy service. They differ from most bargain retailers in that they do not feature low prices. Like bargain retailers, however, they control prices by keeping in-store service levels to a minimum.

Changes in Retailing: The Wheel of Retailing

The **wheel of retailing** concept shows how retail stores evolve over time. The "wheel" works like this: A new retailer emerges primarily because existing stores have become overpriced. The new retailer initially keeps prices down by providing fewer services, selling unknown brands, or locating in a low-rent area. But as the new retailer gets a foothold in the market, it wants to expand its market share. So it begins to offer more services, sells name-brand merchandise, and upgrades its stores facilities. But this increases costs, so it begins charging higher prices to consumers. This, in turn, creates a gap in the low-price end of the market, and even newer retailers move in to fill that gap.

Kmart is a good example of the wheel of retailing concept. It initially offered low-priced products in converted warehouses. But over the years it built new stores, remodelled others, and began offering higher-quality merchandise. In response, a large number of "bargain barns" have sprung up to fill the gap that was created as Kmart moved up.

---

warehouse club (wholesale club)
Huge, membership-only, combined retail-wholesale operations that sell brand-name merchandise.

convenience stores
Retail stores that offer high accessibility, extended hours, and fast service on selected items.

wheel of retailing
The idea that retail stores evolve over time from low-priced stores that provide few services in simple surroundings to higher-priced stores that provide many services in more upscale surroundings.

In 1993, top management at Costco warehouse clubs began to worry that its American market had become saturated. That particular concern turned out to be unwarranted, but it prompted Costco to expand into other countries. The company now operates 20 warehouse stores in Great Britain, Taiwan, South Korea, and Japan. The Costco concept— low prices on high-quality merchandise available to members only—travels well: This store in the London suburb of Watford, England, is one of the chain's most successful outlets anywhere.

Nonstore and Electronic Retailing

Not all goods and services are sold in stores. In fact, some of the nation's largest retailers sell all or most of their products without bricks-and-mortar stores. For example, certain types of consumer goods—soft drinks, candy, and cigarettes—lend themselves to distribution in vending machines. However, vending machine sales still represent only a small proportion of all retail sales. And so-called "e-tailing" sales are expected to increase sharply during the next few years as people shop online with their personal computers.

In this section, we will survey a few of the more important forms of nonstore retailing. In particular, we will examine **direct-response retailing**, in which firms make direct contact with customers both to inform them about products and to receive sales orders. This type of retailing includes *mail marketing, mail order (catalogue marketing), telemarketing, direct selling*, and *electronic retailing* (including *video shopping*).

direct-response retailing
A type of retailing in which firms make direct contact with customers both to inform them about products and to receive sales orders.

Mail Marketing

Direct-mail marketing results in billions of sales dollars annually in both retail and industrial sales. Direct mail is effective because it targets audiences that have been identified from research lists as likely to be interested in specific products. The single mailings sent by insurance companies, magazine and book publishers, and clothing and furniture stores are expensive direct-mail promotions. These various pamphlets, letters, brochures, and convenient order forms result in high-response sales rates. Charities rely on direct mail as a primary fundraising method. Although mail-order responses are increasing at both for-profit and non-profit organizations, the industry faces difficulties from increasing postal rates and a backlash against the accumulation of unwanted catalogues in customers' mailboxes.

Mail Order (or Catalogue Marketing)

In retailing, the world's largest mail-order business is run by Otto Versand, a privately held company based in Hamburg, Germany. Company founder

Werner Versand began in mail order back in 1950 by pasting pictures of shoes in hand-bound catalogues. Today, with annual sales topping US$13 billion, Otto Versand has used mail order to build itself into one of the world's biggest multinational retailers. In addition to mail-order companies in Hungary, Japan, Italy, France, Britain, and Germany, Otto Versand owns 90 percent of Spiegel and its Eddie Bauer subsidiary in the United States.

mail order (catalogue marketing)
A form of nonstore retailing in which customers place orders for merchandise shown in catalogues and receive their orders via mail.

Firms which, like Versand, sell by **mail order** (or **catalogue marketing**) typically send out splashy colour catalogues describing a variety of merchandise. Although mail-order selling has existed for a long time, computer technology and telephone charge transactions have made it a booming industry in recent years. Advances in communication technologies are permitting mail-order cataloguers to expand by targeting overseas customers. Armed with 24-hour international toll-free phone lines, overnight delivery, inexpensive fax machines, and credit-card offers, catalogue marketers find consumers in many foreign countries.

Telemarketing

telemarketing
Use of the telephone to sell directly to consumers.

Telemarketing is the use of the telephone to sell directly to consumers. WATS (wide area telephone service) lines can be used to receive toll-free calls from consumers responding to television and radio ads. Using live or automated dialling, message delivery, and order taking, telemarketers can also use WATS lines to call consumers to promote products and services. Telemarketing is used not only for consumer goods but also for industrial goods and insurance and accounting services. Currently, telemarketing is experiencing exceptional growth in Canada, the United States, and Great Britain. Sales topped US$600 billion in 2000.[25]

Direct Selling

direct selling
A form of nonstore selling sometimes called door-to-door sales.

The oldest form of retailing, **direct selling** is still used by companies that sell door-to-door or through home-selling parties. Most of us have talked with salespeople from World Book, Avon, or Fuller Brush as they make door-to-door sales calls.

The Fuller Brush Company was started in 1906 by Arthur Fuller, a self-described "country bumpkin" from Nova Scotia. The company used to be well known in door-to-door selling, but sweeping changes in North American society—women leaving the home to work, mass retailing, and the globalization of business—caused the company to fall on hard times. Two of its most famous salesmen were the Reverend Billy Graham and disc jockey Dick Clark. The company has continued to be successful in Mexico and Argentina, where direct selling still works well. In 1999, operating under the House of Fuller name, the company sold more than $200 million worth of goods.[26]

Direct selling is also common in the wholesaling of such industrial goods as commercial photocopying equipment. Although direct selling is convenient and gives customers one-on-one attention, prices are usually driven up by labour costs (salespeople often receive commissions of 40 to 50 cents on every sales dollar). Worldwide, 9 million direct salespeople now generate annual sales of $35 billion. In Japan alone, for instance, 1.2 million distributors have made Amway Corp. second only to Coca-Cola as the most profitable foreign retailer.[27]

Electronic Retailing

Electronic retailing is made possible by communications networks that allow sellers to connect to consumers' computers with digital information about products. With over 1.5 million subscribers, Prodigy Communications Corp., which was formed as a joint venture of IBM and Sears, is among the largest

WEBCONNEXION

Grocery Gateway is geared towards busy professionals who don't have time to go to the grocery store themselves. It offers competitive name-brand grocery products and reasonably priced delivery. Customers order online and indicate a specific time when they would like their groceries delivered. Grocery Gateway employs individuals to actually do the shopping for people. Items are picked from the company's Market Centre in Mississauga, Ontario. When the groceries are delivered, customers can pay by credit card, cash, or cheque at their doors. Visit Grocery Gateway at:

www.grocerygateway.com

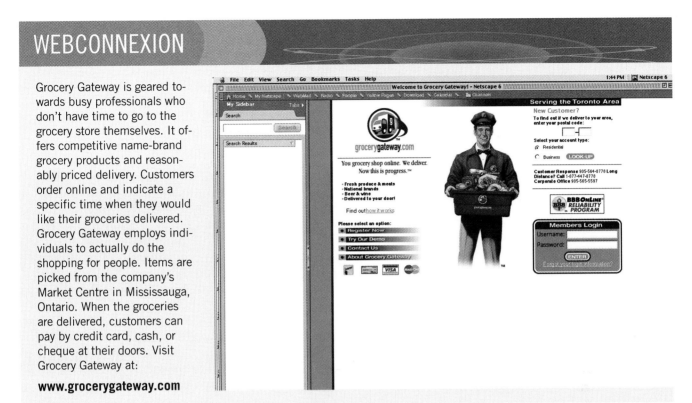

home networks. Customers include individuals as well as small to medium-sized businesses. Prodigy provides members with access to the Internet and displays of available products ranging from travel packages to financial services to consumer goods. The viewer can examine detailed descriptions, compare brands, send for free information, or purchase by credit card from home. As an industry leader in Internet shopping transactions, Prodigy operates with networks throughout the world.[28]

One of the toughest problems e-tailers face is how to get products bought online to customers, particularly when those customers are often not at home. Setting up their own delivery system is too expensive for all but the biggest online retailers. So, partnerships are popping up. Empori.com is one such partnership. Its depots serve as product pickup and return centres for many different online retailers such as Chapters, HMV.com, and the Liquor Control Board of Ontario. Bradley Moseley-Williams, for example bought a bottle of Australian wine, a book, and a compact disc online, and then picked them up at the Empori.com depot in Toronto's Royal Bank Plaza.[29]

Internet-Based Stores.   Use of the Internet to interact with customers—to inform them, to sell to them, and to distribute to them—is starting to grow rapidly. E-retail sales were 13 times higher in 2000 than they were in 1997. However, a study released by Statistics Canada in 2000 showed that e-commerce still accounted for only 20 cents of every $100 of retail sales in 1999.[30] There is a lot of room for growth, and huge growth prospects are fuelling the scramble among firms to position themselves in the e-business industry.[31]

Electronic Catalogues.   **E-catalogues** use the Internet to display products and services for both retail shoppers and business customers. By sending an electronic version (instead of traditional mail catalogues), firms provide millions of users with instant access to pages of products. Naturally, the seller avoids mail distribution and printing costs. Moreover, once the online catalogue is in place, there is little cost in maintaining and accessing it. Recognizing these advantages, about 85 percent of all cataloguers are now on

e-catalogues

Use the Internet to display products and services for both retail shoppers and business customers.

the Internet, with sales via Web sites accounting for 10 percent of all catalogue sales. The top 10 consumer e-catalogues include such names as J.C. Penney (#1), Fingerhut (#3), L.L. Bean (#7), and Victoria's Secret (#8). Top business-to-business e-catalogues include Dell Computer (#1) and Office Depot (#5).[32]

Electronic Storefronts and Cybermalls.   Pioneer Internet shoppers of just five years ago can readily appreciate the friendly browsing offered by today's e-storefronts. A seller's Web site is an **electronic storefront** in which consumers collect information about products and buying opportunities, place sales orders, and pay for their purchases. Sites are also called *virtual storefronts* because digital imaging gives them the appearance of a store that may not exist in real bricks and mortar. Producers of large product lines, such as Dell Computer, have storefronts dedicated to their own product lines. Other sites, such as CDNOW, which offers CDs and audio and video tapes, are category sellers whose storefronts feature products from many manufacturers. Search engines such as Yahoo! serve as **cybermalls**—collections of virtual storefronts representing diverse products. After entering a cybermall, shoppers can navigate easily by choosing from a list of stores (for example, Eddie Bauer), product listings (Pokéman or MP3 players), or departments (apparel or bath and beauty). When your virtual shopping cart is full, you check out and pay your bill. The value-added properties of cybermalls are fairly obvious: speed, convenience, 24-hour access, and, most importantly, an efficient search that avoids the "click-'til-you-drop" syndrome—the endless wandering through cyberspace experienced by early Internet users.

From Door to Door to E-Sales?   Not surprisingly, cyberspace is encroaching on door-to-door distribution channels. Amway, for example, is famous for its **multilevel marketing** channel in which self-employed distributors are paid commissions for recruiting new customers and new Amway representatives. Now Amway is expanding its system of mutilevel marketing onto the Internet with a spinoff called Quixstar. With assistance from Quixstar, you can start your own at-home Internet business. You will be paid for directing new customers to the Quixstar site and for encouraging others to become Quixstar reps. The Internet's huge at-home sales potential is also luring other famous door-to-door names—Tupperware, Avon, and Mary Kay. Such firms are racing to board the Internet even though they are courting potential channel conflict. In all probability, millions of loyal door-to-door sales reps will lose customers to their companies' Internet outlets.[33]

Interactive and Video Marketing.   E-stores no longer provide just numerical data and pictures. Today, both retail and business-to-business customers interact with multimedia Web sites using voice, graphics, animation, film clips, and access to live human advice. One good example of **interactive marketing** is LivePerson, a leading provider of real-time sales and customer service for over 450 Web sites. When customers log onto the Web sites of, say, IgoGolf, they enter a live chat room where a service operator initiates a secure one-on-one text chat. Questions and answers go back and forth to give customers user-friendly personal service during the crucial moments when they have specific questions that must be answered before they decide on a product. Another form of interaction is the so-called *banner ad* that changes as the user's mouse moves about on the Web page, revealing new drop-down boxes, check boxes, and search boxes.[34]

Video marketing, a long-established form of interactive marketing, allows viewers to shop at home from television screens. Most cable systems offer video marketing through home-shopping channels that display and demonstrate products—jewellery, dinnerware, home-accessory items, and even real estate—and allow viewers to phone in or e-mail orders. One home-shopping network, QVC, launched iQVC, its interactive Web site.

electronic storefront
A seller's Web site in which consumers collect information about products and buying opportunities, place sales orders, and pay for their purchases.

cybermalls
Collections of virtual storefronts representing diverse products.

multilevel marketing
A system in which a salesperson earns a commission on their own sales and on the sales of any other salespeople they recruit.

interactive marketing
Selling products and services by allowing customers to interact with multimedia Web sites using voice, graphics, animation, film clips, and access to live human advice.

video marketing
Selling to consumers by showing products on television that consumers can buy by telephone or mail.

PHYSICAL DISTRIBUTION

Physical distribution refers to the activities needed to move products efficiently from manufacturer to consumer. The goals of physical distribution are to keep customers satisfied, to make goods available when and where consumers want them, and to keep costs low. Thus physical distribution includes *customer-service operations* such as order processing, as well as *warehousing* and *transporting operations*.

physical distribution
Those activities needed to move a product from the manufacturer to the end consumer.

Customer-Service Operations

Often the customer's only direct contact with the seller is to place an order. Thus **order processing**—filling orders as they are received—strongly affects how customers view the firm's efficiency and cooperation. The behaviour of order-entry personnel can make or break a firm's reputation.

order processing
In a product's distribution, the receiving and filling of orders.

To please customers and assure repeat business, companies need to offer fast, convenient, and polite service. Bass Pro Shops' (fishing and recreational products) catalogue sales has a toll-free number that is answered quickly by courteous, knowledgeable employees. They offer customers different methods of paying for purchases and indicate when and how an order will arrive.

Many companies set standards for order-cycle times. **Order-cycle time** is the total amount of time from when the order is placed to when the customer receives the goods. Companies that can achieve rapid order-cycle times may have a competitive edge over less efficient firms. Some customers are willing to pay extra to receive their purchases faster, rather than having to wait.

order-cycle time
The total amount of time from order placement to when the customer actually receives the order.

Order Fulfilment and E-Customer Satisfaction

New e-commerce companies often focus on Internet sales, only to discover that after-sale distribution delays cause customer dissatisfaction and discourage repeat sales. Any delay in physical distribution, then, is a breakdown in fulfilment and an obstacle to growth. Order fulfilment begins when the sale is made. It involves getting the product, in good condition and on time, to the customer for each sales transaction. Fulfilment performance has been disappointing for some e-businesses, especially during busy holiday seasons.

To improve on-time deliveries, many businesses, such as Amazon.com, maintain their own distribution centres and ship themselves from their own warehouses near major shipping hubs. Other e-tailers, however, entrust their order-filling services to distribution specialists such as Fingerhut Business Services Inc. and Keystone Fulfillment Inc. Fingerhut, whose clients include Wal-Mart Stores, Levi Strauss, and Etoys, boasts a 1.2-million-square-foot, high-tech distribution centre that employs up to 1200 workers during the holiday peak. Fingerhut processes customer orders, ships items, provides information about product availability, informs customers about the real-time status of orders, and handles returns for their clients. For Fingerhut to do all this, the client e-tailer's computer system must be integrated with the distributor's system.

In deciding whether to build their own distribution centres or to use a third-party distributor, e-tailers must keep in mind the fixed costs as well as the shipping expertise they will need. The capital investment required for a 1-million-square-foot distribution centre is $60 to $80 million; only a high-volume business can afford it. The alternative is to pay a third-party distributor about 10 percent of each sale to fulfil orders, but only after ensuring that they will make reliable on-time deliveries.[35]

Warehousing Operations

Storing or **warehousing** products is a major function of distribution management. In selecting a warehousing strategy, managers must keep in mind the characteristics and costs of warehousing operations.

Types of Warehouses

There are two basic types of warehouses: private and public. Within these categories, we can further divide warehouses according to their use as storage sites or as distribution centres.

The first type, **private warehouses**, are owned by and provide storage for just one company, be it a manufacturer, a wholesaler, or a retailer. Most are used by large firms that deal in mass quantities and need storage regularly.

Public warehouses are independently owned and operated. Companies that use these warehouses pay for the actual space used. Public warehouses are popular with firms that need such storage only during peak business periods. They are also used by manufacturers who want to maintain stock in numerous locations in order to get their products to many markets quickly.

Storage warehouses provide storage for extended periods of time. Producers of seasonal items, such as agricultural crops, most often use this type of warehouse. In contrast, **distribution centres** store products whose market demand is constant and quite high. They are used by retail chains, wholesalers, and manufacturers that need to break large quantities produced or bought into the smaller quantities their stores or customers demand.

Warehousing Costs

All warehouse types involve costs. These costs include obvious expenses such as storage space rental or mortgage payments (usually computed by square foot), insurance, and wages. They also include the costs of inventory control and materials handling. **Inventory control** is a vital part of warehouse operations. It goes beyond keeping track of what is on hand at any time and involves planning to ensure that an adequate supply of a product is in stock at all times—a tricky balancing act.

Materials handling is the transportation, arrangement, and orderly retrieval of goods in inventory. Most warehouse personnel are employed in materials handling. Keeping materials handling costs down requires managers to develop a strategy for storing a company's products that takes into account product locations within the warehouse. One strategy for managing materials is **unitization**, a method that standardizes the weight and form of materials and makes storage and handling more systematic. To reduce the high costs of materials handling, more and more warehouses are automating. Computerized systems can move, store, and retrieve items from storage in the warehouse.

Transportation Operations

Transportation, for both passengers and freight is big business, with the top 50 transportation companies generating over $400 billion in sales revenue each year. The major transportation modes are rail, water, truck, air, and pipelines. In the early part of the twentieth century, railroads dominated the Canadian transportation system, but by the 1970s, truck and air transportation had become much more important.

Cost is a major factor when a company chooses a transportation method. The difference in cost among the various transportation modes is directly

warehousing
That part of the distribution process concerned with storing goods.

private warehouses
Warehouses owned and used by just one company.

public warehouses
Independently owned and operated warehouses that store the goods of many firms.

storage warehouses
Warehouses used to provide storage of goods for extended periods of time.

distribution centres
Warehouses used to provide storage of goods for only short periods before they are shipped to retail stores.

inventory control
The part of warehouse operations that keeps track of what is on hand and ensures adequate supplies of products in stock at all times.

materials handling
The transportation and arrangement of goods within a warehouse and orderly retrieval of goods from inventory.

unitization
A materials handling strategy in which goods are transported and stored in containers with a uniform size, shape, and/or weight.

related to the speed of delivery. The higher the speed of delivery, the greater the cost. But cost is not the only consideration. A company must also consider the nature of its products, the distance the product must travel, timeliness, and customers' needs and wants. A company shipping orchids or other perishable goods will probably use air transport, while a company shipping sand or coal will use rail or water transport.

Trucks

The advantages of trucks include flexibility, fast service, and dependability. Nearly all sections of Canada, except the far north, can be reached by truck. Trucks are a particularly good choice for short-distance distribution and more expensive products. Large furniture and appliance retailers in major cities, for example, use trucks to shuttle merchandise between their stores and to make deliveries to customers. Trucks can, however, be delayed by bad weather. They also are limited in the volume they can carry in a single load.

More and more manufacturers are using **expedited transportation**, which involves paying a higher-than-normal fee for truck delivery in return for guaranteed delivery times. Even this higher fee is still cheaper than air freight.[36]

expedited transportation
Paying a higher-than-normal fee for truck delivery for guaranteed delivery times.

Planes

Air is the fastest available transportation mode. In Canada's far north, it may be the only available transportation. Other advantages include greatly reduced costs in packing, handling, unpacking, and final preparations necessary for sale to the consumer. Also, inventory-carrying costs can be reduced by eliminating the need to store certain commodities. Fresh fish, for example, can be flown to restaurants each day, avoiding the risk of spoilage that comes with packaging and storing. However, air freight is the most expensive form of transportation. In recent years a whole new industry has evolved to meet the customer's need to receive important business papers and supplies "overnight."

Railroads

Railroads have been the backbone of our transportation system since the late 1800s. Until the 1960s, when trucking firms lowered their rates and attracted many customers, railroads were fairly profitable. They are now used primarily to transport heavy, bulky items such as cars, steel, and coal.

A container train crosses the Salmon River bridge in New Brunswick.

Water Carriers

Of all the transportation modes, water transportation is the least expensive. Unfortunately, water transportation is also the slowest way to ship. Boats and barges are mainly used for extremely heavy, bulky materials and products (like sand, gravel, oil, and steel) for which transit times are unimportant. Manufacturers are beginning to use water carriers more often because many ships are now specially constructed to load and store large standardized containers. The St. Lawrence Seaway is a vital link in Canada's water transportation system.

Water transportation is particularly important in Canada's far north. Northern Transportation Co. Ltd. has 90 barges, 9 seagoing tugboats, and 250 employees. The company uses barges to deliver commodities such as fuel oil to various isolated hamlets along the western edge of Hudson's Bay during the summer months. Each barge has a capacity of 4000 tonnes.[37]

Pipelines

Like water transportation, pipelines are slow in terms of overall delivery time. They are also completely inflexible, but they do provide a constant flow of the product and are unaffected by weather conditions. Traditionally, this delivery system has transported liquids and gases. Lack of adaptability to other products and limited routes make pipelines a relatively unimportant transportation method for most industries.

Intermodal Transportation

intermodal transportation
The combined use of different modes of transportation.

containerization
The use of standardized heavy-duty containers in which many items are sealed at the point of shipment and opened only at the final destination.

Intermodal transportation—the combined use of different modes of transportation—has come into widespread use. For example, shipping by a combination of truck and rail ("piggy-back"), water and rail ("fishy back"), or air and rail ("birdyback") has improved flexibility and reduced costs.

To make intermodal transport more efficient, **containerization** uses standardized heavy-duty containers in which many items are sealed at points of shipment and opened only at final destinations. On the trip, containers may be loaded onto ships for ocean transit, transferred onto trucks, loaded on railcars, and delivered to final destinations by other trucks. The containers are then unloaded and returned for future use. International Cargo Management Systems has developed a device that is attached to the inside of containers being shipped. The device pulls in signals from global positioning satellites to determine the container's latitude and longitude. The device then transmits this information to computers at a tracking centre. Customers can call the tracking centre to determine where their package is at any moment.[38]

Companies Specializing in Transportation

The major modes of transportation are available from one or more of four types of transporting companies: common carriers, freight forwarders, contract carriers, and private carriers. Table 17.3 shows the top 10 transportation companies in Canada.

common carriers
Transportation companies that transport goods for any firm or individual wishing to make a shipment.

The nation's **common carriers** transport merchandise for any shipper—manufacturers, wholesalers, retailers, and even individual consumers. They maintain regular schedules and charge competitive prices. The best examples of common carriers are truck lines and railroads.

In 1897, the *Crow's Nest Pass Agreement* established the rate that railways could charge for hauling grain. This agreement was essentially a freight subsidy that helped prairie farmers pay some of their transportation costs to distant ports. But in 1995, the Liberal government abolished the Crow

Table 17.3	The Top 10 Transportation Companies in Canada (ranked by revenues)	

Company	Annual Revenues (in billions)
1. Air Canada	$6.5
2. Canada Post Corp.	5.3
3. Canadian National Railway Co.	5.2
4. Laidlaw Inc.	3.4
5. Canadian Airlines Corp.	3.2
6. NAV CANADA	0.9
7. Trimac Corp.	0.6
8. Fednav Ltd.	0.5
9. Vitran Corp. Inc.	0.4
10. British Columbia Rail Co.	0.4

subsidy. Freight rates increased for prairie farmers, which caused them to reduce their emphasis on growing wheat and increase their emphasis on raising livestock.[39] Since the Crow rate was eliminated, livestock production and agricultural processing have increased on the prairies.

Not all transportation companies own their own vehicles. A **freight forwarder** is a common carrier that leases bulk space from other carriers, such as railroads or airlines. It then resells parts of that space to smaller shippers. Once it has enough contracts to fill the bulk space, the freight forwarder picks up whatever merchandise is to be shipped. It then transports the goods to the bulk carrier, which makes delivery to an agreed-on destination, and handles billing and any inquiries concerning the shipment.

Some transportation companies will transport products for any firm for a contracted amount and time period. These **contract carriers** are usually self-employed operators who own the vehicle that transports the products. When they have delivered a contracted load to its destination, they generally try to locate another contract shipment (often with a different manufacturer) for the return trip.

A few manufacturers and retailers maintain their own transportation systems (usually a fleet of trucks) to carry their own products. The use of such **private carriers** is generally limited to very large manufacturers such as Kraft Foods and Canada Safeway.

freight forwarders

Common carriers that lease bulk space from other carriers and resell that space to firms making small shipments.

contract carriers

Independent transporters who contract to serve as transporters for industrial customers only.

private carriers

Transportation systems owned by the shipper.

Distribution as a Marketing Strategy

Distribution is an increasingly important way of competing for sales. Instead of just offering advantages in product features and quality, price, and promotion, many firms have turned to distribution as a cornerstone of their business strategies. This approach means assessing and improving the entire stream of activities—wholesaling, warehousing, transportation—involved in getting products to customers.

Distribution is an increasingly important way of competing for sales. Instead of just offering advantages in product features and quality, price, and promotion, many firms have turned to distribution as a cornerstone of their business strategies. This approach means assessing and improving the entire stream of activities (wholesaling, warehousing, and transportation) involved in getting products to customers. Its importance is illustrated at Molex, a large manufacturer of electronic connectors and switches. The firm's 100 000 products are used by manufacturers of cars, computers, and consumer products who not only want fast, just-in-time delivery but who are becoming more and more globalized. To meet its customers' needs, Molex became the first connector manufacturer to sign distribution agreements on a global basis. Its relationships with Arrow Electronics and Avnet, the world's largest distributors of electronic components, allow Molex to better service customers who want a single worldwide source for their products.

One approach to streamlining is the use of **hubs**: central distribution outlets that control all or most of a firm's distribution activities. Two contrasting strategies have emerged from this approach: *supply-side and "pre-staging" hubs* on the one hand and *distribution-side hubs* on the other.

hub
Central distribution outlet that controls all or most of a firm's distribution activities.

Supply-Side and "Pre-Staging" Hubs

Supply-side hubs make the most sense when large shipments of supplies flow regularly to a single industrial user, such as a large manufacturer. They are used, for example, by automobile factories, where thousands of incoming supplies can arrive by train, truck, and air. The chief job of the hub is to coordinate the customer's materials needs with supply-chain transportation. If the hub is successful, the factory's inventories are virtually eliminated, storage-space requirements are reduced, and long-haul trucks, instead of lining up at the customer's unloading dock, keep moving.

Distribution-Side Hubs

Whereas supply-side hubs are located near industrial customers, distribution-side hubs may be located much farther away, especially if customers are geographically dispersed. National Semiconductor, one of the world's largest chip makers, is an example. National's finished products, silicon microchips, are produced in plants throughout the world and shipped to customers such as IBM, Toshiba, Siemens, Ford, and Compaq at factory locations around the globe. On the journey from producer to customer, chips originally sat waiting at one location after another—on factory floors, at customs, in distributors' facilities, and in customers' warehouses. Typically, they travelled 20 000 different routes on as many as 12 airlines and spent time in 10 warehouses before reaching their customers. National has streamlined its delivery system by shutting down six warehouses around the world. Now it airfreights microchips worldwide from a single distribution centre in Singapore. All of its activities—storage, sorting, shipping—are run by Federal Express. As a result, distribution costs have fallen, delivery times have been reduced by half, and sales have increased.

SUMMARY OF LEARNING OBJECTIVES

1. **Identify the various *pricing objectives* that govern pricing decisions and describe the price-setting tools used in making these decisions.** A firm's *pricing decisions* reflect the *pricing objectives* set by its management. Although these objectives vary, they all reflect the goals that a seller hopes to reach in selling a product. They include *profit maximizing* (pricing to sell the number of units that will generate the highest possible total profits) and *meeting market share goals* (ensuring continuous sales by maintaining a strong percentage of the total sales for a specific product type). Other considerations include the need to survive in a competitive marketplace, social and ethical concerns, and even a firm's image.

    Price-setting tools are chosen to meet a seller's pricing objectives. *Cost-oriented pricing* recognizes the need to cover the variable costs of producing a product (costs that change with the number of units produced or sold). In determining the price level at which profits will be generated, *break-even analysis* also considers *fixed costs* (costs, such as facilities and salaries, that are unaffected by the number of items produced or sold).

2. **Discuss *pricing strategies* and tactics for existing and new products.** Either a *price-skimming strategy* (pricing very high) or *a penetration-pricing strategy* (pricing very low) may be effective for new products. Depending on the other elements in the marketing mix, existing products may be priced at, above, or below prevailing prices for similar products. Guided by a firm's pricing strategies, managers set prices using tactics such as *price lining* (offering items in certain categories at a set number of prices), *psychological pricing* (appealing to buyers' perceptions of relative prices), and *discounting* (reducing prices to stimulate sales).

   The electronic marketplace has introduced two competing pricing systems—dynamic versus fixed. *Dynamic pricing* is feasible because the flow of information on the Internet notifies millions of buyers around the world of instantaneous changes in product availability. Sellers can also alter prices privately, on a customer-to-customer basis, to attract sales that might be lost under traditional fixed-price structures.

3. **Identify the different *channels of distribution* and explain different *distribution strategies*.** In selecting a *distribution mix*, a firm may use all or any of eight *distribution channels*. The first four are aimed at getting products to consumers, the fifth is for consumers or business customers, and the last three are aimed at getting products to business customers. Channel 1 involves direct sales to consumers. Channel 2 includes a *retailer*. Channel 3 involves both a retailer and a *wholesaler*, and Channel 4 includes an *agent* or *broker* who enters the system before the wholesaler and retailer. Channel 5 includes only an agent between the producer and the customer. Channel 6, which is used extensively for e-commerce, involves a direct sale to an industrial user. Channel 7, which is used infrequently, entails selling to business users through wholesalers. Channel 8 includes retail superstores that get products from producers or wholesalers (or both) for re-selling to business customers. *Distribution strategies* include *intensive*, *exclusive*, and *selective distribution*, which differ in the number of products and channel members involved and in the amount of service performed in the channel.

4. **Explain the differences between *merchant wholesalers* and *agents/brokers*.** *Wholesalers* act as distribution *intermediaries*. They may extend credit as well as store, repackage, and deliver products to other members of the channel. *Full-service* and *limited-function merchant wholesalers* differ in the number and types of distribution functions they offer. Unlike wholesalers, *agents* and *brokers* never take legal possession of products. Rather, they function as sales and merchandising arms of manufacturers who do not have their own sales forces. They may also provide such services as advertising and display merchandising. In e-commerce, *e-agents* assist Internet users in finding products and best prices.

5. **Identify the different types of *retailing* and *retail stores*.** *Retailers* can be described according to two classifications: *product line retailers* and *bargain retailers*. Product line retailers include *department stores*, *supermarkets*, *hypermarkets*, and *specialty stores*. Bargain retailers include *discount houses*, *off-price stores, catalogue showrooms, factory outlets, warehouse clubs*, and *convenience stores*. These retailers differ in terms of size, goods and services offered, and pricing. Some retailing also takes place without stores.

   Nonstore retailing may use *direct mail catalogues, vending machines, video marketing, telemarketing, electronic shopping*, and *direct selling*. Internet retail shopping includes *electronic storefronts* where customers can examine a store's products, receive information about sellers and their products, place orders, and make payments electronically. Customers can also visit *cybermalls*—collections of virtual storefronts representing a variety of product lines on the Internet.

6. **Describe the major activities in the *physical distribution process*.** *Physical distribution* includes all the activities needed to move a product from manufacturers to consumers, including *customer service, warehousing,* and *transportation* of products. Warehouses may be *public* or *private* and may function either as long-term *storage warehouses* or as *distribution centres*. In addition to storage, insurance, and wage-related costs, the cost to warehouse goods also includes *inventory control* (maintaining adequate but not excessive supplies) and *materials handling* (transporting, arranging, and retrieving supplies).

7. **Compare the five basic forms of *transportation* and identify the types of firms that provide them.** Trucks, railroads, planes, water carriers (boats and barges), and pipelines are the major *transportation modes* used in the distribution process. They differ in cost, availability, reliability, speed, and number of points served. Air is the fastest but most expensive mode; water carriers are the slowest but least expensive. Since transport companies were deregulated in 1980, they have become more cost-efficient and competitive by developing such innovations as *intermodal transportation* and *containerization*. Transportation in any form may be supplied by *common carriers, freight forwarders, contract carriers,* or *private carriers*.

KEY TERMS

pricing, 540
market share, 541
variable costs, 543
fixed costs, 543
break-even analysis, 543
break-even point, 543
price leadership, 545
price-skimming strategy, 545
penetration-pricing strategy, 545
price lining, 547
psychological pricing, 547
odd-even psychological pricing, 547
threshold pricing, 548
discount, 548
cash discount, 548
seasonal discount, 548
trade discount, 548
quantity discount, 548
distribution mix, 548
intermediary, 549
wholesalers, 549
retailers, 549
distribution channel, 549

direct channel, 550
agent/broker, 551
industrial distribution, 552
sales offices, 553
intensive distribution, 554
exclusive distribution, 554
selective distribution, 555
channel captain, 555
vertical marketing system (VMS), 555
merchant wholesaler, 555
full-service merchant wholesaler, 555
limited-function merchant wholesaler, 555
drop shipper, 555
rack jobber, 556
e-intermediaries, 557
syndicated selling, 557
shopping agent (e-agent), 558

department stores, 560
supermarkets, 560
hypermarkets, 561
scrambled merchandising, 561
specialty stores, 561
category killers, 561
bargain retailers, 561
discount houses, 561
catalogue showroom, 561
factory outlets, 561
warehouse club (wholesale club), 562
convenience stores, 562
wheel of retailing, 562
direct-response retailing, 563
mail order (catalogue marketing), 564
telemarketing, 564
direct selling, 564
e-catalogues, 565
electronic storefront, 566
cybermalls, 566
multilevel marketing, 566

interactive marketing, 566
video marketing, 566
physical distribution, 567
order processing, 567
order-cycle time, 567
warehousing, 568
private warehouses, 568
public warehouses, 568
storage warehouses, 568
distribution centres, 568
inventory control, 568
materials handling, 568
unitization, 568
expedited transportation, 569
intermodal transportation, 570
containerization, 570
common carriers, 570
freight forwarders, 571
contract carriers, 571
private carriers, 571
hub, 572

STUDY QUESTIONS AND EXERCISES

Review Questions

1. How do cost-oriented pricing and break-even analysis help managers measure the potential impact of prices?
2. Identify four types of discounting and give an example for each that is different from the examples in the text.
3. What is the overall goal of price skimming? Of penetration pricing?
4. From the manufacturer's point of view, what are the advantages and disadvantages of using intermediaries to distribute products? From the end-user's point of view?
5. Identify the eight channels of distribution. In what key ways do the four channels used only for consumer products differ from the channels used only for industrial products?
6. Identify and explain the differences between the three distribution strategies.
7. Explain the different roles played by merchant wholesalers and agents/brokers.
8. Explain how the activities of e-agents (Internet shopping agents) or brokers differ from those of traditional agents/brokers.
9. Identify the five modes of transportation used in product distribution. What factors lead companies to choose one mode over the others to deliver products to end-users?

Analysis Questions

10. Suppose that a small publisher selling to book distributors has fixed operating costs of $600 000 each year and variable costs of $3 per book. How many books must the firm sell to break even if the selling price is $6? If the company expects to sell 50 000 books next year and decides on a 40 percent markup, what will the selling price be?

11. Suppose that your company produces industrial products for other firms. How would you go about determining the prices of your products? Describe the method you would use to arrive at a pricing decision.
12. Give three examples (other than those provided in the chapter) of products that use intensive distribution. Do the same for products that use exclusive distribution and selective distribution. For which category was it easiest to find examples? Why?
13. Consider the various kinds of nonstore retailing. Give examples of two products that typify the products sold to at-home shoppers through each form of nonstore retailing. Explain why different products are best suited to each form of nonstore retailing.
14. If you could own a firm that transports products, would you prefer to operate an intermodal transportation business or one that specializes in a single mode of transportation (say, truck or air)? Explain your choice.

Application Exercises

15. Select a product with which you are familiar and analyze various possible pricing objectives for it. What information would you want to have if you were to adopt a profit-maximizing objective? A market share objective? An image objective?
16. Interview the manager of a local manufacturing firm. Identify the firm's distribution strategy and the channels of distribution that it uses. Where applicable, describe the types of wholesalers or retail stores used to distribute the firm's products.
17. Choose any consumer item at your local supermarket and trace the chain of physical distribution activities that brought it to the store shelf.

Building Your Business Skills

Are You Sold on the Internet?

Goal

To encourage students to consider the value of online retailing as an element in a company's distribution system.

Situation

As the distribution manager of a privately owned clothing manufacturer specializing in camping gear and outdoor clothing, you are convinced that your product line is perfect for online distribution. However, the owner of the company is reluctant to expand distribution from a successful network of retail stores and a catalogue operation. Your challenge is to convince the boss that retailing via the Internet can boost sales.

Method

Step 1:
Join together with four or five classmates to research the advantages and disadvantages of an online distribution system for your company. Among the factors to consider are the following:

- The likelihood that target consumers are Internet shoppers. Camping gear is generally purchased by young, affluent consumers who are comfortable with the Web.
- The industry trend to online distribution. Are similar companies doing it? Have they been successful?
- The opportunity to expand inventory without increasing the cost of retail space or catalogue production and mailing charges.

- The opportunity to have a store that never closes.
- The lack of trust many people have about doing business on the Web. Many consumers are reluctant to provide credit card data over the Web.
- The difficulty that electronic shoppers have in finding a Web site when they do not know the store's name.
- The frustration and waiting time involved in Web searches.
- The certainty that the site will not reach consumers who do not use computers or who are uncomfortable with the Web.

Step 2:

Based on your findings, write a persuasive memo to the company's owner stating your position about expanding to an online distribution system. Include information that will counter expected objections.

Follow-Up Questions

1. What place does online distribution have in the distribution network of this company?
2. In your view, is online distribution the wave of the future? Is it likely to increase in importance as a distribution system for apparel companies? Why or why not?

Exploring the Net

To find out what a real-world company can do to assist e-commerce retailers, log on to the Web site of Keystone Internet Services Inc. at:

www.kfulfillment.com

After you have browsed Keystone's home page and visited the supporting pages, respond to the following items:

1. Consider Keystone's description of "Product Fulfillment" services. List all the activities and services that Keystone identifies for product fulfilment. How does Keystone's description of product fulfilment compare with the definition given in this textbook?
2. Look at the page entitled "E-Commerce." Describe the services that Keystone provides to its clients. Describe the resources that Keystone employs to create customer satisfaction.
3. Examine the page for "Customized Services" and describe the types of services Keystone offers. Are these services solely for online businesses, or might they also be used by non–e-businesses?
4. Examine Keystone's "Telemarketing" services. What kinds of telemarketing services does the firm provide? What resources are available at Keystone for delivering these services?

Concluding Case 17-1

Napster

How about that latest Jennifer Lopez album? Prefer the Metabolics? What about Violent Femmes or maybe Elvis Costello? How about all of it for free? The Internet is changing the way we get our musical entertainment—everything from when we buy, to whom we get it from, to what we pay, to how it gets from sellers to consumers. Consider some of the latest trends. Just five years ago, record stores were the standard sites for finding CDs and audiotapes. You could save some money by going from store to store and comparing prices. In fact, browsing display stands for artists and labels was a way of life for many music buyers.

Then came Internet stores, many of them offering discount prices. For example, you can go to a site such as www.cdhitlist.com, which offers more than 55 000 titles among CDs, cassettes, and VHS/DVD movies. You can search lists, place orders electronically or over the phone, and then receive your music or movie by mail. You can still browse, of course—electronically, at home—and compare prices without burning gasoline or wearing out shoe leather going from store to store. Web sites such as www.evenbetter.com will even do your comparison shopping for you, listing prices from low to high for any product offered by as many as 50 different e-stores.

Now there's an online music service called Napster. When you register at www.napster.com, you get access to "the world's largest online music community." What do you do once you're in? Basically, you can exchange music with other Napster users, sending your albums to others on the Internet and receiving albums from them. For free. Napster is accessible 24 hours per day, and there's no need to wait for the mail because albums are transmitted digitally and downloaded onto your computer in just a few minutes.

A 19-year-old music lover named Shawn Fanning invented the software that got Napster rolling in 1999. By early 2000, officials at several different universities noticed that much of the institution's Internet bandwidth (system capacity) was consumed by students using Napster to trade music online. The universities' servers were so clogged that filters had to be installed to block Napster. By March 2000—just six months after its launch—more than 5 million people had downloaded Napster software

and its user base was growing at a rate between 5 and 25 percent daily. "I love Napster," says one 15-year-old fan. "I'm never buying a CD again."

The music itself is not actually traded on Napster's Web site. Instead, you go to the Web site to obtain the Napster software, which you can download for free onto your computer. The software finds albums you've stored on your hard disk and publishes that information on Napster's Web site, along with lists of millions of other users. Then, using an MP3 format (digital file), you can start trading with anyone else who's live on the Internet at the same time. You get what you want from their hard drives and they get what they want from yours. "Napster," boasts the company's site, "is music at Internet speed." You can enjoy music from your computer speakers or copy it onto an MP3 player, such as the Compressor Personal Jukebox, and listen to as much as 80 hours of stored music while you work, jog, or even sit in your favourite classroom.

What does all this mean for the music industry—for artists, album producers, distributors, and retail stores? According to Stewart Alsop, a partner with the venture capital firm New Enterprise Associates, it means that "the music business as we know it today is hosed.... If I were a music-biz exec ... I'd be singing the blues."

The Napster phenomenon underscores three features of contemporary commerce which, when taken together, go a long way towards explaining why battle lines are forming in the music industry:

1. As long as they can be converted into digital format, products can be transmitted on the Internet rather than by mail. This in itself is nothing new. JAVA, for example, has been delivering software products for years on the Internet. In March 2000, best-selling novelist Stephen King announced that his latest work, *Riding the Bullet*, would be found only on the Internet and not in bookstores.

2. At present, Napster users get the service for free. The availability of such a large menu of free products is revolutionary.

3. The enormous number of participants is significant. It's little wonder, then, that music-industry businesses—members of the traditional distribution channel—are up in arms.

Music artists, of course, earn their livings from royalties on the sales of their albums. Revenues from those royalties are denied them each time a Napster user gets a free album instead of buying it from a legitimate vendor, such as a record store. Without revenues, how can the costs of production be recovered? And at a market price of zero dollars for an album, how can record stores hope to stay in business when, obviously, they cannot lower their prices to zero? It comes as no surprise, therefore, that an industry trade organization, the Recording Industry Association of America (RIAA), has filed suit claiming that Napster's main function is to violate copyright regulations. Napster, claims the RIAA, is "operating a haven for music piracy on an unprecedented scale." Napster proclaims its innocence, arguing that it does nothing more than supply software. It neither takes possession of albums nor does it buy or sell them. The trading of albums occurs solely among individuals on the open market.

Some observers have charged that Napster is being hypocritical; while it is eager to help its users share music, Napster won't share anything it owns. When the alternative band The Offspring started selling T-shirts featuring the Napster logo, Napster immediately told the group to stop. Napster backed off when some Web sites openly commented on the hypocrisy of the move.

While the battle heats up, some companies are preparing to sell albums via MP3 technology (though not for free, of course). They see the Internet as a new distribution alternative. Meanwhile, Napster CEO Eileen Richardson thinks that record companies would be better off joining her firm instead of fighting it. She proposes that Napster would be a terrific asset for selling T-shirts and concert tickets to promote recording artists and albums, as well as a

means of providing exposure for new musicians. Says Richardson: "I don't want to say we're the MTV of the Internet, but—oops—there, I just did!"

RIAA attorney Cary Sherman replies that working with Napster would be basically wrong. Performers and recording companies would be forfeiting their rights to make money. Says Sherman, it's like telling artists that "they're only good enough to sell advertising or maybe a T-shirt." Meanwhile, back on college campuses, students are rising up in protest when administrators free up bandwidth by blocking out Napster.

CASE QUESTIONS

1. What do you think of Napster as an approach for distributing music?
2. Consider the more traditional channels of distribution for music albums. Which channel elements are most affected by the presence of Napster-like services? Explain how those elements are affected.
3. What other products, besides music albums, are the most likely candidates for distribution on the Internet, now and in the future?
4. Why is the music industry so concerned about Internet distribution? In addition to threats, do you see any opportunities for the industry in Internet distribution?
5. Identify the major legal issues that the music industry faces from Napster's presence. Develop a legal argument against Napster. Then take the reverse position and develop an argument in Napster's defence.
6. Aside from legal arguments, does Napster's emergence raise any ethical issues or social responsibility concerns? ◆

Concluding Case 17-2

New Ways to Buy a Car

You know the routine: You walk into a car dealership, find a car that looks interesting, and then start negotiating with a salesperson. But you feel terribly insecure because you really have no idea of what constitutes a "good deal." Even if you are able to reach an agreement about which car to purchase and what you are willing to pay, there is always that nagging feeling that you paid too much. Is there a solution to this problem?

In the mid-1980s, the Saturn division of General Motors implemented a revolutionary pricing strategy. Saturn would take the hassle and heartache out of the dealer–consumer relationship by selling vehicles for a fixed low price that would make negotiation unnecessary. Pricing experts believed that this "no-haggle" approach to auto pricing would appeal to consumers who hated to negotiate and who believed that traditional dealers maximized commissions by keeping prices high. Meanwhile, salespeople working for fixed-price dealers would be paid by the sale, not by a sliding scale commission linked to profit.

Unfortunately, good ideas don't always work in the marketplace, and many auto dealers now believe that the fixed-price approach has some basic flaws. For example, although thousands of consumers have embraced the fixed-price concept, many more continue to seek dealers who are willing to negotiate price.

Moreover, no-haggle dealers found themselves squeezed by competitors willing to undercut close-to-the-bone fixed prices to make sales and reduce inventories. The most aggressive competition is in cities where consumers routinely comparison-shop at several dealers. Fixed-price dealers do best in areas—mostly rural—where they face few rivals.

What is the situation in Canada? The Saturn one-price idea has been tried at various places in Canada. For example, you can visit a one-price dealership in Richmond Hill, Ontario. The North York Chevrolet Geo Oldsmobile dealership began offering one-price selling after its general manager visited a one-price dealership in Michigan. When the new system was implemented, the two top salespeople at the dealership left for greener pastures. And sales staff have let some people walk out the door because they were as little as $8 apart on the price. Sales numbers have not risen since the new system was implemented. But the dealership does get a lot fewer calls from dissatisfied customers after the sale is made.

If you want to take a high-tech approach, you can purchase a no-haggle car on the Internet from Auto-By-Tel. You simply click onto Auto-By-Tel's Web site and make a purchase order. Within 48 hours, one of the 90 Canadian Auto-By-Tel dealers phones you with a no-haggle price. The system requires that consumers know exactly what they want, but most of those who use this system do know.

You can also take the traditional, haggling approach to buying a car on the Internet. When you click on a site, your request and how much you are offering are referred to a dealer located near you. The dealer is then supposed to give you a no-obligation quote. If you're interested, you can then go to the dealer to finish the negotiations and sign the papers. In theory, you can "visit" several dealers to see who has the best price.

Unfortunately, improvements are needed in the system. The biggest problem is dealers who don't respond with a quote. In one study, six Internet car-buying services were sent an identical vehicle request (for a 1999 Jeep Grand Cherokee Limited). One of the services responded within a half-day. A second site channelled the request to its nearest Jeep dealer and a salesman called the following week. One site was down on the day the request was made; after it was back up someone called and said there were no Jeep dealers in the area (as did a fourth site a few days later). The fifth and sixth sites didn't respond at all.

Things are changing so rapidly in this business that it is hard to predict where it will eventually end up. For example, CarsDirect.com lets would-be car buyers see in seconds the manufacturer's retail price, the invoice, and the price that it can get through its connections. It takes almost no interaction with a dealer to close the deal. And Microsoft has joined forces with Ford to create a build-to-order system that someday could allow online shoppers to order a car directly from the factory much like they order a PC now.

CASE QUESTIONS

1. What are the various objectives a business might be pursuing when it prices its products? What objective(s) are automobile dealers pursuing when they price their products?

2. What are the advantages and disadvantages of the one-price system for buying automobiles?

3. Would you prefer to buy an automobile from a one-price dealer or from a traditional dealer? Explain the reasons for your choice. ◆

Chrysler
www.chrysler.com

Auto-By-Tel
www.autobytel.com

CBC Video Case

V-1   CBC ⬤

Spinmaster Toys

In 1993, Anton Rabie and a couple of friends from business school began manufacturing the Earth Buddy—a sawdust and grass-seed filled novelty that competed with products like Chia Pet. The firm had some early successes selling Earth Buddies to large Canadian retail operations like Zellers. Then the U.S. retail giant Kmart indicated that they would like to place an order for half a million units. Although Anton did not have a firm purchase order in hand, he decided to take the risk and began manufacturing hundreds of thousands of Earth Buddies in the hope that Kmart would actually send in an order. To achieve the production volume that was required, Anton had to hire an additional 140 people and had to manage a production system that was producing at a far higher level than anything the company had experienced before.

What has happened to Anton's company since 1993? Well, the news is very positive. The company eventually got the Kmart order and made $500 000 profit from it. By the end of 1998, the company—now called Spinmaster Toys—was selling several different lines of toys, and its annual sales had reached the $10 million mark. During December 1998, Spinmaster had another mega Christmas hit toy on its hands, and Anton was scrambling to try to fill orders from retailers across North America who were desperate to stock the product on their shelves. The product was Air Hogs, a toy plane powered by compressed air that is manufactured in China. Spinmaster never planned for a toy that would be so in demand, so the company has had to dramatically increase output at the Chinese factory where it is made.

In February 1999 Spinmaster took part in the Toy Fair in New York City. The idea was to push the toys that Spinmaster was selling, and to look for new toy ideas. The latest product (an obvious extension of Air Hogs) is an air pressure-powered toy car, which Spinmaster demonstrated to retailers at the Toy Fair. Wal-Mart, Toys 'R' Us, and Costco all expressed a lot of interest in the various air-powered toys that Spinmaster had available.

Yet another twist has developed. Spinmaster is now looking at a water-powered rocket that uses the same basic propulsion idea as the air-powered cars and airplanes. Toys 'R' Us thinks it can sell a couple million units of the water-powered rocket. It wants a partnership with Spinmaster, and will commit to an Air-Hogs toy section in its retail outlets. Sales for these products could reach $50 to $60 million. That scale would be far greater than anything Spinmaster has seen so far. Anton's dream is to have an Air Hogs section in every toy store.

In December 1999, Spinmaster produced yet another hit toy. This one was called finger bikes, which are miniature (collectible) models of real bikes. Anton Rabie is always looking for that next hit toy product. So far, he has been very successful.

STUDY QUESTIONS

1. Briefly describe each of the external environmental factors that marketing managers must take into account when they develop marketing strategies. Which of these factors are particularly important for Spinmaster?

2. What are the variables in the marketing mix? Which of these variables is most important to Spinmaster? Explain.

3. Explain how the various methods of gathering marketing research might be useful to Spinmaster.

4. What are the three categories of consumer products? Which category do the toys that Spinmaster sells fit into?

5. What is the product life cycle, and what are its main phases? Explain the relevance and importance of the product life cycle to Spinmaster Toys.

6. What are the four basic types of promotional tools? Which of these tools would likely be most important to Spinmaster? Why?

Video Resources: "High Flyers," *Venture* #739 (February 15, 2000).

CBC Video Case

Grocery.com

A lot of people thought that the e-commerce revolution was going to take the retail sector by storm. However, so far the revolution is struggling. Consider what is happening in the retail grocery industry. Grocery Gateway is an e-commerce company that wants to revolutionize the retail food sector by selling groceries online. Customers simply visit Gateway's Web site and click on the groceries they want. Then employees at Gateway's warehouse pick customer orders, pack them, and deliver them to customers' doors.

The retail grocery industry is a nearly $60 billion a year business, and Gateway hopes to become a billion-dollar business by changing the way that traditional food retailing works. However, profitably selling and delivering groceries online has turned out to be difficult. Here's why: In a traditional grocery operation, the consumer goes to the grocery store, picks out items, pays for them, and takes them home. In other words, the customer does all the work. In online selling of groceries, by contrast, the company has to do all the work.

It is well known that the retail grocery business has low margins, so observers have wondered why Gateway picked this business. CEO Bill DiNardo says the answer is simple: everyone needs groceries. That may be true, but it is going to be hard to make a profit in a low-margin business like this when the company has to do all the work. David Dunne, a professor at the University of Toronto, says that few online grocery sellers are making money. He notes that in the U.S., investors have become very impatient with the lack of profitability of online grocers, and have driven down the stock prices of such companies. He expects that Gateway will soon face the same investor impatience.

Cash flow is also a problem for Gateway; it is quickly burning through the $70 million it has raised so far. So far, Canadians are resisting grocery e-commerce. Buying online means trusting someone else to pick out your merchandise, and most consumers won't do this, particularly when it comes to perishable items like fruits and vegetables.

These are not the only roadblocks Gateway faces. The company must also achieve efficient logistics and deliver top-flight service to customers. Gateway currently receives about 1 complaint per 20 deliveries it makes. Bill DiNardo, CEO of Gateway, says the company must strive to be right 99.9 percent of the time. However, Gateway must do more than simply get the orders right. It has to achieve efficiencies in delivery if it hopes to make a profit. To gain those efficiencies, it needs to win over entire neighbourhoods so it can minimize driving time for deliveries. Gateway will have to increase its customer base tenfold to achieve those efficiencies.

If Gateway's strategy works, the company will expand and sell other products online as well. Gateway wants to be the e-commerce company of choice, but first it will have to prove it can deliver the groceries. Gateway will also have to cope with competition from another company that is using a different twist on Internet selling. Montreal-based Peachtree Networks works with traditional retailers to help them get online sales. Peachtree gathers the orders online and the retail stores then fill and deliver the orders using their own employees. Peachtree thus avoids the need for expensive warehouses. Peachtree's idea is a good one, but everyone recognizes this model will work only as a sideline because traditional stores can't fill thousands of online orders unless they hire a lot more people. This business model is also a low-risk one, but it won't revolutionize the retail grocery sector.

What are Canada's retail grocery giants doing about online selling? At the moment, they are assessing the threat to their traditional operations. They recognize that if they develop a big online presence, they will undermine their bricks-and-mortar operations. They are reluctant to do that, given all the new superstores they have built during the last few years.

STUDY QUESTIONS

1. Why do intermediaries exist? How is a firm like Gateway different than traditional intermediaries? How is it similar?

2. Consider the various channels of distribution shown in Figure 17.2 (see page 550). Where does an e-retailer like Gateway fit?

3. What are the advantages and disadvantages of electronic storefronts like Gateway?

4. What is the future of food retailing? Will it become a major force in the industry, or will it continue to account for only a small percentage of industry sales? Defend your answer.

Video Resource: "Grocery.com," *Venture #758* (October 3, 2000).

Managing Financial Issues

Management of the financial transactions of a business firm is absolutely critical to its survival. Whether it involves raising money to start a new firm, assessing the riskiness of the firm's investments, managing the firm's cash, or monitoring the firm's activities in securities markets, financial management is a key business activity. The opening cases of the chapters in this section describe the importance of financial management to companies such as the Royal Bank of Canada, the Bank of Montreal, RT Capital Management, and Eaton's.

Part Six, Managing Financial Issues, provides an overview of business finance, including how firms raise and manage money, how they define and manage risk, and how they use Canadian and international securities markets to meet their financial needs.

- We begin in **Chapter 18, Understanding Money and Banking**, by exploring the nature of money, its creation through the banking system, and the role of the Bank of Canada in the nation's financial system. We also describe other important financial services organizations.

- Next, in **Chapter 19, Understanding Securities and Investments**, we consider the markets in which firms raise long-term funds by examining how these markets operate and how they are regulated.

- Finally, in **Chapter 20, Financial Decisions and Risk Management**, we look at three reasons businesses need funds and how financial managers raise both long- and short-term funds. We also examine the kinds of risks businesses encounter and the ways in which they deal with such risks.

CHAPTER 18

UNDERSTANDING MONEY AND BANKING

Banking Behemoths

In 1998, two mega-mergers were proposed by Canadian banks: Royal Bank wanted to merge with the Bank of Montreal, and the Toronto-Dominion Bank wanted to merge with the Canadian Imperial Bank of Commerce. These banks wanted to merge so they could become larger and more competitive in international markets. The federal government blocked both mergers on the grounds that they would reduce domestic competition and harm consumers.

The banks were motivated to merge because they knew that Canadian banks are slipping in the world rankings. In 1998, the CEO of the Bank of Montreal said that the failure to merge would be equivalent to the corner hardware store simply waiting to be put out of business by Home Depot.

Consider some dramatic statistics: In 1984, Canada's largest bank—Royal Bank—was the twenty-second-largest bank in the world, as measured by shareholder equity. By 1998, Royal Bank had slipped to forty-ninth place. The other "Big Six" Canadian banks have also lost ground in the rankings. In 1984, *all* of Canada's "Big Six" banks were ranked in the top 40. By 1998, *none* of them were in the top 40.

There are three main reasons why Canada's banks have slipped so badly in the rankings. First, the Canadian dollar began dropping in value in the early 1980s, and has never recovered. Second, Canadian banks have, until recently, focused more on increasing profits than they have on increasing size. Third, and more important, Canadian banks have not been al-

lowed to merge as banks in other countries have, and this can have a big effect. For example, U.S.-based Fleet Financial Group Inc. ranked only 112th in 1994, but after it merged with Shawmut National Corp. it jumped to 61st place. By 1998, it ranked forty-first, which put it ahead of all major Canadian banks.

A spokesman for the Canadian Bankers Association says that the international stature of Canada's banks has fallen sharply during the last 20 years. He argues that consumers benefit from the international activity of Canadian banks, noting that while they earn 40 percent of their profit outside of Canada, they pay 80 percent of their taxes in Canada, and keep 90 percent of their staff here. But a spokeswoman for the Consumers Association of Canada says that it doesn't make sense that a country like Canada, with its small population, would have banks that are among the world's largest. She says that the banks should stop worrying about how big they are and start improving the way they operate within Canada.

The extremely large profits that Canadian banks have made in the last few years also does not help their public relations with consumers. Canadian banks may be having problems on the size front, but they are doing fine in terms of profits, even compared to their international competitors. A *Globe and Mail* ranking of 11 banks in North America, Europe, and Japan showed that the "Big Six" Canadian banks ranked fifth in terms of average return on equity. British banks ranked first, and Japanese banks ranked last. ◆

The issues of money and banking are important to each of us as we go about our daily lives, and to business firms as they conduct their day-to-day activities. In this chapter, we describe what money is, explain the different definitions of the money supply, and show why money is essential for every business. We also describe the major financial institutions in Canada, and the way in which they facilitate business activity.

By focusing on the learning objectives of this chapter, you will better understand the environment for banking in Canada, and the different kinds of financial institutions that are important. After reading this chapter, you should be able to:

1. Define *money* and identify the different forms it takes in the nation's money supply.

2. Describe the different kinds of *financial institutions* that make up the Canadian financial system and explain the services they offer.

3. Explain how banks create money and identify the means by which they are regulated.

4. Explain the functions of the *Bank of Canada* and describe the tools it uses to control the money supply.

5. Identify ways in which the banking industry is changing.

6. Understand some of the key activities in *international banking and finance*.

LEARNING OBJECTIVES

MONEY

When someone asks you how much money you have, what do you say? Do you count the bills and coins in your pockets? Do you mention the funds in your chequing and savings accounts? What about stocks, bonds, or your car? Taken together, the value of everything you own is your personal *wealth*. Not all of it, however, is *money*. In this section, we will consider what money is and what it does.

What Is Money?

The Canadian bills and coins you carry every day are money. So are U.S. dollars, British pound notes, French francs, and Japanese yen. Modern money often takes the form of printed paper or stamped metal issued by a government. But over the centuries, items as diverse as stone wheels, salt, wool, livestock, shells, and spices have been used as money. **Money** is any object generally accepted by people as payment for goods and services.

Thousands of years ago, people began to accept certain agreed-upon objects in exchange for goods or services. As early as 1100 B.C., the Chinese were using metal money that represented the objects they were exchanging (for example, bronze spades and knives). Coins probably came into use sometime around 600 B.C. and paper money around 1200 A.D.

money
Any object generally accepted by people as payment for goods and services.

Desirable Characteristics of Money

Any object can serve as money if it is portable, divisible, durable, and stable.[1] To understand why these qualities are important, imagine using as money something valuable that lacks them—a 35-kilogram salmon, for example.

Throughout the ages, humans have used many monetary devices. Two interesting ones that were in common circulation are the Iroquois wampum belt (early nineteenth century) from eastern North America and this ancient Greek coin (circa 375 B.C.).

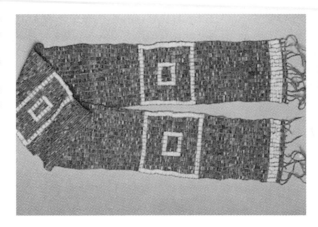

Portability

If you wanted to use the salmon to buy goods and services, you would have to lug a 35-kilogram fish from shop to shop. Modern currency, by contrast, is lightweight and easy to handle.

Divisibility

Suppose you wanted to buy a hat, a book, and some milk from three different stores—all using the salmon as money. How would you divide the fish? First, out comes a cleaver at each store. Then, you would have to determine whether a kilogram of its head is worth as much as a kilogram from its middle. Modern currency is easily divisible into smaller parts with fixed values for each unit. In Canada, for example, a dollar can be exchanged for 4 quarters, 10 dimes, 20 nickels, 100 pennies, or any combination of these coins. It is easy to match units of money with the value of all goods.

Durability

Fish seriously fail the durability test. Each day, whether or not you "spend" it, the salmon will be losing value (and gaining scents). Modern currency, on the other hand, does not spoil, it does not die, and, if it wears out, it can be replaced with new coins and paper money.

Stability

Fish are not stable enough to serve as money. If salmon were in short supply, you might be able to make quite a deal for yourself. But in the middle of a salmon run, the market would be flooded with fish. Since sellers would have many opportunities to exchange their wares for salmon, they would soon have enough fish and refuse to trade for salmon. While the value of the paper money we use today has fluctuated over the years, it is considerably more stable than salmon.

The Functions of Money

Imagine a successful fisherman who needs a new sail for his boat. In a *barter economy*—one in which goods are exchanged directly for one another—he would have to find someone who not only needs fish but who is willing to exchange a sail for it. If no sailmaker wants fish, the fisherman must find someone else—say, a shoemaker—who wants fish and will trade for it. Then the fisherman must hope that the sailmaker will trade for his new shoes. In a money economy, the fisherman would sell his catch, receive money, and exchange the money for such goods as a new sail.

The barter economy is quite inefficient, but it is still used in various places around the world. It is active in Russia, where major problems have arisen as the country tries to move towards a market-based system and away from the command economy that existed under communism. An official survey of 210 companies that form the backbone of the Russian economy found that barter, debt swaps, and other non-monetary deals accounted for a staggering 73 percent of their business transactions in 1996 and 1997.[2]

In broad terms, money serves three functions:

- *Medium of exchange*. Like the fisherman "trading" money for a new sail, we use money as a way of buying and selling things. Without money, we would be bogged down in a system of barter.

- *Store of value*. Pity the fisherman who catches a fish on Monday and wants to buy a few bars of candy on, say, the following Saturday. By then, the fish would have spoiled and be of no value. In the form of currency, however, money can be used for future purchases and therefore "stores" value.

- *Unit of account*. Finally, money lets us measure the relative values of goods and services. It acts as a unit of account because all products can be valued and accounted for in terms of money. For example, the concepts of "$1000 worth of clothes" or "$500 in labour costs" have universal meaning because everyone deals with money every day.

The Money Supply: M-1

For money to serve as a medium of exchange, a store of value, or a unit of account, buyers and sellers must agree on its value. The value of money, in turn, depends in part on its supply, that is, how much money is in circulation. When the money supply is high, the value of money drops. When the money supply is low, the value of money increases.

Unfortunately, it is not easy to measure the supply of money, nor is there complete agreement on exactly how it should be measured. The "narrow" definition of the money supply is called M-1. **M-1** counts only the most liquid forms of money: currency and demand deposits (chequing accounts) in banks.

M-1
Only the most liquid forms of money (currency and demand deposits).

Currency

Currency is paper money and coins issued by the Canadian government. It is widely used to pay small bills. Canadian currency states clearly: "This note is legal tender." Legal tender is money the law requires a creditor to accept in payment of a debt.

currency
Paper money and coins issued by the government.

Demand Deposits

The majority of Canadian households have chequing accounts against which millions of cheques are written each year. A **cheque** is an order instructing the bank to pay a given sum to a specified person or firm. Although not all sellers accept cheques in payment for goods and services, many do. Cheques enable buyers to make large purchases without having to carry large amounts of cash. Sellers gain a measure of safety because the cheques they receive are valuable only to them and can later be exchanged for cash. Money in chequing accounts, known as **demand deposits**, is counted in M-1 because such funds may be withdrawn at any time without notice.

cheque
An order instructing the bank to pay a given sum to a specified person or firm.

demand deposit
Money in chequing accounts; counted as M-1 because such funds may be withdrawn at any time without notice.

The Money Supply: M-2

M-2

Everything in M-1 plus savings deposits, time deposits, and money market mutual funds.

M-2 includes everything in M-1 plus items that cannot be spent directly but that are easily converted to spendable forms: *time deposits, money market mutual funds*, and *savings deposits*. M-2 accounts for nearly all of the nation's money supply. It thus measures the store of monetary value that is available for financial transactions. As this overall level of money increases, more is available for consumer purchases and business investment. When the supply is tightened, less money is available; financial transactions, spending, and business activity thus slow down.

Time Deposits

time deposit

A deposit that requires prior notice to make a withdrawal; cannot be transferred to others by cheque.

Unlike demand deposits, **time deposits** require prior notice of withdrawal and cannot be transferred by cheque. On the other hand, time deposits pay higher interest rates. The supply of money in time deposits—such as *certificates of deposit (CDs)* and *savings certificates*—grew rapidly in the 1970s and 1980s as interest rates rose to 15 percent. But in the 1990s, interest rates dropped sharply and consumers began putting more of their money in mutual funds.

Money Market Mutual Funds

money market mutual funds

Funds operated by investment companies that bring together pools of assets from many investors.

Money market mutual funds are operated by investment companies that bring together pools of assets from many investors. The fund buys a collection of short-term, low-risk financial securities. Ownership of and profits (or losses) from the sale of these securities are shared among the fund's investors.

These funds attracted many investors in the 1980s and 1990s because of high payoffs and because they often allow investors to write cheques against their shares. Mutual funds pay higher returns than most individuals can get on their own because:

1. Funds can buy into higher-paying securities that require larger investments than most individuals can afford.

2. They are managed by professionals who monitor changing investment opportunities.

Savings Deposits

In the wake of new, more attractive investments, traditional savings deposits, such as passbook savings accounts, have declined in popularity.

Credit Cards

Although not included in M-1 or M-2, credit—especially credit cards—has become a major factor in the purchase of consumer goods in Canada. The use of MasterCard, Visa, American Express, Discover, and credit cards issued by individual businesses has become so widespread that many people refer to credit cards as "plastic money." Nevertheless, credit cards do not qualify as money. Rather, they are a *money substitute*; they serve as a temporary medium of exchange but are not a store of value.

Credit cards are big business for two reasons. First, they are quite convenient. Second, credit cards are extremely profitable for issuing companies. Profits derive from two sources:

1. Some cards charge annual fees to holders. All charge interest on unpaid balances. Depending on the issuer, cardholders pay interest rates ranging from 11 to 20 percent.

Credit cards are used to purchase very diverse products. They are profitable for the companies that issue them, and they are convenient for consumers.

2. Merchants who accept credit cards pay fees to card issuers. Depending on the merchant's agreement with the issuer, 2 to 5 percent of total credit-sales dollars goes to card issuers.

THE CANADIAN FINANCIAL SYSTEM

Many forms of money, especially demand deposits and time deposits, depend on the existence of financial institutions to provide a broad spectrum of services to both individuals and businesses. Just how important are reliable financial institutions to both businesses and individuals? Try asking financial consumers in a country in which banking can be an adventure.

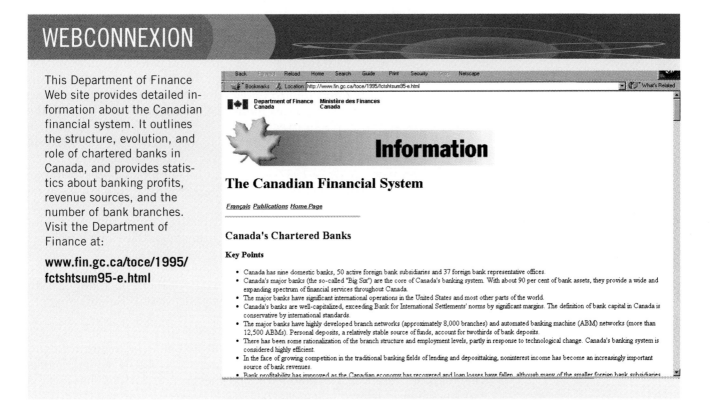

WEBCONNEXION

This Department of Finance Web site provides detailed information about the Canadian financial system. It outlines the structure, evolution, and role of chartered banks in Canada, and provides statistics about banking profits, revenue sources, and the number of bank branches. Visit the Department of Finance at:

**www.fin.gc.ca/toce/1995/
fctshtsum95-e.html**

In Russia, for example, there is almost no banking regulation and no way to distinguish qualified from unscrupulous bankers in the thousands of different financial institutions, large and small, that exist. Businesses need stable financial institutions to underwrite modernization and expansion, and individuals need them to handle currency. The Moscow City Bank has no deposit insurance, and only recently added a customer service desk, loan officers, and a cash machine. Imagine, then, just before these new steps towards modernization, the disappointment of Vladimir Shcherbakov, who needed to withdraw US$500 from his account to buy a car but was turned away by a sign announcing that no withdrawals would be allowed for 10 days. "I'm resigned to losing my money," sighed Shcherbakov. "But if I do get it back, I'll change my rubles into dollars and hold on to it myself."

In the sections that follow, we describe the major types of financial institutions, explain how they work, and survey some of the special services they offer. We also explain their role as creators of money and discuss the regulation of the Canadian banking system.

Financial Institutions

The main function of financial institutions is to ease the flow of money from sectors with surpluses to those with deficits. They do this by issuing claims against themselves and using the proceeds to buy the assets of—and thus invest in—other organizations. A bank, for instance, can issue financial claims against itself by making available funds for chequing and savings accounts. In turn, its assets will be mostly loans invested in individuals and businesses and perhaps in government securities.

There are a variety of financial intermediaries in Canada. They vary in size, in importance, in the types of sources they appeal to, in the form of the claim they give to sources of funds, in the users they supply credit to, and in the type of claim they make against the users of funds.

Until recently, the financial community in Canada was divided rather clearly into four distinct legal areas. Often called the "four financial pillars," they were: (1) chartered banks; (2) alternate banks, such as trust companies and *caisses populaires* or credit unions; (3) life insurance companies and other specialized lending and saving intermediaries, such as factors, finance companies, venture capital firms, mutual funds, and pension funds; and (4) investment dealers. We will discuss the role of these four financial divisions in a moment, but it is important to understand that so many changes have taken place in the financial services industry that the differences across the four divisions are now very blurred.

The crumbling of the four financial pillars began in 1980 when several changes were made to the *Bank Act*. The process accelerated when additional changes were made in 1987 and 1992. Canadian banks, for example, are now permitted to own securities dealers (in 1996, Royal Bank purchased investment dealer Richardson Greenshields); they are also permitted to sell commercial paper and to own insurance companies (although they are not allowed to sell insurance in their own bank branches). Banks have also established subsidiaries to sell mutual funds.

The changes to the *Bank Act* have also allowed subsidiaries of U.S. banks to set up business in Canada, and over 40 of them have done so. In 1997, legislation was changed again to allow *branches* of U.S. banks to conduct business in Canada.

Trust companies have declined in importance during the last few years, and many trust companies have been bought by banks or insurance companies. Insurance companies are facing increased challenges since banks can now sell insurance. The mutual fund business is booming and has created many new jobs during the last decade.

All of these significant changes must be kept in mind as we now turn to a discussion of the four financial pillars of the Canadian economy.

FINANCIAL PILLAR #1—CHARTERED BANKS

A **chartered bank** is a privately owned, profit-seeking firm that serves individuals, nonbusiness organizations, and businesses as a financial intermediary. Chartered banks offer chequing and savings accounts, make loans, and provide many other services to their customers. They are the main source of short-term loans for business firms.

chartered bank
A privately owned, profit-seeking firm that serves individuals, nonbusiness organizations, and businesses as a financial intermediary.

Chartered banks are the largest and most important financial institution in Canada. They offer a unique service. Their liability instruments (the claims against their assets) are generally accepted by the public and by business as money or as legal tender. Initially, these liability instruments took the form of bank notes issued by individual banks. The *Bank Act* amendments of 1944 removed the right to issue bank notes.

Canada has a branch banking system. Unlike the United States, where there are hundreds of banks, each with a few branches, in Canada there are only a few banks, each with hundreds of branches. The largest chartered banks in Canada are shown in Table 18.1.

The 1980 *Bank Act* requires Schedule A banks to be Canadian-owned and have no more than 10 percent of voting shares controlled by a single interest. It also permits Schedule B banks, which may be domestically owned banks that do not meet the 10 percent limit or may be foreign controlled. Schedule B banks are initially limited to one main office and one branch. Since the passing of the Act, several foreign banks have set up Schedule B subsidiaries. The Act limits foreign-controlled banks to deposits that do not exceed 8 percent of the total domestic assets of all banks in Canada.

The five largest Schedule A banks account for about 90 percent of total bank assets. Some of them also have branches in other countries. There are thousands of branch bank offices in Canada, about one for every 3300 people.

Services Offered by Banks

The banking business today is a highly competitive industry. No longer is it enough for banks to accept deposits and make loans. Most, for example, now

Table 18.1	The Top 10 Banks in Canada (ranked by revenues)
Company	**Annual Revenues (in billions)**
1. Canadian Imperial Bank of Commerce	$20.1
2. Royal Bank of Canada	19.6
3. Bank of Montreal	16.6
4. The Bank of Nova Scotia	16.6
5. The Toronto-Dominion Bank	15.6
6. National Bank of Canada	4.7
7. HSBC Bank of Canada	1.8
8. Deutsche Bank Canada	1.1
9. Laurentian Bank of Canada	0.9
10. Alberta Treasury Branches	0.7

offer bank-issued credit cards and safe-deposit boxes. In addition, many offer pension, trust, international, and financial advice, and electronic money transfer.

Pension Services

Most banks help customers establish savings plans for retirement. Banks serve as financial intermediaries by receiving funds and investing them as directed by customers. They also provide customers with information on investment possibilities.

Trust Services

trust services
The management of funds left in the bank's trust.

Many banks offer **trust services**—the management of funds left "in the bank's trust." In return for a fee, the trust department will perform such tasks as making your monthly bill payments and managing your investment portfolio. Trust departments also manage the estates of deceased persons.

International Services

The three main international services offered by banks are *currency exchange, letters of credit,* and *banker's acceptances.* Suppose, for example, that a Canadian company wants to buy a product from a French supplier. For a fee, it can use one or more of three services offered by its bank:

1. It can exchange Canadian dollars for French francs at a Canadian bank and then pay the French supplier in francs.

letter of credit
A promise by a bank to pay money to a business firm if certain conditions are met.

2. It can pay its bank to issue a **letter of credit**—a promise by the bank to pay the French firm a certain amount if specified conditions are met.

banker's acceptance
A promise that the bank will pay a specified amount of money at a future date.

3. It can pay its bank to draw up a **banker's acceptance**, which promises that the bank will pay some specified amount at a future date.

A banker's acceptance requires payment by a particular date; letters of credit are payable only after certain conditions are met. The French supplier, for example, may not be paid until shipping documents prove that the merchandise has been shipped from France.

Financial Advice

Many banks, both large and small, help their customers manage their money. Depending on the customer's situation, the bank may recommend different investment opportunities. The recommended mix might include guaranteed investment certificates, mutual funds, stocks, and bonds. Today, bank advertisements often stress the role of banks as financial advisers.

Electronic Technologies

electronic funds transfer (EFT)
A combination of computer and communications technology that transfers funds or information into, from, within, and among financial institutions.

Chartered banks and some other financial institutions now use electronic funds transfer (EFT) to provide many basic financial services. **Electronic funds transfer** combines computer and communication technology to transfer funds or information into, from, within, and among financial institutions. Examples include the following:

■ Automated teller machines (ATMs), or 24-hour tellers, are electronic terminals that let you bank at almost any time of day or night. Generally, you insert a special card and enter your own secret identification number to withdraw cash, make deposits, or transfer funds between accounts. Increasingly, ATMs are becoming global fixtures. In fact, of the world's 708 000 ATMs, 32 percent are located in Asia, 31 percent are in North America, 25 percent are in Western Europe, and 8 percent are in Latin America.

- Pay-by-phone systems let you telephone your financial institution and instruct it to pay certain bills or to transfer funds between accounts merely by pushing the proper buttons on your telephone.

- Direct deposits or withdrawals allow you to authorize in advance specific, regular deposits and withdrawals. You can arrange to have paycheques and social assistance cheques automatically deposited and recurring expenses, such as insurance premiums and utility bills, automatically paid.

- Point-of-sale transfers let you pay for retail purchases with your debit card. A **debit card** is a type of plastic money that immediately reduces the balance in the user's bank account when it is used. For example, if you use a debit card at a grocery store, the clerk simply runs the card through the machine and asks you to punch in a personal identification number on a keypad beside the cash register. The price of the groceries is then deducted electronically from your chequing account, and money moves from your chequing account to the grocery store's account. In 1992, consumers in Quebec and B.C. were the first to have widespread access to the debit card. A Royal Bank study predicted that the use of debit cards would increase to 100 million transactions by 1995. (The actual number of transactions in 1995 was nearly 400 million, and by 1998 the number was 1.3 billion.)[3]

debit card
A type of plastic money that immediately on use reduces the balance in the user's bank account and transfers it to the store's account.

- The so-called **smart card** is a credit card–sized computer that can be programmed with "electronic money." Also known as "electronic purses" or "stored-value cards," smart cards have existed for nearly a decade. Shoppers in Europe and Asia are the most avid users, holding the majority of the 1.5 billion cards in circulation in 1999. Analysts expect that 4 billion cards will be in use by 2002.[4]

smart card
A credit card–sized computer that can be programmed with "electronic money."

   Why are smart cards increasing in popularity today? For one thing, the cost of producing them has fallen dramatically—from as much as $10 to as little as $1. Convenience is equally important, notes Donald J. Gleason, president of Electronic Payment Services' Smart Card Enterprise division. "What consumers want," Gleason contends, "is convenience, and if you look at cash, it's really quite inconvenient."[5]

Automated Teller Machines (ATMs) have revolutionized the way we do our banking. Now we have access to our money almost everywhere we go—shopping malls, grocery stores, even roadside "minibanks."

   Smart cards can be loaded with money at ATM machines or, with special telephone hookups, even at home. After using your card to purchase an item, you can check an electronic display to see how much money your card has left. Analysts predict that in the near future, smart cards will function as much more than electronic purses. For example, travel industry experts predict that people will soon book travel plans at home on personal computers and then transfer their reservations onto their smart cards. The cards will then serve as airline tickets and boarding passes. As an added benefit, they will allow travellers to avoid waiting in lines at car rental agencies and hotel front desks.

A new, revolutionary world of electronic money has begun to emerge with the rapid growth of the Internet. Electronic money, known as **E-cash**, is money that moves along multiple channels of consumers and businesses via digital electronic transmissions. E-cash moves outside the established network of banks, cheques, and paper currency. How does E-cash work? Traditional currency is used to buy electronic funds, which are downloaded over phone lines into a PC or a portable "electronic wallet" that can store and transmit E-cash. E-cash is purchased from any company that issues (sells) it, including banks. When shopping online—say, to purchase jewellery—a shopper sends digital money to the merchant instead of using traditional cash, cheques, or credit cards. Businesses can purchase supplies and services electronically from any merchant that accepts E-cash. E-cash flows from the buyer's into the seller's E-cash funds, which are instantaneously updated and stored on a microchip.

Although E-cash transactions are cheaper than handling cheques and the paper records involved with conventional money, there are some potential problems. Hackers, for example, may break into E-cash systems and drain them instantaneously. Moreover, if the issuer's computer system crashes, it is conceivable that money "banked" in memory may be lost forever. Finally, regulation and control of E-cash systems remains largely nonexistent; there is virtually none of the protection that covers government-controlled money systems.[6] The "It's a Wired World" box addresses some larger issues in e-banking.

E-cash
Money that moves among consumers and businesses via digital electronic transmissions.

WEBCONNEXION

Marrying the speed and convenience of e-mail with the security of online banking, CertaPay's system integrates into banks' Internet services, enabling customers to send money to anyone with an e-mail address. Unlike the E-cash systems described above, CertaPay offers an Internet payment service that draws funds directly from existing bank accounts. E-mail carries the notifications of payment, while the banks clear the transactions with existing clearing processes. Visit CertaPay at:

www.certapay.com

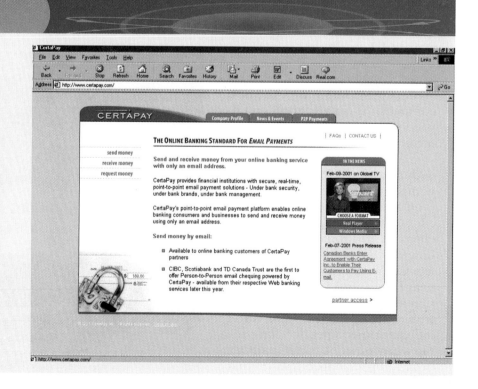

IT'S A WIRED WORLD

To E-Bank or Not to E-Bank

Is banking ready for e-business? It depends on whom you talk to, but based on results to date, bankers have a long way to go before they'll be completely wired. This centuries-old industry isn't yet set up for Internet retail-customer transactions. Commenting on the relatively poor success of Internet banks, one Dutch banker notes: "We underestimate the value of the trust we have built up. It is one of the highest barriers to entry to our business." In other words, consumers are skeptical about trusting personal financial matters to impersonal Internet acquaintances. They're accustomed to dealing with a particular bank, usually at a local facility. Think of the typical services you use—chequing, loans, trusts, investments. Think about face-to-face transactions in a familiar environment. Now contrast that image with an image of Internet transactions with your bank. What if it's a remote bank? What if your contact with your bank is a cyberspace third party?

E-banking raises a basic question that bankers have not encountered before: Should the bank be the party to whom the customer entrusts all of his or her financial activities? Or, from a strictly financial point of view, would a third party be a better choice? This choice has emerged because the Internet, though introducing a third party into the relationship, offers global access to financial products and services beyond the reach of any single bank. As a nonbank third party, for example, OnMoney.com allows you to see and manage all your accounts at one Web location. Banks can't match this service. You can receive and pay bills, prepare and file taxes, check out financial news, and get good deals on financial products from leading vendors (some tailored to your particular needs), all by storing your financial data with—and putting your trust in—a single Web destination. The third party also provides interactive financial management and access to services but does not sell financial products such as car or mortgage loans or stocks and bonds. As a traditional banker, you may like the idea that your customers are linked to a third party that can provide them with a better range of consolidated services. Unfortunately, of course, your customer also gains access to better deals from competing banks and financial services providers.

The alternative is to sell customers on the idea of a centralized bank, but that approach can make customers worry about a bank's objectivity in promoting its own financial products. The customer is likely to ask: If I buy all my products from this bank, how good a deal am I getting on any one of them? The strategic question for the bank, therefore, is how to position itself to win the customer relationship. Bankers disagree on the best approach. The e-Citi unit of Citigroup is hedging its Web strategy by offering a mixture of both Citibank and non-Citibank products for both kinds of customers—those who want one bank to supply all their needs and those who may prefer more diverse offerings. Meanwhile, other banks, especially smaller ones, are leaning towards the option of serving as an adviser that puts customers in touch with outside (third-party) experts for financial advice. Its choice in this matter will undoubtedly have a huge impact on a bank's Web services and customer relationships in the future.

For the present, many bankers are convinced that banks are still dependent on traditional financial products with bank customers who want access to branch locations and human interaction via phone, video, or e-mail. The first generation of Web banks still needs human support and must furnish access to a physical infrastructure (bricks and mortar). Many industry analysts fear that too much technology may push customers into the hands of competitors who still offer face-to-face service.

Figure 18.1 summarizes the services that chartered banks offer. Banks are chartered by the federal government and are closely regulated when they provide these services.

Bank Deposits

Chartered banks provide a financial intermediary service by accepting deposits and making loans with this money. Banks make various types of loans to businesses. When applying for a business loan, it is wise for the manager to remember that the banker is interested in making money for the bank through the loan. The banker is also interested in how the loan will be repaid and how it will be secured. A brief written statement accompanied by a cash-flow analysis is a useful approach when applying for a loan.

Figure 18.1
Examples of services by many chartered banks and trust companies.

chequable deposit
A chequing account.

One type of deposit a customer can make in a bank is a chequable, or demand, deposit. A **chequable deposit** is a chequing account. Customers who deposit coins, paper currency, or other cheques in their chequing accounts can write cheques against the balance in their accounts. Their banks must honour these cheques immediately; this is why chequing accounts are also called demand deposits.

term deposit
Money that remains with the bank for a period of time with interest paid to the depositor.

The other type of deposit a customer can make in a chartered bank is a term deposit. A **term deposit** is one that remains with the bank for a period of time. Interest is paid to depositors for the use of their funds. There are two types of term deposits. The most popular is the regular passbook savings account. Although banks can require notice before withdrawals can be made, they seldom do. These accounts are intended primarily for small individual savers and non-profit organizations.

Another type of term deposit is the guaranteed investment certificate. This deposit is made for a specified period of time ranging from 28 days to several years. These certificates are available to all savers. The interest rate paid on a guaranteed investment certificate is higher than that paid on a regular savings account, but many GICs cannot be cashed in before their maturity dates, so they are less flexible than a savings account.

Bank Loans

Banks are the major source of short-term loans for business. Although banks make long-term loans to some firms, they prefer to specialize in providing short-term funds to finance inventories and accounts receivable.

A *secured* loan is backed by collateral such as accounts receivable or a life insurance policy. If the borrower cannot repay the loan, the bank sells the collateral. An *unsecured* loan is backed only by the borrower's promise to repay it. Only the most creditworthy borrowers can get unsecured loans.

prime rate of interest
The lowest rate charged to borrowers.

Borrowers pay interest on their loans. Large firms with excellent credit records pay the prime rate of interest. The **prime rate of interest** is the lowest rate charged to borrowers. This rate changes constantly owing to changes in the demand for and supply of loanable funds as well as to policies of the Bank of Canada. The so-called "Big Six" Canadian banks (Royal Bank, CIBC, Bank of Montreal, Bank of Nova Scotia, Toronto-Dominion, and National Bank of Canada) typically act in concert with respect to the prime rate.

Banks as Creators of Money

In the course of their activities, financial institutions provide a special service to the economy—they create money. This is not to say that they mint bills and coins. Rather, by taking in deposits and making loans, they *expand the money supply*. We will first look at how this expansion process works, assuming that banks have a **reserve requirement**, that is, that they must keep a portion of their chequable deposits in vault cash or as deposits with the Bank of Canada. (This reserve requirement was dropped in 1991, and the implications of this change are described later.)

reserve requirement
The requirement (until 1991) that banks keep a portion of their chequable deposits in vault cash or as deposits with the Bank of Canada.

Suppose that you saved $100, took it to a bank, and opened a chequing account. Some portion of your $100 is likely to stay in your account, so your bank can earn interest by lending some of it to other borrowers. Let's assume that there is a reserve requirement, and that it is 10 percent. Your bank must therefore keep $10 of your $100 deposit in reserve, so it has only $90 to lend.

Now suppose that a person named Jennifer Leclerc borrows $90 from your bank. She now has $90 added to her chequing account. Assume that she writes a cheque for $90 payable to Canadian Tire. Canadian Tire's bank ends up with a $90 deposit, and that bank is also required to keep $9 in reserve. It therefore has $81 to lend out to someone else.

This process of deposit expansion can continue as shown in Figure 18.2. As you can see, your original deposit of $100 could result in an increase of $1000 in new deposits for all banks in the system. However, what happens if there is no reserve requirement? At the extreme, it means that banks could (theoretically) create infinite amounts of money because they don't have to keep any in reserve. But banks will not do this because it is risky. So, in practice, the dropping of the reserve requirement simply means that banks will be able to create more money than they did when there was a reserve requirement.

Why was the reserve requirement changed? Partly because banks claimed that in the new, deregulated financial services industry it was going to be difficult for them to compete with trust and insurance companies, who have no reserve requirements. The change in reserve requirements could cost the federal government millions of dollars each year in lost interest; it will also lead to increased bank profits or lower loan rates to consumers, or some combination of both.[7]

Other Changes in Banking

Fundamental changes in addition to those already described are taking place in banking. For example, deregulation has caused banks to shift away from their historical role as intermediaries between depositors and borrowers. Canada's banks are diversifying to provide a wider array of financial products to their clients. Training bankers to be effective in this environment is necessary. For example, over 100 executives at Toronto-Dominion Bank attended a Harvard University course that taught them to think like investment bankers. The Bank of Montreal conducted a similar course for over 400 executives.

In the last few years, large companies have reduced their use of bank loans. To compensate for this loss, banks are setting up money market operations. For example, until deregulation, only securities firms were allowed to sell commercial paper (see Chapter 20), but banks expect to dominate in this area before too long. (Commercial paper is usually issued by blue-chip companies that pay a fee to investment dealers or banks to sell the security.) Banks have been allowed to sell commercial paper since June 1987, when deregulation opened up this possibility. The Bank of Montreal and the Toronto-Dominion Bank have been the most active in this market.

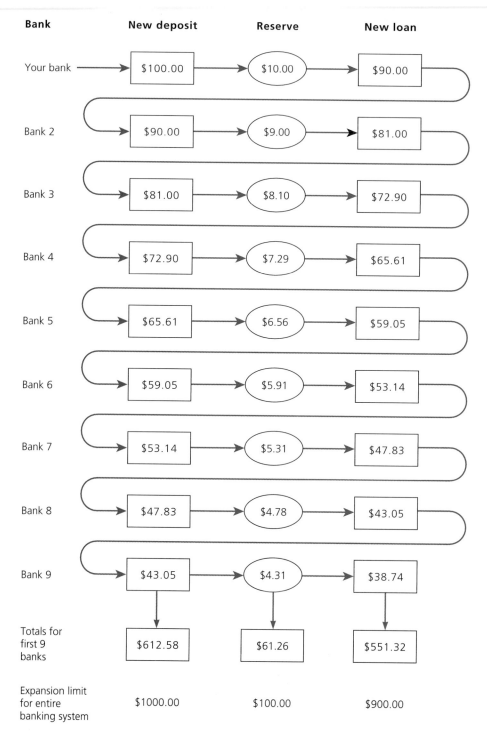

Bank	New deposit	Reserve	New loan
Your bank	$100.00	$10.00	$90.00
Bank 2	$90.00	$9.00	$81.00
Bank 3	$81.00	$8.10	$72.90
Bank 4	$72.90	$7.29	$65.61
Bank 5	$65.61	$6.56	$59.05
Bank 6	$59.05	$5.91	$53.14
Bank 7	$53.14	$5.31	$47.83
Bank 8	$47.83	$4.78	$43.05
Bank 9	$43.05	$4.31	$38.74
Totals for first 9 banks	$612.58	$61.26	$551.32
Expansion limit for entire banking system	$1000.00	$100.00	$900.00

Figure 18.2
How the chartered banking system creates money.

In Canada, about 200 companies have a credit rating good enough for commercial paper. Banks want to use commercial paper more because they do not have to keep capital reserves on hand for commercial paper as they do for acceptances.

Changes are also taking place in banking because consumers are no longer content to simply keep money in a bank when they can get more for it elsewhere. Banks are responding by selling a growing array of corporate and government securities through their branches.

All of this activity is transforming the profit base of banks. In the past, they made most of their money from the spread between interest rates paid to depositors and the rates charged on loans. Investment banking, on the other hand, is fee-based. Banks are making a larger proportion of their profits from fees, and this is blurring the traditional boundary between banks and securities firms.

Another change concerns international banking. Because U.S. and other foreign banks are now allowed to do business in Canada, Canada's "Big Six" banks are going to experience increased competition. They are responding to this threat with a variety of tactics, including cooperating to spread their fixed costs. Syncor Services, for example, is a joint venture between three of the "Big Six" banks that provides cheque-clearing services across Canada.[8] The "Business Today" box describes some key differences between Canadian and U.S. banks.

The Bank of Canada

The **Bank of Canada**, formed in 1935, is Canada's central bank. It has a crucial role to play in managing the Canadian economy and in regulating certain aspects of chartered bank operations.

Bank of Canada
Canada's central bank; formed in 1935.

BUSINESS TODAY

Consumer Satisfaction with Banks: Canada vs. the U.S.

How satisfied are you with the Canadian banking system? Bank bashing is the second most popular sport in Canada after politician bashing. Consumers feel that even while banks are making multibillion-dollar profits, they provide poor service and do a poor job of listening to customer concerns. But bank customers are even less happy in the U.S.

A survey by the Gallup Organization and *American Banker* magazine found that:

- only slightly more than half the respondents were satisfied with their bank
- the banks' most desirable customers—young, university-educated people with above-average incomes—are the most unhappy
- the larger the bank, the less satisfied the customers

Why would this be so? One reason is competition. Even though there are far more banks in the U.S. than in Canada, there is typically less competition in a given U.S. market than there is in Canada. Each of the "Big Six" banks in Canada competes in virtually every market, but in the U.S. a given market may have only two

or three banks. This means, in effect, that service fees are higher in the U.S. because there is less competition there. The service fees charged for ATMs are illustrative.

Consumer groups in the U.S. are on the warpath over rapidly rising ATM fees. Access to ATMs had been free until 1997, but now most banks—particularly the large ones—are charging users on both ends of the transaction. Customers pay about $1.25 to their own bank every time they use another institution's ATM, but they also pay up to $2.50 to the machine's owner. That is three or four times higher than what a Canadian customer would pay for a similar transaction.

Other differences exist between the U.S. and Canadian banking systems. For example, Canadians expect that if they write or cash a cheque, it will clear overnight, but in the U.S. it may take a week to clear. And other services that Canadians take for granted—currency exchange or the ability to pay bills at ATMs—may not even be available at a given bank in the U.S.

All of these specific issues are reasons why U.S. customers are unhappy with their banks. But perhaps the most fundamental advantage of the Canadian banking system is its stability. Since the early 1980s, there have been only two bank failures in Canada, while there have been 1600 bank failures in the U.S.

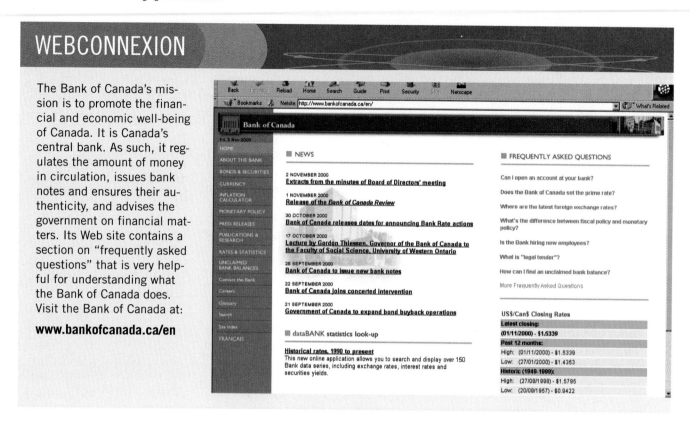

The Bank of Canada is managed by a board of governors composed of a governor, a deputy governor, and 12 directors appointed from different regions of Canada. The directors, with cabinet approval, appoint the governor and deputy governor. The deputy minister of finance is also a nonvoting member of the board. Between meetings of the board, normally held eight times per year, an executive committee acts for the board. This committee is composed of the governor, the deputy governor, two directors, and the deputy minister of finance. The executive committee meets at least once a week.

Operation of the Bank of Canada

The Bank of Canada plays an important role in managing the money supply in Canada. (See Figure 18.3.) If the Bank of Canada wants to increase the money supply, it can buy government securities. The people selling these bonds deposit the proceeds in their banks. These deposits increase banks' reserves and their willingness to make loans. The Bank of Canada can also lower the bank rate; this action will cause increased demand for loans from businesses and households because these customers borrow more money when interest rates drop.

If the Bank of Canada wants to decrease the money supply, it can sell government securities. People spend money to buy bonds, and these withdrawals bring down banks' reserves and reduce their ability to make loans. The Bank of Canada can also raise the bank rate; this action will cause decreased demand for loans from businesses and households because these customers borrow less money when interest rates rise.

Member Bank Borrowing from the Bank of Canada

bank rate
The rate at which chartered banks can borrow from the Bank of Canada.

The Bank of Canada is the lender of last resort for chartered banks. The rate at which chartered banks can borrow from the Bank of Canada is called the **bank**, or rediscount, **rate**. It serves as the basis for establishing the

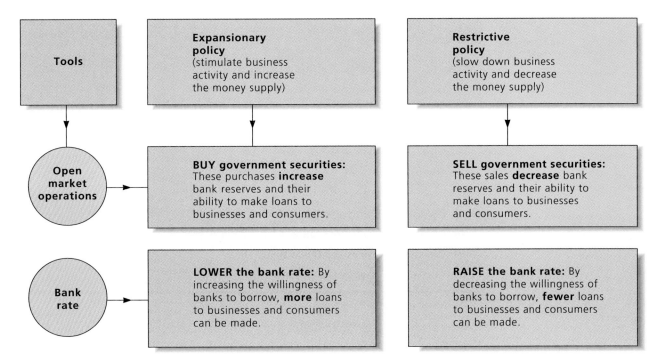

Figure 18.3
Bank of Canada monetary policy actions.

chartered banks' prime interest rates. By raising the bank rate, the Bank of Canada depresses the demand for money; by lowering it, the demand for money increases. In practice, chartered banks seldom have to borrow from the Bank of Canada. However, the bank rate is an important instrument of monetary policy as a determinant of interest rates.

FINANCIAL PILLAR #2—ALTERNATE BANKS

Trust Companies

Another financial intermediary that serves individuals and businesses is the alternate, or near, bank: the trust company. A **trust company** safeguards property—funds and estates—entrusted to it; it may also serve as trustee, transfer agent, and registrar for corporations and provide other services.

    A corporation selling bonds to many investors appoints a trustee, usually a trust company, to protect the bondholders' interests. A trust company can also serve as a transfer agent and registrar for corporations. A transfer agent records changes in ownership of a corporation's shares of stock. A registrar certifies to the investing public that stock issues are correctly stated and comply with the corporate charter. Other services include preparing and issuing dividend cheques to shareholders and serving as trustee for employee profit-sharing funds. Trust companies also accept deposits and pay interest on them.

trust company
Safeguards funds and estates entrusted to it; may also serve as trustee, transfer agent, and registrar for corporations.

Credit Unions/Caisses Populaires

Credit unions (called *caisses populaires* in Quebec) are also alternate banks. They are important to business because they lend money to consumers to buy durable goods such as cars and furniture. They also lend money to businesses. **Credit unions** and caisses populaires are cooperative savings and lending associations formed by a group with common interests. Members

credit union
Cooperative savings and lending association formed by a group with common interests.

Table 18.2	The Top 10 Credit Unions in Canada (ranked by revenues)
Company	**Annual Revenues (in millions)**
1. Le Mouvement des caisses Desjardins	$5485
2. Vancouver City Savings Credit Union	462
3. Credit Union Central of Saskatchewan	189
4. Credit Union Central of B.C.	173
5. Surrey Metro Savings Credit Union	160
6. Richmond Savings Credit Union	135
7. Pacific Coast Savings Credit Union	116
8. Credit Union Central of Ontario	86
9. Capital City Savings and Credit Union Ltd.	86
10. Westminister Savings Credit Union	79

(owners) can add to their savings accounts by authorizing deductions from their paycheques or by making direct deposits. They can borrow short-term, long-term, or mortgage funds from the credit union. Credit unions also invest substantial amounts of money in corporate and government securities. The largest credit unions in Canada are listed in Table 18.2.

FINANCIAL PILLAR #3—SPECIALIZED LENDING AND SAVINGS INTERMEDIARIES

Life Insurance Companies

life insurance company

A mutual or stock company that shares risk with its policyholders for payment of premiums.

An important source of funds for individuals, nonbusiness organizations, and businesses is the life insurance company. A **life insurance company** is a mutual or stock company that shares risk with its policyholders in return for payment of a premium. It lends some of the money it collects from premiums to borrowers. Life insurance companies are substantial investors in real estate mortgages and in corporate and government bonds. Next to chartered banks, they are the largest financial intermediaries in Canada. We discuss insurance companies in more detail in Chapter 20.

Credit unions (caisses populaires) are cooperative saving and lending organizations that loan money to both consumers and businesses.

Factoring Companies

An important source of short-term funds for many firms is factoring companies. **A factoring company** (or factor) buys accounts receivable (amounts due from credit customers) from a firm. It pays less than the face value of the accounts but collects the face value of the accounts. The difference, minus the cost of doing business, is the factor's profit.

A firm that sells its accounts receivable to a factor without recourse shifts the risk of credit loss to the factor. If an account turns out to be uncollectable, the factor suffers the loss. However, a factor is a specialist in credit and collection activities. Using a factor may enable a business firm to expand sales beyond what would be practical without the factor. The firm trades accounts receivable for cash. The factor then notifies the firm's customers to make their overdue payments to the factor.

Financial Corporations

There are two types of financial corporations: sales finance companies and consumer finance companies.

A major source of credit for many firms and their customers is the sales finance company. **A sales finance company** specializes in financing instalment purchases made by individuals and firms. When you buy durable goods from a retailer on an instalment plan with a sales finance company, the loan is made directly to you. The item itself serves as security for the loan. Sales finance companies enable many firms to sell on credit, even though the firms could not afford to finance credit sales on their own.

General Motors Acceptance Corporation (GMAC) is a sales finance company. It is a captive company because it exists to finance instalment contracts resulting from sales made by General Motors. Industrial Acceptance Corporation is a large Canadian sales finance company.

Sales finance companies also finance instalment sales to business firms. Many banks have instalment loan departments.

An important source of credit for many consumers is the consumer finance company. **A consumer finance company** makes personal loans to consumers. Often the borrower pledges no security (collateral) for the loan. For larger loans, collateral may be required, such as a car or furniture.

These companies do not make loans to businesses but they do provide the financing that turns many people into actual paying customers. Household Finance Corporation is an example of a consumer finance company.

Venture Capital or Development Firms

A venture capital firm, or development firm, will provide funds for new or expanding firms thought to have significant potential. Venture capital firms obtain their funds from initial capital subscriptions, from loans from other financial intermediaries, and from retained earnings.

Venture capital firms may provide either equity or debt funds to firms. Financing new, untested businesses is risky, so venture capital firms want to earn a higher-than-normal return on their investment. The ideal situation is an equity investment in a company that becomes very successful and experiences substantial increases in its stock value.

Pension Funds

A pension fund accumulates money that will be paid out to plan subscribers at some time in the future. The money collected is invested in corporate stocks and bonds, government bonds, or mortgages until it is to be paid out. Pension funds are discussed in more detail in Chapter 19.

FINANCIAL PILLAR #4—INVESTMENT DEALERS

Investment dealers (called stockbrokers or underwriters) perform two important financial functions. First, they are the primary distributors of new stock and bond issues (underwriting). Second, they facilitate secondary trading of stocks and bonds, both on stock exchanges and on over-the-counter stock and bond markets (the brokerage function). These functions are discussed in more detail in Chapter 19. The 10 largest investment dealers are shown in Table 18.3.

OTHER SOURCES OF FUNDS

Government Financial Institutions and Granting Agencies

In Canada, a number of government suppliers of funds are important to business. In general, they supply funds to new and/or growing companies. However, established firms can also use some of them.

The **Industrial Development Bank (IDB)**, a subsidiary of the Bank of Canada, was created to make loans to business firms. The **Federal Business Development Bank (FBDB)** took over operation of the IDB in 1975. The IDB was set up to make term loans, primarily to smaller firms judged to have growth potential but unable to secure funds at reasonable terms from traditional sources. Its services were expanded by providing proportionally more equity financing and more management counselling services. The FBDB has been especially active in providing loans for small businesses.

A variety of provincial industrial development corporations provide funds to developing business firms in the hope that they will provide jobs in the province. These were discussed in Chapter 7.

The federal government's Export Development Corporation can finance and insure export sales for Canadian companies. The Canada Mortgage and Housing Corporation (CMHC) is involved in providing and guaranteeing mortgages. The CMHC is particularly important to the construction industry.

A number of federal and provincial programs are specifically designed to provide loans to agricultural operators. Most of these, with the exception of farm improvement loans, which guarantee bank loans to farmers, are long-term loans for land purchase.

Industrial Development Bank (IDB)
A subsidiary of the Bank of Canada created to make loans to business firms.

Federal Business Development Bank (FBDB)
Took over operation of the IDB in 1975; particularly active in lending money to small businesses.

Canada Mortgage and Housing Corporation
www.cmhc-schl.gc.ca

Table 18.3	The Top 10 Investment Dealers in Canada (ranked by revenues)
Company	**Annual Revenues (in millions)**
1. The BMMO Nesbitt Burns Group	$2999
2. TD Securities	2100
3. CIBC World Markets Inc.	1992
4. RBC Dominion Securities	1318
5. National Bank Financial	474
6. Fahnestock Viner Holdings Inc.	414
7. TD Waterhouse Investor Services Canada	342
8. Deutsche Bank Securities Ltd.	222
9. Yorkton Securities	93
10. VERSUS Brokerage Services	17

In addition to these activities, governments are involved in providing grants to business operations. For example, the federal government, through the Department of Regional Industrial Expansion (DRIE), gives grants for certain types of business expansion in designated areas of the country. Other federal government grants are available for activities such as new product development.

International Sources of Funds

Not all of the financing requirements of Canadian businesses and governments are met from within Canada. Foreign sources of funds are also important. The financial institutions of Canada play a role in facilitating the flow of funds into the country.

The Canadian capital market is one part of the international capital market. Canadian provinces borrow extensively in foreign markets such as those in London and in New York. Canadian corporations likewise find it attractive to borrow in foreign markets.

Foreign sources of funds have been significant to the economic development of Canada. Although many groups and individuals have expressed concern about foreign ownership of Canadian firms, projections of Canada's future capital requirements indicate that it will continue to need foreign sources of funds. Canadian financial institutions will continue to play a large role in making these funds available.

INTERNATIONAL BANKING AND FINANCE

Each nation tries to influence its currency exchange rates for economic advantage in international trade. The subsequent country-to-country transactions result in an *international payments process* that moves money among buyers and sellers on different continents.

Exchange Rates and International Trade

As we saw in Chapter 4, every country's currency exchange rate affects its ability to buy and sell on the global market. The value of a given currency (say, the Canadian dollar) reflects the overall supply and demand for Canadian dollars both at home and abroad. This value changes with economic conditions. Worldwide, therefore, firms will watch those trends, and decisions about doing business in Canada will be affected by more or less favourable exchange rates. In 2000, for example, the Canadian dollar was valued at US$0.66, whereas in the 1960s U.S. and Canadian dollars were about equal. Thus, with the Canadian dollar trading near historic lows, American companies have been buying Canadian companies at a record pace and at bargain prices. In the first nine months of 1999, U.S. companies bought 181 Canadian firms for US$24 billion—twice the amount for the same period in 1998. Canada, admits one economist at the Toronto securities firm Nesbitt Burns, "has a 'for sale' sign on the lawn, courtesy of a very cheap exchange rate."[9]

The Law of One Price

How do firms determine when exchange rates are favourable? When a country's currency becomes overvalued, its exchange rate is higher than warranted by its economic conditions. Its high costs make it less competitive. Because its products are too expensive to make and buy, fewer are purchased by other countries. The likely result is a trade deficit (see Chapter 3). In contrast, an undervalued currency means low costs and low prices. It attracts purchases by other countries, usually leading to a trade surplus.

How do we know whether a currency is overvalued or undervalued? One method involves a simple concept called the **law of one price**: the principle that identical products should sell for the same price in all countries. In other words, if the different prices of a Rolex watch in different countries were converted into a common currency, the common-denominator price should be the same everywhere.

But what if prices are not equal? In theory, the pursuit of profits should equalize them. Sellers in high-priced countries will have to reduce prices if they are to compete successfully and make profits. As prices adjust, so should the exchange rates between different currencies until the Rolex can be purchased for the same price everywhere.

A simple example that illustrates over- and undervalued currencies is the Big MacCurrencies, an index published annually in the British magazine *The Economist*. The identical product here is always McDonald's Big Mac, which is made locally in many countries. The first two columns in Table 18.4 list several countries and Big Mac prices in terms of local currencies. Each country's price is then converted into U.S. dollars (based on recent exchange rates). As you can see, the Israel price is most expensive, and the Chinese price is the cheapest.

According to the Big Mac index, then, the Israel shekel is the most overvalued currency (against the U.S. dollar), and the Chinese yuan is the most undervalued currency. In theory, this means that you could buy Big Macs in China (using yuan) and resell them in Israel (for shekels) at a handsome profit. In China, therefore, the demand for burgers would increase, driving the price up towards the higher prices in the other countries. In other words, the law of one price would set in. The index also indicates that the exchange rate of Argentina is neither overvalued nor undervalued, and France's franc is barely overvalued against the dollar. Canada's dollar is undervalued against

law of one price
The principle that identical products should sell for the same price in all countries.

The Economist
www.economist.com

Table 18.4			Big Mac Currency Index
Country	Big Mac Prices in Local Currency	Big Mac Prices in Equivalent U.S. Dollars	Local Currency Overvaluation (+) Undervaluation (−)
United States	**$2.51**	**$2.51**	—
Israel	14.50 shekels	3.58	+43%
Switzerland	5.90 S. francs	3.48	+39
Denmark	24.75 krone	3.08	+23
Britain	1.90 pounds	3.00	+20
Japan	294 yen	2.78	+11
S. Korea	3000 won	2.71	+8
France	18.50 F. francs	2.62	+4
Argentina	2.50 A. pesos	2.50	+0
Mexico	20.90 M. pesos	2.22	−11
New Zealand	$3.40 NZ	1.69	−33
Russia	39.50 rubles	1.39	−45
China	9.90 yuan	1.20	−52

the U.S. dollar. Governments and businesses use far more sophisticated methods to measure the purchasing power of different currencies in making much more complex transactions.

Government Influence on Exchange Rates

What happens in reality when a currency becomes overvalued or undervalued? A nation's economic authorities may take action to correct its balance-of-payments conditions. Typically, they will devalue or revalue the nation's currency. The purpose of devaluing is to cause a decrease in the home country's exchange value. It will then be less expensive for other countries to buy the home country's products. As more of its products are purchased, the home country's payment deficit goes down. The purpose of revaluation, of course, is the reverse: to increase the exchange value and reduce the home country's payment surplus.

At the beginning of December 1994, for instance, the exchange rate was 3.5 Mexican pesos per U.S. dollar. Three weeks later, Mexican officials announced a devaluation, and the rate quickly changed to 4.65 pesos per dollar. By May 2000, the rate had gone to 9.53 pesos per dollar on the world market. The more recent exchange rate encourages other countries to buy more Mexican products, thereby reducing Mexico's payments deficit.

The International Payments Process

Now we know why a nation tries to control its balance of payments and what, at least in part, it can do about an unfavourable balance. Exactly how are payments made? Transactions among buyers and sellers in different countries are simplified through the services provided by their banks. For example, payments from buyers flow through a local bank that converts them from the local currency into the foreign currency of the seller. Likewise, the local bank receives and converts incoming money from the banks of foreign buyers. The *payments process* is shown in Figure 18.4.[10]

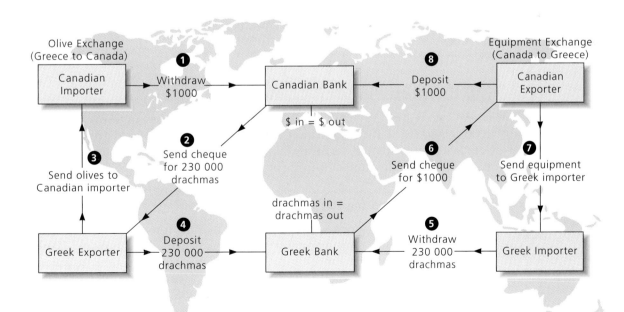

Figure 18.4
The international payments process.

Step 1. A Canadian olive importer withdraws $1000 from its chequing account in order to buy olives from a Greek exporter. The local Canadian bank converts those dollars into Greek drachmas at the current exchange rate (230 drachmas per dollar).

Step 2. The Canadian bank sends the cheque for 230 000 drachmas (230 × 1000) to the exporter in Greece.

Steps 3 and 4. The exporter sends olives to its Canadian customer and deposits the cheque in its local Greek bank. While the exporter now has drachmas that can be spent in Greece, the importer has olives to sell in Canada.

At the same time, a separate transaction is being made between a Canadian machine exporter and a Greek olive oil producer. This time, the importer/exporter roles are reversed between the two countries: The Greek firm needs to *import* a $1000 olive oil press from Canada.

Steps 5 and 6. Drachmas (230 000) withdrawn from a local Greek bank account are converted into $1000 Canadian and sent via cheque to the Canadian exporter.

Steps 7 and 8. The olive oil press is sent to the Greek importer, and the importer's cheque is deposited in the Canadian exporter's local bank account.

In this example, trade between the two countries is *in balance*: Money inflows and outflows are equal for both countries. When such a balance occurs, *money does not actually have to flow between the two countries*. Within each bank, the dollars spent by local importers offset the dollars received by local exporters. In effect, therefore, the dollars have simply flowed from Canadian importers to Canadian exporters. Likewise, the drachmas have moved from Greek exporters to Greek importers.

Interbank Trading

To get a true picture, however, we must multiply this simple illustration by the huge number of daily transactions that take place between countries. Obviously, this system of trade involves banks (or other financial institutions) that buy and sell foreign currencies for their customers. Among these currency trades, the U.S. dollar was by far the most active currency, being involved in 89 percent of all transactions. Next most active were the German mark (34 percent), the Japanese yen (23 percent), and the British pound (9 percent).

The International Bank Structure

There is no worldwide banking system that is comparable, in terms of policy making and regulatory power, to the system of any single industrialized nation. Rather, worldwide banking stability relies on a loose structure of agreements among individual countries or groups of countries.

The World Bank and the IMF

World Bank
A United Nations agency that provides a limited scope of financial services, such as funding national improvements in undeveloped countries.

World Bank
www.worldbank.org

Two United Nations agencies, the World Bank and the International Monetary Fund, help to finance international trade. Unlike true banks, the **World Bank** (technically the International Bank for Reconstruction and Development) actually provides only a very limited scope of services. For instance, it funds national improvements by making loans to build roads, schools, power plants, and hospitals. The resulting improvements eventually enable borrowing countries to increase productive capacity and international trade.

The **International Monetary Fund (IMF)** is a group of some 150 nations that have combined their resources for the following purposes:

- To promote the stability of exchange rates
- To provide temporary, short-term loans to member countries
- To encourage members to cooperate on international monetary issues
- To encourage development of a system for international payments

The IMF makes loans to nations suffering from temporary negative trade balances. By making it possible for these countries to continue buying products from other countries, the IMF facilitates international trade. However, some nations have declined IMF funds rather than accept the economic changes that the IMF demands. For example, some developing countries reject the IMF's requirement that they cut back social programs and spending in order to bring inflation under control.

International Monetary Fund (IMF)
A United Nations agency consisting of about 150 nations who have combined resources to promote stable exchange rates, provide temporary short-term loans, and serve other purposes.

International Monetary Fund
www.imf.org

SUMMARY OF LEARNING OBJECTIVES

1. **Define *money* and identify the different forms it takes in the nation's money supply.** Any item that is portable, divisible, durable, and stable satisfies the four basic characteristics of *money*. Money also serves three functions: it is a medium of exchange, a store of value, and a unit of account. The nation's money supply is often determined by two measures: *M-1* includes liquid (or spendable) forms of money: currency (bills and coins), demand deposits, and other "chequable" deposits (such as chequing accounts and ATM withdrawals). *M-2* includes M-1 plus items that cannot be directly spent but which can be easily converted to spendable forms: time deposits, money market funds, and savings deposits. *Credit* must also be considered as a factor in the money supply.

2. **Describe the different kinds of *financial institutions* that make up the Canadian financial system and explain the services they offer.** The financial intermediaries that form the "four financial pillars" in Canada are chartered banks, alternate banks, specialized lending and savings intermediaries, and investment dealers. The chartered banks, which are at the heart of our financial system, are the most important source of short-term funds for business firms. The chartered banking system creates money in the form of expanding demand deposits. The four kinds of financial institutions offer services like financial advice and brokerage services, electronic funds transfer, pension and trust services, and lending of money.

3. **Explain how banks create money and identify the means by which they are regulated.** By taking in deposits and making loans, banks create money, or more accurately, they expand the money supply. The overall supply of money is controlled by the Bank of Canada.

4. **Explain the functions of the *Bank of Canada* and describe the tools it uses to control the money supply.** The Bank of Canada manages the Canadian economy, controls the money supply, and regulates certain aspects of chartered banking operations. If the Bank of Canada wants to increase the money supply, it can buy government securities or lower the bank rate. If it wants to decrease the money supply, it can sell government securities or increase the bank rate.

5. **Identify ways in which the financial industry is changing.** The clear divisions between the activities of the "four financial pillars" are becoming less obvious. For example, deregulation has allowed banks to begin selling commercial paper. Other financial intermediaries are also beginning to get involved in new financial activities. For example, life insurance companies are starting to take over trust companies so they can get a foothold in the trust business. *Electronic technologies* offer a variety of new financial conveniences to customers. *Debit cards* are plastic cards that permit users to transfer money between bank accounts. *Smart cards* are credit card–sized computers that can be loaded with "electronic money" at ATMs or over special telephone hookups. *E-cash* is money that can be moved among consumers and businesses via digital electronic transmissions.

6. **Understand some of the key activities in *international banking and finance*.** Electronic technologies now permit speedy global financial transactions to support the growing importance of international finance. Country-to-country transactions are conducted according to an *international payment process* that moves money among buyers and sellers in different nations. Each nation tries to influence its *currency exchange* rates to gain advantage in international trade. For example, if its currency is *overvalued*, a higher exchange rate usually results in a *trade deficit*. Conversely, *undervalued* currencies can attract buyers and create *trade surpluses*. Governments may act to influence exchange rates by *devaluing* or *revaluing* their national currencies (that is, by decreasing or increasing them). Devalued currencies make it less expensive for other countries to buy the home country's products.

KEY TERMS

money, 585
M-1, 587
currency, 587
cheque, 587
demand deposit, 587
M-2, 588
time deposit, 588
money market mutual
   funds, 588
chartered bank, 591
trust services, 592
letter of credit, 592

banker's acceptance, 592
electronic funds transfer
   (EFT), 592
debit card, 593
smart card, 593
E-cash, 594
chequable deposit, 596
term deposit, 596
prime rate of interest,
   596
reserve requirement, 597

Bank of Canada, 599
bank rate, 600
trust company, 601
credit union, 601
life insurance company,
   602
factoring company, 603
sales finance company,
   603
consumer finance
   company, 603

venture capital firm, 603
pension fund, 603
Industrial Development
   Bank (IDB), 604
Federal Business
   Development Bank
   (FBDB), 604
law of one price, 606
World Bank, 608
International Monetary
   Fund (IMF), 609

STUDY QUESTIONS AND EXERCISES

Review Questions
1. What is money? What are its ideal characteristics?
2. What are the components of M-1? Of M-2?
3. Describe the structure and operation of the Bank of Canada.
4. List and describe the sources of short-term funds for business firms.

Analysis Questions
5. What kinds of changes in banking are shifting banks away from their historical role?
6. Do we really need all the different types of financial institutions we have in Canada? Could we make do with just chartered banks? Why or why not?

7. Should credit cards be counted in the money supply? Why or why not?
8. Should chartered banks be regulated or should market forces be allowed to set the money supply? Defend your answer.

Application Exercises
9. Interview several consumers to determine which of the new banking services and products they use (debit cards, ATMs, smart cards, etc.). If interviewees are using these services, determine the reasons. If they are not, find out why not.
10. Interview the manager of a local chartered bank. Identify the ways in which the Bank of Canada helps the bank and the ways in which it limits the bank.

Building Your Business Skills

The Risks and Rewards of Credit Cards

Goal
To help students evaluate the risks and rewards associated with excessive credit card use.

Situation
Suppose that you've been out of school for a year and are now working in your first job. Your annual $30 000 salary is enough to support your apartment, car, and the basic necessities of life, but the luxuries are still out of reach. You pay cash for everything until one day you get a preapproved credit card solicitation in the mail, which offers you a $1500 line of credit. You decide to take the offer and begin charging purchases. Within a year, five other credit card companies have contacted you, and you accumulate a total credit card line of $12 000.

Method

Step 1:
Working with three or four classmates, evaluate the advantages and dangers inherent in this situation, both to the consumer and to credit card issuers. To address this issue, research the current percentage of credit card delinquencies and rate of personal bankruptcies. Find out, for example, how these rates compare with those in previous years. In addition, research the profitability of the credit card business.

Step 2:
Evaluate the different methods that credit card companies use to attract new customers. Specifically, look at the following practices:

- Sending unsolicited, preapproved credit card applications to consumers with questionable and even poor credit
- Offering large credit lines to consumers who pay only monthly minimums
- Lowering interest rates on accounts as a way of encouraging revolving payments
- Charging penalties on accounts that are paid in full at the end of every billing cycle (research the GE Rewards MasterCard)
- Sending card holders catalogues of discounted gifts that can be purchased with their charge cards
- Linking credit card use to a program of rewards—say, frequent flier miles linked to amounts charged.

Step 3:
Compile your findings in the form of a set of guidelines designed for consumers receiving unsolicited credit card offers. Your guidelines should analyze the advantages and disadvantages of excessive credit card use.

Follow-Up Questions

1. If you were the person in our hypothetical example, how would you handle your credit situation?
2. Why do you think credit card companies continue to offer cards to people who are financially overextended?
3. What criteria can you suggest to evaluate different credit card offers?
4. How do you know when you have enough credit?

Exploring the Net

More and more financial institutions are utilizing the internet to reach new customers and provide more convenient, less expensive services. Visit President's Choice Financial and ING Direct at:

www.preschoicefinancial.com, www.ingdirect.ca

1. What kind of incentives do both of these online banks offer customers that conventional banks cannot provide? What are the advantages of online banks, according to these sites?
2. Many customers cite anxiety over the intangibility of the process or inhuman nature of banking online as a reason not to use institutions such as these. How do the President's Choice Financial and ING Direct sites try to allay these and other security fears that customers may have?
3. What are some of the services that these banks offer specifically for businesses?

Concluding Case 18-1

Should North America Have a Common Currency?

The introduction of the euro as the common currency of the European Union has started a lot of people thinking that perhaps Canada, the U.S., and Mexico should all have the same currency. A 1999 Angus Reid poll showed that 77 percent of Canadians think that we will, in fact, have a common currency in North America by 2020. This common currency could be achieved by having the three countries simply adopt the U.S. dollar (dollarization), or the three countries could create a new currency (perhaps called the "amero").

Countries as diverse as Bolivia, Uruguay, Peru, Argentina, Laos, Turkey, and Cambodia have already adopted the U.S. dollar as their currency, and some argue that Canada and Mexico should do the same. The three countries would simply fix an exchange rate for the loonie and the peso on a certain date, and after that the U.S. dollar would be the official currency of all three countries. The exchange rate would be fixed so that each country's real income, wealth, and international competitiveness would remain the same. The Bank of Canada would close and the U.S. Federal Reserve Board would have control over monetary policy in the three countries.

The suggestion to either dollarize or adopt the amero comes as a result of Canada's experience with floating exchange rates, which some people feel has been very disappointing. The Canadian dollar has been declining for years in comparison to the U.S. dollar, and no one is quite sure where it will end up. A declining loonie means increased export opportunities, but it may also mean an overreliance on the production of natural resources and an underreliance on high-tech production. Adopting a new currency, it is argued, would bring about greater price stability, lower long-term interest rates, greater productivity, and the creation of more wealth in Canada.

Opponents of a common currency are not hard to find. The C.D. Howe Institute released a study in 1999 saying that Canada's floating exchange rate is working well, and that Canada may have had a recession in 1998 if there had been a common currency and a fixed exchange rate. Gordon Thiessen, the governor of the Bank of Canada, says that the political and economic autonomy that Canada would have to give up when adopting another currency is simply not acceptable. Prime Minister Jean Chrétien is also opposed because the economic power in North America is heavily weighted towards the U.S. In the European Union, power is more balanced between several countries.

Resistance to a common currency does not seem to be as high in Mexico, where the U.S. dollar is already the basis for many business transactions, particularly near the U.S. border. The Mexican Bankers Association supports dollarization, and Mexican president Vicente Fox extolled the virtues of a common North American currency when he visited Canada in 2000.

CASE QUESTIONS

1. What changes would have to take place in Canada before a common currency would become politically and economically acceptable?

2. Those who are in favour of a common North American currency argue that such a currency would be good for Canada because it would lead to lower long-term interest rates, enhanced trade, greater productivity, and the creation of more wealth in Canada. Explain the arguments behind these claims. (You may want to speak with a professor who teaches economics as you develop your answer to this question.)

3. How would dollarization affect the average Canadian? How would creation of the amero affect the average Canadian?

4. Should Canada adopt the U.S. dollar as its currency? Defend your answer. ◆

Concluding Case 18-2

The Canadian Dollar: What's Next?

In the early 1970s, the Canadian dollar was worth about US$1. But in the last 25 years or so, it has moved erratically downwards; and by the end of 2000, it had declined to US$0.65. During one eight-day period in July 1998 the Canadian dollar set a new record low.

The average Canadian probably doesn't pay too much attention to the complexities of currency fluctuations, but does care about the value of the Canadian dollar in terms of the U.S. dollar. Given that the U.S. is close to Canada, is a world power, and is our biggest trading partner, this is not surprising. But the fact is that while the Canadian dollar has *dropped* in value compared to the German mark, the English pound, and the U.S. dollar, it has actually *increased* in value compared to the Indonesian rupiah, the Thai baht, the Malaysian ringgit, and the Japanese yen.

Currency fluctuations create winners and losers. As the value of the Canadian dollar declines, winners are typically exporters (because the prices of our exported goods become cheaper in foreign countries) and tourist operators (more tourists come to Canada since they can get more for their money). Losers are typically importers (who must pay higher prices for foreign goods), Canadians who travel abroad (the cost of their travel will be higher because the value of the dollar is lower), and anyone who has loans that are in foreign currency.

But the creation of winners and losers is not quite that simple. Canadian companies that export their products to the U.S. but get most of their raw materials from within Canada benefit because they pay their bills in Canadian dollars but get revenue in U.S. dollars. MacMillan Bloedel Ltd., for example, gains $3 million a year in increased profits for every one-cent drop in the Canadian dollar. On the other hand, companies whose revenues come from Canadians but whose costs are paid in U.S. dollars are hurt when the Canadian dollar declines (for example, professional sports teams in Canada who pay their players in U.S. dollars).

Whether you are a winner or a loser also depends on the foreign country with which you do the most business. Japanese tourists, for example, used to flock to the Canadian Rockies. But since 1995, the loonie has increased 51 percent in value compared to the Japanese yen, so far fewer Japanese tourists are visiting. Conversely, since the loonie has decreased in value compared to the U.S. dollar, more American tourists are coming to Canada. In Toronto, for example, the number of *conventions* increased only 2 percent from 1996 to 1997, but the number of *people* at those conventions increased 43 percent.

We should not conclude from these statistics that it will be easy for Canadian tourist operators to entice Americans to visit. The trouble lies with the Americans' legendary ignorance about things Canadian. This translates into a lack of knowledge about the good deals Americans can get when they exchange U.S. dollars for Canadian. For example, they might not know that a $100 hotel room will only cost them about US$66.

But while it is true that the U.S. dollar is worth 6 percent more now than just a year ago in Canada, it is worth 70 percent more than the Thai baht, 57 percent more than the Malaysian ringgit, and 23 percent more than the Australian dollar. In other words, the U.S. dollar goes further in many countries Americans might want to visit, so we can't assume they will come to Canada to spend their money.

Even when the Canadian dollar increases in value there can be problems. Many Asian students who used to come to universities in Canada can no longer afford to; the Malaysian ringgit, for example, has dropped 40 percent in relation to the Canadian dollar. The same thing has happened to the currencies of Indonesia and Thailand.

CASE QUESTIONS

1. What are the benefits of a "high" and "low" Canadian dollar? The drawbacks?

2. Compare the level of the Canadian dollar over the last 15 years with Canada's pattern of imports and exports. Is there any relationship among imports, exports, and the level of the Canadian dollar? (The *Bank of Canada Review* contains the information you need to answer this question.)

3. Do you think the government of Canada should intervene to influence the value of the Canadian dollar? Defend your answer. ◆

Visit the *Business* Website at www.pearsoned.ca/griffin
for up-to-date e-business cases!

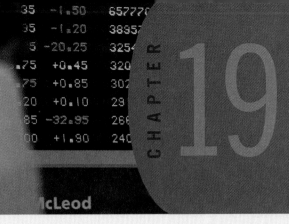

Another Stock Market Scandal

In the summer of 2000, the Ontario Securities Commission (OSC) and the Toronto Stock Exchange (TSE) concluded that the stock prices of many different Canadian companies were being manipulated using a practice called "juicing" or "high-closing." The practice works like this: Just before the stock exchange closes, a trader buys enough shares of a given stock so that the price of that stock rises above the price of the previous trade. This makes it look as if the stock has upward momentum (or, if the stock has been falling, makes it look as if its downward fall has been stopped).

The motivation to juice or high-close a stock is strong for money managers, because they are under intense pressure to increase the value of their portfolios so they can demonstrate high performance and attract more clients. The temptation is particularly strong at year-end because money managers' annual bonuses are tied to their performance.

High-closing activities were detected by a software program that had been specifically designed by the TSE to catch artificially pumped-up stock prices. A surveillance team analyzed computer output to determine whether any stock prices looked suspicious. When they identified several such stocks, the surveillance team requested verification from brokerage houses about who the trader was. Once the surveillance team had received copies of stock orders from various brokers identifying the traders and customers behind each purchase, it became clear that most of the trades had been ordered by one customer, a prominent pension fund manager.

In this case, employees at RT Capital Management Inc., the investment arm of the Royal Bank of Canada, were charged with illegally trading in an attempt to manipulate stock prices (RT Capital Management manages pension funds for many Canadian corporations and governments, including Alcan Aluminum, Noranda, Air Canada, and the province of Newfoundland). Several traders at some major stock brokerages were also charged.

Shortly after the charges were laid, RT Capital Management admitted that it had manipulated the closing price of 26 stocks over 8 days in late 1998 and early 1999. The RT Capital employees who were involved included a senior vice-president and two traders, all of whom were suspended. In July 2000, RT Capital Management was fined $3 million. Twelve traders at 11 different brokerage firms who were also charged agreed to accept fines and suspensions for their illegal actions.

RT Capital Management has lost business to its competitors as a result of the OSC's market manipulation charges. The University of Western Ontario, for example, redirected $1 million of new pension fund contributions to another company, and the city of Toronto did the same with $6 million in new funds.

The activity at RT Capital may have been just the tip of the iceberg. A study by the *Globe and Mail* covering the years 1997, 1998, and 1999 found many examples of unexplained upward jumps in stock prices on the last trading day of a year. These jumps were followed by steep declines early in the new year. For example, MetroNet Communications Corp.'s stock gained $4.45 per share on December 31, 1998, then lost $5.60 per share in early January 1999. The study found that in one year 80 percent of the stocks that had gained 5 percent or more on December 31 (and reached their daily high at the end of the day) also fell early in the new year.

The TSE routinely sends out bulletins to traders reminding them that setting artificial prices is a violation of exchange rules. But high closing cases are difficult to prove because traders can always argue that they bought a certain stock simply because they thought it was a good deal, or because they just happened to be filling a trade order at the end of the day. The TSE policy makes it a trader's responsibility to determine if a client is trying to high-close a stock. ◆

Royal Bank of Canada
www.royalbank.com/rtcp/

Thousands of Canadians regularly invest their money in stocks and bonds. As the opening case demonstrates, activities by stock market professionals can affect typical investors, especially when they are basing their purchasing decisions on the distorted information that is generated by the practice of high-closing.

By focusing on the learning objectives of this chapter, you will better understand the importance of the marketplaces in which securities are traded; the nature of investment vehicles such as stocks and bonds, mutual funds, and commodities; and the reasons for government regulation of securities markets.

After reading this chapter, you should be able to:

LEARNING OBJECTIVES

1. Explain the difference between *primary* and *secondary securities markets*.

2. Discuss the value of *common stock* and *preferred stock* to shareholders and describe the secondary market for each type of security.

3. Distinguish among various types of *bonds* in terms of their issuers, safety, and retirement.

4. Describe the investment opportunities offered by *mutual funds* and *commodities*.

5. Explain the process by which securities are bought and sold.

6. Explain how securities markets are regulated.

SECURITIES MARKETS

Stocks and bonds are known as **securities** because they represent *secured*, or *asset-based*, claims on the part of investors. In other words, holders of stocks and bonds have a stake in the business that issued them. As we saw in Chapter 2, stockholders have claims on some of a corporation's assets (and a say in how the company is run) because each share of stock represents part ownership.

In contrast, *bonds* represent strictly financial claims for money owed to holders by a company. Companies sell bonds to raise long-term funds. The markets in which stocks and bonds are sold are called *securities markets*.

securities
Stocks and bonds (which represent a secured-asset-based claim on the part of investors) that can be bought and sold.

Primary and Secondary Markets for Securities

Primary securities markets handle the buying and selling of new stocks and bonds by firms or governments. New securities are sometimes sold to one buyer or a small group of buyers. These so-called private placements allow the businesses that use them to keep their plans confidential. But because such offerings cannot be resold, buyers demand higher returns from them.

Most new stocks and some bonds are sold to the wider public market. To bring a new security to market, the issuing corporation must obtain approval from a provincial securities commission. It also needs the services of an investment banker. **Investment bankers** serve as financial specialists in issuing new securities. Such well-known firms as RBC Dominion Securities and TD Securities provide three types of investment banking services. They advise the company on the timing and financial terms for the new issue. By *underwriting* (buying) the new securities, investment bankers bear some of the risk of issuing the new security. And, finally, they create the distribution network that moves the new securities through groups of other banks and brokers into the hands of individual investors.

primary securities market
The sale and purchase of newly issued stocks and bonds by firms or governments.

investment banker
Any financial institution engaged in purchasing and reselling new stocks and bonds.

secondary securities market
The sale and purchase of previously issued stocks and bonds.

New securities represent only a small portion of securities traded, however. The market for existing stocks and bonds, the **secondary securities market**, is handled by organizations such as the Toronto Stock Exchange. We will consider the activities of these markets later in this chapter.

Who Invests in Securities Markets?

A variety of investors, ranging from average working citizens to huge cash-rich institutions, buy and sell securities. **Institutional investors**—organizations that invest for themselves and their clients (for example, a mutual fund)—may have the greatest influence on securities markets. But individual investors hold a substantial portion of the stock in Canadian companies.

institutional investors
Organizations whose investments for themselves and their clients are so large that they can influence prices on securities markets.

All investors, large and small, have unique motives and goals that affect their investment *portfolios* (the mix of securities they hold). Young people may be saving for college or university, a car, or a first house. They want relatively safe investments that will preserve their accumulated savings. They also want investments with some liquidity, so that the necessary funds are available when needed.

But people also have long-term goals, such as preparing for retirement. Such individuals are most interested in maximizing their wealth during the next 20 or 30 years. They are largely unconcerned about the ups and downs of investments in any particular year.

Personality differences, too, affect investment decisions. Some people are uncomfortable about taking chances with money, while some *speculators* thrive on the excitement of large gains and losses. Thus, the best types of investments differ depending on investors' goals and attitudes towards the need for safety, income, and growth. As you will see, each type of security offers its own mix of these traits.

STOCKS

Each year, financial managers, along with millions of individual investors, buy and sell the stocks of thousands of companies. This widespread ownership has become possible because of the availability of different types of stocks and because markets have been established for conveniently buying and selling them. In this section, we will focus on the value of *common* and *preferred stoc*k as securities. We will also describe the *stock exchanges* where they are bought and sold.

Common Stock

Individuals and other companies buy a firm's common stock in the hope that the stock will increase in value, affording them a capital gain, and/or will provide dividend income. But what is the value of a common stock? Stock values are expressed in three different ways: as par value, as market value, and as book value.

Par Value

par value
The arbitrary value of a stock set by the issuing company's board of directors and stated on stock certificates; used by accountants but of little significance to investors.

The face value of a share of stock, its **par value**, is set by the issuing company's board of directors. But this arbitrary accounting value has almost nothing to do with the real value of the share.

For example, when United Parcel Service Inc. (UPS), the world's largest express carrier, issued more than 100 million shares of its new Class B Common Stock, the par value was US$0.01 per share. But the stock was sold to the public for US$50 a share.[1] The choice of $50 reflects the price that UPS management believed investors would be willing to pay based on UPS's assets and earnings potential.

Market Value

A stock's real value, then, is its **market value**—the current price of a share in the stock market. UPS shares, for example, sold for up to US$76 a share in 1999, indicating that investors value the stock at much more than the original $50. Market value, therefore, reflects buyers' willingness to invest in a company. It depends on a firm's history of dividend payments, its earnings potential, and on investors' expectations of **capital gains**—profits to be made from selling the stock for more than it cost. Investors, then, are concerned primarily with market value.

In addition to these objective factors, the market price of a stock can be influenced by several subjective factors. *Rumours*, for example, can markedly influence the price of a company's stock, particularly those in the natural resource industries. All it takes is a rumour that a company has made a big gold strike and the price of the stock soars, as it did for Bre-X and Timbuktu Gold Corp. in the 1990s. Both of these "finds" were later proven fraudulent, and many investors lost large amounts of money when the market price of the stock declined sharply.

Investor relations—the art of disseminating information about a company's financial condition—can also influence the price of stock. Investor relations plays up the positive aspects of a company's finances to stockbrokers, financial analysts, and financial institutions in the hope that this will increase the market price of the stock. Toronto-based American Barrick Resources Corp. is well known for its investor relations activities.

The activities of *stockbrokers* can also influence the market price of a stock. If a broker makes a "buy" recommendation for a stock, that recommendation can increase the demand for that stock and cause its price to rise. Conversely, a "sell" recommendation can decrease demand and cause the price to fall. Brokers may also try to "high-close" a stock in an attempt to manipulate its price (see the opening case of this chapter). The brokerage industry has an image problem because of this scandal. Speaking more generally, stockbrokers may also be motivated to put their own financial interests ahead of the financial interests of their clients because stockbrokers are paid on commission. To increase their earnings, brokers may be tempted to pursue a "churn and burn" strategy (buying and selling stock frequently) in order to increase their commissions.

Book Value

The book value of common stock represents stockholders' equity divided by the number of shares. Stockholders' equity is the sum of a company's common stock par value, retained earnings, and additional paid-in capital. In 1999, for example, UPS had stockholders' equity of $11.81 billion. There were 1.15 billion common shares (total of all types) outstanding.[2] Thus, the book value of the stock was $10.27 per share ($11.81/1.15).

Book value is used as a comparison indicator because, for successful companies, the market value is usually greater than its book value. Thus, when market price falls to near book value, some investors buy the stock on the principle that it is underpriced and will increase in the future.

market value
The current price of one share of a stock in the secondary securities market; the real value of a stock.

capital gains
Profits from the sale of an asset (such as stock) for a higher price than that at which it was purchased.

Investment Traits of Common Stock

Common stocks are among the riskiest of all securities. Uncertainties about the stock market itself, for instance, can quickly change a given stock's value. Furthermore, when companies have unprofitable years, they often cannot pay dividends. Shareholder income—and perhaps share price—may both drop. At the same time, however, common stocks offer high growth potential. Naturally the prospects for growth in various industries change from time to time, but the **blue-chip stocks** of well-established, financially sound firms such as IBM and Imperial Oil have historically provided investors with steady income through consistent dividend payouts.

blue-chip stocks
Stocks of well-established, financially sound firms.

What Is a Blue-Chip Stock?   With the proliferation of Internet and start-up dot-coms, it seemed for a while that conventional methods for valuing stocks—a company's history of dividend payouts, steady earnings-per-share growth, and a low price-to-earnings ratio—didn't seem to apply to the "new economy" stocks. In some cases, market prices soared for start-ups that had never earned a dime of profit.

Newcomers like Amazon.com, eBay, and Yahoo! seemed to be viewed as Internet blue-chip stocks even though their financial performance was quite different than that of traditional blue-chip stocks. Consider the differences between Yahoo! and Wal-Mart, for example. If you had invested $10 000 in Wal-Mart stock in June 1995, the market value of this blue-chip stock would have increased to more than $40 000 in just five years. However, the same investment in Yahoo! would have grown to $500 000. (In early 2000, Wal-Mart shares were selling for about US$70 each, while Yahoo! shares were selling for US$250 each.)

This huge difference could not be predicted by using any traditional financial measures, as the numbers in Table 19.1 show. Earnings-per-share (EPS) for 1996–99 shows steady growth for Wal-Mart, but a very uneven pattern for Yahoo! In comparing price-to-earnings ratios, Wal-Mart's 40:1 ratio

Table 19.1					Two Blue-Chip Stocks: Wal-Mart versus Yahoo!	

EARNINGS PER SHARE

	1999	1998	1997	1996	June 2000 Price/ Earnings	January 2000 Book Value/ Share
Wal-Mart	$0.99	0.78	0.67	0.60	40.3	$5.80
Yahoo!	0.10	0.11	−0.53	−0.09	693.1	$2.37

INCOME TREND

	1999 Net Income (in millions)	1-Year Growth	3-Year Growth	5-Year Growth	10-Year Growth
Wal-Mart	$5575	22.9%	20.3%	16.2%	15.8%
Yahoo!	61.1	223.8%	—	—	—

DIVIDEND TREND

	1999 Dividend/ Share	Dividend Growth Rate 3-Year	5-Year	10-Year
Wal-Mart	$0.24	12.0%	15.9%	18.8%
Yahoo!	0.00	0.00	0.00	—

is on the high side, indicating that the stock might be somewhat overpriced. However, Yahoo!'s 693:1 ratio is completely off the scale. As another indicator, Wal-Mart's book value is more than double that of Yahoo!'s, and its net income is nearly 100 times higher. Wal-Mart also has a steady history of dividend payouts to stockholders, while Yahoo! has never paid a dividend.

Overall, then, the traditional measures of stock market value suggest that Wal-Mart should be valued much more highly than Yahoo! However, as we have seen, in early 2000 Yahoo! was valued 12 times higher than Wal-Mart. Why? The most likely explanation is that the stock market had not yet had enough time to determine the real value of high-tech stocks. If we compare Wal-Mart and Yahoo! at the end of 2000, however, we get a much better picture of the true value of the two stocks. On December 14, 2000, Wal-Mart shares were selling for US$50 each, while Yahoo! shares were selling for only US$36.

The drastic change in the price of Yahoo! was illustrative of the sharp drop that occurred in high-tech stocks as 2000 drew to a close. Two Calgary-based high-tech stocks—Cell-Loc and Wi-Lan—also dropped dramatically during 2000. By December 2000, Cell-Loc had dropped 84 percent from its March high, and Wi-Lan had dropped 88 percent.

Preferred Stock

Preferred stock is usually issued with a stated par value, such as $100. Dividends paid on preferred stock are usually expressed as a percentage of the par value. For example, if a preferred stock with a $100 par value pays a 6 percent dividend, shareholders would receive an annual dividend of $6 on each share.

Some preferred stock is *callable*. The issuing firm can require the preferred shareholders to surrender their shares in exchange for a cash payment. The amount of this cash payment, known as the *call price*, is specified in the agreement between the preferred shareholders and the firm.

Investment Traits of Preferred Stock

Because of its preference on dividends, preferred stock's income is less risky than the common stock of the same company. Moreover, most preferred stock is cumulative. With **cumulative preferred stock**, any dividend payments the firm misses must be paid later, as soon as the firm is able. Typically, the firm cannot pay any dividends to its common shareholders until it has made up all late payments to preferred shareholders. If a firm with preferred stock having a $100 par value and paying a 6 percent dividend fails to pay that dividend for two years, it must make up the arrears of $12 per share before it can pay dividends to common shareholders.

Nevertheless, even the income from cumulative preferred stock is not as certain as the corporate bonds of the same company. The company cannot pay dividends if it does not make a profit. The purchase price of the preferred stock can also fluctuate, leading to a capital gain or loss for the shareholder. And the growth potential of preferred stock is limited due to its fixed dividend.

cumulative preferred stock
Preferred stock on which dividends not paid in the past must first be paid up before the firm may pay dividends to common shareholders.

Stock Exchanges

Most of the secondary market for stocks is handled by organized stock exchanges. In addition, a so-called "dealer," or the over-the-counter, market handles the exchange of some stocks. A **stock exchange** is an organization of individuals formed to provide an institutional setting in which stock can be bought and sold. The exchange enforces certain rules to govern its members' trading activities. Most exchanges are non-profit corporations established to serve their members.

stock exchange
A voluntary organization of individuals formed to provide an institutional setting where members can buy and sell stock for themselves and their clients in accordance with the exchange's rules.

To become a member, an individual must purchase one of a limited number of memberships—called "seats"—on the exchange. Only members (or their representatives) are allowed to trade on the exchange. In this sense, because all orders to buy or sell must flow through members, they have a legal monopoly. Memberships can be bought and sold like other assets.

The Trading Floor

Each exchange regulates the places and times at which trading may occur. Trading is allowed only at an actual physical location called the *trading floor*. The floor is equipped with a vast array of electronic communications equipment for conveying buy and sell orders or confirming completed trades. A variety of news services furnish important up-to-the-minute information about world events as well as business developments. Any change in these factors, then, may be swiftly reflected in share prices.

On April 23, 1997, the Toronto Stock Exchange trading floor closed after 145 years of operation. Buy and sell orders are now placed through computers. At its heyday in the 1980s, over 400 traders worked on the floor.[3]

One oft-cited cause of the 1987 panic on the Toronto Stock Exchange is **program trading**—the purchase or sale of a group of stocks valued at $1 million or more, often triggered by computerized trading programs that can be launched without human supervision or control.[4] As market values change during the course of a day, computer programs are busy recalculating the future values of stocks. Once a calculated value reaches a critical point, the program automatically signals a buy or sell order. Program trading could conceivably cause the market to spiral out of control. One way to avoid this is to set up "circuit breakers" that suspend trading for a preset length of time (for example, one hour). The interruption provides a "cooling-off" period that slows down trading activity and allows computer programs to be revised or shut down.

program trading
The purchase or sale of stocks by computerized trading programs that can be launched without human supervision or control.

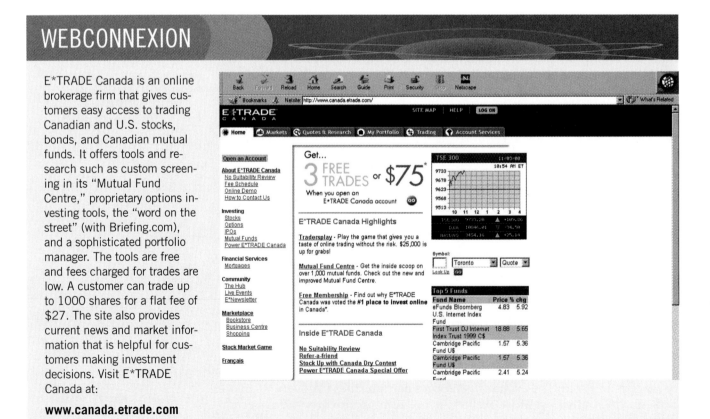

WEBCONNEXION

E*TRADE Canada is an online brokerage firm that gives customers easy access to trading Canadian and U.S. stocks, bonds, and Canadian mutual funds. It offers tools and research such as custom screening in its "Mutual Fund Centre," proprietary options investing tools, the "word on the street" (with Briefing.com), and a sophisticated portfolio manager. The tools are free and fees charged for trades are low. A customer can trade up to 1000 shares for a flat fee of $27. The site also provides current news and market information that is helpful for customers making investment decisions. Visit E*TRADE Canada at:

www.canada.etrade.com

Brokers

Some of the people working on the trading floor are employed by the exchange; others trade stocks for themselves. A large number of those working on the trading floor are brokers. A **broker** receives buy and sell orders from those who are not members of the exchange and executes the orders. In return, the broker earns a commission from the order placer.

broker

An individual licensed to buy and sell securities for customers in the secondary market; may also provide other financial services.

Discount Brokers. Like many services, brokerage assistance can be purchased at either discount or at full-service prices. Buying 200 shares of a $20 stock in 1999 cost an investor only $14.95 at E*Trade, but $116 at a full-service brokerage firm.

Discount brokers offer well-informed individual investors a fast, low-cost way to participate in the market. These customers know what they want to buy or sell, and they usually make trades through personal computers or a telephone order system without talking with a broker. Why are discount brokerage services low cost? For one thing, sales personnel receive fees or salaries, not commissions. Unlike many full-service brokers, they do not offer investment advice or person-to-person sales consultations. They do, however, offer automated online services, such as stock research, industry analysis, and screening for specific types of stocks.

The popularity of online trading stems from convenient access to the Internet, fast no-nonsense transactions, and the opportunity for self-directed investors to manage their own portfolios while paying low fees for trading. The number of equity trades that are executed online is growing so rapidly that online investing is now the Internet's second most popular activity (the most popular is surfing for pornography). As you can see in Figure 19.1, the volume of online trading is increasing as competition among brokers drives prices further downward.

Full Service Brokers. Despite the growth in online investing, an important market remains for full-service brokerages, both for new, uninformed investors and for experienced investors who don't have time to keep up with

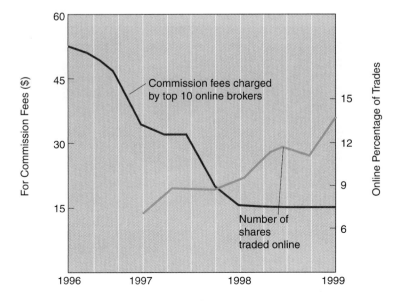

Figure 19.1
The growth of online trading.

all the latest developments. Full-service brokers can offer clients consulting advice in personal financial planning, estate planning, and tax strategies, along with a wider range of investment products. Initial public offerings (IPOs) of stock, for example, are generally not available to the public through online retail brokers. Rather, full-service brokers—who are also the investment bankers that sell the IPO shares—can sell IPO shares to their clients. Financial advisers also do more than deliver information: they offer interpretations of and suggestions on investments that clients might overlook when trying to sift through an avalanche of online financial data.[5]

Canadian Stock Exchanges

The Toronto Stock Exchange. The largest stock exchange in Canada is the Toronto Stock Exchange (TSE). It is made up of about 100 individual members who hold seats. The securities of most major corporations are listed here. A company must pay a fee before it can list its security on the exchange.

The Canadian Venture Exchange. Until recently, there were also stock exchanges in Calgary, Vancouver, and Montreal. In 1999, however, an agreement was reached that (1) created the new Canadian Venture Exchange (CDNX) from the Vancouver and Alberta stock markets, (2) shifted all derivative trading to the Montreal stock exchange, and (3) consolidated all senior equity trading at the TSE.[6] The CDNX now focuses on junior companies.

Foreign Stock Exchanges

Many other countries also have active stock exchanges. In fact, several foreign stock exchanges—most notably those in the U.S. and England—trade far more shares each day than the TSE does.

The New York Stock Exchange. For many people, even those outside the U.S., "the stock market" means the New York Stock Exchange (NYSE). Founded in 1792 and located at the corner of Wall and Broad streets in New York City, the

Canadian Venture Exchange
www.cdnx.ca

The Toronto Stock Exchange is one of several in Canada where shares of stock in Canadian companies are bought and sold.

largest of all U.S. exchanges is the model for exchanges worldwide. An average of 809 million shares valued at US$36 billion change hands each day. About 40 percent of all shares traded on U.S. exchanges are traded at the NYSE.

Only firms meeting certain minimum requirements—earning power, total value of outstanding stock, and number of shareholders—are eligible for listing on the NYSE. The stocks of more than 3000 companies are traded on the NYSE, with a total market value of US$16 trillion. As of March 2000, the common shares of General Electric had the NYSE's highest market value, at US$520 billion. NYSE trading volume in 1999 was more than 204 billion shares.[7]

In Muscat, the capital of Oman, a tiny sultanate on the Arabian peninsula, the tax laws have been changed to encourage more foreign investment. One immediate result has been a 62 percent increase in activity on the Muscat Securities Market, where "high-tech" accoutrements still consist of telephones and (for interested local parties stationed in the gallery) binoculars. There is, of course, a Web site: www.msm-oman.com.

The American Stock Exchange. The second-largest floor-based U.S. exchange, the American Stock Exchange (AMEX), is also located in New York City. It accounts for about 3 percent of all shares traded on U.S. exchanges and, like the NYSE, has minimum requirements for listings. They are, however, less stringent. The minimum number of publicly held shares, for example, is 500 000 versus 1.1 million for the NYSE. The AMEX currently lists about 900 stocks of companies around the world. Indeed, in 1998, foreign stocks made up nearly 7 percent of the total market value of the 32 million shares traded daily on the AMEX.[8] As firms grow, they often transfer their listings from the AMEX to the NYSE.

Other Foreign Stock Exchanges. As recently as 1980, the U.S. market accounted for more than half the value of the world market in traded stocks. As late as 1975, the equity of IBM alone was greater than the national market equities of all but four countries. Market activities, however, have shifted as the value of shares listed on foreign exchanges continues to grow. The annual dollar value of trades on exchanges in London, Tokyo, and other cities is in the trillions. In fact, the London exchange exceeds even the NYSE in the number of stocks listed. In market value, however, transactions on U.S. exchanges remain larger than those on exchanges in other countries. Relatively new exchanges are also flourishing in cities from Shanghai to Warsaw.

Stock markets in Asia have been very volatile during the last few years because of uncertainty about the strength of the economies in the region. The "Business Today" box describes some of the factors that have contributed to this volatility.

The Over-the-Counter Market. The **over-the-counter (OTC) market** is so called because its original traders were somewhat like retailers. They kept supplies of shares on hand and, as opportunities arose, sold them over the counter to interested buyers. Even today, the OTC market has no trading floor. Rather, it consists of many people in different locations who hold an inventory of securities that are not listed on any of the major exchanges. The OTC consists of independent dealers who own the securities that they buy and sell at their own risk. Although OTC activities are of interest from a historical perspective, trading volume is small in comparison to other markets.

over-the-counter (OTC) market
A complex of dealers in constant touch with each other who trade stocks and bonds of some smaller corporations and all fixed-income securities (bonds and debentures).

BUSINESS TODAY

The Asian Crisis

During 1997 and 1998, serious economic and financial problems developed in several Asian countries, including Indonesia, Thailand, Malaysia, and South Korea. Even powerful Japan, once thought to be invincible, was mired in recession. As of mid-1998, Thailand, Indonesia, South Korea, Hong Kong, and Singapore were heading towards a recession. What caused the Asian crisis? Why were so many countries affected? What are the implications for Canada's economy?

Several interrelated factors caused the crisis—reduced economic growth rates in Asia, a sharp drop in the value of Asian currencies, high levels of foreign debt, high levels of bad debts, excess production capacity, a strategy to achieve economic growth by exporting more goods, and governments reluctant to take the steps necessary to resolve the crisis.

The first hint of the problems that lay ahead came in mid-1997, when the currencies of Indonesia, Malaysia, and Thailand began to decline in value. By mid-1998, these currencies had declined by as much as 70 percent against the U.S. dollar. At that point, problems were still limited largely to the countries suffering the currency declines. But the effects soon spread to other countries. As the Indonesian *rupiah*, the Malaysian *ringgit*, and the Thailand *baht* declined in value, these countries found that they could export goods more easily because their products became cheaper on foreign markets. But other countries in Asia then became concerned that they would not be able to be competitive when exporting their goods because the values of the rupiah, ringgit, and baht were so low.

In this same general time period, the value of the South Korean *won* and the Japanese *yen* also dropped because those two countries had economic difficulties of their own. In Japan, for example, banks had loaned large amounts of money on questionable business ventures. Somewhere between half a billion and a billion dollars of bank loans are now thought to be uncollectible. Japan's bad-debt problem could amount to as much as 25 percent of its annual GDP. The same is generally true in South Korea.

As the value of the yen and the won dropped, Japan and South Korea became more competitive in exports, but they also put further downward pressure on the rupiah, ringgit, and baht. China has been able to resist most of these problems so far, but its banks also made many questionable loans. It may have to devalue its currency as well because it is intent on maintaining economic growth by exporting goods.

The International Monetary Fund (IMF) has tried to stabilize the Asian economies by granting multibillion-dollar bailout deals. But the IMF typically grants these bailouts only if the country in question will do some very painful things like closing bankrupt companies and shutting down weak banks. These actions cause increases in unemployment, and governments of the Asian countries have avoided them because they are unpopular with their citizens.

Some critics of the IMF question whether its strategy of imposing austerity measures on these countries is wise. What is really needed, they argue, is acceptance of the fact that billions of dollars in bank loans that were made in the heady days of high economic growth will probably never be collected.

What impact will all this have on Canada? Each year, Canada exports billions of dollars in raw materials such as lumber and coal to Asia. But as those economies go into recession, demand for our raw materials declines. Hence, Canadian companies (who are also very export-oriented) will experience problems selling their products. And we are not alone. Fallout from the Asian crisis has affected family farms in New Zealand, fishers in Alaska, and petrochemical companies in Europe.

Australia, which has focused on exporting to Asia, has been particularly hard hit. Demand for Australian beef fell from 3800 metric tonnes in January 1997 to just 12 tonnes in January 1998. Asian orders for live Australian cattle fell from 31 000 head in January 1997 to zero one year later. That beef, which would have been sent outside Australia, now must be sold within the country, and the increase in supply has depressed beef prices in Australia.

In 1999, the Asian economies began slowly recovering, but in 2000 difficulties were looming again. A possible recession in the U.S., corporate profit warnings, and rising oil prices all threatened to derail the fragile economic recovery.

It's a complicated world!

National Association of Securities Dealers Inc. (NASD)
With more than 5500 member firms, the largest securities-regulation organization in the United States.

NASDAQ and NASD. In the 1960s, a report by the U.S. Securities and Exchange Commission noted that the OTC market was unduly fragmented. One proposal recommended automation of the OTC market, calling for a new system be to implemented by the **National Association of Securities Dealers Inc. (NASD)**. The resulting automated OTC system, launched in

1971, is known as the National Association of Securities Dealers Automated Quotation (NASDAQ) system, the world's first electronic stock market.[9]

With more than 5500 member firms, NASD is the largest securities-regulation organization in the United States. Every broker/dealer in the United States who conducts securities business with the public is required by law to be a member of NASD.[10] NASD includes dealers (not just brokers), who must pass qualification exams and meet certain standards for financial soundness. The privilege of trading in the market is granted by federal regulators and by NASD. The organization's telecommunications system includes the **National Association of Securities Dealers Automated Quotation (NASDAQ)** system, which operates the NASDAQ stock market by broadcasting trading information on an intranet to more than 350 000 terminals worldwide. Whereas orders at the NYSE are paired on the trading floor, NASDAQ orders are paired and executed on a computer network. Currently, NASD is working with officials in an increasing number of countries who want to replace the trading floors of traditional exchanges with electronic networks like NASDAQ.

Although NASD and AMEX have merged to become the NASD-AMEX Market Group, they continue to operate as separate markets (NASDAQ and AMEX). The stocks of 4800 companies are traded by NASDAQ. Newer firms are often listed on NASDAQ when their stocks first become available in the secondary market. Many of these stocks later become well known.

In early 2000, NASDAQ, the fastest-growing U.S. stock market, set a record volume of over 2 billion shares traded in one day. Its 1999 volume of 270 billion shares traded was the industry leader, and it is the leading U.S. market for non-U.S. listings, with a total of 429 non-U.S. companies, including such giants as L.M. Ericsson Telephone Co. (Sweden), NEC Corporation (Japan), and Fuji Photo Film (Japan). Although the volume of shares traded surpasses that of the NYSE, the total market value of NASDAQ's U.S. stocks is only about one-half that of the NYSE. Figure 19.2 shows the number of shares traded on the two floor-based exchanges and the NASDAQ market in the U.S.

National Association of Securities Dealers Automated Quotation (NASDAQ)

A stock market implemented by NASD that operates by broadcasting trading information on an intranet to more than 350 000 terminals worldwide.

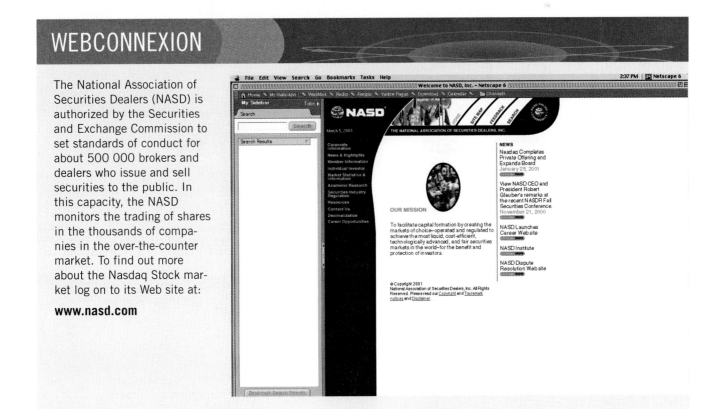

WEBCONNEXION

The National Association of Securities Dealers (NASD) is authorized by the Securities and Exchange Commission to set standards of conduct for about 500 000 brokers and dealers who issue and sell securities to the public. In this capacity, the NASD monitors the trading of shares in the thousands of companies in the over-the-counter market. To find out more about the Nasdaq Stock market log on to its Web site at:

www.nasd.com

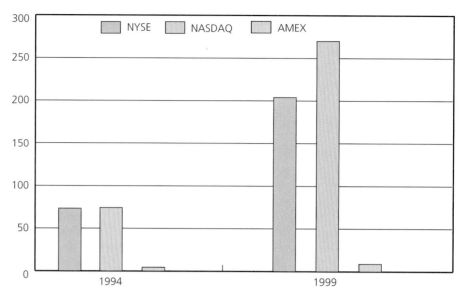

Figure 19.2
Trading levels on U.S. stock exchanges.

In the battle for premier companies, both the New York Stock Exchange and Nasdaq have taken to marketing themselves much more aggresively. Each, for example, has expanded operations at its broadcast centre and permitted more and more TV stations to air real-time stock prices. A virtual high-tech market site, the Nasdaq centre features 100 video monitors and provides a showplace to impress new or prospective companies.

Capitalization

capitalization
The dollar value (market value) of stocks listed on a stock exchange.

Capitalization—the dollar value (market value) of stocks listed on a stock exchange—is another popular measure of stock market size. On March 27, 2000, for instance, the market value of all GE shares was US$520 billion (GE's market price per share on that day multiplied by the number of GE common shares). On that day, GE stock had the largest capitalization of all NYSE listings. You can determine capitalization for any stock exchange by calculating the market value of each stock on the exchange and then totalling the values of all those companies.[11] Because stock prices change every day, so does market capitalization. The top 10 Canadian companies in terms of market capitalization are shown in Table 19.2.

The Most Valuable Companies

Cisco Systems Inc.
www.cisco.com

In late March 2000, Cisco Systems Inc., an Internet networking provider, surpassed Microsoft as the world's most valuable company, a position that Microsoft had held for over a year. Cisco's stock market value was US$555 billion,

Table 19.2	The Top 10 Canadian Companies (based on market capitalization)

Company	Market Capitalization (in billions)
1. Nortel Networks	$221.9
2. BCE Inc.	101.6
3. PMC-Sierra Inc.	36.0
4. The Seagram Co. Ltd.	34.2
5. The Thomson Corp.	32.2
6. The Toronto-Dominion Bank	22.7
7. Bombardier Inc.	19.7
8. Royal Bank of Canada	18.8
9. Imperial Tobacco Canada	17.9
10. Canadian Imperial Bank of Commerce	14.4

followed by Microsoft at nearly US$542 billion and General Electric at US$521 billion. The two leaders are Internet-related firms, and both are listed on the NASDAQ market. GE stock is traded on the NYSE. To better grasp the size of Cisco's market value, consider that its US$555 billion value was larger than the 1998 gross domestic product (GDP) of all but 10 countries in the world. In GDP terms, Cisco would follow Spain and rank ahead of the Netherlands, Mexico, Switzerland, India, and Argentina among the world's richest nations. The combined market value of the three most valuable companies—US$1.6 trillion—would rank fifth in the world, behind only the U.S. Japan, Germany, and France.[12]

The Steps to a Global Stock Market

With its electronic telecommunication system, NASDAQ possesses an infrastructure that could eventually lead to a truly global stock market—one that would allow buyers and sellers to interact from any point in the world. Currently, NASDAQ provides equal access to both the market and market information via simultaneous broadcasts of quotes from more than 1000 participating firms. NASDAQ communication networks enter customer orders and then display new quotes reflecting those orders.

To lay the groundwork for a system that would connect listed companies and investors for worldwide 24-hour-a-day trading, NASDAQ is taking the following steps:

- It has agreed to a deal with the government of Quebec to launch NASDAQ Canada.

- The NASDAQ Japan Market was launched in 2000, in partnership with the Osaka Securities Exchange. This electronic securities market uses a technology that can eventually link Europe and the United States as well.

- Plans are underway for expanding NASDAQ-Europe, an Internet-accessible stock market patterned after NASDAQ. It would offer European traders access to the stocks of listed U.S. and Asian companies.

- An agreement with the Hong Kong Stock Exchange allows some of NASDAQ's shares to trade in Hong Kong, and some of Hong Kong's shares to trade in the U.S.

- News reports indicate that NASDAQ has established relationships with Sydney, Australia's, stock market and that negotiations are underway with South Korea's.[13]

IT'S A WIRED WORLD

Opening the Portals to Cross-Border Trading

In addition to being prominent European cities, what do London, Amsterdam, Frankfurt, Paris, and Stockholm have in common? In the world of business and investments, they are among the many cities with their own stock markets. Some, like Frankfurt, are just one of several stock exchanges in a given country, where trading on any one market is independent of the others. Lately, traditional exchanges have gotten bogged down; they're too cumbersome for today's business world. In Europe, for example, there are so many stock exchanges that the system isn't user-friendly for European investors. For instance, a British trader today is often more interested in trading European stocks by sector (e.g., health care, technology, or minerals) instead of by country (e.g., Spain, Sweden, or Belgium). Traders want a system that makes trades across national boundaries easier and cheaper.

As often happens in the business world, some upstart companies have recognized the gap and are responding to customers' needs. Internet-based newcomers are opening portals all over Europe. NASDAQ-Europe, for example, was launched in November 1999 and targets traders who want to deal in the stocks of technology and start-up firms. Similarly, Jiway, which opened in autumn 2000, is luring retail brokers who want to trade across European borders. Two new Internet-based exchanges—Tradepoint and Easdaq—are just getting started by connecting brokers to a system built for cross-border trading. Easdaq allows transactions in Euros, pounds sterling, or U.S. dollars. Two other Web sites, Posit and E-Crossnet, bypass stock exchanges altogether

and link buyers and sellers directly, allowing them to complete their trades independently.

In addition to technology's influence, some organizational changes are also forcing European exchanges to rethink their traditional roles. In March 2000, three exchanges—the French, Dutch, and Belgian—announced that they were merging into a new exchange called Euronext, thus putting additional pressure on competitors to become more pan-European. As a result, merger negotiations are underway between two of Europe's giant exchanges—London and Frankfurt. For years, the London Stock Exchange (LSE) has held the premier spot among Europe's equities markets, the value of shares listed there being double that of any other European exchange. The Frankfurt exchange has not only worked its way up to the number-two position among Europe's financial centres but is also twice as profitable as the LSE. Now, as the LSE and Frankfurt negotiate a merger, they watch while newer competitors, especially Internet exchanges, encroach on their traditional markets.

Although one consideration involves the kind of technology the merged twosome would use (both parties have agreed to use Frankfurt's Xetra trading system), the problem at present is organizational, not technological: How should the organizational pie be divided? Who will own how much of the merged business? News reports indicate an ownership split as large as 60/40 in Frankfurt's favour, but Frankfurt's latest offer included a concession to a 50/50 split. Just how long negotiations will continue is anybody's guess. Meanwhile, reports indicate that other European exchanges—Milan, Madrid, Ireland, Austria—have approached Frankfurt with a view to joining the newly merged exchange.

Although these initiatives are promising, it will take several years to resolve differences in market regulation and trading practices that currently separate various countries. NASDAQ is not the only organization that is expanding its perspective. The "It's a Wired World" box describes several changes occurring in Europe that will streamline stock market trading there.

BONDS

bond

A written promise that the borrower will pay the lender, at a stated future date, the principal plus a stated rate of interest.

A **bond** is a written promise that the borrower will pay the lender, at some stated future date, a sum of money (the principal) and a stated rate of interest. Bondholders have a claim on a corporation's assets and earnings that comes before the claims of common and preferred shareholders. Bonds differ from one another in terms of maturity, tax status, and level of risk versus potential yield (the interest rate). Potential investors must take these factors into consideration to evaluate which particular bond to buy.

Table 19.3				Bond Ratings
	High Grade	**Medium Grade (Investment Grade)**	**Speculative**	**Poor Grade**
Moody's	Aaa Aa	A Baa	Ba B	Caa to C
Standard & Poor's	AAA AA	A BBB	BB B	CCC to D
Canadian Bond Rating Service	A++	B++	C	B

To help bond investors make assessments, several services rate the quality of bonds from different issuers. Table 19.3 shows ratings by three principal rating services: Standard & Poor's, Moody's, and the Canadian Bond Rating Service. The rating measures the bond's default risk—the chance that one or more promised payments will be deferred or missed altogether.

Although all corporations issue common stock, not all issue bonds. Shareholders provide equity (ownership) capital, while bondholders are lenders (although they are also considered "investors" as far as the securities market is concerned). Stock certificates represent ownership, while bond certificates represent indebtedness. Federal, provincial, and city governments as well as non-profit organizations also issue bonds.

Government Bonds

Government bonds—for example, Canada Savings Bonds—are among the safest investments available. However, securities with longer maturities are somewhat riskier than short-term issues because their longer lives expose them to more political, social, and economic changes. The Canadian government, however, backs all federal bonds. Government securities are sold in large blocks to institutional investors who buy them to ensure desired levels of safety in portfolios. As their needs change, they may buy or sell government securities to other investors.

Provincial and local governments also issue bonds (called municipal bonds) to finance school and transportation systems and a variety of other projects. Banks invest in bonds nearing maturity because they are relatively safe, liquid investments. Pension funds, insurance companies, and private citizens also make longer-term investments in municipal bonds.

Corporate Bonds

Corporate bonds are a major source of long-term financing for Canadian corporations. They have traditionally been issued with maturities ranging from 20 to 30 years. In the 1980s, 10-year maturities came into wider use. As with

Canada Savings Bonds
www.csb.gc.ca

Private corporations are not the only organizations that issue bonds. The government of Canada issues Canada Savings Bonds to finance its debt.

government bonds, longer-term corporate bonds are somewhat riskier than shorter-term bonds. Bond ratings of new and proposed corporate issues are published to keep investors informed of the latest risk evaluations on many bonds. Negative ratings do not preclude a bond's success, but they do raise the interest rate that issuers must offer.

Corporate bonds may be categorized in one of two ways: (1) according to methods of interest payment, and (2) according to whether they are *secured* or *unsecured*.

Interest Payment: Registered and Bearer Bonds

Registered bonds register the names of holders with the company, which simply mails out cheques. Certificates are of value only to registered holders. **Bearer** (or **coupon**) **bonds** require bondholders to clip coupons from certificates and send them to the issuer in order to receive payment. Coupons can be redeemed by anyone, regardless of ownership.

registered bond
The names of holders are registered with the company.

bearer (coupon) bond
Require bondholders to clip coupons from certificates and send them to the issuer in order to receive interest payments.

Secured Bonds

Borrowers can reduce the risk of their bonds by pledging assets to bondholders in the event of default. **Secured bonds** can be backed by first mortgages, other mortgages, or other specific assets. If the corporation does not pay interest when it is due, the firm's assets can be sold and the proceeds used to pay the bondholders.

secured bonds
Bonds issued by borrowers who pledge assets as collateral in the event of nonpayment.

Unsecured Bonds

Unsecured bonds are called **debentures**. No specific property is pledged as security for these bonds. Holders of unsecured bonds generally have claims against property not otherwise pledged in the company's other bonds. Accordingly, debentures have inferior claims on the corporation's assets. Financially strong corporations often use debentures.

debentures
Unsecured bonds.

The Retirement of Bonds

Maturity dates on bonds of all kinds may be very long. But all bonds must be paid off—*retired*—at some point. Most bonds are callable, but others are serial or convertible.

Callable Bonds

Many corporate bonds are callable. The issuer of a **callable bond** has the right at almost any time to call the bonds in and pay them off at a price stipulated in the bond indenture (contract). Usually the issuer cannot call the bond for a certain period of time after issue, but some are callable at any time.

Issuers are most likely to call in existing bonds when the prevailing interest rate is lower than the rate being paid on the bond. But the price the issuer must pay to call in the bond, the *call price*, usually gives a premium to the bondholder. For example, a bond might have a $100 face value and be callable by the firm for $108.67 any time during the first year after

callable bond
A bond that may be paid off by the issuer before the maturity date.

being issued. The call price and the premium decrease annually as the bonds near maturity.

A Notice of Redemption calls for certain bonds to be turned in and paid off by the issuer. The accrual of interest on the selected bonds stops on the redemption date.

Sinking Funds

Bonds are often retired by the use of a **sinking-fund provision** in the bond indenture. This method requires the issuing company to put a certain amount of money into a special bank account each year. At the end of a number of years, the money in this account (including interest) is sufficient to redeem the bonds. Failure to meet the sinking-fund provision places the bond issue in default. Bonds with sinking funds are generally regarded as safer investments than bonds without them.

sinking-fund provision
A clause in the bond indenture (contract) that requires the issuing company to put enough money into a special bank account each year to cover the retirement of the bond issue on schedule.

Serial and Convertible Bonds

As an alternative to sinking funds, some corporations issue serial or convertible bonds. In a **serial bond** issue, the firm retires portions of the bond issue at different predetermined dates. In a $100 million serial bond issue maturing in 20 years, for example, the company may retire $5 million of the issue each year.

Convertible bonds can be paid off in (converted to) common stock of the issuing company, at the option of the bondholder, instead of in cash. Since bondholders have a chance for capital gains, the company can offer lower interest rates when issuing the bonds. However, since bondholders cannot be forced to accept stock in lieu of money, conversion will work only if the corporation is considered a good investment.

To draw a clearer picture of how convertible bonds work, let's consider the following example. In 1999, Canadian Arctic Explorations sold a $100 million issue of 4.5 percent convertible bonds. The bonds were issued in $1000 denominations; they mature in 2009. At any time before maturity, each debenture of $1000 is convertible into 19.125 shares of the company's common stock. Between October 1999 and March 2000, the stock price ranged from a low of $28 to a high of $67. In that time, then, 19.125 common shares had a market value ranging from $535 to $1281. In other words, the bondholder could have exchanged the $1000 bond in return for stock to be kept or sold at a possible profit (or loss).

serial bond
A bond issue in which redemption dates are staggered so that a firm pays off portions of the issue at different predetermined dates.

convertible bond
Any bond that offers bondholders the option of accepting common stock instead of cash in repayment.

Secondary Securities Markets for Bonds

Unlike stocks, nearly all secondary trading in bonds occurs in the OTC market rather than on an organized exchange. As a result, precise statistics about annual trading volumes are not recorded.

Like stocks, however, market values and prices of bonds change from day to day. Prices of bonds with average risks tend to move up or down until the interest rate they yield generally reflects the prevailing interest rate of the economy. That is, the direction of bond prices moves opposite to interest rate changes—as interest rates move up, bond prices tend to go down. The prices of riskier bonds fluctuate more than those of higher-grade bonds and often exceed the interest rate of the economy.

OTHER INVESTMENTS

Although stocks and bonds are very important, they are not the only marketable securities for businesses. Financial managers are also concerned with investment opportunities in mutual funds, commodities, and options.

Mutual Funds

mutual fund

Any company that pools the resources of many investors and uses those funds to purchase various types of financial securities, depending on the fund's financial goals.

no-load fund

A mutual fund in which investors are not charged a sales commission when they buy into or sell out of the fund.

load fund

A mutual fund in which investors are charged a sales commission when they buy into or sell out of the fund.

Companies called **mutual funds** pool investments from individuals and other firms to purchase a portfolio of stocks, bonds, and short-term securities. Investors are part-owners of this portfolio. For example, if you invest $1000 in a mutual fund that has a portfolio worth $100 000, you own 1 percent of the portfolio. Mutual funds usually have portfolios worth many millions of dollars.

Investors in **no-load funds** are not charged a sales commission when they buy into or sell out of the mutual fund. **Load funds** carry a charge of between 2 and 8 percent of the invested funds.

Mutual funds vary by the investment goals they stress. Some stress safety. The portfolios of these mutual funds include treasury bills and other safe issues that offer immediate income (liquidity). Short-term municipal bond funds emphasize tax-exempt, immediate income.

Other funds seek higher current income and are willing to sacrifice some safety. Long-term municipal bond mutual funds, corporate bond mutual funds, and income mutual funds (which invest in common stocks with good dividend-paying records) all fall into this category.

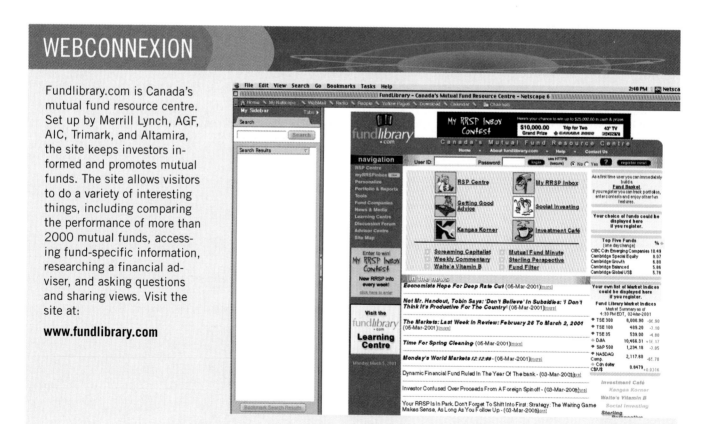

WEBCONNEXION

Fundlibrary.com is Canada's mutual fund resource centre. Set up by Merrill Lynch, AGF, AIC, Trimark, and Altamira, the site keeps investors informed and promotes mutual funds. The site allows visitors to do a variety of interesting things, including comparing the performance of more than 2000 mutual funds, accessing fund-specific information, researching a financial adviser, and asking questions and sharing views. Visit the site at:

www.fundlibrary.com

Still other funds stress growth. Examples include balanced mutual funds, which hold a mixture of bonds, preferred stocks, and common stocks. Growth mutual funds stress common stocks of established firms. Aggressive growth mutual funds seek maximum capital appreciation. To get it, these funds sacrifice current income and safety. They invest in stocks of new companies, troubled companies, and other high-risk securities.

Mutual funds give small investors access to professional financial management. Their managers have up-to-date information about market conditions and the best large-scale investment opportunities. Table 19.4 lists the top 10 mutual funds in Canada.

Commodities

Individuals and businesses can buy and sell commodities as investments. **Futures contracts**—agreements to purchase specified amounts of commodities at given prices on set dates in the future—can be bought and sold in the **commodities market**. These contracts are available not only for stocks but also for commodities including coffee beans, hogs, propane, and platinum. Because selling prices reflect traders' estimates of future events and values, futures prices are volatile and trading is risky.

To clarify the workings of the commodities market, let us look at an example. On March 2, 1999, the price of gold on the open market was $312 per ounce. Futures contracts for June 2000 gold were selling for $320 per ounce. This price reflected investors' judgment that gold prices would be higher the following December. Now suppose that you purchased a 100-ounce gold futures contract in October for $32 000 ($320 x 100). If in December 1999 the June gold futures sold for $345, you could sell your contract for $34 500. Your profit after the two months would be $2500.

futures contract
Agreement to purchase specified amounts of a commodity at a given price on a set future date.

commodities market
Market in which futures contracts are traded.

Margins

Usually, buyers of futures contracts need not put up the full purchase amount. Rather, the buyer posts a smaller amount—the **margin**—that may be as little

margin
The percentage of the total sales price that a buyer must put up to place an order for stock or a futures contract.

Table 19.4	The Top 10 Mutual Funds in Canada (ranked by assets)
Company	**Assets (in billions)**
1. Investors Group	$41.5
2. Royal Mutual Funds Inc.	33.4
3. Mackenzie Financial Corp.	32.0
4. Fidelity Investments Canada Ltd.	30.5
5. TD Asset Management	28.5
6. Trimark Investment Management Inc.	24.4
7. CIBC Securities Inc.	22.2
8. C.I. Mutual Funds	21.9
9. AGF Management Ltd.	20.9
10. Templeton Management Ltd.	20.0

Gold is one of the many commodities for which futures contracts can be bought.

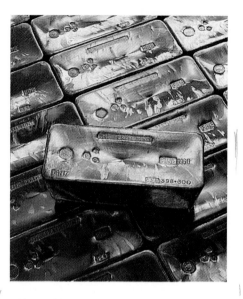

as $3000 for contracts up to $100 000. Let us look again at our gold futures example. As we saw, if you had posted a $3000 margin for your June gold contract, you would have earned a $2500 profit on that investment of $3000 in only two months.

However, you also took a big risk involving two big *if*s: If you had held onto your contract until December, and if gold had dropped, say to $283 (as it really did by June 2000), you would have lost $3700 ($32 000 – 28 300). If you had posted a $3000 margin to buy the contract, you would have lost all of that margin and would owe an additional $700. In fact, between 75 and 90 percent of all small-time investors lose money in the futures market. For one thing, the action is fast and furious, with small investors trying to keep up with professionals ensconced in seats on the major exchanges.

Most investors in commodities markets never intend to take possession of the commodity in question. They merely buy and sell the futures contracts. But some companies buy futures to protect the price of commodities important to their businesses, as when Canada Packers trades in hog futures.

More than 400 "commodity exchanges" have opened up in the former Soviet Union. These exchanges bring together buyers and sellers of many different types of goods. Although they call themselves commodity exchanges, they are in fact far more primitive than commodity exchanges in Canada and the U.S. One trader says they are more like flea markets than commodity exchanges.[14]

Stock Options

stock option
The purchased right to buy or sell a stock.

call option
The purchased right to buy a particular stock at a certain price until a specified date.

put option
The purchased right to sell a particular stock at a certain price until a specified date.

Trading in stock options has become a popular investment activity. A **stock option** is the right to buy or sell a stock. More specifically, a **call option** gives its owner the right to buy a particular stock at a certain price, with that right lasting until a particular date. A **put option** gives its owner the right to sell a particular stock at a specified price, with that right lasting until a particular date. These options are traded on several stock exchanges.

Suppose that you thought the price of Alcan (which sold for $49.10 per share on August 15, 2000) was going to go up. You might buy a call option giving you the right to buy 100 shares of Alcan anytime in the next two months at a so-called strike price of $65. If the stock rose to $75 before October, you would exercise your call option. Your profit would be $10 per share ($75 – $65) less the price you paid to buy the option. However, if the stock price fell instead of rising, you would not exercise your call option because Alcan would be available on the open market for less than $65 per share. You would lose whatever you paid for the option.

In contrast, if you thought the price of Alcan would fall below $49.10 sometime during the two months after August 15, 2000, you might buy a put option. Assume that this option gave you the right to sell 100 shares for $54.10 per share any time before October 2000. If the stock price fell to $44.10, your profit would be $10 per share ($54.10 – $44.10), less whatever you paid for the option. Assume that the price of a put option was $3.00 per share at that time. If the stock price increased, you would not exercise your option to sell, and you would lose what you paid for the put option. The daily prices of put and call options are listed in the financial press.

BUYING AND SELLING SECURITIES

The process of buying and selling stocks, bonds, and other financial instruments is complex. To start, you need to find out about possible investments and match them to your investment objectives. Then you must decide whether you want to use a broker to buy and sell stocks, or whether you want to do it yourself.

Using Financial Information Services

Have you ever looked at the financial section of your daily newspaper and found yourself wondering what all those tables and numbers mean? If you cannot read stock and bond quotations, you probably should not invest in these issues. Fortunately, this skill is easily mastered. More complicated but also important is some grasp of market indexes.

Stock Quotations

Figure 19.3 shows the type of information newspapers provide about daily market transactions of individual stocks. The corporation's name is shown along with the number of shares sold, the high and low prices of the stock for that trading day, the closing price of the stock, and the change from the closing price on the previous day.

Bond Quotations

Bond prices also change from day to day. These changes form the *coupon rate*, which provides information for firms about the cost of borrowing funds.

Prices of domestic corporation bonds, Canadian government bonds, and foreign bonds are reported separately. Bond prices are expressed in terms of 100, even though most have a face value of $1000. Thus, a quote of 85 means that the bond's price is 85 percent of its face value, or $850.

A corporation bond selling at 155 1/4 would cost a buyer $1552.50 ($1000 face value x 1.5525), plus commission. The interest rate on bonds is also quoted as a percentage of par, or face, value. Thus "6 1/2s" pay 6.5 percent of par value per year. Typically, interest is paid semiannually at half of the stated interest or coupon rate.

The market value (selling price) of a bond at any given time depends on its stated interest rate, the "going rate" of interest in the market, and its redemption or maturity date.

A bond with a higher stated interest rate than the going rate on similar quality bonds will probably sell at a premium above its face value—its selling price will be above its redemption price. A bond with a lower stated interest rate than the going rate on similar quality bonds will probably sell at a discount—its selling price will be below its redemption price. How much the premium or discount is depends largely on how far in the future the maturity date is. The maturity date is shown after the interest rate. When more than one year is given, the bond is either retractable or extendible.

Figure 19.4 shows the type of information daily newspapers provide about bond transactions.

- **Stock**
  Inco (Name of Company)

- **Sales**
  376 030
  Total number of shares traded on this date. There were 376 030 shares sold.

- **High**   **Low**
  29.150   28.500
  During the trading day, the highest price was $29.15 and the lowest price was $28.50.

- **Close**
  28.600
  At the close of trading on this date, the last price paid per share was $28.60.

- **Net Change**
  -0.400
  Difference between today's closing price and previous day's closing price. Price decreased by $0.40.

Company	Sales	High	Low	Close	Change
H Bay Co	347 106	34.500	32.000	32.250	-2.500
Humbird	196 310	50.250	47.250	48.850	-2.900
Hy Zels	1 500	4.700	4.700	4.700	-0.100
IBEX T	3 500	5.600	5.250	5.400	-0.200
IITC A	7 000	1.000	1.000	1.000	0.000
IPL eng	38 329	53.000	52.000	52.650	+0.150
ISG Tech	6 583	4.050	3.900	3.950	-0.150
Imasco L	439 447	44.800	44.000	44.250	-0.500
Imax	46 058	35.000	34.000	35.000	+0.500
Imp Metal	22 879	1.630	1.530	1.590	-0.020
Imperial Oil	311 141	87.700	84.750	87.100	+1.100
Inco	**376 030**	**29.150**	**28.500**	**28.600**	**-0.400**
Indochin o	6 100	5.700	5.500	5.500	-0.100
Inex Ph o	8 800	5.250	5.000	5.250	-0.100
Infocorp o	24 400	0.750	0.660	0.740	-0.010
Innova T o	15 000	0.870	0.870	0.870	-0.030
Insulpro	12 000	1.180	1.080	1.130	+0.020

Figure 19.3
How to read a stock quotation.

- **BC Tel**
  Company name is British Columbia Telephone.

- **Coupon**
  The annual rate of interest at face value is 9.65 percent.

- **Maturity**
  The maturity date is April 8, 2022.

- **Price**
  On this date, $138.48 was the price of the last transaction.

- **Yield**
  This is computed by dividing the annual interest paid by the current market price.

- **Change**
  The closing price on this day was up $1.11 from the closing price on the previous day.

Issuer	Coupon	Maturity	Price	Yield	Change
GOVERNMENT OF CANADA					
Canada	4.00	Mar 15-99	100.175	3.865	+0.158
Canada	7.75	Sep 1-99	105.627	4.514	+0.124
Canada	5.50	Feb 1-00	101.897	4.600	+0.155
Canada	8.50	Mar 1-00	108.417	4.648	+0.164
Canada	7.50	Sep 1-00	107.122	4.780	+0.199
PROVINCIALS AND GUARANTEED					
Alta	8.00	Mar 1-00	107.242	4.673	+0.130
BC	9.00	Jan 9-02	114.729	5.046	+0.250
Hy Que	7.00	Jun 1-04	108.100	5.514	+0.460
Man	7.75	Sep 14-00	107.604	4.868	+0.172
Ont Hy	7.75	Nov 3-05	114.086	5.546	+0.493
PEI	8.50	Oct 27-15	123.663	6.285	+0.845
CORPORATE					
Bell	8.80	Aug 24-04	119.790	5.491	+0.490
BC Tel	**9.65**	**Apr 8-22**	**138.489**	**6.488**	**+1.118**
Cdn Util	8.43	Jun 1-05	117.385	5.583	+0.475
Nova Gas	8.30	Jul 15-03	113.508	5.503	+0.386
Royal Bk	5.40	Sep 7-02	100.461	5.289	+0.297
Suncor	6.10	Aug 7-07	100.959	5.967	+0.515

Figure 19.4
How to read a bond quotation.

Bond Yield

Suppose you bought a $1000 par-value bond in 1977 for $650. Its stated interest rate is 6 percent, and its maturity or redemption date is 1997. You therefore receive $60 per year in interest. Based on your actual investment of $650, your yield is 9.2 percent. If you hold it to maturity, you get $1000 for a bond that originally cost you only $650. This extra $350 increases your true, or effective, yield.

Market Indexes

Although they do not indicate how particular securities are doing, **market indexes** provide a useful summary of trends in specific industries and the stock market as a whole. Such information can be crucial in choosing appropriate investments. For example, market indexes reveal bull and bear market trends. **Bull markets** are periods of upward-moving stock prices. The years 1981-89 and 1995-99 featured strong bull markets. Periods of falling stock prices are called **bear markets**. The years 1972-74 and 1991-92 were bear markets.

The TSE 300 Average. The TSE 300 index is an average computed from 300 different top Canadian stocks from 14 different industry groups such as gold and silver, forest products, metals and minerals, transportation, and financial services. The TSE 300 index was the best-performing index in the world in the first half of 2000. It moved sharply upwards during the late 1990s, and topped 11 000 in the summer of 2000, but dropped to 8700 by the end of 2000. For more information on the Toronto Stock Exchange, see Video Case VI-2 on page 676.

The Dow Jones Industrial Average. The most widely cited market index is the Dow Jones Industrial Average (the Dow). The Dow is the sum of market prices for 30 of the largest industrial firms listed on the NYSE. By tradition, the Dow is an indicator of blue-chip stock price movements. Because of the small number of firms it considers, however, it is a limited gauge of the overall stock market.

Over the decades, the Dow has been revised and updated to reflect the changing composition of U.S. companies and industries. The most recent modification occurred in November 1999, when four companies were added—Home Depot, Intel, Microsoft, and SBC Communications—and four companies were dropped—Chevron, Goodyear, Sears, and Union Carbide. These changes not only reflect the increasing importance of technology stocks, but also include for the first time two stocks from the NASDAQ market rather than only companies listed on the NYSE.

Like many other stock indexes, the Dow increased sharply in the late 1990s. It reached 5000 in November 1995, and closed above 11 000 early in 2000. During the rest of 2000, it fluctuated between 10 300 and 10 800.

The Dow's movement has generally been *opposite the trend for interest rates on long-term bonds*. Why? Because as bond rates decrease, investors tend to become more interested in stocks as vehicles for higher financial returns. Furthermore, because lower interest rates mean less expensive borrowing for businesses, business expenses are reduced and businesses become more profitable. Thus, investor hopes for even greater profits continue.

The S&P 500. Because it considers very few firms, the Dow is a limited gauge of the overall U.S. stock market. Standard & Poor's Composite Index (S&P 500) is a broader report. It consists of 500 stocks, including 400 industrial firms, 40 utilities, 40 financial institutions, and 20 transportation companies. Because the index average is weighted according to market capitalization of each stock, the more highly valued companies exercise a greater influence on the index.

The NASDAQ Composite Index.   Some observers regard the NASDAQ Composite Index as the most important of all market indexes. First, unlike the Dow and the S&P 500, it includes not only domestic stocks but also non–U.S.-based common stocks listed on the NASDAQ market. In addition, all NASDAQ-listed companies, not just a select few, are included in the index, for a total of over 5000 firms (both U.S. and non-U.S.)—more than on most other indexes. Like the S&P 500, the NASDAQ Composite is market value–weighted (more highly valued companies have a greater impact). Finally, it includes many new and small companies that, along with technology stocks, have been driving the stock market in recent years. The NASDAQ Composite experienced rapid growth near the end of the 1990s and the index exceeded 5000 at one point. However, the index dropped to only 2500 by the end of 2000.

Buying and Selling Stocks

market order
An order to a broker to buy or sell a certain security at the current market price.

limit order
An order to a broker to buy a certain security only if its price is less than or equal to a given limit.

stop order
An order to a broker to sell a certain security if its price falls to a certain level or below.

round lot
The purchase or sale of stock in units of 100 shares.

odd lots
The purchase or sale of stock in units other than 100 shares.

Based on your own investigations and/or recommendations from your broker, you can place many types of orders. A **market order** requests the broker to buy or sell a certain security at the prevailing market price at the time.

In contrast, both limit and stop orders allow for buying and selling of securities only if certain price conditions are met. A **limit order** authorizes the purchase of a stock only if its price is less than or equal to a given limit. For example, a limit order to buy a stock at $80 per share means that the broker is to buy it if and only if the stock becomes available for a price of $80 or less. Similarly, a **stop order** instructs the broker to sell a stock if its price falls to a certain level. For example, a stop order of $85 on a particular stock means that the broker is to sell it if and only if its price falls to $85 or below.

You can also place orders of different sizes. A **round lot** order requests 100 shares or some multiple thereof. Fractions of a round lot are called **odd lots**. Trading odd lots is usually more expensive than trading round lots, because an intermediary called an odd-lot broker is often involved, which increases brokerage fees.

The business of buying and selling stocks is changing rapidly (see the CBC Video Case on page 675). Formerly, a person had to have a broker in order to buy and sell stocks. However, major changes have occurred in this industry in the last few years. More and more individuals are buying and selling stocks on the Internet, and traditional brokers are worried that before long customers will avoid using their services.

To make matters worse for brokers, it will soon be possible for Canadians to purchase shares of stock directly from the companies that issue them instead of having to go through a broker or the Internet. The fees that customers will have to pay for these direct purchases will be even lower than the fees currently charged by discount brokers. Thus, customers will be able to "cut out the middleman."[15]

Financing Securities Purchases

When you place a buy order of any kind, you must tell your broker how you will pay for the purchase. You might maintain a cash account with your broker. Then, as stocks are bought and sold, proceeds are added into the account and commissions and costs of purchases are withdrawn by the broker. In addition, as with almost every good in today's economy, you can buy shares on credit.

Margin Trading

As with futures contracts, you can buy stocks on *margin*—putting down only a portion of the stock's price. You borrow the rest from your broker, who, in turn, borrows from the banks at a special rate and secures the loans with stock.

Margin trading offers clear advantages to buyers. Suppose you purchased $100 000 worth of stock in Alcan, paying $50 000 of your own money and borrowing the other $50 000 from your broker at 10 percent interest. If, after one year, the shares have risen in value to $115 000, you could sell them, pay your broker $55 000 ($50 000 principal plus $5000 interest), and have $60 000 left over. Your original investment of $50 000 would have earned a 20 percent profit of $10 000. If you had paid the entire price of the stock from your own funds, your investment would have earned only a 15 percent return.

Brokerages benefit from margin trading in two ways. First, it encourages more people to buy more stock, which means more commissions to the brokerage. Second, the firm earns a profit on its loans, since it charges buyers a higher interest rate than it pays the bank.

Although investors often recognize possible profits to be made in margin trading, they sometimes fail to consider that losses, too, can be amplified. Suppose, for example, that you decided on January 4, 1999, to buy 1000 shares of Canadian Petroleum for $53 per share. You put up $26 500 of your own money and borrow $26 500 from your broker. As the stock rises, you reason, the loan will enable you to profit from twice as many shares. Now let us say that shortly after you purchase your stock, its market price begins to fall. You decide to hold on until it recovers. By January 4, 2001, when the price has fallen to $23 per share, you give up hope and sell.

Now let us see how margin trading has amplified your losses. If you had invested your own $26 500 instead of borrowing it, you would recover $23 000 of your $53 000 investment (excluding commissions). Your loss, therefore, would be nearly 57 percent ($30 000 loss ÷ $53 000 invested). By trading on margin, however, even though you still recover $23 000 of your $26 500 investment, you must repay the $26 500 that you borrowed, plus $2650 in loan interest (at a 10 percent annual rate). In this case, your losses total $32 650 ($55 650 in outlays less $23 000 recovered). The percentage loss is 123 percent of your investment ($32 650 loss ÷ $26 500 investment)—much greater than the 57 percent loss you would have suffered without margin trading.

Short Sales

In addition to money, brokerages also lend buyers securities. A **short sale** begins when you borrow a security from your broker and sell it (one of the few times it is legal to sell what you do not own). At a given time in the future, you must restore an equal number of shares of that issue to the brokerage, along with a fee.

For example, suppose that in June you believe the price of Alcan stock will soon fall. You order your broker to sell short 100 shares at the market price of $38 per share. Your broker will make the sale and credit $3800 to your account. If Alcan's price falls to $32 per share in July, you can buy 100 shares for $3200 and give them to your broker, leaving you with a $600 profit (before commissions). The risk is that Alcan's price will not fall but will hold steady or rise, leaving you with a loss.

short sale
Selling borrowed shares of stock in the expectation that their price will fall before they must be replaced, so that replacement shares can be bought for less than the original shares were sold.

SECURITIES REGULATION

Canada, unlike the United States with its Securities and Exchange Commission (SEC), does not have comprehensive federal securities legislation or a federal regulatory body. Government regulation is primarily provincial and there is a degree of self-regulation through the various securities exchanges.

In 1912, the Manitoba government pioneered in Canada laws applying mainly to the sale of new securities. Under these "**blue-sky laws**," corporations issuing securities must back them up with something more than the blue sky. Similar laws were passed in other provinces. Provincial laws also generally require that stockbrokers be licensed and securities be registered before they can be sold. In each province, issuers of proposed new securities must file a prospectus with the provincial securities exchange. A **prospectus** is a detailed registration statement that includes information about the firm, its operation, its management, the purpose of the proposed issue, and any other data helpful to a potential buyer of these securities. The prospectus must be made available to prospective investors.

Ontario is regarded as having the most progressive securities legislation in Canada. The *Ontario Securities Act* contains disclosure provisions for new and existing issues, prevention of fraud, regulation of the Toronto Stock Exchange, and takeover bids. It also prohibits **insider trading**, which is the use of special knowledge about a firm to make a profit in the stock market.

The Toronto Stock Exchange provides an example of self-regulation by the industry. The TSE has regulations concerning listing and delisting of securities, disclosure requirements, and issuing of prospectuses for new securities.

blue-sky laws
Laws regulating how corporations must back up securities.

prospectus
A detailed registration statement about a new stock filed with a provincial securities exchange; must include any data helpful to a potential buyer.

insider trading
The use of special knowledge about a firm to make a profit on the stock market.

SUMMARY OF LEARNING OBJECTIVES

1. **Explain the difference between *primary* and *secondary securities markets*.** *Primary securities markets* involve the buying and selling of new securities, either in public offerings or through *private placements* (sales to single buyers or small groups of buyers). *Investment bankers* specialize in trading securities in primary markets. *Secondary markets* involve the trading of existing stocks and bonds through such familiar bodies as the New York Stock Exchange and Toronto Stock Exchange.

2. **Discuss the value of *common stock* and *preferred stock* to shareholders and describe the secondary market for each type of security.** *Common stock* affords investors the prospect of capital gains, dividend income, or both. Common stock values are expressed in three ways: as *par value* (the face value of a share when it is issued), *market value* (the current market price of a share), and *book value* (the value of shareholders' equity compared with that of other stocks). Market value is the most important value to investors. *Preferred stock* is less risky than common stock; for example, cumulative preferred stock entitles holders to receive missed dividends when the company is financially capable of paying. It also offers the prospect of steadier income than common stock. Shareholders of preferred stock must be paid dividends before shareholders of common stock.

Both common and preferred stock are traded on *stock exchanges* (institutions formed to conduct the trading of existing securities) and in *over-the-counter (OTC) markets* (dealer organizations formed to trade securities outside stock exchange settings). "Members" who hold seats on exchanges act as *brokers*—agents who execute buy-and-sell orders—for nonmembers. Exchanges include the New York Stock Exchange, the Toronto Stock Exchange, and regional and foreign exchanges. In the OTC market, licensed traders serve functions similar to those of exchange members.

3. **Distinguish among various types of *bonds* in terms of their issuers, safety, and retirement.** The safety of bonds issued by various borrowers is rated by such services as Moody's and the Canadian Bond Rating service. *Government bonds* are the safest investment because they are backed by the federal government. *Municipal bonds*, which are offered by provincial and local governments to finance a variety of projects, are also usually safe, and the interest is frequently tax-exempt. *Corporate bonds* are issued by businesses to gain long-term funding. They may be *secured* (backed by pledges of the issuer's assets) or unsecured (*debentures*) and offer varying degrees of safety. *Serial bonds* are retired as portions are redeemed at preset dates; *convertible bonds* are retired by conversion into the issuer's common stock. Government and corporate bonds are callable; that is, they can be paid off by the issuer prior to their maturity dates.

4. **Describe the investment opportunities offered by *mutual funds* and *commodities*.** Like stocks and bonds, *mutual funds*—companies that pool investments to purchase portfolios of financial instruments—offer investors different levels of risk and growth potential. *Load funds* require investors to pay commissions of 2 to 8 percent; *no-load funds* do not charge commissions when investors buy in or out. *Futures contracts*—agreements to buy specified amounts of commodities at given prices on preset dates—are traded in the *commodities market*. Commodities traders often buy on *margins*, percentages of total sales prices that must be put up to order futures contracts.

5. **Explain the process by which securities are bought and sold.** Investors generally use such financial information services as newspaper and online stock, bond, and OTC quotations to learn about possible investments. *Market indexes* such as the Toronto Stock Exchange index, the Dow Jones Industrial Average, the Standard & Poor's Composite Index, and the NASDAQ Composite provide useful summaries of trends, both in specific industries and in the market as a whole. Investors can then place different types of orders. *Market orders* are orders to buy or sell at current prevailing prices. Because investors do not know exactly what prices will be when market orders are executed, they may issue *limit* or *stop orders* that are to be executed only if prices rise to or fall below specified levels. *Round lots* are purchased in multiples of 100 shares. *Odd lots* are purchased in fractions of round lots. Securities can be bought on margin or as part of *short sales*—sales in which investors sell securities that are borrowed from brokers and returned at a later date.

6. **Explain how securities markets are regulated.** To protect investors, provincial securities commissions regulate the public offering of new securities and enforce laws against such practices as *insider trading* (using special knowledge about a firm for profit or gain). Many provincial governments prosecute the sale of fraudulent securities and enforce *blue-sky laws* that require dealers to be licensed and registered where they conduct business.

KEY TERMS

securities, 615
primary securities
    market, 615
investment banker, 615
secondary securities
    market, 616
institutional investors,
    616
par value, 616
market value, 617
capital gains, 617
blue-chip stocks, 618
cumulative preferred
    stock, 619
stock exchange, 619
program trading, 620

broker, 621
over-the-counter (OTC)
    market, 623
National Association of
    Securities Dealers Inc.
    (NASD), 624
National Association of
    Securities Dealers
    Automated Quotation
    (NASDAQ), 625
capitalization, 626
bond, 628
registered bond, 630
bearer (coupon) bond,
    630

secured bonds, 630
debentures, 630
callable bond, 630
sinking-fund provision,
    631
serial bond, 631
convertible bond, 631
mutual fund, 632
no-load fund, 632
load fund, 632
futures contract, 633
commodities market, 633
margin, 633
stock option, 634

call option, 634
put option, 634
market index, 637
bull market, 637
bear market, 637
market order, 638
limit order, 638
stop order, 638
round lot, 638
odd lots, 638
short sale, 639
blue-sky laws, 640
prospectus, 640
insider trading, 640

STUDY QUESTIONS AND EXERCISES

Review Questions

1. What are the purposes of the primary and secondary markets for securities?
2. Which of the three measures of common stock value is most important? Why?
3. What is the difference between callable and convertible bonds?
4. How might an investor lose money in a commodities trade?
5. How do the provincial securities commissions regulate securities markets?

Analysis Questions

6. Which type of stock or bond would be most appropriate for your investment purposes at this time? Why?
7. Which type of mutual fund would be most appropriate for your investment purposes at this time? Why?

8. Choose from a newspaper an example listing of a recent day's transactions for each of the following: a stock on the NYSE; a stock on the TSE; an OTC stock; a bond on the NYSE. Explain what each element in the listing means.

Application Exercises

9. Interview the financial manager of a local business or your school. What are the investment goals of this organization? What mix of securities does it use? What advantages and disadvantages do you see in its portfolio?
10. Contact a broker for information about setting up a personal account for trading securities. Prepare a report on the broker's requirements for placing buy/sell orders, credit terms, cash account requirements, services available to investors, and commissions/fees schedules.

Building Your Business Skills

What Affects the Price of Common Stock?

Goal

To encourage students to understand how a company's internal and external environment affects the price of its common stock.

Method

Step 1:
Research the activity of one of the following common stocks during 2000. In addition, research the internal and external events that affected the company during the year:

- IBM
- Canadian National Railway
- Bank of Montreal
- Yahoo!
- General Motors of Canada
- Air Canada
- Apple Computer
- Chapters

Step 2:
Based on your analysis, answer the following sets of questions:

- What happened to the stock price during the period? What was the high during the year? What was the low?
- What events affected the stock price?
- Which of these events involved internal changes— say, reorganizations, layoffs, a new CEO, a new labour contract, dramatic changes in sales? What were the effects of these events?
- Which of these events involved external factors—say, changes in the competitive environment or an economic downturn? What were the effects of these events?

Follow-Up Questions

1. What were the main factors that influenced the company's stock price?
2. Based on what you learned, can you predict how well the stock will perform over the coming year?

Exploring the Net

Because stock market action can be fast and furious, up-to-date information is a must for most investors. See some of the types of information available on the Internet by accessing the Canoe Money site at the following address:

http://www.canoe.ca/MoneyStocks/index_knowledge.html

1. Use the "Investing Glossary" feature to explain in your own words the following terms: "Arbitrage," "Book Price," "Common shares outstanding," "Over the counter (OTC)," "Rollover," "Scalp," "Umbrella policy."
2. Go to the "Business" section. What coverage would be of interest to the average small business?
3. Find a stock quote for Rogers Cantel. What was the highest price paid that day? What is the difference between today's closing price and the previous day's closing price?
4. Can you find a news release that might influence investors to buy or sell the sock of a particular company? An item that might influence investors to trade the stocks of a company in a particular industry?

Concluding Case 19-1

The Stock Market Roller Coaster

Like a space-age roller coaster ride, today's stock market promises nerve-shattering volatility for anyone with the guts to hop on board. The best advice for the timid—or those prone to motion sickness—is to stay away, especially if the swings that characterized the market recently are here to stay.

Why are today's market swings so violent? Why, for example, did traders sell off US$74 billion in stocks in just one day—55 percent more than during the previous day and 43 percent more than during the next trading day—on the New York Stock Exchange in April 2000? Why did the Dow Jones Industrial Average surge upward 17 percent between October 1999 and January 2000, only to lose those gains during the next two months while the economy remained strong? Market volatility can be traced to several factors, including new Internet stocks, large pools of available cash, new technologies to speed up trading, and global financial interrelationships.

Technology stocks have also added to the market volatility. An abundance of cash-starved e-businesses and high-tech stocks are capturing investor interest and attracting investment dollars as never before, even though many of those firms have yet to turn a profit. High-risk investors, looking beyond today's red ink, are betting on future performance. Thus it's no surprise when economic conditions, political events, or just plain fright stimulate wild ups and downs in the stock market. The technology-heavy NASDAQ Composite, sitting at 2500 in August 1999, suddenly shot up to a record-setting 5100 in March 2000—a gain of more than 100 percent in just seven months—for no clear reason. Then, in a stark turnaround, it fell to 2500 for a nearly 50 percent loss by the end of 2000.

Large pools of available cash also add to market volatility. Few people store their money in savings accounts at local banks the way their parents did. Today, we invest and shift available cash in and out of mutual funds and individual stocks. Split-second decision making by individuals and institutional investors is encouraged by a web of global financial relationships that are instantly reported on 24-hour business television, telephone, and Internet services. Never before in history have the personal finances of Canadians been so inextricably linked to the financial health of countries halfway around the world. When the Indonesian, Korean, and Japanese economies collapsed in 1997 and 1998, investors in Canadian and U.S. companies doing business in those countries added to market volatility by abandoning risky stocks. When concern over economic problems in Southeast Asia eased in the fall of 1998, the stock market rebounded. But in June 2000, with crude oil prices reaching $33 per barrel and gasoline prices topping 75 cents per litre, investors began to worry about a slowdown in the economy. The ups and downs of stock prices—as much as 5 percent a day—remained a fact of life.

Never before have investors had such immediate access to financial market information and analysis. From such sources as Reuters financial news services, we can access real-time securities quotes and financial news from any market in the world on our home PCs. We can plug into Internet-based online brokers for both analysis and full-colour graphic explanations. We can watch CNBC's 24-hour cable operation, or receive a copy of U.S. Federal Reserve chairman Alan Greenspan's latest speech by clicking on the Fed's Web site. The media give us not only instant information but also an instant "feedback loop" through which our reactions to facts, expectations, and rumours have the power to influence market swings.

Media analysts who feel compelled to provide their spin on market changes also affect volatility. Without analysis, the business report would be little more than a recitation of numbers that would sell very few newspapers or hold the attention of very few viewers. It is often difficult to know why the stock market rises or falls, but reporters speculate about the reasons. This speculation is the stuff of which rumours, inflated expectations, and volatility are made.

Immediate media access has turned many avid investors into 24-hour-a-day trade-aholics. Securities are traded among investors in Toronto, New York, Tokyo, London, and Buenos Aires any time of the day or night. When investors wake up in the morning, they can check the latest dollar–yen relationship or Standard & Poor's futures prices. The pace is exhausting, and so is the volatility.

CASE QUESTIONS

1. How do you think stock market volatility will affect today's investors in both the short term and the long term?

2. In a volatile stock market, why is it important for investors to assess their reaction to financial risk and put together short-term and long-term financial plans?

3. Is increasingly more sophisticated computer technology necessarily a good thing for the market? Explain your answer.

4. Computer programs now use mathematical formulas to make buy and sell decisions for large institutions without benefit of human intervention. Is this progress? Explain your answer.

5. What do you think about the media's role in stock market volatility? ◆

Concluding Case 19-2

Institutional Investors Are Getting More Demanding

A fundamental power struggle is being fought between management and the agents who invest the savings of millions of Canadians. The capital pool controlled by organizations such as Jarislowsky Fraser & Co., Canadian National Pension Trust Fund, and the Ontario Municipal Employees Retirement System (OMERS) keeps growing. It now totals over $1 trillion. Because takeovers and mergers have reduced the number of companies they can invest in, institutional investors have taken to watching their investments very closely.

The institutions win some fights and lose others. OMERS holds 6 percent of the common shares of Xerox Canada Inc. When the U.S. head office decided to exchange one common share of the U.S. company for three of the Canadian company, OMERS complained that the price was too low. The plan was approved anyway and OMERS sued Xerox. Since then, the Ontario Securities Commission has developed more stringent rules on directors' responsibilities to shareholders during takeovers.

The same general trend is evident in the U.S. The California Public Employees' Retirement System (CalPERS), with $97 billion in assets to invest, has been very active in trying to get corporations to listen to shareholders. It has tried, for example, to talk to the management of eight publicly traded small and medium-sized companies whose performance has been weak. But most of the companies ignored CalPERS' request. The deputy executive officer of CalPERS says that the corporate governance movement hasn't yet reached smaller companies, and that they just don't understand that shareholders have a right to talk with management.

Sometimes institutional investors have had their representatives elected to the board of directors of companies they are concerned about. Royal Trust Energy Corp. nominated two of its officials to sit on the board of the near-bankrupt Oakwoods Petroleum Ltd. When it became clear that two pension funds—CN's and Central Trust's— would support the Royal Trust nominees, two incumbent management-supported nominees withdrew their names.

Major battles between pension funds and company management often shape up over the issue of poison pills. Poison pills usually give shareholders the right to buy company stock at a below-market price if a would-be purchaser's holdings go beyond a certain level. Management favours poison pills, but institutional investors usually oppose them. In the case of Inco, the institutional investors were major losers when the company persuaded shareholders to adopt the poison pill by offering them a $10 dividend if they would approve the plan.

Management often resents institutional investors, arguing that they do not know how a specific company should be run yet they insist on input anyway. They want institutional investors simply to pick stocks for their clients, not try to tell company management what to do. They point out that institutions generally have no positive advice to offer; rather, they simply veto management plans. When the pension funds of CBC and Investors Group torpedoed a restructuring plan at Unicorp Canada Ltd., they did not offer an alternative. Instead, they insisted that the company come up with proposals for them to accept or reject. Unicorp finally abandoned the restructuring.

Pension fund managers counter by stressing that they are preventing companies' management from taking advantage of small investors. Companies, they argue, too often view small shareholders as a source of cheap money rather than as equal partners in the enterprise.

CASE QUESTIONS

1. What motivates pension fund managers to try to influence the management decisions of companies in which the pension fund holds stock?

2. What are the pros and cons of pension fund managers trying to influence management decisions of the companies in which the pension fund holds stock?

3. Why do institutional investors such as pension funds oppose "poison pills"?

4. Imagine that you are a top manager in a company whose stock is often bought by institutional investors. What kinds of complaints about institutional investors are you likely to have? ◆

Visit the *Business* Website at www.pearsoned.ca/griffin
for up-to-date e-business cases!

It's Finally Over at Eaton's

The last chapter in the colourful history of T. Eaton Co. Ltd. was written late in 1999 when creditors and shareholders agreed to a restructuring plan that gave former arch-rival Sears Canada Inc. control of Eaton's. Many of Eaton's 13 500 employees will lose their jobs as a result of the deal.

The story of Eaton's is the stuff of Canadian legend. Timothy Eaton immigrated to Canada from Ireland in the nineteenth century and built a retailing empire by promising to refund money if customers found the company's goods to be unsatisfactory. In that era, such a guarantee was unheard of. But it worked, and over the next few decades Eaton's prospered. By the 1950s, Eaton's accounted for more than half of all department store spending in Canada.

In the classic tradition, Timothy Eaton passed the presidency of the company to his son John Craig Eaton, who was in turn succeeded by his cousin Robert Young Eaton. John David Eaton (John Craig's son) became president in 1942 and dominated the firm until the 1970s. John Craig Eaton II—the great-grandson of Timothy—is a fourth-generation Eaton. He was in charge from the 1970s onward.

Eaton's emphasis on tradition led to an inability to change in response to shifting markets. In the 1970s, for example, Eaton's refused to get rid of its in-store drug sections in spite of strong evidence that competitors such as Shoppers Drug Mart had stolen this market from them. The company also refused to close some small-town stores that were a drain on profitability.

Massive changes in Canadian retailing during the 1980s and 1990s (including the entry of large U.S. competitors such as Wal-Mart) caused a sharp decline in Eaton's fortunes. As a private corporation, Eaton's was not required to publish its financial statements and was famous for being tight-lipped about its financial condition. By the early 1990s, rumours began to circulate that Eaton's was in trouble. And the rumours turned out to be true. From 1992 to 1997, annual sales revenue declined from $2.1 billion to $1.6 billion. The firm lost $80 million in 1995, and $120 million in 1996. Eaton's shocked the industry in 1997 when it announced that it was seeking bankruptcy protection under the *Companies Creditors Arrangement Act.*

To its credit, Eaton's had actually tried to address some of its more pressing problems. For example, its warehouse outside Toronto had been operating with outdated equipment that caused deliveries to Eaton's retailers across Canada to be delayed. The company responded by modernizing the warehouse with an automated conveyor system. Bar-code readers scanned labels and automatically sent products down conveyors to trucks that took them to the appropriate Eaton's stores. Eaton's also changed the way it dealt with suppliers, and made them comply with packaging, labelling, and shipment accuracy rules. It also reduced the number of suppliers it dealt with and rewarded the remaining suppliers with bigger sales volumes.

But it was not enough, and Eaton's has disappeared as an independent business. The Eaton's name, however, will not disappear. Sears Canada purchased 19 of Eaton's best locations and reopened 7 of them under the Eaton's name. The "new" Eaton's stores are located in Toronto, North York, Calgary, Vancouver, Ottawa, Winnipeg, and Victoria. They will feature pricier, more fashionable brands than those usually carried by Sears Canada. ◆

How a company handles its finances can mean the difference between life and death for the firm. It can also affect the level of interest that investors show in the firm. These fundamental facts apply to both established firms and those that are just starting up.

In this chapter, we will examine the role of financial managers and show why businesses need financial management. We will discuss the sources of short-term funds and how they are put to use, as well as sources and uses of long-term financing. By focusing on the learning objectives in this chapter, you will see how risks arise when companies deploy their funds and how financial managers work to protect their firms from unnecessary financial loss.

After reading this chapter, you should be able to:

1. Describe the responsibilities of a *financial manager*.
2. Identify four sources of *short-term financing* for businesses.
3. Distinguish between the various sources of *long-term financing* and explain the risks entailed by each type.
4. Explain how risk affects business operations and identify the five steps in the *risk-management process*.
5. Explain the distinction between *insurable* and *uninsurable risks*.
6. Distinguish among the different types of *business insurance*.

THE ROLE OF THE FINANCIAL MANAGER

We have seen that production managers are responsible for planning and controlling the output of goods and services. We have noted that marketing managers must plan and control the development and marketing of products. Similarly, **financial managers** plan and control the acquisition and dispersal of the company's financial assets.

The business activity known as **finance** (or corporate finance) typically entails four responsibilities:

- determining a firm's long-term investments
- obtaining funds to pay for those investments
- conducting the firm's everyday financial activities
- helping to manage the risks that the firm takes.

financial managers
Those managers responsible for planning and overseeing the financial resources of a firm.

finance
The business function involving decisions about a firm's long-term investments and obtaining the funds to pay for those investments.

Objectives of the Financial Manager

The overall objective of financial managers is to increase the value of the firm and thus to increase shareholder wealth. To reach this goal, financial managers must ensure that the company's earnings exceed its costs—in other words, that the company earns a profit. For a proprietorship or partnership, profits translate into an increase in the owners' wealth. For a corporation, profits translate into an increase in the value of its common stock.

Responsibilities of the Financial Manager

The various responsibilities of the financial manager in increasing a firm's wealth fall into three general categories: *cash flow management, financial control*, and *financial planning*.

Cash Flow Management

To increase a firm's value, financial managers must ensure that it always has enough funds on hand to purchase the materials and human resources that it needs to produce goods and services. At the same time, of course, there may be funds that are not needed immediately. These must be invested to earn more money for a firm. This activity—**cash flow management**— requires careful planning. If excess cash balances are allowed to sit idle instead of invested, a firm loses the cash returns it could have earned.

How important to a business is the management of its idle cash? One study has revealed that companies averaging $2 million in annual sales typically hold $40 000 in non–interest-bearing accounts. Larger companies hold even larger sums. More and more companies, however, are learning to put their idle funds to work. In 1999, for example, General Electric Co. earned $101 million in interest income during the year by investing otherwise idle incoming cash that was not needed immediately to meet other obligations.[1] By locating idle cash and putting it to work, firms not only gain additional income, but also can avoid having to borrow from outside sources. The savings on interest payments can be substantial.

cash flow management
Managing the pattern in which cash flows into the firm in the form of revenues and out of the firm in the form of debt payments.

Financial Control

Because things never go exactly as planned, financial managers must be prepared to make adjustments for actual financial changes that occur each day. **Financial control** is the process of checking actual performance against plans to ensure that the desired financial status occurs. For example, planned revenues based on forecasts usually turn out to be higher or lower than actual revenues. Why? Simply because sales are unpredictable. Control involves monitoring revenue inflows and making appropriate financial adjustments. Excessively high revenues, for instance, may be deposited in short-term interest-bearing accounts. Or they may be used to pay off short-term debt. Otherwise earmarked resources can be saved or put to better use. In contrast, lower-than-expected revenues may necessitate short-term borrowing to meet current debt obligations.

financial control
The process of checking actual performance against plans to ensure that the desired financial status is achieved.

Budgets are often the backbone of financial control. The budget provides the "measuring stick" against which performance is evaluated. The cash flows, debts, and assets not only of the whole company but also of each department are compared at regular intervals against budgeted amounts. Discrepancies indicate the need for financial adjustments so that resources are used to the best advantage.

Financial Planning

The cornerstone of effective financial management is the development of a **financial plan**. A financial plan describes a firm's strategies for reaching some future financial position. In constructing the plan, a financial manager must ask several questions:

financial plan
A description of how a business will reach some financial position it seeks for the future; includes projections for sources and uses of funds.

- What amount of funds does the company need to meet immediate plans?

- When will it need more funds?

- Where can it get the funds to meet both its short-term and its long-term needs?

To answer these questions, a financial manager must develop a clear picture of *why* a firm needs funds. Managers must also assess the relative costs and benefits of potential funding sources. In the sections that follow, we will examine the main reasons for which companies generate funds and describe the main sources of business funding, for both the short term and the long term.

WHY BUSINESSES NEED FUNDS

Every company needs money to survive. Failure to make a contractually obligated payment can lead to bankruptcy and the dissolution of the firm. However, the successful financial manager must distinguish between two different kinds of financial outlays: *short-term (operating) expenditures* and *long-term (capital) expenditures*.

Short-Term (Operating) Expenditures

A firm incurs short-term expenditures regularly in its everyday business activities. To handle these expenditures, financial managers must pay attention to accounts payable and receivable and to inventories.

Accounts Payable

In drawing up a financial plan, financial managers must pay special attention to accounts payable, for it is the largest single category of short-term debt for most companies. But they must rely on other managers for accurate information about the quantity of supplies that will be required in an upcoming period. Financial managers also need to consider the time period in which they must pay various suppliers. For example, a financial manager for *Maclean's* magazine needs information from production about both the amounts of ink and paper needed to print the magazine and when it will be needed. Obviously, it is in the firm's interest to withhold payment as long as it can without jeopardizing its credit rating.

Accounts Receivable

A sound financial plan requires financial managers to project accurately both the amounts buyers will pay to the firm and when they will make those payments. For example, a manager at Kraft Foods needs to know how many dollars worth of cheddar cheese Safeway supermarkets will order each month and how quickly it pays its bills. Because they represent an investment in products on which the firm has not yet received payment, accounts receivable temporarily tie up some of the firm's funds. It is in the firm's interest to receive payment as quickly as possible.

Given that it is in the self-interest of buyers to delay payment for as long as possible, how can a financial manager predict payment times? The answer lies in the development of a *credit policy*, the set of rules governing the extension of credit to customers. The credit policy sets standards as to which buyers are eligible for what type of credit. Financial managers extend credit to customers who have the ability to pay and honour their obligations to pay. They deny credit to firms with poor repayment histories.

The credit policy also sets payment terms. For example, credit terms of "2/10; net 30" mean that the selling company offers a 2 percent discount if the customer pays within 10 days. The customer has 30 days to pay the regular price. Thus, on a $1000 invoice, the buyer would have to pay only $980 on days 1 to 10 but all $1000 on days 11 to 30. The higher the discount, the more incentive buyers have to pay early. Sellers can thus adjust credit terms to influence when customers pay their bills. Often, however, credit terms can be adjusted only slightly without giving competitors an edge.

Inventories

Between the time a firm buys raw materials and the time it sells finished products, it has funds tied up in **inventory**—materials and goods it will sell within the year. There are three basic types of inventories: raw materials, work-in-process, and finished goods.

The basic supplies a firm buys to use in its production process are its **raw materials inventory**. Levi Strauss's raw materials inventory includes huge rolls of denim. **Work-in-process inventory** consists of goods partway through the production process. Cut-out but not-yet-sewn jeans are part of the work-in-process inventory at Levi's. Finally, the **finished goods inventory** is those items ready for sale. Completed blue jeans ready for shipment to dealers are finished goods inventory.

Failure to manage inventory can have grave financial consequences. Too little inventory of any kind can cost the firm sales. Too much inventory means that the firm has funds tied up that it cannot use elsewhere. In extreme cases, too much inventory may force a company to sell merchandise at low profits simply to obtain needed cash.

inventory
Materials and goods currently held by the company that will be sold within the year.

raw materials inventory
That portion of a firm's inventory consisting of basic supplies used to manufacture products for sale.

work-in-process inventory
That portion of a firm's inventory consisting of goods partway through the production process.

finished goods inventory
That portion of a firm's inventory consisting of completed goods ready for sale.

Long-Term (Capital) Expenditures

Companies need funds to cover long-term expenditures for fixed assets. As noted in Chapter 14, fixed assets are items that have a lasting use or value, such as land, buildings, and machinery. The Hudson Bay Oil and Gas plant in Flin Flon, Manitoba, is a fixed asset.

Long-term expenditures are usually more carefully planned than short-term outlays because they pose special problems. They differ from short-term outlays in the following ways, all of which influence the ways that long-term outlays are funded:

- Unlike inventories and other short-term assets, they are not normally sold or converted into cash.

- Their acquisition requires a very large investment.

- They represent a binding commitment of company funds that continues long into the future.

SOURCES OF SHORT-TERM FUNDS

Firms can call on many sources for the funds they need to finance day-to-day operations and to implement short-term plans. These sources include *trade credit, secured* and *unsecured loans*, and *factoring accounts receivable*.

Trade Credit

Accounts payable are not merely an expenditure. They are also a source of funds to the company, which has the use of both the product purchased and the price of the product until the time it pays its bill. **Trade credit**, the granting of credit by one firm to another, is effectively a short-term loan. Trade credit can take several forms.

- The most common form, **open-book credit**, is essentially a "gentlemen's agreement." Buyers receive merchandise along with invoices stating credit terms. Sellers ship products on faith that payment will be forthcoming.

trade credit
The granting of credit by a selling firm to a buying firm.

open-book credit
Form of trade credit in which sellers ship merchandise on faith that payment will be forthcoming.

promissory note
Form of trade credit in which buyers sign promise-to-pay agreements before merchandise is shipped.

trade draft
Form of trade credit in which buyers must sign statements of payment terms attached to merchandise by sellers.

trade acceptance
Trade draft that has been signed by the buyer.

secured loan
A short-term loan in which the borrower is required to put up collateral.

collateral
Any asset that a lender has the right to seize if a borrower does not repay a loan.

- When sellers want more reassurance, they may insist that buyers sign legally binding **promissory notes** before merchandise is shipped. The agreement states when and how much money will be paid to the seller.

- The **trade draft** is attached to the merchandise shipment by the seller and states the promised date and amount of payment due. To take possession of the merchandise, the buyer must sign the draft. Once signed by the buyer, the document becomes a trade acceptance. Trade drafts and **trade acceptances** are useful forms of credit in international transactions.

Secured Short-Term Loans

For most firms, bank loans are a vital source of short-term funding. Such loans almost always involve a promissory note in which the borrower promises to repay the loan plus interest. In **secured loans**, banks also require the borrower to put up **collateral**—to give the bank the right to seize certain assets if payments are not made as promised. Inventories, accounts receivable, and other assets may serve as collateral for a secured loan.

Perhaps the biggest disadvantages of secured borrowing are the paperwork and administrative costs. Agreements must be written, collateral evaluated, and the terms of the loans enforced. But secured loans do enable borrowers to get funds when they might not qualify for unsecured credit. And even creditworthy borrowers benefit by borrowing at lower rates than with unsecured loans.

Inventory Loans

When a loan is made with inventory as a collateral asset, the lender loans the borrower some portion of the stated value of the inventory. Inventory is more attractive as collateral when it provides the lender with real security for the loan amount: For example, if the inventory can be readily converted into cash, it is relatively more valuable as collateral. Other inventory—say, boxes full of expensive, partially completed lenses for eyeglasses—is of little value on the open market. Meanwhile, a thousand crates of boxed, safely stored canned tomatoes might well be convertible into cash.

The inventory in this auto parts warehouse is good collateral because it is neatly stored, accessible, can be readily evaluated, and is quickly disposable.

Accounts Receivable

When accounts receivable are used as collateral, the process is called **pledging accounts receivable**. In the event of nonpayment, the lender may seize the receivables—that is, funds owed the borrower by its customers. If these assets are not enough to cover the loan, the borrower must make up the difference. This option is especially important to service companies such as accounting firms and law offices. Because they do not maintain inventories, accounts receivable are their main source of collateral.

Typically, lenders who will accept accounts receivable as collateral are financial institutions with

pledging accounts receivable
Using accounts receivable as collateral for a loan.

credit departments capable of evaluating the quality of the receivables. Loans are granted only when lenders are confident that they can recover funds from the borrower's debtors. (We will discuss the companies that specialize in these loans, called *factors*, later in the chapter.)

Unsecured Short-Term Loans

With an **unsecured loan**, the borrower does not have to put up collateral. In many cases, however, the bank requires the borrower to maintain a *compensating balance*: The borrower must keep a portion of the loan amount on deposit with the bank in a non–interest-bearing account.

unsecured loan
A short-term loan in which the borrower is not required to put up collateral.

The terms of the loan—amount, duration, interest rate, and payment schedule—are negotiated between the bank and the borrower. To receive an unsecured loan, then, a firm must ordinarily have a good banking relationship with the lender. Once an agreement is made, a promissory note will be executed and the funds transferred to the borrower. Although some unsecured loans are one-time-only arrangements, many take the form *of lines of credit, revolving credit agreements*, or *commercial paper*.

Lines of Credit

A standing agreement with a bank to lend a firm a maximum amount of funds on request is called a **line of credit**. With a line of credit, the firm knows the maximum amount it will be allowed to borrow if the bank has sufficient funds. The bank does not guarantee that the funds will be available when requested, however.

line of credit
A standing agreement between a bank and a firm in which the bank specifies the maximum amount it will make available to the borrower for a short-term unsecured loan; the borrower can then draw on those funds, when available.

For example, suppose that the Toronto-Dominion Bank gives Sunshine Tanning Inc. a $100 000 line of credit for the coming year. By signing promissory notes, Sunshine's borrowings can total up to $100 000 at any time. The bank may not always have sufficient funds when Sunshine needs them. However, Sunshine benefits from the arrangement by knowing in advance that the bank regards the firm as creditworthy and will loan funds to it on short notice.

Revolving Credit Agreements

Revolving credit agreements are similar to bank credit cards for consumers. Under a **revolving credit agreement**, a lender agrees to make some amount of funds available on demand to a firm for continuing short-term loans. The lending institution guarantees that funds will be available when sought by the borrower. In return, the bank charges a *commitment fee*—a charge for holding open a line of credit for a customer even if the customer does not borrow any funds. The commitment fee is often expressed as a percentage of the loan amount, usually 0.5 to 1 percent of the committed amount.

revolving credit agreement
A guaranteed line of credit for which the firm pays the bank interest on funds borrowed as well as a fee for extending the line of credit.

For example, suppose that the Toronto-Dominion Bank agrees to lend Sunshine Tanning up to $100 000 under a revolving credit agreement. If Sunshine borrows $80 000, it still has access to $20 000. If it pays off $50 000 of the debt, reducing its debt to $30 000, then it has $70 000 available to it. Sunshine pays interest on the borrowed funds and also pays a fee on the unused funds in the line of credit.

Commercial Paper

Some firms can raise funds in the short run by issuing commercial paper. Since **commercial paper** is backed solely by the issuing firm's promise to pay, it is an option for only the largest and most creditworthy firms.

commercial paper
A method of short-run fundraising in which a firm sells unsecured notes for less than the face value and then repurchases them at the face value within 270 days; buyers' profits are the difference between the original price paid and the face value.

How does commercial paper work? Corporations issue commercial paper with a face value. Companies that buy commercial paper pay less than that value. At the end of a specified period (usually 30 to 90 days but legally up to 270 days), the issuing company buys back the paper—*at the face value*. The difference between the price the buying company paid and the face value is the buyer's profit.

For example, if Noranda needs to borrow $10 million for 90 days it might issue commercial paper with a face value of $10.2 million. Insurance companies with $10 million excess cash will buy the paper. After 90 days, Noranda would pay $10.2 million to the insurance companies.

Commercial paper offers those few corporations able to issue it several advantages. Its cost is usually lower than prevailing interest rates on short-term loans. And it gives the issuing company access to a wide range of lenders, not just financial institutions.

Factoring Accounts Receivable

factoring
Selling a firm's accounts receivable to another company for some percentage of their face value in order to realize immediate cash; the buyer's profits depend on its ability to collect the receivables.

One way to raise funds rapidly is **factoring**, that is, selling the firm's accounts receivable. In this process, the purchaser of the receivables, usually a financial institution, is known as the factor. The factor pays some percentage of the full amount of receivables to the selling firm. The seller gets money immediately.

For example, a factor might buy $40 000 worth of receivables for 60 percent of that sum ($24 000). The factor profits to the extent that the money it eventually collects exceeds the amount it paid. This profit depends on the quality of the receivables, the costs of collecting the receivables, the time until the receivables are due, and interest rates.

SOURCES OF LONG-TERM FUNDS

Firms need long-term funding to finance expenditures on fixed assets—the buildings and equipment necessary for conducting their business. They may seek long-term funds through *debt financing* (that is, from outside the firm) or through *equity financing* (by drawing on internal sources). We will discuss both options in this section, as well as a middle ground called *hybrid financing*. We will also analyze some of the options that enter into decisions about long-term financing, as well as the role of the *risk-return relationship* in attracting investors to a firm.

Debt Financing

debt financing
Raising money to meet long-term expenditures by borrowing from outside the company; usually takes the form of long-term loans or the sale of corporate bonds.

Long-term borrowing from outside the company—**debt financing**—is a major component of most firms' long-term financial planning. The two primary sources of such funding are long-term loans and the sale of bonds.

Long-Term Loans

In some respects, a long-term loan is like a short-term loan. The major difference is that a long-term loan extends for 3 to 10 years, while short-term loans must generally be paid off in a few years or less. Most corporations get their long-term loans from a chartered bank, usually one with which the firm has developed a long-standing relationship. But credit companies, insurance companies, and pension funds also grant long-term business loans.

Interest rates on long-term loans are negotiated between borrower and lender. Although some bank loans have fixed rates, others have floating rates tied to the prime rate (see Chapter 18). A loan at "1 percent above prime," then, is payable at 1 percentage point higher than the prime rate. This rate may fluctuate—"float"—because the prime rate itself goes up and down as market conditions change.

Long-term loans are attractive to borrowers for several reasons:

- Because the number of parties involved is limited, loans can often be arranged very quickly.

- The firm need not make public disclosure of its business plans or the purpose for which it is acquiring the loan. (In contrast, the issuance of corporate bonds requires such disclosure.)

- The duration of the loan can easily be matched to the borrower's needs.

- If the firm's needs change, loans usually contain clauses making it possible to change terms.

Long-term loans also have some disadvantages. Large borrowers may have trouble finding lenders to supply enough funds. Long-term borrowers may also have restrictions placed on them as conditions of the loan. They may have to pledge long-term assets as collateral. And they may have to agree not to take on any more debt until the borrowed funds are repaid.

Corporate Bonds

Like commercial paper, a **corporate bond** is a contract—a promise by the issuing company or organization to pay the holder a certain amount of money on a specified date. Unlike commercial paper, however, bond issuers do not pay off quickly. In many cases, bonds may not be redeemed for 30 years from the time of issue. In addition, unlike commercial paper, most bonds pay the bondholder a stipulated sum of interest semiannually or annually. If it fails to make a bond payment, the company is in default.

The terms of a bond, including the amount to be paid, the interest rate, and the **maturity** (payoff) **date**, differ from company to company and from issue to issue. They are spelled out in the bond contract, or *bond indenture*. The indenture also identifies which of the firm's assets, if any, are pledged as collateral for the bonds.

Corporate bonds are the major source of long-term debt financing for most corporations. Bonds are attractive when companies need large amounts of funds for long periods of time. The issuing company gets access to large numbers of lenders through nationwide bond markets and stock exchanges.

But bonds involve expensive administrative and selling costs. They also may require very high interest payments if the issuing company has a poor credit rating.

corporate bond
A promise by the issuing company to pay the holder a certain amount of money on a specified date, with stated interest payments in the interim; a form of long-term debt financing.

maturity date
The date on or before which a company must pay off the principal of a particular bond issue.

Equity Financing

Although debt financing has strong appeal in some cases, looking inside the company for long-term funding is preferable under other circumstances. In small companies, the founders may increase their personal investment in the firm. In most cases, however, **equity financing** takes the form of issuing common stock or of retaining the firm's earnings. As you will see, both options involve putting the owners' capital to work.

equity financing
Raising money to meet long-term expenditures by issuing common stock or by retaining earnings.

Common Stock

As noted in Chapter 2, when shareholders purchase common stock, they seek profits in the form of both dividends and appreciation. Overall, shareholders hope for an increase in the market value of their stock because the firm has profited and grown. By selling shares of stock, the company gets the funds it needs for buying land, buildings, and equipment.

For example, suppose that Sunshine Tanning's founders invested $10 000 by buying the original 500 shares of common stock (at $20 per share) in 1994. If the company used these funds to buy equipment and succeeded financially, by 2000 it might need funds for expansion. A pattern of profitable operations and regularly paid dividends might allow Sunshine to raise $50 000 by selling 500 new shares of stock for $100 per share. This additional paid-in capital would increase the total shareholders' equity to $60 000, as shown in Table 20.1.

It should be noted that the use of equity financing via common stock can be expensive because paying dividends is more expensive than paying bond interest. Why? Interest paid to bondholders is a business expense and, hence, a tax deduction for the firm. Stock dividends are not tax-deductible.

Retained Earnings

Another approach to equity financing is to use retained earnings. As we saw in Chapter 14, these earnings represent profits not paid out in dividends. Using retained earnings means that the firm will not have to borrow money and pay interest on loans or bonds. A firm that has a history of eventually reaping much higher profits by successfully reinvesting retained earnings may be attractive to some investors. But the smaller dividends that can be paid to shareholders as a result of retained earnings may decrease demand for—and thus the price of—the company's stock.

For example, if Sunshine Tanning had net earnings of $50 000 in 2000, it could pay a $50-per-share dividend on its 1000 shares of common stock. But if it plans to remodel at a cost of $30 000 and retains $30 000 of earnings to finance the project, only $20 000 is left to distribute for stock dividends ($20 per share).

Financial Burden on the Firm

If equity funding can be so expensive, why don't firms rely instead on debt capital? Because long-term loans and bonds carry fixed interest rates and represent a fixed promise to pay, regardless of economic changes. If the firm defaults on its obligations, it may lose its assets and even go into bankruptcy.

Table 20.1	Shareholders' Equity for Sunshine Tanning Inc.
Common Shareholders' Equity, 1994:	
Initial common stock (500 shares issued @ $20 per share, 1994)	$10 000
Total shareholders' equity	$10 000
Common Shareholders' Equity, 2000:	
Initial common stock (500 shares issued @ $20 per share, 1994)	$10 000
Additional paid-in capital (500 shares issued @ $100 per share, 2000)	50 000
Total shareholders' equity	$60 000

During the 1997 Asian financial crisis, Korean banks suffered when borrowers (large companies) could not repay outstanding debt. Borrower companies went bankrupt, frightened foreign investors pulled their money out of the country, and borrowing costs soared as global lenders demanded higher returns for the increased risks of loaning funds to Korean firms. As more and more borrowers teetered on the verge of default, the Korean economy weakened. Hyundai Motor Co., for example, was forced to halt car production because of lack of parts from Mando Machinery, which had to file for court protection from creditors. With so much investor pessimism, firms were unable to raise badly needed funds to pay their debts. Thus the Korean government had to issue bonds with guaranteed payment to lenders. But even with government assistance, investor confidence dwindled and, without access to additional loans for business expansion, the Korean economy remained dormant until initial signs of recovery began emerging in late 1999.

Because of the risk of bankruptcy, debt financing appeals most strongly to companies in industries that have predictable profits and cash flow patterns. For example, demand for electric power is steady from year to year and predictable from month to month. So provincial electric utility companies, with their stable stream of income, can carry a substantial amount of debt.

Hyundai Motor Co.
www.hyundai.com

Hybrid Financing: Preferred Stock

Falling somewhere between debt and equity financing is the *preferred stock* (see Chapter 2). Preferred stock is a hybrid because it has some of the features of corporate bonds and some features of common stocks. As with bonds, payments on preferred stock are for fixed amounts, such as $6 per share per year. Unlike bonds, however, preferred stock never matures. It can be held indefinitely, like common stock. And dividends need not be paid if the company makes no profit. If dividends are paid, preferred shareholders receive them first in preference to dividends on common stock.

A major advantage of preferred stock to the issuing corporation is its flexibility. It secures funds for the firm without relinquishing control, since preferred shareholders have no voting rights. It does not require repayment of principal or the payment of dividends in lean times.

Choosing Between Debt and Equity Financing

Part of financial planning involves striking a balance between debt and equity financing to meet the firm's long-term need for funds. Because the mix of debt versus equity provides the firm's financial base, it is called the *capital structure* of the firm. Financial plans contain targets for the capital structure, such as 40 percent debt and 60 percent equity. But choosing a target is not easy. A wide range of debt-versus-equity mixes is possible.

The most conservative strategy would be to use all equity financing and no debt. Under this strategy, a company has no formal obligations for financial payouts. But equity is a very expensive source of capital. The most risk-filled strategy would be to use all debt financing. While less expensive than equity funding, indebtedness increases the risk that a firm will be unable to meet its obligations and will go bankrupt. Magna International, for example, has had a high debt-to-equity ratio in the recent past. Industry analysts believe that increased demand for automobiles will allow the firm to make large profits and pay off much of the debt, causing its debt-to-equity ratio to fall.[2] Somewhere between the two extremes, financial planners try to find a mix that will maximize shareholders' wealth. Figure 20.1 summarizes the factors management must take into account when deciding between debt and equity financing.

Magna International
www.magnaint.com

Debt financing

Equity financing

When must it be repaid?

Fixed deadline	No limit

Will it make claims on income?

Yes, regular and fixed	Only residual claim

Will it have claims on assets?

In liquidation, creditors come first	In liquidation, shareholders must wait until creditors are paid and preferred equity precedes common equity

Will it affect management control?

No	May cause challenge for corporation control

How are taxes affected?

Bond interest is deductible	Dividends are not deductible

Will it affect management flexibility?

Yes, many constraints	No, few constraints

Figure 20.1
Comparing debt and equity financing.

Indexes of Financial Risk

To help understand and measure the amount of financial risk they face, financial managers often rely on published indexes for various investments. *Financial World*, for example, publishes independent appraisals of mutual funds (see Chapter 19), using risk-reward ratings of A (very good) to E (poor) to indicate each fund's riskiness in comparison to its anticipated financial returns. An A-rated fund is judged to offer very good returns relative to the amount of risk involved. An E-rated fund carries the greatest risk with smaller returns. Similarly, Standard & Poor's publishes various indexes for numerous funds and for stocks that are available for purchase by financial managers.

By using such indexes, financial managers can determine how a particular investment compares to other opportunities in terms of its stability. A bond, for example, is considered to be investment grade if it qualifies for

WEBCONNEXION

ERisk.com is the first integrated online resource for risk professionals. Current issues and risk trends are addressed throughout the ERisk.com portal, from dynamic editorial content to state-of-the-art enterprise risk management tools to risk transfer opportunities. With over 12 000 registered users, ERisk.com represents one of the leading risk management communities in the world. In addition, it is a full-service provider of strategic risk management solutions including ASP-based analytics, risk transfer advisory, and consulting services. Visit ERisk.com at:

www.erisk.com

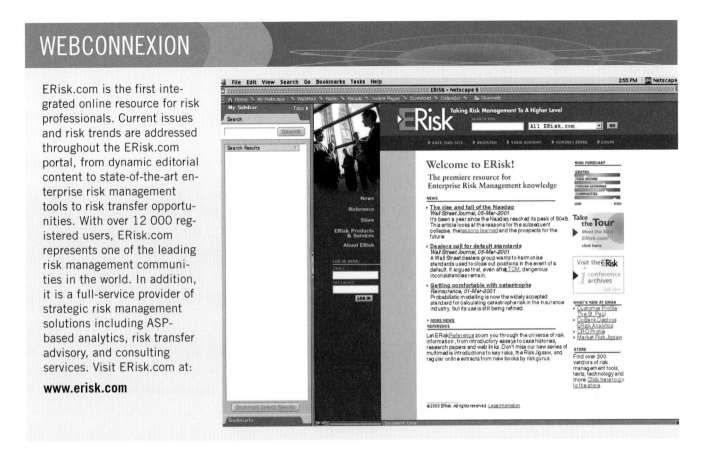

one of the top four ratings of either S&P or Moody's. Bonds below investment grade are called junk bonds because they have unusually high default rates. Nonetheless, junk bonds appeal to many investors because they promise uncommonly high yields.

The Risk-Return Relationship

While developing plans for raising capital, financial managers must be aware of the different motivations of individual investors. Why, for example, do some individuals and firms invest in stocks while others invest only in bonds? Investor motivations, of course, determine who is willing to buy a given company's stocks or bonds. Everyone who invests money is expressing a personal preference for safety versus risk. Investors give money to firms and, in return, anticipate receiving future cash flows.

Some cash flows are more certain than others. Investors generally expect to receive higher payments for higher uncertainty. They generally do not expect large returns for secure investments such as government-insured bonds. Each type of investment, then, has a **risk-return relationship**. Figure 20.2 shows the general risk-return relationship for various financial instruments. High-grade corporate bonds, for example, rate low in terms of risk on future returns but also low on size of expected returns. The reverse is true of junk bonds, those with a higher risk of default.

Risk-return differences are recognized by financial planners, who try to gain access to the greatest funding at the lowest possible cost. By gauging investors' perceptions of their riskiness, a firm's managers can estimate how much it must pay to attract funds to their offerings. Over time, a company can reposition itself on the risk continuum by improving its record on dividends, interest payments, and debt repayment.

risk-return relationship
Shows the amount of risk and the likely rate of return on various financial instruments.

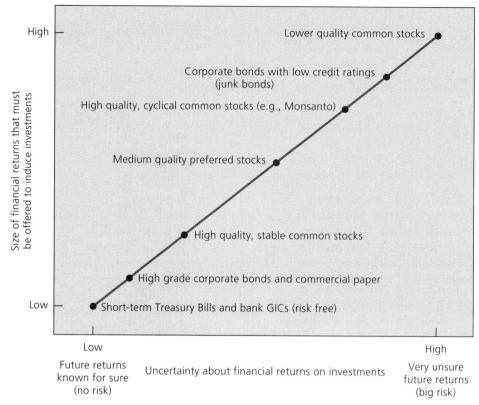

Figure 20.2
Investors expect a chance at greater financial returns for riskier investments.

FINANCIAL MANAGEMENT FOR SMALL BUSINESSES

Most new businesses have inadequate funding. An Ontario government study found that the average investment needed to start a new enterprise was about $58 000, but that more than half of all new companies had less than $15 000 invested.[3] Another study of nearly 3000 new companies revealed a survival rate of 84 percent for new businesses with initial investments of at least $50 000. Those with less funding had a much lower survival rate.[4] Why are so many start-ups underfunded? For one thing, entrepreneurs often underestimate the value of establishing *bank credit* as a source of funds and use *trade credit* ineffectively. In addition, they often fail to consider *venture capital* as a source of funding, and they are notorious for not *planning cash-flow needs* properly.

Establishing Bank Credit and Trade Credit

Banks differ greatly in willingness to assume risk, ability to give professional advice, loyalty to customers, and maximum size of loans offered.[5] Some have liberal credit policies. Some offer financial analysis, cash flow planning, and suggestions based on experience with other local small businesses. Some provide loans to small businesses in bad times and work to keep them going. Others do not.

Credit-seekers must be prepared to show they are worthy of the bank's help. A sound financial plan, a good credit history, and proven capability on the part of the entrepreneur can all convince bankers and other potential financiers that the business can succeed.

Once it has obtained a line of credit, the small business can then attempt to gain more liberal credit policies from other businesses. Sometimes, suppliers will give customers longer credit periods, such as 45 or 60 days net rather than 30 days. Such liberal trade credit terms with suppliers allow the firm to increase its own short-term funds and avoid additional borrowing from banks.

The Business Plan as a Tool for Credit

Start-up firms without proven financial success usually must present a business plan to demonstrate that the firm is a good credit risk.[6] The business plan is a document that tells potential lenders why the money is needed, the amount needed, how the money will be used to improve the company, and when it will be paid back.

Photographer David Cupp, for example, needed $50 000 funding for his new firm, Photos Online Inc., which displays and sells photos over the Internet. His business plan had to be rewritten many times until it became understandable, in financial terms, to potential lenders. The plan eventually reached 35 pages and contained information on the competition as well as cash flow projections. After four failed attempts, the fifth bank approved a $26 000 term loan and granted a $24 000 line of credit, to be used for computers, software, and living expenses to get the business started.[7]

Venture Capital

Many newer businesses—especially those undergoing rapid growth—cannot get the funds they need through borrowing alone. They may, therefore, turn to venture capital—outside equity funding provided in return for part ownership of the borrowing firm. As we saw in Chapter 7, venture capital firms actively seek chances to invest in new firms with rapid growth potential. Because failure rates are high, they typically demand high returns, which are now often 20 to 30 percent. The "It's a Wired World" box notes how Chapters Inc. used both common stock and venture capital funds to support its aggressive expansion plans.

IT'S A WIRED WORLD

It's Hard to Make a Profit Selling Books Online

Chapters Inc. was created by the merger of two entrepreneurial companies—SmithBooks and Coles Book Stores. SmithBooks (originally called W.H. Smith) opened in Toronto in 1950. Coles Book Stores opened in Toronto in 1940, then expanded across Canada, bringing an innovative style of book retailing with stores that were accessible and exciting. Coles also created the world-famous Coles Notes student study guides. In 1980, Coles opened one of the original book superstores, the 67 000-square-foot World's Biggest Bookstore in downtown Toronto.

Chapters is the largest book retailer in Canada and the third-largest in North America. It operates 311 bookstores across the country; 244 of these are traditional bookstores under the banner of Coles or SmithBooks, and 67 are superstores under the Chapters name. The superstores are unique in layout and ambience, and include Starbucks cafés and extended hours of operation. Some of the superstores have Internet cafés, community rooms, and Hear

Music departments where customers can choose from over 15 000 CDs. Computer stations will be installed in all stores to give retail customers access to the same inventory of books that is available to online shoppers.

Chapters decided to begin selling books on the Internet after observing the success of Amazon.com in the U.S. To finance the venture, Chapters raised $51 million through an IPO and another $15 million from a U.S. venture capital fund. Shares of Chapters Online, the company's new Internet book-selling operation, opened at $13.50 in the fall of 1999 and reached a peak of $25 in December 1999. However, by the end of 2000 the share price had dropped back sharply to less than $5.

What happened? While sales are booming at Chapters, the company can't seem to make a profit on its Internet operation, and stockholders have largely abandoned the stock. Amazon.com is having the same type of problem, leading some industry observers to conclude that Internet selling is much kinder to consumers than it is to business, and that it might not be possible to make a profit selling books online.

Planning for Cash-Flow Requirements

Although all businesses should plan for their cash flows, it is especially important for small businesses to do so. Success or failure may hinge on anticipating times when cash will be short and when excess cash is expected.

Figure 20.3 shows possible cash inflows, cash outflows, and net cash position (inflows minus outflows), month by month, for Slippery Fish Bait Supply. In this highly seasonal business, bait stores buy heavily from Slippery during the spring and summer months. Revenues outpace expenses, leaving surplus funds that can be invested. During the fall and winter, expenses exceed revenues. Slippery must borrow funds to keep going until sales revenues pick up again in the spring. Comparing predicted cash inflows from sales with outflows for expenses shows the firm's monthly cash-flow position.

By anticipating shortfalls, a financial manager can seek funds in advance and minimize their cost. By anticipating excess cash, a manager can plan to put the funds to work in short-term, interest-earning investments.

RISK MANAGEMENT

Risk is a factor in every manager's job, and because nearly every managerial action involves risk—that is, the possibility of either desirable outcomes or negative results—risk management is essential.[8] Not surprisingly, then, firms devote considerable resources not only to recognizing potential risks but also to positioning themselves to make the most advantageous decisions.

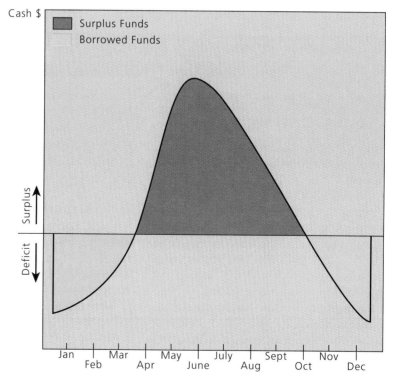

Figure 20.3
Cash flow for Slippery Fish Bait Supply Company.

Coping with Risk

Businesses constantly face two basic types of **risk**—that is, uncertainty about future events. **Speculative risks**, such as financial investments, involve the possibility of gain or loss. **Pure risks** involve only the possibility of loss or no loss. Designing and distributing a new product, for example, is a speculative risk: the product may fail or it may succeed and earn high profits. The chance of a warehouse fire is a pure risk.

For a company to survive and prosper, it must manage both types of risk in a cost-effective manner. We can thus define the process of **risk management** as "conserving the firm's earning power and assets by reducing the threat of losses due to uncontrollable events."[9] In every company, each manager must be alert for risks to the firm and their impact on profits. The risk-management process usually entails the five steps outlined in Figure 20.4.

Step 1: Identify Risks and Potential Losses

Managers analyze a firm's risks to identify potential losses. For example, a firm with a fleet of delivery trucks can expect that one of them will eventually be involved in an accident. The accident may cause bodily injury to the driver or others, may cause physical damage to the truck or other vehicles, or both.

Step 2: Measure the Frequency and Severity of Losses and Their Impact

To measure the frequency and severity of losses, managers must consider both past history and current activities. How often can the firm expect the loss to occur? What is the likely size of the loss in dollars? For example, our firm with the fleet of delivery trucks may have had two accidents per year in the past. If it adds trucks, however, it may reasonably expect the frequency of accidents to increase.

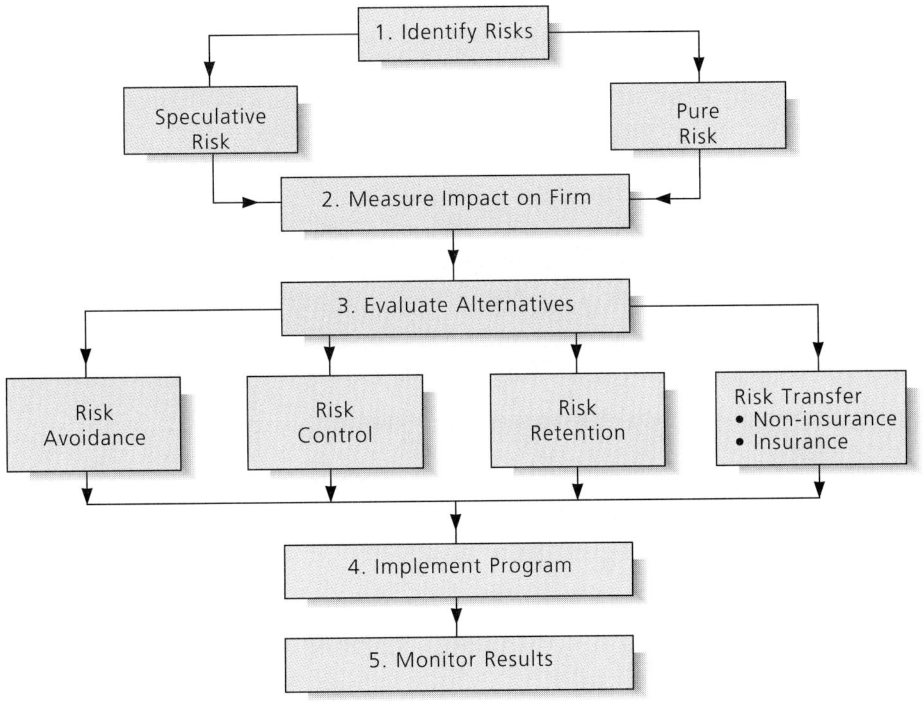

risk
Uncertainty about future events.

speculative risk
An event that offers the chance for either a gain or a loss.

pure risk
An event that offers no possibility of gain; it offers only the chance of a loss.

risk management
Conserving a firm's (or an individual's) financial power or assets by minimizing the financial effect of accidental losses.

Figure 20.4
The risk-management process.

Step 3: Evaluate Alternatives and Choose the Techniques That Will Best Handle the Losses

Having identified and measured potential losses, managers are in a better position to decide how to handle them. With this third step, they generally have four choices: *risk avoidance, control, retention,* or *transfer.*

risk avoidance

Stopping participation in or refusing to participate in ventures that carry any risk.

Risk Avoidance.   A firm opts for **risk avoidance** by declining to enter or by ceasing to participate in a risky activity. For example, the firm with the delivery trucks could avoid any risk of physical damage or bodily injury by closing down its delivery service. Similarly, a pharmaceutical maker may withdraw a new drug for fear of liability suits.

risk control

Techniques to prevent, minimize, or reduce losses or the consequences of losses.

Risk Control.   When avoidance is not practical or desirable, firms can practice **risk control**—say, the use of loss-prevention techniques to minimize the frequency of losses. A delivery service, for instance, can prevent losses by training its drivers in defensive-driving techniques, mapping out safe routes, and conscientiously maintaining its trucks.

risk retention

The covering of a firm's unavoidable losses with its own funds.

Risk Retention.   When losses cannot be avoided or controlled, firms must cope with the consequences. When such losses are manageable and predictable, they may decide to cover them out of company funds. The firm is thus said to "assume" or "retain" the financial consequences of the loss: hence the practice known as **risk retention**. For example, the firm with the fleet of trucks may find that vehicles suffer vandalism totalling $100 to $500 per year. Depending on its coverage, the company may find it cheaper to pay for repairs out of pocket rather than to submit claims to its insurance company.

risk transfer

The transfer of risk to another individual or firm, often by contract.

Risk Transfer.   When the potential for large risks cannot be avoided or controlled, managers often opt for **risk transfer**. They transfer the risk to another firm—namely, an insurance company. In transferring risk to an insurance company, a firm pays a sum called a premium. In return, the insurance company issues an insurance policy—a formal agreement to pay the policyholder a specified amount in the event of certain losses. In some cases, the insured party must also pay a deductible—an agreed-upon amount of the loss that the insured must absorb prior to reimbursement. Thus, our hypothetical company may buy insurance to protect itself against theft, physical damage to trucks, and bodily injury to drivers and others involved in an accident. Table 20.2 lists the top 10 insurance companies in Canada.

Step 4: Implement the Risk-Management Program

The means of implementing risk-management decisions depends on both the technique chosen and the activity being managed. For example, risk

Losses are reduced or prevented when this security specialist uses electronic surveillance (left), when valuables are stored under lock and key (top right), and when workers are reminded to wear safety gear at this construction site (bottom right)

Table 20.2	The Top 10 Life Insurance Companies in Canada (ranked by revenues)

Company	Annual Revenues (in billions)
1. Sun Life Financial Services of Canada	$14.7
2. Manulife Financial Corp.	14.0
3. The Great-West Life Assurance Co.	13.3
4. Canada Life Financial Corp.	7.5
5. Clarica Life Insurance Co.	5.5
6. Industrial-Alliance Life Insurance Co.	2.8
7. The Maritime Life Assurance Co.	1.8
8. Desjardins-Laurentian Life Assurance	1.3
9. Independent Order of Foresters	0.8
10. The Imperial Life Assurance Co. of Canada	0.7

avoidance for certain activities can be implemented by purchasing those activities from outside providers, such as hiring delivery services instead of operating delivery vehicles. Risk control might be implemented by training employees and designing new work methods and equipment for on-the-job safety. For situations in which risk retention is preferred, reserve funds can be set aside out of revenues. When risk transfer is needed, implementation means selecting an insurance company and buying the right policies.

Step 5: Monitor Results

Because risk management is an ongoing activity, follow-up is always essential. New types of risks, for example, emerge with changes in customers, facilities, employees, and products. Insurance regulations change, and new types of insurance become available. Consequently, managers must continually monitor a company's risks, re-evaluate the methods used for handling them, and revise them as necessary.

The Contemporary Risk-Management Program

Virtually all business decisions involve risks having financial consequences. As a result, the company's chief financial officer, along with managers in other areas, usually has a major voice in applying the risk management process. In some industries, most notably insurance, the companies' main line of business revolves around risk-taking and risk management for themselves and their clients.

Today, many firms are taking a new approach to risk management.[10] The key to that approach is developing a program that is both comprehensive and company-wide. In the past, risk management was often conducted by different departments or by narrowly focused financial officers. Now, however, more and more firms have not only created high-level risk-management positions, but, at the same time, stressed the need for middle managers to practise risk management on a daily basis.

INSURANCE AS RISK MANAGEMENT

To deal with some risks, both businesses and individuals may choose to purchase one or more of the products offered by insurance companies. Buyers find insurance appealing for a very basic reason: In return for a relatively small sum of money, they are protected against certain losses, some of them potentially devastating. In this sense, buying insurance is a function of risk management. To define it as a management activity dealing with insurance, we can thus amplify our definition of *risk management* to say that it is the logical development and implementation of a plan to deal with chance losses.

With insurance, then, individuals and businesses share risks by contributing to a fund out of which those who suffer losses are paid. But why are insurance companies willing to accept these risks for other companies? Insurance companies make profits by taking in more **premiums** than they pay out to cover policyholders' losses. Quite simply, although many policyholders are paying for protection against the same type of loss, by no means will all of them suffer such a loss.

premiums

Money paid to an insurance company by customers in return for being covered for certain types of losses should they occur.

Insurable versus Uninsurable Risks

Like every business, insurance companies must avoid certain risks. Insurers thus divide potential sources of loss into *insurable* and *uninsurable risks*.[11] Obviously, they issue policies only for insurable risks. Although there are some exceptions, an insurable risk must satisfy the criteria of predictability, casualty, unconnectedness, and verifiability. As the "Business Today" box illustrates, some insurable risks are very interesting.

Predictability

The insurer must be able to use statistical tools to forecast the likelihood of a loss. For example, an auto insurer needs information about the number of car accidents in the past year to estimate the expected number of accidents for the following year. With this knowledge, the insurer can translate expected numbers and types of accidents into expected dollar losses. The same forecast, of course, also helps insurers determine premiums charged to policyholders.

Casualty

A loss must result from an accident, not from an intentional act by the policyholder. Obviously, insurers do not have to cover damages if a policyholder deliberately sets fire to corporate headquarters. To avoid paying in cases of fraud, insurers may refuse to cover losses when they cannot determine whether policyholders' actions contributed to them.

Unconnectedness

Potential losses must be random and must occur independently of other losses. No insurer can afford to write insurance when a large percentage of those who are exposed to a particular kind of loss are likely to suffer such a loss. One insurance company, for instance, would not want all the hail coverage in Saskatchewan or all the earthquake coverage in Vancouver. By carefully choosing the risks it will insure, an insurance company can reduce its chances of a large loss or even insolvency.

Verifiability

Finally, insured losses must be verifiable as to cause, time, place, and amount. Did an employee develop emphysema because of a chemical to which she was exposed or because she smoked 40 cigarettes per day for 30 years? Did the policyholder pay the renewal premium before the fire destroyed his factory? Were the goods stolen from company offices or from the president's home? What was the insurable value of the destroyed inventory? When all these points have been verified, payment by the insurer goes more smoothly.

BUSINESS TODAY

Entertainment Insurance

The business of insuring entertainment productions and entertainers is very entertaining. Consider the experiences of Chubb Corp. and American Insurance Group.

Chubb Corp. This company is the lead insurer for the Broadway musical "Titanic." The producers of the show paid about $400 000 for insurance to cover things such as a member of the audience being hit by a flying deck chair, or a cast member being injured during the performance. Interestingly, Chubb also covered the real *Titanic*, the one that sank on April 15, 1912, claiming 1523 lives. That real disaster cost the insurance company $100 000, but if the Broadway Titanic sinks, Chubb could be out as much as $14 million.

Chubb's man on the scene is Jim Titterton, who has a degree in fire science and experience as a fire inspector. His first experience with theatre insurance came when he was asked to do a loss-control inspection for the Stephen Sondheim musical "Into the Woods." When Titterton does an inspection, he looks for anything that might cause injury to the actors or the audience. In the Titanic production, for example, powerful motors beneath the stage raise sections of the ship high above the stage, and in the most dramatic moment of the production, these motors tilt the ship just like the real *Titanic* tilted moments before it sank. It is at this point that the actors are in the greatest danger of injury.

Titterton's work is not just an idle exercise. A few years ago, a worker on the set of "Phantom of the Opera" was injured when he was knocked into the orchestra pit by a swinging light fixture. That settlement cost Chubb Corp. well into six figures to settle.

American Insurance Group Inc. (AIG) The producers of the musical "Victor/Victoria" purchased an insurance policy on Julie Andrews. The policy premium—$157 985—insured the producers of the show for up to $2 million if Andrews missed some performances, and up to $8.5 million if she had to leave the show. AIG shared the risk with several other insurance companies, but it was the lead underwriter.

Producers routinely buy this kind of insurance because if a star is unable to perform on a given night, many patrons who have bought tickets want their money back. As it happened, Andrews missed many performances because of various illnesses, and an unusually large number of patrons requested refunds. Total losses to the producers exceeded $1 million.

But when the producers tried to collect their money from the insurance companies, the companies refused to pay, arguing that Andrews had given false answers to questions about her medical history. AIG rescinded the policy on Andrews, and has filed a suit against her, claiming that she gave misleading answers on the insurance policy covering her for the production of "Victor/Victoria."

Insurance is relevant for other show business activities as well. Consider the case of rap music. Well-known rap artists such as Snoop Doggy Dogg can earn more than $50 000 per night on a multi-city concert tour. But national tours by rap artists have been virtually nonexistent since the late 1980s. Why? Because stabbings and gunfire were becoming all too common at these shows. Even when occasional live shows were staged, violence often erupted. Most rap artists have therefore had to rely on videos and radio-station promotions to sell their records and keep their names prominently before their fans.

All of this was supposed to change in 1997, when many rappers planned to take their acts on the road. Bad Boy Entertainment, the record label for rapper Biggie Smalls (also known as Notorious B.I.G.), planned a national tour of up to 30 cities starting in May 1997. But in March, Biggie Smalls was killed in a gangland-style hit. This killing occurred only six months after rapper Tupac Shakur was also gunned down.

Reliance National Insurance is one of the largest underwriters of music events. It also insures many concerts by crooners and rappers. When musicians perform live, insurance costs are usually shared by the performer, the concert promoter, and the arena where the event is being held. Music companies also take out "key man" insurance on musicians. With the killings of Smalls and Shakur, insurance premiums on concerts are expected to skyrocket.

Insuring an all-rapper concert, particularly a "gangsta rap" concert, is seen by industry experts as being nearly impossible, given the violence that has occurred in the past. Eric Wilson, the president of Famous Artists Agency, says that insurance is either impossible to get or so expensive that it is difficult to make a profit on a concert. Some rap bands like the Fugees are seen as more insurable because they perform "feel-good rap."

In the wake of the killings of Smalls and Shakur, record companies are trying to convince rap artists to beef up their security. Insurance companies say they will have to raise premiums if concert promoters don't improve security. Metal detectors at entrances, security guards (one for every 100 people), and reserved seating may all be required before insurance can be purchased for rap concerts.

Chubb Corp.
www.chubb.com

American Insurance Group
www.aig.com

The Insurance Product

Insurance companies are often distinguished by the types of insurance coverage they offer. Whereas some insurers offer only one area of coverage—life insurance, for example—others offer a broad range. In this section, we briefly describe three major categories of business insurance: *liability, property,* and *life.* A more detailed description of insurance products is presented in Appendix B.

Liability Insurance

liability insurance
Covers losses resulting from damage to people or property when the insured party is judged liable.

As we will see in Appendix B, *liability* means responsibility for damages in case of accidental or deliberate harm to individuals or property. **Liability insurance** covers losses resulting from damage to people or property when the insured party is judged liable.

workers' compensation coverage
Compensation for medical expenses, loss of wages, and rehabilitation services for injuries arising from activities related to occupation.

A business is liable for any injury to an employee when the injury arises from activities related to occupation. When workers are permanently or temporarily disabled by job-related accidents or disease, employers are required by law to provide **workers' compensation coverage** for medical expenses, loss of wages, and rehabilitation services.

There is growing concern about fraudulent claims submitted by people who buy liability insurance. One popular scam is the "staged accident." The swindler purposely (but carefully) runs into a telephone pole, and then everyone in the car claims "whiplash." After the accident is reported, the insurance company contacts the car occupants and sends them accident benefit packages. Sometimes people who aren't even insured are paid benefits because they use counterfeit "proof of insurance" cards.[12]

The insurance industry estimates that between $10 and $15 of every $100 dollars you pay in premiums goes to cover fraud losses. The Canadian Coalition Against Insurance Fraud (CCAIF) estimates that insurance fraud costs insurers in Canada more than $1 billion each year. Across Canada, the CCAIF is working with Crime Stoppers; it offers a reward to tipsters who provide information leading to the discovery of fraud.

Property Insurance

property insurance
Covers injuries to firms resulting from physical damage to or loss of real estate or personal property.

Firms purchase **property insurance** to cover injuries to themselves resulting from physical damage to or loss of real estate or personal property. Property losses may result from fire, lightning, wind, hail, explosion, theft, vandalism, or other destructive forces.

business interruption insurance
Covers lost income due to unavoidable interruptions in a firm's business.

In some cases, loss to property is minimal in comparison to loss of income. A manufacturer, for example, may have to close down for an extended time while repairs to fire damage are being completed. During that time, of course, the company is not generating income. Even so, however, certain expenses—such as taxes, insurance premiums, and salaries for key personnel—may continue. To cover such losses, a firm may buy **business interruption insurance**.

Life Insurance

life insurance
Insurance that pays benefits to survivors of a policyholder.

Insurance can also protect a company's human assets. As part of their benefits packages, many businesses purchase **life insurance** for employees. Life insurance companies accept premiums in return for the promise to pay beneficiaries after the death of insured parties. A portion of the premium is used to cover the insurer's own expenses. The remainder is invested in various types of financial instruments such as corporate bonds and stocks.

Most companies buy **group life insurance**, which is underwritten for groups as a whole rather than for each individual member. The insurer's assessment of potential losses and its pricing of premiums are based on the characteristics of the entire group.

group life insurance
Life insurance underwritten for a group as a whole rather than for each individual member.

Special Forms of Business Insurance

Many forms of insurance are attractive to both businesses and individuals. For example, homeowners are as concerned about insuring property from fire and theft as are businesses. Businesses, however, have some special insurable concerns. In this section, we will discuss two forms of insurance that apply to the departure or death of key employees or owners.

Key Person Insurance

Many businesses choose to protect themselves against loss of the talents and skills of key employees. For example, if a salesperson who annually rings up $2.5 million dies or takes a new job, the firm will suffer loss. It will also incur recruitment costs to find a replacement and training expenses once a replacement is hired. **Key person insurance** is designed to offset both lost income and additional expenses.[13]

key person insurance
Insurance that protects a company against loss of the talents and skills of key employees.

Business Continuation Agreements

Who takes control of a business when a partner or an associate dies? Surviving partners are often faced with the possibility of having to accept an inexperienced heir as a management partner. This contingency can be handled in **business continuation agreements**, whereby owners make plans to buy the ownership interest of a deceased associate from his or her heirs. The value of the ownership interest is determined when the agreement is made. Special policies can also provide survivors with the funds needed to make the purchase.

business continuation agreement
An agreement in which owners of a business make plans to buy the ownership interest of a deceased associate from his or her heirs.

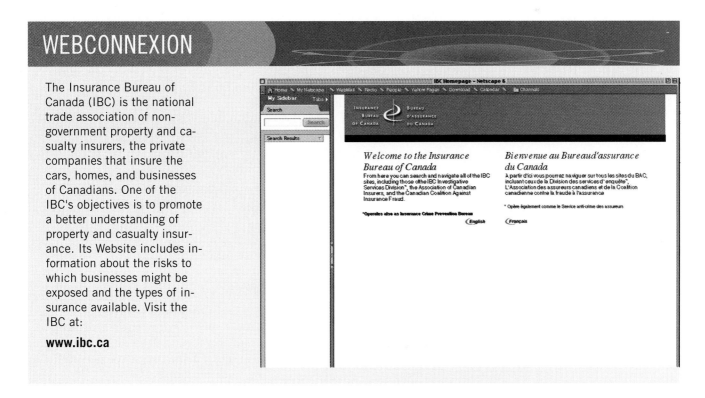

WEBCONNEXION

The Insurance Bureau of Canada (IBC) is the national trade association of non-government property and casualty insurers, the private companies that insure the cars, homes, and businesses of Canadians. One of the IBC's objectives is to promote a better understanding of property and casualty insurance. Its Website includes information about the risks to which businesses might be exposed and the types of insurance available. Visit the IBC at:

www.ibc.ca

SUMMARY OF LEARNING OBJECTIVES

1. **Describe the responsibilities of a *financial manager*.** The job of the financial manager is to increase a firm's value by planning and controlling the acquisition and dispersal of its financial assets. This task involves two key responsibilities: (1) *cash flow management*—ensuring that a firm has enough available money to purchase the materials it needs to produce goods and services, and (2) *financial planning*—devising strategies for reaching future financial goals.

2. **Identify four sources of *short-term financing* for businesses.** To finance short-term expenditures, firms rely on *trade credit*—credit extended by suppliers—and on loans. *Secured loans* require *collateral*—the legal interest in assets that may include inventories or accounts receivable. *Unsecured loans* may be in the form of *lines of credit* or *revolving credit agreements*. Some very large firms issue *commercial paper*—short-term promises to pay. Smaller firms may choose to *pledge accounts receivable*—that is, sell them to financial institutions.

3. **Distinguish between the various sources of *long-term financing* and explain the risks entailed by each type.** Long-term sources of funds include debt financing, equity financing, and the use of preferred stock. *Debt financing* uses long-term loans and *corporate bonds* (promises to pay holders specified amounts by certain dates), both of which obligate the firm to pay regular interest. *Equity financing* involves the use of owners' capital, either from the sale of common stock or from retained earnings. *Preferred stock* is a "hybrid" source of funding that has some of the features of both common stock and bonds. Financial planners must choose the proper mix of long-term funding. *All-equity financing* is the most conservative, least risky, and most expensive strategy. *All-debt financing* is the most speculative option.

4. **Explain how risk affects business operations and identify the five steps in the *risk-management process*.** Businesses operate in an environment pervaded by risk. *Speculative risks* involve the prospect of gain or loss. *Pure risks* involve only the prospect of loss or no loss. Firms manage their risks by following some form of a five-step process: identifying risks, measuring possible losses, evaluating alternative techniques, implementing chosen techniques, and monitoring programs on an ongoing basis. There are generally four methods of handling risk: *risk avoidance, control, retention,* and *transfer*.

5. **Explain the distinction between *insurable* and *uninsurable risks*.** Insurance companies issue policies only for insurable risks—those that meet four criteria. First, the risk must be *predictable* in a statistical sense; the insurer must be able to use statistical tools to forecast the likelihood of a loss. A loss must also pass the test of *casualty*, which indicates that the loss is accidental rather than intentional. Potential losses must also display *unconnectedness*—they must be random and occur independently of other losses. Finally, losses must be *verifiable* in terms of cause, time, place, and amount.

6. **Distinguish among the different types of *business* insurance.** *Liability insurance* covers losses resulting from damage to the persons or property of other people or firms. *Property insurance* covers losses to a firm's own buildings, equipment, and financial assets. *Life insurance* pays benefits to the survivors of a policyholder and has a cash value that can be claimed before the policyholder's death.

KEY TERMS

financial managers, 648
finance, 648
cash flow management, 649
financial control, 649
financial plan, 649
inventory, 651
raw materials inventory, 651
work-in-process inventory, 651
finished goods inventory, 651
trade credit, 651

open-book credit, 651
promissory note, 652
trade draft, 652
trade acceptance, 652
secured loan, 652
collateral, 652
pledging accounts receivable, 652
unsecured loan, 653
line of credit, 653
revolving credit agreement, 653
commercial paper, 653
factoring, 654

debt financing, 654
corporate bond, 655
maturity date, 655
equity financing, 655
risk-return relationship, 659
risk, 663
speculative risk, 663
pure risk, 663
risk management, 663
risk avoidance, 664
risk control, 664
risk retention, 664
risk transfer, 664

premiums, 666
liability insurance, 668
workers' compensation coverage, 668
property insurance, 668
business interruption insurance, 668
life insurance, 668
group life insurance, 669
key person insurance, 669
business continuation agreement, 669

STUDY QUESTIONS AND EXERCISES

Review Questions

1. What are four short-term sources of funds for financing day-to-day business operations? Identify the advantages and disadvantages of each.
2. In what ways do the two sources of debt financing differ from each other? How do they differ from the two sources of equity financing?
3. Describe the relationship between investment risk and return. In what ways might the risk–return relationship affect a company's financial planning?
4. Give two examples of risks that are uninsurable. Why are they uninsurable?
5. Describe the risk management process. What are the major roles of a company's risk manager?

Analysis Questions

6. How would you decide on the best mix of debt, equity, and preferred stock for a company?

7. Why is liability insurance important to business firms?
8. As a risk manager of a large firm, what risks do you think your firm faces? How does this differ for a small firm? What accounts for the most important differences?

Application Exercises

9. Interview the owner of a small local business. Identify the types of short-term and long-term funding this firm typically uses. Why has the company made the financial management decisions it has?
10. Interview the owner of a small local business. Ask this person to describe the risk management process he or she follows. What role, for example, does risk transfer play? Why has the company made the risk management decisions it has?

Building Your Business Skills

Understanding Risk Management Issues

Goal

To encourage students to gain a better understanding of the major financial and risk-management issues that have faced large companies in the mid-1990s.

Method

During the last few years, all of the following companies reported financial problems relating to risk management:

- Levi Strauss
- Eaton's
- Canadian Airlines International
- Sony
- Compaq Computer

Step 1:

Working alone, research one of the companies listed above to learn more about the financial risks that were reported in the news.

Step 2:

Write a short explanation of the risks and financial-management issues that were faced by the firm you researched.

Step 3:

Join in teams with students who researched other companies and compare your findings.

Follow-Up Questions

1. Were there common themes in the "big stories" in financial management?
2. What have the various companies done to minimize future risks and losses?

Exploring the Net

Many tools and resources are available on Canadian business Web sites to help business managers improve financial decision making. One such site is run by the Canadian Business Service Centres. Check out the site at:

http://www.cbsc.org

1. What types of financing sources are available through the government?
2. What type of information can be accessed through this site? Is there a bias toward one type of business or another?
3. What are the various legal issues that must be faced when starting your own business? Does this site provide the means to overcome these obstacles?
4. Go through the "Interactive Business Planner" section. How would you rate this feature? Does it paint an accurate picture of what should be considered for new entrepreneurs?

Concluding Case 20-1

Brascan Sticks to Its Strategy

During the last few years, many companies have been pouring money into fibre optics and dot-com companies. Not Jack Cockwell, the CEO of Brascan Ltd., the Toronto-based conglomerate that owns companies such as Noranda, Brookfield Properties Corp., Great Lakes Power Inc., and Trilon Financial Corp. He recently paid nearly $20 million for two Brazilian cattle ranches and 25 000 steers. They were cheap because of the collapse of the Brazilian currency.

Cockwell is a legendary bargain hunter and his latest purchase continues his long-standing strategy of buying undervalued companies. In the early 1990s, he took $20 million of Seagram Co. Ltd. stock owned by Peter and Edward Bronfman and parlayed it into Canada's most powerful and controversial conglomerate—Edper Group Ltd.

Edper Group Ltd. had serious financial troubles in the early 1990s. When real estate prices dropped dramatically, Edper faced bankruptcy because it was unable to pay its debts. The company sold assets to stay alive, and in 1996 a major financial restructuring of the company took place. In that restructuring, some well-known assets were sold, including John Labatt Ltd., MacMillan Bloedel Ltd., and Royal Trustco Ltd. Edper also sold debt securities through U.S. investment bankers to raise money. The restructuring was watched very carefully by senior Canadian bankers such as John Hunkin (currently CIBC chairman) and Charles Baillie (TD Bank chairman), who visited Edper's offices to check on how things were going.

In fact, things went pretty well. By the mid-1990s, Edper had sold nearly $5 billion in assets and had raised $6.6 billion in new equity financing. It also had reduced its total debt by $10 billion. Renamed Brascan in 2000, the company is continuing its emphasis on Old Economy activity. Because of that strategy, it is seen by many industry observers as out of date and ineffective, and its stock has been very much out of favour among analysts. Brascan's performance has lagged behind that of the TSE 300 Index since 1998.

In spite of this, Cockwell is committed to retaining the company's "holding company" structure, and he has turned down many break-up proposals by investment bankers. By organizing the company into counter-cyclical sectors such as real estate, hydroelectricity, mining, and financial services, he argues that the company won't suffer if there is a downturn in any one of those sectors.

In the mid-1990s, Cockwell became convinced that the overpriced high-tech stock market would experience a big decline, so during 1997 and 1998 Brascan sold assets, reduced its debt, and stockpiled cash. The decline of dot-com stocks during 2000 was exactly what he had predicted, and he now thinks that once the market correction is over, investors will be much more interested in companies like Brascan. If he is wrong, he will retire in 2002 and be remembered as the last of a dying breed of conglomerate moguls who once ruled the Canadian business scene. However, if he is right, he will be remembered as the first of a new breed of successful managers in the post-dot-com era.

In November 2000, Brascan announced that it had achieved its seventh consecutive quarter of increased profit.

CASE QUESTIONS

1. Why might a profitable company like Brascan be out of favour with investment analysts? What can a company do to regain favour?

2. What are the advantages and disadvantages of debt and equity financing? How did these advantages and disadvantages manifest themselves in the Brascan/Edper case?

3. What are the two basic sources of long-term funds? Explain Brascan/Edper's strategy with regard to long-term funding.

4. Discuss the risk-return relationship as it applies to Brascan. ◆

Concluding Case 20-2

A Failure in Risk Management

Stephen Humphries, 25, worked as a trader at Sussex Futures Ltd. in England. One afternoon in August 1999, Humphries engaged in so much fraudulent trading activity that he destroyed the company he worked for. Humphries bet that U.S. unemployment figures were going to go up, but when data were published showing no change in the U.S. unemployment rate, this made U.S. interest rates more likely to rise, which in turn reduced the value of fixed-interest investments such as government bonds. Humphries continued to buy bonds in the hope that things would somehow turn around, but in the end he lost $US1.1 million in about 90 minutes. Sussex Futures ceased operations three months later, and 70 brokers lost their jobs. Ironically, Humphries had lost his job at a previous trading firm when another rogue trader bankrupted that firm.

Humphries is not the only rogue trader who has received publicity lately. Nicholas Leeson, age 28, worked for Barings PLC, a British merchant bank. Leeson's job involved buying and selling futures contracts, particularly investments known as derivatives.

Barings was widely regarded as a conservative institution. Thus, the financial world was astounded when it was revealed that Leeson had incurred staggering trading losses of nearly $1 billion. Over a three-week period, Leeson bought $27 billion in futures contracts and wagered that the sluggish Japanese Nikkei stock index would go up. If the Nikkei rose as he predicted, Leeson would cash in and profit. How? The contract price on which he had originally agreed would be lower than the actual level of the index when the contract came due. He would profit by the amount of the difference. But the Nikkei fell below Leeson's contract price, and Barings was obligated to pay the difference. Leeson tried to reverse his losses, but he was forced to put up cash for margin calls. In other words, he had to pay to maintain a certain percentage of the daily value of his contract—which was dropping along with the Nikkei.

Leeson convinced Barings officials in London to advance him more cash by claiming that he was trading on behalf of a client who would soon be depositing funds with the bank. But it was not enough, and when losses spiralled out of control, Leeson fled, and Barings had to declare bankruptcy. A Dutch banking and insurance company—ING—paid a nominal sum of one British pound in exchange for all of Barings' liabilities and assets. ING announced that it would provide an immediate cash infusion of more than $1 billion to allow Barings to continue its operations.

How could a single trader have racked up such losses? The problem, experts agreed, was a lack of internal risk management controls. In a very general sense, Leeson's activities were subject to control by risk-management officials at Barings, but Leeson was, in essence, supervising and settling his own trading activities. Another reason may have been internal rivalries and turf battles pitting Barings' London-based banking operations against the company's trading divisions world wide. In the weeks following Leeson's arrest, there was a flurry of accusations regarding which Barings executive should have been responsible for preventing the fiasco. "The great shame," lamented one Barings official, "is that we're very conservatively run. The one thing that we were trying to minimize—risk taking—is what blew us out of the water."

What happened to Nick Leeson? After his arrest in Germany, he was kept in jail while awaiting extradition to Singapore. After his trial, he was sentenced to 6.5 years in prison.

CASE QUESTIONS

1. Discuss the activities of Humphries and Leeson in terms of the risk-reward relationship.

2. What kind of risk were Humphries and Leeson facing in their financial dealings?

3. Using the framework developed in this chapter, explain how a risk-management plan could help a financial institution prevent a disaster of the magnitude described in the Humphries and Leeson cases.

4. What are some of the risks and challenges ING faces as the new owner of Barings? ◆

Visit the *Business* Website at www.pearsoned.ca/griffin
for up-to-date e-business cases!

CBC Video Case

VI-1 CBC

Brokers

Once upon a time, the stockbroker was king. Consumers couldn't buy or sell shares of stock unless they went through a broker, and every time they bought or sold stocks they paid a transaction fee. For example, if a customer bought 1000 shares of a blue-chip company, broker commissions at full-service brokers could be as high as $800. In good economic times, brokers made a lot of money and had a fine lifestyle.

But the fairy tale is over. With the advent of online stock buying, massive changes are confronting stockbrokers, and there are tough times ahead. In 2000, about 40 percent of all trades were done online, and it only cost about $27 dollars to purchase 1000 shares of stock. Because of the dramatically lower fees, many consumers are hanging up on their brokers and going online themselves.

Colleen Moorehead used to be full-service broker, but she quit that job and is now president of E-trade Canada. Not surprisingly, she thinks that the future of stock trading is online. Her company spends $10 million on advertising annually, including a spot on the 2000 Super Bowl. All online companies are marketing like crazy.

The term "broker" is quickly becoming outdated. It is now fashionable for people in the business to call themselves "investment advisers." However, to make money, they need to get out of the commission game. Instead, they must position themselves as advisers who receive a fee for services actually rendered. The problem is that brokers are not trained to be financial advisers, so it is a case of trying to fit square pegs into round holes.

Canada's big banks run 75 percent of the brokerage industry. They are scrambling to hold on to customers by starting online services of their own, but they are finding that the profit margins are much lower than they used to be because of price competition. The Bank of Montreal has set up a hybrid service where customers can trade online and receive advice from human beings if they need it. Customers can make as many trades as they want in a year for a flat commission charge of $1500.

The Bank of Montreal has a discount brokerage operation of its own called Investor Line, but this activity actually undercuts its traditional (and more lucrative) brokerage operations. The Bank of Montreal thinks it can grow the online brokerage business fast enough to make up for the fact that margins are much smaller than at traditional brokers. However, critics argue that once the hot stock market cools off, there will be massive layoffs in the brokerage industry as the move to online trading continues.

The bottom line is that online stock buying is saving customers money and putting pressure on traditional brokers to provide more service. Customers are starting to ask themselves, "Why should I go to a traditional broker and pay high fees unless that broker provides extra services that are worth something to me? It's a good question.

STUDY QUESTIONS

1. What is the difference between a primary securities market and a secondary securities market? In which market do brokers work?

2. What is the difference between a full-service broker and a discount broker? Would a person who buys stocks online use either type of broker? Why or why not?

3. Can you think of any unexpected negative consequences of online stock buying? Any unexpected positive consequences?

4. Explain the move to online buying of stocks from a "channels of distribution" perspective (review the relevant material in Chapter 17 before answering this question). Include in your discussion the issue of the functions that intermediaries perform and the value they must add.

Video Resource: "Brokers," *Venture #737* (February 1, 2000).

CBC Video Case   VI-2   CBC ◉

Is the Toronto Stock Exchange in Trouble?

That venerable financial institution called the Toronto Stock Exchange (TSE) is under pressure from a growing number of competitors, and from a failure to solve some of its own internal problems. While speaking to the media just after an embarrassing computer crash, Barbara Stymiest, the president of the TSE, explained that the system froze up due to heavy trading in Nortel Networks. She is unhappy with the all-too-frequent computer glitches on the TSE, and says that her top priority is to ensure that the technology is working well. But, she cautions, electronic systems have their glitches. The technology problems at the TSE are obviously not Stymiest's favourite subject.

There was a time when the TSE was on top of world in technology. In the glory days, the TSE was the first exchange in the world to install a computerized trading system in 1977. Later, other exchanges like Paris and Madrid invested in the system. But the world has moved too fast (or perhaps the TSE has moved too slowly). Morgan McCague, a big customer who represents the Ontario Teachers Pension Fund with assets of $72 billion, says that the TSE's reliance on past glory has put it in jeopardy. He says that if the TSE wants to survive, it will have to make a lot of good moves in the future. Tom Caldwell, a brokerage owner, is also not impressed with the TSE. His former loyalty has turned to cynicism. He thinks that the TSE is dismantling itself, and that customers will increasingly gravitate to the U.S.

Technology is not the only threat to the TSE. Competition is also looming. NASDAQ has opened an office in Montreal, and wants Canadian companies to sell their shares of stock on NASDAQ. They'll be chasing after both first-timers and companies that are already listed on the TSE. NASDAQ is a force to be reckoned with. And there's more bad news on the competitive front. E-traders will soon be able to trade stock with each other instead of going through the TSE. Critics worry that the TSE is oblivious to the fact that they are in a do-or-die situation because of increased competition.

Barbara Stymiest claims that the TSE is working on its problems, and she points to the new corporate structure, new management, and new strategy of the TSE. She also mentions the Global Equity Markets alliance that the TSE has joined, which will market itself to traders. The TSE is also developing new products to interest large institutional buyers. Stymiest points out that the TSE actually outperformed the other major exchanges in 2000. Critics, however, say that the high performance was due to the companies that were listed on the exchange, not because of anything the TSE did.

All of these problems are very unfortunate, because the future of the TSE matters to a lot of Canadians. Consider Steve Arliss. His biotech company isn't big enough to raise money on the NYSE, but he was able to raise 40 million on the TSE. Arliss says there is a "home field advantage" in his dealing with the TSE. His company can attract coverage and a following here in Canada that wouldn't be possible in the U.S. because his firm is simply too small by U.S. standards. He therefore wants to see the TSE stay competitive.

Will the actions the TSE has taken be enough? Time will tell.

STUDY QUESTIONS

1. Why would computer glitches on the TSE cause such unhappiness among brokers and customers?

2. What additional actions might the TSE take to ensure its competitive position?

3. Consider the information provided in Chapter 19 in the section titled "Steps to a Global Stock Market" and in the "It's a Wired World" box on page 628. Will these trends facilitate or inhibit the success of the TSE?

4. Do you think the TSE will survive and prosper, or is it going to go out of business? Defend your answer.

Video Resource: "Troubles at the TSE," Venture #766 (November 28, 2000).

BUSINESS LAW

THE ROLE OF LAW IN CANADIAN SOCIETY

Law is the set of rules and standards that a society agrees upon to govern the behaviour of its citizens. Both the British and the French influenced the development of law in Canada. In 1867, the *British North America (BNA) Act* created the nation of Canada. The *BNA Act* was "patriated" to Canada in 1982 and is known as the *Constitution Act*. This act divides legislative powers in Canada between the federal and provincial governments.

law
The set of rules and standards that a society agrees upon to govern the behaviour of its citizens.

Sources of Law

The law in Canada has evolved and changed in response to our norms and values. Our laws have arisen from three sources: (1) customs and judicial precedents (the source of common law), (2) the actions of provincial and federal legislatures (the source of statutory law), and (3) rulings by administrative bodies (the source of administrative law).

Common law is the unwritten law of England, derived from ancient precedents and judges' previous legal opinions. Common law is based on the principle of equity, the provision to every person of a just and fair remedy. Canadian legal customs and traditions derive from British common law. All provinces except Quebec, which uses the French Civil Code, have laws based on British common law, and court decisions are often based on precedents from common law. That is, decisions made in earlier cases that involved the same legal point will guide the court.

common law
The unwritten law of England, derived from precedent and legal judgments.

Statutory law is written law developed by city councils, provincial legislatures, and parliament. Most law in Canada today is statutory law.

Administrative law is the rules and regulations that government agencies and commissions develop based on their interpretations of statutory laws. For example, Consumer and Corporate Affairs Canada develops regulations on false advertising using federal legislation.

statutory law
Written law developed by city councils, provincial legislatures, and parliament.

administrative law
Rules and regulations that government agencies develop based on their interpretations of statutory law.

The Court System

In Canada, the judiciary branch of government has the responsibility of settling disputes among organizations or individuals by applying existing laws. Both provincial and federal courts exist to hear both criminal and civil cases. The Supreme Court of Canada is the highest court in Canada. It decides whether to hear appeals from lower courts.

BUSINESS LAW

Business firms, like all other organizations, are affected by the laws of the country. **Business law** refers to laws that specifically affect how business firms are managed. Some laws affect all businesses, regardless of size, industry, or location. For example, the *Income Tax Act* requires businesses to pay income tax. Other laws may have a greater impact on one industry than on others. For example, pollution regulations are of much greater concern to Inco than they are to Carlson Wagonlit Travel.

business law
Laws that specifically affect how businesses are managed.

Business managers must have at least a basic understanding of eight important concepts in business law:

- contracts
- warranty
- agency
- torts
- bailment
- negotiable instruments
- property
- bankruptcy

Contracts

Agreements about transactions are common in a business's day-to-day activity. A **contract** is an agreement between two parties to act in a specified way or to perform certain acts. A contract might, for example, apply to a customer buying a product from a retail establishment or to two manufacturers agreeing to buy products or services from each other. A valid contract includes several elements:

- *an agreement*—All parties must consciously agree about the contract.

- *consideration*—The parties must exchange something of value (e.g., time, products, services, money, etc.).

- *competence*—All parties to the contract must be legally able to enter into an agreement. Individuals who are below a certain age or who are legally insane, for example, cannot enter into legal agreements.

- *legal purpose*—What the parties agree to do for or with each other must be legal. An agreement between two manufacturers to fix prices is not legal.

The courts will enforce a contract if it meets the criteria described above. Most parties honour their contracts, but occasionally one party does not do what it was supposed to do. **Breach of contract** occurs when one party to an agreement fails, without legal reason, to live up to the agreement's provisions. The party who has not breached the contract has three alternatives under the law in Canada: (1) discharge, (2) sue for damages, or (3) require specific performance.

An example will demonstrate these three alternatives. Suppose that Barrington Farms Inc. agrees to deliver 100 dozen long-stemmed roses to the Blue Violet Flower Shop the week before Mother's Day. One week before the agreed-upon date, Barrington informs Blue Violet that it cannot make the delivery until after Mother's Day. Under the law, the owner of Blue Violet can choose among any of the following:

Discharge

Blue Violet can also ignore its obligations in the contract. That is, it can contract with another supplier.

Sue for Damages

Blue Violet can legally demand payment for losses caused by Barrington's failure to deliver the promised goods. Losses might include any increased price Blue Violet would have to pay for the roses or court costs incurred in the damage suit.

---

contract
An agreement between two parties to act in a specified way or to perform certain acts.

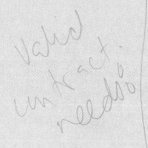
Valid contract needs

breach of contract
When one party to an agreement fails, without legal reason, to live up to the agreement's provisions.

Require Specific Performance

If monetary damages are not sufficient to reimburse Blue Violet, the court can force Barrington's to live up to its original contract.

Agency

In many business situations, one person acts as an agent for another person. Well-known examples include actors and athletes represented by agents who negotiate contracts for them. An **agency–principal relationship** is established when one party (the agent) is authorized to act on behalf of another party (the principal).

    The agent is under the control of the principal and must act on behalf of the principal and in the principal's best interests. The principal remains liable for the acts of the agent as long as the agent is acting within the scope of authority granted by the principal. A salesperson for IBM, for example, is an agent for IBM, the principal.

agency–principal relationship
When one party (the agent) is authorized to act on behalf of another party (the principal).

Bailment

Many business transactions are not covered by the agency–principal relationship. For example, suppose that you take your car to a mechanic to have it repaired. Because the repair shop has temporary possession of something you own, it is responsible for your car. This is a **bailor–bailee relationship**. In a bailor–bailee relationship, the bailor (the car owner) gives possession of his or her property to the bailee (the repair shop) but retains ownership of the item. A business firm that stores inventory in a public warehouse is in a bailor–bailee relationship. The business firm is the bailor and the warehouse is the bailee. The warehouse is responsible for storing the goods safely and making them available to the manufacturer upon request.

bailor–bailee relationship
When a bailor, a property owner, gives possession of the property to a bailee, a custodian, but retains ownership of the property.

property
Anything of tangible or intangible value that the owner has the right to possess and own.

The Law of Property

Property includes anything of tangible or intangible value that the owner has the right to possess and use. **Real property** is land and any permanent buildings attached to that land. **Personal property** is tangible or intangible assets other than real property. Personal property includes cars, clothing, furniture, money in bank accounts, stock certificates, and copyrights.

real property
Land and any permanent buildings attached to that land.

personal property
Tangible or intangible assets other than real property.

Transferring Property

From time to time, businesses and individuals need to transfer property to another person or business. A **deed** is a document that shows ownership of real property. It allows the transfer of title of real property.

    A **lease** grants the use of an asset for a specified period of time in return for payment. The business or individual granting the lease is the lessor and the tenant is the lessee. For example, a business (the lessee) may rent space in a mall for one year from a real estate development firm (the lessor).

    A **title** shows legal possession of personal property. It allows the transfer of title of personal property. When you buy a snowmobile, for example, the former owner signs the title over to you.

deed
A document that shows ownership of real property.

lease
A document that grants the use of an asset for a specified period of time in return for payment.

title
A document that shows legal possession of personal property.

Warranty

When you buy a product or service, you want some assurance that it will perform satisfactorily and meet your needs. A **warranty** is a promise that the product or service will perform as the seller has promised it will.

warranty
A promise that the product or service will perform as the seller has promised it will.

express warranty
A specific claim that a manufacturer makes about a product.

implied warranty
An assumption that a product will perform as the manufacturer claims it will.

There are two kinds of warranties—express and implied. An **express warranty** is a specific claim that the manufacturer makes about a product. For example, a warranty that a screwdriver blade is made of case-hardened steel is an express warranty. An **implied warranty** suggests that a product will perform as the manufacturer claims it will. Suppose that you buy an outboard motor for your boat and the engine burns out in one week. Because the manufacturer implies by selling the motor that it will work for a reasonable period of time, you can return it and get your money back.

Because opinions vary on what is a "reasonable" time, most manufacturers now give limited time warranties on their products. For example, they will guarantee their products against defects in materials or manufacture for six months or one year.

Torts

tort
A wrongful civil act that one party inflicts on another.

intentional tort
A wrongful act intentionally committed.

A **tort** is a wrongful civil act that one party inflicts on another and that results in injury to the person, to the person's property, or to the person's good name. An **intentional tort** is a wrongful act intentionally committed. If a security guard in a department store suspects someone of shoplifting and uses excessive force to prevent him or her from leaving the store, the guard might be guilty of an intentional tort. Other examples are libel, embezzlement, and patent infringement.

negligence
A wrongful act that inadvertently causes injury to another person.

product liability
The liability of businesses for injuries caused to product users because of negligence in design or manufacture.

strict product liability
The liability of businesses for injuries caused by their products even if no evidence of negligence in the product's design or manufacture exists.

Negligence is a wrongful act that inadvertently causes injury to another person. For example, if a maintenance crew in a store mops the floors without placing warning signs in the area, a customer who slips and falls might bring a negligence suit against the store.

In recent years, the most publicized area of negligence has been product liability. **Product liability** means that businesses are liable for injuries caused to product users because of negligence in design or manufacturing. **Strict product liability** means that a business is liable for injuries caused by their products even if there is no evidence of negligence in the design or manufacture of the product.

Negotiable Instruments

negotiable instrument
Types of commercial paper that can be transferred among individuals and business firms.

Negotiable instruments are types of commercial paper that can be transferred among individuals and business firms. Cheques, bank drafts, and certificates of deposit are examples of negotiable instruments.

The *Bills of Exchange Act* specifies that a negotiable instrument must

- be written
- be signed by the person who puts it into circulation (the maker or drawer)
- contain an unconditional promise to pay a certain amount of money
- be payable on demand
- be payable to a specific person (or to the bearer of the instrument).

endorsement
Signing your name to a negotiable instrument making it transferable to another person or organization.

Negotiable instruments are transferred from one party to another through an endorsement. An **endorsement** means signing your name to a negotiable instrument; this makes it transferable to another person or organization. If you sign only your name on the back of a cheque, you are making a *blank* endorsement. If you state that the instrument is being transferred to a specific person, you are making a *special* endorsement. A *qualified* endorsement limits your liability if the instrument is not backed up by sufficient funds. For example, if you get a cheque from a friend and want to use it to buy a new stereo, you can write "without recourse" above your name. If your friend's cheque bounces, you have no liability. A *restrictive* endorsement limits the negotiability of the instrument. For example, if you write "for deposit only" on the back of a cheque and it is later stolen, no one else can cash it.

Bankruptcy

At one time, individuals who could not pay their debts were jailed. Today, however, both organizations and individuals can seek relief by filing for **bankruptcy**—the court-granted permission not to pay some or all debts.

> **bankruptcy**
> *Permission granted by the courts to individuals and organizations not to pay some or all of their debts.*

Thousands of individuals and businesses file for bankruptcy each year. Why do individuals and businesses file for bankruptcy? Cash-flow problems and drops in farm prices caused many farmers and small businesses to go bankrupt. In recent years, large enterprises such as Eaton's and Olympia & York have sought the protection of bankruptcy laws.

Three main factors account for the increase in bankruptcy filings:

1. The increased availability of credit

2. The "fresh-start" provisions in current bankruptcy laws

3. The growing acceptance of bankruptcy as a financial tactic

In some cases, creditors force an individual or firm into **involuntary bankruptcy** and press the courts to award them payment of at least part of what they are owed. Far more often, however, a person or business chooses to file for court protection against creditors. In general, individuals and firms whose debts exceed total assets may file for **voluntary bankruptcy**.

> **involuntary bankruptcy**
> *Bankruptcy proceedings initiated by the creditors of an indebted individual or organization.*

> **voluntary bankruptcy**
> *Bankruptcy proceedings initiated by an indebted individual or organization.*

Business Bankruptcy

A business bankruptcy may be resolved by one of three plans:

- Under a *liquidation plan*, the business ceases to exist. Its assets are sold and the proceeds are used to pay creditors.

- Under a *repayment plan*, the bankruptcy company works out a new payment schedule to meet its obligations. The time frame is usually extended, and payments are collected and distributed by a court-appointed trustee.

- *Reorganization* is the most complex form of business bankruptcy. The company must explain the sources of its financial difficulties and propose a new plan for remaining in business. Reorganization may include a new slate of managers and a new financial strategy. A judge may also reduce the firm's debts to ensure its survival. Although creditors naturally dislike debt reduction, they may agree to the proposal, since 50 percent of what you are owed is better than nothing at all.

INSURANCE

WHY INSURANCE COMPANIES EXIST—AND THRIVE

The reason why companies often find insurance appealing is clear—in return for a sum of money, they are protected against certain potentially devastating losses. But why are insurance companies willing to accept these risks for other companies?

Like all firms, insurance companies are in business to make a profit. They do so by taking in more premiums than they pay out to cover policyholder losses. They profit because they have many policyholders paying them for protection against the same type of loss, yet not all policyholders will experience a loss.

The Statistical Basis of Insurance

For example, consider a town with 5000 insured houses. Based on past history, insurers know that about 50 of these will be involved in a fire each year and that damages will average $40 000 per house involved. That is, insurance companies can expect to pay $2 million ($40 000 x 50) to cover their policyholders. By charging each household in the town $500 per year for fire insurance the company effectively spreads out the risk. It also earns a gross profit of $500 000 ($2.5 million in premiums versus $2 million in damages). This is the insurer's gain for providing risk-spreading services.

To earn a profit, insurance companies must know the likelihood of a particular loss. The more they know, the better their predictions and the fairer the rates they set will be. Insurance companies also benefit from a statistical principle called the **law of large numbers**. As the number of people who seek insurance rises, so does the chance that the actual loss rate will be the same as the statistically calculated rate.

To help them properly price insurance policies, insurers use a system of classification that rates possible losses based on certain characteristics. The frequency of loss from an automobile accident varies with the number of kilometres driven per year, whether the driving is done in a rural or urban area, and with the driver's experience. An individual driving under 5000 kilometres per year on uncongested roads with many years of experience will probably have fewer accidents than someone in the opposite situation. Therefore, individuals with a lower probability of accidents as determined by these classification characteristics should pay a relatively lower premium. If insurance companies did not try to make rates equitable, so few customers might buy policies that the insurance company could not cover its costs.

The ultimate purpose of insurance is to *indemnify* policyholders. That is, policyholders should be brought back to their financial position before the loss. No policyholder should gain financially from insurance. To remain financially viable, an insurance company must be sure never to pay for losses not covered by the policy nor to pay too much for each loss.

law of large numbers
The statistical principle that the larger the number of cases involved, the more closely the actual rate will match the statistically calculated rate.

Types of Insurance Companies

Insurance firms can be either private or public (government).

Private Insurance Companies

Private insurers may be shareholder-owned or mutually owned. **Stock insurance companies**, as the former are known, are like any other corporation. They sell stock to the public, which hopes to earn a profit on its investment. Shareholders can be, but do not have to be, policyholders of the insurance company.

    Mutual insurance companies are owned by their policyholders, for whom they seek to provide insurance at lower rates. As cooperative operations, they divide profits among policyholders, either by issuing dividends or by reducing premiums. In other words, the company's profits are generated for the direct benefit of policyholders rather than for outside shareholders. As non-profit operations, they divide any profit among policyholders at the end of the year.

    Two of the most important activities of private insurers are the underwriting and marketing of insurance offerings. **Underwriting** involves two basic tasks:

1. determining which applications for insurance to accept and which ones to reject

2. deciding what rates the insurer will charge.

    These decisions are made by *underwriters*—experts who gather information and tabulate data, assess loss probabilities, and decide which applications will be accepted. The purpose of all these functions, of course, is to maximize the insurer's profits.

    Agents and brokers are the people who market insurance. An **insurance agent** represents and is paid a commission by an insurance company. The agent, then, represents the insurance seller. An **insurance broker**, on the other hand, is a freelance agent who represents insurance buyers rather than sellers. Brokers work for clients by seeking the best coverage for them. The insurers that they recommend to their clients then pay them commissions. Some brokers also offer risk-management advice for clients.

Public Insurers

Most insurance that businesses buy is written by private insurance companies. But some—and a great deal of individual insurance—is issued by government agencies.

    Provincial governments administer workers' compensation insurance and the federal government administers the employment insurance program. Employers, employees, and the government share the cost of these programs. The federal government also operates the Social Insurance program. It has become an important part of our economic life and is a major means of protecting older, disabled, and poor citizens from economic hardship.

INSURANCE PRODUCTS TO MEET DIVERSE NEEDS

Insurance companies are often distinguished by the types of insurance coverage they offer. While some insurers offer only one area of coverage—life insurance, for example—others offer a broad range. In this section, we describe three major categories of business insurance: *liability, property*, and *life*. Each of these broad categories includes a wide variety of coverage plans and options.

---

stock insurance company
Any insurance company whose stock is held by members of the public, who may or may not be policyholders of the company.

mutual insurance company
Any insurance company that is owned by its policyholders, who share in its profits.

underwriting
Determining which applications for insurance to accept and deciding what rates the insurer will charge.

insurance agent
A person who markets insurance and is paid a commission by the insurance company.

insurance broker
A freelance agent who represents insurance buyers rather than insurance sellers.

Liability Insurance

Liability means responsibility for damages in case of accidental or deliberate harm to individuals or property. Who, for example, might be financially responsible—liable—for the medical expenses, lost wages, and pain and suffering incurred by an individual temporarily or permanently disabled because of another's actions? **Liability insurance** covers losses resulting from damage to people or property when the insured party is judged liable.

General Liability

General liability policies protect business policyholders in cases involving four types of problems:

- **Personal liability** coverage would protect a firm if one of its truck drivers runs over a customer's foot.

- **Professional liability** coverage would protect a surgeon who leaves a pair of scissors inside a patient.

- **Product liability** coverage would protect the maker of a new hair conditioner that causes users' hair to fall out.

- **Premises liability** coverage would protect a firm if a customer slips on a wet floor and suffers a severe concussion.

Selected Types of Liability Coverage

Businesses often choose to purchase comprehensive general liability policies, which provide coverage for all these problems and more. In this section, we will focus on three types of such coverage: *umbrella policies*, *automobile policies*, and *workers' compensation*.

Umbrella Policies. Because the dollar value of a liability loss can be huge, many insurers will write coverage only up to a certain limit. Moreover, many liability contracts exclude certain types of losses. To cover financial consequences that exceed the coverage of standard policies, some businesses buy **umbrella insurance**: insurance intended to cover losses in addition to or excluded by an underlying policy.

For example, suppose that a business has an automobile policy with the following coverage:

- a limit of $500 000 for bodily injury and property damage

- a premises liability policy with a limit of $500 000

- a product liability policy with a limit of $750 000.

Figure B.1 shows how an umbrella policy might double the coverage in each area. Another umbrella policy might extend product liability coverage to items not covered by the firm's existing policy.

Automobile Policies. A firm that owns and maintains automobiles for business use needs a *business automobile policy*. This policy will protect it against liability for bodily injury and property damage inflicted by its vehicles. Typically, such policies provide the following types of coverage:

- *Bodily injury and property damage.* Coverage that pays the firm if it is held legally liable for bodily injury or property damage.

- *Medical.* Coverage that pays for medical expenses incurred by persons in an insured vehicle.

---

liability insurance
Insurance covering losses resulting from damage to persons or property of other people or firms.

personal liability
For a business, responsibility for certain actions of those who work for the business.

professional liability
For a business or a business person, responsibility for an individual's actions in working at the business or profession.

product liability
For a business, responsibility for the actions of its products.

premises liability
For a business, responsibility for occurrences on its premises.

umbrella insurance
Insurance that covers losses over and above those covered by a standard policy as well as losses excluded by a standard policy.

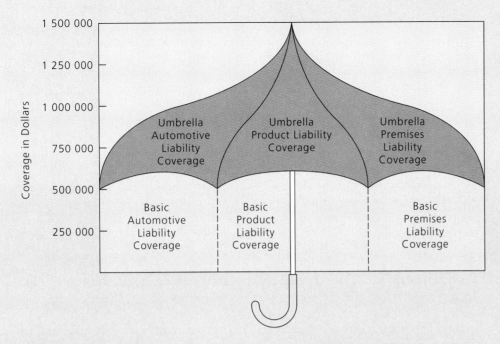

Figure B.1
Umbrella insurance coverage.

- *Uninsured motorists.* Coverage that pays bodily-injury expenses when injury to an insured driver is caused by an uninsured motorist, a hit-and-run driver, or a driver whose employer is insolvent.

Workers' Compensation.   A business is liable for any injury to an employee when the injury arises from activities related to occupation. When workers are permanently or temporarily disabled by job-related accidents or disease, employers are required by law to provide **workers' compensation** coverage for medical expenses, loss of wages, and rehabilitation services.

workers' compensation
A business's liability for injury to its employee(s) resulting from any activities related to the occupation.

Property Insurance

Firms purchase **property insurance** to cover injuries resulting from physical damage to or loss of real personal property. Property losses might result from fire, lightning, wind, hail, explosion, theft, vandalism, or other destructive forces. Many different forms of property insurance exist to cover the many types of property losses.

property insurance
Insurance covering losses resulting from physical damage to real estate or personal property.

Fire and Allied Lines

The typical fire insurance policy covers damage to specified property caused by fire, lightning, or theft. Coverage can be extended to cover other perils such as windstorm, hail, riot, smoke, aircraft, vehicles, explosion, vandalism, malicious mischief, and sonic boom. Some policies also include special provisions insuring the firm's property against sprinkler leakage, earthquake, or flood.

Marine Insurance

Another area of property insurance is **marine insurance**, a form of transportation insurance. Marine insurance includes two distinct areas: ocean marine and inland marine. *Ocean marine insurance* has been around for more than 500 years. Medieval shippers used a system of insurance to protect

marine insurance
A form of transportation insurance covering both the act of transportation (by water, land, or air) the transported goods.

their cargoes from loss. As commerce grew, so did the need for specialized services to guarantee financial solvency in the face of navigation disasters.[1] Today's ocean marine insurance covers the liability and loss of or damage to ships and their cargo.

Waterborne commerce was the most important method of transporting goods for centuries. As industry moved inland, land transportation of cargo became important and the inland marine policies were created. Although *inland marine insurance* sounds like a contradiction in terms, it is truly an extension of the ocean marine form, since it covers transportation (whether by truck, rail, or plane) and transported property. There are four main categories of inland marine insurance: property in transit (such as parcel post), bailee liability (such as dry cleaners), instrumentalities of transportation (such as bridges), and mobile property (such as farm animals).

Title Insurance

title insurance
Insurance that guarantees a seller has clear title to a property.

When real property is purchased, it is customary to research the *title* (ownership) of that property to determine whether it is free of defects such as tax liens. The easiest way for a purchaser to verify that the seller has a clear legal right to convey the property is through the purchase of **title insurance**. A title insurance company will search a variety of sources and guarantee that the seller is the proper owner and that there are no unknown debts or liens against the property. For instance, if the person selling the property owned it with a former spouse, a title search would verify whether the seller has the legal right to sell the property. If the title insurance company erroneously indicates that the title is free of defects and the policyholder subsequently suffers a loss, then the insurance company must reimburse the insured to an amount specified in the policy.

Business Interruption Insurance

business interruption insurance
Insurance to cover potential losses incurred during times when a company is unable to conduct its business.

In some cases the loss to property may be minimal in comparison to the loss of income suffered as a result of the property damage. A manufacturer may be required to close down for an extended period of time while repairs are being completed. During that time the company is not generating income. However, certain expenses—taxes, insurance premiums, and salaries for key personnel—may continue to accrue. The company may also need to keep running advertisements to make customers aware that repairs are progressing so they do not take their business elsewhere permanently. To cover these potential losses a firm may buy **business interruption insurance**.

Credit Insurance

credit insurance
Insurance to protect against customers' failure to pay their bills.

In addition to protecting its physical assets, a firm may also purchase **credit insurance** to protect its financial assets. If a customer does not pay its bills to the business, the selling company loses the value of the goods or services that it sold to the customer on credit. Linda Lingerie Inc. (LLI) bought credit insurance when it heard rumours that Eaton's was in financial trouble. The premium was high—$200 000—but LLI's president, Carolyn Farha, says it gave her peace of mind knowing that her firm would not lose money if Eaton's went bankrupt and was unable to pay its bills to suppliers.[2]

Coinsurance

Because a total loss of property is not likely, property owners have traditionally bought less than the total value in coverage. This practice results in coverage of losses on all parts of the property, but the insurer receives a premium for only a fraction of the property's value. To counter this problem, policies include a coinsurance provision requiring policyholders to insure to a certain minimum percentage of the total value of the property. If the policyholder fails to insure to the required percentage, the insurance company's payment will not cover the entire loss. Instead, insurance pays a smaller amount, as determined by the following formula:

$$\frac{\text{Amount of insurance owned}}{\text{Amount of insurance required}} \times \text{Amount of property loss}$$

$$= \text{Insurance company's payment}$$

If, for example, a building has a replacement value of $80 000 and the insurance policy has an 80 percent coinsurance requirement, the required amount of insurance coverage is $64 000 ($80 000 × 0.8). If the owner carries $64 000 worth of insurance coverage, then a $25 000 loss will be paid in full, as will any other loss up to $64 000. However, if the owner carries only $50 000 of insurance coverage, the insurance company will pay only $19 531.25 of the $25 000 loss, as the following calculation shows:

$$\frac{\$50\ 000}{\$64\ 000} \times \$25\ 000 = \$19\ 531.25$$

The policyholder bears the remainder of the loss ($25 000 − $19 531.25 = $5468.75), in effect, a penalty for underinsuring the property.

Multi-Line Policies

Because companies have many risks, they may need many kinds of insurance. Rather than purchasing many separate policies, firms may elect to buy one of the *multi-line package policies* now offered. These policies combine coverage for property losses with coverage for liability losses. Examples of multi-line policies include the Special Multi-Peril Policy (SMP) for owners of large businesses and the Business Owners Policy (BOP) designed for small to medium-sized retail stores, office buildings, apartment buildings, and similar firms.

Life Insurance

Insurance can protect not only a company's physical and capital assets but its labour assets as well. As part of their benefits packages, many businesses buy **life insurance** for their employees. Life insurance companies accept premiums from policyholders in return for the promise to pay a **beneficiary** after the death of the policyholder. A portion of the premium is used for current losses and expenses. The remainder is invested in various types of financial instruments such as corporate bonds and stocks. A portion of the investment income generated offsets the premium paid by the policyholder. Therefore, an insurance company with a high investment return theoretically should charge less than one with a lower investment return, assuming that both companies have similar loss experience and expenses.

Life insurance is a profitable business in Canada. In 1994, the top 10 insurance companies received over $28.9 billion in premiums from policyholders; net profit for the top 10 firms combined was almost $1.4 billion.[3] Among the many products life insurance companies offer are whole life, term insurance, endowment, and universal life policies.

Whole Life Insurance

In **whole life insurance**, a business or individual pays a sum that is sufficient to keep the policy in force for the whole of the person's life. This sum can

life insurance
Insurance that pays benefits to survivors of a policyholder.

beneficiary
The person to whom benefits of a life insurance policy are paid.

whole life insurance
Insurance coverage in force for the whole of a person's life, with a build-up of cash value.

be paid every year for life or for a stated period of years (such as 20 years). For example, Evita Guard may pay $115 each year and be assured that her beneficiary, her husband, will receive the stated face value upon her death. Alternatively, she could pay $198 each year for 20 years and receive the same benefit. In both cases, the policy is said to be paid-up.

Whole life policies have an internal build-up called a *cash value*. This value can never be forfeited even if the policyholder chooses to stop paying the premium. In some cases, the policyholder can borrow against this value. Or a policyholder can surrender (discontinue) the insurance policy and receive its cash value from the insurance company. Cash value makes whole life policies attractive to some insurance purchasers.

Term Insurance

term insurance
Insurance coverage for a fixed period of time, often 1, 5, 10, or 20 years.

As its name suggests, **term insurance** provides coverage for a term (a temporary time period) stated in the policy. The term can be for 1, 5, 10 or 20 years. Term insurance has no cash value and is less expensive than any of the other forms discussed in this section. A policyholder receives maximum death protection for the premium paid. An individual who has a limited insurance budget but a significant need for death protection should consider term insurance. Term insurance is also the form of life insurance companies supply most often to their employees.

Endowments

endowment
Insurance that pays face value after a fixed period of time whether the policyholder is alive or dead.

A type of policy called an **endowment** pays the face value of the policy whether the policyholder is dead or alive. The purpose of an endowment is to allow accumulation of a fund. For example, a father might buy a $20 000, 10-year endowment in order to accumulate $20 000 within a 10-year period for his daughter's university education. If he dies before the 10 years are up, the insurance company will pay his beneficiary (his daughter). However, if the father lives to the tenth year, the company turns the accumulated $20 000 over to him. Table B.1 compares these three types of policies with regard to premiums, benefits, and use.

Universal Life Insurance

The life insurance industry was very profitable for many years selling only the three policies described above. Whole life was the backbone of the industry. But as interest rates spiralled in the 1960s and 1970s, many policyholders became disillusioned with the very low rate of interest they earned in whole life and endowment policies. Policyholders began surrendering their policies and investing their funds in higher-yielding instruments such as guaranteed investment certificates. This withdrawal of funds, coupled with the difficulty of selling new policies, caused serious problems for life insurance companies. They responded by developing a new product to lure policyholders back to buying insurance: **universal life policies**.

universal life policy
A term insurance policy with a savings component.

Universal life policies combine a term insurance product with a savings component. Although this product may require a high initial premium, premium payments are flexible and interest earned on the savings component is competitive with other money market instruments.

Variable Life Insurance

variable life insurance (VLI)
A modified form of life insurance where the policyholder chooses the minimum face value of the policy.

Another new form of life insurance is a modified form of whole life insurance. **Variable life insurance (VLI)** allows flexibility regarding the minimum face value of the policy, the types of investments supporting it, and even the amount and timing of the premiums.

| Table B.1 | | | Comparison of Basic and Common Life Insurance Contracts | | |

Basic type	Protection period	When benefits are payable	Approximate costs for $10 000 at age 20*	How long premiums are paid	Uses
1. Whole Life	Permanent	At death, any time	—	—	Combination of moderate savings and protection
a. Straight or ordinary life	II	II	$115	Throughout life	II
b. 20-payment life	II	II	$198	For 20 years	Paying up premiums during working life
c. Life paid up at 65	II	II	$127	To age 65	
2. Term	Temporary	At death, only during term	—	—	Protection only
a. Yearly renewable term	II	II	$25 increasing each year	Varies—can be to age 60-70	Maximum protection
b. Five-year level term (renewable and convertible)	II	II	$53	5 years	Very high protection for limited period
3. Endowment	Temporary or long term	At death, or if living, at end of endowment period	—	—	Combination of higher savings and protection
a. 20-year endowment	II	II	$426	20 years	II
b. Retirement income at 65	II	II	$177	To age 65	II

*Costs are necessarily approximate for such general comparisons. Participating policies would be slightly higher, with net costs reduced by annual dividends. Nonparticipating policies would be somewhat lower. Smaller policies under $10 000 will be slightly higher; those over this amount may have a lower rate per $1000. Those insuring women will also be somewhat lower in cost. Extra policy features such as waiver of premium, accidental death benefits, and so on, would increase these estimates.

How does VLI work? Instead of buying a whole life policy with a fixed face value of $100 000, a policyholder may choose a variable life policy with a $100 000 *minimum* face value. The actual face value can exceed the minimum, depending on the market performance of the VLI investment portfolio. VLI policyholders can stipulate the portfolio mix, choosing among a variety of investment instruments such as common stocks, short-term bonds, and high-yield money market securities. The increase in the policy's face value depends on the success of the underlying investments. VLIs are a growing segment of the insurance market because they offer more flexibility than traditional policies.

Group Life Insurance

Most companies buy **group life insurance**, which is underwritten for groups as a whole rather than for each individual member. The insurer's assessment of potential losses and its pricing of premiums are based on the characteristics of the whole group. Johnson & Johnson's benefit plan, for example, includes group life coverage with a standard program of protection and benefits—a master policy purchased by J&J—that applies equally to all employees.

group life insurance
Life insurance written for a group of people rather than an individual.

Key Insurance

Many businesses choose to protect themselves against the loss of the talents and skills of key employees. If a salesperson who brings in $2.5 million in sales every year dies or takes a new job elsewhere, the firm will suffer loss. Moreover, the firm will incur recruitment costs to find a replacement and training expenses once a replacement is hired. *Key person insurance* can offset the lost income and the additional expenses.

A related matter is who takes control of a business when a partner or associate dies. At issue is whether the surviving business partners are willing to accept an inexperienced heir as a management partner in the business. Business continuation agreements are traditionally used to plan for this situation. The business owners can plan to buy the ownership interest of the deceased associate from his or her heirs. The value of the ownership interest is determined when the agreement is made. Special business insurance policies can provide the funds needed to make the purchase.

Reference Notes

Chapter 1

1. Karen Howlett, "Bank Profits Continue to Soar," *The Globe and Mail*, June 5, 2000, pp. B1, B4.

2. See Robert A. Collinge and Ronald M. Ayers, *Economics by Design: Principles and Issues*, 2nd ed. (Upper Saddle River, NJ: Prentice Hall, 2000), pp. 41–42; Michael J. Mandel, "The New Economy," *Business Week*, January 31, 2000, pp. 73–77.

3. Howard W. French, "On the Street, Cubans Fondly Embrace Capitalism," *The New York Times*, February 3, 1994, p. A4.

4. James Kynge, "Private Firms' Growth in China Striking: Report," *The National Post*, May 11, 2000, p. C14.

5. Richard I. Kirkland, Jr., "The Death of Socialism," *Fortune*, January 4, 1988, pp. 64–72.

6. Patrick Martin, "Cash-Strapped Kibbutz Jettisons Socialist Values," *The Globe and Mail*, September 14, 1992, pp. A1–A2.

7. See Karl E. Case and Ray C. Fair, *Principles of Economics*, 5th ed. (Upper Saddle River, NJ: Prentice Hall, 1999), pp. 69–74; Robert A. Collinge and Ronald M. Ayers, *Economics by Design: Principles and Issues*, 2nd ed. (Upper Saddle River, NJ: Prentice Hall, 2000), pp. 51–52.

8. Cait Murphy, "Will the Future Belong to Germany?" *Fortune*, August 2, 1999, pp. 129–36. Also see http://www.inter-shop.com, accessed March 8, 2000.

9. Deborah Orr, "The Post Office with a Ticker," *Forbes*, November 29, 1999, pp. 77–78; Matthew L. Wald, "Canada's Private Control Towers," *The New York Times*, October 23, 1999, p. C1. See also National Center for Policy Analysis, "Privatization," http://www.public-policy.org/~ncpa/pd/private/privat.html, accessed March 8, 2000.

10. Keith McArthur, "Air Canada Accused of Predatory Pricing," *The Globe and Mail*, September 8, 2000, p. B3.

11. Barrie McKenna, "Hyundai Gorged on Federal Funds," *The Globe and Mail*, March 25, 1994, p. B3.

12. See Karl E. Case and Ray C. Fair, *Principles of Economics*, 5th ed. (Upper Saddle River, NJ: Prentice Hall, 1999), pp. 70–90; Robert A. Collinge and Ronald M. Ayers, *Economics by Design: Principles and Issues*, 2nd ed. (Upper Saddle River, NJ: Prentice Hall, 2000), pp. 74–77.

13. E.S. Browning and Greg Ip, "Reality Check," *The Wall Street Journal*, October 16, 2000. pp. A1, A14.

14. Adam Smith, *The Wealth of Nations* (New York: Modern Library, 1937).

15. Cait Murphy, "Will the Future Belong to Germany?" *Fortune*, August 2, 1999, p. 130.

16. Nicholas C. Siropolis, *Small Business Management*, 4th ed. (Boston: Houghton Mifflin, 1990).

17. G. Pascal Zachary, "Let's Play Oligopoly!" *The Wall Street Journal*, March 8, 1999, pp. B1, B10.

18. "Big G Is Growing Fat on Oat Cuisine," *Business Week*, September 18, 1989, p. 29.

19. John Partridge and Lawrence Surtees, "Rogers Faces Assault from Telcos," *The Globe and Mail*, March 28, 1994, pp. B1–B2.

20. Steve Hamm et al., "So What's in the Cards?" *Business Week*, November 22, 1999, pp. 44–50.

21. "Where Global Growth Is Going," *Fortune*, July 31, 1989, pp. 71–92.

22. Barry Marquardson, "GDP Fails as a Measurement," *The Globe and Mail*, July 16, 1998, p. B2.

23. Bruce Little, " The Whopping Surplus Explained," *The Globe and Mail*, September 25, 2000, p. B9.

24. Dan Lett and John Douglas, "Too Often to the Well," *Winnipeg Free Press*, February 17, 1995, p. B10.

25. Michael J. Mandel et al., "The 21st Century Economy," *Business Week*, August 31, 1998, pp. 58–67. See also David Fairlamb and Gail Edmondson, "Work in Progress—Signs Abound of a Nascent New Economy," *Business Week*, January 31, 2000, pp. 80–87.

26. See also Brian Bremner and Moon Ihlwan, "Edging Toward the Information Age," *Business Week*, January 31, 2000, pp. 90–91.

27. Brian Bremner and Moon Ihlwan, "Edging Toward the Information Age," *Business Week*, January 31, 2000, p. 91.

Chapter 2

1. Madelaine Drohan, "Ottawa Targets Interprovincial Barriers," *The Globe and Mail*, May 14, 1991, p. B5.

2. U.S. Small Business Administration, "Selecting the Legal Structure for Your Firm," *Management Aid No. 6.004* (Washington, DC: U.S. Government Printing Office, 1985).

3. Madelaine Drohan, "Lloyd's Ends Tradition of Unlimited Liability," *The Globe and Mail*, April 30, 1993, pp. B1, B8; "Investors Revel in Lloyd's Suit Win," *Winnipeg Free Press*, October 5, 1994, p. C12; "Lloyd's Offers $6 Billion Solution," *The Globe and Mail*, May 24, 1995, p. B8.

4. Quoted in Lowell B. Howard, *Business Law* (Woodbury, NY: Barron's Woodbury Press, 1965), p. 332.

5. Julie Demers, "In the Public Eye," *CGA Magazine*, May 2000, pp. 25–28.

6. Richard Blackwell, "TSE Mulls Early Share Issue," *The Globe and Mail*, February 9, 2000, pp. B1, B16.

7. Ann Gibbon, "Pattison Keeps Deals Spinning," *The Globe and Mail*, June 9, 1997, pp. B1, B5.

8. See also IPOs on the Net (http://trad-ingday.com/ipos/) and TradingDay.com (http://advocacy-net.com/ipomks.htm), accessed March 17, 2000.

9. David F. Scott, Jr. et al., *Basic Financial Management*, 8th ed. (Upper Saddle River, NJ: Prentice Hall, 1999), p. 439.

10. See Nelson D. Schwartz, "The Ugly Truth About IPOs," *Fortune*, November 23, 1998, pp. 190–92+.

11. John Heinzl, "Dual Share Structures Targeted," *The Globe and Mail*, January 9, 1997, pp. B1, B10.

12. Gayle Macdonald, "Board Seat a Hotter Place to Sit," *The Financial Post*, November 19, 1990, p. 36; Arthur Johnson, "Directors: New Breed in a Hot Seat," *Canadian Business*, June 1991, pp. 74–83.

13. Stratford P. Sherman, "How Philip Morris Diversified Right," *Fortune*, October 23, 1989, pp. 120–28.

14. Bill Redekop, "Co-op Withers as Pool Goes Public," *Winnipeg Free Press*, July 15, 1994, p. 1.

15. Lawrence Surtees, "Takeover Concern Prompts BCE Poison Pill Plan," *The Globe and Mail*, February 25, 2000, p. B5.

16. Margot Gibb-Clark, "Share Plans Can Benefit More Than Employees," *The Globe and Mail*, February 14, 2000, p. B6.

Chapter 3

1. See Ricky W. Griffin and Michael W. Pustay, *International Business: A Managerial Perspective*, 2nd ed. (Reading, MA: Addison-Wesley, 1999), pp. 431–33; John J. Wild, Kenneth L. Wild, and Jerry C.Y. Han, *International Business: An Integrated Approach* (Upper Saddle River, NJ: Prentice Hall, 2000), pp. 456–58.

2. Ricky W. Griffin and Michael W. Pustay, *International Business: A Managerial Perspective*, 2nd ed. (Reading, MA: Addison-Wesley, 1999), pp. 44–45. See also Warren J. Keegan, *Global Marketing Management*, 6th ed. (Upper Saddle River, NJ: Prentice Hall, 1999), pp. 42–45.

3. David Fairlamb and Gail Edmondson, "Work in Progress," *Business Week*, January 31, 2000, pp. 80–81+.

4. David Fairlamb and Gail Edmondson, "Work in Progress," *Business Week*, January 31, 2000, pp. 80–81+.

5. See Edmund L. Andrews, "The Metamorphosis of Germany Inc.," *The New York Times*, March 12, 2000, section 3, pp. 1, 12.

6. See Mark Landler, "Mapping Out Silicon Valley East," *The New York Times*, April 5, 1999, pp. C1, C10; Bruce Einhorn with Cathy Yang, "Portal Combat," *Business Week*, January 17, 2000, pp. 96–97.

7. See Ricky W. Griffin and Michael W. Pustay, *International Business: A Managerial Perspective*, 2nd ed. (Reading, MA: Addison-Wesley, 1999), ch. 3. See also Dominick Salvatore, *International Economics*, 6th ed. (Upper Saddle River, NJ: Prentice Hall, 1998), pp. 27–33; Karl E. Case and Ray C. Fair, *Principles of Economics*, 5th ed. (Upper Saddle River, NJ: Prentice Hall, 1999), pp. 813–17.

8. This section is based on Michael Porter, *The Competitive Advantage of Nations* (Boston: Harvard Business School Press, 1990), chs. 3 and 4. See also Warren J. Keegan, *Global Marketing Management*, 6th ed. (Upper Saddle River, NJ: Prentice Hall, 1999), pp. 312–21; John J. Wild, Kenneth L. Wild, and Jerry C.Y. Han, *International Business: An Integrated Approach* (Upper Saddle River, NJ: Prentice Hall, 2000), pp. 175–78.

9. Madelaine Drohan, "Dependency on U.S. Leaves Canada 'Vulnerable': WTO," *The Globe and Mail*, November 20, 1996.

10. See Karl E. Case and Ray C. Fair, *Principles of Economics*, 5th ed. (Upper Saddle River, NJ: Prentice Hall, 1999), pp. 818–21.

11. Robyn Meredith, "Dollar Makes Canada a Land of the Spree," *The New York Times*, August 1, 1999, sec. 3, pp. 1, 11.

12. Heather Scoffield, "Move Toward Common Currency Speeds Up," *The Globe and Mail*, April 22, 2000, pp. B1, B5.

13. Marian Stinson, "Keep Canadian Dollar: Economist," *The Globe and Mail*, April 14, 2000, p. B3.

14. "Exports, Eh?" *Canadian Business*, January 1997, p. 21.

15. Peggy Berkowitz, "You Say Potato, They Say McCain," *Canadian Business*, December 1991, pp. 44–48.

16. Daniel Stoffman, "Cross-Border Selling," *Report on Business Magazine*, November 1991, pp. 61–68.

17. See Ray August, *International Business Law: Text, Cases, and Readings*, 3rd ed. (Upper Saddle River, NJ: Prentice Hall, 2000), pp. 192–97.

18. Jeremy Kahn, "The Fortune Global 500—The World's Largest Corporations," *Fortune*, August 2, 1999, pp. 144–46; F-1–F-22.

19. See Warren J. Keegan, *Global Marketing Management*, 6th ed. (Upper Saddle River, NJ: Prentice Hall, 1999), pp. 290–92; Ricky W. Griffin and Michael W. Pustay, *International Business: A Managerial Perspective*, 2nd ed. (Reading, MA: Addison-Wesley, 1999), pp. 427–31; John J. Wild, Kenneth L. Wild, and Jerry C.Y. Han, *International Business: An Integrated Approach* (Upper Saddle River, NJ: Prentice Hall, 2000), pp. 454–56.

20. See Ricky W. Griffin and Michael W. Pustay, *International Business: A Managerial Perspective*, 2nd ed. (Reading, MA: Addison-Wesley, 1999), pp. 431–33; John J. Wild, Kenneth L. Wild, and Jerry C.Y. Han, *International Business: An Integrated Approach* (Upper Saddle River, NJ: Prentice Hall, 2000), pp. 456–58.

21. See Warren J. Keegan, *Global Marketing Management*, 6th ed. (Upper Saddle River, NJ: Prentice Hall, 1999), pp. 292–94; John J. Wild, Kenneth L. Wild, and Jerry C.Y. Han, *International Business: An Integrated Approach* (Upper Saddle River, NJ: Prentice Hall, 2000), pp. 461–66.

22. See John J. Wild, Kenneth L. Wild, and Jerry C.Y. Han, *International Business: An Integrated Approach* (Upper Saddle River, NJ: Prentice Hall, 2000), ch. 7; Ricky W. Griffin and Michael W. Pustay, *International Business: A Managerial Perspective*, 2nd ed. (Reading, MA: Addison-Wesley, 1999), pp. 436–39.

23. Eric Reguly, "The Devouring of Corporate Canada," *The Globe and Mail*, September 4, 1999, pp. B1, B4.

24. Eric Reguly, "The Devouring of Corporate Canada," *The Globe and Mail*, September 4, 1999, pp. B1, B4.

25. Shawn McCarthy, "Business Sounds Alarm on Vulnerability," *The Globe and Mail*, May 8, 2000, pp. B1, B3.

26. Konrad Yakabuski and Heather Scoffield, "Canada, Brazil Claim Victory Over Decision," *The Globe and Mail*, August 3, 1999, pp. B1–B2.

27. Heather Scoffield and Shawn McCarthy, "WTO Backs Canada in Jet Market Dogfight with Brazil," *The Globe and Mail*, April 1, 2000, pp. B1, B5.

28. Konrad Yakabuski, "Quebec Courts Margarine War," *The Globe and Mail*, October 14, 1997, pp. B1, B4.

29. Neville Nankivell, "Spilled Milk Over Provincial Trade," *The National Post*, April 24, 2000, p. C9.

30. Dawn Walton, "Builders Most Likely to Bribe, Report Finds," *The Globe and Mail*, January 21, 2000, p. B5.

31. Nicholas Bray, "OECD Ministers Agree to Ban Bribery as Means for Companies to Win Business," *The Wall Street Journal*, May 27, 1997, p. A2.

32. Barrie McKenna, "Aluminum Producers Whispering Dirty Word," *The Globe and Mail*, March 5, 1994, pp. B1, B5.

33. Jalil Hamid, "Coffee Rally Reignited," *The Globe and Mail*, May 22, 1997, p. B9.

34. Oliver Bertin, "Coffee Cartel Moves Fast on Price," *Globe and Mail*, May 20, 2000, p. B3.

35. "Ottawa Confirms Dumping," *The Globe and Mail*, July 4, 2000, p. B15.

36. "Bike Makers Win Dumping Case," *The Globe and Mail*, December 11, 1997, p. B6.

37. "New Global Trade Regulator Starts Operations Tomorrow," *Winnipeg Free Press*, December 31, 1994, p. A5.

38. Helene Cooper and Bhushan Bahree, "World's Best Hope for Global Trade Topples Few Barriers," *The Wall Street Journal*, December 3, 1996, pp. A1, A8.

39. Heather Scoffield and Greg Keenan, "Canada Told to Scrap Auto Pact," *The Globe and Mail*, October 14, 1999, pp. A1, A2.

40. Andrew Purvis, "Super Exporter," *Time*, April 28, 1997, p. 36.

41. Andrew Purvis, "Super Exporter," *Time*, April 28, 1997, p. 36.

42. Robert Russo, "NAFTA Report Calls Canada a Winner," *Winnipeg Free Press*, July 12, 1997, p. B24; "NAFTA 'Bad Thing' for United States," *Winnipeg Free Press*, June 27, 1997, p. A11.

43. Bruce Little, "Free Trade 10 Years Later: Who Won?" *The Globe and Mail*, October 3, 1997, pp. B1, B6.

44. Peter Cook, "Free Trade Free-for-All Causes Confusion," *Globe and Mail*, December 5, 1994, p. B7.

Chapter 4

1. This section follows the logic of Gerald F. Cavanaugh, *American Business Values with International Perspectives*, 4th ed. (Upper Saddle River, NJ: Prentice Hall, 1998), ch. 3.

2. See Patricia Sellers, "Crunch Time for Coke," *Fortune*, July 19, 1999, pp. 72–74+.

3. Mark Schwartz, "Heat's on to Get an Effective Code," *The Globe and Mail*, November 27, 1997, p. B2.

4. See Quentin Hardy, "All Carly All the Time," *Forbes*, December 13, 1999, pp. 138–44; Peter Burrows with Peter Elstrom, "The Boss," *Business Week*, August 2, 1999, pp. 76–80+.

5. Julie Schmit, "Nike's Image Problem," *USA Today*, October 4, 1999, pp. 1B, 2B.

6. Jeffrey S. Harrison and R. Edward Freeman, "Stakeholders, Social Responsibility, and Performance: Empirical Evidence and Theoretical Perspectives," *Academy of Management Journal*, 42(5), pp. 479–85. See also David P. Baron, *Business and Its Environment*, 3rd ed. (Upper Saddle River, NJ: Prentice-Hall, 2000), ch. 17.

7. James R. Healey, "Ford to Reveal Plans for Think Brand," *USA Today*, January 10, 2000, p. 1B; Gwen Kinkead, "In the Future, People Like Me Will Go to Jail," *Fortune*, May 24, 1999, pp. 190–200.

8. Jeremy Main, "Here Comes the Big New Cleanup," *Fortune*, November 21, 1988, pp. 102–118.

9. Catherine Collins, "The Race for Zero," *Canadian Business*, March 1991, pp. 52–56.

10. Allan Robinson and Allan Freeman, "Mining's Dam Problem," *The Globe and Mail*, May 16, 1998, pp. B1–B2.

11. Charles Davies, "Strategy Session 1990," *Canadian Business*, January 1990, p. 48.

12. "Room Service and the Recyclable Rubber Chicken," *Canadian Business*, May 1991, p. 19.

13. Casey Mahood, "Bell Zeros in on Waste," *The Globe and Mail*, May 4, 1992, p. B1.

14. Martin Mittelstaedt, "Greenpeace Takes on Cameco Shares," *The Globe and Mail*, June 10, 1991, p. B10.

15. John Fox, "No Eluding the Enviro-Sleuths—Not Even Abroad," *The Financial Post*, April 8, 1991, p. 5.

16. See note 15.

17. Bruce Livesey, "Stuck with the Cleanup," *Canadian Business*, February 1991, pp. 92–96.

18. Geoffrey Scotton, "Cleanups Can Hurt, Companies Warned," *The Financial Post*, June 25, 1991, p. 4.

19. Marc Huber, "A Double-Edged Endorsement," *Canadian Business*, January 1990, pp. 69–71.

20. Daniel Machalaba, "As Old Pallets Pile Up, Critics Hammer Them as New Eco-Menace," *The Wall Street Journal*, April 1, 1998, p. A1.

21. John Saunders, "Polar Plastic Plot Flops," *The Globe and Mail*, June 10, 1994, p. B1.

22. Jayne O'Donnell, "U.S. Fines Drug Companies $725M for Price Fixing," *USA Today*, May 21, 1999, p. B1.

23. Michael McCarthy and Lorrie Grant, "Sears Drops Benetton after Controversial Death Row Ads," *USA Today*, February 18, 2000, p. 2B.

24. Shona McKay, "Willing and Able," *Report on Business*, October 1991, pp. 58–63.

25. "Why Business Is Hiring the Mentally Abled," *Canadian Business*, May 1991, p. 19.

26. J. Southerst, "In Pursuit of Drugs," *Canadian Transportation*, November 1989, pp. 58–65.

27. G. Bylinsky, "How Companies Spy on Employees," *Fortune*, November 4, 1991, pp. 131–40.

28. See David P. Baron, *Business and Its Environment*, 3rd ed. (Upper Saddle River, NJ: Prentice-Hall, 2000), pp. 704–06; Jerald Greenberg and Robert A. Baron, *Behavior in Organizations: Understanding and Managing the Human Side of Work*, 7th ed. (Upper Saddle River, NJ: Prentice Hall, 2000), pp. 374–75.

29. Rick Lyman, "A Tobacco Whistle-Blower's Life Is Transformed," *The New York Times*, October 15, 1999, p. A24.

30. Michael McHugh, "Blowing Whistle on Company Can Be a Risky Venture," *The Financial Post*, August 26, 1991, p. 2.

31. Andy Pasztor, "Whistle-Blower in Toshiba Case Stands to Gain," *The Wall Street Journal*, November 9, 1999, pp. B1, B4.

32. Dan Seligman, "Blowing Whistles, Blowing Smoke," *Forbes*, September 6, 1999, pp. 158–62.

33. Richard Blackwell, "OSC Scores Trading Conviction," *The Globe and Mail*, July 22, 2000, pp. B1–B2; "CEO Jailed for Insider Trading," *Winnipeg Free Press*, September 19, 2000, p. B8.

34. Daniel Stoffman, "Good Behavior and the Bottom Line," *Canadian Business*, May 1991, pp. 28–32.

35. Tom Kierans, "Charity Begins at Work," *Report on Business Magazine*, June 1990, p. 23.

36. Theresa Ebden and Dawn Walton, "Walkerton Recipient of New-Style Corporate Giving," *The Globe and Mail*, June 3, 2000, pp. B1, B6.

37. Theresa Ebden and Dawn Walton, "Walkerton Recipient of New-Style Corporate Giving," *The Globe and Mail*, June 3, 2000, pp. B1, B6.

Chapter 5

1. Robert Williamson, "Motivation on the Menu," *The Globe and Mail*, November 24, 1995, p. B7.

2. Charles W.L. Hill and Gareth Jones, *Strategic Management: An Analytical View*, 2nd ed. (Boston: Houghton Mifflin, 1992).

3. William Carley, "To Keep GE's Profits Rising, Welch Pushes Quality-Control Plan," *The Wall Street Journal*, January 13, 1997, pp. A1, A8.

4. Janet Guyon, "Getting the Bugs Out at VW," *Fortune*, March 29, 1999, pp. 96–102.

5. Melanie Wells, "Red Baron," *Forbes*, July 3, 2000, pp. 150–60; Andrew Ross Sorkin, "Taking Virgin's Brand into Internet Territory," *The New York Times*, February 14, 2000, pp. C1, C17.

6. Dave Ulrich and Dale Lake, "Organizational Capability: Creating Competitive Advantages," *The Academy of Management Executive*, February 1991, pp. 77–83.

7. Shaifali Puri, "A Cut Above," *Fortune*, August 4, 1997, pp. 55–59.

8. Michael Porter, *Competitive Strategy: Techniques for Analyzing Industries and Competitors* (New York: The Free Press, 1980).

9. "Cruise-Ship Delays Leave Guests High and Dry," *The Wall Street Journal*, October 24, 1997, pp. B1, B10; *Hoover's Handbook of American Business 2000* (Austin, TX: Hoover's Business Press, 2000), pp. 1512–13.

10. John Markoff, "A Disruptive Virus Invades Computers around the World," *The New York Times*, May 5, 2000, pp. A1, C9; John Markoff, "Law Officials Seek Origins of the Virus," *The New York Times*, May 6, 2000, pp. C1, C3; Kevin Maney, "Tainted Love," *USA Today*, May 5, 2000, pp. 1B, 2B.

11. Peter Burrows, "The Hottest Property in the Valley?" *Business Week*, August 30, 1999, pp. 69–74.

12. Alex Taylor III, "How a Top Boss Manages His Day," *Fortune*, June 19, 1989, pp. 95–100.

13. Jennifer Reingold, "Executive Pay," *Business Week*, April 17, 2000, p. 101.

14. See Kamal Fatehi, *International Management: A Cross-Cultural and Functional Perspective* (Upper Saddle River, NJ: Prentice Hall, 1996), pp. 5–8, 153–64.

15. "MBAs are Hotter Than Ever," *Business Week*, March 9, 1987, pp. 46–48.

16. Ric Dolphin, "Magna Force," *Canadian Business*, May 1988.

17. Isadore Sharp, "Quality for All Seasons," *Canadian Business Review*, Spring 1990, pp. 21–23.

18. Bruce McDougall, "The Thinking Man's Assembly Line," *Canadian Business*, November 1991, pp. 40–44.

19. Peter Verburg, "Prepare for Takeoff," *Canadian Business*, December 25, 2000, pp. 95–99.

20. Doug Nairne, "Mounties Riding the Vision Thing," *Winnipeg Free Press*, September 16, 1996, p. A5.

21. Gabriella Stern, "How a Young Manager Shook Up the Culture at Old Chrysler Plant," *The Wall Street Journal*, April 21, 1997, pp. A1, A6.

22. Katrina Brooker, "Can Procter & Gamble Change Its Culture, Protect Its Market Share, and Find the Next Tide?" *Fortune*, April 26, 1999, pp. 146–52.

Chapter 6

1. Robert L. Simison, "Ford Rolls Out New Model of Corporate Culture," *The Wall Street Journal*, January 13, 1999, pp. B1, B4.

2. See John A. Wagner and John R. Hollenbeck, *Management of Organizational Behavior* (Englewood Cliffs, NJ: Prentice Hall, 1992), pp. 563–65.

3. "Lucent to Break Up into Four Divisions," Associated Press news story reported in *The Houston Chronicle*, October 27, 1999, p. B2.

4. Jay Diamond and Gerald Pintel, *Retailing*, 6th ed. (Upper Saddle River, NJ: Prentice Hall, 1996), pp. 83–84.

5. Jacquie McNish, "A Chairman with Worries Lots of Others Would Like," *The Globe and Mail*, April 14, 1990, p. B6.

6. Peter Larson, "Winning Strategies," *Canadian Business Review*, Summer 1989, p. 41.

7. Ian Allaby, "The Search for Quality," *Canadian Business*, May 1990, pp. 31–42.

8. Donna Fenn, "Redesign Work," *Inc.*, June 1999, pp. 75–83.

9. Donna Fenn, "The Buyers," *Inc.*, June 1996, pp. 46–48+.

10. Robert Berner and Kevin Helliker, "Heinz's Worry: 4,000 Products, Only One Star," *The Wall Street Journal*, September 17, 1999, pp. B1, B4.

11. J. Galbraith, "Matrix Organization Designs: How to Combine Functional and Project Forms," *Business Horizons*, 1971, pp. 29–40; H.F. Kolodny, "Evolution to a Matrix Organization," *Academy of Management Review*, 4, 1979, pp. 543–53.

12. Interview with Tom Ward, operations manager for Genstar Shipyards.

13. Lawton R. Burns, "Matrix Management in Hospitals: Testing Theories of Matrix Structure and Development," *Administrative Science Quarterly*, 34, 1989, pp. 48–50.

14. Glenn Rifkin, "Digital Dumps Matrix Management," *The Globe and Mail*, July 21, 1994, pp. B1, B4.

15. Gail Edmondson, "Danone Hits Its Stride," *Business Week*, February 1, 1999, pp. 52–53.

16. Frank Rose, "Think Globally, Script Locally," *Fortune*, November 8, 1999, pp. 156–60.

17. Thomas A. Stewart, "See Jack. See Jack Run," *Fortune*, September 27, 1999, pp. 124–27+.

18. See Jerald Greenberg and Robert A. Baron, *Behavior in Organizations: Understanding and Managing the Human Side of Work*, 7th ed. (Upper Saddle River, NJ: Prentice Hall, 2000), pp. 308–09.

19. Tyler Hamilton, "Welcome to the World Wide Grapevine," *The Globe and Mail*, May 6, 2000, pp. B1, B6.

Chapter 7

1. Strategis, Industry Canada, http://strategis.ic.gc.ca.

2. Natalie Southworth, "Canada Gets Top-Tier Ranking," *The Globe and Mail*, November 14, 2000, p. B9.

3. See also Paulette Thomas, "A New Generation ReWrites the Rules," *The Wall Street Journal*, May 22, 2000, p. R4.

4. Gayle MacDonald, "War Stories from the World's Top Female Owners," *The Globe and Mail*, May 2, 1997, p. B9; Murray McNeill, "Women Step Out on Their Own," *The Winnipeg Free Press*, December 8, 1994, p. C10.

5. Alan M. Cohen, "Entrepreneur and Entrepreneurship: The Definition Dilemma," Working Paper Series No. NC89-08, National Centre for Management Research and Development, The University of Western Ontario, London, February 1989.

6. *The State of Small Business 1989, Annual Report on Small Business in Ontario* (Toronto: Ministry of Industry, Trade and Technology, 1990), pp. 24–27.

7. *The State of Small Business 1989, Annual Report on Small Business in Ontario* (Toronto: Ministry of Industry, Trade and Technology, 1990), p. 29.

8. Recent Canadian textbooks include D. Wesley Balderson, *Canadian Small Business Management: Text, Cases and Incidents* (Homewood, IL: Richard D. Irwin, 1990); Raymond W.Y. Kao, *Entrepreneurship and Enterprise Development* (Toronto: Holt, Rinehart and Winston of Canada, 1989); Andrew J. Szonyi and Dan Steinhoff, *Small Business Management Fundamentals*, 3rd Canadian ed. (Scarborough, ON: McGraw-Hill Ryerson, 1987); K. Gersick, *Generation to Generation: Life Cycles of the Family Business* (Boston: Harvard Business School, 1997); L. Shaw, *100 Ways to Market Yourself and Your Small Business* (New York: Berkeley Publishing, 1997).

9. Allan Gould, *The New Entrepreneurs: 80 Canadian Success Stories* (Toronto: Seal Books, 1986); Kenneth Barnes and Everett Banning, *Money Makers: The Secrets of Canada's Most Successful Entrepreneurs* (Toronto: McClelland and Stewart, 1985); Matthew Fraser, *Quebec Inc.: French-Canadian Entrepreneurs and the New Business Elite* (Toronto: Key Porter Books, 1987); J.B. Miner, *The Four Routes to Entrepreneurial Success* (Barrett-Koehler Publishing, 1996); D.L. Sexton and R.W. Smilor, *Entrepreneurship 2000* (Chicago: Upstart Publishing, 1997).

10. Paul Waldie, "Small Business Hits Out," *The Financial Post*, September 4–6, 1993, pp. 1, 10–11.

11. Many models of organizational growth have been developed. One that is often described in management books is in Larry E. Greiner, "Evolution and Revolution as Organizations Grow," *Harvard Business Review*, 50, 4, July/August 1972, pp. 37–46. One example of a growth model developed for small business is Mel Scott and Richard Bruce, "Five Stages of Growth In Small Business," *Long Range Planning*, 20, 3, 1987, pp. 45–52.

12. The statistics in this section are from *Small Business in Canada: Growing to Meet Tomorrow* (Ottawa: Supply and Services Canada), Cat. No. C28-12 1989E; D.P. Moore and E.H. Buttner, *Women Entrepreneurs: Moving Beyond the Glass Ceiling* (Thousand Oaks, CA: Sage Publishing, 1997); *The State of Small Business 1989, Annual Report on Small Business in Ontario* (Toronto: Ministry of Industry, Trade and Technology, 1990).

Chapter 8

1. See Angelo S. DeNisi and Ricky W. Griffin, *Human Resource Management* (Boston: Houghton Mifflin, 2001) for a complete overview.

2. Elizabeth Church, "Store Owners Struggle with Staffing," *The Globe and Mail*, November 25, 1996, p. B6.

3. Caroline Alphonso, "Job Fairs Draw a Crowd," *The Globe and Mail*, August 25, 2000, p. B7.

4. Elizabeth Church, "Nortel Recruits to a Different Beat," *The Globe and Mail*, August 23, 2000, p. M1.

5. Malcolm MacKillop, "An Employer's Guide to Drug Testing," *The Globe and Mail*, April 9, 1998, p. B13.

6. Margot Gibb-Clark, "Ruling Narrows Options for Drug Testing," *The Globe and Mail*, July 28, 1998, p. B11.

7. Jane Allen, "Literacy at Work," *Canadian Business*, February 1991, pp. 70–73.

8. Charles Davies, "Strategy Session 1990," *Canadian Business*, January 1990, p. 50.

9. Scott Feschuk, "Phi Beta Cuppa," *The Globe and Mail*, March 6, 1993, pp. B1, B4.

10. Abby Ellin, "Training Programs Often Miss the Point on the Job," *The New York Times*, March 29, 2000, p. C12.

11. Roma Luciw, "U.S. Wealth Gap Far Wider Than Canada's." *The Globe and Mail*, July 29, 2000, p. B3.

12. Elizabeth Church, "Nortel Workers Pick Tailor-Made Perks," *The Globe and Mail*, December 8, 2000, p. B11.

13. David Roberts, "A Long Way From Cambodia," *The Globe and Mail*, July 5, 1994, p. B18.

14. Ken Kilpatrick and Dawn Walton, "What a Joy to Work for Dofasco," *The Globe and Mail*, February 23, 2000, pp. B1, B8.

15. Peter Verburg, "The Man of Steel's Fed Up," *Canadian Business*, June 26/July 10, 1998, p. 69.

16. Bruce McDougall, "The Thinking Man's Assembly Line," *Canadian Business*, November 1991, p. 40.

17. John Partridge, "B of M Lauded for Promoting Women's Careers," *The Globe and Mail*, January 7, 1994, p. B3.

18. Vivian Smith, "Breaking Down the Barriers," *The Globe and Mail*, November 17, 1992, p. B24.

19. Bob Cox, "Women Gaining on Men's Wages," *The Globe and Mail*, January 18, 1994, p. B4.

20. Gordon Pitts, "Equal Pay Issue: Business Uneasy," *The Financial Post*, August 31, 1985, pp. 1–2.

21. Bruce Little, "Male Earning Power Wanes," *The Globe and Mail*, September 18, 1997, pp. B1, B4.

22. Margot Gibb-Clark, "Harassment Cases Can Also Hurt Employees," *The Globe and Mail*, September 16, 1991, p. B4.

23. Ted Kennedy, "Beware of Health and Safety Law: It Could Bite You," *Canadian Business*, December 1990, p. 19.

24. Virginia Galt and Caroline Alphonso, "Mandatory Retirement Review Launched," *The Globe and Mail*, July 28, 2000, pp. B1–B2.

25. "Canadians Are Retiring Earlier," *Winnipeg Free Press*, June 12, 1997, p. B12.

26. Michael Moss, "For Older Employees, On-the-Job Injuries Are More Often Deadly," *The Wall Street Journal*, June 17, 1997, pp. A1, A10.

27. Max Boisot, *Knowledge Assets* (Oxford: Oxford University Press, 1998).

28. Thomas Stewart, "In Search of Elusive Tech Workers," *Fortune*, February 16, 1998, pp. 171–72.

29. Matt Richtel, "Need for Computer Experts Is Making Recruiters Frantic," *The New York Times*, December 18, 1999, p. C1.

30. Aaron Bernstein, "When Is a Temp Not a Temp?" *Business Week*, December 7, 1998, pp. 90–92.

Chapter 9

1. For a detailed treatment of this entire subject area, see Gregory Moorhead and Ricky W. Griffin, *Organizational Behavior*, 6th ed. (Boston: Houghton Mifflin, 2001).

2. Michael Stern, "Empowerment Empowers Employees," *The Globe and Mail*, December 9, 1991, p. B4.

3. Margot Gibb-Clark, "Canadian Workers Need Some Respect," *The Globe and Mail*, September 4, 1991, pp. B1, B6.

4. Margot Gibb-Clark, "Frustrated Workers Seek Goals," *The Globe and Mail*, May 2, 1991, p. B7.

5. Margot Gibb-Clark, "Family Ties Limit Workers," *The Globe and Mail*, January 22, 1991, pp. B1–B2.

6. Virginia Galt, "Worker Stress Costing Economy Billions, Panel Warns," *The Globe and Mail*, July 21, 2000, p. B9.

7. Frederick W. Taylor, *Principles of Scientific Management* (New York: Harper and Brothers, 1911).

8. Douglas McGregor, *The Human Side of Enterprise* (New York: McGraw-Hill, 1960).

9. Abraham Maslow, "A Theory of Human Motivation," *Psychological Review*, July 1943, pp. 370–96.

10. Frederick Herzberg, Bernard Mausner, and Barbara Bloch Snyderman, *The Motivation to Work* (New York: Wiley, 1959).

11. Victor Vroom, *Work and Motivation* (New York: Wiley, 1964); Craig Pinder, *Work Motivation* (Glenview, IL: Scott, Foresman, 1984).

12. Edwin Locke, "Toward a Theory of Task Performance and Incentives," *Organizational Behavior and Human Performance*, 3 (1968), pp. 157–89.

13. Interviews with Sterling McLeod and Wayne Walker, senior vice-presidents of sales for Investors Group Financial Services.

14. Margot Gibb-Clark, "BC Telecom Managers Get an Overhaul," *The Globe and Mail*, July 23, 1994, p. B3.

15. Wilfred List, "On the Road to Profit," *The Globe and Mail*, July 10, 1991, pp. B1, B3.

16. Ralph King, Jr., "Levi's Factory Workers Are Assigned to Teams, and Morale Takes a Hit," *The Wall Street Journal*, May 20, 1998, pp. A1, A6.

17. Jon R. Katzenbach, *Teams at the Top* (Boston: Harvard Business School Press, 1998).

18. See Gregory Moorhead and Ricky W. Griffin, *Organizational Behavior*, 6th ed. (Boston: Houghton Mifflin, 2001), Chapter 7.

19. Robert White, "Changing Needs of Work and Family: A Union Response," *Canadian Business Review*, Autumn 1989, pp. 31–33.

20. Margot Gibb-Clark, "Banks' Short Work Week Improves Service," *The Globe and Mail*, September 23, 1991, p. B4.

21. "Telecommuting Causing Work Condition Worries," *The Globe and Mail*, January 7, 2000, p. B8.

22. Margot Gibb-Clark, "What Shaped the Workplace in 1998," *The Globe and Mail*, December 29, 1998, p. B6.

23. Margot Gibb-Clark, "Satellite Office a Hit with Staff," *The Globe and Mail*, November 18, 1991, p. B4.

24. "Slaves of the New Economy," *Canadian Business*, April 1996, pp. 86–92.

25. Dawn Walton, "Survey Focuses on Job Sharing," *The Globe and Mail*, June 10, 1997, p. B4.

26. "Insanity, Inc.," *Fast Company*, January 1999, pp. 100–108.

27. Madelaine Drohan, "What Makes a Canadian Manager?" *The Globe and Mail*, February 25, 1997, p. B18.

28. Natalie Southworth, "Canadian Team Builders Turn U.S. Heads," *The Globe and Mail*, August 28, 2000, p. B8.

29. See Gregory Moorhead and Ricky W. Griffin, *Organizational Behavior*, 6th ed. (Boston: Houghton Mifflin, 2001), Chapters 13 and 14.

30. See Gregory Moorhead and Ricky W. Griffin, *Organizational Behavior*, 6th ed. (Boston: Houghton Mifflin, 2001), Chapters 13 and 14.

31. "A Better Workplace," *Time*, April 17, 2000, p. 87.

32. Stephanie Armour, "More Dads Tap into Family Benefits at Work," *USA Today*, June 16, 2000, p. 1B.

Chapter 10

1. David Lipsky and Clifford Donn, *Collective Bargaining in American Industry* (Lexington, MA: Lexington Books, 1981).

2. Aaron Bernstein, "Welch's March to the South," *Business Week*, December 6, 1999, pp. 74, 78.

3. James Houghton, "Automaker's Stealth Move Heightens Labor Tensions," *USA Today*, June 4, 1998, pp. 1B, 2B.

4. Susan Bourette, "Organized Labour Lures Growing Number of Youth," *The Globe and Mail*, July 4, 1997, pp. B1, B4;

Susan Bourette, "Women Make Strides in Union Movement," *The Globe and Mail*, August 29, 1997, pp. B1–B2.

5. Greg Keenan, "CAW Targets Honda, Toyota," *The Globe and Mail*, June 15, 1999, pp. B1, B8.

6. Sarah Binder, "McDonald's Store Closes, Union Wails," *The Globe and Mail*, February 14, 1998, p. B23.

7. Andrew Nikiforuk, "Why Safeway Struck Out," *Canadian Business*, September 1997, p. 27.

8. Margot Gibb-Clark, "Wounds Left by Strike Require Healing," *The Globe and Mail*, September 30, 1991, p. B4.

9. Jeffrey Ball, Glenn Burkins, and Gregory White, "Why Labor Unions Have Grown Reluctant to Use the S-word," *The Wall Street Journal*, December 16, 1999, pp. A1, A8.

10. Phil Taylor, "To the Victor Belongs the Spoils," *Sports Illustrated*, January 18, 1999, pp. 48–52.

11. Peter Verburg, "The Man of Steel's Fed Up," *Canadian Business*, June 26/July 10, 1998, p. 68.

12. Paul McKie, "Goldcorp Workers Accept Offer, Dismantle Union," *Winnipeg Free Press*, April 22, 2000, p. A6.

Chapter 11

1. Ira Sager, "Inside IBM: Internet Business Machines," *Business Week*, December 13, 1999, pp. EB 20+; Gene Bylinsky, "Hot New Technologies for America's Factories," *Fortune*, July 5, 1999, p. 169(N).

2. Eryn Brown, "America's Most Admired Companies," *Fortune*, March 1, 1999, pp. 68, 70–73; www.walmartstores.com, accessed April 24, 2000.

3. Judy Strauss and Raymond Frost, *Marketing on the Internet* (Upper Saddle River, NJ: Prentice Hall, 1999), pp. 266–71.

4. "Digital and Intel Complete Sale of Digital Semi-conductor Manufacturing Operations," Intel press release, May 18, 1998.

5. Keith Bradsher, "General Motors Plans to Build New, Efficient Assembly Plants," *The New York Times*, August 6, 1998, pp. A1, D3.

6. Don Marshall, "Time for Just in Time," *P&IM Review*, June 1991, pp. 20–22. See also Gregg Stocker, "Quality Function Deployment: Listening to the Voice of the Customer," *APICS: The Performance Advantage*, September 1991, pp. 44–48.

7. Kevin Ferguson, "Purchasing in Packs," *Business*, November 1, 1999, p. EB 33.

8. "The Disney Institute," http://www.dis-ney.go.com/DisneyWorld/DisneyInstitute/

ProfessionalPrograms/DisneyDifference/index.html, accessed April 25, 2000.

9. *The Art & Science of Harley-Davidson: 1998 Annual Report* (Milwaukee, WI: Harley-Davidson, Inc., 1998); Gina Imperato, "Harley Shifts Gears," *Fast Company*, June–July 1997, pp. 104–105+.

10. Bruce Little, "Stock Answers," *The Globe and Mail*, June 6, 1995, p. B12.

11. Bruce McDougall, "The Thinking Man's Assembly Line," *Canadian Business*, November 1991, p. 40.

12. Alan Freeman, "Why Firms Avoid Taking Inventory," *The Globe and Mail*, December 12, 1994, pp. B1, B4.

Chapter 12

1. Bart VanArk and Robert McGuckin, "International Comparisons of Labor Productivity and Per Capita Income," *Monthly Labor Review* (Washington, DC: U.S. Dept. of Labor, July 1999), pp. 33–41.

2. Harvey Enchin, "Canada Urged to Stop Living Off Fat of the Land," *The Globe and Mail*, October 25, 1991, pp. B1, B6.

3. Estimated from VanArk and McGuckin, "International Comparisons of Labor Productivity and Per Capita Income," pp. 33–41; and *Survey of Current Business* (Washington, DC: U.S. Dept. of Commerce, April 2000), p. 85.

4. Shawn McCarthy, "Productivity Grows, but Lags U.S.," *The Globe and Mail*, May 2, 2000, pp. B1, B12.

5. John Sheridan, "More Steel Productivity Gains Ahead?" *Industry Week*, September 15, 1997, pp. 86–96.

6. Peter Kennedy, "Canfor Goes High Teach to Cut Costs," *The Globe and Mail*, July 29, 2000, p. 3.

7. "Canadian Business Schools Seek New Research and Operating Funds to Boost Contribution to Innovation," *Research Money*, September 1, 2000, pp. 1–2.

8. Matt Hamblen, "Tools Boost Company's Sales Productivity More Than 20%," *Computerworld*, September 13, 1999, p. 24; Weld Royal, "Stryker Corp.," *Industry Week*, October 19, 1998, pp. 72–74.

9. From Lee J. Krajewski and Larry P. Ritzman, *Operations Management: Strategy and Analysis*, 5th ed. (Reading, MA: Addison-Wesley, 1999), pp. 229–30.

10. Bruce McDougall, "The Thinking Man's Assembly Line," *Canadian Business*, November 1991, p. 40.

11. Joel Kurtzman, "Is Your Company Off Course? Now You Can Find Out Why," *Fortune*, February 17, 1997, p. 133.

12. Ted Wakefield, "No Pain, No Gain," *Canadian Business*, January 1993, pp. 50–54.

13. Margot Gibb-Clark, "Hospital Managers Gain Tool to Compare Notes," *The Globe and Mail*, September 9, 1996, p. B9

14. "Customer Service You Can Taste," *Canadian Business*, July 1991, pp. 19–20.

15. Gordon Pitts, "Stepping on the Quality Ladder," *The Globe and Mail*, June 30, 1992, pp. 64–65.

16. Cathryn Motherwell, "How to Fix a Model of a Muddle," *The Globe and Mail*, November 22, 1994, p. B30.

17. Catherine Greenman, "An Old Craft Learns New Tricks," *The New York Times*, June 10, 1999, pp. G1, G7.

18. "Motorola," http://www.motorola.com, accessed May 24, 2000.

19. Leonard L. Berry, A. Parasuraman, and Valarie A. Zeithaml, "Improving Service Quality in America: Lessons Learned," *Academy of Management Executive*, 8, 2, 1994, pp. 32–45.

Chapter 13

1. Terence P. Paré, "How to Find Out What They Want," *Fortune*, Autumn–Winter 1993, pp. 39–41.

2. Kenneth C. Laudon and Jane P. Laudon, *Essentials of Management Information Systems*, 3rd ed. (Upper Saddle River, NJ: Prentice Hall, 1999), p. 267.

3. Kenneth C. Laudon and Jane P. Laudon, *Essentials of Management Information Systems*, 3rd ed. (Upper Saddle River, NJ: Prentice Hall, 1999), p. 270

4. David Kirkpatrick, "Why Have Investors Ignored Lycos for So Long?" *Fortune*, February 1, 1999, p. 150.

5. Kenneth C. Laudon and Jane P. Laudon, *Essentials of Management Information Systems*, 3rd ed. (Upper Saddle River, NJ: Prentice Hall, 1999), p. 273.

6. Mary J. Cronin, "Ford's Intranet Success," *Fortune*, March 30, 1998, p. 158.

7. Joshua Macht, "The Ultimate Head Trip," *Inc. Technology*, 3 (1997), p. 77.

8. Gene Bylinsky, "Industry's Amazing Instant Prototypes," *Fortune*, January 12, 1998, pp. 120(B–D).

9. Geoffrey Rowan, "Unique Software Thinks Like a Human, " *The Globe and Mail*, December 31, 1996, pp. B1, B4.

10. Kenneth C. Laudon and Jane P. Laudon, *Essentials of Management Information Systems*, 3rd ed. (Upper Saddle River, NJ: Prentice Hall, 1999), pp. 383–88. See also E. Wainwright Martin et al., *Managing Information Technology: What Managers Need to Know*, 3rd ed.

(Upper Saddle River, NJ: Prentice Hall, 1999), pp. 225–27.

11. Emily Smith, "Turning an Expert's Skills into Computer Software," *Business Week*, October 7, 1985, pp. 104–107.

12. Heather Green et al., "It's Time for Rules in Wonderland," *Business Week*, February 21, 2000, pp. 82–88+; Ira Sager et al., "Cyber Crime," *Business Week*, February 21, 2000, pp. 36–42; Ira Sager, Neil Gross, and John Carey, "Locking Out the Hackers," *Business Week*, February 28, 2000, pp. 32–34.

13. See E. Wainwright Martin et al., *Managing Information Technology: What Managers Need to Know*, 3rd ed. (Upper Saddle River, NJ: Prentice Hall, 1999), pp. 61–68.

14. See Larry Long and Nancy Long, *Computers*, 6th ed. (Upper Saddle River, NJ: Prentice Hall, 1999), pp. 165–69.

15. John Cox, "Hospital Marries Wireless Net with Thin Clients," *Network World*, May 15, 2000, pp. 27, 34.

Chapter 14

1. Ronald Hilton, *Managerial Accounting*, 2nd ed. (New York: McGraw-Hill, 1994), p. 7.

2. Mark Heinzl, "Noranda to Shed Interests in Forestry and Energy, Refocusing on Mining," *The Wall Street Journal*, November 19, 1997, pp. A3, A6.

3. Elizabeth MacDonald, "Accounting Sleuths Ferret Hidden Assets," *The Wall Street Journal*, December 18, 1996, pp. B1–B2.

4. Philip Mathias, "Non-Profits Fight Move to GAAP Accounting," *The Financial Post*, March 5, 1994, p. 15.

5. L.A. Nikolai, J.D. Bazley, and J.C. Stallman, *Principles of Accounting*, 3rd ed. (Boston: PWS-Kent, 1990).

6. C.T. Horngren and G.I. Sundem, *Introduction to Financial Accounting* (Englewood Cliffs, NJ: Prentice-Hall, 1987).

7. Larry Light, "Goodwill Accounting: Go Figure," *Business Week*, August 30, 1999, p. 188.

8. Ronald Hilton, *Managerial Accounting*, 2nd ed. (New York: McGraw-Hill, 1994), pp. 402–403.

9. Billie Cunningham, Loren Nikolai, and John Bazley, *Accounting: Information for Business Decisions* (Fort Worth, TX: Dryden, 2000), pp. 133–34.

10. *WorldCom 1999 Annual Report* (Clinton, MS: WorldCom Inc., 2000), pp. 27, 40.

11. *Philip Morris Companies Inc. 1999 Annual Report* (New York: Philip Morris Companies Inc., 2000), p. 19.

12. See Charles T. Horngren, Walter T. Harrison, Jr., and Linda Smith Bamber, *Accounting*, 4th ed. (Upper Saddle River, NJ: Prentice Hall, 1999), pp. 562–63; Arthur J. Keown et al., *The Foundations of Finance: The Logic and Practice of Financial Management*, 2nd ed. (Upper Saddle River, NJ: Prentice Hall, 1998), pp. 89–95.

13. See Charles T. Horngren, Walter T. Harrison, Jr., and Linda Smith Bamber, *Accounting*, 4th ed. (Upper Saddle River, NJ: Prentice Hall, 1999), pp. 201–202.

14. See Loren Nikolai and John Bazley, *Intermediate Accounting*, 7th ed. (Cincinnati: South-Western, 1997), pp. 16-17, 303, 899.

Chapter 15

1. From "AMA Board Approves New Marketing Definition," *Marketing News*, March 31, 1985, p. 1, published by the American Marketing Association.

2. See Philip Kotler, *Marketing Management*, Millennium ed. (Upper Saddle River, NJ: Prentice Hall, 2000), pp. 50–54.

3. Ricardo Sookdeo, "Golfing Gear for Women," *Fortune*, November 14, 1994, p. 257.

4. Jonathan Kapstein, Thaine Peterson, and Lois Therrien, "Look Out World, Philips Is on a War Footing," *Business Week*, January 15, 1990, pp. 44–45.

5. Margot Gibb-Clark, "Customers Have a Say on IBM Managers' Pay," *The Globe and Mail*, April 1, 1991, p. B4.

6. "Above the Crowd," *Canadian Business*, April 1990, p. 76.

7. Philip Kotler, *Marketing Management: Analysis, Planning, Implementation, and Control*, 7th ed. (Englewood Cliffs, NJ: Prentice-Hall, 1991).

8. "Microwaves, VCRs Seen as Comforts of Home Now," *Winnipeg Free Press*, March 20, 1998, p. A15.

9. Robert D. Hof, Steve Hamm, and Ira Sager, "Sunpower," *Business Week*, January 18, 1999, pp. 64–68+.

10. "R/3 Database Server," www.sap.com/solutions/business, accessed March 1, 2000.

11. John Heinzl, "Crayon Maker Draws in an Older Kid," *The Globe and Mail*, March 5, 1998; Shawna Steinberg, "Have Allowance, Will Transform Economy," *Canadian Business*, March 13, 1998, pp. 59–71.

12. Lisa Bannon, "Little Big Spenders," *The Wall Street Journal*, October 13, 1998, pp. A1, A6.

13. Sheryl Ubelacker, "Magazines Target Over-50 Crowd," *Winnipeg Free Press*, April 9, 2000, p. B3.

14. Allen St. John, "Baseball's Billion Dollar Question: Who's on Deck?"

American Demographics, October 1998, pp. 60–62, 65–69.

15. Lauren Goldstein, "Dressing Up an Old Brand," *Fortune*, November 9, 1998, pp. 154–56.

16. Jane Perlez, "Joy of Debts: Eastern Europe on Credit Fling," *The New York Times*, May 30, 1998, p. A3.

17. John Morton, "How to Spot the Really Important Prospects," *Business Marketing*, January 1990, pp. 62–67.

18. Paul Sutter, "How to Succeed in Bubble Gum without Really Trying," *Canadian Business*, January 1992, pp. 48–50.

19. Marina Strauss, "First You Have to Get Their Attention," *The Globe and Mail*, July 12, 1991, p. B1.

20. Sean Silcoff, "2nd Time Trendy," *Canadian Business*, May 29, 2000, pp. 34–39.

21. Oliver Bertin, "John Deere Reaps the Fruits of its Labors," *The Globe and Mail*, September 2, 1991, pp. B1, B3.

22. Stephen Barr, "Trading Places: Barter Re-Enters Corporate America," *Management Review*, August 1993, p. 30; John J. McDonald, "Barter Can Work," *Chief Executive (U.S.)*, June 1994, p. 40.

23. William J. Stanton, Michael J. Etzel, and Bruce J. Walker, *Fundamentals of Marketing*, 10th ed. (New York: McGraw-Hill, 1994), Chapter 5.

24. Thomas Russell, Glenn Verrill, and W. Ronald Lane, *Kleppner's Advertising Procedure*, 11th ed. (Englewood Cliffs, NJ: Prentice-Hall, 1990); James Engel, Martin Warshaw, and Thomas Kinnear, *Promotional Strategy*, 6th ed. (Homewood, IL: Richard D. Irwin, 1987).

Chapter 16

1. Patricia Lush, "From Pipe Dream to Profit," *The Globe and Mail*, December 12, 1994, p. B6.

2. Rebecca Blumenstein, "Auto Industry Reaches Surprising Consensus: It Needs New Engines," *The Wall Street Journal*, January 5, 1998, pp. A1, A10.

3. Kalpana Srinivasan, "Digital TRV Faces Uneasy Revolution," *Winnipeg Free Press*, April 11, 2000, pp. B5, B10.

4. Richard Chase and Nick Aquilano, *Production and Operations Management*, 6th ed. (Homewood, IL: Irwin, 1992), Chapter 4.

5. Leonard E. Berry, A. Parasuraman, and Valerie A. Zeithaml, "Improving Service Quality in America," *Academy of Management Executive*, 8, 2, 1994, pp. 37–38.

6. Joel Baumwell, "Life Cycle for Brands? Forget It!" *Advertising Age*, March 17, 1986, p. 18.

7. See Kevin Lane Keller, *Strategic Brand Management: Building, Measuring, and Managing Brand Equity* (Upper Saddle River, NJ: Prentice Hall, 1998), pp. 2–7; Kotler, *Marketing Management*, pp. 404–18.

8. Paul C. Judge et al., "The Name's the Thing," *Business Week*, November 15, 1999, pp. 36–39.

9. Eileen Kinsella, "Corporate Names Go Quirky," *The Globe and Mail*, May 20, 1997, p. B12.

10. Cyndee Miller, "Little Relief Seen for New Product Failure Rate," *Marketing News*, June 21, 1993, p. 1; Nancy J. Kim, "Back to the Drawing Board," *The Bergen (New Jersey) Record*, December 4, 1994, pp. B1, B4.

11. Brian Milner, "Canada's Franklin the Turtle Heads South," *The Globe and Mail*, February 14, 2000, pp. B1, B10.

12. Marina Strauss, "Holt Renfrew Brands a Strategy," *The Globe and Mail*, March 20, 1997, p. B13.

13. David Square, "Mouse Pad Gets Oodles of Nibbles," *The Winnipeg Free Press*, July 26, 1997, p. B10.

14. Marina Strauss, "Packaging Is a Marketer's Last Chance to Say 'Buy Me'," *The Globe and Mail*, September 17, 1991, p. B4.

15. William Pride and O.C. Ferrell, *Marketing*, 5th ed. (Boston: Houghton Mifflin, 1987).

16. John B. Clark, *Marketing Today: Successes, Failures, and Turnarounds* (Englewood Cliffs, NJ: Prentice-Hall, 1987), p. 32.

17. Robert Berner, "The Rolls-Royce of Leather Jackets is Hard to Come By," *The Wall Street Journal*, November 22, 1996, pp. A1, A10.

18. John Heinzl, "Buckley Wants U.S. to Swallow Its Bad Taste," *The Globe and Mail*, November 11, 1999, pp. B1, B12.

19. John Heinzl, "Advertising Has Its Limits—Ask Eaton's, Canadian," *The Globe and Mail*, August 25, 1999, p. M1.

20. Marina Strauss, "Towel War Turns to Name-Naming," *The Globe and Mail*, December 5, 1995, pp. B1, B10.

21. "Regulators Wary of Ads Rapping Rivals," *The Globe and Mail*, May 23, 1991, p. B4.

22. Stuart Elliot, "Topsy-turvey Becomes Darling of Print Ads," *The Globe and Mail*, February 25, 1992, pp. B1, B6.

23. Marina Strauss, "This Billboard Wants to Pass You By," *The Globe and Mail*, February 27, 1992, p. B4.

24. Laurie Ward, "Big Rock Brews Strong U.S. Growth," *The Financial Post*, September 25, 1993, p. 7.

25. Hilary Stout, "Ad Budget: Zero. Buzz: Defeaning," *The Wall Street Journal*, December 29, 1999, p. B1.

26. Simon Tuck, "Security Rated Top On-Line Fear," *The Globe and Mail*, July 5, 1999, p. B5.

27. Stuart Elliott, "Real or Virtual? You Call It," *The New York Times*, October 1, 1999, pp. C1, C6.

28. See William Wells, John Burnett, and Sandra Moriarty, *Advertising: Principles and Practice*, 5th ed. (Upper Saddle River, NJ: Prentice Hall, 2000), pp. 77–83.

29. Marina Strauss, "Small Shops Quake Over IBM's Earth-Shaking Move," *The Globe and Mail*, May 26, 1994, p. B4.

30. Ann Gibbon, "Ad Group Tries to Demystify Quebec," *Globe and Mail*, November 25, 1993, p. B6.

31. "Regulators Wary of Ads Rapping Rivals," *The Globe and Mail*, May 23, 1991, p. B4.

32. Raju Narisetti, "Move to Drop Coupons Puts Procter & Gamble in a Sticky PR Situation," *The Wall Street Journal*, April 17, 1997, pp. A1, A10.

33. "Point-of-Purchase Rush Is On," *Advertising Age*, February 8, 1988, p. 47.

34. Lois Therrien, "Want Shelf Space at the Supermarket? Ante Up," *Business Week*, August 7, 1989, pp. 60–61.

35. Jennifer Lawrence, "Free Samples Get Emotional Reaction," *Advertising Age*, September 30, 1991, p. 10.

36. "Pageant Runner-Up Looks for Compensation," *Winnipeg Free Press*, February 3, 1998, p. A4.

37. Joseph Periera, "Toy Story: How Shrewd Marketing Made Elmo a Hit," *The Wall Street Journal*, December 16, 1996, pp. B1, B8.

38. Caroline Alphonso, "Roots Going for Gold Again at Olympics," *The Globe and Mail*, August 16, 2000, pp. B1–B2; John Heinzl, "Logos an Olympic Event," *The Globe and Mail*, October 20, 1997, pp. B1, B6; John Heinzl, "How Roots Plants Its Products," *The Globe and Mail*, May 28, 1998, p. B10.

39. Wendy Stueck, "Olympics Still Golden to Marketers," *The Globe and Mail*, September 8, 2000, p. M1.

40. "Does the 'Special Relationship' Include Ketchup and Cola?" *Adweek*, December 13, 1993, p. 17.

41. "DDB Wins Global Corporate Bayer Account Outside U.S.," *Advertising Age International: International Daily*, June 16, 1997, www.adage.com, accessed March 10, 2000; "Nickelodeon Mounts First Brand Campaign in Brazil," *Advertising Age International: International Daily*, March 13, 2000, www.adage.com, accessed March 13, 2000.

Chapter 17

1. Rahul Jacob, "Beyond Quality and Value," *Fortune*, Autumn–Winter 1993, pp. 8–11.

2. Calmetta Y. Coleman, "How Burger King Finally Became a Contender," *The Wall Street Journal*, February 27, 1997, pp. B1, B4.

3. Stephen Kindel, "Tortoise Gains on Hare," *Financial World*, February 23, 1988, pp. 18–20.

4. Constance L. Hays, "Coke Tests Weather-Linked Pricing," *The Globe and Mail*, October 29, 1999, p. B11.

5. Robert D. Hof, "The Buyer Always Wins," *Business Week*, March 22, 1999, pp. EB26, EB28.

6. See Charles T. Horngren, Walter T. Harrison, and Linda Smith Bamber, *Accounting*, 4th ed. (Upper Saddle River, NJ: Prentice Hall, 1999), pp. 957–64.

7. Stewart A. Washburn, "Establishing Strategy and Determining Cost in the Pricing Decision," *Business Marketing*, July 1985, pp. 64–78.

8. Scott McCartney, "Gap Grows Between Business, Leisure Fares," *The Globe and Mail*, November 12, 1997, pp. A16, A18.

9. See Judy Strauss and Raymond Frost, *Marketing on the Internet: Principles of Online Marketing* (Upper Saddle River, NJ: Prentice Hall, 1999), pp. 139–44.

10. "Odd Prices Hurt Image of Prices," *Business Month*, July 1987, p. 23.

11. Duncan Stewart, "Say Goodbye to the Middleman," *The Globe and Mail*, April 19, 2000, p. B14.

12. Randall Litchfield, "The Pressure on Prices," *Canadian Business*, February 1992, pp. 30–35.

13. Ahmad Diba, "An Old-Line Agency Finds an Online Niche," *Fortune*, April 3, 2000, p. 258.

14. Brian Bremner and Moon Ihlwan, "Edging Toward the Information Age," *Business Week*, January 31, 2000; "Staples.com," www.staples.com, and "CCBN.com," www.corporate-ir.net, accessed April 18, 2000.

15. Keith McArthur, "Para Paints' Bold Stroke," *The Globe and Mail*, October 18, 1999, p. M1.

16. Stephanie Anderson Forest, "The Education of Michael Dell," *Business Week*, March 22, 1993, pp. 82–86; Lois Therrien, "Why Gateway Is Racing to Answer on the First Ring," *Business Week*, September 13, 1993, pp. 92–93; Peter Burrows, "The Computer Is in the Mail (Really)," *Business Week*, January 23, 1995, pp. 76–77; Scott McCartney, "Michael Dell—and His Company—Grow Up," *Wall Street Journal*, January 31, 1994, pp. B1, B2.

17. Dale M. Lewison, *Retailing*, 5th ed. (New York: Macmillan, 1994), p. 454; Louis Stern and Adel I. El-Ansary, *Marketing Channels*, 4th ed. (Englewood Cliffs, NJ: Prentice Hall, 1992), pp. 129–30.

18. Leigh Buchanan, "The Best of the Small Business Web," *Inc. Tech*, 1999, no. 4, pp. 67, 72.

19. "Expedia.com," www.expedia.com, accessed April 19, 2000.

20. Judy Strauss and Raymond Frost, *Marketing on the Internet* (Upper Saddle River, NJ: Prentice Hall, 1999), pp. 14, 153–55; Ahmad Diba, "An Old-Line Agency Finds an Online Niche," *Fortune*, April 3, 2000, p. 258.

21. Diane Brady, "From Nabisco to Tropicana to . . . EFDEX?" *Business Week*, September 20, 1999, p. 100; "Efdex,™" www.efdex.com, accessed April 19, 2000.

22. Marina Strauss, "American Eagle Snares Chains from Dylex," *The Globe and Mail*, August 25, 2000, pp. B1, B2.

23. Dana Canedy, "Need Asparagus? Just Click It," *The New York Times*, September 10, 1999, pp. C1, C18.

24. Shelly Branch, "Inside the Cult of Cosco," *Fortune*, September 6, 2000, pp. 184–86+.

25. Gene Gray, "The Future of the Teleservices Industry—Are You Aware," *Telemarketing*, January 1999, pp. 90–96.

26. Rodney Ho, "Fuller Brush Just Won't Bite the Dust," *The Wall Street Journal*, November 3, 1999, pp. B1, B4.

27. Philip Kotler and Gary Armstrong, *Marketing: An Introduction*, 3rd ed. (Englewood Cliffs, NJ: Prentice Hall, 1993), p. 362; Scott Donaton and Joe Mandese, "GM, Hachette to Test TV Show," *Advertising Age*, September 13, 1993, p. 1.

28. "Prodigy.com,™" www.prodigy.com, accessed April 19, 2000.

29. Marina Strauss, "Depots Aim to Solve Delivery Dilemma," *The Globe and Mail*, July 28, 2000, p. M1.

30. Simon Tuck, "Internet Rings Up Puny Sales," *The Globe and Mail*, August 11, 2000, pp. B1, B4.

31. "efdex Launches the First Global e-Market for the Food & Drink Industry," press release from Connors Communications, www.connors.com/press/efdx, accessed April 19, 2000; Dana Canedy, "Need Asparagus? Just Click It," *The New York Times*, September 10, 1999, pp. C1, C18.

32. "Did You Know?" www.catalog-news.com, Maxwell Sroge Publishing, accessed April 19, 2000; Judy Strauss and Raymond Frost, *Marketing on the Internet: Principles of Online Marketing* (Upper Saddle River, NJ: Prentice Hall, 1999), p. 140.

33. Peter Elkind, "Shhhhh! Amway's on the Web," *Fortune*, March 6, 2000, p. 76; Dennis Berman, "Is the Bell Tolling for Door-to-Door Selling?" *Business Week*, November 1, 1999, pp. EB 58–EB 60.

34. "LivePerson.com,™" www.liveper-son.com, accessed April 19, 2000.

35. Saul Hansell, "As Sales Boom Online, Some Customers Boo," *The New York Times*, December 17, 1999, pp. C1, C10; Bob Tedeschi, "E-Commerce Report," *The New York Times*, September 27, 1999, p. C4.

36. Andrew Tausz, "Getting There Fast—By Truck," *The Globe and Mail*, March 1, 1994, p. B23.

37. Andrew Allentuck, "Arctic Delivery Tough Sailing," *The Globe and Mail*, March 1, 1994, p. B23.

38. Rick Tetzeli, "Cargo That Phones Home," *Fortune*, November 15, 1993, p. 143.

39. Bill Redekop, "The Crow Subsidy Is History," *Winnipeg Free Press*, February 28, 1995, p. 1.

Chapter 18

1. P.S. Rose and D.R. Fraser, *Financial Institutions*, 3rd ed. (Plano, TX: Business Publications, Inc., 1988).

2. Andrew Higgins, "Lacking Money to Pay, Russian Firms Survive on Deft Barter System," *The Wall Street Journal*, August 27, 1998, pp. A1, A6.

3. Casey Mahood, "Canadians Embrace the Debit Card," *The Globe and Mail*, June 14, 1999, pp. B1, B4.

4. *Statistical Abstract of the United States* (1999), p. 528; Lisa Daigle, "Beyond Expectations," *Credit Card Management*, May 2000, pp. 50–52; Rutrell Yasin, "U.S. Slow to Play Smart Card Hand," *Internetweek*, October 4, 1999, pp. 33–34.

5. Kelly Holland and Greg Burns, "Plastic Talks," *Business Week*, February 14, 1994, pp. 105–107; Saul Hansell, "An End to the 'Nightmare' of Cash," *New York Times*, September 6, 1994, pp. D1, D5; Thomas McCarroll, "No Checks. No Cash. No Fuss?" *Time*, May 9, 1994, pp. 60–62; Marla Matzer, "Plastic Mania," *Forbes*, October 24, 1994, pp. 281–82.

6. Kelly Holland and Amy Cortese, "The Future of Money," *Business Week*, June 12, 1995, pp. 66–72+.

7. Grep Ip, "Ottawa Set to Lose Millions When Reserve Rules Dropped," *The Financial Post*, July 17, 1991, p. 3.

8. Karen Horcher, "Reconstruction Zone," *CGA Magazine*, June 1997, p. 19.

9. James Brooke, "Is the Dollar Leaving Canada Feeling Drained?" *The New York Times*, November 13, 1999, pp. C1, C4.

10. Robert J. Carbaugh, *International Economics*, 5th ed. (Cincinnati: South-Western, 1995), Chapter 11.

Chapter 19

1. *Prospectus* (United Parcel Service Inc., November 9, 1999).

2. Quicken.com, www.quicken.elogic.com/sec_financials.asp?ticker=UPS&Mod=1&S1=N, accessed June 21, 2000.

3. George G. Kaufman, *The U.S. Financial System: Money, Markets, and Institutions*, 6th ed. (Englewood Cliffs, NJ: Prentice Hall, 1995), p. 432.

4. *NYSE Fact Book: 1995 Data* (New York: New York Stock Exchange, 1996), pp. 7, 43.

5. Saul Hansell, "Low-Cost Trading Is Planned by Merrill Lynch," *The New York Times*, June 2, 1999, A1, C26.

6. Richard Blackwell, "TSE Sees Few Gains from Realignment," *The Globe and Mail*, May 23, 2000, p. 12.

7. The New York Stock Exchange, www.nyse.com, accessed June 23, 2000.

8. NASDAQ, www.nasdaq.com, accessed June 23, 2000.

9. NASDAQ, www.nasdaq.com/about/timeline.stm, accessed June 25, 2000.

10. NASD, www.nasd.com, accessed June 25, 2000.

11. Deborah Solomon, "Internet Firm Cisco Topples Microsoft as World's No. 1," *USA Today*, March 28, 2000, p. 1.

12. *Statistical Abstract of the United States* (Washington, DC: Bureau of the Census, 1999).

13. "The World in Its Hands," *The Economist*, May 6, 2000, p. 77; "The Nasdaq Japan Market Launches First Day of Trading; First Step in Creating Nasdaq Global Platform is Achieved," www.nasdaq.co.uk/reference, accessed June 19, 2000; "Globalization and International Reach," *Nasdaq Initiatives*, www.nasdaq.com, accessed June 23, 2000.

14. Steven Greenhouse, "Exchanges thrive as Russians pursue market economy," *Winnipeg Free Press*, November 3, 1991, p. B13.

15. Rob Carrick, "Direct Plans Cut Brokers Out," *The Globe and Mail*, August 21, 1999, p. B8.

Chapter 20

1. *GE Annual Report 1999* (Fairfield, CT: General Electric Co., 2000), p. 58.

2. John Heinzl, "Good Strategy Gone Awry, Top Retailer's Tale of Woe," *The Globe and Mail*, March 7, 1992, pp. B1, B4.

3. *The State of Small Business, 1989 Annual Report on Small Business in*

Ontario (Toronto: Ministry of Industry, Trade and Technology, 1990).

4. J.W. Duncan, *D&B Reports*, September–October 1991, p. 8.

5. E.F. Brigham, *Fundamentals of Financial Management*, 5th ed. (Chicago: Dryden, 1989).

6. See Norman M. Scarborough and Thomas W. Zimmerer, *Effective Small Business Management: An Entrepreneurial Approach*, 6th ed. (Upper Saddle River, NJ: Prentice Hall, 2000), pp. 298–300.

7. Susan Hodges, "One Big Step Toward a Loan," *Nation's Business*, August 1997, pp. 34–36.

8. Richard S. Boulton, Barry D. Libert, and Steve M. Samek, "Managing Risk in an Uncertain World," *Upside*, June 2000, pp. 268–78.

9. Thomas P. Fitch, *Dictionary of Banking Terms*, 2nd ed. (Hauppauge, NY: Barron's, 1993), p. 531.

10. This section is based on Phillip L. Zweig et al., "Managing risk," *Fortune*, October 31, 1994, pp. 86–90+.

11. See Mark S. Dorfman, *Introduction to Risk Management and Insurance*, 6th ed. (Upper Saddle River, NJ: Prentice Hall, 2000), Ch. 1.

12. Denyse O'Leary, "The Scams That Drive Up Premiums," *The Globe and Mail*, May 2, 1995, p. B1; Denyse O'Leary, "Insurers United Against Fraud Face Serious Obstacles," *The Globe and Mail*, May 2, 1995, p. B1.

13. See Mark S. Dorfman, *Introduction to Risk Management and Insurance*, 6th ed. (Upper Saddle River, NJ: Prentice Hall, 2000), pp. 420–21.

Appendix B

1. Figure estimated from *1988-89 Property/Casualty Fact Book*, p. 19.

2. Gayle MacDonald, "How an Eaton's Supplier Cut Risk," *The Globe and Mail*, March 17, 1997, p. B7.

3. *The Financial Post*, July 1995, p. 172.

Source Notes

Chapter 1

The Saga of Voisey's Bay James Stevenson, "Inco Grilled Despite Impressive Rebound," *Winnipeg Free Press*, April 20, 2000, p. B7; "Giant Newfoundland Nickel Project May Soon Proceed," *Winnipeg Free Press*, November 23, 1999, p. B8; Allan Robinson, "Inco President Willing to Compromise on Voisey's Bay," *The Globe and Mail*, April 29, 1999, pp. B1, B4; Allan Robinson, "Inco to Halt Voisey's Bay Work," *The Globe and Mail*, July 28, 1998, pp. B1, B6; Allan Robinson, "Inco Chairman Defends Actions," *The Globe and Mail*, April 23, 1998, p. B3. **It's a Wired World** Summarized from Dawn Walton, "Net B2B Soaring to Lofty Heights," *The Globe and Mail*, April 28, 2000, p. B10. See also Oracle Corp., "Partner Solutions," http://www.oracle.com/partners/content. html, accessed March 8, 2000; Ford Motor Co., "Inside the Company Newsroom," http://www.ford.com/default.asp?pageid=106&storyid=695, accessed March 8, 2000. See also John Partridge, "Two Banks, Bell Part of Big E-Commerce Venture," *The Globe and Mail*, September 27, 2000, pp. B1, B11. **Figure 1.2** John J. Wild, Kenneth L. Wild, and Jerry C.Y. Jan, *International Business: An Integrated Approach* (Upper Saddle River, NJ: Prentice Hall, 2000). **Business Today** Summarized from Bill Redekop, "Private Wine Stores Cheesed with MLCC," *Winnipeg Free Press*, July 8, 2000, p. A6; David Menzies, "Sour Grapes," *Canadian Business*, February 26, 1999, pp. 28–35. **Table 1.1** *National Post Business 500*, June 2000, pp. 138–39. Reprinted with permission. **WebConnexion** "Home Page." *Petro-Canada*. http://www.petro-canada.ca. November 2000. Reprinted with permission of Petro-Canada. **WebConnexion** "Home Page." *VA Linux Systems.* http://www.valinux.com. November 2000. Reproduced with permision of VA Linux System. **Figure 1.8** *Bank of Canada Banking and Financial Statistics*, June 2000. **Figure 1.9** *Bank of Canada Banking and Financial Statistics*, June 2000, Table H5, p. 599. **WebConnexion** "Home Page." http://www.un.org/english. *United Nations*. November 2000. Reprinted with permission of the United Nations. **WebConnexion** "Economics Home Page." *Bank of Montreal*. http://www.bmo.com/economics. November 2000. Reprinted with permission. **Figure 1.10** Michael J. Mandel, "The New Economy," *Business Week*, January 31, 2000, 75. Data *from Computer Industry Almanac*. **Figure 1.11** Mandel, "The New Economy," 77. Data from International Data Corp. **Figure 1.12** Mandel, "The New Economy," 75. Data from Standard & Poor's DRI.

Chapter 2

Unsung Heroes of Canadian Business Summarized from Jeff Buckstein, "Co-op Confidential," *CGA Magazine*, February 1999, pp. 11–16. **WebConnexion** "Home Page." *Hudson's Bay Company.* http://www.hbc.com/hbconline/home.asp. February 2001. © Hudson's Bay Company. All rights reserved. Reprinted with permission. **Table 2.3** *National Post Business 500*, June 2000, p. 94. Reprinted with permission. **Business Today** Summarized from John Partridge, "1999: The Year the Insurers Went Public," *The Globe and Mail*, December 30, 1999, pp. B1, B5; John Partridge, "Insurer Unveils Demutualization Details," *The Globe and Mail*, May 3, 1999, p. B4. **WebConnexion** "CEO of the Year." *The Caldwell Partners*. http://www.ceoaward-canada.org. November 2000. Reprinted with permission of The Caldwell Partners. **Table 2.5** *National Post Business 500*, June 2000, pp. 94–107. **WebConnexion** "Home Page." *Tembec*. http://www.tembec.ca. February 2001. Reprinted with permission. **Concluding Case 2-1** Summarized from Richard Blackwell, "Banks Give Shareholders a Voice," *The Globe and Mail*, March 3, 2000, p. B10; John Saunders, "Can We Stop Meeting Like This?" *The Globe and Mail*, March 15, 1997, pp. B1, B5; "How to Get the Most Out of an Annual Meeting," *The Globe and Mail*, March 15, 1997, p. B5. **Concluding Case 2-2** Summarized from Peter Verburg, "Prepare for Takeoff," *Canadian Business*, December 25, 2000, pp. 95–99.

Chapter 3

Next Stop: The World Heather Scoffield and Shawn McCarthy, "WTO Backs Canada in Jet Market Dogfight with Brazil," *The Globe and Mail*, April 1, 2000, pp. B1, B5; Konrad Yakabuski and Heather Scoffield, "Canada, Brazil Claim Victory Over Decision," *The Globe and Mail*, August 3, 1999, pp. B1, B4; Konrad Yakabuski, "Bombardier Soars on Jet Orders, but Turbulence May Loom Ahead," *The Globe and Mail*, February 22, 1999, pp. B1, B5; Heather Scoffield, "Bombardier-Embraer Dogfight Heats Up," *The Globe and Mail*, February 15, 1999, pp. B1, B6. **WebConnexion** Used with permission of LetsBuyIt.com. **It's a Wired World** *Hoover's Handbook of World Business 2000* (Austin, TX: Hoover's Business Press, 2000), 410-11; Justin Fox, "Nokia's Secret Code," *Fortune*, May 1, 2000, 160-174; "It Takes a Cell Phone," *Wall Street Journal*, June 25, 1999, B1, B4. **Figure 3.4** *Bank of Canada Banking and Financial Statistics*, June 2000, Table J1, p. S106. **Table 3.1** *Market Research Handbook*, 63-224, 1999, pp. 125–26. **Figure 3.6** Griffin/Ebert, *Business*, Fourth Edition (Englewood Cliffs, NJ: Prentice Hall, 1996). **Business Today** Summarized from Gayle MacDonald, "Purdy's Test Asia's Sweet Tooth," *The Globe and Mail*, June 9, 1997, p. B7. **Table 3.3** *National Post*, June 2000, p. 130. **Table 3.4** *National Post*, June 2000, p. 40. **WebConnexion** Used with permission of Shenyang Shawnee Cowboy Food Co. Ltd. **WebConnexion** "The Canadian Financial System." *Department of Finance Canada*. http://www.fin.gc.ca/toce/1995/fctshtsum95-e.html. November 2000. Reproduced with the permission of the Minister of Public Works and Government Services Canada, 2001. **Concluding Case 3-2** Summarized from Geoffrey York, "Russians Accuse McDonald's of Union Bashing," *The Globe and Mail*, June 14, 1999, p. A17; Geoffrey York, "Beeg Maks on a Roll," *The Globe and Mail*, September 12, 1996, pp. B1, B17; Peter Foster, "McDonald's Excellent Soviet Venture?" *Canadian Business*, May 1991, pp. 51–64.

Chapter 4

The Bubble Bursts at Cinar Susanne Craig, John Partridge, and Bertrand Marotte, "Cinar Co-Founder Okayed Investment," *The Globe and Mail*, March 22, 2000, pp. B1, B4; Richard Finlay, "Cinar Hurt by Poor governance," *The Globe and Mail*, March 15, 2000, p. B15; Susanne Craig, "Cinar Co-Founders Pushed Out," *The Globe and Mail*, March 15, 2000, pp. B1, B9; Dawn Walton, "When There's a Rogue Within the Ranks," *The Globe and Mail*, March 14, 2000, p. B15; Gayle MacDonald and Keith McArthur, "Power Couple Falls from Grace," *The Globe and Mail*, March 7, 2000, p. B9; Susanne Craig, Bertrand Marotte, "Cinar to Take Hit Following Probe," *The Globe and Mail*, February 21, 2000, pp. B1, B3. **Business Today** Summarized from Michael J. McCarthy, "Virtual Morality: A New Workplace Quandary," *The Wall Street Journal*, October 21, 1999, pp. B1, B4; Marina Strauss, "E-Tailers Mix Alcohol with Internet," *The Globe and Mail*, July 21, 2000, p. M1. **Figures 4-1 and 4-2** Based on Gerald S. Cavanaugh, American Business Values: With International Perspectives, 4th ed. (Upper Saddle River, NJ: Prentice Hall, 1998), 71 and 84. **It's a Wired World** Michael Schrage, "If You Passed Notes in School, You'll Love This Idea," *Fortune*, May 1, 2000, 340; Michael J. McCarthy, "Your Manager's Policy on Employees' E-Mail May Have a Weak Spot," *Wall Street Journal*, April 25, 2000, A1, A10; "It's Time for Rules in Wonderland," *Time*, March 20, 2000, 83-96. **WebConnexion** Used with permission of Privada, Inc. **Figure 4.3** Guiding Principles of Great West Life Assurance Company, Winnipeg, Manitoba. Reproduced with permission. **Figure 4-4** David Baron, *Business and Its Environment*, 3rd ed. (Upper Saddle River, NJ: Prentice Hall, 2000), 669. **WebConnexion** "Home Page." *Mountain Equipment Canada*. http://www.mec.ca.

November 2000. Reprinted with permission of Mountain Equipment Canada. **Concluding Case 4-1** Summarized from Terence Corcoran, "Corporate Ungiving," *The National Post*, April 1, 2000, p. D5; "Nortel's New Style Giving," *The National Post*, April 1, 2000, p. D5. **Concluding Case 4-2** Kevin Kelly and Kathleen Kerwin, "There's another side to the López saga," *Business Week*, August 23, 1993, p. 26; John Templeman and Peggy Salz-Trautman, "VW figures its best defense may be a good offense," *Business Week*, August 9, 1993, p. 29; Templeman and David Woodruff, "The aftershock from the López affair," *Business Week*, August 19, 1993, p. 31; Doron Levin, "Executive who left G.M. denies taking documents and sues," *The New York Times*, May 25, 1993, pp. A1, D21; Ferdinand Protzman, "VW hums tight-fisted López tune," *The New York Times*, April 30, 1994, pp. 39, 47; Gabriella Mitchener, "VW Agrees To Big Settlement with GM," *The Wall Street Journal*, January 10, 1997, p. A3; "López Indicted for Taking from GM," *The Globe and Mail*, May 23, 2000, p. B9.

Chapter 5

Seagram's Final Strategy Brian Milner, "Bronfmans Win in Seagram Deal," *The Globe and Mail*, June 15, 2000, pp. B1, B17; Brian Milner, "Seagram Dynasty Down the Hatch," *The Globe and Mail*, June 20, 2000, pp. A1, A7; Allan Swift, "Polygram Bid Heats UP," *Winnipeg Free Press*, November 5, 1998, p. B12; Brian Milner, "Seagram's Top Gun Shoots for the Stars," *The Globe and Mail*, June 6, 1998, pp. B1, B6; Brian Milner, "Seagram Snares Polygram," *The Globe and Mail*, May 22, 1998, pp. B1, B4. **WebConnexion** Used with permission of Virgin Group PLC. **Business Today** Summarized from Henry Mintzberg, *The Nature of Managerial Work* (New York: Harper and Row, 1973), Chapter 3. **Table 5.1** "How to Be a Great e-CEO," *Fortune*, May 24, 1999, 107. **Concluding Case 5-2** Summaried from Sandra Cordon, "Feds Rein in Air Monopoly," *Winnipeg Free Press*, February 18, 2000, pp. B1–B2; Gillian Livingstone, "Done Deal: Canadian Airlines Sold January 5," *Winnipeg Free Press*, December 24, 1999, p. B1; Gillian Livingstone, "Air Canada's Cards on Table," *Winnipeg Free Press*, November 16, 1999, p. B3; Conway Daly, "Air Canada Strikes Back," *Winnipeg Free Press*, October 20,.1999, pp. B1–B2; Jacquie McNish, "CAI Lashes Out at Air Canada," *The Globe and Mail*, September 25, 1999, pp. B1, B9; Andrew Willis, "Institutions Favour Merged Airline," *The Globe and Mail*, August 25, 1999, pp. B1, B6.

Chapter 6

Restructuring at Bata Shoe Ltd. Summarized from Marina Strauss, "Bata to Revamp Worldwide Operations," *The Globe and Mail*, January 17, 2000, pp. B1–B2; Robert Collison, "How Bata Rules the World," *Canadian Business*, September, 1990, pp. 28–34. **WebConnexion** Used with permission of PurchasingCenter.com Inc. **It's a Wired World** David Welch, "At Ford, e-Commerce Is Job 1," *Business Week*, February 28, 2000, 74-78; Eryn Brown, "Nine Ways to Win on the Web," *Fortune*, May 24, 1999, 112-25. **WebConnexion** "Home Page." *Mouvement des caisses populaires et d'économie Desjardins du Québec.* http://www.desjardins.com/ang. February 2001. Reprinted with permission. **Business Today** Summarized from Owen Edwards, "Leak soup," *GQ*, April 1989, pp. 224+; see also Beatryce Nivens, "When to Listen to the office grapevine," *Essence*, March 1989, p. 102; John S. Tompkins, "Gossip: Silicon Valley's secret weapon," *Science Digest*, August 1986, pp. 58+; see also "Why you need the grapevine," *Glamour*, August 1986, pp. 126+.

Chapter 7

A Dysfunctional Family Summarized from Gordon Pitts, "The Cuddy Situation Is an Extreme Case of Family Company Dysfunctionality," *The Globe and Mail*, April 17, 2000, p. B9; David Berman, "Carving Up Cuddy," *Canadian Business*, March 27, 1998, pp. 39–44. **WebConnexion** "Home Page." *Ingenuity.com Inc.* http://www.pht-suite.com. January 2001. Reprinted with permission. **Figure 7.1** Quality of Work in the Service Sector, Statistics Canada, 11-612E, No. 6, 1992. **Figure 7.2** *Hoover's Handbook of World Business 2000* (Austin, TX: Hoover's Business Press, 2000). **Table 7.1** Marc J. Dollinger, *Entrepreneurship: Strategies and Resour*ce*s*, 2ⁿᵈ ed. (Upper Saddle River, NJ: Prentice Hall, 1999), 9. Adapted from Tom Richman, "The Evolution of the Professional Entrepreneur," *Inc.'s The State of Small Business* (1997). 50-53. **Figure 7.3** Allan J. Magrath, "The Thorny Management Issues in Family-Owned Business," *Business Quarterly*, Spring 1988, p. 73. Reprinted with permission of *Business Quarterly*, published by the Western Business School, The University of Western Ontario, London, Ontario. **Business Today** Ann Gibbon, "Gut Instinct Leads Pattison on His Prowl," *The Globe and Mail*, December 6, 1999, p. B11. **WebConnexion** "Home Page." *Amsdell Inc.* http://www.amsdell.com. November 2000. © Amsdell Inc. All Rights Reserved. Reprinted with permission. **Table 7.3** Starke/Sexty, *Contemporary Management in Canada*, Scarborough: Prentice Hall Canada (1995); Gina Gillespie, "Incubators Spell Relief for Startups," *The Globe and Mail*, July 4, 2000, p. B14; Susan Greco, "get$$$now.com," *Inc.*, September 1999, pp. 35–38. **Table 7.5** Mel Scott and Richard Bruce, "Five stages of growth in small business," *Long Range Planning*, 20, 1987, p. 48. **It's a Wired World** Steven Chase, "Corporate Canada Takes to Palm Reading," *The Globe and Mail*, August 31, 2000, pp. B1–B2. **Concluding Case 7-1** Summarized from John Southerst, "Ontario Proposals Hit Sore Point with Franchisors," *The Globe and Mail*, November 25, 1996, p. B6; Ellen Roseman, "Flowering Firm Faces Branch Battles," *The Globe and Mail*, November 28, 1995, p. B13; John Lorinc, "War and Pizza," *Canadian Business*, November 1995, pp. 87–97; John Lorinc, *Opportunity Knocks*. Scarborough: Prentice-Hall Canada Inc., 1995; John Southerst, "Struggle for Franchise Law Ends in Compromise," *The Globe and Mail*, June 27, 2000, p. B14; John Southerst, "Franchise Legislation May Snare Entrepreneurs," *The Globe and Mail*, July 5, 2000, p. B9. **Concluding Case 7-2** CBC *Venture*, November 21, 2000.

Chapter 8

More Cracks in the Glass Ceiling Summarized from Elizabeth Church, "Where Is Canada's Carly?" *The Globe and Mail*, December 30, 1999, p. B8; Andrea Orr, "H-P Names Carly Fiorino CEO," *The Globe and Mail*, July 20, 1999, p. B12; Anita Lahey, "Homegrown," *Canadian Business*, August 13, 1999, pp. 33–35; Belle Rose Ragins, "Gender Gap in the Executive Suite: CEOs and Female Executives Report on Breaking the Glass Ceiling," *Academy of Management Executive*, February 1998, pp. 28–42; Greg Keenan, "Ford Canada Gets New CEO," *The Globe and Mail*, April 9, 1997, p. B1; Joseph White and Carol Hymowitz, "Watershed Generation of Women Executives Is Rising to the Top," *The Globe and Mail*, February 10, 1997, p. A1, A6; Greg Keenan and Janet McFarland, "The Boys' Club," *The Globe and Mail*, September 27, 1997, pp. B1, B5; John Heinzl, "Women Take Charge at Canadian Units," *The Globe and Mail*, November 29, 1996, p. B10; Greg Keenan, "Woman at the Wheel," *The Globe and Mail*, July 8, 1995, pp. B1, B6; Elizabeth Church, "Women Still Shut Out of Many Top Posts," *The Globe and Mail*, February 10, 2000, p. B15. **Table 8.1** *National Post Business 500*, June 2000, p. 132. Reprinted with permission. **It's a Wired World** Summarized from Rose Fisher, "Screen Test," *Canadian Business*, May 1992, pp. 62–64. **WebConnexion** Used with permission of ManagedOps.com. **WebConnexion** Used with permission of American Society for Training and Development. **Business Today** "The Highest Paid Executives," *The National Post*, April 22, 2000, p. E14; "Richest Entertainers," *The National Post*, April 22, 2000, p. E16; Alexander Ross, "Sixty-Five and Ouch," *Canadian Business*, July 1992, p. 44; Janet McFarland, "Mintzberg Takes Aim at Business-Style Government," *The Globe and Mail*, April 19, 1996, p. B9. WebConnexion Used with permission of the Cheesecake Factory. **Concluding Case 8-2** Summarized from Mark Brender, "Free Isn't Easy," *The Globe and Mail*, August 9, 1994, p.B18; Margot Gibb-Clark, "Temps Take on New Tasks," *The Globe and Mail*, December 22, 1993, p. B1; Merle MacIsaac, "New Broom Sweeps Schools," *The Globe and Mail*, March 22, 1994, p. B22; Robert Williamson, "Tradition Gives Way to World of Freelancers," *The Globe and Mail*, January 15, 1993, pp. B1, B4; Sally Ritchie, "Rent-a-Manager," *The Globe and Mail*, August 17, 1993, p. B22.

Chapter 9

Motivating and Leading at PanCanadian Petroleum Ltd. Mary Gooderham, "Oil Firm Looks for Clear Path in Leadership Jungle," *The Globe and Mail*, August 17, 1999, p. B9. **Figure 9.2** Griffin/Ebert, *Business*, Second Edition (Englewood Cliffs, NJ: Prentice Hall, 1996). **It's a Wired World** "Hire Now, Pay Later?" *Forbes*, August 23, 1999, 62; Net Start-Ups Pull Out of the Garage," *USA Today*, October 1, 1999. 1B, 2B. WebConnexion "Home Page." *SaskTel*. http://www.sasktel.com. November 2000. Pearson Education Canada is grateful to SaskTel for granting permission to reproduce their Web page. **Business Today** Summarized from Bruce McDougall, "Perks with Pizzazz," *Canadian Business*, June 1990, pp. 78-79; Don Champion, "Quality—A Way of Life at B.C. Tel," *Canadian Business Review*, Spring 1990, p. 33; Margot Gibb-Clark, "Companies Find Merit in Using Pay as a Carrot," *The Globe and Mail*, May 9, 1990, p. B1; Margot Gibb-Clark, "The Right Reward," *The Globe and Mail*, August 10, 1990, p. B5; Peter Matthews, "Just Rewards—The Lure of Pay for Performance," *Canadian Business*, February 1990, pp. 78-79; Ian Allaby, "Just Rewards," *Canadian Business*, May 1990, p. 39; David Evans, "The Myth of Customer Service," *Canadian Business*, March 1991, pp. 34-39; Bud Jorgensen, "Do Bonuses Unscrupulous Brokers Make?" *The Globe and Mail*, May 28, 1990, p. B5; Wayne Gooding, "Ownership Is the Best Motivator," *Customer Business*, March 1990, p. 6. **WebConnexion** Used with permission of Growth and Leadership Center. **Concluding Case 9-1** Anne Howland, "There's No Place Like Work," *CGA Magazine*, July–August 2000, pp. 21–25.

Chapter 10

A Changing Approach to Labour Relations? Summarized from Greg Keenan, "GM and CAW Forge an Improved Relationship," *The Globe and Mail*, October 23, 1999, pp. B1, B14; Greg Keenan, "CAW Face Declining Numbers in Auto Sector," *The Globe and Mail*, October 23, 1999, p. B14. **Table 10.1** Labour Canada, *Labour Organizations in Canada*, 1989, pp. xiii and xiv. Used by permission of the Minister of Supply and Services Canada. **Figure 10.1** *Labour Organizations in Canada*, 1996, p. xiv. **Business Today** Zena Olijnyk, "CAW Walks Away from Wal-Mart," *The National Post*, April 20, 2000, p. C5; Susan Bourette, "Wal-Mart Staff Want Out of Union," *The Globe and Mail*, April 23, 1998, p. B9; John Heinzl and Marina Strauss, "Wal-Mart's Cheer Fades," *The Globe and Mail*, February 15, 1997, pp. B1, B4; Margot Gibb-Clark, "Why Wal-Mart Lost the Case," *The Globe and Mail*, February 14, 1997, p. B10. **WebConnexion** "The Canadian Labour Code." *Human Resources Development Canada*. http://www.hrdc-drhc.gc.ca/dept.guide/labour5. November 2000. Reproduced with the permission of the Minister of Public Works and the Government Services Canada, 2001. **WebConnexion** "Home Page." *CAW/TCA Canada*. http://www.cwa.ca. November 2000. Reprinted with permission of the Canadian Auto Workers. **It's a Wired World** L.M. Sixel, "Networking on the Web: Union Leaders Turn to Internet for Recruiting, Doing Research," *Houston Chronicle*, March 30, 2000, B1; Bill Leonard, "Disgruntled Employees Take Their Beefs to the World Wide Web," *HRMagazine*, November 1999, 89-94. **Table 10.2** *Labour Organizations in Canada*, 1998, p. 19. **Figure 10.2** Griffin/Ebert, *Business*, Second Edition (Englewood Cliffs, NJ: Prentice Hall, 1996). **WebConnexion** Used with permission of the Institute of Industrial Relations, University of California, Berkeley. **Figure 10.4** Labour Canada, *Labour Organizations in Canada*, 1991, p. xxv. Used by permission of the Minister of Supply and Services Canada. **Concluding Case 10-1** Summarized from "Posties Return to Work; Vow to Sabotage Service," *Winnipeg Free Press*, December 5, 1997, p. B4; Paul Samyn, "Back-to-Work Legislation in the Mail," *Winnipeg Free Press*, December 2, 1997, p. B1; Nahiah Ayed, "Postal Workers Picket Manning's Residence," *Winnipeg Free Press*, December 1, 1997, p. B1; Jennifer Ditchburn, "Commons Passes Back-to-Work Law," *Winnipeg Free Press*, December 3, 1997, p. B3. **Concluding Case 10-2** Summarized from Aaron Bernstein and Wendy Zellner, "Detroit vs. the UAW: At Odds Over Teamwork," *Business Week*, August 24, 1987, pp. 54+; Peter Downs, "Drudgery at Wentzville: The Team Concept Strikes Out," *Commonweal*, September 9, 1988, pp. 453+; John Hoerr, "Is Teamwork," *Business Week*, July 10, 1989, pp. 56+; John Holusha, "A New Spirit at U.S. Auto Plants," *New York Times*, December 29, 1987, p. D1+.

Chapter 11

Natural Capitalism Summarized from Andrew Nikiforuk, "Pure Profit," *Canadian Business*, April 3, 2000, pp. 70–76. **Business Today** Summarized from Marian Stinson, "Assembly Line Robots Taking Workers' Jobs: UN Report," *The Globe and Mail*, February 8, 2000, p. B6; Wally Dennison, "Robotics Paint System Makes Splash at CN," *Winnipeg Free Press*, October 6, 1988, p. 30; "Robots Aren't for Burning," *Canadian Business*, September 1984, p. 45. **WebConnexion** Used with permission of Lightning Rod Software. **WebConnexion** "Home Page." *Dell Canada*. http://www.dell.ca. November 2000. Reprinted with permission. **It's a Wired World** Michael Dornheim, "No Kisses for SAP," *Aviation Week & Space Technology*, November 15, 1999, 21; Craig Stedman, "Failed ERP Gamble Haunts Hershey," *Computerworld*, November 1, 1999, 1, 89; Charles Waltner, "New Recipe for IT Implementation," *Informationweek*, September 27, 1999, 169-17; Peter Galuszka and Stephanie Forest-Anderson, "Just-in-Time Manufacturing Is Working Overtime," *Business Week*, November 8, 1999, 36, 37; Tim Minahan, "Enterprise Resource Planning: Strategies Not Included," *Purchasing*, July 16, 1998, 112-127. **Concluding Case 11-1** Summarized from Alex Taylor, "How Toyota Defies Gravity," *Fortune*, December 8, 1997, pp. 100–108. **Concluding Case 11-2** Summarized from Greg Keenan, "Honda Betting on Speed and Efficiency," *The Globe and Mail*, October 10, 2000, pp. B1, B4; Valerie Reitman, "Honda Sees Performance and Profits From New Accord," *The Wall Street Journal*, August 27, 1997, p. B4; Keith Naughton et al., "Can Honda Build a World Car?" *Business Week*, September 8, 1997, pp. 100–108.

Chapter 12

Coke's Quality Controls Fizzle Summarized from "Anatomy of a Recall: How Coke's Controls Fizzled Out In Europe," *The Wall Street Journal*, June 29, 1999, pp. A1, A6. **WebConnexion** Used with permission of the Canadian Manufacturers and Exporters. **Figure 12.1** Bart Van Ark and Robert McGuckin, "International Comparisons of Labor Productivity and Per Capita Income," *Monthly Labor Review*, July 1999, pp. 33–41. **WebConnexion** "Tradition of Innovation Continues." *Telecom Innovation Centre. Siemens Worldwide*. http://www.tic.siemens.ca/20.html. February 2001. Reprinted with permission. **Figure 12.2** Adapted from D. Daryl Wickoff, "New Tools for Achieving Service Quality." *The Cornell Hotel and Restaurant Administrative Quarterly*, November 1984, 89. " Cornell HRA

Quarterly. Used by permission. All rights reserved. **Business Today** Ebert/Griffin, *Business Essentials* (Englewood Cliffs, NJ: Prentice Hall, 1995), pp. 272-73. **Figure 12.5** Adapted from Richard B. Chase, Nicholas J. Aquilano, and F. Robert Jacobs, *Production and Operations Management*, 8th ed. (Boston: Irwin McGraw-Hill, 1998), p. 771. **It's a Wired World** Philip Siekman, "Mercury Marine: Focusing on the Demand Side, *Fortune [Industrial Management & Technology]*, November 8, 1999, 272N-272O; Mercury: The Water Calls." Accessed May 22, 2000 at www.mercurymarine.com/mercury-home/merchome.cfm; Lynne M. Almvig, "Robotics Milling Department," *Robotics Today*, First Quarter 2000, 1-4. **Concluding Case 12-1** Brian S. Moskal, "Born to Be Real," *Industry Week*, August 2, 1993, pp. 14–18; Robert L. Rose, "Vrooming Back: After Nearly Stalling, Harley-Davidson Finds New Crowd of Riders," *The Wall Street Journal*, August 31, 1990, pp. A1, A6; Peter C. Reid, *Well Made in America* (New York: McGraw-Hill, 1990); John Holusha, "How Harley Outfoxed Japan with Exports," *The New York Times*, August 12, 1990, Sec. 3, p. 5. **Concluding Case 12-2** "Bridgestone Faults Self, Ford for Separations," *Winnipeg Free Press*, December 20, 2000, p. B8; Todd Zaun, Kanji Ishibashi, and Timothy Aeppel, "Firestone Tire Sales Plummet," *The Globe and Mail*, November 13, 2000, p. B8; Timothy Aeppel, Norihiko Shirouzu, and Michael Williams, "Pit Crew," *The Wall Street Journal*, October 11, 2000, pp. A1, A10; "Answers Still Elusive in Tire Crisis," *The Wall Street Journal*, September 15, 2000, pp. B1, B4; Barrie McKenna, "Canada Joins Firestone Tire Fray," *The Globe and Mail*, September 8, 2000, pp. B1, B5; Barrie McKenna, "Companies Accused of Delaying Tire Recall," *The Globe and Mail*, September 7, 2000, pp. B1, B12; Timothy Aeppel, Clare Ansberry, Milo Geyelin, and Robert L. Simison, "Road Signs," *The Wall Street Journal*, September 6, 2000, pp. A1, A16; Robert L. Simison, Karen Lundegaard, Norihiko Shirouzu, and Jenny Heller, "Blowout," *The Wall Street Journal*, August 10, 2000, pp. A1, A16.

Chapter 13

High-Tech Information Processing Summarized from Shawna Steinberg, "Playing for Keeps," *Canadian Business*, June 12, 1998, pp. 74–78. **Table 13.1** *National Post Business 500*, June 2000, p. 144. Reprinted with permission. **It's a Wired World** Sally C. Pipes, "AOL's Access Saga," *Chief Executive*, March 2000, 18; Associated Press, "Media Deal Biggest Ever," *Columbia Daily Tribune*, January 10, 2000, B1; Associated Press, "Merger Gives AOL Fast Track to Speedy Net," *Columbia Daily Tribune*, January 11, 2000, B6; Vicki Zunitch, "Principal Deal Makers Less Than Forthcoming,"

Columbia Daily Tribune, January 11, 2000, B6. **Figure 13.4** Adapted from Kenneth C. Laudon and Jane Laudon, *Essentials of Management Information Systems*, 3rd ed. (Upper Saddle River, NJ: Prentice Hall, 1999), 15. **WebConnexion** Used with permission of National Confectioners Association. **WebConnexion** Used with permission of Acumins. **Figure 13.6** Adapted from Laudon and Laudon, *Essentials of Management Information Systems*, 39. **Figure 13.8** Adapted from Laudon and Laudon, *Essentials of Management Information Systems*, 43. **WebConnexion** Used with permission of Silicon Graphics Inc. **Business Today** Summarized from Michael J. McCarthy, "You Assumed 'Erase' Wiped Out That Rant Against the Boss? Nope," *The Wall Street Journal*, March 7, 2000, pp. A1, A16; G. Bylinsky, "How Companies Spy on Employees," *Fortune*, November 4, 1991, pp. 131–40. **Concluding Case 13-1** Joel Brinkley, "PC Makers Challenge Broadcasters over Format for Digital Television," *New York Times*, April 8, 1997; Joel Brinkley, "Who Will Build Your Next TV? Industries Fight for $150 Billion Prize," *New York Times*, March 28, 1997; Neil Gross, "Defending the Living Room: How TV Makers Intend to Find Off Cyberlopers," *Business Week*, June 24, 1996, pp. 96–98; Frank Rose, "The End of TV as We Knnow It," *Fortune*, December 23, 1996, pp. 58–68; Robert D. Hof and Gary McWilliams, "Digital TV: What Will It Be?" *Business Week*, April 21, 1997; Kyle Pope and Mark Robichaux, "Waiting for HDTV? Don't Go Dumping Your Old Set Just Yet," *Wall Street Journal*, September 12, 1997, p. 1; David Bank, "Changing Picture," *Wall Street Journal*, September 11, 1997, p. R15. **Concluding Case 13-2** Summarized from Gary Lamphier, "Flower Power," *The Globe and Mail*, March 29, 1994, p. B30.

Chapter 14

The Arcane Art of Accounting in Russia Summarized from Andrew Higgins, "At Russian Companies, Hard Numbers Often Are Hard to Come By," *The Wall Street Journal*, August 20, 1998, pp. A1, A9. **Table 14.1** *National Post Business 500*, June 2000, p. 164. Reprinted with permission. **Concluding Case 14-1** Summarized from Richard Blackwell, "OSC Targets Tech Accounting," *The Globe and Mail*, September 26, 2000, pp. B1, B6. **WebConnexion** "Home Page." *CMA Canada*. http://www.cma-canada.org. February 2001. Reprinted with permission. **It's a Wired World** David LeonHardt, "Consultants Are Putting a New Price on Advice," *New York Times*, January 19, 2000, C1, C10; Floyd Norris, "Accounting Firm Is Said to Violate Rules Routinely," *New York Times*, January 7, 2000, A1, C6; Norris, "Rules That Only an Accountant Could Fail to Understand?"

New York Times, January 8, 2000, C1, C14. **WebConnexion** Used with permission of International Accounting Standards Committee. **Concluding Case 14-2** Reed Abelson, "The Shell Game of Hollywood 'Net Profits,'" *New York Times*, March 4, 1996, pp. D1, D6; Elizabeth Lesly, "Fatal Subtraction?" *Business Week*, March 11, 1996, pp. 66–68; Tim Carvell, "Accounting, Hollywood-Style," *Fortune*, November 11, 1996, p. 48.

Chapter 15

Tracking Web Users and Television Watchers Summarized from Nick Wingfield, "The Nielsen of the Internet Faces Growing Questions About Measuring Methods," *The Wall Street Journal*, November 22, 1999, pp. B1, B6; Elizabeth Jensen, "Networks Blast Nielsen, Blame Faulty Ratings for Drop in Viewership," *The Wall Street Journal*, November 22, 1996, pp. A1, A8. **WebConnexion** Used with permission of Harley-Davidson of Dallas. **WebConnexion** "Home Page." *Apple*. http://www.apple.com/ca. November 2000. Reprinted with permission. **WebConnexion** "Home Page." *High Road Communications*. http://www.highroad.com. November 2000. Reprinted with permission. **Business Today** Summarized from Shawn Tully, "Teens: The Most Global Market of All," *Fortune*, May 16, 1994, pp. 90–97. **It's a Wired World** *Costpredict: Organizational Health Cost Analysis* (Columbia, MO: Network Health Systems®, 2000); "*Health & Lifestyle Assessment Handbook* (Columbia, MO: Network Health Systems © 1999). **Concluding Case 15-2** Summarized from William M. Bulkeley, "Wring in the New: Washers That Load from Front Are Hot," *The Wall Street Journal*, April 29, 1997, pp. A1, A5.

Chapter 16

Clodhoppers Summarized from Geoff Kirbyson, "Candy Firm Finds U.S. Hungry For Product," *Winnipeg Free Press*, January 25, 2000, p. C11; Casey Mahood, "Madeover Clodhoppers Stepping Out," *The Globe and Mail*, January 7, 2000, p. M1; "Sweet Love," *Ciao*, Spring 2000, p. 32; Geoff Kirbyson, "Success Sweet for Krave's," *Winnipeg Free Press*, November 30, 2000, p. B7. **WebConnexion** Used with permission of IDEO Product Development. **WebConnexion** Used with permission of Boo.com. **Table 16.1** Philip Kotler and Gary Armstrong, *Marketing: An Introduction*, 3rd ed. (Englewood Cliffs, NJ: Prentice Hall), p. 274; William J. Stanton, Michael J. Etzel, and Bruce J. Walker, *Fundamentals of Marketing*, 10th ed. (New York: McGraw-Hill, 1994), p. 247; William P. Pride and O.C. Ferrell, *Marketing: Concepts and Strategies*, 9th ed. (Boston: Houghton Mifflin, 1995), pp. 307–13. **Table 16.2** "Total measured U.S.

ad spending by category and media," *Advertising Age*, September 28, 1994, p. 8. **Table 16.3** *National Post Business 500*, June 2000, p. 164. Reprinted with permission. **Figure 16.9** *Marketing Magazine*, April 15, 1996, p. 1. **It's a Wired World** Summarized from John Heinzl, "Advertisers Call on Wireless World," *The Globe and Mail*, April 21, 2000, p. B8. **Business Today** Daniel Cremin, "Hosers with Attitude," *Canadian Business*, May 15, 2000, pp. 70–72; Shona McKay, "Make Room, Madison Avenue," *Canadian Business*, January 1993, pp. 33–36. **WebConnexion** "Home Page." *FabulousSavings.com*. http://www. faboulussavings.com. November 2000. Reprinted with permission.

Chapter 17

Reinventing Canadian Retailing Summarized from Sean Silcoff, "Winners Take Everything," *Canadian Business*, September 24, 1999, pp. 47–50; Sean Silcoff, "Life After Eaton's," *Canadian Business*, September 10, 1999, pp. 30–64; Sean Silcoff, "Move Over, Timothy Eaton," *Canadian Business*, June 26/July 10, 1998, pp. 59–64. **Business Today** Summarized from Brian Milner, "Charge More for Movies, Bronfman Urges Industry," *The Globe and Mail*, April 1, 1998, pp. B1, B4; Bruce Orwall, "Bronfman's 'Real-World' a Tough Sell in Hollywood," *The Wall Street Journal*, April 3, 1998, p. B9. **It's a Wired World** Shawn Tully, "The B2B Tool That Really Is Changing the World," *Fortune*, March 20, 2000, 132-34+. **WebConnexion** "Home Page." *The Globe and Mail*. http://www.globeandmail.com. November 2000. Reprinted with permission from The Globe and Mail. **WebConnexion** Used with permission of razorfish.com. **Table 17.2** *National Post*, June 2000, p. 144. **WebConnexion** "Home Page." *grocerygateway.com*. http://www. grocerygateway.com. February 2001. Reprinted with permission. **Table 17.3** *National Post*, June 2000, p. 146. **Concluding Case 17-1** Lee Gomes, "When Its Own Assets Are Involved, Napster Is No Fan of Sharing," *The Wall Street Journal*, July 26, 2000, pp. A1, A10. **Concluding Case 17-2** Fara Warner, "New Tactics Shake Up Online Auto Retailing," *The Wall Street Journal*, October 18, 1999, p. B1; Rob Carrick, "On-Line Autos Need a Tune-Up," *The Globe and Mail*, June 19, 1999, p. B5; Greg Keenan, "Revolution on the Car Lot," *The Globe and Mail*, March 22, 1997, p. B1, B4; Keith Bradsher, "Sticker Shock: Car Buyers Miss Haggling Ritual," *New York Times*, June 13, 1996, pp. D1, D23; Bradley J. Fikes, "Haggling Over Price Is No Longer Automatic," *San Diego Business Journal*, October 3, 1994, pp. 17–18.

Chapter 18

Banking Behemoths Summarized from Mark MacKinnon, "Canadian Banks Have Fallen Many Storeys in Worldwide Ranking," *The Globe and Mail*, August 9, 1999, pp. B1, B4; Mark MacKinnon, "Canadian Banks, If Not the Biggest, Are Among the Most Profitable," *The Globe and Mail*, August 4, 1999, p. B4. **WebConnexion** "The Canadian Trade Commissioner Service." Department of Foreign Affairs and International Trade Canada. http://www.infoexport.gc.ca/ men-e.asp. November 2000. Reprinted with permission of the Minister of Public Works and Government Services Canada, 2001. **Table 18.1** *National Post*, June 2000, p. 152. **WebConnexion** "Home Page." *CertaPay.Com*. http://www.certa-pay.com. February 2001. Reprinted with permission. All rights reserved. **It's a Wired World** Bill Streeter, "Who's in Charge: The Dot-Coms vs. the Banks," *ABA Banking Journal*, February 2000, 43, 45, 46; "You and Your Bank on the Net: The Next Generation and the 'Nyet' Generation," *ABA Banking Journal*, February 2000, S13-S15; Bill Orr, "Easy Money," *ABA Banking Journal*, March 2000, 41, 42, 46, 47; Alex Sheshunoff, "Internet Banking—An Update from the Frontlines," *ABA Banking Journal*, January 2000, 51-55. **Business Today** Summarized from Barrie McKenna, "U.S. Banking Industry Riles Consumers," *The Globe and Mail*, October 13, 1997, pp. B1, B6. **WebConnexion** "Home Page." *Bank of Canada*. http://www.bankofcanada.ca/en/. November 2000. Reprinted with permission from the Bank of Canada. **Table 18.2** *National Post*, June 2000, p. 152. **Table 18.3** *National Post*, June 2000, p. 164. **Table 18.4** *The Economist*, April 29, 2000, 75. **Concluding Case 18-1** Gundi Jeffrey, "Dollar Decisions," *CGA Magazine*, November–December, 2000, pp. 30–33. **Concluding Case 18-2** Summarized from Bruce Little and Chad Skelton, "The Flip Side of the Languishing Loonie," *The Globe and Mail*, June 20, 1998, pp. B1, B7.

Chapter 19

Another Stock Market Scandal David Paddon and Hollie Shaw, "Top Heads Roll at Royal After Scandal," *Winnipeg Free Press*, July 21, 2000, pp. B7, B12; Karen Howlett, Janet McFarland, and Dawn Walton, "Stock Rigging Appears Widespread," *The Globe and Mail*, July 1, 2000, pp. B1, B4; Keith McArthur, "Business Seeps Away from Royal Pensions, " *The Globe and Mail*, July 1, 2000, pp. B1, B5; Richard Blackwell and Jacquie McNish, "OSC Prepared to Deal with RT," *The Globe and Mail*, July 1, 2000, pp. B5; Jacquie McNish, "How the High-Closing High Fliers Got Caught," *The Globe and Mail*, July 3, 2000, pp. B1, B3. **WebConnexion** "Home Page." *E*TRADE Canada™*.

http://www.canada.etrade.com. November 2000. E*TRADE Canada is a trademark of E*TRADE Securities, Inc. and is used with its permission. **Figure 19.1** Leah Nathans Spiro and Edward C. Baig, "Who Needs a Broker?" Business Week, February 22, 1999, 113-116+. **Business Today** Jon Hilsenrath and Jason Booth, "Asia's Recovery Under Attack from Abroad," *The Globe and Mail*, October 16, 2000, p. B6. **WebConnexion** Used with permission of National Association of Securities Dealers, Inc. **Table 19.2** *National Post*, June 2000, p. 92. **It's a Wired World** "Grappling with Change," *The Economist*, April 29, 2000, 71-72; "The World at Its Hands," *The Economist*, May 6, 2000, 77. **Table 19.3** *National Post*, June 2000, p. 168. **WebConnexion** "Home Page." *fundlibrary.com*. http://www. fundlibrary. com. November 2000. Reprinted with permission. Fundlibrary.com is owned and operated by Street Views Inc. Visit www.streetviews.com to freely explore thousands of Canadian equity research reports from major investment dealers. **Concluding Case 19-2** Summarized from Daniel Stoffman, "Look Who's Calling the Shots," *Canadian Business*, July 1990, pp. 45–47.

Chapter 20

It's Finally Over at Eaton's Summarized from Sean Silcoff, "2nd Time Trendy," *Canadian Business*, May 29, 2000, pp. 34–39; Marina Strauss, "Eaton's Sees Final Chapter Being Written," *The Globe and Mail*, November 20, 1999, p. B3; Karen Howlett, "Sears Canada Bags Eaton's," *The Globe and Mail*, September 21, 1999, pp. B1, B16; "Eaton's Stuns Nation," *Winnipeg Free Press*, February 28, 1997, pp. A1, A3; John Heinzl and Paul Waldie, "Eaton's Drowning in Red Ink," *The Globe and Mail*, February 28, 1997, p. B1; Rob Ferguson, "Eaton's Gets on With It," *Winnipeg Free Press*, September 9, 1997, p. B3; Ian McGugan, "Eaton's on the Brink," *Canadian Business*, March 1996, pp. 38–48. **WebConnexion** "Home Page." *ERisk*. http://www.erisk.com. March 2001. Reprinted with permission. **It's a Wired World** Summarized from Eric Reguly, "Shareholders Closed the Book on Chapters Online Long Ago," *The Globe and Mail*, April 15, 2000, p. B9; www.chaptersinc.com/corppro.htm. **Table 20.2** *National Post*, June 2000, p. 154. **Business Today** Summarized from Leslie Scism, "If Disaster Strikes This 'Titanic', Chubb Could Lose Millions," *The Wall Street Journal*, April 9, 1997, pp. A1, A4; Leslie Scism, "Maybe Julie Andrews Could Offer Insurers a Spoonful of Sugar," *The Wall Street Journal*, April 4, 1997, pp. A1, A4; Patrick Reilly, "Insurers Are Downbeat on Rap Concert Tours," *The Wall Street Journal*, March 26, 1997, pp. B1, B12. **WebConnexion** "Business and Commercial Insurance." *Insurance Bureau of Canada*. http://www.ibc.ca. March 2001. Reprinted with permission. **Concluding Case 20-1** Summarized from Jacquie McNish, "Brascan Sticks with Its Vision," *The Globe and Mail*, November 13, 2000, pp. B1, B7. **Concluding Case 20-2** Summarized from Jill Lawless, "Rogue Broker Ruins Firm in 92 Minutes," *The Globe and Mail*, October 4, 2000, p. B9; Sara Webb et al.,

"A Royal Mess: Britain's Barings PLC Bets on Derivatives—and the Cost Is Dear," *The Wall Street Journal*, February 27, 1995, pp. A1, A6; Marcus W. Brauchli, Nicholas Bray, and Michael R. Sesit, "Broken Bank: Barings PLC Officials May Have Been Aware of Trader's Position," *The Wall Street Journal*, March 6, 1995, pp. A1, A7; Richard W. Stevenson, "Markets Shaken as a British Bank Takes a Big Loss," *The New York Times*,

February 27, 1995, pp. A1, A5; Paula Dwyer et al., "The Lesson from Barings' Straits," *Business Week*, March 13, 1995, pp. 30–32; Glenn Whitney, Dutch Concern Agrees to Buy Barings Assets," *The Wall Street Journal*, March 5, 1995, pp. A3, A5; "Leeson's Six-and-a-Half Year Sentence Greeted with Mixed Reviews," *The Globe and Mail*, December 4, 1995, pp. B1, B10.

Photo Credits

Chapter 1 Owen Broad/Image Network, pages 2 and 3; Voisey Bay Mills/Advantage Productions, page 4; Susan McCartney; Al Harvey/The Slide Farm; Bettman Archives; Junebug Clark, page 9; Thomas Sandberg, page 12; Angela Baur; Al Harvey/The Slide Farm, page 21; Kathleen Bellesiles/Little Apple Studio, page 24; SABA Press Photos, Inc./Ricardo Azoury, page 30

Chapter 2 Calgary's Cooperative Association Ltd., page 40; The Granger Collection, page 44; First Light/D. Pollack, page 48; Imperial Oil Limited, page 56; Al Harvey/The Slide Farm, page 58; courtesy BASF, page 61

Chapter 3 Bombardier Inc., page 69; Thomas J. Mueller, page 71; Heimo Aga, page 75; Stone/Paul Chesley, page 77; CP Picture Archive (Fabrice Coffrini), page 86; Canapress/Jacques Boissinot, page 93; Palliser Furniture, page 97

Chapter 4 CP Picture Archive, page 103; AP/World Wide Photos, page 110; David R. Frazier/Photo Researchers, 116; Courtesy of Construction Association of Ontario, page 119; McDonald's Restaurant, page 124

Chapter 5 Real Life/Image Bank, pages 134 and 135; CP Picture Archive (Laurent Rebours), page 136; Bastienne Schmidt , page 139; IT Stock/First Light, page 147; Kharen Hill/Image Network, page 149 (top); David DeLossy/ Image Bank, page 149 (middle); Jeff Smith/Image Bank, page 149 (bottom); Chuck Savage/First Light, page 156; courtesy of Mainframe Entertainment Inc., page 158

Chapter 6 Dick Hemingway, page 165; Nelvana Studios, page 169; Eaton's, page 199; Telus Corporation, page 178; Bob Scott/Image Bank, page 185

Chapter 7 A.M. Cuddy, page 193; S. Houston, page 196; Dick Hemingway, page 200; Canapress, page 202; Midas Canada Inc., page 208

Chapter 8 Chuck Keeler/Stone, pages 222 and 223; Canapress/Frank Gunn, page 224; Hunt Personnel, page 232; Zigy Kaluzny/Stone, page 236; The Stock Market/John Madere, page 251; Mark Richards, page 252

Chapter 9 PanCanadian Petroleum Limited, page 260; Corbis, page 264; Courtesy Western Electric, page 265; Financial Post/Peter Redman, page 267;

Chapter 10 CP Picture Archive (Mike Conley), page 289; Prentice Hall Archives, page 291; Canapress/Adrian Wyld, page 309

Chapter 11 Andy Sacks/Stone, pages 318 and 319; Interface Inc., page 320; Canapress Photo Service, page 326 (top two right, bottom left photos); Plus Pix/First Light, page 326 (top left photo); PhotoDisc, page 326 (bottom right photo); Toyota Motor Manufacturing Canada Inc., page 336; Liaison Agency, Inc./Joe Traver, page 343

Chapter 12 CP Picture Archive (Michael Spingler), page 352; UPI/Corbis-Bettman, page 359; Brownie Harris/First Light, page 363; Dofasco Canada, page 371

Chapter 13 CP Picture Archive (Keith Beaty), page 379; Bruce Ayers/Stone, page 382; Robert Houser Photography, page 390; Photofest, page 407; Brownie Harris, page 409

Chapter 14 Walt Hodges/Tony Stone Images, page 418; PhotoDisc, page 421

Chapter 15 Jon Riley/Stone, pages 454 and 455; Ed Bock/First Light, page 456; Loblaws Brands Limited; Toronto Zoo; Chiat Day/Ill. Doug Martin, page 460;

Grand & Toy, page 466; Al Harvey/The Slide Farm, page 476; Prentice Hall Archives, page 479; The Body Shop Canada, page 480; Feathercraft Products Ltd., page 483

Chapter 16 Krave's Candy, page 492; PhotoDisc, page 497; Ali Kabas, page 504; Dick Hemingway, page 505; Boy Scouts of Canada (top right); Joseph Rodriguez/Black Star (middle left); Duncan Roban/Alpha (top left); CP Picture Archive (Didier Debusschere) (middle right), CP Picture Archive (Fred Chartrand) (bottom), page 512; Microcell Solutions Inc. (left); used with permission of Kellogg Canada Inc., copyright 1995 (right); page 520; Paul Barton/The Stock Market, page 524; Network Aspen/Jeffrey Aaronson, page 530

Chapter 17 Southworks Outlet Mall Inc., page 539; Richard Hutchings/Photo Researchers, page 548; Apple Canada, page 555; Liaison Agency, Inc./Porter Gifford, page 560; David Gamble, page 563; Canadian National, page 569

Chapter 18 Dick Hemingway, pages 582 and 583; Royal Bank Corporate Headquarters, page 584; The Granger Collection, page 586; Dick Hemingway, page 589; Kathleen Bellesiles, page 593; Bob Carroll/Leucar, page 596; Prentice Hall Archives, page 602

Chapter 19 CP Picture Archive (Aaron Harris), page 614; Toronto Star/D. Loek, page 622; SABA Press Photos Inc., page 623; Richard B. Levine/Frances M. Roberts, page 626; Reproduced with permission of the Minister of Finance, page 629; Canapress Photo Service, page 634

Chapter 20 Canapress/Jeff Goode, page 647; David Pollack/The Stock Market, page 652; Lawrence Migdale; Ulrich Welch; Eunice Harris/Photo Researchers, page 664

Each key term, and the page on which is defined, is set in boldface type.